סדר תפלות כל השנה

THE AUTHORISED

Daily Prayer Book

REVISED EDITION

HEBREW TEXT, ENGLISH TRANSLATION
WITH COMMENTARY AND NOTES

BY

DR. JOSEPH H. HERTZ

THE LATE

CHIEF RABBI OF THE BRITISH EMPIRE

NEW YORK

BLOCH PUBLISHING COMPANY

THE AUTHORISED

DAILY PRAYER BOOK

REVISED EDITION

HEBREW TEXT, ENGLISH TRANSLATION

WITH COMMENTARY AND NOTES

PREFATORY NOTE TO THE FIRST EDITION

At the urgent request of several teachers, I have consented to issue this edition of the Authorised Prayer Book in parts. A comprehensive Preface explaining the plan of the work, and giving full acknowledgement of all help received, will appear on its completion.

I cannot, however, delay thanking the Jewish Religious Education Board for granting me the use of the Hebrew text ; and Mr. and Mrs. HENRY FREEDMAN, of Leeds, whose idealism and wise-hearted generosity, in endowing this edition of the Prayer Book, will place it within the reach of all.

" It would be well for the Jewish religion if the beauty and devotional power so largely manifested in its prayers, were more intelligently appreciated by its adherents to-day ", said a well-known theologian not so long ago. The purpose of this work is to render possible such an intelligent appreciation on the part of the ordinary worshipper ; and it is the fervent prayer of the author that, with the help of God, his labours lead to a deepening of devotion in the tents and sanctuaries of Israel in English-speaking lands.

J. H. H.

Rosh Chodesh Cheshvan, 5702.
London, 21st Oct., 1941.

PREFATORY NOTE TO THE ONE VOLUME EDITION

The Chief Rabbi, Dr. J. H. Hertz, C.H., ז״צל, was not spared to see the completion of this one-volume edition of his Prayer Book. He had, however, carried out all the proof corrections until p. 1064, "Confession on Death-bed," which happened to be the last page he corrected ; closing there his great Jewish leadership.

It is hoped that this work—the first of its kind in English—will enable the prayers of its distinguished author to be fulfilled, that his labours therein " lead to a deepening of devotion in the tents and sanctuaries of Israel in English-speaking lands ".

S. H.

Av 5706
July 1946

TABLE OF CONTENTS

THE JEWISH PRAYER BOOK

I.

ITS PARAMOUNT IMPORTANCE

The Jewish Prayer Book, or the *Siddur*, is of paramount importance in the life of the Jewish people. To Israel's faithful hosts in the past, as to its loyal sons and daughters of the present, the Siddur has been the Gate to communion with their Father in Heaven; and, at the same time, it has been a mighty spiritual bond that united them to their scattered brethren the world over. No other book in the whole range of Jewish literature that stretches over three millenia and more, comes so close to the life of the Jewish masses as does the Prayer Book. The Siddur is a daily companion, and the whole drama of earthly existence— its joys and sorrows; workdays, Sabbaths, historic and Solemn Festivals; birth, marriage and death—is sanctified by the formulae of devotion in that holy book. To millions of Jews, every word of it is familiar and loved; and its phrases and Responses, especially in the sacred melodies associated with them, can stir them to the depths of their being. No other volume has penetrated the Jewish home as has the Siddur; or has exercised, and continues to exercise, so profound an influence on the life, character and outlook of the Jewish people, as well in the sphere of personal religion as of moral conduct.

FOR
UNDERSTANDING
OF THE JEW

Surely the story and nature of such a book should be known not only to Jews, but to all who are interested in the classics of Religion. Yet the Jewish Liturgy is the one branch of religious literature that is generally neglected by Christian scholars; and as to Jews of Western lands, a well-known theologian not so long ago wrote, "it would be well for the Jewish religion if the beauty and emotional power so largely manifested in its prayers were more intelligently appreciated by its adherents to-day". As it is, they know that the Shema and the Reading of the Torah constitute the central portions of the Synagogue Service, and are also vaguely aware of some differences between Sephardim and Ashkenazim as regards pronunciation and rendering of their Hebrew Prayers. For the rest, they do not know their bearings in the realm of Jewish Devotion, and move " in worlds not realized ". It is a most regrettable fact. For none can truly know the Jew—the Jew cannot know himself —without a clear grasp of the religious truths enshrined in his Prayer

Book, or of the spiritual forces that were responsible for its rise and development.

AND OF   Just as indispensable is the study of the Siddur for the under-
JUDAISM   standing of Judaism itself. It has been well said that its
       liturgy is the soul-index of a Religion. " You can tell from
a man's prayers, whether he be a man of religious culture, or a man of no
spiritual breeding ", declares a Talmudic teacher. In the same manner,
nothing reveals better the moral worth and message of a religious community, nothing is a truer confessional of its deepest thoughts and
loftiest aspirations, than the historic prayers of that community. This
is certainly so in regard to the Jewish Prayer Book. It is the liturgical
expression of the hopes and convictions that had been accepted by the
Jewish people as a whole. Furthermore, an investigation into the
origins of the Siddur vindicates afresh, and from a new angle, the
supreme place of Judaism among the religions of the world. It discloses
the astounding fact that Israel, over and above its contribution of
Monotheism and Prophetic ideals to the treasure-house of Humanity,
has taught both *true prayer* and *congregational worship* to the children of
men in producing the Psalms, the Synagogue, and the Jewish Liturgy—
each of them a unique achievement in the annals of the Human Spirit.
All this will become clear after a brief examination of the meaning
of Prayer, the place of Prayer in Israel, the rise and significance of the
Synagogue, and the history of the Jewish Liturgy.

II.

PRAYER

LINK BETWEEN   Prayer is a universal phenomenon in the soul-life of
GOD AND MAN   man. It is the soul's reaction to the terrors and joys, the
       uncertainties and dreams of life. " The reason why we
pray ", says William James, " is simply that we cannot help praying ".
It is an instinct that springs eternally from man's unquenchable faith
in a living God, almighty and merciful, Who heareth prayer, and
answereth those who call upon Him in truth ; and it ranges from half-
articulate petition for help in distress to highest adoration, from
confession of sin to jubilant expression of joyful fellowship with
God, from thanksgiving to the solemn resolve to do His will as if
it were our will. Prayer is a Jacob's ladder joining earth to heaven ;
and, as nothing else, wakens in the children of men the sense of

kinship with their Father on High. It is " an ascent of the mind to God "; and, in ecstasies of devotion, man is raised above all earthly cares and fears. The Jewish Mystics compare the action of prayer upon the human spirit to that of the flame on the coal. "As the flame clothes the black, sooty clod in a garment of fire, and releases the heat imprisoned therein, even so does prayer clothe a man in a garment of holiness, evoke the light and fire implanted within him by his Maker, illumine his whole being, and unite the Lower and the Higher Worlds " (Zohar).

PRAYER IN ISRAEL Prayer reaches its loftiest levels in our Sacred Scriptures. Every form of prayer is there found in perfect utterance, and in unsurpassed nobility and splendour. The Scriptural narrative is interspersed with prayer—individual prayers, as well as ritual prayers, such as the Priestly Blessing in Numbers 6. 22. Organized prayer was sufficiently established by the time of Isaiah to have drifted into conventionality, and thereby aroused the indignation of the Prophet (chapter 1. 15). However, no other people had the trust in God, or maintained it so unfalteringly from century to century, as had Israel amid all the tragic vicissitudes of its history : the darker the night, the brighter did Prayer shine in the soul of Israel. Israel's motto might well have been Job's " Though He slay me, yet will I trust in Him "

Hebrew prayer shows no trace of magic and incantation, and is free from the vain repetitions in primitive and heathen cults. It is a true " outpouring of the soul ", a veritable cry " out of the depths " to our Father in Heaven. Prayer in Israel, furthermore, assumed new forms, alongside of adoration, petition, and thanksgiving. If in Greek the root-meaning of the verb " to pray " signifies " to wish "; and if in German it means " to beg "; in Hebrew, the principal word for prayer comes from the root, " to judge ", and the usual reflexive form (hithpallel) means literally, " to judge oneself ". The word *tefillah*, " prayer ", has therefore been understood as " self-examination "—whether we are worthy of addressing the Holy One, who demands righteousness and holiness of life from His worshippers. Thus, Job protests, " There is no violence in my hands, and my prayer is pure "; and one of the best-known synagogue Responses proclaims, " Prayer turns aside doom, but only if it is associated with Repentance and Charity ". Another explanation of the word *tefillah* is, " an invocation of God as judge ", an appeal for justice. Such was the prayer of Abraham when, pleading for the sinners of Sodom, he asked :

" Shall not the Judge of all the earth do right ? " (Genesis 18. 25). And of this nature mostly are the prayers of the Prophets. " Thou art of purer eyes than to behold evil, and Thou canst not look on perverseness, wherefore lookest Thou upon them that deal treacherously and holdest Thy peace when the wicked swalloweth up the man that is more righteous than he " ? is the fearless question of Habakkuk (1. 13).

Jewish prayer is as old as Israel. It is not generally known, that, while sacrifice in Israel was invariably accompanied by prayer, prayer itself was quite independent of sacrifice. The significance of this latter fact cannot be overstated. Consider that even Plato speaks of prayer and sacrifice as *inseparably* linked together ; and then go to the pages of Scripture, and you will find that Jacob prays for delivery from the hands of Esau, Moses intercedes for his People after the apostasy of the Golden Calf, Samson utters his agonized last petition, and the Prophet Jeremiah communes with God—all without sacrifice or the thought of sacrifice. Not that the place of sacrifice in the religious development of mankind is to be under-valued. But, as the Rabbis declare, prayer is greater than sacrifice ; and pure spiritual prayer arose in Israel. Even a detractor of Judaism, like Julius Wellhausen, admits that " Israel is the creator of true prayer ".

THE PSALMS The climax of the Hebrew genius for prayer is the Book of Psalms. Adoration can rise no higher than we find it in the five collections of ancient Hebrew hymns, known as the " Book of Praises ", *Sefer Tehillim*. It translates into simple speech the spiritual passion of the profound scholar ; and it also gives utterance, with the beauty born of truth, to the humble longing and petition of the unlettered peasant. It early found its way into the Temple as part of the daily service ; and to-day, after thousands of years, it is still the inspiration both of Jew and of Christian. In its words, believers have throughout the ages told God their woe, made confession of sin, asked for pardon and help, and rejoiced in the renewal of Divine favour. It is the hymn-book of Humanity.

The main data in regard to the Book of Psalms—its structure and teaching—must be sought elsewhere. Here it is sufficient to remark that much of the discussion as to the authorship of the Book of Psalms has been singularly unhelpful. Negative dogmatism would deny any of the psalms to be older than the Babylonian Exile, and therefore their Davidic origin. Yet a critical historian of the People of Israel acknowledges : " David is the most luminous figure and the most gifted personage in Israelitish history, surpassed in ethical greatness and general historical importance only by Moses, the Man of God. He is one of those phenomenal men such as Providence gives but once to a people, in whom a whole nation with its history reaches once for all its high-water mark " (Cornill). Furthermore, David's noble lament over Saul and Jonathan—the most moving elegy in literature—proves him to have had the gift of true poesy ; and immemorial tradition, as early as the days of Amos, regarded King David as the most eminent religious poet of his nation. And, besides, there was psalm-writing long before the days of David. Hymns, distantly akin to the Psalms, exist in Babylonian and Egyptian literature ; and, in Israel, Moses sang his Song of Deliverance at the Red Sea, and Deborah her Ode of Triumph in the age of the Judges. There is thus no valid reason for doubting the essential truth of the tradition which declares David to have been the founder of the Psalter.

Equally liberating is the recognition that the supposed date or historical background behind a psalm, hardly affects the meaning of the psalm itself. Sometimes that historical background put forward by some moderns, as in the so-called Maccabean psalms, is purely imaginary : thus, we find no allusion to enforced idolatry or to a faithless priesthood in those psalms which are alleged to be the product of the Maccabean period. The fact is, that the sacred singers deal with the great simplicities of religion as reflected in the general experience of man ; and, being lyrical poets in the highest sense, they utter in the voice of one person a universal cry of the human soul. Humiliation for sin, thankfulness for mercies received, vows of constancy in spite of distress, burning faith that in the end it is well with the godly, submission to the will of God—all this is set forth in words expressive of similar emotions in every clime and nation. This is the reason why " the Psalter is the one body of religious poetry which has gone on, irrespective of time and place, race and language, speaking with a voice of power to the heart of men " (Ernest Rhys).

POST-
BIBLICAL
PRAYER
It is only necessary to add that the post-Biblical singers in Israel continued the work of the Prophets and Psalmists. Like the Psalmists, they give voice to the sufferings of Israel, recall memories of the nation's past, and are unwearied in their hopes of the mercy and justice of God. Theirs are the martyr-songs and

penitential prayers (*selichoth*) which the Congregation of Israel chanted during fifteen hundred years of wandering and woe ; while in the hymns (*piyyutim*) they expressed Israel's unremitting cry for God throughout the ages.

III.

THE SYNAGOGUE

But Judaism's greatest contribution to humanity is in the domain of public worship, where alone man develops the wings and the capacity to soar into an invisible world. This it made through the *synagogue*. The synagogue represents something without precedent in antiquity ; and its establishment, as we shall see, forms one of the most important landmarks in the history of Religion. It meant the introduction of a mode of public worship conducted in a manner hitherto quite unknown, but destined to become the mode of worship of civilized humanity.

ITS ORIGIN IN BABYLONIAN EXILE The origins of the synagogue, as of everything living and elemental, are shrouded in obscurity ; and opinions differ widely in regard to the time and land of its birth. Some maintain that it existed in the days of the First Temple ; others hold that it grew out of the lay devotional services which accompanied the daily sacrifices in the rebuilt Temple after the Exile ; still others, that it is a product of the Jewries in Greek-speaking lands. However, most scholars, both Jewish and non-Jewish, are of opinion that the synagogue and the beginnings of regularly recurring congregational Services, first arose in the Babylonian Exile (597—538). During those fateful years in Israel's life, something happened that had never before happened in history. Nations do not survive dispersion ; yet a fragment of a small subjugated people, forcibly transported to a distant land, remains there for a lifetime and does not disintegrate. After two generations, it not only returns unimpaired to its own land, but does so with its national identity heightened, and its religious life immeasurably strengthened—a reborn Israel.

How was this miraculous transformation brought about ? It is not impossible to reconstruct the situation, though no contemporary account of it has come down to us. After the final catastrophe in 586 B.C.E., the exiles—torn from home, and weeping by the rivers of Babylon over their ruined land, their destroyed Holy City and Temple—must have been dumbfounded by the unutterable calamity that had overtaken them " God hath forgotten us ; Israel's story is at an end ; we are a valley of dry bones ", they repeated. This might well have proved to be the literal truth, had they not been accompanied by Prophets of Judah and Jerusalem who shared those sufferings. We are near to certainty, if we assume that Ezekiel, for example, would gather his brethren around him on Sabbaths and Festivals ; and that, by Scripture reading and exposition, and the singing of psalms they had heard in the now burnt Temple, he would fan the sparks of hope amid the ashes of their despair. They would listen with a new understanding to the Sacred Words read and spoken to them, and contritely repent the sins that had wrought the undoing of Israel. They would passionately proclaim both their utter rejection of idolatry and their devotion to the Holy God Whom they would henceforth serve with all their heart, all their soul, and all their might. Thereupon, the very Prophet who had foretold the fall of Jerusalem— and they had seen his prophecy fulfilled—would announce the salvation of a purified Zion, and proclaim the sure return of her repentant children to the Land of their Fathers.

The Prophet's group of followers thus became a body of worshippers. The proved value of these Sabbath and Festival gatherings in re-awakening the national and religious consciousness, would lead to the spread of the custom among other groups of uprooted Judeans. And the regular recurrence of these devotional occasions would, on the one hand, of necessity give rise to some scheme of prayer—outlines of theme, form and expression—to be used at such gatherings ; and, on the other hand, lead to resurrection in the Valley of Dry Bones ! James Darmesteter, the renowned Orientalist, relates that, when in India, he met a rabbi from Jerusalem who told him that, in the course of his wanderings through Persia, he had found a village entirely peopled with Jews descended from the bones resuscitated by Ezekiel. Little did he realize, remarks Darmesteter, that he himself, the wandering Jerusalem rabbi, was one of these descendants ; and that all Israel are the children of the corpses revived by the religious activity of the Prophets during the Babylonian Exile.

ITS SPREAD TO PALESTINE AND THE DIASPORA — Now, the memory of these religious assemblies was not forgotten when the exiles returned to the Homeland. Indeed, we find that within a century after Ezra, pious Jews throughout Palestine would meet on Sabbaths for the purpose of Scripture instruction, followed by religious devotion, and they would do so in a definite place set aside for that purpose. A century thereafter, in the year 247 B.C.E., we have the earliest contemporary non-Jewish mention of a synagogue building in the suburbs of Alexandria. The Hebrew and the Greek names for such " places of assembly " have remained the same to this day ; they are *beth ha-kenesseth* and *synagogue*. By the time the Second Temple fell at the hands of Titus, in the year 70, there seems to have been a synagogue throughout the Roman world wherever Jews dwelt. In Jerusalem, they are said to have been 480 in number ; and ruins of beautiful ancient synagogues in Galilee have survived to this day. So fundamental had the institution become to the religious life, that Philo, Josephus, and the Rabbis, looked upon it as going back to a hoary past. However, as it does not seem to have arisen before the Exile, there are no references to the synagogue in the pre-Exilic parts of Scripture, and but few in the later portions. It is generally agreed that in Psalm 74. 8 (" they have burned up all the *mo-adey El* in the land ") there is such a reference. The literal meaning of the words *mo-adey El* is, " places of assembly ", and the Midrash and the ancient Versions translate them by " synagogues ". At any rate, it is ominous that the only Biblical mention of the synagogue should refer to its burning. That connection has, alas, remained typical in Jewish history. Every attempt to annihilate the Jew has included the wholesale destruction of his places of worship. One need but recall the ghastly aftermath of the Black Death in 1349 ; the 581 synagogues burned in Nazi Germany on November 10th, 1938 ; and the destruction of the Jewish houses of worship throughout France, that culminated in the bombing of six Paris synagogues on October 2nd, 1941.

ITS SERVICE SPIRITUAL AND DEMOCRATIC   The new mode of worship inaugurated by the synagogue was democratic. The men who from the very first read and expounded the Torah and other Scriptural lessons, or led the worshippers in prayer, were rarely drawn from the priestly class. Anyone who possessed sufficient knowledge, and commanded the respect of his fellows, might do so. And that worship was spiritual. Sacrifices could not, of course, be offered anywhere outside the Temple. The Sacred Word, and not any sacramental or ritual act, was now the centre of worship ; and that Sacred Word was the seat of religious authority and the source of religious instruction. Here we have something new under the sun. " With the synagogue there began a new type of worship in the history of humanity ", says a noted non-Jewish scholar, " the type of congregational worship without priest or ritual, still maintained substantially in its ancient form in the modern Synagogue ; and still to be traced in the forms of Christian worship, though overlaid and distorted by many non-Jewish elements. In all their long history, the Jewish people have done scarcely anything more wonderful than to create the synagogue. No human institution has a longer continuous history, and none has done more for the uplifting of the human race " (R. T. Herford).

COPIED BY CHRISTIANITY AND ISLAM After the Maccabean period the synagogue gradually eclipsed the Temple as a dynamic religious force, and spread with the Jew all over the world. Its service of prayer and religious instruction was taken over by both Christendom and Islam ; the Church, in addition, embodying Song—the Psalms—in its worship. The language and formulae of the early Christian devotions follow Jewish models, and the forms and phrases of the Synagogue liturgy reappear in the most sacred prayers of the Church.

ITS PLACE IN JUDAISM In Judaism itself, the synagogue proved of incalculable importance. Through it, the Sabbath and the Festivals penetrated more deeply into the Jewish soul, and the Torah became the common property of the entire people. Because of it, the cessation of the sacrificial cult, which cessation would in any other ancient religion have meant the end of that religion, was not in Judaism an overwhelming disaster. The reason is clear. Long before the fall of the Second Temple the synagogue had become the real pivot of Jewish religious life, especially so among the Jews outside of Palestine. The synagogue became the " home " of the Jew : a Midrashic teacher applies the words (Psalm 90. 1) " Lord, thou hast been *our dwelling-place* in all generations ", to the synagogue. With the centuries, its scope broadened ; and—together with the *beth ha-midrash*, the house of learning, attached to it—functioned also socially, as a school, religious court-house, public hall, and even as a hostel. Since the Middle Ages, the synagogue has been the visible expression of Judaism ; it has kept the Jew in life, and enabled him to survive to the present day. With a truer application than that made by Macaulay in his day, we may declare that the Synagogue, like the Ark in Genesis, carried the Jew through the deluges of history, and that within it are the seeds of a nobler and holier human life, of a better and higher civilization.

IV.

THE LITURGY

THE MEN OF We must now consider the prayers that were spoken in
THE GREAT the synagogue. These are ascribed to the Men of the Great
ASSEMBLY .Assembly—the Prophets, Sages, Scribes and Teachers who,
in the centuries after the return from Babylon, continued
the work of spiritual regeneration begun by Ezra and his fellow-leaders
in the Restoration. They laid down the lines on which all Jewish con-
gregational and individual prayer has moved ever since. They made
the ברכה, the Blessing or Benediction, the unit of Jewish prayer; each
Blessing beginning with the six Hebrew words for, " Blessed art Thou, O
Lord our God, King of the Universe ". God is thus addressed in *direct*
speech, " face to face " ; and He is conceived not as a
LAY THE local or tribal deity, but as " King of the universe " (or,
FOUNDATION " of eternity "). The *Shema* had long before their day
OF SERVICE come to be looked upon as the corner-stone of Judaism
and Israel's confession of Faith. To the Shema, the Men
of the Great Assembly added the daily Litany of prayers, known as
the *Eighteen Benedictions*. In it, the voice of Judaism speaks with the
accent of the Prophets and Psalmists. In simple form, it unites praise
and gratitude to God with spiritual longings and personal petitions.

The Men of the Great Assembly also introduced worship into the
home, by instituting the Kiddush and the Havdolah for the incoming and
outgoing of Sabbath and Festivals—the *Kiddush* re-affirming God as
Creator, Deliverer and Lawgiver ; and the *Havdolah* stressing the everlasting distinction between holy and unholy, light and darkness, which
it is the mission of Israel to proclaim. In the scheme of the Rabbis,
prayer covered the whole existence of the Jew. It was offered at the
beginning and end of every meal, and every activity and human experience were hallowed by the thought of God. And they made devotion
part of the very life of the people by ordaining it as the daily duty of the
Jew ; because they knew—as an Anglo-Jewish student of our Liturgy
well put it—" that what can be done at any time and in any manner, is
apt to be done in no time and in no manner " (Abrahams). This linking
of the earthly with the Heavenly by means of a consecrated morning
hour, this uplifting of everyday existence through communion with the
Divine in prayer, has indeed proved an agency of immeasurable worth
in the life of the spirit—as Jewish and Christian devotion throughout
2,000 years amply testifies (Elbogen).

CONGREGA-
TIONAL
PRAYER
Two things of lasting influence must be noted in regard to this activity of the Men of the Great Assembly. The first is, they conceived the Service as primarily *congregational* ; *i.e.* the worshipper prays not as an individual, but as a member of a Brotherhood ; and his petitions are couched in the plural, so as to include the needs of his neighbour. " In the synagogue there was no room for egoistic prayers ; and, even in the prayers for the congregation, requests for material good were subordinated to petitions for the enlightenment of the spirit and for moral power " (Perles). The most impassioned prayers in the Service are those which express the Israelite's yearning for mankind's recognition of God's sovereignty, and for the final victory of righteousness in the universe.

Judaism attaches great importance to congregational prayer. Aside from the fact that public prayer is the strongest agency for maintaining the religious consciousness of a community, such prayer creates, maintains and intensifies devotion : the congregation, united in the proclamation of the Unity and holiness of God, has the ardent conviction that its prayers will be answered. " Wherever ten persons pray ", says Rabbi Yitzchak, " the *Shechinah*, the Divine Presence, dwells among them ".

And the second matter concerns the language in which Jewish congregational worship is held. Although the speech of
IN HEBREW the masses in Palestine at that time was Aramaic, the prayers of the synagogue were formulated in classical Hebrew; the vernacular, however, not being excluded ; *e.g.* the Kaddish, then purely a prayer for the speedy coming of the Kingdom of God, remained in the Aramaic. The Hebrew language had withdrawn from secular life, and was looked upon as *leshon ha-kodesh*, the Holy Tongue. Apart from the sense of mystery in the Service by the use of the Holy Tongue, increasing both the solemnity and emotional appeal of the Service, the Men of the Great Assembly rightly felt that the Synagogue Service must be essentially the expression of Universal Israel ; and therefore, must be in Israel's historic language, which is the depository of the soul-life of Israel. Hellenistic Jewry did not share this view, and it dispensed with the Sacred Language in its religious life. In its synagogues, the Torah was read in translation, and the prayers were in Greek. " The result was death. It withered away, and ended in total apostasy from Judaism " (Schechter). And those who in our own day

seek the virtual elimination of Hebrew from our Services, aim, consciously or unconsciously, at the destruction of the strongest link both with our wonderful past and with our brethren in the present and future.

V.

HISTORY OF THE LITURGY

It is not the purpose of this introduction to follow the story of the Liturgy in its development across the ages, and take note of its additions, modifications and ramifications in succeeding centuries. Many of them will be dealt with in the commentary on the different portions of the Service. The student who desires a comprehensive survey must consult the standard Jewish books of reference ; and, for deeper study, go to the pioneering works of Leopold Zunz (1794–1886), the founder of the New Jewish Learning, or those of Ismar Elbogen (1874–1943).

Only the most outstanding facts in the history of the Prayer Book will here be mentioned. In the generation after the AFTER THE Destruction of the Temple by the Romans, the Synagogue DESTRUCTION Service was in essentials identical with the Service as we have it to-day. The principal prayer had long been the Shema. Its reading was now understood to be " the taking upon oneself the yoke of the Kingdom of Heaven " ; i.e. the obligation of absolute and loving obedience to the Torah. And the Shema was preceded by two Benedictions—one in praise of the Creator of light ; and the other, of the Giver of the Torah. It was followed by the Redemption prayer. The Eighteen Benedictions that had hitherto been largely in a fluid state—save as to their number, and the concluding formula of each Benediction—had their wording officially fixed. Also, a nineteenth Benediction was added, in order to purge the congregations of sectaries and apostates. The Eighteen Benedictions (the *Amidah*) had become part of the Morning and Afternoon Services. The Responses (" Amen ", " Blessed be He and blessed be His Name ") and Doxologies (lit. " glory-words ", like " Blessed be the Lord, the God of Israel, from everlasting to everlasting ") had been taken over by the people from the Temple worship ; so were the Psalms, recited by the pious as an introduction to their morning devotions ; besides the Hallel (Psalms 113—118) which distinguished the Joyous Festivals, New Moon and Chanukah. On Mondays and Thursdays, there was a short Reading of the Torah ; and on Sabbaths, Festivals and Fasts, also a Lesson from the Prophets.

STATUTORY PRAYER The prayers had become *statutory*, and were no longer spontaneous outbursts of devotion. But be it remembered that only divinely-favoured individuals are capable of spontaneous prayer ; the overwhelming majority of mankind must have their prayers—if these are to serve a spiritual and ethical purpose —written or spoken for them in fixed, authoritative forms. Prescribed prayers, moreover, have their real, lasting and irreplaceable value. Heiler, the greatest authority on the psychology and history of Prayer, writes : " Formularies of prayer can kindle, strengthen and purify the religious life. Even in prayers recited without complete understanding, the worshipper is conscious that he has to do with something holy ; that the words which he uses bring him into relation with God. In spite of all externalism, prescribed prayer has acted at all times as a mighty lever in the spiritual life ". And Bousset truly says :—" One must not underestimate what the regular order of worship and fixed prayers must have meant to the ordinary man, what this saturation and transfusion of everyday life with the thought of God must have meant to a whole religious community." Furthermore, fixed prayer alone prevented chaos at the individual centres of worship, and rendered possible *uniformity* in the Service of the various groups—something of vital importance in Jewry, with its children scattered to the four winds of heaven. At the same time, private prayer and the free effusion of the heart were duly esteemed ; and a special section of the Service, the " Supplications ", was set apart for that purpose.

The regulations concerning the minutiae of prayer are many : the opening treatise of the Talmud, *Berachoth,* is entirely devoted to that subject. Schürer and other Christian theologians contend that these regulations must have stifled the whole spirit of prayer. But this is a controversial fiction ; as if *discipline* in an army, or *laws* in a country, necessarily suppressed patriotism. In fact, rule and discipline in worship *increase* devotion : without them, the noblest forms of adoration are unknown. The same is seen in the kindred realm of poetry. Elaborate schemes of metre and rhyme alone—witness the Greek poets, or Shelley, Goethe, Hugo—seem to render the highest poetry possible. With it all, none realized better than the Rabbis the need for prayer to be true " service of the heart ". He who prays must remember before Whom he stands, they said ; and it was neither the length, nor the brevity, nor the language of the prayer that mattered, but the sincerity. " The All-merciful demands the heart ", is their teaching.

Even two brief individual prayers of that period show that the fountain of devotional inspiration had not become dry. Rabbi Eliezer used to pray, " Let Thy will be done in Heaven above ; grant tranquility of spirit to those that reverence Thee below ; and do that which is good in Thy sight. Blessed art Thou, who hearest prayer ". Rabbi Chiyya's prayer was, " Keep us far from what Thou hatest; bring us near to what Thou lovest ; and deal mercifully with us for Thy Name's sake ". Legal ordinances and casuistical discussions on the rules of prayer did not grow less with the centuries—only to stimulate the rise of the synagogal poesy, the wonderful hymnology of an Ibn Gabirol and Yehudah Hallevi, the burning fervour of the Jewish Mystics, and the naïveté and originality of the Chassidim, both in their Hebrew prayers and those in their vernacular. One of the Chassidic Masters prayed " Lord of the Universe, I desire neither Thy paradise nor Thy bliss in the world to come ; I desire Thee and Thee alone ". This vernacular prayer is clearly in line with the rapturous cry of the sacred singer : " Whom have I in heaven but Thee ? And there is none upon earth that I desire beside Thee " (Psalm 73. 25). Spiritual religion has never found expression more living than in these utterances of Psalmist and Chassid.

But to return to the history of the Liturgy. The Talmudic age (200–500) added several prayers of genius to the Liturgy, notably those of the great Babylonian teacher, Rabh (175–247). The Gaonim, the heads of the later Babylonian academies (600–1040), sanctioned various enlargements of the Service ; and, in the ninth century, produced the first collection of the entire Prayer Book, the Siddur of Amram Gaon. In the twelfth century, Moses Maimonides left a similar authoritative collection of Prayers of the Jewish Year. In the course of time, there arose two main streams of liturgical tradition : the Babylonian,

SEPHARDIM AND ASHKENAZIM

which was transmitted to Spain, became the *Sephardi Rite* ; and the Palestinian, which spread over Northern Europe, and is the *Ashkenazi Rite*. This latter has a Western branch, the German *minhag* proper ; and an Eastern branch, the *minhag* of the Jews of Poland. The Polish *minhag* of the Ashkenazi Rite is now dominant in English-speaking lands.

It is quite beyond the scope of this introduction or commentary to deal with tributary Rites of smaller Jewries—such as, the Italian, Byzantine, North African, Yemenite—or with local Rites, like those of Avignon, Corfu or Tripoli. In all Rites, the foundation prayers are practically the same ; the divergences being mainly in regard to the voluntary " Supplications " in the daily Service, the *piyyutim* for Festivals, the *selichoth* on Penitential days, and the *kinnoth* on the Fast of Av. The first printed Prayer Book was the Ashkenazi Siddur in 1490. Scholarly editions of this Siddur are those of W. Heidenheim in 1800, and of S. Baer in 1868. The latter was the basis of S. Singer's Prayer Book, which first appeared in 1890 under the sanction of Chief Rabbi Nathan Adler. It has been repeatedly reprinted, and, since 1915, has been enlarged by the writer of this commentary. Its text is embodied, with revised translation, in this annotated edition of the Authorised Prayer Book of the United Hebrew Congregations of the British Empire.

THE JEWISH PRAYER BOOK   The Jewish Prayer Book is, we have seen, not the work of one man, one body, or one age. It is the gradual growth of many centuries—" one of the greatest products of the Jewish genius " (Hermann Cohen). There is, of course, nothing religiously *new* in the Siddur ; its phrases and teachings alike are either culled from Scripture and the Rabbinic Writings, or are a devotional paraphrase of them. This but makes it the truer an expression of the Jewish spirit, and but heightens its effectiveness as a summary of the Jewish Faith : the fundamental religious institutions, the basic doctrines of Judaism, as well as its millennial hopes, are ever afresh brought home to the conscience of the Jew in his daily, Sabbath and Festival worship. Only in the Psalter can we parallel the invincible faith, and unfaltering trust in God, the ardent desire to understand and obey God's declared will, that we find in the Siddur. " When we come to view the half-dozen or so great Liturgies of the world purely as religious documents, and to weigh their values as devotional classics, the incomparable superiority of the Jewish convincingly appears. The Jewish Liturgy occupies its pages with the One Eternal Lord ; holds ever true, confident, and direct speech with Him ; exhausts the resources of language in songs of praise, in utterances of loving gratitude, in rejoicing at His nearness, in natural outpourings of grief for sin ; never so much as a dream of intercessors or of hidings from His blessed punishments ; and, withal, such a sweet sense of the divine accessibility every moment to each sinful, suffering child of earth. Certainly the Jew has cause to thank God, and the fathers before him, for the noblest Liturgy the annals of faith can show" (G. E. Biddle in *Jewish Quarterly Review*, 1907).

THE WEEKDAY SERVICE

THE SERVICE FOR
SABBATHS AND FESTIVALS

THE LIFE OF MAN

"LET MAN STRENGTHEN HIMSELF LIKE A LION, AND ARISE IN THE EARLY MORN TO RENDER SERVICE TO HIS CREATOR; AS DAVID SAID (Psalm 57. 9). 'I WILL AWAKE THE DAWN'" (Shulchan Aruch 1. 1).

GLOSS. "'I have set the Lord always before me' (Psalm 16. 8): this is a leading principle in Religion, and in the upward strivings of the righteous who walk ever in the presence of God. For a man's mode of life, his demeanour and his deeds, his speech and his movements, when alone in the house, or in the intimate circle of his family and friends, are unlike those which he would exhibit when in the presence of a great king. And how much more considered will his demeanour be, if he reflect that there stands over him the King of kings, the Holy One, blessed be He, Whose glory fills the whole earth, watching his conduct and surveying his deeds; even as it is written: 'Can any hide himself in secret places that I shall not see him? saith the Lord' (Jeremiah 23. 24). Such contemplation must perforce imbue him with a true sense of reverence and humility, prompted by a feeling of unworthiness, before the Holy Name; and he will be heedless of whoever may scoff at him because of his devotions" (R. Moses Isserles).

Isaac Luria (1534–1572), the great Jewish mystic, opened his daily devotions with the invocation: "Lo! I hold myself ready to fulfil the divine behest, THOU SHALT LOVE THY NEIGHBOUR AS THYSELF" (Leviticus 19. 18). One of his later followers added the words, "and the behest, TO JUDGE ALL MY FELLOW-MEN CHARITABLY" (Leviticus 19. 15; Sayings of the Fathers 1. 6).

One of the leaders of Chassidim, Rabbi Elimelech of Lizansk (1717–1786), began his morning devotions with the following prayer:

"May it be Thy will to remove all barriers between our souls and Thee, our Father Who art in Heaven. Keep us from all haughtiness, anger, and ill-temper, and from all evil thoughts which debase the holy worship that we long to offer unto Thee in purity and love. Plant Thy holy spirit within us, and save us from all envy and jealousy. Endow us with the vision to see in everyone his good qualities, and to close our eyes to his defects. Then shall our prayers cause us to rise to higher and higher spiritual levels, and bring us nearer and nearer unto Thee."

THE MORNING SERVICE

The Morning Service on weekdays consists of :—

I. PRELIMINARIES TO THE SERVICE :—

A. MORNING HYMNS AND BLESSINGS—a miscellany of private
devotion prior to the Service proper ; and   p. 4

B. PSALMS AND " PASSAGES OF SONG "—psalms, Scriptural verses,
songs and Responses of adoration (" doxologies "), intended as a
preparation for public congregational worship.   p. 50

II. THE SHEMA.

THE SHEMA is the Declaration of Israel's Faith. Its reading is
preceded by two Benedictions on God as the Creator of light,
and as the Giver of the Torah ; and is followed by praises of
God as the Redeemer of Israel.   p. 108

III. THE " EIGHTEEN BENEDICTIONS."

A series of short prayers spoken standing and in silence. The
SHEMA and the EIGHTEEN BENEDICTIONS (or Amidah)— constitute the Morning Service proper, and their recital goes back
to Temple times.   p. 130

IV. ADDITIONS TO THE SERVICE :—

A. SUPPLICATIONS—Elegies and propitiatory prayers, especially for
Mondays and Thursdays, on which days there is also a short
Reading from the Torah ; and   p. 161

B. CONCLUSION—the whole Service terminating with Psalms 145
and 20, ובא לציון, Oleynu, and Mourner's Kaddish. There
follow some supplementary Recitations, and voluntary Readings.
                                                         p. 198

תְּפִלַּת שַׁחֲרִית :

On entering the Synagogue say the following:—

מַה־טֹּבוּ אֹהָלֶיךָ יַעֲקֹב מִשְׁכְּנֹתֶיךָ יִשְׂרָאֵל : וַאֲנִי בְּרֹב חַסְדְּךָ אָבוֹא בֵיתֶךָ אֶשְׁתַּחֲוֶה אֶל־הֵיכַל קָדְשְׁךָ בְּיִרְאָתֶךָ : יְיָ אָהַבְתִּי מְעוֹן בֵּיתֶךָ וּמְקוֹם מִשְׁכַּן כְּבוֹדֶךָ : וַאֲנִי אֶשְׁתַּחֲוֶה וְאֶכְרָעָה אֶבְרְכָה לִפְנֵי־יְיָ עֹשִׂי : וַאֲנִי תְפִלָּתִי לְךָ יְיָ עֵת רָצוֹן אֱלֹהִים בְּרָב־חַסְדֶּךָ עֲנֵנִי בֶּאֱמֶת יִשְׁעֶךָ :

I. PRELIMINARIES TO MORNING SERVICE

A. HYMNS AND BLESSINGS

(בִּרְכוֹת הַשַּׁחַר)

The first section of the Preliminaries to the Morning Service consists of hymns, blessings, and meditations suggested by the change from night to day, from sleep to wakefulness ; together with readings from the Torah and the Rabbinical Writings, selected for the purpose of attuning the soul to worship. This miscellany of beautiful prayers was at first intended merely to be read at home, before going to the synagogue and joining the congregation in prayer.

MAH TOVU. *how goodly.* These Scriptural verses express the feelings of reverence and joy on entering the House of God.
tents. Tradition explains this to mean "synagogues" ; and *dwelling-places,* " schools " for religious instruction.

MORNING SERVICE

ENTERING THE HOUSE OF GOD

Numbers 24. 5

Psalm 5. 8

Psalm 26. 8

Psalm 69. 14

On entering the Synagogue say the following :

How goodly are thy tents, O Jacob, thy dwelling places, O Israel ! As for me, in the abundance of thy lovingkindness will I come into thy house : I will worship toward thy holy temple in the fear of thee. Lord, I love the habitation of thy house, and the place where thy glory dwelleth. I will worship and bow down : I will bend the knee before the Lord, my Maker. May my prayer unto thee, O Lord, be in an acceptable time : O God, in the abundance of thy lovingkindness, answer me with thy sure salvation.

———————

in the fear of thee. In reverent awe. This verse is followed by " Lord, I *love*, etc." : both fear and love are basic elements of true religion. The Hebrew word usually translated by *fear*, when applied to God, is the feeling of awesome veneration that keeps the worshipper from presumptuous familiarity ; *love* prevents fear from sinking into cringing dread.

I love . . thy house. The ancient Israelite loved the House of God with a passionate love. " How lovely are thy tabernacles, O Lord of hosts ; my soul longeth, yea, fainteth for the courts of the Lord ", sang the Psalmist (84. 2, 3). The feeling of affection became intensified in the Middle Ages. The following is a modern instance. " In 1939, a boat carrying 120 Jews bound for Bolivia had to stop over a week-end in Baltimore, and the Jewish passengers were invited to be the guests of the different synagogues. The happiness of the refugees at being again able to attend Divine Worship after the burning of their synagogues in the preceding November, was overwhelming. It brought tears into the eyes of their hosts, and they could hardly speak for emotion " (Elbogen).

in an acceptable time. " Which is the most acceptable time ? At the hour of congregational worship " (Talmud).

salvation. Liberation from distress, deliverance.

יִגְדַּל אֱלֹהִים חַי וְיִשְׁתַּבַּח · נִמְצָא וְאֵין עֵת אֶל־מְצִיאוּתוֹ :

אֶחָד וְאֵין יָחִיד כְּיִחוּדוֹ · נֶעְלָם וְגַם אֵין סוֹף לְאַחְדּוּתוֹ :

אֵין לוֹ דְּמוּת הַגּוּף וְאֵינוֹ גוּף · לֹא נַעֲרוֹךְ אֵלָיו קְדֻשָּׁתוֹ :

קַדְמוֹן לְכָל־דָּבָר אֲשֶׁר נִבְרָא · רִאשׁוֹן וְאֵין רֵאשִׁית לְרֵאשִׁיתוֹ :

הִנּוֹ אֲדוֹן עוֹלָם · לְכָל־נוֹצָר יוֹרֶה גְדֻלָּתוֹ וּמַלְכוּתוֹ :

שֶׁפַע נְבוּאָתוֹ נְתָנוֹ אֶל־אַנְשֵׁי סְגֻלָּתוֹ וְתִפְאַרְתּוֹ :

לֹא קָם בְּיִשְׂרָאֵל כְּמֹשֶׁה עוֹד נָבִיא · וּמַבִּיט אֶת־תְּמוּנָתוֹ :

תּוֹרַת אֱמֶת נָתַן לְעַמּוֹ אֵל · עַל יַד נְבִיאוֹ נֶאֱמַן בֵּיתוֹ :

לֹא יַחֲלִיף הָאֵל וְלֹא יָמִיר דָּתוֹ לְעוֹלָמִים לְזוּלָתוֹ :

צוֹפֶה וְיוֹדֵעַ סְתָרֵינוּ · מַבִּיט לְסוֹף דָּבָר בְּקַדְמָתוֹ :

גּוֹמֵל לְאִישׁ חֶסֶד כְּמִפְעָלוֹ · נוֹתֵן לְרָשָׁע רַע כְּרִשְׁעָתוֹ :

יִשְׁלַח לְקֵץ יָמִין מְשִׁיחֵנוּ · לִפְדּוֹת מְחַכֵּי קֵץ יְשׁוּעָתוֹ :

מֵתִים יְחַיֶּה אֵל בְּרֹב חַסְדּוֹ · בָּרוּךְ עֲדֵי עַד שֵׁם תְּהִלָּתוֹ :

אֲדוֹן עוֹלָם · אֲשֶׁר מָלַךְ בְּטֶרֶם כָּל־יְצִיר נִבְרָא :

לְעֵת נַעֲשָׂה בְחֶפְצוֹ כֹּל אֲזַי מֶלֶךְ שְׁמוֹ נִקְרָא :

YIGDAL. Its author is Daniel ben Judah, Dayan in Rome, circa 1300. Its theme is the Jewish Creed as formulated by Moses Maimonides (1135–1204). For its explanation, see pp. 248–255.

This hymn opens the Morning Service. We start our devotions as *faithful* Jews, believing in the existence of a Creator—one, spiritual and eternal; believing in Prophecy and the Torah of Moses; in the

YIGDAL:
THE PRIN-
CIPLES OF
THE
JEWISH
FAITH

The living God we praise, exalt, adore !
He was, He is, He will be evermore !
No unity like unto His can be :
Eternal, inconceivable is He.

No form, or shape has the incorporeal One,
Most holy He, past all comparison.

He was, ere aught was made in heaven, or earth,
But His existence has no date, or birth.

Lord of the Universe is He proclaimed,
Teaching His power to all His hand has framed.

He gave His gift of prophecy to those
In whom He gloried, whom He loved and chose.

No prophet ever yet has filled the place
Of Moses, who beheld God face to face.

Through him (the faithful in His house) the Lord
The law of truth to Israel did accord.

This Law God will not alter, will not change
For any other through time's utmost range.

He knows and heeds the secret thoughts of man :
He saw the end of all ere aught began.

With love and grace doth He the righteous bless,
He metes out evil unto wickedness.

He at the last will His anointed send,
Those to redeem, who hope, and wait the end.

God will the dead to life again restore.
Praised be His glorious Name for evermore !

ADON
OLOM

Lord of the world, He reigned alone
While yet the universe was naught,
When by His will all things were wrought,
Then first His sov'ran name was known.

rule of justice in God's universe ; in the Messiah, and in the immortality of the soul. The translation is by Mrs. Alice Lucas (1852–1935).

ADON OLOM is the most popular hymn added to our Liturgy since
Bible times. Because of its beauty of form, simplicity of language and
sublimity of religious thought, it has been embodied in the various
Rites all over the world. Its author is said by some to be Solomon ibn
Gabirol (1021–1058), the renowned Spanish-Jewish poet and
philosopher. The translation is by Israel Zangwill (1864–1926).

וְאַחֲרֵי כִּכְלוֹת הַכֹּל ׃ לְבַדּוֹ יִמְלוֹךְ נוֹרָא ׃

וְהוּא הָיָה · וְהוּא הֹוֶה · וְהוּא יִהְיֶה בְּתִפְאָרָה ׃

וְהוּא אֶחָד · וְאֵין שֵׁנִי לְהַמְשִׁיל לוֹ לְהַחְבִּירָה ׃

בְּלִי רֵאשִׁית בְּלִי תַכְלִית · וְלוֹ הָעֹז וְהַמִּשְׂרָה ׃

וְהוּא אֵלִי · וְחַי גוֹאֲלִי · וְצוּר חֶבְלִי בְּעֵת צָרָה ׃

וְהוּא נִסִּי וּמָנוֹס לִי · מְנָת כּוֹסִי בְּיוֹם אֶקְרָא ׃

בְּיָדוֹ אַפְקִיד רוּחִי · בְּעֵת אִישַׁן וְאָעִירָה ׃

וְעִם־רוּחִי גְּוִיָּתִי · יְיָ לִי וְלֹא אִירָא ׃

בָּרוּךְ אַתָּה יְיָ אֱלֹהֵינוּ מֶלֶךְ הָעוֹלָם · אֲשֶׁר קִדְּשָׁנוּ בְּמִצְוֹתָיו וְצִוָּנוּ עַל נְטִילַת יָדָיִם ׃

Its appeal is universal. " Every fresh discovery confirms the fact that in all Nature's infinite variety there is one single Principle at work, One Power that is of no beginning and no end ; that has existed before all things were formed, and will remain when all is gone ; the Source and Origin of all, and yet in Itself beyond any conception or image that man can form " (Haffkine). Adon Olom is at the same time the supreme expression of absolute trust in God. The Creator of the universe, and its eternal Ruler, is also man's Guardian, Friend and Redeemer. In life and death, we confidently place our destiny in His hands.

He is the living God to save. The Hebrew phrase is based on Job 19. 25, " I know that my Redeemer liveth ".

my Rock. Like a mountain-stronghold, an impregnable Refuge.

banner. The figure is that of a rallying-point fixed on one of those mountain strongholds.

cup. Stands for all the wants of the worshipper ; Psalm 23. 5.

within His palm. Based on Psalm 31. 6 (" Into Thy hand I commend my spirit ; Thou hast redeemed me, O Lord God of truth ").

in fearless calm. Adon Olom is the closing hymn of the Prayers before Retiring to Rest at night, and is often sung by those who watch the last moments of one who is departing this life.

ADON OLOM

And when the All shall cease to be,
In dread lone splendour He shall reign,
He was, He is, He shall remain
In glorious eternity.

For He is one, no second shares
His nature or His loneliness ;
Unending and beginningless,
All strength is His, all sway He bears.

He is the living God to save,
My Rock while sorrow's toils endure,
My banner and my stronghold sure,
The cup of life whene'er I crave.

I place my soul within His palm
Before I sleep as when I wake,
And though my body I forsake,
Rest in the Lord in fearless calm.

ON WASHING THE HANDS

Blessed art thou, O Lord our God, King of the universe, who hast hallowed us by thy commandments, and given us command concerning the washing of the hands.

BORUCH ATTOH. *Blessed art thou, O Lord our God, King of the universe.* Every prayer beginning with these six Hebrew words is called a *berochah* (ברכה), a Blessing, or Benediction. It represents the oldest unit of Synagogue prayer. A *berochah* gives expression to thanksgiving for personal benefits or enjoyments, and to grateful recognition of God's goodness and providence as shown in Israel's Faith and the phenomena of life and nature.

Anyone in whose presence a Blessing is being formally recited responds with " Blessed be He, and blessed be His Name ", ברוך הוא וברוך שמו, as he hears the Name of God—the third word in every Hebrew Blessing—pronounced. At the end of the Benediction, he says אמן " Amen."

blessed. Or, " praised " ; i.e. revered, worthy of being extolled and glorified. This meaning of *blessed* is based on the root-meaning of *boruch* which is, " to fall on the knees " in adoration. Several of the classical commentators on the Liturgy point out that the word *blessed*, when applied to God, is an adjective similar in grammatical form to חנון ורחום " merciful and gracious ", which denote that mercy and grace are permanent and inherent elements in His nature ; i.e. He constantly bestows mercy and grace. " In the same way *blessed* signifies that He is the Source and Fountain of blessings " (Albo). Consequently, before partaking of any enjoyment, we declare that God is ברוך, " blessing-granting " in that, e.g., He bringeth forth bread from the soil.

בָּרוּךְ אַתָּה יְיָ אֱלֹהֵינוּ מֶלֶךְ הָעוֹלָם · אֲשֶׁר יָצַר אֶת־
הָאָדָם בְּחָכְמָה וּבָרָא בוֹ נְקָבִים נְקָבִים חֲלוּלִים חֲלוּלִים ·
גָּלוּי וְיָדוּעַ לִפְנֵי כִסֵּא כְבוֹדֶךָ שֶׁאִם יִפָּתֵחַ אֶחָד מֵהֶם
אוֹ יִסָּתֵם אֶחָד מֵהֶם אִי אֶפְשַׁר לְהִתְקַיֵּם וְלַעֲמוֹד לְפָנֶיךָ :
בָּרוּךְ אַתָּה יְיָ · רוֹפֵא כָל־בָּשָׂר וּמַפְלִיא לַעֲשׂוֹת :

blessed *ari thou*. Or, " blessed be thou ". Just as between man
and man " to bless " means to confer well-being upon, or prosper, a
cause ; so, in the relation of man to God, " to bless " means to prosper
His cause by our consecration of heart, soul, and might to the advancement of His kingdom. The opening of every *berochah* is thus a declaration of loyalty to God.

thou. We address God as a Person. That is a fact of fundamental
importance. Our God is not a mere physical Force, an unconscious
Being chained in mechanical laws and deaf to prayer. Judaism proclaims a God Who is a conscious Personality, Who made and knows the
human heart, Who hears and answers those why cry unto Him. The
use of " thou " further signifies that each individual worshipper
approaches God in *direct* speech, as his Father, Guide, Friend.

Lord. This is the usual translation of the Divine Name of Four
Letters corresponding to the four Hebrew letters for Y H W H. That
Hebrew Name is never pronounced *as written*. Whether it is printed in
full, or represented by two *yods* as above, it is *always* read " Adonoy ".
That Divine Name is by some translated " Eternal " ; others take it to
mean, " Life-giver " or " Creator ".

God. Heb. *Elohim*. is the general designation of the Divine Being.
The Hebrew word is a plural form, to denote plenitude of might that
comprehends all the forces of eternity and infinity.

our God. We pray not as individuals in isolation, but in the fellowship of Israel. Therefore when reciting statutory prayers, we address
them to the " Lord, *our God* ".

King of the universe. Judaism believes in a living God at work in
both nature and history as Creator, Ruler, Guide and Benefactor. He
is the God not merely of one sect, people, race or land : He is the
God of the spirits of all flesh, the King of the universe.

hallowed us by thy commandments, and given us command. These
words form part of every Blessing, whenever such Blessing is spoken in
connection with the *performance* of a religious precept.

hallowed us. Through obedience to God's will, we become " holy " ;
i.e. separated from the things that are ignoble and vile, and at one with all
things that make for righteousness and humanity. The commandments,
mitzvoth, are means of such hallowing ; their main purpose being
to teach the children of men moral discipline and self-restraint.

THE WON-
DERFUL
COM-
PLEXITY
OF THE
HUMAN
FRAME

Blessed art thou, O Lord our God, King of the universe, who hast formed man in wisdom, and created in him many passages and vessels. It is well known before thy glorious throne, that if but one of these be opened, or one of those be closed, it would be impossible to exist and stand before thee. Blessed art thou O Lord, who art the wondrous healer of all flesh.

It has been pointed out by a medieval commentator on the Prayer Book—Abdurham—that the word (קדשנו) translated "hallowed us" is that used in connection with the Marriage ceremony; and can be translated, "wedded us"; because, in very truth, the observance of the commandments binds us unto God, and keeps us "God-minded". It is impossible to convey to those who have not experienced it, the feeling of holy joy diffused in the humblest Jewish home by such ceremonies as the Kiddush or the Seder. Both the home and those that dwell in it, become hallowed by their observance.

given us command. There is no command concerning the washing of the hands in the Torah. And yet the words, "given us command", are fully justified. Their use is based on Deuteronomy 17. 11, which declares, "According to the law which they [the religious authorities] shall teach thee, thou shalt do". The precept concerning washing of the hands is an early rabbinic institution; and thus, in carrying out what the Rabbis prescribed, we obey the express command of the Torah.

washing of the hands. Just as the priest began his daily service in the Temple by washing his hands (Exodus 30. 20), even so does the Israelite when he is "preparing to meet his God" in prayer. Washing the hands is at once an elementary act of hygiene, as well as a rite of consecration. Personal cleanliness has rightly been held by Jewish pietists to be the door to spiritual purity. "'Cleanliness is next to godliness,' in quite a secular and unlevitical sense, is not a bad proverb, and in full accordance with the Rabbinic spirit" (Montefiore). George Eliot put her finger on one of the chief characteristics of Judaism when she appreciatively speaks of its "reverence for the human body, which lifts the need of the animal life into religion".

ASHER YOTZAR. *who hast formed man.* The blessing over physical cleanliness is followed by thanksgiving for physical health, and the marvellous laws by which physical health is preserved. Man is "fearfully and wonderfully made", and his higher life is dependent upon the regular discharge of bodily functions.

passages. lit. "orifices", or "apertures".

wondrous healer of all flesh. lit. "Who healest all flesh, and workest wondrously".

תְּפִלַּת שַׁחֲרִית

בָּרוּךְ אַתָּה יְיָ אֱלֹהֵינוּ מֶלֶךְ הָעוֹלָם · אֲשֶׁר קִדְּשָׁנוּ
בְּמִצְוֹתָיו וְצִוָּנוּ לַעֲסוֹק בְּדִבְרֵי תוֹרָה :

וְהַעֲרֶב-נָא יְיָ אֱלֹהֵינוּ אֶת דִּבְרֵי תוֹרָתְךָ בְּפִינוּ וּבְפִי
עַמְּךָ בֵּית יִשְׂרָאֵל · וְנִהְיֶה אֲנַחְנוּ וְצֶאֱצָאֵינוּ וְצֶאֱצָאֵי
עַמְּךָ בֵּית יִשְׂרָאֵל כֻּלָּנוּ יוֹדְעֵי שְׁמֶךָ וְלוֹמְדֵי תוֹרָתֶךָ ·
בָּרוּךְ אַתָּה יְיָ · הַמְלַמֵּד תּוֹרָה לְעַמּוֹ יִשְׂרָאֵל :

OCCUPY . . TORAH. The word Torah is usually rendered by
" Law ". This rendering is inadequate and misleading. It overlooks
the element of " teaching ", religious and moral " guidance ", indicated
by the literal meaning of the word *Torah*. Again, *Torah* denotes not
only the Five Books of Moses, but often the entire body of Jewish
religious teaching and practice—the never-failing stream of moral and
spiritual truth that has its fountain and origin in the Pentateuch.
It is the absolute conviction of the teachers of Judaism that habitual
reading and study of the Sacred Literature has a purifying influence.
Jewish learning is part of the Jewish religion ; and to the Rabbis,
study of the Torah constituted an act of Divine Worship. A certain
atoning efficacy was ascribed to such study.

VE-HAAREV. And now we come to the first petition in the Morning
Devotions. It is a petition not for daily bread or for success in worldly
affairs, but *for religious knowledge,* so that all may know God's Name,
and lovingly learn His Message to the children of men.

make pleasant. The study of the Torah is to be a pleasant duty,
and not a burden forced upon us. We must be *happy* in our Judaism ;
and we cannot be happy in our Judaism if we do not know it. Only by
study will our eyes be opened to its spiritual wonders, and shall we
be enabled to spread a knowledge of God's teachings and His dealings
with Israel to those near and dear to us. Popular books on Judaism

Blessed art thou, O Lord our God, King of the universe, who hast hallowed us by thy commandments, and commanded us to occupy ourselves with the words of the Torah.

Make pleasant, therefore, we beseech thee, O Lord our God, the words of thy Torah in our mouth and in the mouth of thy people, the house of Israel, so that we with our offspring and the offspring of thy people, the house of Israel, may all know thy Name and learn thy Torah. Blessed art thou, O Lord, who teachest the Torah to thy people Israel.

and Jewish History are now available in the vernacular. There is, therefore, no excuse for ignorance in regard to the fundamentals of our Faith, the nature of its man-redeeming ideals, or the story of Israel—the knowledge of all of these being essential to the *joyful* fulfilment of God's commandments.

the house of Israel. This is the usual term in the Prayer Book for *Israel* or *Israelite*. It stresses the *religious* consciousness of the Jew, as well as the fact that Religion is not merely a matter between God and the individual. The word *Jew* or *Jews* occurs only in a quotation from the Book of Esther, or in phrases concerning Purim.

may all know. The word *all* is emphatic. Knowledge of the Torah is not to be the exclusive prerogative of any caste or class. " And *all* thy children shall be taught of the Lord ", is the Divine promise (Isaiah 54. 13). Israel is thus the pioneer in what is called universal education. " The Jewish religion, because it was a literature-sustained religion, led to the first effort to provide elementary instruction for all the children of the community " (H. G. Wells). As a consequence, we do not find, until quite recent generations, any " lower classes " in Jewry. The poor, those who toiled all their days for barest subsistence, consecrated their hours of leisure at night to religious study. (Hermann Cohen).

know thy Name. *i.e.* God's nature—" merciful and gracious, slow to anger and abounding in lovingkindness and truth ", that all may imitate His ways of lovingkindness and truth ; Jeremiah 22. 16. " To know Thee is perfect righteousness ; yea, to know Thy power is the root of immortality " (Wisdom of Solomon 15. 3). The " Name " of God means in Scripture all that God has revealed concerning Himself to, and His demands from, the children of man.

בָּרוּךְ אַתָּה יְיָ אֱלֹהֵינוּ מֶלֶךְ הָעוֹלָם · אֲשֶׁר בָּחַר־
בָּנוּ מִכָּל־הָעַמִּים וְנָתַן־לָנוּ אֶת־תּוֹרָתוֹ · בָּרוּךְ אַתָּה יְיָ ·
נוֹתֵן הַתּוֹרָה :

יְבָרֶכְךָ יְיָ וְיִשְׁמְרֶךָ : יָאֵר יְיָ פָּנָיו אֵלֶיךָ וִיחֻנֶּךָּ : יִשָּׂא
יְיָ פָּנָיו אֵלֶיךָ וְיָשֵׂם לְךָ שָׁלוֹם :

מִשְׁנָה פֵּאָה פ׳א

אֵלּוּ דְבָרִים שֶׁאֵין לָהֶם שִׁעוּר · הַפֵּאָה וְהַבִּכּוּרִים

ASHER BOCHAR. *who hast chosen ... Torah.* These simple but sublime words are the formal Blessing recited by him who is "called" to the Reading of the Torah at a congregational Service. It stresses the Selection of Israel (Exodus 19. 5) and the great fact of Revelation. God is the Father of all mankind; but He has chosen Israel to be His in a special degree, not to privilege and rulership, but to be "a light unto the nations," to proclaim and testify to the spiritual values of life; see pp. 798–800.

Giver of the Torah. One would expect some concluding words like, "to Thy people Israel". But the Torah is not for Israel alone. It is for all mankind. As the Talmud says: "'These are the ordinances by which if a *man* do, he shall live by them' (Leviticus 18. 5)—not priest, not Levite, not Israelite, but *man*" (Jacob Emden).

Every *berochah* must be followed by some action referred to in its wording; otherwise, it is uttered "in vain" (לבטלה). Therefore, the Blessing over the Torah having been recited, the following readings are given for its fulfilment: (*a*) a selection from the Bible, (*b*) a Mishna, and (*c*) a comment thereon from the Talmud. Seeing that many loyal Jews are disabled by poverty or lack of talent for deep and continuous study of the Torah, these selections from the Sources of Judaism made it possible for everyone to do some "learning" every day.

(*a*) The first selection, that from the Bible, is the Priestly Blessing, Numbers 6. 24–26. Every child of Israel should daily recall the solemn fact that he is a member of the priest-people, and that he is to be a blessing to his fellow-men. For a full explanation, see the comments on the Order of the Blessing of the Priests; p. 836.

BENEDIC-   Blessed art thou, O Lord our God, King of the universe,
TION OVER
THE   who hast chosen us from all peoples and given us thy
TORAH
Torah. Blessed art thou, O Lord, Giver of the Torah.

Numbers   The Lord bless thee, and keep thee : the Lord make his
6. 24–26
face to shine upon thee, and be gracious unto thee : the
THE
PRIESTLY   Lord turn his face unto thee, and give thee peace.
BLESSING

Mishna, Peah i.

IMMEAS-   These are the commandments which have no fixed
URABLE
DUTIES   measure: the corners of the field, the first fruits, the offerings

The Bible passages chosen at this juncture differ in the various Rites.
Thus, instead of the Priestly Blessing, Rabbi Solomon Luria (1510–1573)
read three verses from the Pentateuch, three from Joshua (1. 7–9), and
the first three verses of Psalm 1. The three Pentateuchal verses which
he chose were :
  " Thou shalt not go up and down as a talebearer among thy
people ; neither shalt thou stand idly by the blood of thy neighbour
[*i.e.* when he is in mortal danger] ; I am the Lord.
  Thou shalt not hate thy brother in thine heart ; thou shalt
surely rebuke thy neighbour, and not suffer sin because of him.
  Thou shalt not take vengeance, nor bear any grudge against the
children of thy people, but thou shalt love thy neighbour as thyself :
I am the Lord " (Leviticus 19. 16–18).

(*b*) The selection from the Mishna is the opening paragraph of its
second tractate, Peah 1. 1. It calls attention to duties that cannot be
measured, and to duties that are of lasting worth both in this life and
in the Hereafter.

THESE ARE THE COMMANDMENTS. *no fixed measure. i.e.* by enactment of the Torah. Though in regard to some of these a minimum
was fixed by Tradition, the amount to be given was left to a man's
own generous impulse.
  corners of the field. In reaping the harvest, they were to be left for
the poor and stranger (Leviticus 23. 22). The Torah does not indicate
how much of the field should be left as " corner ". Tradition fixed the
minimum to be one-sixtieth of the field.
  first fruits. That were taken to the Temple and presented to the
priests (Deuteronomy 26. 1–11).
  offerings . . . three festivals. See Deuteronomy 16 16–17.

וְהָרָאָיוֹן וּגְמִילוּת חֲסָדִים וְתַלְמוּד תּוֹרָה: אֵלּוּ דְבָרִים
שֶׁאָדָם אוֹכֵל פֵּרוֹתֵיהֶם בָּעוֹלָם הַזֶּה וְהַקֶּרֶן קַיֶּמֶת לוֹ
לָעוֹלָם הַבָּא · וְאֵלּוּ הֵן · כִּבּוּד אָב וָאֵם וּגְמִילוּת חֲסָדִים
וְהַשְׁכָּמַת בֵּית הַמִּדְרָשׁ שַׁחֲרִית וְעַרְבִית וְהַכְנָסַת
אוֹרְחִים וּבִקּוּר חוֹלִים וְהַכְנָסַת כַּלָּה וּלְוָיַת הַמֵּת וְעִיּוּן
תְּפִלָּה וַהֲבָאַת שָׁלוֹם בֵּין אָדָם לַחֲבֵרוֹ · וְתַלְמוּד
תּוֹרָה כְּנֶגֶד כֻּלָּם:

practice of charity. The Hebrew term גמילות חסדים, lit. " bestowal
of lovingkindnesses ", is much wider than the word denoting " charity ",
tzedokoh. *Charity* can be shown only to the living and the poor, and
for charity, there *is* a maximum limit in rabbinic Law : a man should not
devote more than one-fifth of his income to almsgiving. Not so *lovingkindness* : it has no measure, and can be shown to all, even to the dead ;
and it can be shown by all, for he that has no money may possess
the noble impulse to kindly action and charitable thought. In
addition to the provision of food and raiment, it demands sym-
pathetic consideration for the feelings of the needy, patience with their
shortcomings, forbearance with their faults, as well as all manner of
tactful provision for the wants of those who are too sensitive to accept
charity. In a word, *Rachmonus*. " Anyone devoid of *Rachmonus* and
human fellow-feeling with sufferers, is not a descendant of Abraham "
(Talmud).

study of the Torah. Another unlimited duty. The pious Israelite
is a life-long learner. And such study of the Torah is vital to the continuance of Israel as a spiritual entity in the world. Both Judaism and
the Jew wither away wherever sacred study is not instilled in home,
school and synagogue.

(c) The third selection, from the Talmud, Sabbath 127a, gives a
list of ten good deeds that bear fruit here on earth and procure bliss
in the Future Life.

these are things . . . the fruits. Every act of filial piety, reverence
and goodwill makes the world a better place. And the man who
performs such an act, himself shares in the moral amelioration that
follows in the wake of noble, human conduct. The ethical virtues here
enumerated became engrained in the Jewish character, largely owing
to the prominence given them in this portion of the Daily Prayers.

brought on appearing before the Lord at the three festivals, the practice of charity and the study of the Torah. —These are the things, of which a man enjoys the fruits in this world, while the stock remains for him for the world to come : viz., honouring father and mother, deeds of lovingkindness, timely attendance at the house of study morning and evening, hospitality to wayfarers, visiting the sick, dowering the bride, attending the dead to the grave, devotion in prayer, and making peace between man and his fellow ; but the study of the Torah leadeth to them all.

stock . . . world to come. The reference is to the reward in the Hereafter ; but in the performance of these duties we experience the bliss of eternity even on earth. See Sayings of the Fathers IV, 22. On the meaning of World-to-come, see p. 255.

honouring father and mother. No excellence in other directions can atone for the lack of reverence towards parents ; see p. 244.

deeds of lovingkindness. See preceding page, on *practice of charity.* " The Jew has suffered so much hurt, he has endured so many injustices, experienced so completely the misery of life, that pity for the poor and the humiliated has become second nature to him. And in his agonized wanderings, he has seen at close range so many men of all races, and of all countries, different everywhere and everywhere alike, that he has understood, he has felt in the flesh of his flesh, that Man is one as God is One. Thus was formed a race which may have the same vices and the same virtues as other races, but which is without doubt the most *human* of all races " (Edmond Fleg).

timely attendance. It was the rule for many centuries, and is followed to this day by the pious, to attend the *beth hamidrash,* the " house of study ", morning and evening. Those engaged in daily labour and worldly occupations thus participated for a brief time in religious study before joining in *public* worship. The latter is greater than private worship, as the holiness of the synagogue and the union with fellow-worshippers intensify devotion. " Congregational prayer contributes to the awakening, intensification and vitalization of the religious feelings, and lifts the individual to a higher stage of devotion " (Heiler).

hospitality to wayfarers. Shelters and hostels for the stranger and " refugee ", have at all times been a necessity in Jewish communities.

dowering the bride. Befriending friendless girls and helping them to establish a home, is a sacred charity that does not to-day everywhere receive the attention it calls for. " He that doeth righteousness *at all times* " (Psalm 106. 3) and whose life is one continuous act of beneficence

אֱלֹהַי · נְשָׁמָה שֶׁנָּתַתָּ בִּי טְהוֹרָה הִיא · אַתָּה
בְרָאתָהּ אַתָּה יְצַרְתָּהּ אַתָּה נְפַחְתָּהּ בִּי · וְאַתָּה מְשַׁמְּרָהּ
בְּקִרְבִּי · וְאַתָּה עָתִיד לְטַלָה מִמֶּנִּי וּלְהַחֲזִירָהּ בִּי לֶעָתִיד
לָבֹא : כָּל־זְמַן שֶׁהַנְּשָׁמָה בְּקִרְבִּי מוֹדֶה אֲנִי לְפָנֶיךָ יְיָ
אֱלֹהַי וֵאלֹהֵי אֲבוֹתַי רִבּוֹן כָּל־הַמַּעֲשִׂים אֲדוֹן כָּל־
הַנְּשָׁמוֹת : בָּרוּךְ אַתָּה יְיָ · הַמַּחֲזִיר נְשָׁמוֹת לִפְגָרִים
מֵתִים :

בָּרוּךְ אַתָּה יְיָ אֱלֹהֵינוּ מֶלֶךְ הָעוֹלָם · אֲשֶׁר נָתַן
לַשֶּׂכְוִי בִינָה לְהַבְחִין בֵּין יוֹם וּבֵין לָיְלָה :
בָּרוּךְ אַתָּה יְיָ אֱלֹהֵינוּ מֶלֶךְ הָעוֹלָם · שֶׁלֹּא עָשַׂנִי נָכְרִי :

is, according to the Rabbis, the man who adopts and bestows parental care upon a female orphan till she is married.

attending the dead. The most disinterested of all deeds of loving-kindness. It is showing reverence to man's humanity as such. In larger communities, a *Chevra Kadisha* ("Holy Brotherhood") exists, whose members attend to the last rites in connection with the dying and the dead, and perform offices of condolence to the mourners.

devotion in prayer. The worshipper must purify his heart before he prays, concentrate his whole being on the service of God, and banish all other thoughts from his mind and heart. This is *kavanah*—a concept that is found in no other ancient language.

making peace between man and his fellow. Peace-making between parted friends, or in personal home-frictions, is a duty of far-reaching importance. Even greater is the prevention of strife and emnity by kind word or judicious counsel. A vital element in the fulfilment of this duty is to be charitable in judging our neighbour (Rashi).

leadeth to them all. Because knowledge of the will of God leads to the practice of the righteous acts enumerated above. It is the soul of them all.

ELOHOY NESHOMOH. *O my God, the soul.* This prayer is an expression of gratitude for the soul's awakening from sleep to new life. The realization of the Divine Source of his soul strengthens man to meet the tasks and temptations of daily life.

is pure. Because "Thou didst create it". Man is made in the Divine Image, and his soul is a spark of the Divine nature. All

PURITY AND IM-MORTAL-ITY OF THE SOUL

O my God, the soul which thou gavest me is pure ; thou didst create it, thou didst form it, thou didst breathe it into me. Thou preservest it within me, and thou wilt take it from me, but wilt restore unto me hereafter. So long as the soul is within me, I will give thanks unto thee, O Lord my God and God of my fathers, Sovereign of all works, Lord of all souls ! Blessed art thou, O Lord, who restorest souls unto the dead.

EARLY MORNING BLESSINGS

Blessed art thou, O Lord our God, King of the universe, who hast given to the mind understanding to distinguish between day and night.

Blessed art thou, O Lord our God, King of the universe, who hast not made me a heathen.

the more solemn is the injunction, " Even as the soul is pure when entering upon its earthly career, so let man return it pure to his Maker " (Midrash). Judaism rejects the dogma of Original Sin. There is no fatal necessity for man to sin : the commandments of God are a bulwark against all animalism and godlessness. Though sin and guilt and crime poison much of human life, the antidote to such poison has been made known to man, enabling him, through repentance, to regain his God-given purity.

restore it unto me. Here the doctrine of the immortality of the soul is affirmed. " The dust returneth to the earth as it was, but the spirit returneth to God Who gave it " (Ecclesiastes 12. 7).

INDIVIDUAL BLESSINGS. After thanking God for enabling us to rise with bodies refreshed by sleep, we thank Him for restoring us to full consciousness, evidenced by our clear discrimination between light and darkness.

mind. The Hebrew word used here, שכוי, occurs only in Job 38. 36. In the Talmud, that word is interpreted to mean " cock ". Some take it in that sense in this Blessing, and connect it with the fact that the service at the Temple began with the cleansing of the Altar at cock-crow. This Blessing would then praise God for the wonderful animal-instinct which acts as an unfailing herald of the morning, rousing us to His service and our daily duties.

After the reawakening of consciousness, comes the reawakening of self-consciousness as Jews, and as free men and women.

heathen. Heb. גוי. In Scripture this word means " nation," but in later Hebrew, " heathen ". In recent times, גוי has been changed in many editions of the Prayer Book to נכרי, lit. " a foreigner ".

In the Talmud, we find the Blessing worded in a positive form, " Blessed art thou, O Lord our God, King of the Universe, *who hast me an Israelite* ", שעשני ישראל העולם מלך אלהינו ד׳ אתה ברוך.

בָּרוּךְ אַתָּה יְיָ אֱלֹהֵינוּ מֶלֶךְ הָעוֹלָם · שֶׁלֹּא עָשַׂנִי עָבֶד :

Men say :—

בָּרוּךְ אַתָּה יְיָ אֱלֹהֵינוּ מֶלֶךְ הָעוֹלָם · שֶׁלֹּא עָשַׂנִי אִשָּׁה :

Women say :—

בָּרוּךְ אַתָּה יְיָ אֱלֹהֵינוּ מֶלֶךְ הָעוֹלָם · שֶׁעָשַׂנִי כִּרְצוֹנוֹ :

בָּרוּךְ אַתָּה יְיָ אֱלֹהֵינוּ מֶלֶךְ הָעוֹלָם · פּוֹקֵחַ עִוְרִים :

It is still so worded to-day in the Italian Rite, as well as in
many older editions of the Ashkenazi Prayer Books. Several high
rabbinic authorities of modern days, including Rabbi Elijah, the Gaon
of Vilna (1720—1797), pronounced in favour of the positive formulation.
But however expressed, grateful consciousness of the privilege of having
been born in the Faith of Israel is essential. He who would serve
humanity, must first of all to himself be true.

bondman. For over 1800 years this Benediction was spoken by a
people oppressed as none other, but endowed with *inner freedom* that
rendered it unconquerable in spirit. This ancient Benediction has a
very real meaning for contemporary Jewry. The Israelite in free
countries has good reason to thank God daily for living in lands where
his life, liberty and human personality are respected.

not made me a woman. There is no derogation of woman implied in
this Benediction ; just as little as, for example, the Blessing of the
Priests, thanking God for having chosen them to perform priestly
functions, implies any derogation of the lay Israelites. The meaning of
this Blessing is merely, " Blessed art thou, O Lord our God, King of the
universe, Who hast set upon me the obligations of a man ". There
can be no doubt as to this, because the author of this Benediction
concerning woman has himself told us his reason for formulating it.
It was, so that men thank God for the privilege which is theirs of performing *all* the precepts of the Torah, many of these precepts not
being incumbent upon women. For the same reason, we thank God
for not being heathens or bondmen, and can thus fulfil all the duties
of Israelites.

The Persians and Greeks had formulae of thanks similar to these three
Benedictions. Plato expressed his gratitude that he was a man and
not one of the lower animals, a man and not a woman, a Greek and not
a barbarian. Nevertheless, the difference between the attitude of the
Greek and that of the Israelite towards the alien, the bondman and
woman remained immeasurable. To the Greek, every foreigner was a
barbarian ; whereas the Israelite was bidden, " Love ye the stranger "

Blessed are thou, O Lord our God, King of the universe, who hast not made me a bondman.

Men say :—

Blessed art thou, O Lord our God, King of the universe, who hast not made me a woman.

Women say :—

Blessed art thou, O Lord our God, King of the universe who hast made me according to thy will.

Blessed art thou, O Lord our God, King of the universe who openest the eyes of the blind.

(Deuteronomy 10. 19). Unlike Israel, Greece did not accord human rights to the slave, and even in the eyes of Aristotle the slave was but an " animated tool ". Furthermore, Judaism did not and does not make the worth of human personality dependent on birth or social position, but on the spirit in which anyone performs the duties of his station in life—be those duties few and the station humble, or be those duties many and the station high. Solemnly does a Midrashic teacher declare : *I call heaven and earth to witness that, whether it be Jew or heathen, man or woman, free or bondman—only according to their acts does the Divine Spirit rest upon them.*

In view of the perennial misunderstandings to which the above three Blessings have given rise, the late Prof. Berliner, urged the re-introduction of the positive wording שעשני ישראל, " Who hast made me an Israelite," to replace the three Blessings concerning the heathen, bondman, and woman. He rightly maintained that " to be filled with gratitude to God for having allotted to me the distinction of participating in Israel's mission and destiny, is surely far more expressive than the present negative formula ".

who hast made me according to thy will. These words were introduced when, in the Middle Ages, many women began to recite the whole of the Morning Service. The true spirit of these words is well conveyed in the following homiletic expansion : " *Who hast made me a woman, to win hearts for Thee by motherly love or wifely devotion; and to lead souls to Thee, by daughter's care or sisterly tenderness and loyalty* " (Mendes).

The eleven Blessings that now follow are brief expressions of thanks to God for the miracle of man's daily resurrection after sleep. In their origin, each one of them accompanied the performance of an act subsequent to rising. At a later date their significance was idealized, and each Blessing was given a wider, in addition to its literal, meaning. The comments that follow, by the late H. P. Mendes, are in the manner of these idealizations.

openest the eyes of the blind. See Psalm 146. 8. " *May we walk*

בָּרוּךְ אַתָּה יְיָ אֱלֹהֵינוּ מֶלֶךְ הָעוֹלָם · מַלְבִּישׁ עֲרֻמִּים :

בָּרוּךְ אַתָּה יְיָ אֱלֹהֵינוּ מֶלֶךְ הָעוֹלָם · מַתִּיר אֲסוּרִים :

בָּרוּךְ אַתָּה יְיָ אֱלֹהֵינוּ מֶלֶךְ הָעוֹלָם · זוֹקֵף כְּפוּפִים :

בָּרוּךְ אַתָּה יְיָ אֱלֹהֵינוּ מֶלֶךְ הָעוֹלָם · רוֹקַע הָאָרֶץ עַל־
הַמָּיִם :

בָּרוּךְ אַתָּה יְיָ אֱלֹהֵינוּ מֶלֶךְ הָעוֹלָם · שֶׁעָשָׂה לִי כָּל־
צָרְכִּי :

בָּרוּךְ אַתָּה יְיָ אֱלֹהֵינוּ מֶלֶךְ הָעוֹלָם · אֲשֶׁר הֵכִין מִצְעֲדֵי־
גָבֶר :

בָּרוּךְ אַתָּה יְיָ אֱלֹהֵינוּ מֶלֶךְ הָעוֹלָם · אוֹזֵר יִשְׂרָאֵל
בִּגְבוּרָה :

בָּרוּךְ אַתָּה יְיָ אֱלֹהֵינוּ מֶלֶךְ הָעוֹלָם · עוֹטֵר יִשְׂרָאֵל
בְּתִפְאָרָה :

בָּרוּךְ אַתָּה יְיָ אֱלֹהֵינוּ מֶלֶךְ הָעוֹלָם · הַנּוֹתֵן לַיָּעֵף כֹּחַ :

בָּרוּךְ אַתָּה יְיָ אֱלֹהֵינוּ מֶלֶךְ הָעוֹלָם · הַמַּעֲבִיר שֵׁנָה
מֵעֵינָי וּתְנוּמָה מֵעַפְעַפָּי :

*open-eyed through life—never blind to our responsibilities and duties towards
those near and dear unto us ; and towards those not so near unto us, but
who are our fellowmen, made in the Divine image ".*

who settest free them that are bound. See Psalm 146. 7.

*" How many of us, alas, are prisoners of misfortune, passion, sin.
With the help of God, we may each of us open the doors of our prison-house.
We need but pray, ' Help me, O Father, to break all bonds that imprison*

Blessed art thou, O Lord our God, King of the universe, who clothest the naked.

Blessed art thou, O Lord our God, King of the universe, who settest free them that are bound.

Blessed art thou, O Lord our God, King of the universe, who raisest up them that are bowed down.

Blessed art thou, O Lord our God, King of the universe, who spreadest forth the earth above the waters.

Blessed art thou, O Lord our God, King of the universe, who providest my every want.

Blessed art thou, O Lord our God, King of the universe, who hast made firm the steps of man.

Blessed art thou, O Lord our God, King of the universe, who girdest Israel with might.

Blessed art thou, O Lord our God, King of the universe, who crownest Israel with glory.

Blessed art thou, O Lord our God, King of the universe, who givest strength to the weary.

Blessed art thou, O Lord our God, King of the universe, who removest sleep from mine eyes and slumber from mine eyelids.

---

the soul. *Help me to set my heart free from selfishness, hatred, jealousy, and thus enable me to reveal my better nature '.*"

raisest up . . . bowed down. See Psalm 145. 14. "*When bowed down in grief, anxiety, fear, give us courage to meet sorrows and trials of any kind.*"

providest my every want. "*If we enjoy prosperity, we thank Thee. If we are in want, we trust in Thee. And may we never harden our heart or shut our hand in the face of human want or suffering.*"

made firm the steps of man. Another form of the root of the Hebrew word for " made firm " is כון, which has the meaning of decision, intention, choice. In this light, the blessing is a reminder that God planted within the soul of man the power of choosing the way of his life, and that he go forward with conscious purpose towards the goal which God sets before him.

girdest Israel with might. God works through human agents; and each day of loving obedience towards God, loyalty to Israel and steadfastness in Right, augments the spiritual health and strength of Israel.

crownest Israel with glory. In similar manner, each noble act on our part increases the honour of our Faith and People. We cannot therefore be too often reminded that *every Israelite holds the honour of Israel in his hands.*

וִיהִי רָצוֹן מִלְפָנֶיךָ יְיָ אֱלֹהֵינוּ וֵאלֹהֵי אֲבוֹתֵינוּ ·
שֶׁתַּרְגִּילֵנוּ בְּתוֹרָתֶךָ וְדַבְּקֵנוּ בְּמִצְוֹתֶיךָ · וְאַל תְּבִיאֵנוּ לֹא
לִידֵי חֵטְא וְלֹא לִידֵי עֲבֵרָה וְעָוֹן וְלֹא לִידֵי נִסָּיוֹן וְלֹא
לִידֵי בִזָּיוֹן · וְאַל תַּשְׁלֶט־בָּנוּ יֵצֶר הָרָע · וְהַרְחִיקֵנוּ מֵאָדָם
רַע וּמֵחָבֵר רָע · וְדַבְּקֵנוּ בְּיֵצֶר הַטּוֹב וּבְמַעֲשִׂים טוֹבִים ·
וְכֹף אֶת יִצְרֵנוּ לְהִשְׁתַּעְבֶּד־לָךְ · וּתְנֵנוּ הַיּוֹם וּבְכָל־יוֹם
לְחֵן וּלְחֶסֶד וּלְרַחֲמִים בְּעֵינֶיךָ וּבְעֵינֵי כָל־רוֹאֵינוּ ·
וְתִגְמְלֵנוּ חֲסָדִים טוֹבִים : בָּרוּךְ אַתָּה יְיָ · גּוֹמֵל חֲסָדִים
טוֹבִים לְעַמּוֹ יִשְׂרָאֵל :

AND MAY IT BE THY WILL. A freer translation is :
" May it be Thy will, O Lord our God and God of our fathers, to
make us familiar with Thy Torah, so that we loyally perform Thy commandments. O lead us not into sin, deliberate wrong-doing, temptation,
or shame ; let not the impulse to evil rule over us : keep us far
from evil-minded men and worthless companions ; help us to cling
to the will to do good ; break our evil desires, and bend our will to
Thine. May we find this day, and every day, grace, favour and mercy in
Thine eyes, and in the eyes of our fellowmen ; and continue to bestow
Thy many kindnesses upon us ".

accustom us to walk in. lit. " accustom us in ". It is well to remember
the vital part played by *habit* in moral and religious education. Ninety-
nine hundredths of our normal activity—such as dressing, walking,
eating, and the routine of our daily avocations—are performed without
effort, because they are habits, and have become part of our very
selves. One of the primary aims in the training of the child and adoles-
cent is to turn as many moral and useful actions as we can into *habits*,
so that they become second nature. " There is no more miserable
human being than one in whom nothing is habitual but indecision "
(William James).

cleave. Because the performance of the precepts of Torah is to be
habitual, it is not on that account to become mechanical. It must
be transfused with the love of God.

sin. As a general term, *sin* embraces all acts or feelings that are
contrary to the laws of God and man. It thus includes both *crime*,
which is an assault on the personality of others ; and *vice*, which is an
assault on our own personality. Here it appears· in the narrower

THE TWO
NATURES
OF MAN :
PRAYER
FOR
DIVINE
HELP IN
DAILY
LIFE

And may it be thy will, O Lord our God and God of our fathers, to accustom us to walk in thy Torah, and to make us cleave to thy commandments. O lead us not into sin, or transgression, iniquity, temptation, or disgrace : let not the evil inclination have sway over us : keep us far from a bad man and a bad companion : make us cleave to the good inclination and to good works : subdue our inclination so that it may submit itself to thee : and let us obtain this day, and every day, grace, favour, and mercy in thine eyes, and in the eyes of all who behold us ; and bestow loving-kindnesses upon us. Blessed art thou, O Lord, who bestowest lovingkindnesses upon thy people Israel.

meaning of an involuntary lapse into wrong.

transgression. A conscious disregard of a moral or religious law.

iniquity. Deliberate persistence in such disregard of the Divine commandments.

temptation. Any lure to break a religious duty ; any enticement of the will to make an evil, instead of a good, choice. Temptation is always a test of a man's stamina ; and, if overcome, is a strengthening of his moral character.

disgrace. The word בזיון signifies any action that brings humiliation or contempt upon the doer.

let not the evil inclination have sway over us. " It is because man is half angel, half brute, that his inner life witnesses such a bitter warfare ", said Rabbi Moses of Coucy. Our better nature—*yetzer hatov*—is constantly opposed by an evil inclination—*yetzer hara*—the wilful impulse that tempts to passion, hatred, and selfish desire. Man's heart is thus a battle-field between his better self and the passions which play an essential part in human self-preservation, but must be controlled and used for life's nobler aims. If man yields ever so little to the promptings of the evil inclination, it soon has him in its power. " The cobweb grows into a cable, the passing stranger becomes the master of the house ", as the Rabbis expressed it. Victory over the lower passions is never easy, and often their strength is well-nigh overwhelming. Man is conscious of his weakness, and hence this daily prayer for Divine help in temptation. By such prayer, and by the grace of God flowing in upon him through the channels of heredity, of sacred teaching, and of religious observance, man can resist the evil inclination, and free himself from its sway. Instead of being the slave of his desires, he then becomes master of himself. Self-conquest, self-control, self-discipline, are the very basis of the religious life.

submit itself to thee. This thought is as profound as it is sublime. Even the evil desires—*e.g.* passion, selfishness, ambition—are an

יְהִי רָצוֹן מִלְּפָנֶיךָ יְיָ אֱלֹהַי וֵאלֹהֵי אֲבוֹתַי · שֶׁתַּצִּילֵנִי
הַיּוֹם וּבְכָל־יוֹם מֵעַזֵּי פָנִים וּמֵעַזּוּת פָּנִים · מֵאָדָם רַע
וּמֵחָבֵר רַע וּמִשָּׁכֵן רַע וּמִפֶּגַע רַע וּמִשָּׂטָן הַמַּשְׁחִית ·
מִדִּין קָשֶׁה וּמִבַּעַל דִּין קָשֶׁה · בֵּין שֶׁהוּא בֶן־בְּרִית וּבֵין
שֶׁאֵינוֹ בֶן־בְּרִית :

לְעוֹלָם יְהֵא אָדָם יְרֵא שָׁמַיִם בַּסֵּתֶר וּבַגָּלוּי · וּמוֹדֶה עַל־
הָאֱמֶת וְדוֹבֵר אֱמֶת בִּלְבָבוֹ וַיַּשְׁכֵּם וְיֹאמַר :

רִבּוֹן כָּל־הָעוֹלָמִים · לֹא עַל־צִדְקוֹתֵינוּ אֲנַחְנוּ מַפִּילִים
תַּחֲנוּנֵינוּ לְפָנֶיךָ כִּי עַל רַחֲמֶיךָ הָרַבִּים · מָה אֲנַחְנוּ מֶה
חַיֵּינוּ מֶה חַסְדֵּנוּ מַה־צִּדְקֵנוּ מַה־יְשׁוּעָתֵנוּ מַה־כֹּחֵנוּ מַה־

essential element of human nature, and are necessary to human life and progress. Without them—the Rabbis truly say—there would be neither building, marrying, nor trading. The moral task of man consists not in eradicating, but in *controlling*, these desires, and in using them to do God's work in the world. Man then harnesses his very passions to a Divine purpose.

This prayer, like all prayers which are not distinctly personal petitions, is in the plural. "He who fails to include his fellowman in his prayers is a sinner" (Talmud). "Many a one prays, but is not heard; because he remained heedless of the woe or needs of others, and thereby has transgressed the Divine command, *Thou shalt love thy neighbour as thyself*" (Sefer Chassidim).

MAY IT BE THY WILL. This is a prayer to be saved from moral hindrances in daily life. Its author is Rabbi Judah the Prince, who edited the Mishna towards the end of the second century. It is in the singular, because it is a personal petition. "As this is a private prayer, the worshipper may insert after it a supplication concerning any hindrance or difficulty of his own dealings with others" (Tur).

arrogant men. Hardened or shameless people who trample on the rights and feelings of others. Throughout the Scriptures there is a positive horror of human insolence. "Where impudence is abundant, there is absence of all human dignity", is a Midrashic saying.

arrogance. Lit. "boldness of face", impudence. After praying to be

PRAYER AGAINST MORAL HINDRANCE

May it be thy will, O Lord my God and God of my fathers, to deliver me this day, and every day, from arrogant men and from arrogance, from a bad man, from a bad companion and from a bad neighbour, and from any mishap or evil hindrance ; from a hard judgment, and from a hard opponent, be he a son of the covenant or be he not a son of the covenant.

At all times let a man revere God in private as in public, acknowledge the truth, and speak the truth in his heart ; and let him rise early and say :

FRAILTY OF MAN
Daniel 9. 18

Sovereign of all worlds ! Not because of our righteous acts do we lay our supplications before thee, but because of thine abundant mercies. What are we ? What is our life ? What is our piety ? What is our righteousness ? What

saved from arrogance in others, we pray to be saved from the same failing in ourselves.

evil hindrance. Or, " destructive hindrance "—malevolent suggestion and corrupting desires ; see p. 312.

hard judgment. Upon us ; a harsh decree, or baneful litigation.

hard opponent. One who is implacable in his demands.

a son of the covenant. An Israelite.

AT ALL TIMES. This was originally a rubric prefixed to the paragraphs following, and exhorts the worshipper to inward religiousness.

According to medieval authorities, the following prayers down to, " your captivity before your eyes, saith the Lord ", are an agonizing cry of a generation passing through the fires of persecution, at a time when Jewish *public* worship was forbidden. (Probably under the Persian ruler, Yazdegerd II, who, in the year 456 of the Christian Era, prohibited the observance of the Sabbath, and the public reading of the Shema). These prayers, being a substitute for the whole of the Morning Service, start with the exhortation to be God-fearing in secret ; give expression to gratitude to God that ours is the privilege of proclaiming the " Hear, O Israel " ; and end with a petition for the fulfilment of the Messianic prophecies of redemption and peace.

not because of our righteous acts. Man has no *claim* on the favour of God.

what are we ? . . . for all is vanity. This part of the prayer is taken from the Neilah Service on the Day of Atonement.

After, " for all is vanity ", the following beautiful addition is found in the Sephardi Rite, " save only the pure soul, which must hereafter render account in judgment before the throne of Thy glory ".

גְּבוּרָתֵנוּ · מַה־נֹּאמַר לְפָנֶיךָ יְיָ אֱלֹהֵינוּ וֵאלֹהֵי אֲבוֹתֵינוּ · הֲלֹא כָּל־הַגִּבּוֹרִים כְּאַיִן לְפָנֶיךָ וְאַנְשֵׁי הַשֵּׁם כְּלֹא הָיוּ וַחֲכָמִים כִּבְלִי מַדָּע וּנְבוֹנִים כִּבְלִי הַשְׂכֵּל · כִּי רֹב מַעֲשֵׂיהֶם תֹּהוּ וִימֵי חַיֵּיהֶם הֶבֶל לְפָנֶיךָ · וּמוֹתַר הָאָדָם מִן־הַבְּהֵמָה אָיִן כִּי הַכֹּל הָבֶל :

אֲבָל אֲנַחְנוּ עַמְּךָ בְּנֵי בְרִיתֶךָ · בְּנֵי אַבְרָהָם אֹהַבְךָ שֶׁנִּשְׁבַּעְתָּ לּוֹ בְּהַר הַמֹּרִיָּה · זֶרַע יִצְחָק יְחִידוֹ שֶׁנֶּעֱקַד עַל־גַּב הַמִּזְבֵּחַ · עֲדַת יַעֲקֹב בִּנְךָ בְכוֹרֶךָ שֶׁמֵּאַהֲבָתְךָ שֶׁאָהַבְתָּ אֹתוֹ וּמִשִּׂמְחָתְךָ שֶׁשָּׂמַחְתָּ־בּוֹ קָרָאתָ אֶת־שְׁמוֹ יִשְׂרָאֵל וִישֻׁרוּן :

לְפִיכָךְ אֲנַחְנוּ חַיָּבִים לְהוֹדוֹת לָךְ וּלְשַׁבֵּחַךְ וּלְפָאֶרְךָ וּלְבָרֶךְ וּלְקַדֵּשׁ וְלָתֶת־שֶׁבַח וְהוֹדָיָה לִשְׁמֶךָ : אַשְׁרֵינוּ מַה־טּוֹב חֶלְקֵנוּ וּמַה־נָּעִים גּוֹרָלֵנוּ זּמַה־יָּפָה יְרֻשָּׁתֵנוּ · אַשְׁרֵינוּ שֶׁאֲנַחְנוּ מַשְׁכִּימִים וּמַעֲרִיבִים עֶרֶב וָבֹקֶר וְאוֹמְרִים פַּעֲמַיִם בְּכָל־יוֹם ·

NEVERTHELESS WE ARE THY PEOPLE. Life is a frail and transitory thing, but it has been given a higher purpose and dignity through the revelation of God's Teaching to Israel, and the resulting dedication of an entire people to God's service.

thy covenant. The covenant at Sinai.

thy friend. See Isaiah 41. 8 ; II Chronicles 20. 7.

bound upon the altar. Ready to make the supreme sacrifice. The *Akedah,* the story of the binding of Isaac, taught the ideal of martyrdom in Israel ; see p. 256.

firstborn son. A title of affection ; Exodus 4. 22.

FRAILTY OF MAN our helpfulness ? What our strength ? What our might ? What shall we say before thee, O Lord our God and God of our fathers ? Are not all the mighty men as nought before thee, the men of renown as though they had not been, the wise as if without knowledge, and the men of understanding as if without discernment ? For most of their works are void, and the days of their lives are vanity before thee, and the pre-eminence of man over the beast is nought : for all is vanity.

PRE-EMINENCE AND MISSION OF ISRAEL Nevertheless we are thy people, the children of thy covenant, the children of Abraham, thy friend, to whom thou didst swear on Mount Moriah ; the seed of Isaac, his only son, who was bound upon the altar ; the congregation of Jacob, thy firstborn son, whose name thou didst call Israel and Jeshurun by reason of the love wherewith thou didst love him, and the joy wherewith thou didst rejoice in him.

It is therefore, our duty to thank, praise and glorify thee, to bless, to sanctify and to offer praise and thanksgiving unto thy Name. Happy are we ! how goodly is our portion, how pleasant our lot, and how beautiful our heritage ! Happy are we who, early and late, morning and evening, twice every day, declare :

Israel. The name bestowed upon Jacob, " for thou hast striven with God and with men, and hast prevailed " ; Genesis 32. 29. *Jeshurun.* " The Upright One "—a poetic term of endearment for Israel ; Deuteronomy 32. 15. These titles he achieved by his self-conquest, and by his firm determination to free himself from past failings, and to live the truly upright life.
    thou didst love him. See Isaiah 44. 2.

It is therefore. As children of such fathers, we are under the sacred obligation of following in their footsteps, and by our lives glorify God's Name.
    happy are we ! This prayer strikingly expresses Israel's blessedness in the extraordinary distinction of having been chosen to proclaim the Unity of God. Unlike other peoples, Israel deemed neither power nor enjoyment to be the aim and purpose of its national existence ; but yearned after Truth and the service of God and humanity. And

שְׁמַע יִשְׂרָאֵל יְהוָֹה אֱלֹהֵינוּ יְהוָֹה אֶחָד :

בָּרוּךְ שֵׁם כְּבוֹד מַלְכוּתוֹ לְעוֹלָם וָעֶד :

אַתָּה הוּא עַד שֶׁלֹּא נִבְרָא הָעוֹלָם · אַתָּה הוּא
מִשֶּׁנִּבְרָא הָעוֹלָם · אַתָּה הוּא בָּעוֹלָם הַזֶּה · וְאַתָּה הוּא
לְעוֹלָם הַבָּא · קַדֵּשׁ אֶת שִׁמְךָ עַל מַקְדִּישֵׁי שְׁמֶךָ וְקַדֵּשׁ
אֶת שִׁמְךָ בְּעוֹלָמֶךָ · וּבִישׁוּעָתְךָ תָּרוּם וְתַגְבִּהַּ קַרְנֵנוּ ·
בָּרוּךְ אַתָּה יְיָ · מְקַדֵּשׁ אֶת־שִׁמְךָ בָּרַבִּים :

אַתָּה הוּא יְיָ אֱלֹהֵינוּ בַּשָּׁמַיִם וּבָאָרֶץ וּבִשְׁמֵי הַשָּׁמַיִם
הָעֶלְיוֹנִים · אֱמֶת אַתָּה הוּא רִאשׁוֹן וְאַתָּה הוּא אַחֲרוֹן
וּמִבַּלְעָדֶיךָ אֵין אֱלֹהִים · קַבֵּץ קֹוֶיךָ מֵאַרְבַּע כַּנְפוֹת
הָאָרֶץ · יַכִּירוּ וְיֵדְעוּ כָּל־בָּאֵי עוֹלָם כִּי אַתָּה־הוּא
הָאֱלֹהִים לְבַדְּךָ לְכֹל מַמְלְכוֹת הָאָרֶץ · אַתָּה עָשִׂיתָ
אֶת־הַשָּׁמַיִם וְאֶת־הָאָרֶץ אֶת־הַיָּם וְאֵת כָּל־אֲשֶׁר בָּם ·

this has remained the yearning of the loyal portion in Jewry in all ages, even in our own day. " If God had appeared to our pious mothers and said to them, as He did to Solomon of old, ' Ask, what shall I give thee '—they would have answered, ' I ask for no riches nor honours to myself ; but O may it be Thy will, Lord of the Universe, that Thou give my children an understanding heart in Torah and Wisdom, so as to discern the eternal difference between good and evil ' " (Bialik.)

our heritage. Our destiny and mission in the world.

Hear, O Israel. The Jewish Declaration of Faith, see p. 116. As stated above, this section seems to date from a period of persecution ; and *Hear, O Israel* was inserted here because the open profession of Judaism by public or regular prayer was prohibited.

blessed be His Name. The acknowledgment of God's sovereignty and of the triumph of His Kingdom on earth ; see p. 113.

HEAR, O ISRAEL : THE LORD IS OUR GOD, THE LORD IS ONE.

Blessed be His Name, whose glorious kingdom is for ever and ever.

GOD'S DOMINION IN THE HEAVENS AND ALL ETERNITY

Thou wast the same ere the world was created ; thou hast been the same since the world hath been created ; thou art the same in this world, and thou wilt be the same in the world to come. Sanctify thy Name upon them that sanctify it, yea, sanctify thy Name throughout thy world ; and through thy saving power raise up and uphold our strength. Blessed art thou, O Lord, who sanctifiest thy Name before the whole world.

THE COMING OF HIS KINGDOM ON EARTH

Thou art the Lord our God in heaven and on earth, and in the highest heavens. Of a truth thou art the first and thou art the last, and beside thee there is no God. O gather them that hope in thee from the four corners of the earth. Let all the inhabitants of the world perceive and know that thou art God, thou alone, over all the kingdoms of the earth. Thou hast made the heavens and the earth, the sea and all that is therein ; and which among all the works of thy hands, whether among those above or among

THOU WAST THE SAME. This is taken from the Midrash, where it is a eulogy of God spoken by the heavenly hosts in antiphonal song with Israel. It emphasizes the absolute uniqueness and eternity of God in time and space, and is an extension of the declaration concerning God's Kingdom.

sanctify thy Name. Make manifest Thy holiness and righteousness by revealing before all the nations Thy saving power on behalf of Israel, the People who sanctify Thee.. When, as in the persecution that gave rise to this prayer, Israel suffers, such suffering is misunderstood by the heathen. Instead of seeing in it a means to purify and lead Israel back to God, they take it as a sign that He is not able to save His people ; in brief, that Might alone is right, and that there is no such thing as moral rule in the universe. Thus, the Name of God, the knowledge of His true Nature—that He is holy, righteous and omnipotent—is inseparably linked with the destinies of Israel. Therefore, Israel prays with the psalmist, " Not unto us, O Lord, not unto us, but unto thy Name give glory " (115. 1).

that sanctify it. May well mean in Hebrew, " that suffer martyrdom for it ".

before the whole world. lit. " amongst the many " : *i.e.* publicly.

וּמִי בְּכָל־מַעֲשֵׂה יָדֶיךָ בָּעֶלְיוֹנִים אוֹ בַתַּחְתּוֹנִים שֶׁיֹּאמַר

לְךָ מַה־תַּעֲשֶׂה: אָבִינוּ שֶׁבַּשָּׁמַיִם עֲשֵׂה עִמָּנוּ חֶסֶד

בַּעֲבוּר שִׁמְךָ הַגָּדוֹל שֶׁנִּקְרָא עָלֵינוּ · וְקַיֶּם־לָנוּ יְיָ אֱלֹהֵינוּ

מַה־שֶׁכָּתוּב · בָּעֵת הַהִיא אָבִיא אֶתְכֶם וּבָעֵת קַבְּצִי

אֶתְכֶם · כִּי־אֶתֵּן אֶתְכֶם לְשֵׁם וְלִתְהִלָּה בְּכֹל עַמֵּי הָאָרֶץ

בְּשׁוּבִי אֶת־שְׁבוּתֵיכֶם לְעֵינֵיכֶם אָמַר יְיָ:

Our Father who art in heaven. The phrase is never " *the* Father in Heaven ", which might merely express God's relation to the universe. The words " Who art in Heaven " have in them no suggestion of the remoteness of God, but merely distinguish between God and an earthly father. Moore points out that the phrase " Father in Heaven " is peculiar to Rabbinical sources and those Greek writings that are dependent on them, in distinction to the other literature produced in contemporary Palestine or Alexandria.

thy great Name which is called over us. See Deuteronomy 28. 10. God's Name is called over Israel; i.e. Israel belongs to God. He will protect His possession, and save Israel; Ezekiel 36. 22, 23.

at that time . . . saith the Lord. This is the concluding verse of the Book of Zephaniah. ZEPHANIAH is one of the so-called Minor Prophets. He flourished during the reign of Josiah, shortly before the first Destruction of the Jewish state. He was the prophet of world-judgment, but also of universal salvation. Perhaps his most striking utterance is in Chap. 3. 9, in which is implied that the peoples of the earth were now dimly groping after the true God, and only stammering His praise; but the time would come when they would adore Him with a full knowledge of Him, and, with one consent, form a universal chorus to chant His praise. In that day would Israel and Israel's Divine redemption be " a name and a praise among all the peoples of the earth ".

SACRIFICES

The Scriptural selections, Numbers 28, and Leviticus 11, as well as the chapter from Mishna Zebachim, deal with sacrifices. Study of the precepts concerning the daily sacrifices was deemed, when the Temple was no more, as meritorious as the actual offering. This interpretation found support in the words of Hosea 14. 3, " We will render the offering of our lips in place of bullocks ". These selections were also accounted as further material for a daily portion of Torah to be learned by each Israelite.

Only scholars can have a full understanding of these additional

THE
COMING
OF HIS
KINGDOM

Zephaniah
3. 20

those beneath, can say unto thee, What doest thou ? Our Father who art in heaven, deal kindly with us for the sake of thy great Name by which we are called ; and fulfil unto us, O Lord our God, that which is written, At that time will I bring you in, and at that time will I gather you ; for I will make you a name and a praise among all the peoples of the earth, when I bring back your captivity before your eyes, saith the Lord.

Rabbinical selections ; and, because of this, they have been printed without vowels in many editions of the Prayer Book. As for the ordinary worshipper to-day, it must be admitted that this portion of the Liturgy has little attraction for him. Such lack of interest is partly due to a mistaken view of sacrifice. The institution of sacrifice is as old as the human race, and is an elementary and universal fact in the history of Religion. This being so, it was in the highest interests of mankind that such universal method of worship be raised to a purely spiritual plane (Maimonides). This was done in the Mosaic legislation. Magic and incantation were banished from the sacrificial cult, and everything idolatrous or unholy was rigorously proscribed. And Jewish sacrificial worship was neither narrow nor exclusive. The Temple was conceived as a House of Prayer for all Nations. At the Dedication of the Temple, King Solomon prayed : " Moreover concerning the stranger that is not of Thy people Israel, when he shall come out of a far country . . . and pray toward this house ; hear Thou in heaven, and do according to all that the stranger calleth to Thee for " (I Kings 8. 41–43). Therefore, while there are resemblances between sacrifice in Israel and sacrifice among other peoples, the fundamental differences between them transform sacrifice as ordained in the Pentateuch into a vehicle of lofty religious communion and truth. The *burnt-offering* expressed the individual's homage to God and entire self-surrender to His will ; the *peace-offering*, gratitude to God for His bounties and mercies ; the *sin-offering*, sorrow at having erred from the way of God and the firm resolve to be reconciled with Him. *The congregational sacrifices*, furthermore, taught the vital lesson of the interdependence of all members of the congregation as a sacred Brotherhood. It is clear that such spiritual and ethical ideals remain for all time the kernel and basis of Religion.

Moderns do not always realize the genuine hold that the sacrificial service had upon the affections of the people in ancient Israel. The Central Sanctuary was the axis round which the national life revolved. The people *loved* the Temple, its pomp and ceremony, the music and song of the Levites and the ministrations of the priests, the High Priest as he stood and blessed' the prostrate worshippers amid profound silence on the Atonement Day. And the choicer spirits were no less ardent in their affection. Their passionate devotion found expression in words like those of the Psalmist (42. 2, 3 ; 43. 3, 4) :—

וַיְדַבֵּר יְהֹוָה אֶל־מֹשֶׁה לֵּאמֹר : צַו אֶת־בְּנֵי יִשְׂרָאֵל
וְאָמַרְתָּ אֲלֵהֶם אֶת־קָרְבָּנִי לַחְמִי לְאִשַּׁי רֵיחַ נִיחֹחִי
תִּשְׁמְרוּ לְהַקְרִיב לִי בְּמוֹעֲדוֹ : וְאָמַרְתָּ לָהֶם זֶה הָאִשֶּׁה
אֲשֶׁר תַּקְרִיבוּ לַיהֹוָה כְּבָשִׂים בְּנֵי־שָׁנָה תְמִימִם שְׁנַיִם
לַיּוֹם עֹלָה תָמִיד : אֶת־הַכֶּבֶשׂ אֶחָד תַּעֲשֶׂה בַבֹּקֶר וְאֵת
הַכֶּבֶשׂ הַשֵּׁנִי תַּעֲשֶׂה בֵּין הָעַרְבָּיִם : וַעֲשִׂירִית הָאֵיפָה
סֹלֶת לְמִנְחָה בְּלוּלָה בְּשֶׁמֶן כָּתִית רְבִיעַת הַהִין : עֹלַת
תָּמִיד הָעֲשֻׂיָה בְּהַר סִינַי לְרֵיחַ נִיחֹחַ אִשֶּׁה לַיהֹוָה :
וְנִסְכּוֹ רְבִיעִת הַהִין לַכֶּבֶשׂ הָאֶחָד בַּקֹּדֶשׁ הַסֵּךְ נֶסֶךְ
שֵׁכָר לַיהֹוָה : וְאֵת הַכֶּבֶשׂ הַשֵּׁנִי תַּעֲשֶׂה בֵּין הָעַרְבָּיִם
כְּמִנְחַת הַבֹּקֶר וּכְנִסְכּוֹ תַּעֲשֶׂה אִשֵּׁה רֵיחַ נִיחֹחַ לַיהֹוָה :

" As the hart panteth after the water brooks,
So panteth my soul after Thee, O God.
My soul thirsteth for God, for the living God ;
When shall I come and appear before God ?

" O send out Thy light and Thy truth : let them lead me ;
Let them bring me unto Thy holy hill,
And to Thy tabernacles.
Then will I go unto the altar of God,
Unto God, my exceeding joy ".

Religious ecstasy has rarely found nobler expression than in these lines of the Psalmist. That words like these reflected the sincere and earnest faith of pious men is beyond question. However, bad men thought of sacrifice merely as an effective means of placating God, just as a gift might serve to corrupt a judge. And when the Prophets of Israel saw sacrifice being held to excuse iniquity, heartlessness and impurity, they gave expression to their burning indignation in the impassioned language of vehement emotion. But it is only against the immoral conception of sacrifice, and not against sacrifice itself, that

SACRI-
FICES
*THE
DAILY
BURNT-
OFFERING*

Numbers xxviii. 1—8.

¹And the Lord spake unto Moses, saying, ²Command the children of Israel, and say unto them, My oblation, my food for my offerings made by fire, of a sweet savour unto me, shall ye observe to offer unto me in its due season. ³And thou shalt say unto them, This is the offering made by fire which ye shall offer unto the Lord ; he-lambs of the first year without blemish, two day by day, for a daily burnt offering. ⁴The one lamb shalt thou offer in the morning, and the other lamb shalt thou offer at even ; ⁵and the tenth part of an ephah of fine flour for a meal offering, mingled with the fourth part of an hin of beaten oil. ⁶It is a continual burnt offering, which was ordained in mount Sinai for a sweet savour, an offering made by fire unto the Lord. ⁷And the drink offering thereof shall be the fourth part of an hin for the one lamb : in the holy place shalt thou pour out a drink offering of strong drink unto the Lord. ⁸And the other lamb shalt thou offer at even : as the meal offering of the morning, and as the drink offering thereof, thou shalt offer it, an offering made by fire, of a sweet savour unto the Lord.

they waged merciless war. As for the later Teachers of Israel, they spiritualized the details of the sacrificial laws, gave them deep symbolical meaning, and drew from them ethical and religious inspiration. Thus, they held that the sacrificial ordinances proved that God was with the persecuted : cattle are chased by lions, goats by panthers, sheep by wolves ; but God commanded, " Not them that persecute, but them that are persecuted, offer ye up to Me ". After the Destruction of the Temple—Rabbi Johanan ben Zakkai taught—deeds of beneficence definitely took the place of the Sacrificial Service.

DAILY BURNT-OFFERING. The daily continual sacrifice was called *tamid*. Offered twice daily throughout the year, it was the centre of public worship in Temple times. And it is in the prayers in connection with the *tamid* that some have sought the beginnings of our historic Liturgy.

RABBI ISHMAEL SAYS. The centre and circumference of Jewish life is the Torah, God's inexhaustible revelation to Israel. But the real Torah is not merely the written Text of the Five Books of Moses ; the real Torah is the meaning enshrined in that Text, as expounded, interpreted, and unfolded in ever greater fullness by successive generations

וִיקרא א' , י'א

וְשָׁחַט אֹתוֹ עַל יֶרֶךְ הַמִּזְבֵּחַ צָפֹנָה לִפְנֵי יְהֹוָה
וְזָרְקוּ בְּנֵי אַהֲרֹן הַכֹּהֲנִים אֶת־דָּמוֹ עַל־הַמִּזְבֵּחַ סָבִיב :

On Sabbath the following is added:—

במדבר כ'ח , ט' י'

וּבְיוֹם הַשַּׁבָּת שְׁנֵי־כְבָשִׂים בְּנֵי־שָׁנָה תְּמִימִם וּשְׁנֵי
עֶשְׂרֹנִים סֹלֶת מִנְחָה בְּלוּלָה בַשֶּׁמֶן וְנִסְכּוֹ : עֹלַת שַׁבַּת
בְּשַׁבַּתּוֹ עַל־עֹלַת הַתָּמִיד וְנִסְכָּהּ :

On New Moon the following is added:—

במדבר כ'ח , י'א-ט'ו

וּבְרָאשֵׁי חָדְשֵׁיכֶם תַּקְרִיבוּ עֹלָה לַיהֹוָה פָּרִים בְּנֵי־בָקָר
שְׁנַיִם וְאַיִל אֶחָד כְּבָשִׂים בְּנֵי־שָׁנָה שִׁבְעָה תְּמִימִם :
וּשְׁלֹשָׁה עֶשְׂרֹנִים סֹלֶת מִנְחָה בְּלוּלָה בַשֶּׁמֶן לַפָּר הָאֶחָד
וּשְׁנֵי עֶשְׂרֹנִים סֹלֶת מִנְחָה בְּלוּלָה בַשֶּׁמֶן לָאַיִל הָאֶחָד :
וְעִשָּׂרֹן עִשָּׂרוֹן סֹלֶת מִנְחָה בְּלוּלָה בַשֶּׁמֶן לַכֶּבֶשׂ הָאֶחָד
עֹלָה רֵיחַ נִיחֹחַ אִשֶּׁה לַיהֹוָה : וְנִסְכֵּיהֶם חֲצִי הַהִין יִהְיֶה
לַפָּר וּשְׁלִישִׁת הַהִין לָאַיִל וּרְבִיעִת הַהִין לַכֶּבֶשׂ יָיִן זֹאת
עֹלַת חֹדֶשׁ בְּחָדְשׁוֹ לְחָדְשֵׁי הַשָּׁנָה : וּשְׂעִיר עִזִּים אֶחָד
לְחַטָּאת לַיהֹוָה עַל־עֹלַת הַתָּמִיד יֵעָשֶׂה וְנִסְכּוֹ :

of Sages and Teachers in Israel. This selection enumerates the principles
of exegesis by which the Rabbis made the *implicit* teaching of the Torah
explicit, and disclosed the Divine thought therein imparted. *Sifra* is the

SACRIFICES

Leviticus i. 11.

And he shall slay it on the side of the altar northward before the Lord : and Aaron's sons, the priests, shall sprinkle its blood upon the altar round about.

On Sabbath the following is added :—

Numbers xxviii. 9, 10.

FOR THE SABBATH DAY

⁹And on the sabbath day two he-lambs of the first year without blemish, and two tenth parts of an ephah of fine flour for a meal offering, mingled with oil, and the drink offering thereof : ¹⁰this is the burnt offering of every sabbath, beside the daily burnt offering, and the drink offering thereof.

On New Moon the following is added :—

Numbers xxviii. 11—15.

FOR THE NEW MOON

¹¹And in the beginnings of your months ye shall offer a burnt offering unto the Lord ; two young bullocks, and one ram, seven he-lambs of the first year without blemish ; ¹²and three tenth parts of an ephah of fine flour for a meal offering, mingled with oil, for each bullock ; and two tenth parts of fine flour for a meal offering, mingled with oil, for the one ram ; ¹³and a several tenth part of fine flour mingled with oil for a meal offering unto every lamb ; for a burnt offering of a sweet savour, an offering made by fire unto the Lord. ¹⁴And their drink offerings shall be half an hin of wine for a bullock, and the third part of an hin for the ram, and the fourth part of an hin for a lamb : this is the burnt offering of every month throughout the months of the year. ¹⁵And one he goat for a sin offering unto the Lord ; it shall be offered beside the daily burnt offering, and the drink offering thereof.

oldest commentary on Leviticus. Its author, Rabbi Ishmael, was of High Priestly descent, a contemporary of Rabbi Akiba, and helped to consolidate Judaism in the period after the destruction of the Second Temple. He died a martyr in the last War of Jewish Independence in the year 135. A generation ago, a renowned scholar, Rector Schwarz of Vienna, demonstrated the profundity and originality of R. Ishmael's logical system.

משנה זבחים פ״ה

א אֵיזֶהוּ מְקוֹמָן שֶׁל־זְבָחִים קָדְשֵׁי קָדָשִׁים שְׁחִיטָתָן בַּצָּפוֹן פָּר וְשָׂעִיר שֶׁל־יוֹם הַכִּפּוּרִים שְׁחִיטָתָן בַּצָּפוֹן וְקִבּוּל דָּמָן בִּכְלִי שָׁרֵת בַּצָּפוֹן וְדָמָן טָעוּן הַזָּיָה עַל־בֵּין הַבַּדִּים וְעַל הַפָּרֹכֶת וְעַל־מִזְבַּח הַזָּהָב מַתָּנָה אַחַת מֵהֶן מְעַכֶּבֶת שְׁיָרֵי הַדָּם הָיָה שׁוֹפֵךְ עַל יְסוֹד מַעֲרָבִי שֶׁלַּמִּזְבֵּחַ הַחִיצוֹן אִם־לֹא נָתַן לֹא עִכֵּב:

ב פָּרִים הַנִּשְׂרָפִים וּשְׂעִירִים הַנִּשְׂרָפִים שְׁחִיטָתָן בַּצָּפוֹן וְקִבּוּל דָּמָן בִּכְלִי שָׁרֵת בַּצָּפוֹן וְדָמָן טָעוּן הַזָּיָה עַל־הַפָּרֹכֶת וְעַל־מִזְבַּח הַזָּהָב מַתָּנָה אַחַת מֵהֶן מְעַכֶּבֶת שְׁיָרֵי הַדָּם הָיָה שׁוֹפֵךְ עַל יְסוֹד מַעֲרָבִי שֶׁלַּמִּזְבֵּחַ הַחִיצוֹן אִם־לֹא נָתַן לֹא עִכֵּב אֵלּוּ וָאֵלּוּ נִשְׂרָפִין בְּבֵית הַדֶּשֶׁן:

ג חַטֹּאת הַצִּבּוּר וְהַיָּחִיד אֵלּוּ הֵן חַטֹּאת הַצִּבּוּר שְׂעִירֵי רָאשֵׁי חֳדָשִׁים וְשֶׁל־מוֹעֲדוֹת שְׁחִיטָתָן בַּצָּפוֹן וְקִבּוּל דָּמָן בִּכְלִי שָׁרֵת בַּצָּפוֹן וְדָמָן טָעוּן אַרְבַּע מַתָּנוֹת עַל אַרְבַּע קְרָנוֹת: כֵּיצַד · עָלָה בַכֶּבֶשׁ וּפָנָה לַסּוֹבֵב וּבָא־לוֹ לְקֶרֶן דְּרוֹמִית מִזְרָחִית · מִזְרָחִית צְפוֹנִית · צְפוֹנִית מַעֲרָבִית · מַעֲרָבִית דְּרוֹמִית · שְׁיָרֵי הַדָּם הָיָה שׁוֹפֵךְ עַל יְסוֹד דְּרוֹמִי · וְנֶאֱכָלִין לִפְנִים מִן־הַקְּלָעִים לְזִכְרֵי כְהֻנָּה בְּכָל־מַאֲכָל לְיוֹם וָלַיְלָה עַד־חֲצוֹת:

ד הָעוֹלָה קֹדֶשׁ קָדָשִׁים שְׁחִיטָתָהּ בַּצָּפוֹן וְקִבּוּל דָּמָהּ בִּכְלִי שָׁרֵת בַּצָּפוֹן וְדָמָהּ טָעוּן שְׁתֵּי מַתָּנוֹת שֶׁהֵן אַרְבַּע וּטְעוּנָה הַפְשֵׁט וְנִתּוּחַ וְכָלִיל לָאִשִּׁים:

Mishna, Zebachim v.

RABBINIC
LESSON ON
PLACES
OF
VARIOUS
SACRI-
FICES

1. Which were the places of sacrifice in the Temple ? The most holy offerings were slaughtered on the north side of the altar, as were also the bull and the he-goat for the Day of Atonement. Their blood was there received in a vessel of service to be sprinkled between the staves of the Ark before the veil of the Holy of Holies and upon the golden altar. The omission of a sprinkling invalidated the atonement ceremonial. The priest poured out the remaining blood on the western base of the outer altar, but if he omitted to do so the atonement ceremony was not invalidated.

2. The bulls and the he-goats which were to be entirely burnt were slaughtered on the north side of the altar, and their blood was there received in a vessel of service to be sprinkled before the veil and upon the golden altar. The omission of a sprinkling invalidated the atonement ceremonial. The priest poured out the remaining blood at the western base of the outer altar ; but if he omitted to do so the atonement ceremony was not invalidated. These as well as the preceding offerings were burnt in the repository of ashes.

3. As to the sin-offerings of the whole congregation and of an individual, the he-goats offered on the New Moon and on festivals are the sin-offerings of the whole congregation. These were slaughtered on the north side of the altar, and their blood was there received in a ritual vessel. It was requisite to make four sprinklings of that blood, one upon each of the four corners of the altar. How was this done ? The priest went up the ascent to the altar and went around its ledge successively to its southeast, northeast, northwest and southwest corners. He poured out the remaining blood at the south side of the base of the outer altar. These sacrifices, prepared for food after any manner, were eaten within the hangings of the court only by the males of the priesthood during that day and evening until midnight.

4. The burnt-offering was classed among the most holy of the offerings. It was slain, on the north side of the altar, and its blood was there received in a ritual vessel. It was requisite to make two doubled sprinklings of that blood so as to constitute four. That offering had to be flayed and dismembered and consumed by fire.

5. As to the peace-offerings of the whole congregation and the trespass-offerings, the following are the trespass-offerings : for robbery, for the profane appropriation of sanctified things, for violating a betrothed handmaid, that which was brought by the

ה זִבְחֵי שַׁלְמֵי צִבּוּר וַאֲשָׁמוֹת׳ אֵלּוּ הֵן אֲשָׁמוֹת אָשָׁם גְּזֵלוֹת
אָשָׁם מְעִילוֹת אָשָׁם שִׁפְחָה חֲרוּפָה אֲשַׁם נָזִיר אֲשַׁם מְצוֹרָע
אָשָׁם תָּלוּי׳ שְׁחִיטָתָן בַּצָּפוֹן וְקִבּוּל דָּמָן בִּכְלֵי שָׁרֵת בַּצָּפוֹן
וְדָמָן טָעוּן שְׁתֵּי מַתָּנוֹת שֶׁהֵן אַרְבַּע׳ וְנֶאֱכָלִין לִפְנִים מִן
הַקְּלָעִים לְזִכְרֵי כְהֻנָּה בְּכָל־מַאֲכָל לְיוֹם וָלַיְלָה עַד חֲצוֹת :

ו הַתּוֹדָה וְאֵיל נָזִיר קָדָשִׁים קַלִּים שְׁחִיטָתָן בְּכָל־מָקוֹם
בָּעֲזָרָה וְדָמָן טָעוּן שְׁתֵּי מַתָּנוֹת שֶׁהֵן אַרְבַּע׳ וְנֶאֱכָלִין בְּכָל
הָעִיר לְכָל אָדָם בְּכָל־מַאֲכָל לְיוֹם וָלַיְלָה. עַד חֲצוֹת : הַמּוּרָם
מֵהֶם כַּיּוֹצֵא בָהֶם אֶלָּא שֶׁהַמּוּרָם נֶאֱכָל לַכֹּהֲנִים לִנְשֵׁיהֶם
וְלִבְנֵיהֶם וּלְעַבְדֵיהֶם :

ז שְׁלָמִים קָדָשִׁים קַלִּים שְׁחִיטָתָן בְּכָל־מָקוֹם בָּעֲזָרָה וְדָמָן
טָעוּן שְׁתֵּי מַתָּנוֹת שֶׁהֵן אַרְבַּע וְנֶאֱכָלִין בְּכָל־הָעִיר לְכָל־אָדָם
בְּכָל־מַאֲכָל לִשְׁנֵי יָמִים וְלַיְלָה אֶחָד : הַמּוּרָם מֵהֶם כַּיּוֹצֵא
בָהֶם אֶלָּא שֶׁהַמּוּרָם נֶאֱכָל לַכֹּהֲנִים לִנְשֵׁיהֶם וְלִבְנֵיהֶם
וּלְעַבְדֵיהֶם :

ח הַבְּכוֹר וְהַמַּעֲשֵׂר וְהַפֶּסַח קָדָשִׁים קַלִּים שְׁחִיטָתָן בְּכָל־
מָקוֹם בָּעֲזָרָה וְדָמָן טָעוּן מַתָּנָה אֶחָת׳ וּבִלְבַד שֶׁיִּתֵּן כְּנֶגֶד
הַיְסוֹד : שִׁנָּה בַּאֲכִילָתָן הַבְּכוֹר נֶאֱכָל לַכֹּהֲנִים וְהַמַּעֲשֵׂר לְכָל־
אָדָם וְנֶאֱכָלִין בְּכָל־הָעִיר בְּכָל־מַאֲכָל לִשְׁנֵי יָמִים וְלַיְלָה אֶחָד׳
הַפֶּסַח אֵינוֹ נֶאֱכָל אֶלָּא בַלַּיְלָה וְאֵינוֹ נֶאֱכָל אֶלָּא עַד־חֲצוֹת
וְאֵינוֹ נֶאֱכָל אֶלָּא לִמְנוּיָו וְאֵינוֹ נֶאֱכָל אֶלָּא צָלִי :

nazirite who had become defiled by a dead body, by the leper at his cleansing, and that brought for the sin-offering about which there was a doubt whether it should be atoned for by a sin-offering. All these were slaughtered on the north side of the altar, and the blood was received there in a ritual vessel. It was requisite to make two doubled sprinklings of that blood so as to constitute four. These sacrifices, prepared for food after any manner, were eaten only within the hangings of the court by the males of the priesthood during that day and evening until midnight.

6. The thanksgiving-offering of individuals and the ram offered by the nazirite at the close of his vow, were of a minor degree of holiness. These might be killed in any part of the court of the Temple. It was requisite to make two doubled sprinklings of their blood so as to constitute four. They might be eaten, prepared for food after any manner, in any part of the city by any person during the whole of that day and evening until midnight. The same rules were observed with the portions of them appertaining to the priests, except that these might be eaten only by the priests, their wives, their children and their servants.

7. The peace-offerings also were holy in a minor degree of holiness. These might be killed in any part of the court of the Temple, and it was requisite to make two doubled sprinklings of their blood so as to constitute four. They might be eaten, prepared for food after any manner, in any part of the city by any person during two days and the intervening night. Their portions appertaining to the priests were subject to the same rules, except that they were to be eaten only by the priests, their wives, their children and their servants.

8. The first-born of beasts, the tithe of cattle, and the paschal lamb were also holy in a minor degree. These might be killed in any part of the court of the Temple. Only one sprinkling of their blood was requisite, but that had to be done towards the base of the altar. In the eating of them, however, the following distinction was made : the first-born animal was eaten by the priests only, but the tithe could be eaten by anyone. Both the first-born animal and the tithe might be eaten prepared for food in any manner, in any part of the city during two days and the intervening night, whereas the paschal lamb had to be eaten on that night only and not later than midnight. Nor might it be eaten except by those of a previously constituted group, nor prepared in any way other than roasted.

בריתא דרבי ישמעאל

רַבִּי יִשְׁמָעֵאל אוֹמֵר · בִּשְׁלֹשׁ עֶשְׂרֵה מִדּוֹת הַתּוֹרָה נִדְרֶשֶׁת:

1 מִקַּל וָחֹמֶר : 2 וּמִגְּזֵרָה שָׁוָה :

3 מִבִּנְיַן אָב מִכָּתוּב אֶחָד וּמִבִּנְיַן אָב מִשְּׁנֵי כְתוּבִים :

4 מִכְּלָל וּפְרָט : 5 וּמִפְּרָט וּכְלָל :

6 כְּלָל וּפְרָט וּכְלָל אִי אַתָּה דָן אֶלָּא כְּעֵין הַפְּרָט :

7 מִכְּלָל שֶׁהוּא צָרִיךְ לִפְרָט וּמִפְּרָט שֶׁהוּא צָרִיךְ לִכְלָל :

8 כָּל־דָּבָר שֶׁהָיָה בִּכְלָל וְיָצָא מִן־הַכְּלָל לְלַמֵּד לֹא לְלַמֵּד
עַל־עַצְמוֹ יָצָא אֶלָּא לְלַמֵּד עַל־הַכְּלָל כֻּלּוֹ יָצָא :

9 כָּל־דָּבָר שֶׁהָיָה בִּכְלָל וְיָצָא לִטְעוֹן טֹעַן אֶחָד שֶׁהוּא
כְעִנְיָנוֹ יָצָא לְהָקֵל וְלֹא לְהַחֲמִיר :

10 כָּל־דָּבָר שֶׁהָיָה בִּכְלָל וְיָצָא לִטְעוֹן טֹעַן אַחֵר שֶׁלֹּא כְעִנְיָנוֹ
יָצָא לְהָקֵל וּלְהַחֲמִיר :

11 כָּל־דָּבָר שֶׁהָיָה בִּכְלָל וְיָצָא לִדּוֹן בְּדָבָר הֶחָדָשׁ אִי אַתָּה
יָכוֹל לְהַחֲזִירוֹ לִכְלָלוֹ עַד שֶׁיַּחֲזִירֶנּוּ הַכָּתוּב לִכְלָלוֹ
בְּפֵרוּשׁ :

12 דָּבָר הַלָּמֵד מֵעִנְיָנוֹ · וְדָבָר הַלָּמֵד מִסּוֹפוֹ :

13 וְכֵן שְׁנֵי כְתוּבִים הַמַּכְחִישִׁים זֶה אֶת־זֶה עַד שֶׁיָּבוֹא
הַכָּתוּב הַשְּׁלִישִׁי וְיַכְרִיעַ בֵּינֵיהֶם :

יְהִי רָצוֹן לְפָנֶיךָ יְיָ אֱלֹהֵינוּ וֵאלֹהֵי אֲבוֹתֵינוּ שֶׁיִּבָּנֶה בֵּית
הַמִּקְדָּשׁ בִּמְהֵרָה בְיָמֵינוּ וְתֵן חֶלְקֵנוּ בְּתוֹרָתֶךָ : וְשָׁם נַעֲבָדְךָ
בְּיִרְאָה כִּימֵי עוֹלָם וּכְשָׁנִים קַדְמֹנִיּוֹת :

In some Congregations קַדִּישׁ דְּרַבָּנָן, *p. 236 is recited here.*

Sifra i.

Rabbi Ishmael says the Torah may be expounded by these thirteen principles of logic :

1. Inference from minor to major, or from major to minor.
2. Inference from similarity of phrases in texts.
3. A comprehensive principle derived from one text, or from two related texts.
4. A general proposition followed by a specifying particular.
5. A particular term followed by a general proposition.
6. A general law limited by a specific application, and then treated again in general terms, must be interpreted according to the tenor of the specific limitation.
7. A general proposition requiring a particular or specific term to explain it, and conversely, a particular term requiring a general one to complement it.
8. When a subject included in a general proposition is afterwards particularly excepted to give information concerning it, the exception is made not for that one instance alone, but to apply to the general proposition as a whole.
9. Whenever anything is first included in a general proposition and is then excepted to prove another similar proposition, this specifying alleviates and does not aggravate the law's restriction.
10. But when anything is first included in a general proposition and is then excepted to state a case that is not a similar proposition, such specifying alleviates in some respects, and in others aggravates, the law's restriction.
11. Anything included in a general proposition and afterwards excepted to determine a new matter, can not be applied to the general proposition unless this be expressly done in the text.
12. An interpretation deduced from the text or from subsequent terms of the text.
13. In like manner when two texts contradict each other, the meaning can be determined only when a third text is found which harmonises them.

May it be thy will, O Lord our God and God of our fathers, that the temple be speedily rebuilt in our days, and grant that our portion be in thy Torah. And there we will serve thee with awe as in the days of old, and as in ancient years.

In some Congregations, the Kaddish on p. 237 is recited here.

Before putting on the טַלִּית, *say the following :—*

חִנְנִי מִתְעַטֵּף בְּטַלִּית שֶׁל־צִיצִת כְּדֵי לְקַיֵּם מִצְוַת בּוֹרְאִי ·
כַּכָּתוּב בַּתּוֹרָה · וְעָשׂוּ לָהֶם צִיצִת עַל־כַּנְפֵי בִגְדֵיהֶם לְדֹרֹתָם ·
וּכְשֵׁם שֶׁאֲנִי מִתְכַּסֶּה בְּטַלִּית בָּעוֹלָם הַזֶּה כֵּן תִּזְכֶּה נִשְׁמָתִי
לְהִתְלַבֵּשׁ בְּטַלִּית נָאָה לְעוֹלָם הַבָּא בְּגַן עֵדֶן · אָמֵן :

On putting on the טַלִּית, *say :—*

בָּרוּךְ אַתָּה יְיָ אֱלֹהֵינוּ מֶלֶךְ הָעוֹלָם · אֲשֶׁר
קִדְּשָׁנוּ בְּמִצְוֹתָיו וְצִוָּנוּ לְהִתְעַטֵּף בַּצִּיצִת :

מַה־יָּקָר חַסְדְּךָ אֱלֹהִים וּבְנֵי אָדָם בְּצֵל כְּנָפֶיךָ יֶחֱסָיוּן :
יִרְוְיֻן מִדֶּשֶׁן בֵּיתֶךָ וְנַחַל עֲדָנֶיךָ תַשְׁקֵם :
כִּי עִמְּךָ מְקוֹר חַיִּים בְּאוֹרְךָ נִרְאֶה־אוֹר :
מְשֹׁךְ חַסְדְּךָ לְיֹדְעֶיךָ וְצִדְקָתְךָ לְיִשְׁרֵי־לֵב :

May it be thy will . . . years. These words are taken from Sayings
of the Fathers, v, 23. "After the recitation of the Temple service, the
prayer for its restoration is a natural sequence" (I. Abrahams).
"Even those laws which have been enacted by human authority
remain in force till they are repealed in a regular and legal manner.
Whether any of these laws of the Torah will ever be abrogated we do
not know, but we are sure that, in case of such abrogation taking place,
it will be done by a revelation as convincing as that on Mount Sinai.
On the other hand, the revival of the Sacrificial Service must, likewise,
be sanctioned by the divine voice of a Prophet" (M. Friedländer).

TALLITH

Like the mezuzah and the tefillin, the fringes are an outward
expression of an inward thought—the duty of holding the Torah and its
commandments in constant remembrance, so that we keep far from the
allurements of sin, and be not entangled in the net of temptation.
The aim of the precept is thus the furtherance of holiness in the life of
the individual and the nation (Numbers 15. 39, 40) ; see further p. 124.
In later generations, the law of the fringes was carried out by means
of the *arba kanfos* and the *tallith*. The *arba kanfos* (lit. "four corners") or
tallith koton (טלית קטון), is an under-garment consisting of a rectangular

THE
TALLITH

MEDITA-
TION
Numbers
15. 38

Before putting on the Tallith, say the following :—

I am here enwrapping myself in this fringed robe, in fulfilment of the command of my Creator, as it is written in the Torah, They shall make them a fringe upon the corners of their garments throughout their generations. And even as I cover myself with the Tallith in this world, so may my soul deserve to be clothed with a beauteous spiritual robe in the world to come, in the garden of Eden. Amen.

On putting on the Tallith, say :—

BLESSING

Blessed art thou, O Lord our God, King of the universe, who hast hallowed us by thy commandments, and hast commanded us to enwrap ourselves in the fringed garment.

Psalm xxxvi. 8—11.

THE IN-
EXHAUST-
IBLE
LOVING-
KINDNESS
OF GOD

[8]How precious is thy lovingkindness, O God ! And the children of men take refuge under the shadow of thy wings. [9]They sate themselves with the abundance of thy house ; and thou givest them to drink of the stream of thy delights. [10]For with thee is the fountain of life : in thy light do we see light. [11]O continue thy lovingkindness unto them that know thee, and thy righteousness to the upright in heart.

piece of cloth, about three feet long and one foot wide, with an aperture in the centre sufficient to let it pass over the head. To its four corners are fastened the tzitzis. The benediction over the *arba kanfos* concludes with the words על מצות ציצת, " concerning the commandment of tzitzis " ; while that over the *tallith* ends with the words להתעטף בציצת, " to enwrap ourselves in the fringed garment " (or, a garment provided with tzitzis).

The *tallith* is a woollen or silken mantle worn by men over the garments during worship by day (except on the eve of Atonement when it is put on some minutes before night-fall). The Reader wears the tallith during every service, except on the morning of the Fast of Av. In some congregations, mourners wear it when they recite the Kaddish.

" By the thirteenth century it had become unusual for Jews to mark their ordinary outward garments by wearing fringes. But the fringed garment had become too deeply associated with Israel's religious life to be discarded entirely at the dictates of fashion in dress. Pope Innocent III in 1215 compelled the Jew to wear a degrading badge ; the fringed garment became all the more an honourable uniform marking at once God's love for Israel and Israel's determination to ' remember to do all God's commandments and be holy unto his God ' " (Abrahams).

Meditation before the תְּפִלִּין.

הִנְנִי מְכַוֵּן בְּהַנָּחַת תְּפִלִּין לְקַיֵּם מִצְוַת בּוֹרְאִי שֶׁצִּוָּנוּ לְהָנִיחַ
תְּפִלִּין · כַּכָּתוּב בַּתּוֹרָה · וּקְשַׁרְתָּם לְאוֹת עַל יָדֶךָ וְהָיוּ לְטֹטָפֹת
בֵּין עֵינֶיךָ · וְהֵם אַרְבַּע פָּרָשׁוֹת אֵלּוּ · שְׁמַע · וְהָיָה אִם שָׁמֹעַ ·
קַדֶּשׁ · וְהָיָה כִּי יְבִאֲךָ · שֶׁיֵּשׁ בָּהֶם יִחוּדוֹ וְאַחְדוּתוֹ יִתְבָּרַךְ
שְׁמוֹ · וְשֶׁנִּזְכֹּר נִסִּים וְנִפְלָאֹת שֶׁעָשָׂה עִמָּנוּ בְּהוֹצִיאוֹ אֹתָנוּ
מִמִּצְרָיִם · וַאֲשֶׁר לוֹ הַכֹּחַ וְהַמֶּמְשָׁלָה בָּעֶלְיוֹנִים וּבַתַּחְתּוֹנִים
לַעֲשׂוֹת בָּהֶם כִּרְצוֹנוֹ · וְצִוָּנוּ לְהָנִיחַ עַל הַיָּד לְזִכְרוֹן זְרֹעוֹ
הַנְּטוּיָה · וְשֶׁהִיא נֶגֶד הַלֵּב לְשַׁעְבֵּד בָּזֶה תַּאֲוַת וּמַחְשְׁבוֹת לִבֵּנוּ
לַעֲבֹדָתוֹ יִתְבָּרַךְ שְׁמוֹ · וְעַל הָרֹאשׁ נֶגֶד הַמֹּחַ שֶׁהַנְּשָׁמָה
שֶׁבְּמֹחִי עִם חוּשַׁי וְכֹחוֹתַי כֻּלָּם יִהְיוּ מְשֻׁעְבָּדִים לַעֲבֹדָתוֹ
יִתְבָּרַךְ שְׁמוֹ · וּמִשֶּׁפַע מִצְוַת תְּפִלִּין יִתְמַשֵּׁךְ עָלַי לִהְיוֹת לִי
חַיִּים אֲרֻכִּים וְשֶׁפַע קֹדֶשׁ וּמַחְשָׁבוֹת קְדוֹשׁוֹת בְּלִי הִרְהוּר חֵטְא
וְעָוֹן כְּלָל · וְשֶׁלֹּא יְפַתֵּנוּ וְלֹא יִתְגָּרֶה בָּנוּ יֵצֶר הָרָע וְיַנִּיחֵנוּ
לַעֲבֹד אֶת יְיָ כַּאֲשֶׁר עִם לְבָבֵנוּ · אָמֵן :

The Meditation (" I am enwrapping myself ") is an instance of the
spiritualization of ceremonial performance in which the Jewish Mystics
excelled. The Benediction is followed by Psalm 36. 8–11, which
verses are recited by the worshipper on putting on the tallith.

8. *children of men*. Frail and mortal as they are, the children of
men seek refuge in God. God's love is all-embracing, and is not limited
to any tribe or nation.

9. *abundance of thy house*. God is more than a Protector. He is a
bountiful Host : cf. Psalm 23. 5, 6. All these figures refer solely to the
spiritual and the unseen

stream of thy delights. lit. " river of Thy pleasures ". These great
sentences touch on the rim of infinite things.

10. *fountain of life*. One of the sublimest utterances in Scripture.
God is the Source of all life, both animal and spiritual.

TEFILLIN

MEDITA-
TION ON
MEANING
OF
TEFILLIN

Deuteronomy
6. 8

Meditation before putting on the Tefillin.

I am now intent upon the act of putting on the Tefillin, in fulfilment of the command of my Creator, who hath commanded us to lay the Tefillin, as it is written in the Torah, And thou shalt bind them for a sign upon thine hand, and they shall be for frontlets between thine eyes. Wi*hin these Tefillin are placed four sections of the Torah, that declare the absolute unity of God, and remind us of the miracles and wonders which he wrought for us when he brought us forth from Egypt, even he who hath power over the highest and the lowest to deal with them according to his will. He hath commanded us to lay the Tefillin upon the hand as a memorial of his outstretched arm ; opposite the heart, to indicate the duty of subjecting the longings and designs of our heart to his service, blessed be he ; and upon the head over against the brain, thereby teaching that the mind, whose seat is in the brain, together with all senses and faculties, is to be subjected to his service, blessed be he. May the effect of the precept thus observed be to extend to me long life with sacred influences and holy thoughts, free from every approach, even in imagination, to sin and iniquity. May the evil inclination not mislead or entice us, but may we be led to serve the Lord as it is in our hearts to do. Amen.

in thy light. God is the light of all our seeing. The thought of God opens the eyes of man to see the purity, joy and holiness that are within man's reach. The marvellous simplicity of the Psalmist's words expresses that highest joy and peace which spring from the sense of fellowship with God.

11. *continue thy lovingkindness.* The bliss that comes from the nearness of God must be more than a momentary feeling.

them that know thee. With an effective knowledge that issues in loving obedience ; see bottom of p. 13.

TEFILLIN

Tefillin appears to be a late Heb. plural of תפלה, prayer. " Four sections from the Torah (Exodus 13. 1–10 ; 11. 16 ; Deuteronomy 6. 4–9; and 11. 13–21) are in the tefillin; and these four sections have been chosen in preference to all the other passages of the Torah, because they contain the command of the tefillin : at the same time they embrace the recognition of the kingship of God, the unity of the Creator, and the exodus from Egypt—fundamental doctrines of Judaism " (Sefer Ha-Chinnuch). The purpose of the tefillin is given in the Meditation.

On putting on the תְּפִלָּה שֶׁל יָד, *say:—*

בָּרוּךְ אַתָּה יְיָ אֱלֹהֵינוּ מֶלֶךְ הָעוֹלָם · אֲשֶׁר
קִדְּשָׁנוּ בְּמִצְוֹתָיו וְצִוָּנוּ לְהָנִיחַ תְּפִלִּין :

On putting on the תְּפִלָּה שֶׁל רֹאשׁ, *say:—*

בָּרוּךְ אַתָּה יְיָ אֱלֹהֵינוּ מֶלֶךְ הָעוֹלָם · אֲשֶׁר
קִדְּשָׁנוּ בְּמִצְוֹתָיו וְצִוָּנוּ עַל־מִצְוַת תְּפִלִּין :

בָּרוּךְ שֵׁם כְּבוֹד מַלְכוּתוֹ לְעוֹלָם וָעֶד :

The רְצוּעָה *is placed thrice round the middle finger, and the following is said:—*

וְאֵרַשְׂתִּיךְ לִי לְעוֹלָם · וְאֵרַשְׂתִּיךְ לִי בְּצֶדֶק וּבְמִשְׁפָּט
וּבְחֶסֶד וּבְרַחֲמִים · וְאֵרַשְׂתִּיךְ לִי בֶּאֱמוּנָה וְיָדַעַתְּ אֶת יְיָ :

The tefillin are not worn on Sabbaths or Festivals, as these are themselves called " signs " of the great truths symbolized by the tefillin. The commandment of tefillin applies to all male persons from their thirteenth birthday, when they attain their religious majority (*Barmitzvah*).

whose glorious kingdom. By such solemn consecration of arm and mind—of every *act* and *thought* in God's service—we advance the Kingdom of Heaven on earth. For the meaning of Kingdom of Heaven, see p. 113.

I will betroth thee. In reciting these verses, the tefillin are compared to the bridal garland, a symbol of the devotion and affection between God and Israel.

The commandment of tefillin is a typical example of the *mitzvoth*, the precepts that encompass the life of the Jew, and serve to strengthen his capacity for moral self-government. As all ceremonies, and especially the tefillin, have been the subject of derision, the following reflections on the place and meaning of symbols and ceremonies in Judaism may be of help.

TEFILLIN
BLESSING

On placing the phylactery on the arm, say :—

Blessed art thou, O Lord our God, King of the universe, who hast hallowed us by thy commandments, and hast commanded us to put on the Tefillin.

On placing the phylactery on the forehead, say :—

Blessed art thou, O Lord our God, King of the universe, who hast hallowed us by thy commandments, and hast given us command concerning the precept of the Tefillin.

Blessed be His Name, whose glorious kingdom is for ever and ever.

The retsuah is wound thrice round the middle finger, and the following is said :—

Hosea 2. 21, 22

And I will betroth thee unto me for ever : yea, I will betroth thee unto me in righteousness, and in judgment, and in lovingkindness, and in mercy : I will even betroth thee unto me in faithfulness : and thou shalt know the Lord.

" You have heard that in Egypt the waters of the Nile, overflowing its banks, take the place of rain ; and that these fructifying waters are led by various channels into the remote fields to irrigate them. Now, the Nile with its precious floods would be of no benefit to the fields without these channels. Thus it is with the Torah and the *mitzvoth.* The Torah is the mighty stream of spirituality, flowing since ancient times through Israel. It would have caused no useful fruits to grow, and would have produced no spiritual progress, no moral advancement, had the *mitzvah* not been there to lead its Divine floods into the homes, the hearts, and the minds of the individual members of the people, by connecting practical life in all its variety and its activities with the spiritual truths of religion.

" It is the greatest mistake, based on an entire misunderstanding of human nature, to assume that men are capable of living in a world of ideas only, and can dispense with symbols that should embody these ideas and give them tangibility and visible form. Only the *mitzvah* is the ladder connecting heaven and earth. The tefillin, containing among others the commandment : ' Thou shalt love the Lord thy God with all thine heart, with all thy soul, and with all thy might ', are laid on the head, the seat of thought, and on the arm, the instrument of action, opposite to the heart, the seat of feeling ; thus teaching that all our thoughts, feelings, and actions must conform to the will of God. This *mitzvah*, performed daily, has contributed more effectively to preserve and to further the morality of our people than have all the learned books on ethics written by our religious philosophers " (M. Jung).

In many Congregations, Psalm xxx, *p*. 234, *is said before* בָּרוּךְ שֶׁאָמַר

בָּרוּךְ שֶׁאָמַר וְהָיָה הָעוֹלָם · בָּרוּךְ הוּא · בָּרוּךְ עוֹשֶׂה
בְרֵאשִׁית · בָּרוּךְ אוֹמֵר וְעוֹשֶׂה · בָּרוּךְ גּוֹזֵר וּמְקַיֵּם ·
בָּרוּךְ מְרַחֵם עַל הָאָרֶץ · בָּרוּךְ מְרַחֵם עַל הַבְּרִיּוֹת ·
בָּרוּךְ מְשַׁלֵּם שָׂכָר טוֹב לִירֵאָיו · בָּרוּךְ חַי לָעַד וְקַיָּם
לָנֶצַח · בָּרוּךְ פּוֹדֶה וּמַצִּיל בָּרוּךְ שְׁמוֹ · בָּרוּךְ אַתָּה יְיָ
אֱלֹהֵינוּ מֶלֶךְ הָעוֹלָם · הָאֵל הָאָב הָרַחֲמָן הַמְהֻלָּל בְּפִי

I. PRELIMINARIES TO MORNING SERVICE
B. PSALMS AND PASSAGES OF SONG
(פסוקי דזמרא)

This portion of the preliminaries to the Morning Service does not
consist of private devotions as is largely the case in the first portion,
but is a recital of psalms and anthems intended to serve as a transition
to public worship. Tradition tells us of saintly men in the days of
the Second Temple who completed the whole of the Book of Psalms
every day. Obviously their example could not become the rule
for those of the devout who had their avocations to pursue. These
confined themselves to chanting in the synagogue the last six
psalms of the Psalter as a prelude to congregational Morning Prayer.
The custom of including Psalms 145–150 in daily worship eventually
became general. The special blessing above namely, *boruch she-omar*
(" Blessed be He who spake "); was then formulated as an adoration
with which to open the recital, as well as a second blessing, *yishtabbach*
(" Praised be Thy Name "), to form its conclusion, p. 104.

In time, these psalms became the nucleus for further additions of
psalm-like selections both before and after the original group ; so that
to-day Psalms 145-150 are *preceded* by (*a*) I Chronicles 16. 8–36 ; (*b*) a
collection of Scriptural verses; (*c*) Psalm 100 ; and (*d*) a further collection
of Scriptural verses (" Let the glory of the Lord ", p. 82). And they
are *followed* by (*a*) responses of adoration (" doxologies ") ; (*b*) the
benediction of David, I Chronicles 29. 10–13 ; (*c*) the prayer in Nehemiah 9. 6–11 ; and (*d*) the Song of Moses, Exodus 14. 30–15. 18.

There are thus in this Section no *prayers* in the ordinary sense of
the word. "Let the *praise* of God precede any *petition* that we may
address to Him ", say the Rabbis ; and the psalms and anthems of
this portion of the Morning Service are a majestic fulfilment of that

PSALMS
AND
PASSAGES
OF SONG

OPENING
ADORA-
TION :
GOD THE
CREATOR
AND
REDEEMER

*In many Congregations, Psalm xxx, p. 235, is said before
" Blessed be he," etc.*

Blessed be he who spake, and the world came into existence : blessed be he : blessed be he who was the maker of
the world in the beginning : blessed be he who speaketh and
doeth : blessed be he who decreeth and performeth : blessed
be he who hath mercy upon earth : blessed be he who
hath mercy upon his creatures : blessed be who dealeth
bountifully with them that reverence him : blessed be he who
liveth for ever, and endureth to eternity : blessed be he who
redeemeth and delivereth : blessed be his Name.—Blessed
art thou, O Lord our God, King of the universe, O God

principle. It is the merit of a great medieval teacher, poet and martyr
—Rabbi Meir of Rothenburg (1230–1293)—that this Section came
formally to be taken over into the congregational Morning Service.

BORUCH SHE-OMAR, *Blessed be he who spake.* This adoration, which
goes back to the ninth century, enumerates various aspects of the
Divine activity and nature. The words ברוך הוא " blessed be He ", are
thought by some to have been the Response spoken by the congregation
after each new attribute of the Deity enumerated ; the second half of
the Response being וברוך שמו, " and blessed be his Name ", immediately before the formal blessing begins.

he who spake . . . beginning. God is first of all recognized as the
Creator and Author of the universe and all that therein is. The true
Jew firmly believes that the universe was called into existence at the
will of the One, eternal, almighty God, Who is its ultimate Source and
Sustainer. The clearest expression of this fundamental conviction is
the opening page of Scripture, the first chapter of Genesis ; and this
chapter was read in connection with the morning offering at the
Temple.

who hath mercy . . . creatures. The almighty Creator worshipped
and adored by Judaism is a God of mercy and compassion to all.

bountifully . . . reverence him. He is the God of faithfulness, Who
educates, punishes, guides ; Who hears the cry of the oppressed, and
has made known His ways of righteousness unto those who revere His
holy Name.

liveth forever . . . delivereth. He is the Life of all worlds and all
eternities, Who reveals Himself in history as the ever-living God of
redeeming lovingkindness.

blessed . . . King of the universe. Having defined God as the Creator,
as the God of lovingkindness and Redeemer who delights in renewing
life and hope to those who turn in penitence to Him, the benediction
proper over the " Service of Psalmody " now begins.

עַמּוֹ · מְשַׁבֵּחַ וּמְפָאֵר בִּלְשׁוֹן חֲסִידָיו וַעֲבָדָיו · וּבְשִׁירֵי
דָוִד עַבְדֶּךָ נְהַלֶּלְךָ יְיָ אֱלֹהֵינוּ · בִּשְׁבָחוֹת וּבִזְמִירוֹת
נְגַדֶּלְךָ וּנְשַׁבֵּחֲךָ וּנְפָאֶרְךָ וְנַזְכִּיר שִׁמְךָ וְנַמְלִיכְךָ מַלְכֵּנוּ
אֱלֹהֵינוּ יָחִיד חֵי הָעוֹלָמִים · מֶלֶךְ מְשֻׁבָּח וּמְפֹאָר
עֲדֵי-עַד- שְׁמוֹ הַגָּדוֹל · בָּרוּךְ אַתָּה יְיָ · מֶלֶךְ מְהֻלָּל
בַּתִּשְׁבָּחוֹת :

דברי הימים א׳׳ ט׳ז ח׳-לו׳

הוֹדוּ לַיְיָ קִרְאוּ בִשְׁמוֹ הוֹדִיעוּ בָעַמִּים עֲלִילֹתָיו :
שִׁירוּ לוֹ זַמְּרוּ-לוֹ שִׂיחוּ בְּכָל-נִפְלְאֹתָיו : הִתְהַלְלוּ בְּשֵׁם
קָדְשׁוֹ יִשְׂמַח לֵב מְבַקְשֵׁי יְיָ : דִּרְשׁוּ יְיָ וְעֻזּוֹ בַּקְּשׁוּ פָנָיו
תָּמִיד : זִכְרוּ נִפְלְאֹתָיו אֲשֶׁר עָשָׂה מֹפְתָיו וּמִשְׁפְּטֵי-
פִיהוּ : זֶרַע יִשְׂרָאֵל עַבְדּוֹ בְּנֵי יַעֲקֹב בְּחִירָיו : הוּא יְיָ
אֱלֹהֵינוּ בְּכָל-הָאָרֶץ מִשְׁפָּטָיו : זִכְרוּ לְעוֹלָם בְּרִיתוֹ דָּבָר
צִוָּה לְאֶלֶף דּוֹר : אֲשֶׁר כָּרַת אֶת-אַבְרָהָם וּשְׁבוּעָתוֹ
לְיִצְחָק : וַיַּעֲמִידֶהָ לְיַעֲקֹב לְחֹק לְיִשְׂרָאֵל בְּרִית עוֹלָם :
לֵאמֹר לְךָ אֶתֵּן אֶרֶץ-כְּנָעַן חֶבֶל נַחֲלַתְכֶם : בִּהְיוֹתְכֶם

I CHRONICLES 16. 8–36.

HODU. *O give thanks.* The opening benediction having been
recited, the Service continues with an anthem taken from I Chronicles
in celebration of David's bringing the Ark to Zion. The first
part of the selection here quoted is, with slight variants, identical with
Psalm 105. 1–15.

The BOOK OF CHRONICLES is an ecclesiastical review of Israel's history
from Adam to the Proclamation of Cyrus inviting the Jewish exiles in
Babylon to rebuild the Temple in a new Jewish commonwealth. The

PSALMS AND PASSAGES OF SONG

OPENING ADORATION

and merciful Father, praised by the mouth of thy people, lauded and glorified by the tongue of thy pious servants. We also will extol thee, O Lord our God, with the songs of David thy servant ; with the praises and psalms we will magnify, laud and glorify thee. We will call upon thy Name, and proclaim thee our King, O our God, thou the only One, the life of all worlds. O King, lauded and glorified be thy great Name for ever and ever. Blessed art thou, O Lord, a King extolled with psalms of praise.

1 Chronicles xvi. 8—36.

GOD'S LOVING-KINDNESS TO ISRAEL IN THE DAYS OF OLD

⁸O give thanks unto the Lord, call upon his Name ; make known his doings among the peoples. ⁹Sing unto him, sing praises unto him ; tell ye of all his marvellous works. ¹⁰Glory ye in his holy Name : let the heart of them rejoice that seek the Lord. ¹¹Search ye for the Lord and his strength ; seek ye his face evermore. ¹²Remember his marvellous works that he hath done ; his wonders, and the judgments of his mouth ; ¹³O ye seed of Israel, his servant, ye children of Jacob, his chosen ones. ¹⁴He is the Lord our God : his judgments are in all the earth. ¹⁵Remember his covenant for ever, the word which he commanded to a thousand generations ; ¹⁶(the covenant) which he made with Abraham, and his oath unto Isaac ; ¹⁷and established it unto Jacob for a statute, to Israel for an everlasting covenant : ¹⁸saying, Unto thee will I give the land of Canaan, as the lot

story of the response to this " Cyrus Declaration " is told in the Books of Ezra and Nehemiah, which are a continuation of the Books of Chronicles. In all these books, there are wonderful prayers of penitence.

8-22. A survey of the beginnings of Israel's history. It praises God for His faithfulness to Israel in the past, and is intended to quicken Israel's gratitude and sense of duty.

8. *call upon his Name. i.e.* proclaim to the world His Divine character as made known in the facts of Israel's history, His revelation of Himself as a God of Righteousness and Mercy. God's deeds are Israel's message to the world.

12. *the judgments of his mouth.* Such as, the sentence pronounced upon the Egyptians.

מְתֵי מִסְפָּר כִּמְעַט וְגָרִים בָּהּ : וַיִּתְהַלְּכוּ מִגּוֹי אֶל־גּוֹי

וּמִמַּמְלָכָה אֶל־עַם אַחֵר : לֹא־הִנִּיחַ לְאִישׁ לְעָשְׁקָם וַיּוֹכַח

עֲלֵיהֶם מְלָכִים : אַל־תִּגְּעוּ בִּמְשִׁיחָי וּבִנְבִיאַי אַל־תָּרֵעוּ :

שִׁירוּ לַיָי כָּל־הָאָרֶץ בַּשְּׂרוּ מִיּוֹם־אֶל־יוֹם יְשׁוּעָתוֹ : סַפְּרוּ

בַגּוֹיִם אֶת־כְּבוֹדוֹ בְּכָל־הָעַמִּים נִפְלְאֹתָיו : כִּי גָדוֹל יְיָ

וּמְהֻלָּל מְאֹד וְנוֹרָא הוּא עַל־כָּל־אֱלֹהִים : כִּי כָּל־אֱלֹהֵי

הָעַמִּים אֱלִילִים וַיָי שָׁמַיִם עָשָׂה : הוֹד וְהָדָר לְפָנָיו עֹז

וְחֶדְוָה בִּמְקֹמוֹ : הָבוּ לַיָי מִשְׁפְּחוֹת עַמִּים הָבוּ לַיָי כָּבוֹד

וָעֹז : הָבוּ לַיָי כְּבוֹד שְׁמוֹ שְׂאוּ מִנְחָה וּבֹאוּ לְפָנָיו

הִשְׁתַּחֲווּ לַיָי בְּהַדְרַת־קֹדֶשׁ : חִילוּ מִלְּפָנָיו כָּל־הָאָרֶץ

אַף־תִּכּוֹן תֵּבֵל בַּל־תִּמּוֹט : יִשְׂמְחוּ הַשָּׁמַיִם וְתָגֵל הָאָרֶץ

וְיֹאמְרוּ בַגּוֹיִם יְיָ מָלָךְ : יִרְעַם הַיָּם וּמְלֹאוֹ יַעֲלֹז הַשָּׂדֶה

19. *few men in number.* When it seemed utterly improbable that a handful of men would come into possession of the land promised to them.

22. *mine anointed ones. i.e.* Divinely set apart and consecrated to God's service ; lit. *my Messiahs.* Here the reference is to the Fathers of the nation who were themselves consecrated, and became the founders of a consecrated People. But the Rabbis assign to these words a wonderful sense, and make them refer to *little children.* They look upon little children as God's Messiahs sent to erring humanity. In them, mankind is constantly given a chance to free itself from the sins, errors and mistakes of the past ; and, through its little children, to be " born again " to a better and nobler future.

my prophets. The reference is still to the Patriarchs ; see Genesis 20. 7. Here again the Rabbis boldly apply these words to *the schoolmasters* in Israel ; because the schoolmasters, like the Prophets, lead each generation back to the spiritual foundations of Israel's Faith, on which alone the Kingdom of God can be established on earth.

of your inheritance : ¹⁹when ye were but a few men in number ; yea, few, and sojourners in it ; ²⁰and when they were going about from nation to nation, and from one kingdom to another people. ²¹He suffered no man to oppress them ; yea, he rebuked kings for their sakes ; ²²(saying), Touch not mine anointed ones, and do my prophets no harm.

ALL PEOPLES AND ALL NATURE ACCLAIM GOD THE UNIVER- SAL KING

²³Sing unto the Lord, all the earth ; proclaim his salvation from day to day. ²⁴Recount his glory among the heathen, his marvels among all the peoples. ²⁵For great is the Lord, and exceedingly to be praised : he is to be revered above all gods. ²⁶For all the gods of the peoples are things of nought : but the Lord made the heavens. ²⁷Grandeur and majesty are before him : strength and gladness are in his place. ²⁸Ascribe unto the Lord, ye families of the peoples, ascribe unto the Lord glory and strength. ²⁹Ascribe unto the Lord the glory due unto his Name : take an offering, and come before him ; worship the Lord in the beauty of holiness. ³⁰Tremble before him all the earth : the world also is set firm, that it cannot be moved. ³¹Let the heavens rejoice, and let the earth be glad ; and let them say among the heathen, The Lord reigneth. ³²Let the sea roar, and the fulness thereof ; let the

---

SING UNTO THE LORD. The second part of the anthem, verses 23–36, is largely identical with Psalm 96 (see p. 349), and sings of God's dominion extending to all nations, and ushering in the joy and blessing of a renovated earth.

23. *his salvation.* The deliverance which He wrought for Israel.

27. *and gladness are in his place.* In His sanctuary. " In whose abode is joy ", we declare in the Grace after the Wedding Feast, p. 1015.

28. *families of the peoples.* The nations themselves are called upon to take up the song in which Israel has made known to them the marvellous works of God.

29. *in the beauty of holiness.* Or, " the majesty of holiness ". The Greeks regarded beauty as holy : the Hebrews, holiness as beautiful (Rosenbaum.)

וְכָל־אֲשֶׁר־בּוֹ : אָז יְרַנְּנוּ עֲצֵי הַיָּעַר מִלִּפְנֵי יְיָ כִּי־בָא

לִשְׁפּוֹט אֶת־הָאָרֶץ : הוֹדוּ לַיָי כִּי טוֹב כִּי לְעוֹלָם חַסְדּוֹ :

וְאִמְרוּ הוֹשִׁיעֵנוּ אֱלֹהֵי יִשְׁעֵנוּ וְקַבְּצֵנוּ וְהַצִּילֵנוּ מִן־הַגּוֹיִם

לְהֹדוֹת לְשֵׁם קָדְשֶׁךָ לְהִשְׁתַּבֵּחַ בִּתְהִלָּתֶךָ : בָּרוּךְ יְיָ

אֱלֹהֵי יִשְׂרָאֵל מִן־הָעוֹלָם וְעַד־הָעֹלָם וַיֹּאמְרוּ כָל־הָעָם

אָמֵן וְהַלֵּל לַיָי :

רוֹמְמוּ יְיָ אֱלֹהֵינוּ וְהִשְׁתַּחֲווּ לַהֲדֹם רַגְלָיו קָדוֹשׁ

הוּא : רוֹמְמוּ יְיָ אֱלֹהֵינוּ וְהִשְׁתַּחֲווּ לְהַר קָדְשׁוֹ כִּי

קָדוֹשׁ יְיָ אֱלֹהֵינוּ : וְהוּא רַחוּם יְכַפֵּר עָוֹן וְלֹא יַשְׁחִית

וְהִרְבָּה לְהָשִׁיב אַפּוֹ וְלֹא יָעִיר כָּל־חֲמָתוֹ : אַתָּה יְיָ

לֹא־תִכְלָא רַחֲמֶיךָ מִמֶּנִּי חַסְדְּךָ וַאֲמִתְּךָ תָּמִיד יִצְּרוּנִי :

33. *trees of the forest exult.* The psalmist invests heaven and earth, the sea, forest and trees with his own emotions ; and invokes them to acclaim the kingship of God. " The Prophets not only personify nature, they *ethicize* it ; *i.e.* they endow it with the capacity of understanding moral distinctions " (Steinthal). In the eyes of the Psalmists, Nature fully sympathizes with the triumphs of the righteous ; the very hills break into singing, and the trees of the forest clap their hands—they look forward with eager expectation to the establishment of God's righteous government in the world.

to judge the earth. Not for punishment, but for government, for restoring harmony and peace in all creation.

35. *salvation.* Victory, deliverance, restoration.

36. *all the people said, Amen.* This, of course, is not part of the psalm sung by the Levites when the Ark of the Covenant was placed in

GOD THE
UNIVER-
SAL KING

field exult, and all that is therein. [33]Then shall the trees of the forest exult before the Lord, for he cometh to judge the earth. [34]O give thanks unto the Lord ; for he is good : for his lovingkindness endureth for ever. [35]And say ye, Save us, O God of our salvation, and gather us and deliver us from the nations, to give thanks unto thy holy Name, and to triumph in thy praise. [36]Blessed be the Lord, the God of Israel, from everlasting even to everlasting. And all the people said, Amen, and praised the Lord.

Psalm 99, 5, 9

Exalt ye the Lord our God, and worship at his temple : holy is he. Exalt ye the Lord our God, and worship at

Psalm 78. 38

his holy mount ; for the Lord our God is holy. And he, being merciful, forgiveth iniquity, and destroyeth not : yea, many a time he turneth his anger away, and doth not stir

Psalm 40. 12

up all his wrath. Withhold not thou thy tender mercies from me, O Lord : let thy lovingkindness and thy truth

---

the Tent that David had prepared for it ; but is the statement of the Chronicler that all the people whole-heartedly joined in the adoration to which they had listened (Kimchi).

Amen is perhaps the most widely known word in human speech : three great religions have made it the principal " response " in their worship, and thus brought it into the lives of men of all climes, races and cultures. Its original meaning is " So be it "—a solemn affirmation to a preceding declaration. " By it the congregation acknowledge what their representative has spoken in prayer, and identify themselves with his words " (Heiler). Great spiritual value was attached by the Rabbis to the reverent response of Amen in prayer. " Whosoever says Amen with all his heart, to him the gates of Paradise shall be opened " (Talmud).

ROMAMU. *exalt ye . . . bountifully with me.* The twenty-three verses that now follow were deemed particularly noteworthy by the Rabbis. Most of them recur in the Prayer Book in the full psalm from which they are taken, or they are otherwise repeated. Full comments will not therefore be here given.

Psalm 99. 5 : *at his temple.* lit. "at his footstool" ; 1 Chronicles 28. 2.

Psalm 42. 12 : *thy lovingkindness and thy truth.* In most instances where these Divine attributes are mentioned together, God's lovingkindness is mentioned *before* His truth. Let man in his dealings with his fellow-men likewise show lovingkindness and truth, but lovingkindness first. Let him speak and act the truth *in love.*

זְכֹר רַחֲמֶיךָ יְיָ וַחֲסָדֶיךָ כִּי מֵעוֹלָם הֵמָּה: תְּנוּ עֹז לֵאלֹהִים

עַל־יִשְׂרָאֵל גַּאֲוָתוֹ וְעֻזּוֹ בַּשְּׁחָקִים: נוֹרָא אֱלֹהִים

מִמִּקְדָּשֶׁיךָ אֵל יִשְׂרָאֵל הוּא נֹתֵן עֹז וְתַעֲצֻמוֹת לָעָם

בָּרוּךְ אֱלֹהִים: אֵל־נְקָמוֹת יְיָ אֵל נְקָמוֹת הוֹפִיעַ:

הִנָּשֵׂא שֹׁפֵט הָאָרֶץ הָשֵׁב גְּמוּל עַל־גֵּאִים: לַיְיָ הַיְשׁוּעָה

עַל־עַמְּךָ בִרְכָתֶךָ פֶּלָה: יְיָ צְבָאוֹת עִמָּנוּ מִשְׂגָּב־לָנוּ

אֱלֹהֵי יַעֲקֹב סֶלָה: יְיָ צְבָאוֹת אַשְׁרֵי אָדָם בֹּטֵחַ בָּךְ:

יְיָ הוֹשִׁיעָה הַמֶּלֶךְ יַעֲנֵנוּ בְיוֹם־קָרְאֵנוּ: הוֹשִׁיעָה אֶת־עַמֶּךָ

וּבָרֵךְ אֶת־נַחֲלָתֶךָ וּרְעֵם וְנַשְּׂאֵם עַד־הָעוֹלָם: נַפְשֵׁנוּ

חִכְּתָה לַיְיָ עֶזְרֵנוּ וּמָגִנֵּנוּ הוּא: כִּי־בוֹ יִשְׂמַח לִבֵּנוּ כִּי

בְשֵׁם קָדְשׁוֹ בָטָחְנוּ: יְהִי־חַסְדְּךָ יְיָ עָלֵינוּ כַּאֲשֶׁר יִחַלְנוּ

לָךְ: הַרְאֵנוּ יְיָ חַסְדֶּךָ וְיֶשְׁעֲךָ תִּתֶּן־לָנוּ: קוּמָה עֶזְרָתָה

לָּנוּ וּפְדֵנוּ לְמַעַן חַסְדֶּךָ: אָנֹכִי יְיָ אֱלֹהֶיךָ הַמַּעַלְךָ מֵאֶרֶץ

מִצְרָיִם הַרְחֶב־פִּיךָ וַאֲמַלְאֵהוּ: אַשְׁרֵי הָעָם שֶׁכָּכָה לּוֹ

אַשְׁרֵי הָעָם שֶׁיְיָ אֱלֹהָיו: וַאֲנִי בְּחַסְדְּךָ בָטַחְתִּי יָגֵל לִבִּי

בִּישׁוּעָתֶךָ אָשִׁירָה לַיְיָ כִּי גָמַל עָלָי:

Psalm 94. 1: retribution. See on Psalm 94, p. 225.
Psalm 3. 9: Selah. Usually explained to mean *for ever* (Targum, Talmud). Many look upon it as a musical sign, a pause, or a summons to the choir or congregation to take up a refrain.

Psalm 25. 6   continually preserve me. Remember, O Lord, thy tender mercies and thy lovingkindnesses ; for they have been ever

Psalm 68. 35, 36   of old. Ascribe ye strength unto God : his majesty is over Israel, and his strength is in the skies. O God, thou art to be feared out of thy sanctuary : the God of Israel, he giveth

Psalm 94. 1, 2   strength and power unto his people. Blessed be God. O Lord, thou God to whom retribution belongeth, thou God to whom retribution belongeth, shine forth. Lift up thyself, thou Judge of the earth : render to the proud their desert.

Psalm 3. 9   Salvation belongeth unto the Lord : thy blessing be upon

Psalm 46. 8   thy people. (Selah.) The Lord of hosts is with us ; the God

Psalm 84. 13   of Jacob is our stronghold. (Selah.) O Lord of hosts, happy

Psalm 20. 10   is the man that trusteth in thee. Save, Lord : may the King

Psalm 28. 9   answer us on the day when we call. Save thy people, and bless thine inheritance : sustain them, and tend them for

Psalm 33. 20—22   ever. Our soul waiteth for the Lord : he is our help and our shield. For our heart shall rejoice in him, because we have trusted in his holy Name. Let thy lovingkindness, O Lord,

Psalm 85. 8   be upon us, according as we have hoped in thee. Show us thy lovingkindness, O Lord, and grant us thy salvation.

Psalm 44. 27   Rise up for our help, and set us free for thy lovingkindness'

Psalm 81. 11   sake. I am the Lord thy God, who brought thee up out of the land of Egypt : open wide thy mouth, and I will fill it.

Psalm 144. 15   Happy is the people, that is thus favoured : happy is the

Psalm 13. 6   people, whose God is the Lord. And as for me, I have trusted in thy lovingkindness ; my heart shall be glad in thy salvation : I will sing unto the Lord, because he hath dealt bountifully with me.

Psalm 44. 27 : *rise up . . . sake.* Culminating note in a despairing prayer of vanquished Israel.
    Psalm 13. 6 : *and as for . . . with me.* Triumphant declaration of a soul that has found God, the Hope of the oppressed.

The following Psalm is omitted on Sabbaths, Holydays, the day before Passover, the Intermediate days of Passover, and on the day before the Day of Atonement.

תהלים ק'

מִזְמוֹר לְתוֹדָה הָרִיעוּ לַיָי כָּל־הָאָרֶץ : עִבְדוּ אֶת־יְיָ
בְּשִׂמְחָה בְּאוּ לְפָנָיו בִּרְנָנָה : דְּעוּ כִּי יְיָ הוּא אֱלֹהִים הוּא
עָשָׂנוּ וְלֹא (וְלוֹ ק) אֲנַחְנוּ עַמּוֹ וְצֹאן מַרְעִיתוֹ : בְּאוּ
שְׁעָרָיו בְּתוֹדָה חֲצֵרֹתָיו בִּתְהִלָּה הוֹדוּ לוֹ בָּרְכוּ שְׁמוֹ :
כִּי־טוֹב יְיָ לְעוֹלָם חַסְדּוֹ וְעַד־דֹּר וָדֹר אֱמוּנָתוֹ :

On Weekdays continue יְהִי כְבוֹד, *page 82.*

On Sabbaths and Holydays, and on הוֹשַׁעֲנָא רַבָּא, *the following Psalms are said:—*

יט לַמְנַצֵּחַ מִזְמוֹר לְדָוִד : הַשָּׁמַיִם מְסַפְּרִים כְּבוֹד־אֵל

PSALM 100.

A call to all the earth to join in the worship of the God of Israel. It is pre-eminent among songs of thanksgiving : all the peoples of the earth are to serve their Heavenly Maker, and in that joyful worship regain their lost unity.

According to Tradition, this psalm was sung whilst the thank-offering was being sacrificed in the Temple. On the days mentioned in the rubric, no thank-offering was brought, hence the omission of the psalm on those days.

2. *serve the Lord with joy.* The psalm is alone sufficient to banish the notion, spread by non-Jewish theologians, of the Jewish worshipper trembling in fear and mortal dread before a vengeful Deity. The Jew serves God *in* joy, and *with* joy ; and proclaims that God's loving-kindness to all the children of men is everlasting.

3. *and we are his.* This is the translation of the Hebrew text *as read* (קרי). As *written* (כתיב) it means, " He hath made us, and *not we ourselves* ".

4. *give thanks unto him.* Some primitive languages have no word for " to thank " ; and the giving of thanks as an express form of intercourse is not a universal trait of humanity. Not so in Judaism. The Prophets brand ingratitude an unnatural sin, since it reduces man below the level of a dumb animal, which at least gratefully remembers the hand that provides its food. Therefore Judaism sees the need of

The following Psalm is omitted on Sabbaths, Holydays, the day before Passover, the Intermediate days of Passover, and on the day before the Day of Atonement.

Psalm c.   A Psalm of Thanksgiving.

LET ALL THE WORLD JOIN IN THE WORSHIP OF GOD

¹Shout for joy unto the Lord, all ye lands. ²Serve the Lord with joy : come before him with exulting. ³Know ye that the Lord he is God : he hath made us, and we are his, his people and the sheep of his pasture. ⁴Enter into his gates with thanksgiving, and into his courts with praise : give thanks unto him, bless his Name. ⁵For the Lord is good ; his lovingkindness is everlasting ; and his faithfulness from generation to generation.

On Weekdays continue " Let the glory," etc., p. 83.

On Sabbaths and Holydays, and on Hoshana Rabba, the following

SABBATH PSALMS

Psalms are said :—

Psalm xix.   ¹For the Chief Musician.   A Psalm of David.

THE DOUBLE REVELA-TION OF GOD : IN NATURE

²The heavens declare the glory of God, and the firmament showeth his handiwork. ³Day unto day poureth forth

perennial reminders of this duty which is at the root of character. In the Messianic era, the Rabbis tell us, all the sacrifices will cease, having fulfilled their educational mission, except the thankoffering. Thanksgiving will remain an eternal obligation of man.

5. *is good.* Is gracious.

THE SABBATH PSALMS.

The nine psalms that now follow do not form part of the weekday Morning Service. They are reserved for Sabbaths and Festivals, when there is a fuller leisure for devotion.

PSALM 19.

" There are two things that fill my soul with holy reverence and ever-growing wonder—the spectacle of the starry sky that virtually annihilates us as physical beings, and the Moral Law which raises us to infinite dignity as intelligent agents ". These words of the great philosopher Immanuel Kant, are an excellent parallel to this wonderful psalm on the double revelation of God, in Nature and in the Torah. What the sun is in the heavens, Religion is in the soul. Heaven and earth declare the omnipotence, wisdom and love of God : Scripture proclaims His ways of holiness and mercy to the children of men.

1–7.   GOD IN NATURE.

2. *declare.* lit. " are declaring ". In the Hebrew, the participle of the verb is used, to denote *continuous* action : " the heavens are forever declaring the glory of God ".

וּמַעֲשֵׂה יָדָיו מַגִּיד הָרָקִיעַ : יוֹם לְיוֹם יַבִּיעַ אֹמֶר וְלַיְלָה

לְלַיְלָה יְחַוֶּה־דָּעַת : אֵין אֹמֶר וְאֵין דְּבָרִים בְּלִי נִשְׁמָע

קוֹלָם : בְּכָל־הָאָרֶץ יָצָא קַוָּם וּבִקְצֵה תֵבֵל מִלֵּיהֶם

לַשֶּׁמֶשׁ שָׂם אֹהֶל בָּהֶם : וְהוּא כְּחָתָן יֹצֵא מֵחֻפָּתוֹ

יָשִׂישׂ כְּגִבּוֹר לָרוּץ אֹרַח : מִקְצֵה הַשָּׁמַיִם ׀ מוֹצָאוֹ

וּתְקוּפָתוֹ עַל־קְצוֹתָם וְאֵין נִסְתָּר מֵחַמָּתוֹ : תּוֹרַת יְהֹוָה

תְּמִימָה מְשִׁיבַת נָפֶשׁ עֵדוּת יְהֹוָה נֶאֱמָנָה מַחְכִּימַת

פֶּתִי : פִּקּוּדֵי יְהֹוָה יְשָׁרִים מְשַׂמְּחֵי־לֵב מִצְוַת יְהֹוָה בָּרָה

מְאִירַת עֵינָיִם : יִרְאַת יְהֹוָה טְהוֹרָה עוֹמֶדֶת לָעַד

מִשְׁפְּטֵי־יְהֹוָה אֱמֶת צָדְקוּ יַחְדָּו : הַנֶּחֱמָדִים מִזָּהָב וּמִפַּז

רָב וּמְתוּקִים מִדְּבַשׁ וְנֹפֶת צוּפִים : גַּם־עַבְדְּךָ נִזְהָר בָּהֶם

---

firmament. *i.e.* the stars and planets in the firmament (Rashi).

3. *poureth forth speech.* lit. " becomes a well-spring of speech ". Every day the heavens renew their testimony to God's glory.

4. *there is no speech . . . earth.* " No real speech, and no real words —not heard is their voice, yet is their sound gone out to the end of the earth ". It is silent eloquence ; " songs without words ".

5. *their sound.* Heb. קַוָּם, " strain " or " chord ". Ancient and modern versions render it, " their sound " ; Herxheimer and Leeser translate, " their melody ".

to the end of the world. World wide is the message which they proclaim in their silence.

> " What though in solemn silence, all
> Move round the dark terrestrial ball ?
> What though no *real* voice nor sound
> Amid their radiant orbs be found ?
> In Reason's ear they all rejoice,
> And utter forth a glorious voice,
> For ever singing as they shine,
> ' The Hand that made us is divine ' " (Addison).

in them. In the heavens.

6. *as a bridegroom.* In the freshness of strength and happiness.

8–12. Even more wonderful is the revelation of God's Will to humanity. A much fuller, and ever more wonderful, rhapsody of the

speech, and night unto night proclaimeth knowledge. ⁴There is no speech nor language ; their voice cannot be heard. ⁵Their sound is gone out through all the earth, and their words to the end of the world ; in them hath he set a tent for the sun. ⁶And he is as a bridegroom coming out of his chamber, and rejoiceth as a strong man to run his course. ⁷His going forth is from the end of the heaven, and his circuit unto the ends of it : and there is nothing hid from
his heat.—⁸The teaching of the Lord is perfect, restoring the soul : the testimony of the Lord is sure, making wise the simple. ⁹The precepts of the Lord are right, rejoicing the heart : the commandment of the Lord is pure, enlightening the eyes. ¹⁰The fear of the Lord is clean, enduring for ever : the judgments of the Lord are true, righteous altogether. ¹¹More to be desired are they than gold, yea, than much fine gold : sweeter also than honey and the droppings of the honeycomb. ¹²Moreover by them is thy

Torah is given in Psalm 119, as the inexhaustible treasure of Divine teaching and life-giving truth ; see p. 1019.

8. *the teaching of the Lord.* Heb. *Torah*—here the name for the Divine revelation in general.

perfect. lit. " flawless ", without blemish.

restoring the soul. Refreshing the spirit, and invigorating man's true self.

testimony. The Torah regarded as a witness to God's will and man's duty ; often this term denotes the Decalogue as the " Tables of testimony ".

sure. Not variable or uncertain.

making wise the simple. Giving practical guidance to immature minds who, but for it, might be easily beguiled by sin and evil.

10. *fear of the Lord.* This phrase is here equivalent to " true religion, as taught in Scripture."

clean. In contrast to everything impure and heathen.

judgments. The Divine enactments which are based on the fact that man is responsible for his actions.

righteous altogether. Strictly just ; one and all they are in accordance with the standard of absolute justice.

11. *sweeter also than honey.* This is no exaggeration. Men loved, and were happy in the keeping of the commandments. " Let no one believe a word of it if he reads in non-Jewish books that the Law was a burden and a bondage. That is historically false " (C. G. Montefiore).

בְּשָׁמְרָם עֵקֶב רָב : שְׁגִיאוֹת מִי־יָבִין מִנִּסְתָּרוֹת נַקֵּנִי :

גַּם מִזֵּדִים חֲשֹׂךְ עַבְדֶּךָ אַל־יִמְשְׁלוּ־בִי אָז אֵיתָם וְנִקֵּיתִי

מִפֶּשַׁע רָב : יִהְיוּ לְרָצוֹן אִמְרֵי־פִי וְהֶגְיוֹן לִבִּי לְפָנֶיךָ

יְהוָה צוּרִי וְגֹאֲלִי :

לְדָוִד בְּשַׁנּוֹתוֹ אֶת־טַעְמוֹ לִפְנֵי אֲבִימֶלֶךְ וַיְגָרֲשֵׁהוּ

וַיֵּלַךְ :

אֲבָרֲכָה אֶת־יְהוָה בְּכָל־עֵת תָּמִיד תְּהִלָּתוֹ בְּפִי :

בַּיהוָה תִּתְהַלֵּל נַפְשִׁי יִשְׁמְעוּ עֲנָוִים וְיִשְׂמָחוּ :

גַּדְּלוּ לַיהוָה אִתִּי וּנְרוֹמְמָה שְׁמוֹ יַחְדָּו :

דָּרַשְׁתִּי אֶת־יְהוָה וְעָנָנִי וּמִכָּל־מְגוּרוֹתַי הִצִּילָנִי :

הִבִּיטוּ אֵלָיו וְנָהָרוּ וּפְנֵיהֶם אַל־יֶחְפָּרוּ :

זֶה עָנִי קָרָא וַיהוָה שָׁמֵעַ וּמִכָּל־צָרוֹתָיו הוֹשִׁיעוֹ :

חֹנֶה מַלְאַךְ־יְהוָה סָבִיב לִירֵאָיו וַיְחַלְּצֵם :

13–15. PRAYER FOR PRESERVATION AND GUIDANCE.
13. *errors.* Lapses due to heedlessness.
clear thou me. Absolve Thou me.
hidden faults. Those unknown to me.
14. *presumptuous sins.* Deliberate sins. Some translate, " presumptuous *men* ", who are disloyal to the Torah, encourage others to follow their ungodly example, and make life hard for the faithful followers of their Jewish duties.
not have . . . dominion over me. So that the deliberate sins become not a man's master, and rule over him, instead of him ruling over them; Genesis 4. 7. If *them* refers to *presumptuous men*, the prayer is, to be saved from the mockery and religious persecution which, on the part of apostates, is especially heartless.

servant warned : in keeping them there is great reward. [13]Who can discern his errors ? Clear thou me from hidden faults. [14]Keep back thy servant also from presumptuous sins ; let them not have dominion over me : then shall I be blameless, and I shall be clear from great transgression. [15]Let the words of my mouth and the meditation of my heart be acceptable before thee, O Lord, my Rock and my Redeemer.

Psalm xxxiv. [1]A Psalm of David ; when he changed his behaviour before Abimelech, who drove him away, and he departed.

*GOD HELP-
ETH THE
HUMBLE
AND THE
FAITHFUL
IN WELL-
DOING*
[2]I will bless the Lord at all times : his praise shall con-continually be in my mouth. [3]My soul shall make her boast in the Lord : the meek shall hear and rejoice. [4]O magnify the Lord with me, and let us exalt his Name together. [5]I sought the Lord, and he answered me, and delivered me from all my fears. [6]They looked unto him, and shone with joy : and their faces shall not be confounded. [7]This sufferer cried, and the Lord heard him, and saved him out of all his troubles. [8]The angel of the Lord encampeth round about

---

15. *Redeemer.* Heb. *goel.* The *goel* was one's nearest of kin, whose duty it was to help a man in time of difficulty or danger. The Psalmist calls God his *goel,* Who will deliver him from both the tyranny of enemies and the bondage of sin ; cf. " For I know that my Redeemer liveth " (Job 19. 25).

PSALM 34.

One of the psalms in which each verse begins with a letter of the Hebrew alphabet.

1. *changed his behaviour. i.e.* feigned madness, for fear of being recognized at the Philistine court, whither he had fled from the wrath of Saul ; see I Samuel 21. 11. (Abimelech, like Pharaoh, seems to have been the title of the dynasty ; Achish was the personal name.)

3. *the meek.* Those who have learned humility in the school of suffering.

4. *magnify . . . together.* This verse is recited as the Sefer Torah is taken from the Ark in worship ; see pp. 188 and 480.

6. *they looked . . . . confounded.* An impersonal construction meaning, when men look up unto Him, they cheer up, and their faces are freed from disappointment.

טַעֲמוּ וּרְאוּ כִּי־טוֹב יְהוָֹה אַשְׁרֵי הַגֶּבֶר יֶחֱסֶה־בּוֹ :

יְראוּ אֶת־יְהוָֹה קְדֹשָׁיו כִּי אֵין מַחְסוֹר לִירֵאָיו :

כְּפִירִים רָשׁוּ וְרָעֵבוּ וְדֹרְשֵׁי יְהוָֹה לֹא־יַחְסְרוּ כָל־טוֹב :

לְכוּ־בָנִים שִׁמְעוּ־לִי יִרְאַת יְהוָֹה אֲלַמֶּדְכֶם :

מִי־הָאִישׁ הֶחָפֵץ חַיִּים אֹהֵב יָמִים לִרְאוֹת טוֹב :

נְצֹר לְשׁוֹנְךָ מֵרָע וּשְׂפָתֶיךָ מִדַּבֵּר מִרְמָה :

סוּר מֵרָע וַעֲשֵׂה־טוֹב בַּקֵּשׁ שָׁלוֹם וְרָדְפֵהוּ :

עֵינֵי יְהוָֹה אֶל־צַדִּיקִים וְאָזְנָיו אֶל־שַׁוְעָתָם :

פְּנֵי יְהוָֹה בְּעֹשֵׂי רָע לְהַכְרִית מֵאֶרֶץ זִכְרָם :

צָעֲקוּ וַיהוָֹה שָׁמֵעַ וּמִכָּל־צָרוֹתָם הִצִּילָם :

קָרוֹב יְהוָֹה לְנִשְׁבְּרֵי־לֵב וְאֶת־דַּכְּאֵי־רוּחַ יוֹשִׁיעַ :

רַבּוֹת רָעוֹת צַדִּיק וּמִכֻּלָּם יַצִּילֶנּוּ יְהוָֹה :

שֹׁמֵר כָּל־עַצְמוֹתָיו אַחַת מֵהֵנָּה לֹא נִשְׁבָּרָה :

---

9. *consider and see.* lit. " taste and see " ; *i.e.* make but trial, and see.

10. *holy ones.* Members of a holy nation.

12. *I will teach.* I will teach you the essence of religion ; viz., speaking truth, doing good, abhorring evil, and seeking peace even when it seems to flee from us.

13. *life . . . days.* "One expression refers to this life ; the other to the Life to come " (Kimchi).

14. *keep thy tongue from evil.* "Let the honour of thy fellow-man be as dear to thee as thine own" (Sayings of the Fathers 1. 15). In no other religious literature is there such condemnation of לשון הרע " the evil tongue " (*i.e.* speaking ill of others, whether it be a malicious slander, or a hearsay retailed out of love of scandal) as there is in Scripture and, even more so, in the Rabbinical Writings. The Rabbis deem calumny an unpardonable sin. Among the four classes who will not be received into the Divine Presence—they declare—are the retailers of slander. "A world in which men do not speak evil of their fellows, or enjoy hearing

SABBATH
PSALMS
*GOD
HELPETH
THE
HUMBLE
AND THE
FAITHFUL
IN WELL-
DOING*

them that reverence him, and delivereth them. ⁹O consider and see that the Lord is good : happy is the man that taketh refuge in him. ¹⁰O revere the Lord, ye his holy ones : for there is no want to them that revere him. ¹¹Young lions do lack, and suffer hunger : but they that seek the Lord shall not want any good. ¹²Come, ye children, hearken unto me : I will teach you the fear of the Lord. ¹³What man is he that delighteth in life, and loveth many days that he may see good ? ¹⁴Keep thy tongue from evil, and thy lips from speaking guile. ¹⁵Depart from evil and do good ; seek peace and pursue it. ¹⁶The eyes of the Lord are towards the righteous, and his ears are towards their cry. ¹⁷The face of the Lord is against them that do evil, to cut off the remembrance of them from the earth. ¹⁸They cry, and the Lord hearkeneth, and delivereth them out of all their troubles. ¹⁹The Lord is nigh unto them that are of a broken heart, and saveth such as are of a contrite spirit. ²⁰Many are the evil fortunes of the righteous : but the Lord delivereth him out of them all. ²¹He guardeth all his limbs : not

them evil spoken of, is a remoter Utopia than one in which they do not take advantage of one another in business. The Jewish moralists conceive this end as the Divine ideal, revealed not alone as a law of human life but as a constituent factor of religion " (Moore).

guile. Deceit.

15. *depart from evil.* Righteousness is to manifest itself *negatively*, in the avoidance of evil ; and *positively*, in the practice of good ; see Isaiah 1. 16, 17.

18. *they cry. They* is usually understood to mean " the righteous ". But surely the most natural explanation is that it refers to " them that do evil ". God punishes them for their sins ; but, the moment they repent of their evil deeds, He hears their cry and delivers them out of all troubles (Ibn Ezra, Sforno, Jacob Emden, S. R. Hirsch). This is the teaching of Isaiah, Ezekiel and Jonah, and is at the very basis of the Day of Atonement. " Thou delightest in the repentance of the wicked, and hast no pleasure in their death " (Neilah Amidah).

19. *nigh . . . broken heart.* Sorrow purges the human breast of its dross ; and, as nothing else, opens the eyes of the soul to spiritual vision and values.

21. *all his limbs.* Denotes the safe preservation of the man's whole being.

תְּמוֹתֵת רָשָׁע רָעָה וְשֹׂנְאֵי צַדִּיק יֶאְשָׁמוּ :

פֹּדֶה יְהֹוָה נֶפֶשׁ עֲבָדָיו וְלֹא יֶאְשְׁמוּ כָּל־הַחֹסִים בּוֹ :

צ׳ תְּפִלָּה לְמֹשֶׁה אִישׁ־הָאֱלֹהִים אֲדֹנָי מָעוֹן אַתָּה הָיִיתָ

לָּנוּ בְּדֹר וָדֹר : בְּטֶרֶם הָרִים יֻלָּדוּ וַתְּחוֹלֵל אֶרֶץ וְתֵבֵל

וּמֵעוֹלָם עַד־עוֹלָם אַתָּה אֵל : תָּשֵׁב אֱנוֹשׁ עַד־דַּכָּא

וַתֹּאמֶר שׁוּבוּ בְנֵי־אָדָם : כִּי אֶלֶף שָׁנִים בְּעֵינֶיךָ כְּיוֹם

אֶתְמוֹל כִּי יַעֲבֹר וְאַשְׁמוּרָה בַלָּיְלָה : זְרַמְתָּם שֵׁנָה יִהְיוּ

בַּבֹּקֶר כֶּחָצִיר יַחֲלֹף : בַּבֹּקֶר יָצִיץ וְחָלָף לָעֶרֶב יְמוֹלֵל

וְיָבֵשׁ : כִּי־כָלִינוּ בְאַפֶּךָ וּבַחֲמָתְךָ נִבְהָלְנוּ : שַׁתָּ עֲוֹנֹתֵינוּ

לְנֶגְדֶּךָ עֲלֻמֵנוּ לִמְאוֹר פָּנֶיךָ : כִּי כָל־יָמֵינוּ פָּנוּ בְעֶבְרָתֶךָ

22. *evil shall slay the wicked.* Sin overthrows the sinner. His evil ways work out their own doom. There is an inevitable recoil of evil upon the evil-doer.

23. *shall be condemned.* To punishment on earth or in the Hereafter.

PSALM 90.

A PRAYER OF MOSES.

The editorial heading ascribes this psalm to Moses, and there are similarities in phrase to Moses' last Address. The psalm is worthy of the Lawgiver. Its loftiness of tone, its solemnity, its conviction of God's nearness, are tinged with a melancholy natural to a man of such sublime triumphs and disappointments. Nowhere is there a nobler realization that everything human is transitory, and that God alone is everlasting. The psalm is a dirge over the futility of all human effort, and the evanescence of all human achievement ; and yet it opens vistas into that eternal world which knows no defeat and no decay.

1. *our dwelling place.* God is our " home ". Isaac Watts has paraphrased some of the main thoughts of this psalm in his well-known hymn :

" O God, our help in ages past,
Our hope for years to come,

SABBATH
PSALMS one of them is broken. ²²Evil shall slay the wicked ; and they that hate the righteous shall be held guilty. ²³The Lord setteth free the soul of his servants ; and none that take refuge in him shall be condemned.

Psalm xc. ¹A Prayer of Moses, the man of God.

LIFE IS
FLEETING :
GOD
ETERNAL
O Lord, thou hast been a dwelling place unto us in all generations. ²Before the mountains were brought forth, or ever thou gavest birth to the earth and the world, even from everlasting to everlasting thou art God. ³Thou turnest man back to dust, and sayest, Return, ye children of men. ⁴For a thousand years in thy sight are but as yesterday when it is past, and as a watch in the night. ⁵Thou carriest them away as with a flood ; they are in a sleep ; in the morning they are like grass which sprouteth afresh. ⁶In the morning it bloometh, and sprouteth afresh ; in the evening it is cut down, and withereth. ⁷For we are consumed by thine anger, and in thy wrath are we confounded. ⁸Thou hast set our iniquities before thee, our secret sins in the light of thy countenance. ⁹For all our days are passed away in thy wrath, we bring our years to an end like a tale that is told. ¹⁰The

> Our shelter from the stormy blast,
> And our eternal home.
> Before the hills in order stood,
> Or earth received her frame,
> From everlasting Thou art God,
> To endless years the same.
> A thousand ages in Thy sight
> Are like an evening gone ;
> Short as the watch that ends the night
> Before the rising sun.

2. *from everlasting to everlasting.* From eternity in the past to eternity in the future.

3. *return, ye children of men.* Unto Me, the Judge of the human spirit. God, the unchanging, is the refuge of changing and erring man.

4. *watch in the night.* Of which the sleeper is unconscious. One of the three parts into which the night was divided.

7–12. Human life is fleeting ; man's sorrow is due to God's anger, the cause of God's anger being man's sin.

כִּלִּינוּ שָׁנֵינוּ כְמוֹ־הֶגֶה : יְמֵי שְׁנוֹתֵינוּ בָהֶם שִׁבְעִים שָׁנָה

וְאִם בִּגְבוּרֹת שְׁמוֹנִים שָׁנָה וְרָהְבָּם עָמָל וָאָוֶן כִּי

גָז חִישׁ וַנָּעֻפָה : מִי־יוֹדֵעַ עֹז אַפֶּךָ וּכְיִרְאָתְךָ עֶבְרָתֶךָ :

לִמְנוֹת יָמֵינוּ כֵּן הוֹדַע וְנָבִא לְבַב חָכְמָה : שׁוּבָה יְהוָֹה

עַד־מָתָי וְהִנָּחֵם עַל־עֲבָדֶיךָ : שַׂבְּעֵנוּ בַבֹּקֶר חַסְדֶּךָ

וּנְרַנְּנָה וְנִשְׂמְחָה בְּכָל־יָמֵינוּ : שַׂמְּחֵנוּ כִּימוֹת עִנִּיתָנוּ

שְׁנוֹת רָאִינוּ רָעָה : יֵרָאֶה אֶל־עֲבָדֶיךָ פָעֳלֶךָ וַהֲדָרְךָ עַל־

בְּנֵיהֶם :

וִיהִי נֹעַם אֲדֹנָי אֱלֹהֵינוּ עָלֵינוּ וּמַעֲשֵׂה יָדֵינוּ כּוֹנְנָה

עָלֵינוּ וּמַעֲשֵׂה יָדֵינוּ כּוֹנְנֵהוּ :

צ״א יֹשֵׁב בְּסֵתֶר עֶלְיוֹן בְּצֵל שַׁדַּי יִתְלוֹנָן : אֹמַר לַיהוָֹה

מַחְסִי וּמְצוּדָתִי אֱלֹהַי אֶבְטַח־בּוֹ : כִּי הוּא יַצִּילְךָ מִפַּח

יָקוּשׁ מִדֶּבֶר הַוּוֹת : בְּאֶבְרָתוֹ יָסֶךְ לָךְ וְתַחַת כְּנָפָיו

9. *as a tale that is told.* lit. " a sound ", a " thought ".

11. *who knoweth the power.* How few have such a just conception of Thine anger as to lead to reverential awe ? " Who has realized the intensity of God's displeasure against sin in the degree that the ' fear of God ' (*i.e.* true religion) requires " ? (Cheyne).

13–17. PRAYER FOR THE RESTORATION OF GOD'S FAVOUR.

14. *in the morning. i.e.* quickly.

16. *thy work.* Thy saving Providence.

17. *graciousness.* Favour, goodwill.

do thou establish. If we apply these words to the psalmist himself, his prayer has been fulfilled. This psalm is still to-day among the best-known of all the outpourings of man's spirit.

SABBATH PSALMS
LIFE IS FLEETING :
GOD ETERNAL

days of our years are threescore years and ten, or even by reason of strength fourscore years ; yet is their pride but travail and nothingness ; for it is soon gone by, and we fly away. ¹¹Who knoweth the power of thine anger, and thy wrath according to the awe that is due unto thee ? ¹²So teach us to number our days, that we may get us a heart of wisdom. ¹³Return, O Lord ; how long ?—and relent thee concerning thy servants. ¹⁴O satisfy us in the morning with thy lovingkindness ; that we may exult and rejoice all our days. ¹⁵Make us rejoice according to the days wherein thou hast afflicted us, the years wherein we have seen evil. ¹⁶Let thy work be made manifest unto thy servants, and thy majesty upon their children.

¹⁷And let the graciousness of the Lord our God be upon us : and establish thou the work of our hands upon us ; yea, the work of our hands do thou establish.

Psalm xci.

ASSUR-ANCE
OF DIVINE PROTEC-TION

¹He that dwelleth in the shelter of the Most High abideth under the shadow of the Almighty. ²I say of the Lord, He is my refuge and my fortress ; my God, in whom I trust. —³For he shall deliver thee from the snare of the fowler, and from the noisome pestilence. ⁴He shall cover thee

PSALM 91.

This psalm is a consoling answer to the preceding psalm. Not by magic formulae and enchantments were mishaps or calamities to be banished, but by trust in God.

It is best to consider this psalm, with the ancient interpreters, as an antiphonal song, and divide it as follows : one voice chants *v.* 1 and 2, and an answering voice speaks *v.* 3–8 ; the first voice repeats 9*a* (" For thou, O Lord, art my refuge "), and the answering voice responds with 9*b*–13 ; while a third voice, a Levite in the Temple, speaking in the name of God, concludes with *v.* 14–16.

1. *shadow of the Almighty.* The figure suggests the protection which a mother-bird gives her brood, as in *v.* 4.

3–9   THE PROVIDENTIAL CARE OF GOD.

3. *snare of the fowler.* Insidious attempts of malicious foes.
noisome. Old English for " noxious " ; destroying.

תֶּחְפֶּה צִנָּה וְסֹחֵרָה אֲמִתּוֹ : לֹא־תִירָא מִפַּחַד לָיְלָה
מֵחֵץ יָעוּף יוֹמָם : מִדֶּבֶר בָּאֹפֶל יַהֲלֹךְ מִקֶּטֶב יָשׁוּד
צָהֳרָיִם : יִפֹּל מִצִּדְּךָ אֶלֶף וּרְבָבָה מִימִינֶךָ אֵלֶיךָ לֹא
יִגָּשׁ : רַק בְּעֵינֶיךָ תַבִּיט וְשִׁלֻּמַת רְשָׁעִים תִּרְאֶה : כִּי־
אַתָּה יְהֹוָה מַחְסִי עֶלְיוֹן שַׂמְתָּ מְעוֹנֶךָ : לֹא־תְאֻנֶּה אֵלֶיךָ
רָעָה וְנֶגַע לֹא־יִקְרַב בְּאָהֳלֶךָ : כִּי מַלְאָכָיו יְצַוֶּה־לָּךְ
לִשְׁמָרְךָ בְּכָל־דְּרָכֶיךָ : עַל־כַּפַּיִם יִשָּׂאוּנְךָ פֶּן תִּגֹּף בָּאֶבֶן
רַגְלֶךָ : עַל־שַׁחַל וָפֶתֶן תִּדְרֹךְ תִּרְמֹס כְּפִיר וְתַנִּין : כִּי
בִי חָשַׁק וַאֲפַלְּטֵהוּ אֲשַׂגְּבֵהוּ כִּי־יָדַע שְׁמִי : יִקְרָאֵנִי
וְאֶעֱנֵהוּ עִמּוֹ אָנֹכִי בְצָרָה אֲחַלְּצֵהוּ וַאֲכַבְּדֵהוּ : אֹרֶךְ
יָמִים אַשְׂבִּיעֵהוּ וְאַרְאֵהוּ בִּישׁוּעָתִי : *Repeat the last verse.*

קל״ה הַלְלוּיָהּ · הַלְלוּ אֶת־שֵׁם יְהֹוָה הַלְלוּ עַבְדֵי יְהֹוָה :
שֶׁעֹמְדִים בְּבֵית יְהֹוָה בְּחַצְרוֹת בֵּית אֱלֹהֵינוּ : הַלְלוּיָהּ

4. *truth.* Faithfulness.
6. *stalketh in darkness.* Plague and Destruction are personified as
destroying beings.

9–16. RENEWED ASSURANCE OF DIVINE PROTECTION.

11. *angels.* The popular belief of two ministering angels that
accompany each man is based on this *v.*
13. *lion and adder.* Figures for fierce obstacles and unforeseen
dangers. Assaults of open violence are represented by the fury of the
lion ; whilst those of secret malice, by the venomous bite of the serpent.
14. *set him on high.* Beyond the reach of danger.
knoweth my Name. Knoweth My revealed character as a God of
justice and mercy.

SABBATH
PSALMS

*ASSUR-
ANCE
OF DIVINE
PROTEC-
TION*
with his pinions, and under his wings shalt thou take refuge : his truth shall be a˙ shield and armour. ⁵Thou shalt not be afraid of the terror by night, nor of the arrow that flieth by day ; ⁶of the pestilence that stalketh in darkness, nor of the destruction that ravageth at noonday. ⁷A thousand may fall at thy side, and ten thousand at thy right hand, yet it shall not come nigh unto thee. ⁸Only with thine eyes shalt thou look on, and see the retribution of the wicked.—⁹For thou, O Lord, art my refuge.—Thou hast made the Most High thy dwelling place ; ¹⁰there shall no evil befall thee, neither shall any scourge come nigh thy tent. ¹¹For he shall give his angels charge over thee, to keep thee in all thy ways. ¹²They shall bear thee upon their hands, lest thou strike thy foot against a stone. ¹³Thou shalt tread upon the lion and the adder ; upon the young lion and the serpent shalt thou trample.—¹⁴Because he hath set his love upon me, therefore will I deliver him : I will set him on high, because he knoweth my Name. ¹⁵When he calleth upon Me, I will answer him ; I will be with him in trouble : I will deliver him and honour him. ¹⁶With length of days will I satisfy him, and will let him see my salvation.

Repeat the last verse.

Psalm cxxxv.

*GOD'S
OMNI-
POTENCE
SHOWN IN
NATURE
AND
ISRAEL'S
STORY*
¹Praise ye the Lord. Praise ye the Name of the Lord ; praise him, ye servants of the Lord : ²ye that stand in the house of the Lord, in the courts of the house of our God. ³Praise ye the Lord ; for the Lord is good : sing

---

16. *my salvation.* My saving care ; the visible manifestation of My providence.

PSALM 135.

Both in nature and in Israel's Divinely-ordered history, God is mighty and merciful.

1. *praise ye the Lord.* Heb. *Hallelujah* (the j is read y). This term occurs only in the Psalter, and seems to have been the summons addressed by the precentor to the congregation in the Temple to join, or to respond, in the recitation of the psalm (Graetz).

2. *that stand in the house of the Lord.* The priests and Levites who minister therein.

כִּי־טוֹב יְהֹוָה זַמְּרוּ לִשְׁמוֹ כִּי נָעִים: כִּי־יַעֲקֹב בָּחַר לוֹ יָהּ
יִשְׂרָאֵל לִסְגֻלָּתוֹ: כִּי אֲנִי יָדַעְתִּי כִּי־גָדוֹל יְהֹוָה וַאֲדֹנֵינוּ
מִכָּל־אֱלֹהִים: כֹּל אֲשֶׁר־חָפֵץ יְהֹוָה עָשָׂה בַּשָּׁמַיִם וּבָאָרֶץ
בַּיַּמִּים וְכָל־תְּהֹמוֹת: מַעֲלֶה נְשִׂאִים מִקְצֵה הָאָרֶץ בְּרָקִים
לַמָּטָר עָשָׂה מוֹצֵא רוּחַ מֵאוֹצְרוֹתָיו: שֶׁהִכָּה בְּכוֹרֵי
מִצְרָיִם מֵאָדָם עַד־בְּהֵמָה: שָׁלַח אוֹתֹת וּמֹפְתִים בְּתוֹכֵכִי
מִצְרָיִם בְּפַרְעֹה וּבְכָל־עֲבָדָיו: שֶׁהִכָּה גּוֹיִם רַבִּים וְהָרַג
מְלָכִים עֲצוּמִים: לְסִיחוֹן מֶלֶךְ הָאֱמֹרִי וּלְעוֹג מֶלֶךְ הַבָּשָׁן
וּלְכֹל מַמְלְכוֹת כְּנָעַן: וְנָתַן אַרְצָם נַחֲלָה נַחֲלָה לְיִשְׂרָאֵל
עַמּוֹ: יְהֹוָה שִׁמְךָ לְעוֹלָם יְהֹוָה זִכְרְךָ לְדֹר־וָדֹר: כִּי־יָדִין
יְהֹוָה עַמּוֹ וְעַל־עֲבָדָיו יִתְנֶחָם: עֲצַבֵּי הַגּוֹיִם כֶּסֶף וְזָהָב
מַעֲשֵׂה יְדֵי אָדָם: פֶּה־לָהֶם וְלֹא יְדַבֵּרוּ עֵינַיִם לָהֶם וְלֹא
יִרְאוּ: אָזְנַיִם לָהֶם וְלֹא יַאֲזִינוּ אַף אֵין־יֶשׁ־רוּחַ בְּפִיהֶם:
כְּמוֹהֶם יִהְיוּ עֹשֵׂיהֶם כֹּל אֲשֶׁר־בֹּטֵחַ בָּהֶם: בֵּית יִשְׂרָאֵל
בָּרְכוּ אֶת־יְהֹוָה בֵּית אַהֲרֹן בָּרְכוּ אֶת־יְהֹוָה: בֵּית הַלֵּוִי
בָּרְכוּ אֶת־יְהֹוָה יִרְאֵי יְהֹוָה בָּרְכוּ אֶת־יְהֹוָה: בָּרוּךְ
יְהֹוָה מִצִּיּוֹן שֹׁכֵן יְרוּשָׁלָיִם הַלְלוּיָהּ:

5–7. GOD'S GREATNESS SHOWN IN NATURE.

6. *deeps.* The subterranean waters.
7. *lightnings for the rain. i.e.* lightnings accompanying the rain.
treasuries. See Job 38. 22.

SABBATH
PSALMS

*GOD'S
OMNI-
POTENCE
SHOWN IN
NATURE
AND
ISRAEL'S
STORY*

praises unto his Name ; for it is pleasant. ⁴For the Lord hath chosen Jacob unto himself, and Israel for his peculiar treasure. ⁵For I know that the Lord is great, and that our Lord is above all gods. ⁶Whatsoever the Lord pleaseth, that doeth he, in heaven and in earth, in the seas and in all deeps. ⁷He causeth vapours to ascend from the ends of the earth ; he maketh lightnings for the rain ; he bringeth forth the wind out of his treasuries. ⁸It is he who smote the firstborn of Egypt, both of man and beast. ⁹He sent signs and wonders into the midst of thee, O Egypt, upon Pharaoh, and upon all his servants. ¹⁰It is he who smote great nations, and slew mighty kings ; ¹¹Sihon king of the Amorites, and Og king of Bashan, and all the kingdoms of Canaan: ¹²and gave their land for an heritage, an heritage unto Israel his people. ¹³Thy Name, O Lord, endureth for ever ; thy fame, O Lord, throughout all generations. ¹⁴Surely the Lord shall judge his people, and relent towards his servants. ¹⁵The idols of the heathen are silver and gold, the work of men's hands. ¹⁶They have mouths, but they speak not ; eyes have they, but they see not ; ¹⁷they have ears, but they hear not ; neither is there any breath in their mouths. ¹⁸They that make them shall become like unto them ; yea, every one that trusteth in them. ¹⁹O house of Israel, bless ye the Lord : O house of Aaron, bless ye the Lord : O house of Levi, bless ye the Lord : ye that fear the Lord, bless ye the Lord. ²¹Blessed be the Lord out of Zion, who dwelleth at Jerusalem. Praise ye the Lord.

8–14. God's Glory shown in Israel's History.

11. *Sihon . . . Og.* The first formidable enemies whom the Israelites encountered after crossing the Wilderness ; Numbers 21.

13. *fame.* lit. " memorial ", bringing to mind all that He is and does. The Heb. term is a synonym for " Name ", when speaking of God.

15–18. The idols are things of empty uselessness, in contrast to God Who is almighty and ever-enduring ; see p. 763.

19–21. All Israel is Summoned to Praise God.

21. *dwelleth at Jerusalem.* Whose earthly Sanctuary is on Mt. Zion.

קל׳. הוֹדוּ לַיהוָה כִּי־טוֹב   כִּי לְעוֹלָם חַסְדּוֹ:

הוֹדוּ לֵאלֹהֵי הָאֱלֹהִים   כִּי לְעוֹלָם חַסְדּוֹ:

הוֹדוּ לַאֲדֹנֵי הָאֲדֹנִים   כִּי לְעוֹלָם חַסְדּוֹ:

לְעֹשֵׂה נִפְלָאוֹת גְּדֹלוֹת לְבַדּוֹ   כִּי לְעוֹלָם חַסְדּוֹ:

לְעֹשֵׂה הַשָּׁמַיִם בִּתְבוּנָה   כִּי לְעוֹלָם חַסְדּוֹ:

לְרוֹקַע הָאָרֶץ עַל־הַמָּיִם   כִּי לְעוֹלָם חַסְדּוֹ:

לְעֹשֵׂה אוֹרִים גְּדֹלִים   כִּי לְעוֹלָם חַסְדּוֹ:

אֶת־הַשֶּׁמֶשׁ לְמֶמְשֶׁלֶת בַּיּוֹם   כִּי לְעוֹלָם חַסְדּוֹ:

אֶת־הַיָּרֵחַ וְכוֹכָבִים לְמֶמְשְׁלוֹת בַּלָּיְלָה   כִּי לְעוֹלָם חַסְדּוֹ:

לְמַכֵּה מִצְרַיִם בִּבְכוֹרֵיהֶם   כִּי לְעוֹלָם חַסְדּוֹ:

וַיּוֹצֵא יִשְׂרָאֵל מִתּוֹכָם   כִּי לְעוֹלָם חַסְדּוֹ:

בְּיָד חֲזָקָה וּבִזְרוֹעַ נְטוּיָה   כִּי לְעוֹלָם חַסְדּוֹ:

לְגֹזֵר יַם־סוּף לִגְזָרִים   כִּי לְעוֹלָם חַסְדּוֹ:

וְהֶעֱבִיר יִשְׂרָאֵל בְּתוֹכוֹ   כִּי לְעוֹלָם חַסְדּוֹ:

וְנִעֵר פַּרְעֹה וְחֵילוֹ בְיַם־סוּף   כִּי לְעוֹלָם חַסְדּוֹ:

לְמוֹלִיךְ עַמּוֹ בַּמִּדְבָּר   כִּי לְעוֹלָם חַסְדּוֹ:

לְמַכֵּה מְלָכִים גְּדֹלִים   כִּי לְעוֹלָם חַסְדּוֹ:

וַיַּהֲרֹג מְלָכִים אַדִּירִים   כִּי לְעוֹלָם חַסְדּוֹ:

לְסִיחוֹן מֶלֶךְ הָאֱמֹרִי   כִּי לְעוֹלָם חַסְדּוֹ:

וּלְעוֹג מֶלֶךְ הַבָּשָׁן   כִּי לְעוֹלָם חַסְדּוֹ:

SABBATH
PSALMS
*A FESTAL
HALLE-
LUJAH :*
*"HIS
LOVING-
KINDNESS
ENDURETH
FOREVER"*

Psalm cxxxvi.

[1]O give thanks unto the Lord ; for he is good : for his lovingkindness endureth for ever. [2]O give thanks unto the God of gods : for his lovingkindness endureth for ever. [3]O give thanks unto the Lord of lords : for his lovingkindness endureth for ever. [4]To him who alone doeth great marvels : for his lovingkindness endureth for ever. [5]To him that by understanding made the heavens : for his lovingkindness endureth for ever. [6]To him that spread forth the earth above the waters : for his lovingkindness endureth for ever. [7]To him that made great lights : for his lovingkindness endureth for ever : [8]the sun to rule by day : for his lovingkindness endureth for ever : [9]the moon and stars to rule by night : for his lovingkindness endureth for ever. [10]To him that smote the Egyptians in their firstborn : for his lovingkindness endureth for ever : [11]and brought out Israel from among them : for his lovingkindness endureth for ever : [12]with a strong hand, and with a stretched out arm : for his lovingkindness endureth for ever. [13]To him who parted the Red Sea asunder : for his lovingkindness endureth for ever : [14]and made Israel to pass through the midst of it : for his lovingkindness endureth for ever : [15]but overthrew Pharaoh and his host in the Red Sea : for his lovingkindness endureth for ever. [16]To him who led his people through the wilderness : for his lovingkindness endureth for ever. [17]To him who smote great kings : for his lovingkindness endureth for ever : [18]and slew mighty kings : for his lovingkindness endureth for ever : [19]Sihon king of the Amorites : for his lovingkindness endureth for ever : [20]and Og king of Bashan :

PSALM 136.

This Song of Glorification is a Temple song, with a constant refrain, " for His lovingkindness endureth for ever ", that was chanted either by a section of priests, Levites, or by the whole assemblage of worshippers ; cf. II Chronicles 7. 3, 6.

4–9. GOD THE CREATOR.

10–12. GOD THE DELIVERER.

וְנָתַן אַרְצָם לְנַחֲלָה   כִּי לְעוֹלָם חַסְדּוֹ :

נַחֲלָה לְיִשְׂרָאֵל עַבְדּוֹ   כִּי לְעוֹלָם חַסְדּוֹ :

שֶׁבְּשִׁפְלֵנוּ זָכַר־לָנוּ   כִּי לְעוֹלָם חַסְדּוֹ :

וַיִּפְרְקֵנוּ מִצָּרֵינוּ   כִּי לְעוֹלָם חַסְדּוֹ :

נֹתֵן לֶחֶם לְכָל־בָּשָׂר   כִּי לְעוֹלָם חַסְדּוֹ :

הוֹדוּ לְאֵל הַשָּׁמָיִם   כִּי לְעוֹלָם חַסְדּוֹ :

לג רַנְּנוּ צַדִּיקִים בַּיהוָה לַיְשָׁרִים נָאוָה תְהִלָּה : הוֹדוּ

לַיהוָה בְּכִנּוֹר בְּנֵבֶל עָשׂוֹר זַמְּרוּ־לוֹ : שִׁירוּ לוֹ שִׁיר חָדָשׁ

הֵיטִיבוּ נַגֵּן בִּתְרוּעָה : כִּי־יָשָׁר דְּבַר־יְהוָה וְכָל־מַעֲשֵׂהוּ

בֶּאֱמוּנָה : אֹהֵב צְדָקָה וּמִשְׁפָּט חֶסֶד יְהוָה מָלְאָה

הָאָרֶץ : בִּדְבַר יְהוָה שָׁמַיִם נַעֲשׂוּ וּבְרוּחַ פִּיו כָּל־

צְבָאָם : כֹּנֵס כַּנֵּד מֵי הַיָּם נֹתֵן בְּאוֹצָרוֹת תְּהוֹמוֹת :

יִירְאוּ מֵיהוָה כָּל־הָאָרֶץ מִמֶּנּוּ יָגוּרוּ כָּל־יֹשְׁבֵי תֵבֵל :

כִּי הוּא אָמַר וַיֶּהִי הוּא צִוָּה וַיַּעֲמֹד : יְהוָה הֵפִיר

23–26. GOD THE SUPPORTER OF ALL THINGS LIVING.

23. *our low estate.* Our basement during subjection to foreign yoke, as in Egypt or Babylon.

25. 26. *all flesh . . . God of heaven.* The psalm is a national hymn of Deliverance, and yet ends on the highest universalist note. God feedeth *all* flesh : He is the God of heaven.

*"HIS
LOVING-
KINDNESS
ENDURETH
FOREVER"*
for his lovingkindness endureth for ever : ²¹and gave their land for an heritage : for his lovingkindness endureth for ever : ²²even an heritage unto Israel his servant : for his lovingkindness endureth for ever. ²³Who remembered us in our low estate : for his lovingkindness endureth for ever : ²⁴and hath delivered us from our adversaries : for his lovingkindness endureth for ever. ²⁵He giveth food to all flesh : for his lovingkindness endureth for ever. ²⁶O give thanks unto the God of heaven : for his lovingkindness endureth for ever.

Psalm xxxiii.

*PRAISE
FOR
NATIONAL
DELIVER-
ANCE ·*
¹Rejoice in the Lord, O ye righteous : praise is seemly for the upright. ²Give thanks unto the Lord with the lyre : sing praises unto him with the harp of ten strings. ³Sing unto him a new song ; play skilfully with sounds of joy. ⁴For the word of the Lord is right ; and all his work is done in faithfulness. ⁵He loveth righteousness and justice : the earth is full of the lovingkindness of the Lord. ⁶By the word of the Lord the heavens were made ; and all the host of them by the breath of his mouth. ⁷He gathereth the waters of the sea together as a heap : he layeth up the floods in store-houses. ⁸Let all the earth revere the Lord : let all the inhabitants of the world stand in awe of him. ⁹For he spake, and it was ; he commanded, and it stood fast.

PSALM 33.
"Happy is the Nation whose God is the Lord."

1. *ye righteous.* " R. Jeremiah said, it does not say, Rejoice in the Lord, ye Priests, ye Levites, ye Israelites ; but it says, *Rejoice in the Lord, ye righteous*—whether Jew or non-Jew, priest or layman " (Sifra).

3. *new song.* Fresh from the psalmist's heart to celebrate a new deliverance or a new instance of God's goodness and mercy.

4. *faithfulness.* The mainfestation of righteousness in the government of the world.

5. *righteousness.* Here equivalent to " equity ", which implies a due and kindly consideration of all the facts of every case.

7. *store-houses.* Masses of water stored away under the earth.

עֲצַת גּוֹיִם הֵנִיא מַחְשְׁבוֹת עַמִּים : עֲצַת יְהֹוָה לְעוֹלָם

תַּעֲמֹד מַחְשְׁבוֹת לִבּוֹ לְדֹר וָדֹר : אַשְׁרֵי הַגּוֹי אֲשֶׁר־יְהֹוָה

אֱלֹהָיו הָעָם בָּחַר לְנַחֲלָה לוֹ : מִשָּׁמַיִם הִבִּיט יְהֹוָה

רָאָה אֶת־כָּל־בְּנֵי הָאָדָם : מִמְּכוֹן־שִׁבְתּוֹ הִשְׁגִּיחַ אֶל

כָּל־יֹשְׁבֵי הָאָרֶץ : הַיֹּצֵר יַחַד לִבָּם הַמֵּבִין אֶל־כָּל־

מַעֲשֵׂיהֶם : אֵין הַמֶּלֶךְ נוֹשָׁע בְּרָב־חָיִל גִּבּוֹר לֹא־יִנָּצֵל

בְּרָב־כֹּחַ : שֶׁקֶר הַסּוּס לִתְשׁוּעָה וּבְרֹב חֵילוֹ לֹא יְמַלֵּט :

הִנֵּה עֵין יְהֹוָה אֶל־יְרֵאָיו לַמְיַחֲלִים לְחַסְדּוֹ : לְהַצִּיל

מִמָּוֶת נַפְשָׁם וּלְחַיּוֹתָם בָּרָעָב : נַפְשֵׁנוּ חִכְּתָה לַיהֹוָה

עֶזְרֵנוּ וּמָגִנֵּנוּ הוּא : כִּי־בוֹ יִשְׂמַח לִבֵּנוּ כִּי בְשֵׁם קָדְשׁוֹ

בָטָחְנוּ : יְהִי־חַסְדְּךָ יְהֹוָה עָלֵינוּ כַּאֲשֶׁר יִחַלְנוּ לָךְ :

צ״ב מִזְמוֹר שִׁיר לְיוֹם הַשַּׁבָּת : טוֹב לְהֹדוֹת לַיהֹוָה וּלְזַמֵּר

לְשִׁמְךָ עֶלְיוֹן : לְהַגִּיד בַּבֹּקֶר חַסְדֶּךָ וֶאֱמוּנָתְךָ בַּלֵּילוֹת :

עֲלֵי־עָשׂוֹר וַעֲלֵי־נָבֶל עֲלֵי הִגָּיוֹן בְּכִנּוֹר : כִּי שִׂמַּחְתַּנִי

יְהֹוָה בְּפָעֳלֶךָ בְּמַעֲשֵׂי יָדֶיךָ אֲרַנֵּן : מַה־גָּדְלוּ מַעֲשֶׂיךָ

יְהֹוָה מְאֹד עָמְקוּ מַחְשְׁבֹתֶיךָ : אִישׁ בַּעַר לֹא יֵדָע וּכְסִיל

---

10. *heathen.* From creation the Psalmist passes to history; and in
v. 12, to the story of Israel.

17. *horse.* Stands for cavalry. Israel's strength is not in a powerful
army, but in God.

18. *hope in his mercy.* Unlike them who put their trust in human
might, neither sword nor famine shall destroy them.

20–22. These words were chanted by the chorus or full body of
worshippers.

SABBATH
PSALMS

*"HAPPY
IS THE
NATION
WHOSE
GOD IS
THE
LORD"*

¹⁰The Lord bringeth the design of the heathen to nought ; he hath foiled the thoughts of the peoples. ¹¹The counsel of the Lord standeth fast for ever, the thoughts of his heart to all generations. ¹²Happy is the nation whose·God is the Lord ; the people whom he hath chosen for his own inheritance. ¹³The Lord looketh down from heaven ; he beholdeth all the sons of men ; ¹⁴from the place of his habitation he gazeth upon all the inhabitants of the earth ; ¹⁵he that fashioneth the hearts of them all, that giveth heed to all their works. ¹⁶A king is not saved by greatness of power : a mighty man is not delivered by greatness of strength. ¹⁷A horse is a vain thing for safety : neither shall it rescue any by its great power. ¹⁸Behold, the eye of the Lord is upon them that reverence him, upon them that hope in his mercy ; ¹⁹to deliver their soul from death, and to keep them alive in famine. ²⁰Our soul waiteth for the Lord : he is our help and our shield. ²¹For our heart shall rejoice in him, because we have trusted in his holy Name. ²²Let thy lovingkindness, O Lord, be upon us, according as we have hoped in thee.

*THE
JUSTICE
OF GOD*

¹Psalm xcii. A Psalm, a Song for the Sabbath Day.

²It is a good thing to give thanks unto the Lord, and to sing praises unto thy Name, O Most High : ³to declare thy lovingkindness in the morning, and thy faithfulness every night, ⁴with an instrument of ten strings and with a harp, with solemn music upon the lyre. ⁵For thou, O Lord, hast made me rejoice through thy work : I will exult in the works of thy hands. ⁶How great are thy works, O Lord : thy thoughts are very deep. ⁷A brutish man knoweth it not, neither doth a fool understand this : ⁸when the wicked sprang up as the grass, and all the workers of iniquity flourished, it was that they might be destroyed for ever.

---

22. *as we have hoped in thee.* The whole history of Israel, has, indeed, been summed up in Jacob's dying words (Genesis 49. 18), " For thy salvation, I hope, O Lord ".

Psalms 92 and 93 will be explained in connection with the Service for the Eve of Sabbath, pp. 360–3.

לֹא־יָבִין אֶת־זֹאת : בִּפְרֹחַ רְשָׁעִים כְּמוֹ־עֵשֶׂב וַיָּצִיצוּ
כָּל־פֹּעֲלֵי אָוֶן לְהִשָּׁמְדָם עֲדֵי־עַד : וְאַתָּה מָרוֹם לְעֹלָם
יְהוָה : כִּי הִנֵּה אֹיְבֶיךָ יְהוָה כִּי־הִנֵּה אֹיְבֶיךָ יֹאבֵדוּ
יִתְפָּרְדוּ כָּל־פֹּעֲלֵי אָוֶן : וַתָּרֶם כִּרְאֵים קַרְנִי בַּלֹּתִי
בְּשֶׁמֶן רַעֲנָן : וַתַּבֵּט עֵינִי בְּשׁוּרָי בַּקָּמִים עָלַי מְרֵעִים
תִּשְׁמַעְנָה אָזְנָי : צַדִּיק כַּתָּמָר יִפְרָח כְּאֶרֶז בַּלְּבָנוֹן יִשְׂגֶּה :
שְׁתוּלִים בְּבֵית יְהוָה בְּחַצְרוֹת אֱלֹהֵינוּ יַפְרִיחוּ : עוֹד
יְנוּבוּן בְּשֵׂיבָה דְּשֵׁנִים וְרַעֲנַנִּים יִהְיוּ : לְהַגִּיד כִּי־יָשָׁר
יְהוָה צוּרִי וְלֹא־עַוְלָתָה בּוֹ :

צ׳ג יְהוָה מָלָךְ גֵּאוּת לָבֵשׁ לָבֵשׁ יְהוָה עֹז הִתְאַזָּר אַף־
תִּכּוֹן תֵּבֵל בַּל־תִּמּוֹט : נָכוֹן כִּסְאֲךָ מֵאָז מֵעוֹלָם אָתָּה :
נָשְׂאוּ נְהָרוֹת יְהוָה נָשְׂאוּ נְהָרוֹת קוֹלָם יִשְׂאוּ נְהָרוֹת
דָּכְיָם : מִקֹּלוֹת מַיִם רַבִּים אַדִּירִים מִשְׁבְּרֵי־יָם אַדִּיר
בַּמָּרוֹם יְהוָה : עֵדֹתֶיךָ נֶאֶמְנוּ מְאֹד לְבֵיתְךָ נַאֲוָה־קֹדֶשׁ
יְהוָה לְאֹרֶךְ יָמִים :

On Weekdays continue here from p. 60.

יְהִי כְבוֹד יְיָ לְעוֹלָם יִשְׂמַח יְיָ בְּמַעֲשָׂיו : יְהִי שֵׁם יְיָ

WEEKDAY SERVICE RESUMED

The weekday service is resumed with "Let the glory of the
Lord endure for ever". This consists of Scriptural verses, brought
together not only by similarity of ideas, but also of phrase. Each subsequent verse contains some word or idea already contained in the
preceding.

⁹But thou, O Lord, art on high for evermore. ¹⁰For, lo, thine enemies, O Lord, for, lo, thine enemies shall perish ; all the workers of iniquity shall be scattered. ¹¹But my strength hast thou exalted, like that of the wild-ox : I am anointed with fresh oil. ¹²Mine eye also hath seen the defeat of mine enemies ; mine ears have heard the doom of them that rose up against me, doers of evil. ¹³The righteous shall spring up like a palm-tree ; he shall grow tall like a cedar in Lebanon. ¹⁴Planted in the house of the Lord, they shall blossom in the courts of our God. ¹⁵They shall still shoot forth in old age ; they shall be full of sap and green : ¹⁶to declare that the Lord is upright ; he is my Rock, and there is no unrighteousness in him.

Psalm xciii

THE LORD
IS KING

¹The Lord reigneth ; he hath robed him in majesty ; the Lord hath robed him, yea, he hath girded himself with strength : the world also is set firm, that it cannot be moved. ²Thy throne is set firm from of old : thou art from everlasting. ³The streams have lifted up, O Lord, the streams have lifted up their voice ; the streams lift up their roaring. ⁴Than the voices of many waters, mighty waters, breakers of the sea, more mighty is the Lord on high. ⁵Thy testimonies are very sure : holiness becometh thine house, O Lord, for evermore.

WEEKDAY
SERVICE
RESUMED

Psalm 104. 31

Psalm
113. 2, 3, 4

On Weekdays continue here from p. 61.

Let the glory of the Lord endure for ever ; let the Lord rejoice in his works. Let the Name of the Lord be blessed from this time and for evermore. From the rising of the sun unto the going down thereof the Lord's Name is to be praised. The Lord is high above all nations, and his glory

Psalm 135, 13

above the heavens. Thy Name, O Lord, endureth for ever ;

Psalm 103, 13

thy fame, O Lord, throughout all generations. The Lord hath established his throne in the heavens ; and his

I Chron. 16. 31

kingdom ruleth over all. Let the heavens rejoice, and let the earth be glad ; and let them say among the nations, The Lord reigneth. THE LORD IS KING ; THE LORD WAS

מְבֹרָךְ מֵעַתָּה וְעַד־עוֹלָם : מִמִּזְרַח־שֶׁמֶשׁ עַד־מְבוֹאוֹ

מְהֻלָּל שֵׁם יְיָ : רָם עַל־כָּל־גּוֹיִם ׀ יְיָ עַל הַשָּׁמַיִם כְּבוֹדוֹ :

יְיָ שִׁמְךָ לְעוֹלָם יְיָ זִכְרְךָ לְדֹר־וָדֹר : יְיָ בַּשָּׁמַיִם הֵכִין

כִּסְאוֹ וּמַלְכוּתוֹ בַּכֹּל מָשָׁלָה : יִשְׂמְחוּ הַשָּׁמַיִם וְתָגֵל

הָאָרֶץ וְיֹאמְרוּ בַגּוֹיִם יְיָ מָלָךְ : יְיָ מֶלֶךְ יְיָ מָלָךְ יְיָ ׀

יִמְלֹךְ לְעֹלָם וָעֶד : יְיָ מֶלֶךְ עוֹלָם וָעֶד אָבְדוּ גוֹיִם

מֵאַרְצוֹ : יְיָ הֵפִיר עֲצַת גּוֹיִם הֵנִיא מַחְשְׁבוֹת עַמִּים :

רַבּוֹת מַחֲשָׁבוֹת בְּלֶב־אִישׁ וַעֲצַת יְיָ הִיא תָקוּם : עֲצַת

יְיָ לְעוֹלָם תַּעֲמֹד מַחְשְׁבוֹת לִבּוֹ לְדֹר וָדֹר : כִּי הוּא אָמַר

וַיֶּהִי הוּא צִוָּה וַיַּעֲמֹד : כִּי־בָחַר יְיָ בְּצִיּוֹן אִוָּהּ לְמוֹשָׁב

לוֹ : כִּי־יַעֲקֹב בָּחַר לוֹ יָהּ יִשְׂרָאֵל לִסְגֻלָּתוֹ : כִּי לֹא־

יִטֹּשׁ יְיָ עַמּוֹ וְנַחֲלָתוֹ לֹא יַעֲזֹב : וְהוּא רַחוּם יְכַפֵּר עָוֹן

וְלֹא יַשְׁחִית וְהִרְבָּה לְהָשִׁיב אַפּוֹ וְלֹא יָעִיר כָּל־חֲמָתוֹ :

יְיָ הוֹשִׁיעָה הַמֶּלֶךְ יַעֲנֵנוּ בְיוֹם־קָרְאֵנוּ :

אַשְׁרֵי יוֹשְׁבֵי בֵיתֶךָ עוֹד יְהַלְלוּךָ סֶּלָה :

אַשְׁרֵי הָעָם שֶׁכָּכָה לּוֹ אַשְׁרֵי הָעָם שֶׁיְיָ אֱלֹהָיו :

תְּהִלָּה לְדָוִד ·　　קמ״ה

אֲרוֹמִמְךָ אֱלוֹהַי הַמֶּלֶךְ וַאֲבָרְכָה שִׁמְךָ לְעוֹלָם וָעֶד :

בְּכָל־יוֹם אֲבָרְכֶךָּ וַאֲהַלְלָה שִׁמְךָ לְעוֹלָם וָעֶד :

Psalm 10. 16 KING ; THE LORD SHALL BE KING FOR EVER AND EVER. The Lord is King for ever and ever ; the heathen are perished out
Psalm 33. 10 of his land. The Lord bringeth the design of the heathen to
Proverbs 19. 21 nought ; he hath foiled the thoughts of the peoples. Many are the thoughts in a man's heart ; but the counsel of the
Psalm 33. 11, 9 Lord, that shall stand. The counsel of the Lord standeth fast for ever, the thoughts of his heart to all generations. For he spake, and it was ; he commanded, and it stood fast.
Psalm 132. 13 For the Lord hath chosen Zion ; he hath desired it for his
Psalm 135. 4 habitation. For the Lord hath chosen Jacob unto himself,
Psalm 94. 14 Israel for his peculiar treasure. For the Lord will not cast
Psalm 78. 38 off his people, neither will he forsake his inheritance. And he, being merciful, forgiveth iniquity, and destroyeth not : yea, many a time he turneth his anger away, and doth
Psalm 20. 10 not stir up all his wrath. Save, Lord : may the King answer us on the day when we call.
ASHREY YOSHEVEY VEYSECHO Happy are they that dwell in thy house : they will be ever praising thee. (Selah.) Happy is the people, that
Psalm 84. 5 is thus favoured : happy is the people, whose God is the
Psalm 144. 15 Lord.

Psalm cxlv. [1]A Psalm of Praise : of David.

THE GREAT-NESS AND UNENDING GOODNESS OF GOD I will extol thee, my God, O King ; and I will bless thy Name for ever and ever. [2]Every day will I bless thee ; and I will praise thy Name for ever and ever. [3]Great is the

---

The Lord is King, the Lord was King, the Lord shall be King for ever and ever. A liturgical Response, first found in late Rabbinic sources, and compounded of Psalm 10. 16, 93. 1 and Exodus 15. 18. It became one of the most solemn Declarations in Judaism, and forms part of the dying Jew's Confession of Faith (p. 1064). Beautiful Festival hymns (*piyyutim*) have these words as a refrain (p. 875).

PSALM 145.

This triumphant hymn of praise, calling upon all men to glorify the Name of God, is an alphabetical psalm, with one strophe, that of *Nun*, missing. It is the first of the six psalms that close the Psalter, and combine simplicity of thought with sublimity of language in the adoration of God. It is the only psalm called a *tehillah*, " a psalm of praise ", from which the whole Book of Psalms received its name *Tehillim*, lit. " Book of Praises ".

גָּדוֹל יְהוָֹה וּמְהֻלָּל מְאֹד וְלִגְדֻלָּתוֹ אֵין חֵקֶר :

דּוֹר לְדוֹר יְשַׁבַּח מַעֲשֶׂיךָ וּגְבוּרֹתֶיךָ יַגִּידוּ :

הֲדַר כְּבוֹד הוֹדֶךָ וְדִבְרֵי נִפְלְאֹתֶיךָ אָשִׂיחָה :

וֶעֱזוּז נוֹרְאֹתֶיךָ יֹאמֵרוּ וּגְדֻלָּתְךָ אֲסַפְּרֶנָּה :

זֵכֶר רַב־טוּבְךָ יַבִּיעוּ וְצִדְקָתְךָ יְרַנֵּנוּ :

חַנּוּן וְרַחוּם יְהוָֹה אֶרֶךְ אַפַּיִם וּגְדָל־חָסֶד :

טוֹב־יְהוָֹה לַכֹּל וְרַחֲמָיו עַל־כָּל־מַעֲשָׂיו :

יוֹדוּךָ יְהוָֹה כָּל־מַעֲשֶׂיךָ וַחֲסִידֶיךָ יְבָרֲכוּכָה :

כְּבוֹד מַלְכוּתְךָ יֹאמֵרוּ וּגְבוּרָתְךָ יְדַבֵּרוּ :

לְהוֹדִיעַ לִבְנֵי הָאָדָם גְּבוּרֹתָיו וּכְבוֹד הֲדַר מַלְכוּתוֹ :

Great importance was in later times attached to the recital of this psalm. "He who repeats Psalm 145 three times daily is assured of his part in the world to come" (Talmud). It was introduced twice in the Morning, and once in the Afternoon Service. The grandeur of the Psalm fully warrants it. It has rightly been called "the Psalm of Universal Benevolence". It sums up the Jewish doctrine of God, whose Kingdom is universal and eternal; it celebrates His greatness (1–6), goodness (7–10), Kingdom (11–13); and His constant love towards all those who love and reverence Him (14–21). If Israel begins the chorus of praise (v. 1), it will not be content until all mankind joins in it (v. 21).

Since early Rabbinic times two verses (Psalm 84. 5 and 144. 14) have been prefixed to Psalm 145, when it forms part of a Synagogue Service.

dwell in thy house. The Talmud uses these words to enjoin the duty of betaking oneself early to the Synagogue and sitting there for a time, in order to attune one's soul to participation in the Service by preliminary devotions.

thus favoured. Or, "whose lot is thus" (Pool).

7. *pour forth.* The fulness of praise evoked by the *goodness* and *righteousness* of God are represented by two verbs: the first, "pour forth", compares it to the clear waters of a spring bursting up

THE
GREAT-
NESS AND
UNENDING
GOODNESS
OF GOD

Lord, and exceedingly to be praised : and his greatness is
unsearchable. ⁴One generation shall laud thy works to
another, and shall declare thy mighty acts. ⁵On the majestic
glory of thy splendour, and on thy marvellous deeds, will I
meditate. ⁶And men shall speak of the might of thy tremendous acts ; and I will recount thy greatness. ⁷They shall pour
forth the fame of thy great goodness, and shall exult in thy
righteousness. ⁸The Lord is gracious and merciful ; slow to
anger and of great lovingkindness. ⁹The Lord is good to all ;
and his tender mercies are over all his works. ¹⁰All thy works
shall give thanks unto thee, O Lord ; and thy loving ones
shall bless thee. ¹¹They shall speak of the glory of thy
kingdom, and talk of thy power ; ¹²to make known to the
sons of men his mighty acts, and the majestic glory of his

into sunlight, musical and living ; and the other, " exult ", describes
it as like the shrill cries of joy raised by a throng at some festival
(Maclaren).

exult in thy righteousness. The use of the word " exult " is noteworthy. " All, or very nearly all, the nations of mankind have recognized the importance of conduct. They, however, looked at conduct,
not as something full of happiness and joy, but as something one could
not manage to do without. No one has ever come near Israel in feeling,
and in making others feel, that to righteousness belongs happiness ! "
(Matthew Arnold).

8. *merciful and gracious.* This thought, based on the revelation of
God's nature in Exodus 34. 6, 7, became an article of faith for the
pious in Israel.

9. *his tender mercies are over all his works.* Rabbi Judah the Prince
was sorely afflicted for many years because one day, when a terror-
stricken calf that was being prepared for slaughter ran to him for
shelter, he repulsed it with the words, " Go, for such is thy destiny ".
His affliction passed away when he rescued a humble field-creature from
a servant who was about to kill it, saying, " Let the creature live ; for
is it not written, *His tender mercies are over all His works ?* " (Talmud).

10. *thy loving ones shall bless thee.* Judaism bids men bless God's
Name for the evil, as for the good, that may befall them. "The Lord gave,
and the Lord hath taken away ; blessed be the Name of the Lord "
(Job 1. 21). Resignation to God's will is as much a duty as is thanksgiving for His unending mercies. Every creature shows some gratitude
for any good that befalls it ; but it is only the *chassidim*, " those who
love God ", that *bless* His name even in the darkness of woe, sorrow
and suffering.

מַלְכוּתְךָ מַלְכוּת כָּל־עֹלָמִים וּמֶמְשַׁלְתְּךָ בְּכָל־דּוֹר וָדֹר :

סוֹמֵךְ יְהוָֹה לְכָל־הַנֹּפְלִים וְזוֹקֵף לְכָל־הַכְּפוּפִים :

עֵינֵי כֹל אֵלֶיךָ יְשַׂבֵּרוּ וְאַתָּה נוֹתֵן־לָהֶם אֶת־אָכְלָם בְּעִתּוֹ :

פּוֹתֵחַ אֶת־יָדֶךָ וּמַשְׂבִּיעַ לְכָל־חַי רָצוֹן :

צַדִּיק יְהוָֹה בְּכָל־דְּרָכָיו וְחָסִיד בְּכָל־מַעֲשָׂיו :

קָרוֹב יְהוָֹה לְכָל־קֹרְאָיו לְכֹל אֲשֶׁר יִקְרָאֻהוּ בֶאֱמֶת :

רְצוֹן־יְרֵאָיו יַעֲשֶׂה וְאֶת־שַׁוְעָתָם יִשְׁמַע וְיוֹשִׁיעֵם :

שׁוֹמֵר יְהוָֹה אֶת־כָּל־אֹהֲבָיו וְאֵת כָּל־הָרְשָׁעִים יַשְׁמִיד :

תְּהִלַּת יְהוָֹה יְדַבֶּר־פִּי וִיבָרֵךְ כָּל־בָּשָׂר שֵׁם קָדְשׁוֹ לְעוֹלָם וָעֶד :

וַאֲנַחְנוּ נְבָרֵךְ יָהּ מֵעַתָּה וְעַד־עוֹלָם הַלְלוּיָהּ :

קמ״ו הַלְלוּיָהּ הַלְלִי נַפְשִׁי אֶת־יְהוָֹה : אֲהַלְלָה יְהוָֹה בְּחַיָּי אֲזַמְּרָה לֵאלֹהַי בְּעוֹדִי : אַל־תִּבְטְחוּ בִנְדִיבִים בְּבֶן־אָדָם שֶׁאֵין לוֹ תְשׁוּעָה : תֵּצֵא רוּחוֹ יָשֻׁב לְאַדְמָתוֹ בַּיּוֹם הַהוּא

---

13. *thy kingdom.* Thy kingship ; the term is unconnected with any thought of land or area, see p. 113.

15. *the eyes of all wait upon thee . . . living thing.* They mutely appeal to God, with expectant eyes fixed on Him. These verses contain the essence of the Grace for daily meals. *v.* 16 is especially named in the Talmud as the reason for the threefold daily repetition of this Psalm. The word " all " occurs more than eleven times in the latter part of the psalm—suggesting boundless visions of the wide sweep of God's universal mercy.

17. *loving.* The adjective *chossid*, which the Greek Version translates *philanthropos*, denotes goodness that manifests itself in deeds of benevolence.

20. *all the wicked will he destroy.* The infinite goodness of God does not mean that He disregards the eternal distinction between

THE GREAT-NESS AND UNENDING GOODNESS OF GOD kingdom. [13]Thy kingdom is an everlasting kingdom, and thy dominion endureth throughout all generations. [14]The Lord upholdeth all that fall, and raiseth up all those that are bowed down. [15]The eyes of all wait upon thee ; and thou givest them their food in due season. [16]Thou openest thine hand, and satisfiest every living thing with favour. [17]The Lord is righteous in all his ways, and loving in all his works. [18]The Lord is nigh unto all them that call upon him, to all that call upon him in truth. [19]He will fulfil the desire of them that reverence him ; he also will hear their cry, and will save them. [20]The Lord guardeth all them that love him ; but all the wicked will he destroy. [21]My mouth shall speak of the praise of the Lord ; and let all flesh bless his holy Name for ever and ever.

Psalm 115. 18 But we will bless the Lord from this time forth and for evermore. Praise ye the Lord.

Psalm cxlvi.

GOD THE ONLY HELPER [1]Praise ye the Lord. Praise the Lord, O my soul : [2]I will praise the Lord, while I live : I will sing praises unto my God while I have my being. [3]Put not your trust in princes, in a son of man, in whom there is no help. [4]When his

---

right and wrong, and will refrain from retributive punishment. It is true that we cannot always " trace the hidden equities of divine reward and catch sight, through the darkness, of the fateful threads of woven fire that covered error with retribution " (Ruskin). But there are various ways of destroying the wicked. One of them is, by destroying the particular form of wickedness that ensnares them ; *e.g.* with the abolition of the slave-trade, a whole group of inhuman villainies were swept away. See on Psalm 104. 35, p. 588.

but we bless . . . evermore. We is emphatic. Whether all flesh join us in blessing His holy Name, or they do not, Israel will continue to adore Him for ever and ever. This verse is added from Psalm 115. 18, so that 145 should end with *Hallelujah,* " Praise ye the Lord," as do the five psalms that follow.

PSALM 146.
" Put your Trust in God, not in Man."

3. *princes.* Here denotes a class, not an office.

4. *designs.* Schemes, purposes. " The psalmist has a profound sense of the phantasmal character of the solid-seeming realities of . human glory and power " (Maclaren).

אָבְדוּ עֶשְׁתֹּנֹתָיו : אַשְׁרֵי שֶׁאֵל יַעֲקֹב בְּעֶזְרוֹ שִׂבְרוֹ עַל־
יְהוָה אֱלֹהָיו : עֹשֶׂה שָׁמַיִם וָאָרֶץ אֶת־הַיָּם וְאֶת־כָּל־אֲשֶׁר־
בָּם הַשֹּׁמֵר אֱמֶת לְעוֹלָם : עֹשֶׂה מִשְׁפָּט לָעֲשׁוּקִים נֹתֵן
לֶחֶם לָרְעֵבִים יְהוָה מַתִּיר אֲסוּרִים : יְהוָה פֹּקֵחַ עִוְרִים
יְהוָה זֹקֵף כְּפוּפִים יְהוָה אֹהֵב צַדִּיקִים : יְהוָה שֹׁמֵר אֶת־
גֵּרִים יָתוֹם וְאַלְמָנָה יְעוֹדֵד וְדֶרֶךְ רְשָׁעִים יְעַוֵּת : יִמְלֹךְ
יְהוָה לְעוֹלָם אֱלֹהַיִךְ צִיּוֹן לְדֹר וָדֹר הַלְלוּיָהּ :

קמ׳ז הַלְלוּיָהּ כִּי־טוֹב זַמְּרָה אֱלֹהֵינוּ כִּי־נָעִים נָאוָה
תְהִלָּה : בּוֹנֵה יְרוּשָׁלַםִ יְהוָה נִדְחֵי יִשְׂרָאֵל יְכַנֵּס : הָרֹפֵא
לִשְׁבוּרֵי לֵב וּמְחַבֵּשׁ לְעַצְּבוֹתָם : מוֹנֶה מִסְפָּר לַכּוֹכָבִים
לְכֻלָּם שֵׁמוֹת יִקְרָא : גָּדוֹל אֲדוֹנֵינוּ וְרַב־כֹּחַ לִתְבוּנָתוֹ
אֵין מִסְפָּר : מְעוֹדֵד עֲנָוִים יְהוָה מַשְׁפִּיל רְשָׁעִים עֲדֵי־
אָרֶץ : עֱנוּ לַיהוָה בְּתוֹדָה זַמְּרוּ לֵאלֹהֵינוּ בְכִנּוֹר :

7. setteth free the prisoners. To understand the full meaning, we need recall the appalling conditions in Oriental prisons (Jeremiah 38. 6–9), and even in English prisons till well into the nineteenth century.

8. the blind. Blindness, being the most grievous affliction, is used to convey the notion of general helplessness.

bowed down. By adversity.

loveth the righteous. "A man may wish to become a Priest or a Levite, but he cannot, because his father was not one. But, if he wishes to become righteous, he can do so, even if he be a heathen; for righteousness is not a matter of descent" (Midrash).

9. guardeth the strangers. No command is repeated as often as the law not to oppress the stranger; not to injure, annoy or grieve him. These commands are without parallel in the legislation of any ancient people; and, in the practice of modern peoples, the duty of loving the alien is almost universally unheeded. "With the law of shielding the alien from wrong, true Religion begins. The alien was to be

breath goeth forth, he returneth to his earth ; in that very day his designs perish. ⁵Happy is he that hath the God of Jacob for his help, whose hope is in the Lord his God : ⁶who made heaven and earth, the sea, and all that is therein ; who keepeth truth for ever ; ⁷who secureth justice for the oppressed ; who giveth food to the hungry : the Lord setteth free the prisoners ; ⁸the Lord openeth the eyes of the blind ; the Lord raiseth up them that are bowed down ; the Lord loveth the righteous; ⁹the Lord guardeth the strangers; he upholdeth the fatherless and widow ; but the way of the wicked he maketh crooked. ¹⁰The Lord shall reign for ever, thy God, O Zion, unto all generations. Praise ye the Lord.

Psalm cxlvii.

*THE
POWER
AND
PROVI-
DENCE OF
GOD*
¹Praise ye the Lord ; for it is good to sing praises unto our God ; for it is pleasant, and praise is seemly. ²The Lord doth build up Jerusalem ; he gathereth together the dispersed of Israel. ³He healeth the broken in heart, and bindeth up their wounds. ⁴He counteth the number of the stars ; he calleth them all by their names. ⁵Great is our Lord, and mighty in power ; his understanding is infinite. ⁶The Lord upholdeth the meek : he bringeth the wicked down to the ground. ⁷Sing unto the Lord with thanksgiving;

protected not because he was a member of one's clan, community or people ; but because he was a human being. In the alien, man discovered the idea of humanity " (Hermann Cohen).

the fatherless and the widow. Typical of all those who are too weak to defend themselves against injustice and opposition.

maketh crooked. He thwarts the designs of sinners, and causes them to reach a goal which they have not in view. " He frustrateth the devices of the crafty, so that their hands cannot perform their enterprise " (Job 5. 12).

PSALM 147.

God's love and power are displayed in nature and Israel's fortunes. The Lord of all creation healeth the broken-hearted, and feedeth the young ravens when they cry. Moral strength is greater than physical strength ; and an unparalleled distinction has been bestowed upon Israel in the holy teachings and righteous judgments made known unto him.

הַמְכַסֶּה שָׁמַיִם בְּעָבִים הַמֵּכִין לָאָרֶץ מָטָר הַמַּצְמִיחַ
הָרִים חָצִיר : נוֹתֵן לִבְהֵמָה לַחְמָהּ לִבְנֵי עֹרֵב אֲשֶׁר
יִקְרָאוּ : לֹא בִגְבוּרַת הַסּוּס יֶחְפָּץ לֹא־בְשׁוֹקֵי הָאִישׁ
יִרְצֶה : רוֹצֶה יְהֹוָה אֶת־יְרֵאָיו אֶת־הַמְיַחֲלִים לְחַסְדּוֹ :
שַׁבְּחִי יְרוּשָׁלַםִ אֶת־יְהֹוָה הַלְלִי אֱלֹהַיִךְ צִיּוֹן : כִּי־חִזַּק
בְּרִיחֵי שְׁעָרָיִךְ בֵּרַךְ בָּנַיִךְ בְּקִרְבֵּךְ : הַשָּׂם גְּבוּלֵךְ שָׁלוֹם
חֵלֶב חִטִּים יַשְׂבִּיעֵךְ : הַשֹּׁלֵחַ אִמְרָתוֹ אָרֶץ עַד־מְהֵרָה
יָרוּץ דְּבָרוֹ : הַנֹּתֵן שֶׁלֶג כַּצָּמֶר כְּפוֹר כָּאֵפֶר יְפַזֵּר :
מַשְׁלִיךְ קַרְחוֹ כְפִתִּים לִפְנֵי קָרָתוֹ מִי יַעֲמֹד : יִשְׁלַח־
דְּבָרוֹ וְיַמְסֵם יַשֵּׁב רוּחוֹ יִזְּלוּ־מָיִם : מַגִּיד דְּבָרוֹ לְיַעֲקֹב
חֻקָּיו וּמִשְׁפָּטָיו לְיִשְׂרָאֵל : לֹא עָשָׂה כֵן לְכָל־גּוֹי
וּמִשְׁפָּטִים בַּל־יְדָעוּם הַלְלוּיָהּ :
קמ״ח הַלְלוּיָהּ · הַלְלוּ אֶת־יְהֹוָה מִן־הַשָּׁמַיִם הַלְלוּהוּ
בַּמְּרוֹמִים : הַלְלוּהוּ כָל־מַלְאָכָיו הַלְלוּהוּ כָּל־צְבָאָו :

9. *the young ravens when they cry.* In none of the Sacred Books of other nations is there the tender consideration for the animal world that there is in our Sacred Scriptures ; cf. Psalm 104. 10–18, p. 584.

10. *horse.* The war-horse is here meant. It is by spiritual strength that Israel's victories are to be won.

swiftness. Swift-footedness was of vital importance to the ancient warrior.

16. *snow.* Snowstorms are rare in Palestine, and therefore strike the imagination more than in Northern climates. When they do occur, they are very severe.

THE
POWER
AND
PROVI-
DENCE OF
GOD

sing praises upon the harp unto our God : 8who covereth the heaven with clouds, who prepareth rain for the earth, who maketh grass to grow upon the mountains ; 9who giveth to the beast its food, and to the young ravens when they cry. 10He delighteth not in the strength of the horse, he taketh no pleasure in the swiftness of a man. 11The Lord taketh pleasure in them that fear him, in them that hope for his lovingkindness. 12Extol the Lord, O Jerusalem ; praise thy God, O Zion. 13For he hath strengthened the bars of thy gates ; he hath blessed thy children within thee. 14He maketh peace in thy borders ; he satisfieth thee with the full-ripe wheat. 15He sendeth out his commandment to the earth ; his word runneth very swiftly. 16He giveth snow like wool ; he scattereth hoar frost like ashes. 17He casteth forth his ice like morsels : who can stand before his cold ? 18He sendeth out his word, and melteth them : he causeth his wind to blow, and the waters flow. 19He declareth his words unto Jacob, his statutes and his judgments unto Israel. 20He hath not dealt so with any other nation : and as for his judgments, they do not know them. Praise ye the Lord.

Psalm cxlviii.

LET ALL
NATURE
AND ALL
MANKIND
PRAISE
THE
CREATOR

1Praise ye the Lord. Praise ye the Lord from the heavens: praise him in the heights. 2Praise ye him, all his angels : praise ye him, all his hosts. 3Praise ye him, sun and moon :

17. *his ice like morsels.* Hail is meant.
20. *He hath not dealt so with any other nation.* " As long as the world lasts, all who want to make progress in righteousness will come to Israel for inspiration, as to the people who have had the sense for righteousness most glowing and strongest. This does truly constitute for Israel a most extraordinary distinction " (Mathew Arnold).

PSALM 148.

A supreme hymn of praise : the instinct of worship is innate in the whole universe ; let heaven and earth praise the Lord. This psalm has had two notable expansions in later Jewish literature—the Song of the Three Children (in the Apocrypha), and Perek Shirah (a tenth century canticle of Creation).
2. *hosts.* Of heaven—sun, moon, stars, mentioned in the following verse.

הַלְלוּהוּ שֶׁמֶשׁ וְיָרֵחַ הַלְלוּהוּ כָּל־כּוֹכְבֵי אוֹר : הַלְלוּהוּ
שְׁמֵי הַשָּׁמָיִם וְהַמַּיִם אֲשֶׁר מֵעַל הַשָּׁמָיִם : יְהַלְלוּ אֶת־שֵׁם
יְהֹוָה כִּי הוּא צִוָּה וְנִבְרָאוּ : וַיַּעֲמִידֵם לָעַד לְעוֹלָם חָק־
נָתַן וְלֹא יַעֲבוֹר : הַלְלוּ אֶת־יְהֹוָה מִן־הָאָרֶץ תַּנִּינִים וְכָל־
תְּהֹמוֹת : אֵשׁ וּבָרָד שֶׁלֶג וְקִיטוֹר רוּחַ סְעָרָה עֹשָׂה
דְבָרוֹ : הֶהָרִים וְכָל־גְּבָעוֹת עֵץ פְּרִי וְכָל־אֲרָזִים : הַחַיָּה
וְכָל־בְּהֵמָה רֶמֶשׂ וְצִפּוֹר כָּנָף : מַלְכֵי־אֶרֶץ וְכָל־לְאֻמִּים
שָׂרִים וְכָל־שֹׁפְטֵי אָרֶץ : בַּחוּרִים וְגַם־בְּתוּלוֹת זְקֵנִים עִם־
נְעָרִים : יְהַלְלוּ אֶת־שֵׁם יְהֹוָה כִּי־נִשְׂגָּב שְׁמוֹ לְבַדּוֹ הוֹדוֹ
עַל־אֶרֶץ וְשָׁמָיִם : וַיָּרֶם קֶרֶן לְעַמּוֹ תְּהִלָּה לְכָל־חֲסִידָיו
לִבְנֵי יִשְׂרָאֵל עַם קְרֹבוֹ הַלְלוּיָהּ :

קמ״ט הַלְלוּיָהּ • שִׁירוּ לַיהֹוָה שִׁיר חָדָשׁ תְּהִלָּתוֹ בִּקְהַל
חֲסִידִים : יִשְׂמַח יִשְׂרָאֵל בְּעֹשָׂיו בְּנֵי־צִיּוֹן יָגִילוּ
בְמַלְכָּם : יְהַלְלוּ שְׁמוֹ בְמָחוֹל בְּתֹף וְכִנּוֹר יְזַמְּרוּ־לוֹ :
כִּי־רוֹצֶה יְהֹוָה בְּעַמּוֹ יְפָאֵר עֲנָוִים בִּישׁוּעָה : יַעְלְזוּ
חֲסִידִים בְּכָבוֹד יְרַנְּנוּ עַל־מִשְׁכְּבוֹתָם : רוֹמְמוֹת אֵל

---

4. *heavens of heavens*. Hebrew idiom for " highest heaven ".

6. *made a decree*. Or, " He set them boundaries which they shall not
pass " (Moffatt) ; *i.e.* the heavenly bodies can do no other than obey
the Divine behest.

14. *exalted the power*. lit. " lifted up a horn " ; the metaphor is
derived from animals tossing their horns in the air in the consciousness
of vigour, or when under a feeling analogous to human pride.

the people near unto him. Nearer to God than any other people ; " a
nation of priests, having the privilege of access to His presence ; and

LET ALL NATURE AND ALL MANKIND PRAISE THE CREATOR

praise him, all ye stars of light. ⁴Praise him, ye heavens of heavens, and ye waters that are above the heavens. ⁵Let them praise the Name of the Lord : for he commanded, and they were created. ⁶He hath established them for ever and ever : he made a decree which none shall transgress. ⁷Praise the Lord from the earth, ye sea-monsters and all deeps : ⁸fire and hail, snow and smoke ; stormy wind, fulfilling his word : ⁹mountains and all hills ; fruit trees and all cedars : ¹⁰wild beasts and all cattle ; creeping things and winged birds : ¹¹kings of the earth and all peoples ; princes and all judges of the earth : ¹²both young men and maidens ; old men and children : ¹³let them praise the Name of the Lord ; for his Name alone is exalted : his majesty is above the earth and heaven. ¹⁴And he hath exalted the power of his people, to the praise of all his loving ones : even of the children of Israel, the people near unto him : praise ye the Lord.

Psalm cxlix.

THANKS-GIVING AFTER VICTORY

¹Praise ye the Lord. Sing unto the Lord a new song ; his praise in the assembly of those that love him. ²Let Israel rejoice in his Maker : let the children of Zion be glad in their King. ³Let them praise his Name with the dance : let them sing praises unto him with the timbrel and harp. ⁴For the Lord taketh pleasure in his people : he adorneth the meek with victory. ⁵Let those that love him triumph in glory : let them sing for joy upon their beds. ⁶High praises

in the consciousness of this dignity comes forward in this psalm as the leader of all creatures in their praise of God, and strike up a hallelujah that is to be joined in by heaven and earth " (Delitzsch).

PSALM 149.

This psalm seems to have been called forth by some unexpected national triumph that brought with it both elation and gladness.

3. *dance.* In early Religion everywhere, dancing played an important part ; Exodus 15. 20.

4. *the meek.* The humble and afflicted.

with victory. With victorious vindication.

5. *upon their beds.* In tranquil security, fearing no foe.

בִּגְרוֹנָם וְחֶרֶב פִּיפִיּוֹת בְּיָדָם : לַעֲשׂוֹת נְקָמָה בַּגּוֹיִם
תּוֹכֵחוֹת בַּלְאֻמִּים : לֶאְסֹר מַלְכֵיהֶם בְּזִקִּים וְנִכְבְּדֵיהֶם
בְּכַבְלֵי בַרְזֶל : לַעֲשׂוֹת בָּהֶם מִשְׁפָּט כָּתוּב הָדָר הוּא
לְכָל־חֲסִידָיו הַלְלוּיָהּ :

ק״נ הַלְלוּיָהּ · הַלְלוּ־אֵל בְּקָדְשׁוֹ הַלְלוּהוּ בִּרְקִיעַ עֻזּוֹ :
הַלְלוּהוּ בִגְבוּרֹתָיו הַלְלוּהוּ כְּרֹב גֻּדְלוֹ : הַלְלוּהוּ בְּתֵקַע
שׁוֹפָר הַלְלוּהוּ בְּנֵבֶל וְכִנּוֹר : הַלְלוּהוּ בְּתֹף וּמָחוֹל
הַלְלוּהוּ בְּמִנִּים וְעֻגָב : הַלְלוּהוּ בְצִלְצְלֵי־שָׁמַע הַלְלוּהוּ
בְּצִלְצְלֵי תְרוּעָה : כֹּל הַנְּשָׁמָה תְּהַלֵּל יָהּ הַלְלוּיָהּ :

The last verse is repeated.

בָּרוּךְ יְיָ לְעוֹלָם אָמֵן ׀ וְאָמֵן : בָּרוּךְ יְיָ מִצִּיּוֹן שֹׁכֵן
יְרוּשָׁלָ͏ִם הַלְלוּיָהּ : בָּרוּךְ יְיָ אֱלֹהִים אֱלֹהֵי יִשְׂרָאֵל
עֹשֵׂה נִפְלָאוֹת לְבַדּוֹ : וּבָרוּךְ שֵׁם כְּבוֹדוֹ לְעוֹלָם וְיִמָּלֵא
כְבוֹדוֹ אֶת־כָּל־הָאָרֶץ אָמֵן ׀ וְאָמֵן :

---

6. *a two-edged sword in their hand.* These words have been applied
to the Maccabees, and they were on the lips of Cromwell and others.
They have, alas, been misapplied at times to justify harsh retaliation
in religious wars. However, " could it be expected that the warriors
who bled for their religion should bless those who sought to trample
it under foot ? " (Moore).

9. *a written judgment* A formal judicial sentence.

He is the honour of all his loving ones. This is the rendering of the
RV Margin : God is the object of all their honouring.

PSALM 150.

In this burst of jubilant joy, the psalmist calls upon all mankind,
upon all living Creation, to join in praise of the one Divine Father :
" Let everything that hath breath praise the Lord ". This last verse,

of God are in their throat, and a two-edged sword in their hand ; ⁷to execute retribution upon the nations, and punishments upon the peoples : ⁸to bind their kings with chains, and their nobles with fetters of iron, ⁹to execute upon them the judgment which is written. He is the honour of all his loving ones. Praise ye the Lord.

Psalm cl.

A UNIVERSAL HALLELUJAH

¹Praise ye the Lord. Praise God in his sanctuary : praise him in the firmament of his power. ²Praise him for his mighty acts : praise him according to his abundant greatness. ³Praise him with the sound of the horn : praise him with the harp and the lyre. ⁴Praise him with the timbrel and dance : praise him with stringed instruments and the pipe. ⁵Praise him with the clear-toned cymbals : praise him with the loud-sounding cymbals. ⁶Let everything that hath breath praise the Lord : praise ye the Lord.

The last verse is repeated.

DOXOLOGIES

Psalm 89. 53

Psalm 135. 21

Psalm 72. 18, 19

Blessed be the Lord for evermore. Amen, and Amen. Blessed be the Lord out of Zion, who dwelleth in Jerusalem. Praise ye the Lord. Blessed be the Lord God, the God of Israel, who alone doeth wondrous things : and blessed be his glorious Name for ever ; and let the whole earth be filled with glory. Amen, and Amen.

being the close of the Psalter, is repeated ; just as the last verse of each of the Five Books of the Torah is repeated, when the Book is completed in the course of the weekly Sabbath Readings in the Synagogue.

1. *of his power.* In which His power and majesty are displayed.

3. *horn.* Heb. *Shofar*, ram's horn. All the musical instruments mentioned are those used in the Temple. " The triumphant strains resounding in this Hallelujah finale make a noble and fitting conclusion to the Psalms, the grandest symphony of praise to God ever composed on earth " (Oesterley).

Blessed . . . Amen and Amen. These verses are the doxologies, or concluding responses, of Psalms 89 (end of Book III of the Psalter), 135, and 72, (end of Book II of the Psalter).

The reading of the Psalms is now followed by three " Passages of Song "—from I Chronicles ; from Nehemiah ; and the Song of Moses.

The following to מִשְׁתַּחֲוִים, *is said standing.*

ד'ה א" כ'ט י'־'ג

וַיְבָרֶךְ דָּוִיד אֶת־יְיָ לְעֵינֵי כָּל־הַקָּהָל וַיֹּאמֶר דָּוִיד בָּרוּךְ
אַתָּה יְיָ אֱלֹהֵי יִשְׂרָאֵל אָבִינוּ מֵעוֹלָם וְעַד־עוֹלָם : לְךָ
יְיָ הַגְּדֻלָּה וְהַגְּבוּרָה וְהַתִּפְאֶרֶת וְהַנֵּצַח וְהַהוֹד כִּי־כֹל
בַּשָּׁמַיִם וּבָאָרֶץ לְךָ יְיָ הַמַּמְלָכָה וְהַמִּתְנַשֵּׂא לְכֹל ׀ לְרֹאשׁ :
וְהָעֹשֶׁר וְהַכָּבוֹד מִלְּפָנֶיךָ וְאַתָּה מוֹשֵׁל בַּכֹּל וּבְיָדְךָ כֹּחַ
וּגְבוּרָה וּבְיָדְךָ לְגַדֵּל וּלְחַזֵּק לַכֹּל : וְעַתָּה אֱלֹהֵינוּ מוֹדִים
אֲנַחְנוּ לָךְ וּמְהַלְלִים לְשֵׁם תִּפְאַרְתֶּךָ :

נחמיה ט' ו'־'א

אַתָּה הוּא יְיָ לְבַדֶּךָ אַתְּ עָשִׂיתָ אֶת־הַשָּׁמַיִם שְׁמֵי
הַשָּׁמַיִם וְכָל־צְבָאָם הָאָרֶץ וְכָל־אֲשֶׁר עָלֶיהָ הַיַּמִּים וְכָל־
אֲשֶׁר בָּהֶם וְאַתָּה מְחַיֶּה אֶת־כֻּלָּם וּצְבָא הַשָּׁמַיִם לְךָ
מִשְׁתַּחֲוִים : אַתָּה הוּא יְיָ הָאֱלֹהִים אֲשֶׁר בָּחַרְתָּ בְּאַבְרָם
וְהוֹצֵאתוֹ מֵאוּר כַּשְׂדִּים וְשַׂמְתָּ שְּׁמוֹ אַבְרָהָם : וּמָצָאתָ
אֶת־לְבָבוֹ נֶאֱמָן לְפָנֶיךָ

וְכָרוֹת עִמּוֹ הַבְּרִית לָתֵת אֶת־אֶרֶץ הַכְּנַעֲנִי הַחִתִּי
הָאֱמֹרִי וְהַפְּרִזִּי וְהַיְבוּסִי וְהַגִּרְגָּשִׁי לָתֵת לְזַרְעוֹ וַתָּקֶם
אֶת־דְּבָרֶיךָ כִּי צַדִּיק אָתָּה : וַתֵּרֶא אֶת־עֳנִי אֲבֹתֵינוּ
בְּמִצְרָיִם וְאֶת־זַעֲקָתָם שָׁמַעְתָּ עַל־יַם־סוּף : וַתִּתֵּן אֹתֹת
וּמֹפְתִים בְּפַרְעֹה וּבְכָל־עֲבָדָיו וּבְכָל־עַם אַרְצוֹ כִּי יָדַעְתָּ

The following to " worship thee," is said standing.

1 Chronicles xxix. 10—13.

VORDS OF
HOMAGE
BY DAVID

¹⁰And David blessed the Lord in the presence of all the congregation : and David said, Blessed art thou, O Lord, the God of Israel our father, from everlasting to everlasting. ¹¹Thine, O Lord, is the greatness, and the power, and the glory, and the victory, and the majesty : for all that is in the heaven and in the earth is thine ; thine, O Lord, is the kingdom, and the supremacy as head over all. ¹²Riches and honour come of thee, and thou rulest over all ; and in thine hand are might and power ; and in thine hand it is to make great, and to give strength unto all. ¹³Now, therefore, our God, we give thanks unto thee, and praise thy glorious Name.

Nehemiah ix. 6—11.

AND NEHE-
MIAH

⁶Thou art the Lord, even thou alone ; thou hast made the heavens, the heaven of heavens, and all their host, the earth and all things that are thereon, the seas and all that is in them, and thou givest life to them all ; and the host of heaven worship thee. ⁷Thou art the Lord the God, who didst choose Abram, and broughtest him forth out of Ur of the Chaldees, and gavest him the name of Abraham : ⁸and foundest his heart faithful before thee :

And thou madest a covenant with him to give the land of the Canaanite, the Hittite, the Amorite, and the Perizzite, and the Jebusite, and the Girgashite, even to give it unto his seed, and hast performed thy words ; for thou art

I CHRONICLES 29. 10–13.   Taken from David's Prayer when he inaugurated the Building of the Temple.   It declares that it is not in the power of man to add to God's glory.

NEHEMIAH 9. 6–11.   This passage gives a rapid survey of Israel's past, and recalls God's early mercies to the nation till the Crossing of the Red Sea.

6. *heaven of heavens.*   Highest heaven.

their host.   The stars.

givest life to.   Preservest.

10. *dealt arrogantly.*   Defiantly and inhumanly.

כִּי הֵזִידוּ עֲלֵיהֶם וַתַּעַשׂ־לְךָ שֵׁם כְּהַיּוֹם הַזֶּה : וְהַיָּם

בָּקַעְתָּ לִפְנֵיהֶם וַיַּעַבְרוּ בְתוֹךְ־הַיָּם בַּיַּבָּשָׁה וְאֶת־רֹדְפֵיהֶם

הִשְׁלַכְתָּ בִמְצוֹלֹת כְּמוֹ־אֶבֶן בְּמַיִם עַזִּים :

שמות י"ד ל'—ט'ו י"ח

וַיּוֹשַׁע יְהֹוָה בַּיּוֹם הַהוּא אֶת־יִשְׂרָאֵל מִיַּד מִצְרָיִם וַיַּרְא

יִשְׂרָאֵל אֶת־מִצְרַיִם מֵת עַל־שְׂפַת הַיָּם : וַיַּרְא יִשְׂרָאֵל

אֶת־הַיָּד הַגְּדֹלָה אֲשֶׁר עָשָׂה יְהֹוָה בְּמִצְרַיִם וַיִּירְאוּ הָעָם

אֶת־יְהֹוָה וַיַּאֲמִינוּ בַּיהֹוָה וּבְמֹשֶׁה עַבְדּוֹ :

אָז יָשִׁיר מֹשֶׁה וּבְנֵי יִשְׂרָאֵל אֶת־הַשִּׁירָה הַזֹּאת לַיהֹוָה

וַיֹּאמְרוּ לֵאמֹר   אָשִׁירָה לַיהֹוָה כִּי גָאֹה גָּאָה   סוּס

וְרֹכְבוֹ רָמָה בַיָּם :   עָזִּי וְזִמְרָת יָהּ וַיְהִי־לִי

לִישׁוּעָה   זֶה אֵלִי וְאַנְוֵהוּ   אֱלֹהֵי אָבִי

וַאֲרֹמְמֶנְהוּ :   יְהֹוָה אִישׁ מִלְחָמָה יְהֹוָה

שְׁמוֹ :   מַרְכְּבֹת פַּרְעֹה וְחֵילוֹ יָרָה בַיָּם   וּמִבְחַר

THE SONG OF MOSES.

To the Israelite, the Redemption from Egypt is the great evidence
of the rule of God in the universe. The Song of Moses was at first only
recited on Sabbath afternoons, but in medieval times began to form
part of the daily devotions of the pious.

EXODUS 14. 30—15. 18.

30. *the Lord saved Israel.* It was the Lord's doing—neither Israel
nor its Leader claimed any merit or glory for the victory.

31. *and in Moses his servant.* " An experience such as the Exodus
and the passage through the Red Sea, must have been reckoned by all

righteous. ⁹And thou sawest the affliction of our fathers in Egypt, and heardest their cry by the Red Sea ; ¹⁰and shewedst signs and wonders upon Pharaoh, and on all his servants, and on all the people of his land ; for thou knewest that they dealt arrogantly against them ; and didst make thee a name, as it is this day. ¹¹And thou didst divide the sea before them, so that they went through the midst of the sea on the dry land ; and their pursuers thou didst cast into the depths, as a stone into the mighty waters.

Exodus xiv. 30—xv. 18.

THE SONG AT THE RED SEA   ³⁰Thus the Lord saved Israel that day out of the hand of the Egyptians ; and Israel saw the Egyptians dead upon the sea shore. ³¹And Israel saw the great power which the Lord put forth against the Egyptians, and the people revered the Lord : and they believed in the Lord, and in Moses his servant.

¹Then sang Moses and the children of Israel this song unto the Lord, and spake, saying,

I will sing unto the Lord, for he hath been highly ex-alted : the horse and his rider hath he thrown into the sea. ²The Lord is my strength and song, and he is become my salvation : this is my God, and I will glorify him ; my father's God, and I will exalt him. ³The Lord is a man of war : the Lord is his Name. ⁴Pharaoh's chariots

who participated in them as a direct act of God. Moses was thereby authenticated in the eyes of the people " (Kittel).

2. *the Lord.* Heb. *Yah*, the shortened form of the Divine Name of Four Letters, as in *Hallelujah*.

my salvation. My source of deliverance.

this is my God. The redeemed had a unique realization of the Presence, and of the delivering help, of God. The Rabbis say, " A maid-servant at the Red Sea had a more vivid and vitalizing experience of the Divine than many a later Prophet ".

my father's God. Poetical for, " the God of my fathers ".

3. *a man of war.* He victoriously fought the battle of His oppressed children.

שָׁלִישָׁיו טֻבְּעוּ בְיַם־סוּף : תְּהֹמֹת יְכַסְיֻמוּ יָרְדוּ בִמְצוֹלֹת כְּמוֹ־אָבֶן :

יְמִינְךָ יְהֹוָה נֶאְדָּרִי בַּכֹּחַ יְמִינְךָ יְהֹוָה תִּרְעַץ אוֹיֵב : וּבְרֹב גְּאוֹנְךָ תַּהֲרֹס

קָמֶיךָ תְּשַׁלַּח חֲרֹנְךָ יֹאכְלֵמוֹ כַּקַּשׁ : וּבְרוּחַ אַפֶּיךָ נֶעֶרְמוּ מַיִם נִצְּבוּ כְמוֹ־נֵד

נֹזְלִים קָפְאוּ תְהֹמֹת בְּלֶב־יָם : אָמַר אוֹיֵב אֶרְדֹּף אַשִּׂיג אֲחַלֵּק שָׁלָל תִּמְלָאֵמוֹ

נַפְשִׁי אָרִיק חַרְבִּי תּוֹרִישֵׁמוֹ יָדִי : נָשַׁפְתָּ בְרוּחֲךָ כִּסָּמוֹ יָם צָלֲלוּ כַּעוֹפֶרֶת בְּמַיִם

אַדִּירִים : מִי־כָמֹכָה בָּאֵלִם יְהֹוָה מִי כָּמֹכָה נֶאְדָּר בַּקֹּדֶשׁ נוֹרָא תְהִלֹּת עֹשֵׂה

פֶלֶא : נָטִיתָ יְמִינְךָ תִּבְלָעֵמוֹ אָרֶץ : נָחִיתָ בְחַסְדְּךָ עַם־זוּ גָּאָלְתָּ נֵהַלְתָּ בְעָזְּךָ אֶל־נְוֵה

קָדְשֶׁךָ : שָׁמְעוּ עַמִּים יִרְגָּזוּן חִיל אָחַז יֹשְׁבֵי פְּלָשֶׁת : אָז נִבְהֲלוּ אַלּוּפֵי

אֱדוֹם אֵילֵי מוֹאָב יֹאחֲזֵמוֹ רָעַד נָמֹגוּ כֹּל יֹשְׁבֵי כְנָעַן : תִּפֹּל עֲלֵיהֶם אֵימָתָה

וָפַחַד בִּגְדֹל זְרוֹעֲךָ יִדְּמוּ כָּאָבֶן עַד־ יַעֲבֹר עַמְּךָ יְהֹוָה עַד־יַעֲבֹר עַם־זוּ

---

6. *thy right hand.* Thy might.

8. *blast of thy nostrils.* A bold, poetic figure for *wind*.

and his host hath he cast into the sea : and his chosen captains are sunk in the Red Sea. ⁵The floods cover them : they went down into the depths like a stone. ⁶Thy right hand, O Lord, is glorious in power, thy right hand, O Lord, dasheth in pieces the enemy. ⁷And in the greatness of thy majesty thou overthrowest them that rise up against thee : thou sendest forth thy wrath, it consumeth them as stubble. ⁸And with the blast of thy nostrils the waters were piled up, the streams stood upright as an heap ; the floods were congealed in the heart of the sea. ⁹The enemy said, I will pursue, I will overtake, I will divide the spoil : my desire shall be satisfied upon them ; I will draw my sword, my hand shall destroy them. ¹⁰Thou didst blow with thy wind, the sea covered them : they sank as lead in the mighty waters. ¹¹Who is like unto thee, O Lord, amongst the mighty : who is like unto thee, glorious in holiness, revered in praises, doing marvels ? ¹²Thou stretchest out thy right hand, the earth swallowed them. ¹³Thou in thy lovingkindness leadest the people whom thou hast redeemed : thou guidest them in thy strength to thy holy habitation. ¹⁴The peoples have heard it ; they tremble : pangs have taken hold of the habitants of Philistia ¹⁵Then were the dukes of Edom confounded ; the mighty men of Moab, trembling taketh hold of them : all the inhabitants of Canaan are melted away. ¹⁶Terror and dread fall upon them : by the greatness of thine arm they are as still as a stone ; till thy people pass over, O Lord, till the people

---

9. *my desire.* lit. " my soul ", which in Hebrew psychology is the seat of desire, here for vengeance and plunder.

11. *glorious in holiness.* Exalted in the majesty of holiness, which quality is the essential, distinguishing feature of the God of Israel.

13. *guidest them.* " This portion of the Song describes in prophetic images the providence of God for the Israelites, shielding them till they have overcome the dangers of the desert, conquered the nations of Canaan, and erected the sanctuary at Zion " (Kalisch).

14. *peoples have heard.* The story of God's wonders on behalf of Israel.

15. *melted away.* Are helpless through terror and despair.

קָנִיתָ : תְּבִאֵמוֹ וְתִטָּעֵמוֹ בְּהַר נַחֲלָתְךָ מָכוֹן

לְשִׁבְתְּךָ פָּעַלְתָּ יְהֹוָה מִקְּדָשׁ אֲדֹנָי כּוֹנְנוּ יָדֶיךָ :

יְהֹוָה יִמְלֹךְ לְעֹלָם וָעֶד : יְיָ יִמְלֹךְ לְעֹלָם וָעֶד :

כִּי לַייָ הַמְּלוּכָה וּמשֵׁל בַּגּוֹיִם : וְעָלוּ מוֹשִׁיעִים בְּהַר צִיּוֹן

לִשְׁפֹּט אֶת־הַר עֵשָׂו וְהָיְתָה לַייָ הַמְּלוּכָה : וְהָיָה יְיָ לְמֶלֶךְ

עַל־כָּל־הָאָרֶץ · בַּיּוֹם הַהוּא יִהְיֶה יְיָ אֶחָד וּשְׁמוֹ אֶחָד :

On Sabbaths and Holydays continue here נִשְׁמַת, *p.* 416.

יִשְׁתַּבַּח שִׁמְךָ לָעַד מַלְכֵּנוּ · הָאֵל הַמֶּלֶךְ הַגָּדוֹל

וְהַקָּדוֹשׁ בַּשָּׁמַיִם וּבָאָרֶץ · כִּי לְךָ נָאֶה יְיָ אֱלֹהֵינוּ וֵאלֹהֵי

16. *pass over.* On their way to the Promised Land.
17. *mountain of thine inheritance.* Canaan.
18. *the Lord shall reign for ever and ever.* The song closes with the promise of the Kingdom of God. The redemption from Egypt was to be followed by the Revelation on Mt. Sinai, when God's Kingdom would be inaugurated. That Kingdom is eternal.

The additional verses expand the idea of *v.* 18.

The Book of OBADIAH denounces the unbrotherly and cruel conduct of the Edomites in the day of Israel's ruin, when Jerusalem was destroyed by the Babylonians. Other nations in later times played the cruel role of Edom, and manifested wanton hatred towards Israel. Obadiah predicts Israel's triumph over them all : " saviours shall climb Mt. Zion ", and there will be no more " causeless emnity ", blind, senseless hatred, between nation and nation.

The Prophet ZECHARIAH roused the exiles returned from Babylon from their despondency, and led them in the rebuilding of the Temple (537–520). His book contains two wonderful sayings. 1. *Not by might, nor by power, but by my spirit, saith the Lord of hosts,* which may be said to proclaim the lesson of all Jewish history ; and 2. *And the Lord*

THE SONG AT THE RED SEA   pass over, that thou hast acquired. ¹⁷Thou wilt bring them in, and plant them in the mountain of thine inheritance, the place, O Lord, which thou hast made for thee to dwell in, the sanctuary, O Lord, which thy hands have established. ¹⁸The Lord shall reign for ever and ever. THE LORD SHALL REIGN FOR EVER AND EVER.

Psalm 22. 29   For the kingdom is the Lord's : and he is ruler over the
Obadiah 1. 21   nations. And saviours shall come up on mount Zion to judge the mount of Esau ; and the kingdom shall be the
Zechariah 14. 9   Lord's. AND THE LORD SHALL BE KING OVER ALL THE EARTH : IN THAT DAY SHALL THE LORD BE ONE AND HIS NAME ONE.

On Sabbaths and Holydays continue here " The breath," etc., p. 417.

YISHTAB-BACH : CONCLUDING BENEDICTION to "PSALMS AND PASSAGES OF SONG "   Praised be thy Name for ever, O our King, the great and holy God and King, in heaven and on earth ; for unto thee, O Lord our God, and God of our fathers, song and praise are becoming, hymn and psalm, strength and

---

shall be King over all the earth : in that day shall the Lord be One, and His Name One—the Messianic hope of Judaism, and the spiritual goal of human history.

shall the Lord be One. In the undivided and undisputed worship of all men : there will be universal recognition of His sovereignty. " As the heathens shall forsake their idols, He will be One, and no strange god with Him " (Rashi). " The Jews, were the only people in their world who conceived the idea of a universal religion " (Moore).

his Name One. His manifold revelations of Himself shall be acknowledged by all to be merely aspects of the one sole Name by which He made Himself known unto Israel.

This is one of the fundamental verses of the Jewish conception of the Kingdom of Heaven. It proclaims the Providential care of God for all mankind, and the future recognition of the true God by all mankind. It closes all synagogue services.

YISHTABBACH. This is the concluding blessing to the " Psalms and Passages of Song ". It is the benediction *after* the reading, just as *Boruch she-omar*, " Blessed be He who spake " (p. 50) is the benediction *before* the reading of those Psalms. There are similar benedictions before and after the reading of Hallel on New Moons and Festivals.

אֲבוֹתֵינוּ שִׁיר וּשְׁבָחָה הַלֵּל וְזִמְרָה עֹז וּמֶמְשָׁלָה נֶצַח
גְּדֻלָּה וּגְבוּרָה תְּהִלָּה וְתִפְאֶרֶת קְדֻשָּׁה וּמַלְכוּת בְּרָכוֹת
וְהוֹדָאוֹת מֵעַתָּה וְעַד־עוֹלָם : בָּרוּךְ אַתָּה יְיָ · אֵל מֶלֶךְ ·
גָּדוֹל בַּתִּשְׁבָּחוֹת · אֵל הַהוֹדָאוֹת · אֲדוֹן הַנִּפְלָאוֹת ·
הַבּוֹחֵר בְּשִׁירֵי זִמְרָה · מֶלֶךְ אֵל חֵי הָעוֹלָמִים :

Reader. יִתְגַּדַּל וְיִתְקַדַּשׁ שְׁמֵהּ רַבָּא בְּעָלְמָא דִּי־בְרָא
כִרְעוּתֵהּ · וְיַמְלִיךְ מַלְכוּתֵהּ בְּחַיֵּיכוֹן וּבְיוֹמֵיכוֹן וּבְחַיֵּי
דִי־כָל־בֵּית יִשְׂרָאֵל בַּעֲגָלָא וּבִזְמַן קָרִיב · וְאִמְרוּ אָמֵן :

Cong. and Reader. יְהֵא שְׁמֵהּ רַבָּא מְבָרַךְ לְעָלַם
וּלְעָלְמֵי עָלְמַיָּא ·

Reader. יִתְבָּרַךְ וְיִשְׁתַּבַּח וְיִתְפָּאַר וְיִתְרֹמַם וְיִתְנַשֵּׂא
וְיִתְהַדָּר וְיִתְעַלֶּה וְיִתְהַלָּל שְׁמֵהּ דִּי־קֻדְשָׁא · בְּרִיךְ הוּא ·
לְעֵלָּא מִן־כָּל־בִּרְכָתָא וְשִׁירָתָא תֻּשְׁבְּחָתָא וְנֶחֱמָתָא
דִּי־אֲמִירָן בְּעָלְמָא · וְאִמְרוּ אָמֵן :

---

song . . . *and thanksgivings.* Fifteen terms of praise and adoration
are enumerated. Hebrew is remarkably rich in the vocabulary of
adoration and worship. " As Latin is the language of war, Greek that
of oratory, so is Hebrew the language of Prayer " (Midrash).
of all worlds. Or, " of all eternities ".

HALF-KADDISH. *magnified.* Here, as elsewhere in the Liturgy,
the Half-Kaddish marks the end of a distinct section of the Service.
It was originally a doxology, spoken at the conclusion of the religious
discourse of the ancient teacher or preacher. He would in this way
dismiss his hearers with a glorification of God and the Messianic hope
of the speedy coming of His kingdom. The doxology was in Aramaic,
because the discourse was in Aramaic, the language spoken by the
Jews after the Babylonian Exile. In time, the doxology passed from
the School to the Synagogue, where it marked the end of each sub-
division of the Service.

dominion, victory, greatness and might, renown and glory, holiness and sovereignty, blessings and thanksgivings from henceforth even for ever. Blessed art thou, O Lord, God and King, great in praises, God of thanksgivings, Lord of wonders, who makest choice of song and psalm, O King and God, the life of all worlds.

HALF KADDISH

Reader.—Magnified and sanctified be his great Name in the world which he hath created according to his will. May he establish his kindgom during your life and during your days, and during the life of all the house of Israel, even speedily and at a near time, and say ye, Amen.

Cong and Reader.—Let his great Name be blessed for ever and to all eternity.

Reader.—Blessed, praised and glorified, exalted, extolled and honoured, magnified and lauded be the Name of the Holy One, blessed be he ; though he be high above all the blessings and hymns, praises and consolations, which are uttered in the world ; and say ye, Amen.

---

may he establish his kingdom. May He bring about the realization of all spiritual values, and transform things as they are into things as they ought to be.

let his great Name be blessed for ever and to all eternity. This is the principal response of the Kaddish (derived from Daniel 2. 20, and analogous to Psalm 113. 2, and to the Response " Blessed be His Name, whose glorious Kingdom is for ever and ever "). It was deemed to be the hymn of hymns, and gained still greater hold upon the reverent affection of the people when it came to be looked upon as the Orphan's Prayer. In its original form, the Kaddish is of great antiquity. It antedates the Destruction of the Temple, and is echoed in the most famous Christian prayer.

Holy One, blessed be he. The most frequent Name of God in post-Biblical Jewish literature. Holiness is the *essential* attribute of God.

consolations. The Heb. word, in addition to its general meaning of comfort in mourning and sorrow, also denotes both the praises of God in connection with the future Messianic time and the Future Life, as well as the consolatory discourses to which the Kaddish was the conclusion.

Aside from the Half-Kaddish, there is the *Full* (p. 206), the *Orphan's* (p. 212), the *Rabbinical* (p. 236) and the *Burial* (p. 1084), Kaddish.

5

Congregation in an undertone.

Reader.

בָּרְכוּ אֶת־יְיָ הַמְבֹרָךְ :

יִתְבָּרַךְ וְיִשְׁתַּבַּח וְיִתְפָּאַר
וְיִתְרוֹמַם וְיִתְנַשֵּׂא שְׁמוֹ שֶׁל־מֶלֶךְ
מַלְכֵי הַמְּלָכִים הַקָּדוֹשׁ בָּרוּךְ הוּא ·
שֶׁהוּא רִאשׁוֹן וְהוּא אַחֲרוֹן
וּמִבַּלְעָדָיו אֵין אֱלֹהִים · סֹלּוּ לָרֹכֵב
בָּעֲרָבוֹת בְּיָהּ שְׁמוֹ וְעִלְזוּ לְפָנָיו ·
וּשְׁמוֹ מְרוֹמָם עַל־כָּל־בְּרָכָה
וּתְהִלָּה :

בָּרוּךְ שֵׁם כְּבוֹד מַלְכוּתוֹ לְעוֹלָם
וָעֶד : יְהִי שֵׁם יְיָ מְבֹרָךְ מֵעַתָּה וְעַד
עוֹלָם :

Cong. and Reader.

בָּרוּךְ יְיָ הַמְבֹרָךְ לְעוֹלָם
וָעֶד :

בָּרוּךְ אַתָּה יְיָ אֱלֹהֵינוּ
מֶלֶךְ הָעוֹלָם · יוֹצֵר אוֹר
וּבוֹרֵא חֹשֶׁךְ · עֹשֶׂה
שָׁלוֹם וּבוֹרֵא אֶת־הַכֹּל:

הַמֵּאִיר לָאָרֶץ וְלַדָּרִים עָלֶיהָ בְּרַחֲמִים · וּבְטוּבוֹ
מְחַדֵּשׁ בְּכָל־יוֹם תָּמִיד מַעֲשֵׂה בְרֵאשִׁית : מָה רַבּוּ
מַעֲשֶׂיךָ יְיָ · כֻּלָּם בְּחָכְמָה עָשִׂיתָ · מָלְאָה הָאָרֶץ קִנְיָנֶךָ :

II. THE SHEMA
AND THE BLESSINGS BEFORE AND AFTER
(קריאת שמע)

The SHEMA is the heart of the Morning (and Evening) Service,
It is Israel's Confession of Faith. The worshipper who recites it.
proclaims, as the Rabbis explain, his allegiance to the Kingdom of
Heaven, and his joyful submission to God's laws and commandments.
The Shema is preceded by two blessings :—
(a) The *Yotzer* prayer, a thanksgiving for the creation of physical
light, the light of day, and the daily renewal of Creation. (b) The *Ahavah*
prayer, אהבה רבה, a fervent outpouring of exalted thanksgiving for the
moral illumination bestowed upon Israel, the light of the Torah.
And the Shema is followed by :
(a) An attestation of faith in the declarations conveyed in the
Shema, אמת ויציב ("True and firm"). (b) Praises of God as the
Redeemer of Israel, גואל ישראל. All these prayers are of great antiquity
considerably older than the Maccabean period.

BORECHU. The Invocation to prayer with which the Public Service
now opens (" Bless ye the Lord who is to be blessed ") is the ancient

INVOCA-
TION TO
CONGRE-
GATIONAL
PRAYER

Reader — BLESS YE THE LORD WHO IS TO BE BLESSED.

Cong. and Reader.— BLESSED IS THE LORD WHO IS TO BE BLESSED FOR EVER AND EVER.

Congregation, in an undertone.

Blessed, praised, glorified, exalted and extolled be the Name of the supreme King of kings, the Holy One, blessed be he, who is the first and the last, and beside him there is no God. Extol ye him that rideth upon the heavens, whose Name is the Lord, and rejoice before him. His Name is exalted above all blessing and praise. Blessed be His Name, whose glorious kingdom is for ever and ever. Let the Name of the Lord be blessed from this time forth and for ever more.

GOD THE
CREATOR
OF ALL
THINGS

Blessed art thou, O Lord our God, King of the universe, who formest light and createst darkness, who makest peace and createst all things :

Who in mercy givest light to the earth and to them that dwell thereon, and in thy goodness renewest the creation

Psalm 104. 24 every day continually. How manifold are thy works, C

formula for calling people to prayer. The Response ('' Blessed is the Lord who is to be blessed for ever and ever '') associates the congregation with the praise of God to which the Reader summons his fellow-worshippers. The passage recited by the congregation in an undertone, is a later addition.

createst all things. Based on Isaiah 45. 7. '' I am the Lord, and there is none else. I form light and create darkness, I make peace and create evil ''. Some see in this expression of absolute monotheism a protest against the ancient Persian belief in two gods—one a god of light and goodness, and the other, of darkness and evil. Jewish teaching recognizes that nothing coming from God is in itself evil, that even the lower passions may be made agencies for good. Hence the change of '' create evil '' into '' createst all things ''. God is the sole Source of everything.

HA-MEIR. *Who in mercy.* This Distinctive Morning Prayer is a eulogy on the Divine ordering of light and darkness, and the consequent daily renewal of the miracle of Creation. '' Even in times of direst oppression and misery these Prayers continued unchanged, and no outward suffering could dim the eye of the Jew to the wonders of Creation's renewal '' (Sachs). '' The realm of Nature is to the Jew nothing distant, strange, cold or uncanny ; it is the workshop of the Almighty, and is ruled by His beneficent Will '' (Bousset).

הַמֶּלֶךְ הַמְרוֹמָם לְבַדּוֹ מֵאָז · הַמְשֻׁבָּח וְהַמְפֹאָר וְהַמִּתְנַשֵּׂא
מִימוֹת עוֹלָם : אֱלֹהֵי עוֹלָם בְּרַחֲמֶיךָ הָרַבִּים רַחֵם עָלֵינוּ ·
אֲדוֹן עֻזֵּנוּ צוּר מִשְׂגַּבֵּנוּ מָגֵן יִשְׁעֵנוּ מִשְׂגָּב בַּעֲדֵנוּ :

אֵל בָּרוּךְ גְּדוֹל דֵּעָה · הֵכִין וּפָעַל זָהֲרֵי חַמָּה · טוֹב
יָצַר כָּבוֹד לִשְׁמוֹ · מְאוֹרוֹת נָתַן סְבִיבוֹת עֻזּוֹ · פִּנּוֹת
צְבָאָיו קְדוֹשִׁים רוֹמְמֵי שַׁדַּי · תָּמִיד מְסַפְּרִים כְּבוֹד־אֵל
וּקְדֻשָּׁתוֹ : תִּתְבָּרַךְ יְיָ אֱלֹהֵינוּ עַל־שֶׁבַח מַעֲשֵׂה יָדֶיךָ ·
וְעַל־מְאוֹרֵי־אוֹר שֶׁעָשִׂיתָ יְפָאֲרוּךָ סֶּלָה :

תִּתְבָּרַךְ צוּרֵנוּ מַלְכֵּנוּ וְגוֹאֲלֵנוּ בּוֹרֵא קְדוֹשִׁים יִשְׁתַּבַּח
שִׁמְךָ לָעַד מַלְכֵּנוּ · יוֹצֵר מְשָׁרְתִים וַאֲשֶׁר מְשָׁרְתָיו כֻּלָּם
עוֹמְדִים בְּרוּם עוֹלָם וּמַשְׁמִיעִים בְּיִרְאָה יַחַד בְּקוֹל דִּבְרֵי
אֱלֹהִים חַיִּים וּמֶלֶךְ עוֹלָם : כֻּלָּם אֲהוּבִים כֻּלָּם בְּרוּרִים

renewest the creation. God is conceived not as a far-off watcher of
a mechanism which He has created, but as a Living Ruler, guiding the
universe and upholding it continually.

The glorification of God in the visible universe leads to a poetic
description of the mystic worship rendered to Him by the angelic hosts.
They sanctify Him in the words of the Prophet, " Holy, holy, holy
is the Lord of hosts : the whole earth is full of his glory ", and this
sanctification is echoed by the Congregation of Israel.

THE BLESSED GOD. This paragraph opens with 22 words, in the
order of the Hebrew alphabet, and develops the theme, " The heavens
declare the glory and holiness of God ". Its authorship, and that of the
following pieces to the end of the benediction on p. 113, is ascribed to
the Mystics of the eighth century. The Heavenly Throne is conceived
as surrounded by angels and adoring heavenly bodies.

chiefs. Probably refers to the archangels.

of his hosts. The stars and planets. *Hosts* is here a metaphor for
the heavenly bodies, and often for the retinue of angels.

Lord ! In wisdom hast thou made them all : the earth is full of thy creatures. O King, who alone wast exalted from aforetime, praised, glorified and extolled from days of old ; O everlasting God, in thine abundant mercies, have mercy upon us, Lord of our strength, Rock of our stronghold, Shield of our salvation, thou Stronghold of ours !

THE FORMER OF LIGHT   The blessed God, great in knowledge, designed and formed the rays of the sun : it was a boon he produced as a glory to his Name : he set the luminaries round about his strength. The chiefs of his hosts are holy beings that exalt the Almighty, and continually declare the glory of God and his holiness. Be thou blessed, O Lord our God, for the excellency of thy handiwork, and for the bright luminaries which thou hast made : they shall glorify thee for ever.

TISBORACH   Be thou blessed, O our Rock, our King and Redeemer, Creator of holy beings, praised be thy Name for ever, O our King ; Creator of ministering spirits, all of whom stand in the heights of the universe, and with awe proclaim in unison aloud the words of the living God and everlasting King.

---

holy beings. Angels. In Hebrew, the word *angel* means simply " messenger " and includes all the instruments of Divine purpose, whether human, superhuman, or the forces of nature.

bright luminaries . . . glorify thee. This view is ,in opposition to that of heathendom, which looked upon the heavenly bodies as objects of adoration and superstitious worship.

TISBORACH. *be thou blessed.* The angels ecstatically chant the praises and holiness of God, and in antiphonal song acclaim the thrice-holy One whose glory fills the universe.

Creator of holy beings. According to the Mystics of Talmudic times, angels are every day created from the River of Fire ; they utter a hymn of praise, and then cease to be.

" The angels of Wind and Fire
Chant only one hymn, and expire
With the song's irresistible stress."
(Longfellow, *Sandalphon.*)

ministering spirits. Angels are held by the Jewish Mystics to be inferior to man in the scale of spiritual existence ; because man is no mere " messenger ", but is endowed with free-will. Since the time of Maimonides, Jewish thinkers allegorize the whole conception of angelic beings.

beloved. There is no envy, jealousy, or rivalry among them.

כֻּלָּם גִּבּוֹרִים · וְכֻלָּם עֹשִׂים בְּאֵימָה וּבְיִרְאָה רְצוֹן קוֹנָם ·
וְכֻלָּם פּוֹתְחִים אֶת־פִּיהֶם בִּקְדֻשָׁה וּבְטָהֳרָה בְּשִׁירָה
וּבְזִמְרָה וּמְבָרְכִים וּמְשַׁבְּחִים וּמְפָאֲרִים וּמַעֲרִיצִים
וּמַקְדִּישִׁים וּמַמְלִיכִים

אֶת־שֵׁם הָאֵל הַמֶּלֶךְ הַגָּדוֹל הַגִּבּוֹר וְהַנּוֹרָא קָדוֹשׁ
הוּא : וְכֻלָּם מְקַבְּלִים עֲלֵיהֶם עֹל מַלְכוּת שָׁמַיִם זֶה מִזֶּה ·
וְנוֹתְנִים רְשׁוּת זֶה לָזֶה לְהַקְדִּישׁ לְיוֹצְרָם · בְּנַחַת רוּחַ
בְּשָׂפָה בְרוּרָה וּבִנְעִימָה קְדֻשָׁה כֻּלָּם כְּאֶחָד עוֹנִים
וְאוֹמְרִים בְּיִרְאָה ·

קָדוֹשׁ קָדוֹשׁ קָדוֹשׁ יְיָ צְבָאוֹת מְלֹא כָל־הָאָרֶץ כְּבוֹדוֹ :
וְהָאוֹפַנִּים וְחַיּוֹת הַקֹּדֶשׁ בְּרַעַשׁ גָּדוֹל מִתְנַשְּׂאִים לְעֻמַּת
שְׂרָפִים לְעֻמָּתָם מְשַׁבְּחִים וְאוֹמְרִים ·

בָּרוּךְ כְּבוֹד־יְיָ מִמְּקוֹמוֹ :

take upon themselves ... heaven. " Mutually accepting for themselves
His heavenly rule " (Pool). The angels thus perform the function
which it is man's highest privilege to fulfil in this life and in the Hereafter.

the yoke of the kingdom of heaven. " Kingdom " here means *kingship*,
and " heaven " is merely a synonym for *God*. " To take upon oneself
the yoke of the Kingdom of Heaven " means, to recognize the rule of
God in the heart and life of man.

As to " yoke ", it is well to remember that a yoke is not imposed
upon animals in order to torture them. To cause them to work without
a yoke, *that* would be torture—and the field would remain untilled. A
yoke enables the animals to *pull together* in preparing the ground for
human benefit. In the same way, when men in harmony and love
take upon themselves the " yoke of the kingdom of heaven," they
resolve to " pull together "—to labour with their fellowmen—for the
furtherance of God's reign ; and, by means of such united spiritual
endeavour, bring about the betterment and ennoblement of the life
of man on earth. This " yoke of the kingdom " is, borne willingly,

All of them are beloved, pure and mighty ; and all of them in dread and awe do the will of their Master ; and all of them open their mouths in holiness and purity, with song and psalm, while they bless and praise, glorify and reverence, sanctify and ascribe sovereignty to—

THE CHORUS OF ANGELS   The Name of the Divine King, the great, mighty and dreaded One, holy is he ; and they all take upon themselves the yoke of the kingdom of heaven one from the other, and give leave one unto the other to declare the holiness of their Creator : in tranquil joy of spirit, with pure speech and holy melody they all respond in unison, and exclaim with awe :

Isaiah 6. 3   HOLY, HOLY, HOLY IS THE LORD OF HOSTS : THE WHOLE EARTH IS FULL OF HIS GLORY.

And the Ophanim and the holy Chayoth with a noise of great rushing, upraising themselves towards the Seraphim, thus over against them offer praise and say :

Ezekiel 3. 12   BLESSED BE THE GLORY OF THE LORD FROM HIS PLACE.

joyfully by the Israelite, as the emblem of free service. In this prayer such state of soul is figuratively transferred to the angelic host.

" The term *Kingdom of Heaven* is less expressive of an accomplished fact than of an undefined and indefinable ideal. It can be viewed from two aspects : the visible and the invisible Kingdom ".

" In the idea of the visible Kingdom of Heaven were included *national* ideas : the restoration of Israel was a vital prelude to the establishment of God's Kingship on earth. It was *ethical :* God's Kingdom meant the reign of righteousness. The reign was also *universal* : ' and the Lord shall be King over all the earth '."

" As for the invisible Kingdom, that is mainly spiritual, expressive of a certain attitude of mind. Thus, communion with God by means of prayer through the removal of all intruding elements between man and his Maker, and through the implicit acceptance of God's Unity, as well as unconditional surrender of mind and heart to His holy Will, this is what is understood by accepting the yoke of the Kingdom of Heaven " (Schechter).

give leave to one another. They are careful not to precede one another in the praises of the Lord, but to acclaim Him with one voice.

holy . . . glory. " Holy—in the highest Heaven, the place of His divine abode ; holy—upon earth, the work of His might ; holy—for ever and ever unto all eternity " (Targum Jonathan).

Ophanim, Chayoth, Seraphim. Names of classes of angels. The meaning of the terms is uncertain. *Ophanim* probably denotes some

לָאֵל בָּרוּךְ נְעִימוֹת יִתֵּנוּ · לְמֶלֶךְ אֵל חַי וְקַיָּם זְמִירוֹת
יֹאמֵרוּ וְתִשְׁבָּחוֹת יַשְׁמִיעוּ · כִּי הוּא לְבַדּוֹ פּוֹעֵל גְּבוּרוֹת
עֹשֶׂה חֲדָשׁוֹת בַּעַל מִלְחָמוֹת זוֹרֵעַ צְדָקוֹת מַצְמִיחַ
יְשׁוּעוֹת בּוֹרֵא רְפוּאוֹת נוֹרָא תְהִלּוֹת אֲדוֹן הַנִּפְלָאוֹת ·
הַמְחַדֵּשׁ בְּטוּבוֹ בְּכָל־יוֹם תָּמִיד מַעֲשֵׂה בְרֵאשִׁית ·
כָּאָמוּר · לְעֹשֵׂה אוֹרִים גְּדֹלִים כִּי לְעוֹלָם חַסְדּוֹ : אוֹר
חָדָשׁ עַל־צִיּוֹן תָּאִיר · וְנִזְכֶּה כֻלָּנוּ מְהֵרָה לְאוֹרוֹ :
בָּרוּךְ אַתָּה יְיָ · יוֹצֵר הַמְּאוֹרוֹת :

אַהֲבָה רַבָּה אֲהַבְתָּנוּ יְיָ אֱלֹהֵינוּ · חֶמְלָה גְדוֹלָה
וִיתֵרָה חָמַלְתָּ עָלֵינוּ : אָבִינוּ מַלְכֵּנוּ · בַּעֲבוּר אֲבוֹתֵינוּ
שֶׁבָּטְחוּ בְךָ וַתְּלַמְּדֵם חֻקֵּי חַיִּים כֵּן תְּחָנֵּנוּ וּתְלַמְּדֵנוּ :
אָבִינוּ הָאָב הָרַחֲמָן · הַמְרַחֵם · רַחֵם עָלֵינוּ וְתֵן בְּלִבֵּנוּ
לְהָבִין וּלְהַשְׂכִּיל לִשְׁמֹעַ לִלְמֹד וּלְלַמֵּד לִשְׁמֹר וְלַעֲשׂוֹת
וּלְקַיֵּם אֶת־כָּל־דִּבְרֵי תַלְמוּד תּוֹרָתֶךָ בְּאַהֲבָה : וְהָאֵר
עֵינֵינוּ בְּתוֹרָתֶךָ וְדַבֵּק לִבֵּנוּ בְּמִצְוֹתֶיךָ וְיַחֵד לְבָבֵנוּ
לְאַהֲבָה וּלְיִרְאָה שְׁמֶךָ וְלֹא נֵבוֹשׁ לְעוֹלָם וָעֶד : כִּי בְשֵׁם

animated "wheels", conceived in association with the Heavenly
Throne; *Chayoth*, literally means, "living creatures"; and *Seraphim*,
"beings of fire".

reneweth the creation. With these words the note struck at the
opening of the *Yotzer* prayer, p. 109, is resumed; viz., praise of the
Creator of light. Before concluding the eulogy, the touching Messianic
petition, "O cause a new light to shine upon Zion, and may we all be
worthy soon to enjoy its brightness", was included.

AHAVOH RABBOH. *With abounding love.* The second of the Blessings
that precede the Shema is praise of God's goodness in giving us His
Teaching, and prayer for His help in the study of the Torah. It recalls

THE
CHORUS OF
ANGELS   To the blessed God they offer melodious strains ; to the
King, the living and ever-existing God, they utter hymns
and make their praises heard ; for he alone worketh mighty
deeds, and maketh new things ; he is the Lord over struggle,
sowing righteousness, and reaping victory. He createth
healing, and is revered in praises. He is the Lord of wonders,
who in his goodness reneweth the creation every day con-
Psalm 136 7   tinually ; as it is said, (O give thanks) to him that maketh
great lights, for his lovingkindness endureth for ever. O
cause a new light to shine upon Zion, and may we all be
worthy soon to enjoy its brightness. Blessed art thou, O
Lord, Creator of the luminaries.

AHAVOH :
GOD'S
CHOICE OF   With abounding love hast thou loved us, O Lord our God,
ISRAEL   and great and overflowing tenderness hast thou shown us.
O our Father, our King, for our fathers' sake, who trusted in
thee, and whom thou didst teach the statutes of life, be also
gracious unto us and teach us. O our Father, merciful
Father, ever compassionate, have mercy upon us ; O put it
into our hearts to understand and to discern, to mark, learn
and teach, to heed, to do and to fulfil in love all the words
of instruction in thy Torah. Enlighten our eyes in thy
Torah, and let our hearts cleave to thy commandments, and
unify our hearts to love and reverence thy Name, so that we

God's unending love to our fathers in entrusting His sacred Teaching
to them, and in calling them to His service ; may He show similar
love to us their children, by giving us proper understanding of that
Teaching, and steadfastness in obeying it in our lives and the lives of
those that come after us.
    There is a strain of profound affection and passionate love of God in
this prayer, that could only have emanated from large-hearted souls
thrilled with profound devotion and purest piety. None of the petitions
for the material goods of life approach the fervour of this prayer for
knowledge of the Torah. With its stress on the love of God and the
Selection of Israel, on the duty of studying the Divine Message of
Israel and of obeying its precepts, it is an anticipation of the main
teachings of the Shema. After an ardent invocation for the Messianic
gathering of Israel, the prayer closes with the benediction, " Who hast
in love chosen Thy people Israel ".
    enlighten our eyes in thy Torah. So that we may all see and fully
grasp its spiritual wonders.

קָרְשְׁךָ הַגָּדוֹל וְהַנּוֹרָא בָּטָחְנוּ · נָגִילָה וְנִשְׂמְחָה
בִּישׁוּעָתֶךָ : וַהֲבִיאֵנוּ לְשָׁלוֹם מֵאַרְבַּע כַּנְפוֹת הָאָרֶץ
וְתוֹלִיכֵנוּ קוֹמְמִיּוּת לְאַרְצֵנוּ · כִּי אֵל פּוֹעֵל יְשׁוּעוֹת אָתָּה ·
וּבָנוּ בָחַרְתָּ מִכָּל־עַם וְלָשׁוֹן וְקֵרַבְתָּנוּ לְשִׁמְךָ הַגָּדוֹל סֶלָה
בֶּאֱמֶת · לְהוֹדוֹת לְךָ וּלְיַחֶדְךָ בְּאַהֲבָה : בָּרוּךְ אַתָּה יְיָ ·
הַבּוֹחֵר בְּעַמּוֹ יִשְׂרָאֵל בְּאַהֲבָה :

(*When prayers are not said with the Congregation, add :—*

אֵל מֶלֶךְ נֶאֱמָן :)

דברים ו׳ ד׳-ט׳

שְׁמַע יִשְׂרָאֵל יְהוָֹה אֱלֹהֵינוּ יְהוָֹה | אֶחָד :

בָּרוּךְ שֵׁם כְּבוֹד מַלְכוּתוֹ לְעוֹלָם וָעֶד :

וְאָהַבְתָּ אֵת יְהוָֹה אֱלֹהֶיךָ בְּכָל־לְבָבְךָ וּבְכָל־נַפְשְׁךָ

cleave to thy commandments. With a love that nothing can break. The Hebrew word for " cleave " is the one used for clinging affection.

unify our hearts. Make them single-hearted and undivided in our allegiance ; make it our heart's sole purpose to love and reverence Thy Name.

In the Heb. the first and the last word of this ardent prayer is the word, אהבה " love "

THE SHEMA

The Shema consists of three sections of the Torah (Deuteronomy 6. 4–8 ; 11. 13–22 ; and Numbers 15. 37–42). It is a proclamation of the existence and Unity of God ; of Israel's complete loyalty to God and His commandments ; the belief in Divine Justice ; the remembrance of the liberation from Egypt, and its corollary, the Election of Israel. These are foundation pillars of the Jewish Faith. Especially does the opening verse, " Hear, O Israel, the Lord is our

be never put to shame. Because we have trusted in thy holy, great and revered Name, we shall rejoice and be glad in thy saving power. O bring us in peace from the four corners of the earth, and make us go upright to our land, for thou art a God who worketh salvation. Thou hast chosen us from all peoples and tongues, and hast brought us near unto thy great Name for ever in faithfulness, that we might in love give thanks unto thee and proclaim thy unity. Blessed art thou, O Lord, who hast chosen thy people Israel in love.

(*When prayers are not said with the Congregation, say :—*
God, faithful King !)

Deuteronomy vi. 4—9.

THE SHEMA :
HEAR, O ISRAEL

HEAR, O ISRAEL : THE LORD IS OUR GOD, THE LORD IS ONE.

BLESSED BE HIS NAME, WHOSE GLORIOUS KINGDOM IS FOR EVER AND EVER.

THOU SHALT LOVE THE LORD THY GOD

⁵And thou shalt love the Lord thy God with all thine heart, and with all thy soul, and with all thy might. ⁶And these words, which I command thee this day, shall be upon

God, the Lord is One ", sound the keynote of all Judaism. It is, therefore, essential that every Jew should have a clear understanding of the implications of this opening verse, as well as of its influence upon Israel and mankind throughout the ages. See THE SHEMA : ITS MEANING AND HISTORY, p. 263.

God, faithful King. The doxology, " Blessed be His Name, whose glorious kingdom is for ever and ever ", was at first recited only in public worship. The three words, *God, faithful King,* seem to be a shorter expression of such conscious submission to the Divine Kingdom, when prayers are not said with the congregation. Others take them to be the remnant of a special benediction before reciting the Shema.

Hear, O Israel, the Lord is our God, the Lord is One. Other renderings are : " Hear, O Israel, the Lord our God, the Lord is One " ; " Hear, O Israel, the Lord is our God, the Lord alone " (Ibn Ezra) ; and " Hear, O Israel, the Eternal our God is a unique, eternal Being " (Zunz). Utterly unacceptable and meaningless is that of the Authorized Version, " Hear, O Israel, the Lord our God is one Lord ".

blessed . . . ever and ever. This response, first used in the Temple during the Day of Atonement Service, was later made the accompaniment of the opening verse of the Shema. As is well known, the Roman Emperors claimed divine honours, and were accorded such

וּבְכָל־מְאֹדֶךָ ׃ וְהָיוּ הַדְּבָרִים הָאֵלֶּה אֲשֶׁר אָנֹכִי מְצַוְּךָ
הַיּוֹם עַל־לְבָבֶךָ ׃ וְשִׁנַּנְתָּם לְבָנֶיךָ וְדִבַּרְתָּ בָּם בְּשִׁבְתְּךָ
בְּבֵיתֶךָ וּבְלֶכְתְּךָ בַדֶּרֶךְ וּבְשָׁכְבְּךָ וּבְקוּמֶךָ ׃ וּקְשַׁרְתָּם
לְאוֹת עַל־יָדֶךָ וְהָיוּ לְטֹטָפֹת בֵּין עֵינֶיךָ ׃ וּכְתַבְתָּם
עַל־מְזוּזֹת בֵּיתֶךָ וּבִשְׁעָרֶיךָ ׃

honours by their slavish subjects, with the sole exception of the Jews.
This doxology was to proclaim that the Israelite submitted to the
rule of God alone, and acknowledged none but Him as the Sovereign
of his life. He thus took upon himself the " yoke of the Kingdom of
Heaven ".

Hear, O Israel. The last letter of the first word שמע, and the last
letter of אחד, are written large in the Hebrew Bible. These two large
letters form the word עד " witness " ; *i.e.* every Israelite by pronouncing
the Shema becomes one of God's witnesses, testifying to His Unity
before the world.

Jewish custom prescribes that the eyes be closed or covered when
pronouncing the opening verse of the Shema—to shut out all distracting impressions, and to concentrate the whole of one's thought on
God's Unity.

the Lord is One. He, the Father and Sustainer of the lives and spirits
of all flesh, the everlasting Power Who guides the destinies of men
and nations, is One, because there is no other God than He : but He
is also One, because He is wholly unlike anything else in existence. He
is therefore the Sole and Unique God.

Therefore, to Him alone it is right to pray, and not to any
being besides Him. The Christian belief that the Godhead consists of
several personalities, is a departure from the pure conception of the
Unity of God ; and Israel has throughout the ages rejected everything that marred or obscured the pure monotheism which it had
given the world. Rather than abandon that pure monotheism, rather
than admit any weakening of it, Jews were prepared to wander, to
suffer, to die.

5. *and thou shalt love.* This is the first instance in human history
that the *love* of God was demanded in any religion. The worshipper, as
he declares the Unity of God, lovingly and unconditionally surrenders
his mind and heart to God's holy will. If the Unity of God is the basis
of the Jewish Creed, the love of God is to be the basis of the Jewish
life. And the noblest spiritual surrender and love of God, the Rabbis
held, was so to live and act toward our fellowmen as to make God and
His Teaching *beloved in their eyes.*

thine heart : [7]and thou shalt teach them diligently unto thy children, and shalt talk of them when thou sittest in thine house, and when thou walkest by the way, and when thou liest down, and when thou risest up. [8]And thou shalt bind them for a sign upon thine hand, and they shall be for frontlets between thine eyes. [9]And thou shalt write them upon the door-posts of thy house, and upon thy gates.

with all thine heart. The One God demands the whole of man, and his undivided allegiance. The Rabbis explain *with all thine heart*, to mean " with all thy desires, including the evil inclination " ; *i.e.* subject thy earthly passions and ambitions to God's Law, and thus make them instruments in His service.

with all thy soul. The Rabbis take these words to mean " with thy whole life " ; *i.e.* love Him with thy heart's last drop of blood, and give up thy dearest inclinations, nay life itself, for God, should He require it. Rabbi Akiba ever longed for the time when his daily profession of the love of God might be put to the proof and be confirmed by act. That moment came when, after his noble part in the last Jewish War of Independence against Imperial Rome, the executioner was tearing his flesh with combs of iron. " All my days ", Akiba told his weeping disciples, " I have longed for this hour. I have loved God *with all my heart*, and I have loved Him *with all my might* ; now that I can love Him *with my whole life*, complete happiness is mine ". It was such understanding of the words of the Shema that gave Jewish martyrs the courage to lay down their lives for their Faith. A medieval Jewish saint used to pray, " My God, Thou hast given me over to starvation and penury. Into the depth of darkness Thou hast plunged me, and Thy might and strength hast Thou taught me. But even if they burn me with fire, only the more will I love Thee and rejoice in Thee " (Bachya).

with all thy might. With whatever lot Providence has assigned to thee, and despite whatever material sacrifice thy loyalty to God and Torah might entail (Talmud).

7. *teach them diligently.* " Let your children have a clear, and not a confused or stammering, knowledge of the duties and teachings of their Faith " (Sifri).

JEWISH EDUCATION : ITS SCOPE.

In ancient times, the Mishna speaks of the Scripture instruction of sons and daughters as the normal practice.

If in later centuries the standard of education for Jewish girls was immeasurably lower than it was in the case of boys, it did not much matter ; as, in the sheltered life of the olden ghetto, Jewish woman remained unharmed by this narrow educational ideal, " and she could immolate herself as a martyr when the need arose " (M. Joseph). Yet even in those ages, a whole devotional literature in the Judeo-German dialect arose, *e.g.* the *Techinnoth* and the *Tze-ennoh Ure-ennoh*, which were exclusively intended for the use of girls and women. These books enabled them to say their prayers in the vernacular, and acquainted them with Scripture and the teachings of Jewish ritual and ethics.

Earlier than among any other people, Jewish law and custom ordained the provision of elementary instruction to the children of rich and poor alike. " Be ye heedful of the children of the poor, for from them does the Torah go forth ", was the admonition of the Rabbis. And the Jewish knowledge which is to endow every Jewish boy or girl with the Jewish outlook and Jewish loyalty, cannot be acquired in the few hundred hours now allotted to it in the current Religion Classes. It must extend over years, and not end with adolescence. The continuation teaching of the Jewish youth and the Jewish adult need not necessarily be carried on in formal classes. But a deep yearning, and constant striving, for acquaintance with Jewish thought, and the sources of Jewish inspiration, are indispensable for conscious, and not merely accidental, membership in the House of Israel.

JEWISH EDUCATION : ITS CONTENT.

As the aim of Jewish religious education is the consecration of the Jewish child to Judaism and his preparation for a life of beneficence for Israel and humanity, it must include the following four subjects.

(1) *Jewish Religion*—*i.e.* the Jewish beliefs concerning God, the Torah and Israel ; the teachings and practices, the symbols and institutions which have come down to the House of Israel through the ages. Such knowledge does not come of itself, and cannot be satisfactorily picked up from other Jewish studies. The growing boy and girl will in the future be often called upon to state and defend their religious position. They should be helped to a formulation of Jewish belief by means of systematic instruction.

(2) *The Hebrew Language.* Hebrew is Israel's historic language, and the key to all Israel's treasures ; and, being the key and receptacle of Israel's message to mankind, no other language, whether living or dead, has had such a vast and eternal span of influence. It is the most important of human tongues, the language of languages, the Sacred Tongue (*leshon ha-kodesh*). Every Jewish child is entitled to the possession of an intimate, even if not extensive, knowledge of the Sacred Tongue, which shall give that child a lot and portion in the synagogue, the heart of Jewish communal life. A Hebrew-less Jewry has no future, because it cannot fairly be said to have a present.

(3) *The Sacred Scriptures.* The beginnings of Israel's history as related in the Pentateuch should early form part of the child's soul-life. But we must go beyond the Pentateuch, and teach the whole Bible story. The main stress must be laid on the living truths underlying the narration of the facts. It is these truths, enshrined not only in Bible history, but in prophecy, psalm, proverb and moral discourse, that are of transcendent worth to the spiritual development of the child. Through these truths, the Bible is a Tree of Life to them that grasp it.

(4) *Jewish History.* Jewish History is a continuous revelation, with a divine lesson for each generation. Nobody can understand the Jew—

the Jew cannot understand himself—if he knows nothing of Jewish history beyond the *Chumesh*, or the Bible, or even Josephus. Every Jew should know the outstanding events and personalities of every age in Jewish history, with appropriate selections from our imperishable literary monuments. Only he who has wept over the tragedy of Israel and has been inspired by the story of our martyrs, who knows something of the wealth of our literature and of our contributions to the humanization of man, can have the proud Jewish consciousness that he is a member of a holy and indomitable People, or understand the meaning of the Unity of Israel, with its great ethical corollaries, the warning against the profanation of the Jewish Name (*Chillul Hashem*), and the sublime duty of hallowing the Name of God (*Kiddush Hashem*).

talk of them. They are to be a theme of living interest, early and late, at home and abroad.

when thou liest down . . . up. The Rabbis based on these words the institution of Evening and Morning Prayer.

8. *bind them*. For the precept of Tefillin, see p. 46.

9. *upon the door-posts*. By means of the *mezuzah*, placed in a metal or glass case, and fixed to the door-post on one's right when entering a house or room in the house. It contains the first two paragraphs of the Shema. The word שדי, "Almighty," written on the back of the parchment, is made visible by means of a small opening in the case. The *mezuzah* is a symbol of God's watchful care over the house and its dwellers. It is a solemn reminder to all who go out and in, that the house is a Jewish home, devoted to the ideals of the Shema.

THE SHEMA : SECOND PARAGRAPH.

The middle of the Shema teaches the doctrine of Divine Righteousness. Israel shall ever look upon its fortunes, even if these depend upon natural events, like the seasons, as rewards or punishments for righteous or unrighteous living. History corroborates the fact that nations decay when they no longer look upon life as built on moral foundations. " Opinions alter, manners change, creeds rise and fall, but the Moral Law is written on the tablets of Eternity. For every false word or unrighteous deed, for cruelty and oppression, for lust or vanity, the price has to be paid at last, not always by the chief offenders, but paid by someone. Justice and truth alone endure and live. Injustice and falsehood may be long-lived, but doomsday comes at last to them " (Froude). This truth of a Higher Justice should form the theme of daily meditation, and should early be implanted in the soul of the child.

REWARD AND PUNISHMENT IN JUDAISM.

The doctrine that obedience to the will of God is rewarded and disobedience punished, is bound up with the basic belief of Judaism in a God of Justice. Because God is just, He will not treat the righteous and the wicked in the same manner. In some way, it must be better with the former than with the latter, because of the justice of God. But such reward—whether conceived as material blessing or, as in later ages, when it became more and more spiritualized—is not made the *motive* for virtue. That must be love of God and His commandments, a free enthusiasm for doing His will.

How far there is correspondence in the life of the individual between

דברים י״א י״ג-כ״א

וְהָיָה אִם־שָׁמֹעַ תִּשְׁמְעוּ אֶל־מִצְוֹתַי אֲשֶׁר אָנֹכִי מְצַוֶּה
אֶתְכֶם הַיּוֹם לְאַהֲבָה אֶת־יְהוָֹה אֱלֹהֵיכֶם וּלְעָבְדוֹ בְּכָל־
לְבַבְכֶם וּבְכָל־נַפְשְׁכֶם: וְנָתַתִּי מְטַר־אַרְצְכֶם בְּעִתּוֹ יוֹרֶה
וּמַלְקוֹשׁ וְאָסַפְתָּ דְגָנֶךָ וְתִירֹשְׁךָ וְיִצְהָרֶךָ: וְנָתַתִּי עֵשֶׂב
בְּשָׂדְךָ לִבְהֶמְתֶּךָ וְאָכַלְתָּ וְשָׂבָעְתָּ: הִשָּׁמְרוּ לָכֶם פֶּן־
יִפְתֶּה לְבַבְכֶם וְסַרְתֶּם וַעֲבַדְתֶּם אֱלֹהִים אֲחֵרִים
וְהִשְׁתַּחֲוִיתֶם לָהֶם: וְחָרָה אַף־יְהוָֹה בָּכֶם וְעָצַר אֶת־
הַשָּׁמַיִם וְלֹא־יִהְיֶה מָטָר וְהָאֲדָמָה לֹא תִתֵּן אֶת־יְבוּלָהּ
וַאֲבַדְתֶּם מְהֵרָה מֵעַל הָאָרֶץ הַטֹּבָה אֲשֶׁר יְהוָֹה נֹתֵן
לָכֶם: וְשַׂמְתֶּם אֶת־דְּבָרַי אֵלֶּה עַל־לְבַבְכֶם וְעַל־נַפְשְׁכֶם

righteousness and happiness, and between misery and sin, is a recurrent
problem both in Biblical and post-Biblical Judaism. Deuteronomy and
Ezekiel declare that men get in this world exactly what they deserve.
Job, Jeremiah, Habakkuk, the Psalms, and Ecclesiastes courageously
face the bitter facts of life, and point out how often it goes well with
the wicked, and ill with the righteous. This world-riddle becomes less
distracting under the influence of the belief in the immortality of the
soul...

After the days of the Maccabees, the belief in immortality became
well-nigh universal among the masses of the Jewish people. R. Yannai
could thus remain quite unperturbed by his recognition, that " it is
not in our power to explain either the prosperity of the wicked,
or the affliction of the righteous ". " Faithful is thy Employer ", says
R. Tarfon, " to pay thee thy reward of thy labour ; and know that the
grant of reward unto the righteous will be in the future life ". New
spiritual conceptions became prominent : such as the great saying of
the illustrious Babylonian teacher Rabh, " In the world to come there
is neither eating nor drinking . . . but the righteous enjoy the radiance
of the Shechinah ".

In connection with this problem, the Rabbis never lost sight of two
things. One, that suffering is not an absolute evil : it educates, it
purifies, it can be an instrument of Divine love. Through it, Israel

Deuteronomy xi. 13—21.

REWARD
AND
PUNISH-
MENT

¹³And it shall come to pass, if ye shall hearken diligently unto my commandments which I command you this day, to love the Lord your God, and to serve him with all your heart and with all your soul, ¹⁴that I will give the rain of your land in its season, the former rain and the latter rain, that thou mayest gather in thy corn, and thy wine, and thine oil. ¹⁵And I will give grass in thy field for thy cattle, and thou shalt eat and be satisfied. ¹⁶Take heed to yourselves, lest your heart be deceived, and ye turn aside, and serve other gods, and worship them ; ¹⁷and the anger of the Lord be kindled against you, and he shut up the heaven, that there be no rain, and that the land yield not her fruit ; and ye perish quickly from off the good land which the Lord giveth you. ¹⁸Therefore shall ye lay up these my words ın

came into possession of the best gifts—the Torah, the Holy Land, and Eternal Life. And the second thing is, that in the deepest sense, righteousness is its own reward. Ben Azzai taught that, even as one sin begets another, so the reward of a good deed is that it leads to another good deed ! שכר מצוה מצוה. The Rabbis would have rejected the thought that in this world righteousness permanently produces misery, and wickedness invariably leads to happiness, as both irrational and blasphemous. Nevertheless, they taught men to disregard the thought of reward altogether ; and to do their duty לשמה, lishmoh, for its own sake. Antigonos of Socho, said, " Be not like servants who minister to their master upon the condition of receiving a reward ; but be like servants who minister to their master without the condition of receiving a reward ; and let the fear of Heaven be upon you ".

13. *to serve him with all your heart.* " Service of the heart is Prayer " (Sifri).
14. *in its season.* Both rewards and punishments are here connected with the rainfall, which is of vital importance in a land like Palestine.
former rain. The heavy rains towards the end of October. They open the agricultural year. The whole winter is the rainy season.
the latter rain. The heavy showers of March and April. Coming as they do when the grain is ripening, and being the last before the long summer drought, they are of great importance.
15. *grass.* Herbage, for human beings as well as for cattle. From the fact that Scripture here speaks of pasture for the cattle, and then continues " *thou* shalt eat ", the Talmud deduced the duty of a man to feed his animals before himself.
16. *take heed.* Satiety easily induces forgetfulness.

וּקְשַׁרְתֶּם אֹתָם לְאוֹת עַל־יֶדְכֶם וְהָיוּ לְטוֹטָפֹת בֵּין
עֵינֵיכֶם : וְלִמַּדְתֶּם אֹתָם אֶת־בְּנֵיכֶם לְדַבֵּר בָּם בְּשִׁבְתְּךָ
בְּבֵיתֶךָ וּבְלֶכְתְּךָ בַדֶּרֶךְ וּבְשָׁכְבְּךָ וּבְקוּמֶךָ : וּכְתַבְתָּם
עַל־מְזוּזוֹת בֵּיתֶךָ וּבִשְׁעָרֶיךָ : לְמַעַן יִרְבּוּ יְמֵיכֶם וִימֵי
בְנֵיכֶם עַל הָאֲדָמָה אֲשֶׁר נִשְׁבַּע יְהֹוָה לַאֲבֹתֵיכֶם לָתֵת
לָהֶם כִּימֵי הַשָּׁמַיִם עַל־הָאָרֶץ :

במדבר ט״ו ל״ז־ם״א

וַיֹּאמֶר יְהֹוָה אֶל־מֹשֶׁה לֵּאמֹר : דַּבֵּר אֶל־בְּנֵי יִשְׂרָאֵל
וְאָמַרְתָּ אֲלֵהֶם וְעָשׂוּ לָהֶם צִיצִת עַל־כַּנְפֵי בִגְדֵיהֶם
לְדֹרֹתָם וְנָתְנוּ עַל־צִיצִת הַכָּנָף פְּתִיל תְּכֵלֶת : וְהָיָה
לָכֶם לְצִיצִת וּרְאִיתֶם אֹתוֹ וּזְכַרְתֶּם אֶת־כָּל־מִצְוֹת יְהֹוָה
וַעֲשִׂיתֶם אֹתָם וְלֹא תָתוּרוּ אַחֲרֵי לְבַבְכֶם וְאַחֲרֵי עֵינֵיכֶם
אֲשֶׁר־אַתֶּם זֹנִים אַחֲרֵיהֶם : לְמַעַן תִּזְכְּרוּ וַעֲשִׂיתֶם אֶת־

18. *lay up these my words.* These words are taken with those immediately preceding and mean : In the event of your perishing from the land and being driven into captivity, even there in exile, you must carry out the behests contained in the Shema.

21. *as the days of the heavens.* *i.e.* so long as the universe endures.

THE SHEMA : THIRD PARAGRAPH.

The third section of the Shema was introduced because of the clear reference it contains to the Liberation from Egypt—the beginning of Israel's life. It also indicates how all these teachings are constantly to be kept before our eyes, and the eyes of our children, by means of an outward expression of an inward thought, tzitzis. The aim of the precept is the furtherance of holiness in the life of the individual and the nation by its constant warning against straying after the desires of the eye and heart ; see p. 44.

your heart and in your soul ; and ye shall bind them for a sign upon your hand, and they shall be for frontlets between your eyes. ¹⁹And ye shall teach them your children, talking of them when thou sittest in thine house, and when thou walkest by the way, and when thou liest down, and when thou risest up. ²⁰And thou shalt write them upon the doorposts of thine house, and upon thy gates : ²¹that your days may be multiplied, and the days of your children, upon the land which the Lord sware unto your fathers to give them, as the days of the heavens above the earth.

Numbers xv. 37—41.

THE MONITION OF THE TZITZIS

³⁷And the Lord spake unto Moses, saying. ³⁸Speak unto the children of Israel, and bid them that they make them a fringe upon the corners of their garments throughout their generations, and that they put upon the fringe of each corner a cord of blue : ³⁹and it shall be unto you for a fringe, that ye may look upon it, and remember all the commandments of the Lord, and do them ; and that ye go not about after your own heart and your own eyes, after which ye go astray : ⁴⁰that ye may remember and do all my

38. *their garments.* ʿOnly of the men ; because of the general rule, that women, whose duties are more absorbing in the home, are free from all precepts which have to be performed at a specified time (מצות עשה שהזמן גרמא).

cord of blue. To-day only white wool-threads are inserted.

39. *look upon it.* lit. " see it " ; hence the fringes are used in worship during daylight only.

and remember. The tzitzis are to keep alive the consciousness of the special relationship in which the true worshipper stands to God. " The blue cord of the tzitzis resembles the sea," says Rabbi Meir, " the sea reflects the heavens, and the heavens resemble the Throne of Glory ". Thus, the outward act of looking upon the tzitzis led the Israelite to inward spiritual conformity with the precepts of God.

after your own heart. " The heart and the eyes are the agents of sin—the eye seeth, the heart desireth, and the person executeth."

40. *be holy unto your God.* The supreme aim of the precept is therefore the hallowing of life.

EMES VE-YATZIV. *true and firm . . . is the word.* The last words of the Shema (" who brought you out of the land of Egypt, to be your God : I am the Lord your God ") are followed by an expression of our unfaltering faith (אמת ויציב) in the truth, that " the Lord is our God " and in the unchangeable validity of His Torah. The God of eternity is

כָּל־מִצְוֹתָי וִהְיִיתֶם קְדֹשִׁים לֵאלֹהֵיכֶם : אֲנִי יְהֹוָה
אֱלֹהֵיכֶם אֲשֶׁר הוֹצֵאתִי אֶתְכֶם מֵאֶרֶץ מִצְרַיִם לִהְיוֹת
לָכֶם לֵאלֹהִים אֲנִי יְהֹוָה אֱלֹהֵיכֶם :

אֱמֶת וְיַצִּיב וְנָכוֹן וְקַיָּם וְיָשָׁר וְנֶאֱמָן וְאָהוּב וְחָבִיב
וְנֶחְמָד וְנָעִים וְנוֹרָא וְאַדִּיר וּמְתֻקָּן וּמְקֻבָּל וְטוֹב וְיָפֶה
הַדָּבָר הַזֶּה עָלֵינוּ לְעוֹלָם וָעֶד : אֱמֶת אֱלֹהֵי עוֹלָם מַלְכֵּנוּ
צוּר יַעֲקֹב מָגֵן יִשְׁעֵנוּ : לְדוֹר וָדוֹר הוּא קַיָּם וּשְׁמוֹ קַיָּם ׃
וְכִסְאוֹ נָכוֹן וּמַלְכוּתוֹ וֶאֱמוּנָתוֹ לָעַד קַיֶּמֶת : וּדְבָרָיו חָיִים
וְקַיָּמִים נֶאֱמָנִים וְנֶחֱמָדִים לָעַד וּלְעוֹלְמֵי עוֹלָמִים עַל־
אֲבוֹתֵינוּ וְעָלֵינוּ עַל־בָּנֵינוּ וְעַל־דּוֹרוֹתֵינוּ וְעַל כָּל־דּוֹרוֹת
זֶרַע יִשְׂרָאֵל עֲבָדֶיךָ :

עַל־הָרִאשׁוֹנִים וְעַל־הָאַחֲרוֹנִים דָּבָר טוֹב וְקַיָּם לְעוֹלָם
וָעֶד ׃ אֱמֶת וֶאֱמוּנָה חֹק וְלֹא יַעֲבוֹר : אֱמֶת שָׁאַתָּה
הוּא יְיָ אֱלֹהֵינוּ וֵאלֹהֵי אֲבוֹתֵינוּ ׃ מַלְכֵּנוּ מֶלֶךְ אֲבוֹתֵינוּ
גּוֹאֲלֵנוּ גּוֹאֵל אֲבוֹתֵינוּ יוֹצְרֵנוּ צוּר יְשׁוּעָתֵנוּ פּוֹדֵנוּ
וּמַצִּילֵנוּ מֵעוֹלָם הוּא שְׁמֶךָ ׃ אֵין אֱלֹהִים זוּלָתֶךָ :

עֶזְרַת אֲבוֹתֵינוּ אַתָּה הוּא מֵעוֹלָם ׃ מָגֵן וּמוֹשִׁיעַ
לִבְנֵיהֶם אַחֲרֵיהֶם בְּכָל־דּוֹר וָדוֹר : בְּרוּם עוֹלָם מוֹשָׁבֶךָ ׃
וּמִשְׁפָּטֶיךָ וְצִדְקָתְךָ עַד־אַפְסֵי אָרֶץ : אַשְׁרֵי אִישׁ שֶׁיִּשְׁמַע

alone the Source of our strength and salvation. The outstanding proof
of this truth is the crowning act of redemption from Egyptian bondage,

commandments, and be holy unto your God. I am the Lord your God, who brought you out of the Land of Egypt, to be your God : I am the Lord your God.

ATTESTA-
TION TO
TEACH-
INGS OF
THE
SHEMA :
OUR FAITH
IN GOD
AND HIS
TORAH

True and firm, established and enduring, right and faithful, beloved and precious, desirable and pleasant, revered and mighty, well-ordered and acceptable, good and beautiful is this thy word unto us for ever and ever. It is true, the God of the universe is our King, the Rock of Jacob, the Shield of our salvation : throughout all generations he endureth and His Name endureth ; his throne is established, and his kingdom and his faithfulness endure for ever. His words also live and endure ; they are faithful and desirable for ever and to all eternity, as for our fathers so also for us, our children, our generations, and for all the generations of the seed of Israel his servants.

Alike for former and later ages thy word is good and endureth for ever and ever ; it is true and trustworthy, a statute which shall not pass away. True it is that thou art indeed the Lord our God, and the God of our Fathers, our King, our fathers' King, our Redeemer, the Redeemer of our fathers, our Maker, the Rock of our salvation ; our Deliverer and Rescuer from everlasting, such is thy Name ; there is no God beside thee.

GOD THE
HELP
OF OUR
FATHERS

Thou hast been the help of our fathers from of old, a Shield and Saviour to their children after them in every generation : in the heights of the universe is thy habitation,

by which Israel became a nation. It is the symbol of all redemption. Hence the name of this prayer, the *Ge-ulla*, Redemption.

EZRAS. *the help of our fathers.* This is a prayer of joyful thanksgiving for the Divine Deliverance of Israel in the past, and a fervent petition for the establishment of the Divine Kingdom in the future. God is enthroned in the highest heavens, the God of eternity, and yet He works righteousness on earth. " Happy is the man who hearkeneth unto Thy commandments, and layeth up Thy Teaching and Thy word in his heart ". At the deliverance from Egypt, God manifested Himself amid the wonders of the Red Sea as the living, eternal God, exalted and revered, who bringeth low the haughty, and answereth the lowly who cry unto Him. We echo the triumphant faith and gratitude of our fathers, when we repeat *Who is like unto Thee, O Lord ?*

לְמִצְוֹתֶיךָ · וְתוֹרָתְךָ וּדְבָרְךָ יָשִׂים עַל־לִבּוֹ : אֱמֶת אַתָּה
הוּא אָדוֹן לְעַמֶּךָ וּמֶלֶךְ גִּבּוֹר לָרִיב רִיבָם : אֱמֶת אַתָּה
הוּא רִאשׁוֹן וְאַתָּה הוּא אַחֲרוֹן · וּמִבַּלְעָדֶיךָ אֵין לָנוּ
מֶלֶךְ גּוֹאֵל וּמוֹשִׁיעַ : מִמִּצְרַיִם גְּאַלְתָּנוּ יְיָ אֱלֹהֵינוּ וּמִבֵּית
עֲבָדִים פְּדִיתָנוּ · כָּל־בְּכוֹרֵיהֶם הָרָגְתָּ וּבְכוֹרְךָ גָּאָלְתָּ ·
וְיַם־סוּף בָּקַעְתָּ וְזֵדִים טִבַּעְתָּ וִידִידִים הֶעֱבַרְתָּ וַיְכַסּוּ מַיִם
צָרֵיהֶם · אֶחָד מֵהֶם לֹא נוֹתָר : עַל־זֹאת שִׁבְּחוּ אֲהוּבִים
וְרוֹמְמוּ אֵל · וְנָתְנוּ יְדִידִים זְמִירוֹת שִׁירוֹת וְתִשְׁבָּחוֹת
בְּרָכוֹת וְהוֹדָאוֹת לְמֶלֶךְ אֵל חַי וְקַיָּם · רָם וְנִשָּׂא גָּדוֹל
וְנוֹרָא מַשְׁפִּיל גֵּאִים וּמַגְבִּיהַּ שְׁפָלִים מוֹצִיא אֲסִירִים
וּפוֹדֶה עֲנָוִים וְעוֹזֵר דַּלִּים וְעוֹנֶה לְעַמּוֹ בְּעֵת שַׁוְּעָם אֵלָיו ·
תְּהִלּוֹת לְאֵל עֶלְיוֹן בָּרוּךְ הוּא וּמְבֹרָךְ · מֹשֶׁה וּבְנֵי
יִשְׂרָאֵל לְךָ עָנוּ שִׁירָה בְּשִׂמְחָה רַבָּה · וְאָמְרוּ כֻלָּם ·

מִי־כָמֹכָה בָּאֵלִם יְהוָה מִי כָּמֹכָה נֶאְדָּר בַּקֹּדֶשׁ נוֹרָא
תְהִלֹּת עֹשֵׂה פֶלֶא :

שִׁירָה חֲדָשָׁה שִׁבְּחוּ גְאוּלִים לְשִׁמְךָ עַל־שְׂפַת הַיָּם
יַחַד כֻּלָּם הוֹדוּ וְהִמְלִיכוּ וְאָמְרוּ ·

יְהוָה ׀ יִמְלֹךְ לְעֹלָם וָעֶד :

צוּר יִשְׂרָאֵל · קוּמָה בְּעֶזְרַת יִשְׂרָאֵל וּפְדֵה כִנְאֻמְךָ
יְהוּדָה וְיִשְׂרָאֵל · גֹּאֲלֵנוּ יְיָ צְבָאוֹת שְׁמוֹ קְדוֹשׁ יִשְׂרָאֵל ·
בָּרוּךְ אַתָּה יְיָ · גָּאַל יִשְׂרָאֵל :

and thy judgments and thy righteousness reach to the furthest ends of the earth. Happy is the man who hearkeneth unto thy commandments, and layeth up thy Torah and thy word in his heart. True it is that thou art indeed the Lord of thy people, and a mighty King to plead their cause. True it is that thou art indeed the first and thou art the last, and beside thee we have no King, Redeemer and Saviour

THE DELIVER-ANCE FROM EGYPT   From Egypt thou didst redeem us, O Lord our God, and from the house of bondmen thou didst deliver us ; all their first-born thou didst slay, but thy first-born thou didst redeem ; thou didst divide the Red Sea, and drown the proud ; but thou madest the beloved to pass through, while the waters covered their adversaries, not one of whom was left. Wherefore the beloved praised and extolled God, and offered hymns, songs, praises, blessings and thanksgivings to the King, the living and ever-enduring God ; who is high and exalted, great and revered ; who bringeth low the haughty, and raiseth up the lowly, freeth the prisoners, delivereth the meek, helpeth the poor, and answereth his people when they cry unto him ; even praises to the Most High God, blessed is he, and ever to be blessed. Moses and the children of Israel sang a song unto thee with great joy, saying, all of them,

Exodus 15. 11   WHO IS LIKE UNTO THEE, O LORD, AMONG THE MIGHTY ? WHO IS LIKE UNTO THEE, GLORIOUS IN HOLINESS, REVERED IN PRAISES, DOING MARVELS ?

With a new song the redeemed people offered praise unto thy Name at the sea shore : they all gave thanks in unison, and proclaimed thy sovereignty, and said.

Exodus 15. 18   THE LORD SHALL REIGN FOR EVER AND EVER.

GOD OUR ROCK AND RE-DEEMER   O Rock of Israel, arise to the help of Israel, and deliver. according to thy promise, Judah and Israel. Our Redeemer, the Lord of hosts is his Name, the Holy One of Israel. Blessed art thou, O Lord, who hast redeemed Israel.

the Lord shall reign. Like our fathers, we acclaim His sovereignty over our lives. He is our Helper and Redeemer (צור ישראל).

The following prayer, עֲמִידָה, *to* פַּרְמוֹנִיּוֹת, *p.156, is to be said standing.*

אֲדֹנָי שְׂפָתַי תִּפְתָּח וּפִי יַגִּיד תְּהִלָּתֶךָ :

בָּרוּךְ אַתָּה יְיָ אֱלֹהֵינוּ וֵאלֹהֵי אֲבוֹתֵינוּ · אֱלֹהֵי
אַבְרָהָם אֱלֹהֵי יִצְחָק וֵאלֹהֵי יַעֲקֹב · הָאֵל הַגָּדוֹל הַגִּבּוֹר
וְהַנּוֹרָא אֵל עֶלְיוֹן · גּוֹמֵל חֲסָדִים טוֹבִים וְקוֹנֵה הַכֹּל ·
וְזוֹכֵר חַסְדֵי אָבוֹת וּמֵבִיא גוֹאֵל לִבְנֵי בְנֵיהֶם לְמַעַן שְׁמוֹ
בְּאַהֲבָה :

III. THE EIGHTEEN BENEDICTIONS
(שמונה עשרה)

Next to the Shema, the Eighteen Benedictions (*Shemoneh Esreh* in Hebrew) are the most important part of the Morning Service. They were known as " Tefillah ", *the* Prayer. In simple speech, these oldest congregational prayers of the Synagogue satisfy the cravings of a pious heart for communion with God, and give expression to praise, thanksgiving, confession, and petition. They are spoken three times daily, in silence, and standing; hence the name *Amidah* (*i.e.* the prayer to be said standing) among Sephardi Jews.

The eighteen (now nineteen) benedictions composing it, fall into three groups :

A. three opening blessings, " PRAISES "; they glorify the everlasting love, eternal might, and infinite holiness of God.

B. twelve (now thirteen) intermediate blessings, " PETITIONS "; they are brief prayers for individual and national well-being; and

C. three concluding benedictions, " THANKSGIVINGS ".

The first three and the last three are constant for every service—whether morning, afternoon or evening; whether week-day, Sabbath or Festival.

The *Shemoneh Esreh* is not a mere collection of short, independent prayers loosely strung together without inner sequence. Yehudah Hallevi and many others have pointed out the logical order of the Benedictions. In the religious spirit that pervades them they resemble the great devotional utterances of Scripture, and in them the voice of Judaism speaks with the classical accent of the Prophets and Psalmists.

This Prayer is not the product of one mind or even of one period. The opening benedictions, the " Praises ", are the work of the Men of

THE EIGHTEEN BENEDICTIONS

The following prayer (Amidah) to " as in ancient years," p. 157, is to be said standing.

Psalm 51 17   O Lord, open thou my lips, and my mouth shall declare thy praise.

I. THE GOD OF HISTORY   Blessed art thou, O Lord our God and God of our fathers, God of Abraham, God of Isaac, and God of Jacob, the great, mighty and revered God, the most high God, who bestowest lovingkindnesses, and art Master of all things ; who rememberest the pious deeds of the patriarchs, and in love wilt bring a redeemer to their children's children for thy Name's sake.

the Great Assembly, in the fourth pre-Christian century. The concluding benedictions, the " Thanksgivings," are not so old ; but they undoubtedly go back to the Maccabean age, the middle of the second century before the Common Era. Much younger are the " Petitions ", though nearly all of them were in use before the end of the Second Temple. As to origin, some of the Eighteen Benedictions were taken over from the Temple ; some were framed originally for private devotion ; while still others seem to have arisen in the Synagogue itself. The final editing of these prayers took place about the year 100, after the Common Era, at the direction of the Patriarch Gamaliel II, the then head of Jewry in the Holy Land. In congregational worship, the Benedictions were first said in silence, so as to permit unconstrained confession on the part of the individual. Then the Reader recited them aloud, for and on behalf of those who could not themselves say the Prayer. This has remained the usage to the present day.

O Lord, open. Since Talmudic times these words are introductory to the Shemoneh Esreh when it is read in silence.

A. THE OPENING BLESSINGS—" PRAISES ".

1–3. These three benedictions embody the fundamental beliefs of Judaism in God Almighty and All-holy, in His Covenant with the Fathers, the Election of Israel, the Messianic Redemption and the Immortality of the soul.

1. First Benediction : *The God of History.*

In this opening Benediction, God is adored as the God of the Fathers, the God of History, and the God Who in love will bring Messianic redemption to the children of the Patriarchs.

blessed. For the significance of this word, as well as of " Thou " when addressed to the Deity, see p. 10.

It is customary to bow at the word " blessed ", and again stand erect at the word " Lord ".

During the עֲשֶׂרֶת יְמֵי תְשׁוּבָה say :—

זָכְרֵנוּ לַחַיִּים מֶלֶךְ חָפֵץ בַּחַיִּים · וְכָתְבֵנוּ בְּסֵפֶר הַחַיִּים ·
לְמַעַנְךָ אֱלֹהִים חַיִּים :

מֶלֶךְ עוֹזֵר וּמוֹשִׁיעַ וּמָגֵן · בָּרוּךְ אַתָּה יְיָ · מָגֵן אַבְרָהָם :
אַתָּה גִבּוֹר לְעוֹלָם אֲדֹנָי מְחַיֵּה מֵתִים אַתָּה רַב לְהוֹשִׁיעַ ·

From the day after שִׂמְחַת תּוֹרָה until the Eve of פֶּסַח say :—

מַשִּׁיב הָרוּחַ וּמוֹרִיד הַגֶּשֶׁם :

God of our fathers . . . Jacob. These words are drawn from the
revelation at the burning bush (Exodus 3. 15). They are based on
Israel's fundamental conviction of the existence of One God, and take
the mind of the worshipper back to the dawn of Israel's religious
beginnings. In invoking the God of our Fathers, we, as their loyal
children, adore the same God—*our* God.

great, mighty and revered. Deuteronomy 10. 17. The Rabbis strongly
opposed any further heaping of Divine epithets in prayer.

bestowest lovingkindnesses. Or, " lavishest tender love " (Pool).

Master of all things. Or, " Maker of all things " (Genesis 14. 19).

rememberest the pious deeds. Thou causest the virtues of the Fathers
to bring salvation to their children's children. The Jewish doctrine of
the " Merits of the Fathers " (זכות אבות) teaches that the piety of the
fathers is accounted to the children as righteousness. " That man is
best able to advance on the road to moral perfection, who starts with
the accumulated spiritual heritage of righteous ancestors " (S. Levy).

in love. God has chosen, and will redeem, Israel not solely for
Israel's merits, but from love ; Deuteronomy 7. 7, 8.

bring a redeemer. See p. 253.

remember us. " Grant us life, O Thou who delightest in bestowing
the blessings of life "—The words go back to the ninth century, the
Gaonic age. They refer to the Heavenly Judgment, as that thought is
uppermost in Jewish hearts during the Ten Days of Repentance.

For the idea of *Book of Life,* see p. 165.

for thine own sake. *i.e.* to fulfil Thy purposes.

King. The ruler of our destinies.

Helper. In all the fortunes of life.

[*During the Ten Days of Repentance say* :—
Remember us unto life, O King, who delightest in life, and
inscribe us in the book of life, for thine own sake, O living God.]

O King, Helper, Saviour and Shield. Blessed art thou,
O Lord, the Shield of Abraham.

II. THE
GOD OF
NATURE

Thou, O Lord, art mighty for ever, thou revivest the
dead, thou art mighty to save.

[*From the day after Simchas Torah until the Eve of Passover, say* :
Thou causest the wind to blow and the rain to fall.]

Saviour. From destruction, moral and physical.
Shield. He who prevents woe and malevolent influences from overcoming us.
blessed art thou. Of all the Eighteen Benedictions, the first alone
both begins and ends with these words, which are the mark of a
berochah. All the others end, but do not begin, as a blessing ; they
are deemed to be merely continuations of the first Benediction.
shield of Abraham. Genesis 15. 1. If, like Abraham, we are ready
to meet every Divine behest with " Here am I ", He is also a Shield
unto us.
2. Second Benediction : *the God of Nature.*
The appeal to History, the sphere of God's supreme revelation,
is now reinforced by an appeal to Nature as displaying the power and
goodness of God. From the distant past, the worshipper turns to the
distant future, and hails God as the King who alone is mighty to save.
The God of the Past and Future is also the God Who lovingly sustains
the living in all the vicissitudes of earthly existence, and Whose infinite
faithfulness remembers and redeems them that sleep in the dust.
art mighty forever. God's protection does not cease at the portals of
the grave. He is mightier than death, and in His eyes the dead have
not died.
revivest the dead. He awakes the dead to new life. This emphatic
statement concerning the resurrection was directed especially against
the worldlings who disputed the deathlessness of the soul, its return to
God, and its continued separate existence after its reunion with the
Divine Source of being.
wind to blow. Nature's perennial renewal declares the omnipotence
of God. Above all so to an agricultural people, for whom the due
ordering of wind and rain vitally affects existence. To the Rabbis,
the changing panorama of the seasons, the resurrection of life every
spring, was the greatest of miracles. It was their conviction that, even
as the rain wondrously wakes to life the seed slumbering in the soil, so
would God awaken the dead to new life. Nature's wonders, they held,
were the strongest proof that their Author was a God of lovingkindness

מְכַלְכֵּל חַיִּים בְּחֶסֶד מְחַיֶּה מֵתִים בְּרַחֲמִים רַבִּים · סוֹמֵךְ
נוֹפְלִים וְרוֹפֵא חוֹלִים וּמַתִּיר אֲסוּרִים וּמְקַיֵּם אֱמוּנָתוֹ
לִישֵׁנֵי עָפָר · מִי כָמוֹךָ בַּעַל גְּבוּרוֹת וּמִי דּוֹמֶה לָּךְ ·
מֶלֶךְ מֵמִית וּמְחַיֶּה וּמַצְמִיחַ יְשׁוּעָה ·

During the עֲשֶׂרֶת יְמֵי תְשׁוּבָה say :—

מִי כָמוֹךָ אַב הָרַחֲמִים זוֹכֵר יְצוּרָיו לַחַיִּים בְּרַחֲמִים ·

וְנֶאֱמָן אַתָּה לְהַחֲיוֹת מֵתִים · בָּרוּךְ אַתָּה יְיָ · מְחַיֶּה
הַמֵּתִים :

When the Reader repeats the עֲמִידָה, the following קְדֻשָׁה is said —

Reader. נְקַדֵּשׁ אֶת שִׁמְךָ בָּעוֹלָם כְּשֵׁם שֶׁמַּקְדִּישִׁים אוֹתוֹ
בִּשְׁמֵי מָרוֹם כַּכָּתוּב עַל יַד נְבִיאֶךָ · וְקָרָא זֶה אֶל זֶה וְאָמַר ·

Cong. קָדוֹשׁ קָדוֹשׁ קָדוֹשׁ יְיָ צְבָאוֹת · מְלֹא כָל הָאָרֶץ
כְּבוֹדוֹ : Reader. לְעֻמָּתָם בָּרוּךְ יֹאמֵרוּ · Cong. בָּרוּךְ כְּבוֹד

Who supports the falling, heals the sick, and frees His children from
all manner of woe and suffering.

thy faith. His promise ; see Daniel 12. 2.

causest salvation to spring forth. " And in the flowering of Thy saving
power givest life " (Pool).

Father of Mercy. In the clauses inserted in the preceding Benediction during the Solemn Season, God is addressed as " King " ; here
He is invoked as " Father ". Often these two terms are combined,
and then the order is always, " Our Father, Our King " אבינו מלכנו.
In all these insertions, there is a prayer for *life*.

3. Third Benediction : *The Sanctification of God.*

NEKADESH. *we will sanctify.* In the first prayer before the Shema
(p. 109) it is the angels that ecstatically sing the holiness of God. Here

THE GOD
OF
NATURE

Thou sustainest the living with lovingkindness, revivest the dead with great mercy, supportest the falling, healest the sick, freest the bound, and keepest thy faith to them that sleep in the dust. Who is like unto thee, Lord of mighty acts, and who resembleth thee, O King, who orderest death and restorest life, and causest salvation to spring forth ?

[*During the Ten Days of Repentance say :—*
Who is like unto thee, Father of mercy, who in mercy rememberest thy creatures unto life ?]

Yea, faithful art thou to revive the dead. Blessed art thou, O Lord, who revivest the dead.

[*When the Reader repeats the Amidah, the following up to "Thou art holy " p. 137, is said after " who revivest the dead."*

III.
"KE-
DUSHA":
SANCTIFI-
CATION
OF GOD
Isaiah 6. 3

Reader.—We will sanctify thy Name in the world even as they sanctify it in the highest heavens, as it is written by the hand of thy prophet :
And they called one unto the other and said,
Cong.—HOLY, HOLY, HOLY IS THE LORD OF HOSTS : THE WHOLE EARTH IS FULL OF HIS GLORY.

Ezekiel 3. 12

*Reader—*Those over against them say, Blessed—
Cong.—BLESSED BE THE GLORY OF THE LORD FROM HIS PLACE.

the congregation of Israel sanctify God's Name : " We, on earth, will sanctify Thy Name as it is sanctified in the heavens above, fulfilling the words of the Prophet, ' And they called . . . full of his glory ' ".

Holy, holy, holy. This cry out of eternity, proclaiming the ineffable holiness, the supreme majesty, and universal sovereignty of God, is the quintessence of the teachings of all true Religion concerning the Divine Nature.

In Hebrew poetry, three-fold repetition indicates the superlative degree : God is highest, unsearchable and infinite holiness. " *Holy* denotes the awesome and august ethical majesty of God, and His complete freedom from all that makes men imperfect and impure. It denotes more than goodness, more than purity, more than righteousness : it embraces all these in their ideal completeness, but it expresses besides the recoil from everything which is their opposite " (Driver).

full . . . glory. All that is sublime in Nature and History is the outward expression and radiation of Divine Power.

from his place. From heaven. Others translate *from its place,* and understand it to mean, Blessed be the glory of God wherever it is manifested.

יְיָ מִמְּקוֹמוֹ : *Reader.* וּבְדִבְרֵי קָדְשְׁךָ כָּתוּב לֵאמֹר ·

Cong. יִמְלֹךְ יְיָ לְעוֹלָם אֱלֹהַיִךְ צִיּוֹן לְדֹר וָדֹר · הַלְלוּיָהּ :

Reader. לְדוֹר וָדוֹר נַגִּיד גָּדְלֶךָ · וּלְנֵצַח נְצָחִים

קְדֻשָּׁתְךָ נַקְדִּישׁ · וְשִׁבְחֲךָ אֱלֹהֵינוּ מִפִּינוּ לֹא יָמוּשׁ

לְעוֹלָם וָעֶד · כִּי אֵל מֶלֶךְ גָּדוֹל וְקָדוֹשׁ אָתָּה · בָּרוּךְ

אַתָּה יְיָ · הָאֵל הַקָּדוֹשׁ :

During the עֲשֶׂרֶת יְמֵי תְשׁוּבָה *conclude the Blessing thus :—*

הַמֶּלֶךְ הַקָּדוֹשׁ :

אַתָּה קָדוֹשׁ וְשִׁמְךָ קָדוֹשׁ וּקְדוֹשִׁים בְּכָל־יוֹם יְהַלְלוּךָ

סֶּלָה · בָּרוּךְ אַתָּה יְיָ · הָאֵל הַקָּדוֹשׁ :

During the עֲשֶׂרֶת יְמֵי תְשׁוּבָה *conclude the Blessing thus :—*

הַמֶּלֶךְ הַקָּדוֹשׁ :

אַתָּה חוֹנֵן לְאָדָם דַּעַת וּמְלַמֵּד לֶאֱנוֹשׁ בִּינָה ·

חָנֵּנוּ מֵאִתְּךָ דֵּעָה בִּינָה וְהַשְׂכֵּל · בָּרוּךְ אַתָּה יְיָ

חוֹנֵן הַדָּעַת :

thy Holy Words. The traditional division of Scripture is into three parts, the Torah, the Prophets (the earlier histories and the literary Prophets), and the Holy Writings, here called Holy Words (Psalms, Proverbs, Job, Five Scrolls, Daniel, Ezra-Nehemiah, and Chronicles).

the Lord shall reign. The glorification culminates in the proclamation of the eternal kingship of the God of Zion.

ATTOH KODOSH. *Thou art holy.* In the sublime strains of the third Benediction, God is hailed as the Holy God of a Holy People, and His holiness, is proclaimed on earth as it is in heaven.

Reader.—And in thy Holy Words it is written, saying

Psalm 146. 10 *Cong.*—THE LORD SHALL REIGN FOR EVER, THY GOD, O ZION, UNTO ALL GENERATIONS. PRAISE YE THE LORD.

Reader.—Unto all generations we will declare thy greatness, and to all eternity we will proclaim thy holiness, and thy praise, O our God, shall not depart from our mouth for ever, for thou art a great and holy God and King. Blessed art thou, O Lord, | *During the Ten Days of Repentance conclude* the holy God. | *the Blessing thus :—the holy King.*]

When the Shemoneh Esreh is repeated in public worship, this paragraph is omitted.

Thou art holy, and thy Name is holy, and the holy praise thee daily. (Selah.) Blessed art thou, O Lord, the holy God. | *During the Ten Days of Repentance conclude the* | *Blessing thus :—the holy King.*

IV.
PRAYER
FOR
UNDER-
STANDING

Thou favourest man with knowledge, and teachest mortals understanding. O favour us with knowledge,

the holy. i.e. those that strive to live lives of holiness. The reference is to Israel, whose sacred mission is the sanctification of God's Name in word and in deed (Baer).

B.   THE INTERMEDIATE BENEDICTIONS —" PETITIONS ".

There are six petitions (Benedictions 4–9) for our *individual* well-being—for understanding, repentance, and forgiveness of sins ; for deliverance from trouble, from illness, and from want. And there are six petitions for *national* well-being (Benedictions 10–15)—for the re-gathering of Israel, for righteous leadership, and protection from outer and inner foes ; for support of the faithful, the rebuilding of Zion, and the re-establishment of the House of David. The last of the intermediate Benedictions (16) is a petition that God grant our prayers.

4–9.   *Individual Petitions.*

This group of petitions are of a personal nature, though they voice the needs of all men. Note that the worshipper prays for *religious* needs—knowledge, repentance and forgiveness of sins—before he prays for his natural wants. Without an understanding heart, a repentant mind, and a steadfast spirit, he is unworthy of his prayers being heard.

4. Fourth Benediction : *For Understanding.*

The first of the petitions is for knowledge and spiritual insight. Throughout Scripture, " wisdom " is regarded as essential to moral

הֲשִׁיבֵנוּ אָבִינוּ לְתוֹרָתֶךָ · וְקָרְבֵנוּ מַלְכֵּנוּ לַעֲבוֹדָתֶךָ ·

וְהַחֲזִירֵנוּ בִּתְשׁוּבָה שְׁלֵמָה לְפָנֶיךָ · בָּרוּךְ אַתָּה יְיָ ·

הָרוֹצֶה בִּתְשׁוּבָה:

סְלַח־לָנוּ אָבִינוּ כִּי חָטָאנוּ · מְחַל־לָנוּ מַלְכֵּנוּ כִּי

פָשָׁעְנוּ · (on Fast Days סְלִיחוֹת are inserted here.) · כִּי מוֹחֵל

וְסוֹלֵחַ אָתָּה · בָּרוּךְ אַתָּה יְיָ · חַנּוּן הַמַּרְבֶּה לִסְלוֹחַ:

living. And we pray to the Fount of Wisdom, that we grow in true understanding, so as better to fulfil the duties of our lot and station. The knowledge especially referred to is the knowledge of the good that enables us to avoid evil, and gives us the power to do righteous things ; see Solomon's prayer I Kings 3. 7, and Jeremiah 9. 23. Hence the *Havdolah* prayer, which solemnly stresses the everlasting distinction between light and darkness, between holy and profane, is introduced in this Benediction on Saturday nights : see on p. 279.

5. Fifth Benediction : *For Repentance.*

The goal of wisdom is the realization of man's true relationship to his Maker. As our worldly pursuits may make us forgetful of our true vocation and destiny, we pray to God, whenever we have deviated from the right path, to give us strength to return to Him in true penitence. And such is our *daily* petition. Man is to repent one day before his death, and—any day may be his last.

thy Torah . . . thy service. There can be no " serving of God " for the Jew, unless it is preceded by knowledge of his Faith, or, at least, by acknowledgment of its sway over our lives.

delightest in repentance. Repentance (Teshuvah) is " a cardinal doctrine in Judaism—its doctrine of salvation " (Moore). Repentance in Judaism implies such sorrow, regret and contrition for past conduct as result in *turning from a wicked to a God-fearing life,* see pp. 838–40; God holds out His hand to the erring sinner, and leads him back to the paths of righteousness. The truly repentant can come nearer to God than even he who had never strayed and fallen.

6. Sixth Benediction : *For Forgiveness.*

Repentance must become articulate ; and mortal man, who is led into temptation and sin in spite of his understanding, prays for pardon

understanding and discernment from thee. Blessed art thou, O Lord, gracious Giver of knowledge.

V. FOR REPENT-ANCE

Cause us to return, O our Father, unto thy Torah ; draw us near, O our King, unto thy service, and bring us back in perfect repentance unto thy presence. Blessed art thou, O Lord, who delightest in repentance.

VI. FOR FORGIVE NESS

Forgive us, O our Father, for we have sinned.; pardon us, O our King, for we have transgressed ;

(*On Fast Days, Selichoth are inserted here.*)

for thou dost pardon and forgive. Blessed art thou, O Lord, who art gracious, and dost abundantly forgive.

of transgression in thought and deed. "Even if he be the veriest sinner, his supplication fits him to receive the Divine mercy, and so helps him to obtain it " (Albo).

The word " forgiveness " סליחה also denotes, " prayer for forgiveness ". On Fast Days such Prayers of Forgiveness, *Selichoth.* are here inserted during the Repetition of the Shemoneh Esreh.

forgive us. Forgiveness and remission of sins in Judaism can take place only *after* repentance. Hence, the order of the two petitions.

we have sinned. Note that the words are " *we* have sinned ", in the plural. " There is none righteous upon earth, who doeth only good, and sinneth not " (Ecclesiastes 7. 20). And we associate ourselves with the sinners, because we are members of one body and responsible to, and for, one another. Our evil example may have misled others, become a stumbling-block in the way of the blind.

transgressed. There is a broad distinction between the Hebrew terms for *sin* and *transgression* : the former is the result of carelessness, ignorance, or weakness ; the latter is a deliberate disregard of moral or religious duty. Instead of fully realizing their responsibility for their evil actions, many to-day make light of guilt ; some deride all moral inhibitions, and deny altogether the existence of sin. Hence, the basic importance of this prayer.

abundantly forgive. God's mercy never ceases, and His mercy is unending. " Let the wicked forsake his way, and the man of iniquity his thoughts ; and let him return unto the Lord, and He will have compassion upon him ; and to our God, for He will abundantly pardon " (Isaiah 55. 7).

After the petitions for spiritual values come those for earthly blessings—life, food and health ; and Judaism teaches us to pray for these with the same fervour and confidence, seeing that they are vital for the fulfilment of our task on earth.

6

רְאֵה בְעָנְיֵנוּ וְרִיבָה רִיבֵנוּ · וּגְאָלֵנוּ מְהֵרָה לְמַעַן
שְׁמֶךָ · כִּי גּוֹאֵל חָזָק אָתָּה · בָּרוּךְ אַתָּה יְיָ · גּוֹאֵל
יִשְׂרָאֵל :

On Fast Days the Reader here says עֲנֵנוּ, *p.146, and concludes thus :*

בָּרוּךְ אַתָּה יְיָ · הָעוֹנֶה בְּעֵת צָרָה :

רְפָאֵנוּ יְיָ וְנֵרָפֵא · הוֹשִׁיעֵנוּ וְנִוָּשֵׁעָה · כִּי תְהִלָּתֵנוּ
אָתָּה · וְהַעֲלֵה רְפוּאָה שְׁלֵמָה לְכָל־מַכּוֹתֵינוּ · * כִּי
אֵל מֶלֶךְ רוֹפֵא נֶאֱמָן וְרַחֲמָן אָתָּה · בָּרוּךְ אַתָּה יְיָ ·
רוֹפֵא חוֹלֵי עַמּוֹ יִשְׂרָאֵל :

בָּרֵךְ עָלֵינוּ יְיָ אֱלֹהֵינוּ אֶת־הַשָּׁנָה הַזֹּאת וְאֶת־כָּל־
מִינֵי תְבוּאָתָהּ לְטוֹבָה · וְתֵן בְּרָכָה עַל פְּנֵי הָאֲדָמָה

From the 4th December until the First Day of Passover
substitute for the last sentence :—

וְתֵן טַל וּמָטָר לִבְרָכָה עַל פְּנֵי הָאֲדָמָה

---

* The following Prayer for a Sick Person may be introduced here :—

וִיהִי רָצוֹן מִלְּפָנֶיךָ יְיָ אֱלֹהֵינוּ וֵאלֹהֵי אֲבוֹתֵינוּ שֶׁתִּשְׁלַח
מְהֵרָה רְפוּאָה שְׁלֵמָה מִן הַשָּׁמַיִם רְפוּאַת הַנֶּפֶשׁ וּרְפוּאַת הַגּוּף
לַחוֹלֶה פ׳ ב׳ פ׳ בְּתוֹךְ שְׁאָר חוֹלֵי יִשְׂרָאֵל ·

7. Seventh Benediction : *For Deliverance from Affliction.*
The affliction may be that of oppression or religious persecution
such as in the days of Antiochus—the probable date of this prayer.
Later, this bedediction came to be a prayer against all woes and evils
that afflict the secular life of man. In a modern paraphrase it reads :
"Look with compassion on all afflicted among us ; be thou our
Guardian and our Advocate, and redeem us speedily from all evil, for
in thee do we trust as our mighty Redeemer."

VII. FOR DELIVERANCE FROM AFFLICTION

Look upon our affliction and plead our cause, and redeem us speedily for thy Name's sake ; for thou art a mighty Redeemer. Blessed art thou, O Lord,

the Redeemer of Israel.

> On Fast Days the Reader here says "Answer us," etc., p. 147, and concludes thus :—
> Who answerest in time of trouble.

VIII. FOR HEALING

Heal us, O Lord, and we shall be healed ; save us and we shall be saved ; for thou art our praise. Grant a perfect healing to all our wounds ;* for thou, almighty King, art a faithful and merciful Physician. Blessed art thou, O Lord, who healest the sick of thy people Israel.

IX. FOR DELIVERANCE FROM WANT

Bless this year unto us, O Lord our God, together with every kind of the produce thereof, for our welfare ; give [*From the* 4th *December until the First Day of Passover include the words* :—dew and rain for] a blessing upon the face of the earth. O satisfy us with

---

[*The following Prayer for a Sick Person may be introduced here* :—
May it be thy will, O Lord our God, and God of our fathers, speedily to send a perfect healing from heaven, a healing of soul and body unto the sick . . . . . among the other sick of Israel.]

plead thou our cause. In times of " causeless hatred " and malignant ill-will, no argument in defence of Israel, or of the Israelite, though that argument be clear as the sun, is of any avail. We place our cause in the hands of Him Who alone can open the eyes of the blind, and free them from slavery to hatred that prevents them from according justice to the oppressed.

8. Eighth Benediction : *For Healing.*

This is a petition for healing to all who are sick, strength for all who are feeble, and relief for all who suffer pain. In some Rites, the benediction has the briefer concluding phrase *who healest the sick.*

A voluntary prayer may here be introduced for any one specific case of illness.

9. Ninth Benediction : *For Deliverance from Want.*

This is a prayer for the year to be fruitful, for dew and rain in their season, and an abundant harvest ; in brief, for bodily support. Whereas the *praise* of God as rain-giver is inserted in the Second Benediction, the actual *petition* for rain forms part of this, the Ninth, Benediction. This petition varied in the different Jewries of antiquity. Here our Rite follows the Babylonian usage ; and the words *give dew and rain*

וְשַׂבְּעֵנוּ מִטּוּבֶךְ · וּבָרֵךְ שְׁנָתֵנוּ כַּשָּׁנִים הַטּוֹבוֹת · בָּרוּךְ
אַתָּה יְיָ · מְבָרֵךְ הַשָּׁנִים :

תְּקַע בְּשׁוֹפָר גָּדוֹל לְחֵרוּתֵנוּ · וְשָׂא נֵס לְקַבֵּץ
גָּלֻיּוֹתֵינוּ · וְקַבְּצֵנוּ יַחַד מֵאַרְבַּע כַּנְפוֹת הָאָרֶץ · בָּרוּךְ
אַתָּה יְיָ · מְקַבֵּץ נִדְחֵי עַמּוֹ יִשְׂרָאֵל :

הָשִׁיבָה שׁוֹפְטֵינוּ כְּבָרִאשֹׁנָה וְיוֹעֲצֵינוּ כְּבַתְּחִלָּה ·
וְהָסֵר מִמֶּנּוּ יָגוֹן וַאֲנָחָה · וּמְלוֹךְ עָלֵינוּ אַתָּה יְיָ לְבַדְּךָ
בְּחֶסֶד וּבְרַחֲמִים · וְצַדְּקֵנוּ בַּמִּשְׁפָּט · בָּרוּךְ אַתָּה יְיָ ·
מֶלֶךְ אוֹהֵב צְדָקָה וּמִשְׁפָּט :

During the עֲשֶׂרֶת יְמֵי תְשׁוּבָה *conclude the Blessing thus :—*

הַמֶּלֶךְ הַמִּשְׁפָּט :

וְלַמַּלְשִׁינִים אַל־תְּהִי תִקְוָה · וְכָל הָרִשְׁעָה כְּרֶגַע
תֹּאבֵד · וְכָל אוֹיְבֶיךָ מְהֵרָה יִכָּרֵתוּ · וּמַלְכוּת זָדוֹן

for a blessing are said in winter from the sixtieth day after the autumnal
equinox (*i.e.* 4th of December) to the first day of Passover.

10–15. *National Petitions.*

The next six Benedictions are impassioned prayers for Israel's
spiritual life, and Israel's national hope in the present and future.

10. Tenth Benediction : *For the Reunion of Israel.*

Long before the destruction of the Jewish State, long before Mac-
cabean times even, there was a wide-spread Jewish Dispersion in
Mediterranean lands, in Babylonia, and in the neighbouring countries.
No doubt there were those who looked upon these settlements in the
Diaspora as outposts of the true Faith among the heathen, and as
seed-plants of a Universal Church. But to the vast majority of the
loyal and devout (Ecclesiasticus 36. 11), the reunion of Israel in the
Holy Land was ever the object of sincerest prayer.

thy goodness, and bless our year like other good years. Blessed art thou, O Lord, who blessest the years.

X. FOR REUNION OF ISRAEL Sound the great horn for our freedom ; raise the ensign to gather our exiles, and gather us from the four corners of the earth. Blessed art thou, O Lord, who gatherest the dispersed of thy people Israel.

XI. FOR THE RIGHTEOUS REIGN OF GOD Restore our judges as in former times, and our counsellors as at the beginning ; remove from us sorrow and sighing ; reign thou over us, O Lord, thou alone, in lovingkindness and tender mercy, and clear us in judgment. Blessed art Thou, O Lord,

| the King who lovest righteousness and judgment. | *During the Ten Days of Repentance say :—* the King of Judgment. |

XII. AGAINST SLANDER-ERS And for slanderers let there be no hope, and let all wickedness perish as in a moment ; let all thine enemies be

11. Eleventh Benediction : *For the Righteous Reign of God.*

The hope of the reunion of Israel leads to the Prophetic aspiration for the righteous reign of God, for the freeing of human society from iniquitous corruption and oppression ; Isaiah 1. 26.

sorrow and sighing. Few evils are the source of deeper grief and suffering than absence of justice in a land.

clear us. Declare our innocence in the Judgment that is to precede such Reign of God.

judgment. The change to " King of Judgment ", like the change to " holy King " in Benediction IV, is to emphasize, during the days intervening between the solemn festivals of New Year and Day of Atonement, the idea of man's responsibility to God.

12. Twelfth Benediction : *Against slanderers, informers and traitors.*

This petition is an addition to the " eighteen benedictions ", which by it became nineteen. It is directed against Jewish sectaries (*Minim*) in the generation after the Destruction of the Second Temple. They wrought division and havoc in the religious camp of Israel. Especially detestable were their fratricidal activities in the political field. They played the informers for the Roman authorities, and brought many of their brethren to a painful death. The wording of this Benediction has undergone manifold modifications. In its present form it has a universal and timeless application. The statement that in this prayer Jews of to-day utter an imprecation against those of another Faith, is a baseless calumny.

slanderers. This term covers both the disloyal Jews in ancient times

מְהֵרָה תְעַקֵּר וּתְשַׁבֵּר וּתְמַגֵּר וְתַכְנִיעַ בִּמְהֵרָה בְיָמֵינוּ ·
בָּרוּךְ אַתָּה יְיָ · שֹׁבֵר אוֹיְבִים וּמַכְנִיעַ זֵדִים :

עַל־הַצַּדִּיקִים וְעַל־הַחֲסִידִים וְעַל־זִקְנֵי עַמְּךָ בֵּית
יִשְׂרָאֵל וְעַל־פְּלֵיטַת סוֹפְרֵיהֶם וְעַל גֵּרֵי הַצֶּדֶק וְעָלֵינוּ
יֶהֱמוּ רַחֲמֶיךָ יְיָ אֱלֹהֵינוּ · וְתֵן שָׂכָר טוֹב לְכֹל הַבּוֹטְחִים
בְּשִׁמְךָ בֶּאֱמֶת · וְשִׂים חֶלְקֵנוּ עִמָּהֶם לְעוֹלָם וְלֹא נֵבוֹשׁ ·
כִּי־בְךָ בָּטָחְנוּ · בָּרוּךְ אַתָּה יְיָ · מִשְׁעָן וּמִבְטָח לַצַּדִּיקִים :

וְלִירוּשָׁלַיִם עִירְךָ בְּרַחֲמִים תָּשׁוּב · וְתִשְׁכּוֹן בְּתוֹכָהּ
כַּאֲשֶׁר דִּבַּרְתָּ · וּבְנֵה אוֹתָהּ בְּקָרוֹב בְּיָמֵינוּ בִּנְיַן עוֹלָם ·

as well as those apostates in the Middle Ages, who instigated persecutions against their former brethren.

wickedness. Not the wicked, but wickedness ; with the cessation of sin, sinners would be no more ; see p. 588.

speedily cut off. All the internal enemies against whom this prayer seems originally to have been directed, *did* speedily perish. Within a few generations they disappeared from the Jewish body.

13. Thirteenth Benediction : *For the Righteous.*

After the denunciation of slanderers and malignant apostates, comes the petition for the righteous, the leaders of the community, the Scholars, and all those who from conviction join the House of Israel.

the pious. Originally the ancient Chassidim, the loyal followers of the early Maccabees.

elders. The original reference was to members of the Sanhedrin.

scribes. The Jewish teachers in the century before the Maccabees.

true proselytes. In the first century, when this benediction was formulated, the heathen religions had lost their hold on serious-minded men and women. Throughout the Roman Empire, many hundreds of thousands were attracted by the One and Holy God of Israel, and by Judaism's stern condemnation of the cruelties and impurities of heathen life. The contemporary historian Josephus tells, " There is not a single town, Greek, Barbarian, or any other, to which the observance of the Sabbath has not penetrated ; whilst fasting [on the Day of Atonement]

speedily cut off, and the dominion of arrogance do thou uproot and crush; cast down and humble speedily in our days. Blessed art thou, O Lord, who breakest the enemies and humblest the arrogant.

**XIII.
FOR THE
RIGHTEOUS
AND
PROSE-
LYTES**
Towards the righteous and the pious, towards the elders of thy people the house of Israel, towards the remnant of their scribes, towards true proselytes, and towards us also may thy tender mercies be stirred, O Lord our God ; grant a good reward unto all who faithfully trust in thy Name ; set our portion with them for ever, so that we may not be put to shame ; for we have trusted in thee. Blessed art thou, O Lord, the stay and trust of the righteous.

**XIV.
FOR THE
RE-
BUILDING
OF JERU-
SALEM**
And to Jerusalem, thy city, return in mercy, and dwell therein as thou hast spoken ; rebuild it soon in our days as an everlasting building, and speedily set up therein the

---

and the kindling of lights [in honour of the Sabbath] and many of our laws as to meats, are observed ". And the stoic philosopher Seneca bitterly complains that " the conquered have given their laws to the conquerors ". The proselytes hailed from all classes, including the Imperial Court. In the Near East, a whole Royal House (Adiabene, corresponding to ancient Assyria) became fully Jewish. Multitudes of these proselytes proved their sincerity in the persecutions which followed the Jewish Wars of Independence in the years 70 and 135. The Emperor Domitan (81–96) inflicted exile, loss of property, and even death, on high-placed proselytes, and had his own cousin executed for that offence. Similar harsh measures against conversions to Judaism were in force in most European countries throughout the Middle Ages. A famous case in Anglo-Jewish history was that of the Deacon who was put to death at Oxford in 1221 for the " crime " of embracing Judaism. The latest martyr-proselyte was Count Pototzki, burned at the stake at Vilna in 1749. Israel still prays for those of non-Jewish birth who from conviction accept and loyally follow the Jewish creed and life.

good reward. Not necessarily material reward, but increase of moral strength, will-power and courage.

not be put to shame. The worshipper entreats that he be saved from the inner catastrophe of feeling that our trust in God and our struggle for truth have been in vain.

14 and 15. Fourteenth and Fifteenth Benedictions : *The Rebuilding of Jerusalem and the Messianic King.*

These two benedictions were originally one. The rebuilding of Jerusalem as the City of Righteousness would usher in the Messianic era, when the highest teachings of Religion would once more go forth out of Zion, and Jerusalem be the spiritual capital of all Humanity.

וְכִסֵּא דָוִד מְהֵרָה לְתוֹכָהּ תָּכִין · בָּרוּךְ אַתָּה יְיָ · בּוֹנֵה יְרוּשָׁלָיִם :

אֶת־צֶמַח דָּוִד עַבְדְּךָ מְהֵרָה תַצְמִיחַ · וְקַרְנוֹ תָּרוּם בִּישׁוּעָתֶךָ · כִּי לִישׁוּעָתְךָ קִוִּינוּ כָּל־הַיּוֹם · בָּרוּךְ אַתָּה יְיָ · מַצְמִיחַ קֶרֶן יְשׁוּעָה :

שְׁמַע קוֹלֵנוּ יְיָ אֱלֹהֵינוּ · חוּס וְרַחֵם עָלֵינוּ · וְקַבֵּל בְּרַחֲמִים וּבְרָצוֹן אֶת־תְּפִלָּתֵנוּ · כִּי אֵל שׁוֹמֵעַ תְּפִלּוֹת וְתַחֲנוּנִים אָתָּה · וּמִלְּפָנֶיךָ מַלְכֵּנוּ רֵיקָם אַל תְּשִׁיבֵנוּ · *) כִּי אַתָּה שׁוֹמֵעַ תְּפִלַּת עַמְּךָ יִשְׂרָאֵל בְּרַחֲמִים · בָּרוּךְ אַתָּה יְיָ · שׁוֹמֵעַ תְּפִלָּה :

---

* On Fast Days the Congregation here say עֲנֵנוּ.

עֲנֵנוּ יְיָ עֲנֵנוּ בְּיוֹם צוֹם תַּעֲנִיתֵנוּ · כִּי בְצָרָה. גְדוֹלָה אֲנָחְנוּ · אַל־תֵּפֶן אֶל־רִשְׁעֵנוּ וְאַל־תַּסְתֵּר פָּנֶיךָ מִמֶּנּוּ וְאַל־תִּתְעַלַּם מִתְּחִנָּתֵנוּ · הֱיֵה נָא קָרוֹב לְשַׁוְעָתֵנוּ · יְהִי נָא חַסְדְּךָ לְנַחֲמֵנוּ · טֶרֶם נִקְרָא אֵלֶיךָ עֲנֵנוּ · כַּדָּבָר שֶׁנֶּאֱמַר · וְהָיָה טֶרֶם יִקְרָאוּ וַאֲנִי אֶעֱנֶה · עוֹד הֵם מְדַבְּרִים וַאֲנִי אֶשְׁמָע · כִּי אַתָּה יְיָ הָעוֹנֶה בְּעֵת צָרָה · פּוֹדֶה וּמַצִּיל בְּכָל עֵת צָרָה וְצוּקָה : כי אתה וכו'

In that New Jerusalem, the Messianic King would establish his throne. Throughout the days of the Second Temple, this feeling prevailed, and it grew in intensity during the tyranny of the Herods, the Roman puppet-kings of Judea. They were not only usurpers, but strangers. Therefore, the restoration of the House of David would alone mean Israel's glory, and be the surest mark of God's favour. In all subsequent centuries, when the Jew speaks of the "Destruction of the Temple, he means the destruction of his homeland, the massacre of his

throne of David. Blessed art thou, O Lord, who rebuildest
Jerusalem.

XV.
FOR THE
MESSIANIC
KING
Speedily cause the offspring of David, thy servant, to
flourish, and lift up his glory by thy divine help because we
wait for thy salvation all the day. Blessed art thou, O Lord,
who causest the strength of salvation to flourish.

XVI. FOR
HEARING
OF PRAYER
Hear our voice, O Lord our God ; spare us and have
mercy upon us, and accept our prayer in mercy and favour ;
for thou art a God who hearkenest unto prayers and
supplications : from thy presence, O our King, turn us not
empty away* ; for thou hearkenest in mercy to the prayer
of thy people Israel. Blessed art thou, O Lord, who hearkenest unto prayer.

[*On Fast Days, the Congregation here say the following :—*

Answer us, O Lord, answer us on this day of the fast of our
humiliation, for we are in great trouble. Turn not to our wickedness ;
conceal not thy face from us, and hide not thyself from our supplication. Be near, we entreat thee, unto our cry ; let thy lovingkindness
be a comfort to us ; even before we call unto thee answer us, accord-
Isaiah 65. 24 ing as it is said, And it shall come to pass that, before they call, I will
answer ; while they are yet speaking, I will hear ; for thou, O Lord,
art he who answereth in time of trouble, who delivereth and
rescueth in all times of trouble and distress ;]

sons and daughters, and the Exile with all its physical pain and
spiritual suffering. Similarly, when he prays, "O that the Temple be
built!", this is but a short prayer for the ingathering of exiles, and for
complete redemption in his homeland " (W. Jawitz)

we wait for thy salvation all the day. "It is our trust in Thee alone
that sustains us day by day " (Pool).

16. Sixteenth Benediction : *For the Hearing of Prayer.*

Having given utterance to the individual and national petitions, the
group of Intermediate Benedictions closes with a petition that all the
preceding payers be answered.

who hearkenest unto prayer. See p. 160.

turn us not empty away. After these words, the worshipper may
add any private petition, anything that he has upon his heart, and ask
God's help, either for himself, his household, or for the community.

רְצֵה יְיָ אֱלֹהֵינוּ בְּעַמְּךָ יִשְׂרָאֵל וּבִתְפִלָּתָם · וְהָשֵׁב
אֶת־הָעֲבוֹדָה לִדְבִיר בֵּיתֶךָ וְאִשֵּׁי יִשְׂרָאֵל וּתְפִלָּתָם
בְּאַהֲבָה תְקַבֵּל בְּרָצוֹן · וּתְהִי לְרָצוֹן תָּמִיד עֲבוֹדַת
יִשְׂרָאֵל עַמֶּךָ ·

On רֹאשׁ חֹדֶשׁ and חֹל הַמּוֹעֵד of פֶּסַח and of סֻכּוֹת say:—

אֱלֹהֵינוּ וֵאלֹהֵי אֲבוֹתֵינוּ · יַעֲלֶה וְיָבֹא וְיַגִּיעַ וְיֵרָאֶה וְיֵרָצֶה
וְיִשָּׁמַע וְיִפָּקֵד וְיִזָּכֵר זִכְרוֹנֵנוּ וּפִקְדוֹנֵנוּ · וְזִכְרוֹן אֲבוֹתֵינוּ · וְזִכְרוֹן
מָשִׁיחַ בֶּן דָּוִד עַבְדֶּךָ · וְזִכְרוֹן יְרוּשָׁלַיִם עִיר קָדְשֶׁךָ · וְזִכְרוֹן כָּל
עַמְּךָ בֵּית יִשְׂרָאֵל לְפָנֶיךָ · לִפְלֵיטָה וּלְטוֹבָה וּלְחֵן וּלְחֶסֶד
וּלְרַחֲמִים וּלְחַיִּים וּלְשָׁלוֹם בְּיוֹם

say— On רֹאשׁ חֹדֶשׁ | On פֶּסַח— | סֻכּוֹת—On
רֹאשׁ הַחֹדֶשׁ | חַג הַמַּצּוֹת | חַג הַסֻּכּוֹת

הַזֶּה · זָכְרֵנוּ יְיָ אֱלֹהֵינוּ בּוֹ לְטוֹבָה וּפָקְדֵנוּ בוֹ לִבְרָכָה וְהוֹשִׁיעֵנוּ
בוֹ לְחַיִּים · וּבִדְבַר יְשׁוּעָה וְרַחֲמִים חוּס וְחָנֵּנוּ וְרַחֵם עָלֵינוּ
וְהוֹשִׁיעֵנוּ · כִּי אֵלֶיךָ עֵינֵינוּ · כִּי אֵל מֶלֶךְ חַנּוּן וְרַחוּם אָתָּה:

C. CLOSING BENEDICTIONS: THANKSGIVINGS.

These three concluding benedictions consist of prayers for the re-establishment of the Divine Service at Jerusalem; thanksgiving for God's daily wonders towards us; and a prayer for Peace and Prosperity.

"The worshipper concludes the Tefillah with benedictions for the restoration of the Divine Glory which we hope to behold as did our ancestors of old; and then he should bow down in gratitude, as if he indeed were in God's Presence and he witnessed the Israelites prostrating themselves when they beheld the Divine Glory. He should offer thanksgiving to God for all His goodness, and conclude the Tefillah with the benediction for peace that he may depart from the Divine Presence in peace" (Hallevi).

Of these closing benedictions (17–19), only the middle one is an expression of gratitude. It is preceded by a petition for the restoration of the Temple Service, and is followed by the Priestly Blessing. As

XVII. FOR RESTORA- TION OF TEMPLE SERVICE

Accept, O Lord our God, thy people Israel and their prayer ; restore the service to the inner sanctuary of thy house ; receive in love and favour both the offerings of Israel and their prayer ; and may the worship of thy people Israel be ever acceptable unto thee.

[*On New Moon and the Intermediate Days of Passover and Tabernacles the following to " merciful God and King " is added* :—

YAALEH VE-YOVO

Our God and God of our fathers ! May our remembrance ascend, come and be accepted before thee, with the remembrance of our fathers, of Messiah the son of David thy servant, of Jerusalem thy holy city, and of all thy people the house of Israel, bringing deliverance and well-being, grace, lovingkindness and mercy, life and peace on this day of

On New Moon say—the New Moon.

On Passover—the Feast of Unleavened Bread.

On Tabernacles—the Feast of Tabernacles.

Remember us, O Lord our God, thereon for our well-being ; be mindful of us for blessing, and save us unto life : by thy promise of salvation and mercy, spare us and be gracious unto us ; have mercy upon us and save us ; for our eyes are bent upon thee, because thou art a gracious and merciful God and King.]

---

neither of these benedictions is of a personal character, and both deal with matters that are the result of man's gratitude to and dependence on his Maker, they too are denominated " Thanksgivings ".

17. Seventeenth Benediction : *For the Temple Service.*
Even as the truth of pure Monotheism came from the Temple on Mt. Zion, so may that Sanctuary in future be the source from which will spread the true knowledge of God to all children of men.

service. Heb. *avodah* ; originally meant the Temple ritual, and later divine worship generally.

restore the service. This phrase was formulated when the Temple had been destroyed. The concluding words, *who restorest thy divine presence*, were originally *For Thee alone do we serve in reverence.*

YAALEH VE-YOVO. On New Moons and Festivals (except at Mussaf) the additional paragraph ויבא יעלה is here introduced. It petitions that, on the days which God gave us for festive joy, the whole

וְתֶחֱזֶינָה עֵינֵינוּ בְּשׁוּבְךָ לְצִיּוֹן בְּרַחֲמִים · בָּרוּךְ אַתָּה
יְיָ · הַמַּחֲזִיר שְׁכִינָתוֹ לְצִיּוֹן :

The Congregation in an undertone—

מוֹדִים אֲנַחְנוּ לָךְ
שָׁאַתָּה הוּא יְיָ אֱלֹהֵינוּ
וֵאלֹהֵי אֲבוֹתֵינוּ לְעוֹלָם
וָעֶד · צוּר חַיֵּינוּ מָגֵן
יִשְׁעֵנוּ אַתָּה הוּא לְדוֹר
וָדוֹר · נוֹדֶה לְּךָ וּנְסַפֵּר
תְּהִלָּתֶךָ עַל חַיֵּינוּ
הַמְּסוּרִים בְּיָדֶךָ וְעַל
נִשְׁמוֹתֵינוּ הַפְּקוּדוֹת לָךְ

מוֹדִים אֲנַחְנוּ לָךְ שָׁאַתָּה הוּא
יְיָ אֱלֹהֵינוּ וֵאלֹהֵי אֲבוֹתֵינוּ אֱלֹהֵי
כָל־בָּשָׂר · יוֹצְרֵנוּ יוֹצֵר בְּרֵאשִׁית ·
בְּרָכוֹת וְהוֹדָאוֹת לְשִׁמְךָ הַגָּדוֹל
וְהַקָּדוֹשׁ · עַל שֶׁהֶחֱיִיתָנוּ וְקִיַּמְתָּנוּ ·
כֵּן תְּחַיֵּנוּ וּתְקַיְּמֵנוּ · וְתֶאֱסוֹף
גָּלֻיּוֹתֵינוּ לְחַצְרוֹת קָדְשֶׁךָ לִשְׁמֹר
חֻקֶּיךָ וְלַעֲשׂוֹת רְצוֹנֶךָ וּלְעָבְדְּךָ
בְּלֵבָב שָׁלֵם עַל שֶׁאֲנַחְנוּ מוֹדִים
לָךְ · בָּרוּךְ אֵל הַהוֹדָאוֹת :

וְעַל נִסֶּיךָ שֶׁבְּכָל־יוֹם עִמָּנוּ וְעַל נִפְלְאוֹתֶיךָ וְטוֹבוֹתֶיךָ
שֶׁבְּכָל־עֵת עֶרֶב וָבֹקֶר וְצָהֳרָיִם · הַטּוֹב כִּי לֹא־כָלוּ
רַחֲמֶיךָ · וְהַמְרַחֵם כִּי לֹא־תַמּוּ חֲסָדֶיךָ מֵעוֹלָם קִוִּינוּ
לָךְ :

On חֲנֻכָּה and פּוּרִים *the following is added:*—

עַל הַנִּסִּים וְעַל הַפֻּרְקָן וְעַל הַגְּבוּרוֹת וְעַל הַתְּשׁוּעוֹת וְעַל
הַמִּלְחָמוֹת שֶׁעָשִׂיתָ לַאֲבוֹתֵינוּ בַּיָּמִים הָהֵם בַּזְּמַן הַזֶּה :

House of Israel be remembered by Him for good and blessing, so that
we may celebrate the Sacred Festival in gladness. When the Reader
utters the phrases, " remember us, O Lord our God, thereon for our
well-being ", and " be mindful of us for blessing ", and " save us unto
life ", the congregation each time responds with " Amen ".

18. Eighteenth Benediction : *Thanksgiving for God's Mercies.*
We give thanks. A singularly beautiful anthem of gratitude for
God's manifold mercies to us.

And let our eyes behold thy return in mercy to Zion. Blessed art thou, O Lord, who restorest thy divine presence unto Zion.

*XVIII.
THANKS-
GIVING
FOR GOD'S
UNFAIL-
ING
MERCIES*

We give thanks unto thee, for thou art the Lord our God and the God of our fathers for ever and ever ; thou art the Rock of our lives, the Shield of our salvation through every generation. We will give thanks unto thee and declare thy praise for our lives which are committed unto thy hand, and for our souls which are in thy charge, and for thy miracles, which are daily with us, and for thy wonders and thy benefits, which are wrought at all times, evening, morn and noon. O thou who art all-good, whose mercies fail not ; thou, merciful Being, whose lovingkindnesses never cease, we have ever hoped in thee.

The Congregation, in an undertone—

We give thanks unto thee, for thou art the Lord our God and the God of our fathers, the God of all flesh, our Creator and the Creator of all things in the beginning. Blessings and thanksgivings be to thy great and holy Name, because thou hast kept us in life and hast preserved us : so mayest thou continue to keep us in life and to preserve us. O gather our exiles to thy holy courts to observe thy statutes, to do thy will, and to serve thee with a perfect heart ; seeing that we give thanks unto thee. Blessed be the God to whom thanksgivings are due.

[*On Chanukah and Purim the following is added* :—

We thank thee also for the miracles, for the redemption, for the mighty deeds and saving acts, wrought by thee, as well as for the wars which thou didst wage for our fathers in days of old, at this season.

The *Modim* said by the congregation, in an undertone, when the Amidah is repeated, is an abstract of several Rabbinical prayers.

also for the miracles. In the Chanukah Prayer special prominence is given to the miracle of the *spiritual revival* of Judaism. The prayer is a summary of the story of the Maccabees, but it stops with the re-conquest of the Temple. It passes over in silence the military glories of the many years of warfare that followed, as of altogether transitory importance. The creators of the Liturgy viewed things under the aspect of eternity.

On חֲנֻכָּה.

בִּימֵי מַתִּתְיָהוּ בֶן־יוֹחָנָן כֹּהֵן גָּדוֹל חַשְׁמוֹנַאי וּבָנָיו כְּשֶׁעָמְדָה
מַלְכוּת יָוָן הָרְשָׁעָה עַל־עַמְּךָ יִשְׂרָאֵל לְהַשְׁכִּיחָם תּוֹרָתֶךָ
וּלְהַעֲבִירָם מֵחֻקֵּי רְצוֹנֶךָ ' וְאַתָּה בְּרַחֲמֶיךָ הָרַבִּים עָמַדְתָּ לָהֶם
בְּעֵת צָרָתָם ' רַבְתָּ אֶת־רִיבָם דַּנְתָּ אֶת־דִּינָם נָקַמְתָּ אֶת־נִקְמָתָם '
מָסַרְתָּ גִבּוֹרִים בְּיַד חַלָּשִׁים וְרַבִּים בְּיַד מְעַטִּים וּטְמֵאִים בְּיַד
טְהוֹרִים וּרְשָׁעִים בְּיַד צַדִּיקִים וְזֵדִים בְּיַד עוֹסְקֵי תוֹרָתֶךָ ' וּלְךָ
עָשִׂיתָ שֵׁם גָּדוֹל וְקָדוֹשׁ בְּעוֹלָמֶךָ וּלְעַמְּךָ יִשְׂרָאֵל עָשִׂיתָ תְּשׁוּעָה
גְדוֹלָה וּפֻרְקָן כְּהַיּוֹם הַזֶּה ' וְאַחַר כֵּן בָּאוּ בָנֶיךָ לִדְבִיר בֵּיתֶךָ
וּפִנּוּ אֶת־הֵיכָלֶךָ וְטִהֲרוּ אֶת־מִקְדָּשֶׁךָ וְהִדְלִיקוּ נֵרוֹת בְּחַצְרוֹת
קָדְשֶׁךָ ' וְקָבְעוּ שְׁמוֹנַת יְמֵי חֲנֻכָּה אֵלּוּ לְהוֹדוֹת וּלְהַלֵּל לְשִׁמְךָ
הַגָּדוֹל :

On פּוּרִים.

בִּימֵי מָרְדְּכַי וְאֶסְתֵּר בְּשׁוּשַׁן הַבִּירָה כְּשֶׁעָמַד עֲלֵיהֶם הָמָן
הָרָשָׁע ' בִּקֵּשׁ לְהַשְׁמִיד לַהֲרֹג וּלְאַבֵּד אֶת־כָּל־הַיְּהוּדִים מִנַּעַר
וְעַד זָקֵן טַף וְנָשִׁים בְּיוֹם אֶחָד ' בִּשְׁלוֹשָׁה־עָשָׂר לְחֹדֶשׁ שְׁנֵים־
עָשָׂר הוּא־חֹדֶשׁ אֲדָר וּשְׁלָלָם לָבוֹז ' וְאַתָּה בְּרַחֲמֶיךָ הָרַבִּים
הֵפַרְתָּ אֶת־עֲצָתוֹ וְקִלְקַלְתָּ אֶת־מַחֲשַׁבְתּוֹ וַהֲשֵׁבוֹתָ גְּמוּלוֹ
בְּרֹאשׁוֹ וְתָלוּ אֹתוֹ וְאֶת־בָּנָיו עַל־הָעֵץ :

וְעַל־כֻּלָּם יִתְבָּרַךְ וְיִתְרוֹמַם שִׁמְךָ מַלְכֵּנוּ תָּמִיד לְעוֹלָם
וָעֶד :

During the עֲשֶׂרֶת יְמֵי תְשׁוּבָה say:—

וּכְתוֹב לְחַיִּים טוֹבִים כָּל־בְּנֵי בְרִיתֶךָ :

וְכֹל הַחַיִּים יוֹדוּךָ סֶּלָה · וִיהַלְלוּ אֶת־שִׁמְךָ בֶּאֱמֶת ·

On Chanukah.

THANKS-
GIVING ON
CHANU-
KAH

In the days of the Hasmonean, Mattathias son of Johanan, the High Priest, and his sons, when the iniquitous power of Greece rose up against thy people Israel to make them forgetful of thy Torah, and to force them to transgress the statutes of thy will, then didst thou in thine abundant mercy rise up for them in the time of their trouble ; thou didst plead their cause, thou didst judge their suit, thou didst avenge their wrong ; thou deliveredst the strong into the hands of the weak, the many into the hands of the few, the impure into the hands of the pure, the wicked into the hands of the righteous, and the arrogant into the hands of them that occupied themselves with thy Torah : for thyself thou didst make a great and holy name in thy world, and for thy people Israel thou didst work a great deliverance and redemption as at this day. And thereupon thy children came into the inner sanctuary of thy house, cleansed thy temple, purified thy holy place, kindled lights in thy sacred courts, and appointed these eight days of Chanukah in order to give thanks and praises unto thy great Name.

On Purim.

AND
PURIM

In the days of Mordecai and Esther, in Sushan the capital, when the wicked Haman rose up against them, and sought to destroy, to slay and cause to perish all the Jews, both young and old, women and little children, on one day, on the thirteenth day of the twelfth month, which is the month Adar, and to take the spoil of them for a prey,—then didst thou in thine abundant mercy bring his counsel to nought, didst frustrate his design, and return his recompense upon his own head ; and they hanged him and his sons upon the gallows.]

For all these acts thy Name, O our King, shall be continually blessed and exalted for ever and ever.

[*During the Ten days of Repentance say :—*
O inscribe all the children of thy covenant for a happy life.]

And everything that liveth shall give thanks unto thee for ever, and shall praise thy Name in truth, O God, our salvation and our help. (Selah.) Blessed art thou, O Lord,

the High Priest. The title was later applied to Mattathias, because his son Simon became High Priest in 141 B.C.E.
Purim. This prayer is a brief summing up of the Book of Esther.

הָאֵל יְשׁוּעָתֵנוּ וְעֶזְרָתֵנוּ סֶלָה · בָּרוּךְ אַתָּה יְיָ · הַטּוֹב שִׁמְךָ וּלְךָ נָאֶה לְהוֹדוֹת :

At the repetition of the עֲמִידָה *by the Reader, the following is introduced :—*

אֱלֹהֵינוּ וֵאלֹהֵי אֲבוֹתֵינוּ · בָּרְכֵנוּ בַּבְּרָכָה הַמְשֻׁלֶּשֶׁת בַּתּוֹרָה · הַכְּתוּבָה עַל יְדֵי מֹשֶׁה עַבְדֶּךָ · הָאֲמוּרָה מִפִּי אַהֲרֹן וּבָנָיו כֹּהֲנִים · עַם קְדוֹשֶׁךָ כָּאָמוּר · יְבָרֶכְךָ יְיָ וְיִשְׁמְרֶךָ : יָאֵר יְיָ פָּנָיו אֵלֶיךָ וִיחֻנֶּךָּ : יִשָּׂא יְיָ פָּנָיו אֵלֶיךָ וְיָשֵׂם לְךָ שָׁלוֹם :

שִׂים שָׁלוֹם טוֹבָה וּבְרָכָה חֵן וָחֶסֶד וְרַחֲמִים עָלֵינוּ וְעַל כָּל־יִשְׂרָאֵל עַמֶּךָ · בָּרְכֵנוּ אָבִינוּ כֻּלָּנוּ כְּאֶחָד בְּאוֹר פָּנֶיךָ · כִּי בְאוֹר פָּנֶיךָ נָתַתָּ לָנוּ יְיָ אֱלֹהֵינוּ תּוֹרַת חַיִּים וְאַהֲבַת חֶסֶד וּצְדָקָה וּבְרָכָה וְרַחֲמִים וְחַיִּים וְשָׁלוֹם · וְטוֹב בְּעֵינֶיךָ לְבָרֵךְ אֶת־עַמְּךָ יִשְׂרָאֵל בְּכָל־עֵת וּבְכָל־שָׁעָה בִּשְׁלוֹמֶךָ ·

בָּרוּךְ אַתָּה יְיָ ·
During the say :— עֲשֶׂרֶת יְמֵי תְשׁוּבָה
בְּסֵפֶר חַיִּים בְּרָכָה וְשָׁלוֹם וּפַרְנָסָה
הַמְבָרֵךְ אֶת־עַמּוֹ
טוֹבָה נִזָּכֵר וְנִכָּתֵב לְפָנֶיךָ אֲנַחְנוּ וְכָל־
עַמְּךָ בֵּית יִשְׂרָאֵל לְחַיִּים טוֹבִים
יִשְׂרָאֵל בַּשָּׁלוֹם :
וּלְשָׁלוֹם · בָּרוּךְ אַתָּה יְיָ · עוֹשֵׂה הַשָּׁלוֹם :

three-fold blessing. Consisting of three clauses.
19. Nineteenth Benediction : *For Peace.*
The prayer for Peace is the last of the " Thanksgiving " benedictions.

whose Name is All-good, and unto whom it is becoming to give thanks.

[At the repetition of the Amidah by the Reader, the following is introduced, but is omitted in the house of mourning.

Our God and God of our fathers, bless us with the three-fold blessing of thy Torah written by the hand of Moses thy servant, which was spoken by Aaron and his sons, the priests, thy holy people, as it is said, THE LORD BLESS THEE, AND KEEP THEE : THE LORD MAKE HIS FACE TO SHINE UPON THEE, AND BE GRACIOUS UNTO THEE : THE LORD TURN HIS FACE UNTO THEE, AND GIVE THEE PEACE.]

Numbers 6. 24-26

XIX. FOR PEACE

Grant peace, welfare, blessing, grace, lovingkindness and mercy unto us and unto all Israel, thy people. Bless us, O our Father, even all of us together, with the light of thy countenance ; for by the light of thy countenance thou hast given us, O Lord our God, the Torah of life, lovingkindness and righteousness, blessing, mercy, life and peace ; and may it be good in thy sight to bless thy people Israel at all times and in every hour with thy peace.

Blessed art thou, O Lord, who blessest thy people Israel with peace.

[During the Ten Days of Repentance say :— In the book of life, blessing, peace and good sustenance may we be remembered and inscribed before thee, we and all thy people the house of Israel, for a happy life and for peace. Blessed art thou, O Lord, who makest peace.]

There can be no Peace, unless it is preceded by thankfulness to God ; even as there can be no true thankfulness, unless that is preceded by service to God. " Only that peace has lasting worth, which is the fruit of common gratitude and common devotion to God's Torah " (Hirsch).

In the Mishnah this benediction is called the " Benediction of the Priests ", because the Priestly Blessing was here daily recited in the Temple. At the present day, this is done by the Reader in the paragraph preceding this benediction, except at those Mussaf Services when the Priests bless the Congregation.

grant peace. The prayer for peace is a Congregational restatement of the Priestly Benediction in the form of a prayer.

אֱלֹהַי · נְצוֹר לְשׁוֹנִי מֵרָע וּשְׂפָתַי מִדַּבֵּר מִרְמָה ·
וְלִמְקַלְלַי נַפְשִׁי תִדּוֹם וְנַפְשִׁי כֶּעָפָר לַכֹּל תִּהְיֶה : פְּתַח
לִבִּי בְּתוֹרָתֶךָ וּבְמִצְוֹתֶיךָ תִּרְדּוֹף נַפְשִׁי · וְכֹל הַחוֹשְׁבִים
עָלַי רָעָה מְהֵרָה הָפֵר עֲצָתָם וְקַלְקֵל מַחֲשַׁבְתָּם · עֲשֵׂה
לְמַעַן שְׁמֶךָ עֲשֵׂה לְמַעַן יְמִינֶךָ עֲשֵׂה לְמַעַן קְדֻשָּׁתֶךָ עֲשֵׂה
לְמַעַן תּוֹרָתֶךָ · לְמַעַן יֵחָלְצוּן יְדִידֶיךָ הוֹשִׁיעָה יְמִינְךָ
וַעֲנֵנִי : יִהְיוּ לְרָצוֹן אִמְרֵי־פִי וְהֶגְיוֹן לִבִּי לְפָנֶיךָ יְיָ צוּרִי
וְגֹאֲלִי : עֹשֶׂה שָׁלוֹם בִּמְרוֹמָיו הוּא יַעֲשֶׂה שָׁלוֹם עָלֵינוּ
וְעַל כָּל־יִשְׂרָאֵל · וְאִמְרוּ אָמֵן :

יְהִי רָצוֹן לְפָנֶיךָ יְיָ אֱלֹהֵינוּ וֵאלֹהֵי אֲבוֹתֵינוּ שֶׁיִּבָּנֶה בֵּית
הַמִּקְדָּשׁ בִּמְהֵרָה בְיָמֵינוּ · וְתֵן חֶלְקֵנוּ בְּתוֹרָתֶךָ : וְשָׁם נַעֲבָדְךָ
בְּיִרְאָה כִּימֵי עוֹלָם וּכְשָׁנִים קַדְמוֹנִיּוֹת : וְעָרְבָה לַיְיָ מִנְחַת
יְהוּדָה וִירוּשָׁלַםִ כִּימֵי עוֹלָם וּכְשָׁנִים קַדְמוֹנִיּוֹת :

O MY GOD. This is a private meditation of Mar, the son of Rabina, a famous rabbi of the fourth century. It is therefore written in the singular. Through its beauty it found a place in all Rites, and became a pendant to the Amidah when spoken silently. As the evil tongue is the most insidious enemy of peace, this prayer follows naturally upon the concluding petition for Peace ; Psalm 34. 14.

let my soul be dumb. " Grant me forbearance unto those who deal ill towards me, and a calm disposition unto all my fellowmen " a prayer at once humble and dignified, marked by solemn simplicity and true greatness (N. Remy). Even in thought we are not to hate those that curse us. " Whosoever does not persecute them that persecute him, whosoever takes an offence in silence, he who does good because of love, he who is cheerful under his sufferings--they are the friends of God " (Talmud).

as the dust. This is victory over self, and has nothing in common with self-contempt. " Be not wicked in thine own esteem ", remains a primary duty for individuals as for communities ; see p. 642.

CONCLUD
ING MEDI-
TATION O my God ! guard my tongue from evil and my lips from
speaking guile ; and to such as curse me let my soul be
dumb, yea, let my soul be unto all as the dust. Open my
heart to thy Torah, and let my soul pursue thy commandments. If any design evil against me, speedily make their
counsel of no effect, and frustrate their designs. Do it for
the sake of thy Name, do it for the sake of thy power, do it
for the sake of thy holiness, do it for the sake of thy Torah.
Psalm 60. 7 In order that thy beloved ones may be delivered, O save
Psalm 19. 15 by thy power, and answer me. Let the words of my mouth
and the meditation of my heart be acceptable before thee,
O Lord, my Rock and my Redeemer. He who maketh peace
in his high places, may he make peace for us and for all
Israel, and say ye, Amen.

May it be thy will, O Lord our God and God of our fathers, that
the temple be speedily rebuilt in our days, and grant our portion in
thy Torah. And there we will serve thee with awe, as in the days of
Malachi 3 4 old, and as in ancient years. Then shall the offering of Judah and
Jerusalem be pleasant unto the Lord, as in the days of old, and as
in ancient years.

open my heart to thy Torah. " Open my heart to Thy sacred
teachings, so that my conduct may be evidence of the fulfilment of
Thy commandments." Only knowledge of God's Will will equip us with
the moral insight and strength for such heroic conduct.
frustrate their designs. Defeat their purposes. This ends the prayer
of Mar, the son of Rabina.
for thy power. lit. " for thy right hand ", *i.e.* to vindicate Thy power.
He who maketh peace. " Creator of the harmony of the spheres,
mayest Thou in Thy tender love create peace for us and for all Israel."
Three steps backwards, with accompanying inclinations to the left
and right, formed the respectful mode of retiring from a superior. This
form was transferred to the concluding verse of the Amidah, as if
retiring from the presence of God (Pool).
The end of the Amidah was accounted an appropriate place for
silent individual prayer ; and many a devotional gem, characterized by
special tenderness and fervour, has come down to us as the outpouring
of great spirits at this stage of the Daily Service.
Rabbi Elazar, when he had finished the Tefillah, used to add : " May
it be Thy will, O Lord our God, to cause love and brotherhood, peace
and comradeship, to abide in our lot ; to enlarge our border with

In illness, or when time is lacking, the following shortened form of the עֲמִידָה *may be said :—*

אֲדֹנָי, p. 130, to הַקָּדוֹשׁ, p. 136

הֲבִינֵנוּ יְיָ אֱלֹהֵינוּ לָדַעַת דְּרָכֶיךָ · וּמוֹל אֶת־לְבָבֵנוּ לְיִרְאָתֶךָ · וְתִסְלַח לָנוּ לִהְיוֹת גְּאוּלִים · וְרַחֲקֵנוּ מִמַּכְאוֹב · וְדַשְּׁנֵנוּ בִּנְאוֹת אַרְצֶךָ · וּנְפוּצוֹתֵינוּ מֵאַרְבַּע כַּנְפוֹת הָאָרֶץ תְּקַבֵּץ · וְהַתּוֹעִים עַל דַּעְתְּךָ יִשָּׁפֵטוּ · וְעַל הָרְשָׁעִים תָּנִיף יָדֶךָ · וְיִשְׂמְחוּ צַדִּיקִים בְּבִנְיַן עִירֶךָ וּבְתִקּוּן הֵיכָלֶךָ וּבִצְמִיחַת קֶרֶן לְדָוִד עַבְדֶּךָ וּבַעֲרִיכַת נֵר לְבֶן־יִשַׁי מְשִׁיחֶךָ · טֶרֶם נִקְרָא אַתָּה תַעֲנֶה · בָּרוּךְ אַתָּה יְיָ · שׁוֹמֵעַ תְּפִלָּה :

Continue —

רְצֵה, p. 148, to קַדְמוֹנִיּוֹת, p. 156.

On רֹאשׁ חֹדֶשׁ חוֹל הַמּוֹעֵד *and* חֲנֻכָּה *say* הַלֵּל, *p.* 756

---

disciples ; to prosper our goal with happy ends and fulfilment of hope. May we be of those who have a portion in the Life to Come. Strengthen us with good companionship, and fortify our good impulses in this life ; so that the reverence of Thy Name be ever the longing of our heart. And may this our happiness in reverencing Thee be remembered by Thee for good ".

R. Zera was in the habit of adding : " May it be Thy will, O Lord our God, that we return to Thee in perfect repentance ; so that we may not be ashamed to meet our fathers in the Life to Come ".

R. Alexander is the author of this additional prayer : " May it be Thy will, O Lord our God, to place us in light, and not in darkness ; and may not our heart grow faint, nor our eyes dim. Lord of the Universe ! It is revealed and known before Thee that it is our desire to perform Thy will ; but what stands in the way ? The Evil Inclination and the oppression of the kingdoms. May it be Thy will to deliver us from their hand, so that we may again perform Thy statutes with a perfect heart ".

R. Pedath and R. Chiyya used to add : " May it be Thy will, O Lord our God and God of our Fathers, that none hate or envy us, and that neither hatred nor envy of any man find place in our hearts. May thy Torah be our occupation, and make us wholehearted in reverencing Thee. Keep us far from what Thou hatest ; bring us near to what Thou lovest ; and deal mercifully with us for Thy Name's sake ".

*In illness, or when time is lacking, the following shortened form of
the Amidah may be said :—*
" O Lord ", p. 131, to " holy God ", p. 137.

Give us understanding, O Lord our God, to know thy
ways ; open our hearts to fear thee, and forgive us so that
we may be redeemed. Keep us far from sorrow ; satisfy our
needs on the produce of thy land, and gather our scattered
ones from the four corners of the earth. Let them that go
astray be judged according to thy will, and bring thy hand
upon the wicked. Let the righteous rejoice in the rebuilding
of thy city, and in the establishment of thy temple, and in
the flourishing of the might of David thy servant, and in
the clear shining light of the son of Jesse, thine anointed.
Even before we call, do thou answer. Blessed art thou,
O Lord, who hearkenest unto prayer.

Continue—

Accept ", p. 149, to "ancient years ", p. 157.
*On New Moon, the Intermediate Days of Passover and Tabernacles,
and on Chanukah, say Hallel, p. 757.*

THE EIGHTEEN BENEDICTIONS
SHORTENED FORM
(הביננו)

Since early times a briefer version of the Amidah has been known.
One of Ben Sira's hymns reads like such an abbreviation, and leading
rabbis of the Mishna and Talmud favoured the use of shortened
forms of the Eighteen Benedictions. These abbreviations, sometimes
in verse, appeared down to the Middle Ages. One of them gained
general recognition in the Liturgy ; namely, the *Havinenu* prayer
ascribed to Mar Samuel, the renowned Babylonian teacher of the third
century. In it, the first three of the Benedictions of the Amidah are
repeated in full, and so are the last three ; but the thirteen " Petitions "
are condensed into one paragraph, as above. Each phrase skilfully
represents one of the Petitions. The following is a recent paraphrase in
verse :—

Cause us, O Lord ! to understand Thy ways,
And fill our hearts with rev'rent fear, all our days.
Forgive us, we entreat Thee, each sin,
That redemption we may hope to win.

In Thy merciful goodness pain and suff'ring allay,
And satisfy us with Thine abundance, we pray.
With Thine all-powerful and tremendous hand
Our scattered ones gather together to our own land.
Transgressors, O mighty Being, judge Thou,
Sinners to Thy just wrath shall submissively bow.
When Thy sacred city with joy we rebuild
And Thy Sanctuary with Thy glorious presence be fill'd,
Then with a loud and exultant voice
Will the righteous, O God of Israel, rejoice.
Let it be Thy divine will speedily to restore
The House of David, Thy servant, as of yore.
And may the light of the son of Jesse blaze
As in reverence Thy hallowed Name we praise.
For Thou who hearkenest to the voice of Prayer,
Art blessed Thy people, O Lord ! declare (J. F. Stern).

Still shorter forms of Prayer were prescribed for times and places of imminent danger to life. In such cases, neither the opening nor the closing Benedictions of the Amidah were recited. One of the best known of these prayers is that of Rabbi Eliezer : " Let Thy will be done in Heaven above ; grant tranquility of spirit to those that reverence Thee below ; and do that which is good in Thy sight. Blessed art Thou, O Lord, Who hearest prayer ". Another of these " short prayers " is : " O God, the needs of Thy people are many, their knowledge slender Give every one of Thy creatures his daily bread, and grant him his urgent needs. Blessed art Thou, O Lord, Who hearest prayer."

who hearkenest unto prayer. lit. " who art a hearkener unto prayer ". The selection of this phrase with which to conclude the condensed Amidah is not accidental. Those words express the infinite difference between the Living God of Judaism—the loving Father who hears prayer—and the Unbelief which declares that the Power behind Nature is a force which is impersonal, an It, and deaf to prayer.

to fear thee. To reverence Thee.

go astray. All sin, transgression, even defiant wickedness, when viewed from a higher plane, are seen to be but folly, blindness.

thy will. lit. " Thy understanding ". God, and not man, is to be their Judge. " He who knows the heart of the sinner, judges mercifully and justly " (Baer).

bring thy hand. Punish.

IV. ADDITIONS TO THE MORNING SERVICE

A. SUPPLICATIONS

(תחנונים)

Supplications is the general name of the prayers between the Shemoneh Esreh and the conclusion of the Service. The statutory congregational prayer having been completed with the recital of the Eighteen Benedictions, each man was now free to pour out the burden of his heart in silent private devotion (Amram). Such seems to have been the usage for many centuries. Only very gradually were the improvisations of the individual replaced by set supplications. These differed greatly in the various Rites ; and—with the exception of אבינו מלכנו " Our Father, our King ", during the Ten Days of Repentance—most of them are to this day repeated by each worshipper for himself. Only with the hymn before the last paragraph of the penitential selections p. 184, is the chanting resumed by the Reader.

In our Rite, these set private devotions appear in two forms in a longer and in a briefer series. The longer series is for Mondays and Thursdays, and consists of (1) seven prayers of supplication ; and (2) brief confession, penitential psalm, and elegies. On other week-days, only the brief confession, the penitential Psalm 6, and one of the elegies are retained. No supplications, litanies or penitential prayers are recited on Sabbaths and Festivals (except on the Day of Atonement, even when it falls on the Sabbath). They are also omitted at occasions of domestic joy, as well as in a house of mourning, so as not to dampen the joy, or heighten the grief, of those affected.

On Monday and Thursday mornings there is, at a congregational service, a short Reading of the Torah.

1. OVINU MALKENU.

During the Ten Days of Repentance, *Ovinu Malkenu* (" Our Father, Our King ") is recited immediately after the Shemoneh Esreh. It is the oldest and the most moving of all the litanies of the Jewish Year. It is of gradual growth. The Talmud assigns some of its lines to Rabbi Akiba, who spoke them on a fast-day in a time of drought. When these moving invocations were taken over for daily recital during the Ten Days of Repentance, prayers for *life* and *pardon* were introduced. New invocations were added in the course of the centuries. Some of these additions give voice to the normal tribulations and needs of human existence ; while others, like the grim refrains towards the end, are the echo of the terrible massacres that accompanied the Black Death in the fourteenth century, when in the whole of Germany only three communities escaped total annihilation. In our Rite, *Ovinu Malkenu* consists of 44 invocations. As some of them are substantially similar to the petitions in the Shemoneh Esreh, the *Ovinu Malkenu* is omitted on days when the Petitions of the Shemoneh Esreh are not said, as on Sabbaths.

During the עֲשֶׂרֶת יְמֵי תְּשׁוּבָה, *morning and afternoon,* אָבִינוּ מַלְכֵּנוּ *is said.*
It is omitted on Friday afternoon and Sabbath, and on עֶרֶב יוֹם כִּפּוּר,
except if such day be a Friday. In that case, אָבִינוּ מַלְכֵּנוּ *is recited at*
שַׁחֲרִית.

אָבִינוּ מַלְכֵּנוּ ־ חָטָאנוּ לְפָנֶיךָ :

אָבִינוּ מַלְכֵּנוּ ־ אֵין לָנוּ מֶלֶךְ אֶלָּא אָתָּה :

אָבִינוּ מַלְכֵּנוּ ־ עֲשֵׂה עִמָּנוּ לְמַעַן שְׁמֶךָ :

אָבִינוּ מַלְכֵּנוּ ־ חַדֵּשׁ עָלֵינוּ שָׁנָה טוֹבָה :

אָבִינוּ מַלְכֵּנוּ ־ בַּטֵּל מֵעָלֵינוּ כָּל־גְּזֵרוֹת קָשׁוֹת :

אָבִינוּ מַלְכֵּנוּ ־ בַּטֵּל מַחְשְׁבוֹת שׂנְאֵינוּ :

אָבִינוּ מַלְכֵּנוּ ־ הָפֵר עֲצַת אוֹיְבֵינוּ :

אָבִינוּ מַלְכֵּנוּ ־ כַּלֵּה כָּל־צָר וּמַשְׂטִין מֵעָלֵינוּ :

אָבִינוּ מַלְכֵּנוּ ־ סְתוֹם פִּיּוֹת מַשְׂטִינֵינוּ וּמְקַטְרְגֵינוּ :

אָבִינוּ מַלְכֵּנוּ ־ כַּלֵּה דֶבֶר וְחֶרֶב וְרָעָב וּשְׁבִי וּמַשְׁחִית מִבְּנֵי
בְרִיתֶךָ :

אָבִינוּ מַלְכֵּנוּ ־ מְנַע מַגֵּפָה מִנַּחֲלָתֶךָ :

אָבִינוּ מַלְכֵּנוּ ־ סְלַח וּמְחַל לְכָל־עֲוֹנוֹתֵינוּ :

אָבִינוּ מַלְכֵּנוּ ־ מְחֵה וְהַעֲבֵר פְּשָׁעֵינוּ מִנֶּגֶד עֵינֶיךָ :

1–3. Introductory.

1. *our Father.* He that formed the stars and fashioned the tiniest
flower, that Almighty Power is our loving Father, Friend and
Redeemer.

our King. Many men and women believe so much in the love of
God that they imagine He permits the wanton breaking of His commandments to go unpunished. In this characteristic prayer we are
taught that God is our Father, but He is also *our King*, Who has given
us His Law of life, and decreed an everlasting difference between right
and wrong.

During the Ten Days of Repentance, morning and afternoon, the following to " and save us ", p. 167, *is said. It is omitted on Friday afternoon and Sabbath, and on the day previous to the Day of Atonement, except if such day be a Friday. In that case, this prayer is recited at the Morning Service.*

OVINU MALKENU LITANY

Our Father, our King ! we have sinned before thee.

Our Father, our King ! we have no King but thee.

Our Father, our King ! deal with us for the sake of thy Name.

Our Father, our King ! let a happy year begin for us.

⁵Our Father, our King ! nullify all evil decrees against us.

Our Father, our King ! nullify the designs of those that hate us.

Our Father, our King ! make the counsel of our enemies of none effect.

Our Father, our King ! rid us of every oppressor and adversary.

Our Father, our King ! close the mouths of our adversaries and accusers.

¹⁰Our Father, our King ! of pestilence and the sword, of famine, captivity and destruction, rid the children of thy covenant.

Our Father, our King ! withhold the plague from thine inheritance.

Our Father, our King ! forgive and pardon all our iniquities.

Our Father, our King ! blot out our transgressions, and make them pass away from before thine eyes.

we have sinned. It is not a self-righteous Israel that offers its supplications before the Throne of mercy. " As soon as a man has the moral strength to see himself as he is, and make the confession ' I have sinned ', the powers of evil lose their hold on him " (Midrash).

2. *we have no King but thee.* To Rabbi Akiba and his circle fighting against Roman tyranny, this may at first have been also a declaration of defiance against the Roman oppressor. However, the words soon lost their political meaning, and acquired a purely religious significance.

4–5. For a Happy Year free from evil decrees.

5. *evil decrees.* Designed by malicious enemies of Israel to shatter over-night the life of a prosperous Jewry, and doom it to exile or extinction.

6–9. Against False Accusations.

9. *accusers.* Those who level libellous charges against Jews, and are largely responsible for those evil decrees.

10. Against Pestilence.

12–15. For Forgiveness of sins.

אָבִינוּ מַלְכֵּנוּ ‧ מְחוֹק בְּרַחֲמֶיךָ הָרַבִּים כָּל־שִׁטְרֵי חוֹבוֹתֵינוּ :

אָבִינוּ מַלְכֵּנוּ ‧ הַחֲזִירֵנוּ בִּתְשׁוּבָה שְׁלֵמָה לְפָנֶיךָ :

אָבִינוּ מַלְכֵּנוּ ‧ שְׁלַח רְפוּאָה שְׁלֵמָה לְחוֹלֵי עַמֶּךָ :

אָבִינוּ מַלְכֵּנוּ ‧ קְרַע רוֹעַ גְּזַר דִּינֵנוּ :

אָבִינוּ מַלְכֵּנוּ ‧ זָכְרֵנוּ בְּזִכָּרוֹן טוֹב לְפָנֶיךָ :

* אָבִינוּ מַלְכֵּנוּ ‧ כָּתְבֵנוּ בְּסֵפֶר חַיִּים טוֹבִים :

אָבִינוּ מַלְכֵּנוּ ‧ כָּתְבֵנוּ בְּסֵפֶר גְּאֻלָּה וִישׁוּעָה :

אָבִינוּ מַלְכֵּנוּ ‧ כָּתְבֵנוּ בְּסֵפֶר פַּרְנָסָה וְכַלְכָּלָה :

אָבִינוּ מַלְכֵּנוּ ‧ כָּתְבֵנוּ בְּסֵפֶר זְכִיּוֹת :

אָבִינוּ מַלְכֵּנוּ ‧ כָּתְבֵנוּ בְּסֵפֶר סְלִיחָה וּמְחִילָה :

אָבִינוּ מַלְכֵּנוּ ‧ הַצְמַח לָנוּ יְשׁוּעָה בְּקָרוֹב :

אָבִינוּ מַלְכֵּנוּ ‧ הָרֵם קֶרֶן יִשְׂרָאֵל עַמֶּךָ :

אָבִינוּ מַלְכֵּנוּ ‧ הָרֵם קֶרֶן מְשִׁיחֶךָ :

אָבִינוּ מַלְכֵּנוּ ‧ מַלֵּא יָדֵינוּ מִבִּרְכוֹתֶיךָ :

אָבִינוּ מַלְכֵּנוּ ‧ מַלֵּא אֲסָמֵינוּ שָׂבָע :

אָבִינוּ מַלְכֵּנוּ ‧ שְׁמַע קוֹלֵנוּ חוּס וְרַחֵם עָלֵינוּ :

אָבִינוּ מַלְכֵּנוּ ‧ קַבֵּל בְּרַחֲמִים וּבְרָצוֹן אֶת־תְּפִלָּתֵנוּ :

אָבִינוּ מַלְכֵּנוּ ‧ פְּתַח שַׁעֲרֵי שָׁמַיִם לִתְפִלָּתֵנוּ :

אָבִינוּ מַלְכֵּנוּ ‧ נָא אַל־תְּשִׁיבֵנוּ רֵיקָם מִלְּפָנֶיךָ :

---

* At the נְעִילָה Service on the Day of Atonement, חָתְמֵנוּ is substituted for כָּתְבֵנוּ in this and the following sentences.

14. *records of our guilt.* The Biblical metaphor of a Book in which men's doings are entered was much developed by the Rabbis. Our prayer is, that any evidences of our guilt in that Book be destroyed, so that naught remains to recall our transgression.

16–23. For fulfilment of Prayers.

Our Father, our King ! erase in thine abundant mercies all the records of our gilt.

¹⁵Our Father, our King ! bring us back in perfect repentance unto thee.

Our Father, our King ! send a perfect healing to the sick of thy people.

Our Father, our King ! rend the evil judgment decreed against us.

Our Father, our King ! let thy remembrance of us be for good.

Our Father, our King ! *inscribe us in the book of happy life.

²⁰Our Father, our King ! inscribe us in the book of redemption and salvation.

Our Father, our King ! inscribe us in the book of maintenance and sustenance.

Our Father, our King ! inscribe us in the book of merit.

Our Father, our King ! inscribe us in the book of forgiveness and pardon.

Our Father, our King ! let salvation soon spring forth for us.

²⁵Our Father, our King ! raise up the strength of Israel, thy people.

Our Father, our King ! raise up the strength of thine anointed.

Our Father, our King ! fill our hands with thy blessings.

Our Father, our King ! fill our storehouses with plenty.

Our Father, our King ! hear our voice, spare us, and have mercy upon us.

³⁰Our Father, our King ! receive our prayer in mercy and in favour.

Our Father, our King ! open the gates of heaven unto our prayer.

Our Father, our King ! we pray thee, turn us not back empty from thy presence.

---

*At the Conclusion Service on the Day of Atonement, "seal us" is substituted for " inscribe us " in this and the following sentences.

19. *book of happy life.* " *The Book of Life* was a spiritual fancy corresponding to a material fact. In ancient Judea to be enrolled in the Book of Life, would imply membership of the Holy Commonwealth ; to be blotted out, would be to suffer disfranchisement. This idea was carried over into the spiritual world " (Abrahams).

24–26. For Israel's Welfare.

27–28. For Prosperity.

29–34. For Hearing of Prayers.

אָבִינוּ מַלְכֵּנוּ · זְכוֹר כִּי עָפָר אֲנָחְנוּ :

אָבִינוּ מַלְכֵּנוּ · תְּהִי הַשָּׁעָה הַזֹּאת שְׁעַת רַחֲמִים וְעֵת רָצוֹן
מִלְּפָנֶיךָ :

אָבִינוּ מַלְכֵּנוּ · חֲמוֹל עָלֵינוּ וְעַל־עוֹלָלֵינוּ וְטַפֵּנוּ :

אָבִינוּ מַלְכֵּנוּ · עֲשֵׂה לְמַעַן הֲרוּגִים עַל־שֵׁם קָדְשֶׁךָ :

אָבִינוּ מַלְכֵּנוּ · עֲשֵׂה לְמַעַן טְבוּחִים עַל־יִחוּדֶךָ :

אָבִינוּ מַלְכֵּנוּ · עֲשֵׂה לְמַעַן בָּאֵי בָאֵשׁ וּבַמַּיִם עַל־קִדּוּשׁ שְׁמֶךָ :

אָבִינוּ מַלְכֵּנוּ · נְקוֹם לְעֵינֵינוּ נִקְמַת דַּם־עֲבָדֶיךָ הַשָּׁפוּךְ :

אָבִינוּ מַלְכֵּנוּ · עֲשֵׂה לְמַעַנְךָ אִם־לֹא־לְמַעֲנֵנוּ :

אָבִינוּ מַלְכֵּנוּ · עֲשֵׂה לְמַעַנְךָ וְהוֹשִׁיעֵנוּ :

אָבִינוּ מַלְכֵּנוּ · עֲשֵׂה לְמַעַן רַחֲמֶיךָ הָרַבִּים :

אָבִינוּ מַלְכֵּנוּ · עֲשֵׂה לְמַעַן שְׁמְךָ הַגָּדוֹל הַגִּבּוֹר וְהַנּוֹרָא שֶׁנִּקְרָא
עָלֵינוּ :

אָבִינוּ מַלְכֵּנוּ · חָנֵּנוּ וַעֲנֵנוּ כִּי אֵין בָּנוּ מַעֲשִׂים עֲשֵׂה עִמָּנוּ צְדָקָה
וָחֶסֶד וְהוֹשִׁיעֵנוּ :

35. " For our Children's sake."

36–39. " For our Martyrs' sake."

37. *slaughtered for the Unity.* In medieval massacres of Jews, as in those scientifically organised by the Nazis, none were spared. Women and infants, the aged and the ailing, all were mercilessly slain.

38. *for the sanctification of thy Name.* As persecution deepened during the Middle Ages, Jewish men and women might at any moment be given the dread alternative of apostasy or death. With rarely an exception, they chose the path of martyrdom. During the First Crusade, when the Jewish communities in the Rhine region were decimated by massacre, or by self-immolation in order to escape baptism, Kalonymos ben Yehudah wrote as an eye-witness :—

" Yea, they slay us and they smite,
Vex our souls with sore affright :

Our Father, our King ! remember that we are but dust.

Our Father, our King ! let this hour be an hour of mercy and a time of favour with thee.

[35]Our Father, our King ! have compassion upon us and upon our children and our infants.

Our Father, our King ! do this for the sake of them that were slain for thy holy Name.

Our Father, our King ! do it for the sake of them that were slaughtered for thy Unity.

Our Father, our King ! do it for the sake of them that went through fire and water for the sanctification of thy Name.

Our Father, our King ! avenge before our eyes the blood of thy servants that hath been shed.

[40]Our Father, our King ! do it for thy sake, if not for ours.

Our Father, our King ! do it for thy sake, and save us.

Our Father, our King ! do it for the sake of thine abundant mercies.

Our Father, our King ! do it for the sake of thy great, mighty and revered Name by which we are called.

Our Father, our King ! be gracious unto us and answer us, for we have no good works of our own ; deal with us in charity and kindness, and save us.

All the closer cleave we, Lord,
To Thine everlasting Word.
Not a line of all their Mass
Shall our lips in homage pass ;
Though they curse, and bind, and kill,
The living God is with us still.
We still are Thine, though limbs are torn ;
Better death than life forsworn.
The fair and young lie down to die
In witness of Thy Unity ;
From dying lips the accents swell,
' Thy God is One, O Israel ; '
And bridegroom answers unto bride,
' The Lord is God, and none beside,'
And, knit with bonds of holiest faith,
They pass to endless Life through death."
40–44. " For Thy mercy's sake ".

On Mondays and Thursdays the following, from וְהוּא רַחוּם *lo* אֶחָד, *p.*178
is added. On other Weekdays continue וַיֹּאמֶר דָּוִד, *p.*180. *Both these
prayers are omitted on* רֹאשׁ חֹדֶשׁ, *during the whole month of* נִיסָן,
on ל'ג בָּעוֹמֶר, *from* רֹאשׁ חֹדֶשׁ סִיוָן *until after* אִסְרוּ חַג שָׁבְעוֹת, *on*
עֶרֶב יוֹם כִּפּוּר, *from* עֶרֶב רֹאשׁ הַשָּׁנָה *and* ט'ו בְּאָב, ט' בְּאָב, *until
after* אִסְרוּ חַג, *on* חֲנֻכָּה, ט'ו בִּשְׁבַט, *on* פּוּרִים *and on the two
days of* פּוּרִים קָטָן. *These prayers are also omitted on the celebration
of a marriage, in the house of an* אָבֵל, *and on the occasion of a*
בְּרִית מִילָה, *if the father,* סַנְדָּק, *or* מוֹהֵל *be present in the synagogue.*

וְהוּא רַחוּם יְכַפֵּר עָוֹן וְלֹא יַשְׁחִית וְהִרְבָּה לְהָשִׁיב
אַפּוֹ וְלֹא יָעִיר כָּל־חֲמָתוֹ: אַתָּה יְיָ לֹא־תִכְלָא רַחֲמֶיךָ
מִמֶּנּוּ חַסְדְּךָ וַאֲמִתְּךָ תָּמִיד יִצְּרוּנוּ: הוֹשִׁיעֵנוּ יְיָ אֱלֹהֵינוּ
וְקַבְּצֵנוּ מִן־הַגּוֹיִם · לְהוֹדוֹת לְשֵׁם קָדְשֶׁךָ לְהִשְׁתַּבֵּחַ
בִּתְהִלָּתֶךָ: אִם־עֲוֹנוֹת תִּשְׁמָר־יָהּ אֲדֹנָי מִי יַעֲמֹד: כִּי־

2. Vehu Rachum.

This group of sombre elegies, popularly known as " the long *Vehu
Rachum* " is recited in the Morning Service on Mondays and Thursdays
only, these having been observed in ancient times by some people as
fast days.

The origin of these seven prayers, brimful with woe over the
suffering that Israel undergoes for its Faith, is shrouded in legend.
Zunz believes them to be contemporary with the terrible persecutions
at the hands of the Goths in seventh century Spain. There is no unity
of authorship. The first two of the prayers (*a* and *b*) consist of Bible
verses ; the others (*c* to *g*) are Biblical in style, and are marked by
purity and simplicity of language. Consciousness of sin is the opening
note, passing into lamentation because of persecution. In all of them,
the love of God and His forgiveness are the hope and trust of the
worshipper. Medieval Israel had fully taken to heart the transcendent spiritual discovery of the Biblical teachers, that the will
of God is revealed in suffering and tribulation, even more than in
conquest and victory. " The Jews have always been the classic people
of self-criticism. Thus our propensity for self-accusation fosters
prejudice against us. Often the opinion is rife (as with Goethe) that
Jews must be so much worse than other people, because their Prophets
and leaders have always, rebuked them for their wickedness. It is not

FOR
MONDAYS
AND
THURS-
DAYS

*On Mondays and Thursdays the following is said to " the Lord is On(",
p. 179. On other Weekdays continue, "And David said", etc., p. 181.
Both these prayers are omitted on New Moon, during the whole month
of Nisan, on the thirty-third day of Counting the Omer, from the first
day of Sivan until the second day after Pentecost, on the 9th and 15th
of Av, on the day before New Year, from the day before the Day of
Atonement until the second day after Tabernacles, on Chanukah,
on the 15th of Shevat, on the two days of Purim, and on the two
days of Purim Koton, i.e., the 14th and 15th of Adar Rishon.
These prayers are also omitted on the celebration of a marriage, in the
house of a mourner during the week of mourning, and on the occasion
of a circumcision if the father, the godfather, or the Mohel be present
in the synagogue.*

*ELEGIES
AND
PENITEN-
TIAL
PRAYERS*

Psalm 78. 38

Psalm 40. 12

‹

Psalm 106. 47

Psalm 130. 3, 4

[And he, being merciful, forgiveth iniquity and destroyeth
not : yea, many a time he turneth his anger away, and doth
not stir up all his wrath. Withhold not thou thy tender
mercies from us, O Lord : let thy lovingkindness and thy
truth continually preserve us. Save us, O Lord our God,
and gather us from amongst the nations, to give thanks unto
thy holy Name, and to triumph in thy praise. If thou shouldst

that our faults have been greater than other peoples', but that our
condemnation of them has been more severe " (M. Lazarus).

Until quite recently these prayers seemed decidedly out of place in
modern life. Little wonder that both friendly and unfriendly critics
of the Jewish Prayer Book urged the excision of these prayers as
obsolete, and as no longer in accord with political and social conditions
in enlightened lands. Recent events have, alas, once again shown the
folly of those who take short views in Jewry.

Fifty years ago a noble proselyte wrote :   " Whoever can read this
long *Vehu Rachum* prayer without emotion, has lost all feeling for
what is great and noble. Despite all the repetitions in these cries for
forgiveness, mercy, help, protection, the effect is not tiring ; because
to witness the stirrings of a deeply moved, struggling soul, cannot be
wearisome to a true lover of mankind. And here it is not merely an
individual soul, but the soul of an entire people, that utters these
elegies and supplications, that gives voice to this woe of a thousand
years. Here is nothing of make-believe, but everything comes from the
furnace of suffering and life " (Nahida Remy).

(a) AND HE, BEING MERCIFUL. The infinite trust in the mercy of
God overflows in all these prayers.

עִמְּךָ הַסְּלִיחָה לְמַעַן תִּוָּרֵא : לֹא כַחֲטָאֵינוּ תַּעֲשֶׂה־לָּנוּ

וְלֹא כַעֲוֹנֹתֵינוּ תִּגְמוֹל עָלֵינוּ : אִם־עֲוֹנֵינוּ עָנוּ בָנוּ יְיָ עֲשֵׂה

לְמַעַן שְׁמֶךָ : זְכֹר רַחֲמֶיךָ יְיָ וַחֲסָדֶיךָ כִּי מֵעוֹלָם הֵמָּה :

יַעַנְנוּ יְיָ בְּיוֹם צָרָה יְשַׂגְּבֵנוּ שֵׁם אֱלֹהֵי יַעֲקֹב : יְיָ הוֹשִׁיעָה

הַמֶּלֶךְ יַעֲנֵנוּ בְיוֹם־קָרְאֵנוּ : אָבִינוּ מַלְכֵּנוּ חָנֵּנוּ וַעֲנֵנוּ כִּי

אֵין בָּנוּ מַעֲשִׂים · צְדָקָה עֲשֵׂה עִמָּנוּ לְמַעַן שְׁמֶךָ : אֲדוֹנֵנוּ

אֱלֹהֵינוּ שְׁמַע קוֹל תַּחֲנוּנֵינוּ וּזְכָר־לָנוּ אֶת־בְּרִית אֲבוֹתֵינוּ

וְהוֹשִׁיעֵנוּ לְמַעַן שְׁמֶךָ : וְעַתָּה אֲדֹנָי אֱלֹהֵינוּ אֲשֶׁר

הוֹצֵאתָ אֶת־עַמְּךָ מֵאֶרֶץ מִצְרַיִם בְּיָד חֲזָקָה וַתַּעַשׂ־לְךָ

שֵׁם כַּיּוֹם הַזֶּה חָטָאנוּ רָשָׁעְנוּ : אֲדֹנָי כְּכָל־צִדְקֹתֶיךָ

יָשָׁב־נָא אַפְּךָ וַחֲמָתְךָ מֵעִירְךָ יְרוּשָׁלַיִם הַר קָדְשֶׁךָ כִּי

בַחֲטָאֵינוּ וּבַעֲוֹנוֹת אֲבוֹתֵינוּ יְרוּשָׁלַיִם וְעַמְּךָ לְחֶרְפָּה

לְכָל־סְבִיבוֹתֵינוּ : וְעַתָּה שְׁמַע אֱלֹהֵינוּ אֶל־תְּפִלַּת עַבְדְּךָ

וְאֶל־תַּחֲנוּנָיו וְהָאֵר פָּנֶיךָ עַל־מִקְדָּשְׁךָ הַשָּׁמֵם לְמַעַן אֲדֹנָי :

הַטֵּה אֱלֹהַי | אָזְנְךָ וּשֲׁמָע פְּקַח עֵינֶיךָ וּרְאֵה שֹׁמְמֹתֵינוּ

וְהָעִיר אֲשֶׁר־נִקְרָא שִׁמְךָ עָלֶיהָ · כִּי לֹא עַל־צִדְקֹתֵינוּ

אֲנַחְנוּ מַפִּילִים תַּחֲנוּנֵינוּ לְפָנֶיךָ כִּי עַל־רַחֲמֶיךָ הָרַבִּים :

אֲדֹנָי | שְׁמָעָה אֲדֹנָי | סְלָחָה אֲדֹנָי הַקְשִׁיבָה וַעֲשֵׂה אַל־

תְּאַחַר · לְמַעַנְךָ אֱלֹהַי כִּי־שִׁמְךָ נִקְרָא עַל־עִירְךָ וְעַל־

עַמֶּךָ : אָבִינוּ הָאָב הָרַחֲמָן · הַרְאֵנוּ אוֹת לְטוֹבָה · וְקַבֵּץ

נְפוּצוֹתֵינוּ מֵאַרְבַּע כַּנְפוֹת הָאָרֶץ · יַכִּירוּ וְיֵדְעוּ כָּל־הַגּוֹיִם

ELEGIES   mark iniquities, O Lord, who could stand ? But there is
Psalm 103. 10 forgiveness with thee, that thou mayest be feared.
Deal not with us, according to our sins, nor requite us
Jeremiah 41 7 according to our iniquities. If our iniquities testify against
Psalm 25. 6   us, act mercifully, O Lord, for thy Name's sake. Remember,
O Lord, thy tender mercies and thy lovingkindnesses ; for
Psalm 20. 2, 10 they have been ever of old. May the Lord answer us in the
day of trouble, the Name of the God of Jacob set us up on
high. Save, Lord : may the King answer us on the day when
we call. Our Father, our King, be gracious unto us and
answer us, for we have no good works of our own ; deal
with us in charity for thy Name's sake. Our Lord, our God,
hearken to the voice of our supplications, and remember
unto us the covenant of our fathers, and save us for thy
Daniel   Name's sake. And now, O Lord our God, thou hast brought
9. 15-17   thy people forth out of the land of Egypt with a mighty
hand, and hast made thee a name as at this day ; we have
sinned, we have done wickedly. O Lord, according to all
thy righteous acts, let thine anger and thy fury, I pray thee,
be turned away from thy city Jerusalem, thy holy mountain;
because for our sins and for the iniquities of our fathers,
Jerusalem and thy people are become a byword with all that
are round about us. Now therefore, hearken, O our God,
unto the prayer of thy servant and to his supplications, and
cause thy face to shine upon thy sanctuary that is desolate,
for the Lord's sake.

Daniel   Incline thine ear, O my God, and hear ; open thine
9. 18, 19   eyes, and behold our desolations, and the city which is
DESOLA-
TION OF
ZION AND   called by thy Name : for we do not lay our supplications
DISPER-   before thee because of our righteous acts, but because of
SION OF
ISRAEL   thine abundant mercies. O Lord, hear ; O Lord, forgive ;
O Lord, hearken and do ; defer not ; for thine own sake,
O my God, because thy city and thy people are called by
thy Name. O our Father, merciful Father, show us a sign for
good, and gather our scattered ones from the four corners of
the earth. Let all the nations perceive and know that thou

7

כִּי אַתָּה יְיָ אֱלֹהֵינוּ : וְעַתָּה יְיָ אָבִינוּ אָתָּה • אֲנַחְנוּ
הַחֹמֶר וְאַתָּה יֹצְרֵנוּ וּמַעֲשֵׂה יָדְךָ כֻּלָּנוּ : הוֹשִׁיעֵנוּ לְמַעַן
שְׁמֶךָ צוּרֵנוּ מַלְכֵּנוּ וְגוֹאֲלֵנוּ : חוּסָה יְיָ עַל־עַמֶּךָ וְאַל־תִּתֵּן
נַחֲלָתְךָ לְחֶרְפָּה לִמְשָׁל־בָּם גּוֹיִם • לָמָה יֹאמְרוּ בָעַמִּים •
אַיֵּה אֱלֹהֵיהֶם : יָדַעְנוּ כִּי חָטָאנוּ וְאֵין מִי יַעֲמֹד בַּעֲדֵנוּ •
שִׁמְךָ הַגָּדוֹל יַעֲמָד־לָנוּ בְּעֵת צָרָה : יָדַעְנוּ כִּי אֵין בָּנוּ
מַעֲשִׂים • צְדָקָה עֲשֵׂה עִמָּנוּ לְמַעַן שְׁמֶךָ : כְּרַחֵם אָב עַל־
בָּנִים כֵּן תְּרַחֵם יְיָ עָלֵינוּ וְהוֹשִׁיעֵנוּ לְמַעַן שְׁמֶךָ : חֲמוֹל
עַל־עַמֶּךָ רַחֵם עַל־נַחֲלָתֶךָ חוּסָה־נָא כְּרֹב רַחֲמֶיךָ •
חָנֵּנוּ וַעֲנֵנוּ כִּי לְךָ יְיָ הַצְּדָקָה עֲשֵׂה נִפְלָאוֹת בְּכָל־עֵת :

הַבֶּט־נָא רַחֶם־נָא עַל־עַמְּךָ מְהֵרָה לְמַעַן שְׁמֶךָ
בְּרַחֲמֶיךָ הָרַבִּים • יְיָ אֱלֹהֵינוּ חוּס וְרַחֵם וְהוֹשִׁיעָה צֹאן
מַרְעִיתֶךָ • וְאַל־יִמְשָׁל־בָּנוּ קֶצֶף כִּי לְךָ עֵינֵינוּ תְלוּיוֹת •
הוֹשִׁיעֵנוּ לְמַעַן שְׁמֶךָ : רַחֵם עָלֵינוּ לְמַעַן בְּרִיתֶךָ • הַבִּיטָה
וַעֲנֵנוּ בְּעֵת צָרָה • כִּי לְךָ יְיָ הַיְשׁוּעָה • בְּךָ תוֹחַלְתֵּנוּ
אֱלוֹהַּ סְלִיחוֹת • אָנָּא סְלַח־נָא אֵל טוֹב וְסַלָּח • כִּי אֵל
מֶלֶךְ חַנּוּן וְרַחוּם אָתָּה :

(b) INCLINE THINE EAR.

we are the clay. One of the most beautiful *piyyutim* of the Atonement
Service is built on the metaphor of the human clay in the hands of the
Divine Potter.

wherefore should they say among the peoples. Such would be the
taunt of the heathen, with a consequent desecration of the Divine Name,

Isaiah 64. 7

PENITEN-
TIAL
PRAYERS

Joel 2. 17

"HAVE
MERCY
UPON THY
PEOPLE"

art the Lord our God. And now, O Lord, thou art our Father ; we are the clay, and thou art our Potter, yea, we are all the work of thy hand. Save us for thy Name's sake, our Rock, our King, and our Redeemer. Spare thy people, O Lord, and give not thine inheritance over to reproach, that the nations should make a by-word of them. Wherefore should they say among the peoples, Where is their God ? We know that we have sinned, and there is none to stand up in our behalf ; let thy great Name stand for our defence in time of trouble. We know that we have no good works of our own ; deal with us in charity for thy Name's sake. As a father hath mercy upon his children, so, O Lord, have mercy upon us, and save us for thy Name's sake. Have pity upon thy people ; have mercy upon thine inheritance ; spare, we pray thee, according to the abundance of thy tender mercies ; be gracious unto us and answer us, for charity is thine, O Lord ; thou doest wondrous things at all times.

Look, we beseech thee, and speedily have mercy upon thy people for thy Name's sake in thine abundant mercies. O Lord our God, spare and be merciful ; save the sheep of thy pasture ; let not wrath prevail over us, for our eyes are bent upon thee ; save us for thy Name's sake. Have mercy upon us for the sake of thy covenant ; look, and answer us in time of trouble, for salvation is thine, O Lord. Our hope is in thee, O God of forgiveness. We beseech thee, forgive, O good and forgiving God, for thou art a gracious and merciful God and King.

Chillul Hashem. God cannot forsake His people, for then He would betray His own cause.

(c) LOOK, WE BESEECH. These are suppliant pleadings of men in constant danger of death to themselves and their dear ones. Hence the agonized repetitions.

אָנָּא מֶלֶךְ חַנּוּן וְרַחוּם · זְכוֹר וְהַבֵּט לִבְרִית בֵּין
הַבְּתָרִים · וְתֵרָאֶה לְפָנֶיךָ עֲקֵדַת יָחִיד לְמַעַן יִשְׂרָאֵל :
אָבִינוּ מַלְכֵּנוּ חָנֵּנוּ וַעֲנֵנוּ כִּי שִׁמְךָ הַגָּדוֹל נִקְרָא עָלֵינוּ ·
עֲשֵׂה נִפְלָאוֹת בְּכָל־עֵת · עֲשֵׂה עִמָּנוּ כְּחַסְדֶּךָ · חַנּוּן
וְרַחוּם הַבִּיטָה וַעֲנֵנוּ בְּעֵת צָרָה · כִּי לְךָ יְיָ הַיְשׁוּעָה :
אָבִינוּ מַלְכֵּנוּ מַחֲסֵנוּ · אַל־תַּעַשׂ עִמָּנוּ כְּרוֹעַ מַעֲלָלֵינוּ ·
זְכֹר רַחֲמֶיךָ יְיָ וַחֲסָדֶיךָ · וּכְרֹב טוּבְךָ הוֹשִׁיעֵנוּ וַחֲמָל־נָא
עָלֵינוּ · כִּי אֵין לָנוּ אֱלוֹהַּ אַחֵר מִבַּלְעָדֶיךָ צוּרֵנוּ : אַל־
תַּעַזְבֵנוּ יְיָ אֱלֹהֵינוּ אַל־תִּרְחַק מִמֶּנּוּ · כִּי נַפְשֵׁנוּ קָצְרָה
מֵחֶרֶב וּמִשֶּׁבִי וּמִדֶּבֶר וּמִמַּגֵּפָה וּמִכָּל־צָרָה וְיָגוֹן · הַצִּילֵנוּ
כִּי לְךָ קִוִּינוּ וְאַל־תַּכְלִימֵנוּ יְיָ אֱלֹהֵינוּ וְהָאֵר פָּנֶיךָ בָּנוּ
וּזְכָר־לָנוּ אֶת־בְּרִית אֲבוֹתֵינוּ וְהוֹשִׁיעֵנוּ לְמַעַן שְׁמֶךָ ·
רְאֵה בְּצָרוֹתֵינוּ וּשְׁמַע קוֹל תְּפִלָּתֵנוּ · כִּי אַתָּה שׁוֹמֵעַ
תְּפִלַּת כָּל־פֶּה :

אֵל רַחוּם וְחַנּוּן · רַחֵם עָלֵינוּ וְעַל כָּל־מַעֲשֶׂיךָ · כִּי אֵין
כָּמוֹךָ יְיָ אֱלֹהֵינוּ · אָנָּא שָׂא נָא פְשָׁעֵינוּ אָבִינוּ מַלְכֵּנוּ
צוּרֵנוּ וְגוֹאֲלֵנוּ אֵל חַי וְקַיָּם הַחָסִין בַּכֹּחַ הֶחָסִיד וְטוֹב עַל
כָּל־מַעֲשֶׂיךָ · כִּי אַתָּה הוּא יְיָ אֱלֹהֵינוּ : אֵל אֶרֶךְ אַפַּיִם
וּמָלֵא רַחֲמִים · עֲשֵׂה עִמָּנוּ כְּרֹב רַחֲמֶיךָ וְהוֹשִׁיעֵנוּ לְמַעַן
שְׁמֶךָ · שְׁמַע מַלְכֵּנוּ תְּפִלָּתֵנוּ וּמִיַּד אוֹיְבֵינוּ הַצִּילֵנוּ ·

We beseech thee, O gracious and merciful King, remember and give heed to the Covenant between the Pieces (with Abraham), and let the binding (upon the altar) of his only son appear before thee, to the welfare of Israel. Our Father, our King, be gracious unto us and answer us, for we are called by thy great Name. Thou who doest wondrous things at all times, deal with us according to thy lovingkindness. O gracious and merciful Being, look, and answer us in time of trouble, for salvation is thine, O Lord. Our Father, our King, our Refuge, deal not with us according to the evil of our doings ; remember, O Lord, thy tender mercies and thy lovingkindnesses ; save us according to thine abundant goodness, and have pity upon us, we beseech thee, for we have no other God beside thee, our Rock. Forsake us not, O Lord our God, be not far from us ; for our soul is shrunken by reason of the sword and captivity and pestilence and plague, and of every trouble and sorrow. Deliver us, for we hope in thee ; put us not to shame, O Lord our God ; make thy countenance to shine upon us ; remember unto us the covenant of our fathers and save us for thy Name's sake. Look upon our troubles, and hear the voice of our prayer, for thou hearest the prayer of every mouth.

Merciful and gracious God ! Have mercy upon us and upon all thy works, for there as none like unto thee, O Lord our God. We beseech thee, forgive our transgressions, O our Father, our King, our Rock and our Redeemer, O living and everlasting God, mighty in strength, loving and good to all thy works ; for thou art the Lord our God. O God, who art slow to anger and full of mercy, deal with us according to the abundance of thy tender mercies, and save us for thy˙ Name's sake. Hear our prayer, O our King, and deliver us from the hand of our enemies ; hear our prayer, O our King,

(d) WE BESEECH THEE.
covenant between the pieces. Genesis 15.
(e) MERCIFUL AND GRACIOUS GOD. God is addressed as Father, King, Rock, Redeemer, " O living and everlasting God, mighty in strength, loving and good to all Thy works ".

שְׁמַע מַלְכֵּנוּ תְּפִלָּתֵנוּ וּמִכָּל־צָרָה וְיָגוֹן הַצִּילֵנוּ : אָבִינוּ

מַלְכֵּנוּ אַתָּה וְשִׁמְךָ עָלֵינוּ נִקְרָא אַל־תַּנִּיחֵנוּ : אַל־תַּעַזְבֵנוּ

אָבִינוּ וְאַל־תִּטְּשֵׁנוּ בּוֹרְאֵנוּ וְאַל־תִּשְׁכָּחֵנוּ יוֹצְרֵנוּ · כִּי

אֵל מֶלֶךְ חַנּוּן וְרַחוּם אָתָּה :

אֵין כָּמְוֹךָ חַנּוּן וְרַחוּם יְיָ אֱלֹהֵינוּ · אֵין כָּמוֹךָ אֵל אֶרֶךְ

אַפַּיִם וְרַב־חֶסֶד וֶאֱמֶת · הוֹשִׁיעֵנוּ בְּרַחֲמֶיךָ הָרַבִּים מֵרַעַשׁ

וּמֵרֹגֶז הַצִּילֵנוּ : זְכֹר לַעֲבָדֶיךָ לְאַבְרָהָם לְיִצְחָק וּלְיַעֲקֹב ·

אַל־תֵּפֶן אֶל־קָשְׁיֵנוּ וְאֶל־רִשְׁעֵנוּ וְאֶל־חַטָּאתֵנוּ : שׁוּב

מֵחֲרוֹן אַפֶּךָ וְהִנָּחֵם עַל־הָרָעָה לְעַמֶּךָ · וְהָסֵר מִמֶּנּוּ מַכַּת

הַמָּוֶת כִּי רַחוּם אָתָּה · כִּי כֵן דַּרְכֶּךָ עֹשֶׂה חֶסֶד חִנָּם

בְּכָל־דּוֹר וָדוֹר : חֽוּסָה יְיָ עַל־עַמֶּךָ וְהַצִּילֵנוּ מִזַּעְמֶךָ ·

וְהָסֵר מִמֶּנּוּ מַכַּת הַמַּגֵּפָה וּגְזֵרָה קָשָׁה · כִּי אַתָּה שׁוֹמֵר

יִשְׂרָאֵל : לְךָ אֲדֹנָי הַצְּדָקָה וְלָנוּ בֹּשֶׁת הַפָּנִים : מַה־

נִּתְאוֹנֵן מַה־נֹּאמַר מַה־נְּדַבֵּר וּמַה־נִּצְטַדָּק : נַחְפְּשָׂה

דְרָכֵינוּ וְנַחְקֹרָה וְנָשׁוּבָה אֵלֶיךָ · כִּי יְמִינְךָ פְּשׁוּטָה לְקַבֵּל

שָׁבִים : אָנָּא יְיָ הוֹשִׁיעָה נָּא · אָנָּא יְיָ הַצְלִיחָה נָא : אָנָּא

יְיָ עֲנֵנוּ בְיוֹם קָרְאֵנוּ : לְךָ יְיָ חִכִּינוּ לְךָ יְיָ קִוִּינוּ לְךָ יְיָ

נְיַחֵל · אַל־תֶּחֱשֶׁה וּתְעַנֵּנוּ · כִּי נָאֲמוּ גוֹיִם אָבְדָה

תִקְוָתָם · כָּל־בֶּרֶךְ וְכָל־קוֹמָה לְךָ לְבַד תִּשְׁתַּחֲוֶה :

(f) THERE IS NONE . . . LIKE THEE.
from fierceness and rage deliver us. Enemies would work up the
multitudes into a homicidal mania against the Jews.

and deliver us from all trouble and sorrow. Thou art our Father, our King, and we are called by thy Name ; abandon us not. Forsake us not, our Father, and cast us not off, O our Creator, and forget us not, O our Maker, for thou art a gracious and merciful God and King.

"FROM FIERCE-NESS AND RAGE DELIVER US"

There is none gracious and merciful like thee, O Lord our God ; there is none like thee, O God, slow to anger and abounding in lovingkindness and truth. Save us in thine abundant mercies ; from fierceness and rage deliver us. Remember thy servants, Abraham, Isaac and Jacob ; look not unto our stubbornness and our wickedness and our sin. Turn from thy fierce anger, and relent of the evil against *Exodus* 32. 12 thy people. Remove from us the stroke of death, for thou art merciful, for such is thy way—showing lovingkindness freely throughout all generations. Spare thy people, O Lord, and deliver us from thy wrath, and remove from us the stroke of the plague, and harsh decrees, for thou art the Guardian of Israel. Unto thee, O Lord, belongeth righteousness, but unto us confusion of face. How may we complain ? What can we say, what can we speak, or how can we justify ourselves ? We will search our ways and try them, and turn again to thee ; for thy right hand is stretched out to *Psalm* 118. 25 receive the penitent. Save, we beseech thee, O Lord ; we beseech thee, O Lord, send prosperity. We beseech thee, O Lord, answer us on the day when we call. For thee, O Lord, we wait ; for thee, O Lord, we hope ; in thee O Lord, we trust ; be not silent, nor let us be oppressed ; for the nations say, Their hope is lost. Let every knee and all that is lofty bow down to thee alone.

---

stroke of the plague and harsh decrees. Harsh disasters usually followed a plague, for which the Jews were blamed ; as at the time of the Black Death when throughout Central and Western Europe the most gruesome cruelties were perpetrated against the Jewish population.

their hope is lost. Funeral orations on Jews have been heard in every century ; yet it is Israel who eventually stands at the graveside of his oppressors.

הַפּוֹתֵחַ יָד בִּתְשׁוּבָה לְקַבֵּל פּוֹשְׁעִים וְחַטָּאִים · נִבְהֲלָה
נַפְשֵׁנוּ מֵרֹב עִצְבוֹנֵנוּ · אַל־תִּשְׁכָּחֵנוּ נֶצַח · קוּמָה
וְהוֹשִׁיעֵנוּ כִּי חָסִינוּ בָךְ: אָבִינוּ מַלְכֵּנוּ אִם אֵין בָּנוּ
צְדָקָה וּמַעֲשִׂים טוֹבִים זְכָר־לָנוּ אֶת־בְּרִית אֲבוֹתֵינוּ
וְעֵדוֹתֵנוּ בְּכָל־יוֹם יְיָ אֶחָד: הַבִּיטָה בְעָנְיֵנוּ כִּי רַבּוּ
מַכְאוֹבֵינוּ וְצָרוֹת לְבָבֵינוּ: חוּסָה יְיָ עָלֵינוּ בְּאֶרֶץ שְׁבִינוּ
וְאַל־תִּשְׁפּוֹךְ חֲרוֹנְךָ עָלֵינוּ · כִּי אֲנַחְנוּ עַמְּךָ בְּנֵי בְרִיתֶךָ:
אֵל הַבִּיטָה דַּל כְּבוֹדֵנוּ בַּגּוֹיִם וְשִׁקְּצוּנוּ כְּטֻמְאַת הַנִּדָּה:
עַד־מָתַי עֻזְּךָ בַּשְּׁבִי וְתִפְאַרְתְּךָ בְּיַד־צָר: עוֹרְרָה גְבוּרָתְךָ
וְקִנְאָתְךָ עַל־אוֹיְבֶיךָ · הֵם יֵבוֹשׁוּ וְיֵחַתּוּ מִגְּבוּרָתָם · וְאַל־
יִמְעֲטוּ לְפָנֶיךָ תְלָאוֹתֵינוּ: מַהֵר יְקַדְּמוּנוּ רַחֲמֶיךָ בְּיוֹם
צָרָתֵנוּ · וְאִם־לֹא לְמַעֲנֵנוּ לְמַעַנְךָ פְּעַל · וְאַל־תַּשְׁחִית
זֵכֶר שְׁאֵרִיתֵנוּ: וְחֹן אִם הַמְיַחֲדִים שְׁמְךָ פַּעֲמַיִם בְּכָל־
יוֹם תָּמִיד בְּאַהֲבָה וְאוֹמְרִים · שְׁמַע יִשְׂרָאֵל יְיָ אֱלֹהֵינוּ
יְיָ ׀ אֶחָד:

(g) O Thou, who openest thy hand to repentance. God, with
the Outstretched Arm to receive the repentant sinner, is a favourite
figure in Jewish penitential literature, as in the Neilah Prayer.

PENITEN-
TIAL
SUPPLICA-
TION

O thou, who openest thy hand to repentance, to receive transgressors and sinners—our soul is sore vexed through the greatness of our grief : forget us not for ever ; arise and save us, for we trust in thee. Our Father, our King, though we be without righteousness and good deeds, remember unto us the covenant of our fathers, and the testimony we bear every day that the Lord is One. Look upon our affliction, for many are our griefs and the sorrows of our heart. Have pity, upon us, O Lord, in the land of our captivity, and pour not out thy wrath upon us, for we are thy people, the children of thy covenant. O God, look, sunken is our glory among the nations, and they held us in abomination, as of utter defilement. How long shall thy strength remain in captivity, and thy glory in the hand of the foe ? Arouse thy might and thy zeal against thine enemies, that they may be put to shame and broken down in their might. O let not our travail seem little in thy sight. Let thy tender mercies speedily come to meet us in the day of our trouble ; and if not for our sake, do it for thine own sake, and destroy not the remembrance of our remnant ; but be gracious unto a people, who in constant love proclaim the

Deuteronomy
6. 4

unity of thy Name twice every day, saying, HEAR, O ISRAEL: THE LORD IS OUR GOD, THE LORD IS ONE.]

held us in abomination. It is the cry of an outraged heart. Nazi savagery has in our own day again reduced the Jew to the level of untouchables.

strength . . . glory. Psalm 78. 61. The reference is probably to the Ark of the Covenant and the Temple.

in constant love. A noble climax to a remarkable devotional outpouring on the part of tortured generations.

וַיֹּאמֶר דָּוִד אֶל־גָּד צַר־לִי מְאֹד נִפְּלָה־נָּא בְיַד־יְהוָֹה כִּי־רַבִּים רַחֲמוּ וּבְיַד אָדָם אַל־אֶפֹּלָה :

רַחוּם וְחַנּוּן חָטָאתִי לְפָנֶיךָ יְיָ מָלֵא רַחֲמִים רַחֵם עָלַי · וְקַבֵּל תַּחֲנוּנָי :

תהלים ו'

יְיָ אַל־בְּאַפְּךָ תוֹכִיחֵנִי וְאַל־בַּחֲמָתְךָ תְיַסְּרֵנִי : חָנֵּנִי יְיָ כִּי־אֻמְלַל אָנִי רְפָאֵנִי יְיָ כִּי נִבְהֲלוּ עֲצָמָי : וְנַפְשִׁי נִבְהֲלָה מְאֹד וְאַתָּ יְיָ עַד־מָתָי : שׁוּבָה יְיָ חַלְּצָה נַפְשִׁי הוֹשִׁיעֵנִי לְמַעַן חַסְדֶּךָ : כִּי אֵין בַּמָּוֶת זִכְרֶךָ בִּשְׁאוֹל מִי יוֹדֶה־לָּךְ : יָגַעְתִּי בְּאַנְחָתִי אַשְׂחֶה בְכָל־לַיְלָה מִטָּתִי בְּדִמְעָתִי עַרְשִׂי אַמְסֶה : עָשְׁשָׁה מִכַּעַס עֵינִי עָתְקָה בְּכָל־צוֹרְרָי : סוּרוּ

3. Tachanun—Supplication for Pardon.

The daily Petition for grace and pardon consists of two portions : one is spoken by the individual in silence, and the other recited by the Reader.

The silent portion begins with II Samuel 24. 14. Though a quite modern inclusion in these prayers, it is a most appropriate introduction to the supplication. It continues with a confession, and Psalm 6.

Whenever this opening of Tachanun is said in the presence of a Sefer Torah, it is recited in the attitude known as " falling on the face " נפילת אפים. At one time, this entailed prostration of the whole body ; but to-day, and especially in Western Countries, the worshipper merely rests his brow on his arm. Such prostration is symbolic of complete humiliation before God, and the committing of our destinies entirely into His hands. This is the moment for the worshipper to give utterance before God to his most secret hopes and needs. The exact content of the psalm or prayer recited is here of secondary importance, as is evidenced by the great variety of psalms and prayers to be found in the different Rites.

II Samuel 24. 14   And David said unto Gad, I am troubled exceedingly ; let us fall, I pray thee, into the hand of the Lord, for his mercies are many ; but let me not fall into the hand of man.

DAILY CON- FESSION   O THOU WHO ART MERCIFUL AND GRACIOUS, I HAVE SINNED BEFORE THEE. O LORD, FULL OF MERCY, HAVE MERCY UPON ME AND RECEIVE MY SUPPLICATIONS.

Psalm vi. 2–11.

ENTREATY IN MORTAL DISTRESS   ²O Lord, rebuke me not in thine anger : neither chasten me in thy hot displeasure. ³Be gracious unto me, O Lord ; for I am withered away ; O Lord, heal me ; for my bones are troubled. ⁴My soul also is sore troubled : and thou, O Lord, how long ? ⁵Return, O Lord, deliver my soul : save me for thy lovingkindness' sake. ⁶For in death there is no remembrance of thee : in the grave who shall give thee thanks ? ⁷I am weary with my groaning ; every night I make my bed to swim ; I melt away my couch with my tears. ⁸Mine eye wasteth away because of grief ; it waxeth

---

The second portion of the Tachanun consists of a *piyyut* (on Mondays and Thursdays, it consists of two *piyyutim*) and a collection of Bible verses.

And David said. David's immortal utterance spoken to the Prophet Gad who was commissioned to offer the erring king a choice of punishments ; one, at the direct hand of God ; or the other, through the agency of man. David in a truly penitential spirit, throws himself on the gracious mercies of God.

O thou who art merciful. These words constitute the Confession of the individual.

PSALM 6.

The psalmist has stood at the brink of the grave. In his anguish he cried to God ; and he ends with the triumphant anticipation of answered prayer.

2. *in thine anger.* He pleads for fatherly chastisement in love, and fears the severe punishment of Divine wrath.

3. *my bones.* The whole physical framework of the body.

6. *in the grave.* Heb. " in Sheol ". Sheol is the Semitic name for the nether-world, conveying the idea of a gloomy region where the disembodied spirits lead a dim and shadowy existence. This view of the life after death long survived in the consciousness of the ancients. Quite other is Israel's conception of the Hereafter : " Thou wilt not abandon my soul to the grave. Thou wilt make known to me the path of life. In Thy presence is fulness of joy ; at Thy right hand, bliss for evermore " (Psalm 16. 10, 11).

מִמֶּנִּי כָּל־פְּעֲלֵי אָוֶן כִּי־שָׁמַע יְיָ קוֹל בִּכְיִי: שָׁמַע יְיָ
תְּחִנָּתִי יְיָ תְּפִלָּתִי יִקָּח: יֵבֹשׁוּ וְיִבָּהֲלוּ מְאֹד כָּל־אֹיְבָי
יָשֻׁבוּ יֵבֹשׁוּ רָגַע:

On Monday and Thursday Mornings the following is added. On other Weekdays, continue שׁוֹמֵר יִשְׂרָאֵל, *p.*184.

Reader and Cong. יְיָ אֱלֹהֵי יִשְׂרָאֵל · שׁוּב מֵחֲרוֹן אַפֶּךָ ·
וְהִנָּחֵם עַל־הָרָעָה לְעַמֶּךָ:

Cong. הַבֵּט מִשָּׁמַיִם וּרְאֵה כִּי הָיִינוּ לַעַג וָקֶלֶס
בַּגּוֹיִם · נֶחְשַׁבְנוּ כְּצֹאן לַטֶּבַח יוּבָל לַהֲרוֹג וּלְאַבֵּד
וּלְמַכָּה וּלְחֶרְפָּה:

Cong. and Reader. וּבְכָל־זֹאת שִׁמְךָ לֹא שָׁכָחְנוּ · נָא
אַל־תִּשְׁכָּחֵנוּ: יְיָ

Cong. זָרִים אוֹמְרִים אֵין תּוֹחֶלֶת וְתִקְוָה · חֹן אֹם
לְשִׁמְךָ מְקַוֶּה · טָהוֹר יְשׁוּעָתֵנוּ קָרְבָה · יָגַעְנוּ וְלֹא
הוּנַח־לָנוּ · רַחֲמֶיךָ יִכְבְּשׁוּ אֶת־כַּעַסְךָ מֵעָלֵינוּ:

Cong. and Reader. אָנָּא שׁוּב מֵחֲרוֹנְךָ · וְרַחֵם סְגֻלָּה
אֲשֶׁר בָּחָרְתָּ: יְיָ

Cong. חוּסָה יְיָ עָלֵינוּ בְּרַחֲמֶיךָ · וְאַל־תִּתְּנֵנוּ בִּידֵי
אַכְזָרִים · לָמָּה יֹאמְרוּ הַגּוֹיִם · אַיֵּה נָא אֱלֹהֵיהֶם · לְמַעַנְךָ
עֲשֵׂה עִמָּנוּ חֶסֶד וְאַל־תְּאַחַר:

8. *waxeth old.* The plotting of his adversaries " ages " him.
9. *hath heard.* The psalmist uses the prophetic past; his is the

old because of all mine adversaries. ⁹Depart from me, all ye workers of iniquity ; for the Lord hath heard the voice of my weeping. ¹⁰The Lord hath heard my supplication ; the Lord will receive my prayer. ¹¹All mine enemies shall be ashamed and sore troubled : they shall turn back, they shall be ashamed suddenly.

On Monday and Thursday Mornings the following is added. On other Weekdays continue, "O Guardian of Israel", p. 185.

IN TIME
OF
MARTYR-
DOM AND
DEFAMA-
TION OF
ISRAEL

[*Reader and Cong.*—O Lord God of Israel, turn from thy fierce wrath, and relent of the evil against thy people

Cong.—Look from heaven and see how we have become a scorn and a derision among the nations ; we are accounted as sheep brought to the slaughter, to be slain and destroyed, or to be smitten and reproached.

Cong. and Reader.—Yet, despite all this, we have not forgotten thy Name : we beseech thee, forget us not.

Cong.—Strangers say, There is no hope or expectancy for you. Be gracious unto a people that trust in thy Name. O thou who art most pure, bring our deliverance near. We are weary, and no rest is granted us. Let thy tender mercies subdue thine anger from us.

Cong. and Reader.—We beseech thee, turn from thy wrath, and have mercy upon the treasured people whom thou hast chosen.

Cong.—O Lord, spare us in thy tender mercies, and give us not into the hands of the cruel. Wherefore should the nations say, Where now is their God ? For thine own sake deal kindly with us, and delay not.

---

certainty of faith, that his prayer will be heard.

the voice of my weeping. "What a fine Hebraism! Weeping is the eloquence of sorrow, and our tears are liquid prayers " (Spurgeon).

O LORD GOD OF ISRAEL. On Monday and Thursday these stanzas from an eleventh century *selichah*, or penetential hymn, with soul-stirring refrains, are recited. As in a lightning flash, they enable us to visualise the horrors of persecution and moral outlawry that were so often the lot of the Jew in the Dark Ages.

yet, despite all this. This refrain gives striking expression to the steadfastness of the Jew amid all the agony and martyrdom.

אָנָא שׁוּב מֵחֲרוֹנֶךָ · וְרַחֵם סְגֻלָּה *Cong. and Reader.*

אֲשֶׁר בָּחָרְתָּ : יי

קוֹלֵנוּ תִשְׁמַע וְתָחוֹן וְאַל־תִּטְּשֵׁנוּ בְּיַד אוֹיְבֵינוּ *Cong.*

לִמְחוֹת אֶת־שְׁמֵנוּ · זְכוֹר אֲשֶׁר נִשְׁבַּעְתָּ לַאֲבוֹתֵינוּ ·

כְּכוֹכְבֵי הַשָּׁמַיִם אַרְבֶּה אֶת־זַרְעֲכֶם · וְעַתָּה נִשְׁאַרְנוּ

מְעַט מֵהַרְבֵּה :

וּבְכָל־זֹאת שִׁמְךָ לֹא שָׁכָחְנוּ · נָא *Cong. and Reader.*

אַל־תִּשְׁכָּחֵנוּ : יי

עָזְרֵנוּ אֱלֹהֵי יִשְׁעֵנוּ עַל־דְּבַר כְּבוֹד־שְׁמֶךָ · *Cong.*

וְהַצִּילֵנוּ וְכַפֵּר עַל־חַטֹּאתֵינוּ לְמַעַן שְׁמֶךָ :

יְיָ אֱלֹהֵי יִשְׂרָאֵל · שׁוּב מֵחֲרוֹן אַפֶּךָ · *Cong. and Reader.*

וְהִנָּחֵם עַל־הָרָעָה לְעַמֶּךָ :

שׁוֹמֵר יִשְׂרָאֵל · שְׁמוֹר שְׁאֵרִית יִשְׂרָאֵל · וְאַל־יֹאבַד

יִשְׂרָאֵל · הָאוֹמְרִים שְׁמַע יִשְׂרָאֵל :

שׁוֹמֵר גּוֹי אֶחָד · שְׁמוֹר שְׁאֵרִית עַם אֶחָד · וְאַל־יֹאבַד

גּוֹי אֶחָד · הַמְיַחֲדִים שִׁמְךָ יְיָ אֱלֹהֵינוּ יְיָ אֶחָד :

שׁוֹמֵר גּוֹי קָדוֹשׁ · שְׁמוֹר שְׁאֵרִית עַם קָדוֹשׁ · וְאַל־יֹאבַד

גּוֹי קָדוֹשׁ · הַמְשַׁלְּשִׁים בְּשָׁלוֹשׁ קְדֻשָּׁה לְקָדוֹשׁ :

מִתְרַצֶּה בְּרַחֲמִים וּמִתְפַּיֵּס בְּתַחֲנוּנִים · הִתְרַצֵּה וְהִתְפַּיֵּס

לְדוֹר עָנִי כִּי אֵין עוֹזֵר :

Cong. and Reader.—We beseech thee, turn from thy wrath, and have mercy upon the treasured people whom thou hast chosen.

Cong.—Hear our voice, and be gracious, and abandon us not into the hand of our enemies to blot out our name ; remember what thou hast sworn to our fathers, I will multiply your seed as the stars of heaven :—and now we are left a few out of many.

Cong. and Reader.—Yet, despite all this, we have not forgotten thy Name : we beseech thee, forget us not.

Cong.—Help us, O God of our salvation, for the sake of the glory of thy Name ; and deliver us, and pardon our sins for thy Name's sake.

Cong. and Reader.—O Lord God of Israel, turn from thy fierce wrath, and relent of the evil against thy people.]

O Guardian of Israel, guard the remnant of Israel, and suffer not Israel to perish, who say, Hear, O Israel.

O Guardian of a unique nation, guard the remnant of a unique nation, and suffer not them to perish, who proclaim the unity of Thy Name, saying, The Lord is our God, the Lord is One.

O Guardian of a holy people, guard the remnant of a holy people, and suffer not them to perish, who thrice repeat the three-fold sanctification unto the Holy One.

O Thou who art propitiated by prayers for mercy, and art conciliated by supplications, be thou propitious and reconciled to an afflicted generation ; for there is none that helpeth.

GUARDIAN OF ISRAEL. *Shomer Yisroel.* These beautiful lines were in recent centuries taken over from the Fast Day prayers into the Daily Service. They are a plea to the love and mercy of God, that Israel who proclaims throughout the ages the Unity and Holiness of God, be saved from destruction. Israel has none other Helper.

אָבִינוּ מַלְכֵּנוּ חָנֵּנוּ וַעֲנֵנוּ כִּי אֵין בָּנוּ מַעֲשִׂים · עֲשֵׂה

עִמָּנוּ צְדָקָה וָחֶסֶד וְהוֹשִׁיעֵנוּ :

וַאֲנַחְנוּ לֹא נֵדַע מַה־נַּעֲשֶׂה כִּי עָלֶיךָ עֵינֵינוּ : זְכֹר

רַחֲמֶיךָ יְיָ וַחֲסָדֶיךָ כִּי מֵעוֹלָם הֵמָּה : יְהִי־חַסְדְּךָ יְיָ עָלֵינוּ

כַּאֲשֶׁר יִחַלְנוּ לָךְ : אַל תִּזְכָּר־לָנוּ עֲוֹנֹת רִאשֹׁנִים מַהֵר

יְקַדְּמוּנוּ רַחֲמֶיךָ כִּי דַלּוֹנוּ מְאֹד : חָנֵּנוּ יְיָ חָנֵּנוּ כִּי־רַב

שָׂבַעְנוּ בוּז : בְּרֹגֶז רַחֵם תִּזְכּוֹר : כִּי הוּא יָדַע יִצְרֵנוּ זָכוּר

כִּי־עָפָר אֲנָחְנוּ : עָזְרֵנוּ אֱלֹהֵי יִשְׁעֵנוּ עַל־דְּבַר כְּבוֹד־שְׁמֶךָ

וְהַצִּילֵנוּ וְכַפֵּר עַל־חַטֹּאתֵינוּ לְמַעַן שְׁמֶךָ :

The Reader says חֲצִי קַדִּישׁ, *p.* 106.

On Mondays and Thursdays אֵל אֶרֶךְ אַפַּיִם *is added. This prayer is,
however, omitted on the following days:—* רֹאשׁ חֹדֶשׁ, *the day before*
פֶּסַח, *on* תִּשְׁעָה בְּאָב, *on the day before* יוֹם כִּפּוּר, *during* חֲנֻכָּה,
the two days of פּוּרִים קָטָן, *and of* פּוּרִים.

אֵל אֶרֶךְ אַפַּיִם וְרַב־חֶסֶד וֶאֱמֶת אַל־בְּאַפְּךָ תוֹכִיחֵנוּ :

חוּסָה יְיָ עַל־עַמֶּךָ וְהוֹשִׁיעֵנוּ מִכָּל־רָע : חָטָאנוּ לְךָ אָדוֹן

סְלַח־נָא כְּרֹב רַחֲמֶיךָ אֵל :

אֵל אֶרֶךְ אַפַּיִם וְרַב־חֶסֶד וֶאֱמֶת אַל־תַּסְתֵּר פָּנֶיךָ

מִמֶּנּוּ : חוּסָה יְיָ עַל־יִשְׂרָאֵל עַמֶּךָ וְהַצִּילֵנוּ מִכָּל־רָע :

חָטָאנוּ לְךָ אָדוֹן סְלַח־נָא כְּרֹב רַחֲמֶיךָ אֵל :

PRAYERS
FOR FOR-
GIVENESS Our Father, our King, be gracious unto us and answer us, for we have no good works of our own ; deal with us in charity and lovingkindness, and save us.

II Chronicles 20. 12 As for us, we know not what to do ; but our eyes are

Psalm 25. 6 upon thee. Remember, O Lord, thy tender mercies and thy

Psalm 33. 22 lovingkindnesses ; for they have been ever of old. Let thy lovingkindness, O Lord, be upon us, according as we have

Psalm 79. 8 hoped in thee. Remember not against us the iniquities of our ancestors : let thy tender mercies speedily come to

Psalm 123. 4 meet us ; for we are brought very low. Be gracious unto us, O Lord, be gracious unto us ; for we are sated to the

Habakkuk 3. 2 full with contempt. In wrath remember to be merciful.

Psalm 103. 14 For he knoweth our frame ; he remembereth that we are

Psalm 79. 9 dust. Help us, O God of our salvation, for the sake of the glory of thy Name ; and deliver us, and pardon our sins for thy Name's sake.

The Reader says Half-Kaddish, p. 107.

[*On Mondays and Thursdays the following two paragraphs are added. They are, however, omitted on the following days :—New Moon, the day before Passover, the Fast of Av, the day before the Day of Atonement, during Chanukah, the two days of Purim, and of Purim Koton, the 14th and 15th of Adar Rishon.*

O God, slow to anger and abounding in lovingkindness and truth, rebuke us not in thine anger. Have pity upon thy people, O Lord, and save us from all evil. We have sinned against thee, O Lord ; forgive, we beseech thee according to the abundance of thy tender mercies, O God.

O God, slow to anger and abounding in lovingkindness and truth, hide not thy face from us. Have pity upon Israel, thy people, and deliver us from all evil. We have sinned against thee, O Lord ; forgive, we beseech thee, according to the abundance of thy tender mercies, O God.]

As FOR US. A shortened form of Tachanun ; originally for late comers, so that they could attend the Reading of the Torah.

Of the two concluding paragraphs, at first one was read by the. Reader, and the second was the Response of the congregation—closing the " Supplications ".

סדר קריאת התורה :

The following to בְּקֶרֶם, *p.* 196, *forms part of the Service when Prayers are said with a Congregation on Mondays and Thursdays, and also, with the exception of* יְהִי רָצוֹן, *pp.* 192, 194, *on Sabbath Afternoons,* חוֹל הַמּוֹעֵד, רֹאשׁ חֹדֶשׁ, *and on a* תַּעֲנִית צִבּוּר (*Mornings and Afternoons*).

The Ark is opened.
Reader and Congregation.

וַיְהִי בִּנְסֹעַ הָאָרֹן וַיֹּאמֶר מֹשֶׁה · קוּמָה | יְיָ וְיָפֻצוּ
אֹיְבֶיךָ וְיָנֻסוּ מְשַׂנְאֶיךָ מִפָּנֶיךָ : כִּי מִצִּיּוֹן תֵּצֵא תוֹרָה
וּדְבַר־יְיָ מִירוּשָׁלָםִ :

בָּרוּךְ שֶׁנָּתַן תּוֹרָה לְעַמּוֹ יִשְׂרָאֵל בִּקְדֻשָּׁתוֹ :

The Reader takes the סֵפֶר תּוֹרָה, *and says:—*

גַּדְּלוּ לַיְיָ אִתִּי · וּנְרוֹמְמָה שְׁמוֹ יַחְדָּו :

Reader and Congregation :—

לְךָ יְיָ הַגְּדֻלָּה וְהַגְּבוּרָה וְהַתִּפְאֶרֶת וְהַנֵּצַח וְהַהוֹד ·
כִּי־כֹל בַּשָּׁמַיִם וּבָאָרֶץ לְךָ יְיָ הַמַּמְלָכָה וְהַמִּתְנַשֵּׂא לְכֹל ׀
לְרֹאשׁ : רוֹמְמוּ יְיָ אֱלֹהֵינוּ וְהִשְׁתַּחֲווּ לַהֲדֹם רַגְלָיו קָדוֹשׁ
הוּא : רוֹמְמוּ יְיָ אֱלֹהֵינוּ וְהִשְׁתַּחֲווּ לְהַר קָדְשׁוֹ כִּי קָדוֹשׁ
יְיָ אֱלֹהֵינוּ :

אַב הָרַחֲמִים · הוּא יְרַחֵם עַם עֲמוּסִים · וְיִזְכּוֹר בְּרִית
אֵיתָנִים · וְיַצִּיל נַפְשׁוֹתֵינוּ מִן־הַשָּׁעוֹת הָרָעוֹת · וְיִגְעַר
בְּיֵצֶר הָרַע מִן הַנְּשׂוּאִים · וְיָחֹן אוֹתָנוּ לִפְלֵיטַת עוֹלָמִים ·
וִימַלֵּא מִשְׁאֲלוֹתֵינוּ בְּמִדָּה טוֹבָה יְשׁוּעָה וְרַחֲמִים :

ORDER OF READING THE TORAH.

When Prayers are said with a Congregation on Monday and Thursday Mornings, and also (with the exception of "May it be the Will", etc., to "Amen", pp. 193, 194) *on Sabbath Afternoons, New Moon, the Intermediate Days of Passover and Tabernacles, Purim, and Fast Days (Mornings and Afternoons).*

The Ark is opened.

Numbers 10. 35, 36   **Reader and Cong.**—And it came to pass, when the ark set forward, that Moses said, Rise up, O Lord, and thine enemies shall be scattered, and they that hate thee shall flee *Isaiah 2. 3* before thee. For out of Zion shall go forth the Torah, and the word of the Lord from Jerusalem.

Blessed be he who in his holiness gave the Torah to his people Israel.

The Reader takes the Scroll of the Torah, and says :—

Psalm 34. 4   Magnify the Lord with me, and let us exalt his Name together.

I Chronicles 29. 11   **Reader and Cong.**—Thine, O Lord, is the greatness, and the power, and the glory, and the victory, and the majesty : for all that is in the heaven and in the earth is thine ; thine, O Lord, is the kingdom, and the supremacy as head over all. Exalt ye the *Psalm 99. 5, 9* Lord our God, and worship at his temple : holy is he. Exalt ye the Lord our God, and worship at his holy mount ; for the Lord our God is holy.

May the Father of mercy have mercy upon a people that have been borne by him. May he remember the covenant with the patriarchs, deliver our souls from evil hours, check the evil inclination in them that have been carried by him, grant us of his grace an everlasting deliverance, and in his lovingkindness fulfil our desires by salvation and mercy.

4. ORDER OF READING OF THE TORAH.

Mondays and Thursdays were market-days in ancient Palestine ; and the villagers would come to the neighbouring town to attend the Law Courts and Markets. As they had no synagogue congregational worship, the Liturgy was enlarged for those days, and a Reading of a short portion from the first section of the Sidrah for the following Sabbath was included. This has remained the universal usage.

The prayers in connection with the Reading of the Torah will be explained in the Sabbath Service, p. 474f.

As the Reader unrolls the סֵפֶר תּוֹרָה *he says :—*

וְתִגָּלֶה וְתֵרָאֶה מַלְכוּתוֹ עָלֵינוּ בִּזְמַן קָרוֹב · וְיָחוֹן פְּלֵיטָתֵנוּ

וּפְלֵיטַת עַמּוֹ בֵּית יִשְׂרָאֵל לְחֵן וּלְחֶסֶד לְרַחֲמִים וּלְרָצוֹן

וְנֹאמַר אָמֵן : הַכֹּל הָבוּ גֹדֶל לֵאלֹהֵינוּ וּתְנוּ כָבוֹד לַתּוֹרָה :

Here the Reader names the Person who is to be called to the Reading.

כֹּהֵן קְרַב יַעֲמֹד פ׳ בֶּן פ׳ הַכֹּהֵן

בָּרוּךְ שֶׁנָּתַן תּוֹרָה לְעַמּוֹ יִשְׂרָאֵל בִּקְדֻשָּׁתוֹ : תּוֹרַת יְיָ

תְּמִימָה מְשִׁיבַת נָפֶשׁ עֵדוּת יְיָ נֶאֱמָנָה מַחְכִּימַת פֶּתִי :

פִּקּוּדֵי יְיָ יְשָׁרִים מְשַׂמְּחֵי־לֵב מִצְוַת יְיָ בָּרָה מְאִירַת

עֵינָיִם : יְיָ עֹז לְעַמּוֹ יִתֵּן יְיָ | יְבָרֵךְ אֶת עַמּוֹ בַשָּׁלוֹם :

הָאֵל תָּמִים דַּרְכּוֹ אִמְרַת יְיָ צְרוּפָה · מָגֵן הוּא לְכֹל

הַחוֹסִים בּוֹ :

Congregation and Reader :—

וְאַתֶּם הַדְּבֵקִים בַּיְיָ אֱלֹהֵיכֶם חַיִּים כֻּלְּכֶם הַיּוֹם :

Those who are called to the Reading say the following Blessing :—

בָּרְכוּ אֶת־יְיָ הַמְבֹרָךְ :

Congregation :— : בָּרוּךְ יְיָ הַמְבֹרָךְ לְעוֹלָם וָעֶד :

The Response is repeated and the Blessing continued :—

בָּרוּךְ אַתָּה יְיָ אֱלֹהֵינוּ מֶלֶךְ הָעוֹלָם · אֲשֶׁר בָּחַר־

בָּנוּ מִכָּל־הָעַמִּים וְנָתַן־לָנוּ אֶת־תּוֹרָתוֹ · בָּרוּךְ אַתָּה

יְיָ · נוֹתֵן הַתּוֹרָה :

After the Reading, the following Blessing is said :—

בָּרוּךְ אַתָּה יְיָ אֱלֹהֵינוּ מֶלֶךְ הָעוֹלָם · אֲשֶׁר נָתַן־

As the Reader unrolls the Scroll, he says :—

And may his kingdom be soon revealed and made visible unto us, and may he be gracious unto our remnant and unto the remnant of his people, the house of Israel, granting them grace, kindness, mercy and favour ; and let us say Amen. Ascribe, all of you, greatness unto our God, and render honour to the Torah.

Here the Reader names the Person who is to be called to the Reading.

Blessed be he, who in his holiness gave the Torah unto his people Israel. The teaching of the Lord is perfect, restoring the soul : the testimony of the Lord is faithful, making wise the simple. The precepts of the Lord are right, rejoicing the heart : the commandment of the Lord is pure, enlightening the eyes. The Lord will give strength unto his people : the Lord will bless his people with peace. As for God, his way is perfect : the word of the Lord is tried : he is a shield unto all them that trust in him.

·Psalm 19 8, 9

Psalm 29. 10
Psalm 18. 31

Deuteronomy 4. 4

Cong. and Reader.—And ye that cleave unto the Lord your God, are alive every one of you this day.

Those who are called to the Reading say the following Blessing :—

BLESS YE THE LORD WHO IS TO BE BLESSED.

Cong.—Blessed be the Lord, who is to be blessed, for ever and ever.

The Response is repeated and the Blessing continued :—

BLESSED ART THOU, O LORD OUR GOD, KING OF THE UNIVERSE, WHO HAST CHOSEN US FROM ALL PEOPLES, AND HAST GIVEN US THY TORAH. BLESSED ART THOU, O LORD, GIVER OF THE TORAH.

After the Reading, the following Blessing is said :—

BLESSED ART THOU, O LORD OUR GOD, KING OF THE UNIVERSE, WHO HAST GIVEN US THE TORAH OF TRUTH, AND HAST PLANTED EVERLASTING LIFE IN OUR MIDST. BLESSED ART THOU, O LORD, GIVER OF THE TORAH.

לָנוּ תּוֹרַת אֱמֶת · וְחַיֵּי עוֹלָם נָטַע בְּתוֹכֵנוּ · בָּרוּךְ
אַתָּה יְיָ · נוֹתֵן הַתּוֹרָה :

Persons who have been in peril of their lives, during journeys by sea or
land, in captivity or sickness, upon their deliverance or recovery
say the following, after the conclusion of the last Blessing :—

בָּרוּךְ אַתָּה יְיָ אֱלֹהֵינוּ מֶלֶךְ הָעוֹלָם · הַגּוֹמֵל לְחַיָּבִים
טוֹבוֹת · שֶׁגְּמָלַנִי כָּל־טוֹב :

The Congregation respond :—

מִי שֶׁגְּמָלְךָ כָּל־טוֹב · הוּא יִגְמָלְךָ כָּל־טוֹב סֶלָה :

After the Reading, the סֵפֶר תּוֹרָה *is held up, and the*
Congregation say the following :—

וְזֹאת הַתּוֹרָה אֲשֶׁר־שָׂם מֹשֶׁה לִפְנֵי בְּנֵי יִשְׂרָאֵל עַל־פִּי
יְיָ בְּיַד־מֹשֶׁה : עֵץ־חַיִּים הִיא לַמַּחֲזִיקִים בָּהּ וְתֹמְכֶיהָ
מְאֻשָּׁר : דְּרָכֶיהָ דַרְכֵי־נֹעַם וְכָל־נְתִיבֹתֶיהָ שָׁלוֹם : אֹרֶךְ
יָמִים בִּימִינָהּ בִּשְׂמֹאלָהּ עֹשֶׁר וְכָבוֹד : יְיָ חָפֵץ לְמַעַן
צִדְקוֹ יַגְדִּיל תּוֹרָה וְיַאְדִּיר :

On those Mondays and Thursdays when תַּחֲנוּן *is said, p.168 to p.186,*
the Reader adds the following, previous to the סֵפֶר תּוֹרָה *being re-*
turned to the Ark :—

יְהִי רָצוֹן מִלִּפְנֵי אָבִינוּ שֶׁבַּשָּׁמַיִם · לְכוֹנֵן אֶת־בֵּית חַיֵּינוּ
וּלְהָשִׁיב אֶת־שְׁכִינָתוֹ בְּתוֹכֵנוּ בִּמְהֵרָה בְיָמֵינוּ · וְנֹאמַר אָמֵן :
יְהִי רָצוֹן מִלִּפְנֵי אָבִינוּ שֶׁבַּשָּׁמַיִם · לְרַחֵם עָלֵינוּ וְעַל פְּלֵיטָתֵנוּ
וְלִמְנוֹעַ מַשְׁחִית וּמַגֵּפָה מֵעָלֵינוּ וּמֵעַל כָּל־עַמּוֹ בֵּית יִשְׂרָאֵל ·
וְנֹאמַר אָמֵן :
יְהִי רָצוֹן מִלִּפְנֵי אָבִינוּ שֶׁבַּשָּׁמַיִם · לְקַיֵּם־בָּנוּ חַכְמֵי יִשְׂרָאֵל ·

[*Persons who have been in peril of their lives, during journeys by sea or land, in captivity or sickness, upon their deliverance or recovery say the following, after the conclusion of the last Blessing* :—

THANKS-GIVING FOR DELIVER-ANCE FROM DANGER

Blessed art thou, O Lord our God, King of the universe, who doest good unto the undeserving, and who hast dealt kindly with me.

The Congregation respond :—

He who hath shown thee kindness, may he deal kindly with thee for ever.]

After the Reading, the Scroll is held up, and the Congregation say :—

Deuteronomy 4. 44

And this is the Torah which Moses set before the children of Israel, according to the commandment of the Lord by

Proverbs 3. 18 17, 16

the hand of Moses. It is a tree of life to them that grasp it, and of them that uphold it every one is rendered happy. Its ways are ways of pleasantness, and all its paths are peace. Length of days is in its right hand ; in its left

Isaiah 42. 21

hand are riches and honour. It pleased the Lord, for his righteousness' sake, to magnify the Torah and to glorify it.

On those Mondays and Thursdays when the Prayers, pp. 169 *to* 187 *are said, the Reader adds the following, previous to the Scroll of the Torah being returned to the Ark* :—

SUPPLICA-TIONS : FOR TEMPLE

May it be the will of our Father who is in heaven to establish the Temple, the house of our life, and to restore his divine presence in our midst, speedily in our days ; and let us say, Amen.

FOR SAFETY FROM PLAGUE

May it be the will of our Father who is in heaven to have mercy upon us and upon our remnant, and to keep destruction and the plague from us and from all his people, the house of Israel ; and let us say, Amen.

FOR THE SAGES

May it be the will of our Father who is in heaven to preserve among us the wise men of Israel ; them, their wives, their sons and

YEHI ROTZON. MAY IT BE THE WILL. A prayer for the protection of all Jewish communities, for scholars, for captives and travellers on land and sea. It is recited while the Sefer Torah is being prepared for return to the Ark.

wise men of Israel. A touching prayer of the community that men

הֵם וּנְשֵׁיהֶם וּבְנֵיהֶם וּבְנוֹתֵיהֶם וְתַלְמִידֵיהֶם וְתַלְמִידֵי
תַלְמִידֵיהֶם בְּכָל־מְקוֹמוֹת מוֹשְׁבוֹתֵיהֶם ' וְנֹאמַר אָמֵן :

יְהִי רָצוֹן מִלִּפְנֵי אָבִינוּ שֶׁבַּשָּׁמַיִם ' שֶׁנִּשְׁמַע וְנִתְבַּשֵּׂר בְּשׂוֹרוֹת
טוֹבוֹת יְשׁוּעוֹת וְנֶחָמוֹת ' וִיקַבֵּץ נִדָּחֵינוּ מֵאַרְבַּע כַּנְפוֹת
הָאָרֶץ ' וְנֹאמַר אָמֵן :

אַחֵינוּ כָּל־בֵּית־יִשְׂרָאֵל הַנְּתוּנִים בְּצָרָה וּבְשִׁבְיָה ' הָעוֹמְדִים
בֵּין בַּיָּם וּבֵין בַּיַּבָּשָׁה ' הַמָּקוֹם יְרַחֵם עֲלֵיהֶם וְיוֹצִיאֵם מִצָּרָה
לִרְוָחָה ' וּמֵאֲפֵלָה לְאוֹרָה ' וּמִשִּׁעְבּוּד לִגְאֻלָּה ' הַשְׁתָּא בַּעֲגָלָא
וּבִזְמַן קָרִיב ' וְנֹאמַר אָמֵן :

On returning the סֵפֶר *to the Ark, the Reader says:—*

יְהַלְלוּ אֶת־שֵׁם יְהוָה כִּי־נִשְׂגָּב שְׁמוֹ לְבַדּוֹ ·

Congregation:—

הוֹדוֹ עַל־אֶרֶץ וְשָׁמָיִם · וַיָּרֶם קֶרֶן לְעַמּוֹ
תְּהִלָּה לְכָל־חֲסִידָיו לִבְנֵי יִשְׂרָאֵל עַם קְרֹבוֹ · הַלְלוּיָהּ :

of Jewish Learning dwell among them. *They* were the aristocracy that
were the pride of the Jewries in former days. Without respect for
Learning, there can be no enduring Judaism.

captivity . . . the sea. We can have some conception of the hideous
ordeal that the victims of medieval persecution had to undergo, if we
recall but two incidents in connection with the Spanish expulsion in 1492
and the Nazi decrees of 1939. In 1492, multitudes fleeing from Spain fell
into the hands of Moorish pirates who plundered them of all they had
and reduced them to slavery ; large numbers died of famine or plague.
Many were cast on Christian shores, but found the gates of mercy shut
on them. In 1939, thousands of men, women and children were dumped
into " no-man's lands ", to sleep in streets and open fields till they could
find some country willing to receive them. But never before was it so
difficult for a Jewish emigrant to find a place of refuge. In May of that

daughters, their disciples and the disciples of their disciples in all the places of their habitation ; and let us say, Amen.

FOR TIDINGS OF SALVATION

May it be the will of our Father who is in heaven that good tidings of salvation and comfort may be heard and announced, and that he may gather our banished ones from the four corners of the earth ; and let us say, Amen.

FOR WANDERERS AND CAPTIVES

As for our brethren, the whole house of Israel, such of them as are given over to trouble or captivity, whether they be on the sea or on the dry land—may the All-present have mercy upon them, and bring them forth from trouble to deliverance, from darkness to light, and from subjection to redemption, now speedily and at a near time ; and let us say, Amen.

On returning the Scroll of the Torah to the Ark, the Reader says :—

Psalm 148. 13, 14

Let them praise the Name of the Lord ; for his Name alone is exalted :

Congregation.—His majesty is above the earth and heaven ; and he hath exalted the power of his people, to the praise of all his loving ones, even of the children of Israel, the people near unto him. Praise ye the Lord.

year, the steamship *St. Louis*, bearing 922 Jewish refugees who spent their last pennies to escape from the Third Reich, was refused landing at Havana, though permits had been issued by the Cuban Commissioner for immigration. Jewish relief organizations thereupon offered to deposit £100 guarantee for each refugee. In vain. After weeks of wandering in Caribbean waters, the ship was returning to Hamburg, the passengers to be sent to concentration camps. It stopped at Antwerp. And there, at the last moment, the Consuls of the governments of England, France, Holland and Belgium agreed to divide the refugees among the four countries. During that year there were on the Mediterranean, many ships, like the *St. Louis*, sailing from port to port, the passengers undergoing fantastic sufferings, but everywhere refused permission to land their human cargoes. *Did* all of them at last land them ?

the All-present. lit. " The Place ", Absolute Space, to indicate God's omnipresence. " As space encompasses all things, so does God encompass the universe, instead of being encompassed by it " (Talmud).

תהלים כ״ד

לְדָוִד מִזְמוֹר · לַיהֹוָה הָאָרֶץ וּמְלוֹאָהּ תֵּבֵל וְיֹשְׁבֵי בָהּ :
כִּי הוּא עַל־יַמִּים יְסָדָהּ וְעַל־נְהָרוֹת יְכוֹנְנֶהָ : מִי־יַעֲלֶה
בְהַר יְהֹוָה וּמִי־יָקוּם בִּמְקוֹם קָדְשׁוֹ : נְקִי כַפַּיִם וּבַר לֵבָב
אֲשֶׁר לֹא־נָשָׂא לַשָּׁוְא נַפְשׁוֹ וְלֹא נִשְׁבַּע לְמִרְמָה : יִשָּׂא
בְרָכָה מֵאֵת יְהֹוָה וּצְדָקָה מֵאֱלֹהֵי יִשְׁעוֹ : זֶה דּוֹר דֹּרְשׁוֹ
מְבַקְשֵׁי פָנֶיךָ יַעֲקֹב סֶלָה : שְׂאוּ שְׁעָרִים רָאשֵׁיכֶם וְהִנָּשְׂאוּ
פִּתְחֵי עוֹלָם וְיָבוֹא מֶלֶךְ הַכָּבוֹד : מִי זֶה מֶלֶךְ הַכָּבוֹד יְהֹוָה
עִזּוּז וְגִבּוֹר יְהֹוָה גִּבּוֹר מִלְחָמָה : שְׂאוּ שְׁעָרִים רָאשֵׁיכֶם
וּשְׂאוּ פִּתְחֵי עוֹלָם וְיָבֹא מֶלֶךְ הַכָּבוֹד : מִי הוּא זֶה מֶלֶךְ
הַכָּבוֹד יְהֹוָה צְבָאוֹת הוּא מֶלֶךְ הַכָּבוֹד סֶלָה :

While the סֵפֶר *is being placed in the Ark, the following, to* כְּקֶדֶם,
is said :—

וּבְנֻחֹה יֹאמַר · שׁוּבָה יְהֹוָה רִבְבוֹת אַלְפֵי יִשְׂרָאֵל :
קוּמָה ׀ יְהֹוָה לִמְנוּחָתֶךָ אַתָּה וַאֲרוֹן עֻזֶּךָ : כֹּהֲנֶיךָ יִלְבְּשׁוּ־
צֶדֶק וַחֲסִידֶיךָ יְרַנֵּנוּ : בַּעֲבוּר דָּוִד עַבְדֶּךָ אַל־תָּשֵׁב פְּנֵי
מְשִׁיחֶךָ : כִּי לֶקַח טוֹב נָתַתִּי לָכֶם תּוֹרָתִי אַל־תַּעֲזֹבוּ :
עֵץ־חַיִּים הִיא לַמַּחֲזִיקִים בָּהּ וְתֹמְכֶיהָ מְאֻשָּׁר : דְּרָכֶיהָ
דַרְכֵי־נֹעַם וְכָל־נְתִיבוֹתֶיהָ שָׁלוֹם : הֲשִׁיבֵנוּ יְהֹוָה אֵלֶיךָ
וְנָשׁוּבָה חַדֵּשׁ יָמֵינוּ כְּקֶדֶם :

Psalm xxiv.   ¹A Psalm of David.

THE TRUE
WORSHIP-
PER

The earth is the Lord's, and the fulness thereof ; the world, and they that dwell therein. ²For it is he that hath founded it upon the seas, and established it upon the floods. ³Who may ascend the mountain of the Lord ? And who may stand in his holy place ? ⁴He that hath clean hands and a pure heart ; who hath not set his desire upon vanity, and hath not sworn deceitfully. ⁵He shall receive a blessing from the Lord, and righteousness from the God of his salvation. ⁶Such is the generation of them that seek after him, that seek thy face, (O God of) Jacob ! (Selah.) ⁷Lift up your heads, O ye gates ; and be lifted up, ye ever-lasting doors, that the King of glory may come in. ⁸Who is the King of glory ? The Lord strong and mighty, the

TRI-
UMPHAL
ENTRY
INTO
SANCTU-
ARY

Lord mighty in battle. ⁹Lift up your heads, O ye gates ; yea, lift them up, ye everlasting doors, that the King of glory may come in. ¹⁰Who, then, is the King of glory ? The Lord of hosts, he is the King of glory. (Selah.)

While the Scroll of the Torah is being placed in the Ark, the following to " as of old " is said :—

Numbers
10. 36
Psalm
132. 8-10

And when it rested, he said, Return, O Lord, unto the ten thousands of the families of Israel. Arise, O Lord, unto thy resting place ; thou, and the ark of thy strength· Let thy priests be clothed with righteousness ; and let thy loving ones shout for joy. For the sake of David thy

Proverbs 4. 2

servant, turn not away the face of thine anointed. For I

Proverbs
3. 18, 17

give you good doctrine ; forsake ye not my Torah. It is a tree of life to them that grasp it, and of them that uphold it every one is rendered happy. Its ways are ways of pleasant-

Lamentations
5. 21

ness, and all its paths are peace. Turn thou us unto thee, O, Lord, and we shall return : renew our days as of old.

THE EARTH IS THE LORD'S. For explanation, see p. 220.
his desire. This rendering is based on the Kethib, which is נפשו.

אַשְׁרֵי יוֹשְׁבֵי בֵיתֶךָ עוֹד יְהַלְלוּךָ סֶּלָה :

אַשְׁרֵי הָעָם שֶׁכָּכָה לּוֹ אַשְׁרֵי הָעָם שֶׁיְיָ אֱלֹהָיו :

קמ׳ה תְּהִלָּה לְדָוִד ·

אֲרוֹמִמְךָ אֱלוֹהַי הַמֶּלֶךְ וַאֲבָרְכָה שִׁמְךָ לְעוֹלָם וָעֶד :

בְּכָל־יוֹם אֲבָרֲכֶךָּ וַאֲהַלְלָה שִׁמְךָ לְעוֹלָם וָעֶד :

גָּדוֹל יְהוָה וּמְהֻלָּל מְאֹד וְלִגְדֻלָּתוֹ אֵין חֵקֶר :

דּוֹר לְדוֹר יְשַׁבַּח מַעֲשֶׂיךָ וּגְבוּרֹתֶיךָ יַגִּידוּ ·

הֲדַר כְּבוֹד הוֹדֶךָ וְדִבְרֵי נִפְלְאֹתֶיךָ אָשִׂיחָה :

וֶעֱזוּז נוֹרְאֹתֶיךָ יֹאמֵרוּ וּגְדֻלָּתְךָ אֲסַפְּרֶנָּה :

זֵכֶר רַב־טוּבְךָ יַבִּיעוּ וְצִדְקָתְךָ יְרַנֵּנוּ :

חַנּוּן וְרַחוּם יְהוָה אֶרֶךְ אַפַּיִם וּגְדָל־חָסֶד :

טוֹב־יְהוָה לַכֹּל וְרַחֲמָיו עַל־כָּל־מַעֲשָׂיו :

יוֹדוּךָ יְהוָה כָּל־מַעֲשֶׂיךָ וַחֲסִידֶיךָ יְבָרְכוּכָה :

כְּבוֹד מַלְכוּתְךָ יֹאמֵרוּ וּגְבוּרָתְךָ יְדַבֵּרוּ :

לְהוֹדִיעַ לִבְנֵי הָאָדָם גְּבוּרֹתָיו וּכְבוֹד הֲדַר מַלְכוּתוֹ :

מַלְכוּתְךָ מַלְכוּת כָּל־עֹלָמִים וּמֶמְשַׁלְתְּךָ בְּכָל־דּוֹר וָדֹר :

סוֹמֵךְ יְהוָה לְכָל־הַנֹּפְלִים וְזוֹקֵף לְכָל־הַכְּפוּפִים :

עֵינֵי כֹל אֵלֶיךָ יְשַׂבֵּרוּ וְאַתָּה נוֹתֵן־לָהֶם אֶת־אָכְלָם בְּעִתּוֹ :

פּוֹתֵחַ אֶת־יָדֶךָ וּמַשְׂבִּיעַ לְכָל־חַי רָצוֹן :

צַדִּיק יְהוָה בְּכָל־דְּרָכָיו וְחָסִיד בְּכָל־מַעֲשָׂיו :

ASHREY
YOSHEVEY
VEYSECHO

Psalm 84. 5

Psalm 144. 15

Happy are they that dwell in thy house : they will be ever praising thee. (Selah.) Happy is the people, that is thus favoured : happy is the people, whose God is the Lord.

Psalm cxlv. ¹A Psalm of Praise : of David.

THE
GREAT-
NESS AND
UNENDING
GOODNESS
OF GOD

I will extol thee, my God, O King ; and I will bless thy Name for ever and ever. ²Every day will I bless thee ; and I will praise thy Name for ever and ever. ³Great is the Lord, and exceedingly to be praised : and his greatness is unsearchable. ⁴One generation shall laud thy works to another, and shall declare thy mighty acts. ⁵On the majestic glory of thy splendour, and on thy marvellous deeds, will I meditate. ⁶And men shall speak of the might of thy tremendous acts ; and I will recount thy greatness. ⁷They shall pour forth the fame of thy great goodness, and shall exult in thy righteousness. ⁸The Lord is gracious and merciful ; slow to anger and of great lovingkindness. ⁹The Lord is good to all ; and his tender mercies are over all his works. ¹⁰All thy works shall give thanks unto thee, O Lord ; and thy loving ones shall bless thee. ¹¹They shall speak of the glory of thy kingdom, and talk of thy power ; ¹²to make known to the sons of men his mighty acts, and the majestic glory of his kingdom. ¹³Thy kingdom is an everlasting kingdom, and thy dominion endureth throughout all generations. ¹⁴The Lord upholdeth all that fall, and raiseth up all those that are bowed down. ¹⁵The eyes of all wait upon thee ; and thou givest them their food in due season. ¹⁶Thou openest thine hand, and satisfiest every living thing with favour. ¹⁷The Lord is righteous in all is ways, and loving in all

IV. ADDITIONS TO THE SERVICE.
B. CONCLUSION OF THE SERVICE.

In our Rite, the Service ends with Psalms 145 and 20, a Prophetic lesson with a second Sanctification, and Oleynu. Where prayers are said with a congregation, Oleynu is preceded by Full Kaddish and followed by Mourner's Kaddish. The " Hymn of Glory," the Day's Psalm, and various optional Readings are supplements to the Service.

קָרוֹב יְהֹוָה לְכָל־קֹרְאָיו לְכֹל אֲשֶׁר יִקְרָאֻהוּ בֶאֱמֶת :

רְצוֹן־יְרֵאָיו יַעֲשֶׂה וְאֶת־שַׁוְעָתָם יִשְׁמַע וְיוֹשִׁיעֵם :

שׁוֹמֵר יְהֹוָה אֶת־כָּל־אֹהֲבָיו וְאֵת כָּל־הָרְשָׁעִים יַשְׁמִיד :

תְּהִלַּת יְהֹוָה יְדַבֶּר־פִּי וִיבָרֵךְ כָּל־בָּשָׂר שֵׁם קָדְשׁוֹ
לְעוֹלָם וָעֶד :

וַאֲנַחְנוּ נְבָרֵךְ יָהּ מֵעַתָּה וְעַד־עוֹלָם · הַלְלוּיָהּ :

On the following days לַמְנַצֵּחַ is omitted: רֹאשׁ חֹדֶשׁ, the day before
חֲנֻכָּה, on פֶּסַח, תִּשְׁעָה בְּאָב, the day before יוֹם כִּפּוּר, during
פּוּרִים קָטָן and פּוּרִים·

תהלים כ׳

לַמְנַצֵּחַ מִזְמוֹר לְדָוִד : יַעַנְךָ יְהֹוָה בְּיוֹם צָרָה יְשַׂגֶּבְךָ
שֵׁם אֱלֹהֵי יַעֲקֹב : יִשְׁלַח עֶזְרְךָ מִקֹּדֶשׁ וּמִצִּיּוֹן יִסְעָדֶךָ :
יִזְכֹּר כָּל־מִנְחֹתֶיךָ וְעוֹלָתְךָ יְדַשְּׁנֶה־סֶלָה : יִתֶּן־לְךָ כִלְבָבֶךָ
וְכָל־עֲצָתְךָ יְמַלֵּא : נְרַנְּנָה בִּישׁוּעָתֶךָ וּבְשֵׁם־אֱלֹהֵינוּ נִדְגֹּל
יְמַלֵּא יְהֹוָה כָּל־מִשְׁאֲלוֹתֶיךָ : עַתָּה יָדַעְתִּי כִּי הוֹשִׁיעַ
יְהֹוָה מְשִׁיחוֹ יַעֲנֵהוּ מִשְּׁמֵי קָדְשׁוֹ בִּגְבוּרוֹת יֵשַׁע יְמִינוֹ :
אֵלֶּה בָרֶכֶב וְאֵלֶּה בַסּוּסִים וַאֲנַחְנוּ בְּשֵׁם־יְהֹוָה אֱלֹהֵינוּ
נַזְכִּיר : הֵמָּה כָּרְעוּ וְנָפָלוּ וַאֲנַחְנוּ קַמְנוּ וַנִּתְעוֹדָד : יְהֹוָה
הוֹשִׁיעָה הַמֶּלֶךְ יַעֲנֵנוּ בְיוֹם־קָרְאֵנוּ :

1. PSALM 145.

Ashrey. For an explanation of Psalm 145, see p. 85.

2. PSALM 20.

The confidence in the Lord's salvation that this psalm expresses,
makes it an appropriate transition to the passage (" And a redeemer
shall come unto Zion ") that immediately follows. This psalm was

THE GREAT-NESS AND UNENDING GOODNESS OF GOD

his works. [18]The Lord is nigh unto all them that call upon him, to all that call upon him in truth. [19]He will fulfil the desire of them that reverence him ; he also will hear their cry, and will save them. [20]The Lord guardeth all them that love him ; but all the wicked will he destroy. [21]My mouth shall speak of the praise of the Lord ; and let all flesh bless his holy Name for ever and ever.

Psalm 115. 18   But we will bless the Lord from this time forth and for evermore. Praise ye the Lord.

> *On the following days Psalm xx is omitted : New Moon, the day before Passover, on the Fast of Av, the day before the Day of Atonement, during the Chanukah, and on Purim Koton.*

> Psalm xx. [1]For the Chief Musician. A Psalm of David.

PRAYER FOR HELP IN DAY OF NEED

[2]The Lord answer thee in the day of trouble ; the Name of the God of Jacob set thee up on high ; [3]send thee help from the sanctuary, and uphold thee out of Zion ; [4]remember all thy offerings, and accept thy sacrifice (Selah) ; [5]grant thee thy heart's desire, and fulfil all thy purpose. [6]We will shout for joy in thy victory, and in the Name of our God we will set up our banners ; the Lord fulfil all thy petitions. [7]Now know I that the Lord saveth his anointed ; he will answer him from his holy heaven with the mighty saving acts of his right hand. [8]Some trust in chariots and some in horses : but we will make mention of the Name of the Lord our God. [9]They are bowed down and fallen : but we are

---

deemed a part of the Tachanun, and is therefore, not read whenever the latter is omitted.

4. *all thy offerings.* The sacrifice of the warrior-king who was going out to meet his enemies.

6. *set up our banners.* Or, " wave our banners ", in token of triumph.

7. *his anointed.* The king, as consecrated to God's service.

8. *some trust in chariots.* " In later ages, when Israel could use no secular arm, these words became the expression of faith in God's powers to save ; and they were made the war-cry of spiritual loyalty in face of a hostile world " (Abrahams).

make mention. As our watchword.

וּבָא לְצִיּוֹן גּוֹאֵל וּלְשָׁבֵי פֶשַׁע בְּיַעֲקֹב נְאֻם יְיָ : וַאֲנִי

זֹאת בְּרִיתִי אֹתָם אָמַר יְיָ רוּחִי אֲשֶׁר עָלֶיךָ וּדְבָרַי אֲשֶׁר־

שַׂמְתִּי בְּפִיךָ לֹא יָמוּשׁוּ מִפִּיךָ וּמִפִּי זַרְעֲךָ וּמִפִּי זֶרַע זַרְעֲךָ

אָמַר יְיָ מֵעַתָּה וְעַד־עוֹלָם :

וְאַתָּה קָדוֹשׁ יוֹשֵׁב תְּהִלּוֹת יִשְׂרָאֵל : וְקָרָא

זֶה אֶל־זֶה וְאָמַר קָדוֹשׁ קָדוֹשׁ קָדוֹשׁ יְיָ צְבָאוֹת

מְלֹא כָל־הָאָרֶץ כְּבוֹדוֹ : וּמְקַבְּלִין דֵּן מִן־דֵּן וְאָמְרִין

קַדִּישׁ בִּשְׁמֵי מְרוֹמָא עִלָּאָה בֵּית שְׁכִינְתֵּהּ · קַדִּישׁ עַל־

אַרְעָא עוֹבַד גְּבוּרְתֵּהּ · קַדִּישׁ לְעָלַם וּלְעָלְמֵי עָלְמַיָּא · יְיָ

צְבָאוֹת מַלְיָא כָל־אַרְעָא זִיו יְקָרֵהּ: וַתִּשָּׂאֵנִי רוּחַ וָאֶשְׁמַע

אַחֲרַי קוֹל רַעַשׁ גָּדוֹל בָּרוּךְ כְּבוֹד־יְיָ מִמְּקוֹמוֹ : וּנְטָלַתְנִי

רוּחָא וְשִׁמְעֵת בַּתְרַי קָל זִיעַ שַׂגִּיא דִּי מְשַׁבְּחִין וְאָמְרִין ·

בְּרִיךְ יְקָרָא דִי יְיָ מֵאֲתַר בֵּית שְׁכִינְתֵּהּ : יְיָ ׀ יִמְלֹךְ לְעֹלָם

וָעֶד : יְיָ מַלְכוּתֵהּ קָאֵם לְעָלַם וּלְעָלְמֵי עָלְמַיָּא : יְיָ אֱלֹהֵי

אַבְרָהָם יִצְחָק וְיִשְׂרָאֵל אֲבוֹתֵינוּ · שָׁמְרָה־זֹּאת לְעוֹלָם

3. AND A REDEEMER SHALL COME TO ZION.

Pious men of old desired to close their morning devotions with readings and expositions from the Prophets, in the same manner as, originally, a Prophetical lesson, the Haftorah, closed the Sabbath Morning Service. Stress of life, however, compelled the utmost shortening of these daily readings and expositions. In our Rite, this daily Prophetical lesson consists merely of Isaiah 59. 20–21. These two verses contain a promise of Redemption ; as well as an assurance of an

risen and stand upright. ¹⁰Save, Lord : may the King answer us on the day when we call.

Isaiah 59. 20, 21   And a redeemer shall come to Zion and to them that turn from transgression in Jacob, saith the Lord. And as for me, this is my covenant with them, saith the Lord : my spirit that is upon thee, and my words which I have put in thy mouth, shall not depart out of thy mouth, nor out of the mouth of thy seed, nor out of the mouth of thy seed's seed, saith the Lord, from henceforth and for ever.

Psalm 22. 4   But thou art holy, O thou that dwellest amid the praises

Isaiah 6, 3   of Israel. And one cried unto another, and said, Holy, holy,

A SECOND KEDU-SHAH   holy is the Lord of hosts : the whole earth is full of his glory *And they receive sanction the one from the other, and say, Holy in the highest heavens, the place of his divine abode ; holy upon earth, the work of his might ; holy for ever and to all eternity is the Lord of hosts ; the whole earth is full of the radiance of his

Ezekiel 3. 12 glory. Then a wind lifted me up, and I heard behind me the voice of a great rushing (saying), Blessed be the glory of the Lord from his place. *Then a wind lifted me up, and I heard behind me the voice of a great rushing, of those who uttered praises, and said, Blessed be the glory of the Lord from

Exodus 15. 18 the region of his divine abode. The Lord shall reign for ever and ever. *The kingdom of the Lord endureth for ever and to all eternity.

*The Aramaic paraphrase of the preceding verse

eternal Covenant that shall link the generations in the sacred resolve' to preserve the spirit and letter of God's Revelation to Israel. Then follows the Sanctification (Kedushah)—Isaiah 6. 3, Ezekiel 3. 12, Exodus 15. 18. As the repetition of the Sanctification is merely the accompaniment of a private Biblical exposition (קדושא דסדרא), it is not recited *congregationally*, but by each worshipper for himself. In this private recital of the Kedushah, a vernacular translation, in Aramaic, was added, in order that even those ignorant of Hebrew understand the sacred words.

The Kedushah is followed by two prayers. The first is a petition that God direct our hearts unto Him, and an acknowledgment of His redeeming grace in all ages. The second prayer is a fervent expression of gratitude for Jewish duty. It concluded the Bible exposition.

לְיֵצֶר מַחֲשָׁבוֹת לְבַב עַמֶּךָ וְהָכֵן לְבָבָם אֵלֶיךָ : וְהוּא רַחוּם

יְכַפֵּר עָוֹן וְלֹא יַשְׁחִית וְהִרְבָּה לְהָשִׁיב אַפּוֹ וְלֹא יָעִיר כָּל־

חֲמָתוֹ : כִּי־אַתָּה אֲדֹנָי טוֹב וְסַלָּח וְרַב־חֶסֶד לְכָל־קֹרְאֶיךָ :

צִדְקָתְךָ צֶדֶק לְעוֹלָם וְתוֹרָתְךָ אֱמֶת : תִּתֵּן אֱמֶת לְיַעֲקֹב

חֶסֶד לְאַבְרָהָם אֲשֶׁר־נִשְׁבַּעְתָּ לַאֲבֹתֵינוּ מִימֵי קֶדֶם : בָּרוּךְ

אֲדֹנָי יוֹם ׀ יוֹם יַעֲמָס־לָנוּ הָאֵל יְשׁוּעָתֵנוּ סֶלָה : יְיָ צְבָאוֹת

עִמָּנוּ מִשְׂגָּב־לָנוּ אֱלֹהֵי יַעֲקֹב סֶלָה : יְיָ צְבָאוֹת אַשְׁרֵי

אָדָם בֹּטֵחַ בָּךְ : יְיָ הוֹשִׁיעָה • הַמֶּלֶךְ יַעֲנֵנוּ בְיוֹם־קָרְאֵנוּ :

בָּרוּךְ אֱלֹהֵינוּ שֶׁבְּרָאָנוּ לִכְבוֹדוֹ וְהִבְדִּילָנוּ מִן־הַתּוֹעִים

וְנָתַן לָנוּ תּוֹרַת אֱמֶת וְחַיֵּי עוֹלָם נָטַע בְּתוֹכֵנוּ • הוּא

יִפְתַּח לִבֵּנוּ בְּתוֹרָתוֹ וְיָשֵׂם בְּלִבֵּנוּ אַהֲבָתוֹ וְיִרְאָתוֹ

וְלַעֲשׂוֹת רְצוֹנוֹ וּלְעָבְדוֹ בְּלֵבָב שָׁלֵם • לְמַעַן לֹא נִיגַע לָרִיק

וְלֹא נֵלֵד לַבֶּהָלָה : יְהִי רָצוֹן מִלְּפָנֶיךָ יְיָ אֱלֹהֵינוּ וֵאלֹהֵי

אֲבוֹתֵינוּ • שֶׁנִּשְׁמוֹר חֻקֶּיךָ בָּעוֹלָם הַזֶּה • וְנִזְכֶּה וְנִחְיֶה

וְנִרְאֶה וְנִירַשׁ טוֹבָה וּבְרָכָה לִשְׁנֵי יְמוֹת הַמָּשִׁיחַ וּלְחַיֵּי

הָעוֹלָם הַבָּא : לְמַעַן יְזַמֶּרְךָ כָבוֹד וְלֹא יִדֹּם • יְיָ אֱלֹהַי

לְעוֹלָם אוֹדֶךָ : בָּרוּךְ הַגֶּבֶר אֲשֶׁר יִבְטַח בַּייָ וְהָיָה יְיָ

מִבְטַחוֹ : בִּטְחוּ בַייָ עֲדֵי־עַד כִּי בְּיָהּ יְיָ צוּר עוֹלָמִים :

וְיִבְטְחוּ בְךָ יוֹדְעֵי שְׁמֶךָ כִּי לֹא־עָזַבְתָּ דֹרְשֶׁיךָ יְיָ :

יְיָ חָפֵץ לְמַעַן צִדְקוֹ יַגְדִּיל תּוֹרָה וְיַאְדִּיר :

PRAYER
FOR
FIDELITY
TO GOD
I Chronicles
29. 18
Psalm 78. 38

Psalm 86. 5

Psalm
119. 142

Micah 7. 20

Psalm 68. 20

Psalm 46. 8

Psalm 84. 13

Psalm 20. 10

AND
LOYALTY
TO THE
TORAH

O Lord, the God of Abraham, of Isaac and of Israel, our fathers, keep this for ever as the inward thought in the heart of thy people, and direct their heart unto thee. And he, being merciful, forgiveth iniquity and destroyeth not : yea, many a time he turned his anger away, and doth not stir up all his wrath. For thou, O Lord, art good and forgiving, and abounding in lovingkindness to all them that call upon thee. Thy righteousness is an everlasting right- eousness, and Thy Torah is truth. Thou wilt show truth to Jacob and lovingkindness to Abraham, according as thou hast sworn unto our fathers from the days of old. Blessed be the Lord, day by day he beareth our burden, even the God who is our salvation. (Selah.) The Lord of hosts is with us ; the God of Jacob is our stronghold. (Selah.) O Lord of hosts, happy is the man who trusteth in thee. Save, Lord : may the King answer us on the day when we call.

Blessed is our God, who hath created us for his glory, and hath separated us from them that go astray, and hath given us theTorah of truth and planted everlasting life in our midst. May he open our heart unto his Torah, and place his love and fear within our hearts, that we may do his will and serve him with a perfect heart, that we may not labour in vain, nor bring forth for confusion. May it be thy will, O Lord our God and God of our fathers, that we may keep thy statutes in this world, and be worthy to live to witness and inherit happiness and blessing in the days of the Messiah

Psalm 30. 13

and in the life of the world to come. To the end that my glory may sing praise unto thee, and not be silent : O Lord

Jeremiah 17. 7

my God, I will give thanks unto thee for ever. Blessed is the man that trusteth in the Lord, and whose trust the Lord is.

keep this forever . . . people : i.e. keep the mind and purpose of Thy people ever in this spirit.
labour in vain. i.e. without any result.
for confusion. May we be saved from the disaster of merely increasing confusion in the world.
days of the Messiah . . . world to come. See pp. 254–5.

On the days when מוּסָף is said, the Reader here says חֲצִי קַדִּישׁ,
i. e., to בְּעָלְמָא ∙ וְאָמְרוּ אָמֵן ; on other days, the whole Kaddish,
as follows :—

Reader. יִתְגַּדַּל וְיִתְקַדַּשׁ שְׁמֵהּ רַבָּא בְּעָלְמָא דִּי־בְרָא

כִרְעוּתֵהּ ∙ וְיַמְלִיךְ מַלְכוּתֵהּ בְּחַיֵּיכוֹן וּבְיוֹמֵיכוֹן וּבְחַיֵּי

דִי־כָל־בֵּית יִשְׂרָאֵל בַּעֲגָלָא וּבִזְמַן קָרִיב ∙ וְאָמְרוּ אָמֵן :

Cong. and Reader יְהֵא שְׁמֵהּ רַבָּא מְבָרַךְ לְעָלַם וּלְעָלְמֵי

עָלְמַיָּא ∙

Reader. יִתְבָּרַךְ וְיִשְׁתַּבַּח וְיִתְפָּאַר וְיִתְרֹמַם וְיִתְנַשֵּׂא

וְיִתְהַדָּר וְיִתְעַלֶּה וְיִתְהַלָּל שְׁמֵהּ דִּי־קֻדְשָׁא ∙ בְּרִיךְ הוּא ∙

לְעֵלָּא מִן־כָּל־בִּרְכָתָא וְשִׁירָתָא תֻּשְׁבְּחָתָא וְנֶחֱמָתָא

דִּי־אֲמִירָן בְּעָלְמָא ∙ וְאָמְרוּ אָמֵן :

Congregation. אָמֵן :

Reader. תִּתְקַבַּל צְלוֹתְהוֹן וּבָעוּתְהוֹן דִּי־כָל־יִשְׂרָאֵל

קֳדָם אֲבוּהוֹן דִּי בִשְׁמַיָּא ∙ וְאָמְרוּ אָמֵן :

Congregation. אָמֵן :

Reader. יְהֵא שְׁלָמָא רַבָּא מִן־שְׁמַיָּא וְחַיִּים עָלֵינוּ

וְעַל־כָּל־יִשְׂרָאֵל ∙ וְאָמְרוּ אָמֵן :

Congregation. אָמֵן :

Reader. עֹשֶׂה שָׁלוֹם בִּמְרוֹמָיו הוּא יַעֲשֶׂה שָׁלוֹם

עָלֵינוּ וְעַל־כָּל־יִשְׂרָאֵל ∙ וְאָמְרוּ אָמֵן :

Isaiah 26. 4   Trust ye in the Lord for ever ; for the Lord is God, an
Psalm 9. 11   everlasting rock. And they that know thy Name will put
their trust in thee ; for thou hast not forsaken them that
Isaiah 42, 21   seek thee, Lord. It pleased the Lord, for his righteousness'
sake, to magnify the Torah and to glorify it.

KADDISH   *On the days when the Mussaf Service is said, the Reader here says*
TISKAB-
BAL   *Half-Kaddish, to " in the world ; and say ye, Amen " ; on other*
days, the whole Kaddish, as follows :—

Reader.—Magnified and sanctified be his great Name in
the world which he hath created according to his will.
May he establish his kingdom during your life and during
your days, and during the life of all the house of Israel,
even speedily and at a near time, and say ye, Amen.

Cong. and Reader.—Let his great Name be blessed for
ever and to all eternity.

Reader.—Blessed, praised and glorified, exalted, extolled
and honoured, magnified and lauded be the Name of the
Holy One, blessed be he ; though he be high above all the
blessings and hymns, praises and consolations, which are
uttered in the world ; and say ye, Amen.

Congregation.—Amen.

Reader.—May the prayers and supplications of all Israel
be accepted by their Father who is in heaven ; and say ye,
Amen.

Congregation.—Amen.

Reader.—May there be abundant peace from heaven, and
life for us and for all Israel ; and say ye, Amen.

Congregation.—Amen.

Reader.—He who maketh peace in his high places, may
he make peace for us and for all Israel ; and say ye, Amen.

4. KADDISH TISKABBAL.

Its distinguishing feature in contrast with the Mourner's and other
forms of the Kaddish, are the words, " May the prayers and supplications of all Israel be accepted by their Father Who is in heaven ".

עָלֵינוּ לְשַׁבֵּחַ לַאֲדוֹן הַכֹּל לָתֵת גְּדֻלָּה לְיוֹצֵר

בְּרֵאשִׁית · שֶׁלֹּא עָשָׂנוּ כְּגוֹיֵי הָאֲרָצוֹת וְלֹא שָׂמָנוּ

כְּמִשְׁפְּחוֹת הָאֲדָמָה · שֶׁלֹּא שָׂם חֶלְקֵנוּ כָּהֶם וְגֹרָלֵנוּ

כְּכָל־הֲמוֹנָם · וַאֲנַחְנוּ כֹּרְעִים וּמִשְׁתַּחֲוִים וּמוֹדִים לִפְנֵי

מֶלֶךְ מַלְכֵי הַמְּלָכִים הַקָּדוֹשׁ בָּרוּךְ הוּא · שֶׁהוּא נוֹטֶה

5. CONCLUDING ADORATION—OLEYNU.

Since the 14th century, the Oleynu prayer—the proclamation of God as Supreme King of the Universe, and as God of a United Humanity—closes *all* congregational services on week-days, Sabbaths and Festivals. In the first half of this sublime prayer, Israel solemnly acknowledges the Selection of Israel for the service of the supreme King of kings. In the second half, it voices Israel's undying hope for the day when all idolatry shall have disappeared; when human activities that are now directed away from God, or counter to God, shall be turned *to* Him and *to* His service; when the reign of Righteousness shall be established among the children of men, and mankind be one united body under the Kingship of God. " The establishment of the Kingdom of the One and Only God throughout the entire world constitutes the Divine Plan of Salvation towards which, according to Jewish teaching, the efforts of all the ages are tending " (Kohler). " It was of the highest religious significance that the idea of the future reunion of humanity in the recognition of One God, became the culminating prayer in the Daily Service " (Elbogen).

Oleynu is not only one of the noblest of our prayers, but also one of the oldest, " a proof of its age being the fact, that there is no mention in it of the restoration of the Temple and the Jewish State, which would scarcely have been omitted had it been composed after their destruction " (Moses Mendelssohn).

Oleynu has had a strange fate, almost typical of Israel's story. The most universalist of prayers, it has yet been the victim of slanderous accusation and persecution, and has repeatedly been suppressed and mutilated. Miserable apostates pretended to see an attack on Christianity in a phrase based on Isaiah 30. 7 and 45. 20 that originally formed part of the first paragraph (" they worship vain things and emptiness, and pray unto God that cannot save ", before the words

OLEYNU :
ISRAEL'S
SELECTION
TO PRO-
CLAIM
GOD AS
SUPREME
KING OF
THE
UNIVERSE

It is our duty to praise the Lord of all things, to ascribe greatness to him who formed the world in the beginning, since he hath not made us like the nations of other lands, and hath not placed us like other families of the earth, since he hath not assigned unto us a portion as unto them, nor a lot as unto all their multitude. For we bend the knee and offer worship and thanks before the supreme King of kings, the Holy One, blessed be he, who stretched forth the

for we bend the knee. Learned Rabbis protested against such misinterpretation, and pointed out that both the quotation from Isaiah and the Prayer itself were pre-Christian ; that Rabh, the renowned Babylonian teacher of the third century, who edited the New Year Mussaf Amidah in which Oleynu is incorporated, lived in an environment where there were no Christians at all. In vain. As late as 1656, Manasseh ben Israel deemed it necessary to devote a whole chapter in his *Vindiciae Judaeorum* to its defence. He relates that the Sultan Selim, on reading the Oleynu in a Turkish translation of the Jewish Prayer Book, said : " Truly this prayer is sufficient for all purposes ; there is no need of any other." Nevertheless, a half-century later, the Prussian Government ordered the elimination of the words from Isaiah, and prohibited the recitation of the uncensored form. Those words do not now occur in the Ashkenazi Rite.

Because of its firm proclamation of the Divine Unity, Oleynu was a favourite prayer of Jewish martyrs. " During the persecution of the Jews of Blois (France) in 1171, where many Masters of the Torah died at the stake, an eye-witness wrote that the death of the saints was accompanied by a solemn song resounding through the stillness of the night, causing the Churchmen who heard it from afar to wonder at the melodious strains, the like of which they had never heard before. It was ascertained afterwards that the martyred saints had made use of the Oleynu as their dying song " (Joseph ha-Cohen in his *Vale of Tears*). These martyrs were the spiritual descendants of Rabbi Akiba—Teacher, warrior, martyr—who died with the declaration of the Unity on his lips.

not made us like the nations. Pool translates, " He has not made us heathens ". The power of a religion does not lie in what it has in common with others, but in what is peculiar to itself. There are certainly similarities between Israel's religious ideals and those of the Western peoples who have learned what is best in their religion from Israel. But it is the *differences* between them—the special emphasis and accent in the promulgation of their Message concerning the great problems and duties of life—that constitute their essential character. These differences are of such transcendent importance that millions of their followers have been, and are willing, to agonize and die for them.

supreme King of kings. lit. "the King of the kings of kings". This formula goes back to the Persian period of Jewish history in the 4th pre-Christian Century. The rulers of Persia bore the title "king of kings ".

שָׁמַיִם וַיֹּסֵד אָרֶץ · וּמוֹשַׁב יְקָרוֹ בַּשָּׁמַיִם מִמַּעַל וּשְׁכִינַת

עֻזּוֹ בְּגָבְהֵי מְרוֹמִים: הוּא אֱלֹהֵינוּ · אֵין עוֹד · אֱמֶת

מַלְכֵּנוּ · אֶפֶס זוּלָתוֹ · כַּכָּתוּב בְּתוֹרָתוֹ · וְיָדַעְתָּ הַיּוֹם

וַהֲשֵׁבֹתָ אֶל־לְבָבֶךָ כִּי יְיָ הוּא הָאֱלֹהִים בַּשָּׁמַיִם מִמַּעַל

וְעַל־הָאָרֶץ מִתָּחַת אֵין עוֹד:

עַל־כֵּן נְקַוֶּה לְךָ יְיָ אֱלֹהֵינוּ לִרְאוֹת מְהֵרָה בְּתִפְאֶרֶת

עֻזֶּךָ · לְהַעֲבִיר גִּלּוּלִים מִן הָאָרֶץ וְהָאֱלִילִים כָּרוֹת יִכָּרֵתוּן ·

לְתַקֵּן עוֹלָם בְּמַלְכוּת שַׁדַּי וְכָל־בְּנֵי בָשָׂר יִקְרְאוּ בִשְׁמֶךָ ·

לְהַפְנוֹת אֵלֶיךָ כָּל־רִשְׁעֵי אָרֶץ: יַכִּירוּ וְיֵדְעוּ כָּל־יוֹשְׁבֵי

תֵבֵל כִּי לְךָ תִּכְרַע כָּל־בֶּרֶךְ תִּשָּׁבַע כָּל־לָשׁוֹן: לְפָנֶיךָ יְיָ

אֱלֹהֵינוּ יִכְרְעוּ וְיִפֹּלוּ · וְלִכְבוֹד שִׁמְךָ יְקָר יִתֵּנוּ · וִיקַבְּלוּ

כֻלָּם אֶת־עֹל מַלְכוּתֶךָ · וְתִמְלוֹךְ עֲלֵיהֶם מְהֵרָה לְעוֹלָם

וָעֶד · כִּי הַמַּלְכוּת שֶׁלְּךָ הִיא וּלְעוֹלְמֵי עַד תִּמְלֹךְ

בְּכָבוֹד: כַּכָּתוּב בְּתוֹרָתֶךָ · יְיָ l יִמְלֹךְ לְעֹלָם וָעֶד:

וְנֶאֱמַר · וְהָיָה יְיָ לְמֶלֶךְ עַל־כָּל־הָאָרֶץ בַּיּוֹם הַהוּא יִהְיֶה

יְיָ אֶחָד וּשְׁמוֹ אֶחָד:

turn unto thyself all the evil-doers upon the earth. All men and nations
shall abandon idolatry and wickedness, falsehood and violence, and
become united in their recognition of the sovereignty of God, the Holy
One, as proclaimed by Israel. The Messianic hope is thus not to destroy
the wicked, but to win them over to God's service ; see on Psalm 104.
35. p. 588. The later Jewish Mystics dreamt of the time when Satan
himself would become a good angel.

yoke of thy kingdom. The rule of Thy Kingship.

OLEYNU   heavens and laid the foundations of the earth, the seat of whose glory is in the heavens above, and the abode of whose might is in the loftiest heights. He is our God ; there is none else : in truth he is our King ; there is none besides

Deuteronomy 4. 39   him ; as it is written in his Torah, And thou shalt know this day, and lay it to thine heart, that the Lord he is God in heaven above and upon the earth beneath : there is none else.

ISRAEL'S HOPE : HUMANITY UNITED IN RECOGNI- TION OF THE ONE GOD   We therefore hope in thee, O Lord our God, that we may speedily behold the glory of thy might, when thou wilt remove the abominations from the earth, and heathendom will be utterly destroyed, when the world will be perfected under the kingdom of the Almighty, and all the children of flesh will call upon thy Name, when thou wilt turn unto thyself all the evil-doers upon earth. Let all the inhabitants of the world perceive and know that unto thee every knee must bow, every tongue must swear allegiance. Before thee, O Lord our God, let them bow and worship ; and unto thy glorious Name let them give honour ; let them all accept the yoke of thy kingdom, and do thou reign over them speedily, and for ever and ever. For the kingdom is thine, and to all eternity thou wilt reign in glory ; as it is written

Exodus 15. 18   in thy Torah, THE LORD SHALL REIGN FOR EVER AND EVER.

Zechariah 14. 9   And it is said, AND THE LORD SHALL BE KING OVER ALL THE EARTH : IN THAT DAY SHALL THE LORD BE ONE, AND HIS NAME ONE.

---

shall the Lord be One. In the undivided and undisputed worship of all men : there will be universal recognition of His sovereignty. " As the heathens shall forsake their idols, He will be One, and no strange god with Him " (Rashi). " The Jews were the only people in their world who conceived the idea of a universal religion " (Moore).

his Name One. His manifold revelations of Himself shall be acknow- ledged by all to be merely aspects of the one sole Name by which He made Himself known unto Israel.

This is one of the fundamental verses of the Jewish conception of the Kingdom of Heaven. It is the Messianic hope of Judaism, and the spiritual goal of human history.

קַדִּישׁ יָתוֹם

Mourner. יִתְגַּדַּל וְיִתְקַדַּשׁ שְׁמֵהּ רַבָּא בְּעָלְמָא דִּי־בְרָא

כִרְעוּתֵהּ • וְיַמְלִיךְ מַלְכוּתֵהּ בְּחַיֵּיכוֹן וּבְיוֹמֵיכוֹן וּבְחַיֵּי

דִּי־כָל־בֵּית יִשְׂרָאֵל בַּעֲגָלָא וּבִזְמַן קָרִיב • וְאִמְרוּ אָמֵן :

Cong. and Mourner. יְהֵא שְׁמֵהּ רַבָּא מְבָרַךְ לְעָלַם

וּלְעָלְמֵי עָלְמַיָּא •

Mourner. יִתְבָּרַךְ וְיִשְׁתַּבַּח וְיִתְפָּאַר וְיִתְרֹמַם וְיִתְנַשֵּׂא

וְיִתְהַדָּר וְיִתְעַלֶּה וְיִתְהַלָּל שְׁמֵהּ דִּי־קֻדְשָׁא • בְּרִיךְ הוּא •

לְעֵלָּא מִן־כָּל־בִּרְכָתָא וְשִׁירָתָא תֻּשְׁבְּחָתָא וְנֶחֱמָתָא

דִּי־אֲמִירָן בְּעָלְמָא • וְאִמְרוּ אָמֵן :

Cong. יְהִי שֵׁם יְיָ מְבֹרָךְ מֵעַתָּה וְעַד עוֹלָם :

Mourner. יְהֵא שְׁלָמָא רַבָּא מִן־שְׁמַיָּא וְחַיִּים עָלֵינוּ

וְעַל־כָּל־יִשְׂרָאֵל • וְאִמְרוּ אָמֵן :

Cong. עֶזְרִי מֵעִם יְיָ עֹשֵׂה שָׁמַיִם וָאָרֶץ :

Mourner. עֹשֶׂה שָׁלוֹם בִּמְרוֹמָיו הוּא יַעֲשֶׂה שָׁלוֹם עָלֵינוּ

וְעַל־כָּל־יִשְׂרָאֵל • וְאִמְרוּ אָמֵן :

---

6 MOURNER'S KADDISH.

The Kaddish points forward to the establishment of the Messianic Kingdom of God, with its promise of Resurrection and assurance of Immortality ; see p. 254–5. Great religious significance was attached by the Rabbis to the Congregation repeating in unison the words, *Let His great Name be blessed for ever and to all eternity.* " As the assembly proclaim these words, the Holy One forgives " (Midrash). The son, reciting the Kaddish, is thus instrumental in calling forth the most important Response in the Service. For the rise and significance of this prayer, see on THE MOURNER'S KADDISH, p. 268.

Mourner's Kaddish.

MOURN-
ER'S
KADDISH

Mourner.—Magnified and sanctified be his great Name in the world which he hath created according to his will. May he establish his kingdom during your life and during your days, and during the life of all the house of Israel, even speedily and at a near time, and say ye, Amen.

Cong. and Mourner.—Let his great Name be blessed for ever and to all eternity.

Mourner.—Blessed, praised and glorified, exalted, extolled and honoured, magnified and lauded be the Name of the Holy One, blessed be he ; though he be high above all the blessings and hymns, praises and consolations, which are uttered in the world ; and say ye, Amen.

Congregation.—Amen.

Mourner.—May there be abundant peace from heaven, and life for us and for all Israel ; and say ye, Amen.

Congregation.—Amen.

Mourner.—He who maketh peace in his high places, may he make peace for us and for all Israel ; and say ye, Amen.

---

may he establish his kingdom. May He bring about the realization of all spiritual values, and transform things as they are into things as they ought to be.

let his great Name be blessed for ever and to all eternity. This is the principal response of the Kaddish (derived from Daniel 2. 20, and analogous to Psalm 113. 2, and to the Response " Blessed be His Name whose glorious Kingdom is for ever and ever "). It was deemed to be the hymn of hymns, and gained still greater hold upon the reverent affection of the people when it came to be looked upon as the Orphan's Prayer. In its original form the Kaddish is of great antiquity. It antedates the Destruction of the Temple, and is echoed in the most famous Christian prayer.

Holy One, blessed be he. The most frequent Name of God in post-Biblical Jewish literature. Holiness is the *essential* attribute of God.

consolations. The Heb. word, in addition to its general meaning of comfort in mourning and sorrow, also denotes both the praises of God in connection with the future Messianic time and the Future Life, as well as the consolatory discourses to which the Kaddish was the conclusion.

שיר הכבוד:

The Ark is opened and the following Hymn is chanted in alternate verses by the Reader and Congregation.

אַנְעִים זְמִירוֹת וְשִׁירִים אֶאֱרוֹג ּ כִּי אֵלֶיךָ נַפְשִׁי תַעֲרוֹג :

נַפְשִׁי חִמְּדָה בְּצֵל יָדֶךָ ּ לָדַעַת כָּל רָז סוֹדֶךָ :

מִדֵּי דַבְּרִי בִּכְבוֹדֶךָ ּ הוֹמֶה לִבִּי אֶל דּוֹדֶיךָ :

עַל כֵּן אֲדַבֵּר בְּךָ נִכְבָּדוֹת ּ וְשִׁמְךָ אֲכַבֵּד בְּשִׁירֵי יְדִידוֹת :

אֲסַפְּרָה כְבוֹדְךָ וְלֹא רְאִיתִיךָ ּ אֲדַמְּךָ אֲכַנְּךָ וְלֹא יְדַעְתִּיךָ :

בְּיַד נְבִיאֶיךָ בְּסוֹד עֲבָדֶיךָ ּ דִּמִּיתָ הֲדַר כְּבוֹד הוֹדֶךָ :

גְּדֻלָּתְךָ וּגְבוּרָתֶךָ ּ כִּנּוּ לְתֹקֶף פְּעֻלָּתֶךָ :

דִּמּוּ אוֹתְךָ וְלֹא כְפִי יֶשְׁךָ ּ. וַיְשַׁוּוּךָ לְפִי מַעֲשֶׂיךָ :

הִמְשִׁילוּךָ בְּרֹב חֶזְיוֹנוֹת ּ הִנְּךָ אֶחָד בְּכָל דִּמְיוֹנוֹת :

7. Supplements.

These consist of the Hymn of Glory and the Day's Psalm. They are followed by a repetition of the Mourner's Kaddish.

(a) *Hymn of Glory*. This hymn found a place in the Service against the opposition of men like Solomon Luria, Jacob Emden and the Gaon of Wilna. They deemed it too sublime for hurried daily recital, and would have had it restricted to Sabbaths and Solemn Festivals. In some communities, it is recited on the Eve of the Day of Atonement alone.

Of the author, Judah the Pious (died 1217), who was at once philosopher and poet, saint and mystic, Zunz says, " To bring to fruition whatever is noble in human endeavour, to vindicate whatever is highest in Israel's aspirations, to discover the innermost truths indicated in

HYMN OF GLORY.

The Ark is opened, and the following Hymn is chanted in alternate verses by the Reader and Congregation.

I

"HYMN OF GLORY"

Sweet hymns shall be my chant and woven songs,
For Thou art all for which my spirit longs—

To be within the shadow of Thy hand
And all thy mystery to understand.

The while Thy glory is upon my tongue,
My inmost heart with love of Thee is wrung.

So though Thy mighty marvels I proclaim,
'Tis songs of love wherewith I greet Thy Name.

II

I have not seen Thee, yet I tell Thy praise,
Nor known Thee, yet I image forth Thy ways.

For by Thy seers' and servants' mystic speech
Thou didst Thy sov'ran splendour darkly teach.

And from the grandeur of Thy work they drew
The measure of Thy inner greatness, too.

They told of Thee, but not as Thou must be,
Since from Thy work they tried to body Thee.

To countless visions did their pictures run,
Behold, through all the visions Thou art one.

Holy Scripture—this seemed to be the aim of a soul in which the poetical, the moral and the saintly were blended together ". " The *Hymn of Glory* well deserves the title. As to its poetic beauty," says Abrahams, " there can be no doubt. Its images are possibly too direct for modern tastes, as they sometimes reach the verge of anthropomorphic licence." Several of these are here omitted from I. Zangwill's stirring version of the poem. In regard to such bold metaphors applied to the Divine Being, it is well to note what a radical Bible critic remarked on their employment by the Psalmists. " So far from being a proof of barbarism, it is proof of Israel's complete emergence from barbarism. It is proof of the sense of religious security which animates the psalmists. They have no expectation of being taken literally. And how much nearer these metaphors bring God to the heart than would a mere list of Divine attributes ! Read the fine *Hymn of Glory* which closes the daily Prayer Book of the Synagogue " (Cheyne).

וַיֶּחֱזוּ בְךָ זִקְנָה וּבַחֲרוּת · וּשְׂעַר רֹאשְׁךָ בְּשֵׂיבָה וְשַׁחֲרוּת :

זִקְנָה בְּיוֹם דִּין וּבַחֲרוּת בְּיוֹם קְרָב · כְּאִישׁ מִלְחָמוֹת יָדָיו

רָב :

חָבַשׁ כּוֹבַע יְשׁוּעָה בְּרֹאשׁוֹ · הוֹשִׁיעָה לּוֹ יְמִינוֹ וּזְרוֹעַ קָדְשׁוֹ :

טַלְלֵי אוֹרוֹת רֹאשׁוֹ נִמְלָא · וּקְוֻצּוֹתָיו רְסִיסֵי לָיְלָה :

יִתְפָּאַר בִּי כִּי חָפֵץ בִּי · וְהוּא יִהְיֶה־לִּי לַעֲטֶרֶת צְבִי :

כֶּתֶם טָהוֹר פָּז דְּמוּת רֹאשׁוֹ · וְחָק עַל מֵצַח כְּבוֹד שֵׁם קָדְשׁוֹ :

לְחֵן וּלְכָבוֹד צְבִי תִפְאָרָה · אֻמָּתוֹ לוֹ עִטְּרָה עֲטָרָה :

מַחְלְפוֹת רֹאשׁוֹ כְּבִימֵי בַחֲרוּת · קְוֻצּוֹתָיו תַּלְתַּלִּים שְׁחֹרוֹת :

נְוֵה הַצֶּדֶק צְבִי תִפְאַרְתּוֹ · יַעֲלֶה־נָּא עַל רֹאשׁ שִׂמְחָתוֹ :

סְגֻלָּתוֹ תְּהִי בְיָדוֹ עֲטֶרֶת · וּצְנִיף מְלוּכָה צְבִי תִפְאֶרֶת :

עֲמוּסִים נְשָׂאָם עֲטֶרֶת עִנְּדָם · מֵאֲשֶׁר יָקְרוּ בְעֵינָיו כִּבְּדָם :

פְּאֵרוֹ עָלַי וּפְאֵרִי עָלָיו · וְקָרוֹב אֵלַי בְּקָרְאִי אֵלָיו :

צַח וְאָדוֹם לִלְבוּשׁוֹ אָדֹם · פּוּרָה בְדָרְכוֹ בְּבוֹאוֹ מֵאֱדוֹם :

* קֶשֶׁר תְּפִלִּין הֶרְאָה לֶעָנָו · תְּמוּנַת יְיָ לְנֶגֶד עֵינָיו :

רוֹצֶה בְעַמּוֹ עֲנָוִים יְפָאֵר · יוֹשֵׁב תְּהִלּוֹת בָּם לְהִתְפָּאֵר :

רֹאשׁ דְּבָרְךָ אֱמֶת · קוֹרֵא מֵרֹאשׁ דּוֹר וָדוֹר עַם דּוֹרֶשְׁךָ דְּרוֹשׁ :

שִׁית הֲמוֹן שִׁירַי נָא עָלֶיךָ · וְרִנָּתִי תִּקְרַב אֵלֶיךָ :

תְּהִלָּתִי תְּהִי לְרֹאשְׁךָ עֲטֶרֶת · וּתְפִלָּתִי תִּכּוֹן קְטֹרֶת :

---

* The Midrashic interpretation of וְרָאִיתָ אֶת אֲחֹרָי, Exod. xxxiv. 23.

III

In Thee old age and youth at once were drawn,*
The grey of eld, the flowing locks of dawn,

The ancient Judge, the youthful Warrior,
The Man of Battles, terrible in war,

The helmet of salvation on His head,
And by His hand and arm the triumph led.

I glorify Him, for He joys in me,
My crown of beauty He shall ever be !

And be His treasured people in His hand
A diadem His kingly brow to band.

By Him they were uplifted, carried, crowned,
Thus honoured inasmuch as precious found.

IV

His glory is on me, and mine on Him,
And when I call He is not far or dim.

Phylacteried the vision Moses viewed
The day he gazed on God's similitude.

He loves His folk ; the meek will glorify,
And, shrined in prayer, draw their rapt reply.

V

Truth is Thy primal word ; at Thy behest
The generations pass—O aid our quest

For Thee, and set my host of songs on high,
And let my psalmody come very nigh.

My praises as a coronal account,
And let my prayer as Thine incense mount.

Deem precious unto Thee the poor man's song,
As those that to Thine altar did belong.

Rise, O my blessing, to the lord of birth,
The breeding, quickening, righteous force of earth.

---

*In regard to these and the following expressions, compare Daniel 7. 9 ; Exod. 15. 3 ; Song of Solomon 5. 2, 14 ; Isaiah 59. 17 ; Psalm 98. 1 (Singer).

תִּיקַר שִׁירַת־רָשׁ בְּעֵינֶיךָ ־ כְּשִׁיר יוֹשֵׁר עַל קָרְבְּנֶיךָ :
בִּרְכָתִי תַעֲלֶה לְרֹאשׁ מַשְׁבִּיר ־ מְחוֹלֵל, וּמוֹלִיד צַדִּיק כַּבִּיר :
וּבְבִרְכָתִי תְנַעֲנֵעַ לִי רֹאשׁ ־ וְאוֹתָהּ קַח לְךָ כִּבְשָׂמִים רֹאשׁ :
יֶעֱרַב־נָא שִׂיחִי עָלֶיךָ ־ כִּי נַפְשִׁי תַעֲרוֹג אֵלֶיךָ :

Reader and Congregation :—

לְךָ יְיָ הַגְּדֻלָּה וְהַגְּבוּרָה וְהַתִּפְאֶרֶת וְהַנֵּצַח וְהַהוֹד ־
כִּי־כֹל בַּשָּׁמַיִם וּבָאָרֶץ לְךָ יְיָ הַמַּמְלָכָה וְהַמִּתְנַשֵּׂא לְכֹל
לְרֹאשׁ : מִי יְמַלֵּל גְּבוּרוֹת יְיָ יַשְׁמִיעַ כָּל־תְּהִלָּתוֹ :

קַדִּישׁ יָתוֹם, *p.*212.

Psalm for the First Day of the Week.

הַיּוֹם יוֹם רִאשׁוֹן בְּשַׁבָּת שֶׁבּוֹ הַלְוִיִּם הָיוּ אוֹמְרִים בַּמִּקְדָּשׁ :
תהלים כ׳ד

לְדָוִד מִזְמוֹר ־ לַיהוָֹה הָאָרֶץ וּמְלוֹאָהּ תֵּבֵל וְיֹשְׁבֵי בָהּ :
כִּי הוּא עַל־יַמִּים יְסָדָהּ וְעַל־נְהָרוֹת יְכוֹנְנֶהָ : מִי־יַעֲלֶה
בְהַר יְהוָֹה וּמִי־יָקוּם בִּמְקוֹם קָדְשׁוֹ : נְקִי כַפַּיִם וּבַר לֵבָב
אֲשֶׁר לֹא־נָשָׂא לַשָּׁוְא נַפְשׁוֹ וְלֹא נִשְׁבַּע לְמִרְמָה : יִשָּׂא
בְרָכָה מֵאֵת יְהוָֹה וּצְדָקָה מֵאֱלֹהֵי יִשְׁעוֹ : זֶה דּוֹר דֹּרְשָׁו
מְבַקְשֵׁי פָנֶיךָ יַעֲקֹב סֶלָה : שְׂאוּ שְׁעָרִים רָאשֵׁיכֶם וְהִנָּשְׂאוּ

(b) *The Day's Psalm.* The custom of reciting a special psalm for
each day of the week was taken over from the Temple. These psalms
have their message for men and women of to-day. Sunday's psalm
(24) asks, " Who can stand on God's holy hill ? " The answer is,
" He that is clean of hand and pure of heart ". Monday's (Psalm 48)
declares, " As is Thy Name, O God, so is Thy renown unto the ends of

Do Thou receive it with acceptant nod,
My choicest incense offered to my God.

And let my meditation grateful be,
For all my being is athirst for Thee.

*1 Chronicles
29. 11*

Reader and Cong.—Thine, O Lord, is the greatness, and the power, and the glory, and the victory, and the majesty : for all that is in the heaven and in the earth is thine ; thine, O Lord, is the kingdom, and the supremacy as head over

Psalm 106. 2 all. Who can utter the mighty acts of the Lord, or shew forth all his praise ?

The Mourner's Kaddish, p. 213.

Psalm for the First Day of the Week.

THE
DAY'S
PSALM

This is the first day of the Week, on which the Levites in the Temple used to say :—

Psalm xxiv. ¹A Psalm of David.

*THE TRUE
WORSHIP-
PER*

The earth is the Lord's, and the fulness thereof ; the world, and they that dwell therein. ²For it is he that hath founded it upon the seas, and established it upon the floods. ³Who may ascend the mountain of the Lord ? And who may stand in his holy place ? ⁴He that hath clean hands and a pure heart ; who hath not set his desire upon vanity, and hath not sworn deceitfully. ⁵He shall receive a blessing from the Lord, and righteousness from the God of his salvation. ⁶Such is the generation of them that seek after him, that seek thy face, (O God of) Jacob ! (Selah.) ⁷Lift

the earth : Thy might is full of righteousness ". Tuesday's (Psalm 82) demands : " Defend the poor and the fatherless ; do justice to the afflicted and the destitute ". Wednesday's (Psalm 94) asks those who doubt the moral government of the world, " He that planted the ear, shall He not hear ? He that formed the eye, shall He not see ? " Thursday's (Psalm 81) expresses the hope, " O that my people would hearken unto Me ! " Friday's (Psalm 93) proclaims that, though the heaving waves of heathendom lash themselves against the rock of God's Throne, that Throne stands eternally unmoved.

FOR SUNDAY : PSALM 24.

When David conquered Jerusalem, he made it the home for the Ark of the Covenant (II Samuel 6. 17). This psalm reflects the joy and enthusiasm that attended the removal of the Ark to Mt. Zion.

פִּתְחֵי עוֹלָם וְיָבוֹא מֶלֶךְ הַכָּבוֹד : מִי זֶה מֶלֶךְ הַכָּבוֹד יְהֹוָה

עִזּוּז וְגִבּוֹר יְהֹוָה גִּבּוֹר מִלְחָמָה : שְׂאוּ שְׁעָרִים רָאשֵׁיכֶם

וּשְׂאוּ פִּתְחֵי עוֹלָם וְיָבֹא מֶלֶךְ הַכָּבוֹד : מִי הוּא זֶה מֶלֶךְ

הַכָּבוֹד יְהֹוָה צְבָאוֹת הוּא מֶלֶךְ הַכָּבוֹד סֶלָה :

Psalm for the Second Day of the Week.

הַיּוֹם יוֹם שֵׁנִי בְּשַׁבָּת שֶׁבּוֹ הַלְוִיִּם הָיוּ אוֹמְרִים בַּמִּקְדָּשׁ :

תהלים מ׳ח

שִׁיר מִזְמוֹר לִבְנֵי־קֹרַח : גָּדוֹל יְהֹוָה וּמְהֻלָּל מְאֹד

בְּעִיר אֱלֹהֵינוּ הַר־קָדְשׁוֹ : יְפֵה נוֹף מְשׂוֹשׂ כָּל־הָאָרֶץ

הַר־צִיּוֹן יַרְכְּתֵי צָפוֹן קִרְיַת מֶלֶךְ רָב : אֱלֹהִים בְּאַרְמְנוֹתֶיהָ

נוֹדַע לְמִשְׂגָּב : כִּי־הִנֵּה הַמְּלָכִים נוֹעֲדוּ עָבְרוּ יַחְדָּו : הֵמָּה

רָאוּ כֵּן תָּמָהוּ נִבְהֲלוּ נֶחְפָּזוּ : רְעָדָה אֲחָזָתַם שָׁם חִיל

כַּיּוֹלֵדָה : בְּרוּחַ קָדִים תְּשַׁבֵּר אֳנִיּוֹת תַּרְשִׁישׁ : כַּאֲשֶׁר

שָׁמַעְנוּ כֵּן רָאִינוּ בְּעִיר יְהֹוָה־צְבָאוֹת בְּעִיר אֱלֹהֵינוּ

1. *the earth is the Lord's.* This and the following verse were sung as the procession was winding up the hill towards the ancient fortress of Zion.

2. *founded it upon the seas.* See Genesis 1. 9.

3. *who may ascend.* Who is worthy to join the procession of worshippers ? Who is worthy to worship on God's holy hill ?

4. *clean hands.* See Psalm 15. The requirements are purely ethical and spiritual The true worshipper is a man of sinless hands, unsoiled by acts of violence or dishonesty.

pure heart. A pure conscience. His desires and motives are free from anything mean, hateful or defiling.

not set up his desire upon vanity. He does not direct his desires to

THE
DAY'S
PSALM

*TRI-
UMPHAL
ENTRY
INTO
SANCTU-
ARY*

*JERU-
SALEM
THE
BEAUTI-
FUL*

up your heads, O ye gates ; and be ye lifted up, ye ever-lasting doors, that the King of glory may come in. ⁸Who is the King of glory ? The Lord strong and mighty, the Lord mighty in battle. ⁹Lift up your heads, O ye gates ; yea, lift them up, ye everlasting doors, that the King of glory may come in. ¹⁰Who, then, is the King of glory ? The Lord of hosts, he is the King of glory. (Selah.)

Psalm for the Second Day of the Week.

This is the Second Day of the Week, on which the Levites in the Temple used to say :—

Psalm xlviii. ¹A Song ; a Psalm of the Sons of Korah.

²Great is the Lord, and highly to be praised, in the city of our God, in his holy mountain. ³Beautiful in elevation, the joy of the whole earth is mount Zion,—at the sides of the north, the city of the great king. ⁴God hath made himself known in her palaces as a stronghold. ⁵For, lo, the kings assembled, they passed on together. ⁶They saw it ; then were they amazed ; they were confounded, they hasted away. ⁷Trembling took hold of them there ; pangs as of a woman in travail. ⁸With the east wind thou breakest the ships of Tarshish. ⁹As we have heard, so have

falsehood, and strive after empty and frivolous things. The text *as read* (Keri) " has not taken My soul unto vanity " ; which means, has not sworn falsely.

5. *righteousness.* The reward which God in His righteousness gives to those who deserve a reward.

7. *lift up your heads.* The hoary gates of the old fortress are repre-sented as unwilling to receive the Ark ; or, as too low and mean for the entrance of the Ark, " which is called by the Name, even the Name of the Lord of hosts " (II Sam. 6. 2). Now that the procession has reached the barred gates of the citadel, a voice summons them to open.

everlasting doors. lit. " ancient doors ", whose story stretches into the past.

8. *who is.* The warders at the gates ask, or perhaps the poet conceives the gates themselves to ask, who it is that thus demands entrance.

10. *Lord of hosts.* The choir in the procession responds that He claims to enter not only as a victorious warrior, but as the King of the Universe.

אֱלֹהִים יְכוֹנְנֶהָ עַד־עוֹלָם סֶלָה: דִּמִּינוּ אֱלֹהִים חַסְדֶּךָ
בְּקֶרֶב הֵיכָלֶךָ: כְּשִׁמְךָ אֱלֹהִים כֵּן תְּהִלָּתְךָ עַל קַצְוֵי־אֶרֶץ
צֶדֶק מָלְאָה יְמִינֶךָ: יִשְׂמַח הַר־צִיּוֹן תָּגֵלְנָה בְּנוֹת יְהוּדָה
לְמַעַן מִשְׁפָּטֶיךָ: סֹבּוּ צִיּוֹן וְהַקִּיפוּהָ סִפְרוּ מִגְדָּלֶיהָ:
שִׁיתוּ לִבְּכֶם לְחֵילָה פַּסְּגוּ אַרְמְנוֹתֶיהָ לְמַעַן תְּסַפְּרוּ
לְדוֹר אַחֲרוֹן: כִּי זֶה ׀ אֱלֹהִים אֱלֹהֵינוּ עוֹלָם וָעֶד הוּא
יְנַהֲגֵנוּ עַל־מוּת:

Psalm for the Third Day of the Week.

הַיּוֹם יוֹם שְׁלִישִׁי בְּשַׁבָּת שֶׁבּוֹ הַלְוִיִּם הָיוּ אוֹמְרִים בַּמִּקְדָּשׁ:
תהלים פ״ב

מִזְמוֹר לְאָסָף אֱלֹהִים נִצָּב בַּעֲדַת־אֵל בְּקֶרֶב אֱלֹהִים
יִשְׁפֹּט: עַד מָתַי תִּשְׁפְּטוּ־עָוֶל וּפְנֵי רְשָׁעִים תִּשְׂאוּ־סֶלָה:
שִׁפְטוּ־דָל וְיָתוֹם עָנִי וָרָשׁ הַצְדִּיקוּ: פַּלְּטוּ־דַל וְאֶבְיוֹן

FOR MONDAY: PSALM 48.

Celebrates Zion's marvellous deliverance from the hosts of the Assyrian conqueror in the year 700 B.C.E.; see Isaiah 37.

3. *beautiful in elevation.* "It must always have presented the appearance beyond any other capital of the then known world of a mountain city, breathing, as compared with the sultry plains of the Jordan, a mountain air; enthroned, as compared with Jericho or Damascus, Gaza or Tyre, on a mountain fastness" (Stanley).

at the sides of the north. Describes the situation of Mt. Zion to the north.

5. *the kings.* The Assyrian vassal-princes.

6. *they saw it.* Its beauty was paralyzing, and a nameless terror came over them.

8. *ships of Tarshish.* Tarshish was in Spain, and ships of special build were required for making that long journey. (Some maintain that this psalm was called forth by an invasion by sea: the ships of Tarshish were broken, and the would-be invaders never reached Jerusalem.)

9. *as we have heard.* This verse was sung by the choir on behalf of the people. Israel's past lives again in their own history.

THE DAY'S PSALM

we seen in the city of the Lord of hosts, in the city of our God : God will establish it for ever. (Selah.) ¹⁰We have thought on thy lovingkindness, O God, in the midst of thy temple. ¹¹As is thy Name, O God, so is thy renown unto the ends of the earth : thy might is full of righteousness. ¹²Let Mount Zion rejoice, let the daughter cities of Judah be glad, because of thy judgments. ¹³Walk about Zion, and go round about her : count the towers thereof. ¹⁴Mark ye well her ramparts, traverse her palaces ; that ye may tell a later generation, ¹⁵that this God is our God for ever and ever : he will guide us eternally.

Psalm for the Third Day of the Week.

This is the Third Day of the Week, on which the Levites in the Temple used to say :—

Psalm lxxxii. ¹A Psalm of Asaph.

GOD THE JUDGE OF JUDGES

God standeth in the congregation of the mighty ; he judgeth among the judges. ²How long will ye judge unjustly, and respect the persons of the wicked ? (Selah.) ³Defend the lowly and fatherless : do justice to the afflicted

---

will establish it forever. Jerusalem has been preserved and shall be preserved. Jerusalem, the hearth of pure religion, the home of prophecy, the sacred fountain of the word of God, has remained the very emblem of the deathlessness of the spirit. A score of conquerors have held it as their choicest prize ; and more than a dozen times has it been utterly destroyed. The Babylonians burnt it, and deported its population ; the Romans slew a million of its inhabitants, razed it to the ground, passed the ploughshare over it, and strewed its furrows with salt ; Hadrian banished its very name from the lips of men, changed it to "Aelia Capitolina ", and prohibited any Jew from entering its precincts on pain of death. Persians and Arabs, Barbarians and Crusaders and Turks, took it and retook it, ravaged it and burnt it ; and yet, marvellous to relate, it ever rises from its ashes to renewed life and glory. It is the Eternal City of the Eternal People.

10–14. *The lessons of the deliverance.*
11. *thy might.* lit. " thy right hand."
righteousness. Righteous or saving deeds ; hence, victory.
12. *judgments.* As executed on the enemy.
14. *mark ye well.* Convince yourselves that, through the mercy of God, they remained untouched.
15. *eternally.* lit. " even unto death ". The words may also mean *youthfulness* : " the blessed life beyond death is the life of immortality, the life of eternal youth " (Delitzsch).

מִיַּד רְשָׁעִים הַצִּילוּ : לֹא יָדְעוּ׳ וְלֹא יָבִינוּ בַּחֲשֵׁכָה

יִתְהַלָּכוּ יִמּוֹטוּ כָּל־מוֹסְדֵי אָרֶץ : אֲנִי אָמַרְתִּי אֱלֹהִים

אַתֶּם וּבְנֵי עֶלְיוֹן כֻּלְּכֶם : אָכֵן כְּאָדָם תְּמוּתוּן וּכְאַחַד

הַשָּׂרִים תִּפֹּלוּ : קוּמָה אֱלֹהִים שָׁפְטָה הָאָרֶץ כִּי־אַתָּה

תִנְחַל בְּכָל־הַגּוֹיִם :

Psalm for the Fourth Day of the Week.

הַיּוֹם יוֹם רְבִיעִי בְּשַׁבָּת שֶׁבּוֹ הַלְוִיִּם הָיוּ אוֹמְרִים בַּמִּקְדָּשׁ :

תהלים צ״ד

אֵל־נְקָמוֹת יְהֹוָה אֵל נְקָמוֹת הוֹפִיעַ : הִנָּשֵׂא שֹׁפֵט

הָאָרֶץ הָשֵׁב גְּמוּל עַל־גֵּאִים : עַד־מָתַי רְשָׁעִים׳ יְהֹוָה עַד־

מָתַי רְשָׁעִים יַעֲלֹזוּ : יַבִּיעוּ יְדַבְּרוּ עָתָק יִתְאַמְּרוּ כָּל־פֹּעֲלֵי

אָוֶן : עַמְּךָ יְהֹוָה יְדַכְּאוּ וְנַחֲלָתְךָ יְעַנּוּ : אַלְמָנָה וְגֵר יַהֲרֹגוּ

וִיתוֹמִים יְרַצֵּחוּ : .וַיֹּאמְרוּ לֹא יִרְאֶה־יָּהּ וְלֹא יָבִין אֱלֹהֵי

יַעֲקֹב : בִּינוּ בֹּעֲרִים בָּעָם וּכְסִילִים מָתַי תַּשְׂכִּילוּ : הֲנֹטַע

For Tuesday : Psalm 82.

Oppression is rife, and the depressed classes can get no justice.

1. *standeth.* The psalmist represents God as taking His stand among the arraigned judges whom He had summoned for trial.

judges. Hebrew, " elohim " ; see on *v.* 6.

2. *respect the persons.* Show partiality to the powerful oppressor.

5. *they know not.* They are unheeding and unwilling to ascertain the truth so as to render right judgment.

are moved. With such " judges of Sodom," the very foundations of society are shaken.

6. *I said.* To myself ; I thought, says the psalmist.

godlike beings Because pronouncing sentence in the name of God, immemorial usage called them " gods " (elohim) ; Exodus 21. 6.

8. *thy possession.* As the nations are God's possession, the psalmist closes with the appeal to Him to take the government of the whole earth into His own hands.

THE
DAY'S
PSALM

and destitute. ⁴Rescue the lowly and needy: deliver them out of the hand of the wicked. ⁵They know not, neither do they understand; they walk about in darkness: all the foundations of the earth are moved. ⁶I said, Ye are godlike beings, and all of you sons of the Most High. ⁷Nevertheless ye shall die like men, and fall as one man, O princes. ⁸Arise O God, judge the earth: for all the nations are thy possession.

Psalm for the Fourth Day of the Week.

This is the Fourth Day of the Week, on which the Levites in the Temple used to say :—

Psalm xciv.

CRY FOR
RETRIBU-
TION

¹O Lord, thou God to whom retribution belongeth, thou God to whom retribution belongeth, shine forth. ²Lift up thyself, thou Judge of the earth : render to the proud their desert. ³Lord, how long shall the wicked, how long shall the wicked triumph ? ⁴They prate, they speak arrogantly : all the workers of iniquity are boastful. ⁵They crush thy people, O Lord, and afflict thine heritage. ⁶They slay the widow and the stranger, and murder the fatherless. ⁷And they say, The Lord will not see, neither will the God of Jacob give

FOR WEDNESDAY : PSALM 94.

1–7. Prophet-like, the psalmist cries out to God to put an end to the cruel violence against the weak.

1. *to whom retribution belongeth.* The repetitions show the intense feeling of the psalmist at the legalized iniquity he is witnessing. He calls on God to punish evil, and vindicate the right. The moment we recognize righteousness to be an essential quality of the Divine Nature, it is impossible to overlook the *penal* activity of the Divine government. A righteous God cannot condone sin, crime and inhumanity. When the righteous were oppressed and the wicked triumphant, the psalmists deemed it not only allowable, but their sacred duty, to pray for the destruction of insolent rulers who poisoned the fountains of justice, and crushed the poor, the widow and the orphan.

shine forth. Reveal Thyself as the Ruler of human affairs.

2. *lift up thyself.* In judicial majesty.

4. *are boastful.* Or, " bear themselves loftily ".

5. *crush.* By extortionate and violent dealings.

heritage. Israel.

6. *widow, stranger, fatherless.* Those who cannot defend themselves are especially the victims of their callous cruelty.

אֲזֶן הֲלֹא יִשְׁמָע אִם־יֹצֵר עַיִן הֲלֹא יַבִּיט : הֲיֹסֵר גּוֹיִם הֲלֹא

יוֹכִיחַ הַמְלַמֵּד אָדָם דָּעַת : יְהוָה יֹדֵעַ מַחְשְׁבוֹת אָדָם כִּי

הֵמָּה הָבֶל : אַשְׁרֵי הַגֶּבֶר אֲשֶׁר־תְּיַסְּרֶנּוּ יָּהּ וּמִתּוֹרָתְךָ

תְלַמְּדֶנּוּ : לְהַשְׁקִיט לוֹ מִימֵי רָע עַד יִכָּרֶה לָרָשָׁע שָׁחַת :

כִּי לֹא־יִטֹּשׁ יְהוָה עַמּוֹ וְנַחֲלָתוֹ לֹא יַעֲזֹב : כִּי־עַד־צֶדֶק

יָשׁוּב מִשְׁפָּט וְאַחֲרָיו כָּל־יִשְׁרֵי־לֵב : מִי־יָקוּם לִי עִם־

מְרֵעִים מִי־יִתְיַצֵּב לִי עִם־פֹּעֲלֵי אָוֶן : לוּלֵי יְהוָה עֶזְרָתָה

לִּי כִּמְעַט שָׁכְנָה דוּמָה נַפְשִׁי : אִם־אָמַרְתִּי מָטָה רַגְלִי

חַסְדְּךָ יְהוָה יִסְעָדֵנִי : בְּרֹב שַׂרְעַפַּי בְּקִרְבִּי תַּנְחוּמֶיךָ

יְשַׁעַשְׁעוּ נַפְשִׁי : הַיְחָבְרְךָ כִּסֵּא הַוּוֹת יֹצֵר עָמָל עֲלֵי־

חֹק : יָגוֹדּוּ עַל־נֶפֶשׁ צַדִּיק וְדָם נָקִי יַרְשִׁיעוּ : וַיְהִי יְהוָה

לִי לְמִשְׂגָּב וֵאלֹהַי לְצוּר מַחְסִי : וַיָּשֶׁב עֲלֵיהֶם ׀ אֶת־

אוֹנָם וּבְרָעָתָם יַצְמִיתֵם יַצְמִיתֵם יְהוָה אֱלֹהֵינוּ :

לְכוּ נְרַנְּנָה לַיהוָה נָרִיעָה לְצוּר יִשְׁעֵנוּ :

8-11. The psalmist rebukes the atheism of the oppressors, and refutes their delusion of impunity.

8. " Consider ye, that act as brutes among the people ; and, ye dullards, when will ye get to understand ? "

9. The Maker of men's eyes cannot be blind! The English philosopher John Stuart Mill said, that this verse contained the strongest argument for the existence of God.

10. He who guides men and nations, shall He not hold judgment ? There is a divine education of the nations. Thinkers like Herder and Leibniz recognized the importance of *v.* 8–10 for the history of the philosophy of religion.

11. *thoughts. i.e.* the delusion that they can.sin on with impunity. *that they.* The thoughts.

12-15. The sufferings of the righteous are only for a time, and .are educational in purpose. Happy is the man who endures patiently until

THE
DAY'S
PSALM

heed. ⁸Give heed, ye brutish among the people : and ye fools, when will ye be wise ? ⁹He that planted the ear, shall he not hear ? He that formed the eye, shall he not see ? ¹⁰He that instructeth the nations, shall not he correct, even he that teacheth man knowledge ? ¹¹The Lord knoweth the thoughts of men, that they are vanity. ¹²Happy is the man whom thou chastenest, O Lord, and teachest out of thy Torah ; ¹³that thou mayest give him rest from the days

CONFID-
ENCE
IN GOD'S
JUSTICE

of evil, until the pit be digged for the wicked. ¹⁴For the Lord will not cast off his people, neither will he forsake his inheritance. ¹⁵For right shall return unto justice : and all the upright in heart shall follow it. ¹⁶Who will rise up for me against the evil-doers, who will stand up for me against the workers of iniquity ? ¹⁷Unless the Lord had been my help, my soul had soon dwelt in silence. ¹⁸When I say, My foot slippeth, thy lovingkindness, O Lord, holdeth me up. ¹⁹In the multitude of my thoughts within me, thy consolations delight my soul. ²⁰Shall the tribunal of wickedness have fellowship with thee, which frameth mischief by statute ? ²¹They gather themselves together against the soul of the righteous, and condemn the innocent blood. ²²But the Lord is become my stronghold ; and my God the rock of my refuge. ²³And he bringeth back upon them their own iniquity, and in their own evil shall cut them off ; the Lord our God shall cut them off.

Psalm 95. 1

O come, let us sing unto the Lord : let us shout for joy to the Rock of our salvation.

Right once more triumphs.
12. *chasteneth.* Instructest through suffering. Life is conceived as a discipline.
16–19. Experience of the Psalmist : human aid failed, but God's help was his salvation.
17. *silence.* The Land of silence.
19. *thoughts.* Distracting thoughts.
20–23. The end of unjust judges. God cannot be the ally of in-justice, but will defend His people.
21. *condemn the innocent blood.* Condemn the innocent to death.
22. *upon them.* Their wrong-doing recoils on their own heads.

Psalm for the Fifth Day of the Week.

הַיּוֹם יוֹם חֲמִישִׁי בְּשַׁבָּת שֶׁבּוֹ הַלְוִיִּם הָיוּ אוֹמְרִים בַּמִּקְדָּשׁ :

תהלים פ״א

לַמְנַצֵּחַ עַל־הַגִּתִּית לְאָסָף : הַרְנִינוּ לֵאלֹהִים עוּזֵּנוּ
הָרִיעוּ לֵאלֹהֵי יַעֲקֹב : שְׂאוּ־זִמְרָה וּתְנוּ־תֹף כִּנּוֹר נָעִים
עִם־נָבֶל : תִּקְעוּ בַחֹדֶשׁ שׁוֹפָר בַּכֶּסֶה לְיוֹם חַגֵּנוּ : כִּי חֹק
לְיִשְׂרָאֵל הוּא מִשְׁפָּט לֵאלֹהֵי יַעֲקֹב : עֵדוּת בִּיהוֹסֵף
שָׂמוֹ בְּצֵאתוֹ עַל־אֶרֶץ מִצְרָיִם שְׂפַת לֹא־יָדַעְתִּי אֶשְׁמָע :
הֲסִירוֹתִי מִסֵּבֶל שִׁכְמוֹ כַּפָּיו מִדּוּד תַּעֲבֹרְנָה : בַּצָּרָה
קָרָאתָ וָאֲחַלְּצֶךָּ אֶעֶנְךָ בְּסֵתֶר רָעַם אֶבְחָנְךָ עַל־מֵי
מְרִיבָה סֶלָה : שְׁמַע עַמִּי וְאָעִידָה בָּךְ יִשְׂרָאֵל אִם־
תִּשְׁמַע־לִי : לֹא־יִהְיֶה בְךָ אֵל זָר וְלֹא תִשְׁתַּחֲוֶה לְאֵל
נֵכָר : אָנֹכִי ׀ יְהֹוָה אֱלֹהֶיךָ הַמַּעַלְךָ מֵאֶרֶץ מִצְרָיִם הַרְחֶב־
פִּיךָ וַאֲמַלְאֵהוּ : וְלֹא־שָׁמַע עַמִּי לְקוֹלִי וְיִשְׂרָאֵל לֹא־אָבָה
לִי : וָאֲשַׁלְּחֵהוּ בִּשְׁרִירוּת לִבָּם יֵלְכוּ בְּמוֹעֲצוֹתֵיהֶם : לוּ

FOR THURSDAY : PSALM 81.

A call to a festal assembly. Jewish Tradition associates the psalm
with the New Year, and *v.* 4 (" Blow the *shofar* on the New Moon, in the
time appointed for our day of festival ") together with *v.* 5 appear in
the Liturgy for that occasion. Its burden is : unwavering fidelity and
consecration to the One God as the indispensable condition of prosperity.

1–5. Summons to keep the Festival.

4. *the new moon.* Of Tishri.

in the time appointed. This is Rashi's rendering, followed by the
Authorized Version.

6–8. God's salvation in Egypt and Sinai.

Psalm for the Fifth Day of the Week.

THE DAY'S PSALM

This is the Fifth Day of the Week, on which the Levites in the Temple used to say :—

Psalm lxxxi.

[1]To the Chief Musician.   Set to the Gittith.   A Psalm of Asaph.

WARNING AGAINST DISOBEDI-ENCE

[2]Sing aloud unto God our strength : shout for joy unto the God of Jacob. [3]Raise the song, and strike the timbrel, the pleasant lyre with the harp. [4]Blow the horn on the new moon, in the time appointed, for our day of festival. [5]For it is a statute for Israel, a decree of the God of Jacob. [6]He appointed it in Joseph for a testimony, when he went forth over the land of Egypt : where I heard the speech of one that I knew not. [7]I removed his shoulder from the burden : his hands were freed from the basket. [8]Thou callest in trouble and I delivered thee ; I answered thee in the secret place of thunder, I proved thee at the waters of Meribah. (Selah.) [9]Hear, O my people, and I will testify against thee : O Israel, if thou wilt hearken unto me. [10]There shall be no strange god in thee ; neither shalt thou worship any foreign god. [11]I am the Lord thy God, who brought thee out of the land of Egypt : open wide thy mouth, and I will fill it. [12]But my people hearkened not to my voice ; and Israel was not willing towards me. [13]So I let them go in the

6. *Joseph.*   Poetic name for " Israel ".

testimony.   Solemn admonition.

speech . . . I knew not. When God revealed Himself to the children of Israel in Egypt, He was largely unknown to them. Israel began to hear God speaking in the wondrous Deliverance from Egypt and the Revelation at Sinai.

7. *basket.* For carrying clay or bricks. These baskets were suspended from each end of a yoke laid across the shoulders.

8. *secret place of thunder.* A reference to the storm at Sinai, when the Torah was given.

Meribah. When Israel's faith in God and obedience to Him were tested ; Exodus 17. 7.

9-11. Israel in the Wilderness is addressed, but Israel of every age is included.

עַמִּי שְׁמַע לִי יִשְׂרָאֵל בִּדְרָכַי יְהַלֵּכוּ : כִּמְעַט אוֹיְבֵיהֶם
אַכְנִיעַ וְעַל־צָרֵיהֶם אָשִׁיב יָדִי : מְשַׂנְאֵי יְהֹוָה יְכַחֲשׁוּ־לוֹ
וִיהִי עִתָּם לְעוֹלָם : וַיַּאֲכִילֵהוּ מֵחֵלֶב חִטָּה וּמִצּוּר דְּבַשׁ
אַשְׂבִּיעֶךָ :

Psalm for the Sixth Day of the Week.

הַיּוֹם יוֹם שִׁשִּׁי בְּשַׁבָּת שֶׁבּוֹ הַלְוִיִּם הָיוּ אוֹמְרִים בַּמִּקְדָּשׁ :

(*See* תהלים צ'ג, *p.*362)

On the days when תַּחֲנוּן (*p.*180 *to p.*186) *is said, the following is added after the Psalm of the Day :—*

תהלים פ'ג

שִׁיר מִזְמוֹר לְאָסָף : אֱלֹהִים אַל־דֳּמִי־לָךְ אַל־תֶּחֱרַשׁ
וְאַל־תִּשְׁקֹט אֵל : כִּי־הִנֵּה אוֹיְבֶיךָ יֶהֱמָיוּן וּמְשַׂנְאֶיךָ נָשְׂאוּ
רֹאשׁ : עַל־עַמְּךָ יַעֲרִימוּ סוֹד וְיִתְיָעֲצוּ עַל־צְפוּנֶיךָ : אָמְרוּ
לְכוּ וְנַכְחִידֵם מִגּוֹי וְלֹא־יִזָּכֵר שֵׁם־יִשְׂרָאֵל עוֹד : כִּי נוֹעֲצוּ
לֵב יַחְדָּו עָלֶיךָ בְּרִית יִכְרֹתוּ : אָהֳלֵי אֱדוֹם וְיִשְׁמְעֵאלִים
מוֹאָב וְהַגְרִים : גְּבָל וְעַמּוֹן וַעֲמָלֵק פְּלֶשֶׁת עִם־יֹשְׁבֵי צוֹר :

13–16. God's mercy is inexhaustible.
13. *stubbornness.* "God punishes men by leaving them to their own self-willed courses of action, which prove their ruin " (Kirkpatrick).
16. *their time.* Israel's time of prosperity.

THE
DAY'S
PSALM

stubbornness of their heart, that they might walk in their own counsels. ¹⁴O that my people would hearken unto me, that Israel would walk in my ways. ¹⁵I would soon subdue their enemies, and turn my hand against their adversaries. ¹⁶The haters of the Lord should submit themselves unto him : so that their time might endure for ever. ¹⁷He would feed them also with the fat of wheat : and with honey out of the rock would I satisfy thee.

Psalm for the Sixth Day of the Week.

This is the Sixth Day of the Week, on which the Levites in the Temple used to say :—(Psalm xciii. p. 363.)

On the days when Tachanun (p. 181 to p. 187) is said, the following is added after the Psalm of the day :—

Psalm lxxxiii. ¹A Song ; a Psalm of Asaph.

THE
ENEMIES
OF JUDAH
AND THEIR
DESTRUC-
TION

²O God, keep not thou silence : hold not thy peace, and be not still, O God. ³For, lo, thine enemies make a tumult : and they that hate thee have lifted up the head. ⁴They take crafty counsel against thy people, and consult together against thy treasured ones. ⁵They have said, Come and let us cut them off from being a nation ; that the name of Israel may be remembered no more. ⁶For they have consulted together with one consent ; against thee do they make a covenant. ⁷The tents of Edom and the Ishmaelites, Moab and the Hagarenes ; ⁸Gebal, and Ammon, and Amalek; Philistia with the inhabitants of Tyre : ⁹Assyria also is

For Friday : Psalm 93.
On Psalm 93 ; see p. 362.
Psalm 83.

A public prayer against an invasion of heathen tribes who were resolved to blot out the name of Israel from the memory of man. Such occasions often recurred in Jewish history ; see Judges 6–8, II Chronicles 20, and I Maccabees 5. Some modernists regret the harsh tone of this psalm ; but " if we had been where the psalmist was, we might well have felt and spoken as he did " (Oesterley).

7–9. List of the confederate peoples.

7. *Hagarenes.* Arabs of different stocks.

8. *Gebal.* A Phoenician city ; *Ammon,* east of the Jordan ; and *Amalek,* in the south. Israel is attacked from three sides.

גַּם־אַשּׁוּר נִלְוָה עִמָּם הָיוּ זְרוֹעַ לִבְנֵי־לוֹט סֶלָה׃ עֲשֵׂה־

לָהֶם כְּמִדְיָן כְּסִיסְרָא כְיָבִין בְּנַחַל קִישׁוֹן׃ נִשְׁמְדוּ בְעֵין־

דֹּאר הָיוּ דֹּמֶן לָאֲדָמָה׃ שִׁיתֵמוֹ נְדִיבֵמוֹ כְּעֹרֵב וְכִזְאֵב

וּכְזֶבַח וּכְצַלְמֻנָּע כָּל־נְסִיכֵמוֹ׃ אֲשֶׁר אָמְרוּ נִירְשָׁה־לָּנוּ

אֵת נְאוֹת אֱלֹהִים׃ אֱלֹהַי שִׁיתֵמוֹ כַגַּלְגַּל כְּקַשׁ לִפְנֵי־

רוּחַ׃ כְּאֵשׁ תִּבְעַר־יָעַר וּכְלֶהָבָה תְּלַהֵט הָרִים׃ כֵּן

תִּרְדְּפֵם בְּסַעֲרֶךָ וּבְסוּפָתְךָ תְבַהֲלֵם׃ מַלֵּא פְנֵיהֶם קָלוֹן

וִיבַקְשׁוּ שִׁמְךָ יְהוָה׃ יֵבֹשׁוּ וְיִבָּהֲלוּ עֲדֵי־עַד וְיַחְפְּרוּ

וְיֹאבֵדוּ׃ וְיֵדְעוּ כִּי־אַתָּה שִׁמְךָ יְהוָה לְבַדֶּךָ עֶלְיוֹן עַל־

כָּל־הָאָרֶץ׃

On רֹאשׁ חֹדֶשׁ, *Psalm civ. p. 582 is read.*

From ר'ח אֱלוּל *till* הוֹשַׁעְנָא רַבָּא, *the following Psalm is read every Morning and Evening. Until the day before the Eve of New Year, or until the Eve of New Year if that day be a Friday, the Shofar is sounded before the reading of the Psalm*

תהלים כ'ז

לְדָוִד יְהוָה אוֹרִי וְיִשְׁעִי מִמִּי אִירָא יְהוָה מָעוֹז חַיַּי מִמִּי

אֶפְחָד׃ בִּקְרֹב עָלַי מְרֵעִים לֶאֱכֹל אֶת־בְּשָׂרִי צָרַי וְאֹיְבַי לִי

הֵמָּה כָּשְׁלוּ וְנָפָלוּ׃ אִם־תַּחֲנֶה עָלַי מַחֲנֶה לֹא־יִירָא לִבִּי אִם־

תָּקוּם עָלַי מִלְחָמָה בְּזֹאת אֲנִי בוֹטֵחַ׃ אַחַת שָׁאַלְתִּי מֵאֵת

יְהוָה אוֹתָהּ אֲבַקֵּשׁ שִׁבְתִּי בְּבֵית יְהוָה כָּל־יְמֵי חַיַּי לַחֲזוֹת

בְּנֹעַם־יְהוָה וּלְבַקֵּר בְּהֵיכָלוֹ׃ כִּי יִצְפְּנֵנִי בְּסֻכֹּה בְּיוֹם רָעָה

10. *Midian.* See Judges 4.
12. *Oreb . . . Zalmunna.* Judges 7 and 8.
13. *habitations of God.* The Holy Land.
17. *that they may seek thy Name.* That they may be drawn to appeal to Thee; that the wicked turn unto Thee in recognition of Thy righteous kingship.

OCCA-
SIONAL
PSALMS

joined with them ; they have been an arm of help to the children of Lot. (Selah.) ¹⁰Do thou unto them as unto Midian ; as to Sisera, as to Jabin, at the brook Kishon. ¹¹They were destroyed at Endor ; they became as dung for the earth. ¹²Make their nobles like Oreb and Zeeb ; yea, all their princes like Zebah and Zalmunna : ¹³who said, Let us take to ourselves in possession the habitations of God. ¹⁴O my God, make them like the whirling dust, as stubble before the wind ; ¹⁵as the fire that burneth the forest, and as the flame that setteth the mountains on fire : ¹⁶so pursue them with thy storm, and confound them with thy hurricane. ¹⁷Fill their faces with confusion ; that they may seek thy Name, O Lord. ¹⁸Let them be ashamed and confounded for ever ; yea, let them be abashed and perish. ¹⁹That they may know that thou, of whom alone the Name is the Lord, art Most High over all the earth.

On New Moon, Psalm civ. p. 583 is read.

From the Second Day of the New Moon of Ellul until Hoshana Rabba, the following Psalm is read every Morning and Evening. Until the day before the Eve of New Year, or until the Eve of New Year if that day be a Friday, the Shofar is sounded before the reading of the Psalm.

Psalm xxvii. ¹A Psalm of David.

DIVINE
LIGHT AND
STRENGTH

The Lord is my light and my salvation ; whom shall I fear ? The Lord is the stronghold of my life ; of whom shall I be afraid ? ²When evil-doers drew nigh against me to eat up my flesh, even my adversaries and my foes, they stumbled and fell. ³Though an host should encamp against me, my heart would not fear ; though war should rise against me, even then would I be confident. ⁴One

PSALM 27.

1. *my light.* In the darkness of affliction, anxiety and danger. The Midrash takes this psalm as the special reading for the Ellul month. It accordingly explains *the Lord is my light*—" through the teachings of Rosh Hashonah " ; *and my salvation*—" through Yom Kippur ". The message of New Year illumines life for us ; and that of the Day of Atonement rescues us from the grasp of sin and despair.

2. *eat up.* They are determined to make an utter end of him.

they. Is emphatic.

יַסְתִּירֵנִי בְּסֵתֶר אָהֳלוֹ בְּצוּר יְרוֹמְמֵנִי : וְעַתָּה יָרוּם רֹאשִׁי עַל
אֹיְבַי סְבִיבוֹתַי וְאֶזְבְּחָה בְאָהֳלוֹ זִבְחֵי תְרוּעָה אָשִׁירָה וַאֲזַמְּרָה
לַיהֹוָה : שְׁמַע־יְהֹוָה קוֹלִי אֶקְרָא וְחָנֵּנִי וַעֲנֵנִי : לְךָ אָמַר לִבִּי
בַּקְּשׁוּ פָנָי אֶת־פָּנֶיךָ יְהֹוָה אֲבַקֵּשׁ : אַל־תַּסְתֵּר פָּנֶיךָ מִמֶּנִּי אַל־
תַּט בְּאַף עַבְדֶּךָ עֶזְרָתִי הָיִיתָ אַל־תִּטְּשֵׁנִי וְאַל־תַּעַזְבֵנִי אֱלֹהֵי
יִשְׁעִי : כִּי־אָבִי וְאִמִּי עֲזָבוּנִי וַיהֹוָה יַאַסְפֵנִי : הוֹרֵנִי יְהֹוָה
דַּרְכֶּךָ וּנְחֵנִי בְּאֹרַח מִישׁוֹר לְמַעַן שׁוֹרְרָי : אַל־תִּתְּנֵנִי בְּנֶפֶשׁ
צָרָי כִּי קָמוּ־בִי עֵדֵי־שֶׁקֶר וִיפֵחַ חָמָס : לוּלֵא הֶאֱמַנְתִּי לִרְאוֹת
בְּטוּב־יְהֹוָה בְּאֶרֶץ חַיִּים : קַוֵּה אֶל־יְהֹוָה חֲזַק וְיַאֲמֵץ לִבֶּךָ
וְקַוֵּה אֶל־יְהֹוָה :

In some Congregations the following Psalm is said daily before
בָּרוּךְ שֶׁאָמַר, *p.* 50 :—

תהלים ל'

מִזְמוֹר שִׁיר חֲנֻכַּת הַבַּיִת לְדָוִד : אֲרוֹמִמְךָ יְהֹוָה כִּי דִלִּיתָנִי
וְלֹא־שִׂמַּחְתָּ אֹיְבַי לִי : יְהֹוָה אֱלֹהָי שִׁוַּעְתִּי אֵלֶיךָ וַתִּרְפָּאֵנִי :

4. *dwell in the house of the Lord.* Have the privilege of habitual
attendance there.
inquire. Meditate.
7. The *tehillah,* " song of praise," now becomes a *tephillah,* " a
prayer." The psalmist is in deep distress.
10. *though my father. i.e.* should my father and mother have forsaken me. The word כי is purely hypothetical, conveying a strong
expression of loneliness and friendlessness.
12. *violence.* Cruelty.
14. *wait for the Lord.* The psalmist's faith rebukes his faintness.

PSALM 30.

There are various Rabbinic explanations of the title. Fundamentally
this is hymn of gratitude for recovery from an almost fatal sickness.
It has also been taken, on the one hand, as a thanksgiving song of one
whose life has been greatly endangered by malignant foes ; and, on the
other hand, it has at various times been applied to Israel's national life.
It seems to have been used at the Dedication of the Second Temple (Ezra
6. 16), and almost certainly so at the reconsecration of the Temple on
the first Chanukah. In Maccabean days, " the very existence of the

OCCA-
SIONAL
PSALMS

thing have I asked of the Lord, that will I seek after : that I may dwell in the house of the Lord all the days of my life, to behold the pleasantness of the Lord, and to inquire in his temple. ⁵For in the day of trouble he will hide me in his pavilion : in the shelter of his tabernacle will he conceal me ; he will lift me up upon a rock. ⁶And now shall mine head be lifted up above my enemies round about me ; and I will offer in his tabernacle sacrifices of joyful shouting ; I will sing, yea, I will sing praises unto the Lord. ⁷Hear, O Lord, when I cry with my voice ; have pity upon me, and answer me. ⁸My heart saith unto thee, (since thou hast said), Seek ye my face, Thy face, Lord, will I seek. ⁹Hide not thy face from me ; thrust not thy servant away in anger: thou hast been my help ; cast me not off, neither forsake me, O God of my salvation. ¹⁰For though my father and my mother have forsaken me, the Lord will take me up. ¹¹Teach me thy way, O Lord ; and lead me on an even path, because of them that lie in wait for me. ¹²Give me not up to the will of mine adversaries : for false witnesses have risen up against me, and such as breathe out violence. ¹³(I should despair), unless I believed to see the goodness of the Lord in the land of the living. ¹⁴Wait for the Lord ; be strong and let thine heart take courage ; yea, wait thou for the Lord.

In some Congregations the following Psalm is said daily before
"Blessed be he", p. 51.

Psalm xxx.

THANKS-
GIVING
FOR
DELIVER-
ANCE

¹A Psalm ; a Song at the Dedication of the House ; a Psalm of David.

²I will extol thee, O Lord ; for thou hast drawn me up, and hast not made my foes to rejoice over me. ³O Lord, my God, I cried

nation had been at stake ; it had been suddenly and unexpectedly freed from a crushing tyranny and, as it were, restored to life ; and this Psalm supplied it with fitting language in which to give thanks for its deliverance. The experience of the individual had been repeated in that of the nation " (Kirkpatrick).

2. *drawn me up.* As from the depths of trouble and utmost danger. The figure is that of drawing a bucket from a deep well.

יְהֹוָה הֶעֱלִיתָ מִן־שְׁאוֹל נַפְשִׁי חִיִּיתַנִי מִיָּרְדִי־בוֹר : זַמְּרוּ לַיהֹוָה
חֲסִידָיו וְהוֹדוּ לְזֵכֶר קָדְשׁוֹ : כִּי רֶגַע בְּאַפּוֹ חַיִּים בִּרְצוֹנוֹ בָּעֶרֶב
יָלִין בֶּכִי וְלַבֹּקֶר רִנָּה : וַאֲנִי אָמַרְתִּי בְשַׁלְוִי בַּל־אֶמּוֹט לְעוֹלָם :
יְהֹוָה בִּרְצוֹנְךָ הֶעֱמַדְתָּה לְהַרְרִי עֹז הִסְתַּרְתָּ פָנֶיךָ הָיִיתִי
נִבְהָל : אֵלֶיךָ יְהֹוָה אֶקְרָא וְאֶל־אֲדֹנָי אֶתְחַנָּן : מַה־בֶּצַע בְּדָמִי
בְּרִדְתִּי אֶל שָׁחַת הֲיוֹדְךָ עָפָר הֲיַגִּיד אֲמִתֶּךָ : שְׁמַע־יְהֹוָה
וְחָנֵּנִי יְהֹוָה הֱיֵה עֹזֵר לִי : הָפַכְתָּ מִסְפְּדִי לְמָחוֹל לִי פִּתַּחְתָּ
שַׂקִּי וַתְּאַזְּרֵנִי שִׂמְחָה : לְמַעַן יְזַמֶּרְךָ כָבוֹד וְלֹא יִדֹּם יְהֹוָה
אֱלֹהַי לְעוֹלָם אוֹדֶךָ :

קַדִּישׁ דְּרַבָּנָן

Reader. יִתְגַּדַּל וְיִתְקַדַּשׁ שְׁמֵהּ רַבָּא בְּעָלְמָא דִי־בְרָא כִרְעוּתֵהּ ·
וְיַמְלִיךְ מַלְכוּתֵהּ בְּחַיֵּיכוֹן וּבְיוֹמֵיכוֹן וּבְחַיֵּי דִי־כָל־בֵּית יִשְׂרָאֵל
בַּעֲגָלָא וּבִזְמַן קָרִיב · וְאִמְרוּ אָמֵן :

Cong. and Reader. יְהֵא שְׁמֵהּ רַבָּא מְבָרַךְ לְעָלַם וּלְעָלְמֵי עָלְמַיָּא ·

Reader. יִתְבָּרַךְ וְיִשְׁתַּבַּח וְיִתְפָּאַר וְיִתְרוֹמַם וְיִתְנַשֵּׂא וְיִתְהַדָּר
וְיִתְעַלֶּה וְיִתְהַלָּל שְׁמֵהּ דִּי־קֻדְשָׁא בְּרִיךְ הוּא · לְעֵלָּא מִן־כָּל־
בִּרְכָתָא וְשִׁירָתָא תֻּשְׁבְּחָתָא וְנֶחֱמָתָא דִּי־אֲמִירָן בְּעָלְמָא ·
וְאִמְרוּ אָמֵן :

4. *from the grave.* His sickness had been desperate.
5. An invitation to the godly to join in thanksgiving.
6. *tarry for the night.* Sorrow is but a passing wayfarer, who may
claim his temporary lodging, but who with the dawn is supplanted by joy.
8. *my mountain.* "Thou hadst made me stand upon strong
mountains" (Targum)—a figure of security.
10. *blood.* The psalmist had been in danger of a violent death.
can the dust give thanks to thee. For the moment, he shares the
sombre views of the Hereafter that are expressed in Psalm 6, and not
those of Psalm 16.

unto thee, and thou didst heal me. [4]O Lord, thou broughtest up my soul from the grave : thou hast kept me alive, that I should not go down to the pit. [5]Sing praise unto the Lord, O ye his loving ones, and give thanks to his holy Name. [6]For his anger is but for a moment ; his favour is for a lifetime : weeping may tarry for the night, but joy cometh in the morning. [7]As for me, I said in my prosperity, I shall never be moved. [8]Thou, Lord, of thy favour hadst made my mountain to stand strong : thou didst hide thy face ; I was confounded. [9]I cried unto thee, O Lord ; and unto the Lord I made supplication : [10]What profit is there in my blood if I go down to the pit ? Can the dust give thanks to thee ? Can it declare thy truth ? [11]Hear, O Lord, and be gracious unto me ; Lord, be thou my helper. [12]Thou hast turned for me my mourning into dancing ; thou hast loosed my sackcloth, and girded me with gladness : [13]to the end that my glory may sing praise to thee, and not be silent : O Lord my God, I will give thanks unto thee for ever.

Kaddish to be said by the Reader or Mourner after reading Lessons from the Works of the Rabbis :—

THE RAB-
BINICAL
KADDISH

Reader.—Magnified and sanctified be his great Name in the world which he hath created according to his will. May he establish his kingdom during your life and during your days, and during the life of all the house of Israel, even speedily and at a near time, and say ye, Amen.

Cong. and Reader.—Let his great Name be blessed for ever and to all eternity.

Reader.—Blessed, praised, and glorified, exalted, extolled and honoured, magnified and lauded be the Name of the Holy One, blessed be he ; though he be high above all the blessings and hymns, praises and consolations, which are uttered in the world ; and say ye, Amen.

12–13. The result of the psalmist's prayer.
13. *my glory.* My soul.

THE RABBINICAL KADDISH.

When ten or more men have studied the Mishna or any of the Rabbinical Writings, one of them recites at the close of the Lesson the above form of the Kaddish. A short section of the Mishna is often read and interpreted at the end of the regular Service, so as to give mourners an opportunity to recite this Kaddish.

עַל יִשְׂרָאֵל וְעַל רַבָּנָן וְעַל תַּלְמִידֵיהוֹן וְעַל כָּל־תַּלְמִידֵי
תַלְמִידֵיהוֹן וְעַל כָּל־מָן דִּי עָסְקִין בְּאוֹרַיְתָא דִּי בְּאַתְרָא הָדֵן
וְדִי בְּכָל־אֲתַר וַאֲתַר יְהֵא לְהוֹן וּלְכוֹן שְׁלָמָא רַבָּא חִנָּא וְחִסְדָּא
וְרַחֲמִין וְחַיִּין אֲרִיכִין וּמְזוֹנָא רְוִיחָא וּפֻרְקָנָא מִן־קֳדָם אֲבוּהוֹן
דִּי בִשְׁמַיָּא · וְאִמְרוּ אָמֵן :

Cong. יְהִי שֵׁם יְיָ מְבֹרָךְ מֵעַתָּה וְעַד עוֹלָם :

Reader. יְהֵא שְׁלָמָא רַבָּא מִן־שְׁמַיָּא וְחַיִּים טוֹבִים עָלֵינוּ וְעַל־
כָּל־יִשְׂרָאֵל · וְאִמְרוּ אָמֵן :

Cong. עֶזְרִי מֵעִם יְיָ עֹשֵׂה שָׁמַיִם וָאָרֶץ :

Reader. עֹשֶׂה שָׁלוֹם בִּמְרוֹמָיו הוּא בְּרַחֲמָיו יַעֲשֶׂה שָׁלוֹם
עָלֵינוּ וְעַל־כָּל־יִשְׂרָאֵל · וְאִמְרוּ אָמֵן :

תפלה על הפרנסה :

עֶזְרִי מֵעִם יְיָ עֹשֵׂה שָׁמַיִם וָאָרֶץ : הַשְׁלֵךְ עַל־יְיָ יְהָבְךָ
וְהוּא יְכַלְכְּלֶךָ : שְׁמָר־תָּם וּרְאֵה יָשָׁר כִּי אַחֲרִית לְאִישׁ שָׁלוֹם :
בְּטַח בַּייָ וַעֲשֵׂה טוֹב שְׁכָן־אֶרֶץ וּרְעֵה אֱמוּנָה : הִנֵּה אֵל יְשׁוּעָתִי
אֶבְטַח וְלֹא אֶפְחָד · כִּי עָזִּי וְזִמְרָת יָהּ יְיָ וַיְהִי־לִי לִישׁוּעָה :
רִבּוֹנוֹ שֶׁל־עוֹלָם · בְּדִבְרֵי קָדְשְׁךָ כָּתוּב לֵאמֹר · הַבּוֹטֵחַ בַּייָ
חֶסֶד יְסוֹבְבֶנּוּ · וְכָתוּב וְאַתָּה מְחַיֶּה אֶת־כֻּלָּם : יְיָ אֱלֹהִים
אֱמֶת · תֵּן בְּרָכָה וְהַצְלָחָה בְּכָל־מַעֲשֵׂה יָדָי · כִּי בָטַחְתִּי בָךְ

PRAYER FOR SUSTENANCE.

Holy Words. The third division of the Hebrew Scriptures—Torah,
Prophets, and Holy Writings (or Holy Words).

The following is an alternative form for this supplication :

O God, Who providest food and raiment to every creature, open
Thy loving hand unto me, and sustain and give me nourishment in a
useful and honourable calling. Help me to support my household by

THE RAB-
BINICAL
KADDISH

Unto Israel, and unto the Rabbis, and unto their disciples, and unto all the disciples of their disciples, and unto all who engage in the study of the Torah in this or in any other place, unto them and unto you be abundant peace, grace, lovingkindness, mercy, long life, ample sustenance and salvation from the Father who is in heaven, and say ye, Amen.

Congregation.—Amen.

Reader.—May there be abundant peace from heaven, and a happy life for us and for all Israel ; and say ye, Amen.

Congregation.—Amen.

Reader.—He who maketh peace in his high places, may he in his mercy make peace for us and for all Israel ; and say ye, Amen.

---

*PRAYER
FOR SUS-
TENANCE*

PRAYER FOR SUSTENANCE.

Psalm
121. 2 ; 55. 23   My help is from the Lord, who made heaven and earth. Cast thy
Psalm 37. 37   burden upon the Lord, and he shall sustain thee. Mark the innocent man, and behold the upright ; for the latter end of that man is peace.

Psalm 37. 3   Trust in the Lord, and do good ; dwell in the land, and feed upon
Isaiah 12. 2   faithfulness. Behold, God is my salvation ; I will trust, and will not be afraid : for the Lord God is my strength and song, and he is become my salvation.—O Sovereign of the universe, in thy Holy Words it is
Psalm 32. 10   written, saying, He that trusteth in the Lord, lovingkindness shall compass him about ; and it is written, And thou gavest life to them all. O Lord God of truth, send blessing and prosperity upon all the work of my hands, for I trust in thee that thou wilt so bless me

lawful and not forbidden means, and in a manner free from all shame, disgrace, or dependence on mortals. Let me walk in the way of the upright before Thee, and deserve Thy blessing of prosperity upon my undertakings. May I be enabled to assist all sacred causes, and be privileged to extend help and hospitality to others who are in need. Shield my home from all evil ; let peace and well-being abide in it ; and in me may the Scripture be fulfilled, *Thou openest thine hand, and satisfiest every living thing with favour.* Amen.

שֶׁעַל־יְדֵי מַשָּׂא וּמַתָּן וַעֲסָקִים שֶׁלִּי תִּשְׁלַח לִי בְּרָכָה כְּדֵי
שֶׁאוּכַל לְפַרְנֵס אֶת־עַצְמִי וּבְנֵי בֵיתִי בְּנַחַת וְלֹא בְצַעַר בְּהֶתֵּר
וְלֹא בְאִסוּר לְחַיִּים וּלְשָׁלוֹם · וִיקֻיַּם בִּי מִקְרָא שֶׁכָּתוּב · הַשְׁלֵךְ
עַל־יְיָ יְהָבְךָ וְהוּא יְכַלְכְּלֶךָ · אָמֵן :

עשרת הדברות :

שמות כ' א'-י'

וַיְדַבֵּר אֱלֹהִים אֵת כָּל־הַדְּבָרִים הָאֵלֶּה לֵאמֹר :
א אָנֹכִי יְהֹוָה אֱלֹהֶיךָ אֲשֶׁר הוֹצֵאתִיךָ מֵאֶרֶץ מִצְרַיִם
מִבֵּית עֲבָדִים :

8. READINGS FROM SCRIPTURE AND THE MORALISTS.

These Devotional Readings are optional, and are nowhere strictly
defined. The chapter on the Akedah, the Binding of Isaac, is in some
Rites read in the early part of the Service, among the Morning Blessings.
In ..ddition to the Ten Commandments, many Prayer Books print the
chapter on the Manna (Exodus 16. 4–43), the section on the Fear of
God (Deuteronomy 10–12), and various other selections from Scripture
and the writings of the Jewish Moralists.

THE TEN COMMANDMENTS
EXODUS 20. '1—14

In the Temple, the Ten Commandments formed an essential part of
the daily Morning Service. They were recited just before the Shema.

The Ten Commandments are a sublime summary of human duties
binding upon all mankind ; a summary unequalled for simplicity,
comprehensiveness and solemnity ; a summary which bears divinity on
its face, and cannot be antiquated as long as the world endures.

FIRST TABLE : DUTIES TOWARDS GOD
FIRST COMMANDMENT.
RECOGNITION OF THE SOVEREIGNTY OF GOD

2. *I am the* LORD *thy God.* The Jewish Traditional view considers
this verse as the first of the Ten Words, and deduces from it the positive
precept, *To believe in the existence of God.*

I. The *personal* pronoun teaches a lesson of vital significance. The
God adored by Judaism is not an impersonal Force, an It, whether
spoken of as " Nature " or " World-Reason ". God is the Source not
only of power and life, but of consciousness, personality, and ethical
action.

thy God. The emphasis is on *thy.* This refers to Israel collectively,

through my occupation and calling, that I may be enabled to support
myself and the members of my household with ease and not with
pain, by lawful and not by forbidden means, unto life and peace.
Psalm 55. 23 In me also let the scripture be fulfilled, Cast thy burden upon the
Lord, and he shall sustain thee. Amen.

THE TEN COMMANDMENTS.
Exodus xx. 1—17.

THE TEN COMMAND-MENTS
¹And God spake all these words, saying.

I. ²I am the Lord thy God, who brought thee out of the
land of Egypt, out of the house of bondage.

II. ³Thou shalt have no other gods before me. ⁴Thou
shalt not make unto thee a graven image ; nor the form

and at the same time to each Israelite individually. " Even as thousands
may look at a great portrait and each one feel that it looks at *him*, so
every Israelite at Horeb felt that the Divine Voice was addressing *him* "
(Midrash).

who brought thee out of the land of Egypt. God is not here designated,
" Creator of heaven and earth ". Israel's God is seen not merely in
Nature, but in the destinies of man. He revealed Himself to Israel
in a great historic deed, the greatest in the life of any people.

The reference to the Deliverance from Egypt is of deepest significance,
not only to Israel, but to all mankind. The primal word of the Divine
Message is the proclamation of the One God as the God of Freedom.
The recognition of God as the God of Freedom illumines the whole of
human history for us. In the light of this truth, history becomes one
continuous Divine revelation of the gradual growth of freedom and
justice on earth.

SECOND COMMANDMENT.

THE UNITY AND SPIRITUALITY OF GOD

3. *thou shalt have no other gods.* Because there are no other
gods besides God. The fundamental dogma of Israel's religion, as of
all higher religion, is the Unity of God. It alone can be the basis for
the teaching of the Unity of mankind, and the consequent Brotherhood
of man, since the one God must be the God of the whole of humanity.

before me. Or, " besides me ". Neither angels nor saintly men or
women, are to receive adoration as Divine beings ; and the Jew is
forbidden to pray to them. This Commandment also forbids belief in
evil spirits, witchcraft, and similar evil superstitions. Furthermore, he
who believes in God will not put his trust in Chance or " luck ".

4. *a graven image.* Judaism alone, from the very beginning, taught
that God was a Spirit ; and made it an unpardonable sin to worship

ב לֹא־יִהְיֶה לְךָ אֱלֹהִים אֲחֵרִים עַל־פָּנָי : לֹא־תַעֲשֶׂה

לְךָ פֶסֶל וְכָל־תְּמוּנָה אֲשֶׁר בַּשָּׁמַיִם מִמַּעַל וַאֲשֶׁר בָּאָרֶץ

מִתַּחַת וַאֲשֶׁר בַּמַּיִם מִתַּחַת לָאָרֶץ : לֹא־תִשְׁתַּחֲוֶה לָהֶם

וְלֹא תָעָבְדֵם כִּי אָנֹכִי יְהֹוָה אֱלֹהֶיךָ אֵל קַנָּא פֹּקֵד עֲוֹן

אָבֹת עַל־בָּנִים עַל־שִׁלֵּשִׁים וְעַל־רִבֵּעִים לְשֹׂנְאָי : וְעֹשֶׂה

חֶסֶד לַאֲלָפִים לְאֹהֲבַי וּלְשֹׁמְרֵי מִצְוֹתָי :

ג לֹא תִשָּׂא אֶת־שֵׁם־יְהֹוָה אֱלֹהֶיךָ לַשָּׁוְא כִּי לֹא יְנַקֶּה

יְהֹוָה אֵת אֲשֶׁר־יִשָּׂא אֶת־שְׁמוֹ לַשָּׁוְא :

God under any external form that human hands can fashion, or under
any image, graven, or un-graven which the human mind can conceive.
5. a jealous God. God desires to be all in all to His children, and
claims an exclusive right to their love and obedience. He hates cruelty
and unrighteousness, and loathes impurity and vice ; and, even as a
mother is jealous of all evil influences that rule her children, He is
jealous when, instead of purity and righteousness, it is idolatry and
unholiness that command their heart-allegiance. Outside Israel, the
ancients believed that the more gods the better ; the richer the pantheon
of a people, the greater its power. It is because the heathen deities
were free from " jealousy " and, therefore, tolerant of one another and
all their abominations, that heathenism was spiritually so degrading
and morally so devastating.

visiting the iniquity of the fathers upon the children. The Torah does
not teach here or elsewhere that the sins of the guilty fathers shall be
visited upon their innocent children. *The soul that sinneth,* it *shall die*
proclaims the Prophet Ezekiel. And in the administration of justice
by the state, the Torah distinctly lays down, " The fathers shall not
be put to death for the children, neither shall the children be put to
death for the fathers ; every man shall be put to death for his own sin "
(Deut. 24. 16). However, human experience all too plainly teaches
the moral interdependence of parents and children. Only in exceptional
cases are children immune from the corrupting influence of sinful
parents.

Another translation is, " *remembering* the iniquity of the fathers " ;
i.e. God *remembers* the sins of the fathers when about to punish
the children. He distinguishes between the moral responsibility

of anything that is in heaven above, or that is in the earth beneath, or that is in the water under the earth ; ⁵thou shalt not bow down thyself unto them, nor serve them : for I the Lord thy God am a jealous God, visiting the iniquity of the fathers upon the children, upon the third and upon the fourth generation, unto them that hate me : ⁶and shewing lovingkindness to the thousandth generaticn, unto them that love me and keep my commandments.

III. ⁷Thou shalt not take the Name of the Lord thy God in vain ; for the Lord will not hold him guiltless that taketh his Name in vain.

which falls exclusively upon the sinful parents, and the natural predisposition to sin that is inherited by the descendants. He takes into account the evil environment and influence. He, therefore, tempers justice with mercy ; and He does so to the third and fourth generation.

of them that hate me. The Rabbis refer these words to the children. The sins of the fathers will be visited upon them, only if they too transgress God's commandments.

6. *and shewing mercy to the thousandth generation.* Contrast the narrow limits, three or four generations, within which the sin is visited, with the thousand generations that His mercy is shown to those who love God and keep His commandments. In His providence, the beneficent consequences of a life of goodness extend indefinitely further than the retribution which is the penalty of persistence in sin.

that love me. Love of God is the essence of Judaism, and from love of God springs obedience to His will.

THIRD COMMANDMENT.
AGAINST PERJURY AND PROFANE SWEARING

The Third Commandment forbids us to dishonour God by invoking His Name to attest what is untrue, or by joining His Name to anything frivolous or insincere.

7. *take the Name of the* Lord. Upon the lips ; *i.e.* to utter.

in vain. lit. " for vanity ", or " falsehood " ; for anything that is unreal or groundless.

God is holy and His Name is holy. His Name, therefore, must not be used profanely to testify to anything that is untrue, insincere or empty. We are to swear by God's Name, only when we are fully convinced of the truth of our declaration, and then only when we are required to do so in a Court of law.

will not hold him guiltless. i.e. will not leave him unpunished. Perjury is an unpardonable offence, which, unless repressed by severest penalties, would destroy human society. The Rabbis ordained a special solemn warning to be administered to any one about to take an oath in a Court of law. In various ages, saintly men avoided swearing

ד זָכוֹר אֶת־יוֹם הַשַּׁבָּת לְקַדְּשׁוֹ : שֵׁשֶׁת יָמִים תַּעֲבֹד

וְעָשִׂיתָ כָּל־מְלַאכְתֶּךָ : וְיוֹם הַשְּׁבִיעִי שַׁבָּת לַיהוָה

אֱלֹהֶיךָ לֹא־תַעֲשֶׂה כָל־מְלָאכָה אַתָּה ׀ וּבִנְךָ וּבִתֶּךָ

עַבְדְּךָ וַאֲמָתְךָ וּבְהֶמְתֶּךָ וְגֵרְךָ אֲשֶׁר בִּשְׁעָרֶיךָ : כִּי

שֵׁשֶׁת־יָמִים עָשָׂה יְהוָה אֶת־הַשָּׁמַיִם וְאֶת־הָאָרֶץ אֶת־

הַיָּם וְאֶת־כָּל־אֲשֶׁר־בָּם וַיָּנַח בַּיוֹם הַשְּׁבִיעִי עַל־כֵּן בֵּרַךְ

יְהוָה אֶת־יוֹם הַשַּׁבָּת וַיְקַדְּשֵׁהוּ :

ה כַּבֵּד אֶת־אָבִיךָ וְאֶת־אִמֶּךָ לְמַעַן יַאֲרִכוּן יָמֶיךָ עַל

הָאֲדָמָה אֲשֶׁר־יְהוָה אֱלֹהֶיךָ נֹתֵן לָךְ :

ו לֹא תִרְצָח ·

altogether. The Essenes, a Jewish Sect in the days of the Second Temple, held that " he who cannot be believed without swearing is already condemned ". " Let thy yea be yea, and thy nay, nay ", says the Talmud.

FOURTH COMMANDMENT.
THE SABBATH DAY

See p. 338.

FIFTH COMMANDMENT.
HONOUR OF PARENTS

This Commandment follows the Sabbath Command, because the Sabbath is the source and the guarantor of family life ; and it is among the Commandments engraved on the First Table, the laws of piety towards God, because the parents stand in the place of God, so far as their children are concerned.

12. *honour thy father and thy mother.* By showing them respect, obedience and love. And this obligation extends beyond the grave. The child must revere the memory of the departed parent in act and feeling. Respect to parents is among the primary human duties ; and no excellence can atone for the lack of such respect. Only in cases of extreme rarity (*e.g.* where godless parents would guide children towards crime) can disobedience be justified. Proper respect to parents may at times involve immeasurable hardship ; yet the duty remains. The greatest achievement open to parents is to be ever worthy of their children's reverence and trust and love.

IV. [8]Remember the sabbath day to keep it holy. [9]Six days shalt thou labour, and do all thy work : [10]but the seventh day is a sabbath unto the Lord thy God : in it thou shalt not do any work, thou, nor thy son, nor thy daughter, thy manservant, nor thy maidservant, not thy cattle, nor thy stranger that is within thy gates : [11]for in six days the Lord made heaven and earth, the sea and all that is therein, and rested on the seventh day : wherefore the Lord blessed the sabbath day and hallowed it.

V. [12]Honour thy father and thy mother : that thy days may be long upon the land which the Lord thy God giveth thee.

VI. [13]Thou shalt not murder.

that thy days may be long. i.e. honouring one's parents will be rewarded by happiness and blessing. This is not always seen in the life of the individual ; but the Commandment is addressed to the individual as a member of society, as the child of a people. Filial respect is the basis of national permanence and prosperity.

SECOND TABLE : DUTIES TOWARDS FELLOW MEN

These duties have their root in the precept " Thou shalt love thy neighbour as thyself ", applied to life, home, property and honour.

THE SIXTH COMMANDMENT.

THE SANCTITY OF HUMAN LIFE

13. *thou shalt not murder.* The infinite worth of human life is based on the fact that man is created " in the image of God ". The intentional killing of any human being, apart from capital punishment legally imposed by a judicial tribunal, or in a war for the defence of national and human rights, is absolutely forbidden. This applies also to self-murder ; and child-life is as sacred as that of an adult. In Greece, weak children were *exposed* ; that is, abandoned on a lonely mountain to perish. Jewish horror of child-murder was long looked upon as a contemptible prejudice. " It is a crime among the Jews to kill any child ", sneered the Roman historian Tacitus.

Hebrew law carefully distinguishes homicide from wilful murder. It saves the involuntary slayer of his fellow-man from vendetta ; and does not permit composition, or money-fine, for the life of the murderer. Jewish ethics enlarge the meaning of murder so as to include both the doing of anything by which the health and well-being of a fellow-man is undermined, as well as the omission of any act by which a fellow-man could be saved in peril, distress or despair.

ז לֹא תִנְאָף ׃

ח לֹא תִגְנֹב ׃

ט לֹא־תַעֲנֶה בְרֵעֲךָ עֵד שָׁקֶר ׃

י לֹא תַחְמֹד בֵּית רֵעֶךָ לֹא־תַחְמֹד אֵשֶׁת רֵעֶךָ
וְעַבְדּוֹ וַאֲמָתוֹ וְשׁוֹרוֹ וַחֲמֹרוֹ וְכֹל אֲשֶׁר־לְרֵעֶךָ ׃

SEVENTH COMMANDMENT.

THE SANCTITY OF MARRIAGE

adultery. " Is an execrable and God-detested wrong-doing " (Philo). This Commandment against infidelity warns husband and wife alike against profaning the sacred Covenant of Marriage. It involves the prohibition of immoral speech, immodest conduct, or association with persons who scoff at the sacredness of purity. The traditional Jewish translation of the great saying of Micah is : " It hath been told thee, O man, what is good, and what the Lord doth require of thee : only to do justly, to love mercy and *walk in purity* with the God ". Among no people has there been a purer home-life than among the Jewish people. No woman enjoyed greater respect than the Jewish woman ; and she fully merited that respect ; *see* Marriage and the Position of Woman in Judaism, p. 1006.

EIGHTH COMMANDMENT.

THE SANCTITY OF PROPERTY

thou shalt not steal. Property represents the fruit of industry and intelligence. Any aggression on the property of our neighbour is, therefore, an assault on his human personality. This Commandment forbids every illegal acquisition of property by cheating, embezzlement or forgery. " There are transactions which are legal and do not involve any breach of law, which are yet base and disgraceful. Such are all transactions in which a person takes advantage of the ignorance or embarrassment of his neighbour for the purposes of increasing his own property " (M. Friedländer).

VII. ¹⁴Thou shalt not commit adultery.

VIII. ¹⁵Thou shalt not steal.

IX. ¹⁶Thou shalt not bear false witness against thy neighbour.

X. ¹⁷Thou shalt not covet thy neighbour's house, thou shalt not covet thy neighbour's wife, nor his manservant nor his maidservant, nor his ox, nor his ass, nor any thing that is thy neighbour's.

NINTH COMMANDMENT.

AGAINST BEARING FALSE WITNESS

The three preceding Commandments are concerned with wrongs inflicted upon our neighbour by actual deed : this Commandment is concerned with wrong inflicted by word of mouth.

thou shalt not bear false witness. The prohibition embraces all forms of slander, defamation and misrepresentation, whether of an individual, a group, a people, a race, or a Faith. None have suffered so much from slander, defamation and misrepresentation as Judaism and the Jew. Thus, modernist theologians still repeat that, according to this Commandment, the Israelite is prohibited only from slandering a fellow-Israelite ; because, they allege, the Hebrew word for "neighbour" (רֵעַ) here, and in " Thou shalt love *thy neighbour* as thyself " (Leviticus 19. 18), does not mean fellow-man, but only fellow-Israelite. This is a glaring instance of bearing false witness against Judaism. In this Commandment, as in all moral precepts in the Torah, the Hebrew word *neighbour* is equivalent to *fellow-man.*

TENTH COMMANDMENT.

AGAINST COVETOUS DESIRES

14. *covet. i.e.* to long for the possession of anything that we cannot get in an honest and legal manner. This Commandment goes to the root of all evil actions—the unholy instincts and impulses of predatory desire, which are the spring of nearly every sin against a neighbour. The man who does not covet his neighbour's goods will not bear false witness against him ; he will neither rob nor murder, nor will he commit adultery. It commands self-control ; for every man has it in his power to determine whether his desires are to master him, or he is to master his desires. Without such self-control, there can be no worthy human life ; it alone is the measure of true manhood or womanhood. " Who is strong ? " asked Rabbi Ben Zoma. " He who controls his passions " ; see p. 666.

שְׁלשָׁה עָשָׂר עִקָרִים :

א אֲנִי מַאֲמִין בֶּאֱמוּנָה שְׁלֵמָה שֶׁהַבּוֹרֵא יִתְבָּרַךְ שְׁמוֹ
הוּא בּוֹרֵא וּמַנְהִיג לְכָל־הַבְּרוּאִים • וְהוּא לְבַדּוֹ עָשָׂה
וְעוֹשֶׂה וְיַעֲשֶׂה לְכָל־הַמַּעֲשִׂים :

PRINCIPLES OF THE JEWISH FAITH.

Judaism is a system of spiritual truths, moral laws and religious practices. The moral laws and religious practices have been duly classified, codified and clothed with binding authority. Not so the spiritual doctrines. No formulation of these exists which enjoys universal recognition by the House of Israel. There are various reasons for this One of them is the fact that Judaism never made salvation dependent upon doctrine *in itself*, apart from its influence on conduct.

Yet the need for enumerating the fundamentals of Judaism that distinguished it from the heathen way of life, arose at an early date.

Thus, during the Babylonian exile, when proselytes began to join the ranks of Judaism, such doctrines as the Unity and Spirituality of God, and the Moral Government of the World, must have been pointed out to them as the new Message that Judaism brought to the children of men.

In later centuries, we find that some of the Rabbis declared one, or more, of the teachings of Judaism to be of pre-eminent importance. Hillel's selection of " Thou shalt love thy neighbour as thyself " (Leviticus, 19. 18) as " the whole " of the Torah, is well-known. Akiba, likewise, looked upon that Golden Rule as the Great Commandment. His companion, Ben Azzai, dissented from him, and selected for that eminence the truth contained in Genesis 5. 1. " This is the book of the generations of *man* "—not black, not white, not heathen, not Hebrew, but MAN. These words, he maintained, proclaimed the Unity of the Human Race, the Brotherhood of Man, as well as the God-likeness of the soul, and hence the infinite value of each human life. Other Jewish teachers, both ancient and modern, held the Ten Commandments to be the Principles of the Faith and the Pillars of the Jewish Life.

Philo seems to have been the first to have drawn up *articles* of Creed. He was followed by Saadya, Yehudah Hallevi, Bachya and many others, with Moses Maimonides the foremost of them all. Every one of these thinkers formulated his series of the fundamental doctrines of Judaism ; and of these it is the Thirteen Principles of Maimonides that attained the widest and the most lasting fame. They appear in two forms in our Rite : poetical, in *Yigdal*, and prose, here. Not that either his contemporaries or those who came after him have all of them endorsed his Thirteen Principles. Thus, Chasdai Crescas (1340–1410), the acutest thinker among his critics, objected that in them there

THIRTEEN PRINCIPLES OF THE FAITH.

1. I believe with perfect faith that the Creator, blessed be his Name, is the Author and Guide of everything that has been created, and that he alone has made, does make, and will make all things.

is no differentiation between *essential beliefs* of Judaism, without which Judaism is inconceivable, and other doctrines, the denial of which does not destroy Judaism. Joseph Albo, in the 15th century, found the number of Maimonides' articles too large ; and he reduced the Jewish Creed to three—the Existence of God, Revelation, and Reward and Punishment. It is not, therefore, a matter for surprise that strictures on Maimonides' list continued in modern times. It could not be otherwise. The various formulations of the Creed have in the past been influenced by the dominant ideas of their age, or by the aberrations of that age which the exponents of Judaism deemed it their duty to combat. It is thus obvious that in a *Creed* which should fully meet the problems of our own day, several new articles would, on the one hand, have to be added to those of Maimonides ; and, on the other hand, several of his articles would have to be restated. Reformulations of the Fundamental Principles of the Jewish Faith have in fact been several times undertaken during the last one hundred and fifty years. It must, however, be added that for every Jew who would be prepared unquestioningly to subscribe to any one of these reformulations, the Articles of Maimonides muster hundreds, and probably thousands, of adherents.

There have also been attempts to deny altogether the existence of Jewish articles of belief ; but eminent scholars of all shades of opinion —Leopold Löw, S. Schechter, K. Kohler—have shown that such contention is not borne out by Jewish history. One need but recall the Unity of God, and the part that it has played in the life of Israel, to see that Judaism *does* possess essential principles of belief. Besides, is not the very name " Jew "—just like " Christian " or " Buddhist "— a creed in a nutshell ? There may also be much truth in the saying, " The catechism of the Jew is his calendar " (S. R. Hirsch) ; and many Jews find a more adequate expression of Judaism in the web of poetic symbol and historic memory that the changing months of the Jewish Year bring in their train, than they do in any metaphysical articles of belief drawn up by our philosophers. Nevertheless, Judaism has dogmas, in the sense of *clear, settled opinions*, which are fundamental to its continued existence. When it is urged that in Judaism " religion means not creed but life ", our reply must be " that a life without guiding principles and thoughts, is a life not worth living " (Schechter). Only an ephemeral religious fad, with neither a history nor a philosophy, can exist without *dogma*, *i.e.* some authoritative statement of its principles ; or without a *theology*, *i.e.* organised religious thought derived from its sacred books, traditions, and institutions. And, unless we are prepared to declare that there is no religious content to our Faith, we must follow Maimonides and our other great religious thinkers, and courageously proclaim the *affirmations* of Judaism.

ב אֲנִי מַאֲמִין בֶּאֱמוּנָה שְׁלֵמָה שֶׁהַבּוֹרֵא יִתְבָּרַךְ שְׁמוֹ

הוּא יָחִיד · וְאֵין יְחִידוּת כָּמוֹהוּ בְּשׁוּם פָּנִים · וְהוּא

לְבַדּוֹ אֱלֹהֵינוּ הָיָה הֹוֶה וְיִהְיֶה :

ג אֲנִי מַאֲמִין בֶּאֱמוּנָה שְׁלֵמָה שֶׁהַבּוֹרֵא יִתְבָּרַךְ שְׁמוֹ

אֵינוֹ גוּף · וְלֹא יַשִּׂיגוּהוּ מַשִּׂיגֵי הַגּוּף · וְאֵין לוֹ שׁוּם

דִּמְיוֹן כְּלָל :

ד אֲנִי מַאֲמִין בֶּאֱמוּנָה שְׁלֵמָה שֶׁהַבּוֹרֵא יִתְבָּרַךְ שְׁמוֹ

הוּא רִאשׁוֹן וְהוּא אַחֲרוֹן :

ה אֲנִי מַאֲמִין בֶּאֱמוּנָה שְׁלֵמָה שֶׁהַבּוֹרֵא יִתְבָּרַךְ שְׁמוֹ

לוֹ לְבַדּוֹ רָאוּי לְהִתְפַּלֵּל · וְאֵין רָאוּי לְהִתְפַּלֵּל לְזוּלָתוֹ :

י אֲנִי מַאֲמִין בֶּאֱמוּנָה שְׁלֵמָה שֶׁכָּל־דִּבְרֵי הַנְּבִיאִים

אֱמֶת :

ז אֲנִי מַאֲמִין בֶּאֱמוּנָה שְׁלֵמָה שֶׁנְּבוּאַת מֹשֶׁה רַבֵּינוּ

עָלָיו הַשָּׁלוֹם הָיְתָה אֲמִתִּית · וְשֶׁהוּא הָיָה אָב לַנְּבִיאִים

The thirteen Principles fall into three groups.

I. The first group (1–5) includes the opening five which declare the
EXISTENCE OF GOD. He is the Creator, One, incorporeal, eternal, and
alone worthy of man's worship ; See ON THE SHEMA, p. 263.

1. *I believe.* Faith is the implicit belief in the truth of the communi
cation made to us, and in the trustworthiness of him who makes it to us
(Friedländer). "And (Abraham) *believed* in the Lord, and He reckoned
it to him as righteousness " (Genesis 15. 6). "And Israel saw the great
work . . . and they *believed* in the Lord, and in Moses His servant "
(Exodus 14. 31).

Some translate the words *ani maamin* by, " I am firmly convinced ".
While all our great religious thinkers, from Saadya Gaon down to
Hermann Cohen, have endeavoured to demonstrate the truths of
Judaism by means of reasoning and logical argument, the words
אני מאמין and אמונה in the above mean, " I believe " and " faith ", in
the same sense that we attach to these words to-day.

2. I believe with perfect faith that the Creator, blessed be his Name, is a Unity, and that there is no unity in any manner like unto his, and that he alone is our God, who was, is, and will be.

3. I believe with perfect faith that the Creator, blessed be his Name, is not a body, and that he is free from all the properties of matter, and that he has not any form whatsoever.

4. I believe with perfect faith that the Creator, blessed be his Name, is the first and the last.

5. I believe with perfect faith that to the Creator, blessed be his Name, and to him alone, it is right to pray, and that it is not right to pray to any being besides him.

6. I believe with perfect faith that all the words of the prophets are true.

3. *not a body.* He is a spiritual being. When God is spoken of in Scripture as, *e.g.*, having eyes, hands, or as being swayed by anger or hate, these expressions are not to be taken in their literal meaning. They are *anthropomorphisms*, *i.e.* attempts to make intelligible to the finite mind that which relates to God, by using expressions that apply only to human beings. The Rabbinic saying, " The Torah speaks in the language of mortals ", became a leading principle of Jewish interpretation of Scripture.

properties. Or, " accidents," in the philosophical sense.

4. *first and the last.* Asserts the eternity of God.

5. *it is right to pray.* There is spiritual communion between the human soul and its Maker. For He is not only all-mighty and eternal, but He is " merciful and gracious, slow to anger and abounding in lovingkindness and truth ; keeping lovingkindness unto the thousandth generation, forgiving iniquity and transgression and sin ". He is an ethical Personality, worthy, and alone worthy, of the worshipful homage of the children of men ; see p. 10.

to any being besides him. Whether deemed to be an angel, saint or intercessor.

II. The second group of principles (**6–9**) deals with Revelation. Revelation means the unveiling of the character of God to the children of men, accompanied by a binding announcement of the Divine will. All this is implied in the Theistic position. If we think of the Universe as merely an aggregate of blind forces, then there is, of course, no room for communication of any kind between God and man. But the moment we assert the existence of a Supreme Mind who

לַקּוֹדְמִים לְפָנָיו וְלַבָּאִים אַחֲרָיו :

ח אֲנִי מַאֲמִין בֶּאֱמוּנָה שְׁלֵמָה שֶׁכָּל־הַתּוֹרָה הַמְּצוּיָה

עַתָּה בְּיָדֵינוּ הִיא הַנְּתוּנָה לְמֹשֶׁה רַבֵּינוּ עָלָיו הַשָּׁלוֹם :

ט אֲנִי מַאֲמִין בֶּאֱמוּנָה שְׁלֵמָה שֶׁזֹּאת הַתּוֹרָה לֹא

תְהִי מָחֳלֶפֶת · וְלֹא תְהִי תוֹרָה אַחֶרֶת מֵאֵת הַבּוֹרֵא

יִתְבָּרַךְ שְׁמוֹ :

י אֲנִי מַאֲמִין בֶּאֱמוּנָה שְׁלֵמָה שֶׁהַבּוֹרֵא יִתְבָּרַךְ שְׁמוֹ

יוֹדֵעַ כָּל־מַעֲשֵׂה בְנֵי אָדָם וְכָל־מַחְשְׁבֹתָם · שֶׁנֶּאֱמַר ·

הַיֹּצֵר יַחַד לִבָּם הַמֵּבִין אֶל־כָּל־מַעֲשֵׂיהֶם :

יא אֲנִי מַאֲמִין בֶּאֱמוּנָה שְׁלֵמָה שֶׁהַבּוֹרֵא יִתְבָּרַךְ שְׁמוֹ

גּוֹמֵל טוֹב לְשׁוֹמְרֵי מִצְוֹתָיו וּמַעֲנִישׁ לְעוֹבְרֵי מִצְוֹתָיו :

is the Fountain and Soul of all the infinite forms of matter and life—
Revelation, or communication between God and man, becomes a logical
and ethical necessity. The exact manner of this super-natural communication between God and man, will be conceived differently by
different groups of believers. Some will follow the Biblical accounts
of Revelation in their literal sense ; others will accept the interpretation
of these Biblical accounts by Rabbis of Talmudic days, Jewish philosophers of the Middle Ages, or Jewish religious thinkers of modern
times. No interpretation, however, is valid or in consonance with the
Jewish Theistic position, which makes human reason or the human
personality the *source* of such revelation. "*All* Revelation is super-
natural. There can be no such thing as a purely natural revelation.
We cannot really know God except as He desires to be known and
makes Himself apprehensible. No view of God that grew up ' of itself '
in the human mind, owing nothing to God's self-disclosing action, could
have any value " (Wobbermin).

Revelation is thus but the obvious inference and corollary of the
character of the Deity held by all who believe in a Personal God and
Father in Heaven ; in prayer to Whom, in worship of Whom, and in
communion with Whom, the highest moments of our lives are passed

7. I believe with perfect faith that the prophecy of Moses our teacher, peace be unto him, was true, and that he was the chief of the prophets, both of those that preceded and of those that followed.

8. I believe with perfect faith that the whole Torah, now in our possession, is the same that was given to Moses our teacher, peace be unto him.

9. I believe with perfect faith that this Torah will not be changed, and that there will never be any other Law from the Creator, blessed be his Name.

10. I believe with perfect faith that the Creator, blessed be his Name, knows every deed of the children of men, and *Psalm 33. 15* all their thoughts, as it is said, It is he that fashioneth the hearts of them all, that giveth heed to all their works.

11. I believe with perfect faith that the Creator, blessed be his Name, rewards those that keep his commandments, and punishes those that transgress them.

and lived. This close relationship between God and man, this interplay of spiritual forces and energies, whereby the human soul responds to the Self-manifesting Life of all Worlds, attains in Israel's Prophets such overmastering *certainty*, that it enables them to declare, " Thus saith the Lord ". Maimonides compared Revelation to illumination by lightning on a dark night. Some Prophets were in their life granted only one such lightning-flash from the Divine ; in the case of others, these lightning-flashes were oft repeated ; whereas to Moses was accorded continuous, unintermittent Light. He was the Teacher of Israel, and the Torah that he taught Israel is Divine. There will be no other Dispensation given unto Israel by the Creator.

III. The third group of Principles (**10–13**) deals with REWARD AND PUNISHMENT, or the Moral Government of the Universe ; see p. 121.

10–11. Jewish ethics is based on the conviction of human responsibility—*freedom of the will* in the choice between good and evil. That choice may be limited for us by heredity and environment ; but just as the earth follows the sun in its vast sweep through celestial space, and yet at the same time daily turns on its axis, even so man, in the midst of the larger national and cultural whole of which he is a part, is a free agent in all fundamental matters of right and wrong in his life. God has given the reins of his conduct into man's own hands. And if he sin, God has taught him Repentance ; and that brings him, when led astray by error, back to his heavenly Father.

יב אֲנִי מַאֲמִין בֶּאֱמוּנָה שְׁלֵמָה בְּבִיאַת הַמָּשִׁיחַ · וְאַף

עַל פִּי שֶׁיִּתְמַהְמֵהַּ עִם כָּל־זֶה אֲחַכֶּה־לּוֹ בְּכָל־יוֹם שֶׁיָּבֹא :

יג אֲנִי מַאֲמִין בֶּאֱמוּנָה שְׁלֵמָה שֶׁתִּהְיֶה תְּחִיַּת הַמֵּתִים

בְּעֵת שֶׁתַּעֲלֶה רָצוֹן מֵאֵת הַבּוֹרֵא יִתְבָּרַךְ שְׁמוֹ וְיִתְעַלֶּה

זִכְרוֹ לָעַד וּלְנֵצַח נְצָחִים :

לִישׁוּעָתְךָ קִוִּיתִי יְיָ · קִוִּיתִי יְיָ לִישׁוּעָתְךָ · יְיָ לִישׁוּעָתְךָ

קִוִּיתִי :

---

12. The salvation of the individual Israelite is indissolubly
linked with the salvation of Israel; and through Israel, with the
triumph of righteousness in the coming of the Messianic Kingdom.
This belief in a Messianic Age has its roots in the Divine promise
to Abraham—"In thee shall all the families of the earth be
blessed" (Genesis 12. 3). The consciousness that Israel has the distinction and the mission to be a source of blessing to all mankind,
led its seers, teachers and thinkers to proclaim a United Humanity as
the Divine goal of human history.

To the overwhelming majority of the House of Israel in every
generation, the Messianic Hope has meant the belief in the coming of a
Messiah (lit. "the Anointed One")—an exalted Personality, upon
whom shall rest the spirit of the Lord. He will restore the glories of
Israel in Israel's ancient land. In his days, the peoples will unite in
acknowledging the unity of God, and there will be cessation of warfare
and the spread of freedom and righteousness over all the earth. In no
sense, however, will he have a hand in the forgiveness of sins. He is
but a mortal leader who, through the restoration of Israel, will usher in
the regeneration of mankind.

Endless have been the sufferings which the Jewish People has
undergone because of this belief. Israel rejects the Christian Messiah,
not only because it will not give up its belief in *One* God, but because
peace and justice have certainly not reigned universally since his
appearance 1,900 years ago. Nevertheless, Judaism fully acknowledges
the good work done by both Christianity and Mohammedanism.
"Through them"—says Maimonides—"the knowledge of the Bible
has spread even unto the remotest islands, and unto many nations
sunk in heathen errors and inhuman practices".

Some have held that Israel himself is the Messiah, God's chosen
and suffering Servant among the nations. The later Mystics added that
each Israelite was an atom, a spark, of the Messiah; and that it was
the Jew's most sacred duty to save that spark from extinction, and
fan it into a flame of holiness and righteousness.

12. I believe with perfect faith in the coming of the Messiah ; and, though he tarry, I will wait daily for his coming .

13. I believe with perfect faith that there will be a revival of the dead at the time when it shall please the Creator, blessed be his Name, and exalted be his fame for ever and ever.

Genesis 49. 18   For thy salvation I hope, O Lord !

---

13. Man is a citizen of two worlds—This world and the World to Come עולם הבא. God hath set eternity in our hearts, and only in Eternity can we reach our full development. This world is the vestibule ; the Future World is man's true home. " The dust returneth to the dust as it was, but the spirit returneth unto God who gave it " (Ecclesiastes 12. 7). Man is then brought into judgment for his deeds on earth ; and in-mortality is the lot of *all*—Jew and non-Jew alike—who in their earthly life do justly, love mercy, and walk in humility with their Maker. " The righteous of all nations have a portion in the World to Come ", say our Sages.

Many and various are the folk-beliefs and poetic fancies in the Rabbinical Writings concerning Heaven, *Gan Eden,* and Hell, *Gehinnom.* Our most authoritative religious guides, however, proclaim that no eye hath seen, nor can mortal fathom, what awaiteth us in the Hereafter ; but that even the tarnished soul will not forever be denied spiritual bliss. Judaism rejects the doctrine of eternal damnation.

" If a man die shall he live again ? " asks Job. Since Maccabean times, the pious have ever believed not only in the soul's survival of death and decay, but that, in God's unfathomable wisdom and in His own time, the body will be reunited with the soul. Many people find Resurrection incredible ; yet it is not more of a mystery than birth, or the stupendous miracle of the annual resurrection of plant-life after winter. " If what never before existed, exists ; why cannot that which once existed, exist again ? " asked Gabiha ben Pasissa. Maimonides and Hallevi make the doctrine of תחית המתים, lit. " revival of the dead ", identical with that of the immortality of the soul, and explain the Talmudic sayings to the contrary as figurative language.

The above are brief summaries of eternal problems. Fuller treatment would require a treatise. Every Jew is in duty bound to make careful study of some scholarly presentation of the Jewish Faith, in which these solemn questions are lucidly and reverently set forth.

פרשת עקדה:

בראשית כ'ב א'-י'ט

וַיְהִי אַחַר הַדְּבָרִים הָאֵלֶּה וְהָאֱלֹהִים נִסָּה אֶת־אַבְרָהָם וַיֹּאמֶר אֵלָיו אַבְרָהָם וַיֹּאמֶר הִנֵּנִי : וַיֹּאמֶר קַח־נָא אֶת־בִּנְךָ אֶת־יְחִידְךָ אֲשֶׁר־אָהַבְתָּ אֶת־יִצְחָק וְלֶךְ־לְךָ אֶל־אֶרֶץ הַמֹּרִיָּה וְהַעֲלֵהוּ שָׁם לְעֹלָה עַל אַחַד הֶהָרִים אֲשֶׁר אֹמַר אֵלֶיךָ : וַיַּשְׁכֵּם אַבְרָהָם בַּבֹּקֶר

THE AKEDAH (THE BINDING OF ISAAC)
The Ideal of Martyrdom

The aged Patriarch who had longed for a rightful heir, and who had had his longing fulfilled in the birth of Isaac, is bidden to offer up this child as a burnt offering unto the Lord. The purpose of the command was to apply a supreme test to Abraham's faith, thus strengthening his faith by the heroic exercise of it. It was a test safe only in a Divine hand, capable of intervening as He did intervene, and as it was His purpose from the first to intervene, as soon as the spiritual end of the trial was accomplished.

In Abraham's age, it was astounding that God should have interposed *to prevent* the sacrifice, not that He should have asked for it. A primary purpose of this command, therefore, was to demonstrate to Abraham and his descendants after him that God abhorred human sacrifice with an infinite abhorrence. Unlike the cruel heathen deities, *it was the spiritual surrender alone that God required.* Moses warns his people not to serve God in the manner of the surrounding nations. " For every abomination to the LORD which He hateth have they done unto their gods ; for even their sons and their daughters they have burnt in the fire to their gods " (Deuteronomy 12. 31). The Prophets shudder at this hideous aberration of man's sense of worship, and they do not rest till all Israel shares their horror of this savage custom. The story of the Binding of Isaac opens the long warfare of Israel against the abomination of child sacrifice which was rife among the Semitic peoples, as well as their Egyptian and Aryan neighbours.

A new meaning and influence begins for the *Akedah* and its demand for man's unconditional surrender to God's will and the behests of God's Law, with the Maccabean revolt, when Jews were first called upon to die for their Faith. Abraham's readiness to sacrifice his most sacred affections on the altar of his God, evoked and developed a new ideal in Israel, *the ideal of martyrdom.* The story of Hannah and her seven Sons, immortalized in the Second Book of Maccabees, has come down to us in many forms. In one of these, the martyr mother says to her youngest child, " Go to Abraham our Father, and tell him that I have bettered his instruction. He offered one child to God ; I offered seven. He merely bound the sacrifice ; I performed it " (Midrash). Allusions

*THE
AKEDAH*

Genesis xxii. 1—19.

[1]And it came to pass after these things, that God did prove Abraham, and said unto him, Abraham ; and he said, here am I. [2]And he said, Take now thy son, thine only son, whom thou lovest, even Isaac, and get thee into the land of Moriah ; and offer him there for a burnt offering upon one of the mountains which I will tell thee of. [3]And Abraham rose early in the morning, and saddled

to the Akedah early found their way into the Liturgy ; and in time a whole cycle of synagogue hymns (*piyyutim*) grew round it. In the Middle Ages, it gave fathers and mothers the superhuman courage to immolate themselves and their children, rather than see them fall away to idolatry or baptism. English Jews need but think of the soul-stirring tragedy enacted at York Castle in the year 1190, to understand the lines of the modern Jewish poet :

" We have sacrificed all. We have given our wealth,
Our homes, our honours, our land, our health,
Our lives—like Hannah her children seven—
For the sake of the Torah that came from Heaven " (J. L. Gordon).

Many to-day have little understanding for martyrdom. They fail to see that it represents the highest moral triumph of humanity— unwavering steadfastness to principle, even at the cost of life. They equally fail to see the lasting influence of such martyrdoms upon the life and character of the nation whose history they adorn ; that such nation is henceforth a stronger and more vital organism, endowed with new powers of the spirit, and above all with a heightened self-consciousness which nothing can daunt. In all human history, there is not a single noble cause, movement or achievement that did not call for sacrifice, nay sacrifice of life itself. Science, Liberty, Humanity, all took their toll of martyrs ; and so did and does Judaism. Israel is the classical people of martyrdom. No other people has made similar sacrifices for Truth, Conscience, Honour and Human Freedom. Few chapters of the Bible have had a more potent and more far-reaching influence on the lives and souls of men than the Akedah.

---

1. *prove. i.e.* test. All the other trials of Abraham's faith were to be crowned by his willingness to sacrifice his dearest hope to the will of God.

2. *thy son, thine only son, whom thou lovest, even Isaac.* The repetition indicates the intense strain that was being placed upon Abraham's faith, and the greatness of the sacrifice demanded of him.

the land of Moriah. Jewish tradition identifies the locality with the Temple Mount (II Chronicles 3, 1).

and offer him there. lit. " lift him up " (upon the altar) ; not the word which signifies the *slaying* of the sacrificial victim. From the outset, therefore, there was no intention of accepting a human sacrifice, although Abraham was at first not aware of this.

וַיַּחֲבשׁ אֶת־חֲמֹרוֹ וַיִּקַּח אֶת־שְׁנֵי נְעָרָיו אִתּוֹ וְאֵת יִצְחָק בְּנוֹ
וַיְבַקַּע עֲצֵי עֹלָה וַיָּקָם וַיֵּלֶךְ אֶל־הַמָּקוֹם אֲשֶׁר־אָמַר־לוֹ הָאֱלֹהִים :
בַּיּוֹם הַשְּׁלִישִׁי וַיִּשָּׂא אַבְרָהָם אֶת־עֵינָיו וַיַּרְא אֶת־הַמָּקוֹם מֵרָחֹק :
וַיֹּאמֶר אַבְרָהָם אֶל־נְעָרָיו שְׁבוּ־לָכֶם פֹּה עִם־הַחֲמוֹר וַאֲנִי וְהַנַּעַר
נֵלְכָה עַד־כֹּה וְנִשְׁתַּחֲוֶה וְנָשׁוּבָה אֲלֵיכֶם : וַיִּקַּח אַבְרָהָם אֶת־עֲצֵי
הָעֹלָה וַיָּשֶׂם עַל־יִצְחָק בְּנוֹ וַיִּקַּח בְּיָדוֹ אֶת־הָאֵשׁ וְאֶת־הַמַּאֲכֶלֶת
וַיֵּלְכוּ שְׁנֵיהֶם יַחְדָּו : וַיֹּאמֶר יִצְחָק אֶל־אַבְרָהָם אָבִיו וַיֹּאמֶר אָבִי
וַיֹּאמֶר הִנֶּנִּי בְנִי וַיֹּאמֶר הִנֵּה הָאֵשׁ וְהָעֵצִים וְאַיֵּה הַשֶּׂה לְעֹלָה :
וַיֹּאמֶר אַבְרָהָם אֱלֹהִים יִרְאֶה־לּוֹ הַשֶּׂה לְעֹלָה בְּנִי וַיֵּלְכוּ שְׁנֵיהֶם
יַחְדָּו : וַיָּבֹאוּ אֶל־הַמָּקוֹם אֲשֶׁר אָמַר־לוֹ הָאֱלֹהִים וַיִּבֶן שָׁם אַבְרָהָם
אֶת־הַמִּזְבֵּחַ וַיַּעֲרֹךְ אֶת־הָעֵצִים וַיַּעֲקֹד אֶת־יִצְחָק בְּנוֹ וַיָּשֶׂם אֹתוֹ
עַל־הַמִּזְבֵּחַ מִמַּעַל לָעֵצִים : וַיִּשְׁלַח אַבְרָהָם אֶת־יָדוֹ וַיִּקַּח אֶת־
הַמַּאֲכֶלֶת לִשְׁחֹט אֶת־בְּנוֹ : וַיִּקְרָא אֵלָיו מַלְאַךְ יְהֹוָה מִן־הַשָּׁמַיִם
וַיֹּאמֶר אַבְרָהָם ׀ אַבְרָהָם וַיֹּאמֶר הִנֵּנִי : וַיֹּאמֶר אַל־תִּשְׁלַח יָדְךָ
אֶל־הַנַּעַר וְאַל־תַּעַשׂ לוֹ מְאוּמָה כִּי עַתָּה יָדַעְתִּי כִּי־יְרֵא אֱלֹהִים
אַתָּה וְלֹא חָשַׂכְתָּ אֶת־בִּנְךָ אֶת־יְחִידְךָ מִמֶּנִּי : וַיִּשָּׂא אַבְרָהָם אֶת־
עֵינָיו וַיַּרְא וְהִנֵּה־אַיִל אַחַר נֶאֱחַז בַּסְּבַךְ בְּקַרְנָיו וַיֵּלֶךְ אַבְרָהָם
וַיִּקַּח אֶת־הָאַיִל וַיַּעֲלֵהוּ לְעֹלָה תַּחַת בְּנוֹ : וַיִּקְרָא אַבְרָהָם שֵׁם־
הַמָּקוֹם הַהוּא יְהֹוָה ׀ יִרְאֶה אֲשֶׁר יֵאָמֵר הַיּוֹם בְּהַר יְהֹוָה יֵרָאֶה :

5. *abide ye here.* Desiring to be alone with Isaac at the dread
moment of sacrifice.

and come again. Was there an undercurrent of conviction that God
would not exact His demand of him? The Rabbis declare that at the
moment the Spirit of Prophecy entered into him, and he spoke more
truly than he knew.

6. *the fire. i.e.* the vessel containing the glowing embers, by means
of which the wood on the altar was to be kindled.

7. *the lamb for a burnt offering.* This simple expression of boyish
curiosity heightens the intense pathos of the situation.

8. *went both of them together.* This phrase is repeated from *v.* 6.
Abraham's answer caused the truth to dawn upon Isaac's mind that
he was to be the offering.

his ass, and took two of his young men with him, and Isaac his son ; and he clave the wood for the burnt offering, and rose up, and went unto the place of which God had told him. ⁴On the third day Abraham lifted up his eyes, and saw the place afar off. ⁵And Abraham said unto his young men, Abide ye here with the ass, and I and the lad will go yonder, and we will worship, and come again to you. ⁶And Abraham took the wood of the burnt offering, and laid it upon Isaac his son ; and he took in his hand the fire and the knife ; and they went both of them together. ⁷And Isaac spoke unto Abraham his father, and said, My father : and he said, Here am I, my son. And he said, Behold, the fire and the wood : but where is the lamb for a burnt offering ? ⁸And Abraham said, God will provide himself the lamb for a burnt offering, my son : so they went both of them together. ⁹And they came to the place which God had told him of ; and Abraham built the altar there, and laid the wood in order, and bound Isaac his son, and laid him upon the altar, upon the wood. ¹⁰And Abraham stretched forth his hand, and took the knife to slay his son. ¹¹And the angel of the Lord called unto him out of heaven, and said, Abraham, Abraham : and he said here am I. ¹²And he said, Lay not thine hand upon the lad, neither do thou anything unto him : for now I know that thou fearest God, seeing thou hast not withheld thy son, thine only son, from me. ¹³And Abraham lifted up his eyes, and looked, and behold, behind him a ram caught in the thicket by his horns : and Abraham went and took the ram, and offered him up for a burnt offering in the stead of his son. ¹⁴And Abraham called the name of ˏthat place Adonai-yireh : as it is said to this day, In the mount where the Lord is seen. ¹⁵And the angel of the Lord called unto Abraham a second

11. *Abraham, Abraham.* This exclamation ("Abraham, Abraham ! ") reflects the anxiety of the angel of the Lord to hold Abraham back at the very last moment.

12. *now I know.* All that God desired was proof of Abraham's *willingness* to obey His command ; and the moral surrender had been complete.

14. *Adonai-yireh.* *i.e.* " God will see ".

to this day. *i.e.* it has become a proverbial expression.

in the mount where the Lord *is seen.* *i.e.* where He reveals himself—referring to the Temple which was afterwards erected on this mount.

17. *possess the gate of his enemies.* The " gate " of the city was its most important site, and its capture gave one command of the city.

וַיִּקְרָא מַלְאַךְ יְהוָֹה אֶל־אַבְרָהָם שֵׁנִית מִן־הַשָּׁמָיִם: וַיֹּאמֶר בִּי
נִשְׁבַּעְתִּי נְאֻם־יְהוָֹה כִּי יַעַן אֲשֶׁר עָשִׂיתָ אֶת־הַדָּבָר הַזֶּה וְלֹא
חָשַׂכְתָּ אֶת־בִּנְךָ אֶת־יְחִידֶךָ: כִּי־בָרֵךְ אֲבָרֶכְךָ וְהַרְבָּה אַרְבֶּה
אֶת־זַרְעֲךָ כְּכוֹכְבֵי הַשָּׁמַיִם וְכַחוֹל אֲשֶׁר עַל־שְׂפַת הַיָּם וְיִרַשׁ
זַרְעֲךָ אֵת שַׁעַר אֹיְבָיו: וְהִתְבָּרֲכוּ בְזַרְעֲךָ כֹּל גּוֹיֵי הָאָרֶץ עֵקֶב
אֲשֶׁר שָׁמַעְתָּ בְּקֹלִי: וַיָּשָׁב אַבְרָהָם אֶל־נְעָרָיו וַיָּקֻמוּ וַיֵּלְכוּ
יַחְדָּו אֶל־בְּאֵר שָׁבַע וַיֵּשֶׁב אַבְרָהָם בִּבְאֵר שָׁבַע:

SELECTIONS FROM JEWISH MORALISTS.

In many of the larger editions of the Prayer Book, there are extracts
from Jewish ethical literature for daily reading. The following selections from medieval Jewish Moralists are from I. *The Paths of Life* of
R. Eliezer ben Isaac (11th century); II. *The Ethical Will* of R. Asher
ben Yechiel (13th century); and III. and IV. *Rokeach* of R. Elazar of
Worms (died 1238).

For further selections, see pp. 722–4 and 1112–5.

I

" My son, give God all honour and the gratitude which is His due.
Thou hast need of Him, but He needs thee not. Put no trust in thy
mere physical well-being here below. Many a one has lain down to
sleep at nightfall, but at morn has not risen again. See that thou guard
well thy soul's holiness; let the thought of thy heart be saintly, and
profane not thy soul with words of impurity.

" Visit the sick and suffering man, and let thy countenance be cheerful when he sees it, but not so that thou oppress the helpless one with
gaiety. Comfort those that are in grief; let piety where thou seest it
affect thee even to tears; and then it may be that thou wilt be spared
the grief of weeping over the death of thy children.

" Respect the poor man by gifts whose hand he knows not of; be
not deaf to his beseechings, deal not hard words out to him. From
a wicked neighbour, see that thou keep aloof, and spend not much
of thy time among the people who speak ill of their brother-man; be
not as the fly that is always seeking sick and wounded places; and tell
not of the faults and failings of those about thee.

" Take no one to wife unworthy to be thy life's partner, and keep
thy sons close to the study of Divine things. Dare not to rejoice when

time out of heaven, [16]and said, By myself have I sworn, saith the Lord, because thou hast done this thing, and hast not withheld thy son, thine only son : [17]that I will surely bless thee, and I will surely multiply thy seed as the stars of the heaven, and as the sand which is upon the sea shore ; and thy seed shall possess the gate of his enemies ; [18]and through thy seed shall all the nations of the earth bless themselves ; because thou hast obeyed my voice. [19]So Abraham returned unto his young men, and they rose up and went together to Beer-sheba ; and Abraham dwelt at Beer-sheba.

---

thine enemy comes to the ground ; but give him food when he hungers. Be on thy guard lest thou give pain to the widow and the orphan ; and beware lest thou ever set thyself up to be both witness and judge against an other.

" Never enter thy house with abrupt and startling step, and bear not thyself so that those who dwell under thy roof shall dread thy presence. Purge thy soul of angry passion, that inheritance of fools; love wise men, and strive to know more and more of the works and the ways of the Creator ".

II

" Be not ready to quarrel ; avoid oaths and passionate adjurations, excess of laughter and outbursts of wrath : they disturb and confound the reason of man. Avoid dealings wherein there is a lie ; and make not gold the foremost longing of thy life ; for that is the first step to idolatry. Rather give money than words ; and as to ill words, see that thou place them in the scale of understanding before they leave thy lips.

" What has been uttered in thy presence, even though not told as secret, let it not pass from thee to others. And if one tell thee a tale, say not to him that thou hast heard it all before. Do not fix thine eyes too much on one who is far above thee in wealth, but on those who are behind thee in worldly fortune.

" Put no one to open shame ; misuse not thy power against any one ; who can tell whether thou wilt not some day be powerless thyself ?

" Do not struggle vaingloriously for the small triumph of showing thyself in the right and a wise man in the wrong ; thou art not one whit the wiser therefor. Be not angry or unkind to anyone for trifles, lest thou make thyself enemies unnecessarily.

" Do not refuse things out of mere obstinancy. Avoid, as much as may be, bad men, men of persistent angry feelings, fools ; thou canst get nothing from their company but shame. Be the first to extend courteous greeting to every one, whatever be his faith ; provoke not to wrath one of another belief than thine ".

III

" No crown carries such royalty with it as doth humility ; no monument gives such glory as an unsullied name ; no worldly gain can equal that which comes from observing God's laws. The highest sacrifice is a broken and contrite heart ; the highest wisdom is that which is found in the Torah ; the noblest of all ornaments is modesty ; and the most beautiful thing that man can do, is to forgive a wrong.

" Cherish a good heart when thou findest it in any one ; hate, for thou mayest hate it, the haughtiness of the overbearing man, and keep the boaster at a distance. There is no skill or cleverness to be compared to that which avoids temptation ; there is no force, no strength, that can equal piety.

" Let thy dealings be of such sort that a blush need never cover thy cheek ; be sternly dumb to the voice of passion ; commit no sin, saying to thyself that thou wilt repent and make atonement at a later time. Follow not the desire of the eyes, banish carefully all guile from thy soul, all unseemly self-assertion from thy bearing and thy temper.

" Speak never mere empty words ; enter into strife with no man ; place no reliance on men of mocking lips ; wrangle not with evil men ; cherish no too fixed good opinion of thyself, but lend thine ear to remonstrance and reproof. Be not weakly pleased at demonstrations of honour ; strive not anxiously for distinction ; be never enviously jealous of others, or too eager for money.

" Honour thy parents ; make peace whenever thou canst among people, lead them gently into the good path ; place thy trust in, give thy company to, those who fear God.

IV

" If the means of thy support in life be measured out scantily to thee, remember that thou hast to be thankful and grateful even for the mere privilege to breathe, and that thou must look upon that suffering as a test of thy piety and a preparation for better things. But if worldly wealth be lent to thee, exalt not thyself above thy brother ; for both of you came naked into the world, and both of you will surely have to sleep at last together in the dust.

" Bear well thy heart against the assaults of envy, which kills even sooner than death itself ; and know no envy at all, save such envy of the merits of virtuous men as shall lead thee to emulate the beauty of their lives. Surrender not thyself a slave to hate, that ruin of all the heart's good resolves, that destroyer of the very savour of food, of our sleep, of all reverence in our souls.

" Keep peace both within the city and without, for it goes well with all those who are counsellors of peace. Be wholly sincere ; mislead no one by prevarications or words smoother than intention, as little as by direct falsehood. For God the Eternal is a God of Truth.

" If thou hadst lived in the dread days of martyrdom, and the peoples had fallen on thee to force thee to apostatize from thy faith, thou wouldst surely, as did so many, have given thy life in its defence. Well then, fight now the fight laid on thee in the better days, the fight with evil desire ; fight and conquer, and seek for allies in this warfare of your soul, seek them in the fear of God and the study of the Torah. Forget not that God recompenses according to the measure wherewith we withstand the evil in our heart. Be a man in thy youth ; but if thou wert then defeated in the struggle, return, return at last to God, however old thou mayest be ".

ON THE SHEMA

ITS MEANING AND HISTORY

THE MEANING OF THE SHEMA.

THE SHEMA
    " Hear, O Israel, the Lord is our God, the Lord is One." These words enshrine Judaism's greatest contribution to the religious thought of mankind. They constitute the primal confession of Faith in the religion of the Synagogue, declaring that the Holy God worshipped and proclaimed by Israel is One ; and that He alone is God, Who was, is, and ever will be. That opening sentence of the Shema rightly occupies the central place in Jewish religious thought, for every other Jewish belief turns upon it : all goes back to it ; all flows from it.

ITS NEGATIONS

ITS NEGA-TIONS
    Polytheism. This sublime pronouncement of absolute monotheism was a declaration of war against all *polytheism*, the worship of many deities, and *paganism*, the deification of any finite thing or being or natural force. It scornfully rejected the star-cults and demon-worship of Babylonia, the animal-worship of Egypt, the Nature-worship of Greece, the emperor-worship of Rome, as well as the stone, tree, and serpent idolatries of other heathen religions, with their human sacrifices, lustful rites, their barbarism and inhumanity. Polytheism breaks the moral unity of man, and involves a variety of moral standards ; that is to say, no standard at all. The study of Comparative Religion clearly shows that, in polytheism, " side by side with a High God of Justice and Truth, the cults of a goddess of sensual love, a god of intoxicating drink, or of thieves and liars might be maintained " (Farnell). It certainly is not the soil on which a high and consistent ethical system grows. This is true of even its highest forms, such as the heathenism of the Greeks. " The Olympian divinities merely copied and even exaggerated the pleasures and pains, the perfections and imperfections, the loftiness and baseness of life on earth. Man could not receive any moral guidance from them. The Greeks possessed nothing even remotely resembling a Decalogue to restrain and bind them " (Kastein). Despite the love of beauty that characterized the Greeks, and despite their iridescent minds, they remained barbarians religiously and morally ; and their race was held up by their pupils, the Romans of Imperial days, as the prototype of everything that was mendacious, cruel, grasping and unjust. The fruit of Greek heathen teaching is, in fact, best seen in the horrors of the arena, the wholesale crucifixions, and the unspeakable bestialities of these same pupils, the Romans of Imperial days.

Quite other were the works of Hebrew Monotheism. Its preaching *ITS NEGA-* of the One, Omnipotent God liberated man from slavery to nature ; *TIONS* from fear of demons and goblins and ghosts ; from all creatures of man's infantile or diseased imagination. And that One God is One who " is sanctified by righteousness ", who is of purer eyes than to endure the sight of evil, or to tolerate wrong. This has been named *ethical monotheism*. There may have been independent recognition of the unity of the Divine nature among some peoples ; *e.g.* the unitary sun-cult of Ikhnaton in Egypt, or some faint glimpses of it in ancient Babylon. But neither in Egypt nor in Babylon was that monotheism essentially ethical, transfused with the Moral Law, and holding moral conduct to be the beginning and end of the religious life. Likewise, moral thinking and moral practices had indeed existed from immemorial times everywhere ; but the sublime idea that *morality* is something Divine, *spiritual in its inmost essence*—this is the distinctive teaching of the Hebrew Scriptures. In Hebrew monotheism, ethical values are not only the highest of human values, but exclusively the only values of eternal worth. " There is none upon earth that I desire beside Thee ", exclaims the Hebrew Psalmist. These words are but a poetic translation of the Shema in terms of religious experience.

Dualism. The Shema excludes *dualism*, and assumption of two rival powers of Light and Darkness, of the universe being regarded as the arena of a perpetual conflict between the principles of Good and Evil. This was the religion of Zoroaster, the seer of ancient Persia. His teaching was far in advance of all other heathen religions. Yet it was in utter contradiction to the belief in One, Supreme Ruler of the World, shaping the light, and at the same time controlling the darkness (Isaiah 45. 7). In the Jewish view, the universe, with all its conflicting forces, is marvellously harmonized in its totality ; and, in the sum, evil is overruled and made a new source of strength for the victory of the good. " He maketh peace in His high places ". Zoroastrianism is alleged by some to the responsible for many folklore elements in Jewish theology, especially for its angelogy. But though later generations in Judaism did speak of Satan and a whole hierarchy of angels, these were invariably thought of as absolutely the *creatures* of God. To attribute Divine powers to any of these beings, and deem them independent of God, or in any way on a par with the Supreme Being, would at all times have been deemed in Jewry to be wild blasphemy. It is noteworthy that the Jewish Mystics placed man—because he is endowed with free will—higher in the scale of spiritual existence than any mere " messenger ", which is the literal meaning of the word *angel*, and its Hebrew original.

Pantheism. And the Shema excludes *pantheism*, which considers the totality of things to be the Divine. The inevitable result of believing that all things are divine, and are equally divine, is that the distinction between right and wrong, between holy and unholy, loses its meaning. Pantheism, in addition, robs the Divine Being of conscious personality. In Judaism, on the contrary, though God pervades the universe, He transcends it. " The heavens are the work of Thy hands. They shall perish, but Thou shalt endure ; yea, all of them shall wax old like a garment ; as a vesture Thou shalt change them, and they shall be

changed. But Thou art the same, and Thy years shall have no end "
(Psalm 102. 26–28). The Rabbis expressed the same thought when they
said : " The Holy One, blessed be He, encompasses the universe, but
the universe does not encompass Him ". And so far from submerging
the Creator in His created universe, they would have endorsed the
lines of Emily Brontë,
> " Though earth and man were gone
> And suns and universes ceased to be,
> And Thou wert left alone,
> Every existence would exist in Thee ".

Judaism recognizes no *intermediary* between God and man ; and
declares that prayer is to be 'directed to God alone, and to no other
being in the heavens above or on earth beneath.

Its Positive Implications

ITS
AFFIRM-
ATIONS

Brotherhood of Man. The belief in the unity of the human race is
the natural corollary of the Unity of God, since the One God must be
the God of the whole of humanity. It was impossible for polytheism to
reach the conception of One Humanity. It could no more have written
the tenth chapter of Genesis, which traces the descent of all the races
of man to a common ancestry, than it could have written the first
chapter of Genesis, which proclaims the One God as the Creator of the
universe and all that is therein. Through Hebrew monotheism alone
was it possible to teach the Brotherhood of Man ; and it was Hebrew
monotheism which first declared, " Thou shalt love thy neighbour as
thyself. And the stranger that sojourneth with you shall be unto you
as the homeborn among you, and thou shalt love him as thyself "
(Leviticus 19. 18, 34).

Unity of the Universe. The conception of Monotheism has been
the basis of modern science, and of the modern world-view. Belief in
the Unity of God opened the eyes of man to the unity of Nature; " that
there is a unity and harmony in the *structure* of things, because of the
unity of their *Source* " (L. Roth). Likewise, A. N. Whitehead declares
that the conception of absolute cosmic regularity is monotheistic in
origin. And " every fresh discovery confirms the fact that in all Nature's
infinite variety there is one single Principle at work ; that there is one
controlling Power which—in the words of our Adon Olam hymn—is of
no beginning and no end, existing before all things were formed, and
remaining when all are gone " (Haffkine).

Unity of History. And this One God—Judaism teaches—is the
righteous and omnipotent Ruler of the universe. History, the scene of
His revelation, and the deeds of redemption it records, are the firm
foundation of all faith in the upward rise of man. In polytheism, it
was practically impossible to arrive at " the conception of a single
Providence ruling the world by fixed laws ; the multitude of divinities
suggests the possibility of discord in the divine cosmos ; and instils a
sense of the capricious and incalculable in the unseen world " (Farnell).
Not so Judaism, with its passionate belief in a Judge of all the earth,
who *can* and will do right. Israel's Teachers saw the world as one
magnificent unity, from the beginning even to everlasting; and history,
as the march of a Divine purpose across the abyss of time. In clarion

voice they proclaimed that Right was irresistible ; that what *ought to be, will be ;* and taught men to see the vision of " the kingdom of God ", *i.e.* human society based on righteousness, as the Messianic goal of history. As early as the days of the Second Temple, the idea of the Sovereignty of God was linked with the Shema. The Rabbis ordained that the words, " Hear, O Israel, the Lord is our God, the Lord is One ", should be immediately followed by ברוך שם כבוד מלכותו לעולם ועד, " Blessed be His name, Whose glorious kingdom is for ever and ever "— the proclamation of the ultimate triumph of justice on earth. Jewish monotheism thus stresses the supremacy of the will of God for righteousness over the forces of history : "*One* will rules all to *one* end—the world as it ought to be " (Moore).

THE HISTORY OF THE SHEMA

The work of the Rabbis. Who unveiled to the masses of the Jewish people the spiritual wonders enshrined in the Shema ? It is the immortal merit of the Rabbis in the centuries immediately before and after the Common Era, that these religious treasures did not remain the possession of the few, but became the heritage of the whole House of Israel. Thanks to the Rabbis, the fulness of that sacred truth gradually saturated the souls of the lowliest, as of the highest, in Israel. The recitation of the Shema was part of the daily worship in the Temple. The Rabbis took it over to the Synagogue, and gave it central place in the morning and evening prayers of every Jew. We may judge the important part it played in the rabbinic consciousness from the fact that the whole Mishna opens with the question, " From what hour is the evening Shema to be read ? " It is the Rabbis who raised the six words שמע ישראל ד' אלהינו ד' אחד to a confession of Faith ; who ordained that they be repeated by the entire body of worshippers when the Torah is taken out on Sabbaths and Festivals ; in the Sanctification (*Kedusha*) on these sacred occasions ; after the Neilah service, as the culmination of the great Day of Atonement ; and in man's last hour, when he is setting out to meet his Heavenly Father face to face. In this way, the Shema became the soul-stirring, collective self-expression of Israel's spiritual being. But even in the private prayer of the individual Jew, the Rabbis spared no effort to enhance the solemnity of its utterance. It is to be said audibly, they ordained, the ear hearing what the lips utter ; and its last word *echod* (" One ") is to be pronounced with special emphasis. All thoughts other than God's Unity must be shut out. It must be spoken with entire collection and concentration of heart and mind (כוונה) ; the reading of the Shema may not be interrupted, even to respond to the salutation of a king. If the words of the Shema are uttered devoutly and reverently—the Rabbis taught—they thrill the very soul of the worshipper, and bring him a realization of communion with the Most High. " When men in prayer declare the Unity of the Holy Name in love and reverence, the walls of earth's darkness are cleft in twain, and the face of the Heavenly King is revealed, lighting up the universe " (Zohar).

The Shema and martyrdom. The Shema became the first prayer of innocent childhood, and the last utterance of the dying. It was the rallying-cry by which a hundred generations in Israel were welded

ITS HISTORY

together to do the will of their Father in heaven ; it was the watchword for the myriads of martyrs who agonized and died for the Unity, " as the *ultima ratio* of their religion " (Herford). During every persecution and massacre, from the time of the Crusades to the wholesale slaughter of the Jewish population in the Ukraine in the years 1919 to 1921, *Shema Yisroel* has been the last sound on the lips of the victims. All the Jewish martyrologies are written round the Shema. In the Middle Ages, the Jewish Teachers introduced a regular Benediction for the recital of the Shema at the hour of " sanctification of the Name " : *i.e.* when a man is facing martyrdom. It is as follows : " Blessed art Thou, O Lord our God, King of the Universe, who hast hallowed us by Thy commandments, and bade us sanctify Thy glorious and awful Name in public. Blessed art Thou, O Lord, Who sanctifiest Thy Name amongst the many " (Recanati). Numberless were the dire occasions when this Benediction was spoken. One instance will suffice. When the hordes of the Crusaders reached Xanten, near the Rhine (June 27, 1096), the Jews of that place were partaking of their Sabbath-eve meal together. The arrival of the Crusaders meant, of course, certain death to them, and the meal was discontinued. But they did not leave the hall, until the saintly R. Moses ha-Cohen first said Grace, enlarging the regular text with prayers appropriate to the awful moment. The Grace was concluded with the Shema. Thereupon they went to the Synagogue, where they all met with martyrdom. The reading of the Shema indeed fulfilled the promise of the Rabbis, that it clothes man with invincible lion-strength. It endowed the Jew with the double-edged sword of the spirit against the unutterable terrors of his long night of suffering and exile

Defence of the Unity. The Rabbis not only trained Israel to the understanding of the vital significance of the Divine Unity ; they also defended the Jewish God-idea whenever its purity was threatened by enemies from without or within. They permitted no toying with polytheism, be its disguises ever so ethereal ; they brooked no departure, even by a hair's breadth, from the most rigorous Monotheism ; and rejected absolutely everything that might weaken or obscure it. The fight against idolatory and paganism begun by the Prophets was continued by the Pharisees. Abraham, the father of the Hebrew people, they taught, started on his career as an idol-wrecker. In legends, parables, and discourses, they showed forth the folly and futility of idol-worship, and pointed to the infamy and moral degradation evidenced by the Roman deification of the reigning Emperor. The Rabbis defended the Unity of God against the Jewish Gnostics, those ancient heretics who blasphemed the God of Israel, ridiculed the Scriptures, and asserted a duality of Divine Powers. And they defended it against the Jewish Christians, who darkened the sky of Israel's Monotheism by teaching a novel doctrine of God's " sonship " ; by identifying a man, born of woman, with God ; and by advocating the doctrine of a Trinity.

In the Middle Ages. Throughout the Middle Ages, the Jewish Teachers continued the religious education of the people begun in earlier centuries. They upheld the cause of pure Monotheism at the Religious Disputations in which they were compelled to participate by the triumphant and all-powerful Church. Of especial importance is the DEFENCE work of the Jewish philosophers, whose effort represents a distinct OF SHEMA enrichment of the world's religious thinking. Saadya, Gabirol, Bachya, Hallevi, Maimonides purge the concept of God of all anthropomorphism, and vindicate the unity and uniqueness of Israel's God-conception. Solomon Ibn Gabirol, renowned alike as philosopher and Synagogue poet, begins his *Royal Crown*, with the words, " Thou art One, the first great Cause of all : Thou art One, and none can penetrate—not even the wisest in heart—the unfathomable mystery of Thy Unity. Thou art One ; Thy Unity can neither be lessened nor increased, for neither plurality, nor change nor any attribute, can be applied to Thee. Thou art One, but the imagination fails in any attempt to define or limit Thee. Therefore I said, ' I will take heed to my ways, that I sin not with my tongue '."

In the present day. The long and arduous warfare begun by the Prophets and continued by the Rabbis is not yet ended. The Unity of God has its antagonists in the present day, as in former ages. Even advanced non-Jewish writers on religion are, as a rule, but hesitating witnesses to the Unity of God ; and liberal Christian theologians wax quite eloquent in depicting the amenities of life under polytheism. They plead that it helped to interfuse the whole of life with " religion " : to intensify the " joy of life " and delight in the world of Nature : and that it made for religious tolerance.

On closer examination, these partisan claims collapse entirely. As for tolerance, even enlightened Greek polytheism permitted three of its greatest thinkers—Socrates, Protagoras, and Anaxagoras—to be put to death on religious grounds. The Jews came into contact with Greek polytheism in its later stages. But neither Antiochus Epiphanes who attempted to drown . Judaism in the blood of its faithful children, nor Apion, the frenzied spokesman of the anti-Semites in Alexandria, displayed particular tolerance.

Again, the alleged interfusion under polytheism of the whole of life with " religion " did not save the votaries of Greek polytheism from moral laxity, licentiousness and *inhuman* behaviour both in war and in peace. As to intensifying the " joy of life "—that " joy of life ", even among Greeks, seems to have been the prerogative of the few. Thus, Greek society was broad-based on unrighteousness, *i.e.* on human slavery ; and in Greece, "the animated tool", as Aristotle defined the slave, was denied all human rights. It is, furthermore, difficult to see wherein the " joy of life " consisted for the human sacrifices regularly offered by the heathen Semites and Slavs, Germans and Greeks. In regard to the last named, it is not generally remembered that we find traces of human sacrifice throughout the Hellenic world, in the cult of almost every god, and in all periods of the independent Greek states. In the Roman Empire, this hideous accompaniment of polytheism continued till the fourth century of our present era ; while in India the burning of widows was officially abolished only in the year 1826 !

The other claims on behalf of polytheism are seen to be equally untenable. Delight in the world of Nature was not confined to polytheists. It could not have been alien to the people that produced the Song of Songs. "Aesthetic contemplation of nature only began when

DEFENCE
OF SHEMA

the landscape was freed from its gods, and men could rejoice in nature's own greatness and beauty " (Humboldt).

Various secular writers on religion go far beyond modernist theologians in their depreciation of monotheism. Unlike those theologians, they do not halt between two opinions, and they know no hesitancies. Ernest Renan ascribed the rise of belief in One God to the desert surroundings of the early Hebrews. " The desert is monotheistic ", he announced. He omitted, however, to explain why, if so, the other Semitic desert-dwellers had remained polytheists ; or why the primeval inhabitants of the Sahara, Gobi and Kalahari deserts were not monotheists. Anti-Semites go further still. In order to belittle Israel's infinite glory as the Prophet of Monotheism, they decry the Unity of God as " a bare, barren, arithmetical idea " ; as merely " the minimum of religion ". (It is strange that the alleged " minimum of religion " should have given the Decalogue to the world ; should have produced the Psalms, the book of devotion of civilized humanity ; should have succeeded in shattering all idols, turning the course of history, and freeing the children of men from the stone heart of heathen antiquity). Some of these anti-Semites contrast the bountiful abundance displayed by Greece in its hundreds of gods and goddesses, by India in its multitude of fantastic deities, with the one God of Israel. " *Only* one God—how mean, how meagre ! "—they exclaim. It is evident that these men deem it necessary to be neither logical nor fair when attacking Jews ; and that one may say anything of Jews and Judaism so long as it covers them with ridicule. But Truth is on the march ; and the number of those non-Jewish thinkers is growing who recognize that " the Shema is the basis of all higher, ethical, spiritual religion ; an imperishable pronouncement, reverberating to this day in every idealistic conception of the universe " (Gunkel).

Conclusion. " It was undeniably a stroke of true religious genius— a veritable prompting by the Holy Spirit, רוּחַ הַקֹּדֶשׁ,—to select, as Prof. Steinthal reminds us, out of the 5,845 verses of the Pentateuch this one verse (Deuteronomy 6. 4) as the inscription for Israel's banner of victory. Throughout the entire realm of literature, secular or sacred, there is probably no utterance to be found that can be compared in its intellectual and spiritual force, or in the influence it exerted upon the whole thinking and feeling of civilized mankind, with the six words which have become the battle-cry of the Jewish People for more than twenty-five centuries " (Kohler).

THE MOURNER'S KADDISH.

The Kaddish prayer is daily recited by hundreds of thousands old and young, rich and poor, learned and ignorant, throughout the world. The tenderest threads of filial feeling and recollection are entwined about this prayer. Even those Jews who are lax and indifferent in religious observance deem it a sacred act of reverence towards their departed father or mother to say Kaddish every day for a year and then one day a year, on the Yahrzeit.

I.

Its origin is mysterious. We find foreshadowings of it in the Biblical books ; prayers for the dead are mentioned in the Books of Maccabees ; snatches of the Kaddish reach us in the legends of Talmudic teachers ; and echoes of it in the writings of the early Mystics : but the Prayer in its entirety we find neither in the Bible, nor in the Mishna, nor in the vast Talmudic and Midrashic literatures. It seems to be a gradual growth, continued from generation to generation, from age to age, until in the period of the Gaonim, some twelve centuries ago, it attained the form which we have before us in our Prayer Books.

So much as to the history of the Kaddish. What of its content ?

The Kaddish exhausts itself in glorification of God, in supplication for God's Kingdom, and for peace upon the House of Israel ; but there is no reference to death, in this Prayer, or to the Hereafter !

A well-known story in the Talmud supplies the key with which to unlock the secret of the Kaddish. Rabbi Meir, the Talmud records, lost both his sons on one day. It was on Sabbath afternoon, when he was in the House of Learning. His wife, the brilliant Beruria, did not on his return break the news to him, in order not to sadden his Sabbath-joy. She waited till the evening, and then timidly approaching her husband, she said : " I have a question to ask of thee. Some time ago, a friend gave me some jewels to keep for him. To-day he demands them back. What shall I do ? " " I cannot understand thee asking such a question. Un-hesitatingly thou shalt return the jewels." Thereupon she led him to the room where their children lay dead. " These are the jewels I must return." Rabbi Meir could but sob forth the words of Job : ד' נתן וד' " The Lord hath given, and the Lord hath taken ; blessed be the Name of the LORD."

The Kaddish is but an amplification of these words of Job ; it is but a summons for us all to imitate the example of Job, Beruria, and Rabbi Meir. When the dark grave swallows what was dearest to us on earth, it is then that Judaism bids us say : " It was God Who gave this joy unto us ; it is God Who hath taken it from us to Himself. We will not wail, nor murmur, nor complain. We will exclaim, ' Blessed be the Name of the LORD '."

Can any faith be higher than this ? Can we conceive a fuller submission to the will of God ? *Such* faith, *such* submission to God's eternal will, is ours when during the months of mourning we recite before the Congregation : יתגדל ויתקדש שמה רבא " Magnified and hallowed be the great Name of God." Precisely at the moment when it is hardest so to do, we lift up our voice to assert the essential holiness and goodness of the Infinite. We rise to the level of Isaiah, and with him declare that, " God's ways are not our ways, His thoughts are not our thoughts ; for as the heavens are higher than the earth, so are His ways higher than our ways, and His thoughts than our thoughts ". In such attitude alone can mortal find peace ; and, therefore, this prayer of sanctification ends with the thought : " May the God of peace in the High Heavens send peace to all whose hearts have been saddened by death." And the congregation answers, *Amen*—Amen for peace in the high heavens, Amen for peace on earth ; peace for the departed, peace for the sorrowing.

II.

So far as to the meaning of the Kaddish to the living. There is another side of the Kaddish—best seen in a folk legend concerning Akiba, the great rabbi, warrior, and martyr. It tells that he once beheld the shadowy figure of a man that carried a load of wood upon his shoulders, and groaning under his load. " What aileth thee ? " asked the Rabbi. " I am one of those forlorn souls condemned for his sins to the agony of hell-fire. I must procure the wood, and myself prepare my place of torment." " And is there no hope for thee ? " " Yes, if my little son, whom I left behind an infant, is taught to utter the Kaddish and cause the assembly of worshippers to respond אמן יהא שמה רבא מברך לעלם ולעלמי עלמיא ' Amen, may God's great Name be praised for ever and ever ' ". Rabbi Akiba resolved to search for the family and infant son of the deceased. He found that the mother had married again, this time a heathen ; and that the child had not even been initiated into the Covenant of Abraham. Rabbi Akiba took the child under his care, and taught him to lisp the Kaddish. Soon— the legend continues—a heavenly message assured him that, through the son's Prayer, the father had obtained salvation.

Now the soundest and saintliest thinkers in Israel have always maintained that all detailed descriptions of Hell or Heaven are but poetic symbols, intended to make abstract conceptions intelligible to mortal minds. Our God is a God of Mercy, who is also a God of Justice. He therefore, rewards the righteous and punishes the wicked. *That* this is done is in the everlasting nature of things ; but *how* this is done, is beyond the ken of mortals. הנסתרות לד׳ אלהינו. " The secret things belong to God alone."

And yet, this legend of Rabbi Akiba and the child saving his father from hell-torments, contains a wonderful truth. It teaches that parent and child are *one*. No man has altogether died, even to this world, if he knows that those he leaves behind him will read this Prayer after him, wherever they be scattered in this wide world ; that they will reverence his memory as their dearest inheritance, and through- out their days, consider the recital of the Kaddish in his memory as a sacred act. מה זרעו בחיים אף הוא בחיים. " No one can be called dead whose children continue his work ", say the Rabbis. And the Kaddish is the vow which the children pronounce that it is their holiest resolve to live in unity of soul with the parent who departed this life ; that the God of the parents shall be their God ; and, therefore, in the face of death they exclaim יתגדל ויתקדש שמה רבא.

Thus is the Kaddish a bond strong enough to chain earth to heaven. It keeps the living together, and forms the bridge across the chasm of the grave to the mysterious Realm of those whose bodies sleep in the dust, but whose souls repose in the shadows of the Almighty. It teaches our soul to cling in trust and hope to One Whose decree obtains in the daily happenings of our individual lives as well as in the larger destinies of mankind, nay, of the universe. This prayer, in short, is the thread in Israel that binds the generations " each to each in natural piety ", and makes the hearts of parents and children beat in eternal unison.

תְּפִלַּת מִנְחָה לְחוֹל :

אַשְׁרֵי יוֹשְׁבֵי בֵיתֶךָ עוֹד יְהַלְלוּךָ פֶּלָה :

אַשְׁרֵי הָעָם שֶׁכָּכָה לּוֹ אַשְׁרֵי הָעָם שֶׁיְיָ אֱלֹהָיו :

קמ״ה   תְּהִלָּה לְדָוִד ·

אֲרוֹמִמְךָ אֱלוֹהַי הַמֶּלֶךְ וַאֲבָרְכָה שִׁמְךָ לְעוֹלָם וָעֶד :

בְּכָל־יוֹם אֲבָרְכֶךָ וַאֲהַלְלָה שִׁמְךָ לְעוֹלָם וָעֶד :

גָּדוֹל יְהוָה וּמְהֻלָּל מְאֹד וְלִגְדֻלָּתוֹ אֵין חֵקֶר :

דּוֹר לְדוֹר יְשַׁבַּח מַעֲשֶׂיךָ וּגְבוּרֹתֶיךָ יַגִּידוּ :

הֲדַר כְּבוֹד הוֹדֶךָ וְדִבְרֵי נִפְלְאֹתֶיךָ אָשִׂיחָה :

וֶעֱזוּז נוֹרְאֹתֶיךָ יֹאמֵרוּ וּגְדֻלָּתְךָ אֲסַפְּרֶנָּה :

זֵכֶר רַב־טוּבְךָ יַבִּיעוּ וְצִדְקָתְךָ יְרַנֵּנוּ :

חַנּוּן וְרַחוּם יְהוָה אֶרֶךְ אַפַּיִם וּגְדָל־חָסֶד :

טוֹב־יְהוָה לַכֹּל וְרַחֲמָיו עַל־כָּל־מַעֲשָׂיו :

יוֹדוּךָ יְהוָה כָּל־מַעֲשֶׂיךָ וַחֲסִידֶיךָ יְבָרְכוּכָה :

כְּבוֹד מַלְכוּתְךָ יֹאמֵרוּ וּגְבוּרָתְךָ יְדַבֵּרוּ :

לְהוֹדִיעַ לִבְנֵי הָאָדָם גְּבוּרֹתָיו וּכְבוֹד הֲדַר מַלְכוּתוֹ :

THE AFTERNOON SERVICE.

(תְּפִלַּת מִנְחָה)

The *Minchah*, or Afternoon, Service consists of Psalm 145, the *Amidah*, *Tachanun*, and *Oleynu*. There is no Shema, as that was to be read only " when thou liest down, and when thou risest up "; *i.e.* at night and in the morning. In consequence, the Benedictions before and after the Shema find no place in the Afternoon Prayer. There are also slight divergences in the Amidah from that of the Morning Service, especially on Fast Days. Furthermore, *Tachanun* is often omitted when Minchah is recited near nightfall. *Oleynu* and

THE AFTERNOON SERVICE

ASHREY YOSHEVEY VEYSECHO

Psalm 84. 5
Psalm 144. 15

THE GREAT-NESS AND UNENDING GOODNESS OF GOD

See p. 85

Happy are they that dwell in thy house : they will be ever praising thee. (Selah.) Happy is the people that is thus favoured : happy is the people, whose God is the Lord.

Psalm cxlv. ¹A Psalm of Praise : of David.

I will extol thee, my God, O King ; and I will bless thy Name for ever and ever. ²Every day will I bless thee ; and I will praise thy Name for ever and ever. ³Great is the Lord, and exceedingly to be praised : and his greatness is unsearchable. ⁴One generation shall laud thy works to another, and shall declare thy mighty acts. ⁵On the majestic glory of thy splendour, and on thy marvellous deeds, will I meditate. ⁶And men shall speak of the might of thy tremendous acts; and I will recount thy greatness. ⁷They shall pour forth the fame of thy great goodness, and shall exult in thy righteousness. ⁸The Lord is gracious and merciful ; slow to anger and of great lovingkindness. ⁹The Lord is good to all ; and his tender mercies are over all his works. ¹⁰All thy works shall give thanks unto thee, O Lord ; and thy loving ones shall bless thee. ¹¹They shall speak of the glory of thy kingdom, and talk of thy power ; ¹²to make known to the

Mourner's Kaddish are likewise omitted in the Minchah preceding a Sabbath or Festival, whenever the Sabbath Service, or that of the Festival, immediately follows.

The time for Minchah is from 12.30 to an hour and a quarter before sunset. The earlier hour is, as a rule, adhered to only on Sabbaths and Festivals. On weekdays, Minchah is usually joined to the Evening Service. When this is done, *Oleynu* is omitted at the end of the Minchah.

The Rabbis stressed the importance of the Minchah prayer. It was associated with the Prophet Elijah and his sublime contest with the priests of Baal on Mt. Carmel. " And it came to pass at the time of the offering of the *minchah*, that Elijah the prophet came near and said, Lord God of Abraham, Isaac and Jacob, let it be known this day that Thou art God in Israel " (I Kings 18. 36). The Minchah prayer is thus linked with the day when all the people fell on their faces, and exclaimed, " The Lord, He is God ; the Lord, He is God "—words which form the conclusion of the Atonement Service, and are among the last words of the dying Israelite.

מַלְכוּתְךָ מַלְכוּת כָּל־עֹלָמִים וּמֶמְשַׁלְתְּךָ בְּכָל־דּוֹר וָדֹר :

סוֹמֵךְ יְהֹוָה לְכָל־הַנֹּפְלִים וְזוֹקֵף לְכָל־הַכְּפוּפִים :

עֵינֵי כֹל אֵלֶיךָ יְשַׂבֵּרוּ וְאַתָּה נוֹתֵן־לָהֶם אֶת־אָכְלָם בְּעִתּוֹ :

פּוֹתֵחַ אֶת־יָדֶךָ וּמַשְׂבִּיעַ לְכָל־חַי רָצוֹן :

צַדִּיק יְהֹוָה בְּכָל־דְּרָכָיו וְחָסִיד בְּכָל־מַעֲשָׂיו :

קָרוֹב יְהֹוָה לְכָל־קֹרְאָיו לְכֹל אֲשֶׁר יִקְרָאֻהוּ בֶאֱמֶת :

רְצוֹן־יְרֵאָיו יַעֲשֶׂה וְאֶת־שַׁוְעָתָם יִשְׁמַע וְיוֹשִׁיעֵם :

שׁוֹמֵר יְהֹוָה אֶת־כָּל־אֹהֲבָיו וְאֵת כָּל־הָרְשָׁעִים יַשְׁמִיד :

תְּהִלַּת יְהֹוָה יְדַבֶּר־פִּי וִיבָרֵךְ כָּל־בָּשָׂר שֵׁם קָדְשׁוֹ לְעוֹלָם וָעֶד :

וַאֲנַחְנוּ נְבָרֵךְ יָהּ מֵעַתָּה וְעַד־עוֹלָם הַלְלוּיָהּ :

The following prayer, קַדְמוֹנִיּוֹת, to עֲמִידָה, p. 294 is to be said standing.

אֲדֹנָי שְׂפָתַי תִּפְתָּח וּפִי יַגִּיד תְּהִלָּתֶךָ :

בָּרוּךְ אַתָּה יְיָ אֱלֹהֵינוּ וֵאלֹהֵי אֲבוֹתֵינוּ · אֱלֹהֵי אַבְרָהָם אֱלֹהֵי יִצְחָק וֵאלֹהֵי יַעֲקֹב · הָאֵל הַגָּדוֹל הַגִּבּוֹר וְהַנּוֹרָא אֵל עֶלְיוֹן · גּוֹמֵל חֲסָדִים טוֹבִים וְקוֹנֵה הַכֹּל · וְזוֹכֵר חַסְדֵי אָבוֹת וּמֵבִיא גוֹאֵל לִבְנֵי בְנֵיהֶם לְמַעַן שְׁמוֹ בְּאַהֲבָה :

During the עֲשֶׂרֶת יְמֵי תְשׁוּבָה say :—

זָכְרֵנוּ לַחַיִּים מֶלֶךְ חָפֵץ בַּחַיִּים · וְכָתְבֵנוּ בְּסֵפֶר הַחַיִּים · לְמַעַנְךָ אֱלֹהִים חַיִּים :

THE GREAT-NESS AND UNENDING GOODNESS OF GOD

sons of men his mighty acts, and the majestic glory of his kingdom. ¹³Thy kingdom is an everlasting kingdom, and thy dominion endureth throughout all generations. ¹⁴The Lord upholdeth all that fall, and raiseth up all those that are bowed down. ¹⁵The eyes of all wait upon thee ; and thou givest them their food in due season. ¹⁶Thou openest thine hand, and satisfiest every living thing with favour. ¹⁷The Lord is righteous in all his ways, and loving in all his works. ¹⁸The Lord is nigh unto all them that call upon him, to all that call upon him in truth. ¹⁹He will fulfil the desire of them that reverence him ; he also will hear their cry, and will save them. ²⁰The Lord guardeth all them that love him ; but all the wicked will he destroy. ²¹My mouth shall speak of the praise of the Lord ; and let all flesh bless his holy Name for ever and ever.

Psalm 115. 18   But we will bless the Lord from this time forth and for evermore.   Praise ye the Lord.

AMIDAH :   *The following prayer (Amidah) to " as in ancient years," p. 295, is to be said standing.*

Psalm 51. 17   O Lord, open thou my lips, and my mouth shall declare thy praise.

I. THE GOD OF HISTORY

Blessed art thou, O Lord our God and God of our fathers, God of Abraham, God of Isaac, and God of Jacob, the great, mighty and revered God, the most high God, who bestowest lovingkindnesses, and art Master of all things ; who re-

See p. 131 memberest the pious deeds of the patriarchs, and in love wilt bring a redeemer to their children's children for thy Name's sake.

[During the Ten Days of Repentance say :—

Remember us unto life, O King, who delightest in life, and inscribe us in the book of life, for thine own sake, O living God.]

מֶלֶךְ עוֹזֵר וּמוֹשִׁיעַ וּמָגֵן ‧ בָּרוּךְ אַתָּה יְיָ ‧ מָגֵן אַבְרָהָם ‧

אַתָּה גִבּוֹר לְעוֹלָם אֲדֹנָי מְחַיֵּה מֵתִים אַתָּה רַב לְהוֹשִׁיעַ ‧

From the day after שִׂמְחַת תּוֹרָה *until the Eve of* פֶּסַח *say :—*

מַשִּׁיב הָרוּחַ וּמוֹרִיד הַגָּשֶׁם ‧

מְכַלְכֵּל חַיִּים בְּחֶסֶד מְחַיֵּה מֵתִים בְּרַחֲמִים רַבִּים ‧ סוֹמֵךְ

נוֹפְלִים וְרוֹפֵא חוֹלִים וּמַתִּיר אֲסוּרִים וּמְקַיֵּם אֱמוּנָתוֹ

לִישֵׁנֵי עָפָר ‧ מִי כָמוֹךְ בַּעַל גְּבוּרוֹת וּמִי דּוֹמֶה לָּךְ ‧

מֶלֶךְ מֵמִית וּמְחַיֶּה וּמַצְמִיחַ יְשׁוּעָה ‧

During the עֲשֶׂרֶת יְמֵי תְשׁוּבָה *say :—*

מִי כָמוֹךְ אַב הָרַחֲמִים זוֹכֵר יְצוּרָיו לַחַיִּים בְּרַחֲמִים ‧

וְנֶאֱמָן אַתָּה לְהַחֲיוֹת מֵתִים ‧ בָּרוּךְ אַתָּה יְיָ ‧ מְחַיֵּה

הַמֵּתִים :

When the Reader repeats the עֲמִידָה, *the following* קְדוּשָׁה *is said :—*

Reader. נְקַדֵּשׁ אֶת שִׁמְךָ בָּעוֹלָם כְּשֵׁם שֶׁמַּקְדִּישִׁים אוֹתוֹ

בִּשְׁמֵי מָרוֹם כַּכָּתוּב עַל יַד נְבִיאֶךָ ‧ וְקָרָא זֶה אֶל זֶה וְאָמַר ‧

Cong. קָדוֹשׁ קָדוֹשׁ קָדוֹשׁ יְיָ צְבָאוֹת ‧ מְלֹא כָל הָאָרֶץ

כְּבוֹדוֹ : *Reader.* לְעֻמָּתָם בָּרוּךְ יֹאמֵרוּ ‧ *Cong.* בָּרוּךְ כְּבוֹד

יְיָ מִמְּקוֹמוֹ : *Reader.* וּבְדִבְרֵי קָדְשְׁךָ כָּתוּב לֵאמֹר ‧

Cong. יִמְלֹךְ יְיָ לְעוֹלָם אֱלֹהַיִךְ צִיּוֹן לְדֹר וָדֹר ‧ הַלְלוּיָהּ :

Reader. לְדוֹר וָדוֹר נַגִּיד גָּדְלֶךָ ‧ וּלְנֵצַח נְצָחִים

קְדֻשָּׁתְךָ נַקְדִּישׁ ‧ וְשִׁבְחֲךָ אֱלֹהֵינוּ מִפִּינוּ לֹא יָמוּשׁ

O King, Helper, Saviour and Shield. Blessed art thou, O Lord, the Shield of Abraham.

II. THE GOD OF NATURE

Thou, O Lord, art mighty for ever, thou revivest the dead, thou art mighty to save.
[*From the day after Simchas Torah until the Eve of Passover, say* : Thou causest the wind to blow and the rain to fall.]

See p. 133

Thou sustainest the living with lovingkindness, revivest the dead with great mercy, supportest the falling, healest the sick, freest the bound, and keepest thy faith to them that sleep in the dust. Who is like unto thee, Lord of mighty acts, and who resembleth thee, O King, who orderest death and restorest life, and causest salvation to spring forth ?
[*During the Ten Days of Repentance say* :— Who is like unto thee, Father of mercy, who in mercy rememberest thy creatures unto life ?]

Yea, faithful art thou to revive the dead. Blessed art thou, O Lord, who revivest the dead.

III. "KEDU-SHA" SANCTIFI-CATION OF GOD

[*When the Reader repeats the Amidah, the following up to "Thou art holy" p. 279, is said after " who revivest the dead."*

Reader.—We will sanctify thy Name in the world even as they sanctify it in the highest heavens, as it is written

See p. 134

by the hand of thy prophet :

Isaiah 6. 3

And they called one unto the other and said,

Cong.—HOLY, HOLY, HOLY IS THE LORD OF HOSTS : THE WHOLE EARTH IS FULL OF HIS GLORY.

Reader.—Those over against them say, Blessed—

Ezekiel 3. 12

Cong.—BLESSED BE THE GLORY OF THE LORD FROM HIS PLACE.

Reader.—And in thy Holy Words it is written, saying,

Psalm 146. 10

Cong.—THE LORD SHALL REIGN FOR EVER, THY GOD, O ZION, UNTO GENERATIONS. PRAISE YE THE LORD.

Reader —Unto all generations we will declare thy great-

בָּרוּךְ · אַתָּה וְקָדוֹשׁ · גָּדוֹל מֶלֶךְ אֵל כִּי · וָעֶד לְעוֹלָם

During the עֲשֶׂרֶת יְמֵי תְּשׁוּבָה אַתָּה יְיָ · הָאֵל הַקָּדוֹשׁ :

conclude the Blessing thus :—

הַמֶּלֶךְ הַקָּדוֹשׁ :

אַתָּה קָדוֹשׁ וְשִׁמְךָ קָדוֹשׁ וּקְדוֹשִׁים בְּכָל־יוֹם יְהַלְלוּךָ

סֶּלָה · בָּרוּךְ אַתָּה יְיָ · הָאֵל הַקָּדוֹשׁ : עֲשֶׂרֶת יְמֵי תְּשׁוּבָה *During the*

conclude the Blessing thus :—

הַמֶּלֶךְ הַקָּדוֹשׁ :

אַתָּה חוֹנֵן לְאָדָם דַּעַת וּמְלַמֵּד לֶאֱנוֹשׁ בִּינָה ·

In the Evening Service at the conclusion of Sabbath or of a Festival add :—

אַתָּה חוֹנַנְתָּנוּ לְמַדַּע תּוֹרָתֶךָ · וַתְּלַמְּדֵנוּ לַעֲשׂוֹת חֻקֵּי

רְצוֹנֶךָ · וַתַּבְדֵּל יְיָ אֱלֹהֵינוּ בֵּין קֹדֶשׁ לְחוֹל בֵּין אוֹר לְחֹשֶׁךְ

בֵּין יִשְׂרָאֵל לָעַמִּים בֵּין יוֹם הַשְּׁבִיעִי לְשֵׁשֶׁת יְמֵי הַמַּעֲשֶׂה ·

אָבִינוּ מַלְכֵּנוּ · הָחֵל עָלֵינוּ הַיָּמִים הַבָּאִים לִקְרָאתֵנוּ לְשָׁלוֹם

חֲשׂוּכִים מִכָּל־חֵטְא וּמְנֻקִּים מִכָּל־עָוֹן וּמְדֻבָּקִים בְּיִרְאָתֶךָ :

(וְ)חָנֵּנוּ מֵאִתְּךָ דֵּעָה בִּינָה וְהַשְׂכֵּל · בָּרוּךְ אַתָּה יְיָ ·

חוֹנֵן הַדָּעַת :

הֲשִׁיבֵנוּ אָבִינוּ לְתוֹרָתֶךָ · וְקָרְבֵנוּ מַלְכֵּנוּ לַעֲבוֹדָתֶךָ ·

וְהַחֲזִירֵנוּ בִּתְשׁוּבָה שְׁלֵמָה לְפָנֶיךָ · בָּרוּךְ אַתָּה יְיָ ·

הָרוֹצֶה בִּתְשׁוּבָה :

Thou hast favoured. Just as on Friday eve, special prayers mark the coming in of the Sabbath, note is taken of the departure of the Sabbath in the first of the weekday petitions. We acknowledge that God has in His mercy taught us everlasting distinctions in the moral universe, even as He has done in the world of nature and history. We pray that

ness, and to all eternity we will proclaim thy holiness, and thy praise, O our God, shall not depart from our mouth for ever, for thou art a great and holy God and King. Blessed art thou, O Lord, the holy God. | *During the Ten Days of Repentance conclude the Blessing thus :—the holy King.]*

Thou art holy, and thy Name is holy, and the holy praise thee daily. (Selah.) Blessed art thou, O Lord, the holy God. | *During the Ten Days Repentance conclude the Blessing thus :—the holy King.*

IV.
PRAYER
FOR
UNDER-
STANDING
See p. 137

Thou favourest man with knowledge, and teachest mortals understanding.

[In the Evening Service, at the conclusion of Sabbath or of a Festival, add :—

Thou hast favoured us with a knowledge of thy Torah, and hast taught us to perform the statutes of thy will. Thou hast made a distinction, O Lord our God, between holy and profane, between light and darkness, between Israel and other nations, between the seventh day and the six working days. O our Father, our King, grant that the days which are approaching us may begin for us in peace, and that we may be withheld from all sin and cleansed from all iniquity, and cleave to the reverence of thee.]

PRAYER
FOR NEW
WEEK

O favour us with knowledge, understanding and discernment from thee. Blessed art thou, O Lord, gracious Giver of knowledge.

V. FOR RE-
PENTANCE

Cause us to return, O our Father, unto thy Torah ; draw us near, O our King, unto thy service, and bring us back in perfect repentance unto thy presence. Blessed art thou, O Lord, who delightest in repentance.

See p 138

through our observance of the Sabbath, a new realization of the infinite difference between holy and profane, between light and darkness, between Israel and the heathen, abide with us throughout the coming week ; and that such realization lead to peace of soul, freedom from sin, and fervent attachment to the God-fearing life ; see the Havdolah Service, p. 744.

reverence of thee. True and heartfelt religious loyalty.

סְלַח־לָנוּ אָבִינוּ כִּי חָטָאנוּ · מְחַל־לָנוּ מַלְכֵּנוּ כִּי
פָשָׁעְנוּ · כִּי מוֹחֵל וְסוֹלֵחַ אָתָּה · בָּרוּךְ אַתָּה יְיָ ·
חַנּוּן הַמַּרְבֶּה לִסְלוֹחַ :

רְאֵה בְעָנְיֵנוּ וְרִיבָה רִיבֵנוּ · וּגְאָלֵנוּ מְהֵרָה לְמַעַן
שְׁמֶךָ · כִּי גּוֹאֵל חָזָק אָתָּה · בָּרוּךְ אַתָּה יְיָ · גּוֹאֵל
יִשְׂרָאֵל : *On Fast Days the Reader here says* עֲנֵנוּ , *p. 286,*
and concludes thus: הָעוֹנֶה בְּעֵת צָרָה :

רְפָאֵנוּ יְיָ וְנֵרָפֵא · הוֹשִׁיעֵנוּ וְנִוָּשֵׁעָה · כִּי תְהִלָּתֵנוּ
אָתָּה · וְהַעֲלֵה רְפוּאָה שְׁלֵמָה לְכָל־מַכּוֹתֵינוּ · * כִּי
אֵל מֶלֶךְ רוֹפֵא נֶאֱמָן וְרַחֲמָן אָתָּה · בָּרוּךְ אַתָּה יְיָ ·
רוֹפֵא חוֹלֵי עַמּוֹ יִשְׂרָאֵל :

בָּרֵךְ עָלֵינוּ יְיָ אֱלֹהֵינוּ אֶת־הַשָּׁנָה הַזֹּאת וְאֶת־כָּל־
מִינֵי תְבוּאָתָהּ לְטוֹבָה · וְתֵן בְּרָכָה

From the 4th December until the day before Passover
substitute for the last two words —

וְתֵן טַל וּמָטָר לִבְרָכָה

עַל פְּנֵי הָאֲדָמָה וְשַׂבְּעֵנוּ מִטּוּבֶךָ · וּבָרֵךְ שְׁנָתֵנוּ כַּשָּׁנִים
הַטּוֹבוֹת · בָּרוּךְ אַתָּה יְיָ · מְבָרֵךְ הַשָּׁנִים :

---

* *The following Prayer for a Sick Person may be introduced here:—*
וִיהִי רָצוֹן מִלְפָנֶיךָ יְיָ אֱלֹהֵינוּ וֵאלֹהֵי אֲבוֹתֵינוּ שֶׁתִּשְׁלַח
מְהֵרָה רְפוּאָה שְׁלֵמָה מִן הַשָּׁמַיִם רְפוּאַת הַנֶּפֶשׁ וּרְפוּאַת הַגּוּף
לַחוֹלֶה פ׳ ב׳ פ׳ בְּתוֹךְ שְׁאָר חוֹלֵי יִשְׂרָאֵל ·

VI. FOR FORGIVE-NESS

Forgive us, O our Father, for we have sinned ; pardon us, O our King, for we have transgressed ; for thou dost pardon and forgive. Blessed art thou, O Lord, who art gracious, and dost abundantly forgive.

VII. FOR DELIVER-ANCE FROM AFFLIC-TION

Look upon our affliction and plead our cause, and redeem us speedily for thy Name's sake ; for thou art a mighty Redeemer. °Blessed art thou, O Lord,

the Reedemer of | °*On Fast Days the Reader here says,"Answer*
Israel | *us," etc., p.* 287, *and concludes thus :—*
| Who answerest in time of trouble.

VIII. FOR HEALING

Heal us, O Lord, and we shall be healed ; save us and we shall be saved ; for thou art our praise. Grant a perfect healing to all our wounds ;* for thou, almighty King, art a faithful and merciful Physician. Blessed art thou, O Lord, who healest the sick of thy people Israel.

IX. FOR DELIVER-ANCE FROM WANT
See p. 141

Bless this year unto us, O Lord our God, together with every kind of the produce thereof, for our welfare ; give [*From the 4th December until the First Day of Passover include the words :—*dew and rain for] a blessing upon the face of the earth. O satisfy us with thy goodness, and bless our year like other good years. Blessed art thou, O Lord, who blessest the years.

The following Prayer for a Sick Person may be introduced here :-
May it be thy will, O Lord our God, and God of our fathers, speedily to send a perfect healing from heaven, a healing of soul and body unto the sick . . . . . among the other sick of Israel.

תְּקַע בְּשׁוֹפָר גָּדוֹל לְחֵרוּתֵנוּ · וְשָׂא נֵס לְקַבֵּץ
גָּלֻיּוֹתֵינוּ · וְקַבְּצֵנוּ יַחַד מֵאַרְבַּע כַּנְפוֹת הָאָרֶץ · בָּרוּךְ
אַתָּה יְיָ · מְקַבֵּץ נִדְחֵי עַמּוֹ יִשְׂרָאֵל :

הָשִׁיבָה שׁוֹפְטֵינוּ כְּבָרִאשׁוֹנָה וְיוֹעֲצֵינוּ כְּבַתְּחִלָּה ·
וְהָסֵר מִמֶּנּוּ יָגוֹן וַאֲנָחָה · וּמְלוֹךְ עָלֵינוּ אַתָּה יְיָ לְבַדְּךָ
בְּחֶסֶד וּבְרַחֲמִים · וְצַדְּקֵנוּ בַּמִּשְׁפָּט · בָּרוּךְ אַתָּה יְיָ ·
מֶלֶךְ אוֹהֵב צְדָקָה וּמִשְׁפָּט :

During עֲשֶׂרֶת יְמֵי תְּשׁוּבָה say:— הַמֶּלֶךְ הַמִּשְׁפָּט :

וְלַמַּלְשִׁינִים אַל־תְּהִי תִקְוָה · וְכָל הָרִשְׁעָה כְּרֶגַע
תֹּאבֵד · וְכָל אוֹיְבֶיךָ מְהֵרָה יִכָּרֵתוּ · וּמַלְכוּת זָדוֹן
מְהֵרָה תְעַקֵּר וּתְשַׁבֵּר וּתְמַגֵּר וְתַכְנִיעַ בִּמְהֵרָה בְיָמֵינוּ ·
בָּרוּךְ אַתָּה יְיָ · שֹׁבֵר אֹיְבִים וּמַכְנִיעַ זֵדִים :

עַל־הַצַּדִּיקִים וְעַל־הַחֲסִידִים וְעַל־זִקְנֵי עַמְּךָ בֵּית
יִשְׂרָאֵל וְעַל־פְּלֵיטַת סוֹפְרֵיהֶם וְעַל גֵּרֵי הַצֶּדֶק וְעָלֵינוּ
יֶהֱמוּ רַחֲמֶיךָ יְיָ אֱלֹהֵינוּ · וְתֵן שָׂכָר טוֹב לְכֹל הַבּוֹטְחִים
בְּשִׁמְךָ בֶּאֱמֶת · וְשִׂים חֶלְקֵנוּ עִמָּהֶם לְעוֹלָם וְלֹא נֵבוֹשׁ ·
כִּי־בְךָ בָּטָחְנוּ · בָּרוּךְ אַתָּה יְיָ · מִשְׁעָן וּמִבְטָח לַצַּדִּיקִים :

וְלִירוּשָׁלַיִם עִירְךָ בְּרַחֲמִים תָּשׁוּב · וְתִשְׁכּוֹן בְּתוֹכָהּ
כַּאֲשֶׁר דִּבַּרְתָּ · וּבְנֵה אוֹתָהּ בְּקָרוֹב בְּיָמֵינוּ בִּנְיַן עוֹלָם ·

X. FOR THE RE-UNION OF ISRAEL

See p. 142

Sound the great horn for our freedom, raise the ensign to gather our exiles, and gather us from the four corners of the earth. Blessed art thou, O Lord, who gatherest the dispersed of thy people Israel.

XI. FOR THE RIGHT-EOUS REIGN OF GOD

Restore our judges as in former times, and our counsellors as at the beginning ; remove from us sorrow and sighing ; reign thou over us, O Lord, thou alone, in lovingkindness and tender mercy, and clear us in judgment. Blessed art thou, O Lord,

| the King who lovest righteousness and judgment | *During the Ten Days of Repentance say—* the King of Judgment. |

XII. AGAINST SLANDER-ERS

And for slanderers let there be no hope, and let all wickedness perish as in a moment ; let all thine enemies be speedily cut off, and the dominion of arrogance do thou uproot and crush, cast down and humble speedily in our days. Blessed art thou, O Lord, who breakest the enemies and humblest the arrogant.

XIII. FOR THE RIGHT-EOUS

See p. 145

Towards the righteous and the pious, towards the elders of thy people the house of Israel, towards the remnant of their scribes, towards true proselytes, and towards us also may thy tender mercies be stirred, O Lord our God ; grant a good reward unto all who faithfully trust in thy Name ; set our portion with them for ever, so that we may not be put to shame ; for we have trusted in thee. Blessed art thou, O Lord, the stay and trust of the righteous.

XIV. FOR THE RE-BUILDING OF JERU-SALEM

And to Jerusalem, thy city, return in mercy, and dwell therein as thou hast spoken ; rebuild it soon in our days as an everlasting building, and speedily set up therein the

וְכִסֵּא דָוִד מְהֵרָה לְתוֹכָהּ תָּכִין ·· *

בָּרוּךְ אַתָּה יְיָ · בּוֹנֵה יְרוּשָׁלָיִם :

אֶת־צֶמַח דָּוִד עַבְדְּךָ מְהֵרָה תַצְמִיחַ · וְקַרְנוֹ תָּרוּם
בִּישׁוּעָתֶךָ · כִּי לִישׁוּעָתְךָ קִוִּינוּ כָּל־הַיּוֹם · בָּרוּךְ אַתָּה
יְיָ · מַצְמִיחַ קֶרֶן יְשׁוּעָה :

שְׁמַע קוֹלֵנוּ יְיָ אֱלֹהֵינוּ · חוּס וְרַחֵם עָלֵינוּ · וְקַבֵּל בְּרַחֲמִים
וּבְרָצוֹן אֶת־תְּפִלָּתֵנוּ · כִּי אֵל שׁוֹמֵעַ תְּפִלּוֹת וְתַחֲנוּנִים

On the Fast of אָב conclude the Blessing thus :—

נַחֵם יְיָ אֱלֹהֵינוּ אֶת־אֲבֵלֵי צִיּוֹן וְאֶת־אֲבֵלֵי יְרוּשָׁלַיִם וְאֶת־
הָעִיר הָאֲבֵלָה וְהַחֲרֵבָה וְהַבְּזוּיָה וְהַשּׁוֹמֵמָה · הָאֲבֵלָה מִבְּלִי
בָנֶיהָ · וְהַחֲרֵבָה מִמְּעוֹנוֹתֶיהָ · וְהַבְּזוּיָה מִכְּבוֹדָהּ · וְהַשּׁוֹמֵמָה
מֵאֵין יוֹשֵׁב · וְהִיא יוֹשֶׁבֶת וְרֹאשָׁהּ חָפוּי כְּאִשָּׁה עֲקָרָה שֶׁלֹּא
יָלָדָה · וַיְבַלְּעוּהָ לִגְיוֹנוֹת · וַיִּירָשׁוּהָ עוֹבְדֵי זָרִים · וַיַּטִּילוּ
אֶת־עַמְּךָ יִשְׂרָאֵל לֶחָרֶב · וַיַּהַרְגוּ בְזָדוֹן חֲסִידֵי עֶלְיוֹן · עַל־כֵּן
צִיּוֹן בְּמַר תִּבְכֶּה · וִירוּשָׁלַיִם תִּתֵּן קוֹלָהּ · לִבִּי לִבִּי עַל חַלְלֵיהֶם
מֵעַי מֵעַי עַל חַלְלֵיהֶם · כִּי אַתָּה יְיָ בָּאֵשׁ הִצַּתָּהּ · וּבָאֵשׁ אַתָּה
עָתִיד לִבְנוֹתָהּ · כָּאָמוּר · וַאֲנִי אֶהְיֶה־לָּהּ נְאֻם־יְיָ חוֹמַת אֵשׁ
סָבִיב · וּלְכָבוֹד אֶהְיֶה בְּתוֹכָהּ · בָּרוּךְ אַתָּה יְיָ · מְנַחֵם צִיּוֹן
וּבוֹנֵה יְרוּשָׁלָיִם : אֶת צמח וכו'

COMFORT, O LORD. Similar to the brief prayers for Chanukah and
Purim, this supplication for comfort to those that mourn for Zion is
inserted on the Fast of the Ninth of Av. Such Supplications arose

throne of David.* Blessed art thou, O Lord, who rebuildest Jerusalem.

XV. FOR THE MESSIANIC KING   Speedily cause the offspring of David, thy servant, to flourish, and lift up his glory by thy divine help because we wait for thy salvation all the day. Blessed art thou, O Lord, who causest the strength of salvation to flourish.

XVI. FOR HEARING OF PRAYER See p. 147   Hear our voice, O Lord our God ; spare us and have mercy upon us, and accept our prayer in mercy and favour ; for thou art a God who hearkenest unto prayers and supplications : from thy presence, O our King, turn us not

*[On the Fast of the Ninth of Av, conclude the blessing thus :—

THE DESTRUC- TION OF JERU- SALEM   Comfort, O Lord our God, the mourners of Zion, and the mourners of Jerusalem, and the city that is in mourning, laid waste, despised and desolate : in mourning—for that she is childless; laid waste—in her dwellings ; despised—on the downfall of her glory; and desolate—through the loss of her inhabitants : she sitteth with her head covered like a barren woman who hath not borne. Legions have devoured her ; worshippers of strange gods have possessed her : they have put thy people Israel to the sword, and in wilfulness have slain the loving ones of the Most High. Therefore let Zion weep bitterly, and Jerusalem give forth her voice. O my heart, my heart ! how it grieveth for the slain ! how my soul yearneth for the slain ! For thou, O Lord, didst consume her with fire : and *Zechariah 2. 9* with fire thou wilt in future restore her, as it is said, As for me, I will be unto her, saith the Lord, a wall of fire round about, and I will be a glory in the midst of her. Blessed art thou, O Lord, who comfortest Zion and rebuildest Jerusalem.]

Continue with " Speedily cause," etc., above.

soon after the Destruction by the Romans. In its present form, the prayer goes back to Saadya.

legions. The Hebrew uses the same Latin word. Three Roman legions under Titus invested Jerusalem.

אַתָּה ‧ וּמִלְּפָנֶיךָ מַלְכֵּנוּ רֵיקָם אַל תְּשִׁיבֵנוּ ‧‧* כִּי
אַתָּה שׁוֹמֵעַ תְּפִלַּת עַמְּךָ יִשְׂרָאֵל בְּרַחֲמִים ‧ בָּרוּךְ
אַתָּה יְיָ ‧ שׁוֹמֵעַ תְּפִלָּה :

רְצֵה יְיָ אֱלֹהֵינוּ בְּעַמְּךָ יִשְׂרָאֵל וּבִתְפִלָּתָם ‧ וְהָשֵׁב
אֶת־הָעֲבוֹדָה לִדְבִיר בֵּיתֶךָ וְאִשֵּׁי יִשְׂרָאֵל וּתְפִלָּתָם
בְּאַהֲבָה תְקַבֵּל בְּרָצוֹן ‧ וּתְהִי לְרָצוֹן תָּמִיד עֲבוֹדַת
יִשְׂרָאֵל עַמֶּךָ ‧

On רֹאשׁ חֹדֶשׁ and of חֹל הַמּוֹעֵד of פֶּסַח and of סֻכּוֹת say:—

אֱלֹהֵינוּ וֵאלֹהֵי אֲבוֹתֵינוּ ‧ יַעֲלֶה וְיָבֹא וְיַגִּיעַ וְיֵרָאֶה וְיֵרָצֶה
וְיִשָּׁמַע וְיִפָּקֵד וְיִזָּכֵר זִכְרוֹנֵנוּ וּפִקְדוֹנֵנוּ ‧ וְזִכְרוֹן אֲבוֹתֵינוּ ‧ וְזִכְרוֹן
מָשִׁיחַ בֶּן דָּוִד עַבְדֶּךָ ‧ וְזִכְרוֹן יְרוּשָׁלַיִם עִיר קָדְשֶׁךָ ‧ וְזִכְרוֹן כָּל
עַמְּךָ בֵּית יִשְׂרָאֵל לְפָנֶיךָ ‧ לִפְלֵיטָה וּלְטוֹבָה וּלְחֵן וּלְחֶסֶד
וּלְרַחֲמִים וּלְחַיִּים וּלְשָׁלוֹם בְּיוֹם

On סֻכּוֹת—	On פֶּסַח—	On רֹאשׁ חֹדֶשׁ say—
חַג הַסֻּכּוֹת	חַג הַמַּצּוֹת	רֹאשׁ הַחֹדֶשׁ

הַזֶּה ‧ זָכְרֵנוּ יְיָ אֱלֹהֵינוּ בּוֹ לְטוֹבָה וּפָקְדֵנוּ בוֹ לִבְרָכָה וְהוֹשִׁיעֵנוּ
בוֹ לְחַיִּים ‧ וּבִדְבַר יְשׁוּעָה וְרַחֲמִים חוּס וְחָנֵּנוּ וְרַחֵם עָלֵינוּ
וְהוֹשִׁיעֵנוּ ‧ כִּי אֵלֶיךָ עֵינֵינוּ ‧ כִּי אֵל מֶלֶךְ חַנּוּן וְרַחוּם אָתָּה :

וְתֶחֱזֶינָה עֵינֵינוּ בְּשׁוּבְךָ לְצִיּוֹן בְּרַחֲמִים ‧ בָּרוּךְ אַתָּה
יְיָ ‧ הַמַּחֲזִיר שְׁכִינָתוֹ לְצִיּוֹן :

---

* On Fast Days the Congregation here say עֲנֵנוּ, p. 146.

empty away* ; for thou hearkenest in mercy to the prayer of thy people Israel. Blessed art thou, O Lord, who hearkenest unto prayer.

XVII. FOR RESTORA- TION OF TEMPLE SERVICE

Accept, O Lord our God, thy people Israel and their prayer ; restore the service to the inner sanctuary of thy house ; receive in love and favour both the offerings of Israel and their prayer ; and may the worship of thy people Israel be ever acceptable unto thee.

See p. 149

[*On New Moon and the Intermediate Days of Passover and Tabernacles the following to " merciful God and King " is added :—*

YAALEH VE-YOVO

Our God and God of our Fathers ! May our remembrance ascend, come and be accepted before thee, with the remembrance of our fathers, of Messiah the son of David thy servant, of Jerusalem thy holy city, and of all thy people the house of Israel, bringing deliverance and well-being, grace, lovingkindness and mercy, life and peace on this day of

On New Moon say—the New Moon.

On Passover—the Feast of Unleavened Bread.

On Tabernacles—the Feast of Tabernacles.

Remember us, O Lord our God, thereon for our well-being ; be mindful of us for blessing, and save us unto life : by thy promise of salvation and mercy, spare us and be gracious unto us ; have mercy upon us and save us ; for our eyes are bent upon thee, because thou art a gracious and merciful God and King.]

And let our eyes behold thy return in mercy to Zion. Blessed art thou, O Lord, who restorest thy divine presence unto Zion.

On Fast Days the Congregation here say, "Answer us," p. 147.

מוֹדִים אֲנַחְנוּ לָךְ

שָׁאַתָּה הוּא יְיָ אֱלֹהֵינוּ

וֵאלֹהֵי אֲבוֹתֵינוּ לְעוֹלָם

The Congregation in an undertone—

מוֹדִים אֲנַחְנוּ לָךְ שָׁאַתָּה הוּא
יְיָ אֱלֹהֵינוּ וֵאלֹהֵי אֲבוֹתֵינוּ אֱלֹהֵי
כָל־בָּשָׂר · יוֹצְרֵנוּ יוֹצֵר בְּרֵאשִׁית ·
בְּרָכוֹת וְהוֹדָאוֹת לְשִׁמְךָ הַגָּדוֹל
וְהַקָּדוֹשׁ · עַל שֶׁהֶחֱיִיתָנוּ וְקִיַּמְתָּנוּ ·
כֵּן תְּחַיֵּנוּ וּתְקַיְּמֵנוּ · וְתֶאֱסוֹף
גָּלְיּוֹתֵינוּ לְחַצְרוֹת קָדְשֶׁךָ לִשְׁמֹר
חֻקֶּיךָ וְלַעֲשׂוֹת רְצוֹנֶךָ וּלְעָבְדְּךָ
בְּלֵבָב שָׁלֵם עַל שֶׁאֲנַחְנוּ מוֹדִים
לָךְ · בָּרוּךְ אֵל הַהוֹדָאוֹת :

וָעֶד · צוּר חַיֵּינוּ מָגֵן

יִשְׁעֵנוּ אַתָּה הוּא לְדוֹר

וָדוֹר · נוֹדֶה לְךָ וּנְסַפֵּר

תְּהִלָּתֶךָ עַל חַיֵּינוּ

הַמְּסוּרִים בְּיָדֶךָ וְעַל

נִשְׁמוֹתֵינוּ הַפְּקוּדוֹת לָךְ

וְעַל נִסֶּיךָ שֶׁבְּכָל־יוֹם עִמָּנוּ וְעַל נִפְלְאוֹתֶיךָ וְטוֹבוֹתֶיךָ
שֶׁבְּכָל־עֵת עֶרֶב וָבֹקֶר וְצָהֳרָיִם · הַטּוֹב כִּי לֹא־כָלוּ
רַחֲמֶיךָ · וְהַמְרַחֵם כִּי לֹא־תַמּוּ חֲסָדֶיךָ מֵעוֹלָם קִוִּינוּ
לָךְ :

On חֲנֻכָּה *and* פּוּרִים *the following is added:—*

עַל הַנִּסִּים וְעַל הַפֻּרְקָן וְעַל הַגְּבוּרוֹת וְעַל הַתְּשׁוּעוֹת וְעַל
הַמִּלְחָמוֹת שֶׁעָשִׂיתָ לַאֲבוֹתֵינוּ בַּיָּמִים הָהֵם בַּזְּמַן הַזֶּה :

On חֲנֻכָּה.

בִּימֵי מַתִּתְיָהוּ בֶן־יוֹחָנָן כֹּהֵן גָּדוֹל חַשְׁמוֹנַאי וּבָנָיו כְּשֶׁעָמְדָה
מַלְכוּת יָוָן הָרְשָׁעָה עַל־עַמְּךָ יִשְׂרָאֵל לְהַשְׁכִּיחָם תּוֹרָתֶךָ
וּלְהַעֲבִירָם מֵחֻקֵּי רְצוֹנֶךָ · וְאַתָּה בְּרַחֲמֶיךָ הָרַבִּים עָמַדְתָּ לָהֶם
בְּעֵת צָרָתָם · רַבְתָּ אֶת־רִיבָם דַּנְתָּ אֶת־דִּינָם נָקַמְתָּ אֶת־נִקְמָתָם ·
מָסַרְתָּ גִבּוֹרִים בְּיַד חַלָּשִׁים וְרַבִּים בְּיַד מְעַטִּים וּטְמֵאִים בְּיַד
טְהוֹרִים וּרְשָׁעִים בְּיַד צַדִּיקִים וְזֵדִים בְּיַד עוֹסְקֵי תוֹרָתֶךָ · וּלְ

XVIII.
THANKS-
GIVING
FOR GOD'S
UNFAIL-
ING
MERCIES

See p. 151

We give thanks unto thee, for thou art the Lord our God and the God of our fathers for ever and ever ; thou art the Rock of our lives, the Shield of our salvation through every generation. We will give thanks unto thee and declare thy praise for our lives which are committed unto thy hand, and for our souls which are in thy charge, and for thy miracles, which are daily with us, and for thy wonders and thy benefits, which are wrought at all times, evening, morn and noon. O thou who art all-good, whose mercies fail not ; thou, merciful Being, whose lovingkindnesses never cease, we have ever hoped in thee.

The Congregation, in an under tone—

We give thanks unto thee, for thou art the Lord our God and the God of our fathers, the God of all flesh, our Creator and the Creator of all things in the beginning. Blessings and thanksgivings be to thy great and holy Name, because thou hast kept us in life and hast preserved us : so mayest thou continue to keep us in life and to preserve us. O gather our exiles to thy holy courts to observe thy statutes, to do thy will, and to serve thee with a perfect heart ; seeing that we give thanks unto thee. Blessed be the God to whom thanksgivings are due.

[On Chanukah and Purim the following is added :—

We thank thee also for the miracles, for the redemption, for the mighty deeds and saving acts, wrought by thee, as well as for the wars which thou didst wage for our fathers in days of old, at this season.

On Chanukah.

THANKS-
GIVING ON
CHANU-
KAH

In the days of the Hasmonean, Mattathias son of Johanan, the High Priest, and his sons, when the iniquitous power of Greece rose up against thy people Israel to make them forgetful of thy Torah, and to force them to transgress the statutes of thy will, then didst thou in thine abundant mercy rise up for them in the time of their trouble ; thou didst plead their cause, thou didst judge their suit, thou didst avenge their wrong ; thou deliveredst the strong into the hands of the weak, the many into the hands of the few, the impure into the hands of the pure, the wicked into the hands of the righteous, and the arrogant into the hands of them that occupied themselves with

עָשִׂיתָ שֵּׁם גָּדוֹל וְקָדוֹשׁ בְּעוֹלָמֶךָ וּלְעַמְּךָ יִשְׂרָאֵל עָשִׂיתָ תְּשׁוּעָה
גְדוֹלָה וּפֻרְקָן כְּהַיּוֹם הַזֶּה ׳ וְאַחַר כֵּן בָּאוּ בָנֶיךָ לִדְבִיר בֵּיתֶךָ
וּפִנּוּ אֶת־הֵיכָלֶךָ וְטִהֲרוּ אֶת־מִקְדָּשֶׁךָ וְהִדְלִיקוּ נֵרוֹת בְּחַצְרוֹת
קָדְשֶׁךָ ׳ וְקָבְעוּ שְׁמוֹנַת יְמֵי חֲנֻכָּה אֵלּוּ לְהוֹדוֹת וּלְהַלֵּל לְשִׁמְךָ
הַגָּדוֹל :

On פּוּרִים.

בִּימֵי מָרְדְּכַי וְאֶסְתֵּר בְּשׁוּשַׁן הַבִּירָה כְּשֶׁעָמַד עֲלֵיהֶם הָמָן
הָרָשָׁע ׳ בִּקֵּשׁ לְהַשְׁמִיד לַהֲרוֹג וּלְאַבֵּד אֶת־כָּל־הַיְּהוּדִים מִנַּעַר
וְעַד זָקֵן טַף וְנָשִׁים בְּיוֹם אֶחָד ׳ בִּשְׁלוֹשָׁה־עָשָׂר לְחֹדֶשׁ שְׁנֵים־
עָשָׂר הוּא־חֹדֶשׁ אֲדָר וּשְׁלָלָם לָבוֹז ׳ וְאַתָּה בְּרַחֲמֶיךָ הָרַבִּים
הֵפַרְתָּ אֶת־עֲצָתוֹ וְקִלְקַלְתָּ אֶת־מַחֲשַׁבְתּוֹ וַהֲשֵׁבוֹתָ גְּמוּלוֹ
בְּרֹאשׁוֹ וְתָלוּ אֹתוֹ וְאֶת־בָּנָיו עַל־הָעֵץ :

וְעַל־כֻּלָּם יִתְבָּרַךְ וְיִתְרוֹמַם שִׁמְךָ מַלְכֵּנוּ תָּמִיד לְעוֹלָם
וָעֶד :

During the עֲשֶׂרֶת יְמֵי תְּשׁוּבָה *say:*—

וּכְתוֹב לְחַיִּים טוֹבִים כָּל־בְּנֵי בְרִיתֶךָ :

וְכֹל הַחַיִּים יוֹדוּךָ סֶּלָה ׳ וִיהַלְלוּ אֶת־שִׁמְךָ בֶּאֱמֶת ׳
הָאֵל יְשׁוּעָתֵנוּ וְעֶזְרָתֵנוּ סֶלָה ׳ בָּרוּךְ אַתָּה יְיָ ׳ הַטּוֹב
שִׁמְךָ וּלְךָ נָאֶה לְהוֹדוֹת :

At the repetition of the עֲמִידָה *by the Reader, the following is
introduced:*—

אֱלֹהֵינוּ וֵאלֹהֵי אֲבוֹתֵינוּ ׳ בָּרְכֵנוּ בַּבְּרָכָה הַמְשֻׁלֶּשֶׁת בַּתּוֹרָה ׳
הַכְּתוּבָה עַל יְדֵי מֹשֶׁה עַבְדֶּךָ ׳ הָאֲמוּרָה מִפִּי אַהֲרֹן וּבָנָיו
כֹּהֲנִים ׳ עַם קְדוֹשֶׁךָ כָּאָמוּר ׳ יְבָרֶכְךָ יְיָ וְיִשְׁמְרֶךָ : יָאֵר יְיָ פָּנָיו
אֵלֶיךָ וִיחֻנֶּךָּ : יִשָּׂא יְיָ פָּנָיו אֵלֶיךָ וְיָשֵׂם לְךָ שָׁלוֹם :

THANKS-
GIVING
ON
CHANU-
KAH.

thy Torah : for thyself thou didst make a great and holy name in thy world, and for thy people Israel thou didst work a great deliverance and redemption as at this day. And thereupon thy children came into the inner sanctuary of thy house, cleansed thy temple, purified thy holy place, kindled lights in thy sacred courts, and appointed these eight days of Chanukah in order to give thanks and praises unto thy great Name.

On Purim.

AND
PURIM

In the days of Mordecai and Esther, in Sushan the capital, when the wicked Haman rose up against them, and sought to destroy, to slay and cause to perish all the Jews, both young and old, women and little children, on one day, on the thirteenth day of the twelfth month, which is the month Adar, and to take the spoil of them for a prey,—then didst thou in thine abundant mercy bring his counsel to nought, didst frustrate his design, and return his recompense upon his own head : and they hanged him and his sons upon the gallows.]

For all these acts thy Name, O our King, shall be continually blessed and exalted for ever and ever.

[*During the Ten Days of Repentance say* :—
O inscribe all the children of thy covenent for a happy life.]

And everything that liveth shall give thanks unto thee for ever, and shall praise thy Name in truth, O God, our salvation and our help. (Selah.) Blessed art thou, O Lord, whose Name is All-good, and unto whom it is becoming to give thanks.

[*At the repetition of the Amidah by the Reader on Fast Days, the following is introduced* :—
Our God and God of our fathers, bless us with the three-fold blessing of thy Torah written by the hand of Moses thy servant, which was spoken by Aaron and his sons, the priests, thy holy people, as it is said, THE LORD BLESS THEE, AND KEEP THEE : THE LORD MAKE HIS FACE TO SHINE UPON THEE, AND BE GRACIOUS UNTO THEE : THE LORD TURN HIS FACE UNTO THEE, AND GIVE THEE PEACE.]

Numbers
6. 24-26

שָׁלוֹם רָב עַל
יִשְׂרָאֵל עַמְּךָ תָּשִׂים
לְעוֹלָם · כִּי אַתָּה
הוּא מֶלֶךְ אָדוֹן
לְכָל הַשָּׁלוֹם · וְטוֹב
בְּעֵינֶיךָ לְבָרֵךְ אֶת־
עַמְּךָ יִשְׂרָאֵל בְּכָל־
עֵת וּבְכָל־שָׁעָה
בִּשְׁלוֹמֶךָ ·

בָּרוּךְ אַתָּה יְיָ ·
הַמְבָרֵךְ אֶת־עַמּוֹ
יִשְׂרָאֵל בַּשָּׁלוֹם :

On Fast Days, the following is said:—

שִׂים שָׁלוֹם טוֹבָה וּבְרָכָה חֵן
וָחֶסֶד וְרַחֲמִים עָלֵינוּ וְעַל כָּל־יִשְׂרָאֵל
עַמֶּךָ . בָּרְכֵנוּ אָבִינוּ כֻּלָּנוּ כְּאֶחָד בְּאוֹר
פָּנֶיךָ · כִּי בְאוֹר פָּנֶיךָ נָתַתָּ לָּנוּ יְיָ
אֱלֹהֵינוּ תּוֹרַת חַיִּים וְאַהֲבַת חֶסֶד
וּצְדָקָה וּבְרָכָה וְרַחֲמִים וְחַיִּים וְשָׁלוֹם ·
וְטוֹב בְּעֵינֶיךָ לְבָרֵךְ אֶת־עַמְּךָ יִשְׂרָאֵל
בְּכָל־עֵת וּבְכָל־שָׁעָה בִּשְׁלוֹמֶךָ ·

During the עֲשֶׂרֶת יְמֵי תְשׁוּבָה *say:—*

בְּסֵפֶר חַיִּים בְּרָכָה וְשָׁלוֹם וּפַרְנָסָה
טוֹבָה נִזָּכֵר וְנִכָּתֵב לְפָנֶיךָ אֲנַחְנוּ וְכָל־
עַמְּךָ בֵּית יִשְׂרָאֵל לְחַיִּים טוֹבִים
וּלְשָׁלוֹם . בָּרוּךְ אַתָּה יְיָ עוֹשֵׂה הַשָּׁלוֹם:

אֱלֹהַי · נְצוֹר לְשׁוֹנִי מֵרָע וּשְׂפָתַי מִדַּבֵּר מִרְמָה ·
וְלִמְקַלְלַי נַפְשִׁי תִדּוֹם וְנַפְשִׁי כֶּעָפָר לַכֹּל תִּהְיֶה : פְּתַח
לִבִּי בְּתוֹרָתֶךָ וּבְמִצְוֹתֶיךָ תִּרְדּוֹף נַפְשִׁי · וְכֹל הַחוֹשְׁבִים
עָלַי רָעָה מְהֵרָה הָפֵר עֲצָתָם וְקַלְקֵל מַחֲשְׁבוֹתָם · עֲשֵׂה
לְמַעַן שְׁמֶךָ עֲשֵׂה לְמַעַן יְמִינֶךָ עֲשֵׂה לְמַעַן קְדֻשָּׁתֶךָ עֲשֵׂה
לְמַעַן תּוֹרָתֶךָ · לְמַעַן יֵחָלְצוּן יְדִידֶיךָ הוֹשִׁיעָה יְמִינְךָ
וַעֲנֵנִי : יִהְיוּ לְרָצוֹן אִמְרֵי־פִי וְהֶגְיוֹן לִבִּי לְפָנֶיךָ יְיָ צוּרִי
וְגֹאֲלִי : עֹשֶׂה שָׁלוֹם בִּמְרוֹמָיו הוּא יַעֲשֶׂה שָׁלוֹם עָלֵינוּ
וְעַל כָּל־יִשְׂרָאֵל · וְאִמְרוּ אָמֵן :

XIX. FOR PEACE

See p. 154

Grant abundant peace unto Israel thy people for ever ; for thou art the sovereign Lord of all peace ; and may it be good in thy sight to bless thy people Israel at all times and in every hour with thy peace.

Blessed art thou, O Lord, who blessest thy people Israel with peace.

On Fast Days, the following is said :—
Grant peace, welfare, blessing, grace, lovingkindness and mercy unto us and unto all Israel, thy people. Bless us, O our Father, even all of us together, with the light of thy countenance; for by the light of thy countenance thou hast given us, O Lord our God, the Torah of life, lovingkindness and righteousness, blessing, mercy, life and peace ; and may it be good in thy sight to bless thy people Israel at all times and in every hour with thy peace.

[*During the Ten Days of Repentance say :—*
In the book of life, blessing, peace and good sustenance may we be remembered and inscribed before thee, we and all thy people the house of Israel, for a happy life and for peace. Blessed art thou, O Lord, who makest peace.]

CONCLUD-ING MEDITA-TION

See p. 156

Psalm 60. 7
Psalm 19. 5

O my God ! guard my tongue from evil and my lips from speaking guile and to such as curse me let my soul be dumb, yea, let my soul be unto all as the dust. Open my heart to thy Torah, and let my soul pursue thy commandments. If any design evil against me, speedily make their counsel of no effect, and frustrate their designs. Do it for the sake of thy Name, do it for the sake of thy power, do it for the sake of thy holiness, do it for the sake of thy Torah. In order that thy beloved ones may be delivered, O save by thy power, and answer me. Let the words of my mouth and the meditation of my heart be acceptable before thee, O Lord, my Rock and my Redeemer. He who maketh peace in his high places, may he make peace for us and for all Israel, and say ye, Amen.

GRANT ABUNDANT PEACE. This is the shorter form of the corresponding prayer in the Morning Service. It is used on all occasions when there can be no Blessing by the Priests, which Blessing was at one time part of the daily Morning Service, as well as of the Minchah Service on Fast Days ; see p. 154.

יְהִי רָצוֹן לְפָנֶיךָ יְיָ אֱלֹהֵינוּ וֵאלֹהֵי אֲבוֹתֵינוּ שֶׁיִּבָּנֶה בֵּית
הַמִּקְדָּשׁ בִּמְהֵרָה בְיָמֵינוּ ׳ וְתֵן חֶלְקֵנוּ בְּתוֹרָתֶךָ : וְשָׁם נַעֲבָדְךָ
בְּיִרְאָה כִּימֵי עוֹלָם וּכְשָׁנִים קַדְמוֹנִיּוֹת : וְעָרְבָה לַיְיָ מִנְחַת
יְהוּדָה וִירוּשָׁלָם כִּימֵי עוֹלָם וּכְשָׁנִים קַדְמוֹנִיּוֹת :

During the עֲשֶׂרֶת יְמֵי תְשׁוּבָה, say אָבִינוּ מַלְכֵּנוּ *p. 55.*

The following prayer to לְמַעַן שְׁמֶךָ *on page 296 is omitted at*
מִנְחָה, *on* רֹאשׁ חֹדֶשׁ, *on the afternoons preceding Sabbaths and*
רֹאשׁ חֹדֶשׁ, *during the whole month of* נִיסָן, *on* לֹ״ב בָּעוֹמֶר,
and preceding afternoon, from the afternoon before רֹאשׁ חֹדֶשׁ סִיוָן *until*
ט״ו בְּאָב, *and preceding afternoon,* on ט׳ בְּאָב, *on* אִסְרוּ חַג שָׁבֻעוֹת *after*
חֲנֻכָּה, *on* אִסְרוּ חַג *until* עֶרֶב יוֹם כִּפּוּר *from* עֶרֶב רֹאשׁ הַשָּׁנָה,
and preceding afternoon, on פּוּרִים *and* ט״ו בִּשְׁבָט, *on* preceding afternoon,
and on the two days of פּוּרִים קָטָן *and preceding afternoon. This prayer*
is also omitted on the occasion of a בְּרִית מִילָה *if the father, the* סַנְדָק or
the מוֹהֵל, *be present in the synagogue, in the house of an* אָבֵל *during the*
week of mourning, or at the celebration of a marriage.

וַיֹּאמֶר דָּוִד אֶל־גָּד צַר־לִי מְאֹד נִפְּלָה־נָא בְיַד־יְהֹוָה
כִּי־רַבִּים רַחֲמָו וּבְיַד אָדָם אַל־אֶפֹּלָה :

רַחוּם וְחַנּוּן חָטָאתִי לְפָנֶיךָ יְיָ מָלֵא רַחֲמִים רַחֵם
עָלַי וְקַבֵּל תַּחֲנוּנָי :

תהלים ו׳

יְיָ אַל־בְּאַפְּךָ תוֹכִיחֵנִי וְאַל־בַּחֲמָתְךָ תְיַסְּרֵנִי : חָנֵּנִי יְיָ
כִּי־אֻמְלַל אָנִי רְפָאֵנִי יְיָ כִּי נִבְהֲלוּ עֲצָמָי : וְנַפְשִׁי נִבְהֲלָה
מְאֹד וְאַתָּ יְיָ עַד־מָתָי : שׁוּבָה יְיָ חַלְּצָה נַפְשִׁי הוֹשִׁיעֵנִי
לְמַעַן חַסְדֶּךָ : כִּי אֵין בַּמָּוֶת זִכְרֶךָ בִּשְׁאוֹל מִי יוֹדֶה־לָּךְ :
יָגַעְתִּי בְּאַנְחָתִי אַשְׂחֶה בְכָל־לַיְלָה מִטָּתִי בְּדִמְעָתִי עַרְשִׂי

May it be thy will, O Lord our God and God of our fathers, that the temple be speedily rebuilt in our days, and grant our portion in thy Torah. And there we will serve thee with awe, as in the days of *Malachi 3. 4* old, and as in ancient years. Then shall the offering of Judah and Jerusalem be pleasant unto the Lord, as in the days of old\ and as in ancient years.

During the Ten Days of Repentance, Fridays and Sabbaths excepted, say "Our Father, our King," p. 163.

The following prayer to " for thy Name's sake " on p. 297 is omitted at the Afternoon Service on the afternoon preceding Sabbaths and New Moons, on New Moon, during the whole month of Nisan, on the thirty-third day of Omer and preceding afternoon, from the afternoon before New Moon of Sivan until the second day after Pentecost, on the Ninth of Av and preceding afternoon, on the Fifteenth of Av, on the day before New Year, from the day before the Day of Atonement until the second day after Tabernacles, on Chanukah and preceding afternoon, on the Fifteenth of Shevat, on the two days of Purim and preceding afternoon, and on the two days of Purim Koton and preceding afternoon. This prayer is also omitted on the occasion of a circumcision if the father, the godfather, or the Mohel, be present in the synagogue or in the house of a mourner during the week of mourning, or at the celebration of a marriage.

II Samuel 24. 14   And David said unto Gad, I am troubled exceedingly ; let us fall, I pray thee, into the hand of the Lord, for his mercies are many ; but let me not fall into the hand of man.

DAILY CON-FESSION See p. 180   O THOU WHO ART MERCIFUL AND GRACIOUS, I HAVE SINNED BEFORE THEE. O LORD, FULL OF MERCY, HAVE MERCY UPON ME AND RECEIVE MY SUPPLICATIONS.

Psalm vi. 1-11.

ENTREATY IN MORTAL DISTRESS

See p. 181

2O Lord, rebuke me not in thine anger : neither chasten me in thy hot displeasure. 3Be gracious unto me, O Lord ; for I am withered away ; O Lord, heal me ; for my bones are troubled. 4My soul also is sore troubled : and thou, O Lord, how long ? 5Return, O Lord, deliver my soul : save me for thy lovingkindness' sake. 6For in death there is no remembrance of thee : in the grave who shall give thee thanks ? 7I am weary with my groaning ; every night I make my bed to swim ; I melt away my couch with my

אֶמְסֶה : עָשְׁשָׁה מִכַּעַם עֵינִי עָתְקָה בְּכָל־צוֹרְרָי : סוּרוּ

מִמֶּנִּי כָּל־פֹּעֲלֵי אָוֶן כִּי־שָׁמַע יְיָ קוֹל בִּכְיִי : שָׁמַע יְיָ

תְּחִנָּתִי יְיָ תְּפִלָּתִי יִקָּח : יֵבֹשׁוּ וְיִבָּהֲלוּ מְאֹד כָּל־אֹיְבָי

יָשֻׁבוּ יֵבֹשׁוּ רָגַע :

שׁוֹמֵר יִשְׂרָאֵל · שְׁמוֹר שְׁאֵרִית יִשְׂרָאֵל · וְאַל־יֹאבַד

יִשְׂרָאֵל · הָאוֹמְרִים שְׁמַע יִשְׂרָאֵל :

שׁוֹמֵר גּוֹי אֶחָד · שְׁמוֹר שְׁאֵרִית עַם אֶחָד · וְאַל־יֹאבַד

גּוֹי אֶחָד · הַמְיַחֲדִים שִׁמְךָ יְיָ אֱלֹהֵינוּ יְיָ אֶחָד :

שׁוֹמֵר גּוֹי קָדוֹשׁ · שְׁמוֹר שְׁאֵרִית עַם קָדוֹשׁ · וְאַל־יֹאבַד

גּוֹי קָדוֹשׁ · הַמְשַׁלְּשִׁים בְּשָׁלוֹשׁ קְדֻשָּׁה לְקָדוֹשׁ :

מִתְרַצֶּה בְּרַחֲמִים וּמִתְפַּיֵּס בְּתַחֲנוּנִים · הִתְרַצֶּה וְהִתְפַּיֵּס

לְדוֹר עָנִי כִּי אֵין עוֹזֵר :

אָבִינוּ מַלְכֵּנוּ חָנֵּנוּ וַעֲנֵנוּ כִּי אֵין בָּנוּ מַעֲשִׂים · עֲשֵׂה

עִמָּנוּ צְדָקָה וָחֶסֶד וְהוֹשִׁיעֵנוּ :

וַאֲנַחְנוּ לֹא נֵדַע מַה־נַּעֲשֶׂה כִּי עָלֶיךָ עֵינֵינוּ : זְכֹר

רַחֲמֶיךָ יְיָ וַחֲסָדֶיךָ כִּי מֵעוֹלָם הֵמָּה : יְהִי־חַסְדְּךָ יְיָ עָלֵינוּ

כַּאֲשֶׁר יִחַלְנוּ לָךְ : אַל תִּזְכָּר־לָנוּ עֲוֹנֹת רִאשֹׁנִים מַהֵר

יְקַדְּמוּנוּ רַחֲמֶיךָ כִּי דַלּוֹנוּ מְאֹד : חָנֵּנוּ יְיָ חָנֵּנוּ כִּי־רַב

שָׂבַעְנוּ בוּז : בְּרֹגֶז רַחֵם תִּזְכּוֹר : כִּי הוּא יָדַע יִצְרֵנוּ זָכוּר

כִּי־עָפָר אֲנָחְנוּ : עָזְרֵנוּ אֱלֹהֵי יִשְׁעֵנוּ עַל־דְּבַר כְּבוֹד־שְׁמֶךָ

וְהַצִּילֵנוּ וְכַפֵּר עַל־חַטֹּאתֵינוּ לְמַעַן שְׁמֶךָ :

tears. [8]Mine eye wasteth away because of grief ; it waxeth old because of all mine adversaries. [9]Depart from me, all ye workers of iniquity ; for the Lord hath heard the voice of my weeping. [10]The Lord hath heard my supplication ; the Lord will receive my prayer. [11]All mine enemies shall be ashamed and sore troubled : they shall turn back, they shall be ashamed suddenly.

PRAYER FOR PROTECTION See p. 185

O Guardian of Israel, guard the remnant of Israel, and suffer not Israel to perish, who say, Hear, O Israel.

O Guardian of a unique nation, guard the remnant of a unique nation, and suffer not them to perish, who proclaim the unity of Thy Name, saying, The Lord is our God, the Lord is One.

O Guardian of a holy people, guard the remnant of a holy people, and suffer not them to perish, who thrice repeat the three-fold sanctification unto the Holy One.

O Thou who art propitiated by prayers for mercy, and art conciliated by supplications, be thou propitious and reconciled to an afflicted generation ; for there is none that helpeth.

PRAYER FOR FORGIVENESS

Our Father, our King, be gracious unto us and answer us, for we have no good works of our own ; deal with us in charity and lovingkindness, and save us.

II Chronicles 20. 12
Psalm 25. 6
Psalm 33. 22

As for us, we know not what to do ; but our eyes are upon thee. Remember, O Lord, thy tender mercies and thy lovingkindnesses ; for they have been ever of old. Let thy lovingkindness, O Lord, be upon us, according as we have hoped in thee. Remember not against us the iniquities of our ancestors : let thy tender mercies speedily come to meet us ; for we are brought very low. Be gracious unto us, O Lord, be gracious unto us ; for we are sated to the full with contempt. In wrath remember to be merciful. For He knoweth our frame ; he remembereth that we are dust. Help us, O God of our salvation, for the sake of the glory of thy Name ; and deliver us, and pardon our sins, for thy Name's sake.

Psalm 79. 8
Psalm 123. 4
Habakkuk 3. 2
Psalm 103. 14
Psalm 79. 9

עָלֵינוּ לְשַׁבֵּחַ לַאֲדוֹן הַכֹּל לָתֵת גְּדֻלָּה לְיוֹצֵר
בְּרֵאשִׁית · שֶׁלֹּא עָשָׂנוּ כְּגוֹיֵי הָאֲרָצוֹת וְלֹא שָׂמָנוּ
כְּמִשְׁפְּחוֹת הָאֲדָמָה · שֶׁלֹּא שָׂם חֶלְקֵנוּ כָּהֶם וְגֹרָלֵנוּ
כְּכָל־הֲמוֹנָם · וַאֲנַחְנוּ כּוֹרְעִים וּמִשְׁתַּחֲוִים וּמוֹדִים לִפְנֵי
מֶלֶךְ מַלְכֵי הַמְּלָכִים הַקָּדוֹשׁ בָּרוּךְ הוּא · שֶׁהוּא נוֹטֶה
שָׁמַיִם וְיוֹסֵד אָרֶץ · וּמוֹשַׁב יְקָרוֹ בַּשָּׁמַיִם מִמַּעַל וּשְׁכִינַת
עֻזּוֹ בְּגָבְהֵי מְרוֹמִים · הוּא אֱלֹהֵינוּ · אֵין עוֹד · אֱמֶת
מַלְכֵּנוּ · אֶפֶס זוּלָתוֹ · כַּכָּתוּב בְּתוֹרָתוֹ · וְיָדַעְתָּ הַיּוֹם
וַהֲשֵׁבֹתָ אֶל־לְבָבֶךָ כִּי יְיָ הוּא הָאֱלֹהִים בַּשָּׁמַיִם מִמַּעַל
וְעַל־הָאָרֶץ מִתָּחַת אֵין עוֹד :

עַל־כֵּן נְקַוֶּה לְּךָ יְיָ אֱלֹהֵינוּ לִרְאוֹת מְהֵרָה בְּתִפְאֶרֶת
עֻזֶּךָ · לְהַעֲבִיר גִּלּוּלִים מִן הָאָרֶץ וְהָאֱלִילִים כָּרוֹת יִכָּרֵתוּן ·
לְתַקֵּן עוֹלָם בְּמַלְכוּת שַׁדַּי וְכָל־בְּנֵי בָשָׂר יִקְרְאוּ בִשְׁמֶךָ ·
לְהַפְנוֹת אֵלֶיךָ כָּל־רִשְׁעֵי אָרֶץ : יַכִּירוּ וְיֵדְעוּ כָּל־יוֹשְׁבֵי
תֵבֵל כִּי לְךָ תִּכְרַע כָּל־בֶּרֶךְ תִּשָּׁבַע כָּל־לָשׁוֹן : לְפָנֶיךָ יְיָ
אֱלֹהֵינוּ יִכְרְעוּ וְיִפֹּלוּ · וְלִכְבוֹד שִׁמְךָ יְקָר יִתֵּנוּ · וִיקַבְּלוּ
כֻלָּם אֶת־עֹל מַלְכוּתֶךָ · וְתִמְלֹךְ עֲלֵיהֶם מְהֵרָה לְעוֹלָם
וָעֶד · כִּי הַמַּלְכוּת שֶׁלְּךָ הִיא וּלְעוֹלְמֵי עַד תִּמְלֹךְ
בְּכָבוֹד : כַּכָּתוּב בְּתוֹרָתֶךָ · יְיָ ׀ יִמְלֹךְ לְעוֹלָם וָעֶד :
וְנֶאֱמַר · וְהָיָה יְיָ לְמֶלֶךְ עַל־כָּל־הָאָרֶץ בַּיּוֹם הַהוּא יִהְיֶה
יְיָ אֶחָד וּשְׁמוֹ אֶחָד :

The Reader says Kaddish, p. 207.

OLEYNU: ISRAEL'S SELECTION TO PROCLAIM GOD AS SUPREME KING OF THE UNIVERSE

It is our duty to praise the Lord of all things, to ascribe greatness to him who formed the world in the beginning, since he hath not made us like the nations of other lands, and hath not placed us like other families of the earth, since he hath not assigned unto us a portion as unto them, nor a lot as unto all their multitude. For we bend the knee and offer worship and thanks before the supreme King of kings, the Holy One, blessed be he, who stretched forth the heavens and laid the foundations of the earth, the seat of whose glory is in the heavens above, and the abode of whose might is in the loftiest heights. He is our God ; there is none else : in truth he is our King ; there is none besides him ; as it is written in his Torah, And thou shalt know this day, and lay it to thine heart, that the Lord he is God in heaven above and upon the earth beneath : there is none else.

See p. 208

Deuteronomy 4. 39

ISRAEL'S HOPE: HUMANITY UNITED IN RECOGNITION OF THE ONE GOD

We therefore hope in thee, O Lord our God, that we may speedily behold the glory of thy might, when thou wilt remove the abominations from the earth, and heathendom will be utterly destroyed, when the world will be perfected under the kingdom of the Almighty, and all the children of flesh will call upon thy Name, when thou wilt turn unto thyself all the evil-doers upon earth. Let all the inhabitants of the world perceive and know that unto thee every knee must bow, every tongue must swear allegiance. Before thee, O Lord our God, let them bow and worship ; and unto thy glorious Name let them give honour ; let them all accept the yoke of thy kingdom, and do thou reign over them speedily, and for ever and ever. For the kingdom is thine, *Exodus 15. 18* and to all eternity thou wilt reign in glory ; as it is written *Zechariah 14. 9* in thy Torah, THE LORD SHALL REIGN FOR EVER AND EVER. And it is said, AND THE LORD SHALL BE KING OVER ALL THE EARTH : IN THAT DAY SHALL THE LORD BE ONE, AND HIS NAME ONE.

קַדִּישׁ יָתוֹם

Mourner. יִתְגַּדַּל וְיִתְקַדַּשׁ שְׁמֵהּ רַבָּא בְּעָלְמָא דִּי־בְרָא

כִרְעוּתֵהּ · וְיַמְלִיךְ מַלְכוּתֵהּ בְּחַיֵּיכוֹן וּבְיוֹמֵיכוֹן וּבְחַיֵּי

דִי־כָל־בֵּית יִשְׂרָאֵל בַּעֲגָלָא וּבִזְמַן קָרִיב · וְאִמְרוּ אָמֵן :

Cong. and Mourner. יְהֵא שְׁמֵהּ רַבָּא מְבָרַךְ לְעָלַם

וּלְעָלְמֵי עָלְמַיָּא ·

Mourner. יִתְבָּרַךְ וְיִשְׁתַּבַּח וְיִתְפָּאַר וְיִתְרֹמַם וְיִתְנַשֵּׂא

וְיִתְהַדַּר וְיִתְעַלֶּה וְיִתְהַלָּל שְׁמֵהּ דִּי־קֻדְשָׁא · בְּרִיךְ הוּא ·

לְעֵלָּא מִן־כָּל־בִּרְכָתָא וְשִׁירָתָא תֻּשְׁבְּחָתָא וְנֶחֱמָתָא

דִּי־אֲמִירָן בְּעָלְמָא · וְאִמְרוּ אָמֵן :

Congregation. אָמֵן :

Mourner. יְהֵא שְׁלָמָא רַבָּא מִן־שְׁמַיָּא וְחַיִּים עָלֵינוּ

וְעַל־כָּל־יִשְׂרָאֵל · וְאִמְרוּ אָמֵן :

Congregation אָמֵן :

Mourner. עֹשֶׂה שָׁלוֹם בִּמְרוֹמָיו הוּא יַעֲשֶׂה שָׁלוֹם

עָלֵינוּ וְעַל־כָּל־יִשְׂרָאֵל · וְאִמְרוּ אָמֵן :

Mourner's Kaddish.

MOURN-
ER'S
KADDISH

Mourner.—Magnified and sanctified be his great Name in the world which he hath created according to his will. May he establish his kingdom during your life and during your days, and during the life of all the house of Israel,

See p. 254

even speedily and at a near time, and say ye, Amen.

Cong. and Mourner.—Let his great Name be blessed for ever and to all eternity.

Mourner.—Blessed, praised and glorified, exalted, extolled and honoured, magnified and lauded be the Name of the Holy One, blessed be he ; though he be high above all the blessings and hymns, praises and consolations, which are uttered in the world ; and say ye, Amen.

Congregation.—Amen.

Mourner.—May there be abundant peace from heaven, and life for us and for all Israel ; and say ye, Amen.

Congregation.—Amen.

Mourner.—He who maketh peace in his high places, may he make peace for us and for all Israel ; and say ye, Amen.

---

6. MOURNER'S KADDISH.

Great religious significance was attached by the Rabbis to the Congregation repeating in unison the words, *Let His great Name be blessed for ever and to all eternity.* " As the assembly proclaim these words, the Holy One forgives " (Midrash). The son, reciting the Kaddish, is thus instrumental in calling forth the most important response in the Service. For the rise and significance of this prayer, see on THE MOURNER'S KADDISH, p. 268.

may he establish his kingdom. May He bring about the realization of all spiritual values, and transform things as they are into things as they ought to be.

let his great Name be blessed for ever and to all eternity. This is the principal response of the Kaddish. It was deemed to be the hymn of hymns, and gained still greater hold upon the reverent affection of the people when it came to be looked upon as the Orphan's Prayer.

consolations. The Heb. word, in addition to its general meaning of comfort in mourning and sorrow, also denotes both the praises of God in connection with the future Messianic time and the Future Life, as well as the consolatory discourses to which the Kaddish was the conclusion.

עַרְבִית לִימוֹת הַחוֹל וְלְמוֹצָאֵי שַׁבָּת :

On Weekdays, if מַעֲרִיב *is read after nightfall, commence* שִׁיר הַמַּעֲלוֹת.
At the termination of the Sabbath say לְדָוִד בָּרוּךְ *to* אֶרֶץ *then*
continue וְהוּא רַחוּם, *see next page. On Weekdays, if* מַעֲרִיב *is read*
before nightfall, commence וְהוּא רַחוּם.

תהלים קל״ד

שִׁיר הַמַּעֲלוֹת הִנֵּה בָּרְכוּ אֶת־יְיָ כָּל־עַבְדֵי יְיָ הָעֹמְדִים

בְּבֵית יְיָ בַּלֵּילוֹת: שְׂאוּ יְדֵכֶם קֹדֶשׁ וּבָרְכוּ אֶת־יְיָ :

יְבָרֶכְךָ יְיָ מִצִּיּוֹן עֹשֵׂה שָׁמַיִם וָאָרֶץ :

יְיָ צְבָאוֹת עִמָּנוּ מִשְׂגָּב־לָנוּ אֱלֹהֵי יַעֲקֹב סֶלָה:

(*To be said three times.*)

(*To be said three times.*) יְיָ צְבָאוֹת אַשְׁרֵי אָדָם בֹּטֵחַ בָּךְ :

(*To be said three times.*) יְיָ הוֹשִׁיעָה הַמֶּלֶךְ יַעֲנֵנוּ בְיוֹם־קָרְאֵנוּ:

The Reader says חֲצִי קַדִּישׁ, *p.* 106.

EVENING SERVICE.

(תפלת ערבית)

The Evening Service illustrates the fundamental simplicity of the
Jewish Liturgy. Its central part is the Shema, which is both
preceded and followed by two blessings. The benedictions preceding are shorter variants of the Morning blessings for physical light and
for the light of revelation. Of the benedictions succeeding the Shema,
the second is a special Night Prayer. The Amidah was not part of
the Evening Service till the days of Maimonides.

EVENING SERVICE

FOR WEEKDAYS AND THE TERMINATION OF THE SABBATH.

On Weekdays, if the Evening Service is read after nightfall, commence here. At the termination of the Sabbath, say Psalms cxliv, and lxvii, pp. 725–729; then continue "And he being merciful," p. 305. On Weekdays, if the Evening Service is read before nightfall, commence, "And he being merciful."

Psalm cxxxiv. ¹A Pilgrim Song.

"BLESS YE THE LORD"   Behold, bless ye the Lord, all ye servants of the Lord, who stand in the house of the Lord in the night seasons. ²Lift up your hands in holiness, and bless ye the Lord. ³The Lord bless thee out of Zion; even he that made heaven and earth.

Psalm 46. 8   The Lord of hosts is with us : the God of Jacob is our stronghold. (Selah.) *(To be said three times.)*

Psalm 84. 13   O Lord of hosts, happy is the man that trusteth in thee. *(To be said three times.)*

Psalm 20. 10   Save, Lord : may the King answer us on the day when we call. *(To be said three times.)*

The Reader says Half-Kaddish, p. 107.

PSALM 134.

This psalm seems to have been a night-song of the Temple watchmen. Verses 1 and 2 were addressed to the guard going off duty by those who came to relieve them ; and who, in their turn, received the answer in verse 3.

The additional verses after Psalm 134, were introduced by the later Mystics with the recommended threefold repetition ; possibly, in order that they thereby remain imbedded in the memory.

The Lord of hosts . . . stronghold. This is from Psalm 46 (" God is our refuge and strength, a very present help in trouble"). The title "Lord of hosts " describes God as the Great King whom all created things in heaven and earth obey ; while the words, " the God of Jacob ", assure us of the fatherly love which He has revealed unto Israel.

AND HE BEING MERCIFUL. In all Rites, this brief appeal for Divine pardon precedes the Service proper, which begins with the Invocation, " Bless ye the Lord ", when a congregational quorum is present ; otherwise, with " Blessed art Thou ". The 13 Hebrew words in the appeal were held to recall the Thirteen Attributes of Divine mercy (Exodus 34. 6, 7). " Save, O Lord ", is the antiphonal response of the Congregation.

וְהוּא רַחוּם יְכַפֵּר עָוֹן וְלֹא יַשְׁחִית וְהִרְבָּה לְהָשִׁיב
אַפּוֹ וְלֹא יָעִיר כָּל־חֲמָתוֹ : יְיָ הוֹשִׁיעָה הַמֶּלֶךְ יַעֲנֵנוּ
בְיוֹם־קָרְאֵנוּ :

Congregation in an undertone.

יִתְבָּרַךְ וְיִשְׁתַּבַּח וְיִתְפָּאַר
וְיִתְרוֹמַם וְיִתְנַשֵּׂא שְׁמוֹ שֶׁל־מֶלֶךְ
מַלְכֵי הַמְּלָכִים הַקָּדוֹשׁ בָּרוּךְ הוּא •
שֶׁהוּא רִאשׁוֹן וְהוּא אַחֲרוֹן
וּמִבַּלְעָדָיו אֵין אֱלֹהִים • סֹלּוּ לָרֹכֵב
בָּעֲרָבוֹת בְּיָהּ שְׁמוֹ וְעִלְזוּ לְפָנָיו •
וּשְׁמוֹ מְרוֹמָם עַל־כָּל־בְּרָכָה
וּתְהִלָּה :
בָּרוּךְ שֵׁם כְּבוֹד מַלְכוּתוֹ לְעוֹלָם
וָעֶד : יְהִי שֵׁם יְיָ מְבֹרָךְ מֵעַתָּה
וְעַד עוֹלָם :

Reader.

בָּרְכוּ אֶת־יְיָ הַמְבֹרָךְ :

Cong. and Reader.

בָּרוּךְ יְיָ הַמְבֹרָךְ לְעוֹלָם
וָעֶד :

בָּרוּךְ אַתָּה יְיָ אֱלֹהֵינוּ
מֶלֶךְ הָעוֹלָם • אֲשֶׁר
בִּדְבָרוֹ מַעֲרִיב עֲרָבִים
בְּחָכְמָה פּוֹתֵחַ שְׁעָרִים
וּבִתְבוּנָה מְשַׁנֶּה עִתִּים

וּמַחֲלִיף אֶת־הַזְּמַנִּים וּמְסַדֵּר אֶת־הַכּוֹכָבִים בְּמִשְׁמְרוֹתֵיהֶם
בָּרָקִיעַ כִּרְצוֹנוֹ • בּוֹרֵא יוֹם וָלַיְלָה גּוֹלֵל אוֹר מִפְּנֵי־
חֹשֶׁךְ וְחֹשֶׁךְ מִפְּנֵי־אוֹר • וּמַעֲבִיר יוֹם .וּמֵבִיא לַיְלָה
וּמַבְדִּיל בֵּין יוֹם וּבֵין לָיְלָה יְיָ צְבָאוֹת שְׁמוֹ • אֵל חַי
וְקַיָּם תָּמִיד יִמְלֹךְ עָלֵינוּ לְעוֹלָם וָעֶד • בָּרוּךְ אַתָּה
יְיָ • הַמַּעֲרִיב עֲרָבִים :

BLESSED ART THOU. This is the specific Evening Prayer, corresponding to the *yotzer* in the Morning Service. It is a prayer of great
beauty. Jewish piety has ever been moved to adoration by the recurrent phenomena of Nature. The changes of the times, morning,

APPEAL
FOR
PARDON
Psalm 78. 38

Psalm 20. 10

INVOCA-
TION
TO CONGRE-
GATIONAL
PRAYER

GOD THE
CREATOR
OF DAY
AND
NIGHT

And he being merciful, forgiveth iniquity, and destroyeth not : yea, many a time he turneth his anger away, and doth not stir up all his wrath. Save, Lord : may the King answer us on the day when we call.

Reader.— BLESS YE THE LORD WHO IS TO BE BLESSED.

Cong. and Reader.— BLESSED IS THE LORD WHO IS TO BE BLESSED FOR EVER AND EVER.

Congregation, in an undertone.

Blessed, praised, glorified, exalted and extolled be the Name of the supreme King of kings, the Holy One, blessed be he, who is the first and the last, and beside him there is no God. Extol ye him that rideth upon the heavens, whose Name is the Lord, and rejoice before him. His Name is exalted above all blessing and praise. Blessed be His Name, whose glorious kingdom is for ever and ever. Let the Name of the Lord be blessed from this time forth and for evermore.

Blessed art thou, O Lord our God, King of the universe who at thy word bringest on the evening twilight, with wisdom openest the gates of the heavens, and with understanding changest times and variest the seasons, and arrangest the stars in their watches in the sky, according to thy will. Thou createst day and night ; thou rollest away the light from before the darkness, and the darkness from before the light ; thou makest the day to pass and the night to approach, and dividest the day from the night, the Lord of hosts is thy Name ; a God living and enduring continually, mayest thou reign over us for ever and ever. Blessed art thou, O Lord, who bringest on the evening twilight.

noon, and night ; sunshine and the rolling away of light before darkness ; the ranging of the stars in their watches in the sky—all fill the worshipper with reverential wonder and awe ; see p. 991.
at thy word. God's creative word that established the order of day and night ; Genesis 1. 3–5.

אַהֲבַת עוֹלָם בֵּית יִשְׂרָאֵל עַמְּךָ אָהָבְתָּ · תּוֹרָה וּמִצְוֹת
חֻקִּים וּמִשְׁפָּטִים אוֹתָנוּ לִמַּדְתָּ · עַל־כֵּן יְיָ אֱלֹהֵינוּ
בְּשָׁכְבֵּנוּ וּבְקוּמֵנוּ נָשִׂיחַ בְּחֻקֶּיךָ · וְנִשְׂמַח בְּדִבְרֵי תוֹרָתֶךָ
וּבְמִצְוֹתֶיךָ לְעוֹלָם וָעֶד · כִּי הֵם חַיֵּינוּ וְאֹרֶךְ יָמֵינוּ
וּבָהֶם נֶהְגֶּה יוֹמָם וָלָיְלָה · וְאַהֲבָתְךָ אַל־תָּסִיר מִמֶּנּוּ
לְעוֹלָמִים · בָּרוּךְ אַתָּה יְיָ · אוֹהֵב עַמּוֹ יִשְׂרָאֵל :

(*When Prayers are not said with the Congregation, add* :—

(אֵל מֶלֶךְ נֶאֱמָן :)

דברים ו׳ ד׳־ט׳

שְׁמַע יִשְׂרָאֵל יְהוָֹה אֱלֹהֵינוּ יְהוָֹה ׀ אֶחָד :

בָּרוּךְ שֵׁם כְּבוֹד מַלְכוּתוֹ לְעוֹלָם וָעֶד :

וְאָהַבְתָּ אֵת יְהוָֹה אֱלֹהֶיךָ בְּכָל־לְבָבְךָ וּבְכָל־נַפְשְׁךָ
וּבְכָל־מְאֹדֶךָ : וְהָיוּ הַדְּבָרִים הָאֵלֶּה אֲשֶׁר אָנֹכִי מְצַוְּךָ
הַיּוֹם עַל־לְבָבֶךָ : וְשִׁנַּנְתָּם לְבָנֶיךָ וְדִבַּרְתָּ בָּם בְּשִׁבְתְּךָ
בְּבֵיתֶךָ וּבְלֶכְתְּךָ בַדֶּרֶךְ וּבְשָׁכְבְּךָ וּבְקוּמֶךָ : וּקְשַׁרְתָּם
לְאוֹת עַל־יָדֶךָ וְהָיוּ לְטֹטָפֹת בֵּין עֵינֶיךָ : וּכְתַבְתָּם
עַל־מְזֻזוֹת בֵּיתֶךָ וּבִשְׁעָרֶיךָ :

דברים י׳א י׳ג־כ׳א

וְהָיָה אִם־שָׁמֹעַ תִּשְׁמְעוּ אֶל־מִצְוֹתַי אֲשֶׁר אָנֹכִי מְצַוֶּה
אֶתְכֶם הַיּוֹם לְאַהֲבָה אֶת־יְהוָֹה אֱלֹהֵיכֶם וּלְעָבְדוֹ בְּכָל־

WITH EVERLASTING LOVE. A briefer form of the Ahavoh prayer in
the Morning Service, thanking God for the sacred gift of Revelation
that He granted Israel. It breathes the purest idealism. All other
goods and gifts of life are transitory ; the Torah alone is the eternal

GOD THE
TEACHER
OF ISRAEL   With everlasting love thou hast loved the house of Israel, thy people ; a Torah and commandments, statutes and judgments hast thou taught us. Therefore, O Lord our God, when we lie down and when we rise up we will meditate on thy statutes ; yea, we will rejoice in the words of thy Torah and in thy commandments for ever ; for they are our life and the length of our days, and we will meditate on them day and night. And mayest thou never take away thy love from us. Blessed art thou, O Lord, who lovest thy people Israel.

(When prayers are not said with the Congregation, say :— God, faithful King !)*

Deuteronomy vi. 4—9.

THE
SHEMA :   HEAR, O ISRAEL : THE LORD IS OUR GOD, THE LORD IS ONE.

BLESSED BE HIS NAME, WHOSE GLORIOUS KINGDOM IS FOR EVER AND EVER.

THOU
SHALT
LOVE THE
LORD THY
GOD   ⁵And thou shalt love the Lord thy God with all thine heart, and with all thy soul, and with all thy might. ⁶And these words, which I corımand thee this day, shall be upon thine heart : ⁷and thou shalt teach them diligently unto thy children, and shalt talk of them when thou sittest in thine
See p. 116-124 house, and when thou walkest by the way, and when thou liest down, and when thou risest up. ⁸And thou shalt bind them for a sign upon thine hand, and they shall be for frontlets between thine eyes. ⁹And thou shalt write them upon the door-posts of thy house, and upon thy gates.

Deuteronomy xi. 13—21.

REWARD
AND
PUNISH-
MENT   ¹³And it shall come to pass, if ye shall hearken diligently unto my commandments which I command you this day, to love the Lord your God, and to serve him with all your

heritage of the Jewish people. The phrase " everlasting love " is from Jeremiah 31. 3.
our life . . . length of our days. Our continued existence as Jews is dependent on our clinging to the commandments of our Faith. When the " ceremonies " are banished from any Jewish home, it loses touch with Divine things, and is left without God in its life.

לְבַבְכֶם וּבְכָל־נַפְשְׁכֶם: וְנָתַתִּי מְטַר־אַרְצְכֶם בְּעִתּוֹ יוֹרֶה

וּמַלְקוֹשׁ וְאָסַפְתָּ דְגָנֶךָ וְתִירשְׁךָ וְיִצְהָרֶךָ: וְנָתַתִּי עֵשֶׂב

בְּשָׂדְךָ לִבְהֶמְתֶּךָ וְאָכַלְתָּ וְשָׂבָעְתָּ: הִשָּׁמְרוּ לָכֶם פֶּן

יִפְתֶּה לְבַבְכֶם וְסַרְתֶּם וַעֲבַדְתֶּם אֱלֹהִים אֲחֵרִים

וְהִשְׁתַּחֲוִיתֶם לָהֶם: וְחָרָה אַף־יְהוָֹה בָּכֶם וְעָצַר אֶת־

הַשָּׁמַיִם וְלֹא־יִהְיֶה מָטָר וְהָאֲדָמָה לֹא תִתֵּן אֶת־יְבוּלָהּ

וַאֲבַדְתֶּם מְהֵרָה מֵעַל הָאָרֶץ הַטֹּבָה אֲשֶׁר יְהוָֹה נֹתֵן

לָכֶם: וְשַׂמְתֶּם אֶת־דְּבָרַי אֵלֶּה עַל־לְבַבְכֶם וְעַל־נַפְשְׁכֶם

וּקְשַׁרְתֶּם אֹתָם לְאוֹת עַל־יֶדְכֶם וְהָיוּ לְטוֹטָפֹת בֵּין

עֵינֵיכֶם: וְלִמַּדְתֶּם אֹתָם אֶת־בְּנֵיכֶם לְדַבֵּר בָּם בְּשִׁבְתְּךָ

בְּבֵיתֶךָ וּבְלֶכְתְּךָ בַדֶּרֶךְ וּבְשָׁכְבְּךָ וּבְקוּמֶךָ: וּכְתַבְתָּם

עַל־מְזוּזוֹת בֵּיתֶךָ וּבִשְׁעָרֶיךָ: לְמַעַן יִרְבּוּ יְמֵיכֶם וִימֵי

בְנֵיכֶם עַל הָאֲדָמָה אֲשֶׁר נִשְׁבַּע יְהוָֹה לַאֲבֹתֵיכֶם

לָתֵת לָהֶם כִּימֵי הַשָּׁמַיִם עַל־הָאָרֶץ:

במדבר ט"ו ל"זמ"א

וַיֹּאמֶר יְהוָֹה אֶל־מֹשֶׁה לֵּאמֹר: דַּבֵּר אֶל־בְּנֵי יִשְׂרָאֵל

וְאָמַרְתָּ אֲלֵהֶם וְעָשׂוּ לָהֶם צִיצִת עַל־כַּנְפֵי בִגְדֵיהֶם

לְדֹרֹתָם וְנָתְנוּ עַל־צִיצִת הַכָּנָף פְּתִיל תְּכֵלֶת: וְהָיָה

לָכֶם לְצִיצִת וּרְאִיתֶם אֹתוֹ וּזְכַרְתֶּם אֶת־כָּל־מִצְוֹת יְהוָֹה

וַעֲשִׂיתֶם אֹתָם וְלֹא תָתוּרוּ אַחֲרֵי לְבַבְכֶם וְאַחֲרֵי עֵינֵיכֶם

אֲשֶׁר־אַתֶּם זֹנִים אַחֲרֵיהֶם: לְמַעַן תִּזְכְּרוּ וַעֲשִׂיתֶם

REWARD AND PUNISH- MENT

heart and with all your soul, ¹⁴that I will give the rain of your land in its season, the former rain and the latter rain, that thou mayest gather in thy corn, and thy wine, and thine oil. ¹⁵And I will give grass in thy field for thy cattle, and thou shalt eat and be satisfied. ¹⁶Take heed to your-selves, lest your heart be deceived, and ye turn aside, and serve other gods, and worship them ; ¹⁷and the anger of the Lord be kindled against you, and he shut up the heaven, that there be no rain, and that the land yield not her fruit ; and ye perish quickly from off the good land which the Lord giveth you. ¹⁸Therefore shall ye lay up these my words in your heart and in your soul ; and ye shall bind them for a sign upon your hand, and they shall be for frontlets between your eyes. ¹⁹And ye shall teach them your children, talking of them when thou sittest in thine house, and when thou walkest by the way, and when thou liest down, and when thou risest up. ²⁰And thou shalt write them upon the door-posts of thine house, and upon thy gates : ²¹that your days may be multiplied, and the days of your children, upon the land which the Lord sware unto your fathers to give them, as the days of the heavens above the earth.

Numbers xv. 37—41.

THE MONITION OF THE TZITZIS

³⁷And the Lord spake unto Moses, saying, ³⁸Speak unto the children of Israel, and bid them that they make them a fringe upon the corners of their garments throughout their generations, and that they put upon the fringe of each corner a cord of blue : ³⁹and it shall be unto you for a fringe, that ye may look upon it, and remember all the command-ments of the Lord, and do them ; and that ye go not about after your own heart and your own eyes, after which ye go astray : ⁴⁰that ye may remember and do all my

AND THE LORD SPAKE. Although the commandment of *tzitzis* does not apply in the night-time, this third paragraph was eventually intro-duced in the Evening Service, because of the clear enunciation of the duty to remember the Going out of Egypt. That remembrance must be with us all the days of our life ; *all* the days—to include night-time as well as day-time.

אֶת־כָּל־מִצְוֹתָי וִהְיִיתֶם קְדֹשִׁים לֵאלֹהֵיכֶם : אֲנִי יְהֹוָה
אֱלֹהֵיכֶם אֲשֶׁר הוֹצֵאתִי אֶתְכֶם מֵאֶרֶץ מִצְרַיִם לִהְיוֹת
לָכֶם לֵאלֹהִים אֲנִי יְהֹוָה אֱלֹהֵיכֶם :

אֱמֶת וֶאֱמוּנָה כָּל־זֹאת וְקַיָּם עָלֵינוּ כִּי הוּא יְיָ אֱלֹהֵינוּ
וְאֵין זוּלָתוֹ וַאֲנַחְנוּ יִשְׂרָאֵל עַמּוֹ · הַפּוֹדֵנוּ מִיַּד מְלָכִים
מַלְכֵּנוּ הַגּוֹאֲלֵנוּ מִכַּף כָּל־הֶעָרִיצִים · הָאֵל הַנִּפְרָע לָנוּ
מִצָּרֵינוּ וְהַמְשַׁלֵּם גְּמוּל לְכָל־אֹיְבֵי נַפְשֵׁנוּ · הָעֹשֶׂה גְדֹלוֹת
עַד־אֵין חֵקֶר וְנִפְלָאוֹת עַד־אֵין מִסְפָּר · הַשָּׂם נַפְשֵׁנוּ
בַּחַיִּים וְלֹא־נָתַן לַמּוֹט רַגְלֵנוּ · הַמַּדְרִיכֵנוּ עַל־בָּמוֹת
אוֹיְבֵינוּ וַיָּרֶם קַרְנֵנוּ עַל־כָּל־שׂנְאֵינוּ · הָעֹשֶׂה־לָּנוּ נִסִּים
וּנְקָמָה בְּפַרְעֹה אוֹתֹת וּמוֹפְתִים בְּאַדְמַת בְּנֵי־חָם · הַמַּכֶּה
בְעֶבְרָתוֹ כָּל־בְּכוֹרֵי מִצְרַיִם וַיּוֹצֵא אֶת־עַמּוֹ יִשְׂרָאֵל
מִתּוֹכָם לְחֵרוּת עוֹלָם · הַמַּעֲבִיר בָּנָיו בֵּין גִּזְרֵי יַם־סוּף
אֶת־רוֹדְפֵיהֶם וְאֶת־שׂוֹנְאֵיהֶם בִּתְהֹמוֹת טִבַּע · וְרָאוּ בָנָיו
גְּבוּרָתוֹ שִׁבְּחוּ וְהוֹדוּ לִשְׁמוֹ וּמַלְכוּתוֹ בְּרָצוֹן קִבְּלוּ
עֲלֵיהֶם · מֹשֶׁה וּבְנֵי יִשְׂרָאֵל לְךָ עָנוּ שִׁירָה בְּשִׂמְחָה
רַבָּה · וְאָמְרוּ כֻלָּם ·

מִי־כָמֹכָה בָּאֵלִם יְהֹוָה מִי כָּמֹכָה נֶאְדָּר בַּקֹּדֶשׁ
נוֹרָא תְהִלֹּת עֹשֵׂה פֶלֶא :

מַלְכוּתְךָ רָאוּ בָנֶיךָ בּוֹקֵעַ יָם לִפְנֵי מֹשֶׁה · זֶה אֵלִי
עָנוּ · וְאָמְרוּ · יְהֹוָה יִמְלֹךְ לְעֹלָם וָעֶד :

commandments, and be holy unto your God. ⁴¹I am the Lord your God, who brought you out of the land of Egypt, to be your God : I am the Lord your God.

GOD THE RE-DEEMER

True and trustworthy is all this, and it is established with us that he is the Lord our God, and there is none beside him, and that we, Israel, are his people. It is he who redeemed us from the hand of kings, even our King, who delivered us from the grasp of all tyrants ; the God, who *Job* 9. 10 on our behalf dealt out punishment to our adversaries, and requited all our mortal enemies ; who doeth great things *Psalm* 66. 9 past finding out, yea, and wonders without number ; who maintaineth us in life, and hath not suffered our feet to slip ; who made us overcome and conquer our enemies, and exalted our strength above all them that hated us ; who wrought for us miracles and retribution upon Pharaoh, signs and wonders in the land of the children of Ham ; who in his wrath smote all the first-born of Egypt, and brought forth his people Israel from among them to everlasting freedom ; who made his children pass through the divided Red Sea, but sank their pursuers and their enemies in its depths. Then his children beheld his might ; they praised and gave thanks unto his Name, and willingly accepted his sovereignty. Moses and the children of Israel sang a song unto thee with great joy, saying, all of them, *Exodus* 15. 11   WHO IS LIKE UNTO THEE, O LORD, AMONG THE MIGHTY ? WHO IS LIKE UNTO THEE, GLORIOUS IN HOLINESS, REVERED IN PRAISES, DOING WONDERS ?

Thy children beheld thy sovereign power, as thou didst cleave the sea before Moses : they exclaimed, This is my *Exodus* 15. 18 God ! and said, THE LORD SHALL REIGN FOR EVER AND EVER.

TRUE AND TRUSTWORTHY. The Shema is followed, as in the Morning Service, by an Attestation to its truths, passing into a jubilant recollection of the Redemption from Egypt, and of the redeemed triumphantly proclaiming the sovereignty of God.

וְנֶאֱמַר כִּי־פָדָה יְיָ אֶת־יַעֲקֹב וּגְאָלוֹ מִיַּד חָזָק מִמֶּנּוּ ·
בָּרוּךְ אַתָּה יְיָ · גָּאַל יִשְׂרָאֵל :

הַשְׁכִּיבֵנוּ יְיָ אֱלֹהֵינוּ לְשָׁלוֹם וְהַעֲמִידֵנוּ מַלְכֵּנוּ לְחַיִּים ·
וּפְרֹשׂ עָלֵינוּ סֻכַּת שְׁלוֹמֶךָ · וְתַקְּנֵנוּ בְּעֵצָה טוֹבָה
מִלְּפָנֶיךָ · וְהוֹשִׁיעֵנוּ לְמַעַן שְׁמֶךָ · וְהָגֵן בַּעֲדֵנוּ וְהָסֵר
מֵעָלֵינוּ אוֹיֵב דֶּבֶר וְחֶרֶב וְרָעָב וְיָגוֹן · וְהָסֵר שָׂטָן
מִלְּפָנֵינוּ וּמֵאַחֲרֵינוּ · וּבְצֵל כְּנָפֶיךָ תַּסְתִּירֵנוּ כִּי אֵל
שׁוֹמְרֵנוּ וּמַצִּילֵנוּ אָתָּה כִּי אֵל מֶלֶךְ חַנּוּן וְרַחוּם אָתָּה ·
וּשְׁמוֹר צֵאתֵנוּ וּבוֹאֵנוּ לְחַיִּים וּלְשָׁלוֹם מֵעַתָּה וְעַד
עוֹלָם · בָּרוּךְ אַתָּה יְיָ · שׁוֹמֵר עַמּוֹ יִשְׂרָאֵל לָעַד :

בָּרוּךְ יְיָ לְעוֹלָם · אָמֵן וְאָמֵן : בָּרוּךְ יְיָ מִצִּיּוֹן שֹׁכֵן
יְרוּשָׁלָםִ · הַלְלוּיָהּ : בָּרוּךְ יְיָ אֱלֹהִים אֱלֹהֵי יִשְׂרָאֵל עֹשֵׂה
נִפְלָאוֹת לְבַדּוֹ : וּבָרוּךְ שֵׁם כְּבוֹדוֹ לְעוֹלָם וְיִמָּלֵא כְבוֹדוֹ
אֶת־כָּל־הָאָרֶץ · אָמֵן וְאָמֵן : יְהִי כְבוֹד יְיָ לְעוֹלָם יִשְׂמַח

CAUSE US . . . TO LIE DOWN. Or, " grant, O Lord, that we may
lie down ". This is the second of the benedictions that follow the
Shema in the evenings. In it we pray for protection during the night,
when man feels the need of God's watchfulness over him far more
than by day.

the adversary. Heb. *Satan.* Jewish thought conceives of angels
as absolutely subordinate to God. An angel is God's " messenger ",
which is the literal meaning of the Hebrew word מלאך, of the Greek
word *angelos*, and of the English word " angel ", derived from it. In
the Jewish Prayer Book, angels are always instruments of the Divine
beneficence. *Satan* may seem to be an exception, but that name is
not used of a particular personality, but in the general sense of " adversary ". Even when he is personified in poetry, as in Job, he has no
independent power, but is an instrument of the Divine Plan. " The

Jeremiah 31. 11

And it is said, For the Lord hath delivered Jacob, and redeemed him from the hand of him that was stronger than he. Blessed art thou, O Lord, who hast redeemed Israel.

GOD THE . GUARDIAN

Cause us, O Lord our God, to lie down in peace, and raise us up, O our King, unto life. Spread over us the protection of thy peace ; direct us aright through thine own good counsel ; save us for thy Name's sake ; be thou a shield about us ; remove from us every enemy, pestilence, sword, famine and sorrow ; remove also the adversary from before us and from behind us. O shelter us beneath the shadow of thy wings ; for thou, O God, art our Guardian and our Deliverer ; yea, thou, O God, art a gracious and merciful King ; and guard our going and our coming unto life and unto peace from this time forth and for evermore. Blessed are thou, O Lord, who guardest thy people Israel for ever.

Psalm 89. 53   Blessed be the Lord for evermore. Amen, and Amen.

Psalm 135. 21 Blessed be the Lord out of Zion, who dwelleth in Jerusalem.

Psalm 82. 18, 19 Praise ye the Lord. Blessed be the Lord God, the God of Israel, who alone doeth wondrous things : and blessed be his glorious Name for ever ; and let the whole earth be

Psalm 104. 31 filled with his glory. Amen, and Amen. Let the glory of the

whole conception has now no place in Judaism, except in popular folk-lore. In the Prayer Book, Satan is mostly identical with the *evil impulse,* the lower passions which are a hindrance to man's pursuit of the nobler aims of life. It is against the dominance of this impulse that the Israelite still prays " (Abrahams). *The adversary,* therefore, is the man, spirit, or evil impulse that seduces us to do wrong.

BLESSED BE THE LORD. Originally a collection of eighteen verses, and probably intended to be in place of the Eighteen Benedictions before these had been incorporated in the Evening Service. This collection of verses is therefore not recited whenever the week-day *Shemone Esreh* is replaced by the Sabbath or Festival *Amidah.*

The verses proclaim the incomparable glory, love and justice of God ; supplicate for redemption, security and peace ; and pray for the recognition of the Divine Unity by all peoples. Over and above the intrinsic appropriateness of the verses, they are all connected by similarity of idea, as well as by identity of some word or words.

the whole earth. The universalist note prevails throughout the collection.

יְיָ בְּמַעֲשָׂיו : יְהִי שֵׁם יְיָ מְבֹרָךְ מֵעַתָּה וְעַד־עוֹלָם : כִּי

לֹא־יִטֹּשׁ יְיָ אֶת־עַמּוֹ בַּעֲבוּר שְׁמוֹ הַגָּדוֹל כִּי הוֹאִיל יְיָ

לַעֲשׂוֹת אֶתְכֶם לוֹ לְעָם : וַיַּרְא כָּל־הָעָם וַיִּפְּלוּ עַל־

פְּנֵיהֶם וַיֹּאמְרוּ יְיָ הוּא הָאֱלֹהִים יְיָ הוּא הָאֱלֹהִים : וְהָיָה

יְיָ לְמֶלֶךְ עַל־כָּל־הָאָרֶץ בַּיּוֹם הַהוּא יִהְיֶה יְיָ אֶחָד וּשְׁמוֹ

אֶחָד : יְהִי חַסְדְּךָ יְיָ עָלֵינוּ כַּאֲשֶׁר יִחַלְנוּ לָךְ : הוֹשִׁיעֵנוּ

אֱלֹהֵי יִשְׁעֵנוּ וְקַבְּצֵנוּ וְהַצִּילֵנוּ מִן־הַגּוֹיִם לְהוֹדוֹת לְשֵׁם

קָדְשֶׁךָ לְהִשְׁתַּבֵּחַ בִּתְהִלָּתֶךָ : כָּל־גּוֹיִם אֲשֶׁר עָשִׂיתָ

יָבוֹאוּ וְיִשְׁתַּחֲווּ לְפָנֶיךָ אֲדֹנָי וִיכַבְּדוּ לִשְׁמֶךָ : כִּי־גָדוֹל

אַתָּה וְעֹשֵׂה נִפְלָאוֹת אַתָּה אֱלֹהִים לְבַדֶּךָ : וַאֲנַחְנוּ

עַמְּךָ וְצֹאן מַרְעִיתֶךָ נוֹדֶה לְּךָ לְעוֹלָם לְדוֹר וָדֹר

נְסַפֵּר תְּהִלָּתֶךָ :

בָּרוּךְ יְיָ בַּיּוֹם · בָּרוּךְ יְיָ בַּלָּיְלָה · בָּרוּךְ יְיָ

בְּשָׁכְבֵנוּ · בָּרוּךְ יְיָ בְּקוּמֵנוּ : כִּי בְיָדְךָ נַפְשׁוֹת הַחַיִּים

וְהַמֵּתִים : אֲשֶׁר בְּיָדוֹ נֶפֶשׁ כָּל־חָי וְרוּחַ כָּל־בְּשַׂר־

אִישׁ : בְּיָדְךָ אַפְקִיד רוּחִי פָּדִיתָה אוֹתִי יְיָ אֵל אֱמֶת :

אֱלֹהֵינוּ שֶׁבַּשָּׁמַיִם יַחֵד שִׁמְךָ וְקַיֵּם מַלְכוּתְךָ תָּמִיד

וּמְלוֹךְ עָלֵינוּ לְעוֹלָם וָעֶד :

יִרְאוּ עֵינֵינוּ וְיִשְׂמַח לִבֵּנוּ וְתָגֵל נַפְשֵׁנוּ בִּישׁוּעָתְךָ

BLESSED . . . BY DAY. This paragraph concentrates the whole
of human adoration and supplication, and is in itself an ideal Evening
Prayer.

Psalm 113. 2   Lord endure for ever ; Let the Lord rejoice in his works. Let the Name of the Lord be blessed from this time forth and *I Samuel* 12. 22   for evermore. For the Lord will not forsake his people, for his great Name's sake ; because it hath pleased him to *I Kings* 18. 39 make you a people unto himself. And when all the people saw it, they fell on their faces : and they said, The Lord, he *Zechariah* 14. 9   is God ; the Lord, he is God. And the Lord shall be King over all the earth : in that day shall the Lord be One, *Psalm* 33. 22 and his Name One. Let thy lovingkindness, O Lord, be *I Chronicles* 16. 35   upon us, according as we have hoped for thee. Save us, O God of our salvation, and gather us and deliver us from the nations, to give thanks unto thy holy Name, and to *Psalm* 86. 9, 6 triumph in thy praise. All nations whom thou hast made shall come and worship before thee, O Lord ; and they shall glorify thy Name : for thou art great and doest marvellous things ; thou art God alone. But we are thy people *Psalm* 79. 13 and the sheep of thy pasture ; we will give thanks unto thee for ever : we will recount thy praise to all generations.

Blessed be the Lord by day ; blessed be the Lord by night ; blessed be the Lord when we lie down ; blessed be the Lord when we rise up. For in thy hand are the souls *Job* 12. 10   of the living and the dead, as it is said, In his hand is the soul of every living thing, and the spirit of all human flesh. *Psalm* 31. 6   Into thy hand I commend my spirit ; thou hast redeemed me, O Lord God of truth. Our God who art in heaven, assert the unity of thy Name, and establish thy kingdom continually, and reign over us for ever and ever.

May our eyes behold, our hearts rejoice, and our souls

MAY OUR EYES BEHOLD. The benediction at the end of this collection of Scriptural verses expresses the hope of the speedy establishment of God's Kingdom. It is followed by Half-Kaddish, because at one time it marked the end of the Evening Service.

The silent Amidah now follows, and there is no loud Repetition. In olden days, there followed *Tachanun* and supplications of private character. These have totally disappeared from European Rites. For some centuries, Ashkenazi custom has sanctioned the recitation of three Nature psalms after *Oleynu*, whenever *Maariv* is read after nightfall. This innovation was largely due to the desire to give mourners an opportunity to say an additional Kaddish.

בֶּאֱמֶת בֶּאֱמֹר לְצִיּוֹן מָלַךְ אֱלֹהָיִךְ · יְיָ מֶלֶךְ · יְיָ מָלָךְ ·
יְיָ יִמְלֹךְ לְעוֹלָם וָעֶד : כִּי הַמַּלְכוּת שֶׁלְּךָ הִיא וּלְעוֹלְמֵי
עַד תִּמְלֹךְ בְּכָבוֹד כִּי אֵין לָנוּ מֶלֶךְ אֶלָּא אָתָּה · בָּרוּךְ
אַתָּה יְיָ · הַמֶּלֶךְ בִּכְבוֹדוֹ תָּמִיד יִמְלוֹךְ עָלֵינוּ לְעוֹלָם
וָעֶד וְעַל כָּל מַעֲשָׂיו :

עֲמִידָה, *pp.*274—294. חֲצִי קַדִּישׁ, *p.*106.

קַדִּישׁ יָתוֹם, *p.* 300. עָלֵינוּ, *p.* 298. קַדִּישׁ תִּתְקַבַּל, *p.*206.

* *At the termination of the Sabbath* חֲצִי קַדִּישׁ *is said after the* עֲמִידָה.
The Service then continues with וִיהִי נֹעַם,

When מַעֲרִיב בִּזְמַנּוּ *is read, the following three Psalms are said :—*

תהלים כ״ד

לְדָוִד מִזְמוֹר · לַיְיָ הָאָרֶץ וּמְלוֹאָהּ תֵּבֵל וְיֹשְׁבֵי בָהּ :
כִּי־הוּא עַל־יַמִּים יְסָדָהּ וְעַל־נְהָרוֹת יְכוֹנְנֶהָ : מִי־יַעֲלֶה
בְהַר יְיָ וּמִי־יָקוּם בִּמְקוֹם קָדְשׁוֹ : נְקִי כַפַּיִם וּבַר לֵבָב
אֲשֶׁר לֹא נָשָׂא לַשָּׁוְא נַפְשִׁי וְלֹא נִשְׁבַּע לְמִרְמָה :
יִשָּׂא בְרָכָה מֵאֵת יְיָ וּצְדָקָה מֵאֱלֹהֵי יִשְׁעוֹ : זֶה
דּוֹר דֹּרְשָׁו מְבַקְשֵׁי פָנֶיךָ יַעֲקֹב סֶלָה : שְׂאוּ שְׁעָרִים
רָאשֵׁיכֶם וְהִנָּשְׂאוּ פִּתְחֵי עוֹלָם וְיָבוֹא מֶלֶךְ הַכָּבוֹד :
מִי זֶה מֶלֶךְ הַכָּבוֹד יְיָ עִזּוּז וְגִבּוֹר יְיָ גִּבּוֹר מִלְחָמָה :
שְׂאוּ שְׁעָרִים רָאשֵׁיכֶם וּשְׂאוּ פִּתְחֵי עוֹלָם וְיָבֹא מֶלֶךְ
הַכָּבוֹד : מִי הוּא זֶה מֶלֶךְ הַכָּבוֹד יְיָ צְבָאוֹת הוּא
מֶלֶךְ הַכָּבוֹד סֶלָה :

be glad in thy true salvation, when it shall be said unto Zion, Thy God reigneth. THE LORD IS KING ; THE LORD *See p.* 85 WAS KING ; THE LORD SHALL BE KING FOR EVER AND EVER : for the kingdom is thine, and to everlasting thou wilt reign in glory ; for we have no king but thee. Blessed art thou, O Lord, the King, who constantly in his glory will reign over us and over all his works for ever and ever.

Half-Kaddish, p. 107.　　　　　*Amidah, pp.* 275 *to* 295.

Kaddish, p. 207.　"*It is our duty,*" &*c., p.* 299.

The Mourner's Kaddish, p. 301.

At the termination of the Sabbath, Half-Kaddish, p. 107, *is said after the Amidah. Divine Service then continues with "And let the pleasantness " ; p.* 729.

When the Evening Service is read after nightfall, the following three Psalms are said :—

Psalm xxiv. [1]A Psalm of David.

THE TRUE WORSHIP-PER The earth is the Lord's, and the fulness thereof ; the world, and they that dwell therein. [2]For it is he that hath founded it upon the seas, and established it upon the floods. *See p.* 220 [3]Who may ascend the mountain of the Lord ? And who may stand in his holy place ? [4]He that hath clean hands and a pure heart ; who hath not set his desire upon vanity, and hath not sworn deceitfully. [5]He shall receive a blessing from the Lord, and righteousness from the God of his salvation. [6]Such is the generation of them that seek after him, that seek thy face, (O God of) Jacob ! (Selah.) [7]Lift up your heads, O ye gates ; and be ye lifted up, ye everlasting doors, that the King of glory may come in. [8]Who is the King of glory ? The Lord strong and mighty, the TRI-UMPHAL ENTRY INTO SANCTUARY Lord mighty in battle. [9]Lift up your heads, O ye gates ; yea, lift them up, ye everlasting doors, that the King of glory may come in. [10]Who, then, is the King of glory ? The Lord of hosts, he is the King of glory. (Selah.)

תהלים ח׳

לַמְנַצֵּחַ עַל־הַגִּתִּית מִזְמוֹר לְדָוִד : יְיָ אֲדֹנֵינוּ מָה־אַדִּיר
שִׁמְךָ בְּכָל־הָאָרֶץ אֲשֶׁר־תְּנָה הוֹדְךָ עַל־הַשָּׁמָיִם : מִפִּי
עוֹלְלִים וְיֹנְקִים יִסַּדְתָּ עֹז לְמַעַן צוֹרְרֶיךָ לְהַשְׁבִּית אוֹיֵב
וּמִתְנַקֵּם : כִּי־אֶרְאֶה שָׁמֶיךָ מַעֲשֵׂה אֶצְבְּעֹתֶיךָ יָרֵחַ
וְכוֹכָבִים אֲשֶׁר כּוֹנָנְתָּה : מָה־אֱנוֹשׁ כִּי־תִזְכְּרֶנּוּ וּבֶן־אָדָם
כִּי תִפְקְדֶנּוּ : וַתְּחַסְּרֵהוּ מְּעַט מֵאֱלֹהִים וְכָבוֹד וְהָדָר
תְּעַטְּרֵהוּ : תַּמְשִׁילֵהוּ בְּמַעֲשֵׂי יָדֶיךָ כֹּל שַׁתָּה תַחַת־
רַגְלָיו : צֹנֶה וַאֲלָפִים כֻּלָּם וְגַם בַּהֲמוֹת שָׂדָי : צִפּוֹר
שָׁמַיִם וּדְגֵי הַיָּם עֹבֵר אָרְחוֹת יַמִּים : יְיָ אֲדֹנֵינוּ מָה־
אַדִּיר שִׁמְךָ בְּכָל־הָאָרֶץ :

תהלים כ׳ט

מִזְמוֹר לְדָוִד · הָבוּ לַיְיָ בְּנֵי אֵלִים הָבוּ
לַיְיָ כָּבוֹד וָעֹז : הָבוּ לַיְיָ כְּבוֹד שְׁמוֹ הִשְׁתַּחֲווּ
לַיְיָ בְּהַדְרַת־קֹדֶשׁ : קוֹל יְיָ עַל הַמָּיִם אֵל־הַכָּבוֹד

PSALM 8.

PRE-EMINENCE OF MAN AND MAN'S DOMINION OVER NATURE.
1. GITTITH. Either the name of the melody or the instrument.
2. *glorious.* Majestic.
thy Name. " That expression of Thyself in the works of creation
and Providence by which Thy character may be recognized ".
3. *founded a power.* The mystery of man is greater than the mystery
of the heavens. Man, even in the weakness of childhood, is a witness
of the existence and character of God.

Psalm viii.

PRE-
EMINENCE
OF MAN
¹For the Chief Musician ; set to Gittith. A Psalm of David.
²O Lord, our Lord, how gracious is thy Name in all the earth, who hast set thy splendour upon the heavens ! ³Out of the mouth of babes and sucklings hast thou founded a power, because of thine adversaries, that thou mightest still the enemy and the revengeful. ⁴When I look upon thy heavens, the work of thy fingers, the moon and the stars which thou hast ordained ; ⁵what is man that thou art mindful of him, and the son of man that thou givest heed to him, ⁶and madest him little less than divine, and didst crown him with glory and majesty ? ⁷Thou madest him to have dominion over the works of thy hands ; thou hast put all things under his feet ; ⁸all sheep and oxen, yea, and the beasts of the plain ; ⁹the birds of the air and the fish of the sea, whatsoever passeth through the paths of the sea. ¹⁰O Lord, our Lord, how glorious is thy Name in all the earth !

Psalm xxix. ¹A Psalm of David.

GOD'S
MAJESTY
IN THE
STORM
Ascribe unto the Lord, O ye sons of might, ascribe unto the Lord glory and strength. ²Ascribe unto the Lord the glory due unto his Name ; worship the Lord in the beauty of holiness. ³The voice of the Lord is upon the waters :

5. *what is man.* How small, and yet how great, is man !

6. *little less than divine.* Mere atom that man seems, when compared with the infinite vastness of the heavens, he is more marvellous than sun, moon or star ; for *he* has the capacity to feel, and to re-think the Creator's thoughts. " Beloved and pre-eminent is man ", taught Rabbi Akiba, " for he is created in the image of God ; and what is more, he has the consciousness that he is created in the image of God " !

הָרְעִים יְיָ עַל־מַיִם רַבִּים : קוֹל־יְיָ בַּכֹּחַ קוֹל יְיָ
בֶּהָדָר : קוֹל יְיָ שֹׁבֵר אֲרָזִים וַיְשַׁבֵּר יְיָ אֶת־אַרְזֵי
הַלְּבָנוֹן : וַיַּרְקִידֵם כְּמוֹ־עֵגֶל לְבָנוֹן וְשִׂרְיוֹן כְּמוֹ
בֶן־רְאֵמִים : קוֹל־יְיָ חֹצֵב לַהֲבוֹת אֵשׁ : קוֹל
יְיָ יָחִיל מִדְבָּר יָחִיל יְיָ מִדְבַּר קָדֵשׁ : קוֹל יְיָ
יְחוֹלֵל אַיָּלוֹת וַיֶּחֱשֹׂף יְעָרוֹת וּבְהֵיכָלוֹ כֻּלּוֹ אֹמֵר כָּבוֹד :
יְיָ לַמַּבּוּל יָשָׁב וַיֵּשֶׁב יְיָ מֶלֶךְ לְעוֹלָם : יְיָ עֹז לְעַמּוֹ
יִתֵּן יְיָ | יְבָרֵךְ אֶת־עַמּוֹ בַשָּׁלוֹם :

On the days of Omer when תַּחֲנוּן *(see p. 294) is said, one of the*
following Psalms is added:—

On Sunday.

תהלים כ״ה

לְדָוִד אֵלֶיךָ יְהוָה נַפְשִׁי אֶשָּׂא : אֱלֹהַי בְּךָ בָטַחְתִּי
אַל־אֵבוֹשָׁה אַל־יַעַלְצוּ אוֹיְבַי לִי : גַּם כָּל־קוֶֹיךָ לֹא יֵבֹשׁוּ
יֵבֹשׁוּ הַבּוֹגְדִים רֵיקָם : דְּרָכֶיךָ יְהוָה הוֹדִיעֵנִי אֹרְחוֹתֶיךָ
לַמְּדֵנִי : הַדְרִיכֵנִי בַאֲמִתֶּךָ וְלַמְּדֵנִי כִּי־אַתָּה אֱלֹהֵי יִשְׁעִי

8. *beasts of the plain.* In the Psalmist's day, the dominion of man
over nature was most strikingly exercised in his mastery of the animal
creation. Man's mastery over Nature has immeasurably increased with
the ages.

PSALM 29.

Thunder-storms of tropical intensity are frequent in Palestine in
winter, and the Israelite saw in them special manifestations of Divine
might and majesty.

1. *sons of might.* The angels, standing in God's immediate presence
and watching the storm, are called upon by the poet to praise Him
whose glory is seen in the storm.

3–9. Rise, progress and effect of the thunder-storm.

3. *voice of the Lord.* The thunder. The first peal is heard as coming
from the Mediterranean sea, whence storms arise in Palestine. It
bursts over the northern mountain-ranges.

the God of glory thundereth, even the Lord upon the many waters. ⁴The voice of the Lord is powerful ; the voice of the Lord is full of majesty. ⁵The voice of the Lord breaketh the cedars ; yea, the Lord breaketh in pieces the cedars of Lebanon. ⁶He maketh them also to skip like a calf ; Lebanon and Sirion like a young wild-ox. ⁷The voice of the Lord heweth out flames of fire ; ⁸the voice of the Lord shaketh the wilderness ; the Lord shaketh the wilderness of Kadesh. ⁹The voice of the Lord maketh the hinds to calve, and strippeth the forests bare : and in his temple everything saith, Glory. ¹⁰The Lord sat enthroned at the Flood ; yea, the Lord sitteth as King for ever. ¹¹The Lord will give strength unto his people ; the Lord will bless his people with peace.

On the days of Omer when Tachanun (see p. 295)
is said, one of the following Psalms is added :—
On Sunday.
Psalm xxv. A Psalm of David.

PRAYER
FOR
GOD'S
GUID
ANCE

¹Unto thee, O Lord, do I lift up my soul. ²O my God, in thee have I trusted, let me not be ashamed ; let not mine enemies triumph over me. ³Yea, none that wait for thee shall be ashamed : they shall be ashamed who deal treacherously without cause. ⁴Show me thy ways, O Lord ; teach me thy paths. ⁵Guide me in thy truth, and teach

5. *Lebanon.* The very mountains shake to their foundations.
6. *Sirion.* Mt. Hermon.
7. *heweth out.* With every thunder-peal come forked lightning shafts.
8. *wilderness.* The poet sees the mountains in the North leap in terror. The storm has now swept over the whole length of the land, and pours out its fury on the Wilderness of Kadesh in the South.
9. *calve . . . bare.* These are no mere poetical figures ; they are observed facts.
in his temple. His Heavenly Temple.
Glory. This is the chant of the angels.
10. *at the Flood.* He was King then, and is King always.
11. The God who rules and stills the storm, is the same Who blesses His people with moral strength and lasting peace.

אוֹתְךָ קִוִּיתִי כָּל־הַיּוֹם: זְכֹר רַחֲמֶיךָ יְהֹוָה וַחֲסָדֶיךָ כִּי
מֵעוֹלָם הֵמָּה: חַטֹּאות נְעוּרַי וּפְשָׁעַי אַל־תִּזְכֹּר כְּחַסְדְּךָ
זְכָר־לִי־אַתָּה לְמַעַן טוּבְךָ יְהֹוָה: טוֹב וְיָשָׁר יְהֹוָה עַל־כֵּן
יוֹרֶה חַטָּאִים בַּדָּרֶךְ: יַדְרֵךְ עֲנָוִים בַּמִּשְׁפָּט וִילַמֵּד עֲנָוִים
דַּרְכּוֹ: כָּל־אָרְחוֹת יְהֹוָה חֶסֶד וֶאֱמֶת לְנֹצְרֵי בְרִיתוֹ
וְעֵדֹתָיו: לְמַעַן־שִׁמְךָ יְהֹוָה וְסָלַחְתָּ לַעֲוֹנִי כִּי רַב־הוּא:
מִי זֶה הָאִישׁ יְרֵא יְהֹוָה יוֹרֶנּוּ בְּדֶרֶךְ יִבְחָר: נַפְשׁוֹ בְּטוֹב
תָּלִין וְזַרְעוֹ יִירַשׁ אָרֶץ: סוֹד יְהֹוָה לִירֵאָיו וּבְרִיתוֹ
לְהוֹדִיעָם: עֵינַי תָּמִיד אֶל־יְהֹוָה כִּי־הוּא יוֹצִיא מֵרֶשֶׁת
רַגְלִי: פְּנֵה־אֵלַי וְחָנֵּנִי כִּי־יָחִיד וְעָנִי אָנִי: צָרוֹת לְבָבִי
הִרְחִיבוּ מִמְּצוּקוֹתַי הוֹצִיאֵנִי: רְאֵה־עָנְיִי וַעֲמָלִי וְשָׂא
לְכָל־חַטֹּאותַי: רְאֵה אוֹיְבַי כִּי־רָבּוּ וְשִׂנְאַת חָמָס
שְׂנֵאוּנִי: שָׁמְרָה נַפְשִׁי וְהַצִּילֵנִי אַל־אֵבוֹשׁ כִּי־חָסִיתִי

The following five psalms, all of them of a penitential character,
are sometimes recited during Omer, which is a time of semi-
mourning. However, this custom is neither uniform nor general among
congregations.

PSALM 25.

This alphabetical psalm is one of the tenderest and most beautiful
in the Psalter. It is an appeal to the Divine compassion, a heart-felt
human cry and living utterance of personal religion.

2. *ashamed.* Disappointed in the succour hoped for.

3. *without cause.* Wantonly, treachery for the sake of treachery;
like שנאת חנם, " causeless hatred ".

4. *show me thy ways.* He seeks understanding of the Divine purposes
in the events of his life, so that he may order his conduct accordingly.

7. *sins of my youth.* Failures and lapses of frailty; in contrast with
transgressious, i.e. deliberate offences of later years.

me ; for thou art the God of my salvation ; for thee do I wait all the day. ⁶Remember, O Lord, thy tender mercies, and thy lovingkindnesses ; for they have been ever of old. ⁷Remember not the sins of my youth, nor my transgressions ; according to thy lovingkindness remember thou me, for thy goodness' sake, O Lord. ⁸Good and just is the Lord : therefore will he instruct sinners in the way. ⁹The meek will he guide in justice : and the meek will he teach his way. ¹⁰All the paths of the Lord are loving-kindness and truth unto such as keep his covenant and his testimonies. ¹¹For thy Name's sake, O Lord, pardon mine iniquity, for it is great. ¹²Who is the man that feareth the Lord ? Him shall he instruct in the way that he should choose. ¹³His soul shall dwell in happiness ; and his seed shall inherit the land. ¹⁴The secret of the Lord is with them that fear him ; and he will make known to them his covenant. ¹⁵Mine eyes are ever toward the Lord ; for he shall draw my feet out of the net. ¹⁶Turn thee unto me and have pity upon me ; for I am solitary and afflicted. ¹⁷The troubles of my heart are enlarged : O bring thou me out of my distresses. ¹⁸Consider mine affliction and my travail ; and forgive all my sins. ¹⁹Consider mine enemies for they are many ; and they hate me with cruel hatred. ²⁰O guard my soul, and deliver me : let me

8. *good and just is the Lord.* The Rabbis deem this one of the great sayings of Scripture. Because God is good, He is *just* ; *i.e.* sinners must suffer the consequences of their misdeeds And because God is just, He is *good* ; *i.e.* these consequences of men's sins prove in the end to be not vindictive but remedial.

in the way The article is emphatic ; viz , the way of Repentance, known from of old ; Genesis 4. 7 (Kimchi).

9. *the meek* The humble-minded.

in justice In the practice of Right.

11. *for thy Name's sake.* Exodus 34. 5, 6—Merciful and gracious, slow to anger and abounding in lovingkindness and truth.

13. *inherit the land.* His children will follow his example.

14. *secret.* Heb. סוד. The close and intimate communion in which God makes Himself known to the soul ; that higher intimacy with the Eternal Spirit that reveals the meaning of His providential dealings with the children of men.

בָּךְ : תֹּם־וָיֹשֶׁר יִצְּרוּנִי כִּי קִוִּיתִיךָ : פְּדֵה־אֱלֹהִים אֶת־
יִשְׂרָאֵל מִכֹּל צָרוֹתָיו :

On Monday.

תהלים לב

לְדָוִד מַשְׂכִּיל אַשְׁרֵי נְשׂוּי־פֶּשַׁע כְּסוּי חֲטָאָה : אַשְׁרֵי
אָדָם לֹא־יַחְשֹׁב יְהוָה לוֹ עָוֹן וְאֵין בְּרוּחוֹ רְמִיָּה : כִּי
הֶחֱרַשְׁתִּי בָּלוּ עֲצָמָי בְּשַׁאֲגָתִי כָּל־הַיּוֹם : כִּי יוֹמָם וָלַיְלָה
תִּכְבַּד עָלַי יָדֶךָ נֶהְפַּךְ לְשַׁדִּי בְּחַרְבֹנֵי קַיִץ סֶלָה : חַטָּאתִי
אוֹדִיעֲךָ וַעֲוֹנִי לֹא־כִסִּיתִי אָמַרְתִּי אוֹדֶה עֲלֵי פְשָׁעַי
לַיהוָה וְאַתָּה נָשָׂאתָ עֲוֹן חַטָּאתִי סֶלָה : עַל־זֹאת יִתְפַּלֵּל
כָּל־חָסִיד אֵלֶיךָ לְעֵת מְצֹא רַק לְשֵׁטֶף מַיִם רַבִּים אֵלָיו
לֹא יַגִּיעוּ : אַתָּה סֵתֶר לִי מִצַּר תִּצְּרֵנִי רָנֵּי פַלֵּט תְּסוֹבְבֵנִי
סֶלָה : אַשְׂכִּילְךָ וְאוֹרְךָ בְּדֶרֶךְ־זוּ תֵלֵךְ אִיעֲצָה עָלֶיךָ
עֵינִי : אַל־תִּהְיוּ כְּסוּס כְּפֶרֶד אֵין הָבִין בְּמֶתֶג וָרֶסֶן עֶדְיוֹ
לִבְלוֹם בַּל קְרֹב אֵלֶיךָ : רַבִּים מַכְאוֹבִים לָרָשָׁע וְהַבּוֹטֵחַ
בַּיהוָה חֶסֶד יְסוֹבְבֶנּוּ : שִׂמְחוּ בַיהוָה וְגִילוּ צַדִּיקִים
וְהַרְנִינוּ כָּל־יִשְׁרֵי־לֵב :

16. *solitary.* Friendless.

17. *are enlarged* Have become many.

22. *set free.* This verse may have been spoken by the choir (Mendelssohn).

PSALM 32.
THE JOY OF CONFESSION AND RECONCILIATION.

1. *maschil.* " A didactic poem " ; or, " instructive composition."

2. *no guile.* The first condition of forgiveness on man's part is absolute sincerity.

not be ashamed, for I have taken refuge in thee. ²¹Let integrity and uprightness protect me, for I wait for thee. ²²Set Israel free, O God, from all his troubles.

On Monday.

Psalm xxxii. ¹A Psalm of David. Maschil.

THE HAPPI- NESS OF SIN FORGIVEN   Happy is he whose transgression is forgiven, whose sin is pardoned. ²Happy is the man unto whom the Lord reckoneth not iniquity, and in whose spirit there is no guile. ³When I kept silence, my bones wasted away through my moaning all the day long. ⁴For day and night thy hand was heavy upon me : my sap was changed into the droughts of summer. (Selah.) ⁵I acknowledged my sin unto thee and mine iniquity I did not cover : I said, I will confess my transgressions unto the Lord ; and thou forgavest the guilt of my sin. (Selah.) ⁶For this let every one that loveth thee pray unto thee at a time when thou mayest be found : surely when the great waters overflow they shall not reach unto him. ⁷Thou art my hiding place ; thou wilt preserve me from trouble ; thou wilt compass me about with songs of deliverance. (Selah.) ⁸I will instruct thee and teach thee in the way which thou must go : I will give counsel ; mine eye shall be upon thee. ⁹Be ye not as the horse, or as the mule, which hath no understanding : whose mouth must be held in with bit and bridle, that they come not near unto thee. ¹⁰Many are the sorrows of the wicked : but he that trusteth in the Lord, lovingkindness shall compass him about. ¹¹Rejoice in the Lord and be glad, ye righteous : and exult aloud, all ye that are upright in heart.

3. *when I kept silence.* Before he made outspoken confession of his guilt, he was worn away by internal battlings.

4. *hand.* Punishment.

droughts of summer. Outward disease and inward anguish overwhelmed him, and dried up his frame.

5. *forgavest* He poured forth his soul's burden unto God, and that brought an assurance of forgiveness ; Proverbs 28. 13.

6. *For this.* Therefore, he bids all who love God to pray unto Him in their distress.

when thou mayest be found. Cf. Isaiah 55. 6.

On Tuesday.

תהלים ל'ח

מִזְמוֹר לְדָוִד לְהַזְכִּיר: יְהֹוָה אַל־בְּקֶצְפְּךָ תוֹכִיחֵנִי

וּבַחֲמָתְךָ תְיַסְּרֵנִי: כִּי־חִצֶּיךָ נִחֲתוּ־בִי וַתִּנְחַת עָלַי יָדֶךָ:

אֵין־מְתֹם בִּבְשָׂרִי מִפְּנֵי זַעְמֶךָ אֵין־שָׁלוֹם בַּעֲצָמַי מִפְּנֵי

חַטָּאתִי: כִּי־עֲוֹנֹתַי עָבְרוּ רֹאשִׁי כְּמַשָּׂא כָבֵד יִכְבְּדוּ

מִמֶּנִּי: הִבְאִישׁוּ נָמַקּוּ חַבּוּרֹתָי מִפְּנֵי אִוַּלְתִּי: נַעֲוֵיתִי

שַׁחֹתִי עַד־מְאֹד כָּל־הַיּוֹם קֹדֵר הִלָּכְתִּי: כִּי־כְסָלַי

מָלְאוּ נִקְלֶה וְאֵין מְתֹם בִּבְשָׂרִי: נְפוּגֹתִי וְנִדְכֵּיתִי

עַד־מְאֹד שָׁאַגְתִּי מִנַּהֲמַת לִבִּי: אֲדֹנָי נֶגְדְּךָ כָל־תַּאֲוָתִי

וְאַנְחָתִי מִמְּךָ לֹא־נִסְתָּרָה: לִבִּי סְחַרְחַר עֲזָבַנִי כֹחִי

וְאוֹר עֵינַי גַּם־הֵם אֵין אִתִּי: אֹהֲבַי וְרֵעַי מִנֶּגֶד נִגְעִי

יַעֲמֹדוּ וּקְרוֹבַי מֵרָחֹק עָמָדוּ: וַיְנַקְשׁוּ מְבַקְשֵׁי נַפְשִׁי

וְדֹרְשֵׁי רָעָתִי דִּבְּרוּ הַוּוֹת וּמִרְמוֹת כָּל־הַיּוֹם יֶהְגּוּ: וַאֲנִי

כְחֵרֵשׁ לֹא אֶשְׁמָע וּכְאִלֵּם לֹא יִפְתַּח־פִּיו: וָאֱהִי

8. *mine eye shall be upon thee.* The Authorized Version translates, " I will guide thee with mine eye "—one of the notable words of comfort in Scripture. The speaker is God.

9. *not as the horse.* Man, unlike the beast, should not require the bit of calamity to withhold him from sin.

10. *many are the sorrows of the wicked.* " A great religious axiom " (Perowne).

11. *rejoice in the Lord.* This penitential psalm opens and ends in a note of joy—which is characteristic of Judaism.

PSALM 38.

The sufferer is convinced that his is a punishment because of sin. Tortured by pain of body and anguish of mind, deserted by his friends, mocked and menaced by his enemies, he lays his cause before God.

On Tuesday.

Psalm xxxviii.

[1]A Psalm of David, to bring to remembrance.

THE PENITENT ON BED OF SICKNESS

[2]O Lord, rebuke me not in thy wrath : neither chasten me in thy hot displeasure. [3]For thine arrows have sunk into me, and thy hand is come down upon me. [4]There is no soundness in my flesh because of thine indignation ; neither is there any health in my bones because of my sin. [5]For mine iniquities are gone over mine head : as a heavy burden they are too heavy for me. [6]My wounds are noisome, they fester because of my foolishness. [7]I writhe and am bowed down greatly ; I go mourning all the day long. [8]For my loins are filled with burning ; and there is no soundness in my flesh. [9]I am benumbed and crushed exceedingly : I groan through the disquietude of my heart. [10]Lord, all my desire is before thee ; and my sighing is not hid from thee. [11]My heart throbbeth, my strength faileth me : as for the light of mine eyes, it also is no longer mine. [12]My friends and my companions stand aloof from my plague ; and my kinsmen stand afar off. [13]They also that seek after my life lay snares for me ; and they that seek my hurt speak of utter destruction, and meditate deceits all the day long. [14]But I am as a deaf man, I hear not ; and I am as a dumb man that openeth not his mouth. [15]Yea,

---

1. *to bring to remembrance.* " A psalm in which the writer, being in great distress, calls upon God to remember him and save him " (Rashi).

2. *in thy wrath.* Cf. Psalm 6. 2, p. 181 ; and, " In wrath remember mercy ", Habakkuk 3. 2.

3. *arrows.* The different calamaties that befall him.

5. *gone over mine head . . . burden.* " First the rushing flood of sins, then the burden of them ; what a realistic picture these two incompatible ideas present of the mental condition of one who, because of his sins, is sunk in the sea of despair, and bowed down by their weight ! " (Oesterley).

6. *wounds.* lit. " stripes ", scourged as it were, by God.

foolishness. Sinfulness ; sin being essentially foolishness.

7. *I go mourning.* In the guise of a mourner.

כְּאִישׁ אֲשֶׁר לֹא־שֹׁמֵעַ וְאֵין בְּפִיו תּוֹכָחוֹת : כִּי־לְךָ
יְהֹוָה הוֹחָלְתִּי אַתָּה תַעֲנֶה אֲדֹנָי אֱלֹהָי : כִּי־אָמַרְתִּי פֶּן־
יִשְׂמְחוּ־לִי בְּמוֹט רַגְלִי עָלַי הִגְדִּילוּ : כִּי אֲנִי לְצֶלַע נָכוֹן
וּמַכְאוֹבִי נֶגְדִּי תָמִיד : כִּי־עֲוֹנִי אַגִּיד אֶדְאַג מֵחַטָּאתִי :
וְאֹיְבַי חַיִּים עָצֵמוּ וְרַבּוּ שֹׂנְאַי שָׁקֶר : וּמְשַׁלְּמֵי רָעָה
תַּחַת טוֹבָה יִשְׂטְנוּנִי תַּחַת רָדְפִי־טוֹב : אַל־תַּעַזְבֵנִי
יְהֹוָה אֱלֹהָי אַל־תִּרְחַק מִמֶּנִּי : חוּשָׁה לְעֶזְרָתִי אֲדֹנָי
תְּשׁוּעָתִי :

On Wednesday.

תהלים נ"א

לַמְנַצֵּחַ מִזְמוֹר לְדָוִד : בְּבוֹא־אֵלָיו נָתָן הַנָּבִיא כַּאֲשֶׁר־
בָּא אֶל־בַּת־שָׁבַע : חָנֵּנִי אֱלֹהִים כְּחַסְדֶּךָ כְּרֹב רַחֲמֶיךָ
מְחֵה פְשָׁעָי : הֶרֶב כַּבְּסֵנִי מֵעֲוֹנִי וּמֵחַטָּאתִי טַהֲרֵנִי : כִּי־
פְשָׁעַי אֲנִי אֵדָע וְחַטָּאתִי נֶגְדִּי תָמִיד : לְךָ לְבַדְּךָ חָטָאתִי
וְהָרַע בְּעֵינֶיךָ עָשִׂיתִי לְמַעַן־תִּצְדַּק בְּדָבְרֶךָ תִּזְכֶּה

12. *plague.* Some affliction which is regarded as a punishment sent by God ! Hence the unhelpfulness and estrangement of his friends, and the joy of his enemies. Yet deserted by his friends, consumed by a fever, and with failing eyes, he all the closer clings to God.

15. *reproofs.* Retorts, arguments in his defence. He submits to all reviling in silence.

18. *to fall.* lit. " to halt " ; to walk as a lame man.

21. *rendering evil for good.* Being guilty of base ingratitude.

23. *Lord of my salvation.* " True repentance includes faith ; it despairs of itself, but not of God " (Delitzsch).

PSALM 51.

This is the most heart-searching of all the psalms, and the world's

I am as a man that heareth not, and in whose mouth there are no reproofs. ¹⁶For in thee, O Lord, do I hope : thou wilt answer, O Lord my God. ¹⁷For I said, Lest they rejoice over me : when my foot slippeth, they magnify themselves against me. ¹⁸For I am ready to fall, and my pain is continually before me. ¹⁹For I declare my iniquity ; I am troubled because of my sin. ²⁰But mine enemies are full of life, and are strong ; and they that hate me wrongfully are many. ²¹And, rendering evil for good, they are adversaries unto me, because I follow after good. ²²Forsake me not, O Lord ; O my God, be not far from me. ²³Make haste to help me, O Lord my salvation

On Wednesday.

Psalm li.

"HAVE PITY UPON ME" : A PENI-TENT'S SUPPLICA TION

¹For the Chief Musician. A Psalm of David ; ²When Nathan the Prophet came unto him, after he had gone in unto Bath-sheba.

³Have pity upon me, O God, according to thy loving-kindness : according to the multitude of thy tender mercies blot out my transgressions. ⁴Wash me thoroughly from mine iniquity, and cleanse me from my sin. ⁵For I acknowledge my transgressions : and my sin is ever before me. ⁶Against thee, who art the only One, have I sinned, and done that which is evil in thy sight, that thou mayest be justified when thou speakest, and be clear when thou judgest.

noblest penitential hymn. It is the voice of the penitent soul in all ages ; and we only need be human to appreciate it. " Woe unto us, if that passionate cry does not appeal to us " (Montefiore). In the Italian Rite, the Col Nidré Service opens with the reading of this psalm.

The Rabbis looked upon the sin and repentance of David as a parable for Humanity. David was Israel's ideal ruler. Yet Scripture, with an impartiality that is absolutely without parallel in Oriental Literature, neither suppresses nor palliates the temptations and crimes of its royal hero. And not only after his death does it record as a heinous crime what all other national chronicles would pass over as a venial or natural weakness of a ruler. In his own lifetime, nay to his face, is the truth told him. And the fearlessness of the Prophet is rewarded by profoundest penitence: "And David said unto Nathan, I have sinned against the Lord " ; see II Samuel 12.

בְּשָׁפְטֶךָ : הֵן־בְּעָווֹן חוֹלָלְתִּי וּבְחֵטְא יֶחֱמַתְנִי אִמִּי : הֵן
אֱמֶת חָפַצְתָּ בַטֻּחוֹת וּבְסָתֻם חָכְמָה תוֹדִיעֵנִי : תְּחַטְּאֵנִי
בְאֵזוֹב וְאֶטְהָר תְּכַבְּסֵנִי וּמִשֶּׁלֶג אַלְבִּין : תַּשְׁמִיעֵנִי שָׂשׂוֹן
וְשִׂמְחָה תָּגֵלְנָה עֲצָמוֹת דִּכִּיתָ : הַסְתֵּר פָּנֶיךָ מֵחֲטָאַי
וְכָל־עֲוֹנֹתַי מְחֵה : לֵב טָהוֹר בְּרָא־לִי אֱלֹהִים וְרוּחַ
נָכוֹן חַדֵּשׁ בְּקִרְבִּי : אַל־תַּשְׁלִיכֵנִי מִלְּפָנֶיךָ וְרוּחַ קָדְשְׁךָ
אַל־תִּקַּח מִמֶּנִּי : הָשִׁיבָה לִּי שְׂשׂוֹן יִשְׁעֶךָ וְרוּחַ נְדִיבָה
תִסְמְכֵנִי : אֲלַמְּדָה פֹשְׁעִים דְּרָכֶיךָ וְחַטָּאִים אֵלֶיךָ
יָשׁוּבוּ : הַצִּילֵנִי מִדָּמִים ׀ אֱלֹהִים אֱלֹהֵי תְּשׁוּעָתִי תְּרַנֵּן
לְשׁוֹנִי צִדְקָתֶךָ : אֲדֹנָי שְׂפָתַי תִּפְתָּח וּפִי יַגִּיד תְּהִלָּתֶךָ :
כִּי לֹא־תַחְפֹּץ זֶבַח וְאֶתֵּנָה עוֹלָה לֹא תִרְצֶה : זִבְחֵי
אֱלֹהִים רוּחַ נִשְׁבָּרָה לֵב־נִשְׁבָּר וְנִדְכֶּה אֱלֹהִים לֹא

5. *I acknowledge.* The first step of repentance. " Of all acts, is not for man *repentance* the most divine ? The deadliest sin were supercilious consciousness of no sin. David's life and history, as written for us in those Psalms of his, I consider to be the truest emblem ever given of a man's moral progress and warfare here below " (Carlyle).

6. *thee, who art the only One.* (Wessely, Mendelssohn, Lowe-Jennings, Barnes). All sin, as sin, even when against our fellowmen as was David's, is in the first instance and in its deepest sense a rebellion against God and the Divine guidance of His children.

when thou speakest. When Thou pronouncest sentence against me.

7. *brought forth in iniquity.* This is merely the equivalent of, " I am a sinful, human being, the child of sinful, human beings ". The statement is made not to palliate his offence, but to show the greater need for Divine forgiveness and cleansing.

9. *hyssop.* A plant used in the ritual cleansing of a leper.

12. *create . . . pure heart.* He prays for a radical change in mind and character.

steadfast spirit. A spirit not easily swayed hither and thither by blasts of temptation.

There is a story that Voltaire began to parody this psalm. When

⁷Behold, I was brought forth in iniquity, and in sin did my mother conceive me. ⁸Behold, thou desirest truth in the inward parts ; therefore, in mine inmost heart make me to know wisdom, ⁹Purge me with hyssop, and I shall be clean : wash me, and I shall be whiter than snow. ¹⁰Make me to hear gladness and joy, that the bones which thou hast crushed may be glad. ¹¹Hide thy face from my sins, and blot out all mine iniquities. ¹²Create for me a pure heart, O God ; and renew a steadfast spirit within me. ¹³Cast me not away from thy presence ; and take not thy holy spirit from me. ¹⁴Restore unto me the gladness of thy salvation ; and uphold me with a willing spirit. ¹⁵Then will I teach transgressors thy ways ; and sinners shall return unto thee. ¹⁶Deliver me from blood-guiltiness, O God, thou God of my salvation, and my tongue shall exult in thy righteousness. ¹⁷O Lord, open thou my lips, and my mouth shall declare thy praise. ¹⁸For thou delightest not in sacrifice, else would I give it : thou takest no pleasure in burnt offering. ¹⁹The sacrifices of God are a broken spirit : a broken and a contrite heart,

he reached this verse, he could not proceed, and desisted from the blasphemous attempt.

13. *take not thy holy spirit.* As it was withdrawn from Saul, when he felt himself forsaken by God.

14. *gladness of thy salvation.* The glad sense of Thy help.

with a willing spirit. " With Thy freely-bestowed spirit."

15. *will I teach.* By showing God's pity for the penitent, he will be able to reclaim others who have fallen.

shall return unto thee. Usually it is supposed that the wicked must be removed by destruction. David's sin and repentance will demonstrate that a moral change in the sinner, causing him to abandon his wickedness, brings him back to God.

16. *from bloodguiltiness. i.e.* deliver me from the sentence which is passed on those who have shed blood.

God of my salvation. The God who is about to deliver me from the death which I deserve.

thy righteousness. Here the word צְדָקָה approaches its later meaning, " charity ".

17. *open thou my lips.* The lips that had been closed for all acts of worship by alienation of heart and aberration of life. This verse opens the *Shemoneh Esreh* ; it has been similarly used in the Church since the sixth century

תִּבְזֶה : הֵיטִיבָה בִרְצוֹנְךָ אֶת־צִיּוֹן תִּבְנֶה חוֹמוֹת
יְרוּשָׁלָ͏ִם : אָז תַּחְפֹּץ זִבְחֵי־צֶדֶק עוֹלָה וְכָלִיל אָז יַעֲלוּ
עַל־מִזְבַּחֲךָ פָרִים :

On Thursday.

תהלים פ״ו

תְּפִלָּה לְדָוִד הַטֵּה יְהֹוָה אָזְנְךָ l עֲנֵנִי כִּי־עָנִי וְאֶבְיוֹן
אָנִי : שָׁמְרָה נַפְשִׁי כִּי־חָסִיד אָנִי הוֹשַׁע עַבְדְּךָ אַתָּה
אֱלֹהַי הַבּוֹטֵחַ אֵלֶיךָ : חָנֵּנִי אֲדֹנָי כִּי־אֵלֶיךָ אֶקְרָא כָּל־
הַיּוֹם : שַׂמֵּחַ נֶפֶשׁ עַבְדֶּךָ כִּי־אֵלֶיךָ יְהֹוָה נַפְשִׁי אֶשָּׂא :
כִּי־אַתָּה אֲדֹנָי טוֹב וְסַלָּח וְרַב־חֶסֶד לְכָל־קֹרְאֶיךָ :
הַאֲזִינָה יְהֹוָה תְּפִלָּתִי וְהַקְשִׁיבָה בְּקוֹל תַּחֲנוּנוֹתָי : בְּיוֹם
צָרָתִי אֶקְרָאֶךָּ כִּי תַעֲנֵנִי : אֵין־כָּמוֹךָ בָאֱלֹהִים l אֲדֹנָי וְאֵין
כְּמַעֲשֶׂיךָ : כָּל־גּוֹיִם אֲשֶׁר עָשִׂיתָ יָבוֹאוּ וְיִשְׁתַּחֲווּ לְפָנֶיךָ
אֲדֹנָי וִיכַבְּדוּ לִשְׁמֶךָ : כִּי־גָדוֹל אַתָּה וְעֹשֵׂה נִפְלָאוֹת
אַתָּה אֱלֹהִים לְבַדֶּךָ : הוֹרֵנִי יְהֹוָה דַּרְכֶּךָ אֲהַלֵּךְ בַּאֲמִתֶּךָ

---

19. *sacrifices of God.* Those which He desires most.

broken spirit. In which obstinacy of pride has been " broken " and replaced by the humility of repentance. " That which God declares to be a defect in an animal sacrifice, He accounts as an advantage in the heart-sacrifice of a man " (Midrash).

21. *delight in sacrifices.* There is no contradiction between this verse and *v.* 19. The Psalms proclaim the all-sufficiency of repentance, yet the same Psalms were the hymn-book of the Temple Service.

sacrifices of righteousness. Those presented in a right spirit.

PSALM 86.

1–7. An Appeal to the God of Mercy.

1. *poor.* Afflicted.

2. *godly.* Pious, duteous in lovingkindness.

O God, thou wilt not despise. [20]Do good in thy favour
unto Zion : build thou the walls of Jerusalem. [21]Then wilt
thou delight in sacrifices of righteousness, in burnt offering
and whole burnt offering : then will they offer bullocks
upon thine alter.

On Thursday.

Psalm lxxxvi.

[1]A Prayer of David.

PRAYER
FOR HELP,
GUIDANCE
AND
DELIVER-
ANCE

Incline thine ear, O Lord, and answer me ; for I am
poor and needy. [2]Preserve my soul, for I am godly : O
thou my God, save thy servant that trusteth in thee. [3]Be
gracious unto me, O Lord ; for· unto thee do I cry all the
day long. [4]Rejoice the soul of thy servant ; for unto thee,
O Lord, do I lift up my soul. [5]For thou, Lord, art good
and forgiving, and abounding in lovingkindness unto all
them that call upon thee. [6]Give ear, O Lord, unto my
prayer ; and attend to the voice of my supplications. [7]In
the day of my trouble I call upon thee ; for thou wilt
answer me. [8]There is none like unto thee among the gods,
O Lord ; and there are no works like unto thine. [9]All
nations whom thou hast made shall come and worship
before thee, O Lord ; and they shall glorify thy Name :
[10]for thou art great, and doest marvellous things ; thou art
God alone. [11]Teach me thy way, O Lord ; I will walk in

5. *forgiving.* Heb. סלח ; lit. " a Forgiver ", one Whose nature and
character it is to forgive.
8–10. The Greatness of God.
8. *among the gods.* This is here a mere conventional phrase, and does
not ascribe reality to those gods. In the very second verse, the psalmist
exclaims, " Thou art God alone ".
9. *all nations . . . worship.* That all the nations are children of
One God, and will yet grope their way out of hereditary ignorance
towards the Truth, is a fundamental conviction of psalmist, as of
prophet ; *e.g.* Jeremiah 16. 20. In the Liturgy, we have, among others,
the close of the *Oleynu* (Zechariah 14. 9), the wonderful New Year
Amidah, and the ויאתיו hymn on the day of Atonement.

יַחֵד לְבָבִי לְיִרְאָה שְׁמֶךָ : אוֹדְךָ ׀ אֲדֹנָי אֱלֹהַי בְּכָל־לְבָבִי
וַאֲכַבְּדָה שִׁמְךָ לְעוֹלָם : כִּי־חַסְדְּךָ גָּדוֹל עָלָי וְהִצַּלְתָּ
נַפְשִׁי מִשְּׁאוֹל תַּחְתִּיָּה : אֱלֹהִים זֵדִים קָמוּ עָלַי וַעֲדַת
עָרִיצִים בִּקְשׁוּ נַפְשִׁי וְלֹא שָׂמוּךָ לְנֶגְדָּם : וְאַתָּה אֲדֹנָי
אֵל־רַחוּם וְחַנּוּן אֶרֶךְ אַפַּיִם וְרַב־חֶסֶד וֶאֱמֶת : פְּנֵה
אֵלַי וְחָנֵּנִי תְּנָה־עֻזְּךָ לְעַבְדֶּךָ וְהוֹשִׁיעָה לְבֶן־אֲמָתֶךָ :
עֲשֵׂה־עִמִּי אוֹת לְטוֹבָה וְיִרְאוּ שֹׂנְאַי וְיֵבֹשׁוּ כִּי־אַתָּה
יְהֹוָה עֲזַרְתַּנִי וְנִחַמְתָּנִי :

<p. 300. קַדִּישׁ יָתוֹם

11–13. Prayer for guidance.

11. *unite my heart.* Unify my heart, so as to be undivided in its allegiance, and single-hearted in Thy service; Deuteronomy 6. 5.

14–17. " Save, for the danger is great ".

14. *the proud.* The arrogant men who scoff at religion and oppress its followers.

not set thee before them. They have no regard for God's will, and no fear of His judgments.

thy truth : unite my heart to fear thy Name. [12]I will praise thee, O Lord my God, with my whole heart ; and I will glorify thy Name for evermore. [13]For great is thy loving-kindness toward me, and thou hast delivered my soul from the grave beneath. [14]O God, the proud are risen up against me, and a band of violent men have sought after my soul, and have not set thee before them. [15]But thou, O Lord, art a merciful and gracious God, slow to anger, and abounding in lovingkindness and truth. [16]O turn unto me, and have pity upon me ; give thy strength unto thy servant, and save the son of thine handmaid. [17]Work in my behalf a token of good ; that they which hate me may see it and be put to shame, because thou, Lord, hast helped me and comforted me.

Mourner's Kaddish, p. 301.

---

15. *a merciful and gracious God.* Quotation from Exodus 34. 6.

16. *son of thine handmaid.* This phrase is parallel to " servant ". Rashi points out that " the son of thine handmaid " denotes a closer relationship to the master, as those " born in the house " (Gen. 14. 14) were the most trusted dependents.

17. *token.* Some visible, unmistakable sign of Divine favour, so that men realize that God is on his side.

SABBATH SERVICES

שַׁבָּת
שמות כ ח׳-י״א

ד זָכוֹר אֶת־יוֹם הַשַּׁבָּת לְקַדְּשׁוֹ : שֵׁשֶׁת יָמִים תַּעֲבֹד
וְעָשִׂיתָ כָּל־מְלַאכְתֶּךָ : וְיוֹם הַשְּׁבִיעִי שַׁבָּת לַיהוָה
אֱלֹהֶיךָ לֹא־תַעֲשֶׂה כָל־מְלָאכָה אַתָּה ׀ וּבִנְךָ וּבִתֶּךָ

THE SABBATH

1. THE SABBATH COMMANDMENT

Exodus 20. 8–11 forms the Fourth Commandment, that ordains the Sabbath, one of the basic institutions in Israel.

8. *to keep it holy.* To treat it as a day unprofaned by workaday purposes. In addition to being a day of rest, the Sabbath is to be " a holy day set apart for the building up of the spiritual element in man " (Philo). Religious *worship* and religious *instruction*—the renewal of man's spiritual life in God—form an essential part of Sabbath observance. We, therefore, sanctify the Sabbath by a special Sabbath liturgy, by statutory Lessons from the Torah and the Prophets, and by attention to discourse and instruction by religious teachers. Sabbath worship is still the chief bond which unites Jews into a *religious* Brotherhood. Neglect of such worship injures the spiritual life of both the individual and the community; see p. 414.

9. *shalt thou labour.* Work during the six days of the week is as essential to man's welfare as is rest on the seventh. No man or woman, howsoever rich, is freed—say the Jewish Sages—from the obligation of doing some work, as idleness invariably leads to evil thoughts and evil deeds. The Jewish Sages are tireless in their insistence that work ennobles and sanctifies, and that idleness is the door to temptation and sin. They were themselves labourers, earning their daily bread by following some handicraft—masons, tailors, sandal-makers, carpenters. The most renowned of all the Rabbis, Hillel the Elder, was a wood-cutter.

In Israel alone, labour did not mean the bondage of man. The Sabbath gave the toiler every week a day of freedom and leisure. This was quite incomprehensible to the Greeks and Romans. Their writers—Tacitus, Juvenal, Plutarch—make merry over the idea of presenting one day in every seven to the worker ! The far-reaching humanitarian significance of the Sabbath was, of course, undreamt of by them ; and even " our modern spirit, with all its barren theories of

THE SABBATH

Exodus xx. 8–11.

THE FOURTH COMMAND-MENT

⁸Remember the sabbath day to keep it holy. ⁹Six days shalt thou labour, and do all thy work ; ¹⁰but the seventh day is a sabbath unto the Lord thy God : in it thou shalt not do any work, thou, nor thy son, nor thy daughter, thy manservant, nor thy maidservant, nor thy cattle, nor

civic and political rights, and its strivings towards freedom and equality, has not thought out and called into existence a single institution that, in its beneficient effects upon the labouring classes, can in the slightest degree be compared to the Weekly Day of Rest promulgated in the Sinaitic wilderness " (Proudhon). The proportion of one day's rest in seven has been justified by the experience of the last 3,000 years. Physical health suffers without such relief. The first French Republic rejected the idea of desisting from labour on one day in seven, and ordained a rest of one day in ten. The experiment was a complete failure.

10. *a sabbath unto the Lord.* A day specially devoted to God.

thou shalt not do any work. Scripture does not give a list of labours forbidden on Sabbath ; but it incidentally mentions field-labour, buying and selling, travelling, cooking, etc., as forbidden work. The Mishna enumerates, under thirty-nine different heads, all such acts as are in Jewish Law defined as " work," and, therefore, not to be performed on the Sabbath day ; such as ploughing, reaping, carrying loads, kindling a fire, writing, sewing, etc. Certain other things which cannot be brought under any of these 39 categories are also prohibited, because they lead to a breach of Sabbath rest (שבות) ; as well as all acts that would tend to change the Sabbath into an ordinary day. Whatever we are not allowed to do ourselves, we must not have done for us by a fellow-Jew, even by one who is a Sabbath-breaker. All Sabbath laws, however, are suspended as soon as there is the least danger to human life ; פקוח נפש דוחה את השבת say the Rabbis. The Commandments of God are to promote life and well-being—a principle based on Leviticus 18. 5, " and these are the precepts of the Lord, by which *ye shall live* וחי בהם."

thou. The head of the house, responsible for all that dwell therein.

manservant . . . maidservant. Not only our children but also our servants, whether Israelite or heathen, nay even the beasts of burden, are to share in the rest of the Sabbath day. " The Sabbath is a boundless boon for mankind and the greatest wonder of religion. Nothing can appear more simple than this institution, to rest on the seventh day, after six days of work. And yet no legislator in the

עַבְדְּךָ וַאֲמָתְךָ וּבְהֶמְתְּךָ וְגֵרְךָ אֲשֶׁר בִּשְׁעָרֶיךָ : כִּי
שֵׁשֶׁת־יָמִים עָשָׂה יְהֹוָה אֶת־הַשָּׁמַיִם וְאֶת־הָאָרֶץ אֶת־
הַיָּם וְאֶת־כָּל־אֲשֶׁר־בָּם וַיָּנַח בַּיּוֹם הַשְּׁבִיעִי עַל־כֵּן בֵּרַךְ
יְהֹוָה אֶת־יוֹם הַשַּׁבָּת וַיְקַדְּשֵׁהוּ :

world hit upon this idea! To the Greeks and the Romans it was an object of derision, a superstitious usage. But it removed with one stroke the contrast between slaves who must labour incessantly, and their masters who may celebrate continuously " (B. Jacob). " Slavery in the real sense of the word did not exist in Israel. Israel was the only ancient Community whose society did not rest upon the shoulders of slaves; and thus Israel created for the first time a truly ethical civilization " (Baeck).

thy cattle. It is one of the glories of Judaism that, thousands of years ago, it so fully recognized our duties to the dumb friends and helpers of man; see *Deuteronomy* pp. 302–5 (854–5).

11. *for in six days*. By keeping the Sabbath, the Rabbis tell us, we testify to our belief in God as the Creator of the Universe; in a God who is not identical with Nature, but is a free *Personality*, the Creator and Ruler of Nature.

blessed the sabbath. Made it a day of blessing to those who observe it. " The Sabbath was something quite new, which had never before existed in any nation or in any religion—a standing reminder that man can emancipate himself from the slavery of his worldly cares; that man was made for spiritual freedom, peace, and joy " (Ewald). " The Sabbath is one of the glories of our humanity. For if to labour is noble, of our own free will to pause in that labour which may lead to success, to money, to fame is nobler still. To dedicate one day a week to rest and to God, this is the prerogative and the privilege of man alone " (C. G. Montefiore).

and hallowed it. Endowed it with sanctifying powers. The sanctity of the Sabbath is seen in its traces upon the Jewish soul. Isaiah speaks of the Sabbath as " a delight "; and the Liturgy describes Sabbath rest as " voluntary and congenial, happy and cheerful." Joy has ever been the keynote of the Sabbath; and, throughout the centuries, Israel's children have found in it a divinely-given refuge from the withering blasts of an unsympathetic world. The Sabbath banishes care and toil, grief and sorrow. All fasting (except on the Day of Atonement, which as the Sabbath of Sabbaths transcends this rule of the ordinary Sabbath) is forbidden; and *all* mourning is suspended on the Sabbath day. Each of the three Sabbath-meals is an obligatory religious act (מצוה); and is in the olden Jewish home accompanied by זמירות, Table Songs. The spiritual effect of the Sabbath is termed by the Rabbis the " extra-soul," which the Israelite enjoys on that day.

thy stranger that is within thy gates : ¹¹for in six days the Lord made heaven and earth, the sea and all that is therein, and rested on the seventh day : wherefore the Lord blessed the sabbath day and hallowed it.

Ignorant and unsympathetic critics condemn the Rabbinic Sabbath-laws with their numberless minutiae as an intolerable " burden." These restrictions justify themselves in that the Jew who actually and strictly obeys these injunctions, *and only such a Jew*, has a Sabbath. And as to the alleged formalism of all these Sabbath laws, a German Protestant theologian of anti-Semitic tendencies confessed : " Anyone who has had the opportunity of knowing the inner life of Jewish families that observe the Law of the fathers with sincere piety and in all strictness, will have been astonished at the wealth of joyfulness, gratitude and sunshine, undreamt of by the outsider, which the Law animates in the Jewish home. The whole household rejoices on the Sabbath, which they celebrate with rare satisfaction not only as the day of rest, but rather as the day of rejoicing. Jewish prayers term the Sabbath a ' joy of the soul ' to him who hallows it ; *he* ' enjoys the abundance of Thy goodness.' Such expressions are not mere words ; they are the outcome of pure and genuine happiness and enthusiasm " (R. Kittel).

" When dire necessity compels a Jew to break the Sabbath, let him not think that the Sabbath is lost to him, or he to Judaism. So long as Jewish conscientiousness is alive within him, let him endeavour to keep as much of the Sabbath as he is able. He must not say, ' I have broken the Sabbath. How can I join my brethren in the Sabbath Service ! ' Whatever he does conscientiously will be acceptable before God, and he will thus find himself exhorted to watch carefully, and to seize the first opportunity of returning to the full observance of Sabbath. The same principle applies to all the Divine precepts " (M. Friedländer).

Without the observance of the Sabbath, of the olden Sabbath, of the Sabbath as perfected by the Rabbis, the whole of Jewish life would in time disappear. And only if the olden Sabbath is maintained by those who observe it, and regained by those who have lost or abandoned it, is the permanence of Israel assured. The Falashas, that forgotten Jewish tribe in the interior of Abyssinia, who had been cut off for ages from their brethren of the house of Israel, were some generations ago sorely harassed by hired missionaries to name the Saviour and Mediator of the Jews. They spoke wiser than they knew when they answered, " The Saviour of the Jews is the Sabbath." And in our day, Achad Ha-am has rightly said : " Far more than Israel has kept the Sabbath, it is the Sabbath that has kept Israel."

קִבָּלַת שַׁבָּת :

Meditation before kindling the Sabbath lights.

רִבּוֹן הָעוֹלָמִים · הִנֵּה בָאתִי לְהַדְלִיק אֶת הַנֵּרוֹת
לִכְבוֹד הַשַּׁבָּת · כַּכָּתוּב וְקָרָאתָ לַשַּׁבָּת עֹנֶג לִקְדוֹשׁ יְיָ
מְכֻבָּד : וּבִזְכוּת מִצְוָה זוֹ תַּשְׁפִּיעַ עָלַי וְעַל בְּנֵי בֵיתִי
שֶׁפַע הַחַיִּים שֶׁתְּחָנֵּנוּ וּתְבָרְכֵנוּ בְּרֹב בְּרָכוֹת · וְתַשְׁכֵּן
שְׁכִינָתְךָ בְּתוֹכֵנוּ :

אַב הָרַחֲמִים · אָנָּא מְשֹׁךְ חַסְדְּךָ עָלַי וְעַל קְרֹבַי
הָאֲהוּבִים וְזַכֵּנִי (לְגַדֵּל בָּנַי וּבְנוֹתַי) לָלֶכֶת בְּדַרְכֵי
יְשָׁרִים לְפָנֶיךָ דְּבֵקִים בַּתּוֹרָה וּבְמַעֲשִׂים טוֹבִים ·
הַרְחֵק מֵעָלֵינוּ כָּל חֶרְפָּה תּוּגָה וְיָגוֹן · וְשִׂים שָׁלוֹם
אוֹרָה וְשִׂמְחָה בִּמְעוֹנֵנוּ : כִּי עִמְּךָ מְקוֹר הַחַיִּים בְּאוֹרְךָ
נִרְאֶה־אוֹר · אָמֵן :

Continue with the Blessing, p. 344.

2. INAUGURATION OF THE SABBATH

The Sabbath is inaugurated in the Home by the kindling of the Sabbath lights; and in the Synagogue, by special psalms and the *Lechoh Dodi* hymn prior to the Evening Service. In the Evening Service there are some departures—omissions and additions—from the weekday Evening Service.

INAUGURATION OF THE SABBATH.

Meditation before kindling the Sabbath lights.

THE
SABBATH
LIGHTS

Psalm 58. 13

Lord of the Universe, I am about to perform the sacred duty of kindling the lights in honour of the Sabbath, even as it is written : " And thou shalt call the Sabbath a delight, and the holy day of 'the Lord honourable." And may the effect of my fulfilling this commandment be, that the stream of abundant life and heavenly blessing flow in upon me and mine ; that thou be gracious unto us, and cause thy Presence to dwell among us.

Father of Mercy, O continue thy lovingkindness unto me and my dear ones. Make me worthy to (rear my children so that they) walk in the way of the righteous before thee, loyal to thy Torah and clinging to good deeds. Keep thou far from us all manner of shame, grief, and care ; and grant Psalm 36. 10 that peace, light, and joy ever abide in our home. For with thee is the fountain of life ; in thy light do we see light. Amen.

Continue with the Blessing, p. 345.

THE SABBATH LIGHTS

The two lights kindled in the home in honour of the Sabbath are symbolical of the joy and blessing, serenity and peace that always distinguished the Jewish Day of Rest. It has at all times been deemed the solemn duty of the Jewish Woman thus to inaugurate the Sabbath, a duty that she was on no account to neglect. The due observance of this precept, we are told, ensures שלום בית, domestic peace ; and it does so, in giving the light of Sabbatical sanctity to the home. " The Sabbath planted a heaven in every Jewish home, filling it with long-expected and blissfully-greeted peace ; making each home a sanctuary, the father a priest, and the mother who lights the Sabbath candles an angel of light " (B. Jacob).

After the kindling, the hands are spread out before the lights, or over the face, and the blessing is spoken. The sacred ceremony itself has for many centuries been preceded, or followed, by

On kindling the lights, say :—

בָּרוּךְ אַתָּה יְיָ אֱלֹהֵינוּ מֶלֶךְ הָעוֹלָם · אֲשֶׁר קִדְּשָׁנוּ
בְּמִצְוֹתָיו וְצִוָּנוּ לְהַדְלִיק נֵר שֶׁל־שַׁבָּת :

spontaneous or non-statutory words of prayer on the part of the housewife, for the welfare, spiritual and physical, of those entrusted to her care. The vision of the mother thus praying for her loved ones accompanies the loyal Jew or Jewess throughout life. A poet hailing from an Eastern European Jewry sings :

> " From memory's spring flows a vision to-night,
> My mother is kindling and blessing the light ;

> " The light of Queen Sabbath, the heavenly flame,
> That one day in seven quells hunger and shame.

> " My mother is praying and screening her face,
> Too bashful to gaze at the Sabbath light's grace.

> " She murmurs devoutly, ' Almighty, be blessed,
> For sending Thy angel of joy and of rest.

> " 'And may as the candles of Sabbath divine
> The eyes of my son in Thy Law ever shine ' . . .

> " Of childhood, fair childhood, the years are long fled :
> Youth's candles are quenched, and my mother is dead.

> " And yet ev'ry Friday, when twilight arrives,
> The face of my mother within me revives ;

> " A prayer on her lips, ' O Almighty, be blessed,
> For sending us Sabbath, the angel of rest.'

> " And some hidden feeling I cannot control
> A Sabbath light kindles deep, deep in my soul "
>
> (P. M. Raskin).

Such Sabbath prayers are included in the *Techinnoth*, " Meditations for every day, season and occasion ", that have been published in various languages for the use of Jewish women. The special prayer printed in this volume was prepared by the author of this Commentary in 1923.

The institution of the Sabbath light is almost certainly pre-Maccabean. This is clear from the fact that in Mishna times, none ever doubted that the Sabbath light should be kindled ; the only dispute was in regard to the material wherewith it might be lighted. It was a

On kindling the lights, say :—

THE
SABBATH
LIGHTS
Blessed art thou, O Lord our God, King of the universe, who hast hallowed us by thy commandments, and commanded us to kindle the Sabbath light.

ceremony beloved of the people, who saw in the home illumined by the Sabbath lights a foretaste of the ineffable bliss of Life Eternal. To be deprived of the possibility of fulfilling this precept was deemed a grievous affliction. " Even if one has no food, and has to go begging for the money to pay for the oil required for the lighting, it is his bounden duty to do so ", is the ruling of Maimonides.

Enemies of Judaism fully realized the importance of this beautiful symbol in Jewish religious life—from the days of the heathen philosopher Seneca who proposed State prohibition of Sabbath lights, down to the apostates in Soviet Russia who laboured for its extirpation among the Jewish masses. It is interesting to note that sectarians seem never to have observed the kindling of the Sabbath lights. Jewish Christians were soon persuaded to repudiate a ceremony that gave the olden Day of Rest additional sanctity and joy. The Karaites from the very beginning rejected the Sabbath lights, and at one time protested against this sacred immemorial custom by sitting in absolute darkness on Friday nights. A similar blindness is seen among latter-day sectarians. In the Prayer Books of Liberal Jews, there is no reference to the Sabbath light, or any Blessing or Prayer for its kindling.

3. WELCOMING THE SABBATH

(קבלת שבת)

Since the middle of the sixteenth century, psalms and a special hymn are recited before the Evening Service as a welcome to " Queen Sabbath ". This innovation was due to the Jewish mystics at Safed, in Northern Palestine. They were visionaries, ascetics, and poets, who lived in an atmosphere of exaltation. They dreamt of " last things "— the Coming of the Messiah and Judgment Day—and looked for Israel's imminent Redemption. In consequence, the psalms which they selected for welcoming the Sabbath, the six Psalms 95–99 and 29, were a reflection of their mystic mood. These psalms, on the one hand, proclaim that *God is King*, *i.e.* that He has begun to assert His rule on earth, a terror to the wicked, a solace to the righteous ; and, on the other hand, are a summons to worship, calling upon all nature and all nations to join in adoration of the Holy and Righteous Ruler of the Universe. This Welcome to the Sabbath appeared for the first time as a portion of the Friday Eve Service in 1599. The custom of the Safed Cabalists has been taken over, partly or as a whole, in all the Rites.

When a Festival, or one of the Intermediate Days of a Festival, falls on Sabbath. the Inauguration Service commences with מִזְמוֹר שִׁיר, *p.* 360.

תהלים צ'ה

לְכוּ נְרַנְּנָה לַיְיָ נָרִיעָה לְצוּר יִשְׁעֵנוּ : נְקַדְּמָה פָנָיו
בְּתוֹדָה בִּזְמִירוֹת נָרִיעַ לוֹ : כִּי אֵל גָּדוֹל יְיָ וּמֶלֶךְ גָּדוֹל
עַל־כָּל־אֱלֹהִים : אֲשֶׁר בְּיָדוֹ מֶחְקְרֵי־אָרֶץ וְתוֹעֲפוֹת הָרִים
לוֹ : אֲשֶׁר־לוֹ הַיָּם וְהוּא עָשָׂהוּ וְיַבֶּשֶׁת יָדָיו יָצָרוּ : בֹּאוּ
נִשְׁתַּחֲוֶה וְנִכְרָעָה נִבְרְכָה לִפְנֵי־יְיָ עֹשֵׂנוּ : כִּי הוּא אֱלֹהֵינוּ
וַאֲנַחְנוּ עַם מַרְעִיתוֹ וְצֹאן יָדוֹ הַיּוֹם אִם־בְּקֹלוֹ תִשְׁמָעוּ :
אַל־תַּקְשׁוּ לְבַבְכֶם כִּמְרִיבָה כְּיוֹם מַסָּה בַּמִּדְבָּר : אֲשֶׁר
נִסּוּנִי אֲבוֹתֵיכֶם בְּחָנוּנִי גַּם־רָאוּ פָעֳלִי : אַרְבָּעִים שָׁנָה
אָקוּט בְּדוֹר וָאֹמַר עַם תֹּעֵי לֵבָב הֵם וְהֵם לֹא־יָדְעוּ
דְרָכָי : אֲשֶׁר־נִשְׁבַּעְתִּי בְאַפִּי אִם־יְבֹאוּן אֶל־מְנוּחָתִי :

PSALM 95.
"O COME, LET US SING BEFORE THE LORD"

1–7. A call to worship the Creator of the world and Shepherd of Israel.

1. *sing.* lit. "ring out our joy".
shout for joy. A joy which runs beyond all words.
Rock. A synonym for "God".
3. *above all gods.* "Are there any other gods"? asks the Midrash; and triumphantly points to *v.* 5 of the next psalm, "all the gods of the heathens are things of nought".

Psalm xcv.

When a Festival, or one of the Intermediate Days of a Festival, falls on Sabbath, the Inauguration Service commences with " A Psalm, a Song, etc," p. 361.

¹O come, let us sing before the Lord : let us shout for joy to the Rock of our salvation. ²Let us come before his presence with thanksgiving : let us shout for joy unto him with psalms. ³For the Lord is a great God, and a great King above all gods. ⁴In his hand are the deep places of the earth ; the heights of the mountains are his also. ⁵The sea is his, and he made it ; and his hands formed the dry land. ⁶O come, let us worship and bow down ; let us kneel before the Lord our Maker. ⁷For he is our God, and we are the people of his pasture, and the sheep of his hand. To-day, O that ye would hearken to his voice ! ⁸Harden not your hearts as at Meribah, as in the day of Massah in the wilderness : ⁹when your fathers tried me, and proved me, although they had seen my work. ¹⁰Forty years long was I wearied with that generation, and said; It is a people that do err in their heart, and they have not known my ways. ¹¹Wherefore I sware in my wrath, that they should not enter into my rest.

---

4. *heights.* lit. " toilsome heights ", the soaring mountain-peaks upon which man cannot set his foot.

6. *our Maker.* He who made us to be His own people.

7. *of his hand.* Guided by His hand.

to-day. " If Israel came back in true repentance to the Holy One even one day, deliverance would forthwith ensue " (Talmud).

8–11. A warning against disobedience.

8. *Meribah . . . Massah.* The reference is to the murmuring of the children of Israel at the lack of water during the wanderings in the Wilderness ; Exodus 17. 1–7 and Numbers 20. 1–13.

9. *proved me.* Tested me.

10. *that do err in their heart.* Are of an unsteady mind.

11. *my rest.* The Holy Land, the land of rest after your wanderings ; Deuteronomy 12. 9.

תהלים צ׳ו

שִׁירוּ לַיָי שִׁיר חָדָשׁ שִׁירוּ לַיָי כָּל־הָאָרֶץ : שִׁירוּ לַיָי

בָּרֲכוּ שְׁמוֹ בַּשְּׂרוּ מִיּוֹם־לְיוֹם יְשׁוּעָתוֹ : סַפְּרוּ בַגּוֹיִם כְּבוֹדוֹ

בְּכָל־הָעַמִּים נִפְלְאוֹתָיו : כִּי גָדוֹל יְיָ וּמְהֻלָּל מְאֹד נוֹרָא

הוּא עַל־כָּל־אֱלֹהִים : כִּי כָּל־אֱלֹהֵי הָעַמִּים אֱלִילִים וַיָי

שָׁמַיִם עָשָׂה : הוֹד־וְהָדָר לְפָנָיו עֹז וְתִפְאֶרֶת בְּמִקְדָּשׁוֹ :

הָבוּ לַיָי מִשְׁפְּחוֹת עַמִּים הָבוּ לַיָי כָּבוֹד וָעֹז : הָבוּ לַיָי

כְּבוֹד שְׁמוֹ שְׂאוּ־מִנְחָה וּבֹאוּ לְחַצְרוֹתָיו : הִשְׁתַּחֲווּ לַיָי

בְּהַדְרַת־קֹדֶשׁ חִילוּ מִפָּנָיו כָּל־הָאָרֶץ : אִמְרוּ בַגּוֹיִם יְיָ

מָלָךְ אַף־תִּכּוֹן תֵּבֵל בַּל־תִּמּוֹט יָדִין עַמִּים בְּמֵישָׁרִים :

יִשְׂמְחוּ הַשָּׁמַיִם וְתָגֵל הָאָרֶץ יִרְעַם הַיָּם וּמְלֹאוֹ : יַעֲלֹז

שָׂדַי וְכָל־אֲשֶׁר־בּוֹ אָז יְרַנְּנוּ כָּל־עֲצֵי־יָעַר : לִפְנֵי יְיָ כִּי

בָא כִּי בָא לִשְׁפֹּט הָאָרֶץ יִשְׁפֹּט־תֵּבֵל בְּצֶדֶק וְעַמִּים

בֶּאֱמוּנָתוֹ :

PSALM 96.

1–6. Let all the nations praise God, for He is supreme.

1. *new song.* Fresh mercies demand fresh expressions of thanksgiving and homage.

2. *proclaim.* Tell the good news.

5. *things of nought.* Heb. *elilim,* " nothings ". This word is a mocking echo of *elim,* " gods " ; and expresses the vanity of the pretensions of these so-called divinities.

made the heavens. He is the Creator.

7–10. Let all nations worship Him, for as King He will judge the world.

Psalm xcvi.

¹O sing unto the Lord a new song : sing unto the Lord, all the earth. ²Sing unto the Lord, bless his Name : proclaim his salvation from day to day. ³Declare his glory among the nations, his wondrous works among all the peoples. ⁴For great is the Lord, and exceedingly to be praised : he is to be revered above all gods. ⁵For all the gods of the peoples are things of nought : but the Lord made the heavens. ⁶Splendour and majesty are before him : strength and beauty are in his sanctuary. ⁷Ascribe unto the Lord, ye families of the peoples, ascribe unto the Lord glory and strength. ⁸Give unto the Lord the glory due unto his Name: bring an offering and come into his courts. ⁹O worship the Lord in the beauty of holiness ; tremble before him, all the earth. ¹⁰Say among the nations, the Lord reigneth : the world also is set firm that it cannot be moved : he shall judge the peoples with equity. ¹¹Let the heavens rejoice, and let the earth be glad ; let the sea roar, and the fulness thereof ; ¹²let the plain exult and all that is therein ; yea, let all the trees of the forest sing for joy, ¹³before the Lord, for he cometh ; for he cometh to judge the earth : he will judge the world with righteousness, and the peoples in his faithfulness.

---

8. *come into his courts.* The heathen are invited to take their place alongside the Israelites in the Temple courts, that all may unite in one song of praise to the Universal King (Davies).

9. *beauty of holiness.* Or, " majesty of holiness ".

10. *He shall judge the peoples.* A new era is to begin, and all the peoples shall have the boon of His righteous judging.

11–13. Let universal Nature rejoice in the prospect of righteous rule.

12. *trees of the forest.* An appeal for the sympathy of nature, such as we find in Isaiah 44. 23 and 55. 12 ; see p. 56.

13. *He cometh.* The Kingdom of God is at hand !

to judge the earth. "*Judging* has no terrible sound to a Hebrew : ' with righteousness shall He judge (*i.e.* right) the weak ', Isaiah 11. 4. The predominant aspect of judgment here is not punishment but righteous government " (Cheyne).

תהלים צ׳ז

יְיָ מָלָךְ תָּגֵל הָאָרֶץ יִשְׂמְחוּ אִיִּים רַבִּים: עָנָן וַעֲרָפֶל

סְבִיבָיו צֶדֶק וּמִשְׁפָּט מְכוֹן כִּסְאוֹ: אֵשׁ לְפָנָיו תֵּלֵךְ

וּתְלַהֵט סָבִיב צָרָיו: הֵאִירוּ בְרָקָיו תֵּבֵל רָאֲתָה וַתָּחֵל

הָאָרֶץ: הָרִים כַּדּוֹנַג נָמַסּוּ מִלִּפְנֵי יְיָ מִלִּפְנֵי אֲדוֹן כָּל־

הָאָרֶץ: הִגִּידוּ הַשָּׁמַיִם צִדְקוֹ וְרָאוּ כָל־הָעַמִּים כְּבוֹדוֹ:

יֵבשׁוּ כָּל־עֹבְדֵי פֶסֶל הַמִּתְהַלְלִים בָּאֱלִילִים הִשְׁתַּחֲווּ־לוֹ

כָּל־אֱלֹהִים: שָׁמְעָה וַתִּשְׂמַח צִיּוֹן וַתָּגֵלְנָה בְּנוֹת יְהוּדָה

לְמַעַן מִשְׁפָּטֶיךָ יְיָ: כִּי־אַתָּה יְיָ עֶלְיוֹן עַל־כָּל־הָאָרֶץ מְאֹד

נַעֲלֵיתָ עַל־כָּל־אֱלֹהִים: אֹהֲבֵי יְיָ שִׂנְאוּ רָע שֹׁמֵר נַפְשׁוֹת

חֲסִידָיו מִיַּד רְשָׁעִים יַצִּילֵם: אוֹר זָרֻעַ לַצַּדִּיק וּלְיִשְׁרֵי־לֵב

שִׂמְחָה: שִׂמְחוּ צַדִּיקִים בַּיְיָ וְהוֹדוּ לְזֵכֶר קָדְשׁוֹ:

תהלים צ׳ח

מִזְמוֹר שִׁירוּ לַיְיָ שִׁיר חָדָשׁ כִּי־נִפְלָאוֹת עָשָׂה

הוֹשִׁיעָה־לּוֹ יְמִינוֹ וּזְרוֹעַ קָדְשׁוֹ: הוֹדִיעַ יְיָ יְשׁוּעָתוֹ לְעֵינֵי

PSALM 97.

1–6. Let the earth rejoice, because God the King appears in terrible majesty.

1. *The Lord reigneth, i.e.* has become King ; and is manifesting His royal power.

coast-lands. lit. " isles ", lands reached by sea.

2. *clouds . . . righteousness.* Though God shrouds Himself in mystery and might, His Kingdom is founded upon righteousness.

3. *a fire goeth before him.* The coming of God is described in imagery taken from the revelation at Mt. Sinai and the visions of the Prophets.

7–12. The confusion of idolaters and exultation of the faithful.

7. *bow down to him.* A contemptuous challenge to the idols of the

THE
COMING
JUDG-
MENT

Psalm xcvii.

¹The Lord reigneth ; let the earth be glad ; let the many coast-lands rejoice   ²Clouds and darkness are round about him : righteousness and justice are the foundation of his throne. ³A fire goeth before him, and burneth up his adversaries round about. ⁴His lightnings illumine the world : the earth seeth and trembleth. ⁵The mountains melt like wax before the Lord, before the Lord of the whole earth. ⁶The heavens declare his righteousness, and all the peoples behold his glory. ⁷Ashamed be all they that serve graven images, that make their boast of things of nought : bow down to him, all ye gods. ⁸Zion heard and was glad, and the cities of Judah rejoiced, because of thy judgments, O Lord. ⁹For thou, Lord, art most high above all the earth : thou art exalted far above all gods. ¹⁰O ye that love the Lord, hate evil : ne preserveth the souls of his loving ones ; he delivereth them out of the hand of the wicked. ¹¹Light is sown for the righteous, and joy for the upright in heart. ¹²Rejoice in the Lord, ye righteous ; and give thanks to his holy Name.

Psalm xcviii. A ¹Psalm.

HOMAGE
OF
NATURE
AND MAN
TO THE
JUDGE OF
THE
WORLD

O sing unto the Lord a new song ; for he hath done marvellous things : his right hand, and his holy arm, hath wrought salvation for him. ²The Lord hath made known his salvation : his righteousness hath he revealed in the

heathen : they are so devoid of life, that they cannot even prostrate themselves before God.

8. *cities.* lit. " daughters ", the smaller cities.

10. *hate evil.* " The fear of the Lord is to hate evil " (Proverbs 8. 13).

11. *light is sown for the righteous.* It may for the present be hidden like the seed in the earth, but it is sure to spring forth. Let the righteous therefore go on hating evil.

PSALM 98.

1–6. All are to salute God with voice and musical instruments, like men who go forth to meet their monarch.

1. *his right hand . . . arm.* Symbols for, " His might ".

wrought salvation. Worked victory.

הַגּוֹיִם גִּלָּה צִדְקָתוֹ : זָכַר חַסְדּוֹ וֶאֱמוּנָתוֹ לְבֵית יִשְׂרָאֵל
רָאוּ כָל־אַפְסֵי־אָרֶץ אֵת יְשׁוּעַת אֱלֹהֵינוּ : הָרִיעוּ לַיָי כָּל־
הָאָרֶץ פִּצְחוּ וְרַנְּנוּ וְזַמֵּרוּ : זַמְּרוּ לַיָי בְּכִנּוֹר בְּכִנּוֹר וְקוֹל
זִמְרָה : בַּחֲצֹצְרוֹת וְקוֹל שׁוֹפָר הָרִיעוּ לִפְנֵי הַמֶּלֶךְ יְיָ :
יִרְעַם הַיָּם וּמְלֹאוֹ תֵּבֵל וְיֹשְׁבֵי בָהּ : נְהָרוֹת יִמְחֲאוּ־כָף
יַחַד הָרִים יְרַנֵּנוּ : לִפְנֵי יְיָ כִּי בָא לִשְׁפֹּט הָאָרֶץ יִשְׁפֹּט־
תֵּבֵל בְּצֶדֶק וְעַמִּים בְּמֵישָׁרִים :

תהלים צ'ט

יְיָ מָלָךְ יִרְגְּזוּ עַמִּים יֹשֵׁב כְּרוּבִים תָּנוּט הָאָרֶץ : יְיָ
בְּצִיּוֹן גָּדוֹל וְרָם הוּא עַל־כָּל־הָעַמִּים : יוֹדוּ שִׁמְךָ גָּדוֹל
וְנוֹרָא קָדוֹשׁ הוּא : וְעֹז מֶלֶךְ מִשְׁפָּט אָהֵב אַתָּה כּוֹנַנְתָּ
מֵישָׁרִים מִשְׁפָּט וּצְדָקָה בְּיַעֲקֹב אַתָּה עָשִׂיתָ : רוֹמְמוּ
יְיָ אֱלֹהֵינוּ וְהִשְׁתַּחֲווּ לַהֲדֹם רַגְלָיו קָדוֹשׁ הוּא : מֹשֶׁה
וְאַהֲרֹן בְּכֹהֲנָיו וּשְׁמוּאֵל בְּקֹרְאֵי שְׁמוֹ קֹרִאים אֶל־יְיָ
וְהוּא יַעֲנֵם : בְּעַמּוּד עָנָן יְדַבֵּר אֲלֵיהֶם שָׁמְרוּ עֵדֹתָיו
וְחֹק נָתַן־לָמוֹ : יְיָ אֱלֹהֵינוּ אַתָּה עֲנִיתָם אֵל נֹשֵׂא הָיִיתָ

7–9. Let nature join in the loud acclamation, for He shall judge the earth righteously.

8. *clap their hands.* The metaphor suggests the roaring of the waves.

PSALM 99.

1–3. Exhortation to recognize God's holiness.

1. *is moved.* Let the earth quake—as at every manifestation of God in Hebrew poetry.

3. *holy is he.* The words form a choral refrain, as in v. 7 and 9. " Holy " here in the sense of " infinite " and " righteous ".

sight of the nations. ³He hath remembered his lovingkindness and his faithfulness toward the house of Israel : all the ends of the earth have seen the salvation of our God. ⁴Shout for joy unto the Lord, all the earth ; break forth into exultation, and sing praises. ⁵Sing praises unto the Lord with the harp ; with the harp and the voice of melody. ⁶With trumpets and the sound of the horn shout for joy before the king, the Lord. ⁷Let the sea roar and the fulness thereof, the world, and they that dwell therein. ⁸Let the floods clap their hands, let the mountains exult together, ⁹before the Lord, for he cometh to judge the earth : he will judge the world with righteousness, and the peoples with equity.

Psalm xcix.

¹The Lord reigneth ; the peoples stand in awe : he is enthroned upon the cherubim ; the earth is moved. ²The Lord is great in Zion ; and he is high above all the peoples. ³Let them give thanks to thy great and dreaded Name ; holy is he. ⁴The King's strength also loveth justice ; thou didst establish equity ; thou hast wrought justice and righteousness in Jacob. ⁵Exalt ye the Lord our God, and worship at his temple : holy is he. ⁶Moses and Aaron among his priests, and Samuel among them that call upon his Name, called upon the Lord, and he answered them. ⁷He spake unto them in the pillar of cloud : they kept his testimonies, and the statute that he gave them. ⁸Thou didst answer them, O Lord our God : a forgiving God thou wast unto them, though thou didst punish their misdeeds.

4. *the King's strength . . . justice.* God's might is no arbitrary power but expresses itself in justice and retribution. In the words of the medieval poet, He is

> " The Judge who comes in terror,
> The Judge who comes in might,
> To put an end to evil,
> To set the crown on right ".

5. *temple.* lit. " footstool ".

8. *a forgiving God . . . didst punish.* Among the thirteen Attributes of Mercy, we have " . . . forgiving iniquity, transgression and sin, but not clearing the guilty ". He is a righteously zealous God. He judges

לָהֶם וְנֹקֵם עַל־עֲלִילוֹתָם: רוֹמְמוּ יְיָ אֱלֹהֵינוּ וְהִשְׁתַּחֲווּ

לְהַר קָדְשׁוֹ כִּי קָדוֹשׁ יְיָ אֱלֹהֵינוּ:

תהלים כ׳ט

מִזְמוֹר לְדָוִד הָבוּ לַיְיָ בְּנֵי אֵלִים הָבוּ לַיְיָ כָּבוֹד וָעֹז:

הָבוּ לַיְיָ כְּבוֹד שְׁמוֹ הִשְׁתַּחֲווּ לַיְיָ בְּהַדְרַת־קֹדֶשׁ: קוֹל

יְיָ עַל הַמָּיִם אֵל־הַכָּבוֹד הִרְעִים יְיָ עַל־מַיִם רַבִּים:

קוֹל־יְיָ בַּכֹּחַ קוֹל יְיָ בֶּהָדָר: קוֹל יְיָ שֹׁבֵר אֲרָזִים

וַיְשַׁבֵּר יְיָ אֶת־אַרְזֵי הַלְּבָנוֹן: וַיַּרְקִידֵם כְּמוֹ־עֵגֶל לְבָנוֹן

וְשִׂרְיוֹן כְּמוֹ בֶן־רְאֵמִים: קוֹל־יְיָ חֹצֵב לַהֲבוֹת אֵשׁ:

קוֹל יְיָ יָחִיל מִדְבָּר יָחִיל יְיָ מִדְבַּר קָדֵשׁ: קוֹל יְיָ

יְחוֹלֵל אַיָּלוֹת וַיֶּחֱשֹׂף יְעָרוֹת וּבְהֵיכָלוֹ כֻּלּוֹ אֹמֵר

כָּבוֹד: יְיָ לַמַּבּוּל יָשָׁב וַיֵּשֶׁב יְיָ מֶלֶךְ לְעוֹלָם: יְיָ עֹז

לְעַמּוֹ יִתֵּן יְיָ | יְבָרֵךְ אֶת־עַמּוֹ בַשָּׁלוֹם:

and punishes impartially; and does not spare the good when they deserve punishment.

"All these Psalms 95–99 tell of a setting up of a Divine Kingdom on earth. All alike anticipate the event with joy. One universal anthem bursts from the whole world to greet the advent of the righteous King. Even inanimate nature sympathizes with the joy; the sea thunders her welcome, the rivers clap their hands, the trees of the wood break forth into singing before the Lord. In all these Psalms alike, the joy springs from the same source, from the thought that on this earth, where might has triumphed so long over right, a *righteous* King shall reign, and a Kingdom shall be set up which shall be a kingdom of *righteousness* and judgment and truth " (Perowne).

Psalm 99 is not followed by 100—essentially a morning hymn, and more appropriate for weekdays—but by the twenty-ninth psalm, which from early times was associated with the Sabbath. It too is a " royal " psalm, singing of the Lord enthroned as King forever (*v.* 10).

PSALM 29.

Thunder-storms of tropical intensity are frequent in Palestine in winter, and the Israelite saw in them special manifestations of Divine might and majesty.

⁹Exalt ye the Lord our God, and worship at his holy mount ; for the Lord our God is holy.

Psalm ˙xxix.   ¹A Psalm of David.

Ascribe unto the Lord, O ye sons of might, ascribe unto the Lord glory and strength.   ²Ascribe unto the Lord the glory due unto his Name ; worship the Lord in the beauty of holiness.   ³The voice of the Lord is upon the waters : the God of glory thundereth, even the Lord upon the many waters.   ⁴The voice of the Lord is powerful ; the voice of the Lord is full of majesty.   ⁵The voice of the Lord breaketh the cedars ; yea, the Lord breaketh in pieces the cedars of Lebanon.   ⁶He maketh them also to skip like a calf ; Lebanon and Sirion like a young wild-ox.   ⁷The voice of the Lord heweth out flames of fire ;   ⁸the voice of the Lord shaketh the wilderness ; the Lord shaketh the wilderness of Kadesh.   ⁹The voice of the Lord maketh the hinds to calve, and strippeth the forests bare : and in his temple everything saith, Glory.   ¹⁰The Lord sat enthroned at the Flood ; yea, the Lord sitteth as King for ever.   ¹¹The Lord will give strength unto his people ; the Lord will bless his people with peace.

1. *sons of might.* The angels, standing in God's immediate presence and watching the storm, are called upon by the poet to praise Him whose glory is seen in the storm.

3-9. Rise, progress and effect of the thunder-storm.

3. *voice of the Lord.* The thunder. The first peal is heard as coming from the Mediterranean sea, whence storms arise in Palestine. It bursts over the northern mountain-ranges.

5. *Lebanon.* The very mountains shake to their foundations.

6. *Sirion.* Mt. Hermon.

7. *heweth out.* With every thunder-peal come forked lightning shafts.

8. *wilderness.* The poet sees the mountains in the North leap in terror. The storm has now swept over the whole length of the land, and pours out its fury on the wilderness in the South.

9. *calve . . . bare.* These are no mere poetical figures ; they are observed facts.

in his temple. His Heavenly Temple.

Glory. This is the chant of the angels.

10. *at the Flood.* He was King then, and is King always.

11. The God who rules and stills the storm, is the same Who blesses His people with moral strength and lasting peace.

לְכָה דוֹדִי לִקְרַאת כַּלָה · פְּנֵי שַׁבָּת נְקַבְּלָה: לכה

שָׁמוֹר וְזָכוֹר בְּדִבּוּר אֶחָד · הִשְׁמִיעָנוּ אֵל הַמְיֻחָד · יְיָ

אֶחָד וּשְׁמוֹ אֶחָד · לְשֵׁם וּלְתִפְאֶרֶת וְלִתְהִלָּה: לכה

לִקְרַאת שַׁבָּת לְכוּ וְנֵלְכָה · כִּי הִיא מְקוֹר הַבְּרָכָה ·

מֵראשׁ מִקֶּדֶם נְסוּכָה · סוֹף מַעֲשֶׂה בְּמַחֲשָׁבָה

תְּחִלָּה: לכה

מִקְדַּשׁ מֶלֶךְ עִיר מְלוּכָה · קוּמִי צְאִי מִתּוֹךְ הַהֲפֵכָה · רַב

לָךְ שֶׁבֶת בְּעֵמֶק הַבָּכָא · וְהוּא יַחֲמוֹל עָלַיִךְ

חֶמְלָה: לכה

הִתְנַעֲרִי מֵעָפָר קוּמִי · לִבְשִׁי בִּגְדֵי תִפְאַרְתֵּךְ עַמִּי · עַל־

יַד בֶּן־יִשַׁי בֵּית הַלַּחְמִי · קָרְבָה אֶל־נַפְשִׁי גְאָלָהּ: לכה

"Come, my Friend, to Meet the Bride"

In addition to inaugurating the Sabbath by the singing of psalms, the Safed Cabalists, like the Rabbis of old, personified the Sabbath as a Queen, as a Bride, to be welcomed each week with radiant joy. A number of their hymns on this theme have come down to us. The most popular of them is the *Lechoh Dodi* (" Come, my friend, to meet the Bride ") by Rabbi Solomon Halevy Alkabetz composed about the year 1540. (His name appears as an acrostic in the Hebrew ; the translation is by Solomon Solis-Cohen). It is a mere mosaic of Biblical phrases, yet the resulting whole is wonderfully fresh, fragrant and full of new charm.

" It is perhaps one of the finest pieces of religious poetry in exist-ence, and has been translated by Herder and Heine. Universal Israel, whose love for Bride Sabbath and whose hope for final redemption it echoes so well, soon honoured Alkabetz's poem with a prominent place in almost all its rituals ; and the Lechoh Dodi is now sung all over the world on the Sabbath eve, when Queen Sabbath holds her levée in the tents of Israel " (Schechter).

The idea of the welcome underlying the poem goes back to Talmudic times. Rabbi Chanina used to sing, " Come and we will go out to meet the Bride, the Queen " ! and Rabbi Yannai robed himself in festive

"LECHOH DODI"

Come, my beloved, with chorus of praise,
Welcome Bride Sabbath, the Queen of the days.

" Keep and Remember " !—in One divine Word
He that is One, made His will heard ;
One is the name of Him, One is the Lord !
His are the fame and the glory and praise !

Sabbath, to welcome thee, joyous we haste ;
Fountain of blessing from ever thou wast—
First in God's planning, thou fashioned the last,
Crown of His handiwork, chiefest of days.

City of holiness, filled are the years ;
Up from thine overthrow ! Forth from thy fears !
Long hast thou dwelt in the valley of tears,
Now shall God's tenderness shepherd thy ways.

Rise, O my folk, from the dust of the earth,
Garb thee in raiment beseeming thy worth ;
Nigh draws the hour of the Bethlehemite's birth,
Freedom who bringeth, and glorious days.

attire and saluted the Sabbath with the words, " Come, O Bride ; come, O Bride ". In Safed, white robed men and boys went out in procession up the hills and down the dales chanting psalms, and sang in the Sabbath to the strains of the Song of Songs.

keep . . . remember. The command in Exodus 20. 8 begins, " Remember the Sabbath day to keep it holy " ; while in Deuteronomy 5. 12 it says, " Observe the Sabbath day to keep it holy ". Tradition explains the different wording by stating that both forms were communicated by God *simultaneously* ; *i.e.* the Fourth Commandment in Deuteronomy, though differing in form, does not imply anything that was not revealed by God on Mt. Sinai. Moses uses the stronger expression the second time, because in his exhortation he has a practical object in view, viz., the observance of God's command.

first in God's planning, though fashioned the last. Based on the Midrashic simile of the Architect who has plans of the whole structure before beginning the building. The Sabbath is the end and pinnacle of the Creation, for which end everything else was made.

city of holiness. The poet bids Zion rise, and become a fitting abode for the Queen. The Jewish Messianic note grows in volume till the end of the poem.

Bethlehemite. The Messiah is a descendant of David, the son of Jesse, of Bethlehem.

הִתְעוֹרְרִי הִתְעוֹרְרִי · כִּי בָא אוֹרֵךְ קוּמִי אוֹרִי · עוּרִי

עוּרִי שִׁיר דַּבֵּרִי · כְּבוֹד יְיָ עָלַיִךְ נִגְלָה : לכה

לֹא תֵבְשִׁי וְלֹא תִכָּלְמִי · מַה תִּשְׁתּוֹחֲחִי וּמַה תֶּהֱמִי · בָּךְ

יֶחֱסוּ עֲנִיֵּי עַמִּי · וְנִבְנְתָה עִיר עַל־תִּלָּהּ : לכה

וְהָיוּ לִמְשִׁסָּה שֹׁאסָיִךְ · וְרָחֲקוּ כָּל־מְבַלְּעָיִךְ · יָשִׂישׂ עָלַיִךְ

אֱלֹהָיִךְ · כִּמְשׂוֹשׂ חָתָן עַל־כַּלָּה : לכה

יָמִין וּשְׂמֹאל תִּפְרוֹצִי · וְאֶת־יְיָ תַּעֲרִיצִי · עַל יַד־אִישׁ בֶּן

פַּרְצִי · וְנִשְׂמְחָה וְנָגִילָה : לכה

בּוֹאִי בְשָׁלוֹם עֲטֶרֶת בַּעְלָהּ · גַּם בְּשִׂמְחָה וּבְצָהֳלָה · תּוֹךְ

אֱמוּנֵי עַם סְגֻלָּה · בּוֹאִי כַלָּה · בּוֹאִי כַלָּה : לכה

On the entry of Mourners into the Synagogue they are greeted thus :

הַמָּקוֹם יְנַחֵם אֶתְכֶם בְּתוֹךְ שְׁאָר אֲבֵלֵי צִיּוֹן וִירוּשָׁלָיִם :

wake and bestir thee. The imagery and wording in this and the following stanzas is from the triumphant Song of Zion Redeemed, in the second part of Isaiah.

those that despoiled. This stanza is from the version of De Sola Pool.

son of Perez. The ancestor of Boaz, husband of Ruth, from whom David descended (Ruth 4. 18–22).

crown of thy lord. lit. " crown of thy husband ". The husband is Israel ; and the Sabbath, his crown and glory.

GREETING THE MOURNERS.

During the first week of mourning, the bereaved remain at home. All mourning is suspended with the advent of the Sabbath, which is officially assumed to begin at the moment when the Congregation

"LECHOH
DODI"
Wake and bestir thee, for come is thy light !
Up ! With thy shining, the world shall be bright ;
Sing ! For thy Lord is revealed in His might—
    Thine is the splendour His glory displays !

" Be not ashamed ", saith the Lord, " nor distressed ;
Fear not and doubt not. The people oppressed,
Zion, My city, in thee shall find rest—
    Thee, that anew on thy ruins I raise ".

" Those that despoiled thee shall plundered be,
Routed all those who showed no ruth ;
God shall exult and rejoice in thee,
    Joyful as bridegroom with bride of youth ".

Stretch out thy borders to left and to right ;
Fear but the Lord, Whom to fear is delight—
The man, son of Perez, shall gladden our sight,
    And we shall rejoice to the fulness of days.

Come in thy joyousness, Crown of thy lord ;
Come, bringing peace to the folk of the Word ;
Come where the faithful in gladsome accord,
    Hail thee as Sabbath-Bride, Queen of the days.

Come where the faithful are hymning thy praise ;
Come as a bride cometh, Queen of the days !

*GREETING
THE
MOURN-
ERS*
On the entry of Mourners into the Synagogue they are greeted thus :
    May the Almighty comfort you among the other
mourners for Zion and Jerusalem.

have completed *Lechoh Dodi* the hymn of Welcome. On the first Friday
eve after the funeral, the mourners remain in the anteroom till they
are ushered into the Synagogue at the conclusion of *Lechoh Dodi.* They
are met by the Minister, and the above greeting is spoken to them on
behalf of the Congregation. This human custom is not as well-known,
and fully understood, as its touching beauty and sublimity warrant.
For if the Sabbath-psalms prove the interpenetration of Nature and
the Divine, Greeting the Mourners is eloquent testimony that in
Judaism, the whole of life—all its joys and sorrows, its sunshine and
sorrow—is interpenetrated with Religion.

תהלים צ'ב

מִזְמוֹר שִׁיר לְיוֹם הַשַּׁבָּת : טוֹב לְהֹדוֹת לַיהוָה וּלְזַמֵּר
לְשִׁמְךָ עֶלְיוֹן : לְהַגִּיד בַּבֹּקֶר חַסְדֶּךָ וֶאֱמוּנָתְךָ בַּלֵּילוֹת
עֲלֵי־עָשׂוֹר וַעֲלֵי־נָבֶל עֲלֵי הִגָּיוֹן בְּכִנּוֹר : כִּי שִׂמַּחְתַּנִי
יְהוָה בְּפָעֳלֶךָ בְּמַעֲשֵׂי יָדֶיךָ אֲרַנֵּן : מַה־גָּדְלוּ מַעֲשֶׂיךָ
יְהוָה מְאֹד עָמְקוּ מַחְשְׁבֹתֶיךָ : אִישׁ בַּעַר לֹא יֵדָע וּכְסִיל
לֹא־יָבִין אֶת־זֹאת : בִּפְרֹחַ רְשָׁעִים כְּמוֹ־עֵשֶׂב וַיָּצִיצוּ
כָּל־פֹּעֲלֵי אָוֶן לְהִשָּׁמְדָם עֲדֵי־עַד : וְאַתָּה מָרוֹם לְעֹלָם
יְהוָה : כִּי הִנֵּה אֹיְבֶיךָ יְהוָה כִּי־הִנֵּה אֹיְבֶיךָ יֹאבֵדוּ
יִתְפָּרְדוּ כָּל־פֹּעֲלֵי אָוֶן : וַתָּרֶם כִּרְאֵים קַרְנִי בַּלֹּתִי
בְּשֶׁמֶן רַעֲנָן : וַתַּבֵּט עֵינִי בְּשׁוּרָי בַּקָּמִים עָלַי מְרֵעִים
תִּשְׁמַעְנָה אָזְנָי : צַדִּיק כַּתָּמָר יִפְרָח כְּאֶרֶז בַּלְּבָנוֹן יִשְׂגֶּה :

Very much older than the reading of Psalms 95–99, is that of the
two following Psalms, 92 and 93. It is an ancient custom, found in
nearly all the Rites.

PSALM 92.

1-5. It is a good thing to sing praises to God.

1. *Sabbath day.* So universal is the expression of human thanksgiving and devout meditation on the works of God in this psalm, that
some Rabbis—those " poets of Religion ", as Jeremy Taylor calls
them—held that it must have been spoken by Adam when he first
beheld the wonders of Nature ! The psalm can also be interpreted as
an expression of national gratitude for some marvellous deliverance.
It is designated " for the Sabbath day " in the title of the psalm,
because it was sung in the Temple at the Sabbath burnt-offering.

2. *good thing.* A right, delightful thing.

[1]Psalm xcii.   A Psalm, a Song for the Sabbath Day.
[2]It is a good thing to give thanks unto the Lord, and to sing praises unto thy Name, O Most High : [3]to declare thy lovingkindness in the morning, and thy faithfulness every night, [4]with an instrument of ten strings and with a harp, with solemn music upon the lyre. [5]For thou, O Lord, hast made me rejoice through thy work : I will exult in the works of thy hands. [6]How great are thy works, O Lord : thy thoughts are very deep. [7]A brutish man knoweth it not, neither doth a fool understand this : [8]when the wicked sprang up as the grass, and all the workers of iniquity flourished, it was that they might be destroyed for ever. [9]But thou, O Lord, art on high for evermore. [10]For, lo, thine enemies, O Lord, for, lo, thine enemies shall perish ; all the workers of iniquity shall be scattered. [11]But my strength hast thou exalted, like that of the wild-ox : I am anointed with fresh oil. [12]Mine eye also hath seen the defeat of mine enemies ; mine ears have heard the doom of them that rose up against me, doers of evil. [13]The righteous shall

6-9. The brutish man does not know that the wicked flourish only to perish.

6. *works.* The result of Thy working in the moral government of the world.

thoughts. Purposes ; God's designs for the training of Israel.

9. *on high for evermore.* " God is in his Heaven : all's right with the world ".

10-15. The righteous shall triumph, rejoicing at the disappearance of the wicked.

11. *I am . . . fresh oil.* " Thou dost revive my failing strength " (Moffatt).

12. *mine eye.* It is national, not personal, enemies, that are spoken of. Israel's cause was the cause of God against idolatry, falsehood, tyranny. " Who would not rejoice in the victory of the right ? The Israelite did not speak of the defeat of evil and the triumph of good, but of the destruction of the wicked and the prosperity of the righteous " (Kirkpatrick).

enemies. Or, " them that lie in wait for me ".

שְׁתוּלִים בְּבֵית יְהֹוָה בְּחַצְרוֹת אֱלֹהֵינוּ יַפְרִיחוּ : עוֹד

יְנוּבוּן בְּשֵׂיבָה דְּשֵׁנִים וְרַעֲנַנִּים יִהְיוּ : לְהַגִּיד כִּי־יָשָׁר

יְהֹוָה צוּרִי וְלֹא עַוְלָתָה בּוֹ :

תהלים צ״ג

יְהֹוָה מָלָךְ גֵּאוּת לָבֵשׁ לָבֵשׁ יְהֹוָה עֹז הִתְאַזָּר אַף־

תִּכּוֹן תֵּבֵל בַּל־תִּמּוֹט : נָכוֹן כִּסְאֲךָ מֵאָז מֵעוֹלָם אָתָּה :

נָשְׂאוּ נְהָרוֹת יְהֹוָה נָשְׂאוּ נְהָרוֹת קוֹלָם יִשְׂאוּ נְהָרוֹת

דָּכְיָם : מִקֹּלוֹת מַיִם רַבִּים אַדִּירִים מִשְׁבְּרֵי־יָם אַדִּיר

בַּמָּרוֹם יְהֹוָה : עֵדֹתֶיךָ נֶאֶמְנוּ מְאֹד לְבֵיתְךָ נַאֲוָה־קֹדֶשׁ

יְהֹוָה לְאֹרֶךְ יָמִים :

קַדִּישׁ יָתוֹם, *p.* 398

13. *palm-tree.* Symbol of beauty.
cedar in Lebanon. Symbol of strength.
15. *in old age.* Israel, even when it seems to be falling into decay, may be entering upon a second spring-time (Cheyne).
16. *to declare . . . upright.* "Showing how just the Eternal is" (Moffatt).
unrighteousness. Failure of His faithfulness.

PSALM 93.

God Is the Eternal Sovereign who will conquer all His enemies. This psalm is the prelude to Psalms 95–99, whose keynote is : "The Lord is King". They are all Messianic.

THE
JUSTICE
OF GOD
spring up like a palm-tree ; he shall grow tall like a cedar in Lebanon. ¹⁴Planted in the house of the Lord, they shall blossom in the courts of our God. ¹⁵They shall still shoot forth in old age ; they shall be full of sap and green : ¹⁶to declare that the Lord is upright ; he is my Rock, and there is no unrighteousness in him.

Psalm xciii.

THE LORD
IS KING
¹The Lord reigneth ; he hath robed him in majesty ; the Lord hath robed him, yea, he hath girded himself with strength : the world also is set firm, that it cannot be moved. ²Thy throne is set firm from of old : thou art from everlasting. ³The floods have lifted up, O Lord, the floods have lifted up their voice ; the floods lift up their roaring. ⁴Than the voices of many waters, mighty waters, breakers of the sea, more mighty is the Lord on high. ⁵Thy testimonies are very sure : holiness becometh thine house, O Lord, for evermore.

The Mourner's Kaddish, p. 399.

1. *reigneth.* At one time it seemed to the faithful as if God had abdicated His throne ; but now he has become King. By some wondrous self-revelation of God, such as the Return from Babylon, mankind has come to realize that He is clothed in majesty and strength.

world is set firm. The first result of God's reign is that the world, hitherto shaken and tossed, is set firm, and there will be an end to anarchy and confusion. The moral world-order that seemed to be tottering, is restored.

2. *from everlasting.* Though to mankind His sovereignty may appear something new, it is nevertheless from of old, even as He is everlasting.

3. *the floods.* The world-powers, threatening to engulf the nations, are as wild, hungry, ocean-waves that beat against the shore to inundate the land.

4. *than . . . waters.* In vain have the world's Powers tried to resist the reign of God. Insurrection against God ends in noise.

5. *very sure.* As it is vain for man to fight God, so is it vain to attempt to suppress the Religion which God has established by means of His revealed testimonies.

thine house. It shall nevermore be defiled by heathen invaders.

13

בָּרְכוּ אֶת־יְיָ הַמְבֹרָךְ :

בָּרוּךְ יְיָ הַמְבֹרָךְ לְעוֹלָם
וָעֶד :

בָּרוּךְ אַתָּה יְיָ אֱלֹהֵינוּ

מֶלֶךְ הָעוֹלָם · אֲשֶׁר

בִּדְבָרוֹ מַעֲרִיב עֲרָבִים

בְּחָכְמָה פּוֹתֵחַ שְׁעָרִים

וּבִתְבוּנָה מְשַׁנֶּה עִתִּים

יִתְבָּרַךְ וְיִשְׁתַּבַּח וְיִתְפָּאַר
וְיִתְרוֹמַם וְיִתְנַשֵּׂא שְׁמוֹ שֶׁל־מֶלֶךְ
מַלְכֵי הַמְּלָכִים הַקָּדוֹשׁ בָּרוּךְ הוּא ·
שֶׁהוּא רִאשׁוֹן וְהוּא אַחֲרוֹן
וּמִבַּלְעָדָיו אֵין אֱלֹהִים · סֹלּוּ לָרֹכֵב
בָּעֲרָבוֹת בְּיָהּ שְׁמוֹ וְעִלְזוּ לְפָנָיו ·
וּשְׁמוֹ מְרוֹמָם עַל־כָּל־בְּרָכָה
וּתְהִלָּה :

בָּרוּךְ שֵׁם כְּבוֹד מַלְכוּתוֹ לְעוֹלָם
וָעֶד : יְהִי שֵׁם יְיָ מְבֹרָךְ מֵעַתָּה
וְעַד עוֹלָם :

וּמַחֲלִיף אֶת־הַזְּמַנִּים וּמְסַדֵּר אֶת־הַכּוֹכָבִים בְּמִשְׁמְרוֹתֵיהֶם

בָּרָקִיעַ כִּרְצוֹנוֹ · בּוֹרֵא יוֹם וָלַיְלָה גּוֹלֵל אוֹר מִפְּנֵי־

חֹשֶׁךְ וְחֹשֶׁךְ מִפְּנֵי־אוֹר · וּמַעֲבִיר יוֹם וּמֵבִיא לַיְלָה

וּמַבְדִּיל בֵּין יוֹם וּבֵין לַיְלָה יְיָ צְבָאוֹת שְׁמוֹ · אֵל חַי

וְקַיָּם תָּמִיד יִמְלוֹךְ עָלֵינוּ לְעוֹלָם וָעֶד · בָּרוּךְ אַתָּה

יְיָ · הַמַּעֲרִיב עֲרָבִים :

4. SABBATH EVENING SERVICE

The Evening Service itself is, in the main, identical with the week-day liturgy. A variation is introduced in the second benediction after the Shema, *hashkivenu* ("Cause us to lie down in peace"); and the collection of verses that follows it ("Blessed be the Lord for evermore", p. 312) is omitted, as this was originally a substitute for the weekday Amidah. The Sabbath Amidah consists not of nineteen benedictions, but of seven: one central benediction taking the place of the thirteen weekday petitions.

INVOCA-
TION TO
CONGREGA-
TIONAL
PRAYER

Reader.—BLESS YE THE LORD WHO IS TO BE BLESSED.

Cong. and Reader.— BLESSED IS THE LORD WHO IS TO BE BLESSED FOR EVER AND EVER.

Congregation, in an undertone.

Blessed, praised, glorified, exalted and extolled be the Name of the supreme King of kings, the Holy One, blessed be he, who is the first and the last, and beside him there is no God. Extol ye him that rideth upon the heavens, whose Name is the Lord, and rejoice before him. His Name is exalted above all blessing and praise. Blessed be His Name, whose glorious kingdom is for ever and ever. Let the Name of the Lord be blessed from this time forth and for evermore.

GOD THE
CREATOR
OF DAY
AND NIGHT

Blessed art thou, O Lord our God, King of the universe, who at thy word bringest on the evening twilight, with wisdom openest the gates of the heavens, and with understanding changest times and variest the seasons, and arrangest the stars in their watches in the sky, according to thy will. Thou createst day and night ; thou rollest away the light from before the darkness, and the darkness from before the light ; thou makest the day to pass and the night to approach, and dividest the day from the night, the Lord of hosts is thy name ; a God living and enduring continually, mayest thou reign over us for ever and ever. Blessed art thou, O Lord, who bringest on the evening twilight.

BLESSED ART THOU. This is the specific Evening Prayer, corresponding to the *yotzer* in the Morning Service. It is a prayer of great beauty. Jewish piety has ever been moved to adoration by the recurrent phenomena of Nature. The changes of the times, morning, noon, and night ; sunshine and the rolling away of light before darkness ; the ranging of the stars in their watches in the sky—all fill the worshipper with reverential wonder and awe ; see pp. 109 and 991.

at thy word. God's creative word that established the order of day and night ; Genesis 1. 3–5.

אַהֲבַת עוֹלָם בֵּית יִשְׂרָאֵל עַמְּךָ אָהָבְתָּ · תּוֹרָה וּמִצְוֹת
חֻקִּים וּמִשְׁפָּטִים אוֹתָנוּ לִמַּדְתָּ · עַל־כֵּן יְיָ אֱלֹהֵינוּ
בְּשָׁכְבֵּנוּ וּבְקוּמֵנוּ נָשִׂיחַ בְּחֻקֶּיךָ · וְנִשְׂמַח בְּדִבְרֵי תוֹרָתֶךָ
וּבְמִצְוֹתֶיךָ לְעוֹלָם וָעֶד · כִּי הֵם חַיֵּינוּ וְאֹרֶךְ יָמֵינוּ
וּבָהֶם נֶהְגֶּה יוֹמָם וָלָיְלָה · וְאַהֲבָתְךָ אַל־תָּסִיר מִמֶּנּוּ
לְעוֹלָמִים · בָּרוּךְ אַתָּה יְיָ · אוֹהֵב עַמּוֹ יִשְׂרָאֵל :

(When Prayers are not said with the Congregation, add :—

אֵל מֶלֶךְ נֶאֱמָן ;)

דברים ו' ד'-ט'

שְׁמַע יִשְׂרָאֵל יְהֹוָה אֱלֹהֵינוּ יְהֹוָה ׀ אֶחָד :

בָּרוּךְ שֵׁם כְּבוֹד מַלְכוּתוֹ לְעוֹלָם וָעֶד :

וְאָהַבְתָּ אֵת יְהֹוָה אֱלֹהֶיךָ בְּכָל־לְבָבְךָ וּבְכָל־נַפְשְׁךָ
וּבְכָל־מְאֹדֶךָ : וְהָיוּ הַדְּבָרִים הָאֵלֶּה אֲשֶׁר אָנֹכִי מְצַוְּךָ
הַיּוֹם עַל־לְבָבֶךָ : וְשִׁנַּנְתָּם לְבָנֶיךָ וְדִבַּרְתָּ בָּם בְּשִׁבְתְּךָ
בְּבֵיתֶךָ וּבְלֶכְתְּךָ בַדֶּרֶךְ וּבְשָׁכְבְּךָ וּבְקוּמֶךָ : וּקְשַׁרְתָּם
לְאוֹת עַל־יָדֶךָ וְהָיוּ לְטֹטָפֹת בֵּין עֵינֶיךָ : וּכְתַבְתָּם
עַל־מְזֻזוֹת בֵּיתֶךָ וּבִשְׁעָרֶיךָ :

דברים י"א י"ג-כ"א

וְהָיָה אִם־שָׁמֹעַ תִּשְׁמְעוּ אֶל־מִצְוֹתַי אֲשֶׁר אָנֹכִי מְצַוֶּה
אֶתְכֶם הַיּוֹם לְאַהֲבָה אֶת־יְהֹוָה אֱלֹהֵיכֶם וּלְעָבְדוֹ בְּכָל־

WITH EVERLASTING LOVE. A briefer form of the Ahavoh prayer in the Morning Service, thanking God for the sacred gift of Revelation that He granted Israel. It breathes the purest idealism. All other goods and gifts of life are transitory ; the Torah alone is the eternal

GOD THE TEACHER OF ISRAEL With everlasting love thou hast loved the house of Israel, thy people ; the Torah and commandments, statutes and judgments hast thou taught us. Therefore, O Lord our God, when we lie down and when we rise up we will meditate on thy statutes ; yea, we will rejoice in the words of thy Torah and in thy commandments for ever ; for they are our life and the length of our days, and we will meditate on them day and night. And mayest thou never take away thy love from us. Blessed art thou, O Lord, who lovest thy people Israel.

(When prayers are not said with the Congregation, say :— God, faithful King !)

Deuteronomy vi. 4—9.

THE SHEMA : HEAR, O ISRAEL See pp. 116 and 263 HEAR, O ISRAEL : THE LORD IS OUR GOD, THE LORD IS ONE.

BLESSED BE HIS · NAME, WHOSE GLORIOUS KINGDOM IS FOR EVER AND EVER.

THOU SHALT LOVE THE LORD See p. 118 ¹And thou shalt love the Lord thy God with all thine heart, and with all thy soul, and with all thy might. ⁶And these words, which I command thee this day, shall be upon thine heart : ⁷and thou shalt teach them diligently unto thy children, and shalt talk of them when thou sittest in thine house, and when thou walkest by the way, and when thou liest down, and when thou risest up. ⁸And thou shalt bind them for a sign upon thine hand, and they shall be for frontlets between thine eyes. ⁹And thou shalt write them upon the door-posts of thy house, and upon thy gates.

Deuteronomy xi. 13—21.

REWARD AND PUNISH-MENT See p. 121 ¹³And it shall come to pass, if ye shall hearken diligently unto my commandments which I command you this day, to love the Lord your God, and to serve him with all your

heritage of the Jewish people. The phrase " everlasting love " is from Jeremiah 31. 3.

our life . . . length of our days. Our continued existence as Jews is dependent on our clinging to the commandments and statutes of our Faith. When the " ceremonies " are banished from any Jewish home, its members lose touch with Divine things, and are left without God in their lives.

לְבַבְכֶם וּבְכָל־נַפְשְׁכֶם: וְנָתַתִּי מְטַר־אַרְצְכֶם בְּעִתּוֹ יוֹרֶה

וּמַלְקוֹשׁ וְאָסַפְתָּ דְגָנֶךָ וְתִירֹשְׁךָ וְיִצְהָרֶךָ: וְנָתַתִּי עֵשֶׂב

בְּשָׂדְךָ לִבְהֶמְתֶּךָ וְאָכַלְתָּ וְשָׂבָעְתָּ: הִשָּׁמְרוּ לָכֶם פֶּן־

יִפְתֶּה לְבַבְכֶם וְסַרְתֶּם וַעֲבַדְתֶּם אֱלֹהִים אֲחֵרִים

וְהִשְׁתַּחֲוִיתֶם לָהֶם: וְחָרָה אַף־יְהוָה בָּכֶם וְעָצַר אֶת־

הַשָּׁמַיִם וְלֹא־יִהְיֶה מָטָר וְהָאֲדָמָה לֹא תִתֵּן אֶת־יְבוּלָהּ

וַאֲבַדְתֶּם מְהֵרָה מֵעַל הָאָרֶץ הַטֹּבָה אֲשֶׁר יְהוָה נֹתֵן

לָכֶם: וְשַׂמְתֶּם אֶת־דְּבָרַי אֵלֶּה עַל־לְבַבְכֶם וְעַל־נַפְשְׁכֶם

וּקְשַׁרְתֶּם אֹתָם לְאוֹת עַל־יֶדְכֶם וְהָיוּ לְטוֹטָפֹת בֵּין

עֵינֵיכֶם: וְלִמַּדְתֶּם אֹתָם אֶת־בְּנֵיכֶם לְדַבֵּר בָּם בְּשִׁבְתְּךָ

בְּבֵיתֶךָ וּבְלֶכְתְּךָ בַדֶּרֶךְ וּבְשָׁכְבְּךָ וּבְקוּמֶךָ: וּכְתַבְתָּם

עַל־מְזוּזוֹת בֵּיתֶךָ וּבִשְׁעָרֶיךָ: לְמַעַן יִרְבּוּ יְמֵיכֶם וִימֵי

בְנֵיכֶם עַל הָאֲדָמָה אֲשֶׁר נִשְׁבַּע יְהוָה לַאֲבֹתֵיכֶם

לָתֵת לָהֶם כִּימֵי הַשָּׁמַיִם עַל־הָאָרֶץ:

במדבר ט״ו ל״ז-מ״א

וַיֹּאמֶר יְהוָה אֶל־מֹשֶׁה לֵּאמֹר: דַּבֵּר אֶל־בְּנֵי יִשְׂרָאֵל

וְאָמַרְתָּ אֲלֵהֶם וְעָשׂוּ לָהֶם צִיצִת עַל־כַּנְפֵי בִגְדֵיהֶם

לְדֹרֹתָם וְנָתְנוּ עַל־צִיצִת הַכָּנָף פְּתִיל תְּכֵלֶת: וְהָיָה

לָכֶם לְצִיצִת וּרְאִיתֶם אֹתוֹ וּזְכַרְתֶּם אֶת־כָּל־מִצְוֹת יְהוָה

וַעֲשִׂיתֶם אֹתָם וְלֹא תָתוּרוּ אַחֲרֵי לְבַבְכֶם וְאַחֲרֵי עֵינֵיכֶם

אֲשֶׁר־אַתֶּם זֹנִים אַחֲרֵיהֶם: לְמַעַן תִּזְכְּרוּ וַעֲשִׂיתֶם

THE
SHEMA
REWARD
AND
PUNISH-
MENT

heart and with all your soul, [14]that I will give the rain of your land in its season, the former rain and the latter rain, that thou mayest gather in thy corn, and thy wine, and thine oil. [15]And I will give grass in thy field for thy cattle, and thou shalt eat and be satisfied. [16]Take heed to yourselves, lest your heart be deceived, and ye turn aside, and serve other gods, and worship them ; [17]and the anger of the Lord be kindled against you, and he shut up the heaven, that there be no rain, and that the land yield not her fruit ; and ye perish quickly from off the good land which the Lord giveth you. [18]Therefore shall ye lay up these my words in your heart and in your soul ; and ye shall bind them for a sign upon your hand, and they shall be for frontlets between your eyes. [19]And ye shall teach them your children, talking of them when thou sittest in thine house, and when thou walkest by the way, and when thou liest down, and when thou risest up. [20]And thou shalt write them upon the doorposts of thine house, and upon thy gates : [21]that your days may be multiplied, and the days of your children, upon the land which the Lord sware unto your fathers to give them, as the days of the heavens above the earth.

Numbers xv. 37—41.

THE
MONITION
OF THE
TZITZIS
See p. 124

[37]And the Lord spake unto Moses, saying, [38]Speak unto the children of Israel, and bid them that they make them a fringe upon the corners of their garments throughout their generations, and that they put upon the fringe of each corner a cord of blue : [39]and it shall be unto you for a fringe, that ye may look upon it, and remember all the commandments of the Lord, and do them ; and that ye go not about after your own heart and your own eyes, after which ye

AND THE LORD SPAKE. Although the commandment of *tzitzis* does not apply in the night-time, this third paragraph was eventually introduced in the Evening Service, because of the clear enunciation of the duty to remember the Deliverance from Egypt. That remembrance must 'be with us all the days of our life ; *all* the days—to include the night as well as the day-time.

אֶת־כָּל־מִצְוֹתָי וִהְיִיתֶם קְדֹשִׁים לֵאלֹהֵיכֶם: אֲנִי יְהוָֹה
אֱלֹהֵיכֶם אֲשֶׁר הוֹצֵאתִי אֶתְכֶם מֵאֶרֶץ מִצְרַיִם לִהְיוֹת
לָכֶם לֵאלֹהִים אֲנִי יְהוָֹה אֱלֹהֵיכֶם:

אֱמֶת וֶאֱמוּנָה כָּל־זֹאת וְקַיָּם עָלֵינוּ כִּי הוּא יְיָ אֱלֹהֵינוּ
וְאֵין זוּלָתוֹ וַאֲנַחְנוּ יִשְׂרָאֵל עַמּוֹ · הַפּוֹדֵנוּ מִיַּד מְלָכִים
מַלְכֵּנוּ הַגּוֹאֲלֵנוּ מִכַּף כָּל־הֶעָרִיצִים · הָאֵל הַנִּפְרָע לָנוּ
מִצָּרֵינוּ וְהַמְשַׁלֵּם גְּמוּל לְכָל־אֹיְבֵי נַפְשֵׁנוּ · הָעֹשֶׂה גְדֹלוֹת
עַד־אֵין חֵקֶר וְנִפְלָאוֹת עַד־אֵין מִסְפָּר · הַשָּׂם נַפְשֵׁנוּ
בַּחַיִּים וְלֹא־נָתַן לַמּוֹט רַגְלֵנוּ · הַמַּדְרִיכֵנוּ עַל־בָּמוֹת
אוֹיְבֵינוּ וַיָּרֶם קַרְנֵנוּ עַל־כָּל־שׂנְאֵינוּ · הָעֹשֶׂה־לָּנוּ נִסִּים
וּנְקָמָה בְּפַרְעֹה אוֹתֹת וּמוֹפְתִים בְּאַדְמַת בְּנֵי־חָם · הַמַּכֶּה
בְעֶבְרָתוֹ כָּל־בְּכוֹרֵי מִצְרָיִם וַיּוֹצֵא אֶת־עַמּוֹ יִשְׂרָאֵל
מִתּוֹכָם לְחֵרוּת עוֹלָם · הַמַּעֲבִיר בָּנָיו בֵּין גִּזְרֵי יַם־סוּף
אֶת־רוֹדְפֵיהֶם וְאֶת־שׂנְאֵיהֶם בִּתְהֹמוֹת טִבַּע · וְרָאוּ בָנָיו
גְבוּרָתוֹ שִׁבְּחוּ וְהוֹדוּ לִשְׁמוֹ וּמַלְכוּתוֹ בְּרָצוֹן קִבְּלוּ
עֲלֵיהֶם · מֹשֶׁה וּבְנֵי יִשְׂרָאֵל לְךָ עָנוּ שִׁירָה בְּשִׂמְחָה
רַבָּה · וְאָמְרוּ כֻלָּם ·

מִי־כָמֹכָה בָּאֵלִם יְהוָֹה מִי כָּמֹכָה נֶאְדָּר בַּקֹּדֶשׁ
נוֹרָא תְהִלֹּת עֹשֵׂה פֶלֶא:

מַלְכוּתְךָ רָאוּ בָנֶיךָ בּוֹקֵעַ יָם לִפְנֵי מֹשֶׁה · זֶה אֵלִי
עָנוּ · וְאָמְרוּ · יְהוָֹה יִמְלֹךְ לְעֹלָם וָעֶד:

go astray : ⁴⁰that ye may remember and do all my commandments, and be holy unto your God. ⁴¹I am the Lord your God, who brought you out of the land of Egypt, to be your God : I am the Lord your God.

GOD THE REDEEMER   True and trustworthy is all this, and it is established with us that he is the Lord our God, and there is none beside him, and that we, Israel, are his people. It is he who redeemed us from the hand of kings, even our King, who delivered us from the grasp of all tyrants ; the God, who on our behalf dealt out punishment to our adversaries, and *Job* 9.10 requited all our mortal enemies ; who doeth great things *Psalm* 66. 9 past finding out, yea, and wonders without number ; who maintaineth us in life, and hath not suffered our feet to slip ; who made us overcome and conquer our enemies, and exalted our strength above all them that hated us ; who wrought for us miracles and retribution upon Pharaoh, signs and wonders in the land of the children of Ham ; who in his wrath smote all the first-born of Egypt, and brought forth his people Israel from among them to everlasting freedom ; who made his children pass through the divided Red Sea, but sank their pursuers and their enemies in its depths. Then his children beheld his might ; they praised and gave thanks unto his Name, and willingly accepted his sovereignty. Moses and the children of Israel sang a song unto thee with great joy, saying, all of them,

Exodus 15. 11   WHO IS LIKE UNTO THEE, O LORD, AMONG THE MIGHTY ? WHO IS LIKE UNTO THEE, GLORIOUS IN HOLINESS, REVERED IN PRAISES, DOING WONDERS ?

Thy children beheld thy sovereign power, as thou didst cleave the sea before Moses : they exclaimed, This is my *Exodus* 15. 18 God ! and said, THE LORD SHALL REIGN FOR EVER AND EVER.

TRUE AND TRUSTWORTHY. The Shema is followed, as in the Morning Service, by an Attestation to its truths, passing into a jubilant recollection of the Redemption from Egypt, and of the redeemed triumphantly proclaiming the sovereignty of God.

וְנֶאֱמַר כִּי־פָדָה יְיָ אֶת־יַעֲקֹב וּגְאָלוֹ מִיַּד חָזָק מִמֶּנּוּ ·

בָּרוּךְ אַתָּה יְיָ · גָּאַל יִשְׂרָאֵל :

הַשְׁכִּיבֵנוּ יְיָ אֱלֹהֵינוּ לְשָׁלוֹם וְהַעֲמִידֵנוּ מַלְכֵּנוּ לְחַיִּים ·

וּפְרוֹשׂ עָלֵינוּ סֻכַּת שְׁלוֹמֶךָ · וְתַקְּנֵנוּ בְּעֵצָה טוֹבָה

מִלְּפָנֶיךָ · וְהוֹשִׁיעֵנוּ לְמַעַן שְׁמֶךָ · וְהָגֵן בַּעֲדֵנוּ וְהָסֵר

מֵעָלֵינוּ אוֹיֵב דֶּבֶר וְחֶרֶב וְרָעָב וְיָגוֹן · וְהָסֵר שָׂטָן

מִלְּפָנֵינוּ וּמֵאַחֲרֵינוּ · וּבְצֵל כְּנָפֶיךָ תַּסְתִּירֵנוּ כִּי אֵל

שׁוֹמְרֵנוּ וּמַצִּילֵנוּ אָתָּה כִּי אֵל מֶלֶךְ חַנּוּן וְרַחוּם אָתָּה ·

וּשְׁמוֹר צֵאתֵנוּ וּבוֹאֵנוּ לְחַיִּים וּלְשָׁלוֹם מֵעַתָּה וְעַד

עוֹלָם · וּפְרוֹשׂ עָלֵינוּ סֻכַּת שְׁלוֹמֶךָ · בָּרוּךְ אַתָּה יְיָ ·

הַפּוֹרֵשׂ סֻכַּת שָׁלוֹם עָלֵינוּ וְעַל כָּל־עַמּוֹ יִשְׂרָאֵל וְעַל־

יְרוּשָׁלַיִם :

On שַׁבָּת:—

וְשָׁמְרוּ בְנֵי־יִשְׂרָאֵל אֶת־הַשַּׁבָּת לַעֲשׂוֹת אֶת־הַשַּׁבָּת

CAUSE US . . . TO LIE DOWN. Or, "grant, O Lord, that we may
lie down ". This is the second of the benedictions that follow the
Shema in the evenings. In it we pray for protection during the night
when man feels the need of God's watchfulness over him far more than
by day.

the adversary. Heb. *Satan.* Jewish thought conceives of angels
as absolutely subordinate to God. An angel is God's "messenger",
which is the literal meaning of the Hebrew word מַלְאָךְ, of the Greek
word *angelos*, and of the English word "angel", derived from it. In
the Jewish Prayer Book, angels are always instruments of the Divine

Jeremiah
31. 11

And it is said, For the Lord hath delivered Jacob, and redeemed him from the hand of him that was stronger than he. Blessed art thou, O Lord, who hast redeemed Israel.

GOD THE
GUARDIAN

Cause us, O Lord our God, to lie down in peace, and raise us up, O our King, unto life. Spread over us the protection of thy peace ; direct us aright through thine own good counsel ; save us for thy Name's sake ; be thou a shield about us ; remove from us every enemy, pestilence, sword, famine and sorrow ; remove also the adversary from before us and from behind us. O shelter us beneath the shadow of thy wings ; for thou, O God, art our Guardian and our Deliverer ; yea, thou, O God, art a gracious and merciful King ; and guard our going and our coming unto life and unto peace from this time forth and for evermore ; yea, spread over us the protection of thy peace. Blessed art thou, O Lord, who spreadest the protection of peace over us and over all thy people Israel, and over Jerusalem.

On Sabbaths :—

Exodus
31. 16, 17

[16]And the children of Israel shall keep the Sabbath, to observe the Sabbath throughout their generations, for an

beneficence. *Satan* may seem to be an exception, but that name is not used of a particular personality, but in the general sense of " adversary ". Even when he is personified in poetry, as in Job, he has no independent power, but is an instrument of the Divine Plan. " The whole conception has now no place in Judaism, except in popular folklore. In the Prayer Book, Satan is mostly identical with the *evil impulse*, the lower passions which are a hindrance to man's pursuit of the nobler aims of life. It is against the dominance of this impulse that the Israelite still prays " (Abrahams). *The adversary*, therefore, is the man, spirit, or evil impulse that seduces us to do wrong.

who spreadest . . . Jerusalem. This is instead of the week-night ending, " who guardest thy people Israel forever ". The Sabbath itself is Israel's guardian, and so the benediction was changed to express the peace which comes to the Jewish home with Sabbath eve.

לְדֹרֹתָם בְּרִית עוֹלָם : בֵּינִי וּבֵין בְּנֵי יִשְׂרָאֵל אוֹת הִוא
לְעֹלָם כִּי־שֵׁשֶׁת יָמִים עָשָׂה יְהוָֹה אֶת־הַשָּׁמַיִם וְאֶת־
הָאָרֶץ וּבַיּוֹם הַשְּׁבִיעִי שָׁבַת וַיִּנָּפַשׁ :

On סֻכּוֹת and שָׁבֻעוֹת‏, פֶּסַח :—

וַיְדַבֵּר מֹשֶׁה אֶת־מֹעֲדֵי יְהוָֹה אֶל־בְּנֵי יִשְׂרָאֵל :

On רֹאשׁ הַשָּׁנָה :—

תִּקְעוּ בַחֹדֶשׁ שׁוֹפָר בַּכֶּסֶה לְיוֹם חַגֵּנוּ : כִּי חֹק לְיִשְׂרָאֵל
הוּא מִשְׁפָּט לֵאלֹהֵי יַעֲקֹב :

On יוֹם כִּפּוּר :—

כִּי בַיּוֹם הַזֶּה יְכַפֵּר עֲלֵיכֶם לְטַהֵר אֶתְכֶם מִכֹּל חַטֹּאתֵיכֶם
לִפְנֵי יְהוָֹה תִּטְהָרוּ :

p. 106. ‏, חֲצִי קַדִּישׁ

On Festivals say the appropriate עֲמִידוֹת.

אֲדֹנָי שְׂפָתַי תִּפְתָּח וּפִי יַגִּיד תְּהִלָּתֶךָ :

בָּרוּךְ אַתָּה יְיָ אֱלֹהֵינוּ וֵאלֹהֵי אֲבוֹתֵינוּ · אֱלֹהֵי
אַבְרָהָם אֱלֹהֵי יִצְחָק וֵאלֹהֵי יַעֲקֹב · הָאֵל הַגָּדוֹל הַגִּבּוֹר
וְהַנּוֹרָא אֵל עֶלְיוֹן · גּוֹמֵל חֲסָדִים טוֹבִים וְקוֹנֵה הַכֹּל ·

Since Gaonic times the two Biblical verses are here inserted on
Sabbaths ; one verse for the three Pilgrim Festivals, and one each for
New Year and the Day of Atonement.

everlasting covenant. ¹⁷It is a sign between me and the children of Israel for ever, that in six days the Lord made the heavens and the earth, and on the seventh day he ceased from work and rested.

On Passover, Pentecost and Tabernacles, say :—

Leviticus 23. 44   And Moses declared the set feasts of the Lord unto the children of Israel.

On New Year :—

Psalm 81. 4, 5   Blow the horn on the new moon, in the time appointed, for our day of festival. For it is a statute for Israel, a decree of the God of Jacob.

On the Day of Atonement :—

Leviticus 16. 30   For on this day shall atonement be made for you to cleanse you ; from all your sins shall ye be clean before the Lord.

Kaddish, p. 107.
On Festivals say the appropriate Amidah.

Psalm 51. 17   O Lord, open thou my lips, and my mouth shall declare thy praise.

AMIDAH   Blessed art thou, O Lord our God and God of our fathers,
I. THE GOD OF HISTORY   God of Abraham, God of Isaac, and God of Jacob, the great, mighty and revered God, the most high God, who bestowest lovingkindnesses, and art Master of all things ; who rememberest the pious deeds of the patriarchs, and in love

---

blow the horn. See p. 228.
for on this day. See pp. 890 and 891.
an everlasting covenant. The weekly hallowing of the Sabbath is Israel's proclamation of belief in God as the Creator and Ruler of the Universe, and is evidence of our obedience to His Will. Such proclamation is a perennial renewal of the Covenant that God established with the Fathers, Abraham, Isaac and Jacob.

O Lord, open. Since Talmudic times these words are recited as introductory to the Shemoneh Esreh when it is read in silence.

THE AMIDAH.

The opening benedictions embody the fundamental beliefs of Judaism in God Almighty and All-holy, in His Covenant with the Fathers, the Election of Israel, the Messianic Redemption and the Immortality of the soul.

וְזוֹכֵר חַסְדֵי אָבוֹת וּמֵבִיא גוֹאֵל לִבְנֵי בְנֵיהֶם לְמַעַן שְׁמוֹ בְּאַהֲבָה ׃

On שַׁבָּת שׁוּבָה say :—

זָכְרֵנוּ לַחַיִּים מֶלֶךְ חָפֵץ בַּחַיִּים ׳ וְכָתְבֵנוּ בְּסֵפֶר הַחַיִּים ׳ לְמַעַנְךָ אֱלֹהִים חַיִּים ׃

מֶלֶךְ עוֹזֵר וּמוֹשִׁיעַ וּמָגֵן ׳ בָּרוּךְ אַתָּה יְיָ ׳ מָגֵן אַבְרָהָם ׃

אַתָּה גִבּוֹר לְעוֹלָם אֲדֹנָי מְחַיֵּה מֵתִים אַתָּה רַב לְהוֹשִׁיעַ ׳

From שַׁבָּת בְּרֵאשִׁית until the First Day of פֶּסַח, say :—

מַשִּׁיב הָרוּחַ וּמוֹרִיד הַגֶּשֶׁם ׃

מְכַלְכֵּל חַיִּים בְּחֶסֶד מְחַיֵּה מֵתִים בְּרַחֲמִים רַבִּים ׳ סוֹמֵךְ

First Benediction : *The God of History.*

In this benediction, God is adored as the God of the Fathers, the God of History, and the God Who in love will bring Messianic redemption to the children of the Patriarchs.

blessed. For the significance of this word, as well as of " Thou " when addressed to the Deity, see p. 10.

It is customary to bow at the word " blessed ", and again stand erect at the word " Lord ".

God of our fathers . . . Jacob. These words are drawn from the Revelation at the burning bush (Exodus 3. 15). They are based on Israel's fundamental conviction of the existence of One God, and take the mind of the worshipper back to the dawn of Israel's religious beginnings. In invoking the God of our Fathers, we, as their loyal children, adore the same God—*our* God.

great, mighty and revered. Deuteronomy 10. 17. The Rabbis strongly opposed any further heaping of Divine epithets in prayer.

bestowest lovingkindnesses. Or, " lavishest tender love " (Pool).

Master of all things. Or, " Possessor of all things " (Genesis 14. 19).

rememberest the pious deeds. Thou causest the virtues of the Fathers to bring salvation to their children's children. The Jewish doctrine of the " Merits of the Fathers " (זכות אבות) teaches that the piety of the fathers is accounted to the children as righteousness. " That man is best able to advance on the road to moral perfection, who starts with the accumulated spiritual heritage of righteous ancestors " (Levy).

wilt bring a redeemer to their children's children for thy Name's sake.

[*During the Ten Days of Repentance, say* :—

Remember us unto life, O King, who delightest in life, and inscribe us in the book of life, for thine own sake, O living God.]

O King, Helper, Saviour and Shield. Blessed art thou, O Lord, the Shield of Abraham.

II. THE GOD OF NATURE

Thou, O Lord, art mighty for ever, thou revivest the dead, thou art mighty to save.

[*From the day after Simchas Torah until the Eve of Passover, say* :

Thou causest the wind to blow and the rain to fall.]

Thou sustainest the living with lovingkindness, revivest the dead with great mercy, supportest the falling, healest

---

in love. God has chosen, and will redeem, Israel not solely for Israel's merits, but from love ; Deuteronomy 7. 7, 8.

bring a redeemer. See p. 254.

remember us. " Grant us life, O Thou who delightest in dispensing the blessings of life "—The words go back to the ninth century, the Gaonic age. They refer to the Heavenly Judgment, as that thought is uppermost in Jewish hearts during the Ten Days of Repentance.

For the idea of *Book of Life*, see p. 165.

for thine own sake. i.e. to fulfil Thy purposes.

King. The ruler of our destinies.

Helper. In all the fluctuations of life.

Saviour. From destruction, moral and physical.

Shield. He who prevents ills and malevolent influences from overcoming us.

blessed art thou. Of all the Eighteen Benedictions, the first alone both begins and ends with these words, which are the mark of a *berochah*. All the others end, but do not begin, as a blessing ; they are deemed to be merely continuations of the first benediction.

Shield of Abraham. Genesis 15. 1. If, like Abraham, we are ready to meet every Divine behest with " Here I am ", He is also a Shield unto us.

Second Benediction : *the God of Nature.*

The appeal to History, the peculiar sphere of God's revelation, is now reinforced by an appeal to Nature as displaying the power and goodness of God. From the distant past, the worshipper turns to the distant future, and hails God as the King who alone is mighty to save. The God of the Past and Future is also the God Who lovingly sustains the living in all the vicissitudes of earthly existence, and whose infinite faithfulness remembers and redeems them that sleep in the dust.

נוֹפְלִים וְרוֹפֵא חוֹלִים וּמַתִּיר אֲסוּרִים וּמְקַיֵּם אֱמוּנָתוֹ

לִישֵׁנֵי עָפָר · מִי כָמְוֹךָ בַּעַל גְּבוּרוֹת וּמִי דְּוֹמֶה לָּךְ ·

מֶלֶךְ מֵמִית וּמְחַיֶּה וּמַצְמִיחַ יְשׁוּעָה ·

On שַׁבָּת שׁוּבָה say :—

מִי כָמְוֹךָ אַב הָרַחֲמִים זוֹכֵר יְצוּרָיו לַחַיִּים בְּרַחֲמִים ·

וְנֶאֱמָן אַתָּה לְהַחֲיוֹת מֵתִים · בָּרוּךְ אַתָּה יְיָ · מְחַיֵּה

הַמֵּתִים :

אַתָּה קָדוֹשׁ וְשִׁמְךָ קָדוֹשׁ וּקְדוֹשִׁים בְּכָל־יוֹם יְהַלְלוּךָ

סֶּלָה · בָּרוּךְ אַתָּה יְיָ · הָאֵל הַקָּדוֹשׁ :

On שַׁבָּת שׁוּבָה conclude the Blessing thus :—

הַמֶּלֶךְ הַקָּדוֹשׁ :

אַתָּה קִדַּשְׁתָּ אֶת־יוֹם הַשְּׁבִיעִי לִשְׁמֶךָ · תַּכְלִית מַעֲשֵׂה

שָׁמַיִם וָאָרֶץ · וּבֵרַכְתּוֹ מִכָּל־הַיָּמִים וְקִדַּשְׁתּוֹ מִכָּל־

הַזְּמַנִּים · וְכֵן כָּתוּב בְּתוֹרָתֶךָ :

art mighty forever. God's protection does not cease at the portals of the grave. He is mightier than death, and in His eyes the dead have not died.

revivest the dead. He awakes the dead to new life. This emphatic statement concerning the resurrection was directed against the world-lings who disputed the deathlessness of the soul, its return to God, and its continued separate existence after its reunion with the Divine Source of being.

wind to blow. Nature's perennial renewal declares the omnipotence of God This is especially so to an agricultural people, for whom the due ordering of wind and rain alone renders existence possible. To the Rabbis, the changing panorama of the seasons, the resurrection of life every spring, was the greatest of miracles. It was their conviction that, even as the rain wondrously wakes to life the seed slumbering in

the sick, freest the bound, and keepest thy faith to them that sleep in the dust. Who is like unto thee, Lord.of mighty acts, and who resembleth thee, O King, who orderest death and restorest life, and causest salvation to spring forth ?

[*During the Ten Days of Repentance, say* :—
Who is like unto thee, Father of mercy, who in mercy rememberest thy creatures unto life ?]

Yea, faithful art thou to revive the dead. Blessed art thou, O Lord, who revivest the dead.

III. SANCTIFICATION OF GOD   Thou art holy, and thy Name is holy, and holy beings praise thee daily. (Selah.) Blessed art thou, O Lord, the holy God. | *During the Ten Days of Repentance conclude the Blessing thus* :—the holy King.

IV. PREEMINENCE OF THE SABBATH   Thou didst hallow the seventh day unto thy Name, as the end of the creation of heaven and earth ; thou didst bless it above all days, and didst hallow it above all seasons ; and thus it is written in thy Torah :

the soil, so would God awaken the dead to new life. Nature's wonders, they held, were the strongest proof that their Author was a God of lovingkindness Who supports the falling, heals the sick, and frees His children from all manner of woe and suffering.

causest salvation to spring forth. " And in the flowering of Thy saving power givest life " (Pool).

Father of Mercy. In the clauses inserted in the preceding benediction during the Solemn Season, God is addressed as " King " ; here He is invoked as " Father ". Often these two terms are combined, and then the order is always, " Our Father, Our King " אבינו מלכנו. In all these insertions, there is a prayer for *life*.

Third Benediction : *Sanctification.*

ATTOH KODOSH. *Thou art holy.* In the third benediction, God is hailed as the Holy God of a Holy People.

holy beings. i.e. those that strive to live lives of holiness. The reference is to Israel, whose sacred mission is the sanctification of God's Name in word and in deed (Baer).

Fourth Benediction : *Pre-eminence of the Sabbath.*

THOU DIDST HALLOW THE SEVENTH DAY. The first three and the last three of Eighteen Benedictions recur in all Amidahs. They are increased by one special benediction on the Sabbath—varying in form in all services, Evening, Morning, Mussaf and Afternoon.

וַיְכֻלּוּ הַשָּׁמַיִם וְהָאָרֶץ וְכָל צְבָאָם : וַיְכַל אֱלֹהִים בַּיּוֹם
הַשְּׁבִיעִי מְלַאכְתּוֹ אֲשֶׁר עָשָׂה וַיִּשְׁבֹּת בַּיּוֹם הַשְּׁבִיעִי
מִכָּל־מְלַאכְתּוֹ אֲשֶׁר עָשָׂה : וַיְבָרֶךְ אֱלֹהִים אֶת־יוֹם
הַשְּׁבִיעִי וַיְקַדֵּשׁ אֹתוֹ כִּי בוֹ שָׁבַת מִכָּל־מְלַאכְתּוֹ אֲשֶׁר־
בָּרָא אֱלֹהִים לַעֲשׂוֹת :

אֱלֹהֵינוּ וֵאלֹהֵי אֲבוֹתֵינוּ • רְצֵה בִמְנוּחָתֵנוּ קַדְּשֵׁנוּ
בְּמִצְוֹתֶיךָ וְתֵן חֶלְקֵנוּ בְּתוֹרָתֶךָ • שַׂבְּעֵנוּ מִטּוּבֶךָ וְשַׂמְּחֵנוּ

1. AND THE HEAVEN. *host.* lit. " army ' ; the totality of the
universe conceived as an organized whole, a cosmos.
2. *seventh day.* " What did the world lack after the six days' toil ?
Rest. So God finished His labours on the seventh day by the creation
of a day of rest, the Sabbath " (Midrash).
rested. This ascribing of human actions and feelings to God is called
anthropomorphism, and is employed in the Bible to make intelligible to
the finite, human mind that which relates to the Infinite. The Talmudic
saying, דברה תורה כלשון בני אדם. " The Torah speaks the ordinary
language of men," is a leading principle in Scripture interpretation.
3. *God blessed.* The Creator endowed the Sabbath with a blessing
which would be experienced by all who observed it. On the Sabbath,
the Talmud says, the Jew receives an " additional soul," נשמה יתרה ; *i.e.*
his spiritual nature is heightened through the influence of the holy day.
hallowed. The Sabbath demands more than stoppage of work. It is
specifically marked off as a day consecrated to God and the life of the
spirit.
created and made. lit. " which God created to make," *i.e.* to continue
acting (Ibn Ezra, Abarbanel) throughout time by the unceasing operation of Divine laws. As the Rabbis say, the work of creation continues,
and the world is still in the process of creation, so long as the conflict
between good and evil remains undecided. Ethically the world is thus
still " unfinished," and it is man's glorious privilege to help finish it.
He can by his life hasten the triumph of the forces of good in the universe.
OUR GOD. This is the special Sabbath prayer in the Amidah.
The Sabbath Service is for joyful communion with God. No mention
of guilt, sin or wrongdoing, and no thought of want, tribulation or

Genesis 2. 1–3   ¹And the heaven and the earth were finished and all their host. ²And on the seventh day God had finished his work which he had made ; and he rested on the seventh day from all his work which he had made. ³And God blessed the seventh day, and he hallowed it, because he rested thereon from all his work which God had created and made.

SABBATH PRAYER   Our God and God of our fathers, accept our rest ; hallow us by thy commandments, and grant our portion in

sorrow, are to mar the Sabbath serenity of the worshipper. Hence the thirteen intermediate petitions of the weekday Amidah are replaced in all the Sabbath Amidahs by this central prayer of wonderful spirituality and beauty. Its ancient name was, " holiness of the day ".

accept our rest. i.e. may our rest be acceptable to Thee, and be such as will increase our moral strength and deepen our consecration to life's noblest purposes. Sabbath rest is more than mere abstention from physical work ; and, therefore, must include worship and Scripture-reading, with their consequent strengthening of religious habit in life.

hallow us by thy commandments. Through obedience to God's will, we become " holy " ; *i.e.* separated from the things that are ignoble and vile, and at one with all things that make for righteousness and humanity. Thy commandments, *mitzvoth*, the ceremonies and practical duties of Jewish religious life, are means of such hallowing ; their main purpose being " to purge our being of all moral dross ", לצרף בהן את הבריות, and train us to discipline and self-restraint. Observance of the *mitzvoth* binds us to God, and keeps us " God-minded ". It is impossible to convey to those who have not experienced it, the feeling of holy joy diffused in the humblest Jewish home by such ceremonies as the Kiddush, or the kindling of the Chanukah lights. Both the home and those that dwell in it become hallowed by their observance. The Israelite obtains sanctification not through vagaries of his own fancy, nor by following any theological fashion of the hour ; but by loyalty to the historic institutions and teachings of his Faith.

grant our portion. That we participate in the blessings which flow from the observance of the Divine behests of the Torah. The Torah is the possession of the *Congregation* of Israel, and each Israelite should be fully conscious, and in real possession, of his share in the infinite riches of its holiness.

בִּישׁוּעָתֶךָ וְטַהֵר לִבֵּנוּ לְעָבְדְּךָ בֶּאֱמֶת · וְהַנְחִילֵנוּ יְיָ
אֱלֹהֵינוּ בְּאַהֲבָה וּבְרָצוֹן שַׁבַּת קָדְשֶׁךָ · וְיָנוּחוּ בָהּ יִשְׂרָאֵל
מְקַדְּשֵׁי שְׁמֶךָ · בָּרוּךְ אַתָּה יְיָ · מְקַדֵּשׁ הַשַּׁבָּת :

רְצֵה יְיָ אֱלֹהֵינוּ בְּעַמְּךָ יִשְׂרָאֵל וּבִתְפִלָּתָם · וְהָשֵׁב
אֶת-הָעֲבוֹדָה לִדְבִיר בֵּיתֶךָ · וְאִשֵּׁי יִשְׂרָאֵל וּתְפִלָּתָם

thy goodness. The material and spiritual blessings which Thou deemest good for the children of men.

gladden us with thy salvation. There is no happiness comparable to that of the trustful soul which has placed its destinies in the hands of God.

salvation. This word is differently understood by Jews and non-Jews. To the non-Jew, *salvation* means redemption from sin here, and deliverance from its consequences thereafter. (For these conceptions, the Jew uses the words " repentance for sin " and " forgiveness of sin "). In the Psalms and Siddur, however, *salvation* denotes either deliverance from distress and peril, or freedom for the moral expansion of our higher nature. It is something that saves us from our lower self, illumines and regenerates our soul, and makes us willing instruments of God's Eternal plan. The Sabbath is a " fountain " of salvation, because from it such blessed feelings flow.

purify our hearts. With the psalmist we pray, " Create in me a pure heart ", so that every desire within us be obedient to purity, righteousness, and holy living. " Let no pride or self-seeking, no covetousness or revenge, no impure mixture or unhandsome purposes, no little ends and low imaginations, pollute my spirit, and unhallow any of my words and actions " (Jeremy Taylor).

to serve thee in truth. The pure heart renders possible sincere service of God in public or private worship, as in public or private lovingkindness to our fellowmen.

let us inherit. The Sabbath is a noble heritage, to which we are to cling with all our being, and leave nothing undone to enable every Israelite to retain it. In the words of a noble Jew : " If I were asked to

thy Torah ; satisfy us with thy goodness, and gladden us with thy salvation ; purify our hearts to serve thee in truth ; and in thy love and favour, O Lord our God, let us inherit thy holy Sabbath; and may Israel, who sanctify thy Name, rest thereon. Blessed art thou, O Lord, who hallowest the Sabbath.

v.
RESTORA-
TION OF
TEMPLE
SERVICE

Accept, O Lord our God, thy people Israel and their prayer ; restore the service to the inner sanctuary of thy

single out one of the great historical institutions more essential for our preservation than all others, I would not hesitate to declare that it is the observance of the Sabbath. Without this, the home and the Synagogue, the festivals and the holy days, the language and the history of our people, will gradually disappear. If the Sabbath will be maintained by those who have observed it and will be restored to those who have abandoned it, then the permanence of Judaism is assured. To all who are prosperous, the question of the observance of the Sabbath involves the sacrifice of a luxury, nothing more . . . Every Jew who has it within his power should aid in the effort to restore the Sabbath to the man from whom it has been taken away. No deeds of charity or philanthropy, no sacrifices of time or fortune made by any Jew, at all equals in beneficent result the expenditure of time and money looking towards the re-establishment of the Jewish Sabbath among the Jewish people. No amount of prating about morals will ever take the place of rooted habits ruthlessly plucked out " (Cyrus Adler).

who hallowest the Sabbath. In the similar prayer of the Festival Amidah, the phrase is *who hallowest Israel and the sacred seasons.* That mention of Israel is due to the fact that the Festivals are specifically Israelite in character. Not so the Sabbath : it preceded the selection of Israel, and applies to the whole of mankind. Hence the omission of " Israel " in the Sabbath benediction.

The three concluding benedictions consist of prayers for the re-establishment of the Divine Service at Jerusalem ; thanksgiving for God's daily wonders towards us ; and a Prayer for Peace and Prosperity.

Fifth Benediction : *For the Temple Service.*

Even as the truth of pure Monotheism came from the Temple on Mt. Zion, so may that Sanctuary in future be the source from which will spread the true knowledge of God to all the children of men.

service. Heb. *avodah* ; originally meant the Temple ritual, and later divine worship generally.

restore the service. This phrase was formulated when the Temple had been destroyed ; The concluding phrase, *who restorest thy divine presence*, was originally *For Thee alone do we serve in reverence.*

בְּאַהֲבָה תְּקַבֵּל בְּרָצוֹן · וּתְהִי לְרָצוֹן תָּמִיד עֲבוֹדַת
יִשְׂרָאֵל עַמֶּךָ ·

On רֹאשׁ חֹדֶשׁ and of חֹל הַמּוֹעֵד of פֶּסַח and of סֻכּוֹת say אֱלֹהֵינוּ וכו׳,
to אַתָּה, p. 148.

וְתֶחֱזֶינָה עֵינֵינוּ בְּשׁוּבְךָ לְצִיּוֹן בְּרַחֲמִים · בָּרוּךְ אַתָּה
יְיָ · הַמַּחֲזִיר שְׁכִינָתוֹ לְצִיּוֹן:

מוֹדִים אֲנַחְנוּ לָךְ שָׁאַתָּה הוּא יְיָ אֱלֹהֵינוּ וֵאלֹהֵי
אֲבוֹתֵינוּ לְעוֹלָם וָעֶד · צוּר חַיֵּינוּ מָגֵן יִשְׁעֵנוּ אַתָּה הוּא
לְדוֹר וָדוֹר · נוֹדֶה לְּךָ וּנְסַפֵּר תְּהִלָּתֶךָ עַל־חַיֵּינוּ הַמְּסוּרִים
בְּיָדֶךָ וְעַל נִשְׁמוֹתֵינוּ הַפְּקוּדוֹת לָךְ · וְעַל נִסֶּיךָ שֶׁבְּכָל־
יוֹם עִמָּנוּ וְעַל נִפְלְאוֹתֶיךָ וְטוֹבוֹתֶיךָ שֶׁבְּכָל־עֵת עֶרֶב
וָבֹקֶר וְצָהֳרָיִם · הַטּוֹב כִּי לֹא־כָלוּ רַחֲמֶיךָ · וְהַמְרַחֵם
כִּי לֹא־תַמּוּ חֲסָדֶיךָ מֵעוֹלָם קִוִּינוּ לָךְ:

On חֲנֻכָּה say עַל הַנִּסִּים, pp. 150, 152.

וְעַל־כֻּלָּם יִתְבָּרַךְ וְיִתְרוֹמַם שִׁמְךָ מַלְכֵּנוּ תָּמִיד לְעוֹלָם
וָעֶד:

On שַׁבָּת שׁוּבָה say:—

וּכְתוֹב לְחַיִּים טוֹבִים כָּל־בְּנֵי בְרִיתֶךָ:

וְכֹל הַחַיִּים יוֹדוּךָ סֶּלָה · וִיהַלְלוּ אֶת־שִׁמְךָ בֶּאֱמֶת ·
הָאֵל יְשׁוּעָתֵנוּ וְעֶזְרָתֵנוּ סֶלָה · בָּרוּךְ אַתָּה יְיָ · הַטּוֹב
שִׁמְךָ וּלְךָ נָאֶה לְהוֹדוֹת:

1

house ; receive in love and favour both the offerings of Israel and their prayer ; and may the worship of thy people Israel be ever acceptable unto thee.

[*On New Moon and the Intermediate Days of Passover and Tabernacles, the prayer " Our God " to " merciful God and King ", p. 149, is added*]

And let our eyes behold thy return in mercy to Zion. Blessed art thou, O Lord, who restorest thy divine presence unto Zion.

VI. THANKS-GIVING FOR GOD'S UNFAIL-ING MERCIES We give thanks unto thee, for thou art the Lord our God and the God of our fathers for ever and ever ; thou art the Rock of our lives, the Shield of our salvation through every generation. We will give thanks unto thee and declare thy praise for our lives which are committed unto thy hand, and for our souls which are in thy charge, and for thy miracles, which are daily with us, and for thy wonders and thy benefits, which are wrought at all times, evening, morn and noon. O thou who art all-good, whose mercies fail not ; thou, merciful Being, whose lovingkindnesses never cease, we have ever hoped in thee.

[*On Chanukah, add prayers on pp.* 151, 153.]

For all these acts thy Name, O our King, shall be continually blessed and exalted for ever and ever.

[*During the Ten Days of Repentance say* :—
O inscribe all the children of thy covenant for a happy life.]

And everything that liveth shall give thanks unto thee for ever, and shall praise thy Name in truth, O God, our salvation and our help. (Selah.) Blessed art thou, O Lord, whose Name is All-good, and unto whom it is becoming to give thanks.

Sixth Benediction : *Thanksgiving for God's Unfailing Mercies.*
We give thanks. A singularly beautiful anthem of gratitude for God's manifold mercies to us.

שָׁלוֹם רָב עַל יִשְׂרָאֵל עַמְּךָ תָּשִׂים לְעוֹלָם · כִּי אַתָּה
הוּא מֶלֶךְ אָדוֹן לְכָל הַשָּׁלוֹם · וְטוֹב בְּעֵינֶיךָ לְבָרֵךְ אֶת־
עַמְּךָ יִשְׂרָאֵל בְּכָל־עֵת וּבְכָל־שָׁעָה בִּשְׁלוֹמֶךָ :

On שַׁבָּת שׁוּבָה say :—

בָּרוּךְ אַתָּה יְיָ ·
בְּסֵפֶר חַיִּים בְּרָכָה וְשָׁלוֹם וּפַרְנָסָה

הַמְבָרֵךְ אֶת־עַמּוֹ
טוֹבָה נִזָּכֵר וְנִכָּתֵב לְפָנֶיךָ אֲנַחְנוּ וְכָל־
עַמְּךָ בֵּית יִשְׂרָאֵל לְחַיִּים טוֹבִים

יִשְׂרָאֵל בַּשָּׁלוֹם :
וּלְשָׁלוֹם · בָּרוּךְ אַתָּה יְיָ · עוֹשֵׂה
הַשָּׁלוֹם :

אֱלֹהַי · נְצוֹר לְשׁוֹנִי מֵרָע וּשְׂפָתַי מִדַּבֵּר מִרְמָה ·
וְלִמְקַלְלַי נַפְשִׁי תִדּוֹם וְנַפְשִׁי כֶּעָפָר לַכֹּל תִּהְיֶה : פְּתַח
לִבִּי בְּתוֹרָתֶךָ וּבְמִצְוֹתֶיךָ תִּרְדּוֹף נַפְשִׁי · וְכֹל הַחוֹשְׁבִים
עָלַי רָעָה מְהֵרָה הָפֵר עֲצָתָם וְקַלְקֵל מַחֲשְׁבוֹתָם · עֲשֵׂה
לְמַעַן שְׁמֶךָ עֲשֵׂה לְמַעַן יְמִינֶךָ עֲשֵׂה לְמַעַן קְדֻשָּׁתֶךָ עֲשֵׂה
לְמַעַן תּוֹרָתֶךָ · לְמַעַן יֵחָלְצוּן יְדִידֶיךָ הוֹשִׁיעָה יְמִינְךָ
וַעֲנֵנִי : יִהְיוּ לְרָצוֹן אִמְרֵי־פִי וְהֶגְיוֹן לִבִּי לְפָנֶיךָ יְיָ צוּרִי

Seventh Benediction : *For Peace.*

The prayer for Peace is the last of the " Thanksgiving " benedictions.
There can be no Peace, unless it is preceded by thankfulness to God ;
even as there can be no true thankfulness, unless that is preceded by
service to God. " Only that peace has lasting worth, which is the fruit
of common gratitude and common devotion to God's Torah " (Hirsch).

O my God. This is a private meditation of Mar, the scn of Rabina,
a famous rabbi of the fifth century. Through its beauty it found a place
in all Rites, and became a pendant to the Amidah when spoken
silently. As the evil tongue is the most insidious enemy of peace, this
prayer follows naturally upon the concluding petition for peace ;
Psalm 34. 14.

VII. FOR
PEACE

Grant abundant peace unto Israel thy people for ever ; for thou art the sovereign Lord of all peace ; and may it be good in thy sight to bless thy people Israel at all times and in every hour with thy peace.

Blessed art thou, O Lord, who blessest thy people Israel with peace.

[*During the Ten Days of Repentance, say* :— In the book of life, blessing, peace and good sustenance may we be remembered and inscribed before thee, we and all thy people the house of Israel, for a happy life and for peace. Blessed art thou, O Lord, who makest peace.]

CONCLUD-
ING
MEDITA•
TION

O my God ! 'guard my tongue from evil and my lips from speaking guile ; and to such as curse me let my soul be dumb, yea, let my soul be unto all as the dust. Open my heart to thy Torah, and let my soul pursue thy commandments. If any design evil against me, speedily make their counsel of no effect, and frustrate their designs. Do it for the sake of thy Name, do it for the sake of thy power, do it for the sake of thy holiness, do it for the sake of thy Torah.

Psalm 60. 7

Psalm 19. 15

In order that thy beloved ones may be delivered, O save by thy power, and answer me. Let the words of my mouth and the meditation of my heart be acceptable before thee,

---

let my soul be dumb. " Grant me forbearance unto those who deal ill towards me, and a calm disposition unto all my fellowmen " a prayer at once humble and dignified, marked by solemn simplicity and true greatness (N. Remy). " Whosoever does not persecute them that persecute him, whosoever takes an offence in silence, he who does good because of love, he who is cheerful under his sufferings—they are the friends of God " (Talmud).

as the dust. This is victory over self, and has nothing in common with self-contempt. " Be not wicked in thine own esteem ", remains a primary duty for individuals as for communities ; see p. 642.

open my heart to thy Torah. " Open my heart to Thy sacred teachings, so that my conduct may be evidence of the fulfilment of Thy commandments."

frustrate their designs. Defeat their purposes. This ends the prayer of Mar, the son of Rabina.

of thy power. lit. " of thy right hand ", *i.e.* to vindicate Thy power.

וְגֹאֲלִי : עֹשֶׂה שָׁלוֹם בִּמְרוֹמָיו הוּא יַעֲשֶׂה שָׁלוֹם עָלֵינוּ

וְעַל כָּל־יִשְׂרָאֵל · וְאִמְרוּ אָמֵן :

יְהִי רָצוֹן לְפָנֶיךָ יְיָ אֱלֹהֵינוּ וֵאלֹהֵי אֲבוֹתֵינוּ שֶׁיִּבָּנֶה בֵּית

הַמִּקְדָּשׁ בִּמְהֵרָה בְיָמֵינוּ · וְתֵן חֶלְקֵנוּ בְּתוֹרָתֶךָ : וְשָׁם נַעֲבָדְךָ

בְּיִרְאָה כִּימֵי עוֹלָם וּכְשָׁנִים קַדְמוֹנִיּוֹת : וְעָרְבָה לַיְיָ מִנְחַת

יְהוּדָה וִירוּשָׁלָיִם כִּימֵי עוֹלָם וּכְשָׁנִים קַדְמוֹנִיּוֹת :

The Reader and Congregation repeat from וַיְכֻלּוּ *to* לַעֲשׂוֹת, *p.* 380.

From בָּרוּךְ *to* מְקַדֵּשׁ הַשַּׁבָּת, *p.* 390, *is omitted when Prayers are*

not said with a Congregation :—

Reader. בָּרוּךְ אַתָּה יְיָ אֱלֹהֵינוּ וֵאלֹהֵי אֲבוֹתֵינוּ ·

אֱלֹהֵי אַבְרָהָם אֱלֹהֵי יִצְחָק וֵאלֹהֵי יַעֲקֹב · הָאֵל הַגָּדוֹל

הַגִּבּוֹר וְהַנּוֹרָא אֵל עֶלְיוֹן קֹנֵה שָׁמַיִם וָאָרֶץ :

Reader and Congregation. מָגֵן אָבוֹת בִּדְבָרוֹ מְחַיֵּה מֵתִים

בְּמַאֲמָרוֹ הָאֵל (הָאֵל *for* הַמֶּלֶךְ *read* שַׁבַּת שׁוּבָה *On*) הַקָּדוֹשׁ

שֶׁאֵין כָּמֹהוּ הַמֵּנִיחַ לְעַמּוֹ בְּיוֹם שַׁבַּת קָדְשׁוֹ · כִּי

בָם רָצָה לְהָנִיחַ לָהֶם · לְפָנָיו נַעֲבוֹד בְּיִרְאָה וָפַחַד

וְנוֹדֶה לִשְׁמוֹ בְּכָל־יוֹם תָּמִיד מֵעֵין הַבְּרָכוֹת · אֵל הַהוֹדָאוֹת

אֲדוֹן הַשָּׁלוֹם מְקַדֵּשׁ הַשַּׁבָּת וּמְבָרֵךְ שְׁבִיעִי · וּמֵנִיחַ

בִּקְדֻשָּׁה לְעַם מְדֻשְּׁנֵי עֹנֶג · זֵכֶר לְמַעֲשֵׂה בְרֵאשִׁית :

He who maketh peace. "Creator of the harmony of the spheres,
mayest Thou in Thy tender love create peace for us and for all Israel"
(Pool).

O Lord, my Rock and my Redeemer. He who maketh peace in his high places, may he make peace for us and for all Israel, and say ye, Amen.

May it be thy will, O Lord our God and God of our fathers, that the temple be speedily rebuilt in our days, and grant our portion in thy Torah. And there we will serve thee with awe, as in the days of old, and as in ancient years. Then shall the offering of Judah and Jerusalem be pleasant unto the Lord, as in the days of old, and as in ancient years.

The Reader and Congregation repeat from "And the heaven," to " and made," p. 381.

The following three paragraphs, to " the Sabbath," p. 391, *are omitted when Prayers are not said with a Congregation :—*

Reader.—Blessed art thou, O Lord our God and God of our fathers, God of Abraham, God of Isaac and God of Jacob, the great, mighty and revered God, the most High God, Master of heaven and earth.

Reader and Cong.—He with his word was a shield to our forefathers, and by his bidding will revive the dead ; the holy God (*on the Sabbath of Repentance say, "* holy King *"*), like unto whom there is none ; who giveth rest to his people on his holy Sabbath day, because he took pleasure in them to grant them rest. Him we will serve with fear and awe, and daily and constantly we will give thanks unto his Name in the fitting forms of Blessings. He is the God to whom thanksgivings are due, the Lord of peace, who halloweth the Sabbath and blesseth the seventh day, and in holiness giveth rest unto a people sated with delights, in remembrance of the creation.

Malachi 3. 4

SUMMARY
OF
SABBATH
AMIDAH

The silent Amidah is followed, according to Talmudic rule, by the repetition of Genesis 2. 1–3, and the recitation of a condensation of the Sabbath Amidah, that gives the substance of the Seven Benedictions.

HE WITH HIS WORD. *fitting forms of Blessings. i.e.* in benedictions suitable to the sacred occasion.

delights. See Isaiah 58. 13, " and call the Sabbath a delight."

אֱלֹהֵינוּ וֵאלֹהֵי אֲבוֹתֵינוּ · רְצֵה בִמְנוּחָתֵנוּ · *Reader.*

קַדְּשֵׁנוּ בְּמִצְוֹתֶיךָ וְתֵן חֶלְקֵנוּ בְּתוֹרָתֶךָ · שַׂבְּעֵנוּ מִטּוּבֶךָ

וְשַׂמְּחֵנוּ בִּישׁוּעָתֶךָ וְטַהֵר לִבֵּנוּ לְעָבְדְּךָ בֶּאֱמֶת · וְהַנְחִילֵנוּ

יְיָ אֱלֹהֵינוּ בְּאַהֲבָה וּבְרָצוֹן שַׁבַּת קָדְשֶׁךָ וְיָנוּחוּ בָהּ

יִשְׂרָאֵל מְקַדְּשֵׁי שְׁמֶךָ · בָּרוּךְ אַתָּה יְיָ · מְקַדֵּשׁ הַשַּׁבָּת :

קַדִּישׁ תִּתְקַבַּל, *p.* 206.

The following is not said on Festivals, on שַׁבַּת חוֹל הַמּוֹעֵד *or on
the evening after a Festival :—*

משנה שבת פ"ב

(א) בַּמֶּה מַדְלִיקִין וּבַמֶּה אֵין מַדְלִיקִין · אֵין מַדְלִיקִין לֹא
בְלֶכֶשׁ וְלֹא בְחֹסֶן וְלֹא בְכַלָּךְ · וְלֹא בִּפְתִילַת הָאִידָן וְלֹא
בִּפְתִילַת הַמִּדְבָּר · וְלֹא בִירוֹקָה שֶׁעַל פְּנֵי הַמַּיִם · וְלֹא בְזֶפֶת
וְלֹא בְשַׁעֲוָה · וְלֹא בְשֶׁמֶן קִיק וְלֹא בְּשֶׁמֶן שְׂרֵפָה · וְלֹא
בְאַלְיָה וְלֹא בְחֵלֶב · נַחוּם הַמָּדִי אוֹמֵר מַדְלִיקִין בְּחֵלֶב
מְבֻשָּׁל · וַחֲכָמִים אוֹמְרִים אֶחָד מְבֻשָּׁל וְאֶחָד שֶׁאֵינוֹ מְבֻשָּׁל
אֵין מַדְלִיקִין בּוֹ : (ב) אֵין מַדְלִיקִין בְּשֶׁמֶן שְׂרֵפָה בְּיוֹם
טוֹב · רַבִּי יִשְׁמָעֵאל אוֹמֵר אֵין מַדְלִיקִין בְּעִטְרָן מִפְּנֵי כְּבוֹד
הַשַּׁבָּת · וַחֲכָמִים מַתִּירִין בְּכָל הַשְּׁמָנִים בְּשֶׁמֶן שֻׁמְשְׁמִין
בְּשֶׁמֶן אֱגוֹזִים בְּשֶׁמֶן צְנוֹנוֹת בְּשֶׁמֶן דָּגִים בְּשֶׁמֶן פַּקּוּעוֹת
בְּעִטְרָן וּבְנֵפְטְ · רַבִּי טַרְפוֹן אוֹמֵר אֵין מַדְלִיקִין אֶלָּא בְּשֶׁמֶן

The Full Kaddish is a sign that originally the Sabbath Evening
Service was now concluded. The present-day additions are, (a) A

See p. 381

Reader.—Our God and God of our fathers, accept our rest ; hallow us by thy commandments, and grant our portion in thy Torah ; satisfy us with thy goodness, and gladden us with thy salvation ; purify our hearts to serve thee in truth ; and in thy love and favour, O Lord our God, let us inherit thy holy Sabbath ; and may Israel, who sanctify thy name, rest thereon. Blessed art thou, O Lord, who hallowest the Sabbath.

Kaddish, p. 207.

The following is not said on Festivals, on the Intermediate Sabbath of a Festival, or on the evening after a Festival.

Mishna Treatise Sabbath, ch. ii.

REGULA-
TIONS
CONCERN-
ING
SABBATH
LAMP
BAMMEH
MADLIKIN

1. With what materials may the Sabbath lamp be lighted, and with what may it not be lighted ? It may not be lighted with cedar-bast, nor with uncombed flax, nor with floss-silk, nor with willow-fibre, nor with nettle fibre, nor with water-weeds, (all these forming imperfect wicks). It may also not be lighted with pitch, nor with liquid wax, nor with oil made from the seeds of the cotton plant, nor with oil which, having been set apart as a heave-offering and having become defiled, is condemned to be destroyed by burning, nor with the fat from the tails of sheep, nor with tallow. Nahum the Mede says, one may use tallow when it has been boiled ; but the other sages say, that whether so prepared or not, it may not be used.

2. On a festival one may not use such consecrated oil as has been condemned, after defilement, to be burnt. R. Ishmael says, one may not, from respect to the Sabbath, use tar. The sages permit the use of all kinds of oil ; the oil of sesamum, of nuts, of radish seeds, of fish, of colocynth seeds, as well as tar and naphtha. R. Tarphon says, one may use no other than olive oil for lighting the Sabbath lamp.

Mishna chapter, with Haggadic ending; (*b*) Kiddush ; (*c*) Oleynu, with Mourner's Kaddish ; and, in English congregations, (*d*) Yigdal.

The Mishna Chapter. Since the ninth century this chapter, containing the regulations concerning the material proper for the Sabbath light, has been recited. In many Rites this is done *before* the Evening Service, and even before Minchah. Its recitation to-day, in Ashkenazi congregations, is not universal.

זַיִת בִּלְבָד : (ג) כָּל הַיּוֹצֵא מִן הָעֵץ אֵין מַדְלִיקִין בּוֹ אֶלָּא
פִּשְׁתָּן · וְכָל הַיּוֹצֵא מִן הָעֵץ אֵינוֹ מִטַּמֵּא טֻמְאַת אֹהָלִים
אֶלָּא פִשְׁתָּן · פְּתִילַת הַבֶּגֶד שֶׁקִּפְּלָהּ וְלֹא הִבְהֲבָהּ · רַבִּי
אֱלִיעֶזֶר אוֹמֵר טְמֵאָה הִיא וְאֵין מַדְלִיקִין בָּהּ · רַבִּי עֲקִיבָא
אוֹמֵר טְהוֹרָה הִיא וּמַדְלִיקִין בָּהּ : (ד) לֹא יִקֹּב אָדָם
שְׁפוֹפֶרֶת שֶׁל בֵּיצָה וִימַלְאֶנָּה שֶׁמֶן וְיִתְּנֶנָּה עַל פִּי הַנֵּר
בִּשְׁבִיל שֶׁתְּהֵא מְנַטֶּפֶת וַאֲפִלּוּ הִיא שֶׁל חֶרֶס' וְרַבִּי יְהוּדָה
מַתִּיר · אֲבָל אִם חִבְּרָהּ הַיּוֹצֵר מִתְּחִלָּה מֻתָּר מִפְּנֵי שֶׁהוּא
כְּלִי אֶחָד · לֹא יְמַלֵּא אָדָם קְעָרָה שֶׁמֶן וְיִתְּנֶנָּה בְּצַד הַנֵּר
וְיִתֵּן רֹאשׁ הַפְּתִילָה בְּתוֹכָהּ בִּשְׁבִיל שֶׁתְּהֵא שׁוֹאֶבֶת · וְרַבִּי
יְהוּדָה מַתִּיר : (ה) הַמְכַבֶּה אֶת הַנֵּר מִפְּנֵי שֶׁהוּא מִתְיָרֵא
מִפְּנֵי גוֹיִם מִפְּנֵי לִסְטִים מִפְּנֵי רוּחַ רָעָה אוֹ בִּשְׁבִיל הַחוֹלֶה
שֶׁיִּישָׁן פָּטוּר · כְּחָס עַל הַנֵּר כְּחָס עַל הַשֶּׁמֶן כְּחָס עַל
הַפְּתִילָה חַיָּב · רַבִּי יוֹסֵי פּוֹטֵר בְּכֻלָּן חוּץ מִן הַפְּתִילָה
מִפְּנֵי שֶׁהוּא עוֹשָׂהּ פֶּחָם : (ו) עַל שָׁלשׁ עֲבֵרוֹת נָשִׁים
מֵתוֹת בִּשְׁעַת לֵדָתָן · עַל שֶׁאֵינָן זְהִירוֹת בְּנִדָּה בְּחַלָּה
וּבְהַדְלָקַת הַנֵּר : (ז) שְׁלֹשָׁה דְבָרִים צָרִיךְ אָדָם לוֹמַר בְּתוֹךְ
בֵּיתוֹ עֶרֶב שַׁבָּת עִם חֲשֵׁכָה · עִשַּׂרְתֶּם עֵרַבְתֶּם הַדְלִיקוּ
אֶת הַנֵּר · סָפֵק חֲשֵׁכָה סָפֵק אֵינָהּ חֲשֵׁכָה אֵין מְעַשְּׂרִין
אֶת הַוַּדַּאי וְאֵין מַטְבִּילִין אֶת הַכֵּלִים וְאֵין מַדְלִיקִין אֶת
הַנֵּרוֹת · אֲבָל מְעַשְּׂרִין אֶת הַדְּמַאי וּמְעָרְבִין וְטוֹמְנִין אֶת
הַחַמִּין :

Mishna 3, *flax*. Spoken of in Joshua 2. 6 as "the flax of a tree".
Mishna 6 is Haggadic moralising, and stresses in strong terms the
importance of the duties named therein.

3. No part of a tree may be used as a wick for lighting, with the exception of flax ; nor is any part of a tree, if used in the construction of a tent, capable of acquiring pollution according to the law concerning the pollution of tents, except flax. If a slip of cloth has been folded but not singed, R. Eliezer says it may become unclean, and may not be used as a wick for lighting ; R. Akiba says it remains clean, and may be used.

4. One may not perforate an egg-shell, fill it with oil, and place it above the opening of the lamp, so that drops of oil may fall therein ; he may not even employ an earthenware vessel in this manner ; but R. Yehudah permits it. If, however, the potter had originally joined the two parts, then it is allowed, because it is actually only one vessel. A person may not fill a bowl with oil, place it by the side of the lamp, and put the end of the wick into it, so that it may draw the oil to the flame ; but R. Yehudah permits it.

5. He who extinguishes the light, because he is in fear of heathens, of robbers, or of an evil spirit, or to enable a sick person to sleep, is absolved ; if his object is to save the lamp, the oil, or the wick, he is guilty of a breach of the Sabbath law. R. Yosé absolves from such guilt in every case except in that of the one whose object is to save the wick, because by thus extinguishing it, he converts it into a coal.

6. For three transgressions women die in childbirth : because they have been negligent in regard to their periods of separation, in respect to the consecration of *Challah* (the first cake of the dough), and in the lighting of the Sabbath lamp.

7. Three things a man must say to his household on Sabbath eve towards dusk : Have ye separated the tithe ? Have ye made the Erub ? Kindle the Sabbath lamp. If it be doubtful whether it is dark, that which is certainly untithed must not then be tithed, vessels must not be immersed to purify them from their defilement, nor must the Sabbath lamps be lighted ; but that which is doubtfully untithed may be tithed, the Erub may be made, and hot victuals may be covered to retain their heat.

Mishna 7, *Erub* is a symbolical act by which continuity is established ; especially, with reference to preparing meals for the Sabbath on a Holy Day occurring on a Friday.
Mishna 7. *Sabbath Lamp.* See pp. 343-345.

תלמוד מסכת ברכות

אָמַר רַבִּי אֶלְעָזָר אָמַר רַבִּי חֲנִינָא · תַּלְמִידֵי חֲכָמִים
מַרְבִּים שָׁלוֹם בָּעוֹלָם · שֶׁנֶּאֱמַר וְכָל־בָּנַיִךְ לִמּוּדֵי יְיָ וְרַב
שְׁלוֹם בָּנָיִךְ · אַל תִּקְרָא בָּנַיִךְ אֶלָּא בּוֹנָיִךְ :־שָׁלוֹם רָב
לְאֹהֲבֵי תוֹרָתֶךָ וְאֵין לָמוֹ מִכְשׁוֹל : יְהִי־שָׁלוֹם בְּחֵילֵךְ שַׁלְוָה
בְּאַרְמְנוֹתָיִךְ : לְמַעַן אַחַי וְרֵעָי אֲדַבְּרָה־נָּא שָׁלוֹם בָּךְ :
לְמַעַן בֵּית־יְיָ אֱלֹהֵינוּ אֲבַקְשָׁה טוֹב לָךְ : יְיָ עֹז לְעַמּוֹ יִתֵּן
יְיָ וְיָבָרֵךְ אֶת־עַמּוֹ בַשָּׁלוֹם :

The Reader, taking a cup of wine in his hand, says :—

בָּרוּךְ אַתָּה יְיָ אֱלֹהֵינוּ מֶלֶךְ הָעוֹלָם · בּוֹרֵא פְּרִי הַגָּפֶן :

בָּרוּךְ אַתָּה יְיָ אֱלֹהֵינוּ מֶלֶךְ הָעוֹלָם · אֲשֶׁר קִדְּשָׁנוּ
בְּמִצְוֹתָיו וְרָצָה בָנוּ · וְשַׁבַּת קָדְשׁוֹ בְּאַהֲבָה וּבְרָצוֹן
הִנְחִילָנוּ זִכָּרוֹן לְמַעֲשֵׂה בְרֵאשִׁית · כִּי הוּא יוֹם תְּחִלָּה
לְמִקְרָאֵי קֹדֶשׁ זֵכֶר לִיצִיאַת מִצְרָיִם · כִּי־בָנוּ בָחַרְתָּ
וְאוֹתָנוּ קִדַּשְׁתָּ מִכָּל־הָעַמִּים · וְשַׁבַּת קָדְשְׁךָ בְּאַהֲבָה
וּבְרָצוֹן הִנְחַלְתָּנוּ · בָּרוּךְ אַתָּה יְיָ · מְקַדֵּשׁ הַשַּׁבָּת :

Rabbi Elazar said. The Haggadic selection that follows is a typical example of a Rabbinic homily. It is on Peace, and is based on Isaiah 54. 13, which foretells that Zion's peace will be based not on armed force, but on God-fearing lives of all its inhabitants.

sages increase peace throughout the world. This is a memorable pronouncement of the deepest importance. In seeking for a saying wherewith to sum up the spirit of Judaism and of Jewry across the ages, one would always come back to these words. The human ideal is the man of wisdom, wisdom of mind and heart ; the aim of wisdom is to establish peace (Lewissohn). Note that it inculcates peace not merely in the family or in the community, but throughout the world.

read not. A homiletic admonition to understand the word *banayich* as if it were written *bonayich*, so as to remember that the children of a nation are the builders of its future.

Talmud Babli. End of Treatise Berachoth.

HAGGADIC
DISCOURSE
Isaiah 54. 13
R. Elazar said in the name of R. Chanina, The disciples of the sages increase peace throughout the world, as it is said, and all thy children shall be taught of the Lord ; and great shall be the peace of thy children. (Read not here *banayich*, thy children, but *bonayich*,

Psalm
119. 165
Psalm
122. 7, 8, 9
thy builders.)—Great peace have they who love thy Torah ; and there is no stumbling for them. Peace be within thy rampart, prosperity within thy palaces. For my brethren and companions' sakes I would fain speak peace concerning thee. For the sake of the

Psalm 29. 10
house of the Lord our God I would seek thy good. The Lord will give strength unto his people ; the Lord will bless his people with peace.

The Reader, taking a cup of wine in his hand, says :—

SYNA-
GOGUE
KIDDUSH
Blessed art Thou, O Lord our God, King of the universe, who createst the fruit of the vine.

Blessed art thou, O Lord our God, King of the universe, who hast hallowed us by thy commandments and hast taken pleasure in us, and in love and favour hast given us thy holy Sabbath as an inheritance, a memorial of the creation—that day being also the first of the holy convocations, in remembrance of the departure from Egypt. For thou hast chosen us and hallowed us above all nations, and in love and favour hast given us thy holy Sabbath as an inheritance. Blessed art thou, O Lord, who hallowest the Sabbath.

The Synagogue Kiddush. The presence of this home-rite in the Synagogue Service is due to various causes. Wine, an essential element of the Kiddush ceremony, was beyond the reach of most people in Babylon, and arrangements had to be made for a congregational Kiddush. Furthermore, in Babylon and in some medieval European countries, passing strangers were often lodged in the Synagogue building ; and, for their benefit, the Kiddush was recited at the end of the Synagogue Service. The Reader faced the congregation during the Kiddush, as it did not form part of the Service proper. In later generations, when the Synagogue buildings ceased to be the communal inn, the Kiddush nevertheless retained its old place. Its elimination was urged by some literalists, because the original reason for its introduction had ceased. But neither the spiritual leaders nor the communities would agree to that demand.

עָלֵינוּ לְשַׁבֵּחַ לַאֲדוֹן הַכֹּל לָתֵת גְּדֻלָּה לְיוֹצֵר
בְּרֵאשִׁית · שֶׁלֹּא עָשָׂנוּ כְּגוֹיֵי הָאֲרָצוֹת וְלֹא שָׂמָנוּ
כְּמִשְׁפְּחוֹת הָאֲדָמָה · שֶׁלֹּא שָׂם חֶלְקֵנוּ כָּהֶם וְגוֹרָלֵנוּ
כְּכָל-הֲמוֹנָם · וַאֲנַחְנוּ כּוֹרְעִים וּמִשְׁתַּחֲוִים וּמוֹדִים לִפְנֵי
מֶלֶךְ מַלְכֵי הַמְּלָכִים הַקָּדוֹשׁ בָּרוּךְ הוּא · שֶׁהוּא נוֹטֶה
שָׁמַיִם וְיוֹסֵד אָרֶץ · וּמוֹשַׁב יְקָרוֹ בַּשָּׁמַיִם מִמַּעַל וּשְׁכִינַת
עֻזּוֹ בְּגָבְהֵי מְרוֹמִים: הוּא אֱלֹהֵינוּ · אֵין עוֹד · אֱמֶת
מַלְכֵּנוּ · אֶפֶס זוּלָתוֹ · כַּכָּתוּב בְּתוֹרָתוֹ · וְיָדַעְתָּ הַיּוֹם
וַהֲשֵׁבֹתָ אֶל-לְבָבֶךָ כִּי יְיָ הוּא הָאֱלֹהִים בַּשָּׁמַיִם מִמַּעַל
וְעַל-הָאָרֶץ מִתָּחַת אֵין עוֹד:

עַל-כֵּן נְקַוֶּה לְךָ יְיָ אֱלֹהֵינוּ לִרְאוֹת מְהֵרָה בְּתִפְאֶרֶת
עֻזֶּךָ · לְהַעֲבִיר גִּלּוּלִים מִן הָאָרֶץ וְהָאֱלִילִים כָּרוֹת יִכָּרֵתוּן
לְתַקֵּן עוֹלָם בְּמַלְכוּת שַׁדַּי · וְכָל-בְּנֵי בָשָׂר יִקְרְאוּ בִשְׁמֶךָ
לְהַפְנוֹת אֵלֶיךָ כָּל-רִשְׁעֵי אָרֶץ: יַכִּירוּ וְיֵדְעוּ כָּל-יוֹשְׁבֵי
תֵבֵל כִּי לְךָ תִּכְרַע כָּל-בֶּרֶךְ תִּשָּׁבַע כָּל-לָשׁוֹן: לְפָנֶיךָ
אֱלֹהֵינוּ יִכְרְעוּ וְיִפֹּלוּ · וְלִכְבוֹד שִׁמְךָ יְקָר יִתֵּנוּ · וִיקַבְּלוּ
כֻלָּם אֶת-עֹל מַלְכוּתֶךָ · וְתִמְלוֹךְ עֲלֵיהֶם מְהֵרָה לְעוֹלָם
וָעֶד · כִּי הַמַּלְכוּת שֶׁלְּךָ הִיא וּלְעוֹלְמֵי עַד תִּמְלוֹךְ בְּכָבוֹד
כַּכָּתוּב בְּתוֹרָתֶךָ · יְיָ יִמְלֹךְ לְעוֹלָם וָעֶד: וְנֶאֱמַר · וְהָיָה
יְיָ לְמֶלֶךְ עַל-כָּל-הָאָרֶץ בַּיּוֹם הַהוּא יִהְיֶה יְיָ אֶחָד
וּשְׁמוֹ אֶחָד:

OLEYNU :
ISRAEL'S
SELECTION
TO
PROCLAIM
GOD AS
SUPREME
KING OF
THE
UNIVERSE
See p. 208

It is our duty to praise the Lord of all things, to ascribe greatness to him who formed the world in the beginning ; since he hath not made us like the nations of other lands, and hath not placed us like other families of the earth ; since he hath not assigned unto us a portion as unto them, nor a lot as unto all their multitude. For we bend the knee and offer worship and thanks before the supreme King of kings, the Holy One, blessed be he, who stretched forth the heavens and laid the foundations of the earth, the seat of whose glory is in the heavens above, and the abode of whose might is in the loftiest heights. He is our God ; there is none else : in truth he is our King ; there is none besides him ;

Deuteronomy
4. 39

as it is written in the Torah, And thou shalt know this day, and lay it to thine heart, that the Lord he is God in heaven above and upon the earth beneath : there is none else.

ISRAEL'S
HOPE :
HUMANITY
UNITED IN
RECOGNI-
TION OF
THE ONE
GOD

We therefore hope in thee, O Lord our God, that we may speedily behold the glory of thy might ; when thou wilt remove the abominations from the earth, and heathendom will be utterly destroyed ; when the world will be perfected under the kingdom of the Almighty, and all the children of flesh will call upon thy Name ; when thou wilt turn unto thyself all the evil-doers upon earth. Let all the inhabitants of the world perceive and know that unto thee every knee must bow, every tongue must swear allegiance. Before thee, O Lord our God, let them bow and worship ; and unto thy glorious Name let them give honour ; let them all accept the yoke of thy kingdom, and do thou reign over them speedily, and for ever and ever. For the kingdom is thine, and to all eternity thou wilt reign in glory ; as it is written

Exodus 15. 18

in thy Torah, THE LORD SHALL REIGN FOR EVER AND EVER.

Zechariah
14. 9

And it is said, AND THE LORD SHALL BE KING OVER ALL THE EARTH : IN THAT DAY SHALL THE LORD BE ONE, AND HIS NAME ONE.

קַדִּישׁ יָתוֹם

Mourner. יִתְגַּדַּל וְיִתְקַדַּשׁ שְׁמֵהּ רַבָּא בְּעָלְמָא דִּי־בְרָא

כִרְעוּתֵהּ · וְיַמְלִיךְ מַלְכוּתֵהּ בְּחַיֵּיכוֹן וּבְיוֹמֵיכוֹן וּבְחַיֵּי

דִי־כָל־בֵּית יִשְׂרָאֵל בַּעֲגָלָא וּבִזְמַן קָרִיב · וְאִמְרוּ אָמֵן :

Cong. and Mourner. יְהֵא שְׁמֵהּ רַבָּא מְבָרַךְ לְעָלַם וּלְעָלְמֵי

עָלְמַיָּא ·

Mourner. יִתְבָּרַךְ וְיִשְׁתַּבַּח וְיִתְפָּאַר וְיִתְרוֹמַם וְיִתְנַשֵּׂא

וְיִתְהַדַּר וְיִתְעַלֶּה וְיִתְהַלָּל שְׁמֵהּ דִּי־קֻדְשָׁא · בְּרִיךְ הוּא

לְעֵלָּא מִן־כָּל־בִּרְכָתָא וְשִׁירָתָא תֻּשְׁבְּחָתָא וְנֶחֱמָתָא דִּי־

אֲמִירָן בְּעָלְמָא · וְאִמְרוּ אָמֵן :

יְהֵא שְׁלָמָא רַבָּא מִן־שְׁמַיָּא וְחַיִּים עָלֵינוּ וְעַל־

כָּל־יִשְׂרָאֵל · וְאִמְרוּ אָמֵן :

עֹשֶׂה שָׁלוֹם בִּמְרוֹמָיו הוּא יַעֲשֶׂה שָׁלוֹם עָלֵינוּ

וְעַל־כָּל־יִשְׂרָאֵל · וְאִמְרוּ אָמֵן :

6. MOURNER'S KADDISH.

The Kaddish points forward to the establishment of the Messianic Kingdom of God, with its promise of Resurrection and assurance of Immortality; see p. 254. The greatest religious significance was attached by the Rabbis to the congregation repeating in unison the words, *Let His great Name be blessed for ever and to all eternity.* " As the assembly proclaim these words, the Holy One forgives " (Midrash). The son, reciting the Kaddish, is thus instrumental in calling forth the most

Mourner's Kaddish

Mourner.—Magnified and sanctified be his great Name in the world which he hath created according to his will. May he establish his kingdom during your life and during your days, and during the life of all the house of Israel, even speedily and at a near time, and say ye, Amen.

Cong. and Mourner.—Let his great Name be blessed for ever and to all eternity.

Mourner.—Blessed, praised and glorified, exalted, extolled and honoured, magnified and lauded be the Name of the Holy One, blessed be he ; though he be high above all the blessings and hymns, praises. and consolations, which are uttered in the world ; and say ye, Amen.

May there be abundant peace from heaven, and life for us and for all Israel ; and say ye, Amen.

He who maketh peace in his high places, may he make peace for us and for all Israel; and say ye, Amen.

important Response in the Service. This ancient prayer was deemed to be the hymn of hymns, and gained still greater hold upon the reverent affection of the people when it came to be looked upon as the Orphan's Prayer. In its original form, the Kaddish is of great antiquity. It antedates the Destruction of the Temple, and is echoed in the most famous Christian prayer. For its rise and significance, see on THE MOURNER'S KADDISH, p. 269.

may he establish his kingdom. May He bring about the realization of all spiritual values, and transform things as they are into things as they ought to be.

consolations. The Heb. word, in addition to its general meaning of comfort in mourning and sorrow, also denotes the praises of God in connection with the Messianic time and the Future Life, as well as the consolatory discourses to which the Kaddish was the conclusion.

יִגְדַּל אֱלֹהִים חַי וְיִשְׁתַּבַּח · נִמְצָא וְאֵין עֵת אֶל־מְצִיאוּתוֹ :

אֶחָד וְאֵין יָחִיד כְּיִחוּדוֹ · נֶעְלָם וְגַם אֵין סוֹף לְאַחְדּוּתוֹ :

אֵין לוֹ דְּמוּת הַגּוּף וְאֵינוֹ גוּף · לֹא נַעֲרוֹךְ אֵלָיו קְדֻשָּׁתוֹ :

קַדְמוֹן לְכָל־דָּבָר אֲשֶׁר נִבְרָא · רִאשׁוֹן וְאֵין רֵאשִׁית
לְרֵאשִׁיתוֹ :

הִנּוֹ אֲדוֹן עוֹלָם · לְכָל־נוֹצָר יוֹרֶה גְדֻלָּתוֹ וּמַלְכוּתוֹ :

שֶׁפַע נְבוּאָתוֹ נְתָנוֹ אֶל־אַנְשֵׁי סְגֻלָּתוֹ וְתִפְאַרְתּוֹ :

לֹא קָם בְּיִשְׂרָאֵל כְּמשֶׁה עוֹד נָבִיא · וּמַבִּיט אֶת־תְּמוּנָתוֹ :

תּוֹרַת אֱמֶת נָתַן לְעַמּוֹ אֵל · עַל יַד נְבִיאוֹ נֶאֱמַן בֵּיתוֹ :

לֹא יַחֲלִיף הָאֵל וְלֹא יָמִיר דָּתוֹ לְעוֹלָמִים לְזוּלָתוֹ :

צוֹפֶה וְיוֹדֵעַ סְתָרֵינוּ · מַבִּיט לְסוֹף דָּבָר בְּקַדְמָתוֹ :

גּוֹמֵל לְאִישׁ חֶסֶד כְּמִפְעָלוֹ · נוֹתֵן לְרָשָׁע רַע כְּרִשְׁעָתוֹ :

יִשְׁלַח לְקֵץ יָמִין מְשִׁיחֵנוּ · לִפְדּוֹת מְחַכֵּי קֵץ יְשׁוּעָתוֹ :

מֵתִים יְחַיֶּה אֵל בְּרוֹב חַסְדּוֹ · בָּרוּךְ עֲדֵי עַד שֵׁם תְּהִלָּתוֹ :

This hymn opens the Morning Service, and is the concluding hymn on Sabbath and Festival eves. English Jews thus also close their devotions on those sacred occasions as *faithful* Jews, believing in the existence of a Creator—one, spiritual and eternal; believing in Prophecy and the Torah of Moses; in the rule of justice in God's universe; in the Messiah, and in the immortality of the soul; see p. 6.

YIGDAL:
THE
PRIN-
CIPLES OF
THE
JEWISH
FAITH

The living God we praise, exalt, adore !
He was, He is, He will be evermore !
No unity like unto His can be :
Eternal, inconceivable is He.
No form, or shape has the incorporeal One,
Most holy He, past all comparison.
He was, ere aught was made in heaven, or earth,
But His existence has no date, or birth.
Lord of the Universe is He proclaimed,
Teaching His power to all His hand has framed.
He gave His gift of prophecy to those
In whom He gloried, whom He loved and chose.
No prophet ever yet has filled the place
Of Moses, who beheld God face to face.
Through him (the faithful in His house) the Lord
The law of truth to Israel did accord.
This Law God will not alter, will not change
For any other through time's utmost range.
He knows and heeds the secret thoughts of man :
He saw the end of all ere aught began.
With love and grace doth He the righteous bless,
He metes out evil unto wickedness.
He at the last will His anointed send,
Those to redeem, who hope, and wait the end.
God will the dead to life again restore.
Praised be His glorious Name for evermore !

" The minhag of this Synagogue shall be the Polish minhag as used in Hamburg, with the addition of Yigdal to be chanted at the end of every Friday Evening Service ".—Takanah of the Great Synagogue, London, 1722.

The melody of *Yigdal* on Sabbath and Festival eves is of a moving swinging, and triumphant quality. The same is true of Adon Olom at the end of the Sabbath Morning Service ; p. 556.

On the Eve of Sabbaths and of Holydays it is customary for Parents, either at the conclusion of the Service in Synagogue, or upon reaching their Home, to pronounce the following Benediction upon their Children :—

To Sons say :— יְשִׂמְךָ אֱלֹהִים כְּאֶפְרַיִם וְכִמְנַשֶּׁה :

To Daughters :— יְשִׂמֵךְ אֱלֹהִים כְּשָׂרָה רִבְקָה רָחֵל וְלֵאָה :

To Sons and Daughters :— יְבָרֶכְךָ יְיָ וְיִשְׁמְרֶךָ : יָאֵר יְיָ פָּנָיו אֵלֶיךָ וִיחֻנֶּךָ : יִשָּׂא יְיָ פָּנָיו אֵלֶיךָ וְיָשֵׂם לְךָ שָׁלוֹם :

Some say the following in the Home :—

מוֹדָה אֲנִי לְפָנֶיךָ יְיָ אֱלֹהַי וֵאלֹהֵי אֲבוֹתַי עַל־כָּל־הַחֲסָדִים אֲשֶׁר עָשִׂיתָ עִמָּדִי וַאֲשֶׁר אַתָּה עָתִיד לַעֲשׂוֹת עִמִּי וְעִם כָּל־בְּרִיּוֹתֶיךָ : וִיהִי רָצוֹן מִלְּפָנֶיךָ אֲדוֹן הַשָּׁלוֹם אֲבִי הָרַחֲמִים שֶׁתְּבָרְכֵנִי וְתִפְקְדֵנִי לְחַיִּים טוֹבִים וּלְשָׁלוֹם וּתְזַכֵּנִי אוֹתִי (וְאֶת־אִשְׁתִּי וְאֶת־זַרְעִי) לִמְצוֹא חֵן וְשֵׂכֶל טוֹב בְּעֵינֶיךָ וּבְעֵינֵי כָל־רוֹאַי : וְאֶזְכֶּה לְקַבֵּל שַׁבָּתוֹת מִתּוֹךְ רֹב שִׂמְחָה וְכָבוֹד וּמִתּוֹךְ מְעוּט עֲווֹנוֹת : וְתַעֲבִיר מִמֶּנִּי וּמִכָּל־בְּנֵי בֵיתִי כָּל־חֳלִי וּמַדְוֶה וְכָל־עֲנִיּוּת וְדַבְּקֵנוּ בְּיֵצֶר הַטּוֹב לְעָבְדְּךָ בֶּאֱמֶת וּבְיִרְאָה וּבְאַהֲבָה : אָנָּא מֶלֶךְ הַכָּבוֹד אֲדוֹן הַשָּׁלוֹם : צַוֵּה לִי מַלְאָכֶיךָ

5. HOME SERVICE. THE FATHER'S BLESSING.

A parent's blessing is considered in Judaism to be of vital significance; and the custom of blessing children on the Sabbath Eve is the rule since Talmudic times. The placing of both hands on the head of the child became a symbol of transmitting the spirit of God, even as the Blessing itself linked the generations in piety and affection.

as Ephraim and Manasseh. The words of Jacob (Genesis 48.) when, on his death-bed, he blessed his grandchildren, Ephraim and Manasseh. These had voluntarily given up their place in the higher Egyptian aristocracy, and would not barter away their " Jewishness " for the most exalted social position, or the most enviable career, in

BLESSING THE CHILDREN   *On the Eve of Sabbaths and of Holydays it is customary for Parents, either at the conclusion of the Service in Synagogue, or upon reaching their Home, to pronounce the following Benediction upon their Children :—*

To Sons say :—

God make thee as Ephraim and Manasseh.

To Daughters say :—

God make thee as Sarah, Rebekah, Rachel and Leah.

To Sons and Daughters :—

The Lord bless thee, and keep thee : the Lord make his face to shine upon thee, and be gracious unto thee : the Lord turn his face unto thee, and give thee peace.

Some say the following in the Home :—

SABBATH MEDITA- TION   I give thanks unto thee, O Lord my God and the God of my fathers, for all the kindnesses that thou hast shown unto me, and that thou art ready to show unto me and to all thy creatures. May it be thy will, O Lord of peace, Father of mercy, to bless me and to ordain for me a happy and peaceful life. Make me worthy (and my wife and my children) to find favour and good understanding in thine eyes, and in the eyes of all who behold me, so that I be deserving to welcome each Sabbath amid ever-growing joy and ever-waning wrongdoing. Oh, remove from me and

the Egyptian state. Every parent may well pray that his children show the same loyalty to their father's God and People.

Sarah . . . Leah. May they follow Jewish ideals of womanhood. Some aspects of that ideal are given in the Song of the Valorous Woman. It is, of course, understood that the parent may add whatever blessings his heart dictates to him, and in his own phrasing.

" The simple, touching ceremony of the parent placing the hand in blessing on the head of his child, has been a wonderful instrument in fostering the growth and strengthening the power of filial piety in the Jewish home. There can be in the heart of the child no disharmony of spirit, certainly no conflict or revolt against parental teaching, so long as he seeks and receives the father's blessing. This ceremony, therefore, is an Elijah that fulfils the words of Malachi the Prophet : " he shall turn the hearts of the fathers to the children, and the hearts of the children to the fathers ". I deem it to be one of the gravest spiritual losses of modern Jewry that this pious custom, sanctified through a hundred generations, is passing away among us." (M. Lazarus).

The Prayer, " I give thanks unto thee," is of recent date.

מַלְאֲכֵי הַשָּׁלוֹם מְשָׁרְתֵי עֶלְיוֹן שֶׁיִּפְקָדוּנִי בְּיוֹם קָדְשֵׁנוּ

לְטוֹבָה וְלִבְרָכָה לְחַיִּים וּלְשָׁלוֹם מֵעַתָּה וְעַד ־ עוֹלָם ׳ אָמֵן :

שָׁלוֹם עֲלֵיכֶם מַלְאֲכֵי הַשָּׁרֵת מַלְאֲכֵי עֶלְיוֹן ׳ מֶלֶךְ מַלְכֵי

הַמְּלָכִים הַקָּדוֹשׁ בָּרוּךְ הוּא :

בּוֹאֲכֶם לְשָׁלוֹם מַלְאֲכֵי הַשָּׁלוֹם מַלְאֲכֵי עֶלְיוֹן מֶלֶךְ מַלְכֵי

הַמְּלָכִים הַקָּדוֹשׁ בָּרוּךְ הוּא :

בָּרְכוּנִי לְשָׁלוֹם מַלְאֲכֵי הַשָּׁלוֹם מַלְאֲכֵי עֶלְיוֹן מֶלֶךְ מַלְכֵי

הַמְּלָכִים הַקָּדוֹשׁ בָּרוּךְ הוּא :

צֵאתְכֶם לְשָׁלוֹם מַלְאֲכֵי הַשָּׁלוֹם מַלְאֲכֵי עֶלְיוֹן ׳ מֶלֶךְ מַלְכֵי

הַמְּלָכִים הַקָּדוֹשׁ בָּרוּךְ הוּא :

אֵשֶׁת חַיִל מִי יִמְצָא וְרָחֹק מִפְּנִינִים מִכְרָהּ : בָּטַח בָּהּ

לֵב בַּעְלָהּ וְשָׁלָל לֹא יֶחְסָר : גְּמָלַתְהוּ טוֹב וְלֹא־רָע כֹּל

יְמֵי חַיֶּיהָ : דָּרְשָׁה צֶמֶר וּפִשְׁתִּים וַתַּעַשׂ בְּחֵפֶץ כַּפֶּיהָ :

הָיְתָה כָּאֳנִיּוֹת סוֹחֵר מִמֶּרְחָק תָּבִיא לַחְמָהּ : וַתָּקָם בְּעוֹד

לַיְלָה וַתִּתֵּן טֶרֶף לְבֵיתָהּ וְחֹק לְנַעֲרֹתֶיהָ : זָמְמָה שָׂדֶה

GREETING THE SABBATH ANGELS.

The Greeting of the Sabbath Angels was introduced by the Cabalists. It is based on the Talmudic saying that two angels, a good and an evil angel, accompany every man as he returns from welcoming the Sabbath in the Synagogue. If the good angel finds the lights kindled and the table set, he says: " May it be God's will that the next Sabbath be as this one ", and the evil angel has to answer " Amen ". When they find the Sabbath neglected, it is the good angel who is compelled to assent to the evil angel's prediction, " May it be the same next Sabbath ".

THE VALOROUS WOMAN.

After the blessing of the children, the exalted position of the Jewish wife is stressed by the recital of Proverbs 31. 10–31, which is an alphabetic Ode on the Perfect Wife Her nobility of character is matched by her domestic efficiency. She is industrious and sagacious

from my household sickness and suffering and poverty. Strengthen our better nature within us, so that we serve thee in truth, in reverence and in love. I beseech thee, O King of glory, Lord of peace, may the Sabbath angels, the heavenly angels of peace, usher in unto us happiness and blessing, life and peace, from now and for evermore. Amen.

GREETING THE SABBATH ANGELS   " Peace be unto you, ye ministering angels, messengers of the Most High, the supreme King of Kings, holy and blessed is he.

" May your coming be in peace, messengers of the Most High, the supreme King of Kings, holy and blessed is he.

" Bless me with peace, ye messengers of the Most High, the supreme King of Kings, holy and blessed is he.

" May your departure be in peace, ye messengers of peace, messengers of the Most High, the supreme King of Kings, holy and blessed is he ".

"THE WOMAN OF WORTH"   ¹⁰A woman of worth who can find ? For her price is far above rubies. ¹¹The heart of her husband trusteth in her ; and he shall have no lack of gain. ¹²She doeth him good and not evil all the days of her life. ¹³She seeketh wool and flax, and worketh willingly with her hands. ¹⁴She is like the merchant-ships; she bringeth her food from afar. ¹⁵She riseth also while it is yet night, and giveth food to her household, and their task to her maidens. ¹⁶She considereth a field, and buyeth it: with the fruit òf her hands she planteth a vineyard. ¹⁷She girdeth her loins with strength, and maketh strong her arms. ¹⁸ She perceiveth that her merchandise is good : her lamp goeth not out by night. ¹⁹She putteth her hands to the distaff, and her hands hold the spindle. ²⁰She stretcheth out her hand to the poor ; yea, she

kind-hearted and honoured.

10. *a woman of worth.* Heb. *ayshes chayil* ; " a valorous woman ". *who can find ? i.e.* is not easily found.

13. She directs the industrial work of her household. The preparation of garments was a main function of woman in ancient times.

17. *with strength.* All her success is the result of determined energy.

18. *her lamp goeth not out by night.* A Semitic idiom for, " her house is prosperous ".

וַתְּקְחֵהוּ מִפְּרִי כַפֶּיהָ נָטְעָה כָּרֶם : חָגְרָה בְעוֹז מָתְנֶיהָ

וַתְּאַמֵּץ זְרוֹעֹתֶיהָ : טָעֲמָה כִּי־טוֹב סַחְרָהּ לֹא־יִכְבֶּה

בַלַּיְלָה נֵרָהּ : יָדֶיהָ שִׁלְּחָה בַכִּישׁוֹר וְכַפֶּיהָ תָּמְכוּ פָלֶךְ :

כַּפָּהּ פָּרְשָׂה לֶעָנִי וְיָדֶיהָ שִׁלְּחָה לָאֶבְיוֹן : לֹא־תִירָא

לְבֵיתָהּ מִשָּׁלֶג כִּי כָל־בֵּיתָהּ לָבֻשׁ שָׁנִים : מַרְבַדִּים

עָשְׂתָה־לָּהּ שֵׁשׁ וְאַרְגָּמָן לְבוּשָׁהּ : נוֹדָע בַּשְּׁעָרִים בַּעְלָהּ

בְּשִׁבְתּוֹ עִם־זִקְנֵי־אָרֶץ : סָדִין עָשְׂתָה וַתִּמְכֹּר וַחֲגוֹר נָתְנָה

לַכְּנַעֲנִי : עֹז וְהָדָר לְבוּשָׁהּ וַתִּשְׂחַק לְיוֹם אַחֲרוֹן : פִּיהָ

פָּתְחָה בְחָכְמָה וְתוֹרַת־חֶסֶד עַל־לְשׁוֹנָהּ : צוֹפִיָּה הֲלִיכוֹת

בֵּיתָהּ וְלֶחֶם עַצְלוּת לֹא תֹאכֵל : קָמוּ בָנֶיהָ וַיְאַשְּׁרוּהָ

בַּעְלָהּ וַיְהַלְלָהּ : רַבּוֹת בָּנוֹת עָשׂוּ חָיִל וְאַתְּ עָלִית עַל־

כֻּלָּנָה : שֶׁקֶר הַחֵן וְהֶבֶל הַיֹּפִי אִשָּׁה יִרְאַת־יְהוָֹה הִיא

תִתְהַלָּל : תְּנוּ־לָהּ מִפְּרִי יָדֶיהָ וִיהַלְלוּהָ בַשְּׁעָרִים מַעֲשֶׂיהָ :

20–31. She is kind to the poor, and gentle to all; self-respecting and dignified, with Religion as the root and basis of her life.

20. *stretcheth out her hand.* With something in it. Her charitable work is as important as her household activities.

23. *in the gates.* The place where public business was transacted.

25. *strength and dignity are her clothing.* A perfect description of perfect womanhood.

laugheth. She is free from anxiety, having provided for the future.

26. *lovingkindness . . . . tongue.* Perhaps the most beautiful features in the portrait.

28. *rise up.* She gets full recognition from those she lives for.

favour. Attractiveness.

30. *beauty is vain.* Not that beauty is to be despised; but there must be full recognition that it is transitory and passes away, and with it the happiness that is based on beauty alone.

a woman that feareth the Lord. The religious side of her character is given in a mere touch—a touch which depicts everything.

31. *fruit of her hands.* "Give her due credit for her deeds" (Moffatt).

putteth forth her hands to the needy. ²¹She is not afraid of the snow for her household ; for all her household are clothed with scarlet. ²²She maketh for herself coverings of tapestry; her clothing is fine linen and purple. ²³Her husband is known in the gates, when he sitteth among the elders of the land. ²⁴She maketh linen garments and selleth them ; and delivereth girdles unto the merchant. ²⁵Strength and dignity are her clothing ; and she laugheth at the time to come. ²⁶She openeth her mouth with wisdom ; and the law of lovingkindness is on her tongue. ²⁷She looketh well to the ways of her household, and eateth not the bread of idleness. ²⁸Her children rise up and call her blessed; her husband also, and he praiseth her, saying : ²⁹Many daughters have done worthily, but thou excellest them all. ³⁰Favour is false, and beauty is vain ; but a woman that feareth the Lord, she shall be praised. ³¹Give her of the fruit of her hands ; and let her works praise her in the gates.

THE KIDDUSH.

The Kiddush is the formal consecrating of home life. It is the ceremony and prayer by which the holiness of the Sabbath is proclaimed by the Israelite in his own home. At the beginning of the first Sabbath-meal, the wife, children and dependents take part in this ceremony which brings out the double significance of the Sabbath— the religious and the historical. The Sabbath proclaims the basic truth that this universe is not the product of chance, but is the work of a Divine Power. It is also a reminder of the Deliverance from Egypt, and of God as Israel's Redeemer.

" Remember the Sabbath day "—the Traditional explanation of these words is, " remember it over wine ". As wine gladdens the heart of man (Psalm 104. 15), our meal on the eve of Sabbaths and Festivals begins with a cup of wine in honour of the day, accompanied by two Blessings : one over the wine, and one on the holiness of the day.

The Jew recognizes that wine, though liable to abuse, is none the less a divine gift, worthy to be used in acts of adoration of Him who is the bounteous Bestower of all good. Judaism emphasizes the joyous side of life which is not only sanctified, but sanctifies, by lawful use.

If there is no wine, the Blessing over wine is omitted, and the *motzi*, the Blessing over bread, said in its place.

a memorial of the creation. Talmudic legend tells that when the heavens and earth were being called into existence, matter was getting out of hand, and the Divine Voice had to resound, " Enough ! so far

סֵדֶר קִדּוּשׁ לְלֵיל שַׁבָּת:

*The following is said in the Home by the Master of the House,
previous to partaking of the Sabbath Meal :—*

וַיְהִי־עֶרֶב וַיְהִי־בֹקֶר

יוֹם הַשִּׁשִּׁי: וַיְכֻלּוּ הַשָּׁמַיִם וְהָאָרֶץ וְכָל־צְבָאָם: וַיְכַל
אֱלֹהִים בַּיּוֹם הַשְּׁבִיעִי מְלַאכְתּוֹ אֲשֶׁר עָשָׂה וַיִּשְׁבֹּת בַּיּוֹם
הַשְּׁבִיעִי מִכָּל־מְלַאכְתּוֹ אֲשֶׁר עָשָׂה: וַיְבָרֶךְ אֱלֹהִים אֶת־
יוֹם הַשְּׁבִיעִי וַיְקַדֵּשׁ אֹתוֹ כִּי בוֹ שָׁבַת מִכָּל־מְלַאכְתּוֹ
אֲשֶׁר־בָּרָא אֱלֹהִים לַעֲשׂוֹת:

בָּרוּךְ אַתָּה יְיָ אֱלֹהֵינוּ מֶלֶךְ הָעוֹלָם · בּוֹרֵא פְּרִי הַגָּפֶן:

בָּרוּךְ אַתָּה יְיָ אֱלֹהֵינוּ מֶלֶךְ הָעוֹלָם · אֲשֶׁר קִדְּשָׁנוּ
בְּמִצְוֹתָיו וְרָצָה בָנוּ · וְשַׁבַּת קָדְשׁוֹ בְּאַהֲבָה וּבְרָצוֹן
הִנְחִילָנוּ זִכָּרוֹן לְמַעֲשֵׂה בְרֵאשִׁית · כִּי הוּא יוֹם תְּחִלָּה
לְמִקְרָאֵי קֹדֶשׁ זֵכֶר לִיצִיאַת מִצְרָיִם · כִּי־בָנוּ בָחַרְתָּ
וְאוֹתָנוּ קִדַּשְׁתָּ מִכָּל־הָעַמִּים וְשַׁבַּת קָדְשְׁךָ בְּאַהֲבָה
וּבְרָצוֹן הִנְחַלְתָּנוּ · בָּרוּךְ אַתָּה יְיָ · מְקַדֵּשׁ הַשַּׁבָּת:

בָּרוּךְ אַתָּה יְיָ אֱלֹהֵינוּ מֶלֶךְ הָעוֹלָם · הַמּוֹצִיא לֶחֶם
מִן הָאָרֶץ:

KIDDUSH—*continued from preceding page.*
and no further " ! Likewise, in man's little universe matter is constantly getting out of hand, threatening to overwhelm and crush our
soul. By means of the Sabbath, called זכרון למעשה בראשית " a
memorial of Creation ", man, made in the image of God, is endowed
with the Divine power of saying " Enough " ! to all rebellious claims

THE KIDDUSH

KIDDUSH·FOR SABBATH EVENING

The following is said in the Home by the Master of the House, previous to partaking of the Sabbath Meal :—

And it was evening and it was morning,—the sixth day.

Genesis 2. 1–3 ¹And the heaven and the earth were finished and all their host. ²And on the seventh day God had finished his work which he had made ; and he rested on the seventh day *See p. 380* from all his work which he had made. ³And God blessed the seventh day, and he hallowed it, because he rested thereon from all his work which God had created and made.

Blessed art Thou, O Lord our God, King of the universe, who createst the fruit of the vine.

Blessed art thou, O Lord our God, King of the universe, who hast hallowed us by thy commandments and hast taken pleasure in us, and in love and favour hast given us thy holy Sabbath as an inheritance, a memorial of the creation—that day being also the first of the holy convocations, in remembrance of the departure from Egypt. For thou hast chosen us and hallowed us above all nations, and in love and favour hast given us thy holy Sabbath as an inheritance. Blessed art thou, O Lord, who hallowest the Sabbath.

HA-MOTZI BLESSING Blessed art thou, O Lord our God, King of the universe, who bringest forth bread from the earth.

---

of our environment, and is reminded of his potential victory over all forces that would drag him down.

first of the holy convocations. The Sabbath is named first in the list of Holy Days, Leviticus 23.

remembrance of the departure from Egypt. The Israelites in Egypt slaved day after day without a rest. By ceasing from toil one day in seven, we distinguish our work from the drudgery of the slave. Judaism " proclaims a truce once in seven days to all personal anxieties and degrading thoughts about the means of subsistence and success in life. In countries where life is a hard struggle, what more precious, more priceless public benefit can be imagined than this breathing time, this recurring armistice between man and the hostile powers that beset his life, this solemn Sabbatic Festival ? " (J. R. Seeley).

HA-MOTZI. *bread.* Food ; the wording is from Psalm 104. 14.

זְמִירוֹת לְשַׁבָּת :

יָהּ רִבּוֹן עָלַם וְעָלְמַיָּא · אַנְתְּ הוּא מַלְכָּא מֶלֶךְ
מַלְכַיָּא : עוֹבַד גְּבוּרְתֵּךְ וְתִמְהַיָּא · שַׁפִּיר קֳדָמָךְ
לְהַחֲוָיָה : יה רבון

שְׁבָחִין אֲסַדֵּר צַפְרָא וְרַמְשָׁא · לָךְ אֱלָהָא קַדִּישָׁא
דִּי בְרָא כָל-נַפְשָׁא · עִירִין קַדִּישִׁין וּבְנֵי אֱנָשָׁא ·
חֵיוַת בָּרָא וְעוֹפֵי שְׁמַיָּא : יה רבון

רַבְרְבִין עוֹבְדָיךְ וְתַקִּיפִין · מָכֵךְ רָמַיָּא זַקֵף כְּפִיפִין ·
לוּ יְחֵא גְבַר שְׁנִין אַלְפִין · לָא יֵעַל גְּבוּרְתֵּךְ
בְּחֻשְׁבְּנַיָּא : יה רבון

אֱלָהָא דִּי לֵהּ יְקָר וּרְבוּתָא · פְּרֹק יָת-עָנָךְ מִפֻּם
אַרְיָוָתָא · וְאַפֵּק יָת-עַמָּךְ מִגּוֹא גָלוּתָא · עַמָּךְ דִּי
בְחַרְתְּ מִכָּל-אֻמַּיָּא : יה רבון

לְמִקְדָּשֵׁךְ תּוּב וּלְקֹדֶשׁ קֻדְשִׁין · אֲתַר דִּי בֵהּ יֶחֱדוּן
רוּחִין וְנַפְשִׁין · וִיזַמְּרוּן שִׁירִין וְרַחֲשִׁין · בִּירוּשְׁלֵם
קַרְתָּא דִי-שֻׁפְרַיָּא : יה רבון

The Zemiroth—Jewish Table Hymns.

During the meal, Jewish Table Songs are chanted in domestic circles that observe the Sabbath with the olden love and joy—"Songs summing up, in light and jingling metre, the very essence of holy joyousness —neither riotous, nor ascetic : the note of spiritualized common sense which has been the keynote of historical Judaism" (Zangwill). It is the ancient Jewish Mystics who added a touch of ecstasy to the daily

SABBATH TABLE HYMNS

"YOH
RIBBON
OLAM"

God of the World, eternity's sole Lord!
King over kings, be now thy Name adored!
Blessed are we to whom thou dost accord
  This gladsome time thy wondrous ways to scan!
God of the World, etc.

Early and late to thee our praises ring,
Giver of life to every living thing!
Beasts of the field, and birds that heavenward wing,
  Angelic hosts and all the sons of man!
God of the World, etc.

Though we on earth a thousand years should dwell,
Too brief the space, thy marvels forth to tell!
Pride thou didst lower, all the weak who fell
  Thy hand raised up e'er since the world began!
God of the World, etc.

Thine is the power, thine the glory be!
When lions rage, Oh, deign thy flock to free!
Thine exiled sons, Oh, take once more to thee,
  Choose them again as in thine ancient plan!
God of the World, etc.

Turn to thy city, Zion's sacred shrine!
On yon fair mount again let beauty shine!
There, happy throngs their voices shall combine,
  There, present joy all former ill shall ban!
God of the World, etc.

meals by composing and singing gleeful table hymns to the Giver of all things. This saintly custom was in time adopted by the whole House of Israel, albeit only for the Sabbath, which is and must ever remain the central sun in the existence of the faithful Jew.

  The unique combination, in these Table Songs, of adoration of God with genial appreciation of good cheer, is a product of the Jewish genius, which interweaves the secular with the sacred, and spreads over the ordinary facts of life the rainbow of the Divine. Those who sing these beautiful hymns and melodies "make the Sabbath a delight", and

צוּר מִשֶּׁלּוֹ אָכַלְנוּ · בָּרְכוּ אֱמוּנַי · שָׂבַעְנוּ וְהוֹתַרְנוּ ·

כִּדְבַר יְיָ :

הַזָּן אֶת־עוֹלָמוֹ · רוֹעֵנוּ אָבִינוּ · אָכַלְנוּ אֶת־לַחְמוֹ ·

וְיֵינוֹ שָׁתִינוּ · עַל־כֵּן נוֹדֶה לִשְׁמוֹ · וּנְהַלְלוֹ בְּפִינוּ ·

אָמַרְנוּ וְעָנִינוּ אֵין־קָדוֹשׁ כַּיְיָ : צור משלו

בְּשִׁיר וְקוֹל תּוֹדָה · נְבָרֵךְ אֱלֹהֵינוּ · עַל אֶרֶץ חֶמְדָּה ·

שֶׁהִנְחִיל לַאֲבוֹתֵינוּ · מָזוֹן וְצֵידָה · הִשְׂבִּיעַ לְנַפְשֵׁנוּ ·

חַסְדּוֹ גָּבַר עָלֵינוּ · וֶאֱמֶת יְיָ : צור משלו

רַחֵם בְּחַסְדֶּךָ · עַל עַמְּךָ צוּרֵנוּ · עַל צִיּוֹן מִשְׁכַּן

כְּבוֹדֶךָ · זְבוּל בֵּית תִּפְאַרְתֵּנוּ · בֶּן־דָּוִד עַבְדֶּךָ · יָבֹא

וְיִגְאָלֵנוּ · רוּחַ אַפֵּינוּ · מְשִׁיחַ יְיָ : צור משלו

יִבָּנֶה הַמִּקְדָּשׁ · עִיר צִיּוֹן תְּמַלֵּא · וְשָׁם נָשִׁיר שִׁיר

חָדָשׁ · וּבִרְנָנָה נַעֲלֶה · הָרַחֲמָן הַנִּקְדָּשׁ · יִתְבָּרַךְ

וְיִתְעַלֶּה · עַל כּוֹס יַיִן מָלֵא · כְּבִרְכַּת יְיָ : צור משלו

implant in the souls of their children an ineradicable love of the Sacred Day. The Sabbath is to them, as it was to their fathers of old, a foretaste of that " Day which is wholly a Sabbath, and a rest in life everlasting ".

There is no fixed number to the number of Table Songs recited, nor any fixed order for their recital.

GOD OF THE WORLD. It is in Aramaic, and its author is Israel Najara, of Safed, in the sixteenth century. It has been set to many beautiful melodies. The translation is by I. Abrahams.

Rock from whose store we have eaten—
Bless him, my faithful companions.
Eaten have we and left over—
    This was the word of the Lord.

Feeding his world like a shepherd—
Father whose bread we have eaten,
Father whose wine we have drunken.
Now to his Name we are singing,
Praising him loud with our voices,
Saying and singing for ever :
    Holy is none like the Lord.   *Rock, etc.*

Singing with sound of thanksgiving,
Bless we our God for the good land
Given of old to our fathers ;
Bless we him now who has given
Food for our hunger of spirit ;
Strong over us is his mercy,
    Mighty the truth of the Lord.   *Rock, etc.*

Mercy, O Rock, for thy people !
Pity the place of thy glory,
Zion, the house of our beauty.
Soon shall he come to redeem us—
Offspring of David, thy servant,
He that is breath of our spirit—
    Send thine anointed, O Lord !   *Rock, etc.*

Oh that the Temple were builded,
Filled again Zion our city—
There a new song shall we sing him,
Merciful, holy and blessed,—
Bless we him now and for ever,
Over the full brimming wine cup,
    Blest as we are of the Lord.   *Rock, etc.*

ROCK FROM WHOSE STORE. Of unknown authorship. The translation is by Nina Salaman. The hymn is an introduction to the Grace after meals. For further Table Hymns see pp. 566-569.

MORNING SERVICE FOR SABBATHS

" On the Sabbath day, a spirit of rejoicing is suffused throughout the universe. When the sons of the Holy People, with jubilant hearts and arrayed in Sabbath attire, go to the House of God and pour out their souls in song of praise and prayer, every one of them is adorned with an effulgence from the Divine Crown " (Zohar).

Such, in the language of the Mystics, is the effect of congregational prayer which, even to the pious Israelite, is not as a rule available except on Sabbaths and Festivals. Only on those days does the ordinary Jew join in a public expression of Religion, and in a demonstration of Israel's spiritual identity. This worship is of immeasurable importance. By uniting men in prayer, it strengthens loyalty in the individual, fans and intensifies his religious feelings, and keeps him a worshipping being. It is, therefore, the imperative duty of Jews living together in any place to provide for a house of public devotion.

As congregational prayer is the fervent utterance of the common spiritual need of a religious community, it must be in the con-secrated, historic forms of devotion of that community. At any rate, in Jewry, only the Traditional Service has any hope of continuance, or of living influence in the souls of its men and women. This presupposes that Jewish men and women are *reared* to the Service. Indeed, the bringing up of its coming generation to the full participation in Israel's worship—equipping its youth with a knowledge of the Sacred Language, and familiarizing it with the Liturgy—is among the main aims of Jewish religious education. However, vitally important as is such training, we must beware of over-estimating the intellectual element in worship. Communion with God is not necessarily dependent on the grasp of the *literal* meaning of the prayers ; so long as the worshipper is sustained, though it be but vaguely and indistinctly, by devotional moods and feelings. " Even in prayers recited without complete under-standing, the worshipper is conscious that he has to do with something holy ; that the words which he uses bring him into relation with God " (Heiler).

And the *melody* and *chant* in prayer are often of a far more lasting influence than the verbal message. " The strongest effect of chanted liturgies is independent of detailed verbal meaning. The most powerful prayer seeks for nothing special, but is a yearning to escape from the limitations of our own weakness, and an invocation of all Good to enter and abide with us " (George Eliot). The Mystics and the Chassidim fully understood this ; and so did the common people, who, throughout the centuries, insisted on Chazonus as an essential accompaniment of Synagogue worship. The Mystics taught, "There are halls in the heavens above that open but to the voice of song". This is certainly true of the human soul: it may remain shut to other influences, but it opens to the voice of melody. A great Chassid wisely put it, "The sphere of music is near the sphere of repentance ". And as for the common people, there is much truth in Zangwill's characterization of the worshippers at an East End chevrah—" Their religious consciousness was largely a musical box : the thrill of a ram's horn, the cadenza of a psalmic phrase, the jubilance of a festival ' Amen ', and the sobriety of a workaday ' Amen ', the Passover melodies and the Pentecost, the minor keys of Atonement and the hilarous rapsodies of Rejoicing, the plain chant of the Law and the more ornate intonation of the Prophets." This is in line with the words of that profound student of Man and his Past, J. G. Frazer, " Every faith has its appropriate music, and the difference between the creeds might almost be expressed in musical notation ".

In view of all this, participation in the Traditional Service, even if the worshipper cannot translate all its phrases into his own vernacular, is of irreplaceable value ; seeing that, in addition to all else, it keeps alive in the Jewish heart the sense of worship, the knowledge of membership in the House of Israel, and the feeling of sympathy with every good cause. Therefore, to dismiss such "unthinking" devotion as unworthy of the name of Prayer, is to remain blind to the deep educational values inherent in it. " The great mass of average people ", says Heiler, " need fixed religious forms to which, in their spiritual dependence, they can cling ; they need some stern compulsion to drive them away from the concerns of daily life, and lift them up to a higher world ". In Israel, the Traditional Sabbath Service, is above all others such a fixed religious form. It is an obligatory observance thát remains the strongest agency for awakening and sustaining the religious consciousness of the Jew. It leaves its mark on the souls of them who hallow it, and adorns their life "with an effulgence from the Divine Crown ".

On Sabbaths and Festival Mornings, the Service begins with Yigdal, p. 6. Its earlier portion is substantially the same as on weekdays. Psalm 100 is omitted (as there was no thank-offering in the Temple on Festive days), and nine more psalms (pp. 60–82) are recited in the section " Psalms and Passages of Song ".

These additional Psalms adore God as Creator (Psalms 19 and 90 deal with the wonders of God and His universe) ; proclaim the Sabbath as a memorial of Israel's liberation from Egyptian bondage (Psalms 136 and 138) ; and praise God as the Deliverer from all woe. Psalm 92—"a Song for the Sabbath Day"—was later understood to be the Psalm for the Hereafter, " for the Day which is wholly a Sabbath and rest in Life everlasting ". It is thus a reminder of Immortality.

After the Song at the Red Sea, p. 104, the Service assumes its festive character with the important doxology *Nishmas*.

תְּפִלַּת שַׁחֲרִית לְשַׁבָּת וְיוֹם טוֹב:

Page 6 to אֶחָד, p. 104. Then continue as follows :—

נִשְׁמַת כָּל־חַי תְּבָרֵךְ אֶת־שִׁמְךָ יְיָ אֱלֹהֵינוּ • וְרוּחַ כָּל־
בָּשָׂר תְּפָאֵר וּתְרוֹמֵם זִכְרְךָ מַלְכֵּנוּ תָּמִיד • מִן־הָעוֹלָם
וְעַד־הָעוֹלָם אַתָּה אֵל • וּמִבַּלְעָדֶיךָ אֵין לָנוּ מֶלֶךְ גּוֹאֵל
וּמוֹשִׁיעַ פּוֹדֶה וּמַצִּיל וּמְפַרְנֵס וּמְרַחֵם בְּכָל־עֵת צָרָה
וְצוּקָה • אֵין לָנוּ מֶלֶךְ אֶלָּא אָתָּה : אֱלֹהֵי הָרִאשׁוֹנִים
וְהָאַחֲרוֹנִים • אֱלוֹהַּ כָּל־בְּרִיּוֹת אֲדוֹן כָּל־תּוֹלָדוֹת הַמְהֻלָּל
בְּרֹב הַתִּשְׁבָּחוֹת הַמְנַהֵג עוֹלָמוֹ בְּחֶסֶד וּבְרִיּוֹתָיו בְּרַחֲמִים:
וַיְיָ לֹא־יָנוּם וְלֹא־יִישָׁן • הַמְעוֹרֵר יְשֵׁנִים וְהַמֵּקִיץ נִרְדָּמִים •
וְהַמֵּשִׂיחַ אִלְּמִים • וְהַמַּתִּיר אֲסוּרִים וְהַסּוֹמֵךְ נוֹפְלִים
וְהַזּוֹקֵף כְּפוּפִים : לְךָ לְבַדְּךָ אֲנַחְנוּ מוֹדִים : אִלּוּ פִינוּ
מָלֵא שִׁירָה כַיָּם וּלְשׁוֹנֵנוּ רִנָּה כַּהֲמוֹן גַּלָּיו וְשִׂפְתוֹתֵינוּ

MORNING SERVICE
FOR SABBATHS AND FESTIVALS.

NISHMAS

Even as the number of psalms has been increased for Sabbaths and
Festivals, so has the special Benediction that concludes the daily reading
of the Psalms (*yishtabach*, p. 104) been expanded by prefixing to it the
poetic *Nishmas* prayer. This ancient and beautiful adoration, with its
rich poetical imagery, deserves to be known far beyond the borders of
Jewry. The first part (till " to Thee alone we give thanks ") probably
dates from Temple times : the remainder was known to the Talmudic
teachers. Tradition connects its authorship with the statesman-rabbi
of the Maccabean dynasty, Simeon ben Shatach (p. 620). A curious
legend that was current in medieval Germany and France, declared the
author of *Nishmas* to have been Simon Cephas, *i.e.* the Apostle Peter.
In this Prayer he was to have completed his renunciation of the new

PSALMS
AND
PASSAGES
OF SONG—
Continued

NISHMAS
I. GOD—
THE
KING, RE-
DEEMER,
AND
HELPER

2. NO
HUMAN
TONGUE
CAN
EXHAUST
HIS
PRAISES

MORNING SERVICE
FOR SABBATHS AND FESTIVALS.

Page 7 to " the Lord is One ", p. 105. *Then continue as follows* :

The breath of every living being shall bless thy Name, O Lord our God, and the spirit of all flesh shall ever extol and exalt thy fame, O our King. From everlasting to everlasting thou art God ; and beside thee we have no King, O thou who redeemest and savest, settest free and deliverest, who supportest and pitiest in all times of trouble and distress ; yea, we have no King but thee.

Thou art God of the first and of the last ages, God of all creatures, Lord of all generations, adored in innumerable praises, guiding thy world with lovingkindness and thy creatures with tender mercies. The Lord slumbereth not, nor sleepeth ; he arouseth the sleepers and awakeneth the slumberers ; he maketh the dumb to speak, setteth free the prisoners, supporteth the falling, and raiseth up those who are bowed down.

To thee alone we give thanks. Were our mouths full of song as the sea, and our tongues of exultation as the

Doctrine with which he had been associated. This legend was indignantly repudiated by Rashi and others.

1. The Breath. Let all men bless and glorify Him Who is our sole Saviour and Redeemer.

and exalt thy fame. The usual translation, "and exalt thy memorial," is unintelligible and misleading. זכר is the synonym of שם " Name ", and means title, remembrance, or fame. Cf. Psalm 145. 7 and Psalm 97. 12; pp. 87 and 351.

settest free. Heb. פודה, by arrangement with him who has mastery over you.

and deliverest. Heb. מציל, snatching from mortal danger, like saving the lamb from the wolf.

guiding . . lovingkindness. A characteristic teaching of Judaism. Mercy (מדת הרחמים) accompanies Justice in God's dealings with mankind

arouseth the sleepers. To repentance, or to new life.

2. *were our mouths . . .* Man is incapable of adequately thanking God for His infinite mercies.

שֶׁבַח כְּמֶרְחֲבֵי רָקִיעַ · וְעֵינֵינוּ מְאִירוֹת כַּשֶּׁמֶשׁ וְכַיָּרֵחַ ·
וְיָדֵינוּ פְרוּשׂוֹת כְּנִשְׁרֵי שָׁמָיִם · וְרַגְלֵינוּ קַלּוֹת כָּאַיָּלוֹת ·
אֵין אֲנַחְנוּ מַסְפִּיקִים לְהוֹדוֹת לְךָ יְיָ אֱלֹהֵינוּ וֵאלֹהֵי
אֲבוֹתֵינוּ וּלְבָרֵךְ אֶת־שְׁמֶךָ עַל־אַחַת מֵאֶלֶף אֶלֶף
אַלְפֵי אֲלָפִים וְרִבֵּי רְבָבוֹת פְּעָמִים הַטּוֹבוֹת שֶׁעָשִׂיתָ עִם־
אֲבוֹתֵינוּ וְעִמָּנוּ ׃ מִמִּצְרַיִם גְּאַלְתָּנוּ יְיָ אֱלֹהֵינוּ וּמִבֵּית
עֲבָדִים פְּדִיתָנוּ · בְּרָעָב זַנְתָּנוּ וּבְשָׂבָע כִּלְכַּלְתָּנוּ · מֵחֶרֶב
הִצַּלְתָּנוּ וּמִדֶּבֶר מִלַּטְתָּנוּ וּמֵחֳלָיִם רָעִים וְנֶאֱמָנִים
דִּלִּיתָנוּ ׃ עַד־הֵנָּה עֲזָרוּנוּ רַחֲמֶיךָ · וְלֹא־עֲזָבוּנוּ חֲסָדֶיךָ ·
וְאַל־תִּטְּשֵׁנוּ יְיָ אֱלֹהֵינוּ לָנֶצַח ׃ עַל־כֵּן אֵבָרִים שֶׁפִּלַּגְתָּ
בָּנוּ וְרוּחַ וּנְשָׁמָה שֶׁנָּפַחְתָּ בְּאַפֵּינוּ וְלָשׁוֹן אֲשֶׁר שַׂמְתָּ
בְּפִינוּ · הֵן הֵם יוֹדוּ וִיבָרְכוּ וִישַׁבְּחוּ וִיפָאֲרוּ וִירוֹמְמוּ
וְיַעֲרִיצוּ וְיַקְדִּישׁוּ וְיַמְלִיכוּ אֶת־שְׁמֶךָ מַלְכֵּנוּ ׃ כִּי כָל־פֶּה

as the sea . . . . waves. In the poetic figure, the *sea* indicates the inexhaustibleness ; the *waves*, the countlessness ; and the *skies*, the immeasurable infinity, of God's praises.

were our mouths full of song. These words formed the opening of a prayer of thanks in Talmudic days for timely and copious rain. Two things should be noted in regard to these hyperboles. In the first place, there is a substratum of fact underlying them. " Is not every glance of the eye (woe to the blind!) an ineffable benefit ? every breath of man, and his every step, another opportunity towards blessing and joy " ? (Remy). Moreover, God's grace may be displayed as much, and more so, in the things He denies us, as in what He grants us. And then think of the evil visitations we dreaded that have not befallen us, the catastrophes which threatened our health and happiness, that passed away without our even being aware of them. In the second place, hyperboles are part of Oriental literary manner. Thus, the Pentecost hymn

PSALMS
AND
PASSAGES
OF SONG—
continued

multitude of its waves, and our lips of praise as the wide-extended skies ; were our eyes shining with light like the sun and the moon, and our hands were spread forth like the eagles of the air, and our feet were swift as the wild deer, we should still be unable to thank thee and to bless thy Name, O Lord our God and God of our fathers, for one thousandth or one ten thousandth part of the bounties which thou hast bestowed upon our fathers and upon us.

*OR OUR
GRATI-
TUDE*

Thou didst redeem us from Egypt, O Lord our God, and didst release us from the house of bondage ; during famine thou didst feed us, and didst sustain us in plenty ; from the sword thou didst rescue us, from pestilence thou didst save us, and from sore and lingering diseases thou didst deliver us.

3. *THERE-
FORE WITH
ALL OUR
BEING
SHALL WE
LAUD HIS
NAME*

Hitherto thy tender mercies have helped us, and thy lovingkindnesses have not left us : forsake us not, O Lord our God, for ever. Therefore the limbs which thou hast planted in us, and the spirit and soul which thou hast breathed into us, and the tongue which thou hast set in our mouths, lo, they shall thank, bless, praise, glorify, extol, reverence, hallow and do homage to thy Name, O our King. For every mouth shall give thanks unto thee,

Akdomus, echoing Rabbinic phraseology, declares :
> " Could we with ink the ocean fill,
> Were every blade of grass a quill,
> Were the world of parchment made,
> And every man a scribe by trade—
> To write the love
> Of God above
> Would drain that ocean dry ;
> Nor would the scroll
> Contain the whole,
> Though stretched from sky to sky ! "

like the sun and the moon. So as to see all the wonders of Creation.
like the eagles. To spy out all His mysteries.
swift as the wild deer. To do the will of God. *Wild deer.* lit. " hinds ", noted for fleet movement.
3. Therefore, with all our body and every faculty of soul shall we throughout our lives adore Him.
planted in us. Or, " distributed within us ".

לְךָ יוֹדֶה · וְכָל־לָשׁוֹן לְךָ תִשָּׁבַע · וְכָל־בֶּרֶךְ לְךָ תִכְרַע

וְכָל־קוֹמָה לְפָנֶיךָ תִשְׁתַּחֲוֶה · וְכָל־לְבָבוֹת יִירָאוּךָ · וְכָל־

קֶרֶב וּכְלָיוֹת יְזַמְּרוּ לִשְׁמֶךָ · כַּדָּבָר שֶׁכָּתוּב · כָּל עַצְמוֹתַי

תֹּאמַרְנָה יְיָ מִי כָמוֹךָ : מַצִּיל עָנִי מֵחָזָק מִמֶּנּוּ וְעָנִי וְאֶבְיוֹן

מִגֹּזְלוֹ : מִי יִדְמֶה־לָּךְ וּמִי יִשְׁוֶה־לָּךְ וּמִי יַעֲרָךְ־לָךְ · הָאֵל

הַגָּדוֹל הַגִּבּוֹר וְהַנּוֹרָא אֵל עֶלְיוֹן קֹנֵה שָׁמַיִם וָאָרֶץ :

נְהַלֶּלְךָ וּנְשַׁבֵּחֲךָ וּנְפָאֶרְךָ וּנְבָרֵךְ אֶת־שֵׁם קָדְשֶׁךָ ·

כָּאָמוּר · לְדָוִד · בָּרְכִי נַפְשִׁי אֶת־יְיָ וְכָל־קְרָבַי אֶת־שֵׁם

קָדְשׁוֹ : הָאֵל בְּתַעֲצֻמוֹת עֻזֶּךָ · הַגָּדוֹל בִּכְבוֹד שְׁמֶךָ ·

הַגִּבּוֹר לָנֶצַח וְהַנּוֹרָא בְּנוֹרְאוֹתֶיךָ · הַמֶּלֶךְ הַיּוֹשֵׁב עַל

כִּסֵּא רָם וְנִשָּׂא ·

שׁוֹכֵן עַד · מָרוֹם וְקָדוֹשׁ שְׁמוֹ · וְכָתוּב רַנְּנוּ צַדִּיקִים

בַּיְיָ לַיְשָׁרִים נָאוָה תְהִלָּה :

בְּפִי יְשָׁרִים תִּתְהַלָּל · וּבְדִבְרֵי צַדִּיקִים תִּתְבָּרַךְ ·

וּבִלְשׁוֹן חֲסִידִים תִּתְרוֹמָם · וּבְקֶרֶב קְדוֹשִׁים תִּתְקַדָּשׁ :

וּבְמַקְהֲלוֹת רִבְבוֹת עַמְּךָ בֵּית יִשְׂרָאֵל בְּרִנָּה יִתְפָּאַר

שִׁמְךָ מַלְכֵּנוּ בְּכָל־דּוֹר וָדוֹר · שֶׁכֵּן חוֹבַת כָּל־הַיְצוּרִים

---

innermost being. lit. "inward parts and reins".

needy . . . robbeth. Injustice is to the authors of the Liturgy, as to
Prophet and Psalmist of old, the great blot in the life of humanity;

*WE SHALL
EVER
LAUD HIS
NAME* and every tongue shall swear allegiance unto thee ; every knee shall bow to thee, and whatsoever is lofty shall prostrate itself before thee. All hearts shall revere thee, and our innermost being shall sing unto thy Name, accord-

Psalm 35. 10 ing to the word that is written, All my bones shall say, Lord, who is like unto thee ? Thou deliverest the poor from him that is stronger than he, the poor and the needy from him that robbeth him. Who is like unto thee, who is equal to thee, who can be compared unto thee, O God, great, mighty, and awful, most high God, Maker of heaven and earth ? We will praise, laud and glorify thee, and we will bless thy holy Name, as it is said, (A Psalm of David,)

Psalm 103. 1 Bless the Lord, O my soul ; and all that is within me, bless his holy Name. Thou art God in the vastness of thy power, great in thy glorious Name, mighty for ever and revered by thy awe-inspiring acts, the King who sitteth upon a high and lofty throne.

He inhabiteth eternity, exalted and holy is his Name;
Psalm 33. 1 and it is written, Exult in the Lord, O ye righteous ; praise
4. *AND IN
ASSEM-
BLIES
WORSHIP
HIM* is seemly for the upright.

By the mouth of the upright thou shalt be praised, by the words of the righteous thou shalt be blessed, by the tongue of the pious thou shalt be extolled, and in the midst of the holy thou shalt be hallowed.

In the assemblies also of the tens of thousands of thy people, the house of Israel, thy Name, O our King, shall

and they never weary of proclaiming that the God of Justice will secure the triumph of Right among the children of men.

4. *He inhabiteth eternity.* Based on Isaiah 57. 15.

upright. The first letters of the Hebrew words for *upright, righteous, pious,* and *holy* happen to spell the word יצחק, Isaac ; and by re-arranging the words for *praised, blessed, extolled* and *hallowed,* the third letters of these words form רבקה, Rebekah. " Such fanciful ideas were and still are appreciated by many, whose affectionate ingenuity would play in childlike rapture round the words of the beloved prayers " (Abrahams).

לְפָנֶיךָ יְיָ אֱלֹהֵינוּ וֵאלֹהֵי אֲבוֹתֵינוּ · לְהוֹדוֹת לְהַלֵּל

לְשַׁבֵּחַ לְפָאֵר לְרוֹמֵם לְהַדֵּר לְבָרֵךְ לְעַלֵּה וּלְקַלֵּס עַל כָּל־

דִּבְרֵי שִׁירוֹת וְתִשְׁבְּחוֹת דָּוִד בֶּן־יִשַׁי עַבְדְּךָ מְשִׁיחֶךָ :

יִשְׁתַּבַּח שִׁמְךָ לָעַד מַלְכֵּנוּ · הָאֵל הַמֶּלֶךְ הַגָּדוֹל

וְהַקָּדוֹשׁ בַּשָּׁמַיִם וּבָאָרֶץ · כִּי לְךָ נָאֶה יְיָ אֱלֹהֵינוּ וֵאלֹהֵי

אֲבוֹתֵינוּ שִׁיר וּשְׁבָחָה הַלֵּל וְזִמְרָה עֹז וּמֶמְשָׁלָה נֶצַח

גְּדֻלָּה וּגְבוּרָה תְּהִלָּה וְתִפְאֶרֶת קְדֻשָּׁה וּמַלְכוּת בְּרָכוֹת

וְהוֹדָאוֹת מֵעַתָּה וְעַד־עוֹלָם · בָּרוּךְ אַתָּה יְיָ · אֵל מֶלֶךְ ·

גָּדוֹל בַּתִּשְׁבָּחוֹת · אֵל הַהוֹדָאוֹת · אֲדוֹן הַנִּפְלָאוֹת ·

הַבּוֹחֵר בְּשִׁירֵי זִמְרָה · מֶלֶךְ אֵל חֵי הָעוֹלָמִים :

Reader. יִתְגַּדַּל וְיִתְקַדַּשׁ שְׁמֵהּ רַבָּא בְּעָלְמָא דִּי־בְרָא

כִרְעוּתֵהּ · וְיַמְלִיךְ מַלְכוּתֵהּ בְּחַיֵּיכוֹן וּבְיוֹמֵיכוֹן וּבְחַיֵּי

דִי־כָל־בֵּית יִשְׂרָאֵל בַּעֲגָלָא וּבִזְמַן קָרִיב · וְאִמְרוּ אָמֵן :

YISHTABBACH. *Praised be thy Name*—the Benediction for the
" Psalms and Passages of Song "—the same as on p. 104—is now recited.
It is the benediction *after* the reading, just as *Boruch she-omar*,
"Blessed be He who spake " (p. 50) is the benediction *before* the reading,
of those Psalms. There are similar benedictions before and after the
reading of Hallel on New Moons and Festivals.

song . . . thanksgiving. Fifteen distinct terms of praise and adoration
are enumerated. Hebrew is remarkably rich in the vocabulary of
adoration and worship. " As Latin is the language of war, Greek that
of oratory, so is Hebrew the language of Prayer " (Midrash).

of all worlds. Or, " of all eternities ".

be glorified with joyous song in every generation ; for such is the duty of all creatures before thee, O Lord our God and God of our fathers, to thank, praise, laud, glorify, extol, honour, bless, exalt and acclaim thee, even beyond all the words of song and adoration of David the son of Jesse, thy anointed servant.

CONCLUD-
ING
BENEDIC-
TION to
PSALMS
AND
PASSAGES
OF SONG

Praised be thy Name for ever, O our King, the great and holy God and King, in heaven and on earth ; for unto thee, O Lord our God, and God of our fathers, song and praise are becoming, hymn and psalm, strength and dominion, victory, greatness and might, renown and glory, holiness and sovereignty, blessings and thanksgivings from henceforth even for ever. Blessed art thou, O Lord, God and King, great in praises, God of thanksgivings, Lord of wonders, who makest choice of song and psalm, O King and God, the life of all worlds.

HALF-
KADDISH

Reader.—Magnified and sanctified be his great Name in the world which he hath created according to his will. May he establish his kingdom during your life and during your days, and during the life of all the house of Israel, even speedily and at a near time, and say ye, Amen.

HALF-KADDISH. *magnified.* As elsewhere in the Liturgy, the Half-Kaddish marks the end of a section of the Service; here, of the Preliminary part of the Sabbath Morning Service. It was originally a doxology, or formula of praise, concluding the religious discourse of the ancient teacher. He would in this way dismiss his assembly with a glorification of God and the Messianic hope of the speedy coming of His kingdom. The doxology was in Aramaic, because the discourse was in Aramaic, the language spoken by the Jews after the Babylonian Exile. In time, the doxology passed from the School to the Synagogue.

may he establish his kingdom. May He bring about the realization of all spiritual values; and transform things as they are, into things as they ought to be.

let his great Name be blessed for ever and to all eternity. This is the principal response of the Kaddish (derived from Daniel 2. 20, and analogous to Psalm 113. 2, and to the response, " Blessed be His Name, whose glorious Kingdom is for ever and ever "). It was deemed to be the hymn of hymns, and gained still greater hold upon the reverent

Cong. and Reader.

יְהֵא שְׁמֵהּ רַבָּא מְבָרַךְ לְעָלַם

וּלְעָלְמֵי עָלְמַיָּא ·

Reader.

יִתְבָּרַךְ וְיִשְׁתַּבַּח וְיִתְפָּאַר וְיִתְרוֹמַם וְיִתְנַשֵּׂא

וְיִתְהַדָּר וְיִתְעַלֶּה וְיִתְהַלָּל שְׁמֵהּ דִּי־קֻדְשָׁא · בְּרִיךְ הוּא ·

לְעֵלָּא מִן־כָּל־בִּרְכָתָא וְשִׁירָתָא תֻּשְׁבְּחָתָא וְנֶחֱמָתָא

דִּי־אֲמִירָן בְּעָלְמָא · וְאִמְרוּ אָמֵן :

Congregation in an undertone.

יִתְבָּרַךְ וְיִשְׁתַּבַּח וְיִתְפָּאַר
וְיִתְרוֹמַם וְיִתְנַשֵּׂא שְׁמוֹ שֶׁל־מֶלֶךְ
מַלְכֵי הַמְּלָכִים הַקָּדוֹשׁ בָּרוּךְ הוּא ·
שֶׁהוּא רִאשׁוֹן וְהוּא אַחֲרוֹן
וּמִבַּלְעָדָיו אֵין אֱלֹהִים · סֹלּוּ לָרֹכֵב
בָּעֲרָבוֹת בְּיָהּ שְׁמוֹ וְעִלְזוּ לְפָנָיו ·
וּשְׁמוֹ מְרוֹמָם עַל־כָּל־בְּרָכָה
וּתְהִלָּה :
בָּרוּךְ שֵׁם כְּבוֹד מַלְכוּתוֹ לְעוֹלָם
וָעֶד : יְהִי שֵׁם יְיָ מְבֹרָךְ מֵעַתָּה וְעַד
עוֹלָם :

Reader.

בָּרְכוּ אֶת־יְיָ הַמְבֹרָךְ :

Cong. and Reader.

בָּרוּךְ יְיָ הַמְבֹרָךְ לְעוֹלָם
וָעֶד :

בָּרוּךְ אַתָּה יְיָ אֱלֹהֵינוּ

מֶלֶךְ הָעוֹלָם · יוֹצֵר אוֹר

וּבוֹרֵא חֹשֶׁךְ · עֹשֶׂה

שָׁלוֹם וּבוֹרֵא אֶת־הַכֹּל:

affection of the people when the Kaddish became the Orphan's Prayer.
In its original form, the Kaddish is of great antiquity. It antedates
the Destruction of the Temple, and is echoed in the most famous
Christian prayer.

the Holy One, blessed be he. The most frequent Name of God in post-
Biblical Jewish literature. Holiness is the *essential* attribute of God.

consolations. The Hebrew word, in addition to its general meaning of
comfort in mourning and sorrow, also denotes both the praises of God
in connection with the future Messianic time and the Future Life, as
well as the consolatory discourses to which the Kaddish was the
conclusion.

Cong. and Reader.—Let his great Name be blessed for ever and to all eternity.

Reader.—Blessed, praised and glorified, exalted, extolled and honoured, magnified and lauded be the Name of the Holy One, blessed be he ; though he be high above all the blessings and hymns, praises and consolations, which are uttered in the world ; and say ye, Amen.

INVOCA-TION TO CONGRE-GATIONAL PRAYER

Reader. —BLESS YE THE LORD WHO IS TO BE BLESSED.

Cong. and Reader.— BLESSED IS THE LORD WHO IS TO BE BLESSED FOR EVER AND EVER.

Congregation, in an undertone.

Blessed, praised, glorified, exalted and extolled be the Name of the supreme King of kings, the Holy One, blessed be he, who is the first and the last, and beside him there is no God. Extol ye him that rideth upon the heavens, whose Name is the Lord, and rejoice before him. His Name is exalted above all blessing and praise. Blessed be His Name, whose glorious kingdom is for ever and ever. Let the Name of the Lord be blessed from this time forth and for evermore.

Blessed art thou, O Lord our God, King of the universe, who formest light and createst darkness, who makest peace and createst all things :

THE SHEMA
AND THE BLESSINGS BEFORE AND AFTER
(קריאת שמע)

The SHEMA is the heart of the Morning (and Evening) Service. It is Isreal's Confession of Faith. The worshipper who recites it proclaims, as the Rabbis explain, his allegiance to the Kingship of Heaven, and his joyful submission to God's laws and commandments.

The Shema is preceded by two blessings :—
(*a*) The *Yotzer* prayer, a thanksgiving for the formation of physical light, the light of day, and the daily renewal of Creation. (*b*) The *Ahavah* prayer, אהבה רבה, a fervent outpouring of exalted thanksgiving for the moral illumination bestowed upon Israel, the light of the Torah.

On Sabbaths, and on Festivals falling on Sabbaths, say the following
to פֶּלָה, *p.* 430.

On Festivals falling on Week days say הַמֵּאִיר, *p.* 108, *to* פֶּלָה,
p. 110 *and then continue* תִּתְבָּרַךְ, *p.* 432.

הַכֹּל יוֹדוּךָ וְהַכֹּל יְשַׁבְּחוּךָ ‧ וְהַכֹּל יֹאמְרוּ אֵין קָדוֹשׁ

כַּיָי ‧ הַכֹּל יְרוֹמְמוּךָ פֶּלָה יוֹצֵר הַכֹּל ‧ הָאֵל הַפּוֹתֵחַ בְּכָל־

יוֹם דַּלְתוֹת שַׁעֲרֵי מִזְרָח ‧ וּבוֹקֵעַ חַלּוֹנֵי רָקִיעַ ‧ מוֹצִיא

חַמָּה מִמְּקוֹמָהּ וּלְבָנָה מִמְּכוֹן שִׁבְתָּהּ ‧ וּמֵאִיר לָעוֹלָם

כֻּלּוֹ וּלְיוֹשְׁבָיו שֶׁבָּרָא בְּמִדַּת רַחֲמִים : הַמֵּאִיר לָאָרֶץ

וְלַדָּרִים עָלֶיהָ בְּרַחֲמִים ‧ וּבְטוּבוֹ מְחַדֵּשׁ בְּכָל־יוֹם תָּמִיד

מַעֲשֵׂה בְרֵאשִׁית : הַמֶּלֶךְ הַמְרוֹמָם לְבַדּוֹ מֵאָז ‧ הַמְשֻׁבָּח

וְהַמְפֹאָר וְהַמִּתְנַשֵּׂא מִימוֹת עוֹלָם : אֱלֹהֵי עוֹלָם בְּרַחֲמֶיךָ

הָרַבִּים רַחֵם עָלֵינוּ ‧ אֲדוֹן עֻזֵּנוּ צוּר מִשְׂגַּבֵּנוּ ‧ מָגֵן

יִשְׁעֵנוּ מִשְׂגָּב בַּעֲדֵנוּ : אֵין כְּעֶרְכְּךָ וְאֵין זוּלָתֶךָ ‧ אֶפֶס

And the Shema is followed by :

(a) An attestation of faith in the declarations conveyed in the
Shema, אמת ויציב ("True and firm"). (b) Praises of God as the
Redeemer of Israel, גואל ישראל. All these prayers are of great antiquity,
considerably older than the Maccabean period.

BORECHU. The Invocation to prayer with which the Public Service
now opens (" Bless ye the Lord who is to be blessed ") is the ancient
formula for calling people to prayer. The Response ("Blessed is the
Lord who is to be blessed for ever and ever") associates the
congregation with the praise of God to which the Reader, summons
his fellow-worshippers. The passage that is recited by the congregation in an undertone, is a later addition.

createst all things. Based on Isaiah 45. 7. " I am the Lord, and there
is none else. I form light and create darkness, I make peace and create

On Sabbaths, and on Festivals falling on Sabbaths, say the following to " they shall glorify thee for ever," p. 431.

On Festivals falling on weekdays say, "Who in mercy ", p. 109, to " glorify thee for ever ", p. 111, and then continue, " Be thou blessed ", p. 433.

GOD THE CREATOR OF ALL THINGS

All shall thank thee, and all shall praise thee, and all shall say, There is none holy like the Lord. All shall extol thee for ever, thou Creator of all things, O God who openest every day the door of the gates of the East, and cleavest the windows of the firmament, leading forth the sun from his place, and the moon from her dwelling, giving light to the whole world and to its inhabitants whom thou didst create by the attribute of mercy. In mercy thou givest light to the earth and to them that dwell thereon, and in thy goodness renewest the creation every day continually ; O King, who alone wast exalted from aforetime, praised, glorified and extolled ·from days of old. O everlasting God, in thine abundant mercies, have mercy upon us, Lord of our strength, Rock of our stronghold, Shield of our salvation, thou Stronghold of ours ! There is none to be compared unto thee, neither is there any beside thee ; there

evil ". Some see in this declaration of absolute monotheism a protest against the ancient Persian belief in two gods—one a god of light and goodness, and the other, of darkness and evil. Jewish teaching emphasizes that nothing coming from God is in itself evil, that even the lower passions may be made agencies for good. Hence the change of " create evil " into " createst all things ". God is the sole Source of everything.

ALL SHALL THANK THEE. The week-day *yotzer* prayer (see p. 108) here appears in an expanded form in the Sabbath Service. The opening sentences take up the last word הכל, " all ", in the benediction preceding it, and poetically expand it. The closing words, *There is none to be compared . . . revival of the dead*, are a Midrash-like exposition of the two preceding sentences, phrase by phrase. The dawn of morning shows the rule of God in Nature, and this rule shall continue in all eternity, *in this world and the world to come*. Even in the days of the Messiah, none and not the Messiah himself, shall share dominion with Him.

For the interrelation of man's regeneration *in this life*, and his salvation in the *future life*, see the comments on the corresponding articles of the Jewish Creed, pp. 254 and 255.

בְּלָתֶּךָ וּמִי דוֹמֶה־לָּךְ : אֵין כְּעֶרְכְּךָ יְיָ אֱלֹהֵינוּ בָּעוֹלָם
הַזֶּה • וְאֵין זוּלָתֶךָ מַלְכֵּנוּ לְחַיֵּי הָעוֹלָם הַבָּא : אֶפֶס
בִּלְתֶּךָ גּוֹאֲלֵנוּ לִימוֹת הַמָּשִׁיחַ • וְאֵין דּוֹמֶה־לָּךְ מוֹשִׁיעֵנוּ
לִתְחִיַּת הַמֵּתִים :

אֵל אָדוֹן עַל כָּל־הַמַּעֲשִׂים • בָּרוּךְ וּמְבֹרָךְ בְּפִי כָל־
נְשָׁמָה : גָּדְלוֹ וְטוּבוֹ מָלֵא עוֹלָם • דַּעַת וּתְבוּנָה סוֹבְבִים
אוֹתוֹ : הַמִּתְגָּאֶה עַל־חַיּוֹת הַקֹּדֶשׁ • וְנֶהְדָּר בְּכָבוֹד עַל־
הַמֶּרְכָּבָה : זְכוּת וּמִישׁוֹר לִפְנֵי כִסְאוֹ • חֶסֶד וְרַחֲמִים
לִפְנֵי כְבוֹדוֹ : טוֹבִים מְאוֹרוֹת שֶׁבָּרָא אֱלֹהֵינוּ • יְצָרָם
בְּדַעַת בְּבִינָה וּבְהַשְׂכֵּל : כֹּחַ וּגְבוּרָה נָתַן בָּהֶם • לִהְיוֹת
מוֹשְׁלִים בְּקֶרֶב תֵּבֵל : מְלֵאִים זִיו וּמְפִיקִים נֹגַהּ • נָאֶה
זִיוָם בְּכָל־הָעוֹלָם : שְׂמֵחִים בְּצֵאתָם וְשָׂשִׂים בְּבוֹאָם •
עוֹשִׂים בְּאֵימָה רְצוֹן קוֹנָם : פְּאֵר וְכָבוֹד נוֹתְנִים

GOD, THE LORD OVER ALL WORKS. This alphabetic hymn is a
homage to God for the creation of the heavenly hosts—the sun, moon
and stars. It is based on the middle paragraph of the daily *yotzer*
prayer, p. 110, each of its opening 22 words being here expanded into
a line. Rapoport (1790–1867), one of the pioneers in the revival of
Jewish Learning, ascribed its authorship to the ESSENES, a Jewish sect
at the time of the Second Temple. They were a mystic brotherhood
with quaint ascetic customs, silent common meals, white robes and
lustrations. They so arranged their morning prayers as to finish the
Shema when the sun came out in radiance. They seem always to have
moved on the borderland of ecstasy ; and their life evoked to an unusual
degree the admiration of all. Pliny calls them the marvel of the world.
They numbered a little over 4,000 souls, utterly despising riches,
worldly fame and pleasure, and practising a rare benevolence to one

is none but thee : who is like unto thee ? *There is none to be compared unto thee,* O Lord our God, in this world, *neither is there any beside thee,* O our King, for the life of the world to come ; *there is none but thee,* O our Redeemer, for the days of the Messiah ; *neither is there any like unto thee,* O our Saviour, for the revival of the dead.

A HYMN OF CREATION   God, the Lord over all works, blessed is he, and ever to be blessed by the mouth of everything that hath breath. His greatness and goodness fill the universe ; knowledge and understanding surround him : he is exalted above the holy Chayoth and is adorned in glory above the celestial chariot : purity and rectitude are before his throne, loving-kindness and tender mercy before his glory. The luminaries are good which our God hath created : he formed them with knowledge, understanding and discernment ; he gave them might and power to rule in the midst of the world. They are full of lustre, and they radiate brightness : beautiful is their lustre throughout all the world. They rejoice in their going forth, and are glad in their returning ; they perform with awe the will of their Master. Glory and

another and to mankind in general. They brought the virtue of integrity, both of speech and action, to as high a point as can be reached by human beings. In the sphere of social ethics, they were the first to condemn slavery as an impious attack on the natural rights of men.

   Other scholars maintain that this hymn is the work of a later group of Mystics (the *yoredey Merkabah*) in the eighth and ninth century

   chayoth. See p. 435.

   celestial chariot. This bold figure is derived from the vision of Ezekiel (Chaps. 1 and 10).

   purity and rectitude. Like the *yotzer* prayer of which it is a part this hymn is a praise of God and of His power revealed in His qualities of righteousness and mercy, as well as in the marvels and regularity of the luminaries, the work of His hands.

   formed them with knowledge. i.e., endowed them with knowledge—such was everywhere the belief of the ancients, and even of the medieval thinkers.

לְשֵׁמוֹ · צָהֲלָה וְרִנָּה לְזֵכֶר מַלְכוּתוֹ : קָרָא לַשֶּׁמֶשׁ

וַיִּזְרַח־אוֹר · רָאָה וְהִתְקִין צוּרַת הַלְּבָנָה : שֶׁבַח

נוֹתְנִים־לוֹ כָּל־צְבָא מָרוֹם · תִּפְאֶרֶת וּגְדֻלָּה שְׂרָפִים

וְאוֹפַנִּים וְחַיּוֹת הַקֹּדֶשׁ

לָאֵל אֲשֶׁר שָׁבַת מִכָּל־הַמַּעֲשִׂים · בַּיּוֹם הַשְּׁבִיעִי הִתְעַלָּה

וְיָשַׁב עַל־כִּסֵּא כְבוֹדוֹ · תִּפְאֶרֶת עָטָה לְיוֹם הַמְּנוּחָה עֹנֶג

קָרָא לְיוֹם הַשַּׁבָּת : זֶה שֶׁבַח שֶׁלְּיוֹם הַשְּׁבִיעִי שֶׁבּוֹ שָׁבַת

אֵל מִכָּל־מְלַאכְתּוֹ · וְיוֹם הַשְּׁבִיעִי מְשַׁבֵּחַ וְאוֹמֵר · מִזְמוֹר

שִׁיר לְיוֹם הַשַּׁבָּת טוֹב לְהֹדוֹת לַיָי : לְפִיכָךְ יְפָאֲרוּ וִיבָרְכוּ

לָאֵל כָּל־יְצוּרָיו · שֶׁבַח יְקָר וּגְדֻלָּה יִתְּנוּ לָאֵל מֶלֶךְ יוֹצֵר

כֹּל · הַמַּנְחִיל מְנוּחָה לְעַמּוֹ יִשְׂרָאֵל בִּקְדֻשָּׁתוֹ בְּיוֹם שַׁבָּת

קֹדֶשׁ : שִׁמְךָ יְיָ אֱלֹהֵינוּ יִתְקַדַּשׁ · וְזִכְרְךָ מַלְכֵּנוּ יִתְפָּאַר

בַּשָּׁמַיִם מִמַּעַל וְעַל־הָאָרֶץ מִתָּחַת : תִּתְבָּרַךְ מוֹשִׁיעֵנוּ

עַל־שֶׁבַח מַעֲשֵׂה יָדֶיךָ · וְעַל־מְאוֹרֵי־אוֹר שֶׁעָשִׂיתָ יְפָאֲרוּךָ

סֶּלָה :

Seraphim, Chayoth, Ophanim. Names of classes of angels. The meaning
of the terms is uncertain. *Ophanim* probably denotes some animated
"wheels", conceived in association with the Heavenly Throne; *Chayoth*,
literally means, "living creatures"; and *Seraphim*, "beings of fire".
"Some of the rabbins tell us that the *cherubim* are a set of angels who
know most, and the *seraphim* are a set of angels who love most"
(Joseph Addison).

honour they render unto his Name, exultation and rejoicing at the fame of his kingship. He called unto the sun, and it shone forth in light : he looked, and ordained the figure of the moon. All the hosts on high render praise unto him, the Seraphim, the Ophanim and the holy Chayoth ascribing glory and greatness—

HYMN OF SABBATH DAY

To the God who rested from all his works, and on the seventh day exalted himself and sat upon the throne of his glory. With beauty did he robe the day of rest, and called the Sabbath day a delight. This is the great distinction of the Sabbath day, that God rested thereon from all his work, when the Sabbath day itself offered praise

Psalm 92. 2

and said "A Psalm, a song of the Sabbath day, It is good to give thanks unto the Lord". Therefore let all his creatures glorify and bless God ; let them render praise, honour and greatness to the God and King who is Creator of all things, and who, in his holiness, giveth an inheritance of rest to his people Israel on the holy Sabbath day. Thy Name, O Lord our God, shall be hallowed, and thy fame, O our King, shall be proclaimed in heaven above and on the earth beneath. Be thou blessed, O our Saviour, for the excellency of thy handiwork, and for the bright luminaries which thou hast made : they shall glorify thee for ever.

To THE GOD. This meditation belonged to a group of seven hymns, one for every day of the week, recounting the work of Creation completed on that day. In these hymns, each day proclaimed the praises of God in the words of the psalm set aside for the day. Like the other amplifications of the *yotzer* prayer, they belong to the Talmudic age or very shortly after.

delight. Spiritual delight.

the Sabbath day itself offered praise. Just as the luminaries glorify God, the Sabbath itself becomes the herald of the Lord, proclaiming, It is good to give thanks unto God (Midrash Tillim).

be thou blessed, O our Saviour. Beginning with these words, the prayers before and after the Shema are identical with the weekday form.

תִּתְבָּרַךְ צוּרֵנוּ מַלְכֵּנוּ וְגוֹאֲלֵנוּ בּוֹרֵא קְדוֹשִׁים יִשְׁתַּבַּח

שִׁמְךָ לָעַד מַלְכֵּנוּ • יוֹצֵר מְשָׁרְתִים וַאֲשֶׁר מְשָׁרְתָיו כֻּלָּם

עוֹמְדִים בְּרוּם עוֹלָם • וּמַשְׁמִיעִים בְּיִרְאָה יַחַד בְּקוֹל דִּבְרֵי

אֱלֹהִים חַיִּים וּמֶלֶךְ עוֹלָם: כֻּלָּם אֲהוּבִים כֻּלָּם בְּרוּרִים

כֻּלָּם גִּבּוֹרִים וְכֻלָּם עֹשִׂים בְּאֵימָה וּבְיִרְאָה רְצוֹן קוֹנָם •

וְכֻלָּם פּוֹתְחִים אֶת־פִּיהֶם בִּקְדֻשָּׁה וּבְטָהֳרָה בְּשִׁירָה

וּבְזִמְרָה • וּמְבָרְכִים וּמְשַׁבְּחִים וּמְפָאֲרִים וּמַעֲרִיצִים

וּמַקְדִּישִׁים וּמַמְלִיכִים

אֶת־שֵׁם הָאֵל הַמֶּלֶךְ הַגָּדוֹל הַגִּבּוֹר וְהַנּוֹרָא קָדוֹשׁ

הוּא : וְכֻלָּם מְקַבְּלִים עֲלֵיהֶם עֹל מַלְכוּת שָׁמַיִם זֶה מִזֶּה •

TISBORACH. *be thou blessed.* The angels ecstatically chant the praises and holiness of God, and in antiphonal song acclaim the thrice-holy One whose glory fills the universe.

Creator of holy beings. According to the Mystics of Talmudic times, angels are every day created from the River of Fire ; they utter a hymn of praise, and then cease to be.

> " The angels of Wind and Fire
> Chant only one hymn, and expire
> With the song's irresistible stress."
> (Longfellow, *Sandalphon.*)

ministering spirits. Angels are held by the Jewish Mystics to be inferior to man in the scale of spiritual existence ; because man is no mere " messenger ", but is endowed with free-will. Since the time of Maimonides, Jewish thinkers allegorize the whole conception of angelic beings.

beloved. There is no envy, jealousy, or rivalry among them.

take upon themselves . . . heaven. " Mutually accepting for themselves His heavenly rule " (Pool.) The angels thus perform the function which is man's highest privilege to fulfil.

the yoke of the kingdom of heaven. " Kingdom " here means *kingship*, and " heaven " is merely a synonym for *God*. " Take upon oneself the yoke of the Kingdom of Heaven " means, to recognize the rule of God in the heart and life of man.

THE CHORUS OF ANGELS   Be thou blessed, O our Rock, our King and Redeemer, Creator of holy beings, praised be thy Name for ever, O our King ; Creator of ministering spirits, all of whom stand in the heights of the universe, and with awe proclaim in unison aloud the words of the living God and everlasting King. All of them are beloved, pure and mighty ; and all of them in dread and awe do the will of their Master ; and all of them open their mouths in holiness and purity, with song and psalm, while they bless and praise, glorify and reverence, sanctify and ascribe sovereignty to—

KINGDOM OF HEAVEN   The Name of the Divine King, the great, mighty and dreaded One, holy is he ; and they all take upon themselves the yoke of the kingdom of heaven one from the other, and

---

As to " yoke ", it is well to remember that a yoke is not imposed upon animals in order to torture them. To cause them to work without a yoke, *that* would be torture—and the field would remain untilled. A yoke enables the animals *to pull together* in preparing the ground for human benefit. In the same way, when men in harmony and love take upon themselves the " yoke of the kingdom of heaven," they resolve to " pull together "—to labour *with* their fellowmen—for the furtherance of God's reign ; and, by means of such united spiritual endeavour, bring about the betterment and ennoblement of the life of man on earth. This " yoke of the kingdom " is borne willingly, joyfully by the Israelite, as the emblem of free service. In this prayer such state of soul is figuratively transferred to the angelic host.

" The term *Kingdom of Heaven* is less expressive of an accomplished fact than of an undefined and indefinable ideal. It can be viewed from two aspects : the visible and the invisible Kingdom."

" In the idea of the visible Kingdom of Heaven were included *national* ideas : the restoration of Israel was a vital prelude to the establishment of God's Kingship on earth. It was *ethical :* God's Kingdom meant the reign of righteousness. The reign was also *universal :* ' and the Lord shall be King over all the earth '."

" As for the invisible Kingdom, that is mainly spiritual, expressive of a certain attitude of mind. Thus, communion with God by means of prayer through the removal of all intruding elements between man and his Maker, and through the implicit acceptance of God's Unity, as well as unconditional surrender of mind and heart to His holy Will, this is what is understood by accepting the yoke of the Kingdom of Heaven " (Schechter).

וְנוֹתְנִים רְשׁוּת זֶה לָזֶה לְהַקְדִּישׁ לְיוֹצְרָם · בְּנַחַת רוּחַ
בְּשָׂפָה בְרוּרָה וּבִנְעִימָה קְדֻשָׁה כֻּלָּם כְּאֶחָד עוֹנִים
וְאוֹמְרִים בְּיִרְאָה ·

קָדוֹשׁ קָדוֹשׁ קָדוֹשׁ יְיָ צְבָאוֹת מְלֹא כָל־הָאָרֶץ כְּבוֹדוֹ :
וְהָאוֹפַנִּים וְחַיּוֹת הַקֹּדֶשׁ בְּרַעַשׁ גָּדוֹל מִתְנַשְּׂאִים לְעֻמַּת
שְׂרָפִים לְעֻמָּתָם מְשַׁבְּחִים וְאוֹמְרִים ·

בָּרוּךְ כְּבוֹד־יְיָ מִמְּקוֹמוֹ :

לָאֵל בָּרוּךְ נְעִימוֹת יִתֵּנוּ · לְמֶלֶךְ אֵל חַי וְקַיָּם זְמִירוֹת
יֹאמֵרוּ וְתִשְׁבָּחוֹת יַשְׁמִיעוּ · כִּי הוּא לְבַדּוֹ פּוֹעֵל גְּבוּרוֹת
עֹשֶׂה חֲדָשׁוֹת בַּעַל מִלְחָמוֹת זוֹרֵעַ צְדָקוֹת מַצְמִיחַ יְשׁוּעוֹת
בּוֹרֵא רְפוּאוֹת נוֹרָא תְהִלּוֹת · אֲדוֹן הַנִּפְלָאוֹת · הַמְחַדֵּשׁ
בְּטוּבוֹ בְּכָל־יוֹם תָּמִיד מַעֲשֵׂה בְרֵאשִׁית · כָּאָמוּר · לְעֹשֵׂה
אוֹרִים גְּדֹלִים כִּי לְעוֹלָם חַסְדּוֹ : אוֹר חָדָשׁ עַל־צִיּוֹן תָּאִיר
וְנִזְכֶּה כֻלָּנוּ מְהֵרָה לְאוֹרוֹ : בָּרוּךְ אַתָּה יְיָ · יוֹצֵר
הַמְּאוֹרוֹת :

אַהֲבָה רַבָּה אֲהַבְתָּנוּ יְיָ אֱלֹהֵינוּ · חֶמְלָה גְדוֹלָה וִיתֵרָה
חָמַלְתָּ עָלֵינוּ : אָבִינוּ מַלְכֵּנוּ · בַּעֲבוּר אֲבוֹתֵינוּ שֶׁבָּטְחוּ בְךָ

give leave one unto the other. They are careful not to precede one
another in the praises of the Lord, but to acclaim Him with one voice.
holy . . . glory. "Holy—in the highest Heaven, the place of His
divine abode; holy—upon earth, the work of His might; holy—for
ever and ever unto all eternity" (Targum Jonathan); see p. 453.

give leave one unto the other to declare the holiness of their Creator : in tranquil joy of spirit, with pure speech and holy melody they all respond in unison, and exclaim with awe :

Isaiah 6. 3   HOLY, HOLY, HOLY IS THE LORD OF HOSTS : THE WHOLE EARTH IS FULL OF HIS GLORY.

And the Ophanim and the holy Chayoth with a noise of great rushing, upraising themselves towards the Seraphim, thus over against them offer praise and say :

Ezekiel 3. 12   BLESSED BE THE GLORY OF THE LORD FROM HIS PLACE.

THE CREATOR OF LIGHT   To the blessed God they offer melodious strains ; to the King, the living and ever-existing God, they utter hymns and make their praises heard ; for he alone worketh mighty deeds, and maketh new things ; he is the Lord over struggle, sowing righteousness, and reaping victory. He createth healing, and is revered in praises. He is the Lord of wonders, who in his goodness reneweth the creation every day con-

Psalm 136. 7   tinually ; as it is said, (O give thanks) to him that maketh great lights, for his lovingkindness endureth for ever. O cause a new light to shine upon Zion, and may we all be worthy soon to enjoy its brightness. Blessed art thou, O Lord, Creator of the luminaries.

AHAVAH : GOD'S CHOICE OF ISRAEL   With abounding love hast thou loved us, O Lord our God, and great and overflowing tenderness hast thou shown us. O our Father, our King, for our fathers' sake, who trusted in thee, and whom thou didst teach the statutes of life, be also

---

reneweth the creation. With these words the note struck at the opening of the *yotzer* prayer, p. 426, is resumed ; viz., praise of the Creator of light. Before concluding the eulogy, the touching Messianic petition, " O cause a new light to shine upon Zion, and may we all be worthy soon to enjoy its brightness ", was included.

AHAVOH RABBOH. *With abounding love.* The second of the blessings that precede the Shema is praise of God's goodness in giving us the Torah, and prayer for His help in the study of the Torah. It recalls

וְתַלְמְדֵם חָקֵי הַיִּים כֵּן תְּחָנֵנוּ וּתְלַמְּדֵנוּ : אָבִינוּ הָאָב
הָרַחֲמָן הַמְרַחֵם רַחֵם עָלֵינוּ וְתֵן בְּלִבֵּנוּ לְהָבִין וּלְהַשְׂכִּיל
לִשְׁמֹעַ לִלְמֹד וּלְלַמֵּד לִשְׁמֹר וְלַעֲשׂוֹת וּלְקַיֵּם אֶת־כָּל־דִּבְרֵי
תַלְמוּד תּוֹרָתֶךָ בְּאַהֲבָה : וְהָאֵר עֵינֵינוּ בְּתוֹרָתֶךָ וְדַבֵּק
לִבֵּנוּ בְּמִצְוֹתֶיךָ וְיַחֵד לְבָבֵנוּ לְאַהֲבָה וּלְיִרְאָה שְׁמֶךָ וְלֹא־
נֵבוֹשׁ לְעוֹלָם וָעֶד : כִּי בְשֵׁם קָדְשְׁךָ הַגָּדוֹל וְהַנּוֹרָא
בָּטָחְנוּ · נָגִילָה וְנִשְׂמְחָה בִּישׁוּעָתֶךָ : וַהֲבִיאֵנוּ לְשָׁלוֹם
מֵאַרְבַּע כַּנְפוֹת הָאָרֶץ וְתוֹלִיכֵנוּ קוֹמְמִיּוּת לְאַרְצֵנוּ · כִּי
אֵל פּוֹעֵל יְשׁוּעוֹת אָתָּה · זִבָּנוּ בָחַרְתָּ מִכָּל־עַם וְלָשׁוֹן
וְקֵרַבְתָּנוּ לְשִׁמְךָ הַגָּדוֹל סֶלָה בֶּאֱמֶת · לְהוֹדוֹת לְךָ
וּלְיַחֶדְךָ בְּאַהֲבָה : בָּרוּךְ אַתָּה יְיָ · הַבּוֹחֵר בְּעַמּוֹ יִשְׂרָאֵל
בְּאַהֲבָה :

God's unending love to our fathers in entrusting His sacred Teaching to
them, and in calling them to His service ; may He show similar love
to their children, by giving us proper understanding of that Teaching,
and steadfastness in obeying it in our lives and the lives of those that
come after us.

There is a strain of profound love and zeal for God and Religion
in this prayer, that could only have emanated from souls overflowing
with selfless devotion and purest piety. None of the petitions for
the material goods of life approach in fervour this ancient prayer for
knowledge of the Torah. With its stress on the love of God and the
Selection of Israel, on the duty of studying the Divine Message of
Israel and of obeying its precepts, it is an anticipation of the main
teachings of the Shema. After an ardent invocation for the Messianic
gathering of Israel, the prayer closes with the benediction, " Who hast
chosen Thy people Israel in love ".

enlighten our eyes in thy Torah. So that we may all see and fully
grasp its spiritual wonders.

AHAVAH :
GOD'S
CHOICE
OF ISRAEL

gracious unto us and teach us. O our Father, merciful Father, ever compassionate, have mercy upon us ; O put it into our hearts to understand and to discern, to mark, learn and teach, to heed, to do and to fulfil in love all the words of instruction in thy Torah. Enlighten our eyes in thy Torah, and let our hearts cleave to thy commandments, and unify our hearts to love and reverence thy Name, so that we be never put to shame. Because we have trusted in thy holy, great and revered Name, we shall rejoice and be glad in thy saving power. O bring us in peace from the four corners of the earth, and make us go upright to our land, for thou art a God who worketh salvation. Thou hast chosen us from all peoples and tongues, and has brought us near unto thy great Name for ever in faithfulness, that we might in love give thanks unto thee and proclaim thy unity. Blessed art thou, O Lord, who hast chosen thy people Israel in love.

cleave to thy commandments. With love that nothing can break. The Hebrew word for " cleave " is the one used for clinging affection.

unify our hearts. Make them single-hearted and undivided in our allegiance ; make it our heart's sole purpose to love and reverence Thy Name.

In the Hebrew, the first and the last word of this ardent prayer is the word, אהבה " love ".

THE SHEMA

The Shema consists of three sections of the Torah (Deuteronomy 6. 4–8 ; 11. 13–22 ; and Numbers 15. 37–42). It is a proclamation of the existence and Unity of God ; of Israel's complete loyalty to God and His commandments ; the belief in Divine Justice ; the remembrance of the liberation from Egypt, and its corollary, the Election of Israel. These are foundation pillars of the Jewish Faith. Especially does the opening verse, " Hear, O Israel, the Lord is our God, the Lord is One ", sound the keynote of all Judaism. It is, there-fore, essential that every Jew should have a clear understanding of the implications of this opening verse, as well as of its influence upon Israel and mankind throughout the ages. See THE SHEMA : ITS MEANING AND HISTORY, p. 263.

God, faithful King. The doxology, " Blessed be His Name, whose glorious kingdom is for ever and ever ", was at first recited only in public worship. The three words, *God, faithful King,* seem to be a shorter

(When prayers are not said with the Congregation, say :—

אֵל מֶלֶךְ נֶאֱמָן :)

דברים ו' ד'-ט'

שְׁמַע יִשְׂרָאֵל יְהוָֹה אֱלֹהֵינוּ יְהוָֹה ׀ אֶחָד :

בָּרוּךְ שֵׁם כְּבוֹד מַלְכוּתוֹ לְעוֹלָם וָעֶד :

וְאָהַבְתָּ אֵת יְהוָֹה אֱלֹהֶיךָ בְּכָל־לְבָבְךָ וּבְכָל־נַפְשְׁךָ

וּבְכָל־מְאֹדֶךָ : וְהָיוּ הַדְּבָרִים הָאֵלֶּה אֲשֶׁר אָנֹכִי מְצַוְּךָ

expression of such conscious submission to the Divine Kingdom, when
prayers are not said with the congregation. Others take them to be
the remnant of a special benediction before reciting the Shema.

Hear, O Israel : the Lord is our God, the Lord is One. Other renderings
are : " Hear, O Israel, the Lord our God, the Lord is One " ; " Hear,
O Israel, the Lord is our God, the Lord alone " (Ibn Ezra) ; and " Hear,
O Israel, the Eternal our God is a unique, eternal Being " (Zunz).
Utterly unacceptable and meaningless is that of the Authorized Version,
" Hear, O Israel, the Lord our God is one Lord ".

Hear, O Israel. The last letter of the first word שמע, and the last
letter of אחד, are written large in the Hebrew Bible. These two large
letters form the word עד " witness " ; *i.e.* every Israelite by pronouncing
the Shema becomes one of " God's witnesses," testifying to His Unity
before the world.

Jewish custom prescribes that the eyes be closed or covered when
pronouncing the opening verse of the Shema—to shut out all distracting
impressions, and concentrate the whole of one's thought on God's
Unity.

the Lord is One. He, the Father and Sustainer of the lives and spirits
of all flesh, the everlasting Power Who guides the destinies of men
and nations, is One, because there is no other God than He : but He
is also One, because He is wholly unlike anything else in existence. He
is thus the Sole and unique God.

Therefore, to Him alone it is right to pray, and not to any
being besides Him. The belief that the Godhead consists of several
personalities, is a departure from the pure conception of the Unity of
God ; and Israel has throughout the ages rejected everything that
marred or obscured the conception of pure monotheism which it had
given the world. Rather than abandon that pure monotheism, rather
than admit any weakening of it, Jews were prepared to wander, to
suffer, to die.

(When prayers are not said with the Congregation, say :—
God, faithful King !)

Deuteronomy vi. 4—9.

THE
SHEMA :
HEAR, O
ISRAEL

HEAR, O ISRAEL : THE LORD IS OUR GOD,
THE LORD IS ONE.
BLESSED BE HIS NAME, WHOSE GLORIOUS KINGDOM
IS FOR EVER AND EVER.

THOU
SHALT
LOVE THE
LORD THY
GOD

⁵And thou shalt love the Lord thy God with all thine heart, and with all thy soul, and with all thy might. ⁶And these words, which I command thee this day, shall be upon

blessed . . . ever and ever. This response, first used in the Temple during the Day of Atonement Service, was later made the accompaniment of the opening verse of the Shema. As is well known, the Roman Emperors claimed divine honours, and were accorded such honours by their slavish subjects, with the sole exception of the Jews. This doxology was to proclaim that the Israelite submitted to the rule of God alone, and acknowledged Him as the sole Sovereign Lord of his life. He thus took upon himself the " yoke of the Kingdom of Heaven ".

5. *and thou shalt love.* This is the first instance in human history that the *love* of God was demanded in any religion. The worshipper, as he declares the Unity of God, lovingly and unconditionally surrenders his mind and heart to God's holy will. If the Unity of God is the basis of the Jewish Creed, the love of God is to be the basis of the Jewish life. And the noblest spiritual surrender to the Divine Being, the Rabbis held, was so to live and act toward our fellowmen as to make God and His Teaching *beloved in their eyes.*

with all thine heart. The One God demands the whole of man, and his undivided allegiance. The Rabbis explain *with all thine heart,* to mean " with all thy desires, including the evil inclination " ; *i.e.* subject thy earthly passions and ambitions to God's Law, and thus make them instruments in His service.

with all thy soul. The Rabbis take these words to mean " with thy whole life " ; *i.e.* love Him with thy heart's last drop of blood, and give up thy dearest inclinations, nay, life itself, for God, should He require it. Rabbi Akiba ever longed for the time when his daily profession of the love of God might be put to the proof and be confirmed by act. That moment came when, after his heroic part in the last Jewish War of Independence against Imperial Rome, the executioner was tearing his flesh with combs of iron. " All my days ", Akiba told his weeping disciples, " I have longed for this hour. I have loved God *with all my heart,* and I have loved Him *with all my might* ; now that I can love Him *with my whole life,* complete happiness is mine ". It was such understanding of the words of the Shema that gave Jewish martyrs the courage to lay down their lives

הַיּוֹם עַל־לְבָבֶךָ: וְשִׁנַּנְתָּם לְבָנֶיךָ וְדִבַּרְתָּ בָּם בְּשִׁבְתְּךָ
בְּבֵיתֶךָ וּבְלֶכְתְּךָ בַדֶּרֶךְ וּבְשָׁכְבְּךָ וּבְקוּמֶךָ: וּקְשַׁרְתָּם
לְאוֹת עַל־יָדֶךָ וְהָיוּ לְטֹטָפֹת בֵּין עֵינֶיךָ: וּכְתַבְתָּם
עַל־מְזֻזוֹת בֵּיתֶךָ וּבִשְׁעָרֶיךָ:

דברים י׳א י׳נ־כ׳א

וְהָיָה אִם־שָׁמֹעַ תִּשְׁמְעוּ אֶל־מִצְוֹתַי אֲשֶׁר אָנֹכִי מְצַוֶּה
אֶתְכֶם הַיּוֹם לְאַהֲבָה אֶת־יְהוָֹה אֱלֹהֵיכֶם וּלְעָבְדוֹ בְּכָל־
לְבַבְכֶם וּבְכָל־נַפְשְׁכֶם: וְנָתַתִּי מְטַר־אַרְצְכֶם בְּעִתּוֹ יוֹרֶה
וּמַלְקוֹשׁ וְאָסַפְתָּ דְגָנֶךָ וְתִירֹשְׁךָ וְיִצְהָרֶךָ: וְנָתַתִּי עֵשֶׂב

for their Faith. A medieval Jewish saint used to pray, " My God, Thou
hast given me over to starvation and penury. Into the depth of darkness Thou hast plunged me, and Thy might and strength hast Thou
taught me. But even if they burn me with fire, only the more will
I love Thee and rejoice in Thee " (Bachya).

with all thy might. With whatever lot Providence has assigned to
thee, and despite whatever material sacrifices thy loyalty to God and
Torah might entail (Talmud).

7. *teach them diligently.* " Give thy children a clear, and not a
confused or stammering, knowledge of the duties and teachings of their
Faith " (Sifri).

For JEWISH EDUCATION, its scope and content, see pp. 119–121.

talk of them. They are to be a theme of living interest, early and
late, at home and abroad.

when thou liest down . . . up. The Rabbis based on these words the
institution of Evening and Morning Prayer.

8. *bind them.* For the precept of Tefillin, see p. 46.

9. *upon the door-posts.* By means of the *mezuzah*, placed in a metal
or glass case, and fixed to the door-post on one's right when entering
a house or room in the house. It contains the first two paragraphs
of the Shema. The word שדי, " Almighty," written on the back of
the parchment, is made visible by means of a small opening in the case.
The *mezuzah* is a symbol of God's watchful care over the house and its
dwellers. It is a solemn reminder to all who go out and in, that the
house is a Jewish home, devoted to the ideals of the Shema.

THE
SHEMA

thine heart : 7and thou shalt teach them diligently unto thy children, and shalt talk of them when thou sittest in thine house, and when thou walkest by the way, and when thou liest down, and when thou risest up. 8And thou shalt bind them for a sign upon thine hand, and they shall be for frontlets between thine eyes. 9And thou shalt write them upon the door-posts of thy house, and upon thy gates.

Deuteronomy xi. 13—21.

REWARD
AND
PUNISH-
MENT

13And it shall come to pass, if ye shall hearken diligently unto my commandments which I command you this day, to love the Lord your God, and to serve him with all your heart and with all your soul, 14that I will give the rain of your land in its season, the former rain and the latter rain, that thou mayest gather in thy corn, and thy wine, and thine oil. 15And I will give grass in thy field for thy cattle,

THE SHEMA : SECOND PARAGRAPH.

The middle of the Shema teaches the doctrine of Divine Right-eousness. Israel shall ever look upon its fortunes, even if these depend upon natural events like the seasons, as rewards or punishments for righteous or unrighteous living. History corroborates the fact that nations decay when they no longer look upon life as built on moral foundations. " Opinions alter, manners change, creeds rise and fall, but the Moral Law is written on the tablets of Eternity. For every false word or unrighteous deed, for cruelty and oppression, for lust or vanity, the price has to be paid at last, not always by the chief offenders, but paid by someone. Justice and truth alone endure and live. Injustice and falsehood may be long-lived, but doomsday comes at last to them " (Froude). This truth of a Higher Justice should form the theme of daily meditation, and should early be implanted in the soul of the child.

For REWARD AND PUNISHMENT IN JUDAISM, see pp. 121–123.

13. *to serve him with all your heart.* " What is heart-service ? Service of the heart is Prayer " (Sifri).

14. *in its season.* Both rewards and punishments are here con-nected with the rainfall, which is of vital importance in a land like Palestine.

former rain. The heavy rains towards the end of October. They open the agricultural year. The whole winter is the rainy season.

the latter rain. The heavy showers of March and April. Coming as they do when the grain is ripening, and being the last before the long summer drought, they are of great importance.

15. *grass.* Herbage, for human beings as well as for cattle. From the fact that Scripture here speaks of pasture for the cattle, and then

בְּשָׂדֶךָ לִבְהֶמְתֶּךָ וְאָכַלְתָּ וְשָׂבָעְתָּ: הִשָּׁמְרוּ לָכֶם פֶּן־
יִפְתֶּה לְבַבְכֶם וְסַרְתֶּם וַעֲבַדְתֶּם אֱלֹהִים אֲחֵרִים
וְהִשְׁתַּחֲוִיתֶם לָהֶם: וְחָרָה אַף־יְהֹוָה בָּכֶם וְעָצַר אֶת־
הַשָּׁמַיִם וְלֹא־יִהְיֶה מָטָר וְהָאֲדָמָה לֹא תִתֵּן אֶת־יְבוּלָהּ
וַאֲבַדְתֶּם מְהֵרָה מֵעַל הָאָרֶץ הַטֹּבָה אֲשֶׁר יְהֹוָה נֹתֵן
לָכֶם: וְשַׂמְתֶּם אֶת־דְּבָרַי אֵלֶּה עַל־לְבַבְכֶם וְעַל־נַפְשְׁכֶם
וּקְשַׁרְתֶּם אֹתָם לְאוֹת עַל־יֶדְכֶם וְהָיוּ לְטוֹטָפֹת בֵּין
עֵינֵיכֶם: וְלִמַּדְתֶּם אֹתָם אֶת־בְּנֵיכֶם לְדַבֵּר בָּם בְּשִׁבְתְּךָ
בְּבֵיתֶךָ וּבְלֶכְתְּךָ בַדֶּרֶךְ וּבְשָׁכְבְּךָ וּבְקוּמֶךָ: וּכְתַבְתָּם
עַל־מְזוּזוֹת בֵּיתֶךָ וּבִשְׁעָרֶיךָ: לְמַעַן יִרְבּוּ יְמֵיכֶם וִימֵי
בְנֵיכֶם עַל הָאֲדָמָה אֲשֶׁר נִשְׁבַּע יְהֹוָה לַאֲבֹתֵיכֶם לָתֵת
לָהֶם כִּימֵי הַשָּׁמַיִם עַל־הָאָרֶץ:

במדבר ט"ו לז־מ"א

וַיֹּאמֶר יְהֹוָה אֶל־מֹשֶׁה לֵּאמֹר: דַּבֵּר אֶל־בְּנֵי יִשְׂרָאֵל
וְאָמַרְתָּ אֲלֵהֶם וְעָשׂוּ לָהֶם צִיצִת עַל־כַּנְפֵי בִגְדֵיהֶם
לְדֹרֹתָם וְנָתְנוּ עַל־צִיצִת הַכָּנָף פְּתִיל תְּכֵלֶת: וְהָיָה

continues " *thou* shalt eat ", the Talmud deduced the moral precept that
a man must feed his animals before he himself partakes of his meal.
  16. *take heed.* Satiety easily induces forgetfulness.
  18. *lay up these my words.* These words are taken with those
immediately preceding, and mean : In the event of your perishing from
the land and being driven into captivity, even there in exile, you must
carry out the behests contained in the Shema.

**THE
SHEMA**

and thou shalt eat and be satisfied. ¹⁶Take heed to yourselves, lest your heart be deceived, and ye turn aside, and serve other gods, and worship them ; ¹⁷and the anger of the Lord be kindled against you, and he shut up the heaven, that there be no rain, and that the land yield not her fruit ; and ye perish quickly from off the good land which the Lord giveth you. ¹⁸Therefore shall ye lay up these my words in your heart and in your soul ; and ye shall bind them for a sign upon your hand, and they shall be for frontlets between your eyes. ¹⁹And ye shall teach them your children, talking of them when thou sittest in thine house, and when thou walkest by the way, and when thou liest down, and when thou risest up. ²⁰And thou shalt write them upon the doorposts of thine house, and upon thy gates : ²¹that your days may be multiplied, and the days of your children, upon the land which the Lord sware unto your fathers to give them, as the days of the heavens above the earth.

Numbers xv. 37—41.

*THE
MONITION
OF THE
TZITZIS*

³⁷And the Lord spake unto Moses, saying, ³⁸Speak unto the children of Israel, and bid them that they make them a fringe upon the corners of their garments throughout their generations, and that they put upon the fringe of each

---

21. *as the days of the heavens.* *i.e.* so long as the universe endures.

THE SHEMA : THIRD PARAGRAPH.

The third section of the Shema was introduced because of the clear reference it contains to the Redemption from Egypt—the beginning of Israel's life. It also indicates how all these teachings are constantly to be kept before our eyes, and the eyes of our children, by means of an outward expression of an inward thought, tzitzis. The aim of the precept is the furtherance of holiness in the life of the individual and the nation by its constant warning against straying after the desires of the eye and heart ; see p. 44.

38. *their garments.* Only of the men ; because of the general rule, that women, whose duties are more absorbing in the home, are free from all precepts which have to be performed at a specified time מצות עשה שהזמן גרמא).

לָכֶם לְצִיצִת וּרְאִיתֶם אֹתוֹ וּזְכַרְתֶּם אֶת־כָּל־מִצְוֹת יְהֹוָה
וַעֲשִׂיתֶם אֹתָם וְלֹא תָתוּרוּ אַחֲרֵי לְבַבְכֶם וְאַחֲרֵי עֵינֵיכֶם
אֲשֶׁר־אַתֶּם זֹנִים אַחֲרֵיהֶם ׃ לְמַעַן תִּזְכְּרוּ וַעֲשִׂיתֶם אֶת־
כָּל־מִצְוֹתָי וִהְיִיתֶם קְדֹשִׁים לֵאלֹהֵיכֶם ׃ אֲנִי יְהֹוָה
אֱלֹהֵיכֶם אֲשֶׁר הוֹצֵאתִי אֶתְכֶם מֵאֶרֶץ מִצְרַיִם לִהְיוֹת
לָכֶם לֵאלֹהִים אֲנִי יְהֹוָה אֱלֹהֵיכֶם ׃
אֱמֶת וְיַצִּיב וְנָכוֹן וְקַיָּם וְיָשָׁר וְנֶאֱמָן וְאָהוּב וְחָבִיב
וְנֶחְמָד וְנָעִים וְנוֹרָא וְאַדִּיר וּמְתֻקָּן וּמְקֻבָּל וְטוֹב וְיָפֶה
הַדָּבָר הַזֶּה עָלֵינוּ לְעוֹלָם וָעֶד ׃ אֱמֶת אֱלֹהֵי עוֹלָם מַלְכֵּנוּ
צוּר יַעֲקֹב מָגֵן יִשְׁעֵנוּ ׃ לְדוֹר וָדוֹר הוּא קַיָּם וּשְׁמוֹ קַיָּם ׃
וְכִסְאוֹ נָכוֹן וּמַלְכוּתוֹ וֶאֱמוּנָתוֹ לָעַד קַיָּמֶת ׃ וּדְבָרָיו חָיִים
וְקַיָּמִים נֶאֱמָנִים וְנֶחֱמָדִים לָעַד וּלְעוֹלְמֵי עוֹלָמִים עַל־
אֲבוֹתֵינוּ וְעָלֵינוּ עַל־בָּנֵינוּ וְעַל־דּוֹרוֹתֵינוּ וְעַל כָּל־דּוֹרוֹת
זֶרַע יִשְׂרָאֵל עֲבָדֶיךָ ׃

cord of blue. To-day only white wool-threads are inserted.

39. look upon it. lit. "see it"; hence the fringes are used in worship during daylight only.

and remember. The tzitzis are to keep alive in the Israelite the consciousness of the special relationship in which the true worshipper stands to God. "The blue cord of the tzitzis resembles the sea, the sea reflects the heavens, and the heavens resemble the Throne of Glory" Thus, the outward act of looking upon the tzitzis is to the Israelite an inward act of spiritual conformity with the precepts of God.

after your own heart. "The heart and the eyes are the agents of sin—the eye seeth, the heart desireth, and the person executeth." (Talmud).

40. be holy unto your God. The supreme aim of the precept is therefore the hallowing of life.

THE
SHEMA

corner a cord of blue : ³⁹and it shall be unto you for a fringe, that ye may look upon it, and remember all the commandments of the Lord, and do them ; and that ye go not about after your own heart and your own eyes, after which ye go astray : ⁴⁰that ye may remember and do all my commandments, and be holy unto your God. ⁴¹I am the Lord your God, who brought you out of the land of Egypt, to be your God : I am the Lord your God.

*ATTESTA-
TION TO
TEACHINGS
OF THE
SHEMA :
OUR FAITH
IN GOD
AND HIS
TORAH*

True and firm, established and enduring, right and faithful, beloved and precious, desirable and pleasant, revered and mighty, well-ordered and acceptable, good and beautiful is this thy word unto us for ever and ever. It is true, the God of the universe is our King, the Rock of Jacob, the Shield of our salvation : throughout all generations he endureth and his Name endureth ; his throne is established, and his kingdom and his faithfulness endure for ever. His words also live and endure ; they are faithful and desirable for ever and to all eternity, as for our fathers so also for us, our children, our generations, and for all the generations of the seed of Israel his servants.

EMES VE-YATZIV. *true and firm . . . this thy word.* The last words of the Shema (" who brought you out of the land of Egypt, to be your God : I am the Lord your God ") are followed by an expression of our unfaltering faith (אמת ויציב) in the truth, that " the Lord is our God ", that the God of eternity is forever the Source of Israel's strength and salvation. The outstanding proof of this truth is the Going forth from Egypt, which is the symbol of all redemption.

EZRAS. *Thou hast been the help.* This is a prayer of joyful thanksgiving for the Divine Redemption of Israel in the past, and a fervent petition for the establishment of the Divine Kingdom in the future. God is enthroned in the highest heavens, the God of eternity, and yet He works righteousness on earth. God manifested Himself amid the wonders of the Red Sea as the living, eternal God, exalted and revered, Who bringeth low the haughty, and answereth the lowly that cry unto him. We echo the triumphant faith and gratitude of our fathers, when we repeat *Who is like unto Thee, O Lord ?*

" Prayer in public worship is the living expression of redemption which a religious communion possesses. But redemption is, for Jewish (and Christian) faith, indissolubly bound up with history. The saving acts of God form, therefore, an important subject of praise and thanksgiving. The central deed of redemption in the Jewish Faith, the Exodus of

עַל הָרִאשׁוֹנִים וְעַל הָאַחֲרוֹנִים דָּבָר טוֹב וְקַיָּם לְעוֹלָ
וָעֶד · אֱמֶת וֶאֱמוּנָה חֹק וְלֹא יַעֲבוֹר : אֱמֶת שָׁאַתָּה הוּ
יְיָ אֱלֹהֵינוּ וֵאלֹהֵי אֲבוֹתֵינוּ · מַלְכֵּנוּ מֶלֶךְ אֲבוֹתֵינוּ גּוֹאֲלֵנ
גּוֹאֵל אֲבוֹתֵינוּ יוֹצְרֵנוּ צוּר יְשׁוּעָתֵנוּ פּוֹדֵנוּ וּמַצִּילֵנ
מֵעוֹלָם הוּא שְׁמֶךָ · אֵין אֱלֹהִים זוּלָתֶךָ :

עֶזְרַת אֲבוֹתֵינוּ אַתָּה הוּא מֵעוֹלָם · מָגֵן וּמוֹשִׁי
לִבְנֵיהֶם אַחֲרֵיהֶם בְּכָל־דּוֹר וָדוֹר : בְּרוּם עוֹלָם מוֹשָׁבֶךָ
וּמִשְׁפָּטֶיךָ וְצִדְקָתְךָ עַד־אַפְסֵי אָרֶץ : אַשְׁרֵי אִישׁ שֶׁיִּשְׁמַ
לְמִצְוֹתֶיךָ · וְתוֹרָתְךָ וּדְבָרְךָ יָשִׂים עַל־לִבּוֹ : אֱמֶת אַתָּ
הוּא אָדוֹן לְעַמֶּךָ וּמֶלֶךְ גִּבּוֹר לָרִיב רִיבָם : אֱמֶת אַתָּ
הוּא רִאשׁוֹן וְאַתָּה הוּא אַחֲרוֹן · וּמִבַּלְעָדֶיךָ אֵין לָנ
מֶלֶךְ גּוֹאֵל וּמוֹשִׁיעַ : מִמִּצְרַיִם גְּאַלְתָּנוּ יְיָ אֱלֹהֵינוּ וּמִבֵּי
עֲבָדִים פְּדִיתָנוּ · כָּל־בְּכוֹרֵיהֶם הָרָגְתָּ וּבְכוֹרְךָ גָּאָלְתָּ
וְיַם־סוּף בָּקַעְתָּ וְזֵדִים טִבַּעְתָּ וִידִידִים הֶעֱבַרְתָּ וַיְכַסּוּ מַיִ
צָרֵיהֶם · אֶחָד מֵהֶם לֹא נוֹתָר : עַל־זֹאת שִׁבְּחוּ אֲהוּבִי
וְרוֹמְמוּ אֵל · וְנָתְנוּ יְדִידִים זְמִירוֹת שִׁירוֹת וְתִשְׁבָּחוֹ
בְּרָכוֹת וְהוֹדָאוֹת לְמֶלֶךְ אֵל חַי וְקַיָּם · רָם וְנִשָּׂא גָּדוֹ
וְנוֹרָא מַשְׁפִּיל גֵּאִים וּמַגְבִּיהַּ שְׁפָלִים מוֹצִיא אֲסִירִי
וּפוֹדֶה עֲנָוִים וְעוֹזֵר דַּלִּים וְעוֹנֶה לְעַמּוֹ בְּעֵת שַׁוְּעָם אֵלָיו
תְּהִלּוֹת לָאֵל עֶלְיוֹן בָּרוּךְ הוּא וּמְבֹרָךְ · מֹשֶׁה וּבְנֵ

Alike for former and later ages thy word is good and endureth for ever and ever ; it is true and trustworthy, a statute which shall not pass away. True it is that thou art indeed the Lord our God, and the God of our fathers, our King, our fathers' King, our Redeemer, the Redeemer of our fathers, our Maker, the Rock of our salvation ; our Deliverer and Rescuer from everlasting, such is thy Name ; there is no God beside thee.

GOD THE HELP OF OUR FATHERS

Thou hast been the help of our fathers from of old, a Shield and Saviour to their children after them in every generation : in the heights of the universe is thy habitation, and thy judgments and thy righteousness reach to the furthest ends of the earth. Happy is the man who hearkeneth unto thy commandments, and layeth up thy Teaching and thy word in his heart. True it is that thou art indeed the Lord of thy people, and a mighty King to plead their cause. True it is that thou art indeed the first and thou art the last, and beside thee we have no King, Redeemer and Saviour.

THE DELIVER-ANCE FROM EGYPT

From Egypt thou didst redeem us, O Lord our God, and from the house of bondmen thou didst deliver us ; all their first-born thou didst slay, but thy first-born thou didst redeem ; thou didst divide the Red Sea, and drown the proud ; but thou madest the beloved to pass through, while the waters covered their adversaries, not one of whom was left. Wherefore the beloved praised and extolled God, and offered hymns, songs, praises, blessings and thanksgivings to the King, the living and ever-enduring God ; who is high and exalted, great and revered ; who bringeth low the haughty, and raiseth up the lowly, freeth the prisoners, delivereth the meek, helpeth the poor, and answereth his people when they cry unto him ; even praises to the Most High God, blessed is he, and ever to be blessed. Moses and the children of Israel sang a song unto thee with great joy, saying, all of them,

Israel from Egypt, widens out in liturgical prayer into an epic contemplation of God's creative and redeeming deeds " (Heiler).

יִשְׂרָאֵל לְךָ עָנוּ שִׁירָה בְּשִׂמְחָה רַבָּה · וְאָמְרוּ כֻלָּם ·

מִי־כָמֹכָה בָּאֵלִם יְהֹוָה מִי כָּמֹכָה נֶאְדָּר בַּקֹּדֶשׁ נוֹרָא
תְהִלֹּת עֹשֵׂה פֶּלֶא :

שִׁירָה חֲדָשָׁה שִׁבְּחוּ גְאוּלִים לְשִׁמְךָ עַל־שְׂפַת הַיָּם

יַחַד כֻּלָּם הוֹדוּ וְהִמְלִיכוּ וְאָמְרוּ ·

יְהֹוָה ׀ יִמְלֹךְ לְעֹלָם וָעֶד :

צוּר יִשְׂרָאֵל · קוּמָה בְּעֶזְרַת יִשְׂרָאֵל וּפְדֵה כִנְאֻמֶךָ

יְהוּדָה וְיִשְׂרָאֵל · גֹּאֲלֵנוּ יְיָ צְבָאוֹת שְׁמוֹ קְדוֹשׁ יִשְׂרָאֵל ·

בָּרוּךְ אַתָּה יְיָ · גָּאַל יִשְׂרָאֵל :

The following prayer, עֲמִידָה, *to* קַדְמוֹנִיּוֹת, *p. 468, is to be said
standing. On Festivals, say the appropriate Amidah.*

אֲדֹנָי שְׂפָתַי תִּפְתָּח וּפִי יַגִּיד תְּהִלָּתֶךָ :

בָּרוּךְ אַתָּה יְיָ אֱלֹהֵינוּ וֵאלֹהֵי אֲבוֹתֵינוּ · אֱלֹהֵי
אַבְרָהָם אֱלֹהֵי יִצְחָק וֵאלֹהֵי יַעֲקֹב · הָאֵל הַגָּדוֹל הַגִּבּוֹר
וְהַנּוֹרָא אֵל עֶלְיוֹן · גּוֹמֵל חֲסָדִים טוֹבִים וְקוֹנֵה הַכֹּל ·
וְזוֹכֵר חַסְדֵי אָבוֹת וּמֵבִיא גוֹאֵל לִבְנֵי בְנֵיהֶם לְמַעַן שְׁמוֹ
בְּאַהֲבָה ·

the Lord shall reign. Like our fathers, we acclaim His sovereignty
over our lives. He is our Rock and our Redeemer (צור ישראל).

SABBATH AMIDAH.

Every Sabbath Amidah consists of seven Benedictions, the first
three and the last three being the same as those of the weekday
Amidah. The Intermediate Benediction varies in each of the Sabbath

Exodus 15. 11   WHO IS LIKE UNTO THEE, O LORD, AMONG THE MIGHTY ? WHO IS LIKE UNTO THEE, GLORIOUS IN HOLINESS, REVERED IN PRAISES, DOING MARVELS ?

With a new song the redeemed people offered praise unto thy Name at the sea shore : they all gave thanks in unison, and proclaimed thy sovereignty, and said,

Exodus 15. 18   THE LORD SHALL REIGN FOR EVER AND EVER.

GOD OUR ROCK AND RE-DEEMER   O Rock of Israel, arise to the help of Israel, and deliver, according to thy promise, Judah and Israel. Our Redeemer, the Lord of hosts is his Name, the Holy One of Israel. Blessed art thou, O Lord, who hast redeemed Israel.

THE AMIDAH   *The following prayer (Amidah) to " as in ancient years," p. 469, is to be said standing. On Festivals, say the appropriate Amidah.*

Psalm 51. 17   O Lord, open thou my lips, and my mouth shall declare thy praise.

I. THE GOD OF HISTORY   Blessed art thou, O Lord our God and God of our fathers, God of Abraham, God of Isaac, and God of Jacob, the great, mighty and revered God, the most high God, who bestowest lovingkindnesses, and art Master of all things ; who rememberest the pious deeds of the patriarchs, and in love wilt bring a redeemer to their children's. children for thy Name's sake.

services, as does also the Kedusha. For the history of the Amidah, see the Eighteen Benedictions, pp. 131-2.

O Lord, open. Since Talmudic times these words are introductory to the Amidah when it is read in silence.

1–3. THE OPENING BLESSINGS—" PRAISES "

These three benedictions embody the fundamental beliefs of Judaism in God Almighty and All-holy, in His Covenant with the Fathers, the Election of Israel, the Messianic Redemption and the Immortality of the soul.

1. First Benediction : *The God of History.*

In this opening benediction, God is adored as the God of the Fathers, the God of History, and the God Who in love will bring Messianic redemption to the children of the Patriarchs.

blessed. For the significance of this word, as well as of " Thou " when addressed to the Deity, see p. 10.

It is customary to bow at the word " blessed ", and stand upright at the word " Lord ".

On שַׁבָּת שׁוּבָה say :—

זָכְרֵנוּ לַחַיִּים מֶלֶךְ חָפֵץ בַּחַיִּים ׳ וְכָתְבֵנוּ בְּסֵפֶר הַחַיִּים ׳
לְמַעַנְךָ אֱלֹהִים חַיִּים :

מֶלֶךְ עוֹזֵר וּמוֹשִׁיעַ וּמָגֵן ׳ בָּרוּךְ אַתָּה יְיָ ׳ מָגֵן אַבְרָהָם :

אַתָּה גִבּוֹר לְעוֹלָם אֲדֹנָי מְחַיֵּה מֵתִים אַתָּה רַב לְהוֹשִׁיעַ ׳

From שַׁבַּת בְּרֵאשִׁית until the First Day of פֶּסַח say :—

מַשִּׁיב הָרוּחַ וּמוֹרִיד הַגֶּשֶׁם :

מְכַלְכֵּל חַיִּים בְּחֶסֶד מְחַיֵּה מֵתִים בְּרַחֲמִים רַבִּים ׳ סוֹמֵךְ

God of our fathers . . . Jacob. These words are drawn from the
Revelation at the burning bush (Exodus 3. 15). They are based on
Israel's fundamental conviction of the existence of One God, and take
the mind of the worshipper back to the days of Israel's religious
beginnings. In invoking the God of our Fathers, we, as their loyal
children, adore the same God—*our* God.

great, mighty and revered. Deuteronomy 10. 17. The Rabbis strongly
opposed any further heaping of Divine epithets in prayer.

bestowest lovingkindnesses. Or, " lavishest tender love " (Pool).

Master of all things. Or, " Maker of all things " (Genesis 14. 19).

rememberest the pious deeds. Thou causest the virtues of the Fathers
to bring salvation to their children's children. The Jewish doctrine of
the " Merits of the Fathers " (זכות אבות) teaches that the piety of the
fathers is accounted to the children as righteousness. " That man is
best able to advance on the road to moral perfection, who starts with
the accumulated spiritual heritage of righteous ancestors " (Levy).

in love. God has chosen, and will redeem, Israel not solely because of
Israel's merits, but from love ; Deuteronomy 7. 7, 8.

bring a redeemer. See p. 253.

remember us. " Grant us life, O Thou who delightest in dispensing
the blessings of life "—these words go back to the ninth century, the
Gaonic age. They refer to the Heavenly Judgment, as that thought is
uppermost in Jewish hearts during the Ten Days of Repentance.

For the idea of *Book of Life,* see p. 165.

for thine own sake. *i.e.* to fulfil Thy purposes.

King. The ruler of our destinies.

Helper. In all the fluctuations of life.

Saviour. From destruction, moral and physical.

Shield. He who prevents ills and malevolent influences from overcoming us.

[*On the Sabbath of Repentance say* :—

Remember us unto life, O King who delightest in life, and inscribe us in the book of life, for thine own sake, O living God.]

O King, Helper, Saviour and Shield. Blessed art thou, O Lord, the Shield of Abraham.

II. THE GOD OF NATURE   Thou, O Lord, art mighty for ever, thou revivest the dead, thou art mighty to save.

[*From the Sabbath after Simchas Torah until the First Day of Passover, say* :

Thou causest the wind to blow and the rain to fall.]

Thou sustainest the living with lovingkindness, revivest

---

blessed art thou. Of all the Amidah Benedictions, the first alone both begins and ends with these words, which are the mark of a *berochah*. All the others end, but do not begin, as a Blessing ; they are deemed to be merely continuations of the first Benediction:

Shield of Abraham. Genesis 15. 1. If, like Abraham, we are ready to meet every Divine behest with " Here I am ", He is a Shield unto us also.

2. Second Benediction : *the God of Nature.*

The appeal to History, the peculiar sphere of God's revelation, is now reinforced by an appeal to Nature, as displaying the power and goodness of God. From the distant past, the worshipper turns to the distant future, and hails God as the King who alone is mighty to save. The God of the Past and Future is also the God Who lovingly sustains the living in all the vicissitudes of earthly existence, and whose infinite faithfulness remembers and redeems them that sleep in the dust.

art mighty forever. God's protection does not cease at the portals of the grave. He is mightier than death, and in His eyes the dead have not died.

revivest the dead. He awakes the dead to new life. This emphatic statement concerning the resurrection was directed against the worldlings who disputed the deathlessness of the soul, its return to God, and its continued separate existence after its reunion with the Divine Source of being.

wind to blow. Nature's perennial renewal declares the omnipotence of God. This is especially so to an agricultural people, for whom the due ordering of wind and rain alone renders existence possible. To the Rabbis, the changing panorama of the seasons, the resurrection of life every spring, was the greatest of miracles. It was their conviction that, even as the rain wondrously wakes to life the seed slumbering in the soil, so would God awaken the dead to new life. Nature's wonders, they held, were the strongest proof that their Author was a God of

נוֹפְלִים וְרוֹפֵא חוֹלִים וּמַתִּיר אֲסוּרִים וּמְקַיֵּם אֱמוּנָתוֹ

לִישֵׁנֵי עָפָר · מִי כָמְוֹךָ בַּעַל גְּבוּרוֹת וּמִי דְוֹמֶה לָּךְ ·

מֶלֶךְ מֵמִית וּמְחַיֶּה וּמַצְמִיחַ יְשׁוּעָה ·

On שַׁבַּת שׁוּבָה say :—

מִי כָמְוֹךָ אַב הָרַחֲמִים זוֹכֵר וְצוּרָיו לַחַיִּים בְּרַחֲמִים ·

וְנֶאֱמָן אַתָּה לְהַחֲיוֹת מֵתִים · בָּרוּךְ אַתָּה יְיָ · מְחַיֵּה

הַמֵּתִים :

When the Reader repeats the עֲמִידָה, *the following* קְדוּשָׁה *is said* :—

Reader. נְקַדֵּשׁ אֶת שִׁמְךָ בָּעוֹלָם כְּשֵׁם שֶׁמַּקְדִּישִׁים אוֹתוֹ

בִּשְׁמֵי מָרוֹם כַּכָּתוּב עַל יַד נְבִיאֶךָ · וְקָרָא זֶה אֶל זֶה וְאָמַר ·

Cong. קָדוֹשׁ קָדוֹשׁ קָדוֹשׁ יְיָ צְבָאוֹת · מְלֹא כָל הָאָרֶץ

כְּבוֹדוֹ :

Reader. אָז בְּקוֹל רַעַשׁ גָּדוֹל אַדִּיר וְחָזָק מַשְׁמִיעִים

lovingkindness Who supports the falling, heals the sick, and frees His
children from all manner of woe and suffering.

thy faith : His promise ; see Daniel 12. 2.

causest salvation to spring forth. " And in the flowering of Thy saving
power givest life " (Pool).

Father of mercy. In the clauses inserted in the first Benediction
during the Solemn Season, God is addressed as " King " ; here He is
invoked as " Father ". Often these two terms are combined, and then
the order is always, " Our Father, Our King " אבינו מלכנו. In all these
insertions, there is a prayer for *life*.

3. Third Benediction : *The Sanctification of God.*

WE WILL SANCTIFY. The majestic imagery of the angels proclaiming the ineffable holiness, supreme majesty, and universal

THE GOD
OF
NATURE

the dead with great mercy, supportest the falling, healest the sick freest the bound and keepest thy faith to them that sleep in the dust. Who is like unto thee, Lord of mighty acts, and who resembleth thee, O King, who orderest death and restorest life, and causest salvation to spring forth ?

[*On the Sabbath of Repentance say* :—

Who is like unto thee, Father of mercy, who in mercy rememberest thy creatures unto life ?]

Yea, faithful art thou to revive the dead. Blessed art thou, O Lord, who revivest the dead.

[*When the Reader repeats the Amidah, the following up to "Thou art holy", p.* 455, *is said.*

III. " KE-
DUSHA " :
SANCTIFI-
CATION
OF GOD

Reader.—We will sanctify thy Name in the world, even as they sanctify it in the highest heavens, as it is written by the hand of thy prophet :

Isaiah 6. 3

And they called one unto the other and said,

Cong.—HOLY, HOLY, HOLY IS THE LORD OF HOSTS : THE WHOLE EARTH IS FULL OF HIS GLORY.

Reader.—Then with a noise of great rushing, mighty and strong, they make their voices heard, and, upraising

sovereignty of God, early suggested that a similar proclamation be heard on earth in the synagogues of Israel. Out of these prayers of sanctification by the angels on high, and His loyal worshippers on earth—the Mystics taught—a crown is woven for the Creator. In some of the Rites, the Kedusha accordingly opens with the words כתר יתנו לך. It is a most poetic conception, and has inspired some notable poetry.

Holy, holy, holy. This cry out of eternity is indeed the quintessence of the teachings of all true Religion concerning the Divine Nature.

In Hebrew poetry, three-fold repetition indicates the superlative degree : God is highest, unsearchable and infinite holiness. " *Holy* denotes the awesome and august ethical majesty of God, and His complete freedom from all that makes men imperfect and impure. It denotes more than goodness, more than purity, more than righteousness : it embraces all these in their ideal completeness, but it expresses besides the recoil from everything which is their opposite " (Driver).

full . . . glory. All that is sublime in Nature and History is the outward expression and radiation of Divine Power.

קוֹל מִתְנַשְּׂאִים לְעֻמַּת שְׂרָפִים לְעֻמָּתָם בָּרוּךְ יֹאמֵרוּ ·

Congregation. בָּרוּךְ כְּבוֹד יְיָ מִמְּקוֹמוֹ :

Reader. מִמְּקוֹמְךָ מַלְכֵּנוּ תוֹפִיעַ וְתִמְלוֹךְ עָלֵינוּ כִּי מְחַכִּים

אֲנַחְנוּ לָךְ : מָתַי תִּמְלוֹךְ בְּצִיּוֹן · בְּקָרוֹב בְּיָמֵינוּ לְעוֹלָם וָעֶד

תִּשְׁכּוֹן : תִּתְגַּדַּל וְתִתְקַדַּשׁ בְּתוֹךְ יְרוּשָׁלַיִם עִירְךָ לְדוֹר

וָדוֹר וּלְנֵצַח נְצָחִים : וְעֵינֵינוּ תִרְאֶינָה מַלְכוּתֶךָ כַּדָּבָר

הָאָמוּר בְּשִׁירֵי עֻזֶּךָ עַל יְדֵי דָוִד מְשִׁיחַ צִדְקֶךָ :

Cong. יִמְלֹךְ יְיָ לְעוֹלָם אֱלֹהַיִךְ צִיּוֹן לְדֹר וָדֹר · הַלְלוּיָהּ :

Reader. לְדוֹר וָדוֹר נַגִּיד גָּדְלֶךָ · וּלְנֵצַח נְצָחִים קְדֻשָּׁתְךָ

נַקְדִּישׁ · וְשִׁבְחֲךָ אֱלֹהֵינוּ מִפִּינוּ לֹא יָמוּשׁ לְעוֹלָם וָעֶד ·

כִּי אֵל מֶלֶךְ גָּדוֹל וְקָדוֹשׁ אָתָּה · בָּרוּךְ אַתָּה יְיָ

הָאֵל [הַמֶּלֶךְ] *say:—* [On שַׁבַּת שׁוּבָה] הַקָּדוֹשׁ :

אַתָּה קָדוֹשׁ וְשִׁמְךָ קָדוֹשׁ וּקְדוֹשִׁים בְּכָל־יוֹם יְהַלְלוּךָ

סֶּלָה · בָּרוּךְ אַתָּה יְיָ · הָאֵל [הַמֶּלֶךְ] *say --* [On שַׁבַּת שׁוּבָה

הַקָּדוֹשׁ :

with a noise. Based on Ezekiel 3. 2, the source also of the Response which follows.

from thy place shine forth. The invocation leading up to the Response, *The Lord shall reign for ever . . . unto all generations,* is compact of aspirations for the near restoration of the Divine rule in Jerusalem.

themselves towards the Seraphim, they exclaim over against them, Blessed—

Ezekiel 3. 12 *Cong.*—BLESSED BE THE GLORY OF THE LORD FROM HIS PLACE.

Reader.—From thy place shine forth, O our King, and reign over us, for we wait for thee. When wilt thou reign in Zion ? Speedily, even in our days, do thou dwell there, and for ever. Mayest thou be magnified and sanctified in the midst of Jerusalem thy city throughout all generations and to all eternity. O let our eyes behold thy kingdom, according to the word that was spoken in the songs of thy might by David, thy righteous anointed :

Psalm 146. 10 *Cong.*—THE LORD SHALL REIGN FOR EVER, THY GOD, O ZION, UNTO ALL GENERATIONS. PRAISE YE THE LORD.

Reader.—Unto all generations we will declare thy greatness, and to all eternity we will proclaim thy holiness, and thy praise, O our God, shall not depart from our mouth for ever, for thou art a great and holy God and King. Blessed art thou, O Lord, the holy God. *On the Sabbath of Repentance conclude the Blessing thus :—* the holy King.]

Thou art holy, and thy Name is holy, and the holy praise thee daily. (Selah.) Blessed art thou, O Lord, the holy God. *On the Sabbath of Repentance conclude the Blessing thus :—* the holy King.

---

the Lord shall reign. The whole paean of glorification culminates in the proclamation of the eternal kingship of the God of Zion.

ATTOH KODOSH. *Thou art holy.* This is the permanent portion of the third benediction. God is hailed as the Holy God of a Holy People.

the holy. i.e. those that strive to live lives of holiness. The reference is to Israel, whose sacred mission is the sanctification of God's Name in word and in deed (Baer).

יִשְׂמַח מֹשֶׁה בְּמַתְּנַת חֶלְקוֹ כִּי עֶבֶד נֶאֱמָן קָרָאתָ לּוֹ ·
כְּלִיל תִּפְאֶרֶת בְּרֹאשׁוֹ נָתַתָּ · בְּעָמְדוֹ לְפָנֶיךָ עַל הַר־סִינַי ·
וּשְׁנֵי לֻחֹת אֲבָנִים הוֹרִיד בְּיָדוֹ · וְכָתוּב בָּהֶם שְׁמִירַת
שַׁבָּת · וְכֵן כָּתוּב בְּתוֹרָתֶךָ ·

שמות ל״א ט׳ד״ז

וְשָׁמְרוּ בְנֵי־יִשְׂרָאֵל אֶת־הַשַּׁבָּת לַעֲשׂוֹת אֶת־הַשַּׁבָּת
לְדֹרֹתָם בְּרִית עוֹלָם : בֵּינִי וּבֵין בְּנֵי יִשְׂרָאֵל אוֹת הִוא
לְעֹלָם כִּי־שֵׁשֶׁת יָמִים עָשָׂה יְהֹוָה אֶת־הַשָּׁמַיִם וְאֶת־
הָאָרֶץ וּבַיּוֹם הַשְּׁבִיעִי שָׁבַת וַיִּנָּפַשׁ :

וְלֹא נְתַתּוֹ יְיָ אֱלֹהֵינוּ לְגוֹיֵי הָאֲרָצוֹת · וְלֹא הִנְחַלְתּוֹ
מַלְכֵּנוּ לְעוֹבְדֵי פְסִילִים · וְגַם בִּמְנוּחָתוֹ לֹא יִשְׁכְּנוּ רְשָׁעִים·
כִּי לְיִשְׂרָאֵל עַמְּךָ נְתַתּוֹ בְּאַהֲבָה · לְזֶרַע יַעֲקֹב אֲשֶׁר

4. Fourth Benediction : *Intermediate Benediction.*

The Sabbath Service is for joyful communion with God. No mention of guilt, sin or wrong-doing, and no thought of want, tribulation or sorrow, are to mar the Sabbath serenity of the worshipper. Hence the thirteen intermediate petitions of the weekday Amidah are replaced by a central Sabbath prayer of wonderful spirituality and beauty. Its ancient name was " holiness of the day ".

MOSES REJOICED. This paragraph is the introduction to the Intermediate Sabbath Benediction.

a crown of glory. Some refer this to the halo which shone on the face of Moses, Exodus 34. 28. Abudraham explains the " crown of glory " to consist in the honour expressed in the words, *thou didst call him a faithful servant* (Numbers 12. 7).

thus it says in thy Torah. Exodus 31. 16, 17—one of the ten passages, over and above the Fourth Commandment, that stress the observance of the Sabbath. The reason why the citation is not from the Decalogue, or has replaced that from the Decalogue, is the following. In Temple times, the Ten Commandments formed an essential part of the daily

IV. INTER-
MEDIATE
BENEDIC-
TION

Moses rejoiced at the lot assigned to him, for thou didst call him a faithful servant : a crown of glory didst thou place upon his head, when he stood before thee upon Mount Sinai ; and in his hand he brought down the two tables of stone, on which was written the observance of the Sabbath, and thus it says in thy Torah :

Exodus xxxi. 16, 17

INSTITUT-
ING THE
SABBATH

¹⁶And the children of Israel shall keep the Sabbath, to observe the Sabbath throughout their generations, for an everlasting covenant. ¹⁷It is a sign between me and the children of Israel for ever, that in six days the Lord made the heavens and the earth, and on the seventh day he rested, and ceased from his work.

And thou didst not bestow it, O Lord our God, unto the other nations of the earth, nor didst thou, O our King, make it the heritage of those who worship idols, nor do the unrighteous dwell in its rest ; but unto thy people Israel thou didst give it in love, unto the seed of Jacob

Morning Service. The Sages found themselves forced to remove it from the Service altogether, because the Jewish sectaries were misleading the masses into believing that the Decalogue alone contained the words of the living God. Therefore, when proof-texts for the Sabbath were to be found outside the Ten Commandments, those proof-texts were preferred.'

an everlasting covenant. The weekly hallowing of the Sabbath by the Israelites, being a proclamation of belief in God and obedience of His Torah, effects a perennial renewal of the covenant of God with the Patriarchs.

rested. Scripture often ascribes human feelings and actions to God, in order to make intelligible to finite minds that which relates to the Infinite. " The Torah uses the ordinary language of man " (Talmud).

AND THOU DIDST NOT BESTOW. See p. 340. The Sabbath is God's gift to all mankind : it is part of the Biblical scheme of creation (Genesis 2. 1–3). No small part of Israel's immeasurable gift to mankind is the weekly Day of Rest, and the spiritual communion that it has given to toiling humanity. In contrast to such universal aspect of the Sabbath, this prayer views the Sabbath as a special boon to Israel. This view is found also in the Book of Jubilees, a work of pre-Maccabaen days.

unrighteous. Heb. רשעים. For many centuries most prayer-books had this reading instead of ערלים, which recent editions, through the

בָּם בָּחָרְתָּ · עַם מְקַדְּשֵׁי שְׁבִיעִי כֻּלָּם יִשְׂבְּעוּ וְיִתְעַנְּגוּ

מִטּוּבֶךְ · וְהַשְּׁבִיעִי רָצִיתָ בּוֹ וְקִדַּשְׁתּוֹ חֶמְדַּת יָמִים אוֹתוֹ

קָרָאתָ זֵכֶר לְמַעֲשֵׂה בְרֵאשִׁית:

אֱלֹהֵינוּ וֵאלֹהֵי אֲבוֹתֵינוּ · רְצֵה בִמְנוּחָתֵנוּ · קַדְּשֵׁנוּ

בְּמִצְוֹתֶיךָ וְתֵן חֶלְקֵנוּ בְּתוֹרָתֶךָ · שַׂבְּעֵנוּ מִטּוּבֶךְ וְשַׂמְּחֵנוּ

בִּישׁוּעָתֶךָ · וְטַהֵר לִבֵּנוּ לְעָבְדְּךָ בֶּאֱמֶת · וְהַנְחִילֵנוּ יְיָ

אֱלֹהֵינוּ בְּאַהֲבָה וּבְרָצוֹן שַׁבַּת קָדְשֶׁךָ · וְיָנוּחוּ בָהּ יִשְׂרָאֵל

---

influence of Baer, have reintroduced. Some understand the latter
term as עֲרֵלֵי לֵב, those whose hearts are closed to Divine truth.

call it. Or, "proclaim it". Rashi understands the closing words to
mean, " It is the desirable of days; thou didst proclaim it a memorial
of creation ".

remembrance of creation. Exodus 20. 11. See p. 407.

OUR GOD. *accept our rest. i.e.* may our rest be such as shall increase
our moral strength and deepen our consecration to life's noblest
purposes. Sabbath rest is more than mere abstention from physical
work; and, therefore, must include worship and Scripture-reading, with
their strengthening of Religion as the basis of life.

hallow us by thy commandments. Through obedience to God's will,
we become " holy " ; *i.e.* separated from the things that are ignoble
and vile, and at one with all things that make for righteousness and
humanity. The commandments, *mitzvoth*, the ceremonies and practical
duties of Jewish religious life, are means of such hallowing ; their main
purpose being " to purge our being of all moral dross ", לְצָרֵף בָּהֶן אֶת
הַבְּרִיּוֹת, and train us to discipline and self-restraint. Observance of the
mitzvoth binds us to God, and keeps us " God-minded ". It is impossible to convey to those who have not experienced it, the feeling of
holy joy diffused in the humblest Jewish home by such ceremonies as
the Kiddush, or the kindling of the Chanukah lights. Both the home
and those that dwell in it become hallowed by their observance. The
Israelite obtains sanctification, not through vagaries of his own fancy,
nor by following any "spiritual" fashion of the hour; but by loyalty to
the recognized institutions and teachings of his Faith.

grant our portion. That we participate in the blessings which flow

whom thou didst choose. The people that sanctify the seventh day, even all of them shall be satiated and delighted with thy goodness, seeing that thou didst find pleasure in the seventh day, and didst hallow it ; thou didst call it the desirable of days, in remembrance of the creation.

SABBATH PRAYER

Our God and God of our fathers, accept our rest ; hallow us by thy commandments, and grant our portion in thy Torah ; satisfy us with thy goodness, and gladden us with thy salvation ; purify our hearts to serve thee in truth ; and in thy love and favour, O Lord our God, let us inherit thy holy Sabbath ; and may Israel, who sanctify thy Name,

---

from the observance of the Divine behests of the Torah. The Torah is the possession of the *congregation* of Israel, and each Israelite should be fully conscious, and in real possession, of his share in the infinite riches of its holiness.

thy goodness. The material and spiritual blessings which Thou deemest good for the children of men.

gladden us with thy salvation. There is no happiness like that of the trustful soul which has committed its life into the hands of God.

salvation. This word is differently understood by Jews and non-Jews. To the non-Jew, *salvation* means redemption from sin here, and deliverance from its consequences thereafter. (For these conceptions, the Jew uses the words " repentance for sin " and " forgiveness of sin "). In the Psalms and Siddur, however, *salvation* denotes either deliverance from distress and peril, or freedom for the moral expansion of our higher nature. It is something that saves us from our lower self, illumines and regenerates our soul, and makes us willing instruments of God's Eternal plan. The Sabbath is a " fountain " of salvation, because from it such blessed influences flow.

purify our hearts. With the psalmist we pray, " Create in me a pure heart ", so that every desire within us be obedient to righteousness and holy living. " Let no pride or self-seeking, no covetousness or revenge, no impure mixture or unhandsome purposes, no little ends and low imaginations, pollute my spirit, and unhallow any of my words and actions " (Jeremy Taylor).

to serve thee in truth. The pure heart renders possible sincere service of God in public or private worship, as in public or private lovingkindness to our fellowmen.

let us inherit. The Sabbath is a noble heritage, to which we are to cling with all our being, and leave nothing undone to enable every

16

מְקַדְּשֵׁי שְׁמֶךָ · בָּרוּךְ אַתָּה יְיָ · מְקַדֵּשׁ הַשַּׁבָּת :

רְצֵה יְיָ אֱלֹהֵינוּ בְּעַמְּךָ יִשְׂרָאֵל וּבִתְפִלָּתָם · וְהָשֵׁב

אֶת־הָעֲבוֹדָה לִדְבִיר בֵּיתֶךָ · וְאִשֵּׁי יִשְׂרָאֵל וּתְפִלָּתָם

בְּאַהֲבָה תְקַבֵּל בְּרָצוֹן · וּתְהִי לְרָצוֹן תָּמִיד עֲבוֹדַת יִשְׂרָאֵל

עַמֶּךָ :

On חֹל הַמּוֹעֵד *and* רֹאשׁ חֹדֶשׁ *say* :—

אֱלֹהֵינוּ וֵאלֹהֵי אֲבוֹתֵינוּ · יַעֲלֶה וְיָבֹא וְיַגִּיעַ וְיֵרָאֶה וְיֵרָצֶה

וְיִשָּׁמַע וְיִפָּקֵד וְיִזָּכֵר זִכְרוֹנֵנוּ וּפִקְדוֹנֵנוּ · וְזִכְרוֹן אֲבוֹתֵינוּ · וְזִכְרוֹן

מָשִׁיחַ בֶּן דָּוִד עַבְדֶּךָ · וְזִכְרוֹן יְרוּשָׁלַיִם עִיר קָדְשֶׁךָ · וְזִכְרוֹן כָּל

עַמְּךָ בֵּית יִשְׂרָאֵל לְפָנֶיךָ · לִפְלֵיטָה וּלְטוֹבָה וּלְחֵן וּלְחֶסֶד

וּלְרַחֲמִים וּלְחַיִּים וּלְשָׁלוֹם בְּיוֹם

Israelite to retain it. In the words of a noble Jew : " If I were asked to single out one of the great historical institutions more essential for our preservation than all others, I would not hesitate to declare that it is the observance of the Sabbath. Without this, the home and the Synagogue, the Festivals and the Holy days, the language and the history of our people, would gradually disappear. If the Sabbath will be maintained by those who have observed it, and will be restored to those who have abandoned it, then the permanence of Judaism is assured. To all who are prosperous, the question of the observance of the Sabbath involves the sacrifice of a luxury, nothing more . . . Every Jew who has it within his power, should aid in the effort to restore the Sabbath to the man from whom it has been taken away. No deeds of charity or philanthropy, no sacrifices of time or fortune made by any Jew, at all equals in beneficent result the expenditure of time and money looking towards the re-establishment of the Jewish Sabbath among the Jewish people. No amount of prating about morals will ever take the place of rooted habits ruthlessly plucked out " (Cyrus Adler).

who hallowest the Sabbath. In the similar prayer of the Festival Amidah, the phrase is *who hallowest Israel and the sacred seasons.* That mention of Israel is due to the fact that the Festivals are specifically Israelite in character. Not so the Sabbath : it preceded the selection of Israel, and applies to the whole of mankind. Hence the omission of " Israel " in the Sabbath benediction.

rest thereon. Blessed art thou, O Lord, who hallowest the Sabbath.

V. FOR RESTORA-TION OF TEMPLE SERVICE

Accept, O Lord our God, thy people Israel and their prayer ; restore the service to the inner sanctuary of thy house ; receive in love and favour both the offerings of Israel and their prayer ; and may the worship of thy people Israel be ever acceptable unto thee.

[*On New Moon and the Intermediate Days of Passover and Tabernacles, the following to " merciful God and King " is added :—*

YAALEH VE-YOVO

Our God and God of our fathers ! May our remembrance ascend, come and be accepted before thee, with the remembrance of our fathers, of Messiah the son of David

5–7. CLOSING BENEDICTIONS : THANKSGIVINGS.

Of these closing benedictions (5–7), only the middle one is an expression of gratitude. It is preceded by a petition for the restoration of the Temple Service, and is followed by the Priestly Blessing. As neither of these benedictions is of a personal character, and both deal with matters that are the result of man's gratitude to and dependence on his Maker, they too are denominated " Thanksgivings ".

"The worshipper concludes the Tefillah with benedictions for the restoration of the Divine Glory which we hope to behold as did our ancestors of old ; and then he should bow down in gratitude, as if he indeed were in God's Presence and witnessed the Israelites prostrating themselves when they beheld the Divine Glory. He should offer thanksgiving to God for all His goodness, and conclude the Tefillah with the benediction for Peace, that he may depart from the Divine Presence in peace " (Hallevi).

5. Fifth Benediction : *For the Temple Service.*

Even as the truth of pure Monotheism came from the Temple on Mt. Zion, so may that Sanctuary in future be the source from which will spread the true knowledge of God to all the children of men.

service. Heb. *avodah ;* originally meant the Temple ritual, and later divine worship generally.

restore the service. This phrase was formulated when the Temple had been destroyed.

YAALEH VE-YOVO. On New Moons and Festivals (except at Mussaf) the additional paragraph יעלה ויבא is here introduced. It petitions that, on the days which God gave us for festive joy, the whole House of Israel be remembered by Him for good and blessing, so that we may celebrate the Sacred Festival in gladness. When the Reader utters the phrases, " remember us, O Lord our God, thereon for our

On סֻכּוֹת—	פֶּסַח— On	y ,s רֹאשׁ חֹדֶשׁ On
חַג הַסֻּכּוֹת	חַג הַמַּצּוֹת	רֹאשׁ הַחֹדֶשׁ

הַזֶּה ׳ זָכְרֵנוּ יְיָ אֱלֹהֵינוּ בּוֹ לְטוֹבָה וּפָקְדֵנוּ בוֹ לִבְרָכָה וְהוֹשִׁיעֵנוּ

בוֹ לְחַיִּים ׳ וּבִדְבַר יְשׁוּעָה וְרַחֲמִים חוּס וְחָנֵּנוּ וְרַחֵם עָלֵינוּ

וְהוֹשִׁיעֵנוּ ׳ כִּי אֵלֶיךָ עֵינֵינוּ ׳ כִּי אֵל מֶלֶךְ חַנּוּן וְרַחוּם אָתָּה :

וְתֶחֱזֶינָה עֵינֵינוּ בְּשׁוּבְךָ לְצִיּוֹן בְּרַחֲמִים ׳ בָּרוּךְ אַתָּה

יְיָ ׳ הַמַּחֲזִיר שְׁכִינָתוֹ לְצִיּוֹן :

מוֹדִים אֲנַחְנוּ לָךְ

שָׁאַתָּה הוּא יְיָ אֱלֹהֵינוּ

וֵאלֹהֵי אֲבוֹתֵינוּ לְעוֹלָם

וָעֶד ׳ צוּר חַיֵּינוּ מָגֵן

יִשְׁעֵנוּ אַתָּה הוּא לְדוֹר

וָדוֹר ׳ נוֹדֶה לְּךָ וּנְסַפֵּר

תְּהִלָּתֶךָ עַל חַיֵּינוּ

הַמְּסוּרִים בְּיָדֶךָ וְעַל

נִשְׁמוֹתֵינוּ הַפְּקוּדוֹת לָךְ

The Congregation, in an undertone—

מוֹדִים אֲנַחְנוּ לָךְ שָׁאַתָּה הוּא

יְיָ אֱלֹהֵינוּ וֵאלֹהֵי אֲבוֹתֵינוּ אֱלֹהֵי

כָל בָּשָׂר ׳ יוֹצְרֵנוּ יוֹצֵר בְּרֵאשִׁית ׳

בְּרָכוֹת וְהוֹדָאוֹת לְשִׁמְךָ הַגָּדוֹל

וְהַקָּדוֹשׁ ׳ עַל שֶׁהֶחֱיִיתָנוּ וְקִיַּמְתָּנוּ ׳

כֵּן תְּחַיֵּנוּ וּתְקַיְּמֵנוּ ׳ וְתֶאֱסוֹף

גָּלֻיּוֹתֵינוּ לְחַצְרוֹת קָדְשֶׁךָ לִשְׁמֹר

חֻקֶּיךָ וְלַעֲשׂוֹת רְצוֹנֶךָ וּלְעָבְדְּךָ

בְּלֵבָב שָׁלֵם עַל שֶׁאֲנַחְנוּ מוֹדִים

לָךְ ׳ בָּרוּךְ אֵל הַהוֹדָאוֹת :

וְעַל נִסֶּיךָ שֶׁבְּכָל יוֹם עִמָּנוּ וְעַל נִפְלְאוֹתֶיךָ וְטוֹבוֹתֶיךָ

שֶׁבְּכָל־עֵת עֶרֶב וָבֹקֶר וְצָהֳרָיִם ׳ הַטּוֹב כִּי לֹא־כָלוּ רַחֲמֶיךָ ׳

well-being ", and " be mindful of us for blessing ", and " save us unto
life ", the congregation each time responds with " Amen ".
   6. Sixth Benediction : *Thanksgiving for God's Unfailing Mercies.*
   We give thanks. A singularly beautiful anthem of gratitude for God's
manifold mercies to us.

thy servant, of Jerusalem thy holy .city, and of all thy people the house of Israel, bringing deliverance and well-being, grace, lovingkindness and mercy, life and peace on this day of

On New Moon say—the New Moon.

On Passover—the Feast of Unleavened Bread.

On Tabernacles—the Feast of Tabernacles.

Remember us, O Lord our God, thereon for our well-being ; be mindful of us for blessing, and save us unto life : by thy promise of salvation and mercy, spare us and be gracious unto us ; have mercy upon us and save us ; for our eyes are bent upon thee, because thou art a gracious and merciful God and King.]

And let our eyes behold thy return in mercy to Zion. Blessed art thou, O Lord, who restorest thy divine presence unto Zion.

VI. THANKS-GIVING FOR GOD'S UNFAIL-ING MERCIES

We give thanks unto thee, for thou art the Lord our God and the God of our fathers for ever and ever ; thou art the Rock of our lives, the Shield of our salvation through every generation. We will give thanks unto thee and declare thy praise for our lives which are committed unto thy hand, and for our souls which are in thy charge, and for thy miracles, which are daily with us, and for thy wonders and thy benefits, which are wrought at all times, evening, morn and noon. O thou who art all-good, whose mercies fail not ; thou, merciful Being, whose lovingkindnesses never cease, we have ever hoped in thee.

The Congregation, in an undertone—

We give thanks unto thee,. for thou art the Lord our God and the God of our fathers, the God of all flesh, our Creator and the Creator of all things in the beginning. Blessings and thanksgivings be to thy great and holy Name, because thou hast kept us in life and hast preserved us : so mayest thou continue to keep us in life and to preserve us. O gather our exiles to thy holy courts to observe thy statutes, to do thy will, and to serve thee with a perfect heart ; seeing that we give thanks unto thee. Blessed be the God to whom thanksgivings are due.

וְהַמְרַחֵם כִּי לֹא־תַמּוּ חֲסָדֶיךָ ・ מֵעוֹלָם קִוִּינוּ לָךְ :

On חֲנֻכָּה say עַל הַנִּסִּים, *p.* 150 *and* 152.

וְעַל כֻּלָּם יִתְבָּרַךְ וְיִתְרוֹמַם שִׁמְךָ מַלְכֵּנוּ תָּמִיד לְעוֹלָם

וָעֶד :

On שַׁבַּת שׁוּבָה say :—

וּכְתוֹב לְחַיִּים טוֹבִים כָּל־בְּנֵי בְרִיתֶךָ :

וְכֹל הַחַיִּים יוֹדוּךָ סֶּלָה וִיהַלְלוּ אֶת־שִׁמְךָ בֶּאֱמֶת ・ הָאֵל

יְשׁוּעָתֵנוּ וְעֶזְרָתֵנוּ סֶלָה ・ בָּרוּךְ אַתָּה יְיָ ・ הַטּוֹב שִׁמְךָ

וּלְךָ נָאֶה לְהוֹדוֹת :

At the repetition of the עֲמִידָה *by the Reader the following is*
introduced :—

אֱלֹהֵינוּ וֵאלֹהֵי אֲבוֹתֵינוּ ・ בָּרְכֵנוּ בַּבְּרָכָה הַמְשֻׁלֶּשֶׁת בַּתּוֹרָה

הַכְּתוּבָה עַל יְדֵי מֹשֶׁה עַבְדֶּךָ ・ הָאֲמוּרָה מִפִּי אַהֲרֹן וּבָנָיו

כֹּהֲנִים ・ עַם קְדוֹשֶׁךָ כָּאָמוּר ・ יְבָרֶכְךָ יְיָ וְיִשְׁמְרֶךָ : יָאֵר יְיָ פָּנָיו

אֵלֶיךָ וִיחֻנֶּךָּ : יִשָּׂא יְיָ פָּנָיו אֵלֶיךָ וְיָשֵׂם לְךָ שָׁלוֹם :

שִׂים שָׁלוֹם טוֹבָה וּבְרָכָה חֵן וָחֶסֶד וְרַחֲמִים עָלֵינוּ

וְעַל כָּל יִשְׂרָאֵל עַמֶּךָ ・ בָּרְכֵנוּ אָבִינוּ כֻּלָּנוּ כְּאֶחָד בְּאוֹר

פָּנֶיךָ ・ כִּי בְאוֹר פָּנֶיךָ נָתַתָּ לָנוּ יְיָ אֱלֹהֵינוּ תּוֹרַת חַיִּים

וְאַהֲבַת חֶסֶד וּצְדָקָה וּבְרָכָה וְרַחֲמִים וְחַיִּים וְשָׁלוֹם ・

וְטוֹב בְּעֵינֶיךָ לְבָרֵךְ אֶת־עַמְּךָ יִשְׂרָאֵל בְּכָל־עֵת וּבְכָל־

שָׁעָה בִּשְׁלוֹמֶךָ :

[*On Chanukah say, " We thank thee also,"* pp. 151, 153.]

For all these acts, thy Name, O our King, shall be continually blessed and exalted for ever and ever.

[*On the Sabbath of Repentance say* :—
O inscribe all the children of thy covenant for a happy life.]

And everything that liveth shall give thanks unto thee for ever, and shall praise thy Name in truth, O God, our salvation and our help. (Selah.) Blessed art thou, O Lord, whose Name is All-good, and unto whom it is becoming to give thanks.

[*At the repetition of the Amidah by the Reader, the following is introduced* :—

Our God and God of our fathers, bless us with the three-fold blessing of thy Torah written by the hand of Moses thy servant, which was spoken by Aaron and his sons, the priests, thy holy

Numbers 6. 24-26

people, as it is said, THE LORD BLESS THEE, AND KEEP THEE : THE LORD MAKE HIS FACE TO SHINE UPON THEE, AND BE GRACIOUS UNTO THEE : THE LORD TURN HIS FACE UNTO THEE, AND GIVE THEE PEACE.]

*VII.
FOR PEACE*

Grant peace, welfare, blessing, grace, lovingkindness and mercy unto us and unto all Israel, thy people. Bless us, O our Father, even all of us together, with the light of thy countenance ; for by the light of thy countenance thou hast given us, O Lord our God, the Teaching of life, lovingkindness and righteousness, blessing, mercy, life and peace ; and may it be good in thy sight to bless thy people Israel at all times and in every hour with thy peace.

7. Seventh Benediction : *For Peace.*
The prayer for Peace is the last of the " Thanksgiving " benedictions. There can be no Peace, unless it is preceded by thankfulness to God ; even as there can be no true thankfulness, unless that is preceded by service to God.

The Priestly Blessing was here daily recited in the Temple. At the present day, this is done by the Reader in the paragraph preceding this benediction, except at those Mussaf Services when the Priests bless the Congregation.

three-fold. Because it consists of three clauses.

GRANT PEACE. The prayer for peace is a congregational restatement of the Priestly Benediction in the form of a prayer.

On שַׁבַּת שׁוּבָה say :—

בָּרוּךְ אַתָּה יְיָ ·
בְּסֵפֶר חַיִּים בְּרָכָה וְשָׁלוֹם וּפַרְנָסָה
טוֹבָה נִזָּכֵר וְנִכָּתֵב לְפָנֶיךָ אֲנַחְנוּ וְכָל־
עַמְּךָ בֵּית יִשְׂרָאֵל לְחַיִּים טוֹבִים
וּלְשָׁלוֹם · בָּרוּךְ אַתָּה יְיָ · עוֹשֵׂה
הַשָּׁלוֹם :

הַמְבָרֵךְ אֶת־עַמּוֹ

יִשְׂרָאֵל בַּשָּׁלוֹם :

אֱלֹהַי · נְצוֹר לְשׁוֹנִי מֵרָע וּשְׂפָתַי מִדַּבֵּר מִרְמָה ·
וְלִמְקַלְלַי נַפְשִׁי תִדּוֹם וְנַפְשִׁי כֶּעָפָר לַכֹּל תִּהְיֶה : פְּתַח
לִבִּי בְּתוֹרָתֶךָ וּבְמִצְוֹתֶיךָ תִּרְדּוֹף נַפְשִׁי · וְכֹל הַחוֹשְׁבִים
עָלַי רָעָה מְהֵרָה הָפֵר עֲצָתָם וְקַלְקֵל מַחֲשַׁבוֹתָם · עֲשֵׂה
לְמַעַן שְׁמֶךָ עֲשֵׂה לְמַעַן יְמִינֶךָ עֲשֵׂה לְמַעַן קְדֻשָּׁתֶךָ עֲשֵׂה
לְמַעַן תּוֹרָתֶךָ · לְמַעַן יֵחָלְצוּן יְדִידֶיךָ הוֹשִׁיעָה יְמִינְךָ
וַעֲנֵנִי : יִהְיוּ לְרָצוֹן אִמְרֵי־פִי וְהֶגְיוֹן לִבִּי לְפָנֶיךָ יְיָ צוּרִי
וְגֹאֲלִי : עֹשֶׂה שָׁלוֹם בִּמְרוֹמָיו הוּא יַעֲשֶׂה שָׁלוֹם עָלֵינוּ
וְעַל כָּל־יִשְׂרָאֵל · וְאִמְרוּ אָמֵן :

O MY GOD. This is a private meditation of Mar, the son of Rabina, a famous rabbi of the fifth century. It is therefore written in the singular. Through its beauty it found a place in all Rites, and became a pendant to the Amidah when spoken silently. As the evil tongue is the most insidious enemy of peace, this prayer follows naturally upon the concluding petition for Peace ; Psalm 34. 14.

let my soul be dumb. "Grant me forbearance unto those who deal ill towards me, and a calm disposition unto all my fellowmen"— a prayer at once humble and dignified, marked by solemn simplicity and true greatness (N. Remy). Even in thought we are not to hate those that curse us. "Whosoever does not persecute them that persecute him, whosoever takes an offence in silence, he who does good not because of reward but out of love, he who is cheerful under his sufferings—such are the friends of God" (Talmud).

Blessed art thou, O Lord, who blessest thy people Israel with peace.

[*On the Sabbath of Repentance say* :—
In the book of life, blessing, peace and good sustenance may we be remembered and inscribed before thee, we and all thy people the house of Israel, for a happy life and for peace. Blessed art thou, O Lord, who makest peace.]

CON-CLUDING MEDITA-TION

O my God! guard my tongue from evil, and my lips from speaking guile ; and to such as curse me let my soul be dumb, yea, let my soul be unto all as the dust. Open my heart to thy Torah, and let my soul pursue thy commandments. If any design evil against me, speedily make their counsel of no effect, and frustrate their designs. Do it for the sake of thy Name, do it for the sake of thy power, do it for the sake of thy holiness, do it for the sake of thy Torah. *Psalm* 60. 7 In order that thy beloved ones may be delivered, O save *Psalm* 19. 5. by thy power, and answer me. Let the words of my mouth and the meditation of my heart be acceptable before thee, O Lord, my Rock and my Redeemer. He who maketh peace in his high places, may he make peace for us and for all Israel ; and say ye, Amen.

May it be thy will, O Lord our God and God of our fathers, that the temple be speedily rebuilt in our days, and grant our portion in

---

as the dust. This is victory over self, and has nothing in common with self-contempt. " Be not wicked in thine own esteem ", remains a primary duty for individuals as for communities.

open my heart to thy Torah. " Open my heart to Thy sacred teachings, so that my conduct may be evidence of the fulfilment of Thy commandments." Only knowledge of God's Will will equip us with the moral insight and strength for heroic conduct.

frustrate their designs. Defeat their purposes, and turn their curses into blessings. This ends the prayer of Mar, the son of Rabina. The Hebrew original can be arranged in short poetic lines.

of thy power. lit. " of thy right hand ", *i.e.* to vindicate Thy power.

He who maketh peace. " Creator of the harmony of the spheres, mayest Thou in Thy tender love create peace for us and for all Israel." Three steps backwards, with accompanying inclinations to the left and right, formed the respectful mode of retiring from a superior. This form was transferred to the concluding verse of the Amidah, as if retiring from the presence of God (Pool).

יְהִי רָצוֹן לְפָנֶיךָ יְיָ אֱלֹהֵינוּ וֵאלֹהֵי אֲבוֹתֵינוּ שֶׁיִּבָּנֶה בֵּית
הַמִּקְדָּשׁ בִּמְהֵרָה בְיָמֵינוּ ׳ וְתֵן חֶלְקֵנוּ בְּתוֹרָתֶךָ : וְשָׁם נַעֲבָדְךָ
בְּיִרְאָה כִּימֵי עוֹלָם וּכְשָׁנִים הַדְמוֹנִיּוֹת : וְעָרְבָה לַיְיָ מִנְחַת
יְהוּדָה וִירוּשָׁלָיִם כִּימֵי עוֹלָם וּכְשָׁנִים הַדְמוֹנִיּוֹת :

On רֹאשׁ חֹדֶשׁ, יָמִים טוֹבִים, חוֹל הַמּוֹעֵד and חֲנֻכָּה, הַלֵּל is said
after the Amidah. קַדִּישׁ תִּתְקַבַּל, p. 206.

The end of the Amidah was accounted an appropriate place for silent individual prayer, in the manner of the meditation of Mar, the son of Rabina.

Rabbi Elazar, when he had finished the Amidah, used to add: " May it be Thy will, O Lord our God, to cause love and brotherhood, peace and comradeship to abide in our lot; to enlarge our border with disciples; to prosper our goal with happy ends and fulfilment of hope. May we be of those who have a portion in the Life to Come. Strengthen us with good companionship, and fortify our good impulses in this life; so that the reverence of Thy Name be ever the longing of our heart. And may this our happiness in reverencing Thee be remembered by Thee for good ".

R. Zera was in the habit of adding: " May it be Thy will, O Lord our God, that we return to Thee in perfect repentance; so that we may not be ashamed to meet our fathers in the Life to Come ".

R. Alexander is the author of this additional prayer: " May it be Thy will, O Lord our God, to place us in a corner of light, and not in a corner of darkness; and may not our heart grow faint, nor our eyes dim. Lord of the Universe! It is revealed and known before Thee that it is our desire to perform Thy will; but what stands in the way? The Evil Inclination and the oppression of the kingdoms. May it be Thy will to deliver us from their hand, so that we may again perform Thy statutes with a perfect heart ".

R. Pedath and R. Chiyya used to add: " May it be Thy will, O Lord of God and God of our Fathers, that none hate or envy us, and that neither hatred nor envy of any man find place in our hearts. May thy Torah be our occupation, and make us wholehearted in reverencing Thee. Keep us far from what Thou hatest; bring us near to what Thou lovest; and deal mercifully with us for Thy Name's sake ".

thy Torah. And there we will serve thee with awe, as in the days of
Malachi 3. 4 old, and as in ancient years. Then shall the offering of Judah and
Jerusalem be pleasant unto the Lord, as in the days of old, and as
in ancient years.

*On New Moon, Festivals, the Intermediate Days of Festivals, and on
Chanukah, Hallel is said after the Amidah.*

Kaddish, p. 207

ORDER OF READING THE TORAH ON SABBATHS AND FESTIVALS

READING OF TORAH AND PROPHETS

Its Significance in the History of Religion

"From early times in Israel, we find institutions to bring men, submerged in life's troubles and errors, nearer to the Divine. Sabbath and Festivals, Prayer and Torah-exposition provided consolation to the sinner, help to the weak, and religious instruction to all. The public worship of the Synagogue became the visible banner of Israel's spiritual nationhood" (Leopold Zunz). Jewish congregational worship seems at all times to have included the reading and exposition of the Divine Teaching given to Israel. Thereby the Synagogue became a place of instruction in the truth and duties of Revealed Religion, the imparting or receiving of such instruction being itself regarded as an *act of worship*. Moreover, reading of Scripture on Sabbaths and Festivals was for many centuries accompanied by a translation (*targum*) into the vernacular, which translation was usually a devotional exposition of the portion read. The Weekly and Festival Readings thus familiarized every Jew on the leisure days of the Jewish Calendar with the religious and ethical teachings of his Faith. The Sabbath became the great educator in the highest education of all; namely, in the laws governing human conduct.

The effect of the Sabbath Readings and homilies upon the Jewish people has been incalculable. They moulded Israel into a spiritual democracy, and made the Torah the possession of the *congregation* of Jacob. Zunz has shown that almost the whole of Israel's inner history since the close of Bible times, can be traced in the Synagogue Readings and attendant discourses on the Torah. And eighteen hundred years before Zunz, the immeasurable spiritual value of the Readings and their exposition was fully recognized. Josephus explains to his Roman public: " The Lawgiver showed the Law to be the best and the most necessary means of instruction, by enjoining the people to assemble not once or twice, or frequently, but every week, while abstaining from all other work, in order to hear the Law and learn it in a thorough manner—a thing which all other lawgivers seem to have neglected ".

This endeavour to educate the whole people in its religion had no parallel in the ancient world. In the Synagogue, the foremost place was for the first time in human history given to the reading of a Sacred Book. That Book declared to the assembled congregation the will of God ; and its uninterrupted voice of instruction, exhortation and inspiration has reverberated throughout the generations in Israel. In the fulness of time, it reverberated far beyond Israel. Multitudes of Gentiles were, in the first centuries of the present era, won for Judaism, through the Sabbath-readings of the Torah and the Prophets. The lasting influence of the Scriptural Readings as an agency in the moral education of mankind, is felt to the present day. This unique Jewish institution " determined the type of Christian worship, which in the Greek and Roman world of the day might otherwise easily have taken the form of mere mystery ; and, in part directly, in part through the Church, it furnished a model to Mohammed. Thus Judaism gave to the world not only the fundamental ideas of the great monotheistic religions, but the institutional forms in which they have perpetuated and propagated themselves " (Moore).

A brief survey of the rise and development of the Torah-readings is essential for the understanding of Jewish usage to-day in this sphere of devotion.

As stated, Scripture Readings go back to ancient times. During the Feast of Tabernacles preceding the conclusion of the Sabbatical year, there was a public reading of portions of Deuteronomy at the Sanctuary. " Assemble the people, the men and the women and the little ones, and thy stranger that is within thy gates, that they may hear and that they may learn, and fear the Lord your God, and observe to do all the words of the law " (Deuteronomy 31. 12). It seems that Readings and expositions of Scripture were given by the Prophets to young and old on Sabbaths and Festivals. " Wherefore wilt thou go to him to-day ? "—the Shunammite woman is asked when she is preparing to go to the Prophet Elisha ; " it is neither New Moon nor Sabbath " (II Kings 4. 23). After the Exile, we find that Ezra read from the Torah on every day of Tabernacles ; and, in later generations, the High Priest read selections from the Torah on the Day of Atonement. Such readings were also a feature of the lay devotional services which accompanied the daily sacrifices in the rebuilt Temple. Various portions of the Pentateuch and the Psalms were at an early date introduced into the daily Synagogue Service ; and, since Maccabean days, the set Readings from the Sacred Scroll on Sabbaths and Festivals have been regularly and universally observed.

At first these Readings were quite short on ordinary Sabbaths, as were also the selected passages on Festivals. In time, they grew longer, and, what is of especial importance, the Sabbath Readings became continuous. *Selection* from different parts of the Torah for ordinary Sabbaths was prohibited, and the Five Books of the Torah were completed in three years. This triennial cycle for the completion of the Torah on Sabbath mornings, was for many centuries the usage in Palestine. However, the virile and enthusiastic Jewry of Babylon concluded the Torah in the course of one year. Eventually this became the established rule throughout Israel.

With the coming of the larger Readings, more than one person was "called up" to read aloud the Sacred Text to the congregation. On

סדר קריאת התורה לשבת ויום טוב :

אֵין כָּמוֹךָ בָאֱלֹהִים אֲדֹנָי וְאֵין כְּמַעֲשֶׂיךָ : מַלְכוּתְךָ
מַלְכוּת כָּל־עֹלָמִים וּמֶמְשַׁלְתְּךָ בְּכָל דּוֹר וָדֹר : יְיָ מֶלֶךְ
יְיָ מָלָךְ יְיָ | יִמְלֹךְ לְעֹלָם וָעֶד : יְיָ עֹז לְעַמּוֹ יִתֵּן יְיָ | יְבָרֵךְ
אֶת־עַמּוֹ בַשָּׁלוֹם :

אַב הָרַחֲמִים הֵיטִיבָה בִרְצוֹנְךָ אֶת־צִיּוֹן תִּבְנֶה חוֹמוֹת
יְרוּשָׁלָיִם : כִּי בְךָ לְבַד בָּטָחְנוּ מֶלֶךְ אֵל רָם וְנִשָּׂא אָדוֹן
עוֹלָמִים :

The Ark is opened.

Reader and Congregation :—

וַיְהִי בִּנְסֹעַ הָאָרֹן וַיֹּאמֶר מֹשֶׁה • קוּמָה | יְיָ וְיָפֻצוּ אֹיְבֶיךָ

week-days, the number was three ; on New Moon, four ; on Festivals, five ; on the Day of Atonement, six—and the numbers were not to be exceeded. The largest number—seven—was reserved for the Sabbaths, with possibilities of increasing that number.

The enlarged Readings involved further far-reaching changes. Not everyone of those called to the Torah was able to read the unvowelled Text with the required correctness. In order not to put anyone publicly to shame, the reading of all the portions was before long taken over by the Chazan, or by one specially deputed by the congregation for that purpose, the *baal kore*. Only in the case of a Barmitzvah was an exception made. In consequence of this new arrangement, the humblest and lowliest of the community came to share with the learned the coveted religious privilege of being called to the Torah.

An additional change was now rendered necessary. Originally, one Blessing was recited by the man first called to the Torah ; and the other Blessing was recited at the conclusion of the entire Reading, by the man who was called up seventh. As if still further to ensure personal participation on the part of those called up, the usage arose for each one to recite both Blessings. By means of this innovation, the ceremony of being called to the Law became, in the eyes of the people, even more sacred and endeared than before.

ORDER OF READING THE TORAH ON SABBATHS AND FESTIVALS

Psalm 86. 8   There is none like unto thee among the gods, O Lord ; *Psalm* 145. 13 and there are no works like unto thine. Thy kingdom is an everlasting kingdom, and thy domination endureth throughout all generations. The Lord is King ; the Lord was King ; *Psalm* 29. 11 The Lord shall be King for ever and ever. The Lord will give strength unto his people ; the Lord will bless his people with peace.

Father of mercies, do good in thy favour unto Zion ; build thou the walls of Jerusalem. For in thee alone do we trust, O King, high and exalted God, Lord of worlds.

*OPENING
THE ARK
Numbers
10. 35, 36*

The Ark is opened.

Reader and Cong.—And it came to pass, when the Ark set forward, that Moses said, Rise up, O Lord, and thine

I. OPENING OF THE ARK.

The taking out of the Scroll of the Torah from the Sacred Ark, as well as its return thereto have for over a thousand years formed the solemn and dramatic centre of the public service on Sabbaths and Festivals. The prayers by the Reader, and the congregational participation in those prayers by means of Responses and sacred acts, are the growth of over 1,500 years They are especially elaborate and impressive in the Ashkenazi Rite.

(*A*) *Before* the opening of the Ark, the verses beginning " There is none like unto Thee " are recited. This custom dates from the thirteenth century.

There is none . . . . among the gods. This phrase of the psalmist does not ascribe reality to those gods. In that same psalm (86. 10) he exclaims, "Thou art God alone."

The Lord is King. See p. 85.

וְיָנֻסוּ מְשַׂנְאֶיךָ מִפָּנֶיךָ : כִּי מִצִּיּוֹן תֵּצֵא תוֹרָה וּדְבַר־
יְיָ מִירוּשָׁלָםִ :

The Reader takes the סֵפֶר תּוֹרָה, and says :—

בָּרוּךְ שֶׁנָּתַן תּוֹרָה לְעַמּוֹ יִשְׂרָאֵל בִּקְדֻשָּׁתוֹ :

In some Congregations the following is said :—

זוהר פ' ויקהל

בְּרִיךְ שְׁמֵהּ דְּמָרֵא עָלְמָא בְּרִיךְ כִּתְרָךְ וְאַתְרָךְ · יְהֵא רְעוּתָךְ עִם
עַמָּךְ יִשְׂרָאֵל לְעָלַם · וּפֻרְקַן יְמִינָךְ אַחֲזֵי לְעַמָּךְ בְּבֵית מִקְדְּשָׁךְ
וּלְאַמְטוּיֵא לָנָא מִטּוּב נְהוֹרָךְ וּלְקַבֵּל צְלוֹתָנָא בְּרַחֲמִין : יְהֵא
רַעֲוָא קֳדָמָךְ דְּתוֹרִיךְ לָן חַיִּין בְּטִיבוּתָא · וְלֶהֱוֵא אֲנָא פְּקִידָא
בְּגוֹ צַדִּיקַיָּא לְמִרְחַם עָלַי וּלְמִנְטַר יָתִי וְיַת כָּל־דִּי לִי וְדִי לְעַמָּךְ
יִשְׂרָאֵל : אַנְתְּ הוּא זָן לְכֹלָּא וּמְפַרְנֵס לְכֹלָּא · אַנְתְּ הוּא שַׁלִּיט
עַל כֹּלָּא · אַנְתְּ הוּא דְּשַׁלִּיט עַל מַלְכַיָּא וּמַלְכוּתָא דִּי־לָךְ הִיא :

(B) *At* the opening of the Ark, both Reader and congregation chant ויהי בנסע (" when the Ark is set forward ") and כי מציון (" for out of Zion ").

and it came to pass. This is the invocation prayer (Numbers 10. 35) of the children of Israel in the Wilderness, whenever the Ark of the Covenant went forward. The Ark of the Covenant, guiding the Israelite tribes in their desert wanderings, typified God in front of His people—the Divine Presence—protecting them, and leading them on to victory. We still feel the thrill of sacred enthusiasm that animated our fathers of old when they heard these words.

rise up, O Lord . . . before thee. The impressive war-cry of truth against error, of righteousness against sin. God's enemies are the enemies of Israel. When God arises against the hosts of Israel's enemies, they scatter, as the darkness before the sunlight.

for out of Zion. These words (Isaiah 2. 3) are taken from the Prophet's sublime vision of the Messianic age, when Israel's spiritual teachings shall extend to all humanity and dominate the hearts of men. Right, not might, shall then rule the world; and the energies of man

enemies shall be scattered, and they that hate thee shall flee
before thee. For out of Zion shall go forth the Law, and
the word of the Lord from Jerusalem.

The Reader takes the Scroll, and says :—

Blessed be he who in his holiness gave the Torah to
his people Israel.

[*In some Congregations the following is said :—*
Zohar, Parshath Vayakhel.

*MEDITA-
TION*

Blessed be the Name of the Sovereign of the universe. Blessed
be thy crown and thy abiding-place. Let thy favour rest with thy
people Israel for ever : show them the redemption of thy might in
thy holy temple. Bestow upon us the benign gift of thy light, and
in mercy accept our supplications. May it be thy will to prolong
our life in well-being. Let me also be numbered among the righteous,
so that thou mayest be merciful unto me, and have me in thy keeping,

that are now devoted to purposes of slaughter and destruction, will be
consecrated to ends of constructive human welfare. The Prophet continues: "They shall beat their swords into ploughshares, and their spears
into pruning hooks: nation shall not lift up sword against nation, neither
shall they learn war any more ".

in his holiness. And therefore commanded, " Ye shall be holy, for
I the Lord am holy " (Leviticus 19. 2).

(*C*) Prayers before taking out the Scroll of the Torah.
The opening verses and doxologies in *A* and *B* were originally followed
by the *Shema* and other declarations of faith, p. 481. Since 1600,
many congregations have, under the influence of the Cabalists, introduced here (1) on Sabbaths, a selection from the Zohar ; and, (2) on
Festivals, the recital of the Thirteen Attributes ; followed by (3) a
special Supplication.

1. *Blessed be the Name.* This selection is immediately preceded
in the Zohar by the words, "When the Scroll is taken out in the
congregation to read therein, the gates of the Heavens of Mercy
open, and Celestial Love awakes. It is then fitting for a man to recite
this prayer ".

The ZOHAR, the "Book of Light", ostensibly a commentary on the
Torah, was long believed to be the work of Simeon ben Yochai, of the
second century (concerning him, see p. 654). It first became known in
1290 in Spain, and is the result of a long mystical tradition and the
product of many periods and civilizations. It is a strange work, and

אֲנָא עַבְדָּא דְקוּדְשָׁא בְּרִיךְ הוּא דְּסָגֵידְנָא קַמֵּהּ וּמִקַּמֵּהּ דִּיקַר
אוֹרַיְתֵהּ בְּכָל עִדָּן וְעִדָּן ׳ לָא עַל אֱנָשׁ רָחֵיצְנָא ׳ וְלָא עַל בַּר
אֱלָהִין סָמִיכְנָא ׳ אֶלָּא בֶּאֱלָהָא דִשְׁמַיָּא ׳ דְּהוּא אֱלָהָא קְשׁוֹט ׳
וְאוֹרַיְתֵהּ קְשׁוֹט ׳ וּנְבִיאוֹהִי קְשׁוֹט ׳ וּמַסְגֵּא לְמֶעְבַּד טַבְוָן וּקְשׁוֹט ׳
בֵּהּ אֲנָא רָחֵיץ ׳ וְלִשְׁמֵהּ קַדִּישָׁא יַקִּירָא אֲנָא אָמַר תֻּשְׁבְּחָן :
יְהֵא רַעֲוָא קֳדָמָךְ דְּתִפְתַּח לִבִּי בְּאוֹרַיְתָא ׳ וְתַשְׁלִים ׳ מִשְׁאֲלִין
דְּלִבִּי ׳ וְלִבָּא דְכָל־עַמָּךְ יִשְׂרָאֵל ׳ לְטַב וּלְחַיִּין וְלִשְׁלָם : ־

On Festivals the following is said :—

יְהֹוָה ׀ יְהֹוָה אֵל רַחוּם וְחַנּוּן אֶרֶךְ אַפַּיִם וְרַב חֶסֶד וֶאֱמֶת :
נֹצֵר חֶסֶד לָאֲלָפִים נֹשֵׂא עָוֹן וָפֶשַׁע וְחַטָּאָה וְנַקֵּה :

(To be said three times.)
On Passover, Pentecost and Tabernacles say :—

רִבּוֹן הָעוֹלָם ׳ מַלֵּא מִשְׁאֲלוֹת לִבִּי לְטוֹבָה ׳ וְהָפֵק רְצוֹנִי וְתֵן

the first impression is one of bewildering incoherence, though some of its
utterances are of striking beauty. Characteristic is the place which the
Zohar assigns to man. He is the connecting link between Deity and the
Universe; and man can by his conduct become, as it were, the
collaborator of Divinity. Each new prayer is a strengthening of the
world's spiritual forces; whereas sin stops up the channels of grace,
and brings with it an increase of evil and confusion in the universe. The
Torah has a deeply mystical meaning, but its secrets are revealed to those
only who love it. "The narratives of the Torah", says the Zohar, "are
its garments. More valuable than the garment is the body which carries it;
and more valuable even than that, is the soul enshrined in the body".
It was its teaching of the dignity of man, of his immortality dependent
altogether on conduct, as much as its poetry and mystery, that conquered
such a large portion of the Jewish world for the Zohar.

open my heart unto thy Torah. Direct communion with the Divine
is here combined with loyal obedience to the commandments of the
Torah. The view that the mystic, as such, disregards all ritual or
religious precepts and is a law unto himself, is not borne out by
history.

2. On Festivals, the Ashkenazi Rite has in quite recent centuries
taken over from the Mystics the custom to repeat aloud the Thirteen
Attributes of God's Mercy. The custom saying them three times, first

OPENING THE ARK

with all that belong to me and to thy people Israel. Thou art he that feedeth and sustaineth all ; thou art he that ruleth over all ; thou art he that ruleth over kings, for dominion is thine. I am the servant of the Holy One, blessed be he, before whom and before whose glorious Torah I prostrate myself at all times : not in man do I put my trust, nor upon any angel do I rely, but upon the God of heaven, who is the God of truth, and whose Teaching is truth, and whose prophets are prophets of truth, and who aboundeth in deeds of goodness and truth. In him I put my trust, and unto his holy and glorious Name I utter praises. May it be thy will to open my heart unto thy Teaching, and to fulfil the wishes of my heart and of the hearts of all thy people Israel for good, for life, and for peace.]

[On Festivals the following is said :—

Exodus 34, 6, 7 THE INFINITE MERCIES OF GOD

The Lord, the Lord is a merciful and gracious God, slow to anger and abounding in lovingkindness and truth ; keeping lovingkindness for thousands, forgiving iniquity and transgression and sin, and acquitting the penitent. *(To be said three times.)*

On Passover, Pentecost and Tabernacles, say :—

SUPPLICA-TION

Lord of the universe, fulfil the wishes of my heart for good ;

suggested in 1805 by C. J. D. Azulay, was declared optional by Dr. H. Adler.

THE THIRTEEN ATTRIBUTES. It is a primary task of true religion to convey a pure and lofty conception of the Deity to the soul of the worshipper. Nothing can be more lofty than the revelation of the nature of God in these Thirteen Attributes. Disregarding speculative or mystical aspects of the God-idea, they refer exclusively to the inexhaustible Love and eternal Justice of God. They have stamped themselves upon the Jewish consciousness as the sublimest expression in human language of the essential nature of God. So sacred does Judaism deem them, that they are not recited by the individual when saying his prayers *by himself*, but only in congregational worship on a day when the Scroll of the Torah is taken out, or on Fast days. They became the dominant Refrain on Penitential Days, and especially in the Neilah Service on the Day of Atonement. A superior potency was ascribed to them in such supplications, and no repetition of them—it came to be held—would be without effect. However, great teachers did not fail to point out, that only if one *acts* in accordance with these Divine qualities of mercy, lovingkindness and truth, and imitates them in his conduct, will God forgive all sins. In their awesome solemnity, infinite tenderness, and tremendous affirmation of the Mercy of God, the Attributes are of fundamental importance to all who aim to live the life of religion.

שְׁאֵלָתִי לִי עַבְדְּךָ (פ' בֶּן פ') אֲמָתְךָ (פ' בַּת פ') וְזַכֵּנִי (וְאֶת
אִשְׁתִּי) (וְאֶת־בַּעֲלִי) (וּבָנַי וּבְנוֹתַי) לַעֲשׂוֹת רְצוֹנְךָ בְּלֵבָב שָׁלֵם ·
וּמַלְּטֵנִי מִיֵּצֶר הָרָע · וְתֵן חֶלְקֵנוּ בְּתוֹרָתֶךָ · וְזַכֵּנוּ כְּדֵי שֶׁתִּשְׁרֶה
שְׁכִינָתְךָ עָלֵינוּ · וְהוֹפַע עָלֵינוּ רוּחַ חָכְמָה וּבִינָה רוּחַ עֵצָה
וּגְבוּרָה רוּחַ דַּעַת וְיִרְאַת יְיָ · וְכֵן יְהִי רָצוֹן מִלְּפָנֶיךָ יְיָ
אֱלֹהֵינוּ וֵאלֹהֵי אֲבוֹתֵינוּ שֶׁאֶזְכֶּה לַעֲשׂוֹת מַעֲשִׂים טוֹבִים
בְּעֵינֶיךָ · וְלָלֶכֶת בְּדַרְכֵי יְשָׁרִים לְפָנֶיךָ · וְקַדְּשֵׁנוּ בְּמִצְוֹתֶיךָ
כְּדֵי שֶׁנִּזְכֶּה לְחַיִּים טוֹבִים וַאֲרֻכִּים לְחַיֵּי הָעוֹלָם הַבָּא ·
וְתִשְׁמְרֵנוּ מִמַּעֲשִׂים רָעִים וּמִשָּׁעוֹת רָעוֹת הַמִּתְרַגְּשׁוֹת לָבֹא
לָעוֹלָם · וְהַבּוֹטֵחַ בַּיְיָ חֶסֶד יְסוֹבְבֶנּוּ · אָמֵן :

The Lord, the Lord. The repetition of the Divine Name is explained
by the Rabbis to teach, that God is the same after a man has sinned as
He was before a man has sinned. The change to be wrought is not in
God, but in the heart of man ; Isaiah 55. 6.
merciful. Full of compassion for the sufferings and miseries of
human frailty.
and gracious. In man these qualities manifest themselves fitfully
and temporarily. It is otherwise in God ; in Him, compassion and
grace are permanent, inherent and necessary emanations of His nature.
slow to anger. Waiting even unto the day of the sinner's death for
him to retrace his steps.
plenteous in mercy. Showering His blessings beyond man's deserving.
and truth. God is God of Truth. His righteousness is but His truth

SUPPLICA-
TION

grant my desire, give me my request, even unto me, thy servant,
—— the son of —— (thy maid servant —— the daughter of ——),
and make me worthy (together with my wife,) (my husband,) (my
children,) to do thy will with a perfect heart ; and deliver me from
the evil inclination. O grant our portion in thy Torah ; make us
worthy to have thy divine presence abiding with us ; bestow
upon us the spirit of wisdom and understanding, the spirit of
counsel and might, the spirit of knowledge and fear of the Lord. So
also may it be thy will, O Lord our God and God of our fathers,
that I may be fitted to do such deeds as are good in thy sight, and
to walk in the way of the upright before thee. Sanctify us by thy
commandments, that we may merit the long and blessed life of the
world to come : guard us from evil deeds, and also from evil hours
that visit and afflict this world. As for him who trusteth in the
Lord, let lovingkindness surround him. Amen.

in action. " The Lord your God is Truth " אמת אלהיכם ד׳, is the people's
culmination of the Shema.

lovingkindness for thousands. Remembering the good deeds of the
ancestors to the thousandth generation, and reserving reward and
recompense to the remotest descendants.

forgiving iniquity. Bearing with indulgence the failings of man, his
shortcomings due to heedlessness and error ; yea, forgiving evil deeds
that spring from malice and rebellion against the Divine.

acquitting the penitent. But " not acquitting the impenitent ". This
is the Jewish interpretation of the words ונקה לא ינקה. God is merciful
and gracious and forgiving ; but He does not leave obstinate persistence
in evil unpunished. The sinner must suffer the consequences of his
misdeeds; and the unfailing consequences of sin, help man to perceive
that there is no " chance " in morals. The punishments of sin are thus
not vindictive, but remedial.

3. The recital of the Thirteen Attributes first by Reader, then by
the congregation, and lastly by the Choir, is followed on the Three
Festivals by a silent supplication for personal welfare; (and, on the

יִהְיוּ לְרָצוֹן אִמְרֵי פִי וְהֶגְיוֹן לִבִּי לְפָנֶיךָ יְיָ צוּרִי וְגֹאֲלִי :

וַאֲנִי תְפִלָּתִי לְךָ יְיָ עֵת רָצוֹן אֱלֹהִים בְּרָב־חַסְדֶּךָ עֲנֵנִי

בֶּאֱמֶת יִשְׁעֶךָ :   (*This verse is said three times.*)

The Reader takes the סֵפֶר תּוֹרָה, *and the following is said* :—

Reader and Congregation :—

שְׁמַע יִשְׂרָאֵל יְהֹוָה אֱלֹהֵינוּ יְהֹוָה אֶחָד :

Reader and Congregation :—

אֶחָד אֱלֹהֵינוּ גָּדוֹל אֲדוֹנֵינוּ קָדוֹשׁ שְׁמוֹ :

Reader :—

גַּדְּלוּ לַיְיָ אִתִּי וּנְרוֹמְמָה שְׁמוֹ יַחְדָּו :

Reader and Congregation :—

לְךָ יְיָ הַגְּדֻלָּה וְהַגְּבוּרָה וְהַתִּפְאֶרֶת וְהַנֵּצַח וְהַהוֹד •

New Year and Day of Atonement, by a prayer for forgiveness and pardon). They are by Nathan Hanover, the renowned chronicler of the terrible Cossack massacres which more than decimated Polish Jewry in the years 1648–60. His collection of prayers has furnished some of the best among the recent additions to the Prayer Book.

These prayers, being "supplications", are not said when a Festival (except the Day of Atonement) falls on a Sabbath. Neither are the Thirteen Attributes then recited.

As these Supplications are to be said silently by each one to himself, care should be taken that sufficient time is allowed the worshippers to finish the reading of it either in Hebrew or in English.

(D) The foregoing prayers are said while the Scroll is still in the Ark, even though its doors had been opened. The Reader now takes the Scroll from the hands of him who opened the Ark, and lifting

Psalm 19, 15 Let the words of my mouth and the meditation of my heart be acceptable before thee, O Lord, my Rock and my Redeemer.

Psalm 69, 14 May my prayer unto thee, O Lord, be in an acceptable time : O God, in the abundance of thy lovingkindness, answer me with thy sure salvation. (*This verse is said three times.*)

CONGREGATION'S PROFESSION OF FAITH Deuteronomy 6. 5

The Reader takes the Scroll of the Torah, and the following is said :—

Reader and Congregation:—HEAR, O ISRAEL : THE LORD IS OUR GOD, THE LORD IS ONE.

Reader and Congregation:—ONE IS OUR GOD ; GREAT IS OUR LORD ; HOLY IS HIS NAME.

Psalm 34. 4 *Reader* :—Magnify the Lord with me, and let us exalt his Name together.

Reader and Congregation :—

I Chronicles 29. 11 Thine, O Lord, is the greatness, and the power, and the glory, and the victory, and the majesty : for all that is in

it on high, recites the Shema. The entire body of worshippers then repeats the Proclamation of the Divine Unity. The Reader continues, followed by the Congregation, " One is our God ; great is our Lord ; holy is his Name ". The two declarations repeated on this occasion in such soul-stirring manner, bring home the basic principles of Judaism—the Unity, Omnipotence and Holiness of God—to young and old, women and children, assembled for divine Service on Sabbaths and Festivals. And what more appropriate psychological occasion could there be found for such Profession of Faith than the taking out of the Torah, that both enhances the sanctity of the proclamation, and welds the worshippers into one body ? So effective did this ceremony prove, that enemies of Judaism endeavoured on more than one occasion to have it suppressed. As far back as the year 533, the Emperor Justinian was induced by his ecclesiastical advisers to prohibit this solemn ceremony in all synagogues of the Byzantine Empire (Mann).

ONE IS OUR GOD. This is no Bible verse.

THINE, O LORD. The congregational Response to the Reader's invitation, " Magnify the Lord with me ". With the chanting of this Response, a procession with the Scroll is started round the Synagogue. The procession ends as the Response concludes with the words : " for the Lord our God is holy ".

כִּי כֹל בַּשָּׁמַיִם וּבָאָרֶץ לְךָ יְיָ הַמַּמְלָכָה וְהַמִּתְנַשֵּׂא לְכֹל
לְרֹאשׁ : רוֹמְמוּ יְיָ אֱלֹהֵינוּ וְהִשְׁתַּחֲווּ לַהֲדֹם רַגְלָיו קָדוֹשׁ
הוּא : רוֹמְמוּ יְיָ אֱלֹהֵינוּ וְהִשְׁתַּחֲווּ לְהַר קָדְשׁוֹ כִּי קָדוֹשׁ
יְיָ אֱלֹהֵינוּ :

עַל הַכֹּל יִתְגַּדַּל וְיִתְקַדַּשׁ וְיִשְׁתַּבַּח וְיִתְפָּאַר וְיִתְרוֹמָם
וְיִתְנַשֵּׂא : שְׁמוֹ שֶׁל־מֶלֶךְ מַלְכֵי הַמְּלָכִים הַקָּדוֹשׁ בָּרוּךְ הוּא :
בָּעוֹלָמוֹת שֶׁבָּרָא הָעוֹלָם הַזֶּה וְהָעוֹלָם הַבָּא : כִּרְצוֹנוֹ וְכִרְצוֹן
יְרֵאָיו וְכִרְצוֹן כָּל־בֵּית יִשְׂרָאֵל : צוּר הָעוֹלָמִים אֲדוֹן כָּל־
הַבְּרִיּוֹת אֱלוֹהַּ כָּל־הַנְּפָשׁוֹת : הַיּוֹשֵׁב בְּמֶרְחֲבֵי מָרוֹם הַשּׁוֹכֵן
בִּשְׁמֵי שְׁמֵי קֶדֶם : קְדֻשָּׁתוֹ עַל־הַחַיּוֹת וּקְדֻשָּׁתוֹ עַל־כִּסֵּא
הַכָּבוֹד : וּבְכֵן יִתְקַדַּשׁ שִׁמְךָ בָּנוּ יְיָ אֱלֹהֵינוּ לְעֵינֵי כָּל־חָי :
וְנֹאמַר לְפָנָיו שִׁיר חָדָשׁ כַּכָּתוּב : שִׁירוּ לֵאלֹהִים זַמְּרוּ שְׁמוֹ סֹלּוּ
לָרֹכֵב בָּעֲרָבוֹת בְּיָהּ שְׁמוֹ וְעִלְזוּ לְפָנָיו : וְנִרְאֵהוּ עַיִן בְּעַיִן
בְּשׁוּבוֹ אֶל־נָוֵהוּ כַּכָּתוּב : כִּי עַיִן בְּעַיִן יִרְאוּ בְּשׁוּב יְיָ צִיּוֹן :
וְנֶאֱמַר וְנִגְלָה כְּבוֹד יְיָ וְרָאוּ כָל־בָּשָׂר יַחְדָּו כִּי פִּי יְיָ דִּבֵּר :

אַב הָרַחֲמִים הוּא יְרַחֵם עַם עֲמוּסִים וְיִזְכֹּר בְּרִית אֵיתָנִים
וְיַצִּיל נַפְשׁוֹתֵינוּ מִן־הַשָּׁעוֹת הָרָעוֹת וְיִגְעַר בְּיֵצֶר הָרַע מִן
הַנְּשׂוּאִים וְיָחֹן אוֹתָנוּ לִפְלֵיטַת עוֹלָמִים וִימַלֵּא מִשְׁאֲלוֹתֵינוּ
בְּמִדָּה טוֹבָה יְשׁוּעָה וְרַחֲמִים ·

II. THE READING.

(*A*) Preparing the Scroll. During the preparation and unrolling of
the Scroll, the Reader repeats in silence the seventh century doxology,
Magnified and hallowed . . . hath spoken it.

MAY THE FATHER OF MERCY. This short *piyyut* dates from the
school of Rashi, in twelfth century France. Its continuation is "And
may He help ", p. 485.

PRO-
CESSION
WITH
SCROLL
Psalm 99, 5, 9

the heaven and in the earth is thine ; thine, O Lord, is the kingdom, and the supremacy as head over all. Exalt ye the Lord our God, and worship in his temple : holy is he. Exalt ye the Lord our God, and worship at his holy mount ; for the Lord our God is holy.

DOXOLOGY

Magnified and hallowed, praised and glorified, exalted and extolled above all be the Name of the Supreme King of Kings, the holy One, blessed be he, in the worlds which he hath created,—this world and the world to come,—in accordance with his desire, and with the desire of them that fear him, and of all the house of Israel : the Rock everlasting, the Lord of all creatures, the God of all souls ; who dwelleth in the wide-extended heights, who inhabiteth the heaven of heavens of old ; whose holiness is above the Chayoth and above the throne of glory. Now, therefore, thy Name, O Lord our God, shall be hallowed amongst us in the sight of all living. Let

Psalm 68. 5

us sing a new song before him, as it is written, Sing unto God, sing praises unto his Name, extol ye him that rideth upon the heavens, whose name is the Lord, and rejoice before him. And may we see him, eye to eye, when he returneth to his habitation, as it is written,

Isaiah 52. 8

For they shall see eye to eye, when the Lord returneth unto Zion.

Isaiah 40. 59

And it is said, And the glory of the Lord shall be revealed, and all flesh shall see it together ; for the mouth of the Lord hath spoken it.

PRAYER
INTRO-
DUCTORY
TO CALL-
ING UP TO
THE
TORAH

May the Father of mercy have mercy upon a people that have been borne by him. May he remember the covenant with the patriarchs, deliver our souls from evil hours, check the evil inclination in them that have been carried by him, grant us of his grace an everlasting deliverance, and in the attribute of his goodness fulfil our desires by salvation and mercy.

been borne by him. See Isaiah 46. 3 and also Exodus 19. 4.
check the evil inclination. See p. 25.

(B) Calling up to the Torah. Men are called up to the Torah by their Hebrew names. The first to be called up is a person of priestly descent (*kohen*); and the second, a levite (*levi*.)
    The Scroll from which the statutory Reading takes place is of parchment, made of calf-skin. It is written by hand, in the square Hebrew characters, and is without vowel-points, accents or verse-divisions—

The סֵפֶר תּוֹרָה *is placed upon the desk, and the Reader says*
the following :—

וַיַּעֲזוֹר וְיָגֵן וְיוֹשִׁיעַ לְכֹל הַחוֹסִים בּוֹ וְנֹאמַר אָמֵן ׃ הַכֹּל
הָבוּ גֹדֶל לֵאלֹהֵינוּ וּתְנוּ כָבוֹד לַתּוֹרָה ׃ כֹּהֵן קְרַב ׃ יַעֲמוֹד

Here the Reader names the Person who is called to the Reading
of the תּוֹרָה.

בָּרוּךְ שֶׁנָּתַן תּוֹרָה לְעַמּוֹ יִשְׂרָאֵל בִּקְדֻשָּׁתוֹ ׃ תּוֹרַת יְיָ
תְּמִימָה מְשִׁיבַת נָפֶשׁ עֵדוּת יְיָ נֶאֱמָנָה מַחְכִּימַת פֶּתִי ׃
פִּקּוּדֵי יְיָ יְשָׁרִים מְשַׂמְּחֵי־לֵב מִצְוַת יְיָ בָּרָה מְאִירַת
עֵינָיִם ׃ יְיָ עֹז לְעַמּוֹ יִתֵּן יְיָ ׀ יְבָרֵךְ אֶת־עַמּוֹ בַשָּׁלוֹם ׃ הָאֵל
תָּמִים דַּרְכּוֹ אִמְרַת יְיָ צְרוּפָה מָגֵן הוּא לְכֹל הַחוֹסִים בּוֹ ׃

Congregation and Reader :—

וְאַתֶּם הַדְּבֵקִים בַּיְיָ אֱלֹהֵיכֶם חַיִּים כֻּלְּכֶם הַיּוֹם ׃

Those who are called to the Reading of the תּוֹרָה *say the following*
Blessing :—

בָּרְכוּ אֶת־יְיָ הַמְבֹרָךְ ׃

Congregation :—

בָּרוּךְ יְיָ הַמְבֹרָךְ לְעוֹלָם וָעֶד ׃

these being later additions to the Sacred Text. The Scroll must contain
the whole of the Five Books of the Torah, and not merely a portion of
them.

The Scroll of the Torah is placed upon the desk, and the Reader says the following :—

CALLING UP TO THE TORAH

And may he help, shield and save all who trust in him, and let us say, Amen. Ascribe all of you greatness unto our God, and render honour to the Torah.

Here the Reader names the Person who is to be called to the Reading.

Psalm 19. 8, 9

Blessed be he, who in his holiness gave the Torah unto his people Israel. The Teaching of the Lord is perfect, restoring the soul : the testimony of the Lord is faithful, making wise the simple. The precepts of the Lord are right, rejoicing the heart : the commandment of the Lord is pure, enlighten-

Psalm 29. 10

ing the eyes. The Lord will give strength unto his people :

Psalm 18. 31

the Lord will bless his people with peace. As for God, his way is perfect : the word of the Lord is tried : he is a shield unto all them that trust in him.

Deuteronomy 4. 4

Cong. and Reader.—And ye that cleave unto the Lord your God are alive every one of you this day.

Those who are called to the Reading say the following Blessing :—

BLESSINGS BY THOSE CALLED TO THE TORAH

BLESS YE THE LORD WHO IS TO BE BLESSED.

Cong.—Blessed be the Lord, who is to be blessed, for ever and ever.

The reading of the Sefer Torah is chanted according to the *neginoth*, or " accents ". They give a musical and dramatic interpretation of the Text, representing the modulations and inflections of the living voice in reading Scripture as a portion of the religious service. " It is a kind of melody, half-way between oratory and song, chanted in reading ; and for this melody the *neginoth* serve the purpose of musical notes " (Davidson). In form, most of them are arcs and angles of a circle. Simon Hertz, in his אבני שהם, endeavoured to explain the meaning of the accents, and their interrelation, from their geometric shape and their position in the full circle.

The cantillation of the *neginoth* varies in the different Rites ; and even in the same Rite, Sabbaths, various Festivals, Purim and the Ninth of Av have each their own manner of cantillation.

The two Benedictions that are recited by each one called to the Torah go back to the fourth and seventh centuries respectively.

The Response is repeated, and the Blessing continued :—

בָּרוּךְ אַתָּה יְיָ אֱלֹהֵינוּ מֶלֶךְ הָעוֹלָם · אֲשֶׁר בָּחַר־בָּנוּ
מִכָּל־הָעַמִּים וְנָתַן־לָנוּ אֶת־תּוֹרָתוֹ · בָּרוּךְ אַתָּה יְיָ ·
נוֹתֵן הַתּוֹרָה :

After the Reading, the following Blessing is said :—

בָּרוּךְ אַתָּה יְיָ אֱלֹהֵינוּ מֶלֶךְ הָעוֹלָם · אֲשֶׁר נָתַן־לָנוּ
תּוֹרַת אֱמֶת · וְחַיֵּי עוֹלָם נָטַע בְּתוֹכֵנוּ · בָּרוּךְ אַתָּה יְיָ ·
נוֹתֵן הַתּוֹ־רָ־ה :

*Persons who have been in peril of their lives, during journeys by sea
or land, in captivity or sickness, upon their deliverance or recovery
ay the following after the conclusion of the last Blessing :—*

בָּרוּךְ אַתָּה יְיָ אֱלֹהֵינוּ מֶלֶךְ הָעוֹלָם · הַגּוֹמֵל לְחַיָּבִים
טוֹבוֹת · שֶׁגְּמָלַנִי כָּל־טוֹב :

The Congregation respond :—

מִי שֶׁגְּמָלְךָ כָּל־טוֹב · הוּא יִגְמָלְךָ כָּל־טוֹב סֶלָה :

---

who hast chosen . . . Torah. These simple but sublime words stress
the Selection of Israel (Exodus 19. 5) and the great fact of Revelation.
God is the Father of all mankind; but He has chosen Israel to be His
in a special degree, not to privilege and rulership, but to be "a light
unto the nations," to proclaim and testify to the spiritual values of life.

Giver of the Torah. One would expect some concluding words like,
"to Thy people Israel". But the Law of God is not for Israel alone.
It is for all mankind. As the Talmud says: "'These are the ordinances
by which if a *man* do, he shall live by them' (Leviticus 18. 5)—not
priest, not Levite, not Israelite, but *man*" (Jacob Emden).

The second Benediction expresses Israel's gratitude for the Law of
Truth entrusted to it, and for the everlasting life which thereby
became Israel's portion.

The Response is repeated and the Blessing continued :—

BLESSINGS BY THOSE CALLED TO THE TORAH

BLESSED ART THOU, O LORD OUR GOD, KING OF THE UNIVERSE, WHO HAST CHOSEN US FROM ALL PEOPLES, AND HAST GIVEN US THY TORAH. BLESSED ART THOU, O LORD, GIVER OF THE TORAH.

After the Reading, the following Blessing is said :—

BLESSED ART THOU, O LORD OUR GOD, KING OF THE UNIVERSE, WHO HAST GIVEN US THE LAW OF TRUTH, AND HAST PLANTED EVERLASTING LIFE IN OUR MIDST. BLESSED ART THOU, O LORD, GIVER OF THE TORAH.

GOMEL: THANKS-GIVING FOR DELIVER-ANCE FROM DANGER

[*Persons who have been in peril of their lives, during journeys by sea or land, in captivity or sickness, upon their deliverance or recovery say the following, after the conclusion of the last Blessing :—*

Blessed art thou, O Lord our God, King of the universe, who doest good unto the undeserving, and who hast dealt kindly with me.

The Congregation respond :—

He who hath shown thee kindness, may he deal kindly with thee for ever.]

(*C*) Other Prayers accompanying the Reading.

1. The GOMEL-benediction is laid down in the Talmud as the natural expression of gratitude to God for signal deliverances from mortal peril. It is founded on Psalm 107, wherein deliverance from four dangers is described—travellers who, after terrible dangers, reach their destination (4–9) ; released prisoners of war, or those wrongfully imprisoned and in the shadow of death, who regain their freedom (10–16) ; sick men restored to health (17–22) ; and sailors, all but wrecked in terrific storms that reach land in safety (23–32). The Psalmist concludes each section with the words, " Let them give thanks unto the Lord for His goodness, and for His wonderful works to the children of men ". The Benediction is not limited to the above-mentioned four classes, but is recited after signal escape from any danger.

This Benediction is followed with deepfelt sympathy by the fellow-worshippers. It has been well said that, until recently, every Jewish community was one, united, inquisitive family, all sharing the joys and sorrows of each. Private joys were announced in the course of the Service, and private griefs condoled with during worship, as when the mourners were welcomed into the synagogue on Friday Eve after *Lechoh Dodi.* When a *Gomel*-benediction is recited by an entire community, it is, in the nature of things, of a soul-stirring character. Thus, on Friday evening, December 14th, 1940, enemy bombing of a

After the last person called to the Torah, אַחֲרוֹן, *has recited his second Blessing, and before the Maftir has been called, the* סֵפֶר תּוֹרָה *is covered, and* חֲצִי קַדִּישׁ, *p. 428, is said.*

For a person called to קְרִיאַת הַתּוֹרָה

מִי שֶׁבֵּרַךְ אֲבוֹתֵינוּ אַבְרָהָם יִצְחָק וְיַעֲקֹב הוּא יְבָרֵךְ אֶת־

ר״ ——————— אֲשֶׁר עָלָה לַתּוֹרָה • הַקָּדוֹשׁ בָּרוּךְ

הוּא יְבָרֵךְ אֹתוֹ, וְאֶת־מִשְׁפַּחְתּוֹ • וְיִשְׁלַח בְּרָכָה וְהַצְלָחָה

בְּכָל־מַעֲשֵׂה יָדָיו (וִיזַכֵּהוּ לַעֲלוֹת לְרֶגֶל — :add (on the שָׁלֹשׁ רְגָלִים

עִם־כָּל־יִשְׂרָאֵל אֶחָיו • וְנֹאמַר אָמֵן :

קְרִיאַת הַתּוֹרָה מִי שֶׁבֵּרַךְ *at the conclusion of* General

מִי שֶׁבֵּרַךְ אֲבוֹתֵינוּ אַבְרָהָם יִצְחָק וְיַעֲקֹב הוּא יְבָרֵךְ אֶת־

כָּל־הַקְּרוּאִים אֲשֶׁר עָלוּ לַתּוֹרָה הַיּוֹם • הַקָּדוֹשׁ בָּרוּךְ הוּא

יְבָרֵךְ אוֹתָם וְאֶת־מִשְׁפַּחְתָּם וְיִשְׁלַח בְּרָכָה וְהַצְלָחָה בְּכָל־

מַעֲשֵׂה יְדֵיהֶם • (וִיזַכֵּם לַעֲלוֹת לְרֶגֶל — :add (on the שָׁלֹשׁ רְגָלִים

וְנֹאמַר אָמֵן :

city in England resulted in 587 deaths, among them a number of Jews. Next morning, when the Jewish worshippers repeated in a body the Gomel-thanksgiving for their delivery, there was not a dry eye in the synagogue.

2. *Mi-sheberach.* After each individual reading, it is usual for a Blessing—*mi-sheberach*—to be invoked upon the one called to the Torah. He, in turn, can have Blessings pronounced upon others, whether as a token of friendship or of sympathy in their joy ; or a Memorial Prayer (*El Molé Rachamim* or *Adon Ho-olomim*) in remembrance of those who have gone before us. The recital of these special Blessings for themselves, family and friends, soon came to be regarded by the people as of the greatest importance. As a rule, these Blessings are accompanied by an offering to the congregation or towards some charitable cause or institution. These offerings largely take the place of the contribution box in non-Jewish houses of worship, as no money is handled on Sabbaths and Festivals.

After the last person called to the Torah, has recited his second Benediction, and before the Maftir has been called, the Scroll is covered, and Half-Kaddish, p. 423, is said.

For each person called to the Reading of the Torah.

MI-
SHEBE-
RACHS

May he who blessed our fathers, Abraham, Isaac and Jacob, bless——who has been called to the Reading of the Torah (and offered——for charity). May the Holy One bless him and his family, and send blessing and prosperity on all the work of his hands ; [*On the Three Festivals add* :—may he be found worthy to participate in the Temple rejoicings on the Festival] ;

and let us say, Amen.

———————

General mi-sheberach, at the conclusion of the whole Reading :

May he who blessed our fathers, Abraham, Isaac and Jacob, bless all those who have been called to the Torah this day. May the Holy One bless them and their families, and may he send blessing and prosperity upon all the work of their hands; [*On the Three Festivals add :* may they be found worthy to participate in the Temple rejoicings on this Festival] ;

and let us say, Amen.

The recital of mi-sheberachs for charitable purposes arose in medieval France ; and, though at first confined to the Festivals, it was soon extended to every Sabbath. In the course of time, these offerings as tokens of friendship, as well as for charitable purposes, were greatly multiplied, and often led to an undue lengthening of the Service. Sometimes the donations, or their number and the amounts donated, provoked comment. In this regard, it is well to remember that a free and easy attitude in worship may, in devotional ages, be associated with very sincere piety. Abrahams rightly quotes *Julius Caesar* IV, 2 :
" When love begins to sicken and decay,
It uses an enforced ceremony.
There are no tricks in plain and simple faith ".
Yet we cannot well blame the modern congregations that have, in the interest of decorum, dispensed with offerings, or have considerably curtailed them; though, generous feelings of filial piety and loyal friendship have thereby in a measure, been stifled. As far back as the middle of the thirteenth century, Rabbi Elijah Menachem, of London, the greatest rabbinical scholar of pre-Expulsion Jewry, even disapproved of the practice of reciting the mi-sheberach after each

On the occasion of naming a new-born daughter

מִי שֶׁבֵּרַךְ אַבְרָהָם יִצְחָק וְיַעֲקֹב הוּא יְבָרֵךְ אֶת ———————

וְאֶת־בִּתּוֹ הַנּוֹלְדָה לוֹ וְיִקָּרֵא שְׁמָהּ בְּיִשְׂרָאֵל ———————

אָנָּא בָּרֵךְ אֶת אָבִיהָ וְאֶת־אִמָּהּ וְיִזְכּוּ לְגַדְּלָהּ לְיִרְאָתֶךָ

לְחֻפָּה וּלְמַעֲשִׂים טוֹבִים ׃ וְנֹאמַר אָמֵן ׃

The following is said by the Father of a בַּר מִצְוָה, *when the latter
has concluded the Blessing after having been called to the Reading
of the Torah:—*

בָּרוּךְ שֶׁפְּטָרַנִי מֵעָנְשׁוֹ שֶׁל זֶה ׃

For a בַּר־מִצְוָה

מִי שֶׁבֵּרַךְ אֲבוֹתֵינוּ אַבְרָהָם יִצְחָק וְיַעֲקֹב הוּא יְבָרֵךְ אֶת־

הַבָּחוּר ——————— בַּר־מִצְוָה אֲשֶׁר עָלָה לַתּוֹרָה ׃

הַקָּדוֹשׁ בָּרוּךְ הוּא יִשְׁמְרֵהוּ וְיַצִּילֵהוּ מִכָּל־צָרָה וְצוּקָה

וְיָשֵׂם בְּלִבּוֹ אַהֲבָתוֹ וְיִרְאָתוֹ וְלַעֲשׂוֹת רְצוֹנוֹ וּלְעָבְדוֹ בְּלֵבָב

שָׁלֵם כָּל־הַיָּמִים ׃ וְנֹאמַר אָמֵן ׃

For a חָתָן *and a* כַּלָּה *on the* שַׁבָּת *before their marriage*

מִי שֶׁבֵּרַךְ אֲבוֹתֵינוּ אַבְרָהָם יִצְחָק וְיַעֲקֹב הוּא יְבָרֵךְ אֶת־

הֶחָתָן ——————— וְאֶת־הַכַּלָּה ——————— ׃

הַקָּדוֹשׁ בָּרוּךְ הוּא יַדְרִיכֵם בְּאוֹרוֹ וַאֲמִתּוֹ כָּל־הַיָּמִים וְיִשְׁלַח

בְּרָכָה וְהַצְלָחָה בְּכָל־מַעֲשֵׂה יְדֵיהֶם ׃ וְנֹאמַר אָמֵן ׃

person called to the Torah; and he introduced in its place a general mi-
sheberach at the conclusion of the Reading for all those that had been
called up. In 1847, Chief Rabbi Nathan Adler ruled that only one
mi-sheberach is to be made for each individual, and an additional one
in case only of a special offering to an established charity. He also
shortened the formula of the various mi-sheberachs. In 1892, his son
sanctioned the re-introduction in many British synagogues of the one
comprehensive mi-sheberach at the end of the whole Reading.

On the occasion of naming a new-born daughter.

May he who blessed our fathers, Abraham, Isaac and Jacob, bless——— and his daughter born unto him. May her name be known in Israel as———. O, guard and protect her father and mother, and may they live to rear her in the fear of God, for the nuptial canopy, and for a life of good deeds ; and let us say, Amen.

The following is said by the Father of a Bar-Mitzvah, when the latter has concluded the Blessing after having been called to the Reading of the Torah.

Blessed be he who hath freed me from the responsibility for this child.

Mi-sheberach for a Barmitzvah.

May he who blessed our fathers, Abraham, Isaac and Jacob, bless the lad on his barmitzvah, who was called to the Torah (and offered———for charity). May the Holy One preserve him and save him from all sorrow and distress ; and may He plant in his heart the love and fear of God to do His will and serve Him with a perfect spirit all his days ; and let us say, Amen.

Offering on the occasion of an intended marriage.

May he who blessed our fathers, Abraham, Isaac and Jacob, bless the bridegroom———and his bride, and all those who make offerings on their behalf. May the Holy One guide them with his light and his truth all their days and send happiness and prosperity unto them ; and let us say, Amen.

On the Sabbath after the birth of a child, a mi-sheberach is recited for the health of the mother and babe. If the new-born child is a girl, she is given her Hebrew name in that mi-sheberach.

3. BARMITZVAH. The words spoken by the father are not an expression of relief at being freed from the duty to care for his son, but of his joy that the son enters the community as an independent member. Artom thus paraphrased it : " Blessed be the Almighty who has given me the power of fulfilling my duty towards my son. I have prepared him morally and religiously for this day when the responsibility falls upon his own shoulders ".

On the origin and meaning of the Bar Mitzvah institution, and the prayer of Chacham Artom for the Bar Mitzvah lad, see p. 1042.

On the Sabbath preceding the nuptials, the bridegroom is called

For a sick person

מִי שֶׁבֵּרַךְ אֲבוֹתֵינוּ אַבְרָהָם יִצְחָק וְיַעֲקֹב הוּא יְבָרֵךְ אֶת־

‏———————— אֲשֶׁר נָדַר ————————

לִצְדָקָה ‏————————•

אָנָּא רְפָא נָא אֶת־הַחוֹלֶה (הַחוֹלָה)————

הִמָּלֵא נָא רַחֲמִים עָלָיו (עָלֶיהָ) לְהַחֲלִימוֹ (לְהַחֲלִימָהּ)

וּלְהַחֲיוֹתוֹ (וּלְהַחֲיוֹתָהּ) וְיִשְׁלַח לוֹ (לָהּ) בִּמְהֵרָה רְפוּאָה

שְׁלֵמָה רְפוּאַת הַנֶּפֶשׁ וּרְפוּאַת הַגּוּף • שַׁבָּת הִיא מִלִּזְעֹק

וּרְפוּאָה קְרוֹבָה לָבוֹא • וְנֹאמַר אָמֵן :

Short form of Memorial Prayer

אֲדוֹן הָעוֹלָמִים יִזְכֹּר אֶת־נִשְׁמַת ‏————————

שֶׁהָלַךְ לְעוֹלָמוֹ (שֶׁהָלְכָה לְעוֹלָמָהּ) ‏————————•

נוֹדֵר (נוֹדֶרֶת) ‏———————— לִצְדָקָה לְזִכְרוֹן נִשְׁמָתוֹ

(נִשְׁמָתָהּ) • אָנָּא אַב־הָרַחֲמִים וְהַסְּלִיחוֹת תְּהִי נַפְשׁוֹ

(נַפְשָׁהּ) צְרוּרָה בִּצְרוֹר הַחַיִּים וּתְהִי מְנוּחָתוֹ (מְנוּחָתָהּ)

כָּבוֹד • וְנֹאמַר אָמֵן :

After the Reading of the Torah, the סֵפֶר תּוֹרָה *is held up, and the Congregation say the following :—*

וְזֹאת הַתּוֹרָה אֲשֶׁר־שָׂם מֹשֶׁה לִפְנֵי בְּנֵי יִשְׂרָאֵל עַל־פִּי

יְיָ בְּיַד־מֹשֶׁה : עֵץ־חַיִּים הִיא לַמַּחֲזִיקִים בָּהּ וְתֹמְכֶיהָ

to the Torah. In former generations, a special formula of calling up was used for a bridegroom, giving expression to the joy of his fellow-worshippers in his happiness.

Prayers are also offered in the form of mi-sheberach for any sick person, imploring healing for the sufferer.

A short Memorial Prayer may also be offered either before the Haftorah, or after the Prayer for the King and Royal Family.

For a sick person.

MI-SHEBE-RACH

May he who blessed our fathers, Abraham, Isaac and Jacob, bless the sick person————— May he in his mercy restore him (her) to perfect health, and speedily send him (her) a healing of soul and a healing of body ; and let us say, Amen.

MEMORIAL PRAYER

Short form of Memorial Prayer (to be changed according to sex).

O Lord of Eternity, remember the soul of————who has departed this life. (His son————offers————for charity in his memory). O Father of compassion and forgiveness, may his soul be bound up in the bond of eternal life, and may his rest be in glory ; and let us say, Amen.

HAGBAHA AND GELILAH

Deuteronomy 4. 14

After the Reading, the Scroll is held up, and the Congregation say the following :—

And this is the Torah which Moses set before the children of Israel, according to the commandment of the Lord by

---

(*D*) HAGBAHA—the Lifting up of the Scroll ; and GELILAH—the Rolling up of the Scroll, and covering it with the mantle, as it was when taken from the Ark.

And this is the Torah. Several modern songs of notable beauty celebrate the Lifting up of the Torah. The following are a few lines in translation :

" This is the Flag for which our sires
Mustered their hosts unshaken ;
They went through a thousand fires—
Their Flag was never forsaken " (Haarbleicher).

" The Torah has been our consolation,
Our help in exile and sore privation.
Lost have we all we were wont to prize :
Our holy Temple a ruin lies ;
Laid waste is the land where our songs were sung ;
Forgotten our language, our mother-tongue ;
Of kingdom and priesthood are we bereft ;
Our Faith is our only treasure left.
We have sacrificed all. We have given our wealth,
Our homes, our honours, our land, our health,
Our lives—like Hannah her children seven—
For the sake of the Torah that came from heaven "

(Gordon).

To the pious Jew, the Scroll of the Torah is the most sacred of things, even as the Ark of the Covenant was to the Israelite of old. The sorrow of Eli at the loss of the Ark of the Covenant in the days of old (I Samuel 4. 18) re-echoes in the wonderful elegy of the renowned teacher, martyr

מֵאֻשָּׁר : דְּרָכֶיהָ דַרְכֵי־נֹעַם וְכָל־נְתִיבוֹתֶיהָ שָׁלוֹם : אֹרֶךְ
יָמִים בִּימִינָהּ בִּשְׂמֹאלָהּ עֹשֶׁר וְכָבוֹד : יְיָ חָפֵץ לְמַעַן
צִדְקוֹ יַגְדִּיל תּוֹרָה וְיַאְדִּיר :

Before Reading the הַפְטָרָה *the following is said :—*

בָּרוּךְ אַתָּה יְיָ אֱלֹהֵינוּ מֶלֶךְ הָעוֹלָם · אֲשֶׁר בָּחַר
בִּנְבִיאִים טוֹבִים וְרָצָה בְדִבְרֵיהֶם הַנֶּאֱמָרִים בֶּאֱמֶת :
בָּרוּךְ אַתָּה יְיָ · הַבּוֹחֵר בַּתּוֹרָה וּבְמֹשֶׁה עַבְדּוֹ וּבְיִשְׂרָאֵל
עַמּוֹ וּבִנְבִיאֵי הָאֱמֶת וָצֶדֶק :

After Reading the הַפְטָרָה *the following is said :—*

בָּרוּךְ אַתָּה יְיָ אֱלֹהֵינוּ מֶלֶךְ הָעוֹלָם · צוּר כָּל־
הָעוֹלָמִים צַדִּיק בְּכָל־הַדּוֹרוֹת הָאֵל הַנֶּאֱמָן הָאוֹמֵר

and poet, Rabbi Meir of Rothenburg, over the great Burning of the
Torah in 1244. Many a loyal Jew in Nazi and Nazi-occupied lands
attempted, at the risk of his life, to save the sacred Scrolls from destruction or desecration by the inhuman foe. And " for any community of
people to be, and to remain, Jewish, they must be brought up from their
tenderest childhood to regard the Sefer Torah as the title-deed of their
birthright and pedigree; which they are religiously to hand down
unaltered from generation to generation. For is there a Jewish community
anywhere, however safely domiciled, which has relinquished the Torah
for even one generation and has survived that separation ? "

" The Torah is a fountain of life. In it is protection greater than in
fortresses. Those who forsake the Torah, bringing it into disrepute and
weakening the hold it has on us, are working at the destruction of the
Brotherhood that cradled and sheltered their fathers and forefathers
through all the vicissitudes of the bygone ages, to whom they owe their
own life and presence on earth " (Haffkine).

and this is the Torah. The Bible-quotation ends with the words,
" children of Israel ". The remaining words from Numbers 9. 23 seem
to have been a congregational Response to the first half, that was
uttered by the person who elevated the Sefer.

Proverbs
3. 18, 17, 16

the hand of Moses. It is a tree of life to them that grasp it, and of them that uphold it every one is rendered happy. Its ways are ways of pleasantness, and all its paths are peace. Length of days is in its right hand; in its left hand are

Isaiah **42**. 21

riches and honour. It pleased the Lord, for his righteousness' sake, to magnify the Law and to glorify it.

Before the Lesson from the Prophets the following is said :—

BLESSINGS BEFORE THE HAF-TORAH

Blessed art thou, O Lord our God, King of the universe, who hast chosen good prophets, and hast found pleasure in their words which were spoken in truth.

Blessed art Thou, O Lord, who hast chosen the Torah, and Moses thy servant, and Israel thy people, and prophets of truth and righteousness.

After the Lesson from the Prophets the following is said :—

AFTER THE HAF-TORAH

Blessed art thou, O Lord our God, King of the universe, Rock of all worlds, righteous through all generations, O faithful God, who sayest and doest, who speakest and

---

it is a tree of life. This and the two following verses are in the reverse order from that in the original Text in Proverbs, but the sense is unaffected. Without the Torah, we would sink in the bog of materialism and godlessness. Happy are they who cling to their Judaism.

for his righteousness' sake. For his own everlasting purposes; for the future glorification of Religion by its diffusion among the nations.

III. THE PROPHETICAL READING AND PRAYERS FOLLOWING

(*A*). The Haftorah and Benedictions.

Long before the destruction of the Temple, it had become the rule that the Reading of the Torah was followed by a Reading from the Prophets. This term embraces the " earlier " Prophets—Joshua, Judges, Samuel and Kings, relating the *story* of Israel in the time of the Prophets; and the " later " Prophets—giving the *writings* of Isaiah, Jeremiah, Ezekiel and the Book of the Twelve Prophets (this is the correct name, and not " Minor " Prophets). In the choice of the Prophetical selections, it was sought to find something appropriate or akin to the Reading from the Torah. However, at certain seasons of the year, the Haftorahs have reference to the Festival or Fast of that season. Thus, on the three Sabbaths preceding the Ninth of Av, Haftorahs of " rebuke " are read; and Haftorahs of " consolation " are read on the seven Sabbaths after that Fast. The average length of the

וְעוֹשֶׂה הַמְדַבֵּר וּמְקַיֵּם שֶׁכָּל־דְּבָרָיו אֱמֶת וָצֶדֶק: נֶאֱמָן

אַתָּה הוּא יְיָ אֱלֹהֵינוּ וְנֶאֱמָנִים דְּבָרֶיךָ וְדָבָר אֶחָד

מִדְּבָרֶיךָ אָחוֹר לֹא־יָשׁוּב רֵיקָם · כִּי אֵל מֶלֶךְ נֶאֱמָן

וְרַחֲמָן אָתָּה · בָּרוּךְ אַתָּה יְיָ · הָאֵל הַנֶּאֱמָן בְּכָל־

דְּבָרָיו :

רַחֵם עַל־צִיּוֹן כִּי הִיא בֵּית חַיֵּינוּ וְלַעֲלוּבַת נֶפֶשׁ

תּוֹשִׁיעַ בִּמְהֵרָה בְיָמֵינוּ : בָּרוּךְ אַתָּה יְיָ · מְשַׂמֵּחַ צִיּוֹן

בְּבָנֶיהָ :

שַׂמְּחֵנוּ יְיָ אֱלֹהֵינוּ בְּאֵלִיָּהוּ הַנָּבִיא עַבְדֶּךָ וּבְמַלְכוּת

בֵּית דָּוִד מְשִׁיחֶךָ · בִּמְהֵרָה יָבֹא וְיָגֵל לִבֵּנוּ · עַל־כִּסְאוֹ

לֹא־יֵשֵׁב זָר וְלֹא יִנְחֲלוּ עוֹד אֲחֵרִים אֶת־כְּבוֹדוֹ · כִּי

בְשֵׁם קָדְשְׁךָ נִשְׁבַּעְתָּ לּוֹ שֶׁלֹּא יִכְבֶּה נֵרוֹ לְעוֹלָם וָעֶד ·

בָּרוּךְ אַתָּה יְיָ · מָגֵן דָּוִד :

On שַׁבָּת, including שַׁבַּת חוֹל הַמּוֹעֵד פֶּסַח, say :—

עַל־הַתּוֹרָה וְעַל־הָעֲבוֹדָה וְעַל־הַנְּבִיאִים וְעַל־יוֹם

הַשַּׁבָּת הַזֶּה שֶׁנָּתַתָּ־לָּנוּ יְיָ אֱלֹהֵינוּ לִקְדֻשָּׁה וְלִמְנוּחָה

לְכָבוֹד וּלְתִפְאָרֶת · עַל־הַכֹּל יְיָ אֱלֹהֵינוּ אֲנַחְנוּ מוֹדִים

Haftorah is 21 verses. The *Maftir*—the reader of the Prophetical
selection—is called to the Torah after the statutory seven, and at least
three verses from the end of the Weekly Sidra are repeated. On
Festivals, an appropriate selection is read from a second Scroll. In
this way, the closest connection is indicated between the teaching of

fulfillest, all whose words are truth and righteousness. Faithful art thou, O Lord our God, and faithful are thy words, and not one of thy words shall return void, for thou art a faithful and merciful God and King. Blessed art thou, O Lord, God, who art faithful in all thy words.

Have mercy upon Zion, for it is the home of our life, and save her that is grieved in spirit speedily, even in our days. Blessed art thou, O Lord, who makest Zion joyful through her children.

Gladden us, O Lord our God, with Elijah the prophet, thy servant, and with the kingdom of the house of David, thine anointed. Soon may he come and rejoice our hearts. Suffer not a stranger to sit upon his throne, nor let others any longer inherit his glory ; for by thy holy Name thou didst swear unto him, that his light should not be quenched for ever. Blessed art thou, O Lord, the Shield of David.

On Sabbaths, including the Intermediate Sabbath of Passover, say :—

For the Torah, for the divine service, for the prophets, and for this Sabbath day, which thou, O Lord our God, hast given us for holiness and for rest, for honour and for glory,—for all these we thank and bless thee, O Lord our

the Torah and that of the Prophets. Eternal as is the inspiration of the latter, it is *supplementary* to the Torah, in which the highest teachings of Religion are even more definitely embodied than in the Prophets.

The word הפטרה means, " dismissal ". Another name was אשלמתא " completion ". These names indicate that at one time the Service closed with the Prophetical Lesson.

The Benedictions before and after the Haftorah are derived from the minor Talmudic tractate Soferim in the seventh century.

whose words are truth. A confession of faith in the truth of the Scripture that had been read.

faithful art thou. This was originally spoken as a Response by the congregation standing, thereby repeating the confession and attestation made by the reader of the Haftorah.

suffer not a stranger to sit upon his throne. This phrase may date back to the days of the later Maccabees and the Herodian kings, who were accounted " strangers ", being of Idumean descent. The Chassidim, the Pious, looked upon them as usurpers of the throne that should have been filled by a descendant of David.

לָךְ וּמְבָרְכִים אוֹתָךְ · יִתְבָּרַךְ שִׁמְךָ בְּפִי כָּל־חַי תָּמִיד
לְעוֹלָם וָעֶד · בָּרוּךְ אַתָּה יְיָ · מְקַדֵּשׁ הַשַׁבָּת :

On *say* :— שַׁבָּת חוֹל הַמּוֹעֵד סֻכּוֹת, *as also on* On שְׁלֹשׁ רְגָלִים

עַל־הַתּוֹרָה וְעַל־הָעֲבוֹדָה וְעַל־הַנְּבִיאִים וְעַל־הַיּוֹם (שַׁבָּת on
add הַשַׁבָּת הַזֶּה וְעַל־הַיּוֹם)

On סֻכּוֹת *say* :—	on שָׁבוּעוֹת *say* :—	on פֶּסַח *say* :—
חַג הַסֻּכּוֹת הַזֶּה	חַג הַשָּׁבוּעוֹת הַזֶּה	חַג הַמַּצּוֹת הַזֶּה

הַשְּׁמִינִי חַג הָעֲצֶרֶת הַזֶּה *say*, שְׁמִינִי עֲצֶרֶת on

שֶׁנָּתַתָּ לָּנוּ יְיָ אֱלֹהֵינוּ (*add* on שַׁבָּת לִקְדֻשָּׁה וְלִמְנוּחָה) לְשָׂשׂוֹן
וּלְשִׂמְחָה לְכָבוֹד וּלְתִפְאָרֶת · עַל־הַכֹּל יְיָ אֱלֹהֵינוּ אֲנַחְנוּ מוֹדִים
לָךְ וּמְבָרְכִים אוֹתָךְ · יִתְבָּרַךְ שִׁמְךָ בְּפִי כָּל־חַי תָּמִיד לְעוֹלָם
וָעֶד · בָּרוּךְ אַתָּה יְיָ · מְקַדֵּשׁ (*add* on שַׁבָּת הַשַׁבָּת וְ) יִשְׂרָאֵל
וְהַזְּמַנִּים :

On *say* :— רֹאשׁ הַשָּׁנָה

עַל־הַתּוֹרָה וְעַל־הָעֲבוֹדָה וְעַל־הַנְּבִיאִים וְעַל־הַיּוֹם (שַׁבָּת on
add הַשַׁבָּת הַזֶּה וְעַל יוֹם) הַזִּכָּרוֹן הַזֶּה שֶׁנָּתַתָּ לָּנוּ יְיָ אֱלֹהֵינוּ
(*add* on שַׁבָּת לִקְדֻשָּׁה וְלִמְנוּחָה) לְכָבוֹד וּלְתִפְאָרֶת · עַל־הַכֹּל
יְיָ אֱלֹהֵינוּ אֲנַחְנוּ מוֹדִים לָךְ וּמְבָרְכִים אוֹתָךְ · יִתְבָּרַךְ שִׁמְךָ
בְּפִי כָּל־חַי תָּמִיד לְעוֹלָם וָעֶד · וּדְבָרְךָ אֱמֶת וְקַיָּם לָעַד · בָּרוּךְ
אַתָּה יְיָ · מֶלֶךְ עַל־כָּל־הָאָרֶץ · מְקַדֵּשׁ (*add* on שַׁבָּת הַשַׁבָּת וְ)
יִשְׂרָאֵל וְיוֹם הַזִּכָּרוֹן :

On *say* :— יוֹם כִּפּוּר

עַל־הַתּוֹרָה וְעַל־הָעֲבוֹדָה וְעַל־הַנְּבִיאִים וְעַל־הַיּוֹם (שַׁבָּת on
add הַשַׁבָּת הַזֶּה וְעַל יוֹם) הַכִּפֻּרִים הַזֶּה שֶׁנָּתַתָּ לָּנוּ יְיָ אֱלֹהֵינוּ

VARIA-
TIONS IN
HAF-
TORAH ON
FESTIVALS

God, blessed be thy Name by the mouth of every living being continually and for ever. Blessed art thou, O Lord, who hallowest the Sabbath.

[*On the Three Festivals, as also on the Intermediate Sabbath of Tabernacles, say :*—

For the Torah, for the divine service, for the prophets ;
On the Sabbath : for this Sabbath Day,
On Passover : and for this day of the Feast of Unleavened Bread,
On Pentecost : and for this day of the Feast of Weeks,
On Tabernacles : and for this day of the Feast of Tabernacles.
On the Eighth Day of Solemn Assembly : and for this Eighth-day feast of Solemn Assembly,
which thou, O Lord our God, hast given us (*on Sabbath add,* for holiness and for rest,) for joy and gladness, for honour and glory,— for all these we thank and bless thee, O Lord our God, blessed be thy Name by the mouth of every living being continually and for ever. Blessed art thou, O Lord, who hallowest (*on Sabbath add,* the Sabbath,) Israel and the Festivals.

On the New Year say :—

For the Torah, for the divine service, for the prophets (*on Sabbath add,* and for this Sabbath Day), and for this Day of Remembrance, which thou, O Lord our God, hast given us (*on Sabbath add,* for holiness and for rest,) for honour and glory,—for all these we thank and bless thee, O Lord our God, blessed be thy Name by the mouth of every living being continually and for ever : thy word is true and endureth for ever. Blessed art thou, O Lord, King over the whole earth, who hallowest (*on Sabbath add,* the Sabbath,) Israel and the Day of Remembrance.

On the Day of Atonement say :—

For the Torah, for the divine service, for the prophets (*on Sabbath add,* for this Sabbath Day,) and for this Day of Atonement,

(B) A series of extra prayers follows between the conclusion of the Prophetic Lesson and the Return of the Scroll to the Ark. The first of these is :

YEKUM PURKAN.—Prayer for the Rabbinical Academies and rabbis and students. This Aramaic prayer was composed in Babylonia, some time after the third century. The Exilarch, or "Head of the Exile" (Resh galutha) was the lay ruler of the large Babylonian Jewry, and a dignitary of important considerable importance. The office continued till the

add) שַׁבָּת on לְחַדֵּשָׁה וְלִמְנוּחָתָה) לִסְלִיחָה וְלִמְחִילָה וּלְכַפָּרָה ·
לְכָבוֹד וּלְתִפְאָרֶת · עַל־הַכֹּל יְיָ אֱלֹהֵינוּ אֲנַחְנוּ מוֹדִים לָךְ
וּמְבָרְכִים אוֹתָךְ · יִתְבָּרַךְ שִׁמְךָ בְּפִי כָל־חַי תָּמִיד לְעוֹלָם וָעֶד ·
וּדְבָרְךָ אֱמֶת וְקַיָּם לָעַד · בָּרוּךְ אַתָּה יְיָ · מֶלֶךְ מוֹחֵל וְסוֹלֵחַ
לַעֲוֹנוֹתֵינוּ וְלַעֲוֹנוֹת עַמּוֹ בֵּית יִשְׂרָאֵל · וּמַעֲבִיר אַשְׁמוֹתֵינוּ בְּכָל
שָׁנָה וְשָׁנָה · מֶלֶךְ עַל־כָּל־הָאָרֶץ מְקַדֵּשׁ (add שַׁבָּת on הַשַּׁבָּת וְ)
יִשְׂרָאֵל וְיוֹם הַכִּפֻּרִים :

*The following three paragraphs are not said on Festivals occurring
on Weekdays.*

יְקוּם פֻּרְקָן מִן־שְׁמַיָּא חִנָּא וְחִסְדָּא וְרַחֲמֵי וְחַיֵּי אֲרִיכֵי
וּמְזוֹנֵי רְוִיחֵי וְסַיַּעְתָּא דִי־שְׁמַיָּא וּבַרְיוּת גּוּפָא וּנְהוֹרָא
מַעַלְיָא · זַרְעָא חַיָּא וְקַיָּמָא זַרְעָא דִי לָא־יִפְסַק וְדִי
לָא־יִבְטַל מִפִּתְגָּמֵי אוֹרַיְתָא · לְמָרָנָן וְרַבָּנָן חֲבוּרָתָא
קַדִּישָׁתָא דִי בְּאַרְעָא דִי־יִשְׂרָאֵל דִי בְּבָבֶל וְדִי בְּכָל
אַרְעָת גָּלְוָתָנָא · לְרֵישֵׁי כַלֵּי וּלְרֵישֵׁי גָלְוָתָא וּלְרֵישֵׁי
מְתִיבָתָא וּלְדַיָּנֵי דִי־בָבָא · לְכָל־תַּלְמִידֵיהוֹן וּלְכָל־
תַּלְמִידֵי תַלְמִידֵיהוֹן וּלְכָל־מָן דִי עָסְקִין בְּאוֹרַיְתָא ·
מַלְכָּא דִי־עָלְמָא יְבָרֵךְ יַתְהוֹן יַפִּישׁ חַיֵּיהוֹן וְיַשְׂגֵּא

year 1040. During those centuries, the Rabbinical Academies in the
Babylonian cities of Sura and Pumbeditha continued to dominate
Jewish intellectual life. "We must endeavour to picture a state of
affairs in which scholarship received all the deference which the Middle
Ages paid to Religion ; in which the heads of the two seats of learning
were no less powerful than the Archbishops of Canterbury and of York
in medieval England ; and in which the Masters of the Law did not
hesitate to pit themselves against the civil power—sometimes with conspicuous success. There was no professional class, who studied to qualify

which thou, O Lord our God, hast given us (*on Sabbath add*, for holiness and for rest,) for forgiveness, pardon and atonement, for honour and glory,—for all these we thank and bless thee, O Lord our God, blessed be thy Name by the mouth of every living being continually and for ever : thy word is true and endureth for ever. Blessed art thou, O Lord, thou King, who pardonest and forgivest our iniquities and the iniquities of thy people, the house of Israel, and makest our trespasses to pass away year by year ; King over the whole earth, who hallowest (*on Sabbath add*, the Sabbath,) Israel and the Day of Atonement.]

The following three paragraphs are not said on Festivals occurring on Weekdays.

PRAYERS
FOR
RELIGIOUS
LEADERS

"YEKUM
PURKAN"

May salvation from heaven, with grace, lovingkindness, mercy, long life, ample sustenance, heavenly aid, health of body, a higher enlightenment, and a living and abiding offspring, that will not break with, nor neglect any of the words of the Torah, be granted unto the teachers and rabbins of the holy community, who are in the land of Israel, and in the land of Babylon, and in all the lands of our dispersion ; unto the heads of the academies, the chiefs of the captivity, the heads of the colleges, and the judges in the gates ; unto all their disciples, unto all the disciples of their disciples, and unto all who occupy themselves with the study of the Torah. May the King of the universe bless

for some appointment. To absorb himself in the Law of God was regarded as the privilege and the duty of every man, from the highest to the lowest. The Exilarch himself was sometimes a capable scholar. An artisan or agriculturalist would attend the school each day after the morning and evening services, working in his fields or shop in the interval. During the day, eager students would be unflagging in their attendance on some famous Rabbi, listening to his verdict in cases which were brought him for decision, and mentally noting not only his arguments and precedents but also his small talk, his conduct, his most trivial habits. In the spring and autumn, when agricultural work was suspended, students would flock to the academies from every part of the country, and for a whole month instruction was continuous. This (the *Kallah* as it was termed) corresponded in its way to the modern University extension system, though carried on with an intensity and generality unparalleled in our more sophisticated age " (Roth).

יוֹמֵיהוֹן וְיִתֵּן אַרְכָה לִשְׁנֵיהוֹן · וְיִתְפָּרְקוּן וְיִשְׁתֵּיזְבוּן מִן
כָּל־עָקָא וּמִן כָּל־מַרְעִין בִּישִׁין · מָרָן דִּי בִשְׁמַיָּא יְהֵא
בְסַעְדְּהוֹן כָּל־זְמַן וְעִדָּן · וְנֹאמַר אָמֵן :

*The following two paragraphs are only said when Service is held
with a Congregation.*

יְקוּם פֻּרְקָן מִן־שְׁמַיָּא חִנָּא וְחִסְדָּא וְרַחֲמֵי וְחַיֵּי אֲרִיכֵי
וּמְזוֹנֵי רְוִיחֵי וְסִיַּעְתָּא דִי־שְׁמַיָּא וּבַרְיוּת גּוּפָא וּנְהוֹרָא
מְעַלְּיָא · זַרְעָא חַיָּא וְקַיָּמָא זַרְעָא דִּי לָא־יִפְסַק וְדִי
לָא־יִבְטַל מִפִּתְגָּמֵי אוֹרַיְתָא · לְכָל־קְהָלָא קַדִּישָׁא הָדֵן
רַבְרְבַיָּא עִם זְעֵירַיָּא טַפְלָא וּנְשַׁיָּא · מַלְכָּא דִי־עָלְמָא
יְבָרֵךְ יָתְכוֹן יַפִּישׁ חַיֵּיכוֹן וְיַשְׂגֵּא יוֹמֵיכוֹן וְיִתֵּן אַרְכָה
לִשְׁנֵיכוֹן · וְתִתְפָּרְקוּן וְתִשְׁתֵּיזְבוּן מִן כָּל־עָקָא וּמִן כָּל־
מַרְעִין בִּישִׁין · מָרָן דִּי בִשְׁמַיָּא יְהֵא בְסַעְדְּכוֹן כָּל־זְמַן
וְעִדָּן · וְנֹאמַר אָמֵן :

מִי שֶׁבֵּרַךְ אֲבוֹתֵינוּ אַבְרָהָם יִצְחָק וְיַעֲקֹב הוּא יְבָרֵךְ
אֶת־כָּל־הַקָּהָל הַקָּדוֹשׁ הַזֶּה עִם כָּל־קְהִלּוֹת הַקֹּדֶשׁ ·
הֵם וּנְשֵׁיהֶם וּבְנֵיהֶם וּבְנוֹתֵיהֶם וְכֹל אֲשֶׁר לָהֶם · וּמִי

It has often been maintained that, as the Exilarch and Babylonian
academies are no more, this prayer is an anomaly. This is a mistaken
view. The recent addition of the words, *in all lands of our dispersion,*
after " the teachers who are in the land of Israel and in the land of
Babylon ", makes the prayer applicable to our own times. However,
its omission has been sanctioned in English Synagogues.

PRAYERS them, prolong their lives, increase their days, and add to their years, and may they be saved and delivered from every trouble and mishap. May the Lord of heaven be their help at all times and seasons ; and let us say, Amen.

The following two paragraphs are said only when Service is held with a Congregation.

FOR THE CONGRE- GATION May salvation from heaven, with grace, lovingkindness mercy, long life, ample sustenance, heavenly aid, health of body, a higher enlightenment, and a living and abiding offspring, that will not break with, nor neglect any of the words of the Torah, be granted unto all this holy congregation, great and small, women and children. May the King of the universe bless you, prolong your lives, increase your days and add to your years, and may you be saved and delivered from every trouble and mishap. May the Lord of heaven be your help at all times and seasons ; and let us say, Amen.

FOR THOSE WHO LABOUR FOR COM- MUNITY May he who blessed our fathers, Abraham, Isaac and Jacob, bless all this holy congregation, together with all other holy congregations : them, their wives, their sons and daughters, and all that belong to them ; those also who

The second *Yekum Purkan*, a later composition, is a prayer for each individual member—young and old—of the congregation. The *Misheberach* following goes back to Gaonic times. It calls down the blessing of heaven upon all who labour for the community, or contribute in whatever way to the beauty of the Service.

(C) PRAYER FOR THE GOVERNMENT.

Loyalty to the State is ingrained in the Jewish character. The Jew has often shown himself to be the *intensive* form of any nationality whose language and customs he adopts—" the Piel of the Peoples " (Emma Lazarus). He has at all times placed love of country high among religious precepts. A recent historian points out that Jews are by nature conservative ; and that in all those countries in which persecution has not embittered their life, they are no more radical than the non-Jewish members of the social class to which they belong (Vallentin).

This Jewish feeling of loyalty to King and Country has its roots far in the past. " My son, fear thou the Lord and the king, and meddle not with them that are given to change " (Proverbs 24. 21) is a warning

שֶׁמְּיַחֲדִים בָּתֵּי כְנֵסִיּוֹת לִתְפִלָּה · וּמִי שֶׁבָּאִים בְּתוֹכָם
לְהִתְפַּלֵּל · וּמִי שֶׁנּוֹתְנִים נֵר לַמָּאוֹר וְיַיִן לְקִדּוּשׁ
וּלְהַבְדָּלָה וּפַת לְאוֹרְחִים וּצְדָקָה לַעֲנִיִּים · וְכָל־מִי
שֶׁעוֹסְקִים בְּצָרְכֵי צִבּוּר בָּאֱמוּנָה · הַקָּדוֹשׁ בָּרוּךְ הוּא
יְשַׁלֵּם שְׂכָרָם וְיָסִיר מֵהֶם כָּל־מַחֲלָה וְיִרְפָּא לְכָל־גּוּפָם
וְיִסְלַח לְכָל־עֲוֹנָם · וְיִשְׁלַח בְּרָכָה וְהַצְלָחָה בְּכָל־מַעֲשֵׂה
יְדֵיהֶם עִם כָּל־יִשְׂרָאֵל אֲחֵיהֶם · וְנֹאמַר אָמֵן :

against revolutionary intrigue. "Seek ye the peace of the city
whither I have caused you to be carried away captive, and pray unto
the Lord for it; for in its welfare shall be your peace" (Jeremiah 29. 7)
is the exhortation of the Prophet to the exiles in Babylon. From Ezra
6. 10, it is evident that when the returned exiles rebuilt the Temple,
sacrifices and prayers for the King and the Royal Family formed part
of the cultus. A century later, when Alexander the Great, inflamed
against the Jewish nation by slanderous accusations, was bent on
destroying Jerusalem, he was met by the High Priest and the elders,
who pleaded: "Wilt thou, O mighty king, destroy the Temple
in which sacrifices and prayers are offered for thee and thy land?"
Both Philo and Josephus speak of prayers that were regularly offered
for the Roman Emperor. In their day, the immemorial custom of
praying for the welfare of Ruler and State had become the fixed rule.

It is true that, when the deranged Emperor Caligula (37–41) ordered
his image to be placed in the Temple at Jerusalem, the Jews alone in the
world-wide Roman Empire refused to pay divine honours to him.
They pleaded with the Roman commander that, if he insisted on setting
up the image, he would first have to sacrifice the whole Jewish people;
as they would rather die than transgress the Commandment against
image-worship. At this, the Roman commander "felt both astonishment and pity on account of their invincible regard for their religion,
and their courage which made them ready to die for it" (Josephus).
Only the sudden death of the Imperial madman saved the defenceless
population from fearful massacre. In the next generation, on the very
brink of the War against Rome, Rabbi Chanina taught: "Pray for
the welfare of the government, since but for the fear thereof men would
swallow each other alive"; see p. 647. A hundred and fifty years
later, Mar Samuel of Nehardea laid it down for all time that, in civil
matters, the law of the land is as binding on Jews as the religious
commandments of their own Faith, דִּינָא דְמַלְכוּתָא דִּינָא. Graetz places

FOR THOSE
WHO
LABOUR
FOR COM-
MUNITY
unite to form Synagogues for prayer, and those who enter therein to pray ; those who give the lamps for lighting, and wine for Kiddush and Havdolah, bread to the wayfarers, and charity to the poor, and all such as occupy themselves in faithfulness with the wants of the congregation. May the Holy One, blessed be he, give them their recompense ; may he remove from them all sickness, heal all their body, forgive all their iniquity, and send blessing and prosperity upon all the work of their hands, as well as upon all Israel, their brethren ; and let us say, Amen.

this decision of Mar Samuel on a par with the teaching of Jeremiah. They made it possible for Jewry to exist in the Dispersion.

Strangely enough, the exact wording of these ancient prayers has not come down to us. The earliest formula known is not older than the eleventh century prayer at Worms : " May He who blessed our fathers Abraham, Isaac and Jacob bless our exalted Kaiser. May He bless and prosper his undertakings ; establish his throne in justice, so that righteousness rule in the land ; and grant life and peace to him and his seed after him. And let us say, Amen ". In the communities of Spain, the Prayer for the King was recited even on Mondays and Thursdays, as well as on the Eve of the Atonement (Abudraham). Presumably it was the one which the Spanish Jews brought with them when they came to Holland; namely, " He who giveth salvation unto kings ". It was first printed in 1658; and, as its wording seemed to agree with the oral tradition among the Ashkenazim, it soon found its way into all Prayer Books. How widespread was its use is evidenced by the following fact. When, in 1666, the false Messiah Sabbethai Tsevi appeared in Smyrna, and a tidal wave of hysteria swept over the Jewish communities from Bagdad to Amsterdam, this prayer was adapted to proclaim him ; and Heaven was entreated to " bless, guard, protect, and help, exalt, magnify, and highly aggrandize " the Messianic pretender.

It was the Jews of Napoleon's day who were the first to depart from the generally accepted form of Prayer for the Government. In the new prayers which they composed, they omitted the entreaty that God incline the heart of the rulers to have pity on Israel, and that the time of deliverance of Zion draw near. " This passage was no longer appropriate, in a prayer composed after the emancipation of the Jews ", a French rabbinical apologist wrote fifty years ago. Alas, he could not see that emancipations, even French emancipations, might be repealed.

In 1895, the British Rabbinate was induced to modify the words " put compassion (רחמנות) into the Queen's heart and into the hearts of her counsellors and nobles, that they may deal kindly with us and with all Israel "

The Reader takes the Scroll of the Law, and says the following Prayer for the Government.

הַנּוֹתֵן תְּשׁוּעָה לַמְּלָכִים וּמֶמְשָׁלָה לַנְּסִיכִים. מַלְכוּתוֹ

מַלְכוּת כָּל־עוֹלָמִים. הַפּוֹצֶה אֶת־דָּוִד עַבְדּוֹ מֵחֶרֶב רָעָה.

הַנּוֹתֵן בַּיָּם דֶּרֶךְ וּבְמַיִם עַזִּים נְתִיבָה. הוּא יְבָרֵךְ וְיִשְׁמוֹר

וְיִנְצוֹר וְיַעֲזוֹר וִירוֹמֵם וִיגַדֵּל וִינַשֵּׂא לְמַעֲלָה

אֶת כָּל־שָׂרֵי הַמְּדִינוֹת הָאֵלוּ

מֶלֶךְ מַלְכֵי הַמְּלָכִים בְּרַחֲמָיו יִשְׁמְרֵם וִיחַיֵּם וּמִכָּל צָרָה

וָנֶזֶק יַצִּילֵם: מֶלֶךְ מַלְכֵי הַמְּלָכִים בְּרַחֲמָיו יָרִים וְיַגְבִּיהַּ

כּוֹכַב מַעֲרַכְתָּם וְיַאֲרִיכוּ יָמִים עַל מֶמְשַׁלְתָּם: מֶלֶךְ מַלְכֵי

הַמְּלָכִים בְּרַחֲמָיו יִתֵּן בְּלִבָּם וּבְלֵב כָּל־יוֹעֲצֵיהֶם וְשָׂרֵיהֶם

רַחֲמָנוּת לַעֲשׂוֹת טוֹבָה עִמָּנוּ וְעִם כָּל יִשְׂרָאֵל אַחֵינוּ:

בִּימֵיהֶם וּבְיָמֵינוּ תִּוָּשַׁע יְהוּדָה וְיִשְׂרָאֵל יִשְׁכֹּן לָבֶטַח וּבָא

לְצִיּוֹן גּוֹאֵל. וְכֵן יְהִי רָצוֹן. וְנֹאמַר אָמֵן:

They were changed into

"put a spirit of wisdom and understanding into her heart and into the hearts of all her counsellors . . . that they deal kindly and truly with all Israel".

The elimination of the supplication for רחמנות was in some quarters hailed as a great improvement. Nevertheless, the older form was a truer reflection of reality for millions of Jews, even before the Nazi Terror.

*The Reader takes the Scroll of the Law, and says the
following Prayer for the Government.*

He who giveth salvation unto kings and dominion
unto princes, whose kingdom is an everlasting kingdom,
who delivered his servant David from the hurtful sword,
who maketh a way in the sea and a path in the mighty
waters,—may he bless, guard, protect, and help, exalt,
magnify, and highly aggrandize

THE CONSTITUTED OFFICERS OF THIS GOVERNMENT.

May the Supreme King of Kings in his mercy preserve them in life and deliver them from all trouble and
hurt. May the Supreme King of Kings in his mercy exalt
them and raise them on high, and grant them a long and
prosperous rule. May the Supreme King of Kings in his
mercy inspire them and all their counsellors and officers
with benevolence toward us, and all Israel our brethren.
In their days and in ours may Judah be saved and Israel
dwell securely; and may the redeemer come unto Zion.
O that this may be his will, and let us say, Amen.

Its concluding sentences sound the universalist note—" In his
days and in ours, may our Heavenly Father spread the protection of
peace over all the dwellers on earth ". The Jewish humanist, Azariah
de Rossi (1513–1578) maintained that, like the High Priest of old, Jews
are to pray for the whole of mankind:—" We, who are scattered to the
four winds of heaven, should supplicate Almighty God for the peace of
all the inhabitants of the world ; that no nation lift up sword
against nation ; and that He remove from their hearts all strife and
hatred : for in their peace we too have peace ".

(D) ANNOUNCING THE NEW MOON.

The ordinary Jewish year consists of twelve lunar months of a little
more than $29\frac{1}{2}$ days each, with every new moon (Rosh Chodesh) a
minor festival. As, on the one hand, twelve lunar months total only a
little more than $354\frac{1}{4}$ days, which is eleven days less than the solar year
of $365\frac{1}{4}$ days ; and, on the other hand, the Festivals had to be celebrated in their seasons according to the *solar* year—Passover in spring,
Pentecost in summer and Tabernacles in autumn ; it was essential to
harmonize the lunar and solar years. This was done by the introduction,
in some years, of an extra month Adar, which made that year a leap

On the Sabbath preceding רֹאשׁ חֹדֶשׁ *the following is said:—*

יְהִי רָצוֹן מִלְּפָנֶיךָ יְיָ אֱלֹהֵינוּ וֵאלֹהֵי אֲבוֹתֵינוּ שֶׁתְּחַדֵּשׁ
עָלֵינוּ אֶת־הַחֹדֶשׁ הַזֶּה לְטוֹבָה וְלִבְרָכָה ׃ וְתִתֶּן־לָנוּ חַיִּים
אֲרֻכִּים חַיִּים שֶׁל־שָׁלוֹם חַיִּים שֶׁל־טוֹבָה חַיִּים שֶׁל־
בְּרָכָה חַיִּים שֶׁל־פַּרְנָסָה חַיִּים שֶׁל־חִלּוּץ עֲצָמוֹת ׃ חַיִּים
שֶׁיֵּשׁ בָּהֶם יִרְאַת שָׁמַיִם וְיִרְאַת חֵטְא חַיִּים שֶׁאֵין בָּהֶם
בּוּשָׁה וּכְלִמָּה ׃ חַיִּים שֶׁל־עֹשֶׁר וְכָבוֹד ׃ חַיִּים שֶׁתְּהֵי בָנוּ

year. In our fixed calendar, there are seven such leap years, of thirteen months each, in every cycle of nineteen years. But years, whether ordinary years or leap years, have not a uniform duration in the Jewish reckoning. Ordinary years vary between 353, 354 and 355 days; and leap years between 383, 384 and 385 days. Religious considerations once decided which year was to be a leap year, as well as when the months of Kislev and Cheshvan were to be " long " (having 30 days) or " short " (29 days). These months vary, in order that the first day of Rosh Hashonah never fall on a Sunday, Wednesday or Friday (לא אדו ראש השנה); which rule secures, among other things, that the Day of Atonement does not either immediately precede or immediately follow the Sabbath.

The proclamation of the New Moon was in ancient times the supreme function of the Sanhedrin at Jerusalem. At first the exact time of the New Moon was decided on by actual observation, and the date was announced by kindling fire-signals on the hill-tops. " A man would wave the fire-signal on the Mount of Olives, until he could see his fellow doing the like on the top of the next hill. And so too on top of the third hill, until one could see the whole Exile before him like a sea of fire " (Mishna). Later, the Patriarch of Palestine Jewry determined the dates of the Festivals by astronomical calculation according to rules that long remained the tradition of the Patriarchate (סוד העבור). Eventually in the fourth century, the Patriarch Hillel II published the rules for the computation of the Calendar. The learned could now, without difficulty, find out for themselves the dates of the Festivals; but it was still necessary to inform the masses of the exact beginning of each month. Therefore, it became the universal custom to proclaim in the

On the Sabbath preceding New Moon the following is said :—

May it be thy will, O Lord our God and God of our fathers, to renew unto us this coming month for good and for blessing. O grant us long life, a life of peace, of good, of blessing, of sustenance, of bodily vigour, a life marked by the fear of Heaven and the dread of sin, a life free from shame and reproach, a life of prosperity and honour, a life in which the love of the Torah and the fear of

Synagogue, on the Sabbath preceding the New Moon, the day on which the coming month would. begin. The third paragraph in the present form of the Prayer constituted such announcement. In nearly all Rites, the Announcement is preceded by a fervent petition for Redemption and a United Israel.

In the course of time, this prayer underwent a striking change. Instead of the *announcement of the new moon* it came to be regarded as the *blessing of the coming month* (" Rosh Chodesh benshen "). It is not more than two centuries ago, that some of the editions of the Ashkenazi Prayer Book printed as an introduction to the Announcing of the New Moon, the private prayer which the great Babylonian teacher Rabh recited after the daily Eighteen Benedictions. Chazanim give it a musical setting that touches the hearts of the worshippers, to whom it has become the most solemn prayer on the Sabbath preceding the New Moon.

to renew unto us. These words were inserted into Rabh's prayer in order to adapt it for the occasion.

dread of sin. In the Talmud the phrase is not found in this part of the prayer, only towards the end. The expression " dread of sin " may be negative, but the meaning is intensely positive. It is not merely to refrain from wrong acts, but the religious readiness of mind to do at any moment what at the moment would be the truest service of God.

shame and reproach. These words follow " dread of sin ". It is evident that where there is " dread of sin ", there is no danger of " shame and reproach ".

prosperity. So as to secure a life freed from all dependence on the gifts or charity of mortals. " It is a sign of healthy naturalness, as well as freedom from rationalism and ascetic pessimism, that the devout can pray for life, food and health with the same conviction, fervour and confidence as for pardon for his sins and for the coming of the Kingdom of God " (Heiler).

אַהֲבַת תּוֹרָה וְיִרְאַת שָׁמַיִם · חַיִּים שֶׁיִּמָּלְאוּ מִשְׁאֲלוֹת
לִבֵּנוּ לְטוֹבָה · אָמֵן סֶלָה :

Reader :—

מִי שֶׁעָשָׂה נִסִּים לַאֲבוֹתֵינוּ וְגָאַל אוֹתָם מֵעַבְדוּת
לְחֵרוּת · הוּא יִגְאַל אוֹתָנוּ בְּקָרוֹב וִיקַבֵּץ נִדְחֵינוּ
מֵאַרְבַּע כַּנְפוֹת הָאָרֶץ · חֲבֵרִים כָּל־יִשְׂרָאֵל · וְנֹאמַר אָמֵן :

(naming the day or רֹאשׁ חֹדֶשׁ)יְהְיֶה בַּיּוֹם(naming the month)

הַבָּא (הַבָּאִים) עָלֵינוּ וְעַל כָּל יִשְׂרָאֵל לְטוֹבָה : (days

Congregation and Reader.

יְחַדְּשֵׁהוּ הַקָּדוֹשׁ בָּרוּךְ הוּא עָלֵינוּ וְעַל כָּל־עַמּוֹ בֵּית
יִשְׂרָאֵל לְחַיִּים וּלְשָׁלוֹם · לְשָׂשׂוֹן וּלְשִׂמְחָה · לִישׁוּעָה
וּלְנֶחָמָה · וְנֹאמַר אָמֵן :

In many Congregations the following is said only on the Sabbaths
preceding שָׁבֻעוֹת and תִּשְׁעָה בְּאָב :—

אַב הָרַחֲמִים שׁוֹכֵן מְרוֹמִים בְּרַחֲמָיו הָעֲצוּמִים · הוּא
יִפְקוֹד בְּרַחֲמִים הַחֲסִידִים וְהַיְשָׁרִים וְהַתְּמִימִים · קְהִלּוֹת

for good. When God wishes to punish a man—say the Rabbis—He grants him *all* his desires. The meaning is : It is God and not the man, who knows whether the things prayed for are a real boon ; and we pray for a life in which the desires of our heart that tend to our good, shall be fulfilled.

HE WHO WROUGHT MIRACLES. These sentences probably embody the very words used two thousand years ago, when the proclamation of the New Moon by the Sanhedrin was accompanied by blessings and praises.

For obvious reasons, there is no announcement of the New Moon in regard to the month of Tishri, of which the first day is Rosh Hashonah. Long before the Sabbath preceding it, the day of the New Year is common knowledge to young and old alike.

BLESSING THE COMING MONTH

Heaven shall cleave to us, a life in which the desires of our heart shall be fulfilled for good. Amen. (Selah.)

Reader.—He who wrought miracles for our fathers, and redeemed them from slavery unto freedom, may he speedily redeem us, and gather our exiles from the four corners of the earth, even all Israel united in fellowship; and let us say, Amen.

The New Moon of (*naming the month*) will be on (*naming the day or days*). May it come to us and to all Israel for good.

Cong. and Reader.—May the Holy One, blessed be he, renew it unto us and unto all his people, the house of Israel, for life and peace, for gladness and joy, for salvation and consolation; and let us say, Amen.

In many Congregations the following is said only on the Sabbaths preceding Pentecost and the Fast of the Ninth of Av :—

REQUIEM FOR THE MARTYRS

II. Samuel 1. 23

May the Father of mercies, who dwelleth on high, in his mighty compassion, remember those loving, upright, and blameless ones, the holy congregations, who laid down their lives for the

(E) In Memoriam Prayers for the Departed.

Prayers for the departed have been known since ancient times (II Maccabees 12. 43–45). But as part of the Sabbath Service, they only date from the twelfth century, and then usually in connection with a promise to assist in charitable undertakings. A special Memorial Service for the Dead takes place on four days of the year—the Day of Atonement, the eighth days of Passover and Tabernacles, and the second day of Pentecost.

Requiem for the Martyrs.

May the Father of Mercies. Probably composed soon after the First Crusade in 1096, when a large number of communities in Germany were annihilated through massacre, or through self-immolation to escape baptism. Its recital originally followed the reading of the list of martyrs. This prayer occurs only in the Ashkenazi Rite; and, in Western countries, is recited on the Sabbath before Pentecost—which Sabbath concludes the Sefirah season, the anniversary of the massacres —as well as on the Sabbath before the Fast of Av, that commemorates the Destruction of Jerusalem.

sanctification of the Divine Name. Heb. *Kiddush Hashem.* Martyrs who lay down their lives for their Faith are the supreme example

הַקֹּדֶשׁ שֶׁמָּסְרוּ נַפְשָׁם עַל קְדֻשַּׁת הַשֵּׁם · הַנֶּאֱהָבִים וְהַנְּעִימִים
בְּחַיֵּיהֶם וּבְמוֹתָם לֹא נִפְרָדוּ · מִנְּשָׁרִים קַלּוּ וּמֵאֲרָיוֹת גָּבֵרוּ
לַעֲשׂוֹת רְצוֹן קוֹנָם וְחֵפֶץ צוּרָם : יִזְכְּרֵם אֱלֹהֵינוּ לְטוֹבָה עִם
שְׁאָר צַדִּיקֵי עוֹלָם · וְיִנְקוֹם נִקְמַת דַּם עֲבָדָיו הַשָּׁפוּךְ : כַּכָּתוּב
בְּתוֹרַת מֹשֶׁה אִישׁ הָאֱלֹהִים · הַרְנִינוּ גוֹיִם עַמּוֹ כִּי דַם-עֲבָדָיו
יִקּוֹם · וְנָקָם יָשִׁיב לְצָרָיו וְכִפֶּר אַדְמָתוֹ עַמּוֹ : וְעַל יְדֵי עֲבָדֶיךָ
הַנְּבִיאִים כָּתוּב לֵאמֹר · וְנִקֵּיתִי דָמָם לֹא נִקֵּיתִי · וַיְיָ שֹׁכֵן
בְּצִיּוֹן : וּבְכִתְבֵי הַקֹּדֶשׁ נֶאֱמַר · לָמָּה יֹאמְרוּ הַגּוֹיִם אַיֵּה
אֱלֹהֵיהֶם : יִוָּדַע בַּגּוֹיִם לְעֵינֵינוּ נִקְמַת דַּם עֲבָדֶיךָ הַשָּׁפוּךְ :

of those who hallow the Name of God by resisting every kind of temptation to turn away from Judaism. *Kiddush Hashem* is the positive counterpart of *Chillul Hashem*, the Profanation of the Divine Name by conduct unworthy of our Faith. These two conceptions are of fundamental importance in Jewish ethics. They have exerted a marvellous power in curbing self-indulgence in the individual, and in spurring him on to the greatest possible self-sacrifice and suffering for Israel's cause. " As every good and noble man must ever bear in mind that the dignity of humanity is in his hands, so should each earnest adherent of the Jewish Faith remember that the glory of God is entrusted to his care " (Perles).

the righteous of the world. i.e. the righteous among the followers of other Faiths. This is a truly wonderful touch. The author of this agonizing prayer on behalf of his slaughtered brethren did not despair of humanity; and he did not, because of the misdeeds of some of his contemporaries, exclude the righteous among them from participation in Future Life. Similarly, the recital of these dirges and martyrologies generated not vindictiveness, but heroic endurance in the worshippers. It inspired ordinary men and women with the courage to suffer all things for that which they held to be dearer than life. As to the Prayer itself, it might well end here, with the usual formula, "and may their souls be bound up in the bond of eternal life; the Lord is their inheritance, and let us say, Amen ".

The remaining portion of this Prayer consists of proof-texts, which are later additions, and differ in the various usages of the Ashkenazi Rite. As printed above, they give expression to the bitter cry for Divine retribution. " Let us not fail to realize the conditions which brought forth such prayers, and which, in a measure, constitute their justification. They were wrung from a people's agony. But were they anything more than words, however fervent ? No. Vengeance

REQUIEM FOR THE MARTYRS   sanctification of the divine Name, who were lovely and pleasant in their lives, and in their death were not divided ; swifter than eagles, stronger than lions to do the will of their Master and the desire of their Rock. May our God remember them for good with the other righteous of the world, and render retribution for the blood of his servants which hath been shed ; as it is written in the Torah of Moses, *Deuteronomy 32. 43* the man of God, Rejoice, O ye nations, with his people, for he will avenge the blood of his servants, and will render retribution to his adversaries, and will make expiation for the land of his people. And *Joel 4. 21* by the hands of thy servants, the Prophets, it is written saying, I will

was prayed for—and left to God " (M. Joseph). Above all else, it is well to remember that the cry for retribution is very human, and is the ethical reaction of righteous indignation against inhuman wrong. Israel Abrahams aptly recalls the story of the Waldenses. In the early months of 1655, these stalwart Protestants were ordered by the then King of Savoy to embrace the Roman Catholic Faith. On their resistance, they were subjected to imprisonment, torture and massacre ; while hundreds of families who escaped, perished miserably of famine and exposure on the snow-covered mountains. These dreadful atrocities moved John Milton to indite his famous lines,
> " Avenge, O Lord, thy slaughtered saints, whose bones
> Lie scattered on the Alpine mountains cold ".

There is surely nothing irreligious in this attitude of the poet. When the wicked are triumphant, it is not only allowable, but it is our sacred duty to pray for the destruction of the iniquitous authors of calculated inhumanity. The same considerations explain this portion of the Dirge of the Martyrs. The sufferings of the Jews immeasurably exceeded those of the Waldenses. The Jewish poets of the Middle Ages would have been callous indeed had they remained unmoved by the destruction of their brethren. In the second chapter of his *Synagogal Poetry of the Middle Ages*, Zunz has given a wonderful survey of Jewish Martyrdom. " If there exists a ladder in suffering, Israel has reached the highest rung. If the duration of sorrows and the patience with which they are borne ennoble, the Jews may challenge the aristocracy of every land. If a literature is called rich which possesses a few classical tragedies, what place then is due to a Tragedy lasting 1,500 years, written and acted by the heroes themselves ? " And, alas, the end is not yet. The twentieth century opened for the Jew with Kishineff ; and, in its fourth decade, five million Jews have been annihilated by the Germans in Poland, aside from cycles of mass-massacres in Nazi-occupied lands that are unparalleled in the blood-stained annals of Europe.

rejoice, O ye nations. This is from the Farewell Song of Moses. The dying Lawgiver calls upon the heathen to rejoice in Israel's deliverance. The justice and faithfulness of God manifested in that vindication, give men new confidence in the moral character of the forces which rule the universe

וָאוֹמַר כִּי דוֹרֵשׁ דָּמִים אוֹתָם זָכָר לֹא שָׁכַח צַעֲקַת עֲנָוִים :

וָאוֹמַר יָדִין בַּגּוֹיִם מָלֵא גְוִיּוֹת מָחַץ רֹאשׁ עַל אֶרֶץ רַבָּה :

מִנַּחַל בַּדֶּרֶךְ יִשְׁתֶּה עַל כֵּן יָרִים רֹאשׁ :

אַשְׁרֵי יוֹשְׁבֵי בֵיתֶךָ עוֹד יְהַלְלוּךָ סֶּלָה :

אַשְׁרֵי הָעָם שֶׁכָּכָה לּוֹ אַשְׁרֵי הָעָם שֶׁיְיָ אֱלֹהָיו :

תהלים קמ״ה

תְּהִלָּה לְדָוִד ·

אֲרוֹמִמְךָ אֱלוֹהַי הַמֶּלֶךְ וַאֲבָרְכָה שִׁמְךָ לְעוֹלָם וָעֶד :

בְּכָל־יוֹם אֲבָרְכֶךָ וַאֲהַלְלָה שִׁמְךָ לְעוֹלָם וָעֶד :

גָּדוֹל יְהוָֹה וּמְהֻלָּל מְאֹד וְלִגְדֻלָּתוֹ אֵין חֵקֶר :

דּוֹר לְדוֹר יְשַׁבַּח מַעֲשֶׂיךָ וּגְבוּרֹתֶיךָ יַגִּידוּ :

הֲדַר כְּבוֹד הוֹדֶךָ וְדִבְרֵי נִפְלְאֹתֶיךָ אָשִׂיחָה :

וֶעֱזוּז נוֹרְאוֹתֶיךָ יֹאמֵרוּ וּגְדֻלָּתְךָ אֲסַפְּרֶנָּה :

זֵכֶר רַב־טוּבְךָ יַבִּיעוּ וְצִדְקָתְךָ יְרַנֵּנוּ :

he shall judge. David is promised complete victory over the blood-stained "King" (Moloch) of the Ammonites.

lift up the head. Wearied with the pursuit, the warrior refreshes himself by drinking of the torrent rushing by, and finds new vigour till full victory is his.

PSALM 145.

This triumphant hymn of praise, calling upon all men to glorify the majesty of God, is an alphabetical psalm, with one strophe, that of *Nun,* missing. It combines simplicity of thought with sublimity of language in the adoration of God.

It has rightly been called " the Psalm of universal benevolence ". It sums up the Jewish doctrine of God; it celebrates His greatness (1–6), goodness (7–10), Kingdom (11–13), and His constant love towards all those who love and reverence Him (14–21). If Israel begins the chorus of praise (*v.* 1), it will not be content until all mankind joins in it (*v.* 21).

hold (the heathen) innocent, but not in regard to the blood which they have shed : for the Lord dwelleth in Zion. And in the Holy *Psalm 79. 10* Writings it is said, Wherefore should the heathen say, Where then is their God ? Let there be made known among the nations in our sight the rendering of retribution for the blood of thy servants *Psalm 9. 13* which hath been shed. And it is said, For he that rendereth retribution for blood remembereth them ; he forgetteth not the cry of the *Psalm* humble. And it is further said. He shall judge among the nations. *110. 6, 7* The places are full of dead bodies: he shall smite rulers over a wide land. Of the brook shall he drink in the way : therefore shall he lift up the head.

ASHREY SHEVEY VEYSECHO Happy are they that dwell in thy house : they will be *Psalm 84. 5* ever praising thee. (Selah.) Happy is the people, that *Psalm 144. 15* is thus favoured : happy is the people, whose God is the Lord.

Psalm cxlv. ¹A Psalm of Praise : of David.

THE GREAT-NESS AND UNENDING GOODNESS OF GOD I will extol thee, my God, O King ; and I will bless thy Name for ever and ever. ²Every day will I bless thee ; and I will praise thy Name for ever and ever. ³Great is the Lord, and exceedingly to be praised : and his greatness is unsearchable. ⁴One generation shall laud thy works to another, and shall declare thy mighty acts. ⁵On the majestic glory of thy splendour, and on thy marvellous deeds, will I meditate. ⁶And men shall speak of the might of thy tremendous acts ; and I will recount thy greatness. ⁷They shall pour forth the fame of thy great goodness, and shall exult in thy

Since early Rabbinic times two verses (Psalm 84. 5 and 144. 14) have been prefixed to Psalm 145, when it forms part of a Morning or Afternoon Service.

7. *pour forth.* The fulness of praise evoked by the *goodness* and *righteousness* of God are represented by two verbs : the first, " pour forth ", compares its gush to the clear waters of a spring bursting up into sunlight, musical and living ; and the other, " exult ", describes it as like the shrill cries of joy raised by a throng at some festival (Maclaren).

exult in thy righteousness. The use of the word " exult " is noteworthy. " All, or very nearly all, the nations of mankind have recognized the importance of conduct. They, however, looked at conduct not as something full of happiness and joy, but as something one could

חַנּוּן וְרַחוּם יְהֹוָה אֶרֶךְ אַפַּיִם וּגְדָל־חָסֶד :

טוֹב־יְהֹוָה לַכֹּל וְרַחֲמָיו עַל־כָּל־מַעֲשָׂיו :

יוֹדוּךָ יְהֹוָה כָּל־מַעֲשֶׂיךָ וַחֲסִידֶיךָ יְבָרְכוּכָה :

כְּבוֹד מַלְכוּתְךָ יֹאמֵרוּ וּגְבוּרָתְךָ יְדַבֵּרוּ :

לְהוֹדִיעַ לִבְנֵי הָאָדָם גְּבוּרֹתָיו וּכְבוֹד הֲדַר מַלְכוּתוֹ :

מַלְכוּתְךָ מַלְכוּת כָּל־עֹלָמִים וּמֶמְשַׁלְתְּךָ בְּכָל־דּוֹר וָדֹר :

סוֹמֵךְ יְהֹוָה לְכָל־הַנֹּפְלִים וְזוֹקֵף לְכָל־הַכְּפוּפִים :

עֵינֵי כֹל אֵלֶיךָ יְשַׂבֵּרוּ וְאַתָּה נוֹתֵן־לָהֶם אֶת־אָכְלָם בְּעִתּוֹ :

פּוֹתֵחַ אֶת־יָדֶךָ וּמַשְׂבִּיעַ לְכָל־חַי רָצוֹן :

צַדִּיק יְהֹוָה בְּכָל־דְּרָכָיו וְחָסִיד בְּכָל־מַעֲשָׂיו :

קָרוֹב יְהֹוָה לְכָל־קֹרְאָיו לְכֹל אֲשֶׁר יִקְרָאֻהוּ בֶאֱמֶת :

רְצוֹן־יְרֵאָיו יַעֲשֶׂה וְאֶת־שַׁוְעָתָם יִשְׁמַע וְיוֹשִׁיעֵם :

שׁוֹמֵר יְהֹוָה אֶת־כָּל־אֹהֲבָיו וְאֵת כָּל־הָרְשָׁעִים יַשְׁמִיד :

not manage to do without. No one has ever come near Israel in feeling, and in making others feel, that to righteousness belongs happiness!" (Matthew Arnold).

8. *gracious and merciful.* This thought, based on the revelation of God's nature in Exodus 34. 6, 7, became an article of faith for the pious in Israel.

9. *his tender mercies are over all his works.* Rabbi Judah the Prince was sorely afflicted for many years because one day, when a terror-stricken calf, that was being prepared for slaughter, ran to him for shelter, he repulsed it with the words "Go, for such is thy destiny". His affliction passed away when he rescued a humble field-creature from a servant who was about to kill it, saying, "Let the creature live; for is it not written, *His tender mercies are over all His works?*" (Talmud).

10. *thy loving ones shall bless thee.* Judaism bids men bless God's Name for the evil, as for the good, that may befall them. "The Lord gave, and the Lord hath taken away; blessed be the Name of the Lord" (Job 1. 21). Resignation to God's will is as much a duty as is

THE
GREAT-
NESS AND
UNENDING
GOODNESS
OF GOD

righteousness. ⁸The Lord is gracious and merciful ; slow to anger and of great lovingkindness. ⁹The Lord is good to all ; and his tender mercies are over all his works. ¹⁰All thy works shall give thanks unto thee, O Lord ; and thy loving ones shall bless thee. ¹¹They shall speak of the glory of thy kingdom, and talk of thy power ; ¹²to make known to the sons of men his mighty acts, and the majestic glory of his kingdom. ¹³Thy kingdom is an everlasting kingdom, and thy dominion endureth throughout all generations. ¹⁴The Lord upholdeth all that fall, and raiseth up all those that are bowed down. ¹⁵The eyes of all wait upon thee ; and thou givest them their food in due season. ¹⁶Thou openest thine hand, and satisfiest every living thing with favour. ¹⁷The Lord is righteous in all his ways, and loving in all his works. ¹⁸The Lord is nigh unto all them that call upon him, to all that call upon him in truth. ¹⁹He will fulfil the desire of them that reverence him; he also will hear their cry, and will save them. ²⁰The Lord guardeth all them that love him ; but all the wicked will he destroy. ²¹My mouth shall

thanksgiving for His unending mercies. Every creature shows some gratitude for any good that befalls it ; but it is only the *chassidim,* " those who love God ", that *bless* His Name, even in the darkness of woe, sorrow and suffering.

13. *thy kingdom.* Thy kingship ; the term is unconnected with any thought of land or area, see p. 113.

15. *the eyes of all wait upon thee.* . . . *living thing.* They mutely appeal to God, with expectant eyes fixed on Him. These verses contain the essence of the Grace for daily meals; and are especially named in the Talmud as the reason for the threefold daily repetition of this Psalm. The word " all " occurs more than eleven times in the latter part of the psalm—suggesting boundless visions of the wide sweep of God's universal mercy.

17. *loving.* The adjective *chossid,* which the Greek Version translates *philanthropos,* denotes goodness that manifests itself in deeds of benevolence, in the practice of lovingkindness.

20. *all the wicked will he destroy.* The infinite goodness of God does not mean that He disregards the eternal distinction between right and wrong, and will refrain from retributive punishment. It is true that we cannot always " trace the hidden equities of divine reward and catch sight, through the darkness, of the fateful threads of woven fire that covered error with retribution " (Ruskin). But there are various ways of destroying the wicked. One of them is, by destroying

תְּהִלַּת יְהֹוָה יְדַבֶּר־פִּי וִיבָרֵךְ כָּל־בָּשָׂר שֵׁם קָדְשׁוֹ לְעוֹלָם וָעֶד:

וַאֲנַחְנוּ נְבָרֵךְ יָהּ מֵעַתָּה וְעַד־עוֹלָם · הַלְלוּיָהּ:

On returning the סֵפֶר *to the Ark the Reader says :—*

יְהַלְלוּ אֶת־שֵׁם יְהֹוָה כִּי־נִשְׂגָּב שְׁמוֹ לְבַדּוֹ ·

Congregation :—

הוֹדוֹ עַל־אֶרֶץ וְשָׁמָיִם: וַיָּרֶם קֶרֶן לְעַמּוֹ תְּהִלָּה לְכָל־חֲסִידָיו לִבְנֵי יִשְׂרָאֵל עַם קְרֹבוֹ · הַלְלוּיָהּ:

On Sabbaths and on Festivals occurring on Sabbaths say :—

תהלים כ"ט

מִזְמוֹר לְדָוִד · הָבוּ לַיְיָ בְּנֵי אֵלִים הָבוּ לַיְיָ כָּבוֹד וָעֹז: הָבוּ לַיְיָ כְּבוֹד שְׁמוֹ הִשְׁתַּחֲווּ לַיְיָ בְּהַדְרַת־קֹדֶשׁ: קוֹל יְיָ עַל הַמָּיִם אֵל־הַכָּבוֹד הִרְעִים יְיָ עַל־מַיִם רַבִּים: קוֹל יְיָ בַּכֹּחַ קוֹל יְיָ בֶּהָדָר: קוֹל יְיָ שֹׁבֵר אֲרָזִים וַיְשַׁבֵּר יְיָ אֶת־אַרְזֵי הַלְּבָנוֹן: וַיַּרְקִידֵם כְּמוֹ־עֵגֶל לְבָנוֹן וְשִׂרְיוֹן כְּמוֹ בֶן־רְאֵמִים: קוֹל־יְיָ חֹצֵב לַהֲבוֹת אֵשׁ: קוֹל יְיָ יָחִיל

the particular form of wickedness that ensnares them ; *e.g.* with the abolition of the slave-trade, a whole group of inhuman villainies were swept away. See on Psalm 104. 35, p. 588.

but we will bless . . . evermore. We is emphatic. Whether all flesh join us in blessing His holy Name, or they do not, Israel will continue to adore Him for ever and ever.

IV. RETURNING THE SCROLL TO THE ARK.

LET THEM PRAISE. After these verses are recited, the Procession for the return of the Scroll begins. The verses were in use in Gaonic times;

speak of the praise of the Lord ; and let all flesh bless his holy Name for ever and ever.

Psalm 115. 18   But we will bless the Lord from this time forth and for

RETURN-
ING THE
SCROLL
Psalm
148. 13, 14

evermore. Praise ye the Lord.

On returning the Scroll of the Torah to the Ark, the Reader says :—

Let them praise the Name of the Lord ; for his Name alone is exalted :

Congregation.—His majesty is above the earth and heaven ; and he hath exalted the power of his people, to the praise of all his loving ones, even of the children of Israel, the people near unto him. Praise ye the Lord.

On Sabbaths and on Festivals occurring on Sabbaths, say :—

Psalm xxix. ¹A Psalm of David.

GOD'S
MAJESTY

Ascribe unto the Lord, O ye sons of might, ascribe unto the Lord glory and strength. ²Ascribe unto the Lord the glory due unto his Name ; worship the Lord in the beauty of holiness. ³The voice of the Lord is upon the waters : the God of glory thundereth, even the Lord upon the many waters. ⁴The voice of the Lord is powerful ; the voice of the Lord is full of majesty. ⁵The voice of the Lord breaketh the cedars ; yea, the Lord breaketh in pieces the cedars of Lebanon. ⁶He maketh them also to skip like a calf ; Lebanon and Sirion like a young wild-ox. ⁷The voice of the

and, since 1100, Psalm 29 is recited on Sabbaths. Subsequently, Psalm 24 was set aside for Festivals falling on weekdays.

PSALM 29.

Thunder-storms of tropical intensity are frequent in Palestine in winter, and the Israelite saw in them special manifestations of Divine might and majesty.

1. *sons of might.* The angels, standing in God's immediate presence and watching the storm, are called upon by the poet to praise Him whose glory is seen in the storm.

3–9. Rise, progress and effect of the thunder-storm.

3. *voice of the Lord.* The thunder. The first peal is heard as coming from the Mediterranean sea, whence storms arise in Palestine. It bursts over the northern mountain-ranges.

6. *Lebanon.* The very mountains shake to their foundations.

Sirion. Mt. Hermon.

מִדְבָּר יָחִיל יְיָ מִדְבַּר קָדֵשׁ : קוֹל יְיָ יְחוֹלֵל אַיָּלוֹת וַיֶּחֱשֹׂף
יְעָרוֹת וּבְהֵיכָלוֹ כֻּלּוֹ אֹמֵר כָּבוֹד : יְיָ לַמַּבּוּל יָשָׁב וַיֵּשֶׁב
יְיָ מֶלֶךְ לְעוֹלָם : יְיָ עֹז לְעַמּוֹ יִתֵּן יְיָ ׀ יְבָרֵךְ אֶת־עַמּוֹ
בַשָּׁלוֹם :

On Festivals occurring on Week days say :—

תהלים כ"ד

לְדָוִד מִזְמוֹר • לַייָ הָאָרֶץ וּמְלוֹאָהּ תֵּבֵל וְיֹשְׁבֵי בָהּ :
כִּי־הוּא עַל־יַמִּים יְסָדָהּ וְעַל־נְהָרוֹת יְכוֹנְנֶהָ : מִי־יַעֲלֶה
בְהַר יְיָ וּמִי־יָקוּם בִּמְקוֹם קָדְשׁוֹ : נְקִי כַפַּיִם וּבַר לֵבָב
אֲשֶׁר לֹא נָשָׂא לַשָּׁוְא נַפְשׁוֹ וְלֹא נִשְׁבַּע לְמִרְמָה : יִשָּׂא
בְרָכָה מֵאֵת יְיָ וּצְדָקָה מֵאֱלֹהֵי יִשְׁעוֹ : זֶה דּוֹר דֹּרְשָׁו
מְבַקְשֵׁי פָנֶיךָ יַעֲקֹב סֶלָה : שְׂאוּ שְׁעָרִים רָאשֵׁיכֶם וְהִנָּשְׂאוּ
פִּתְחֵי עוֹלָם וְיָבוֹא מֶלֶךְ הַכָּבוֹד : מִי זֶה מֶלֶךְ הַכָּבוֹד יְיָ :

7. *heweth out.* With every thunder-peal come forked lightning shafts.

8. *wilderness.* The poet sees the mountains in the North leap in terror. The storm has now swept over the whole length of the land, and pours out its fury on the Wilderness in the South.

9. *calve . . . bare.* These are no mere poetical figures ; they are observed facts.

in his temple. His Heavenly Temple.

Glory. This is the chant of the angels.

10. *at the Flood.* He was King then, and is King always.

11. The God who rules and stills the storm, is the same Who blesses His people with moral strength and lasting peace.

PSALM 24.

When David conquered Jerusalem, he made it the home for the Ark of the Covenant (II Samuel 6. 17). This psalm reflects the joy and enthusiasm that attended the removal of the Ark to Mt. Zion.

1. *the earth is the Lord's.* This and the following verse were sung

RETURN-
ING THE
SCROLL

Lord heweth out flames of fire ; ⁸the voice of the Lord shaketh the wilderness ; the Lord shaketh the wilderness of Kadesh. ⁹The voice of the Lord maketh the hinds to calve, and strippeth the forests bare : and in his temple everything saith, Glory. ¹⁰The Lord sat enthroned at the Flood ; yea, the Lord sitteth as King for ever. ¹¹The Lord will give strength unto his people ; the Lord will bless his people with peace.

[*On Festivals occurring on Weekdays, say* :—

Psalm xxiv. ¹A Psalm of David.

THE TRUE
WORSHIP-
PER

The earth is the Lord's, and the fulness thereof ; the world, and they that dwell therein. ²For it is he that hath founded it upon the seas, and established it upon the floods. ³Who may ascend the mountain of the Lord ? And who may stand in his holy place ? ⁴He that hath clean hands and a pure heart ; who hath not set his desire upon vanity, and hath not sworn deceitfully. ⁵He shall receive a blessing from the Lord, and righteousness from the God of his salvation. ⁶Such is the generation of them that seek after him, that seek thy face, (O God of) Jacob ! (Selah.) ⁷Lift up your heads, O ye gates ; and be ye lifted up, ye ever-lasting doors, that the King of glory may come in. ⁸Who

as the procession was winding up the hill towards the ancient fortress of Zion.

2. *founded it upon the seas.* See Genesis 1. 9.

3. *who may ascend.* Who is worthy to join the procession of worshippers? Who is worthy to worship on God's holy hill ?

4. *clean hands.* See Psalm 15. The requirements are purely ethical and spiritual. The true worshipper is a man of sinless hands, unsoiled by acts of violence or dishonesty.

pure heart. A pure conscience. His desires and motives are free from anything mean, hateful or defiling.

not set his desire upon vanity. He does not direct his desires to falsehood, and strive after empty and frivolous things. The translation is based on the Written Text (Kethib).

5. *righteousness.* The reward which God in His righteousness gives to those who deserve a reward.

7. *lift up your heads.* The hoary gates of the old fortress are

עִזּוּז וְגִבּוֹר יְיָ גִּבּוֹר מִלְחָמָה: שְׂאוּ שְׁעָרִים רָאשֵׁיכֶם
וּשְׂאוּ פִּתְחֵי עוֹלָם וְיָבֹא מֶלֶךְ הַכָּבוֹד: מִי הוּא זֶה מֶלֶךְ
הַכָּבוֹד יְיָ צְבָאוֹת הוּא מֶלֶךְ הַכָּבוֹד סֶלָה:

While the סֵפֶר *is being placed in the Ark, the following to* בְּקֶדֶם
is said :—

וּבְנֻחֹה יֹאמַר שׁוּבָה יְיָ רִבְבוֹת אַלְפֵי יִשְׂרָאֵל:
קוּמָה יְיָ לִמְנוּחָתֶךָ אַתָּה וַאֲרוֹן עֻזֶּךָ: כֹּהֲנֶיךָ יִלְבְּשׁוּ־צֶדֶק
וַחֲסִידֶיךָ יְרַנֵּנוּ: בַּעֲבוּר דָּוִד עַבְדֶּךָ אַל־תָּשֵׁב פְּנֵי
מְשִׁיחֶךָ: כִּי לֶקַח טוֹב נָתַתִּי לָכֶם תּוֹרָתִי אַל־תַּעֲזֹבוּ:
עֵץ חַיִּים הִיא לַמַּחֲזִיקִים בָּהּ וְתֹמְכֶיהָ מְאֻשָּׁר: דְּרָכֶיהָ
דַרְכֵי־נֹעַם וְכָל־נְתִיבוֹתֶיהָ שָׁלוֹם: הֲשִׁיבֵנוּ יְיָ אֵלֶיךָ
וְנָשׁוּבָה חַדֵּשׁ יָמֵינוּ כְּקֶדֶם:

חֲצִי קַדִּישׁ, p . 422.

represented as unwilling to receive the Ark ; or, as too low and mean
for the entrance of the Ark, " which is called by the Name, even the
Name of the Lord of hosts " (II Sam. 6. 2). Now that the procession has
reached the barred gates of the citadel, a voice summons them to open.

everlasting doors. lit. " ancient doors ", whose story stretches into
the past, far and dim.

8. *who is.* The warders at the gates ask, or perhaps the poet
conceives the gates themselves to ask, Who is it that thus demands
entrance.

10. *Lord of Hosts.* The choir in the procession responds that He
claims to enter not only as a victorious warrior, but as the King of the
Universe.

is the King of glory ?. The Lord strong and mighty, the

TRIUMPH- Lord mighty in battle. ⁹Lift up your heads, O ye gates ;
AL ENTRY
INTO yea, lift them up, ye everlasting doors, that the King of
SANCTU-
ARY glory may come in. ¹⁰Who, then, is the King of glory ? The

Lord of hosts, he is the King of glory. (Selah.)]

While the Scroll is being placed in the Ark, the following is said :—

Numbers And when it rested, he said, Return, O Lord, unto the
10. 36
Psalm ten thousands of the families of Israel. Arise, O Lord,
132. 8-10 unto thy resting place ; thou, and the ark of thy strength.

Let thy priests be clothed with righteousness ; and let thy

loving ones shout for joy. For the sake of David thy servant,

Proverbs 4. 2 turn not away the face of thine anointed. For I give you

Proverbs good doctrine ; forsake ye not my Teaching. It is a tree of
3. 18, 17 life to them that grasp it, and of them that uphold it every

one is rendered happy. Its ways are ways of pleasantness,

Lamentations and all its paths are peace. Turn thou us unto thee, O
5. 21 Lord, and we shall return : renew our days as of old.

Kaddish p. 423.

AND WHEN IT RESTED. As at the Opening of the Ark, our minds go
back to our fathers in the Wilderness. We well might take to heart these
immortal ancient words ; and at the beginnings and endings of all our
efforts, not only of our Readings of the Torah, offer up these old prayers
—the prayer which asks for the Divine Presence in the incipiency of our
labours, and the prayer which asks for the Divine Presence at the completion of our work.

arise, O Lord. See p. 474.

turn thou us unto thee. An ideal close of the sublime Service of the
Reading of the Torah.

A community, like an individual, is unable to emerge from religious
apathy by a mere fiat of the will. " No prisoner can by himself free
himself from prison ", say the Rabbis. The prerequisite of his being
freed at all, is a longing for liberty—the conviction that freedom is
better than bondage. The same is true of spiritual renewal. There
must first of all be the desire for the life illumined and transformed by
Religion. When that desire finds articulate expression in words like,
" Turn Thou us unto Thee, and we shall return ", it carries its own
fulfilment with it.

renew our days as of old. Originally these words were spoken 2,500
years ago after the burning of Jerusalem by the Babylonians. From

the depths, Israel then prayed for the soul-communion with God that had marked its life in the olden days. In our times, likewise, Israel feels deeply humiliated by the causeless hatreds and venomous slanders that everywhere assail it ; bewildered by the horrible annihilation of millions of innocent victims, simply because they are Jews ; alarmed at the estrangement from 'God of such large sections of the Jewish people. " May our God be with us, as He was with our fathers ; let Him not leave us, not forsake us ! " And, we will not leave nor forsake *Him*. Our prayer for spiritual renewal is the expression of our readiness, like our fathers of old, to live for eternal things. Like unto our fathers, Religion will be a living reality, ennobling and sanctifying.

> " For in the background figures vague and vast
> Of patriarchs and prophets rose sublime,
> And all the great traditions of the Past
>
> They saw reflected in the coming time.
> And thus forever with reverted look
> The mystic volume of the world they read,
> Spelling it backward like a Hebrew book . . . "
>
> (Longfellow).

V. SERMON.

After the Service in connection with the Reading of the Torah, and before the Mussaf Service, the sermon is preached, in Western congregations.

The SERMON—*i.e.* the religious or moral discourse at congregational worship—is, like congregational worship itself, one of Israel's great contributions to mankind. At least a century before the Destruction of Jerusalem in the year 70, the institution of the pulpit was traced back to Moses himself, and the sermon seems to have formed an essential part of the Sabbath Service. Philo writes :

" Innumerable schools of practical wisdom, self-control, manliness, uprightness and the other virtues are opened every Sabbath day in all cities. In these schools, the people listen with the utmost attention out of a thirst for a refreshing discourse, while one of the best-qualified stands up, and instructs them in what is best and most conducive to welfare, things by which their whole life may be made better ".

It is to be regretted that the vital importance of the sermon in Jewish worship is not as universally understood as it should be. It has its confirmed detractors, who assert that pulpit instruction is a comparatively modern practice which has been borrowed from our Christian neighbours. Nothing could be further from the true historical facts. We need but recall the passionate pleadings of the Prophets for a higher life of righteousness and purity, as well as the exposition of Scripture and religious instruction that date at the latest from the Babylonian

Exile. As to the preachers of the Rabbinic ages, from the creators of the Midrashim that embody the sermon-heads preached in Talmudic generations, down to thé Maggid of Dubno (1741-1804)—whose parables, *meshalim*, are still on the lips of Jews in, or hailing from, Slavonic lands—it is difficult to over-estimate the part which preachers·played in keeping the Jewish soul strong and hopeful by means of the ever-flowing fountains of idealism and consolation that they opened for the faithful. In the later Middle Ages, the custom of regular synagogal instruction may have somewhat fallen into abeyance ; yet there were always wandering *maggidim*, who had a strange power to enkindle in the hearts of their hearers the fire of faith and devotion ; to comfort, to warn and recall the backslider to the paths of purity and righteousness.

And such is still the vocation of the present-day preacher. Like the priest of old, he is the sleepless guardian of Israel's sanctuary, the consecrated custodian of Israel's Teaching, and zealous defender of its eternal validity. Undisturbed by ephemeral aberrations of opinion, he is to hand down Israel's spiritual. treasures undiminished in power, purity, and lustre. By similitudes from nature, history, and the vast ocean of Jewish lore, he proves to his hearers that the teachings of Judaism are in accordance with humanity's highest ideals—nay, that these teachings have helped to shape these ideals ; that " the fear of the Lord is the beginning of wisdom," the foundation on which alone all human happiness can be built. " The supreme object of preaching must ever be to lead souls unto God ; to wean men and women from the pursuit of low and earthly aims to all that is good, pure and true ; to build up within them the grace of patience, the power of self-discipline, and the instinct of loving helpfulness, the spirit of sacrifice and of service. The preacher must feel deep sympathy with every single individual whom he addresses, regarding every upturned face, and none the less the faces turned away from him, as the countenances of never-dying souls whom he has to help on their earthly pilgrimage " (Hermann Adler).

תפלת מוסף לשבת:

For מוסף שַׁבָּת וְחוֹל הַמּוֹעֵד see Service for שָׁלוֹשׁ רְגָלִים‎, p. 814.

The following קְדֻמוֹנִיוֹת to עֲמִידָה, p. 540, is said standing

אֲדֹנָי שְׂפָתַי תִּפְתָּח וּפִי יַגִּיד תְּהִלָּתֶךָ :

בָּרוּךְ אַתָּה יְיָ אֱלֹהֵינוּ וֵאלֹהֵי אֲבוֹתֵינוּ · אֱלֹהֵי
אַבְרָהָם אֱלֹהֵי יִצְחָק וֵאלֹהֵי יַעֲקֹב · הָאֵל הַגָּדוֹל הַגִּבּוֹר
וְהַנּוֹרָא אֵל עֶלְיוֹן · גּוֹמֵל חֲסָדִים טוֹבִים וְקוֹנֵה הַכֹּל ·
וְזוֹכֵר חַסְדֵי אָבוֹת וּמֵבִיא גוֹאֵל לִבְנֵי בְנֵיהֶם לְמַעַן שְׁמוֹ
בְּאַהֲבָה ·

On שַׁבָּת שׁוּבָה say :—

זָכְרֵנוּ לְחַיִּים מֶלֶךְ חָפֵץ בַּחַיִּים · וְכָתְבֵנוּ בְּסֵפֶר הַחַיִּים ·
לְמַעַנְךָ אֱלֹהִים חַיִּים :

מֶלֶךְ עוֹזֵר וּמוֹשִׁיעַ וּמָגֵן · בָּרוּךְ אַתָּה יְיָ · מָגֵן אַבְרָהָם :
אַתָּה גִּבּוֹר לְעוֹלָם אֲדֹנָי מְחַיֵּה מֵתִים אַתָּה רַב לְהוֹשִׁיעַ ·

From פֶּסַח until the First Day of שַׁבָּת בְּרֵאשִׁית say :—

מַשִּׁיב הָרוּחַ וּמוֹרִיד הַגֶּשֶׁם :

מְכַלְכֵּל חַיִּים בְּחֶסֶד מְחַיֵּה מֵתִים בְּרַחֲמִים רַבִּים · סוֹמֵךְ

THE MUSSAF SERVICE

On Sabbaths and Festivals, there were in the Temple *additional* offerings, over and above the regular daily morning sacrifices. It is usually assumed that an additional (" Mussaf ") Prayer was, in consequence, introduced into the Sabbath and Festival Liturgies. This is by no means certain. The oldest sources speak of the Mussaf Prayer quite apart from sacrifice. This shows that the Mussaf arose independently of the Temple cultus (Elbogen).

MUSSAF SERVICE FOR SABBATHS.

For the Additional Service on the Intermediate Sabbath of a Festival,
see Service for the Festivals, p. 815.

MUSSAF
AMIDAH

The following prayer (Amidah) to " as in ancient years," p. 541, is to
be said standing.

Psalm 51. 17 — O Lord, open thou my lips, and my mouth shall declare thy praise.

I. THE
GOD OF
HISTORY
See p. 449

Blessed art thou, O Lord our God and God of our fathers, God of Abraham, God of Isaac, and God of Jacob, the great, mighty and revered God, the most high God, who bestowest lovingkindnesses, and art Master of all things ; who rememberest the pious deeds of the patriarchs, and in love wilt bring a redeemer to their children's children for thy Name's sake.

[*On the Sabbath of Repentance say :—*
Remember us unto life, O King, who delightest in life, and inscribe us in the book of life, for thine own sake, O living God.]

O King, Helper, Saviour and Shield. Blessed art thou, O Lord, the Shield of Abraham.

II. THE
GOD OF
NATURE
See p. 451

Thou, O Lord, art mighty for ever, thou revivest the dead, thou art mighty to save.

[*From the day after Simchas Torah until the Eve of Passover, say :*
Thou causest the wind to blow and the rain to fall.]

Thou sustainest the living with lovingkindness, revivest the dead with great mercy, supportest the falling, healest

---

At first the Mussaf prayers were said only when one worshipped with a congregation. In time, it was made obligatory upon every individual to recite it, as much as the Morning Service.

In the Amidah of the Mussaf Service, the opening and closing benedictions are, as in the Sabbath Morning Service, the invariable first three and the last three of the daily Amidah. The Intermediate Benediction includes the Scriptural words from the Book of Numbers concerning the additional Sabbath (or Festival) offerings.

In some congregations (especially among Sefardim), the Reader recites the first three benedictions aloud with the congregation ; the Intermediate Benediction is recited in silence ; and the last three are again read aloud with the congregation. After the Mussaf Amidah, the Service closes in English congregations with En Kelohenu, Oleynu and Adon Olom.

נוֹפְלִים וְרוֹפֵא חוֹלִים וּמַתִּיר אֲסוּרִים וּמְקַיֵּם אֱמוּנָתוֹ
לִישֵׁנֵי עָפָר · מִי כָמְוֹךָ בַּעַל גְּבוּרוֹת וּמִי דְוֹמֶה לָּךְ ·
מֶלֶךְ מֵמִית וּמְחַיֶּה וּמַצְמִיחַ יְשׁוּעָה ·

On שַׁבַּת שׁוּבָה say :—

מִי כָמְוֹךָ אַב הָרַחֲמִים זוֹכֵר יְצוּרָיו לְחַיִּים בְּרַחֲמִים ·

וְנֶאֱמָן אַתָּה לְהַחֲיוֹת מֵתִים · · בָּרוּךְ אַתָּה יְיָ · מְחַיֶּה
הַמֵּתִים :

When the Reader repeats the עֲמִידָה, *the following* קְדוּשָׁה *is said.*

Reader. נַעֲרִיצְךָ וְנַקְדִּישְׁךָ כְּסוֹד שִׂיחַ שַׂרְפֵי קְדֶשׁ
הַמַּקְדִּישִׁים שִׁמְךָ בַּקֹּדֶשׁ · כַּכָּתוּב עַל יַד נְבִיאֶךָ · וְקָרָא
זֶה אֶל זֶה וְאָמַר ·

Cong. קָדוֹשׁ קָדוֹשׁ קָדוֹשׁ יְיָ צְבָאוֹת מְלֹא כָל הָאָרֶץ
כְּבוֹדוֹ :

Reader. כְּבוֹדוֹ מָלֵא עוֹלָם מְשָׁרְתָיו שׁוֹאֲלִים זֶה לָזֶה
אַיֵּה מְקוֹם כְּבוֹדוֹ · לְעֻמָּתָם בָּרוּךְ יֹאמֵרוּ ·

Cong. בָּרוּךְ כְּבוֹד יְיָ מִמְּקוֹמוֹ ·

The Kedusha. The Mussaf Sanctification has distinctive features
of its own. It dwells even more sublimely than does the Sabbath Morning
Kedusha on the majestic conception of the angels in heaven glorifying

the sick, freest the bound, and keepest thy faith to them that sleep in the dust. Who is like unto thee; Lord of mighty acts, and who resembleth thee, O King, who orderest death and restorest life, and causest salvation to spring forth ?

[*During the Ten Days of Repentance say* :—
Who is like unto thee, Father of mercy, who in mercy rememberest thy creatures unto life ?]

Yea, faithful art thou to revive the dead. Blessed art thou, O Lord, who revivest the dead.

[*When the Reader repeats the Amidah, the following up to " Thou art holy," p.* 531, *is said.*

III. "KE-DUSHA" : SANCTIFICATION OF GOD

Isaiah 6. 3

See p. 453

Ezekiel 3. 12

Reader.—We will reverence and sanctify thee according to the mystic utterance of the holy Seraphim, who sanctify thy Name in holiness, as it is written by the hand of thy prophet, And they called one unto the other and said,

Cong.—HOLY, HOLY, HOLY IS THE LORD OF HOSTS : THE WHOLE EARTH IS FULL OF HIS GLORY.

Reader.—His glory filleth the universe : his ministering angels ask one another, Where is the place of his glory ? Those over against them say, Blessed—

Cong.—BLESSED BE THE GLORY OF THE LORD FROM HIS PLACE.

the Eternal King, and it introduces Israel—the unique people on earth—proclaiming, in response to the angelic choir, the holiness and glory, the unity and sovereignty, of God's Name. This is largely done by making " Shema Yisroel ", the congregation's confession of faith, part of the Mussaf Kedusha.

The origin of this congregational proclamation is as follows. During a sixth century persecution in the Byzantine Empire, Jews were forbidden to recite the *Shema* in public worship. Government spies used to attend the synagogues on Sabbaths and Festivals, so as to prevent it forming part of the Morning Service. Chazanim would then introduce it in the Mussaf Kedusha ; and it remained an integral part of that Kedusha even when better days dawned. The people loved this public and solemn repetition of the Shema, and would not give it up, after it had once become established usage. And no wonder. " The congregational recital of the Shema Yisroel is one of the most dramatically meaningful practices of Judaism. It is a supreme occasion for expressing the thrill of being a Jew " (Kaplan).

Reader. מִמְּקוֹמוֹ הוּא יִפֶן בְּרַחֲמִים וְיָחוֹן עַם הַמְיַחֲדִים

שְׁמוֹ עֶרֶב וָבֹקֶר בְּכָל יוֹם תָּמִיד פַּעֲמַיִם בְּאַהֲבָה שְׁמַע

אוֹמְרִים ·

Cong. שְׁמַע יִשְׂרָאֵל יְיָ אֱלֹהֵינוּ יְיָ אֶחָד :

Reader. אֶחָד הוּא אֱלֹהֵינוּ הוּא אָבִינוּ הוּא מַלְכֵּנוּ הוּא

מוֹשִׁיעֵנוּ · וְהוּא יַשְׁמִיעֵנוּ בְּרַחֲמָיו שֵׁנִית לְעֵינֵי כָּל־חַי

לִהְיוֹת לָכֶם לֵאלֹהִים : *Cong.* אֲנִי יְיָ אֱלֹהֵיכֶם :

Reader. וּבְדִבְרֵי קָדְשְׁךָ כָּתוּב לֵאמֹר ·

Cong. יִמְלֹךְ יְיָ לְעוֹלָם אֱלֹהַיִךְ צִיּוֹן לְדֹר וָדֹר · הַלְלוּיָהּ :

Reader. לְדוֹר וָדוֹר נַגִּיד גָּדְלֶךָ וּלְנֵצַח נְצָחִים קְדֻשָּׁתְךָ

נַקְדִּישׁ · וְשִׁבְחֲךָ אֱלֹהֵינוּ מִפִּינוּ לֹא יָמוּשׁ לְעוֹלָם וָעֶד ·

כִּי אֵל מֶלֶךְ גָּדוֹל וְקָדוֹשׁ אָתָּה · בָּרוּךְ אַתָּה יְיָ

הָאֵל [הַמֶּלֶךְ *say* שַׁבָּת שׁוּבָה *On*] הַקָּדוֹשׁ :

אַתָּה קָדוֹשׁ וְשִׁמְךָ קָדוֹשׁ וּקְדוֹשִׁים בְּכָל־יוֹם יְהַלְלוּךָ

סֶּלָה · בָּרוּךְ אַתָּה יְיָ · הָאֵל [הַמֶּלֶךְ *say* שַׁבָּת שׁוּבָה *On*]

הַקָּדוֹשׁ :

On שַׁבָּת וְרֹאשׁ חֹדֶשׁ, *continue on p.* 542.

תִּכַּנְתָּ שַׁבָּת רָצִיתָ קָרְבְּנוֹתֶיהָ · צִוִּיתָ פֵּרוּשֶׁיהָ עִם

Whenever a Sabbath coincides with the New Moon, there is a
variation in the Intermediate Benediction. Its opening then assumes
a form quite different from that of the ordinary Sabbath; see p. 542.

SANCTIFI-CATION OF GOD   *Reader.*—From his place may he turn in mercy and be gracious unto a people who, evening and morning, twice every day, proclaim with constancy the unity of his Name, saying in love, Hear—

Deuteronomy 6. 5   *Cong.*—HEAR, O ISRAEL : THE LORD IS OUR GOD, THE LORD IS ONE.

Reader.—One is our God ; he is our Father ; he is our King ; he is our Saviour ; and he of his mercy will let us hear a second time, in the presence of all living (his promise), " To be to you for a God."

Cong.—" I AM THE LORD YOUR GOD."

Reader.—And in thy Holy Words it is written, saying,

Psalm 146. 10   *Cong.*—THE LORD SHALL REIGN FOR EVER, THY GOD, O ZION, UNTO ALL GENERATIONS. PRAISE YE THE LORD.

Reader.—Unto all generations we will declare thy greatness, and to all eternity we will proclaim thy holiness, and thy praise, O our God, shall not depart from our mouth for ever, for thou art a great and holy God and King. Blessed art thou, O Lord, | *On the Sabbath of Repentance* the holy God. | *conclude the last Blessing thus :—* | the holy King.]

Thou art holy, and thy Name is holy, and holy beings praise thee daily. (Selah.)   Blessed art thou, O Lord, the holy God.   [*On the Sabbath of Repentance, say,* the holy King.]

On Sabbath and New Moon, continue with, "Thou didst form," *p.* 543.

Thou didst institute the Sabbath, and didst favourably

THOU DIDST INSTITUTE. The Intermediate Benediction was originally the same as in the Morning Service. Only since the third century, has formal mention been made in it of the additional Sabbath sacrifices. Some centuries later, this was preceded by a prayer (יהי רצון) for the Restoration of the Temple. This prayer was in turn eventually prefaced by a brief recital (תכנת שבת) of the institution of the Sabbath and its Service. In this devotional recital each word begins with a different

סִדּוּרֵי נְסָכֶיהָ · מֵעֲנָגֶיהָ לְעוֹלָם כָּבוֹד יִנְחָלוּ · טוֹעֲמֶיהָ

חַיִּים זָכוּ · וְגַם הָאוֹהֲבִים דְּבָרֶיהָ גְּדֻלָּה בָּחָרוּ · אָז מִסִּינַי

נִצְטַוּוּ עָלֶיהָ · וַתְּצַוֵּנוּ יְיָ אֱלֹהֵינוּ לְהַקְרִיב בָּהּ קָרְבַּן מוּסַף

שַׁבָּת כָּרָאוּי : יְהִי רָצוֹן מִלְּפָנֶיךָ יְיָ אֱלֹהֵינוּ וֵאלֹהֵי

אֲבוֹתֵינוּ שֶׁתַּעֲלֵנוּ בְשִׂמְחָה לְאַרְצֵנוּ וְתִטָּעֵנוּ בִּגְבוּלֵנוּ ·

וְשָׁם נַעֲשֶׂה לְפָנֶיךָ אֶת־קָרְבְּנוֹת חוֹבוֹתֵינוּ · תְּמִידִים

כְּסִדְרָם וּמוּסָפִים כְּהִלְכָתָם · וְאֶת־מוּסַף יוֹם הַשַּׁבָּת הַזֶּה

נַעֲשֶׂה וְנַקְרִיב לְפָנֶיךָ בְּאַהֲבָה כְּמִצְוַת רְצוֹנֶךָ כְּמוֹ

שֶׁכָּתַבְתָּ עָלֵינוּ בְּתוֹרָתֶךָ עַל־יְדֵי מֹשֶׁה עַבְדֶּךָ מִפִּי כְבוֹדֶךָ

כָּאָמוּר : וּבְיוֹם הַשַּׁבָּת שְׁנֵי־כְבָשִׂים בְּנֵי־שָׁנָה תְּמִימִם

וּשְׁנֵי עֶשְׂרֹנִים סֹלֶת מִנְחָה בְּלוּלָה בַשֶּׁמֶן וְנִסְכּוֹ : עֹלַת

שַׁבָּת בְּשַׁבַּתּוֹ עַל־עֹלַת הַתָּמִיד וְנִסְכָּהּ :

יִשְׂמְחוּ בְמַלְכוּתְךָ שׁוֹמְרֵי שַׁבָּת וְקוֹרְאֵי עֹנֶג · עַם

מְקַדְּשֵׁי שְׁבִיעִי כֻּלָּם יִשְׂבְּעוּ וְיִתְעַנְּגוּ מִטּוּבֶךָ · וְהַשְּׁבִיעִי

letter of the Hebrew alphabet, but in an inverted order, beginning with
the last letter *tav*, and continuing backwards with *shin, resh, kuph,* etc.

This portion of the Mussaf Prayer has been much assailed in modern
times. " References to the sacrificial Service, and especially prayers
for its restoration, are disliked by some," wrote the Principal of Jews
College, the saintly Dr. M. Friedlander, over fifty years ago. In view of
the late origin of this prayer and in view, furthermore, that for a long
time the whole Mussaf Prayer was deemed to be voluntary for the
individual worshipper, we can quite endorse his decision : " Let
him whose heart is not with his fellow-worshippers in any of their

*IV. INTER-
MEDIATE
BENEDIC-
TION*

accept its offerings ; thou didst command its special duties with the order of its drink offerings. They that delight in it shall inherit everlasting glory; they that enjoy its happiness merit eternal life; while such as love its teachings have chosen true greatness. Already from Sinai they were commanded concerning it ; and thou hast also commanded us, O Lord our God, to bring thereon the additional offering of the Sabbath in due form. May it be thy will, O Lord our God and God of our fathers, to lead us in joy unto our land, and to plant us within our borders, where we will prepare unto thee the offerings that are obligatory for us, the daily offerings according to their order, and the additional offerings according to their rule ; and the additional offering of this Sabbath day we will prepare and offer up unto thee in love, according to the behest of thy will, as thou hast prescribed for us in thy Torah through Moses thy servant, from the mouth of thy glory, as it is said :

Numbers 28. 9

And on the Sabbath day two he-lambs of the first year without blemish, and two tenth parts of an ephah of fine flour for a meal offering, mingled with oil, and the drink offering thereof : this is the burnt offering of every Sabbath, beside the daily burnt offering and the drink offering thereof.

See p. 458

They that keep the Sabbath and call it a delight shall rejoice in thy kingdom ; the people that hallow the seventh

supplications, silently substitute his own prayers for them ; but let him not interfere with the devotion of those to whom 'the statutes of the Lord are right, rejoicing the heart; the commandments of the Lord pure, enlightening the eyes ; the judgments of the Lord true and righteous altogether' (Ps. 19. 9, 10), and who yearn for the opportunity of fulfilling Divine commandments which they cannot observe at present ". See also SACRIFICES p. 32–35.

רָצִיתָ בּוֹ וְקִדַּשְׁתּוֹ · חֶמְדַּת יָמִים אוֹתוֹ קָרָאתָ זֵכֶר
לְמַעֲשֵׂה בְרֵאשִׁית :

אֱלֹהֵינוּ וֵאלֹהֵי אֲבוֹתֵינוּ · רְצֵה בִמְנוּחָתֵנוּ · קַדְּשֵׁנוּ
בְּמִצְוֹתֶיךָ וְתֵן חֶלְקֵנוּ בְּתוֹרָתֶךָ · שַׂבְּעֵנוּ מִטּוּבֶךָ וְשַׂמְּחֵנוּ
בִּישׁוּעָתֶךָ · וְטַהֵר לִבֵּנוּ לְעָבְדְּךָ בֶּאֱמֶת · וְהַנְחִילֵנוּ יְיָ
אֱלֹהֵינוּ בְּאַהֲבָה וּבְרָצוֹן שַׁבַּת קָדְשֶׁךָ · וְיָנוּחוּ בָהּ יִשְׂרָאֵל
מְקַדְּשֵׁי שְׁמֶךָ · בָּרוּךְ אַתָּה יְיָ · מְקַדֵּשׁ הַשַּׁבָּת :

רְצֵה יְיָ אֱלֹהֵינוּ בְּעַמְּךָ יִשְׂרָאֵל וּבִתְפִלָּתָם · וְהָשֵׁב
אֶת־הָעֲבוֹדָה לִדְבִיר בֵּיתֶךָ · וְאִשֵּׁי יִשְׂרָאֵל וּתְפִלָּתָם
בְּאַהֲבָה תְקַבֵּל בְּרָצוֹן · וּתְהִי לְרָצוֹן תָּמִיד עֲבוֹדַת
יִשְׂרָאֵל עַמֶּךָ :

וְתֶחֱזֶינָה עֵינֵינוּ בְּשׁוּבְךָ לְצִיּוֹן בְּרַחֲמִים · בָּרוּךְ אַתָּה
יְיָ · הַמַּחֲזִיר שְׁכִינָתוֹ לְצִיּוֹן :

CLOSING BENEDICTIONS : THANKSGIVINGS.

These three concluding benedictions consist of prayers for the
re-establishment of the Divine Service at Jerusalem ; thanksgiving for
God's daily wonders towards us ; and a prayer for Peace and Prosperity.

"The worshipper concludes the Tefillah with benedictions for the
restoration of the Divine Glory which we hope to behold as did our
ancestors of old ; and then he should bow down in gratitude, as if he
indeed were in God's Presence and he witnessed the Israelites prostrating themselves when they beheld the Divine Glory. He should offer
thanksgiving to God for all His goodness, and conclude the Tefillah
with the benediction for peace that he may depart from the Divine
Presence in peace " (Hallevi).

day, even all of them shall be satiated and delighted with thy goodness, seeing that thou didst find pleasure in the seventh day, and didst hallow it ; thou didst call it the desirable of days, in rememberance of the creation.

SABBATH PRAYER

See p. 458

Our God and God of our fathers, accept our rest ; hallow us by thy commandments, and grant our portion in thy Torah ; satisfy us with thy goodness, and gladden us with thy salvation ; purify our hearts to serve thee in truth ; and in thy love and favour, O Lord our God, let us inherit thy holy Sabbath ; and may Israel, who sanctify thy Name, rest thereon. Blessed art thou, O Lord, who hallowest the Sabbath.

V. FOR RESTORA- TION OF TEMPLE SERVICE

See p. 461

Accept, O Lord our God, thy people Israel and their prayer ; restore the service to the inner sanctuary of thy house ; receive in love and favour both the fire offerings of Israel and their prayer ; and may the service of thy people Israel be ever acceptable unto thee.

And let our eyes behold thy return in mercy to Zion. Blessed art thou, O Lord, who restorest thy divine presence unto Zion.

Of these closing benedictions only the middle one is an expression of gratitude. It is preceded by a petition for the restoration of the Temple Service, and is followed by the Priestly Blessing. As neither of these benedictions is of a personal character, and both deal with matters that are the result of man's gratitude to and dependence on his Maker, they too are classed among the " Thanksgivings ".

V.   Fifth Benediction : *For the Temple Service.*

Even as the truth of pure Monotheism came from the Temple on Mt. Zion, so may that Sanctuary in future be the source from which will spread the true knowledge of God to all the children of men.

service. Heb. *avodah* ; originally meant the Temple ritual, and later divine worship generally.

restore the service. This phrase was formulated when the Temple had been destroyed. The concluding phrase, *who restorest thy divine presence*, was originally *For thee alone do we serve in reverence.*

מוֹדִים אֲנַחְנוּ לָךְ
שָׁאַתָּה הוּא יְיָ אֱלֹהֵינוּ
וֵאלֹהֵי אֲבוֹתֵינוּ לְעוֹלָם
וָעֶד ׳ צוּר חַיֵּינוּ מָגֵן
יִשְׁעֵנוּ אַתָּה הוּא לְדוֹר
וָדוֹר ׳ נוֹדֶה לְּךָ וּנְסַפֵּר
תְּהִלָּתֶךָ עַל חַיֵּינוּ
הַמְּסוּרִים בְּיָדֶךָ וְעַל
נִשְׁמוֹתֵינוּ הַפְּקוּדוֹת לָךְ ׳

The Congregation in an undertone—

מוֹדִים אֲנַחְנוּ לָךְ שָׁאַתָּה הוּא
יְיָ אֱלֹהֵינוּ וֵאלֹהֵי אֲבוֹתֵינוּ אֱלֹהֵי
כָל בָּשָׂר ׳ יוֹצְרֵנוּ יוֹצֵר בְּרֵאשִׁית ׳
בְּרָכוֹת וְהוֹדָאוֹת לְשִׁמְךָ הַגָּדוֹל
וְהַקָּדוֹשׁ עַל שֶׁהֶחֱיִיתָנוּ וְקִיַּמְתָּנוּ ׳
כֵּן תְּחַיֵּנוּ וּתְקַיְּמֵנוּ ׳ וְתֶאֱסוֹף
גָּלֻיּוֹתֵינוּ לְחַצְרוֹת קָדְשֶׁךָ לִשְׁמוֹר
חֻקֶּיךָ וְלַעֲשׂוֹת רְצוֹנֶךָ וּלְעָבְדְּךָ
בְּלֵבָב שָׁלֵם עַל שֶׁאֲנַחְנוּ מוֹדִים
לָךְ ׳ בָּרוּךְ אֵל הַהוֹדָאוֹת ׃

וְעַל כֻּלָּם יִתְבָּרַךְ וְיִתְרוֹמַם שִׁמְךָ מַלְכֵּנוּ תָּמִיד לְעוֹלָם
וָעֶד ׃

On עַל הַנִּסִּים *say* חֲנֻכָּה, *pp.* 150, 152.

וְעַל כֻּלָּם יִתְבָּרַךְ וְיִתְרוֹמַם שִׁמְךָ מַלְכֵּנוּ תָּמִיד לְעוֹלָם
וָעֶד ׃

On שַׁבָּת שׁוּבָה *say :—*

וּכְתוֹב לְחַיִּים טוֹבִים כָּל־בְּנֵי בְרִיתֶךָ ׃

וְכֹל הַחַיִּים יוֹדוּךָ סֶּלָה וִיהַלְלוּ אֶת־שִׁמְךָ בֶּאֱמֶת הָאֵל
יְשׁוּעָתֵנוּ וְעֶזְרָתֵנוּ סֶלָה ׳ בָּרוּךְ אַתָּה יְיָ ׳ הַטּוֹב שִׁמְךָ
וּלְךָ נָאֶה לְהוֹדוֹת ׃

VI.
THANKS-
GIVING
FOR GOD'S
UN-
FAILING
MERCIES

We give thanks unto thee, for thou art the Lord our God and the God of our fathers for ever and ever ; thou art the Rock of our lives, the Shield of our salvation through every generation. We will give thanks unto thee and declare thy praise for our lives which are committed unto thy hand, and for our souls which are in thy charge, and for thy miracles, which are daily with us, and for thy wonders and thy benefits, which are wrought at all times, evening, morn and noon. O thou who art all-good, whose mercies fail not ; thou, merciful Being, whose loving-kindnesses never cease, we have ever hoped in thee.

Congregation, in an undertone—
We give thanks unto thee, for thou art the Lord our God and the God of our fathers, the God of all flesh, our Creator and the Creator of all things in the beginning. Blessings and thanksgivings be to thy great and holy Name, because thou hast kept us in life and hast preserved us : so mayest thou continue to keep us in life and to preserve us. O gather our exiles to thy holy courts to observe thy statutes, to do thy will, and to serve thee with a perfect heart ; seeing that we give thanks unto thee. Blessed be the God to whom thanksgivings are due.

[*On Chanukah say* :—
"We thank thee also," *etc., pp.* 151, 153.]

For all these things thy Name, O our King, shall be continually blessed and exalted for ever and ever.

[*On the Sabbath of Repentance say* :—
O inscribe all the children of thy covenant for a happy life.]

And everything that liveth shall give thanks unto thee for ever, and shall praise thy Name in truth, O God, our salvation and our help. Blessed art thou, O Lord, whose Name is All-good, and unto whom it is becoming to give thanks.

At the repetition of the עֲמִידָה *by the Reader, the following is introduced* :—

אֱלֹהֵינוּ וֵאלֹהֵי אֲבוֹתֵינוּ ׳ בָּרְכֵנוּ בַּבְּרָכָה הַמְשֻׁלֶּשֶׁת בַּתּוֹרָה הַכְּתוּבָה עַל יְדֵי מֹשֶׁה עַבְדֶּךָ ׳ הָאֲמוּרָה מִפִּי אַהֲרֹן וּבָנָיו כֹּהֲנִים עַם קְדוֹשֶׁךָ ׳ כָּאָמוּר ׳ יְבָרֶכְךָ יְיָ וְיִשְׁמְרֶךָ : יָאֵר יְיָ פָּנָיו אֵלֶיךָ וִיחֻנֶּךָּ : יִשָּׂא יְיָ פָּנָיו אֵלֶיךָ וְיָשֵׂם לְךָ שָׁלוֹם :

שִׂים שָׁלוֹם טוֹבָה וּבְרָכָה חֵן וָחֶסֶד וְרַחֲמִים עָלֵינוּ וְעַל כָּל יִשְׂרָאֵל עַמֶּךָ ׳ בָּרְכֵנוּ אָבִינוּ כֻּלָּנוּ כְּאֶחָד בְּאוֹר פָּנֶיךָ ׳ כִּי בְאוֹר פָּנֶיךָ נָתַתָּ לָּנוּ יְיָ אֱלֹהֵינוּ תּוֹרַת חַיִּים וְאַהֲבַת חֶסֶד וּצְדָקָה וּבְרָכָה וְרַחֲמִים וְחַיִּים וְשָׁלוֹם ׳ וְטוֹב בְּעֵינֶיךָ לְבָרֵךְ אֶת־עַמְּךָ יִשְׂרָאֵל בְּכָל־עֵת וּבְכָל־ שָׁעָה בִּשְׁלוֹמֶךָ :

On שַׁבָּת שׁוּבָה *conclude the prayer thus* :

בְּסֵפֶר חַיִּים בְּרָכָה וְשָׁלוֹם וּפַרְנָסָה טוֹבָה נִזָּכֵר וְנִכָּתֵב לְפָנֶיךָ אֲנַחְנוּ וְכָל־עַמְּךָ בֵּית יִשְׂרָאֵל לְחַיִּים טוֹבִים וּלְשָׁלוֹם ׳ בָּרוּךְ אַתָּה יְיָ ׳ עוֹשֵׂה הַשָּׁלוֹם :

בָּרוּךְ אַתָּה יְיָ ׳ הַמְבָרֵךְ אֶת־עַמּוֹ יִשְׂרָאֵל בַּשָּׁלוֹם :

אֱלֹהַי ׳ נְצוֹר לְשׁוֹנִי מֵרָע וּשְׂפָתַי מִדַּבֵּר מִרְמָה ׳ וְלִמְקַלְלַי נַפְשִׁי תִדּוֹם וְנַפְשִׁי כֶּעָפָר לַכֹּל תִּהְיֶה : פְּתַח לִבִּי בְּתוֹרָתֶךָ וּבְמִצְוֹתֶיךָ תִּרְדּוֹף נַפְשִׁי ׳ וְכֹל הַחוֹשְׁבִים

Concluding Benediction : *For Peace.*

The prayer for Peace is the last of the "Thanksgiving" benedictions. There can be no Peace, unless it is preceded by thankfulness to God ;

[*At the repetition of the Amidah by the Reader, the following
is introduced .—*

Our God and God of our fathers, bless us with the three-fold
blessing of thy Torah written by the hand of Moses thy servant,
which was spoken by Aaron and his sons, the priests, thy holy
people, as it is said, THE LORD BLESS THEE, AND KEEP THEE : THE
LORD MAKE HIS FACE TO SHINE UPON THEE, AND BE GRACIOUS UNTO
THEE : THE LORD TURN HIS FACE UNTO THEE, AND GIVE THEE
PEACE.]

VII.
PRAYER
FOR PEACE

Grant peace, welfare, blessing, grace, lovingkindness and
mercy.unto us and unto all Israel, thy people. Bless us,
O our Father, even all of us together, with the light of thy
countenance ; for by the light of thy countenance thou
hast given us, O Lord our God, the Law of life, lovingkindness and righteousness, blessing, mercy, life and peace ;
and may it be good in thy sight to bless thy people Israel
at all times and in every hour with thy peace.

Blessed art
thou O Lord,
who blessest thy
people Israel with
peace.

On the Sabbath of Repentance say :—

In the book of life, blessing, peace and
good sustenance may we be remembered
and inscribed before thee, we and all thy
people the house of Israel, for a happy life
and for peace. Blessed art thou, O Lord, who
makest peace.

O my God ! guard my tongue from evil and my lips
from speaking guile ; and to such as curse me let my soul
be dumb, yea, let my soul be unto all as the dust. Open

even as there can be no true thankfulness, unless that is preceded by
service to God. " Only that peace has lasting worth, which is the fruit
of common gratitude and common devotion to God's Torah " (Hirsch).

In the Mishna this benediction is called the " Benediction of the
Priests ", because the Priestly Blessing was here daily recited in the
Temple. At the present day, this is done by the Reader in the paragraph preceding this benediction, except at those Mussaf Services when
the Priests bless the Congregation.

three-fold. Because it consists of three clauses.

grant peace. The prayer for peace is a Congregational restatement of
the Priestly Benediction in the form of a prayer.

עָלַי רָעָה מְהֵרָה הָפֵר עֲצָתָם וְקַלְקֵל מַחֲשְׁבוֹתָם ׃ עֲשֵׂה
לְמַעַן שְׁמֶךָ עֲשֵׂה לְמַעַן יְמִינֶךָ עֲשֵׂה לְמַעַן קְדֻשָּׁתֶךָ עֲשֵׂה
לְמַעַן תּוֹרָתֶךָ ׃ לְמַעַן יֵחָלְצוּן יְדִידֶיךָ הוֹשִׁיעָה יְמִינְךָ
וַעֲנֵנִי ׃ יִהְיוּ לְרָצוֹן אִמְרֵי־פִי וְהֶגְיוֹן לִבִּי לְפָנֶיךָ יְיָ צוּרִי
וְגֹאֲלִי ׃ עֹשֶׂה שָׁלוֹם בִּמְרוֹמָיו הוּא יַעֲשֶׂה שָׁלוֹם עָלֵינוּ
וְעַל כָּל־יִשְׂרָאֵל ׃ וְאִמְרוּ אָמֵן ׃

יְהִי רָצוֹן לְפָנֶיךָ יְיָ אֱלֹהֵינוּ וֵאלֹהֵי אֲבוֹתֵינוּ שֶׁיִּבָּנֶה בֵּית
הַמִּקְדָּשׁ בִּמְהֵרָה בְיָמֵינוּ וְתֵן חֶלְקֵנוּ בְּתוֹרָתֶךָ ׃ וְשָׁם נַעֲבָדְךָ
בְּיִרְאָה כִּימֵי עוֹלָם וּכְשָׁנִים קַדְמוֹנִיּוֹת ׃ וְעָרְבָה לַיְיָ מִנְחַת
יְהוּדָה וִירוּשָׁלָ͏ִם כִּימֵי עוֹלָם וּכְשָׁנִים קַדְמוֹנִיּוֹת ׃

קַדִּישׁ תִּתְקַבַּל, *p.* 206.

Continue with אֵין כֵּאלֹהֵינוּ, *p.* 544.

O my God. This is a private meditation of Mar, the son of Rabina
a famous rabbi of the fourth century. It is therefore written in the
singular. Through its beauty it found a place in all Rites, and became
a pendant to every Amidah when spoken silently. As the evil tongue is
the most insidious enemy of peace, this prayer follows naturally upon
the concluding petition for peace ; Psalm 34. 14.

let my soul be dumb. " Grant me forbearance unto those who deal
ill towards me, and a calm disposition unto all my fellowmen "
a prayer at once humble and dignified, marked by solemn simplicity
and true greatness (N. Remy). Even in thought we are not to hate
those that curse us. " Whosoever does not persecute them that
persecute him, whosoever takes an offence in silence, he who does
good not because of reward but out of love, he who is cheerful under
his sufferings—such are the friends of God " (Talmud).

my heart to thy Torah, and let my soul pursue thy commandments. If any design evil against me, speedily make their counsel of none effect, and frustrate their designs. Do it for the sake of thy Name, do it for the sake of thy power, do it for the sake of thy holiness, do it for the sake of thy Torah. In order that thy beloved ones may be delivered, O save by thy power, and answer me. Let the words of my mouth and the meditation of my heart be acceptable before thee, O Lord, my Rock and my Redeemer. He who maketh peace in his high places, may he make peace for us and for all Israel, and say ye, Amen.

May it be thy will, O Lord our God and God of our fathers, that the temple be speedily rebuilt in our days, and grant our portion in thy Torah. And there we will serve thee with awe, as in the days of old, and as in ancient years. Then shall the offering of Judah and Jerusalem be pleasant unto the Lord, as in the days of old, and as in ancient years.

Kaddish, p. 207.

Continue with, " There is none like our God " p. 545.

---

as the dust. This is victory over self, and has nothing in common with self-contempt. " Be not wicked in thine own esteem ", remains a primary duty for individuals as for communities ; see p. 642.

open my heart to thy Torah. " Open my heart to Thy sacred teachings, so that my conduct may be evidence of the fulfilment of Thy commandments." Only knowledge of God's Word will equip us with the moral insight and strength for such heroic conduct.

frustrate their designs. Defeat their purposes. This ends the prayer of Mar, the son of Rabina.

for thy power. lit. " for thy right hand ", *i.e.* to vindicate Thy power.

He who maketh peace. " Creator of the harmony of the spheres, mayest Thou in Thy tender love create peace for us and for all Israel." Three steps backwards, with accompanying inclinations to the left and right, formed the respectful mode of retiring from a superior. This form was transferred to the concluding verse of the Amidah, as if retiring from the presence of God (Pool).

On שַׁבָּת וְרֹאשׁ חֹדֶשׁ, this is read in place of תִּכַּנְתָּ שַׁבָּת, p. 530.

אַתָּה יָצַרְתָּ עוֹלָמְךָ מִקֶּדֶם · כִּלִּיתָ מְלַאכְתְּךָ בַּיּוֹם הַשְּׁבִיעִי ·
אָהַבְתָּ אוֹתָנוּ וְרָצִיתָ בָּנוּ וְרוֹמַמְתָּנוּ מִכָּל־הַלְּשׁוֹנוֹת · וְקִדַּשְׁתָּנוּ
בְּמִצְוֹתֶיךָ וְקֵרַבְתָּנוּ מַלְכֵּנוּ לַעֲבוֹדָתֶךָ · וְשִׁמְךָ הַגָּדוֹל וְהַקָּדוֹשׁ
עָלֵינוּ קָרָאתָ · וַתִּתֶּן־לָנוּ יְיָ אֱלֹהֵינוּ בְּאַהֲבָה שַׁבָּתוֹת לִמְנוּחָה
וְרָאשֵׁי חֳדָשִׁים לְכַפָּרָה : וּלְפִי שֶׁחָטָאנוּ לְפָנֶיךָ אֲנַחְנוּ וַאֲבוֹתֵינוּ
חָרְבָה עִירֵנוּ וְשָׁמֵם בֵּית מִקְדָּשֵׁנוּ וְגָלָה יְקָרֵנוּ וְנֻטַּל כָּבוֹד
מִבֵּית חַיֵּינוּ · וְאֵין אֲנַחְנוּ יְכוֹלִים לַעֲשׂוֹת חוֹבוֹתֵינוּ בְּבֵית
בְּחִירָתֶךָ בַּבַּיִת הַגָּדוֹל וְהַקָּדוֹשׁ שֶׁנִּקְרָא שִׁמְךָ עָלָיו מִפְּנֵי הַיָּד
שֶׁנִּשְׁתַּלְּחָה בְּמִקְדָּשֶׁךָ : יְהִי רָצוֹן מִלְּפָנֶיךָ יְיָ אֱלֹהֵינוּ וֵאלֹהֵי
אֲבוֹתֵינוּ שֶׁתַּעֲלֵנוּ בְשִׂמְחָה לְאַרְצֵנוּ וְתִטָּעֵנוּ בִּגְבוּלֵנוּ · וְשָׁם
נַעֲשֶׂה לְפָנֶיךָ אֶת־קָרְבְּנוֹת חוֹבוֹתֵינוּ תְּמִידִים כְּסִדְרָם וּמוּסָפִים
כְּהִלְכָתָם · וְאֶת־מוּסְפֵי יוֹם הַשַּׁבָּת הַזֶּה וְיוֹם רֹאשׁ הַחֹדֶשׁ
הַזֶּה נַעֲשֶׂה וְנַקְרִיב לְפָנֶיךָ בְּאַהֲבָה כְּמִצְוַת רְצוֹנֶךָ · כְּמוֹ
שֶׁכָּתַבְתָּ עָלֵינוּ בְּתוֹרָתֶךָ עַל־יְדֵי מֹשֶׁה עַבְדֶּךָ מִפִּי כְבוֹדֶךָ
כָּאָמוּר : וּבְיוֹם הַשַּׁבָּת שְׁנֵי־כְבָשִׂים בְּנֵי־שָׁנָה תְּמִימִם וּשְׁנֵי
עֶשְׂרֹנִים סֹלֶת מִנְחָה בְּלוּלָה בַשֶּׁמֶן וְנִסְכּוֹ : עֹלַת שַׁבַּת בְּשַׁבַּתּוֹ
עַל־עֹלַת הַתָּמִיד וְנִסְכָּהּ :

וּבְרָאשֵׁי חָדְשֵׁיכֶם תַּקְרִיבוּ עֹלָה לַיָי פָּרִים בְּנֵי־בָקָר שְׁנַיִם
וְאַיִל אֶחָד כְּבָשִׂים בְּנֵי־שָׁנָה שִׁבְעָה תְּמִימִם : וּמִנְחָתָם
וְנִסְכֵּיהֶם כִּמְדֻבָּר · שְׁלֹשָׁה עֶשְׂרֹנִים לַפָּר וּשְׁנֵי עֶשְׂרֹנִים לָאַיִל
וְעִשָּׂרֹן לַכֶּבֶשׂ וְיַיִן כְּנִסְכּוֹ וְשָׂעִיר לְכַפֵּר וּשְׁנֵי תְמִידִים
כְּהִלְכָתָם :

New Moons for atonement. The New Moon sin-offering atoned
for the ritual lapses of the preceding month; see p. 776. Later, the
Cabalists stressed this aspect of the ancient New Moon celebrations,
that had passed out of the consciousness of the Jew in the Dispersion.

On Sabbath and New Moon, in place of " Thou didst institute ", p. 531

IV. INTER-MEDIATE BENEDICTION Thou didst form thy world from of old ; thou hadst finished thy work on the seventh day ; thou hast loved us and taken pleasure in us, hast exalted us above all nations, hast hallowed us by thy commandments, hast brought us near, O our King, unto thy service, and called us by thy great and holy Name. Thou, O Lord our God, also gavest us in love Sabbaths for rest and New Moons for atonement. But because we sinned against thee, both we and our fathers, our city hath been laid waste, our sanctuary is desolate, our splendour hath gone into exile, and the glory hath been removed from the house of our life, so that we are not able to perform our obligations in thy chosen house, in that great and holy house which was called by thy Name, because of the hand of violence that hath been laid upon thy sanctuary. May it be thy will, O Lord our God and God of our fathers, to lead us up in joy unto our land, and to plant us within our borders, where we will prepare unto thee the offerings that are obligatory for us, the daily offerings according to their order, and the additional offerings according to their rule ; and the additional offerings of this Sabbath day and of this New Moon we will prepare and offer up unto thee in love, according to the behest of thy will, as thou hast prescribed for us in thy Torah through Moses thy servant, from the mouth of thy glory, as it

Numbers 28. 9 is said : And on the Sabbath day two he-lambs of the first year without blemish, and two tenth parts of an ephah of fine flour for a meal offering, mingled with oil, and the drink offering thereof : this is the burnt offering of every Sabbath, beside the daily burnt offering and the drink offering thereof.

Numbers 28. 11, 12 And in the beginnings of your months ye shall offer a burnt offering unto the Lord ; two young bullocks and one ram, seven he-lambs of the first year without blemish. And their meal offering and their drink offerings as hath been ordained, three tenth parts of an ephah for each bullock, and two tenth parts for the ram, and one tenth part for each lamb, with wine according to the drink offering thereof, and a he-goat wherewith to make atonement, and the two daily offerings according to their enactment.

> *the house of our life.* Is a rabbinical term for the Temple. Since the thirteenth century this same phrase בית חיים, *house of life,* " came euphemistically, and partly from a fine sense of spiritual fitness, to designate the burial ground " (Abrahams).

יִשְׂמְחוּ בְמַלְכוּתְךָ שׁוֹמְרֵי שַׁבָּת וְקוֹרְאֵי עֹנֶג ׳ עַם מְקַדְּשֵׁי
שְׁבִיעִי כֻּלָּם יִשְׂבְּעוּ וְיִתְעַנְּגוּ מִטּוּבֶךָ ׳ וְהַשְּׁבִיעִי רָצִיתָ בּוֹ
וְקִדַּשְׁתּוֹ ׳ חֶמְדַּת יָמִים אוֹתוֹ קָרָאתָ זֵכֶר לְמַעֲשֵׂה בְרֵאשִׁית :

אֱלֹהֵינוּ וֵאלֹהֵי אֲבוֹתֵינוּ ׳ רְצֵה בִמְנוּחָתֵנוּ וְחַדֵּשׁ עָלֵינוּ
בְּיוֹם הַשַּׁבָּת הַזֶּה אֶת־הַחֹדֶשׁ הַזֶּה לְטוֹבָה וְלִבְרָכָה ׳ לְשָׂשׂוֹן
וּלְשִׂמְחָה ׳ לִישׁוּעָה וּלְנֶחָמָה ׳ לְפַרְנָסָה וּלְכַלְכָּלָה ׳ לְחַיִּים
וּלְשָׁלוֹם ׳ לִמְחִילַת חֵטְא וְלִסְלִיחַת עָוֹן (during Leap Year) וּלְכַפָּרַת
פָּשַׁע) : כִּי בְעַמְּךָ יִשְׂרָאֵל בָּחַרְתָּ מִכָּל־הָאֻמּוֹת ׳ וְשַׁבַּת קָדְשְׁךָ
לָהֶם הוֹדַעְתָּ וְחָקֵּי רָאשֵׁי חֳדָשִׁים לָהֶם קָבַעְתָּ : בָּרוּךְ אַתָּה יְיָ ׳
מְקַדֵּשׁ הַשַּׁבָּת וְיִשְׂרָאֵל וְרָאשֵׁי חֳדָשִׁים :

Continue with רְצֵה, *p.* 534 *to the end of the Amidah, p.* 540.

אֵין כֵּאלֹהֵינוּ ׳ אֵין כֵּאדוֹנֵינוּ ׳ אֵין כְּמַלְכֵּנוּ ׳ אֵין
כְּמוֹשִׁיעֵנוּ : מִי כֵאלֹהֵינוּ ׳ מִי כֵאדוֹנֵינוּ ׳ מִי כְמַלְכֵּנוּ ׳
מִי כְמוֹשִׁיעֵנוּ : נוֹדֶה לֵאלֹהֵינוּ ׳ נוֹדֶה לַאדוֹנֵינוּ ׳
נוֹדֶה לְמַלְכֵּנוּ ׳ נוֹדֶה לְמוֹשִׁיעֵנוּ : בָּרוּךְ אֱלֹהֵינוּ ׳
בָּרוּךְ אֲדוֹנֵינוּ ׳ בָּרוּךְ מַלְכֵּנוּ ׳ בָּרוּךְ מוֹשִׁיעֵנוּ : אַתָּה
הוּא אֱלֹהֵינוּ ׳ אַתָּה הוּא אֲדוֹנֵינוּ ׳ אַתָּה הוּא מַלְכֵּנוּ ׳
אַתָּה הוּא מוֹשִׁיעֵנוּ ׳ אַתָּה הוּא שֶׁהִקְטִירוּ אֲבוֹתֵינוּ
לְפָנֶיךָ אֶת קְטֹרֶת הַסַּמִּים :

---

for good and for blessing. Twelve terms for joy and happiness are
here employed—one for each month of the year.

EN KELOHEYNU. One of the most popular chants of the Jewish
People. Ashkenazim sing it every Sabbath and Festival; while
Sephardim recite it also on weekdays. In the age of the Gaonim, it
was also spoken at evening services. Originally this anthem began with *mi-
kelohenu.* " Who is like our God " ? To this question, the logical answer

See p. 460

They that keep the Sabbath and call it a delight shall rejoice in thy kingdom ; the people that hallow the seventh day, even all of them shall be satiated and delighted with thy goodness, seeing that thou didst find pleasure in the seventh day, and didst hallow it ; thou didst call it the desirable of days, in remembrance of the creation.

SABBATH AND NEW MOON PRAYER

Our God and God of our fathers, accept our rest, and on this Sabbath day renew this New Moon unto us for good and for blessing, for joy and for gladness, for salvation and comfort, for sustenance and maintenance, for life and peace, for pardon of sin and forgiveness of iniquity (*during Leap Year* :—and for atonement of transgression) ; for thou hast chosen thy people Israel from among all nations, and hast made thy holy Sabbath known unto them, and hast appointed unto them statutes for the beginnings of the months. Blessed art thou, O Lord, who sanctifiest the Sabbath, Israel and the beginnings of the months. *Continue with "Accept, O Lord," p.* 535 *to the end of the Amidah, p.* 541.

EN KELO-HEYNU

There is none like our God, none like our Lord, none like our King, none like our Saviour. Who is like our God, who like our Lord, who like our King, who like our Saviour ? We will give thanks unto our God, we will give thanks unto our Lord, we will give thanks unto our King, we will give thanks unto our Saviour. Blessed be our God, blessed be our Lord, blessed be our King, blessed be our Saviour. Thou art our God, thou art our Lord, thou art our King, thou art our Saviour. Thou art he unto whom our fathers burnt the incense of spices.

is, " There is none like our God ". It continues with " Blessed be our God ", and concludes with " Thou art our God ". The later re-arrangement of the first three lines resulted in the initial Hebrew letters of those lines spelling the word אמן ("Amen"). In some communities, *En Keloheynu* is used as a table hymn on Sabbaths and Festivals.

The last line forms a transition to the passage concerning the spices. In English synagogues, the reading of that passage, as well as of the rabbinical selections that follow, is optional.

תלמוד מסכת כריתות ו'

פִּטּוּם הַקְּטֹרֶת הַצֳּרִי וְהַצִּפֹּרֶן וְהַחֶלְבְּנָה וְהַלְּבוֹנָה · מִשְׁקַל
שִׁבְעִים שִׁבְעִים מָנֶה : מֹר וּקְצִיעָה שִׁבֹּלֶת נֵרְדְּ וְכַרְכֹּם · מִשְׁקַל
שִׁשָּׁה עָשָׂר שִׁשָּׁה עָשָׂר מָנֶה · הַקֹּשְׁטְ שְׁנֵים עָשָׂר · וְקִלּוּפָה
שְׁלֹשָׁה · וְקִנָּמוֹן תִּשְׁעָה · בֹּרִית כַּרְשִׁינָה תִּשְׁעָה קַבִּין · יֵין
קַפְרִיסִין סְאִין תְּלָתָא וְקַבִּין תְּלָתָא · וְאִם אֵין לוֹ יֵין קַפְרִיסִין
מֵבִיא חֲמַר חִוַּרְיָן עַתִּיק : מֶלַח סְדוֹמִית לְבַע הַקַּב · מַעֲלֶה
עָשָׁן כָּל שֶׁהוּא : רַבִּי נָתָן אוֹמֵר אַף כִּפַּת הַיַּרְדֵּן כָּל שֶׁהוּא וְאִם
נָתַן בָּהּ דְּבַשׁ פְּסָלָהּ · אִם חִסֵּר אַחַת מִכָּל סַמָּנֶיהָ חַיָּב מִיתָה :
רַבָּן שִׁמְעוֹן בֶּן גַּמְלִיאֵל אוֹמֵר · הַצֳּרִי אֵינוֹ אֶלָּא שְׂרָף הַנּוֹטֵף
מֵעֲצֵי הַקְּטָף : בֹּרִית כַּרְשִׁינָה שֶׁשָּׁפִין בָּהּ אֶת הַצִּפֹּרֶן · כְּדֵי
שֶׁתְּהֵא נָאָה : יֵין קַפְרִיסִין שֶׁשּׁוֹרִין בּוֹ אֶת הַצִּפֹּרֶן · כְּדֵי
שֶׁתְּהֵא עַזָּה :

משנה סוף מסכת תמיד

הַשִּׁיר שֶׁהַלְוִיִּם הָיוּ אוֹמְרִים בְּבֵית הַמִּקְדָּשׁ :
בַּיּוֹם הָרִאשׁוֹן הָיוּ אוֹמְרִים · לַיְיָ הָאָרֶץ וּמְלוֹאָהּ תֵּבֵל
וְיוֹשְׁבֵי בָהּ : (כ"ד)

בַּשֵּׁנִי הָיוּ אוֹמְרִים · גָּדוֹל יְיָ וּמְהֻלָּל מְאֹד בְּעִיר אֱלֹהֵינוּ
הַר־קָדְשׁוֹ : (מ"ח)

בַּשְּׁלִישִׁי הָיוּ אוֹמְרִים · אֱלֹהִים נִצָּב בַּעֲדַת־אֵל בְּקֶרֶב אֱלֹהִים
יִשְׁפֹּט : (פ"ב)

בָּרְבִיעִי הָיוּ אוֹמְרִים · אֵל נְקָמוֹת יְיָ אֵל נְקָמוֹת הוֹפִיעַ :
(צ"ד)

בַּחֲמִישִׁי הָיוּ אוֹמְרִים · הַרְנִינוּ לֵאלֹהִים עוּזֵּנוּ הָרִיעוּ
לֵאלֹהֵי יַעֲקֹב : (פ"א)

**RABBINIC
SELEC-
TIONS :**
INCENSE

Talmud Babli: Treatise Kerithoth 6a.

The compound forming the incense consisted of balm, onycha, galbanum and frankincense, in quantities weighing seventy manehs each ; of myrrh, cassia, spikenard and saffron, each sixteen manehs by weight ; of costus twelve, of aromatic bark three, and of cinnamon nine manehs ; of lye obtained from a species of leek, nine kabs ; of Cyprus wine three seahs and three kabs : though, if Cyprus wine was not procurable, old white wine might be used ; of salt of Sodom the fourth part of a kab, and of the herb Maaleh Ashan a minute quantity. R. Nathan says, a minute quantity was also required of the odoriferous herb Cippath, that grew on the banks of the Jordan ; if, however, one added honey to the mixture, he rendered the incense unfit for sacred use, while he who, in preparing it, omitted one of its necessary ingredients, was liable to the penalty of death. Rabban Simeon, son of Gamaliel, says the balm is a resin that exudes from the wood of the balsam tree. The lye obtained from a species of leek was rubbed over the onycha to improve it, while the Cyprus wine was used to steep it in, so that its odour might be more pungent.

Mishna: End of Treatise Tamid.

*DAILY
PSALMS*

These were the Psalms which the Levites used to recite in the Temple :—

On the first day of the week they used to recite (Psalm 24), The earth is the Lord's and the fulness thereof ; the world and they that dwell therein.

On the second day (Psalm 48), Great is the Lord and exceedingly to be praised, in the city of our God, in his holy mountain.

On the third day (Psalm 82), God standeth in the congregation of the mighty ; he judgeth among the judges.

On the fourth day (Psalm 94), O Lord, thou God to whom retribution belongeth, thou God to whom retribution belongeth, shine forth.

The Day's Psalm. The custom of reciting a special psalm for each day of the week is thus seen to have been taken over from Temple. These psalms have their message for men and women of to-day. Sunday's psalm (24) asks, " Who can stand on God's holy hill ? " The answer is, " He that is clean of hand and pure of heart ". Monday's (Psalm 48) declares, " As is Thy Name, O God, so is Thy renown unto

בַּשִּׁשִּׁי הָיוּ אוֹמְרִים · יְיָ מָלָךְ גֵּאוּת לָבֵשׁ · לָבֵשׁ יְיָ עֹז
הִתְאַזָּר אַף־תִּכּוֹן תֵּבֵל בַּל־תִּמּוֹט : (צ״ב)

בַּשַּׁבָּת הָיוּ אוֹמְרִים · מִזְמוֹר שִׁיר לְיוֹם הַשַּׁבָּת : (צ״ב)
מִזְמוֹר שִׁיר לֶעָתִיד לָבֹא · לְיוֹם שֶׁכֻּלּוֹ שַׁבָּת וּמְנוּחָה
לְחַיֵּי הָעוֹלָמִים :

תלמוד מסכת ברכות

אָמַר רַבִּי אֶלְעָזָר אָמַר רַבִּי חֲנִינָא · תַּלְמִידֵי חֲכָמִים
מַרְבִּים שָׁלוֹם בָּעוֹלָם · שֶׁנֶּאֱמַר וְכָל בָּנַיִךְ לִמּוּדֵי יְיָ וְרַב
שָׁלוֹם בָּנָיִךְ · אַל תִּקְרָא בָּנָיִךְ אֶלָּא בּוֹנָיִךְ :–שָׁלוֹם רָב
לְאֹהֲבֵי תוֹרָתֶךָ וְאֵין לָמוֹ מִכְשׁוֹל : יְהִי־שָׁלוֹם בְּחֵילֵךְ שַׁלְוָה
בְּאַרְמְנוֹתָיִךְ : לְמַעַן אַחַי וְרֵעָי אֲדַבְּרָה־נָּא שָׁלוֹם בָּךְ :
לְמַעַן בֵּית־יְיָ אֱלֹהֵינוּ אֲבַקְשָׁה טוֹב לָךְ : יְיָ עֹז לְעַמּוֹ יִתֵּן
יְיָ יְבָרֵךְ אֶת־עַמּוֹ בַשָּׁלוֹם :

the ends of the earth : Thy might is full of righteousness ". Tuesday's
(Psalm 82) demands : " Defend the poor and the fatherless ; do justice
to the afflicted and the destitute ". Wednesday's (Psalm 94) asks those
who doubt the moral government of the world, " He that planted the
ear, shall He not hear ? He that formed the eye, shall He not see ? "
Thursday's (Psalm 81) expresses the hope, " O that my people would
hearken unto Me, that Israel would walk in My ways ! " Friday's
(Psalm 93) proclaims that, though the heaving waves of all the seas of
heathendom lash themselves in wild fury against the rock of God's
Throne, God reigneth and His Throne stands eternally unmoved. The
Sabbath psalm, Psalm 92, is the song of the Hereafter.

the day which will be wholly a Sabbath. A wonderful description of
the Sabbath day—a foretaste of Heaven as well as of immortality. It
is, of course, symbol and metaphor only. For the immortal life is often
conceived by the Rabbis, not as inactivity, but as continual progress,
a proceeding " from strength to strength ". One of their striking
aphorisms is, " There is no rest for the righteous ", even as there is
no peace for the wicked.

Rabbi Elazar said. The Haggadic selection that follows is a typical
example of a Rabbinic homily. It is on Peace, and is based on Isaiah

On the fifth day (Psalm 81), Exult aloud unto God our strength ; shout for joy unto the God of Jacob.

On the sixth day (Psalm 93), The Lord reigneth ; he hath robed him in majesty ; the Lord hath robed him, yea, he hath girded himself with strength : the world also is set firm, that it cannot be moved.

On the Sabbath (Psalm 92), A psalm, a song for the Sabbath Day. It is the psalm and song also for the hereafter, for the day which will be wholly a Sabbath, and will bring rest in life everlasting.

Talmud Babli.   End of Treatise Berachoth.

ON PEACE
Isaiah 54. 13

R. Elazar said in the name of R. Chanina, The disciples of the sages increase peace throughout the world, as it is said, and all thy children shall be taught of the Lord ; and great shall be the peace of thy children. (Read not here *banayich*, thy children, but *bonayich*,

Psalm 119. 165

thy builders.)—Great peace have they who love thy Torah ; and there is no stumbling for them. Peace be within thy rampart,

Psalm
122. 7, 8, 9

prosperity within thy palaces. For my brethren and companions' sakes I would fain speak peace concerning thee. For the sake of the

Psalm 29. 10

house of the Lord our God I would seek thy good. The Lord will give strength unto his people ; the Lord will bless his people with peace.

54. 13, which foretells that Zion's peace will be based not on armed force, but on the God-fearing lives of all its inhabitants.

increase peace throughout the world. This is a memorable pronouncement of the deepest importance. In seeking for a saying wherewith to sum up the spirit of Judaism and of Jewry across the ages, one would always come back to these words. The human ideal is the man of wisdom, wisdom of mind and heart ; the aim of wisdom is to establish peace (Lewissohn). Note that it demands peace not merely in the family, in the community, but throughout the world. " In God's eyes the man stands high who makes peace between fathers and children, between masters and servants, between neighbour and neighbour. But he stands highest who establishes peace among the nations " (Talmud).

read not. No actual change in the text is intended by the formula, " Read not." It is merely a homiletic admonition to understand the word *banayich* as if it were written *bonayich* ; and remember that the children of a nation are the builders of its future.

עָלֵינוּ לְשַׁבֵּחַ לַאֲדוֹן הַכֹּל לָתֵת גְּדֻלָּה לְיוֹצֵר
בְּרֵאשִׁית · שֶׁלֹּא עָשָׂנוּ כְּגוֹיֵי הָאֲרָצוֹת וְלֹא שָׂמָנוּ
כְּמִשְׁפְּחוֹת הָאֲדָמָה · שֶׁלֹּא שָׂם חֶלְקֵנוּ כָּהֶם וְגֹרָלֵנוּ
בְּכָל הֲמוֹנָם · וַאֲנַחְנוּ כֹּרְעִים וּמִשְׁתַּחֲוִים וּמוֹדִים לִפְנֵי
מֶלֶךְ מַלְכֵי הַמְּלָכִים הַקָּדוֹשׁ בָּרוּךְ הוּא · שֶׁהוּא נוֹטֶה
שָׁמַיִם וְיוֹסֵד אָרֶץ · וּמוֹשַׁב יְקָרוֹ בַּשָּׁמַיִם מִמַּעַל וּשְׁכִינַת
עֻזּוֹ בְּגָבְהֵי מְרוֹמִים : הוּא אֱלֹהֵינוּ · אֵין עוֹד · אֱמֶת
מַלְכֵּנוּ · אֶפֶס זוּלָתוֹ · כַּכָּתוּב בְּתוֹרָתוֹ · וְיָדַעְתָּ הַיּוֹם

CONCLUDING ADORATION—OLEYNU.

Since the 14th century, the Oleynu prayer—the proclamation of
God as Supreme King of the Universe, and as God of a United
Humanity—closes *all* congregational services on weekdays, Sabbaths
and Festivals. In the first half of this sublime prayer, Israel solemnly
acknowledges the Selection of Israel for the service of the Supreme
King of kings. In the second half, it voices Israel's undying hope for
the day when all idolatry shall have disappeared; when human
activities that are now directed away from God, or counter to
God, shall be turned to him and to His service; when the reign of
Righteousness shall be established among the children of men, and
mankind be one united body under the Kingship of God. "The establishment of the Kingdom of the One and Only God throughout the
entire world constitutes the Divine Plan of Salvation towards which,
according to Jewish teaching, the efforts of all the ages are tending"
(Kohler). "It was of the highest religious significance that the idea
of the future reunion of humanity in the recognition of One God, became
the culminating prayer in the Daily Service" (Elbogen).

Oleynu is not the only one of the noblest of our prayers, but also one
of the oldest, "a proof of its age being the fact, that there is no mention
in it of the restoration of the Temple and the Jewish State, which would
scarcely have been omitted had it been composed after their destruction" (Moses Mendelssohn).

Oleynu has had a strange fate, almost typical of Israel's story. The
most universalist of prayers, it has yet been the victim of slanderous
accusation and persecution, and has repeatedly been suppressed and
mutilated. Miserable apostates pretended to see an attack on

OLEYNU :
ISRAEL'S
SELECTION
TO PRO-
CLAIM GOD
AS
SUPREME
KING OF
THE
UNIVERSE

It is our duty to praise the Lord of all things, to ascribe greatness to him who formed the world in the beginning, since he hath not made us like the nations of other lands, and hath not placed us like other families of the earth, since he hath not assigned unto us a portion as unto them, nor a lot as unto all their multitude. For we bend the knee and offer worship and thanks before the supreme King of kings, the Holy One, blessed be he, who stretched forth the

Christianity in a phrase based on Isaiah 30. 7 and 45. 20 that originally formed part of the first paragraph (" they worship vain things and emptiness, and pray unto God that cannot save ", before the words *for we bend the knee*). Learned Rabbis protested against such misinterpretation, and pointed out that both the quotation from Isaiah and the Prayer itself were pre-Christian ; that Rabh, the renowned Babylonian teacher of the third century, who edited the New Year Mussaf Amidah in which Oleynu is incorporated, lived in an environment where there were no Christians at all. In vain. As late as 1656, Manasseh ben Israel deemed it necessary to devote a whole chapter in his *Vindiciae Judaeorum* to its defence. He relates that the Sultan Selim, on reading the Oleynu in a Turkish translation of the Jewish Prayer Book, said : " Truly this prayer is sufficient for all purposes ; there is no need of any other." Nevertheless, a half-century later, the Prussian Government ordered the elimination of the words from Isaiah, and prohibited the recitation of the uncensored form. Those words do not now occur in the Ashkenazi Rite.

Because of its firm proclamation of the Divine Unity, Oleynu was a favourite prayer of Jewish martyrs. " During the persecution of the Jews of Blois (France) in 1171, where many masters of the Torah died at the stake, an eye-witness wrote that the death of the saints was accompanied by a song resounding through the stillness of the night, causing the churchmen who heard it from afar to wonder at the melodious strains, the like of which they had never heard before. It was ascertained afterwards that the martyred saints had made use of the Oleynu as their dying song " (Joseph ha-Cohen in his *Vale of Tears*). These martyrs were the spiritual descendants of Rabbi Akiba—Teacher, warrior, martyr—who died with the declaration of the Unity on his lips.

not made us like the nations. Pool translates, " He has not made us heathens ". The power of a religion does not lie in what it has in common with others, but in what is peculiar to itself. There are certainly similarities between Israel's religious ideals and those of the Western peoples who have learned what is best in their religion from Israel. But it is the *differences* between them—the special emphasis and accent in the promulgation of their Message concerning the great problems and duties of life—that constitute their essential character.

וַהֲשֵׁבֹתָ אֶל־לְבָבֶךָ כִּי יְיָ הוּא הָאֱלֹהִים בַּשָּׁמַיִם מִמַּעַל וְעַל־הָאָרֶץ מִתָּחַת אֵין עוֹד:

עַל־כֵּן נְקַוֶּה לְךָ יְיָ אֱלֹהֵינוּ לִרְאוֹת מְהֵרָה בְּתִפְאֶרֶת עֻזֶּךָ · לְהַעֲבִיר גִּלּוּלִים מִן הָאָרֶץ וְהָאֱלִילִים כָּרוֹת יִכָּרֵתוּן · לְתַקֵּן עוֹלָם בְּמַלְכוּת שַׁדַּי וְכָל־בְּנֵי בָשָׂר יִקְרְאוּ בִשְׁמֶךָ · לְהַפְנוֹת אֵלֶיךָ כָּל־רִשְׁעֵי אָרֶץ: יַכִּירוּ וְיֵדְעוּ כָּל־יוֹשְׁבֵי תֵבֵל כִּי לְךָ תִּכְרַע כָּל־בֶּרֶךְ תִּשָּׁבַע כָּל־לָשׁוֹן: לְפָנֶיךָ יְיָ אֱלֹהֵינוּ יִכְרְעוּ וְיִפּוֹלוּ · וְלִכְבוֹד שִׁמְךָ יְקָר יִתֵּנוּ · וִיקַבְּלוּ כֻלָּם אֶת־עֹל מַלְכוּתֶךָ · וְתִמְלוֹךְ עֲלֵיהֶם מְהֵרָה לְעוֹלָם וָעֶד · כִּי הַמַּלְכוּת שֶׁלְּךָ הִיא וּלְעוֹלְמֵי עַד תִּמְלוֹךְ בְּכָבוֹד: כַּכָּתוּב בְּתוֹרָתֶךָ · יְיָ | יִמְלֹךְ לְעוֹלָם וָעֶד: וְנֶאֱמַר · וְהָיָה יְיָ לְמֶלֶךְ עַל־כָּל־הָאָרֶץ בַּיּוֹם הַהוּא יִהְיֶה יְיָ אֶחָד וּשְׁמוֹ אֶחָד:

These differences are of such transcendant importance that millions of their followers have been, and are willing, to agonize and die for them.

supreme King of kings. lit. " the King of the kings of kings ". This formula goes back to the Persian period of Jewish history. The rulers of Persia bore the title " king of kings ".

turn unto thyself all the wicked of the earth. All men and nations shall abandon idolatry and wickedness, falsehood and violence, and become united in their recognition of the sovereignty of God, the Holy One, as proclaimed by Israel. The Messianic hope is thus not to destroy the wicked, but to win them over to God's service ; see on Psalm 104. 35. p. 588. The Jewish Mystics dreamt of the time when Satan himself would become a good angel.

yoke of thy kingdom. The rule of Thy Kingship.

heavens and laid the foundations of the earth, the seat of whose glory is in the heavens above, and the abode of whose might is in the loftiest heights. He is our God ; there is none else : in truth he is our King ; there is none besides *Deuteronomy 4. 39* him ; as it is written in his Torah, And thou shalt know this day, and lay it to thine heart, that the Lord he is God in heaven above and upon the earth beneath : there is none else.

ISRAEL'S HOPE:
HUMANITY UNITED IN RECOGNI-TION OF THE ONE GOD We therefore hope in thee, O Lord our God, that we may speedily behold the glory of thy might, when thou wilt remove the abominations from the earth, and heathendom will be utterly destroyed, when the world will be perfected under the kingdom of the Almighty, and all the children of flesh will call upon thy Name, when thou wilt turn unto thyself all the evil-doers upon earth. Let all the inhabitants of the world perceive and know that unto thee every knee must bow, every tongue must swear allegiance. Before thee, O Lord our God, let them bow and worship ; and unto thy glorious Name let them give honour ; let them all accept the yoke of thy kingdom, and do thou reign over them speedily, and for ever and ever. For the kingdom is thine, and to all eternity thou wilt reign in glory ; as it is written *Exodus* 15. 18 in thy Torah, THE LORD SHALL REIGN FOR EVER AND EVER. *Zechariah 14. 9* And it is said, AND THE LORD SHALL BE KING OVER ALL THE EARTH : IN THAT DAY SHALL THE LORD BE ONE, AND HIS NAME ONE.

shall the Lord be One. In the undivided and undisputed worship of all men : there will be universal recognition of His sovereignty. " As the heathen shall forsake their idols, He will be One, and no strange god with Him " (Rashi). " The Jews were the only people in their world who conceived the idea of a universal religion " (Moore).

his Name One. His manifold revelations of Himself shall be acknowledged by all to be merely aspects of the one sole Name by which He made Himself known unto Israel.

This is one of the fundamental verses of the Jewish conception of the Kingdom of Heaven. It is the Messianic hope of Judaism, and the spiritual goal of human history.

קַדִּישׁ יָתוֹם

Mourner. יִתְגַּדַּל וְיִתְקַדַּשׁ שְׁמֵהּ רַבָּא בְּעָלְמָא דִּי־בְרָא

כִרְעוּתֵהּ · וְיַמְלִיךְ מַלְכוּתֵהּ בְּחַיֵּיכוֹן וּבְיוֹמֵיכוֹן וּבְחַיֵּי דִּי־

כָל־בֵּית יִשְׂרָאֵל בַּעֲגָלָא וּבִזְמַן קָרִיב · וְאִמְרוּ אָמֵן :

Cong. and Mourner. יְהֵא שְׁמֵהּ רַבָּא מְבָרַךְ לְעָלַם וּלְעָלְמֵי

עָלְמַיָּא ·

Mourner. יִתְבָּרַךְ וְיִשְׁתַּבַּח וְיִתְפָּאַר וְיִתְרֹמַם וְיִתְנַשֵּׂא

וְיִתְהַדַּר וְיִתְעַלֶּה וְיִתְהַלָּל שְׁמֵהּ דִּי־קֻדְשָׁא · בְּרִיךְ הוּא ·

לְעֵלָּא מִן־כָּל־בִּרְכָתָא וְשִׁירָתָא תֻּשְׁבְּחָתָא וְנֶחֱמָתָא דִּי־

אֲמִירָן בְּעָלְמָא · וְאִמְרוּ אָמֵן :

Cong. אָמֵן :

Mourner. יְהֵא שְׁלָמָא רַבָּא מִן־שְׁמַיָּא וְחַיִּים עָלֵינוּ וְעַל־

כָּל־יִשְׂרָאֵל · וְאִמְרוּ אָמֵן :

Cong. אָמֵן :

Mourner. עֹשֶׂה שָׁלוֹם בִּמְרוֹמָיו הוּא יַעֲשֶׂה שָׁלוֹם עָלֵינוּ

וְעַל כָּל־יִשְׂרָאֵל · וְאִמְרוּ אָמֵן :

MOURNER'S KADDISH.

The Kaddish points forward to the establishment of the Messianic Kingdom of God, with its promise of Resurrection and assurance of immortality; see p. 254–5. Great religious significance was attached by the Rabbis to the congregation repeating in unison the words, *Let His great Name be blessed for ever and to all eternity.* "As the assembly proclaim these words, the Holy One forgives" (Midrash). The son, reciting the Kaddish, is thus instrumental in calling forth the most important response in the Service. For the rise and significance of this prayer, see on THE MOURNER'S KADDISH, p. 268.

Mourner's Kaddish.

Mourner.—Magnified and sanctified be his great Name in the world which he hath created according to his will. May he establish his kingdom during your life and during your days, and during the life of all the house of Israel, even speedily and at a near time, and say ye, Amen.

Cong. and Mourner.—Let his great Name be blessed for ever and to all eternity.

Mourner.—Blessed, praised and glorified, exalted, extolled and honoured, magnified and lauded be the Name of the Holy One, blessed be he ; though he be high above all the blessings and hymns, praises and consolations, which are uttered in the world ; and say ye, Amen.

Cong.—Amen.

Mourner.—May there be abundant peace from heaven, and life for us and for all Israel ; and say ye, Amen.

Cong.—Amen.

Mourner.—He who maketh peace in his high places, may he make peace for us and for all Israel ; and say ye, Amen.

may he establish his kingdom. May He bring about the realization of all spiritual values, and transform things as they are into things as they ought to be.

let his great Name be blessed for ever and to all eternity. This is the principal Response of the Kaddish (derived from Daniel 2. 20, and analogous to Psalm 113. 2, and to the response, "Blessed be His Name whose glorious Kingdom is for ever and ever "). The Kaddish was deemed to be the hymn of hymns, and gained still greater hold upon the reverent affection of the people when it came to be looked upon as the Orphan's Prayer. In its original form, the Kaddish is of great antiquity. It antedates the Destruction of the Temple, and is echoed in the most famous Christian prayer.

consolations. The Heb. word, in addition to its general meaning of comfort in mourning, denotes the praises of God in connection with the future Messianic time and the Future Life, as well as the consolatory discourses to which the Kaddish was the conclusion.

אֲדוֹן עוֹלָם · אֲשֶׁר מָלַךְ   בְּטֶרֶם כָּל־יְצִיר נִבְרָא :

לְעֵת נַעֲשָׂה בְחֶפְצוֹ כֹּל   אֲזַי מֶלֶךְ שְׁמוֹ נִקְרָא :

וְאַחֲרֵי כִּכְלוֹת הַכֹּל   לְבַדּוֹ יִמְלוֹךְ נוֹרָא :

וְהוּא הָיָה · וְהוּא הֹוֶה ·   וְהוּא יִהְיֶה בְּתִפְאָרָה :

וְהוּא אֶחָד · וְאֵין שֵׁנִי   לְהַמְשִׁיל לוֹ לְהַחְבִּירָה :

בְּלִי רֵאשִׁית בְּלִי תַכְלִית ·   וְלוֹ הָעֹז וְהַמִּשְׂרָה :

וְהוּא אֵלִי · וְחַי גּוֹאֲלִי ·   וְצוּר חֶבְלִי בְּעֵת צָרָה :

וְהוּא נִסִּי וּמָנוֹס לִי ·   מְנָת כּוֹסִי בְּיוֹם אֶקְרָא :

בְּיָדוֹ אַפְקִיד רוּחִי ·   בְּעֵת אִישַׁן וְאָעִירָה :

וְעִם רוּחִי גְּוִיָּתִי ·   יְיָ לִי וְלֹא אִירָא :

ADON OLOM is the most .popular hymn added, to our Liturgy since Bible times. Because of its beauty of form, simplicity of language, and sublimity of religious thought, it has been embodied in the various Rites all over the world. Its author is said by some to be Solomon ibn Gabirol (1021–1058), the renowned Spanish-Jewish poet, hymn-writer and philosopher. The translation is by Israel Zangwill.

Its appeal is universal. " Every fresh discovery confirms the fact that in all Nature's infinite variety there is one single Principle at work, One Power which is of no beginning and no end ; that has existed before all things were formed, and will remain when all is gone ; the Source and Origin of all, and yet in Itself beyond any conception or image that man can form " (Haffkine). Adon Olom is at the same time the supreme expression of absolute trust in God. The Creator of the universe, and its eternal Ruler, is also man's Guardian, Friend and Redeemer. In life and death we, confidently place our destiny in His hands.

Lord of the world, He reigned alone
While yet the universe was naught,
When by His will all things were wrought,
Then first His sov'ran name was known.

And when the All shall cease to be,
In dread lone splendour He shall reign,
He was, he is, He shall remain
In glorious eternity.

For He is one, no second shares
His nature or His loneliness ;
Unending and beginningless,
All strength is His, all sway He bears.

He is the living God to save,
My Rock while sorrow's toils endure,
My banner and my stronghold sure,
The cup of life whene'er I crave.

I place my soul within His palm
Before I sleep as when I wake,
And though my body I forsake,
Rest in the Lord in fearless calm.

He is the living God to save. The Hebrew phrase is based on Job 19. 25, " I know that my Redeemer liveth ".

my Rock. Like a mountain-stronghold, an impregnable Refuge.

banner. The figure is that of a rallying-point fixed on one of the mountain strongholds.

cup. Symbolic of all the wants of the worshipper ; Psalm 42. 2.

within His palm. Based on Psalm 31. 6 (" Into Thy hand I commend my spirit ; Thou hast redeemed me, O Lord God of truth ").

in fearless calm. Adon Olom is the closing hymn of the Prayers before Retiring to Rest at night, and is often sung by those who watch the last moments of one who is departing this life.

שִׁיר הַיִּחוּד לְיוֹם הַשַּׁבָּת :

n some Congregations the following is said before בָּרוּךְ שֶׁאָמַר, *p.* 50.

אָז בַּיּוֹם הַשְּׁבִיעִי נַחְתָּ • יוֹם הַשַּׁבָּת עַל כֵּן בֵּרַכְתָּ :

וְעַל כָּל פּוֹעַל תְּהִלָּה עֲרוּכָה • חֲסִידֶיךָ בְּכָל עֵת יְבָרְכוּכָה :

בָּרוּךְ יְיָ יוֹצֵר כֻּלָּם • אֱלֹהִים חַיִּים וּמֶלֶךְ עוֹלָם :

כִּי מֵעוֹלָם עַל עֲבָדֶיךָ רֹב רַחֲמֶיךָ וַחֲסָדֶיךָ :

וּבְמִצְרַיִם הַחִלּוֹת לְהוֹדִיעַ כִּי מְאֹד נַעֲלֵיתָ

עַל כָּל אֱלֹהִים • בַּעֲשׂוֹתְךָ בָהֶם שְׁפָטִים גְּדֹלִים וּבֵאלֹהֵיהֶם :

בִּבְקָעֲךָ יַם סוּף עַמְּךָ רָאוּ הַיָּד הַגְּדוֹלָה • וַיִּירָאוּ :

נִחַנְךָ עַמְּךָ לַעֲשׂוֹת לָךְ שֵׁם תִּפְאֶרֶת • לְהַרְאוֹת גָּדְלְךָ :

וְדִבַּרְתָּ עִמָּם מִן הַשָּׁמַיִם • וְגַם הֶעָבִים נָטְפוּ מָיִם :

יָדַעְתָּ לֶכְתָּם בַּמִּדְבָּר • בְּאֶרֶץ צִיָּה אִישׁ לֹא עָבָר :

תַּתָּה לְעַמְּךָ דָּגָן שָׁמַיִם • וּבֶעָפָר שְׁאֵר וּמָצוּר מָיִם :

תְּגָרֵשׁ גּוֹיִם רַבִּים עַמִּים • יִירְשׁוּ אַרְצָם וַעֲמַל לְאֻמִּים :

UNITY HYMN FOR THE SABBATH. There are seven such hymns, one for each day of the week. They are variously attributed to Judah the Pious (see p. 214), or to his father, Samuel. S. J. Rapoport believes the author to have been Berachya ha-Nakdan, whom some hold to be identical with Benedict of Oxford, a thirteenth century Anglo-Jewish fabulist.

The following rendering by Mrs. Lucas reproduces the substance of the poem:—

> Of old Thou didst the Sabbath bless and praise,
> Because thereon Thou didst Thy work behold,
> Completed in the sun's new-kindled rays
> Of old.

UNITY HYMN FOR THE SABBATH DAY.

In some Congregations the following is said before " Blessed be he who spake," p. 51.

HYMN OF
UNITY

Of old thou didst rest on the seventh day ; thou didst therefore bless the Sabbath.

For every work of thine praise is prepared for thee ; thy loving ones bless thee at all times.

Blessed be the Lord, the Maker of them all, the living God and everlasting King.

For from of old there hath rested upon thy servants the abundance of thy mercies and thy lovingkindnesses.

But in Egypt thou didst begin to make known that thou art exalted far

Above all gods, when thou didst execute great judgments upon the Egyptians and upon their gods.

When thou didst cleave the Red Sea, thy people saw thy great hand, and they feared.

Thou didst guide thy people, so that thou mightest make unto thyself a name of glory to manifest thy greatness.

Thou spakest also with them from the heavens, when the clouds dropped water.

Thou knewest their wanderings in the wilderness, in a land of drought where none passed through.'

Thou gavest to thy people the corn of heaven, flesh abundant as the dust, and water from the rock.

Thou didst drive out many nations, and they took possession of their land and of the labour of the peoples ;

Bless Thou this day with mercies manifold
Thy people, that in love and awe obeys
Thy word and chants Thy righteousness untold.

Lord, we desire to do Thy will always !
Make pure our hearts like thrice refined gold,
And these our prayers accept as in the days
Of old.

In the Hymn of Unity for the Third Day, a scribe's error has led to misunderstanding. The correct reading is אַף כֹּל טוֹפָנָא לֹא יִטְמְנוּךְ— " No Flood can sweep Thee away " (Onkelos on Genesis 6. 17 translates מבול by טוֹפָנָא.)

בַּעֲבוּר יִשְׁמְרוּ חֻקִּים וְתוֹרוֹת ׳ אִמְרוֹת יְיָ אֲמָרוֹת טְהוֹרוֹת :

וַיִּתְעַדְּנוּ בְּמִרְעֶה שָׁמֵן ׳ וּמֵחַלָּמִישׁ צוּר פַּלְגֵי שָׁמֶן :

בְּנוּחָם בָּנוּ עִיר קָדְשֶׁךָ ׳ וַיְפָאֲרוּ בֵּית מִקְדָּשֶׁךָ :

נֹתֹאמַר פֹּה אֵשֵׁב לְאֹרֶךְ יָמִים ׳ צֵידָהּ בָּרֵךְ אֲבָרֵךְ :

כִּי שָׁם יִזְבְּחוּ זִבְחֵי צֶדֶק ׳ אַף כֹּהֲנֶיךָ יִלְבְּשׁוּ צֶדֶק :

וּבֵית הַלֵּוִי נְעִימוֹת יְזַמֵּרוּ ׳ לְךָ יִתְרוֹעֲעוּ אַף יָשִׁירוּ :

בֵּית יִשְׂרָאֵל וְיִרְאֵי יְיָ ׳ יְכַבְּדוּ וְיוֹדוּ שְׁמְךָ יְיָ :

הֵטִיבוֹתָ מְאֹד לָרִאשׁוֹנִים ׳ כֵּן תֵּיטִיב גַּם לָאַחֲרוֹנִים :

יְיָ תָּשִׂישׂ נָא עָלֵינוּ ׳ כַּאֲשֶׁר שַׂשְׂתָּ עַל אֲבוֹתֵינוּ ׳

אוֹתָנוּ לְהַרְבּוֹת וּלְהֵיטִיב ׳ וְנוֹדֶה לְךָ לְעוֹלָם כִּי תֵיטִיב :

יְיָ תִּבְנֶה עִירְךָ מְהֵרָה ׳ כִּי עָלֶיהָ שִׁמְךָ נִקְרָא :

וְקֶרֶן דָּוִד תַּצְמִיחַ בָּהּ ׳ וְתִשְׁכּוֹן לְעוֹלָם יְיָ בְּקִרְבָּהּ :

זִבְחֵי צֶדֶק שָׁמָּה נִזְבָּחָה ׳ וְכִימֵי קֶדֶם תֶּעֱרַב מִנְחָה :

וּבְרֵךְ עַמְּךָ בְּאוֹר פָּנֶיךָ ׳ כִּי חֲפֵצִים לַעֲשׂוֹת רְצוֹנֶךָ :

וּכִרְצוֹנְךָ תַּעֲשֶׂה חֲפָצֵנוּ ׳ הַבֶּט נָא עַמְּךָ כֻּלָּנוּ :

בְּחַרְתָּנוּ הֱיוֹת לְךָ לְעַם סְגֻלָּה ׳ עַל עַמְּךָ בִרְכָתְךָ סֶּלָה :

וְתָמִיד נְסַפֵּר תְּהִלָּתֶךָ ׳ וּנְהַלֵּל לְשֵׁם תִּפְאַרְתֶּךָ :

וּמִבְרְכָתְךָ עַמְּךָ יְבֹרָךְ ׳ כִּי אֵת כָּל אֲשֶׁר תְּבָרֵךְ מְבֹרָךְ :

וַאֲנִי בְּעוֹדִי אֲהַלְלָה בּוֹרְאִי ׳ וַאֲבָרְכֵהוּ כָּל יְמֵי צְבָאִי :

יְהִי שֵׁם יְיָ מְבֹרָךְ לְעוֹלָם ׳ מִן הָעוֹלָם וְעַד הָעוֹלָם :

That they might observe thy statutes and laws, the words of the Lord, which are pure words.

And they delighted themselves with fat pastures, and with rivers of oil from the flinty rock.

When they rested, they built thy holy city, and adorned the house of thy sanctuary.

Then thou saidst, Here will I dwell for length of days ; I will surely bless her provision.

There they shall sacrifice sacrifices of righteousness : thy priests also shall be clothed with righteousness.

The house of Levi also shall chant pleasant songs ; they shall shout for joy and sing unto thee.

The house of Israel and they that fear the Lord shall give glory and thanks unto thy Name, O Lord.

Thou hast dealt out exceeding kindness to the earliest ages ; deal thus kindly also with the latest.

O Lord, rejoice over us, even as thou didst rejoice over our fathers,

To multiply us and deal kindly with us ; and we will for ever give thanks unto thee for thy goodness.

O Lord, rebuild thy city speedily, for it is called by thy Name.

And make the might of David to flourish therein, and dwell in the midst thereof for ever, O Lord.

There we will offer sacrifices of righteousness, and there may our oblation be pleasant as in former days.

O bless thy people with the light of thy countenance ; for they desire to do thy will.

And in thy good will fulfil our desire ; look, we beseech thee, we are thy people, all of us.

Thou hast chosen us to be unto thee a treasured people : let thy blessing be upon thy people for ever.

And we will continually declare thy praise, and praise thy glorious Name.

Of thy blessing let thy people be blessed, for every one whom thou blessest is blessed.

As for me, while I have my being, I will praise my Creator, and I will bless him all the days of my appointed time.

Psalm 113. 2   Let the Name of the Lord be blessed for ever, from everlasting even to everlasting.

כְּכָתוּב ׳ בָּרוּךְ יְיָ אֱלֹהֵי יִשְׂרָאֵל מִן הָעוֹלָם וְעַד הָעוֹלָם ׳
וַיֹּאמְרוּ כָל הָעָם אָמֵן וְהַלֵּל לַיָי: עָנֵת דָּנִיֵּאל וְאָמַר ׳ לֶהֱוֵא
שְׁמֵהּ דִּי אֱלָהָא מְבָרַךְ מִן עָלְמָא וְעַד עָלְמָא דִּי חָכְמְתָא
וּגְבוּרְתָּא דִּי לֵהּ הִיא: וְנֶאֱמַר ׳ וַיֹּאמְרוּ הַלְוִיִּם יֵשׁוּעַ וְקַדְמִיאֵל
בָּנִי חֲשַׁבְנְיָה שֵׁרֵבְיָה הוֹדִיָּה שְׁבַנְיָה פְתַחְיָה ׳ קוּמוּ בָּרֲכוּ אֶת
יְיָ אֱלֹהֵיכֶם מִן הָעוֹלָם עַד הָעוֹלָם וִיבָרֲכוּ שֵׁם כְּבוֹדֶךָ וּמְרוֹמַם
עַל כָּל בְּרָכָה וּתְהִלָּה: וְנֶאֱמַר ׳ בָּרוּךְ יְיָ אֱלֹהֵי יִשְׂרָאֵל מִן
הָעוֹלָם וְעַד הָעוֹלָם ׳ וְאָמַר כָּל הָעָם אָמֵן הַלְלוּיָהּ: וְנֶאֱמַר ׳
וַיְבָרֶךְ דָּוִיד אֶת יְיָ לְעֵינֵי כָּל הַקָּהָל וַיֹּאמֶר דָּוִיד ׳ בָּרוּךְ אַתָּה
יְיָ אֱלֹהֵי יִשְׂרָאֵל אָבִינוּ מֵעוֹלָם וְעַד עוֹלָם :

שִׁיר הַכָּבוֹד, p. 214.

מִזְמוֹר שִׁיר לְיוֹם הַשַּׁבָּת, p. 360.

קַדִּישׁ יָתוֹם, p.

1 Chronicles 16. 36 — As it is written: Blessed be the Lord, the God of Israel, from everlasting even to everlasting. And all the people said, Amen, *Daniel 2. 20* — and praised the Lord. Daniel answered and said, Blessed be the Name of God for ever and ever: for wisdom and might are his. *Nehemiah 9. 5* — And it is said: Then the Levites, Jeshua, Kadmiel, Bani, Hashabneiah, Sherebiah, Hodiah, Shebaniah, and Pethahiah said, Stand up and bless the Lord your God from everlasting to everlasting: and let them bless thy glorious Name, that is exalted above all *Psalm 106. 48* — blessing and praise. And it is said: Blessed be the Lord, the God of Israel, from everlasting even to everlasting: and let all the people *1 Chronicles 29. 10* — say, Amen: praise ye the Lord. And it is said, And David blessed the Lord in the presence of all the congregation: and David said, Blessed art thou, O Lord, the God of Israel our father, from everlasting to everlasting.

Hymn of Glory, p. 215.

Psalm 92, A Psalm, a Song for the Sabbath Day, p. 361.

Mourner's Kaddish, p. 555.

AS IT IS WRITTEN. This is a collection of all the doxologies in which occurs the expression from *everlasting to everlasting*—an assertion of immortality.

The Mishna records that in the Temple, the concluding benediction of every prayer contained the phrase מן העולם "from everlasting;" e.g. Blessed art Thou, O Lord, *from everlasting*, Who hearest prayer. "But then the heretics grew bold. They asserted that the words מן העולם meant 'from the world', and declared that there was only *one* world, denying the Hereafter. Thereupon, the Sages ordained that the concluding words of each benediction in the Temple Service shall be, Blessed art thou, O Lord, *from everlasting to everlasting* מן העולם ועד העולם" (Berachoth IX, 5).

סדר קדוש לסעודת שחרית בשבת:

שמות ל'א ט'ד'ז

וְשָׁמְרוּ בְנֵי־יִשְׂרָאֵל אֶת־הַשַּׁבָּת לַעֲשׂוֹת אֶת־הַשַּׁבָּת לְדֹרֹתָם בְּרִית עוֹלָם: בֵּינִי וּבֵין בְּנֵי יִשְׂרָאֵל אוֹת הִוא לְעֹלָם כִּי שֵׁשֶׁת יָמִים עָשָׂה יְהוָה אֶת־הַשָּׁמַיִם וְאֶת־הָאָרֶץ וּבַיּוֹם הַשְּׁבִיעִי שָׁבַת וַיִּנָּפַשׁ:

שמות כ' ח'־י'א

זָכוֹר אֶת־יוֹם הַשַּׁבָּת לְקַדְּשׁוֹ: שֵׁשֶׁת יָמִים תַּעֲבֹד וְעָשִׂיתָ כָּל־מְלַאכְתֶּךָ: וְיוֹם הַשְּׁבִיעִי שַׁבָּת לַיהוָה אֱלֹהֶיךָ לֹא־תַעֲשֶׂה כָל־מְלָאכָה אַתָּה וּבִנְךָ וּבִתֶּךָ עַבְדְּךָ וַאֲמָתְךָ וּבְהֶמְתֶּךָ וְגֵרְךָ אֲשֶׁר בִּשְׁעָרֶיךָ: כִּי שֵׁשֶׁת־יָמִים עָשָׂה יְהוָה אֶת־הַשָּׁמַיִם וְאֶת־הָאָרֶץ אֶת־הַיָּם וְאֶת־כָּל־ אֲשֶׁר בָּם וַיָּנַח בַּיּוֹם הַשְּׁבִיעִי עַל־כֵּן בֵּרַךְ יְהוָה אֶת־יוֹם הַשַּׁבָּת וַיְקַדְּשֵׁהוּ:

בָּרוּךְ אַתָּה יְיָ אֱלֹהֵינוּ מֶלֶךְ הָעוֹלָם · בּוֹרֵא פְּרִי הַגָּפֶן:

בָּרוּךְ אַתָּה יְיָ אֱלֹהֵינוּ מֶלֶךְ הָעוֹלָם · הַמּוֹצִיא לֶחֶם מִן הָאָרֶץ:

KIDDUSH FOR SABBATH MORNING.

Exodus xxxi. 16, 17

And the children of Israel shall keep the Sabbath, to observe the Sabbath throughout their generations, for an everlasting covenant. It is a sign between me and the children of Israel for ever, that in six days the Lord made the heavens and the earth, and on the seventh day he rested, and ceased from his work.

Exodus xx. 8–11.

Remember the sabbath day to keep it holy. Six days shalt thou labour, and do all thy work : but the seventh day is a sabbath unto the Lord thy God : in it thou shalt not do any work, thou, nor thy son, nor thy daughter, thy manservant, nor thy maidservant, nor thy cattle, nor thy stranger that is within thy gates : for in six days the Lord made heaven and earth, the sea and all that is therein, and rested on the seventh day : wherefore the Lord blessed the sabbath day and hallowed it.

Blessed art thou, O Lord our God, King of the universe, who createst the fruit of the vine.

Blessed art thou, O Lord our God, King of the universe, who bringest forth bread from the earth.

KIDDUSH FOR SABBATH MORNING.

In this Kiddush, which is of later origin, and of less importance than the Evening Kiddush, the simple blessing over wine was deemed sufficient. In order to lend it additional significance, Exodus 31. 16, 17 was recited (some add, or substitute, Exodus 20. 8–11), and was known as the " Great Kiddush ". Once again, the Israelite is reminded of the fundamental religious truth, that the universe is not the product of chance, but is the work of a Divine Power that commands both labour and rest unto the children of men.

fruit of the vine. In the absence of wine, another beverage may be used, with its appropriate benediction.

זמירות לשבת :

יוֹם זֶה לְיִשְׂרָאֵל אוֹרָה וְשִׂמְחָה · שַׁבָּת מְנוּחָה :

צִוִּית פִּקּוּדִים בְּמַעֲמַד סִינַי · שַׁבָּת וּמוֹעֲדִים לִשְׁמוֹר

בְּכָל־שָׁנַי · לַעֲרוֹךְ לְפָנַי מַשְׂאֵת וַאֲרוּחָה · שַׁבָּת

מְנוּחָה : יום זה

חֶמְדַּת הַלְּבָבוֹת לְאֻמָּה שְׁבוּרָה · לִנְפָשׁוֹת נִכְאָבוֹת

נְשָׁמָה יְתֵרָה · לְנֶפֶשׁ מְצֵרָה יָסִיר אֲנָחָה · שַׁבָּת

מְנוּחָה : יום זה

קִדַּשְׁתָּ בֵּרַכְתָּ אוֹתוֹ מִכָּל־יָמִים · בְּשֵׁשֶׁת כִּלִּיתָ מְלֶאכֶת

עוֹלָמִים · בּוֹ מָצְאוּ עֲגוּמִים הַשְׁקֵט וּבִטְחָה · שַׁבָּת

מְנוּחָה : יום זה

לְאִסּוּר מְלָאכָה צִוִּיתָנוּ נוֹרָא · אֶזְכֶּה הוֹד מְלוּכָה אִם

שַׁבָּת אֶשְׁמוֹרָה · אַקְרִיב שַׁי לַמּוֹרָא מִנְחָה מֶרְקָחָה ·

שַׁבָּת מְנוּחָה : יום. זה

חַדֵּשׁ מִקְדָּשֵׁנוּ · זָכְרָה נֶחֱרֶבֶת · טוּבְךָ מוֹשִׁיעֵנוּ תְּנָה

לַנֶּעֱצֶבֶת · בְּשַׁבָּת יוֹשֶׁבֶת בְּזֶמִיר וּשְׁבָחָה · שַׁבָּת

מְנוּחָה :

יוֹם זֶה לְיִשְׂרָאֵל אוֹרָה וְשִׂמְחָה · שַׁבָּת מְנוּחָה :

SABBATH TABLE HYMNS.

This day is for Israel light and rejoicing,
A Sabbath of rest.
Thou badest us standing assembled at Sinai
  That all the years through we should keep thy
  behest—
To set out a table full-laden, to honour
  The Sabbath of rest. *This day, etc.*

Treasure of heart for the broken people,
  Gift of new soul for the souls distrest,
Soother of sighs for the prisoned spirit—
  A Sabbath of rest. *This day, etc.*

When the work of the worlds in their wonder was
  finished,
  Thou madest this day to be holy and blest,
And those heavy-laden found safety and stillness,
  A Sabbath of rest. *This day, etc.*

If I keep thy command I inherit a kingdom,
  If I treasure the Sabbath I bring thee the best—
The noblest of offerings, the sweetest of incense—
  A Sabbath of rest. *This day, etc.*

Restore us our shrine—O remember our ruin
  And save now and comfort the sorely opprest
Now sitting at Sabbath, all singing and praising
  The Sabbath of rest. *This day, etc.*

The Sabbath meal is, as a rule, also accompanied by TABLE HYMNS.
Two of these appeared on pp. 410–413. Of the two following the first is
by Isaac Luria, the great sixteenth century mystic.

THIS DAY IS FOR ISRAEL. It describes the delight of the Sabbath,
and the goodly reward for those who honour and keep the Sacred Day.

gift of a new soul. This introduces the idea of the *oversoul*, which
resides in man during the Sabbath; *i.e.* the Sabbatical quietude and
delight raise the soul, as it were, to a higher spiritual sphere; see p. 340.

כִּי אֶשְׁמְרָה שַׁבָּת אֵל יִשְׁמְרֵנִי · אוֹת הִיא לְעוֹלְמֵי

עַד בֵּינוֹ וּבֵינִי :

אָסוּר מְצֹא חֵפֶץ מֵעֲשׂוֹת דְּרָכִים · גַּם מִלְּדַבֵּר בּוֹ

דִּבְרֵי צְרָכִים · דִּבְרֵי סְחוֹרָה אַף דִּבְרֵי מְלָכִים ·

אֶהְגֶּה בְּתוֹרַת אֵל וּתְחַכְּמֵנִי :   כי אשמרה

בּוֹ אֶמְצְאָה תָמִיד נֹפֶשׁ לְנַפְשִׁי · הִנֵּה לְדוֹר רִאשׁוֹן

נָתַן קְדוֹשִׁי מוֹפֵת · בְּתֵת לֶחֶם מִשְׁנֶה בַּשִּׁשִּׁי · כָּכָה

בְּכָל-שִׁשִּׁי יַכְפִּיל מְזוֹנִי :   כי אשמרה

רָשַׁם בְּדָת הָאֵל חוֹק אֶל-סְגָנָיו · בּוֹ לַעֲרוֹךְ לֶחֶם

פָּנִים לְפָנָיו · גַּם בּוֹ לְהִתְעַנּוֹת עַל פִּי נְבוֹנָיו אָסוּר ·

לְבַד מִיּוֹם כִּפּוּר עֲוֹנִי :   כי אשמרה

הוּא יוֹם מְכֻבָּד הוּא יוֹם תַּעֲנוּגִים · לֶחֶם וְיַיִן טוֹב

בָּשָׂר וְדָגִים · מִתְאַבְּלִים בּוֹ הֵם אָחוֹר נְסוּגִים · כִּי

יוֹם שְׂמָחוֹת הוּא וַיְשַׂמְּחֵנִי :   כי אשמרה

מֵחֵל מְלָאכָה בּוֹ סוֹפוֹ לְהַכְרִית · עַל כֵּן אֲכַבֵּס בּוֹ

לִבִּי כְּבֹרִית · אֶתְפַּלְלָה אֶל-אֵל עַרְבִית וְשַׁחֲרִית ·

מוּסָף וְגַם מִנְחָה הוּא יַעֲנֵנִי :   כי אשמרה

If we the Sabbath keep with faithful heart,
The Lord will Israel keep with love divine ;
Of his good grace and our true loyalty,
O let this day for ever prove the sign!

The daily round its restless turmoil ends,
Our ears are closed to worldly battle-cries ;
From toil set free, the hour we dedicate
To ponder on the Law that maketh wise. *If we, etc.*

Then wondrous memories refresh our soul,
Of manna, on our sires conferred of yore ;
For us, as for our fathers, Heaven provides
A double portion for the Sabbath store. *If we, etc.*

The shew-bread every week the Priests arrayed
Anew upon the Table, 'twas God's word ;
So we nor grieve nor fast on Sabbath days,
But feast around the Table of the Lord. *If we, etc.*

O honoured day, that sets our heart aglow !
O day of joy, ordained to make us glad !
With bread and wine we greet thee and good cheer,
A traitor he, whose Sabbath heart is sad ! *If we, etc.*

At eve and morn and noon our prayers ascend,
A loving answer God on us bestows ;
Our heart with Sabbath balsam let us lave,
And find a solace for all earthly woes ! *If we, etc.*

If we the Sabbath. The author is Abraham ibn Ezra (1092–1167),
the famous Spanish-Jewish Bible commentator, grammarian, philosopher, traveller, and poet who enriched the Liturgy with several notable
hymns. He visited England in 1158, and here wrote his famous
" Epistle on the Sabbath ".

תְּפִלַת מִנְחָה לְשַׁבָּת:

אַשְׁרֵי, p. 514.

וּבָא לְצִיּוֹן גּוֹאֵל וּלְשָׁבֵי פֶשַׁע בְּיַעֲקֹב נְאֻם יְיָ: וַאֲנִי זֹאת בְּרִיתִי אוֹתָם אָמַר יְיָ רוּחִי אֲשֶׁר עָלֶיךָ וּדְבָרַי אֲשֶׁר־שַׂמְתִּי בְּפִיךָ לֹא יָמוּשׁוּ מִפִּיךָ וּמִפִּי זַרְעֲךָ וּמִפִּי זֶרַע זַרְעֲךָ אָמַר יְיָ מֵעַתָּה וְעַד־עוֹלָם:

וְאַתָּה קָדוֹשׁ יוֹשֵׁב תְּהִלּוֹת יִשְׂרָאֵל: וְקָרָא זֶה אֶל־זֶה וְאָמַר קָדוֹשׁ קָדוֹשׁ קָדוֹשׁ יְיָ צְבָאוֹת מְלֹא כָל־הָאָרֶץ כְּבוֹדוֹ: וּמְקַבְּלִין דֵּן מִן־דֵּן וְאָמְרִין קַדִּישׁ בִּשְׁמֵי מְרוֹמָא עִלָּאָה בֵּית שְׁכִינְתֵּהּ · קַדִּישׁ עַל־אַרְעָא עוֹבַד גְּבוּרְתֵּהּ · קַדִּישׁ לְעָלַם וּלְעָלְמֵי עָלְמַיָּא · יְיָ צְבָאוֹת מַלְיָא כָל־אַרְעָא זִיו יְקָרֵהּ: וַתִּשָּׂאֵנִי רוּחַ וָאֶשְׁמַע אַחֲרַי קוֹל רַעַשׁ גָּדוֹל בָּרוּךְ כְּבוֹד־יְיָ מִמְּקוֹמוֹ: וּנְטַלְתַּנִי רוּחָא וְשִׁמְעֵת בַּתְרַי קָל זִיעַ שַׂגִּיא דִי מְשַׁבְּחִין וְאָמְרִין · בְּרִיךְ יְקָרָא דִי יְיָ מֵאֲתַר בֵּית שְׁכִינְתֵּהּ: יְיָ ׀ יִמְלֹךְ לְעֹלָם וָעֶד: יְיָ מַלְכוּתֵהּ קָאֵם לְעָלַם וּלְעָלְמֵי עָלְמַיָּא: יְיָ אֱלֹהֵי אַבְרָהָם יִצְחָק וְיִשְׂרָאֵל אֲבוֹתֵינוּ · שָׁמְרָה־זֹּאת לְעוֹלָם לְיֵצֶר מַחְשְׁבוֹת לְבַב עַמֶּךָ וְהָכֵן לְבָבָם אֵלֶיךָ: וְהוּא רַחוּם יְכַפֵּר עָוֹן וְלֹא יַשְׁחִית וְהִרְבָּה לְהָשִׁיב אַפּוֹ וְלֹא יָעִיר כָּל־חֲמָתוֹ: כִּי־אַתָּה אֲדֹנָי טוֹב וְסַלָּח וְרַב־חֶסֶד לְכָל־קֹרְאֶיךָ:

AFTERNOON SERVICE FOR SABBATHS AND FESTIVALS.

MINCHA SERVICE

Say " Happy are they" . . . to the end of Psalm cxlv, p. 515.

Isaiah 59. 20, 21

And a redeemer shall come to Zion and to them that turn from transgression in Jacob, saith the Lord. And as for me, this is my covenant with them, saith the Lord : my *See p. 202* spirit that is upon thee, and my words which I have put in thy mouth, shall not depart out of thy mouth, nor out of the mouth of thy seed, nor out of the mouth of thy seed's *A SECOND KEDUSHA* seed, saith the Lord, from henceforth and for ever.

Psalm 22. 4

But thou art holy, O thou that dwellest amid the praises *Isaiah 6. 3* of Israel. And one cried unto another, and said, Holy, holy, holy is the Lord of hosts : the whole earth is full of his glory. *And they receive sanction the one from the other, and say, Holy in the highest heavens, the place of his divine abode ; holy upon earth, the work of his might ; holy for ever and to all eternity is the Lord of hosts ; the whole earth is full of the radiance of his *Ezekiel 3. 12* glory. Then a wind lifted me up, and I heard behind me the voice of a great rushing (saying), Blessed be the glory of the Lord from his place. *Then a wind lifted me up, and I heard behind me the voice of a great rushing, of those who uttered praises, and said, Blessed be the glory of the Lord from *Exodus 15. 18* the region of his divine abode. The Lord shall reign for ever and ever. *The kingdom of the Lord endureth for ever and to all eternity.

PRAYER FOR FIDELITY TO GOD

O Lord, the God of Abraham, of Isaac and of Israel, our fathers, keep this for ever as the inward thought in the *I Chronicles 29. 18* heart of thy people, and direct their heart unto thee. *Psalm 78. 38* And he, being merciful, forgiveth iniquity and destroyeth not : yea, many a time he turneth his anger away, and doth *Psalm 86. 5* not stir up all his wrath. For thou, O Lord, art good and forgiving, and abounding in lovingkindness to all them that

*The Aramaic paraphrase of the preceding verse.

צִדְקָתְךָ צֶדֶק לְעוֹלָם וְתוֹרָתְךָ אֱמֶת : תִּתֵּן אֱמֶת לְיַעֲקֹב
חֶסֶד לְאַבְרָהָם אֲשֶׁר־נִשְׁבַּעְתָּ לַאֲבֹתֵינוּ מִימֵי קֶדֶם : בָּרוּךְ
אֲדֹנָי יוֹם׀ יוֹם יַעֲמָס־לָנוּ הָאֵל יְשׁוּעָתֵנוּ סֶלָה : יְיָ צְבָאוֹת
עִמָּנוּ מִשְׂגָּב־לָנוּ אֱלֹהֵי יַעֲקֹב סֶלָה : יְיָ צְבָאוֹת אַשְׁרֵי
אָדָם בֹּטֵחַ בָּךְ : יְיָ הוֹשִׁיעָה ‏• הַמֶּלֶךְ יַעֲנֵנוּ בְיוֹם־קָרְאֵנוּ :
בָּרוּךְ אֱלֹהֵינוּ שֶׁבְּרָאָנוּ לִכְבוֹדוֹ וְהִבְדִּילָנוּ מִן־הַתּוֹעִים
וְנָתַן לָנוּ תּוֹרַת אֱמֶת וְחַיֵּי עוֹלָם נָטַע בְּתוֹכֵנוּ ‏• הוּא
יִפְתַּח לִבֵּנוּ בְּתוֹרָתוֹ וְיָשֵׂם בְּלִבֵּנוּ אַהֲבָתוֹ וְיִרְאָתוֹ
וְלַעֲשׂוֹת רְצוֹנוֹ וּלְעָבְדוֹ בְּלֵבָב שָׁלֵם ‏• לְמַעַן לֹא נִיגַע לָרִיק
וְלֹא נֵלֵד לַבֶּהָלָה : יְהִי רָצוֹן מִלְּפָנֶיךָ יְיָ אֱלֹהֵינוּ וֵאלֹהֵי
אֲבוֹתֵינוּ ‏• שֶׁנִּשְׁמוֹר חֻקֶּיךָ בָּעוֹלָם הַזֶּה ‏• וְנִזְכֶּה וְנִחְיֶה
וְנִרְאֶה וְנִירַשׁ טוֹבָה וּבְרָכָה לִשְׁנֵי יְמוֹת הַמָּשִׁיחַ וּלְחַיֵּי
הָעוֹלָם הַבָּא : לְמַעַן יְזַמֶּרְךָ כָבוֹד וְלֹא יִדֹּם ‏• יְיָ אֱלֹהַי
לְעוֹלָם אוֹדֶךָ : בָּרוּךְ הַגֶּבֶר אֲשֶׁר יִבְטַח בַּיְיָ וְהָיָה יְיָ
מִבְטַחוֹ : בִּטְחוּ בַיְיָ עֲדֵי־עַד כִּי בְּיָהּ יְיָ צוּר עוֹלָמִים :
וְיִבְטְחוּ בְךָ יוֹדְעֵי שְׁמֶךָ כִּי לֹא־עָזַבְתָּ דֹרְשֶׁיךָ יְיָ :
יְיָ חָפֵץ לְמַעַן צִדְקוֹ יַגְדִּיל תּוֹרָה וְיַאְדִּיר :

The Reader here says חֲצִי־קַדִּישׁ *p.* 428.

The following is omitted on Festivals when falling on Week days :—

וַאֲנִי תְפִלָּתִי לְךָ יְיָ עֵת רָצוֹן אֱלֹהִים בְּרָב חַסְדֶּךָ
עֲנֵנִי בֶּאֱמֶת יִשְׁעֶךָ :

Psalm 119. 142 call upon thee. Thy righteousness is an everlasting right-
Micah 7. 20 eousness, and thy Torah is truth. Thou wilt show truth to
Jacob and lovingkindness to Abraham, according as thou
Psalm 68. 20 hast sworn unto our fathers from the days of old. Blessed
be the Lord, day by day he beareth our burden, even the
Psalm 46. 8 God who is our salvation. (Selah.) The Lord of hosts is
with us; the God of Jacob is our stronghold. (Selah.)
Psalm 84. 13 O Lord of hosts, happy is the man who trusteth in thee.
Psalm 20. 10 Save, Lord : may the King answer us on the day when we
call.

*AND
LOYALTY
TO THE
TORAH*   Blessed is our God, who hath created us for his glory, and
hath separated us from them that go astray, and hath given
us the Torah of truth and planted everlasting life in our midst.
May he open our heart unto his Torah, and place his love
and fear within our hearts, that we may do his will and serve
him with a perfect heart, that we may not labour in vain,
nor bring forth for confusion. May it be thy will, O Lord
our God and God of our fathers, that we may keep thy
statutes in this world, and be worthy to live to witness and
inherit happiness and blessing in the days of the Messiah
Psalm 30. 13 and in the life of the world to come. To the end that my
glory may sing praise unto thee, and not be silent : O Lord
Jeremiah 17. 7 my God, I will give thanks unto thee for ever. Blessed is the
man that trusteth in the Lord, and whose trust the Lord is.
Isaiah 26. 4 Trust ye in the Lord for ever ; for the Lord is God, an
Psalm 9. 11 everlasting rock. And they that know thy Name will put
their trust in thee ; for thou hast not forsaken them that
Isaiah 42. 21 seek thee, Lord. It pleased the Lord, for his righteousness'
sake, to magnify the Torah and to glorify it.

The Reader here says Half-Kaddish, p. 429.

*The following verse is omitted on Festivals when falling on
Weekdays.*

Psalm 69. 14   And as for me, may my prayer unto thee, O Lord, be
in an acceptable time : O God, in the abundance of thy
lovingkindness, answer me with thy sure salvation.

On Sabbaths the first פָּרָשָׁה *of the* סְדְרָה *of the following Sabbath
is read.*

For סֵדֶר קְרִיאַת הַתּוֹרָה, *see pp.* 188–196.

While the Vestments are being replaced upon the סֵפֶר תּוֹרָה.

מִזְמוֹר שִׁיר לְיוֹם הַשַּׁבָּת, *p.* 360, *is said.*

The Scroll is put back into the Ark, and the Reader recites Kaddish
p. 106, *followed by the Amidah.*

On Festivals, say the appropriate Amidah.

אֲדֹנָי שְׂפָתַי תִּפְתָּח וּפִי יַגִּיד תְּהִלָּתֶךָ :

בָּרוּךְ אַתָּה יְיָ אֱלֹהֵינוּ וֵאלֹהֵי אֲבוֹתֵינוּ · אֱלֹהֵי
אַבְרָהָם אֱלֹהֵי יִצְחָק וֵאלֹהֵי יַעֲקֹב · הָאֵל הַגָּדוֹל הַגִּבּוֹר
וְהַנּוֹרָא אֵל עֶלְיוֹן · גּוֹמֵל חֲסָדִים טוֹבִים וְקוֹנֵה הַכֹּל ·
וְזוֹכֵר חַסְדֵי אָבוֹת וּמֵבִיא גוֹאֵל לִבְנֵי בְנֵיהֶם לְמַעַן
שְׁמוֹ בְּאַהֲבָה ·

On שַׁבָּת שׁוּבָה *say :—*

זָכְרֵנוּ לְחַיִּים מֶלֶךְ חָפֵץ בַּחַיִּים · וְכָתְבֵנוּ בְּסֵפֶר הַחַיִּים ·
לְמַעַנְךָ אֱלֹהִים חַיִּים :

SABBATH AFTERNOON SERVICE.

This Service goes back to ancient times, and seems from the very
first to have included Scriptural Readings and discourses. The Readings
were not taken from the Pentateuch alone, but also from the Prophets
and sometimes from the Kethuvim, the " Holy Writings " that form

On Sabbaths, the first section of the Lesson from the Pentateuch of the following Sabbath is read.

For the Order of Reading the Torah, see pp. 189–197.

While the Vestments are being replaced upon the Scroll, Psalm 92, p. 361, is said. The Scroll is put back into the Ark, and the Reader recites Kaddish, p. 107, followed by the Amidah.

On Festivals, say the appropriate Amidah.

Psalm 51. 17   O Lord, open thou my lips, and my mouth shall declare thy praise.

I. THE GOD OF HISTORY   Blessed art thou, O Lord our God and God of our fathers, God of Abraham, God of Isaac, and God of Jacob, the great, mighty and revered God, the most high God, who bestowest lovingkindnesses, and art Master of all things ; who re-

See p. 449   memberest the pious deeds of the patriarchs, and in love wilt bring a redeemer to their children's children for thy Name's sake.

[*On the Sabbath of Repentance say* :—
Remember us unto life, O King, who delightest in life, and inscribe us in the book of life, for thine own sake, O living God.]

the third section of Scripture. There was a time when they seem to have consisted of *selections* from the current Sidra and Haftorah. Quite different is the custom to-day. All Rites prescribe the reading of the first section of the next week's Sidra. The Readings from the Prophets and " Writings " have long disappeared, but the prayers that originally concluded such Scriptural Readings and discourses (pp. 571–573) remain to this day. They are the *Kedusha de Sidra*—the Kedusha of the Biblical exposition, as explained on pp. 202–203.

מֶלֶךְ עוֹזֵר וּמוֹשִׁיעַ וּמָגֵן · בָּרוּךְ אַתָּה יְיָ · מָגֵן אַבְרָהָ

אַתָּה גִּבּוֹר לְעוֹלָם אֲדֹנָי מְחַיֵּה מֵתִים אַתָּה רַב לְהוֹשִׁי

From שַׁבַּת בְּרֵאשִׁית *until the First Day of* פֶּסַח say :—

מַשִּׁיב הָרוּחַ וּמוֹרִיד הַגָּשֶׁם :

מְכַלְכֵּל חַיִּים בְּחֶסֶד מְחַיֵּה מֵתִים בְּרַחֲמִים רַבִּים · סוֹ

נוֹפְלִים וְרוֹפֵא חוֹלִים וּמַתִּיר אֲסוּרִים וּמְקַיֵּם אֱמוּ

לִישֵׁנֵי עָפָר · מִי כָמוֹךָ בַּעַל גְּבוּרוֹת וּמִי דּוֹמֶה לָּ

מֶלֶךְ מֵמִית וּמְחַיֶּה וּמַצְמִיחַ יְשׁוּעָה ·

On שַׁבַּת שׁוּבָה say :—

מִי כָמוֹךָ אַב הָרַחֲמִים זוֹכֵר יְצוּרָיו לַחַיִּים בְּרַחֲמִים ·

וְנֶאֱמָן אַתָּה לְהַחֲיוֹת מֵתִים : בָּרוּךְ אַתָּה יְיָ · מְחַ

הַמֵּתִים :

When the Reader repeats the עֲמִידָה, *the following* קְדֻשָּׁה *is said :*

Reader. נְקַדֵּשׁ אֶת שִׁמְךָ בָּעוֹלָם כְּשֵׁם שֶׁמַּקְדִּישִׁים אוֹ

בִּשְׁמֵי מָרוֹם כַּכָּתוּב עַל יַד נְבִיאֶךָ · וְקָרָא זֶה אֶל זֶה וְאָמַ

Cong. קָדוֹשׁ קָדוֹשׁ קָדוֹשׁ יְיָ צְבָאוֹת · מְלֹא כָל הָאָ

כְּבוֹדוֹ : Reader לְעֻמָּתָם בָּרוּךְ יֹאמֵרוּ · Cong. בָּרוּךְ כְּב

יְיָ מִמְּקוֹמוֹ : Reader. וּבְדִבְרֵי קָדְשְׁךָ כָּתוּב לֵאמֹ

Cong. יִמְלֹךְ יְיָ לְעוֹלָם אֱלֹהַיִךְ צִיּוֹן לְדֹר וָדֹר · הַלְלוּיָ

O King, Helper, Saviour and Shield. Blessed art thou,
O Lord, the Shield of Abraham.

II. THE
GOD OF
NATURE

Thou, O Lord, art mighty for ever, thou revivest the
dead, thou art mighty to save.

[*From the Sabbath after the Eighth Day of Solemn Assembly until
the First Day of Passover, say* :

See p. 451
Thou causest the wind to blow and the rain to fall.]

Thou sustainest the living with lovingkindness, revivest
the dead with great mercy, supportest the falling, healest
the sick, freest the bound, and keepest thy faith to them
that sleep in the dust. Who is like unto thee, Lord of mighty
acts, and who resembleth thee, O King, who orderest death
and restorest life, and causest salvation to spring forth ?

[*On the Sabbath of Repentance say* :—
Who is like unto thee, Father of mercy, who in mercy rememberest thy creatures unto life ?]
Yea, faithful art thou to revive the dead. Blessed art
thou, O Lord, who revivest the dead.

[*When the Reader repeats the Amidah, the following up to "Thou
art holy " p.* 579, *is said.*

III.
"KEDU-
SHA":
SANCTIFI-
CATION
OF GOD
Isaiah 6. 3

Reader.—We will sanctify thy Name in the world even
as they sanctify it in the highest heavens, as it is written by
the hand of the prophet :
And they called one unto the other and said,
Cong.—HOLY, HOLY, HOLY IS THE LORD OF HOSTS :

See p. 452
THE WHOLE EARTH IS FULL OF HIS GLORY.
Reader.—Those over against them say, Blessed—

Ezekiel 3. 12
Cong.—BLESSED BE THE GLORY OF THE LORD FROM
HIS PLACE.
Reader.—And in thy Holy Words it is written, saying,

Psalm 146. 10
Cong.—THE LORD SHALL REIGN FOR EVER, THY GOD,
O ZION, UNTO ALL GENERATIONS. PRAISE YE THE LORD.

Reader. לְדוֹר וָדוֹר נַגִּיד גָּדְלֶךָ · וּלְנֵצַח נְצָחִים

קְדֻשָּׁתְךָ נַקְדִּישׁ · וְשִׁבְחֲךָ אֱלֹהֵינוּ מִפִּינוּ לֹא יָמוּ

לְעוֹלָם וָעֶד · כִּי אֵל מֶלֶךְ גָּדוֹל וְקָדוֹשׁ אָתָּה · בָּרוּ

אַתָּה יְיָ · הָאֵל [say, On שַׁבַּת שׁוּבָה הַמֶּלֶךְ] הַקָּדוֹשׁ :

אַתָּה קָדוֹשׁ וְשִׁמְךָ קָדוֹשׁ וּקְדוֹשִׁים בְּכָל־יוֹם יְהַלְלוּ

סֶּלָה · בָּרוּךְ אַתָּה יְיָ · הָאֵל [say, On שׁ׳ שׁוּבָה הַמֶּלֶךְ] הַקָּדוֹ

אַתָּה אֶחָד וְשִׁמְךָ אֶחָד · וּמִי כְּעַמְּךָ יִשְׂרָאֵל גּ

אֶחָד בָּאָרֶץ : תִּפְאֶרֶת גְּדֻלָּה · וַעֲטֶרֶת יְשׁוּעָה · יוֹ

מְנוּחָה וּקְדֻשָּׁה לְעַמְּךָ נָתַתָּ : אַבְרָהָם יָגֵל · יִצְחָק יְרַנֵּ

יַעֲקֹב וּבָנָיו יָנוּחוּ בוֹ : מְנוּחַת אַהֲבָה וּנְדָבָה · מְנוּחַ

אֱמֶת וֶאֱמוּנָה · מְנוּחַת שָׁלוֹם וְשַׁלְוָה וְהַשְׁקֵט וָבֶטַה

מְנוּחָה שְׁלֵמָה שָׁאַתָּה רוֹצֶה בָּהּ · יַכִּירוּ בָנֶיךָ וְיֵדְעוּ

מֵאִתְּךָ הִיא מְנוּחָתָם וְעַל מְנוּחָתָם יַקְדִּישׁוּ אֶת שְׁמֶךָ

אֱלֹהֵינוּ וֵאלֹהֵי אֲבוֹתֵינוּ · רְצֵה בִמְנוּחָתֵנוּ · קַדְּשֵׁ

בְּמִצְוֹתֶיךָ וְתֵן חֶלְקֵנוּ בְּתוֹרָתֶךָ · שַׂבְּעֵנוּ מִטּוּבֶךָ וְשַׂמְּחֵ

בִּישׁוּעָתֶךָ · וְטַהֵר לִבֵּנוּ לְעָבְדְּךָ בֶּאֱמֶת · וְהַנְחִילֵנוּ

אֱלֹהֵינוּ בְּאַהֲבָה וּבְרָצוֹן שַׁבַּת קָדְשֶׁךָ · וְיָנוּחוּ בָהּ יִשְׂרָא

מְקַדְּשֵׁי שְׁמֶךָ · בָּרוּךְ אַתָּה יְיָ · מְקַדֵּשׁ הַשַּׁבָּת :

Reader.—Unto all generations we will declare thy great-ness, and to all eternity we will proclaim thy holiness, and thy praise, O our God, shall not depart from our mouth for ever, for thou art a great and holy God and King. Blessed art thou, O Lord, | *On the Sabbath of Repentance, say :—* the holy God. | the holy King.]

Thou art holy, and thy Name is holy, and holy beings praise thee daily. (Selah.) Blessed art thou, O Lord, the holy God. | *On the Sabbath of Repentance, say :—* | the holy King.

IV. INTER MEDIATE BENEDIC-TION

Thou art One and thy Name is One, and who is like thy people Israel, an unique nation on the earth ? Glorious greatness and a crown of salvation, even the day of rest and holiness, thou hast given unto thy people :—Abraham was glad, Isaac rejoiced, Jacob and his sons rested thereon :— a rest granted in generous love, a true and faithful rest, a rest in peace and tranquility, in quietude and safety, a perfect rest wherein thou delightest. Let thy children perceive and know that this their rest is from thee, and by their rest may they hallow thy Name.

SABBATH PRAYER

See p. 459

Our God and God of our fathers, accept our rest ; hallow us by thy commandments, and grant our portion in thy Torah ; satisfy us with thy goodness, and gladden us with thy salvation ; purify our hearts to serve thee in truth ; and in thy love and favour, O Lord our God, let us inherit thy holy Sabbath ; and may Israel, who sanctify thy Name, rest thereon. Blessed art thou, O Lord, who hallowest the Sabbath.

THOU ART ONE. As in the other Sabbath Amidahs, that of the Afternoon Service has its own special introduction to the Intermediate Benediction. Its opening is based on I Chronicles 17. 20–21.

Abraham . . . Isaac . . . Jacob. The Patriarchs are often repre-sented as having observed the Sabbath. " They were all distinguished for their tranquil confidence in God, and this seemed to the Rabbis a prefiguration of the Sabbath calm as enjoined in the Law " (Abrahams).

רְצֵה יְיָ אֱלֹהֵינוּ בְּעַמְּךָ יִשְׂרָאֵל וּבִתְפִלָּתָם · וְהָשֵׁב
אֶת־הָעֲבוֹדָה לִדְבִיר בֵּיתֶךָ · וְאִשֵּׁי יִשְׂרָאֵל וּתְפִלָּתָם
בְּאַהֲבָה תְקַבֵּל בְּרָצוֹן · וּתְהִי לְרָצוֹן תָּמִיד עֲבוֹדַת
יִשְׂרָאֵל עַמֶּךָ ·

On רֹאשׁ חֹדֶשׁ and חֹל הַמּוֹעֵד of פֶּסַח and of סֻכּוֹת, say 'אֱלֹהֵינוּ וכו',
to אַתָּה p. 460.

וְתֶחֱזֶינָה עֵינֵינוּ בְּשׁוּבְךָ לְצִיּוֹן בְּרַחֲמִים · בָּרוּךְ אַתָּ
יְיָ · הַמַּחֲזִיר שְׁכִינָתוֹ לְצִיּוֹן :

Here continue אֲנָחְנוּ מוֹדִים קַדְמֹנִיּוֹת to, p. 384, on p. 388. וּכְשָׁנִים

The following is omitted on such occasions as those on which תַּחֲנוּן
is omitted on Week days (see p. 293).

צִדְקָתְךָ צֶדֶק לְעוֹלָם וְתוֹרָתְךָ אֱמֶת : וְצִדְקָתְךָ אֱלֹהִים
עַד־מָרוֹם אֲשֶׁר עָשִׂיתָ גְדֹלוֹת אֱלֹהִים מִי כָמוֹךָ : צִדְקָתְךָ
כְּהַרְרֵי־אֵל מִשְׁפָּטֶיךָ תְּהוֹם רַבָּה אָדָם וּבְהֵמָה תוֹשִׁיעַ יְיָ :

קַדִּישׁ תִּתְקַבַּל, p. 206.

THY RIGHTEOUSNESS. Some have seen in these verses " a submission
to Divine Judgment ", such as is spoken in connection with the death
of a beloved one. The introduction of such a strange note into a Sabbath
Service is connected with the tradition that Moses died on Sabbath
afternoon (the Zohar adds, also Joseph and David). But such explanation is quite improbable, as there is no mourning of any sort on the
Sabbath day. It is, therefore, best to consider these verses as replacing
the Supplication of the week-day Service (see page 161). This makes
clear the meaning of the rubric.

Accept, O Lord our God, thy people Israel and their prayer; restore the service to the inner sanctuary of thy house ; receive in love and favour both the fire-offerings of Israel and their prayer ; and may the service of thy people Israel be ever acceptable unto thee.

[*On New Moon and the Intermediate Days of Passover and Tabernacles say, "Our God . . . May our remembrance," to " King," p.* 461.]

And let our eyes behold thy return in mercy to Zion. Blessed art thou, O Lord, who restorest thy divine presence unto Zion.

Here continue " We give thanks," p. 383 *to " as in ancient years," p.* 387.

The following is omitted on such occasions as those on which Tachanun is omitted on Weekdays (see p. 294) :—

Psalm 112. 142
Psalm 71. 19
Psalm 36. 7

Thy righteousness is an everlasting righteousness, and thy Law is truth. Thy righteousness also, O God, is very high ; thou who hast done great things, O God, who is like unto thee ? Thy righteousness is like the mountains of God ; thy judgments are a great deep : man and beast thou savest, O Lord.

Kaddish, p. 207.

Since Gaonic times *Aboth*, the *Sayings of the Fathers* have been read either during the Mincha Service or immediately preceding or following it. Later, the reading of sections of Psalms was likewise linked with the Sabbath Afternoon Service ; in our Rite, Aboth is read during the summer months, and the Psalms during the winter. Sabbath afternoon was also the time for examining what the children had learned in Sacred Knowledge during the week. And aside from listening to Synagogue discourses, there was reading of devotional books and the books of the moralists. A selection from these was given on p. 260–263. A second selection is to be found on p. 722, and a third on p. 1112

From שַׁבָּת הַגָּדוֹל until (שִׂמְחַת תּוֹרָה after שַׁבָּת (the שַׁבָּת בְּרֵאשִׁית
(the שַׁבָּת before פֶּסַח), the following Psalms are read :—

תהלים ק'ד

בָּרְכִי נַפְשִׁי אֶת־יְיָ • יְיָ אֱלֹהַי גָּדַלְתָּ מְּאֹד : הוֹ

וְהָדָר לָבָשְׁתָּ : עֹטֶה אוֹר כַּשַּׂלְמָה נוֹטֶה שָׁמַיִם כַּיְרִיעָה

הַמְקָרֶה בַמַּיִם עֲלִיּוֹתָיו • הַשָּׂם־עָבִים רְכוּבוֹ הַמְהַלֵּ

עַל־כַּנְפֵי־רוּחַ : עֹשֶׂה מַלְאָכָיו רוּחוֹת מְשָׁרְתָיו אֵשׁ לֹהֵט

יָסַד אֶרֶץ עַל־מְכוֹנֶיהָ בַּל־תִּמּוֹט עוֹלָם וָעֶד : תְּהוֹ

PSALM 104.

A HYMN TO PROVIDENCE :

GOD THE CREATOR AND SUSTAINER OF NATURE

In this most wonderful of Nature hymns, the worshipping poet is enraptured by the marvels of Creation, and loses himself in adoration of God. The order of thought follows the account of Creation in the first chapter of Genesis. It opens with the calling into existence of light and the formation of the heavens, v. 1–4 ; the dry land, 5–18 ; the heavenly bodies, 19–23 ; fish and food, 24–26 ; man and beast, 27–30 ; and closes with the prayer that evil disappear from earth, 31–35. In the view of the sacred singer, God did not make the world, then leave it to itself. He is constantly renewing the miracle of creation (see p. 110). And the Psalmist not merely enumerates the wonderful works of God, but his is the absolute conviction of the unity of all things on earth and sea and sky as one Divine harmony.

Herder, a pioneer of the appreciation of the Bible as literature, declared, " It is worth while studying the Hebrew language for ten years, in order to read Psalm 104 in the original ". " We are astonished to find, in a lyric poem of such limited compass, the whole universe— the heavens and the earth—sketched with a few bold sketches. The contrast of the labour of man with the animal life of Nature, and the image of the omnipresent, invisible Power, renewing the earth at will, is a grand and solemn poetical creation " (Humboldt).

1–4. God's majesty revealed in Creation. In Hebrew poetry, Nature never becomes the Divine All, but always remains " the work of His hands ".

From the Sabbath after Simchas Torah until the Sabbath before Passover, the following Psalms are read :—

Psalm civ.

HYMN OF
CREATION
AND
PROVID-
ENCE

¹Bless the Lord, O my soul : O Lord my God, thou art very great ; thou hast robed thee in splendour and majesty. ²He covereth himself with light as with a garment ; he stretcheth out the heavens like a curtain : ³he layeth the beams of his upper chambers in the waters ; he maketh the clouds his chariot ; he walketh upon the wings of the wind. ⁴He maketh winds his messengers ; his ministers flaming fire : ⁵he founded the earth upon its bases, that it might not be moved for ever. ⁶Thou didst cover it with the deep as with a vesture ; the waters stood

1. *bless.* The Psalmist's invocation to his soul denotes not thanksgiving merely, but is the outcome of wonder and admiration of God's greatness as displayed in the universe. Among the Benedictions in the Jewish Prayer Book, are those on seeing the ocean or a high mountain, and on first beholding the new blossoms in spring ; see p. 990.

art very great. i.e. Thou didst show thyself very great.

2. *light.* Light, the first created element is, as it were, God's robe, revealing while it conceals Him. It is the condition of life, the source of gladness, the emblem of purity.

covereth himself. In the original Text, participles are used. This in Hebrew indicates *continuance* of action, the continuance of creation in the present.

curtain. The comparison of the skies to a curtain is primitive ; all the grander is the sublime thought which the whole psalm expresses. " The religious elevation of the present psalm is quite inexplicable, unless we allow that this simple folk have been specially guided from Above " (Witton Davies).

4. *messengers.* lit. " angels ". In the Psalms, unlike the later books of Scripture, angels have no names and no personality : an angel is merely a momentary messenger of God. The cosmic forces, wind and lightning, all execute the bidding of God, and serve His purposes in the universe.

flaming fire. The lightning.

5–9. The story of the earth's formation restated in poetic form.

5. *upon its bases.* the earth is compared to a building erect on solid foundations.

כַּלְּבוּשׁ כִּסִּיתוֹ · עַל־הָרִים יַעַמְדוּ מָיִם: מִן־גַּעֲרָתְךָ יְנוּסוּ
מִן־קוֹל רַעַמְךָ יֵחָפֵזוּן: יַעֲלוּ הָרִים יֵרְדוּ בְקָעוֹת אֶל־
מְקוֹם זֶה יָסַדְתָּ לָהֶם: גְּבוּל־שַׂמְתָּ בַּל־יַעֲבֹרוּן · בַּל־
יְשׁוּבוּן לְכַסּוֹת הָאָרֶץ: הַמְשַׁלֵּחַ מַעְיָנִים בַּנְּחָלִים בֵּי
הָרִים יְהַלֵּכוּן: יַשְׁקוּ כָּל־חַיְתוֹ שָׂדָי יִשְׁבְּרוּ פְרָאִים
צְמָאָם: עֲלֵיהֶם עוֹף־הַשָּׁמַיִם יִשְׁכּוֹן מִבֵּין עֳפָאִים יִתְּנוּ
קוֹל: מַשְׁקֶה הָרִים מֵעֲלִיּוֹתָיו · מִפְּרִי מַעֲשֶׂיךָ תִּשְׂבַּ
הָאָרֶץ: מַצְמִיחַ חָצִיר לַבְּהֵמָה וְעֵשֶׂב לַעֲבֹדַת הָאָדָם
לְהוֹצִיא לֶחֶם מִן־הָאָרֶץ: וְיַיִן יְשַׂמַּח לְבַב־אֱנוֹשׁ לְהַצְהִי
פָנִים מִשָּׁמֶן · וְלֶחֶם לְבַב־אֱנוֹשׁ יִסְעָד: יִשְׂבְּעוּ עֲ
יְיָ · אַרְזֵי לְבָנוֹן אֲשֶׁר נָטָע: אֲשֶׁר־שָׁם צִפֳּרִים יְקַנֵּנוּ
חֲסִידָה בְּרוֹשִׁים בֵּיתָהּ: הָרִים הַגְּבֹהִים לַיְּעֵלִים

7. voice of thy thunder. Thy mighty voice. At its bidding, the poet sees the waters flee in terror to their appointed beds.

9. a bound. The sand.

10–18. Springs and brooks created. Bountiful provision is made for the wants of men and animals.

12. branches. Foliage.

13. is satisfied. Has its fill from.

fruit of thy works. i.e. the rain, the issue of God's work.

14. herbs. The term includes wheat, the vine, and the olive tree. Man is thought of as a worker: the special dignity of man is labour.

service of man. Use of man.

bread from the earth. These words form the substance of the best known Benediction, viz., the *Motzi*, over bread.

15. his face to shine. In hot, desert lands, the skin; unless rubbed with oil or fats, becomes rough and scaly.

16. trees of the Lord. The natural growth of the primeval forest, in contrast to trees planted by the hand of man.

above the mountains. ⁷At thy rebuke they fled ; at the voice of thy thunder they hasted away. ⁸The mountains rose, the valleys sank unto the place which thou hadst founded for them. ⁹Thou hast set a bound that they may not pass over ; that they turn not again to cover the earth. ¹⁰He sendeth forth springs into the valleys ; they run among the mountains. ¹¹They give drink to every beast of the plain ; the wild asses quench their thirst. ¹²By them the birds of the heaven have their dwelling, they utter their voice from among the branches. ¹³He giveth drink to the mountains from his upper chambers : the earth is satisfied with the fruit of thy works. ¹⁴He causeth grass to grow for the cattle, and herbs for the service of man ; that he may bring forth bread from the earth ; ¹⁵and wine that maketh glad the heart of man, and oil to make his face to shine, and bread that strengtheneth man's heart. ¹⁶The trees of the Lord are satisfied ; the cedars of Lebanon which he hath planted ; ¹⁷where the birds make their nests : as for the stork, the fir trees are her house . ¹⁸The high mountains

18. *conies*. After the great, come the little. The animal here meant is the rock-badger ; a shy, rabbit-like creature which inhabits places seldom trodden by man.

There are parallels in other ancient literatures to the description in *v*. 14–18. Thus in an Egyptian hymn we read :

" He who created herbs for the cattle,
And the fruit-tree for men ;
He who giveth breath to that which is in the egg,
And maketh to live the son of the worm ;
He who maketh that whereon the gnats live,
The worms and the flies likewise ;
He who maketh what the mice in their holes need,
And sustaineth the birds on all the trees ".

Many unwarranted conclusions have been drawn from these similarities. It must not, however, be forgotten that for Nature poets, there is only one Nature ; and also that, because of the common instincts of mankind, the emotional reactions to Nature are often similar. One fundamental difference remains. To the Egyptian poet the sun is the Creator : the Hebrew declares the Creator to be the God of Righteousness ; see *v*. 35.

סְלָעִים מַחְסֶה לַשְׁפַנִּים : עָשָׂה יָרֵחַ לְמוֹעֲדִים · שֶׁמֶשׁ יָדַ

מְבוֹאוֹ : תָּשֶׁת חֹשֶׁךְ וִיהִי לָיְלָה בּוֹ תִרְמֹשׂ כָּל־חַיְתוֹ־יָעַר

הַכְּפִירִים שֹׁאֲגִים לַטָּרֶף וּלְבַקֵּשׁ מֵאֵל אָכְלָם : תִּזְרַ

הַשֶּׁמֶשׁ יֵאָסֵפוּן וְאֶל־מְעוֹנֹתָם יִרְבָּצוּן : יֵצֵא אָדָם לְפָעֳ

וְלַעֲבֹדָתוֹ עֲדֵי־עָרֶב : מָה־רַבּוּ מַעֲשֶׂיךָ יְיָ · כֻּלָּם בְּחָכְמָ

עָשִׂיתָ · מָלְאָה הָאָרֶץ קִנְיָנֶךָ : זֶה הַיָּם גָּדוֹל וּרְחַ

יָדָיִם · שָׁם רֶמֶשׂ וְאֵין מִסְפָּר חַיּוֹת קְטַנּוֹת עִם־גְּדֹלוֹת

שָׁם אֳנִיּוֹת יְהַלֵּכוּן · לִוְיָתָן זֶה יָצַרְתָּ לְשַׂחֶק־בּוֹ : כֻּלָ

אֵלֶיךָ יְשַׂבֵּרוּן לָתֵת אָכְלָם בְּעִתּוֹ : תִּתֵּן לָהֶם יִלְקֹטוּן

תִּפְתַּח יָדְךָ יִשְׂבְּעוּן טוֹב : תַּסְתִּיר פָּנֶיךָ יִבָּהֵלוּן

תֹּסֵף רוּחָם יִגְוָעוּן · וְאֶל־עֲפָרָם יְשׁוּבוּן : תְּשַׁלַּח רוּחֲ

יִבָּרֵאוּן · וּתְחַדֵּשׁ פְּנֵי אֲדָמָה : יְהִי כְבוֹד יְיָ לְעוֹלָם

יִשְׂמַח יְיָ בְּמַעֲשָׂיו : הַמַּבִּיט לָאָרֶץ וַתִּרְעָד · יִגַּ

19–23. Creation of the heavenly bodies.

19. *for seasons.* Lunar calculations play a predominant role in the fixing of the exact dates of the Festivals.

its going down. i.e. its setting; the sun knows his duty. "Thus simply and even poetically does the Psalmist traverse the early Semitic fancy that Sun and Moon are deities" (Barnes).

20. *move.* Creep forth, or "rove about".

21. *roar.* These beasts are God's unconscious suppliants. In the eyes of the Psalmist, the world is not made merely for man; God feeds the lions as well as the children of men.

24–26. The Sea and all that is therein.

24. *possessions.* Works.

are for the wild goats ; the rocks are a refuge for the conies.
¹⁹He made the moon for seasons : the sun knoweth its
going down. ²⁰Thou makest darkness, and it is night ;
wherein all the beasts of the forest do move. ²¹The young
lions roar after their prey, and seek their food from God.
²²The sun ariseth, they get them away, and lay them down
in their dens. ²³Man goeth forth unto his work and to his
labour until the evening.

²⁴How manifold are thy works, O Lord ! In wisdom
hast thou made them all : the earth is full of thy
possessions. ²⁵Yonder is the sea, great and of wide extent ;
therein are moving things innumerable, living creatures
both small and great. ²⁶There the ships make their
course ; there is leviathan whom thou hast formed to
sport therein. ²⁷These all wait upon thee, that thou mayest
give them their food in due season. ²⁸Thou givest unto
them, they gather ; thou openest thine hand, they are
satisfied with good. ²⁹Thou hidest thy face, they are confounded ; thou gatherest in their breath, they die, and
return to their dust. ³⁰Thou sendest forth thy spirit, they
are created ; and. thou renewest the face of the ground.

³¹Let the glory of the Lord endure for ever ; let the Lord
rejoice in his works. ³²He looketh on the earth, and it
trembleth ; he toucheth the mountains, and they smoke.
³³I will sing unto the Lord as long as I live : I will sing

---

26. *leviathan.* Here probably the whale. Sometimes it stands for
" sea-monster ", or the crocodile.

27-30. God is the Source of life. Life, not death, is the master-
principle of the universe.

29. *hidest thy face.* Withdrawest Thy sustaining power.

31-35. Conclusion : prayers and praise of the Sovereign Judge of
the world.

31. *rejoice.* Cf. Genesis 1. 31 and Proverbs 8. 30.

32. *looketh . . . trembleth.* If His works cease to give Him joy, He
can indeed destroy them ; for, by a look, He causes the earth to
tremble ; and, by a touch, sets the mountains on fire (Delitzsch).

33. Cf. Psalm 146. 2.

בֶּהָרִים וַיֶּעֱשָֽׁנוּ: אָשִֽׁירָה לַיָי בְּחַיָּי · אֲזַמְּרָה לֵאלֹהַי
בְּעוֹדִי: יֶעֱרַב עָלָיו שִׂיחִי · אָנֹכִי אֶשְׂמַח בַּיָי: יִתַּמּוּ
חַטָּאִים מִן־הָאָֽרֶץ וּרְשָׁעִים עוֹד אֵינָם · בָּרְכִי נַפְשִׁי
אֶת־יָי · הַלְלוּיָהּ:

34. sweet. Acceptable. As the highest and the smallest creatures all owe their existence to His will, this fact gives assurance that sin and ungodliness must vanish from a universe which God has made; see next v.

35. let sinners cease on earth. Lit. "out of the earth". This verse is not an imprecation, but a solemn hope. (The translation, "sinners shall be consumed", is quite wrong). To the Hebrew Prophet and Psalmist alike, sin is the great blot on creation—the one glaring disharmony in God's beautiful world. It must disappear, if God is to rejoice in His universe.

The Psalmist speaks of "sinners": "modern thought would say, May sin be banished from the earth" (Kirkpatrick). As a matter of fact, it was so said by Jewish lips 1750 years ago, and in connection with this very verse, (in which the word chattoim, "sinners", can by a slight change in punctuation be read chatoim, "sins"). Rabbi Meir (see p. 704) lived in a neighbourhood of lawless men. They sorely vexed and afflicted him, so much so that one day he wished for their death. Then his brilliant wife Beruria, "opened her mouth in wisdom". She said to him, "How canst thou act thus? The Psalmist says 'let sins cease on earth;' and then he continues, 'and the wicked shall be no more'. This teaches that as soon as sin vanishes, there will be no more sinners. Therefore do thou pray, not for the destruction of these wicked men, but for their repentance". Rabbi · Meir did so and, we are told, they turned from their evil ways. Beruria was the daughter of a renowned Teacher and martyr, Chananya ben Teradyon (see p. 647), and was herself a scholar and renowned rabbinic authority in her learned generation. Her reading of חַטָּאִים (" sinners) ", the crucial word in this verse, as חֲטָאִים ("sins"), was not due to ignorance or feminine wilfulness. The Hebrew Text of Scripture was at that time as yet unvowelled. There are many similar variant readings in the Psalms and Proverbs; and Rabbi Meir himself was famed for a number of variants in the Hebrew text of Scripture. To Beruria thus belongs the glory of having given expression to a great doctrine of religion and humanity; viz. Hate sin, and not the sinner; exterminate crime, i.e. the conditions that make for crime, and there will be no criminals.

Two contemporaries of Beruria gave a similar interpretation of the first two Hebrew words of this verse. Rabbi Judah ben Ilai translated, יתמו חטאים, not by "let sinners cease", but by, "let sinners become

praise to my God while I have my being. ³⁴May my
meditation be sweet unto him : as for me, I will rejoice in
the Lord. ³⁵Let sinners cease on earth, and the wicked
shall be no more. Bless the Lord, O my soul : praise ye
the Lord.

perfect " (by repentance), and in that hour they will no longer be
wicked. Rabbi Nehemiah translated, " let *wickednesses* cease, and the
wicked will be no more ". The words of all these Rabbinic teachers,
Beruria, Judah and Nehemiah, are in accordance with the epoch-
making proclamation of the Prophet, " As I live, saith the Lord God,
I have no pleasure in the death of the wicked ; but that the wicked
turn from his way, and live " (Ezekiel 33. 11).

For an example of Beruria's unique self-possession and resignation
in overwhelming sorrow, see p. 270.

THE PILGRIM PSALMS.

Introductory Note to Psalms 120–134.

Psalms 120–134 are each entitled שיר המעלות, lit. " A song of the
goings-up ". The exact meaning of this title has been variously stated.
It may mean either, (1) song by the exiles returning from Babylon to
the Land of their fathers (Ezra 7. 2) ; or (2) song of the pilgrims
who journeyed up to the Temple mount in Jerusalem. In order to
keep the three Pilgrim Festivals at the National Sanctuary, pious
Israelites would band themselves together, camping out on the journey,
and singing songs as they went.

The title has also been translated, "song of Ascents ", " song of
Degrees ", or " song of the Steps ". This is usually based on the description which the Mishna gives of the Succos festivities on the fifteen
steps leading down from the Israelites' Court in the Temple. However,
the Mishna says nothing concerning the nature of the psalms then
sung, nor does it state that they were recited on those steps.

In view of the above, "Pilgrim Songs" seems a natural explanation of these fifteen שיר המעלות psalms. There is no reference to
the Return from the Exile in some of them ; others seem to be derived
from a collection of hymns for the Pilgrim Festivals ; but all of them
may well have been sung on pilgrimages. They are short; the utterance
of a single thought, feeling or hope; and are of exceeding beauty.
They form a Psalter within the Psalter, speaking the language of
the people, and revealing a sweet, child-like spirit of devotion. This
People's Song Book gives evidence of much pure and bright domestic
life, based upon the fear and love of God, among the rank and file of
Jewish worshippers ; as well as of unquenchable confidence in God's
mercies and deliverances from danger and tribulation, whether national
or personal.

תהלים ק׳כ

שִׁיר הַמַּעֲלוֹת · אֶל־יְיָ בַּצָּרָתָה לִּי קָרָאתִי וַיַּעֲנֵנִי
יְיָ הַצִּילָה נַפְשִׁי מִשְּׂפַת־שֶׁקֶר מִלָּשׁוֹן רְמִיָּה : מַה־יִּתֵּן לְ
וּמַה־יֹּסִיף לָךְ · לָשׁוֹן רְמִיָּה : חִצֵּי גִבּוֹר שְׁנוּנִים עִ
גַּחֲלֵי רְתָמִים : אוֹיָה לִי כִּי־גַרְתִּי מֶשֶׁךְ שָׁכַנְתִּי עִם־אָהֳ
קֵדָר : רַבַּת שָׁכְנָה־לָהּ נַפְשִׁי עִם שׂוֹנֵא שָׁלוֹם : אֲנ
שָׁלוֹם · וְכִי אֲדַבֵּר הֵמָּה לַמִּלְחָמָה :

תהלים קכ׳א

שִׁיר לַמַּעֲלוֹת · אֶשָּׂא עֵינַי אֶל־הֶהָרִים · מֵאַיִן יָב
עֶזְרִי : עֶזְרִי מֵעִם יְיָ עֹשֵׂה שָׁמַיִם וָאָרֶץ : אַל־יִתֵּן לַמּ
רַגְלֶךָ אַל־יָנוּם שֹׁמְרֶךָ : הִנֵּה לֹא יָנוּם וְלֹא יִישָׁן שׁוֹמֵ

PSALM 120.

An exile's distressful cry at his failure to attain to peace in a hostile environment. The collection of Pilgrim Psalms is appropriately opened by one which depicts the hard lot of dispersed Israelites.

1. *in my distress.* The Psalmist lives among unfriendly tribes east of the Jordan, either as a recent exile or a resident alien.

I cried. From the past he draws encouragement for the present. God will again answer him.

2. *deceitful tongue.* Fomenting strife by lying accusations.

3. *shall be given . . . done more.* What punishment upon punishment shall visit the calumniating enemy ?

4. *sharpened arrows.* Most commentators take this to mean that God requites the deceitful tongue—sharp as the arrow, and working like fire—in its own coin. May the arrow and the fire destroy it ! However, this verse may be a further description of the lying tongue.

sharpened Made hard by intense heat.

the mighty man. Warrior.

broom. Makes the hottest fire, and its embers retain the heat for a considerable time.

Psalm cxx.   ¹A Pilgrim Song.

PRAYER FOR DELIVER- ANCE FROM TREACH- EROUS NEIGH- BOURS

In my distress I cried unto the Lord, and he answered me. ²Deliver my soul, O Lord, from a lying lip, and from a deceitful tongue. ³What shall be given unto thee, and what shall be done more unto thee, thou deceitful tongue ? ⁴Sharpened arrows of a mighty man with coals of broom. ⁵Woe is me, that I sojourn in Mesech, that I dwell among the tents of Kedar. ⁶My soul hath full long had her dwelling with him that hateth peace. ⁷I am all peace ; but when I speak, they are for war.

Psalm cxxi.   ¹A Pilgrim Song.

THE GUARDIAN OF ISRAEL

I lift up mine eyes unto the hills : whence will my help come ? ²My help is from the Lord, the maker of heaven and earth. ³He will not suffer my foot to slip : he that guardeth thee will not slumber. ⁴Behold, he that guardeth

---

5. *I sojourn.* lit. " I sojourned " ; here as in *v.* 1, the past has the sense of the present tense.

Mesech . . . Kedar. Arab tribes ; I Chronicles 1. 17 and Genesis 25. 13.

6. *full long.* All too long.

with him that hateth peace. With haters of peace.

7. *I am all peace.* lit. " I am peace ". This experience of the Psalmist has, alas, often been that of the whole of Israel.

PSALM 121.

GOD'S PROVIDENTIAL CARE.

The pilgrims on their way to the Temple gaze for the first glimpse of the hills of Zion. They encourage one another in words of faith and hope. The psalm was probably sung antiphonally.

Unlike the other Pilgrim Psalms, this psalm has the title שִׁיר לַמַּעֲלוֹת, which the Midrash explains as " a song with reference to the steps, upon which God leads the righteous in their upward strivings into the Higher World ".

1. *unto the hills.* Of Jerusalem.

whence will my help come. This question is not one of doubt, but is simply to introduce the answer in the *v.* following.

2. *maker of heaven and earth.* The One, omnipotent Creator of the Universe, in contrast to the false gods that are " things of nought ".

3–4. Another speaker, who continues the thought in *v.* 2.

4. *neither slumber.* Israel's Watchman is not like a human sentinel, who is liable to be overcome by sleep on his watch.

יִשְׂרָאֵל : יְיָ שֹׁמְרֶךָ יְיָ צִלְּךָ עַל־יַד יְמִינֶךָ : יוֹמָם הַשֶּׁמֶשׁ
לֹא־יַכֶּכָּה וְיָרֵחַ בַּלָּיְלָה : יְיָ | יִשְׁמָרְךָ מִכָּל־רָע יִשְׁמֹר אֶת־
נַפְשֶׁךָ : יְיָ יִשְׁמָר־צֵאתְךָ וּבוֹאֶךָ מֵעַתָּה וְעַד־עוֹלָם :

תהלים קכ'ב

שִׁיר הַמַּעֲלוֹת לְדָוִד · שָׂמַחְתִּי בְּאֹמְרִים לִי בֵּית יְ
נֵלֵךְ : עֹמְדוֹת הָיוּ רַגְלֵינוּ בִּשְׁעָרַיִךְ יְרוּשָׁלָ͏ִם : יְרוּשָׁלַ͏ִב
הַבְּנוּיָה כְּעִיר שֶׁחֻבְּרָה־לָּהּ יַחְדָּו : שֶׁשָּׁם עָלוּ שְׁבָטִים
שִׁבְטֵי־יָהּ עֵדוּת לְיִשְׂרָאֵל לְהֹדוֹת לְשֵׁם יְיָ : כִּי שָׁמָּ

5. *thy shade.* Thy protection.
upon thy right hand. The usual side for a friend or an ally.
6. *smite thee.* Sunstroke is a special danger in the East; II Kings 4. 19.
nor the moon. Belief in the baneful influence of the moon in causing intermittent insanity is widespread; cf. our English word, *lunacy.*
7. *thy soul.* Thy life, both inwardly and outwardly.
8. *thy going out . . . coming in.* All thy undertakings—a common Hebrew expression for the whole daily life.
for evermore. Until death and beyond death.
This wonderful psalm has been often put into verse. The following is by Mrs. Alice Lucas :

> " Unto the hills I lift mine eyes,
> Whence comes my help, my help that lies
> In God, enthroned above the skies,
> Who made the heavens and earth to be.

> " He guides thy foot o'er mountain steeps,
> He slumbers not, thy soul Who keeps,
> Behold He slumbers not, nor sleeps,
> Of Israel the guardian He.

> " He is thy Rock, thy shield and stay,
> On thy right hand a shade alway,
> The sun ne'er smiteth thee by day,
> The moon at night ne'er troubles thee.

Israel will neither slumber nor sleep. ⁵The Lord is thy guardian : the Lord is thy shade upon thy right hand. ⁶The sun shall not smite thee by day, nor the moon by night. ⁷The Lord shall guard thee from all evil ; he shall guard thy soul. ⁸The Lord shall guard thy going out and thy coming in, from this time forth and for evermore.

Psalm cxxii.   ¹A Pilgrim Song ; of David.

JOY AND
PRAYER
OF
PILGRIMS

I was glad when they said unto me, Let us go unto the house of the Lord. ²Our feet are standing within thy gates, O Jerusalem, ³Jerusalem that art built up as a city that is compact together : ⁴whither the tribes go up, even the tribes of the Lord, for a testimony unto Israel, to give thanks unto the Name of the Lord. ⁵For there are set

" The Lord will guard thy soul from sin,
Thy life from harm without, within,
Thy going out and coming in,
From this time forth eternally ".

PSALM 122.

The pilgrimage is at an end. The pilgrim poet is now in the sacred City which is to him the symbol of national unity, the seat of justice, and the centre of Israel's historical splendour. " Pray for the welfare of Jerusalem," is the feeling that animates him.

1. *of David.* This pilgrim-song must have come from a collection of Davidic Psalms.

I was glad. He had from the first joyfully welcomed the invitation to join a pilgrimage to the Sanctuary.

2. *are standing.* The Heb. words imply, " have been and are still standing ". When these pilgrims had reached the city gates, they halted for a while, spell-bound by the sight of the city's magnificence and memories of its ancient glories. This verse was sung by those who carried the first-fruits offerings as they entered the gates (Talmud).

3. *compact together.* The rebuilt Jerusalem is " compact ", no more waste places and no more gaps. Coverdale's rendering, " that is at unity with itself ", expresses the mutual harmony of its inhabitants as well as the unity of the nation. The Hebrew words yield an even nobler sense, if rendered, " where fellowship is made " (Mendelssohn, Duhm, Barnes) ; or, " wherein all associate together " (Leeser)—the city that, in the words of Rabbi Joshua ben Levi, makes all Israelites brethren.

4. *a testimony.* i.e. a precept of the Torah—there to give thanks to God (Ibn Ezra). The reference is to Exodus 23. 17, requiring all males to appear at the Sanctuary on the Festivals.

יֵשְׁבוּ כִסְאוֹת לְמִשְׁפָּט כִּסְאוֹת לְבֵית דָּוִד : שַׁאֲלוּ שְׁלוֹם
יְרוּשָׁלָםִ ・ יִשְׁלָיוּ אֹהֲבָיִךְ : יְהִי־שָׁלוֹם בְּחֵילֵךְ שַׁלְוָה
בְּאַרְמְנוֹתָיִךְ : לְמַעַן־אַחַי וְרֵעָי אֲדַבְּרָה־נָּא שָׁלוֹם בָּךְ
לְמַעַן בֵּית־יְיָ אֱלֹהֵינוּ אֲבַקְשָׁה טוֹב לָךְ :

תהלים קכ'ג

שִׁיר הַמַּעֲלוֹת ・ אֵלֶיךָ נָשָׂאתִי אֶת־עֵינַי הַיֹּשְׁבִי
בַּשָּׁמָיִם : הִנֵּה כְעֵינֵי עֲבָדִים אֶל־יַד אֲדוֹנֵיהֶם כְּעֵינֵי
שִׁפְחָה אֶל־יַד גְּבִרְתָּהּ ・ כֵּן עֵינֵינוּ אֶל־יְיָ אֱלֹהֵינוּ עַד
שֶׁיְּחָנֵּנוּ : חָנֵּנוּ יְיָ חָנֵּנוּ כִּי־רַב שָׂבַעְנוּ בוּז : רַבַּת שָׂבְעָה
לָהּ נַפְשֵׁנוּ הַלַּעַג הַשַּׁאֲנַנִּים הַבּוּז לִגְאֵיוֹנִים :

תהלים קכ'ד

שִׁיר הַמַּעֲלוֹת לְדָוִד ・ לוּלֵי יְיָ שֶׁהָיָה לָנוּ יֹאמַר־נָא
יִשְׂרָאֵל : לוּלֵי יְיָ שֶׁהָיָה לָנוּ בְּקוּם עָלֵינוּ אָדָם : אֲזַ

5. *thrones for judgment.* For all the functions of royalty, that included the dispensing of justice. The King was the chief judge (II Samuel 15. 2), and Jerusalem the national seat of justice. In the time of the Second Temple, it was the seat of the Sanhedrin.

8. *speak peace concerning thee.* Pray for thy welfare. The Psalmist is filled with noblest patriotism. He will for all time remain united in love with the Holy City as the goal of his longing, and with those dwelling therein as his brethren and friends.

PSALM 123.

An utterance of deep depression as in 120, but waiting for the salvation of the Almighty. The returned exiles had looked for the realization of Messianic glories—and here they were exposed to the scorn and contempt of the Samaritans who took every opportunity of harassing and insulting them.

thrones for judgment, the thrones of the house of David. ⁶Pray for the peace of Jerusalem ; may they prosper that love thee. ⁷Peace be within thy rampart, prosperity within thy palaces. ⁸For my brethren and companions' sakes I would fain speak peace concerning thee. ⁹For the sake of the house of the Lord our God I would seek thy good.

Psalm cxxiii. ¹A Pilgrim Song.

PRAYER FOR DIVINE PITY

Unto thee do I lift up mine eyes, O thou that dwellest in the heavens. ²Behold, as the eyes of servants look unto the hand of their master, as the eyes of a maiden unto the hand of her mistress, so our eyes look unto the Lord our God, until he have pity upon us. ³Have pity upon us, O Lord, have pity upon us : for we are full sated with contempt. ⁴Our soul is full sated with the mocking of those that are at ease, with the contempt of the proud.

Psalm cxxiv. ¹A Pilgrim Song ; of David.

DELIVER-ANCE IS OF GOD

If it had not been the Lord who was on our side, let Israel now say.: ²if it had not been the Lord who was on

2. *as the eyes of servants.* Watching anxiously the least movement of the master, the eye of hope, looks to God, and to Him alone, for help.

hand. The hand as *giving*, and not as *commanding*, is here meant. In the Rosh Hashanah Prayer, God is thought of not only as Master, but as Father as well. " This day Thou causest all the creatures of the Universe to stand in judgment, as children or as servants. If as children, have pity upon us as a father pitieth his children ; and if as servants, our eyes wait on thee, until Thou be gracious unto us and bring forth our judgment as the light ".

3. *full sated.* It has been their daily food.

4. *are at ease.* Live on in careless security and, therefore, regardless of the feelings of others.

the proud. The haughty. The Text *as read* (Keri) means, "the proud oppressors ".

PSALM 124.

Evidently written while the impression of Israel's escape from some deadly danger was still fresh. Some think of the rule of Babylon that had been broken by Cyrus, and the captives were freed from the meshes of the net which had so long kept them in its toils. Others, of some deliverance of the struggling community in the days of Nehemiah (4. 7–23).

חַיִּים בְּלָעֽוּנוּ בַּחֲרוֹת אַפָּם בָּֽנוּ : אֲזַי הַמַּֽיִם שְׁטָפֽוּנוּ
נַֽחְלָה עָבַר עַל־נַפְשֵֽׁנוּ : אֲזַי עָבַר עַל־נַפְשֵֽׁנוּ הַמַּֽיִם
הַזֵּידוֹנִים : בָּרוּךְ יְיָ שֶׁלֹּא נְתָנָֽנוּ טֶֽרֶף לְשִׁנֵּיהֶם : נַפְשֵֽׁנוּ
כְּצִפּוֹר נִמְלְטָה מִפַּח יוֹקְשִׁים · הַפַּח נִשְׁבָּר וַאֲנַֽחְנוּ
נִמְלָֽטְנוּ : עֶזְרֵֽנוּ בְּשֵׁם יְיָ עֹשֵׂה שָׁמַֽיִם וָאָֽרֶץ :

תהלים קכ׳ה

שִׁיר הַמַּעֲלוֹת · הַבֹּטְחִים בַּיְיָ כְּהַר־צִיּוֹן לֹא־יִמּוֹט
לְעוֹלָם יֵשֵׁב : יְרוּשָׁלַֽםִ הָרִים סָבִיב לָהּ · וַיְיָ סָבִיב לְעַמּוֹ
מֵעַתָּה וְעַד־עוֹלָם : כִּי לֹא יָנֽוּחַ שֵֽׁבֶט הָרֶֽשַׁע עַל גּוֹרַל
הַצַּדִּיקִים · לְמַֽעַן לֹא־יִשְׁלְחוּ הַצַּדִּיקִים בְּעַוְלָֽתָה יְדֵיהֶם :
הֵיטִֽיבָה יְיָ לַטּוֹבִים וְלִישָׁרִים בְּלִבּוֹתָם : וְהַמַּטִּים
עֲקַלְקַלּוֹתָם יוֹלִיכֵם יְיָ אֶת־פֹּעֲלֵי הָאָֽוֶן · שָׁלוֹם עַל־יִשְׂרָאֵל :

3. *swallowed us up alive.* As wild beasts devour their prey.

4. *waters.* The picture of a swollen mountain torrent, devastating and sweeping all before it, is a common figure for sudden attack of enemies.

gone over our soul. Overwhelmed us.

5. *proud waters.* Surging waters.

The last psalm was the sigh of sufferers; this psalm is the joyful thanksgiving for full deliverance. In every generation, Israel has had good cause to sing this song; for in every generation, enemies rise up against us to destroy us. And they would destroy us, but that the God of Heaven is our Deliverer.

PSALM 125.

GOD, ISRAEL'S ABIDING DEFENCE.

2. *the mountains.* They are an ever-present symbol to the dwellers of Jerusalem of God's guardianship.

3. *sceptre.* Symbol of rule.

our side, when men rose up against us, ³then they had swallowed us up alive, when their wrath was kindled against us ; ⁴then the waters had overwhelmed us the stream had gone over our soul ; ⁵then the proud waters had gone over our soul. ⁶Blessed be the Lord, who hath not given us as a prey to their teeth.   ⁷Our soul escaped as a bird out of the snare of the fowlers : the snare was broken and we escaped. ⁸Our help is in the Name of the Lord, who made heaven and earth.

Psalm cxxv.   ¹A Pilgrim Song.

ISRAEL'S ABIDING DEFENCE

They that trust in the Lord are as Mount Zion, which cannot be moved, but abideth for ever.   ²The mountains are round about Jerusalem, and the Lord is round about his people, from this time forth and for evermore.   ³For the sceptre of wickedness shall not rest upon the lot of the righteous, lest the righteous put forth their hands unto iniquity.   ⁴Do good, O Lord, unto those that are good, and to them that are upright in their hearts.   ⁵But as for such as turn aside unto their crooked ways, the Lord will destroy them with the workers of iniquity. Peace be upon Israel.

sceptre of wickedness. Or, " the rod of the ungodly "; some hostile power that was on the march against Judea.
rest upon. Continue to be heavy upon.
the lot of the righteous. The Land of Israel, divided among the Israelites by lot (Joshua 18).
the righteous. The Israelites justly so-called, when contrasted with the heathen.
lest the righteous. The Psalmist does not most of all dread the destruction of Jerusalem, or of its inhabitants. He fears something even more than that; namely, prolonged oppression that might cause the righteous to disbelieve in the reign, and triumph, of Righteousness on earth.
4. *upright.* The loyal and honest Israelites.
5. *as turn aside.* Renegades who forsake their God and People.
with the workers of iniquity. They will be swept away with the heathen foe.
peace be upon Israel. " Finally, the poet, stretching out his hands over all Israel as if blessing them like a priest, embraces all his hopes, petitions and wishes in this prayer. Peace is the end of tyranny, hostility, dismemberment, unrest, anguish ; peace is freedom and harmony, and unity and security and blessedness " (Delitzsch).

תהלים קכ'ו

שִׁיר הַמַּעֲלוֹת ・ בְּשׁוּב יְיָ אֶת־שִׁיבַת צִיּוֹן הָיִינוּ
כְּחֹלְמִים : אָז יִמָּלֵא שְׂחֹק פִּינוּ וּלְשׁוֹנֵנוּ רִנָּה ・ אָז
יֹאמְרוּ בַגּוֹיִם הִגְדִּיל יְיָ לַעֲשׂוֹת עִם־אֵלֶּה : הִגְדִּיל יְיָ
לַעֲשׂוֹת עִמָּנוּ הָיִינוּ שְׂמֵחִים : שׁוּבָה יְיָ אֶת־שְׁבִיתֵנוּ
כַּאֲפִיקִים בַּנֶּגֶב : הַזֹּרְעִים בְּדִמְעָה ・ בְּרִנָּה יִקְצֹרוּ :
הָלוֹךְ יֵלֵךְ וּבָכֹה נֹשֵׂא מֶשֶׁךְ־הַזָּרַע ・ בֹּא־יָבֹא בְרִנָּה
נֹשֵׂא אֲלֻמֹּתָיו :

תהלים קכ'ז

שִׁיר הַמַּעֲלוֹת לִשְׁלֹמֹה ・ אִם־יְיָ לֹא־יִבְנֶה בַיִת שָׁוְא
עָמְלוּ בוֹנָיו בּוֹ ・ אִם־יְיָ לֹא־יִשְׁמָר־עִיר שָׁוְא שָׁקַד שׁוֹמֵר :

PSALM 126.

Israel remembers the marvellous Redemption from Exile and the
triumphant Return from Babylon. That Restoration was a marvel so
astonishing that it could hardly be credited. But adversity has once
more overtaken Israel, and the Psalmist prays that God may again
bless and prosper the nation.

1. *turned again the captivity of Zion.* i.e., brought back Zion's
children that had been in captivity. It may also mean, " turned the
fortunes of Zion ", or, " restored the prosperity of Zion " (Job 42. 10).

unto them that dream. We could not believe our senses, so delighted
were we : the Redemption that suddenly broke upon us, seemed to us
at first to be not a reality but a beautiful dream.

2. *among the nations.* What astonishment this unique historic
event excited among them !

3. *hath done great things for us.* Jewry takes up the words of the
heathen, and recalls the joy of the wonderful time.

4–6. Prayer for a renewal of that redemption.

4. *streams.* Water-courses.

Psalm cxxvi. ¹A Pilgrim Song.

ISRAEL'S
RESTORA-
TION
When the Lord turned again the captivity of Zion, we were like unto them that dream. ²Then was our mouth filled with laughter, and our tongue with exultation : then said they among the nations, The Lord hath done great things for them. ³The Lord had done great things for us ; whereat we rejoiced. ⁴Bring back our captivity, O Lord,

SOWING
IN TEARS
as the streams in the South. ⁵They that sow in tears shall reap in joy. ⁶Though he goeth on his way weeping, bearing the store of seed, he shall come back with joy, bearing his sheaves.

Psalm cxxvii. ¹A Pilgrim Song ; of Solomon.

FROM GOD
ALL
BLESSINGS
COME
Except the Lord build the house, they labour in vain that build it : except the Lord watch over the city, the

in the South. In the *Negeb*, the arid region in the south of Judea. During the summer months the Negeb is a picture of desolation—large tracts of bleak rock with empty ravines and dry river-beds. However, one downpour of torrential rain, peculiar to the semi-tropical region, converts its empty ravines into rushing streams ; as if by magic, a green vegetation is conjured up, and the desert changes into an Eden. Israel and its future have often appeared to many of its children as such a dry land, bleak and dreary and desert. Its seers and patriots, however, have known that, let but the dew of Restoration descend upon it, and the dry river-beds of the Diaspora would be changed into living streams of faith and freedom and righteousness.

5. *sow in tears.* Israel has wept enough : the time of joyous reaping is at hand. " Precisely those undertakings which at first seemed hopeless and were begun under pressing troubles, end in achieving the greatest good " (Gerlach).

6. *though he goeth.* He that bears the trail of seed may go on his way weeping, but he shall assuredly come home with ringing shouts of joy, bearing his sheaves.

store of seed. lit. " trail of seed "—the sower leaves a trail of seed behind him.

PSALM 127.

GOD'S BLESSING ALONE PROSPERS ALL THINGS.

1. House-building is in vain, unless God builds with the builders ; and city-guarding is in vain, unless God keeps guard. House-building and city-guarding are here examples of all human undertakings.

שָׁוְא לָכֶם מַשְׁכִּימֵי קוּם מְאַחֲרֵי־שֶׁבֶת אֹכְלֵי לֶחֶם
הָעֲצָבִים · כֵּן יִתֵּן לִידִידוֹ שֵׁנָא : הִנֵּה נַחֲלַת יְיָ בָּנִים
שָׂכָר פְּרִי הַבָּטֶן : כְּחִצִּים בְּיַד־גִּבּוֹר כֵּן בְּנֵי הַנְּעוּרִים :
אַשְׁרֵי הַגֶּבֶר אֲשֶׁר מִלֵּא אֶת־אַשְׁפָּתוֹ מֵהֶם · לֹא יֵבֹשׁוּ
כִּי־יְדַבְּרוּ אֶת־אוֹיְבִים בַּשָּׁעַר :

תהלים קכ׳ח

שִׁיר הַמַּעֲלוֹת · אַשְׁרֵי כָּל־יְרֵא יְיָ הַהֹלֵךְ בִּדְרָכָיו :
יְגִיעַ כַּפֶּיךָ כִּי תֹאכֵל אַשְׁרֶיךָ וְטוֹב לָךְ : אֶשְׁתְּךָ כְּגֶפֶן
פֹּרִיָּה בְּיַרְכְּתֵי בֵיתֶךָ · בָּנֶיךָ כִּשְׁתִלֵי זֵיתִים סָבִיב
לְשֻׁלְחָנֶךָ : הִנֵּה כִי־כֵן יְבֹרַךְ גָּבֶר יְרֵא יְיָ : יְבָרֶכְךָ יְיָ
מִצִּיּוֹן · וּרְאֵה בְּטוּב יְרוּשָׁלָםִ כֹּל יְמֵי חַיֶּיךָ : וּרְאֵה־
בָנִים לְבָנֶיךָ · שָׁלוֹם עַל־יִשְׂרָאֵל :

2. A warning against over-anxiety in any work.

Some may toil and vex themselves and make little progress ; but God surprises His loved ones with His gifts even while they slumber. The rendering of the Authorized Version, " He giveth His beloved sleep ", is of great beauty.

3. *heritage of the Lord.* All blessings are of God ; above all, the blessing of children.

4. *as arrows.* A natural figure when the building and guarding—as in the days of Nehemiah—had to be carried on in face of opposition from within and without.

children of youth. Of young parents.

5. *the gate.* The place of civil debate and judgment. The man who appeared before the judges attended by a body of stalwart sons, need ear no false accusers, and would secure an attentive hearing.

watchman waketh but in vain. ²It is vain for you to rise up early, and so late take rest, and eat the bread of toil : such things he giveth unto his beloved in sleep. ³Lo, children are an heritage of the Lord : the fruit of the womb is his reward. ⁴As arrows in the hand of a mighty man, so are the children of youth. ⁵Happy is the man that hath filled his quiver with them : they shall not be put to shame, when they speak with enemies in the gate.

Psalm cxxviii. ¹A Pilgrim Song.

A BLESSED HOME   Happy is every one that feareth the Lord, that walketh in his ways. ²When thou shalt eat the labour of thine hands, happy shalt thou be, and it shall be well with thee. ³Thy wife shall be as a fruitful vine, in the recesses of thine house : thy children like olive plants, round about thy table. ⁴Behold thus shall the man be blessed that feareth the Lord. ⁵May the Lord bless thee out of Zion : mayest thou see the good of Jerusalem all the days of thy life. ⁶Yea, mayest thou see thy children's children. Peace be upon Israel.

PSALM 128.

This psalm has been called the " Home, Sweet Home " of Judaism. It teaches that the noblest gift of God to the godly man, who by his honest toil is independent of human support, is a peaceful and happy home life.

1. *walketh in his ways. i.e.* lives a life of probity and lovingkindness.

2. *eat the labour of thine hands.* A wonderful assertion of the dignity of labour.

happy shalt thou be. " In this world ", add the Rabbis ; and *it shall be well with thee,* " in the world to come ".

5. *see the good of Jerusalem.* Or, " see thy desire in the good of Jerusalem ". The man that feareth the Lord hears the call of social and national duty. He identifies himself with the fortunes of his People, and finds his happiness in its welfare.

6. *children's children.* To renew his youth, as he watches the building of the new generations.

peace be upon Israel. This remains the Israelite's highest hope and aim.

תהלים קכ'ט

שִׁיר הַמַּעֲלוֹת · רַבַּת צְרָרוּנִי מִנְּעוּרַי יֹאמַר נָא
יִשְׂרָאֵל : רַבַּת צְרָרוּנִי מִנְּעוּרָי · גַּם לֹא יָכְלוּ-לִי : עַל
גַּבִּי חָרְשׁוּ חֹרְשִׁים · הֶאֱרִיכוּ לְמַעֲנִיתָם : יְיָ צַדִּיק · קִצֵּץ
עֲבוֹת רְשָׁעִים : יֵבֹשׁוּ וְיִסֹּגוּ אָחוֹר כֹּל שֹׂנְאֵי צִיּוֹן : יִהְיוּ
כַּחֲצִיר גַּגּוֹת · שֶׁקַּדְמַת שָׁלַף יָבֵשׁ : שֶׁלֹּא מִלֵּא כַפּוֹ
קוֹצֵר וְחִצְנוֹ מְעַמֵּר : וְלֹא אָמְרוּ הָעֹבְרִים בִּרְכַּת יְיָ
אֲלֵיכֶם · בֵּרַכְנוּ אֶתְכֶם בְּשֵׁם יְיָ :

תהלים ק'ל

שִׁיר הַמַּעֲלוֹת · מִמַּעֲמַקִּים קְרָאתִיךָ יְיָ : אֲדֹנָי שִׁמְעָה
בְקוֹלִי · תִּהְיֶינָה אָזְנֶיךָ קַשֻּׁבוֹת לְקוֹל תַּחֲנוּנָי : אִם-
עֲוֹנוֹת תִּשְׁמָר-יָהּ · אֲדֹנָי מִי יַעֲמֹד : כִּי-עִמְּךָ הַסְּלִיחָה

PSALM 129.

In the days of the writer of this psalm, Israel was surrounded by hatred. But Israel survived her enemies in the past; she would do so again. In times of darkness, the Jew finds solace and strength in the history of his People.

3. *plowed upon my back.* Cf. " I gave my back to the smiters " (Isaiah 51. 23)—bold metaphors for cruel maltreatment. Yet that suffering did not deaden Israel's spiritual life; nay, it deepened it. One is reminded of Heine's confession that to him the message of the Bible was not as clear or luminous as it was to " Uncle Tom "; for Uncle Tom read it *with his back.*

4. *cords.* As when the cords which bind the oxen to the plough are broken, the plougher can no more furrow the earth; so God has cut off from the tyrants the means of the exercise of their tyranny, the bands which fastened the yoke of servitude.

6. *upon the housetops.* Having no depths of soil, it withers prematurely.

Psalm cxxix. [1]A Pilgrim Song.

*ISRAEL'S
OPPRES-
SORS*

To the full have they afflicted me from my youth up,
let Israel now say ; [2]to the full have they afflicted me
from my youth up : yet have they not prevailed against
me. [3]The plowers plowed upon my back, they made long
their furrows. [4]The Lord is righteous : he hath cut asunder the
cords of the wicked. [5]Let them be put to shame and turned
backward, all they that hate Zion. [6]Let them be as the
grass upon the housetops, which withereth before it shooteth
forth : [7]wherewith the reaper filleth not his hand, nor he
that bindeth sheaves his bosom : [8]neither do they which go
by say, The blessing of the Lord be upon you ; we bless
you in the Name of the Lord.

Psalm cxxx. [1]A Pilgrim Song.

*OUT OF
THE
DEPTHS*

Out of the depths have I cried unto thee, O Lord.
[2]Lord, hear my voice : let thine ears be attentive to the
voice of my supplications. [3]If thou, Lord, shouldst mark
iniquities, O Lord, who could stand ? [4]But there is forgiveness with thee, that thou mayest be feared. [5]I wait for the

---

7. *reaper.* The " grass " includes corn springing from grains
accidently dropped on the roof.
  bosom. Lap or loose fold of his garment.
  8. *the blessing . . . you.* The friendly greeting of the passers-by
to the reapers at work ; see Ruth 2. 4.
  we bless you . . . Lord. The Targum takes these words to be the
response of the reapers.

PSALM 130.

One of the most famous Psalms—*De profundis.* God is a God of
forgiveness ; therefore, Israel can hope and trust.
  1. *out of the depths.* It is a cry from the depth of sin and the depth
of calamity. Israel is in danger of being overwhelmed by a sea of
trouble ; it is only his cry out of the depths that is evidence of his life,
and hope of his survival.
  3. *shouldst mark iniquities.* " If thou, Lord, wilt be extreme to mark
what is done amiss " (Coverdale).
  who could stand. Before Thee in judgment.
  4. *with thee.* Israel has no need of a Mediator or Intercessor. Every
sinner has direct access to God, as a child has to its parent. And with
God *alone* is forgiveness.

לְמַעַן תִּוָּרֵא : קִוִּיתִי יְיָ קִוְּתָה נַפְשִׁי · וְלִדְבָרוֹ הוֹחָלְתִּי
נַפְשִׁי לַאדֹנָי מִשֹּׁמְרִים לַבֹּקֶר שֹׁמְרִים לַבֹּקֶר : יַחֵ
יִשְׂרָאֵל אֶל־יְיָ · כִּי־עִם־יְיָ הַחֶסֶד וְהַרְבֵּה עִמּוֹ פְדוּת :
וְהוּא יִפְדֶּה אֶת־יִשְׂרָאֵל מִכֹּל עֲוֹנוֹתָיו :

תהלים קל׳א

שִׁיר הַמַּעֲלוֹת לְדָוִד · יְיָ לֹא־גָבַהּ לִבִּי וְלֹא־רָמוּ עֵינַי
וְלֹא־הִלַּכְתִּי בִּגְדֹלוֹת וּבְנִפְלָאוֹת מִמֶּנִּי : אִם־לֹא שִׁוִּיתִ
וְדוֹמַמְתִּי נַפְשִׁי כְּגָמֻל עֲלֵי אִמּוֹ · כַּגָּמֻל עָלַי נַפְשִׁי : יַחֵ
יִשְׂרָאֵל אֶל־יְיָ מֵעַתָּה וְעַד־עוֹלָם :

תהלים קל׳ב

שִׁיר הַמַּעֲלוֹת · זְכוֹר־יְיָ לְדָוִד אֵת כָּל־עֻנּוֹתוֹ : אֲשֶׁר־
נִשְׁבַּע לַיְיָ נָדַר לַאֲבִיר יַעֲקֹב : אִם־אָבֹא בְּאֹהֶל בֵּיתִ
אִם־אֶעֱלֶה עַל־עֶרֶשׂ יְצוּעָי : אִם־אֶתֵּן שְׁנָת לְעֵינָי לְעַפְעַפַּ

that thou mayest be feared. i.e. be held in reverence. If God were pitiless, man would stand in terror of Him, but could not revere or love Him. God's loving pardon raises the sinner to the higher reverence which is akin to love. The word "feared" here, as in so many places in Scripture, does not mean "dreaded". Thus the Torah speaks of a man's duty to "fear" his mother; i.e. revere and obey her (Leviticus 19. 3).

6. watchmen. The repetition gives a touch of pathetic earnestness. As the tired night watchmen yearn for the break of day—as sentinels, in the bitter cold, guarding some key-position against the enemy, wait for the morning to relieve their duty—so Israel yearns for God to end the night of trouble, and usher in the dawn of a happier day.

7. plenteous deliverance. Manifold ways and means of effecting Israel's deliverance. Anti-Semitic theologians deny that Judaism is a "religion of Redemption". This psalm alone—quite apart from

Lord, my soul doth wait, and in his word do I hope. ⁶My soul waiteth for the Lord, more than watchmen wait for the morning ; yea, more than watchmen for the morning.

HOPE IN THE LORD

⁷O let Israel hope in the Lord ; for with the Lord there is lovingkindness, and with him is plenteous deliverance. ⁸And he shall deliver Israel from all his iniquities.

Psalm cxxxi. ¹A Pilgrim Song ; of David.

CHILD LIKE TRUST

Lord, my heart is not haughty, nor mine eyes lofty ; neither do I exercise myself in great matters, or in things too marvellous for me. ²Surely I have stilled and quieted my soul, like a weaned child with his mother ; my soul is with me like a weaned child. ³O Israel, hope in the Lord from this time forth and for evermore.

Psalm· cxxxii. ¹A Pilgrim Song.

DIVINE PROMISE TO DAVID

Lord, remember unto David all his affliction ; ²how he sware unto the Lord, and vowed unto the Mighty One of Jacob : ³Surely I will not come into the tent of my house, nor go up unto the couch of my rest ; ⁴I will not give sleep

Israel's doctrine of Repentance, and the sacred institution of the Day of Atonement—is an absolute denial of that baseless libel.

PSALM 131.

Its author has learned child-like trust in the school of suffering. He has mastered his tyrannous longings, and, through the discipline of humility, resigned himself contentedly to the will of God.

1. *great matters.* May mean perplexing· questions of religion, such as the suffering of the righteous, or the coming of the Messiah. The Psalmist was not a Job, fearlessly probing religious questions : his humility before God gave him blissful contentment.

2. *a weaned child.* As the weaned child is satisfied by the mere presence of his mother, so the Psalmist is no longer agitated by a desire for earthly prosperities. God is enough for him.

PSALM 132.

The Ancient Promise to David and Zion.

Religion blesses when the generations are bound together in love of its ideals.

1. *unto David.* Unto the Davidic family. This idea of a solidarity of successive generations led to the doctrine of the Merits of the Fathers (Zechuth Ovous) ; see p. 132.

2. *sware.* A poetical way of expressing his determination.

תְּנוּמָה : עַד־אֶמְצָא מָקוֹם לַיָי מִשְׁכָּנוֹת לַאֲבִיר יַעֲקֹב :

הִנֵּה שְׁמַעֲנוּהָ בְאֶפְרָתָה מְצָאנוּהָ בִּשְׂדֵי־יָעַר : נָבוֹאָה

לְמִשְׁכְּנוֹתָיו נִשְׁתַּחֲוֶה לַהֲדֹם רַגְלָיו : קוּמָה יְיָ לִמְנוּחָתֶךָ

אַתָּה וַאֲרוֹן עֻזֶּךָ : כֹּהֲנֶיךָ יִלְבְּשׁוּ־צֶדֶק וַחֲסִידֶיךָ יְרַנֵּנוּ :

בַּעֲבוּר דָּוִד עַבְדֶּךָ אַל־תָּשֵׁב פְּנֵי מְשִׁיחֶךָ : נִשְׁבַּע־יְיָ

לְדָוִד · אֱמֶת לֹא־יָשׁוּב מִמֶּנָּה · מִפְּרִי בִטְנְךָ אָשִׁית

לְכִסֵּא־לָךְ : אִם־יִשְׁמְרוּ בָנֶיךָ בְּרִיתִי וְעֵדֹתִי זוֹ אֲלַמְּדֵם ·

גַּם־בְּנֵיהֶם עֲדֵי־עַד יֵשְׁבוּ לְכִסֵּא־לָךְ : כִּי־בָחַר יְיָ בְּצִיּוֹן

אִוָּהּ לְמוֹשָׁב לוֹ : זֹאת־מְנוּחָתִי עֲדֵי־עַד · פֹּה אֵשֵׁב כִּי

אִוִּתִיהָ : צֵידָהּ בָּרֵךְ אֲבָרֵךְ אֶבְיוֹנֶיהָ אַשְׂבִּיעַ לָחֶם :

וְכֹהֲנֶיהָ אַלְבִּישׁ יֶשַׁע וַחֲסִידֶיהָ רַנֵּן יְרַנֵּנוּ : שָׁם אַצְמִיחַ

קֶרֶן לְדָוִד עָרַכְתִּי נֵר לִמְשִׁיחִי : אוֹיְבָיו אַלְבִּישׁ בֹּשֶׁת ·

וְעָלָיו יָצִיץ נִזְרוֹ :

6–10. The people recall the finding of the Ark, and their enthusiasm at its establishment in Zion : their prayer to bless the priests, the nation, and the King.

6. *we heard it.* The people are the speakers.

Ephrathah. Probably the name of the district in which was situated the village Kiriath-Jearim which harboured the Ark (I Samuel 7. 1, 2) *fields of Jaar.* *i.e.* " the Fields of the Forest " ; the neighbourhood of Kiriath-Jearim.

8. *ark of thy strength.* Heb. idiom for " Thy mighty ark ".

DIVINE
PROMISE
TO DAVID

to mine eyes, or slumber to mine eyelids ; ⁵until I find out a place for the Lord, a habitation for the Mighty One of Jacob. ⁶Lo, we heard of it in Ephrathah : we found it in the fields of Jaar. ⁷Let us go into his habitation ; let us worship at his temple. ⁸Arise, O Lord, unto thy resting-place ; thou, and the ark of thy strength. ⁹Let thy priests be clothed with righteousness ; and let thy loving ones exult. ¹⁰For the sake of David thy servant turn not away the face of thine anointed. ¹¹The Lord hath sworn unto David in truth—he will not turn from it— : of the fruit of thy body will I set upon thy throne. ¹²If thy sons will keep my covenant, and my testimonies that I shall teach them, their sons also shall sit upon thy throne for evermore. ¹³For the Lord hath chosen Zion ; he hath desired it for his habitation. ¹⁴This is my resting-place for ever : here will I dwell ; for I have desired it. ¹⁵I will abundantly bless her provision : I will satisfy her needy with bread. ¹⁶Her priests also will I clothe with salvation : and her loving ones shall exult aloud. ¹⁷There will I make the strength of David to flourish ; I have prepared a lamp for mine anointed. ¹⁸His enemies will I clothe with shame ; but upon him his crown shall shine.

9. *clothed with righteousness.* Be worthy servants of the God of righteousness.

10. *thine anointed.* The anointed King of Israel for the time being.

11–18. The Divine Response.

15. *her needy.* In the early days of the Restoration, when this psalm was probably written, the people suffered much from scarcity.

16. *with salvation.* He will prosper those who minister faithfully.

17. *strength of David.* He will restore the victorious might of the house of David.

a lamp. A natural metaphor for the preservation of the dynasty.

תפלת מנחה לשבת

תהלים קל״ג

שִׁיר הַמַּעֲלוֹת לְדָוִד · הִנֵּה מַה־טּוֹב וּמַה־נָּעִים שֶׁבֶת אַחִים גַּם־יָחַד : כַּשֶּׁמֶן הַטּוֹב עַל־הָרֹאשׁ יֹרֵד עַל־הַזָּקָן זְקַן אַהֲרֹן שֶׁיֹּרֵד עַל־פִּי מִדּוֹתָיו : כְּטַל־חֶרְמוֹן שֶׁיֹּרֵד עַל־הַרְרֵי צִיּוֹן · כִּי־שָׁם צִוָּה יְיָ אֶת־הַבְּרָכָה · חַיִּים עַד־הָעוֹלָם :

תהלים קל״ד

שִׁיר הַמַּעֲלוֹת · הִנֵּה בָּרְכוּ אֶת־יְיָ כָּל־עַבְדֵי יְיָ הָעֹמְדִים בְּבֵית יְיָ בַּלֵּילוֹת : שְׂאוּ־יְדֵכֶם קֹדֶשׁ וּבָרְכוּ אֶת־יְיָ : יְבָרֶכְךָ יְיָ מִצִּיּוֹן עֹשֵׂה שָׁמַיִם וָאָרֶץ :

עָלֵינוּ, *p*. 550.

קַדִּישׁ יָתוֹם, *p*. 554.

Psalm 133.

The Blessing of unity in family, community of worshippers, state, and restored Israel.

2. *goodly oil.* Oil was the symbol of joy and festivity. Here the reference is to the perfumed sacred oil with which the High Priest was anointed.

3. *dew.* " Is a symbol for what is refreshing, quickening, invigorating ; and the Psalmist compares the influence of brotherly unity upon the nation to the effect of the dew upon the vegetation. From such dwelling together, individuals draw fresh energy " (Kirkpatrick).

Psalm cxxxiii. [1]A Pilgrim Song ; of David.

THE BLISS OF UNITY

Behold, how good and pleasant it is for brethren to dwell together in unity ! [2]It is like the goodly oil upon the head, that floweth down upon the beard, even Aaron's beard which cometh down upon the skirt of his garments ; [3]like the dew of Hermon, that falleth upon the mountains of Zion : for there the Lord commanded the blessing, even life for evermore.

Psalm cxxxiv. [1]A Pilgrim Song

" BLESS YE THE LORD "

Behold, bless ye the Lord, all ye servants of the Lord, who stand in the house of the Lord in the night seasons. [2]Lift up your hands in holiness, and bless ye the Lord. [3]The Lord bless thee out of Zion ; even he that made heaven and earth.

Oleynu, p. 551.

Mourner's Kaddish, p. 555.

---

like the dew of Hermon. This means either, plenteous as the dew of Hermon is that which falls on Mt. Zion ; or, the moisture that is borne from snow-capped Hermon and falls in refreshing drops on Zion.

life for evermore. " The days of Israel are innumerable " (Ecclesiasticus 37. 25).

PSALM 134.

This psalm seems to have been a night-song of the Temple watchmen. Verses 1 and 2 were addressed to the guard going off duty by those who came to relieve them ; and they, in their turn, answered in the words of verse 3.

With the sweet interchange of greeting and exhortation to congregational worship, this group of psalms joyously ends.

פִּרְקֵי אָבוֹת:

ABOTH: SAYINGS OF THE FATHERS

"Sayings of the Fathers" is the most widely known of all the sixty-three tractates of the Mishna. It is unique in character. The Mishna is a code of laws governing Jewish life : its subject matter is, therefore, predominantly legal. But this tractate is almost entirely concerned with moral conduct. It consists, for the greater part, of the favourite maxims—being the epitome of their wisdom and experience—of some sixty Rabbis, extending over a period of nearly five hundred years, from 300 B.C.E. to 200 of the Christian era. It also contains anonymous sayings, and touches upon various historical and folk-lore themes.

Aboth is the name by which the tractate was originally designated. It means " Fathers ", *i.e.* the spiritual patriarchs who preserved and developed the Torah as the living tradition of Israel's Faith. In its opening portion, Aboth gives a " chain " of these teachers and a notable saying of each one. *Sayings of the Fathers* is an appropriate English title, as the work preserves and transmits these winged words of wisdom and piety. It is preferable to the current name, " Ethics of the Fathers ", seeing that Aboth is not a systematic ethical treatise. The wisdom of the ages finds in every people its way to the masses, by means only of the proverb, saying, or parable. So was it in Israel. These moral, religious, and folk aphorisms came also to be known as *Mishnath Chassidim*, "the Mishna of the Pious ", *i.e.* a Course of Instruction in Holy Living. The famous teacher Raba (died 352 C.E.) declared, "Whoever would become pious must fulfil the words of Aboth מִילֵּי דְאָבוֹת ". A great non-Jewish scholar of our day endorses that judgment. " The level of these sayings is very high, and for a knowledge of the ideals of rabbinical ethics and piety, no other easily accessible source is equal to Aboth " (Moore).

The appeal of Aboth is widely human and fundamentally Biblical. The Gaon of Wilna and others have shown that every one of the sayings has its roots, or parallel, in Scripture. Aboth is not, however, merely an echo of the gnomic wisdom of the Bible. If, for example, we compare Proverbs 22. 1 (" A good name is rather to be chosen than great riches ") with Aboth IV, 17 (" There are three crowns : the crown of learning, the crown of priesthood, and the crown of royalty ; but the crown of a good name excels them all "), we find that the latter has a distinct beauty of its own. In the same way, many of the ethical teachings of Scripture are given in Aboth a new and ever memorable setting ; *e.g.* " In a place where there are no men, strive thou to be a man ". In brief, Aboth is no unworthy continuation of Scripture.

By a sure religious instinct the entire tractate has been early embodied in the Prayer Book. No other *complete* work of any kind— not even the Book of Psalms—has that distinction. The Gaon Rab Amram, in the eighth century, mentions that it was customary in the Bábylonian Academies to read one of the chapters of Aboth on Sabbath afternoons. In consequence, the people came to speak of the book as *Pirkey Aboth*, " the Chapters of the Fathers " ; or, in conversation simply as *Perek*, " the Chapter ". Ashkenazi communities to-day read a chapter, occasionally two, from the Sabbath after Passover to the Sabbath before the New Year.

" By this excellent practice, a whole body of moral dicta—each one summing up with remarkable conciseness a life's experience and philosophy, each one breathing the spirit of piety, saintliness, justice, and love for humanity—has sunk deeply into the innermost heart and consciousness of the Jewish people " (Gorfinkle). " Aboth takes rank as a classic in Jewish literature ; yet it has never been regarded by Jews as mere literature, as if they had no personal concern with what it said, and were only pleased with the manner of saying it. Aboth speaks to the heart of the Jew in a way and to an extent seldom realized by any non-Jewish reader " (Herford). Sabbath by Sabbath parents studied these wise and edifying maxims with their children, and stressed their moral application ; with the result, that the words became part of both Jewish speech and life. The humblest Jewish workman, who had no opportunity for deep Talmudic study, had his Siddur, and was usually well versed in the contents of Aboth reprinted therein. Its influence in moulding the character of the Jew has consequently been as great as it has been beneficent.

Aboth has been made the subject of popular and of philosophical commentaries more often than any other of the Rabbinical Writings. Full use has been made of that literature in this latest exposition of wonderful sayings that are universal in application, and have not lost their power with the passing of time. They give guidance in human duty ; and the reader of to-day will find in them light upon many problems of life and conduct.

*One of the following chapters is read on each Sabbath from the Sabbath
after פֶּסַח to the Sabbath before* רֹאשׁ הַשָּׁנָה

כָּל־יִשְׂרָאֵל יֵשׁ לָהֶם חֵלֶק לָעוֹלָם הַבָּא · שֶׁנֶּאֱמַר וְעַמֵּךְ כֻּלָּם
צַדִּיקִים לְעוֹלָם יִירְשׁוּ אָרֶץ · נֵצֶר מַטָּעַי מַעֲשֵׂה יָדַי לְהִתְפָּאֵר :

פֶּרֶק רִאשׁוֹן :

(א) מֹשֶׁה קִבֵּל תּוֹרָה מִסִּינַי · וּמְסָרָהּ לִיהוֹשֻׁעַ וִיהוֹשֻׁעַ
לִזְקֵנִים וּזְקֵנִים לִנְבִיאִים וּנְבִיאִים מְסָרוּהָ לְאַנְשֵׁי כְנֶסֶת

ALL ISRAEL. This quotation from Mishna Sanhedrin x, 1 is read
before each chapter of Aboth. By studying the teaching contained in
Aboth and following it in his life, every Israelite can become a worthy
member of "the kingdom of priests and a holy nation", and so earn
the reward which is in store for the righteous.

This dogmatic announcement—ALL ISRAELITES HAVE A PORTION IN
THE WORLD TO COME—closes a long controversy. Many believed that
the number of those who were to share the immortal life was very small.
Sectarian and Jewish-Christian circles held that the vast majority
of mankind were doomed to perdition, unless "saved" by the blood of
a Redeemer. Not so the authoritative Rabbinic opinion as expressed in
this mishna. "The teaching of Hillel concerning the all-sufficing mercy
of God, swept aside the hapless conception that eternal suffering awaits
the average man" (Kohler). Moreover, salvation is not conceived by
the Rabbis as confined to Israel. Any heathen who observed the purely
ethical commandments of the Decalogue (see on Genesis 9. 7 in
Genesis, 81, one vol. ed., 33) was considered "righteous"; and the pronouncement, "The righteous of all peoples have a portion in the World to
come", was early recognized as the universal belief of Judaism.

the world to come. See p. 255.

as it is said. The Sages of Israel did not claim to originate new
religious or ethical doctrines, but to derive them from Scripture : hence
their custom of adding a proof-text. "It must be noted that the Rabbis,
like other preachers, made use of texts for homiletical purposes, and
did not therefore always adhere to the strictly literal meaning of the
Scriptural words" (Singer).

thy people. The people that by its conduct deserves to have the
Divine Name attached to it.

One of the following chapters is read on each Sabbath from the Sabbath after Passover until the Sabbath before the New Year.

aiah 60. 21   All Israel have a portion in the world to come; as it is said, And thy people shall be all righteous; they shall inherit the land for ever, the branch of my planting, the work of my hands, that I may be glorified.

CHAPTER I

1. Moses received the Torah on Sinai, and handed it down to Joshua; Joshua to the elders; the elders to the

---

inherit the land for ever. Employed here in a spiritual sense : the Abode of the righteous, where death is no more.

that I may be glorified. The good life is a hallowing of God, and our acknowledgment of His sovereignty of the universe.

CHAPTER I

1–15. A CHRONOLOGICAL RECORD OF THE ORIGIN AND TRANSMISSION OF THE ORAL TRADITION IN JUDAISM, FROM THE OLDEST RABBINIC AUTHORITIES DOWN TO HILLEL AND SHAMMAI.

1. MOSES. Israel's career as a spiritual force in history begins with the Father of the Prophets, *Mosheh Rabbenu,* " Moses our Teacher ", as his People affectionately names him.

Torah. The word " Torah " is variously used for the Pentateuch, the entire Scriptures, the Oral Tradition, as well as for the whole body of religious truth, study and practice. Often the word " Torah " is equivalent to the word " Religion ". In this mishna, the reference is to the Oral Tradition. To the Rabbis, the real Torah was not merely the Written Text of the Five Books of Moses (תורה שבכתב) ; it also included the meaning enshrined in that Text, as expounded and unfolded by the interpretation of successive generations of Sages who made its implicit Divine teachings explicit. This Oral Teaching was handed down from the earliest days by word of mouth (תורה שבעל פה), until it was codified in the Mishna (*circa* 200 A.C.E.).

on Sinai. *i.e.* from God on Sinai.

handed it down. Tradition is a key-word in the Jewish religious system. The Judaism of to-day is in the direct line of descent from the Revelation on Sinai, the intervening generations of teachers forming links in an unbroken chain of Tradition (A. Cohen).

elders. Men of knowledge and experience who, after the death of Joshua, continued to administer Israel and act as its religious guides ; Joshua, 24. 31. The term here includes the Judges till Samuel.

הַגְּדוֹלָה ‧ הֵם אָמְרוּ שְׁלשָׁה דְבָרִים ‧ הֱווּ מְתוּנִים בַּדִּין

וְהַעֲמִידוּ תַלְמִידִים הַרְבֵּה וַעֲשׂוּ סְיָג לַתּוֹרָה : (ב) שִׁמְעוֹן

הַצַּדִּיק הָיָה מִשְּׁיָרֵי כְּנֶסֶת הַגְּדוֹלָה ‧ הוּא הָיָה אוֹמֵר ‧

עַל־שְׁלשָׁה דְבָרִים הָעוֹלָם עוֹמֵד עַל הַתּוֹרָה וְעַל הָעֲבוֹדָה

וְעַל גְּמִילוּת חֲסָדִים : (ג) אַנְטִיגְנוֹס אִישׁ שׂוֹכוֹ קִבֵּל

מִשִּׁמְעוֹן הַצַּדִּיק ‧ הוּא הָיָה אוֹמֵר ‧ אַל־תִּהְיוּ כַּעֲבָדִים

הַמְשַׁמְּשִׁים אֶת־הָרַב עַל־מְנָת לְקַבֵּל פְּרָס ‧ אֶלָּא הֱווּ כַּעֲבָדִים

הַמְשַׁמְּשִׁים אֶת־הָרַב שֶׁלֹּא עַל־מְנָת לְקַבֵּל פְּרָס ‧ וִיהִי מוֹרָא

prophets. The unique band of interpreters of the Divine will, whose writings are an enduring inspiration to the human race.

Great Assembly. Or, " Great Synagogue ". The Prophets, Scribes, Sages and Teachers who continued the spiritual regeneration of Israel that was begun by Ezra. Tradition states that they laid the foundations of the Liturgy, edited several of the books of Scripture, and all but fixed the Biblical canon. Later generations summed up their religious activity in the words : " They restored the crown of the Torah to its pristine splendour ". The main facts concerning the Great Assembly are unassailable by sober historical criticism.

used to say. Were in the habit of saying : these words were their motto.

be deliberate in judgment. Originally an admonition to judges, warning them against hasty decisions. In the earliest exposition of Aboth, this maxim was given a wider application : every man is to be moderate in judgment ; *i.e.* refrain from haste, anger, impatience and stubbornness in his dealings with his fellow-men (Aboth di Rabbi Nathan).

raise up many disciples. Judaism is a religious democracy ; and the Torah is the heritage of the *congregation* of Israel ; see p. 13.

a fence round the Torah. Surround it with cautionary rules that shall, like a danger signal, halt a man before he gets within breaking distance of the Divine statute itself. On the Sabbath, for example, even the handling of work-tools is forbidden, מוקצה.

2. *Simon the Just.* Either Simon ben Onias I (High Priest from 310 to 291 B.C.E.) ; or, more probably, his grandson (High Priest from 219 to 199). Joshua ben Sira, the contemporary of the latter Simon, speaks of him as, "Great among his brethren and the glory of his people. How glorious was he when he came out of the Sanctuary ! Like the full moon on the feast days, and like the rainbow becoming visible in the cloud " (Ecclesiasticus 50).

prophets; and the prophets handed it down to the Men of the Great Assembly. They said three things: Be deliberate in judgment; raise up many disciples; and make a fence round the Torah.

2. Simon the Just was one of the last survivors of the Great Assembly. He used to say, Upon three things the world is based: upon the Torah, upon Divine service, and upon the practice of charity.

3. Antigonos of Socho received the tradition from Simon the Just. He used to say, Be not like servants who minister to their master upon the condition of receiving a reward; but be like servants who minister to their master without

---

upon three things. i.e. the neglect of these three things would entail the downfall of all Jewish life. They are Religion, Worship and Humanity.

the Torah. God's Word to Man. It is Israel's "tree of life". Saadya Gaon, in the tenth century, declared: "Our nation is a nation only by reason of its Torah".

Divine Service. Originally this meant the Sacrificial cult of the Temple, including the prayers by which it was accompanied. But the term soon came to mean "service of God in the heart", Worship. For the fundamental importance of Prayer—Man's response to God—in Israel, see the Introduction to this Prayer Book.

the practice of charity. Man's recognition of the duties of brotherhood to his fellow-man. The Prophet Micah (6. 8) declared the love of mercy to be one-third of Religion; and the Rabbis held readiness to be helpful to those needing help to be the sign of the Israelite. It is likewise the sign of humanity. "The pitiless man is like the cattle of the field which are indifferent to the sufferings of their kind" (Sefer Chassidim). See pp. 16 and 17.

3. *Antigonos.* The first noted Jew with a Greek name. He lived in the first half of the third pre-Christian century.

Socho. Mentioned in Joshua 15. 35.

received. The Hebrew term קִבֵּל indicates direct transmission of the Traditional Learning (קַבָּלָה).

be not like servants. Serve God from pure motives.

a reward. According to Jewish teaching it is not wrong to hope for God's reward of righteous living; see pp. 121–123. Even a detractor of Judaism admits that "Piety is not content to stretch out its hands to the empty air—it must meet an Arm descending from heaven. It needs a reward; not for the reward's sake, but in order to be sure of its own reality; in order to know that there is a communion of God with

שָׁמַיִם עֲלֵיכֶם: ‏(ד) יוֹסֵי בֶּן־יוֹעֶזֶר אִישׁ צְרֵדָה וְיוֹסֵי בֶּן־

יוֹחָנָן אִישׁ יְרוּשָׁלַיִם קִבְּלוּ מֵהֶם • יוֹסֵי בֶּן־יוֹעֶזֶר אִישׁ

צְרֵדָה אוֹמֵר • יְהִי בֵיתְךָ בֵּית וַעַד לַחֲכָמִים וֶהֱוֵי מִתְאַבֵּק

בַּעֲפַר רַגְלֵיהֶם וֶהֱוֵי שׁוֹתֶה בַצָּמָא אֶת־דִּבְרֵיהֶם: ‏(ה) יוֹסֵי

בֶּן־יוֹחָנָן אִישׁ יְרוּשָׁלַיִם אוֹמֵר • יְהִי בֵיתְךָ פָּתוּחַ לִרְוָחָה

וְיִהְיוּ עֲנִיִּים בְּנֵי בֵיתֶךָ • וְאַל־תַּרְבֶּה שִׂיחָה עִם הָאִשָּׁה •

בְּאִשְׁתּוֹ אָמְרוּ קַל וָחֹמֶר בְּאֵשֶׁת חֲבֵרוֹ • מִכַּאן אָמְרוּ חֲכָמִים

כָּל־הַמַּרְבֶּה שִׂיחָה עִם הָאִשָּׁה גּוֹרֵם רָעָה לְעַצְמוֹ וּבוֹטֵל

---

man, and a road by which to reach it " (Wellhausen). However, Antigonos maintains that, legitimate as the hope of reward may be, it is not to be the *motive* of our obedience. The Law of God should be kept for its own sake. " Blessed is the man who fears the Lord, and in His commandments delights greatly" (Psalm 112. 1); "in His commandments, and not *in the reward* of the commandments ", is the Rabbinic comment.

the fear of Heaven. The Heb. מורא does not mean *dread* of God. It denotes the awe and reverence we feel before the Eye that seeth all things, the Ear that heareth all things, and the Judge before Whom we are to give account for our doings on earth (III, 1). Renan's rendering, " let the dew of Heaven be upon you ", is beautiful but inexact.

4. *José.* An abbreviated form of Joseph. He lived in the first half of the second pre-Christian century.

Zeredah. Mentioned in Joshua 15. 35.

from the preceding. The Heb. is " from them " ; *i.e.,* either from Simon and Antigonos, or from the series of unnamed teachers in the intervening period between Antigonos and José.

From this point to mishna 12, we have the Rabbis named in pairs (*Zugoth*) : one held the office of *Nasi*, the President of the Sanhedrin (in English, this word generally ends in an *m*—which is quite wrong); and the second was *Av Beth Din*," father (chief) of the Court of Law." The appointment of a dual authority seems to have been a revival of an earlier practice ; II Chronicles 19. 11. The SANHEDRIN was the Supreme Court and National Council. It consisted of 71 members, and administered the political, as well as the religious, life of the nation in the later centuries of the Second Temple. It also dealt with the more important civil and criminal cases.

the dust of their feet. Disciples as a rule sat on the ground before their master.

5. *let thy house be open wide.* Wide, as a sign of cordial welcome. Hospitality to the homeless has always been one of the conspicuous

the condition of receiving a reward ; and let the fear of Heaven be upon you.

4. José, the son of Yoezer, of Zeredah, and José, the son of Yochanan, of Jerusalem, received the tradition from the preceding. José, the son of Yoezer, of Zeredah, said, Let thy house be a meeting house for the wise ; sit amidst the dust of their feet ; and drink in their words with thirst.

5. José, the son of Yochanan, of Jerusalem, said, Let thy house be open wide ; let the poor be members of thy household ; and engage not in much gossip with women. This applies even to one's own wife ; how much more then to the wife of one's neighbour. Hence the sages say, Whoso engages in much gossip with women brings evil upon himself, neglects the study of the Torah, and will in the end inherit Gehinnom.

virtues of the Jewish life (Genesis 18). " In the Middle Ages the treatment of poor Jewish travellers was considerate beyond description. Nothing might be done to put the guest to shame " (Abrahams).

members of thy household. The poor are to be treated as if they were part of the family.

much gossip with women. Nothing derogatory to woman is implied here. The words " gossip," and especially " much," should be noted. Some maintain that this maxim belongs to an ethic which modern thought has outgrown ; however, its admonition to avoid not only the occasion to sin, but everything that might lead to it, will ever retain its moral value.

this applies. A later marginal note, added by some one who thought that the maxim needed elucidation.

one's own wife. The reference is here to excessive talk on trivial matters; for the Rabbis urge a man to discuss his serious concerns with his wife and profit by her counsel. For the position of woman in Judaism, see introductory note to the Marriage Service, pp. 1006–9.

how much more. This form of argument is known as *kol v'chomer,* " from minor to major "; see p. 43.

evil. The danger of immoral conduct. This marginal note finds its parallel in Ecclesiasticus 9. 9.

Gehinnom. lit. " the valley of Hinnom," situated S.W. of Jerusalem. In the days of old, it had been the scene of the savage rites connected with the Canaanite worship of Moloch, to whom children were sacrificed. The name became a term for what is loathsome and horrifying ; and popular belief in later times identified the locality with the place where the dead expiate their sins. The name is the opposite of Gan Eden, " Paradise."

מִדִּבְרֵי תוֹרָה וְסוֹפוֹ יוֹרֵשׁ גֵּיהִנֹּם : (ו) יְהוֹשֻׁעַ בֶּן־פְּרַחְיָה

וְנִתַּי הָאַרְבֵּלִי קִבְּלוּ מֵהֶם · יְהוֹשֻׁעַ בֶּן־פְּרַחְיָה אוֹמֵר · עֲשֵׂה

לְךָ רַב וּקְנֵה לְךָ חָבֵר וֶהֱוֵה דָן אֶת־כָּל־הָאָדָם לְכַף זְכוּת :

(ז) נִתַּי הָאַרְבֵּלִי אוֹמֵר הַרְחֵק מִשְּׁכֵן רָע וְאַל־תִּתְחַבֵּר לְרָשָׁע

וְאַל־תִּתְיָאֵשׁ מִן־הַפֻּרְעָנוּת : (ח) יְהוּדָה בֶּן טַבַּי וְשִׁמְעוֹן

בֶּן־שָׁטַח קִבְּלוּ מֵהֶם · יְהוּדָה בֶּן־טַבַּי אוֹמֵר · אַל־תַּעַשׂ

עַצְמְךָ כְּעוֹרְכֵי הַדַּיָּנִים · וּכְשֶׁיִּהְיוּ בַּעֲלֵי הַדִּין עוֹמְדִים לְפָנֶיךָ

---

6. *Arbelite.* A native of Arbel, north of Tiberias.

provide thyself a teacher. So as to learn the truths of Religion under competent guidance, and be saved from error and confusion of mind.

get thee a companion. lit. "acquire a companion". Here companionship is recommended for joint religious study. The commentary on Aboth attributed to Rashi, explains this to mean, " acquire books " —the best of companions, and invaluable for the acquisition of religious knowledge. But the saying has an even larger meaning ; namely, win a friend, " one to whom you can reveal all your secrets " (Aboth di Rabbi Nathan). Friendship develops what is best in man ; and everyone can *make* friends, if he tries hard enough. " Either companionship or death," was the prayer of Choni, the Jewish Rip Van Winkle, when he awoke from his sleep of seventy years, and found himself a friendless man in a strange world. The Bible is the Book of Friendship, both in its profound sayings on friendship and the touching examples of it— David and Jonathan, Ruth and Naomi.

charitably. lit. " in the scale of merit." This is one of the great maxims of ethical conduct. " In righteousness shalt thou judge thy neighbour ", is the Divine command (Leviticus 19. 15). Do not judge your suspected fellow-man by appearances, but give him the benefit of the doubt. When weighing what speaks for and against him, incline the balance in his favour. " Whoever judges his fellow in the scale of merit, will be himself similarly judged by God "—say the Rabbis ; and " Great shall be the punishment of a חושד בכשרים, one who suspects, or causes others to suspect, the innocent " ; see p. 2.

7. *keep thee far . . . wicked.* Cf. the morning prayer : " Keep us from a bad man and a bad companion," p. 24. " Woe to the wicked, woe to his neighbour " ; and " the dry wood sets fire to the green ", are two Rabbinic proverbs. A hundred years before Nittai, Ben Sira taught, " He that toucheth pitch shall be defiled " (Ecclesiasticus 13. 1). Nittai's warning may be connected with the clause that follows : when thou seest the wicked profit from their evil ways and escape punishment, be not thou tempted to join them in the hope of the same immunity. The day of reckoning will come.

6. Joshua, the son of Perachyah, and Nittai, the Arbelite, received the tradition from the preceding. Joshua, the son of Perachyah, said, Provide thyself a teacher ; get thee a companion ; and judge all men charitably.

7. Nittai, the Arbelite, said, Keep thee far from a bad neighbour ; associate not with the wicked ; and abandon not the belief in retribution.

8. Judah, the son of Tabbai, and Simeon, the son of Shatach, received the tradition from the preceding. Judah, the son of Tabbai, said, (In the judge's office) act not the counsel's part ; when the parties to a suit are standing

abandon not the belief in retribution. The doctrine of retribution (see p. 121) follows inevitably from the attribute of Divine justice. The conclusion of a modern historian is noteworthy : " One lesson, and only one, history may be said to repeat with distinctness : that the world is built somehow on moral foundations : that in the long run it is well with the good ; in the long run it is ill with the wicked " (Froude).

8. Judah, the son of Tabbai, was among the teachers who fled to Alexandria, because of the persecution of the Pharisees by king Alexander Jannai (103–76 B.C.E.), a partisan of the Sadducees.

The SADDUCEES were the ruling priestly and aristocratic element during the two centuries preceding the Destruction of Jerusalem in the year 70. They had come under foreign influences, were estranged from the older Jewish life, and chafed under the regulations of the Traditional Law. They denied its authority, as they did the resurrection of the dead, and the continued existence of the soul after death. They were opposed by the PHARISEES—the Scribes and Sages who continued the work of the Men of the Great Assembly. The overwhelming majority of the nation was with the Pharisaic teachers. It is they who built up a purely spiritual worship ; deepened the belief in the immortality of the soul ; and made the Sacred Scriptures the possession of the people. Through their " fences " for the safeguarding of the religious life, they rescued pure monotheism and real morality in their time and for all time. It is unfortunate that these Jewish Puritans have been for 1800 years so maligned by sectarian hatred, that the very name " Pharisee " is often used as a synonym for " hypocrite." Yet they were among the noblest men that ever lived.

act not the counsel's part. Do not suggest to either litigant arguments which he could plead in his behalf : the judge must be impartial. The words may also mean, " Make not thyself like the preparers of the judges " ; *i.e.* men who try to influence the judge before the case is heard, so as to dispose his mind favourably to one party.

are standing before thee. At the hearing of the evidence, the judge must observe equal strictness towards accusers and accused.

21

יִהְיוּ בְעֵינֶיךָ כִּרְשָׁעִים · וּכְשֶׁנִּפְטָרִים מִלְּפָנֶיךָ יִהְיוּ יִהְיוּ בְעֵינֶיךָ
כְּזַכָּאִים כְּשֶׁקִּבְּלוּ עֲלֵיהֶם אֶת־הַדִּין : (ט) שִׁמְעוֹן בֶּן־שָׁטַח
אוֹמֵר · הֱוֵי מַרְבֶּה לַחֲקוֹר אֶת־הָעֵדִים · וֶהֱוֵי זָהִיר בִּדְבָרֶיךָ
שֶׁמָּא מִתּוֹכָם יִלְמְדוּ לְשַׁקֵּר : (י) שְׁמַעְיָה וְאַבְטַלְיוֹן קִבְּלוּ
מֵהֶם · שְׁמַעְיָה אוֹמֵר · אֱהַב אֶת־הַמְּלָאכָה וּשְׂנָא אֶת־הָרַבָּנוּת
וְאַל־תִּתְוַדַּע לָרָשׁוּת : (יא) אַבְטַלְיוֹן אוֹמֵר · חֲכָמִים הִזָּהֲרוּ
בְדִבְרֵיכֶם שֶׁמָּא תָחוּבוּ חוֹבַת גָּלוּת וְתִגְלוּ לִמְקוֹם מַיִם

---

as wicked. Not that he is to assume the accused *guilty* of what he
is charged with doing. In Jewish Law a man is held to be innocent,
until he is *proved* guilty. The judge is merely warned against in any
manner showing favour. "Do not start with the assumption that A is a
man of honour and would not plead falsely ; for, if so, you will not find
him in the wrong, whatever the evidence that comes to light " (Berti-
nora).

Jewish teaching attaches the loftiest ideals to the judicial office.
When acting as judge, a man is the deputy of the Supreme Judge ; and
" he should always imagine that a sword is pointed to his heart, and
Gehinnom yawns at his feet ", should he degrade his sacred office. In
a case of a capital offence, circumstantial evidence was rejected. A
sentence of acquittal might be pronounced at once ; but condemnation
might not be pronounced on the day the trial concluded. A Court that
passed a death sentence once in seven years, was known as a Bloody
Assize.

both as innocent. " The sentence of the Court, if just, is adequate to
the case ; and clears the score against both litigants " (Herford).

9. *Simeon, the son of Shatach.* His sister Queen Salome Alexandra,
the widow of King Jannai, reigned from 76–67 B.C.E. and he then enjoyed
great influence. He opposed the Sadducees, and made the Pharisaic
party dominant in Israel. Two special achievements ensure him a shining
place in the annals of Israel—the restricting of divorce by new regulations in regard to the *Kesubah* (the Marriage Contract), and the opening
of schools for the young. In his days of poverty, he one day commissioned his disciples to buy him a camel from an Arab. When they
brought him the animal, they gleefully announced that they had found
a precious stone in its collar. "Did the seller know of this " ? he
asked. " Do you think me a barbarian that I should take advantage
of the letter of the law by which the gem is mine together with the
camel ? Return the gem to the Arab immediately". When the heathen
received it back, he exclaimed : " Blessed be the God of Simeon ben

before thee, let them both be regarded by thee as wicked;
but when they are departed from thy presence, regard
them both as innocent, the verdict having been acquiesced
in by them.

9. Simeon, the son of Shatach, said, Be very searching
in the examination of witnesses, and be heedful of thy words,
lest through them they learn to falsify.

10. Shemayah and Avtalyon received the tradition from
the preceding. Shemayah said, Love work; hate lordship;
and seek no intimacy with the ruling power.

11. Avtalyon said, Ye sages, be heedful of your words,
lest ye incur the penalty of exile and be exiled to a place

Shatach! Blessed be the God of Israel ". That exclamation of the
heathen, we are told, was dearer to him than all the riches of the world.
It was a Kiddush Hashem—a Sanctification of the Divine Name.

be very searching. This maxim was probably the fruit of a tragic
experience. His son was executed upon a charge which, when too late,
was proved to have been groundless; and closer examination of the
witnesses would have revealed the falsity of their evidence.

be heedful of thy words. An injudicious word can suggest to the
witness a way of distorting his testimony.

10. *Shemayah and Avtalyon.* According to Tradition they were
descendants of proselytes.

love work. Far from looking upon manual labour as a curse,
the Rabbis extolled it as an important factor in man's moral education; and many of the most eminent scholars were manual labourers;
see p. 630. The slowness among Western nations to recognize the
dignity of labour is no doubt due to the fact that, till quite recent
times, classical literature monopolized the education of the governing
classes among European peoples. As with the Greeks and Romans,
idleness was for ages the mark of nobility.

hate lordship. Shun office. Hate domineering, playing the superior
over your fellows. It hardens the heart, and destroys the finer
feelings in him who lords it over others.

the ruling power. He had in mind the local Roman rulers in the
days of the later Hasmoneans and of Herod; but it is never prudent
to come under the notice of a despotic government; see II, 3.

11. *be heedful of your words.* " If sages are to be heedful of their
words, how much the more should those who are not sages " (Talmud).

This saying, like the one immediately preceding, is based on the
political conditions of Roman Palestine. Avtalyon had witnessed the
persecution of the religious teachers under King Alexander Jannai
and during the fratricidal conflict of his successors. Many of the teachers
had suffered death, others had to flee for their lives into distant lands.

הָרָעִים וְיִשְׁתּוּ הַתַּלְמִידִים הַבָּאִים אַחֲרֵיכֶם וְיָמוּתוּ וְנִמְצָא
שֵׁם שָׁמַיִם מִתְחַלֵּל: (יב) הִלֵּל וְשַׁמַּי קִבְּלוּ מֵהֶם · הִלֵּל
אוֹמֵר · הֱוֵה מִתַּלְמִידָיו שֶׁל־אַהֲרֹן אוֹהֵב שָׁלוֹם וְרוֹדֵף שָׁלוֹם
אוֹהֵב אֶת־הַבְּרִיּוֹת וּמְקָרְבָן לַתּוֹרָה: (יג) הוּא הָיָה אוֹמֵר ·
נְגַד שְׁמָא אֲבַד שְׁמָא וּדְלָא מוֹסִיף יָסֵף וּדְלָא יָלֵף קְטָלָא

In such a time—Avtalyon guardedly warns the contemporary teachers
of Judaism—the wise are *circumspect* in their utterances on public
questions.   Aside from the peril to their persons, there was real
danger to the Faith.   Several of the Sages had fled to Alexandria, the
then capital of the intellectual world, and seething with schools of
fantastic speculation.   The disciples of those exiled Sages followed them
to Alexandria ; and there they found a Jewry that had discarded the
Hebrew language, and held the observances and institutions of the
Torah to be mere symbols and allegories.   Many of these disciples
succumbed to this Hellenistic Judaism which left its followers nothing
to live by, and nothing to die for.   To the pious Palestinian Jew,
Alexandria was indeed " a place of evil waters," a fountain of heresy.

and die. A spiritual death ; they became lost to true Judaism.

and the Heavenly Name be profaned. Judaism, as the Revelation
of God, would be discredited by these apostasies—a Chillul Hashem.

12. *Hillel and Shammai.* The last and most famous of the " pairs ".
They were men of different temperament and methods—Hillel being the
embodiment of humility and kindness, while Shammai lacked patience
and was not of a conciliatory nature.   Hillel is the most renowned of the
Rabbis.   He rose from the humblest ranks to the highest place in the
Sanhedrin, and founded a dynasty of scholars.   His active years were
from 30 B.C.E. to 10 of the Common Era.   " He was known as the saint
and the sage who, in his private life and in his dealings with men,
practised the highest virtues of morality and resignation, just as he
taught them in his maxims with unexcelled brevity and earnestness "
(Bacher).   The most famous saying of Hillel is, " What is hateful unto
thee, do it not to thy fellow-man ; this is the whole Torah, the rest
is commentary."   See " The Golden Rule in Judaism," p. 644.

disciples of Aaron. Aaron was the great peace-maker in Rabbinic
legend.   He would, in the case of an open rupture between two men, hasten
first to the one, then to the other, saying to each : " If thou didst but
know how he with whom thou hast quarrelled regrets his hard words
to thee " ! With the result, that the former enemies would in their
hearts forgive each other, and as soon as they were again face to face,
would greet each other as friends.   His kindness led many a man who
was about to commit a sin, to say to himself, "How shall I be able to lift
up my eyes to Aaron's face ! " Thus did Aaron turn away many from
iniquity ; Malachi 2. 6.

loving peace. An everlasting virtue ; see pp. 15–18.

of evil waters, and the disciples who come after you drink thereof and die, and the Heavenly Name be profaned.

12. Hillel and Shammai received the tradition from the preceding. Hillel said, Be of the disciples of Aaron, loving peace and pursuing peace, loving thy fellow-creatures, and drawing them near to the Torah.

13. He used to say, A name made great is a name destroyed ; he who does not increase his knowledge, decreases it ; and he who does not study, deserves to die ; and he who makes a worldly use of the crown (of the Torah), shall pass away.

thy fellow-creatures. The word *beriyyoth* connotes the whole human family: there is one humanity on earth, even as there is but One God in heaven. The term *beriyyoth* often includes even the brute creation; and tq spare animals unnecessary pain is deemed a duty of primary importance צַעַר בַּעֲלֵי חַיִּים מִדְּאוֹרַיְתָא.

drawing them near to the Torah. Hillel did not advocate love of fellow-Jews only, or only of the righteous. He demanded love for all, Jew and non-Jew, those under the Torah and those far from the Torah. Those far from Religion, whether they are within or outside the House of Israel, are to be drawn to it by ways of love and peace. And of such nature was the intensive Jewish propaganda throughout the Roman Empire during the century preceding the fall of Jerusalem. It was primarily the proclamation of the One God, of His Moral Law, and of the Day of Judgment ; see p. 144.

13. *he used to say.* This maxim, like the one in II, 7, is in Aramaic, the language of Babylon, where Hillel was born. ·

a name made great. Fame is usually short-lived, and in his ambition to attain great fame, a man often loses his good name. " Vaulting ambition which o'erleaps itself " (Shakespeare).

increase his knowledge. Study of Torah must be continuous,· otherwise what has been learnt will be forgotten.

he who does not study. If a man deliberately refuses to learn aught of Religion, he commits spiritual suicide, and he cannot be regarded as a living member of the House of Israel. Another reading is, " he who does not teach " ; *i.e.* he fails to impart the religious knowledge he has. This was deemed an unpardonable sin.

a worldly use of the crown. Of Learning ; see IV, 7. A warning against using for worldly advantage any noble gift one possesses. The original word for " crown " is תָּגָא ; and various explanations have been given of its exact meaning. Some believe it to be the Latin word *toga.* Hillel's saying would then be, " Anyone who takes to the *toga* (*i.e.* adopts the Roman manner of living, as many of the upper classes did in his day) passes away " from his Faith and People.

חַיָּב וְדְאִשְׁתַּמֵּשׁ בְּתָגָא חֲלָף : (יד) הוּא הָיָה אוֹמֵר׳ אִם
אֵין אֲנִי לִי מִי לִי וּכְשֶׁאֲנִי לְעַצְמִי מָה אֲנִי וְאִם לֹא עַכְשָׁו
אֵימָתָי : (טו) שַׁמַּי אוֹמֵר׳ עֲשֵׂה תוֹרָתְךָ קֶבַע אֱמוֹר מְעַט
וַעֲשֵׂה הַרְבֵּה וֶהֱוֵי מְקַבֵּל אֶת־כָּל־הָאָדָם בְּסֵבֶר פָּנִים יָפוֹת:
(טז) רַבָּן גַּמְלִיאֵל אוֹמֵר׳ עֲשֵׂה לְךָ רַב וְהִסְתַּלֵּק מִן הַסָּפֵק
וְאַל־תַּרְבֶּה לְעַשֵּׂר אוּמָדוֹת : (יז) שִׁמְעוֹן בְּנוֹ אוֹמֵר׳ כָּל־
יָמַי גָּדַלְתִּי בֵּין הַחֲכָמִים וְלֹא מָצָאתִי לַגּוּף טוֹב מִשְּׁתִיקָה
וְלֹא הַמִּדְרָשׁ עִקָּר אֶלָּא הַמַּעֲשֶׂה וְכָל־הַמַּרְבֶּה דְבָרִים מֵבִיא

14. *for myself.* This is far more than merely a rule of worldly wisdom.
" If I do not rouse my soul to higher things, who will rouse it ? "
(Maimonides). Virtue is victory by the individual himself over temptation that assails him. The battle cannot be fought, nor the victory won,
by another.

if I am only for myself. Helpfulness is the sign of humanity. It
is only a Cain who asks, "Am I my brother's keeper ? "

> " Heaven's gate is shut
> To him who comes alone ;
> Save thou a soul,
> And *it* shall save thine own ! " (Whittier).

if not now, when ? Duty's hour is always now, or the opportunity
may go forever.

The great moral geniuses of the world have understood to clothe
the profoundest truths in simplest language. " Had Hillel left us but
this single saying, we should be for ever grateful to him ; for scarce
anything can be said more briefly, more profoundly, or more earnestly "
(H. Ewald).

15. *fix a period.* The study of Torah must not be something casual
or occasional.

and do much. " The righteous promise little, and perform much ;
the wicked promise much, and do not perform even a little " (Talmud).

receive all men with a cheerful countenance. Have a friendly manner
in all your dealings with men.

I, 16–II, 8. SAYINGS OF THE MEN OF THE SCHOOL OF HILLEL, AND
ADDITIONAL SAYINGS OF HILLEL.

16. *Rabban Gamaliel.* Gamaliel I, who was Hillel's grandson and
President of the Great Sanhedrin in the first century. He is the
first teacher to bear the superior title *Rabban* (" our Master "). Many

14. He used to say, If I am not for myself, who will be for me ? And if I am only for myself, what am I ? And if not now, when ?

15. Shammai said, Fix a period for thy study of the Torah ; say little and do much ; and receive all men with a cheerful countenance.

16. Rabban Gamaliel said, Provide thyself a teacher ; be quit of doubt; and accustom not thyself to give tithes by a conjectural estimate.

17. Simeon, his son, said, All my days I have grown up among the wise, and I have found nought of better service than silence ; not learning but doing is the chief thing ; and whoso is profuse of words causes sin.

beneficent regulations are ascribed to him. Among them, the regulation to visit and heal the heathen sick, to bury the friendless dead of heathens, and support their indigent poor in the same way as was done in regard to the Jewish poor, sick and dead. He also laid down the principle, " One must not impose on the public a restriction which the majority cannot endure ". In the Christian Writings, Paul claims to have sat at Gamaliel's feet ; and, in consequence, the latter figures in many Church legends.

provide thyself a teacher. The same phrase as in mishna 6, but here the advice is addressed to one who is himself a teacher or judge. When formulating decisions on questions of law, he should not rely merely upon his own knowledge and judgment, but have another authority whom to consult.

to give tithes by a conjectural estimate. In apportioning the tithe of the produce to be devoted to priests, levites and the poor, the allocation was to be made by exact measure, not by guesswork. " Leave as little scope as possible for personal bias and the temptations of self-interest " (Taylor).

17. *Simeon, his son.* The son of Rabban Gamaliel I. He belonged to the Peace party in the closing years of the Jewish State.

silence. Warnings against loquacity abound in Rabbinic literature. One aphorism reads : " Silence is good for the wise ; how much more so for the foolish " ; cf. " Even a fool, when he holdeth his peace, is counted wise " (Proverbs 17. 28).

not learning but doing. This saying gives expression to a main characteristic of Judaism ; see III, 12, 19 and 22. It does not dispute the high place assigned to learning the Torah : right doing depends on knowing what to do and how to do it. " Study is most important, because it leads to deed ", was the decision of the historic Synod at Lydda, in 133 A.C.E. The aim of the Torah is practical, not theoretical ; above all else its purpose is to regulate conduct. Not

חִסְמָא : (יח) רַבָּן שִׁמְעוֹן בֶּן־גַּמְלִיאֵל אוֹמֵר • עַל־שְׁלֹשָׁה
דְבָרִים הָעוֹלָם קַיָּם עַל־הָאֱמֶת וְעַל־הַדִּין וְעַל־הַשָּׁלוֹם •
שֶׁנֶּאֱמַר אֱמֶת וּמִשְׁפַּט שָׁלוֹם שִׁפְטוּ בְּשַׁעֲרֵיכֶם :

רַבִּי חֲנַנְיָא בֶּן־עֲקַשְׁיָא אוֹמֵר • רָצָה הַקָּדוֹשׁ בָּרוּךְ הוּא
לְזַכּוֹת אֶת־יִשְׂרָאֵל לְפִיכָךְ הִרְבָּה לָהֶם תּוֹרָה וּמִצְוֹת •
שֶׁנֶּאֱמַר יְיָ חָפֵץ לְמַעַן צִדְקוֹ יַגְדִּיל תּוֹרָה וְיַאְדִּיר :

knowledge, but practice, is of decisive importance; but the practice flows
from knowledge. The Midrash illustrates this by a story, evidently
taken from life, of two muleteers who were enemies. The mule of
one falls beneath its burden; the other sees it, and passes on. But
then he remembers having learned the law of Exodus 23. 5 (" If thou
see the ass of him that hateth thee lying under his burden . . . thou
shalt surely help with him "), and at once he returns and helps the other.
It was the end of their enmity; and it was the knowledge of the Torah
which the one possessed, that yielded this brotherly conduct.

profuse of words causes sin. Based on Proverbs 10. 19, " In
the multitude of words there wanteth not transgression ". A talkative
person is, *e.g.*, liable to become a tale-bearer and slanderer.

18. *Simeon, the son of Gamaliel.* This Gamaliel was the son of
Gamaliel II (who became Patriarch in the year 80) and father of R.
Judah the Prince, the editor of the Mishna. His saying is a variant of
the maxim of Simon the Just (I, 2), and indicates the spiritual forces
by which the social order is held together. Both sayings may be
regarded as new formulations of the Golden Rule.

truth. Truth was called by the Rabbis, " the seal of God . Truthfulness is of fundamental importance. " Let thy yea be yea, and thy
nay, nay ". The liar is an outcast in Heaven ; " he is of those who will
never be admitted to the presence of the Shechinah ". " He who visited
punishment upon the generations of the Flood will call him to account
who breaks his word." The Sages delight in him who is true to his bond,
even when according to the strict letter of the law, he could evade
doing so. " Have thy dealings with thy fellowmen been in truthfulness ? " will be the first question asked on the Judgment Day. Truth
should be spoken *in love :*

   " A truth that's told with bad intent
   Beats all the lies you can invent " (Blake).

18. Rabban Simeon, the son of Gamaliel, said, By three things is the world preserved : by truth, by judgment, and by peace ; as it is said, Judge ye the truth and the judgment of peace in your gates.

Zechariah 8. 16

Rabbi Chananya, the son of Akashya, said, The Holy One, blessed be he, was pleased to make Israel worthy ; wherefore he gave them a copious Torah and many commandments ; as it is said, It pleased the Lord, for his righteousness' sake, to magnify the Torah and make it honourable.

Isaiah 42. 21

judgment. For the place of Justice in human life, see *Deuteronomy,* 212–215 (one-vol. ed., 820–822).

Justice is truth in action, in contrast to lawless might. The tragedy of the Jew throughout history is that he has so often been denied justice. Let no Jew, therefore, deny justice to anyone ; and never deprive anyone of life or health, honour or happiness.

peace. For the meaning of this term, see pp. 835–7. A Talmudical comment points out the sequence of ideas : " The three are really one : if judgment is executed, truth is vindicated, and peace results "

As the reading of each chapter of Aboth is prefaced by the quotation "All Israel " etc., there is also an epilogue to the reading. It is taken from the end of the Mishna tractate *Makkoth.*

Rabbi Chananya. He flourished in the middle of the second century of the Christian Era.

to make Israel worthy. lit. " to make Israel acquire merit ", by giving them opportunity of abundant service and perfect obedience.

copious Torah and many commandments. " These words may be a polemic against the subversive doctrine of Paul concerning the Torah. Here it is asserted that there is no greater proof of God's love to Israel than the multitude of commandments He has given Israel. They were a gracious gift of God, designed to train Israel in moral holiness, and make them all the more worthy in the eyes of the Holy One, blessed be He " (I. Epstein).

his righteousness' sake. Interpreted as " for the sake of Israel's merit."

פֶּרֶק שֵׁנִי:

כָּל יִשְׂרָאֵל וכו׳

(א) רַבִּי אוֹמֵר · אֵיזוֹ הִיא דֶרֶךְ יְשָׁרָה שֶׁיָּבוֹר לוֹ הָאָדָם
כָּל־שֶׁהִיא תִפְאֶרֶת לְעֹשֶׂהָ וְתִפְאֶרֶת לוֹ מִן הָאָדָם · וֶהֱוֵה
זָהִיר בְּמִצְוָה קַלָּה כְּבַחֲמוּרָה שֶׁאֵין אַתָּה יוֹדֵעַ מַתַּן שְׂכָרָן
שֶׁל־מִצְוֹת · וֶהֱוֵה מְחַשֵּׁב הֶפְסֵד מִצְוָה כְּנֶגֶד שְׂכָרָהּ וּשְׂכַר
עֲבֵרָה כְּנֶגֶד הֶפְסֵדָהּ: הִסְתַּכֵּל בִּשְׁלשָׁה דְבָרִים וְאֵין אַתָּה
בָא לִידֵי עֲבֵרָה · דַּע מַה־לְמַעְלָה מִמָּךְ עַיִן רוֹאָה וְאֹזֶן
שׁוֹמַעַת וְכָל־מַעֲשֶׂיךָ בַּסֵּפֶר נִכְתָּבִים : (ב) רַבָּן גַּמְלִיאֵל בְּנוֹ
שֶׁל־רַבִּי יְהוּדָה הַנָּשִׂיא אוֹמֵר · יָפֶה תַלְמוּד תּוֹרָה עִם דֶּרֶךְ

CHAPTER II.

1. Rabbi. Judah the Prince (ha-Nasi), the son of Rabban Simeon the Second (I, 18) and a descendant of Hillel in the seventh generation, was born in 135 A.C.E. on the day on which Rabbi Akiba was martyred by the Romans. He died in 219. He was the learned patrician, possessed of great wealth, and enjoying the friendship of members of the Imperial House. In his day, the dignity of the Patriarch of Palestine was little short of that of an actual monarch. In the sphere of his spiritual labours, he made it his aim to ensure unity of religious observance. He collected the decisions and opinions of earlier Teachers, noted those which were universally agreed to, and those which were not; and thus at last produced a code of the Traditional Laws that soon attained to canonical rank. This is known as the MISHNA. It is divided into six Orders. The Orders are sub-divided into tractates; tractates into chapters; and chapters into paragraphs—which are each spoken of as a mishna. The first Order deals with Agricultural laws, preceded by *Berachoth*, the tractate on Prayer. The second Order is on Festivals; and the third, on laws of Marriage and Divorce. The fourth is on Civil legislation, and is concluded by *Aboth* as an edifying supplement to this juristic section. The fifth deals with Sanctuary and food laws; and the sixth, with the laws of clean and unclean. The Mishna became the basis of elucidation—Gemara—both in the Palestinian schools and those of Babylon. The final recensions of these elucidations constitute the Jerusalem Talmud (ca. 350) and the Babylonian Talmud (ca. 500).

CHAPTER II

"All Israel," etc., p. 613.

1. Rabbi said, Which is the right course that a man should choose for himself ? That which is an honour to him who does it, and which also brings him honour from mankind. Be heedful of a light precept as of a grave one, for thou knowest not the grant of reward for each precept. Reckon the loss incurred by the fulfilment of a precept against the reward secured by its observance, and the gain gotten by a transgression against the loss it involves. Reflect upon three things, and thou wilt not come within the power of sin: Know what is above thee—a seeing Eye, and a hearing Ear, and all thy deeds written in a Book.

2. Rabban Gamaliel, the son of Rabbi Judah the Prince, said, An excellent thing is the study of the Torah combined

So great was the esteem that his uncommon ability, wide culture and lofty character secured for Rabbi Judah the Prince, that he was known simply as " Rabbi ", or " our holy Master ". The first four paragraphs of this second chapter of Aboth were included in the Code of the Mishna by a later editor.

choose. The conviction that man possesses the power of free-will is basic in Judaism ; cf. III, 19.

that which is an honour to him who does it. That which honours the person who follows it, and wins the approval of his fellow-men. Some Texts read " to his Maker ", instead of " to him who does it "—that which has the approval of God.

honour from mankind. The Rabbis stress the importance of a good reputation ; see III, 13 ; IV, 17.

light precept. A command which does not involve much effort and sacrifice ; or, one for which the penalty of infraction can only be slight. Rabbi is here quoting Ben Azzai ; see IV, 2.

the loss. Through self-denial, or monetary sacrifice. Disregard the cost involved in fulfilling a command, and deem any gain accruing from a transgression as a loss.

a seeing Eye . . . Ear. The safeguard against falling into sin is the thought of God, Who seeth all things, heareth all things, and judgeth the children of men according to their doings.

in a Book. The idea of a Heavenly Book of Records is founded on Exodus 32. 32, Malachi 3. 16, and Daniel 7. 10. For the belief that man himself enters his misdeeds in that Book, see on III, 20

2. *Rabban Gamaliel.* The third who bore that name.

אֶרֶץ שֶׁיְּגִיעַת שְׁנֵיהֶם מַשְׁכַּחַת עָוֹן ' וְכָל־תּוֹרָה שֶׁאֵין עִמָּהּ

מְלָאכָה סוֹפָהּ בְּטֵלָה וְגוֹרֶרֶת עָוֹן ' וְכָל־הָעוֹסְקִים עִם־

הַצִּבּוּר יִהְיוּ עוֹסְקִים עִמָּהֶם לְשֵׁם שָׁמַיִם שֶׁזְּכוּת אֲבוֹתָם

מְסַיַּעְתָּם וְצִדְקָתָם עוֹמֶדֶת לָעַד ' וְאַתֶּם מַעֲלֶה אֲנִי עֲלֵיכֶם

שָׂכָר הַרְבֵּה כְּאִלּוּ עֲשִׂיתֶם: (ג) הֱווּ זְהִירִים בָּרָשׁוּת שֶׁאֵין

מְקָרְבִים לוֹ לָאָדָם אֶלָּא לְצֹרֶךְ עַצְמָם ' נִרְאִים כְּאוֹהֲבִים

בִּשְׁעַת הֲנָאָתָם וְאֵין עוֹמְדִים לוֹ לָאָדָם בִּשְׁעַת דָּחֳקוֹ:

(ד) הוּא הָיָה אוֹמֵר ' עֲשֵׂה רְצוֹנוֹ כִּרְצוֹנֶךָ כְּדֵי שֶׁיַּעֲשֶׂה

רְצוֹנְךָ כִּרְצוֹנוֹ ' בַּטֵּל רְצוֹנְךָ מִפְּנֵי רְצוֹנוֹ כְּדֵי שֶׁיְּבַטֵּל רְצוֹן

---

worldly occupation. " The insistence of Jewish Teachers upon the duty of having a trade or occupation is a mark of that practical sanity which is pre-eminent in Jewish ethics " (Herford). " The modern jargon about ' gentlemanly ' occupations gets no countenance from Judaism. All work is noble that is done nobly " (M. Joseph). No honest toil, no matter how hard or repugnant, was deemed beneath the dignity of a scholar, so long as it safeguarded his independence, and saved him from being a burden on others. Like the Prophets of old, the Rabbis would take no pay for their teaching or official activities (see on IV. 7). They were either manual labourers or they followed some calling or craft. Hillel was a wood-cutter ; Shammai, a builder ; R. Joshua, a blacksmith ; R. Chanina, a shoemaker ; R. Huna, a water-carrier ; R. Abba, a tailor ; others were carpenters, tent-makers, farmers, and merchants ; see I. 10.

makes sin to be forgotten. If the day is filled with honest toil and the night with study, temptation is robbed of its power. Whereas complete idleness, the Rabbis rightly hold, leads to wrongdoing and wrong thinking, sometimes even to mental aberration.

must in the end be futile. Since, in order to maintain himself, he will have to search for occasional work, which is both uncertain and unremunerative.

the cause of sin. " He who does not bring up his son to some occupation, is as if he were teaching him robbery " (Talmud).

employed with the congregation. Or, " who occupy themselves with (the affairs of) the community ".

for Heaven's sake. i.e. " for God's sake " ; an exhortation to disinterested labour. Neither self-aggrandizement nor love of wielding authority, but the pure desire to promote the welfare of the community, is to guide them in their labours.

with some worldly occupation, for the labour demanded by them both makes sin to be forgotten. All study of the Torah without work, must in the end be futile and become the cause of sin. Let all who are employed with the congregation act with them for Heaven's sake, for then the merit of their fathers sustains them, and their righteousness endures for ever. And as for you, (God will then say,) I account you worthy of great reward, as if you had wrought it all yourselves.

3. Be ye guarded in your relations with the ruling power; for they who exercise it draw no man near to them except for their own interests; appearing as friends when it is to their own advantage, they stand not by a man in the hour of his need.

4. He used to say, Do His will as if it were thy will, that He may do thy will as if it were His will. Nullify thy will before His will, that He may nullify the will of others before thy will.

merit of their fathers. Zechuth Ovoth, see p. 132. The inspiration drawn from the past is an incentive to right action, and increases the zeal, and the achievement, of those engaged upon good work.

their righteousness. When such are the motives behind their efforts, these efforts will lead to enduring results.

as if you had wrought it all yourselves. The faithful workers will not only receive reward for their own labours, but also for the extra good resulting through the influence of ancestral merit.

3. *be ye guarded*. A warning to the communal workers addressed in the preceding mishna, but applicable to all. The character of the Roman officials who administered the Holy Land at that period was such as fully to warrant this bitter comment. However, it is largely true of every " ruling power " ; see on I, 10.

4. *as if it were thy will*. Obey God readily and joyfully, as if you were carrying out your own desires. " Strive to do the will of God, with a perfect heart and a willing soul ; and efface thy will, even if obeying the will of God entail suffering unto thee " (Machzor Vitry).

that He may do thy will. When there is harmony in the relationship between the soul of man and God, man's desires will be worthy of fulfilment on the part of God.

nullify thy will. Should its promptings run counter to His laws and commandments.

the will of others. Who seek to do thee harm.

אֲחֵרִים מִפְּנֵי רְצוֹנֶךָ : (ה) הִלֵּל אוֹמֵר • אַל־תִּפְרוֹשׁ מִן־

הַצִּבּוּר וְאַל־תַּאֲמֵן בְּעַצְמָךְ עַד יוֹם מוֹתָךְ וְאַל־תָּדִין אֶת־

חֲבֵרָךְ עַד שֶׁתַּגִּיעַ לִמְקוֹמוֹ וְאַל־תֹּאמַר דָּבָר שֶׁאִי אֶפְשָׁר

לִשְׁמוֹעַ שֶׁסּוֹפוֹ לְהִשָּׁמֵעַ וְאַל־תֹּאמַר לִכְשֶׁאֶפָּנֶה אֶשְׁנֶה שֶׁמָּא

לֹא תִפָּנֶה : (ו) הוּא הָיָה אוֹמֵר • אֵין בּוֹר יְרֵא חֵטְא וְלֹא

עַם הָאָרֶץ חָסִיד וְלֹא הַבַּיְשָׁן לָמֵד וְלֹא הַקַּפְּדָן מְלַמֵּד וְלֹא

כָּל־הַמַּרְבֶּה בִסְחוֹרָה מַחְכִּים • וּבַמָּקוֹם שֶׁאֵין אֲנָשִׁים הִשְׁתַּדֵּל

THE ORIGINAL CHRONOLOGICAL SEQUENCE, INTERRUPTED BY
I, 16–II, 4, RESUMED.

5. separate not thyself from the congregation. Identify your individual life with that of the community, and stay not apart from it. Share its weal or woe, and do nothing to undermine its solidarity. Separation is especially unpardonable when the community is in distress. In the conflict with Amalek, the hands of Moses grew weary, and they took a stone and put it under him. " Could they not have given him a chair or a cushion ? " it is asked. But then Moses said, " Since my brethren are in trouble, lo, I will bear my part with them ; for he who bears his portion of the burden, will live to see the hour of consolation " (Talmud).

trust not in thyself. Man must remain on guard against lapse into sin or heresy throughout his life. The Talmud cites the instance of one who held the office of High Priest for eighty years, and then became a Sadducee. Its larger meaning is, " Let no man deem his wisdom perfect, his knowledge all-embracing, his character unassailable, or his fortune unchangeable " (Marti).

judge not thy fellow-man. A humane rule of conduct. Do not judge another till you yourself have come into his circumstances or situation. " Do not harshly condemn a person who succumbed to temptation until, faced by a similar temptation, you overcame it " (Rashi). A later commentator writes, " Do not presume to condemn another, in particular a man who has reached a high office and appears to you not to be acting correctly. If and when you have reached his position, then alone will you be in a position to judge " (Rabbi Jonah).

say not anything. Take pains to make your meaning immediately intelligible to the hearer. A teacher should not utter his doctrine in an enigmatic form, in the hope that its meaning will eventually become clear. The original may also be rendered : " Divulge not things that ought to be kept secret, on the plea that in the end all things are sure to become public knowledge ".

when I have leisure. A specific application of Hillel's general rule, " If not now, when ? " (I, 14).

5. Hillel said, Separate not thyself from the congregation ; trust not in thyself until the day of thy death ; judge not thy fellow-man until thou art come into his place; and say not anything which cannot be understood at once, in the hope that it will be understood in the end ; neither say, When I have leisure I will study ; perchance thou wilt have no leisure.

6. He used to say, An empty-headed man cannot be a sin-fearing man, nor can an ignorant person be truly pious, nor can the diffident learn, nor the passionate teach, nor is everyone who excels in business wise. In a place where there are no men, strive to be a man.

6. *empty-headed man.* lit. " a boorish person "—uncultivated and unmannered.

sin-fearing man. " Fear of sin " is the technical term for " the deliberate avoidance of an action that constituted an offence only for the sensitive, but was for the average Jew not deemed a sin " (Büchler); see comment on *pious.*

ignorant person. Heb. *am ha-aretz.* The usual expression for a vulgar person, or for one unlearned in Torah.

pious. Heb. חסיד. Of saintly character ; one who does more than the strict letter of the law requires. Without the beneficent influence of religious knowledge, the ignorant person remains colour-blind to the finer implications of the spiritual life. In Judaism, ignorance is *not* the mother of devotion : only too often is it the mother of desertion.

nor can the diffident. Because he is afraid to ask questions in regard to what is unintelligible to him.

passionate. If the teacher is quick-tempered, he is lacking in patience when interrupted by his pupil's questions. Under such a teacher, obscure points will pass without sufficient explanation.

excels in business. Or, " engrossed in business ". Combine a worldly occupation with your Torah-study; but overmuch absorption in business is not as a rule the road to spirituality. Many people look upon a " captain of industry " as the highest embodiment of human wisdom. Hillel assures us, and modern experience confirms his view, that this is quite unjustified.

where there are no men. If a task requires to be done, and there are no other men to do it, it is for us to undertake it. However, in a place where there *is* a man, we must refrain from undue self-assertion. The plain duty then is co-operation or *subordination.* Another explanation is given in Midrash Shemuel : " In a place where no man seeth or knoweth thee, say not, I will sin, as no one seeth or knoweth me. Even when alone, strive to be a man, true and God-fearing '

לִהְיוֹת אִישׁ : (ז) אַף הוּא רָאָה גֻּלְגֹּלֶת אַחַת שֶׁצָּפָה עַל־פְּנֵי

הַמָּיִם · אָמַר לָהּ · עַל דַּאֲטֵיפְתְּ אֲטִיפוּךְ וְסוֹף מְטַיְפָיִךְ

יְטוּפוּן : (ח) הוּא הָיָה אוֹמֵר · מַרְבֶּה בָשָׂר מַרְבֶּה רִמָּה ·

מַרְבֶּה נְכָסִים מַרְבֶּה דְאָגָה · מַרְבֶּה נָשִׁים מַרְבֶּה כְשָׁפִים ·

מַרְבֶּה שְׁפָחוֹת מַרְבֶּה זִמָּה · מַרְבֶּה עֲבָדִים מַרְבֶּה גָזֵל ·

מַרְבֶּה תוֹרָה מַרְבֶּה חַיִּים · מַרְבֶּה יְשִׁיבָה מַרְבֶּה חָכְמָה ·

מַרְבֶּה עֵצָה מַרְבֶּה תְבוּנָה · מַרְבֶּה צְדָקָה מַרְבֶּה שָׁלוֹם ·

קָנָה שֵׁם טוֹב קָנָה לְעַצְמוֹ · קָנָה לוֹ דִבְרֵי תוֹרָה קָנָה לוֹ

חַיֵּי הָעוֹלָם הַבָּא : (ט) רַבָּן יוֹחָנָן בֶּן־זַכַּי קִבֵּל מֵהִלֵּל

וּמִשַּׁמַּאי · הוּא הָיָה אוֹמֵר · אִם לָמַדְתָּ תוֹרָה הַרְבֵּה אַל־

---

7. *a skull.* Hillel seems to have known the person whose skull it was, and he had been a brigand.

because thou drownedst others. They who resort to violence become victims of violence. Hillel, and the Rabbis after him, clung to the Biblical belief of retributive justice. " With the measure wherewith a man measures, shall he be measured." Repentance alone, they held, could counter-act the operation of this rule. " There are those who acquire eternal life in years upon years ; there are those who (by repentance) acquire it in an hour ", said Rabbi Judah the Prince.

8. Incisive comments on human nature in the social life of his time.

flesh . . . worms. A denunciation of gluttony.

property . . . anxiety. Lest he lose it by theft, robbery, or a turn in his fortunes.

wives . . . witchcraft. Rival wives resorted to witchcraft in order to retain or regain their husband's affection. Hillel's saying thus condemns polygamy. Although polygamy lingered for many centuries after Hillel, there is no record of a Rabbi having had more than one wife at one time. About the year 1000, the spiritual leader of European Jewry, R. Gershom ben Judah, " the Light of the Exile ", declared it prohibited ; and he issued a *cherem* against anyone who, through fraud or subterfuge, entered upon a polygamous marriage.

maid-servants. Female slaves were not usually of high morality.

men-servants. With rare exceptions, they had no scruples as to robbing their masters.

the more Torah, the more life. Eternal life. Cf. " for length of days, and years of life, and peace, shall they add to thee " (Proverbs 3.

7. Moreover, he saw a skull floating on the surface of the water : he said to it, Because thou drownedst others, they have drowned thee ; and, at the last, they that drowned thee shall themselves be drowned.

8. He used to say, The more flesh, the more worms ; the more property, the more anxiety ; the more wives, the more witchcraft ; the more maid-servants, the more lewdness ; the more men-servants, the more robbery ; —the more Torah, the more life ; the more schooling, the more wisdom ; the more counsel, the more understanding ; the more charity, the more peace. He who has acquired a good name, has acquired it for himself ; he who has acquired for himself words of Torah, has acquired for himself life in the world to come.

9. Rabban Yochanan, the son of Zakkai, received the tradition from Hillel and Shammai. He used to say, If

the more schooling. The more opportunities given for corporate study, the greater the ingenuity developed.

the more charity. In later Hebrew, צדקה means " alms-giving ". In reducing the wants of those in need by monetary aid, the harmony of social life is promoted. If we take צדקה in the Biblical sense, and translate it by " righteousness ", the saying echoes the profound declaration of the Prophet, " The work of righteousness shall be peace ; and the effect of righteousness, quietness and confidence for ever " (Isaiah 32. 17).

a good name. The greatest of treasures, bu. it cannot be transferred to others.

life in the world to come. The effect of Torah-knowledge is the acquisition of merits that outlast this life.

world to come. Heb. *olom ha-bo.* In the Hereafter.

9–21. SAYINGS OF YOCHANAN BEN ZAKKAI AND HIS DISCIPLES.

9. *Yochanan, the son of Zakkai.* When the fall of Jerusalem became certain, he escaped from the city and made his submission to the Romans. He predicted that Vespasian would be elevated to the Imperial throne, and was granted permission to open a school of Rabbinic instruction at Yavneh. This school became the spiritual centre of Jewry ; and by its establishment he rescued Judaism from the shipwreck of the destruction that overwhelmed the Jewish state in the year 70. " Yochanan united within himself the qualities of the prophet Jeremiah and Zerubbabel. Like Jeremiah, he mourned over

תְּחֵזַק טוֹבָה לְעַצְמֶךָ כִּי לְכָךְ נוֹצֵרְתָּ: (י) חֲמִשָּׁה תַלְמִידִים

הָיוּ לוֹ לְרַבָּן יוֹחָנָן בֶּן־זַכַּי ׳ וְאֵלּוּ הֵן ׳ רַבִּי אֱלִיעֶזֶר בֶּן־

הוֹרְקָנוֹס רַבִּי יְהוֹשֻׁעַ בֶּן־חֲנַנְיָא רַבִּי יוֹסֵי הַכֹּהֵן רַבִּי

שִׁמְעוֹן בֶּן־נְתַנְאֵל וְרַבִּי אֶלְעָזָר בֶּן־עֲרָךְ: (יא) הוּא הָיָה

מוֹנֶה שְׁבָחָם ׳ אֱלִיעֶזֶר בֶּן־הוֹרְקָנוֹס בּוֹר סוּד שֶׁאֵינוֹ מְאַבֵּד

טִפָּה ׳ יְהוֹשֻׁעַ בֶּן־חֲנַנְיָא אַשְׁרֵי יוֹלַדְתּוֹ ׳ יוֹסֵי הַכֹּהֵן חָסִיד ׳

שִׁמְעוֹן בֶּן־נְתַנְאֵל יְרֵא חֵטְא ׳ אֶלְעָזָר בֶּן־עֲרָךְ כְּמַעְיָן הַמִּתְגַּבֵּר:

(יב) הוּא הָיָה אוֹמֵר ׳ אִם יִהְיוּ כָּל־חַכְמֵי יִשְׂרָאֵל בְּכַף

מֹאזְנַיִם וֶאֱלִיעֶזֶר בֶּן־הוֹרְקָנוֹס בְּכַף שְׁנִיָּה מַכְרִיעַ אֶת־כֻּלָּם:

אַבָּא שָׁאוּל אוֹמֵר מִשְּׁמוֹ ׳ אִם יִהְיוּ כָּל־חַכְמֵי יִשְׂרָאֵל בְּכַף

מֹאזְנַיִם וֶאֱלִיעֶזֶר בֶּן־הוֹרְקָנוֹס אַף עִמָּהֶם וְאֶלְעָזָר בֶּן־עֲרָךְ

---

the destruction of Jerusalem ; and, like Zerubbabel, he laid the foundation-stone of a new edifice in Judaism " (Graetz).

A disciple of Hillel, Yochanan had a wonderful insight into the
essence of religion. He loved all men, and assigned a supreme place to
charity. To one lamenting the loss of the Temple, he declared : " We
have a means of atonement left that is as effectual as the Temple ;
namely, Lovingkindness. That is now our sin-offering." Again, on his
death-bed, his blessing to his disciples was : " Fear God, as much as
you fear man ". " Not more ? " they asked in surprise. " If you would
but fear Him as much ! " answered the dying sage.

ascribe not any merit to thyself. Although to have acquired knowledge
of Torah was praiseworthy, it should not be an occasion for boastful
self-righteousness.

thereunto wast thou created. Thou hast only achieved a purpose in
life that should be the ambition of every Israelite ; merely done thy
duty, and utilized gifts with which God had endowed thee.

10. *five disciples.* Of special excellence; see mishna 15-19.

11. *praise. i.e.* superiority ; the special quality which distinguished
each of his favourite disciples.

cemented cistern. Figurative of a retentive memory. Eliezer won
fame for his exact knowledge of the Traditional teaching handed down
from earlier ages. He was a teacher of Rabbi Akiba.

thou hast learnt much Torah, ascribe not any merit to thyself, for thereunto wast thou created.

10. Rabban Yochanan, the son of Zakkai, had five disciples; and these are they, Rabbi Eliezer, the son of Hyrcanus, Rabbi Joshua, the son of Chananya, Rabbi José, the Priest, Rabbi Simeon, the son of Nathaniel, and Rabbi Elazar, the son of Arach.

11. He used thus to recount their praise : Eliezer, the son of Hyrcanus, is a cemented cistern, which loses not a drop ; Joshua, the son of Chananya—happy is she that bare him ; José, the Priest, is a pious man ; Simeon, the son of Nathaniel, is a fearer of sin ; Elazar, the son of Arach, is like a spring flowing with ever-sustained vigour.

12. He used to say, If all the sages of Israel were in one scale of the balance, and Eliezer, the son of Hyrcanus, in the other, he would outweigh them all. Abba Saul said in his name, If all the sages of Israel, together with Eliezer, the son of Hyrcanus, were in one scale of the balance, and Elazar, the son of Arach, in the other scale, he would outweigh them all.

---

happy is she that bare him. What a life of benignity and blessing must it have been, to have elicited such praise from a statesman, scholar and saint like Rabban Yochanan !

pious man. i.e., one who shows particular heedfulness in matters of mine and thine ; see mishna 17.

fearer of sin. See mishna 6.

a spring. In contrast to a " cemented cistern ", he had an original mind which overflowed with new ideas.

12. *if all the sages.* Yochanan set the higher value on the accurate preservation of the Traditional lore, as against acute argumentative power ; and, for that reason, praised the pre-eminence of Eliezer.

Abba Saul. He was a contemporary of R. Judah the Prince. "Abba ", Aramaic for " father ", was a title of affection given to several Rabbis. He cited another tradition of Yochanan's estimate, and thus awarded the palm to Elazar ben Arach : the critical and original mind, rather than the retentive memory, was given preference.

בְּכַף שְׁנֵיהּ מַכְרִיעַ אֶת־כֻּלָּם : (יג) אָמַר לָהֶם ' צְאוּ וּרְאוּ
אֵיזוֹ הִיא דֶרֶךְ טוֹבָה שֶׁיִּדְבַּק בָּהּ הָאָדָם ' רַבִּי אֱלִיעֶזֶר
אוֹמֵר עַיִן טוֹבָה ' רַבִּי יְהוֹשֻׁעַ אוֹמֵר חָבֵר טוֹב ' רַבִּי יוֹסֵי
אוֹמֵר שָׁכֵן טוֹב ' רַבִּי שִׁמְעוֹן אוֹמֵר הָרוֹאֶה אֶת־הַנּוֹלָד ' רַבִּי
אֶלְעָזָר אוֹמֵר לֵב טוֹב : אָמַר לָהֶם ' רוֹאֶה אֲנִי אֶת־דִּבְרֵי
אֶלְעָזָר בֶּן־עֲרָךְ מִדִּבְרֵיכֶם שֶׁבִּכְלַל דְּבָרָיו דִּבְרֵיכֶם :
(יד) אָמַר לָהֶם ' צְאוּ וּרְאוּ אֵיזוֹ הִיא דֶרֶךְ רָעָה שֶׁיִּתְרַחֵק
מִמֶּנָּה הָאָדָם ' רַבִּי אֱלִיעֶזֶר אוֹמֵר עַיִן רָעָה ' רַבִּי יְהוֹשֻׁעַ
אוֹמֵר חָבֵר רָע ' רַבִּי יוֹסֵי אוֹמֵר שָׁכֵן רָע ' רַבִּי שִׁמְעוֹן אוֹמֵר
הַלֹּוֶה וְאֵינוֹ מְשַׁלֵּם ' אֶחָד הַלֹּוֶה מִן־הָאָדָם כְּלֹוֶה מִן־הַמָּקוֹם '
שֶׁנֶּאֱמַר לֹוֶה רָשָׁע וְלֹא יְשַׁלֵּם וְצַדִּיק חוֹנֵן וְנוֹתֵן ' רַבִּי
אֶלְעָזָר אוֹמֵר לֵב רָע : אָמַר לָהֶם ' רוֹאֶה אֲנִי אֶת־דִּבְרֵי
אֶלְעָזָר בֶּן־עֲרָךְ מִדִּבְרֵיכֶם שֶׁבִּכְלַל דְּבָרָיו דִּבְרֵיכֶם :
(טו) הֵם אָמְרוּ שְׁלֹשָׁה דְבָרִים ' רַבִּי אֱלִיעֶזֶר אוֹמֵר ' יְהִי
כְבוֹד חֲבֵרְךָ חָבִיב עָלֶיךָ כְּשֶׁלָּךְ וְאַל־תְּהִי נוֹחַ לִכְעוֹס

13. *he said.* *i.e.* Rabban Yochanan.

go forth and see. Or, " behold now " ; a phrase for arousing attention
to a question.

the good way. What good quality shall a man cleave to as the essential
of a good life ? What is the clue to right living ?

a good eye. The kindly eye, blessed with the quality of seeing the
good in other people, and free from envy and ill-will; cf. v, 22.

a good friend. This means primarily, to *be* a good friend.

a good neighbour. *i.e.* the possession of the attributes which make
one a good neighbour, a worthy member of society.

one who foresees. The effect of his actions before performing them.

a good heart. *i.e.* unselfish love in thought, feeling and deed. In
Hebrew the heart is the source of feeling and action, as well as the seat of
understanding. " The heart sees, hears, speaks ; the heart rejoices,
weeps, breaks and rebels ; the heart invents, suspects, desires, loves and

13. He said to them, Go forth and see which is the good
way to which a man should cleave. R. Eliezer said, A good
eye ; R. Joshua said, A good friend ; R. José said, A good
neighbour ; R. Simeon said, One who foresees the fruit of
an action ; R. Elazar said, A good heart. Thereupon he said
to them, I approve the words of Elazar, the son of Arach,
rather than your words, for in his words yours are included.

14. He said to them, Go forth and see which is the evil
way that a man should shun. R. Eliezer said, An evil
eye ; R. Joshua said, A bad friend ; R. José said, A bad
neighbour ; R. Simeon said, One who borrows and does
not repay. (He that borrows from man is the same as if he
Psalm 37. 21 borrowed from God ; as it is said, The wicked borroweth,
and payeth not again, but the righteous dealeth graciously
and giveth) ; R. Elazar said, A bad heart. Thereupon
he said to them, I approve the words of Elazar, the son of
Arach, rather than your words, for in his words yours are
included.

15. They each said three things. R. Eliezer said, Let
the honour of thy fellow-man be as dear to thee as thine
own ; be not easily moved to anger; and repent one

hates ; meditates, schemes and obeys " (Midrash). If the heart is
good, it will prompt only right action.
14. *an evil eye.* Stands for envy, ill-will, niggardliness.
one who borrows and does not repay. Such a one does *not* foresee the
future, and is blind to the consequences of his conduct.
borrows from man. This clause is probably an editorial comment.
One who lacks foresight and incurs responsibilities which he is unable
to meet, borrows from God ; seeing that wealth comes from Him, and
men are merely His stewards.
and giveth. *i.e.* he repays the lender for his act of kindness.
15. *let the honour. . . . own.* A great saying. This sternly
condemns any action or word that injures another man's reputation or
exposes him to contempt or derision. The sin increases in gravity
when one benefits by such disgrace of his fellowman. "He who
elevates himself at the expense of his neighbour's degradation, has no
share in the World to come " (Talmud).

וְשׁוּב יוֹם אֶחָד לִפְנֵי מִיתָתָךְ וֶהֱוֵה מִתְחַמֵּם כְּנֶגֶד אוּרָן

שֶׁל־חֲכָמִים וֶהֱוֵה זָהִיר בְּגַחַלְתָּן שֶׁלֹּא תִכָּוֶה · שֶׁנְּשִׁיכָתָן

נְשִׁיכַת שׁוּעָל וַעֲקִיצָתָן עֲקִיצַת עַקְרָב וּלְחִישָׁתָן לְחִישַׁת

שָׂרָף וְכָל־דִּבְרֵיהֶם כְּגַחֲלֵי אֵשׁ : (טז) רַבִּי יְהוֹשֻׁעַ אוֹמֵר ·

עַיִן הָרַע וְיֵצֶר הָרַע וְשִׂנְאַת הַבְּרִיּוֹת מוֹצִיאִים אֶת־הָאָדָם

מִן־הָעוֹלָם : (יז) רַבִּי יוֹסֵי אוֹמֵר · יְהִי מָמוֹן חֲבֵרְךָ חָבִיב

עָלֶיךָ כְּשֶׁלָּךְ וְהַתְקֵן עַצְמְךָ לִלְמוֹד תּוֹרָה שֶׁאֵינָהּ יְרֻשָּׁה

לָךְ וְכָל־מַעֲשֶׂיךָ יִהְיוּ לְשֵׁם שָׁמָיִם : (יח) רַבִּי שִׁמְעוֹן אוֹמֵר ·

be not easily moved to anger. " Whosoever gives way to anger, if he
is wise, his wisdom leaves him ; if he is a prophet, the spirit of Prophecy
forsakes him. He who breaks anything in his anger, is as if he were
an idolater " (Talmud). Anger is a blind emotional reaction to an
injury received. Thus, when a child hurts its foot against a stone,
it is often so unreasonably angry as to strike the stone. Altogether
different is the moral feeling of *indignation* that sweeps over us whenever we see a great wrong committed; not because it injures *us*, as is
always the case in anger, but because the wrong is an outrage against
justice and right. See also R. Eliezer's prayer, p. xxi.

repent one day before thy death. When R. Eliezer gave this exhortation to his disciples, they asked, " But does a man know the day of
his death ? " He replied, " Let him then repent to-day, lest he die
to-morrow "; see p. 138.

the fire of the wise. One who wishes to warm himself, remains a certain
distance from the fire ; if he approaches too near, he is burned. So,
do not endeavour to become too intimate with the Wise. This admonition reflects personal experience. R. Eliezer was excommunicated by
his colleagues because he refused to accept the ruling of the majority,
and he died under the ban. There is much suppressed passion in his
words, " which do not deny to his opponents a measure of justification "
(Graetz). "As a piece of self-revelation, they awaken sympathy for a
great man suffering in lonely bitterness " (Herford).

16. Rabbi Joshua ben Chananya was the " man of the golden
mean " in the School of Yavneh. Of great gentleness and ready wit,
he was averse to extravagant measures, whether in religion or in life.
He is the author of the universalist doctrine, " The righteous of all
nations have a share in the World to come ". He visited Rome in 95,
and by his balanced and calm character exercised a restraining influence
in all dealings with the authorities. In addition to his Rabbinical
erudition, he was possessed of considerable astronomical knowledge.

day before thy death. And (he further said), Warm thyself by the fire of the wise ; but beware of their glowing coals, lest thou be burnt, for their bite is the bite of the fox, and their sting is the scorpion's sting, and their hiss is the serpent's hiss, and all their words are like coals of fire.

16. R. Joshua said, The evil eye, the evil inclination, and hatred of his fellow-creatures drive a man out of the world.

17. R. José said, Let the property of thy fellow-man be as dear to thee as thine own ; qualify thyself for the study of the Torah, since the knowledge of it is not an inheritance of thine; and let all thy deeds be done for the sake of Heaven.

Thus he seems to have known, and foreseen the reappearance, of what many believe to have been Halley's comet.

the evil eye. An envious disposition ; see on mishna 14.

the evil inclination. See p. 25. Man's natural instincts, when uncontrolled, lead to sin, and ruin a man's life.

hatred of his fellow-creatures. Misanthropy, contempt for your fellow-men. For " fellow-creatures " (*beriyyoth*), see on 1, 12.

drive a man out of the world. Means either shorten his life ; or, preferably, cut him off from human society.

17. *fellow-man.* Another application of the Golden Rule : respect your fellow-man's property rights as you would desire yours to be respected ; see mishna 15 and v, 13.

qualify thyself. Or, " prepare thyself ". As in the case of prayer, the study of the Torah must be approached with a mind properly attuned to a sacred purpose.

not an inheritance of thine. i.e. the actual knowledge may only be acquired by personal effort ; it cannot be bequeathed or inherited.

all thy deeds be done for the sake of Heaven. Even the common actions of daily life should be consecrated to the service of God, and be hallowed by Religion. Thus, Hillel told his disciples that to keep the body physically clean by bathing, was a religious duty. Cf. the English hymn,

> " Teach me, my God and King,
> In all things Thee to see ;
> And what I do in any thing,
> To do it as for Thee.

> A servant with this clause
> Makes drudgery divine ;
> Who sweeps a room as for Thy laws,
> Makes that and the action fine " (Herbert).

הֱוֵה זָהִיר בִּקְרִיאַת שְׁמַע וּבַתְּפִלָּה וּכְשֶׁאַתָּה מִתְפַּלֵּל אַל־
תַּעַשׂ תְּפִלָּתְךָ קֶבַע אֶלָּא רַחֲמִים וְתַחֲנוּנִים לִפְנֵי הַמָּקוֹם ·
שֶׁנֶּאֱמַר כִּי־חַנּוּן וְרַחוּם הוּא אֶרֶךְ אַפַּיִם וְרַב־חֶסֶד וְנִחָם
עַל־הָרָעָה · וְאַל־תְּהִי רָשָׁע בִּפְנֵי עַצְמֶךָ : (יט) רַבִּי אֶלְעָזָר
אוֹמֵר · הֱוֵה שָׁקוּד לִלְמוֹד תּוֹרָה וְדַע מַה־שֶּׁתָּשִׁיב
לְאֶפִּיקוֹרוֹס וְדַע לִפְנֵי מִי אַתָּה עָמֵל וּמִי הוּא בַּעַל מְלַאכְתְּךָ
שֶׁיְּשַׁלֶּם־לְךָ שְׂכַר פְּעֻלָּתֶךָ : (כ) רַבִּי טַרְפוֹן אוֹמֵר · הַיּוֹם
קָצֵר וְהַמְּלָאכָה מְרֻבָּה וְהַפּוֹעֲלִים עֲצֵלִים וְהַשָּׂכָר הַרְבֵּה

---

18. *be careful to read the Shema.* see p. 116 f.

and to say the Amidah. See p. 130.

as a fixed mechanical task. Prescribed prayers are not to be offered in a perfunctory way. The Rabbis who created the Liturgy taught the loftiest conception of prayer. See p. XXI and XXII.

be not wicked in thine own esteem. This saying preaches the duty of self-respect. Do not think yourself so abandoned that it is useless for you to make " an appeal for mercy and grace " before God. " Regard not thyself as wholly wicked, since by so doing thou givest up hope of repentance " (Maimonides). Communities, like individuals, are under the obligation not to be wicked in their own esteem. Achad Ha-am wrote : " Nothing is more dangerous for a nation or for an individual than to plead guilty to imaginary sins. Where the sin is real—by honest endeavour the sinner can purify himself. But when a man has been persuaded to suspect himself unjustly—what *can* he do ? Our greatest need is emancipation from self-contempt, from this idea that we are really worse than all the world. Otherwise, we may in course of time become in reality what we now imagine ourselves to be."

19. *be eager.* Without enthusiasm, the constant application essential for study will wane.

know what answer. It is a duty to fit oneself for the duty of defending the honour of Judaism against ignorant or malicious opponents.

unbeliever. Heb. *apikouros*, the Hebraized Greek form for a follower of Epicurus. That philosopher denied that God took any notice of human beings, or that He cared in the least whether their conduct was righteous or otherwise. Such denial of a Heavenly Judge and a Judgment Day is in Judaism the cardinal sin. Hence his name was chosen as a synonym for sceptic or heretic.

know. Be conscious that you are working "for the Name of Heaven". The quality of your effort will be influenced by that consciousness.

18. R. Simeon said, Be careful to read the Shema, and to say the Amidah ; and when thou prayest, regard not thy prayer as a fixed mechanical task, but as an appeal for mercy and grace before the All-present (as it is said, *Joel 2. 13* For he is gracious and full of mercy, slow to anger, and abounding in lovingkindness, and relenteth him of the evil) ; and be not wicked in thine own esteem.

19. R. Elazar said, Be eager to learn Torah ; know what answer to give to the unbeliever; know also before whom thou toilest, and who thy Employer is, who will pay thee the reward of thy labour.

20. Rabbi Tarfon said, The day is short, and the work is great, and the labourers are sluggish, and the reward is much, and the Master is urgent.

---

20. *Rabbi Tarfon.* Of priestly descent, he had officiated in the Temple. Though not a disciple of Rabban Yochanan, he was his contemporary. Of stern and rigid temperament, his was yet a nature of true religious delicacy and refinement. One Sabbath day, his mother's sandals split ; and as she could not mend them and would have to walk across the courtyard barefoot, Tarfon kept stretching his hands under her feet, so that she might walk over them all the way : he out-did Sir Walter Raleigh in chivalry. His best-known saying, here given, is of great solemnity and beauty.

the day is short. The life of man, or that part of it between childhood (dawn) and old age (evening) when it is possible to work with full vigour, is but of brief duration. But man is neither to despair nor yield to idleness.

the work. The utilization of life's opportunities in the service of God.

is great. Therefore time is too precious to waste.

labourers. God's creatures.

sluggish. There is in man a tendency to negligence and indolence that requires conscious effort to overcome ; see III, 14.

reward. Although the ideal is to work from a sense of duty, reward awaits the loyal toiler ; see on I, 3.

the Master. lit. " the master of the house ", the universal Father Who has the right to demand the labour of the members of His household, mankind.

urgent. It will brook no delay : " If not now, when ? "

It has been suggested that the first clause of the Hebrew might originally have been קָצִיר הַיּוֹם *to-day is harvest time* : the work is great, the labourers are sluggish, the reward is much, and the Master is urgent !

וּבְעַל הַבַּיִת דּוֹחֵק : (כא) הוּא הָיָה אוֹמֵר ׃ לֹא עָלֶיךָ
הַמְּלָאכָה לִגְמוֹר וְלֹא־אַתָּה בֶּן־חוֹרִין לְהִבָּטֵל מִמֶּנָּה ׃ אִם
לָמַדְתָּ תוֹרָה הַרְבֵּה נוֹתְנִים לְךָ שָׂכָר הַרְבֵּה וְנֶאֱמָן הוּא
בַּעַל מְלַאכְתְּךָ שֶׁיְּשַׁלֶּם לְךָ שָׂכַר פְּעֻלָּתֶךָ ׃ וְדַע שֶׁמַּתַּן
שְׂכָרָם שֶׁל־צַדִּיקִים לֶעָתִיד לָבוֹא :

רַבִּי חֲנַנְיָא בֶּן־עֲקַשְׁיָא וכו׳

21. to complete the work. It may not be given thee to complete the task called for, but that is no reason why it should not be attempted. Be not disheartened by the greatness and difficulty of what is before thee. Do as much as is in thy power.

THE " GOLDEN RULE " IN JUDAISM.

The world at large is unaware of the fact that the sublime maxim of morality, " Thou shalt love thy neighbour as thyself" (Leviticus 19. 18)—was first taught by Judaism. No less a thinker than John Stuart Mill expressed his surprise that it came from the Pentateuch. Not only is it Jewish in origin, but, long before the rise of Christianity, Israel's religious Teachers quoted it, either verbally or in paraphrase, as expressing the essence of the moral life. Thus, Ben Sira says, " Honour thy neighbour as thyself "; and, a hundred years later, the Testaments of the Twelve Patriarchs declares, " A man should not do to his neighbour what a man does not desire for himself ". Tobit admonishes his son in the words, " What is displeasing to thyself, that do not unto any other ". Philo and Josephus have sayings similar to the above. As to the Rabbis, there is the well-known story of Hillel and the heathen scoffer who asked him to condense for him the whole Torah in briefest possible form. Hillel's answer is, " Whatever is hateful unto thee, do it not unto thy fellow : this is the whole Torah ; the rest is explanation". In the generation after the Destruction of the Temple, Rabbi Akiba declares, " *Thou shalt love thy neighbour as thyself* is a fundamental rule in the Torah ". " All men are created in the Divine image," says his contemporary Ben Azzai ; " and, therefore, all are our fellowmen, and entitled to love and brotherhood ".

And the command of Leviticus 19. 18 applies to classes and nations as well as to individuals. The Prophets in their day, on the one hand, arraigned the rich for their oppression of the poor ; and, on the other hand, pilloried the nations that were guilty of inhumanity and breach of faith towards one another. Of Rabbinic opinion in all times, the following saying of Judah the Pious (see p. 214) is typical : " On the Judgment Day, the Holy One, blessed be He, will call the nations to account for every violation of- the command ' Thou shalt love

21. He used also to say, It is not thy duty to complete the work, but neither art thou free to desist from it ; if thou hast studied much Torah, much reward will be given thee, for faithful is thy Employer to pay thee the reward of thy labour ; and know that the grant of reward unto the righteous will be in the Time to come.
" Rabbi Chananya ", etc., p. 627.

thy neighbour as thyself' of which they have been guilty in their dealings with one another ".

Though the Founder of Christianity quotes " Thou shalt love thy neighbour as thyself " as the old Biblical command of recognized central importance, nevertheless Christian theologians maintain that its morality is only tribal, alleging that the Hebrew word for "neighbour" (*rea*) refers only to the fellow-Israelite. This is incorrect. One need not be a Hebrew scholar to convince oneself of the fact that *rea* means neighbour of whatever race or creed. Thus, in Exodus 11. 12, " Let them ask every man of his neighbour and every woman of her neighbour "—the Hebrew word for *neighbour* cannot possibly mean " fellow-Israelite ", but distinctly refers to the Egyptians. In order to prevent any possible misunderstanding, the command of love of neighbour is, in *v.* 34 of that same nineteenth chapter of Leviticus, extended to include the homeless alien :—

" The stranger that sojourneth with you shall be unto you as the homeborn among you, and thou shalt love him as thyself."

The word " neighbour " in Leviticus 19. 18 is thus equivalent to "fellow-man ", and it includes in its range every human being by virtue of his humanity. " The commandment to love one's fellow-man", said Rabba, a Babylonian teacher in the third century, " must be observed even in the execution of a criminal, and he should be granted as easy a death as possible ". In Jerusalem, the criminal before being led to execution was given a drugged cup of wine, by which he lost consciousness of what was being done to him. Quite other was the spirit of Rome. The Romans invented the fiendish punishment of crucifixion, which prolonged the death agonies of the victims for days. If Jewish teaching and Jewish example had been heeded, the history of torture in European history would have been far less voluminous than it is.

Christian theologians stress the fact that both the Book of Tobit and Hillel paraphrase Leviticus 19. 18 in a negative way—" Whatever is hateful unto thee, do it not unto thy fellow " : and they, therefore, maintain that the Jewish Golden Rule is merely a " negative " Golden Rule. This argument is illusory. In the oldest Christian literature, the two forms are recorded indiscriminately. The negative Golden Rule occurs in the Western texts of Acts 15. 20, Romans 13. 10, the Teaching of the Twelve Apostles, and the Apostolical Constitutions; and positive forms of the Rule have had a place in Judaism. Thus Hillel says, "Love thy fellow-creatures " ; and Eliezer ben Hyrcanus,

פֶּרֶק שְׁלִישִׁי :

כָּל יִשְׂרָאֵל וכו'

(א) עֲקַבְיָא בֶּן־מַהֲלַלְאֵל אוֹמֵר הִסְתַּכֵּל בִּשְׁלשָׁה דְבָרִים וְאֵין אַתָּה בָא לִידֵי עֲבֵרָה דַּע מֵאַיִן בָּאתָ וּלְאָן אַתָּה הוֹלֵךְ וְלִפְנֵי מִי אַתָּה עָתִיד לִתֵּן דִּין וְחֶשְׁבּוֹן • מֵאַיִן בָּאתָ מִטִּפָּה סְרוּחָה • וּלְאָן אַתָּה הוֹלֵךְ לִמְקוֹם עָפָר רִמָּה וְתוֹלֵעָה • וְלִפְנֵי מִי אַתָּה עָתִיד לִתֵּן דִּין וְחֶשְׁבּוֹן לִפְנֵי מֶלֶךְ מַלְכֵי הַמְּלָכִים הַקָּדוֹשׁ בָּרוּךְ הוּא : (ב) רַבִּי חֲנִינָא סְגַן הַכֹּהֲנִים אוֹמֵר • הֱוֵה מִתְפַּלֵּל בִּשְׁלוֹמָהּ שֶׁל־מַלְכוּת שֶׁאִלְמָלֵא מוֹרָאָהּ אִישׁ אֶת־רֵעֵהוּ חַיִּים בְּלָעוֹ : (ג) רַבִּי חֲנַנְיָא בֶּן־תְּרַדְיוֹן

"Let the honour of thy fellow-man be as dear to thee as thine own". But the mere fact that Leviticus 19. 18 is itself positive, renders all talk of a "negative" Jewish morality in connection with the Golden Rule fatuous.

One word more. Noble as is the Golden Rule, it is only *part* of the ethical and social legislation of the Torah. "Condensations of the essentials of the moral law into one comprehensive rule, are of interest as exhibiting a sound estimate of religious and moral values. For the actual conduct of life, and above all for the practical morals of a community or a people in any age, explicit rules, defining cases and prescribing what is to be done in concrete instances, are indispensable" (Moore).

CHAPTER III.

SAYINGS OF AKIBA AND OTHERS.

The sayings in this chapter are not in chronological order.

1. *Akavya.* A contemporary of Hillel. He was offered the position of Av Beth Din (see on I, 4) after Shammai's death, on condition that he retracted certain opinions he had expressed ; but he refused to do so. "Let not men say that, for the sake of office, I changed my views." When, on his death-bed, his son asked that he recommend him to his friends, he answered : "It is thy deeds that will bring thee near to men, and thy deeds that will drive thee from them".

reflect. Sinfulness is the result of pride, and of thoughtlessness as to what follows death. If a man remembers whence he cometh, he is rendered humble. If he considers whither he is going, he is saved from passion and the lust for money. And if he bears in mind the Tribunal

CHAPTER III

"All Israel", etc., p. 613.

1. Akavya, the son of Mahalalel, said, Reflect upon three things, and thou wilt not come within the power of sin : know whence thou camest, whither thou art going ; and before whom thou wilt in future have to give account and reckoning. Whence thou camest :—from a fetid drop ; whither thou art going :—to a place of dust, worms and maggots ; and before whom thou wilt in future have to give account and reckoning :—before the Supreme King of kings, the Holy One, blessed be he.

2. R. Chanina, the Vice-High Priest, said, Pray for the welfare of the government, since but for the fear thereof men would swallow each other alive.

3. R. Chananya, the son of Teradyon, said, If two sit together and interchange no words of Torah, they are a meeting of scoffers, concerning whom it is said, The godly man sitteth not in the seat of the scoffers ; but if two sit

Psalm 1. 1

before Whom he is to appear, he will flee from sin. See II, 1.
    place of dust. Cf. "dust thou art, and unto dust shalt thou return" (Genesis 3. 19).
    2. *Vice-High Priest.* A deputy for the High Priest, to take his place should the latter be prevented from discharging his functions.
    pray for the welfare of the government. See p. 503. The "government" was Rome ; and, although it was harsh in its administration, he advised his fellow-Jews not to work for a breach with Rome. His seems to have been the attitude of the conservative priesthood in the political controversy which preceded the Great War against Rome in 66-70.
    swallow each other alive. Government stands for order ; and without it there would be the chaos of anarchy; cf. Shakespeare, "You cry against the noble Senate, who . . . . keep you in awe, which else would feed on one another" (Coriolanus I, 1, 188–192).

MISHNA 3, 4 and 7. Conversation must be hallowed in thought and speech by remembrance of the Divine Presence. The texts quoted are applied in the homiletic manner of the Haggadists of that generation
    3. *Chananya.* He was the father of Beruria, the renowned wife of Rabbi Meir ; see p. 588. He suffered martyrdom in the Second War against Rome, after the defeat of Bar Cochba in the year 135, of the Christian era. The Romans were masters in torture. He was wrapped in a Scroll of the Torah, and then set fire to ; and to prolong his sufferings, moist wool was placed over his heart. His dying words were

אוֹמֵר · שְׁנַיִם שֶׁיּוֹשְׁבִים וְאֵין בֵּינֵיהֶם דִּבְרֵי תוֹרָה הֲרֵי זֶה
מוֹשַׁב לֵצִים · שֶׁנֶּאֱמַר וּבְמוֹשַׁב לֵצִים לֹא יָשָׁב · אֲבָל שְׁנַיִם
שֶׁיּוֹשְׁבִים וְיֵשׁ בֵּינֵיהֶם דִּבְרֵי תוֹרָה שְׁכִינָה שְׁרוּיָה בֵּינֵיהֶם ·
שֶׁנֶּאֱמַר אָז נִדְבְּרוּ יִרְאֵי יְיָ אִישׁ אֶל־רֵעֵהוּ וַיַּקְשֵׁב יְיָ וַיִּשְׁמָע
וַיִּכָּתֵב סֵפֶר זִכָּרוֹן לְפָנָיו לְיִרְאֵי יְיָ וּלְחֹשְׁבֵי שְׁמוֹ · אֵין
לִי אֶלָּא שְׁנַיִם · מִנַּיִן אֲפִילוּ אֶחָד שֶׁיּוֹשֵׁב וְעוֹסֵק בַּתּוֹרָה
שֶׁהַקָּדוֹשׁ בָּרוּךְ הוּא קוֹבֵעַ לוֹ שָׂכָר · שֶׁנֶּאֱמַר יֵשֵׁב בָּדָד
וְיִדֹּם כִּי נָטַל עָלָיו : ‏(ד)‏ רַבִּי שִׁמְעוֹן אוֹמֵר · שְׁלֹשָׁה שֶׁאָכְלוּ
עַל שֻׁלְחָן אֶחָד וְלֹא אָמְרוּ עָלָיו דִּבְרֵי תוֹרָה כְּאִלּוּ אָכְלוּ
מִזִּבְחֵי מֵתִים · שֶׁנֶּאֱמַר כִּי כָּל־שֻׁלְחָנוֹת מָלְאוּ קִיא צֹאָה בְּלִי

'The parchment is being burnt, but the letters are soaring upward ",
.e. the Sacred Message written on it is indestructible.

the Divine Presence. Heb. Shechinah, the Holy Spirit that
makes God's presence felt by man. God's majesty descends upon a
group of two, three or ten persons engaged in sacred discourse. " How
many such majesties are there ? " a heretic sneeringly asked of Rabban
Gamaliel II. He replied, " Does not the sun send forth a million rays
upon the earth ? And should not the majesty of God, which is millions
of times brighter, be reflected in every spot on earth ? "

though he sit alone. The Scriptural verse, removed from its context, is
made the basis of the fine thought; namely, that the Spirit of God abides
with the solitary man who allows his mind to dwell upon the holy
teachings of the Torah.

4. Simeon. i.e. R. Simeon ben Yochai (circa 100–160).
A disciple of R. Akiba, and a most eminent Rabbi of his period. He
was a man of confident and independent mind ; a hater of Roman
tyranny and a convinced democrat who declared, " Every Israelite is
to be regarded as of royal descent ". In a wonderful parable, he
taught the solidarity of Israel. "In a boat at sea, one of the men began
to bore a hole in the bottom of the boat. On being remonstrated with,
he answered : ' I am only boring under my own seat.' ' Yes ', said his
comrades, ' but when the sea rushes in, we shall all be drowned with
you '. So it is with Israel. Its weal or its woe is in the hands of every
individual Israelite ". He spent many years in hiding from the Roman
authorities who had sentenced him to death. His life was adorned by
legend. He became the ideal of the Cabalists, and he was for many

together and interchange words of Torah, the Divine Presence
Malachi 3. 16 abides between them; as it is said, Then they that feared the
Lord spake one with the other : and the Lord hearkened
and heard, and a book of remembrance was written before
him, for them that feared the Lord, and that thought upon
his Name. Now, the Scripture enables me to draw this inference in respect to two persons ; whence can it be deduced
that if even one person sedulously occupies himself with the
Torah, the Holy One, blessed be he, appoints unto him a
Lamentations 3. 27 reward ? Because it is said, Though he sit alone, and meditate in stillness, yet he taketh it (the reward) upon him.

4. R. Simeon said, If three have eaten at a table and
have spoken there no words of Torah, it is as if they had
Isaiah 28. 8 eaten of sacrifices to dead idols, of whom it is said, For all
their tables are full of vomit and filthiness ; the All-present

centuries held to be the author of the Zohar, which is deemed sacred by
the Cabalists.   An annual festival is to this day celebrated by the
Mystics in his honour at Meron, in Northern Palestine. See also IV, 13

if three have eaten. Simeon ben Yochai expands the saying of R.
Chananya. In Judaism the meal is regarded as a religious service with
special benedictions before and after it. The act of eating is spiritualized
by prayer, and by being made subservient to the strengthening of the
ties of domestic affection and of interest in higher things.

spoken . . . no words of Torah. A company of three requires the
recital of Grace with a special responsive introduction. The Grace
consisting of thanksgiving for food, coupled with historic and religious
memories, is in itself a fitting fulfilment of the demand for discourse
at table on sacred things ; see pp. 960–971.

sacrifices to dead idols. If they paid no heed to religious matters
and not even recited the Grace, the meal was merely for the satisfaction
of physical needs, with no sacredness whatever surrounding it. " Exag
gerated statements such as this have the purpose of arresting the atten
tion, and of driving home the lesson or the warning given " (Oesterley)

vomit and filthiness.   As his proof-text, R. Simeon chooses
Isaiah's denunciation of the drunkards of ancient Samaria, Chapter
28, in order to express his horror of the revels and feastings among
the Roman ruling classes of his day. These revels were often attended
by indecency, and the disgusting use of emetics in furtherance of
gluttony. Not such—taught R. Simeon—was to be the place of the
meal and its educational mission in the life of the Jew. The family
table was to be the family altar.

מָקוֹם ׳ אֲבָל שְׁלֹשָׁה שֶׁאָכְלוּ עַל שֻׁלְחָן אֶחָד וְאָמְרוּ עָלָיו
דִּבְרֵי תוֹרָה כְּאִלּוּ אָכְלוּ מִשֻּׁלְחָנוֹ שֶׁל־מָקוֹם ׳ שֶׁנֶּאֱמַר וַיְדַבֵּר
אֵלַי זֶה הַשֻּׁלְחָן אֲשֶׁר לִפְנֵי יְיָ: (ה) רַבִּי חֲנִינָא בֶּן־חֲכִינַי
אוֹמֵר ׳ הַנֵּעוֹר בַּלַּיְלָה וְהַמְהַלֵּךְ בַּדֶּרֶךְ יְחִידִי וּמְפַנֶּה לִבּוֹ
לְבַטָּלָה הֲרֵי זֶה מִתְחַיֵּב בְּנַפְשׁוֹ: (ו) רַבִּי נְחוּנְיָא בֶּן־הַקָּנָה
אוֹמֵר ׳ כָּל־הַמְקַבֵּל עָלָיו עֹל תּוֹרָה מַעֲבִירִים מִמֶּנּוּ עֹל
מַלְכוּת וְעֹל דֶּרֶךְ אֶרֶץ ׳ וְכָל־הַפּוֹרֵק מִמֶּנּוּ עֹל תּוֹרָה נוֹתְנִים

the All-present is not (*in their thoughts*). lit. "without a place
makom)"; but in Rabbinic Hebrew, *makom* is a synonym of God
see on II, 14); hence the interpretation, "without the All-present".

this is the table. Referring to the altar, which is said to have been
' three cubits high ", here taken as symbolical of three men seated at
the table. When the table is sanctified by prayer, and is not disgraced
by frivolity, it becomes holy like the altar.

5. *Chanina, the son of Chachinai.* A contemporary of R. Simeon
and disciple of R. Akiba; he lived during the first half of the second
century.

keeps awake at night. Even the waking hours due to sleeplessness
should be spent in serious meditation. " My soul is satisfied . . . when
I remember Thee upon my couch, and meditate on Thee in the night-
watches " (Psalm 63. 6f).

and who goes on his way alone. He is on a journey unaccompanied.
Having no companion with whom to discuss serious topics, there is
more danger of his mind dwelling upon frivolous matters.

turns his heart to idle thoughts. Idle thoughts lead to sin, therefore
the mind must be occupied with words of Torah; see Deuteronomy
3. 7. " Thou shalt talk of them when thou sittest in thine house, and
when thou walkest by the way, and when thou liest down, and when
thou risest up." " This saying is one more illustration of that consecration of the whole of man's waking existence to the service of God,
which was for the Pharisee the ' way of the perfect life ' " (Herford).

sins against himself. Without the protective influence of Religion,
man is in constant danger of a lapse into evil, that might make him
incur guilt of the gravest nature.

6. *Nechunya, son of Ha-kana.* A contemporary of Rabban Yochanan. Later generations looked upon him as a foremost mystic. The
prayer, " We beseech thee ", (p. 945) after the Counting of the Omer, is
attributed to him. In his old age, he declared, " Never in my life have
I sought honour through the degradation of a colleague, nor has my
ill-will against any fellow-man lasted till night-time ".

is not (in their thoughts). But if three have eaten at a table and have spoken there words of Torah, it is as if they had eaten at the table of the All-present, to which the Scripture Ezekiel **41**. **22** may be applied, And he said unto me, This is the table that is before the Lord.

5. R. Chanina, the son of Chachinai, said, He who keeps awake at night, and goes on his way alone, and turns his heart to idle thoughts, such a one sins against himself.

6. R. Nechunya, son of Ha-kana, said, Whoso receives upon himself the yoke of the Torah, from him the yoke of the kingdom and the yoke of worldly care will be removed; but whoso casts off from him the yoke of the Torah, upon him will be laid the yoke of the kingdom and the yoke of worldly care.

yoke of the Torah. The multitude of commandments ordained by God is compared to a yoke (see p. 112), not as the symbol of oppression but of obedience. Like the yoke harnessed to an animal, it provides guidance of right direction and useful service. " The Law will always be a yoke, though a glorious yoke ; and the duty of bending beneath it in humble and glad self-surrender is the characteristic obligation of Israel through the ages " (M. Joseph).

yoke of the kingdom. " Stands for the burdens, such as taxation put upon a man by the government under which he lives, or the oppression which he may suffer at the hands of the great " (Taylor).

worldly care. Heb. *derech eretz*, see on II, 2. The hardships, anxieties, and discontent in connection with the gaining of a livelihood.

will be removed. " Absorption in sacred study frees a man from care over worldly matters, and renders him invulnerable to the vicissitude of time and fortune " (Derenbourg). The Tables of the Law are a charter of freedom ; see VI, 2. " To the man of true ethical and religious culture, civil law and the demands of society have ceased to be a burden to others, it is a yoke " (Geiger). In Büchler's opinion, R. Nechunya addressed himself not to all Jews, but to those who hesitated whether they should divide their time between the study of the Torah and a secular calling. Unlike R. Judah the Prince, who urged each scholar to have some worldly occupation, he advised them to make the study of the Torah their exclusive life-work. We have no evidence that either the Roman government remitted taxation in the case of scholars, or that the communities paid these and provided for their sustenance and that of their families.

casts off from him the yoke. A Heb. expression for rebellion. If a person seeks relief by revolt against God's commandments, the effect is to make the rigour of his mundane concerns more keenly felt.

עָלָיו עַל מַלְכוּת וְעַל דֶּרֶךְ אֶרֶץ : (ז) רַבִּי חֲלַפְתָּא בֶּן־
דּוֹסָא אִישׁ כְּפַר חֲנַנְיָא אוֹמֵר · עֲשָׂרָה שֶׁיּוֹשְׁבִים וְעוֹסְקִים
בַּתּוֹרָה שְׁכִינָה שְׁרוּיָה בֵּינֵיהֶם · שֶׁנֶּאֱמַר אֱלֹהִים נִצָּב בַּעֲדַת־
אֵל · וּמִנַּיִן אֲפִילוּ חֲמִשָּׁה · שֶׁנֶּאֱמַר וַאֲגֻדָּתוֹ עַל־אֶרֶץ יְסָדָהּ ·
וּמִנַּיִן אֲפִילוּ שְׁלשָׁה · שֶׁנֶּאֱמַר בְּקֶרֶב אֱלֹהִים יִשְׁפֹּט · וּמִנַּיִן
אֲפִילוּ שְׁנַיִם · שֶׁנֶּאֱמַר אָז נִדְבְּרוּ יִרְאֵי יְיָ אִישׁ אֶל־רֵעֵהוּ
וַיַּקְשֵׁב יְיָ וַיִּשְׁמָע · וּמִנַּיִן אֲפִילוּ אֶחָד · שֶׁנֶּאֱמַר בְּכָל־הַמָּקוֹם
אֲשֶׁר אַזְכִּיר אֶת־שְׁמִי אָבֹא אֵלֶיךָ וּבֵרַכְתִּיךָ : (ח) רַבִּי אֶלְעָזָר
אִישׁ בַּרְתּוֹתָא אוֹמֵר · תֶּן־לוֹ מִשֶּׁלּוֹ שָׁאַתָּה וְשֶׁלְּךָ שֶׁלּוֹ ·
וְכֵן בְּדָוִד הוּא אוֹמֵר כִּי־מִמְּךָ הַכֹּל וּמִיָּדְךָ נָתַנּוּ לָךְ :
(ט) רַבִּי יַעֲקֹב אוֹמֵר · הַמְהַלֵּךְ בַּדֶּרֶךְ וְשׁוֹנֶה וּמַפְסִיק
מִמִּשְׁנָתוֹ וְאוֹמֵר מַה־נָּאֶה אִילָן זֶה מַה־נָּאֶה נִיר זֶה מַעֲלֶה

---

7. Chalafta, the son of Dosa. His saying continues the thought in mishna 3 and 4, and extends the number to a maximum of ten.

congregation. Heb. *edah*, the same word as in Numbers 14. 27, where it is used of the twelve spies, excluding Joshua and Caleb. This is the basis of the regulation which requires a minimum number (minyan) of ten adult males to constitute an *edah*, a "congregation", for public worship.

band. A collection of articles held together by the five fingers of the hand; hence, the number five.

judges. The minimum number of judges to form a tribunal in Jewish Law is three.

I will come unto thee. The singular "thee" indicates one person.

8. Elazar. He was a disciple of R. Joshua ben Chananya, and a contemporary of R. Akiba.

Bertotha. In Galilee; perhaps identical with Berothah (Ezekiel 47. 16).

give unto Him of what is His. An inspiring concept which ennobles life. All that man is and has, derives from God; body, soul, and life itself are what God has entrusted to him. They should consequently not be employed for self-advantage, but in His service. Rabbi Elazar himself faithfully practised his teaching. He was so generous in his gifts, that the official collectors of charity passed him by, for fear that he would contribute more than his means permitted.

7. R. Chalafta, the son of Dosa, of the village of Chananya, said, When ten people sit together and occupy themselves with the Torah, the Shechinah abides among them ; *Psalm 82. 1* as it is said, God standeth in the congregation of the godly. And whence can it be shown that the same applies to five ? *Amos 9. 6* Because it is said, He hath founded his band upon the earth. And whence can it be shown that the same applies to three ? *Psalm 82. 1* Because it is said, He judgeth among the judges. And whence can it be shown that the same applies to two ? *Malachi 3. 16* Because it is said, Then they that feared the Lord spake one with the other ; and the Lord hearkened, and heard. And whence can it be shown that the same applies even to *Exodus 20. 24* one ? Because it is said, In every place where I cause my Name to be remembered I will come unto thee and I will bless thee.

8. R. Elazar, of Bertotha, said, Give unto Him of what is His, seeing that thou and what thou hast are His : this *1 Chronicles 29. 14* is also found expressed by David, who said, For all things come of Thee, and of Thine own we have given Thee.

9. R. Jacob said, He who is walking by the way and rehearses what he has learnt, and breaks off from his rehearsing and says, How fine is that tree, how fine is that field, him the Scripture regards as if he were guilty against himself.

---

9. *Jacob.* His father's name was Korshai. Some maintain that he was a grandson of Elisha ben Abuya (IV, 25) and a teacher of R. Judah the Prince. His saying states the duty of study of the Torah in extreme form. The Rabbis were certainly not indifferent to the beauty of Nature, as they prescribed various Benedictions on beholding beautiful persons and things ; see p. 991.

breaks off. What is deprecated here is a wilful distraction of the mind from Torah-meditation by the surrounding scenery.

Scripture regards. No text is, or could well be, quoted, in support of the statement.

as if. Actually he does not sin, as the exclamation, " How fine is this tree ", is itself an adoration of God. It is only because learning is so much more important, that the breaking off therefrom deserves condemnation (Machzor Vitry and Tiferéth Yisroel). This mishna has also been interpreted homiletically. "He who turns away from the

עָלָיו הַכָּתוּב כְּאִלּוּ מִתְחַיֵּב בְּנַפְשׁוֹ : (י) רַבִּי דּוֹסְתַּי בַּר

יַנַּי מִשֵּׁם רַבִּי מֵאִיר אוֹמֵר · כָּל־הַשּׁוֹכֵחַ דָּבָר אֶחָד מִמִּשְׁנָתוֹ

מַעֲלֶה עָלָיו הַכָּתוּב כְּאִלּוּ מִתְחַיֵּב בְּנַפְשׁוֹ · שֶׁנֶּאֱמַר רַק

הִשָּׁמֶר לְךָ וּשְׁמֹר נַפְשְׁךָ מְאֹד פֶּן־תִּשְׁכַּח אֶת־הַדְּבָרִים

אֲשֶׁר־רָאוּ עֵינֶיךָ · יָכוֹל אֲפִילוּ תָּקְפָה עָלָיו מִשְׁנָתוֹ · תַּלְמוּד

לוֹמַר וּפֶן־יָסוּרוּ מִלְּבָבְךָ כֹּל יְמֵי חַיֶּיךָ · הָא אֵינוֹ מִתְחַיֵּב

בְּנַפְשׁוֹ עַד־שֶׁיֵּשֵׁב וִיסִירֵם מִלִּבּוֹ : (יא) רַבִּי חֲנִינָא בֶּן־דּוֹסָא

אוֹמֵר · כֹּל שֶׁיִּרְאַת חֶטְאוֹ קוֹדֶמֶת לְחָכְמָתוֹ חָכְמָתוֹ

מִתְקַיֶּמֶת וְכֹל שֶׁחָכְמָתוֹ קוֹדֶמֶת לְיִרְאַת חֶטְאוֹ אֵין חָכְמָתוֹ

מִתְקַיֶּמֶת : (יב) הוּא הָיָה אוֹמֵר · כֹּל שֶׁמַּעֲשָׂיו מְרֻבִּים

מֵחָכְמָתוֹ חָכְמָתוֹ מִתְקַיֶּמֶת וְכֹל שֶׁחָכְמָתוֹ מְרֻבָּה מִמַּעֲשָׂיו

אֵין חָכְמָתוֹ מִתְקַיֶּמֶת : (יג) הוּא הָיָה אוֹמֵר · כֹּל שֶׁרוּחַ

הַבְּרִיּוֹת נוֹחָה הֵימֶנּוּ רוּחַ הַמָּקוֹם נוֹחָה הֵימֶנּוּ · וְכֹל שֶׁאֵין

Torah, *i.e.* gives up belief in Revelation, and seeks his religious inspiration from Nature, that man sins against his own soul " (J. H. Kara,
Boless l'minchah).

10. *Dostai.* An older contemporary of R. Judah the Prince, and
disciple of R. Meir.

whoso forgets. It is probable that this saying was not meant to have
a general application, but was intended for those who were styled
talmide chachamim, " disciples of the sages ". For such as these, forgetfulness was a serious defect; and highly culpable, if due to remissness on
their part.

now, one might suppose. This seems to be R. Dostai's comment on
R. Meir's statement.

too hard for him. Anyone may forget when what he tries to learn
is difficult.

of set purpose removes those lessons. This inference is drawn from the
words " all the days of thy life ". Unintentional forgetfulness can be
overcome by persistent study; but here we have a case where the
student deliberately abandons the study of the Torah. " A man should
be as careful to preserve his Torah as he is in regard to his money; for,
it is hard to get as gold, and perishes easily as glass. He who learns
Torah and does not *repeat* it, is as one who sows and does not reap." (Sifre).

10. R. Dostai, the son of Yannai, said in the name of
R. Meir, Whoso forgets one word of his study, him the
Scripture regards as if he had forfeited his life; for it is said,
Deuteronomy 4. 9 Only take heed to thyself, and keep thy soul diligently, lest
thou forget the things which thine eyes have seen. Now,
one might suppose that the same result follows even if a
man's study has been too hard for him. To guard against
Deuteronomy 4. 9 such an inference, it is said, And lest they depart from thy
mouth all the days of thy life. Thus, a person's guilt is not
established until he deliberately and of set purpose removes
those lessons from his heart.

11. R. Chanina, the son of Dosa, said, He in whom the
fear of sin comes before wisdom, his wisdom shall endure ;
but he in whom wisdom comes before the fear of sin, his
wisdom will not endure.

12. He used to say, He whose deeds exceed his wisdom,
his wisdom shall endure ; but he whose wisdom exceeds his
deeds, his wisdom will not endure.

13. He used to say, He in whom the spirit of his fellow-
creatures takes delight, in him the Spirit of the All-present

---

11. *Chanina, the son of Dosa.* A disciple of Rabban Yochanan.
Renowned as a mystic and wonder-worker. His sayings are amongst
the simplest and sublimest in Aboth.
fear of sin. " A man with wisdom but without fear of Heaven, is
like the man with the key of an inner court, but unable to enter because
he has not the key of the outer court " (Talmud).
12. *he whose deeds exceed his wisdom.* Wisdom is only a means to
an end ; and, unless it fulfils itself in action of the right kind, it serves
no true purpose and so cannot endure. It was a favourite saying of
Raba (279-352) : " The goal of wisdom is repentance and good deeds ;
so that a man shall not learn Torah, and study Mishna, and then contradict his father or master or teacher ; as it is said, 'The fear of the
Lord is the beginning of wisdom'" In the eyes of the Rabbis, the
fear of the Lord was even more : it was the *whole* of wisdom ; (1, 17).
13. *fellow-creatures.* Avoid doing things that even *appear* wrong,
משום מראית עין. If a man so conducts himself as to win the approval
of his fellows, he is assured of gaining the Divine approval. Such a
statement does scant justice to the prophet, or the martyr : human
favour does not, as a rule, shadow *them.* But R. Chanina was a mystic,
and his deeper meaning is, when a man establishes harmonious

רוּחַ הַבְּרִיּוֹת נוֹחָה הֵימֶנּוּ אֵין רוּחַ הַמָּקוֹם נוֹחָה הֵימֶנּוּ:

(יד) רַבִּי דוֹסָא בֶּן־הָרְכִּינַס אוֹמֵר · שֵׁנָה שֶׁל־שַׁחֲרִית וְיַיִן

שֶׁל־צָהֳרַיִם וְשִׂיחַת הַיְלָדִים וִישִׁיבַת בָּתֵּי כְנֵסִיּוֹת שֶׁל־עַמֵּי

הָאָרֶץ מוֹצִיאִים אֶת־הָאָדָם מִן־הָעוֹלָם: (טו) רַבִּי אֶלְעָזָר

הַמּוֹדָעִי אוֹמֵר · הַמְחַלֵּל אֶת־הַקֳּדָשִׁים וְהַמְבַזֶּה אֶת־הַמּוֹעֲדוֹת

וְהַמַּלְבִּין פְּנֵי חֲבֵרוֹ בָּרַבִּים וְהַמֵּפֵר בְּרִיתוֹ שֶׁל־אַבְרָהָם

אָבִינוּ וְהַמְגַלֶּה פָנִים בַּתּוֹרָה שֶׁלֹּא כַהֲלָכָה אַף עַל פִּי שֶׁיֵּשׁ

בְּיָדוֹ תּוֹרָה וּמַעֲשִׂים טוֹבִים אֵין לוֹ חֵלֶק לָעוֹלָם הַבָּא:

(טז) רַבִּי יִשְׁמָעֵאל אוֹמֵר · הֱוֵה קַל לְרֹאשׁ וְנוֹחַ לְתִשְׁחֹרֶת

relations with his associates, any cause for displeasure on the part of God is removed, and thus He too takes delight in him. Cf. I Samuel 2. 26 and Proverbs 3. 4.

14. Dosa, the son of Horkinas. A younger contemporary of Rabban Yochanan. He was a man of wealth, and these warning words were probably addressed to his social circle.

morning sleep. Involves the waste of precious hours of the day that should be spent in work or study ; Proverbs 6. 9–11.

mid-day wine. Wine in Judaism is certainly not forbidden, when in measure and in season. However, mid-day wine indisposes a man alike for Torah and for business. " There are four stages from sobriety to drunkenness. Before drinking, a man is innocent as a lamb; after drinking enough, he is strong as a lion ; in the next stage, he is like a hog ; when thoroughly drunken, he is like an ape, and dances and jests and knows not what he is doing " (Midrash). Cf. Proverbs 23. 29–33.

children's talk. Or. " the babbling of youths ". A warning against wasting too much time in listening to children's prattle, or to the idle chatter of young people.

houses of assembly of the ignorant. See Psalm 1. 1. Frequenting meeting-places of the vulgar, reduces a man to their level.

drive a man from the world. Cf. II, 16. The practices enumerated render a man disinclined towards piety and the company of the learned.

15. Elazar of Modim. The home of the Maccabees. He was a disciple of Rabban Yochanan, and was put to death by Bar Cochba, having been falsely denounced by a Samaritan as a traitor. His saying seems to have been directed against Gnostic and Jewish-Christian sectarians in his day. Many of those " Liberal " Jews rejected all religious authority, and their attitude opened the door to spiritual nihilism. The Rabbis readily granted that some of these men may have been well-meaning, men of considerable learning and social position;

takes delight ; and he in whom the spirit of his fellow-creatures takes not delight, in him the Spirit of the All-present takes not delight.

14. R. Dosa, the son of Horkinas, said, Morning sleep and midday wine, and children's talk, and attending the meeting places of the ignorant, drive a man from the world.

15. R. Elazar of Modim said, He who profanes things sacred, and despises the festivals, and puts his fellow-man to shame in public, and makes void the covenant of Abraham our father, and makes the Torah bear a meaning other than the right, such a one, even though knowledge of the Torah and good deeds be his, has no share in the world to come.

16. R. Ishmael said, Be submissive to a superior, affable to a suppliant, and receive all men with cheerfulness.

but choosing to act as they did, they could not claim to be of the House of Israel.

things sacred. The saying is especially true when the words " things sacred " are taken in their larger, literal sense : he treats holy things as if they were not holy.

despises the festivals. By showing contempt for the Holy Occasions of the Jewish year, he not only violates the Divine commandment, but dissociates himself from Israel's history which is their background ; as well as from the community that finds its consciousness heightened by their celebration.

puts his fellow-man to shame in public. A heinous offence against the Golden Rule (II, 15). These sectarians " heckled " the Jewish teachers, and put them to shame at public discussions or gatherings (Moritz Friedländer).

makes void the covenant. Assimilationist Jews in ancient, as in modern, times sealed their apostasy by their repudiation of the Abrahamic covenant.

a meaning other than the right. A condemnation of arbitrary interpretations that are contrary to the accepted ruling.

though . . . Torah and good deeds be his. Although these are the highest qualifications a Jew can possess, they do not outweigh the serious offences enumerated. Those guilty of them cannot be considered as Israelites.

16. *Ishmael.* Grandson of a High Priest, he was taken captive to Rome after the fall of Jerusalem, and obtained his release through the efforts of R. Joshua ben Chananya; see also p. 37. His system of exegesis differed from that of Rabbi Akiba, and followed the plain meaning of

נֶהֱוֶה מְקַבֵּל אֶת־כָּל־הָאָדָם בְּשִׂמְחָה : (יז) רַבִּי עֲקִיבָא
אוֹמֵר · שְׂחוֹק וְקַלּוּת רֹאשׁ מַרְגִּילִים אֶת־הָאָדָם לְעֶרְוָה :
מָסֹרֶת סְיָג לַתּוֹרָה מַעְשְׂרוֹת סְיָג לָעשֶׁר נְדָרִים סְיָג
לִפְרִישׁוּת סְיָג־לַחָכְמָה שְׁתִיקָה : (יח) הוּא הָיָה אוֹמֵר ·
חָבִיב אָדָם שֶׁנִּבְרָא בְּצֶלֶם חִבָּה יְתֵרָה נוֹדַעַת לוֹ שֶׁנִּבְרָא
בְּצֶלֶם אֱלֹהִים · שֶׁנֶּאֱמַר כִּי בְּצֶלֶם אֱלֹהִים עָשָׂה אֶת־הָאָדָם :
חֲבִיבִים יִשְׂרָאֵל שֶׁנִּקְרְאוּ בָנִים לַמָּקוֹם חִבָּה יְתֵרָה נוֹדַעַת
לָהֶם שֶׁנִּקְרְאוּ בָנִים לַמָּקוֹם · שֶׁנֶּאֱמַר בָּנִים אַתֶּם לַיְיָ

the Text. He was a lovable character. He is the author of the saying, "The daughters of Israel are beautiful, but it is poverty which makes them appear homely"

be submissive to a superior. lit. "be swift (to obey) a chief." Living in a period when the hand of Rome was heavy upon the Jews, and her local rulers were oppressors, he advised his brethren to accept in as cheerful a spirit as possible the harsh conditions of their political existence.

a suppliant. The meaning of the Heb. is uncertain. Some modern authorities render: "Be patient under forced service". Another possible translation is, "Be deferential to your seniors, and affable to your juniors".

receive all men with cheerfulness. A parallel to 1, 15.

17-20. SAYINGS OF RABBI AKIBA.

17. Akiba. In the influence exerted by his teaching, Akiba (60–135) is among the greatest intellectual forces in Israel. Tradition has it that he was forty years old before he began the study of the Torah; and that he had a romantic attachment to his wealthy employer's daughter, who, despite all adversity, remained devoted to him. He joined Bar Cochba in the Second War against the Romans, and met a martyr's death about 135, in the course of his heroic stand for his Faith and People. His principal teachers were Joshua ben Chananya and Eliezer ben Hyrcanus. He held that the Torah was not written in the language of every-day life. Not only every precept, but every word and letter were meaning-laden, and not a dot was superfluous. His arrangement of the Traditional laws was retained by his followers, Meir and Judah the Prince, and is embodied in the Mishna.

Great in intellect, Akiba was no less great in character. In especial he seems to have been conscious of the majesty of God and of His supreme justice—a justice which, he declared, is yet altogether consistent

17. R. Akiba said, Jesting and levity lead a man on to lewdness. The Massorah is a fence to the Torah ; tithes are a fence to riches ; vows are a fence to abstinence ; a fence to wisdom is silence.

18. He used to say, Beloved is man, for he was created in the image of God ; but it was by a special love that it was made known to him that he was created in the image

Genesis 9 6 of God ; as it is said, For in the image of God made he man. Beloved are Israel, for they were called children of the All-present ; but it was by a special love that it was made

with goodness and mercy. " Whatever God doeth is for the best ", was his favourite saying. " That absolute submission to the will of God, which can perceive in suffering only an expression of God's fatherly love and mercy—*that* was the ideal of Akiba " (Schechter).

jesting and levity. Judaism does not denounce merriment as such, and a jester may leave the saintly behind in true merit of life. R. Akiba's saying warns against jesting that leads to undue familiarity between the. sexes. In the sphere of religion and morality, " fences " are necessary safeguards against falling into sin.

Massorah. i.e. " tradition " (see on I, 1). The term is used particularly of the traditional transmission of the Scriptural text, which preserved the Divine Revelation from falsification through accident, ignorance or sectarian bias.

tithes are a fence to riches. Allocating to religious and charitable purposes the ordained portion, does not reduce a man's wealth. It makes the owner conscious that his property is due to a Divine Providence (mishna 8), and this feeling saves him from squandering his possessions unwisely.

vows. A vow serves to keep him who makes it from doing what he might ignorantly or carelessly do without it. Though many have found vows helpful in cultivating self-restraint and shunning over-indulgence, Scripture discourages vowing. See "Vows and Vowing in Judaism," *Numbers*, 310 (one vol. ed., 730).

abstinence. Heb. *perishuth*, lit. " separation " from what defiles the body or contaminates the soul. The term " pharisee " is by some scholars derived from this word.

silence. See on I, 17.

18. *man.* The human being, without limitation of creed and racial origin.

by a special love. It is with God as with man. To declare one's love is a more signal proof of affection than love without such declaration. Divine possibilities have been implanted in man ; but it is an especial mark of God's love to His human children that they have been endowed with the *consciousness* of these Divine possibilities within them.

אֱלֹהֵיכֶם : חֲבִיבִים יִשְׂרָאֵל שֶׁנִּתַּן לָהֶם כְּלִי חֶמְדָּה חִבָּה
יְתֵרָה נוֹדַעַת לָהֶם שֶׁנִּתַּן לָהֶם כְּלִי חֶמְדָּה שֶׁבּוֹ נִבְרָא
הָעוֹלָם ‧ שֶׁנֶּאֱמַר כִּי לֶקַח טוֹב נָתַתִּי לָכֶם תּוֹרָתִי אַל־תַּעֲזֹבוּ :
(יט) הַכֹּל צָפוּי וְהָרְשׁוּת נְתוּנָה וּבְטוֹב הָעוֹלָם נָדוֹן וְהַכֹּל
לְפִי רֹב הַמַּעֲשֶׂה : (כ) הוּא הָיָה אוֹמֵר ‧ הַכֹּל נָתוּן בְּעֵרָבוֹן
וּמְצוּדָה פְרוּשָׂה עַל־כָּל־הַחַיִּים ‧ הֶחָנוּת פְּתוּחָה וְהַחֶנְוָנִי
מַקִּיף וְהַפִּנְקָס פָּתוּחַ וְהַיָּד כּוֹתֶבֶת וְכָל הָרוֹצֶה לִלְווֹת יָבֹא

beloved are Israel. The Selection of Israel is a great world-historic event. Even greater is the fact, that his high calling has been made known to Israel. It is his Jewish Consciousness that lends immortality to the Jew.

children unto the Lord. Every Israelite is a son of God, and he approaches his Heavenly Father in a spirit of child-like trust.

desirable instrument. The Torah, whose commandments are " more to be desired than gold " (Psalm 19. 11) and are of eternal validity.

through which the world was created. The Rabbis held that the Torah existed before the universe, and contained the spiritual design according to which the world was created. " Wisdom," in the Book of Proverbs, is identified with the Torah in such passages as : " The Lord by wisdom founded the earth " (3. 19). In this manner, the Rabbis gave expression to the profound truth that the Creation serves an eternal, spiritual purpose.

19. This saying of Rabbi Akiba is among the most important in Aboth, and lays down a fundamental doctrine of practical religion. Despite the fact that God foresees the course which a man will adopt when faced with the choice of two paths, man has free choice. God's foreknowledge and the freedom of man's will are reconcilable ; so are God's mercy and justice in His dealings with man.

everything is foreseen. Everything past, present and future is seen by God—even as a watchman in a lighthouse tower sees ships in the distance coming and going, and can in a tempest foresee which among them must dash itself to destruction.

by grace. lit. " with goodness ". The Psalmist's declaration, " The Lord is good to all, and His tender mercies are over all His works " (Psalm 145. 9), is a favourite text of the Rabbis. They underline the word " all ", and deduce from it that His goodness extends to animals as well as man (see p. 87), to the Gentile as well as to the Israelite. Akiba's universalist note is probably derived from his teacher Rabbi Joshua ben Chananya.

yet all is according to the amount of work. God is good and merciful,

known to them that they were called children of the All-
Deuteronomy present; as it is said, Ye are children unto the Lord your
14. 1   God. Beloved are Israel, for unto them was given the
desirable instrument ; but it was by a special love that it
was made known to them that that desirable instrument
was theirs, through which the world was created; as it is
Proverbs 4. 2 said, For I give you good doctrine ; forsake ye not my Law.

19. Everything is foreseen, yet freedom of choice is
given ; and the world is judged by grace, yet all is according
to the amount of work.

20. He used to say, Everything is given on pledge, and
a net is spread for all the living : the shop is open ; and the
dealer gives credit ; and the ledger lies open ; and the hand
writes ; and whosoever wishes to borrow may come and
borrow; but the collectors regularly make their daily round;
and exact payment from man, whether he be content or not ;

but He rewards or punishes according to man's doings on earth.
20. *given on pledge.* The doctrine previously stated is now given
in language taken from commerce. The world is likened to the office
of a merchant.

everything. i.e. life and all its opportunities are granted to man
on the " pledge " that he will utilize them wisely and well.

a net is spread for all the living. Nobody can evade his responsibility
for the use he makes of his life, because all are called to account before
the Divine Tribunal.

the shop is open. The world is stocked with what God has provided
for the welfare and happiness of His creatures.

the dealer gives credit. God does not demand immediate payment;
after death will be the reckoning.

and the hand writes. There is a record of every obligation incurred,
expressing the thought of II, 1, "All thy deeds are written in a Book".
Jewish folklore declares that every night, while the body is asleep, the
soul ascends on high, and records whatever sin and transgression had
been committed during the day.

whosoever wishes to borrow. Man makes free use of his share of the
world's goods, and adapts it to his wishes.

their daily round. But man is under supervision, and the manner in
which he disposes of God's bounty is examined. If that bounty has been
abused, His agents exact penalties, such as calamity and suffering.

whether he be content or not. " With his knowledge or without his
knowledge " ; *i.e.* whether he is conscious or not that the troubles
which befall him are a visitation for his misuse of life.

וְיֵלְכָה וְהַגַּבָּאִים מַחֲזִירִים תָּדִיר בְּכָל־יוֹם וְנִפְרָעִים מִן־הָאָדָם

מִדַּעְתּוֹ וְשֶׁלֹּא מִדַּעְתּוֹ וְיֵשׁ לָהֶם עַל מַה־שֶּׁיִּסְמֹכוּ וְהַדִּין

דִּין אֱמֶת • וְהַכֹּל מְתֻקָּן לַסְּעוּדָה : (כא) רַבִּי אֶלְעָזָר בֶּן־

עֲזַרְיָה אוֹמֵר • אִם אֵין תּוֹרָה אֵין דֶּרֶךְ אֶרֶץ אִם אֵין דֶּרֶךְ

אֶרֶץ אֵין תּוֹרָה • אִם אֵין חָכְמָה אֵין יִרְאָה אִם אֵין יִרְאָה

אֵין חָכְמָה • אִם אֵין דַּעַת אֵין בִּינָה אִם אֵין בִּינָה אֵין

דַּעַת • אִם אֵין קֶמַח אֵין תּוֹרָה אִם אֵין תּוֹרָה אֵין קֶמַח :

(כב) הוּא הָיָה אוֹמֵר • כֹּל שֶׁחָכְמָתוֹ מְרֻבָּה מִמַּעֲשָׂיו לְמָה

הוּא דוֹמֶה • לְאִילָן שֶׁעֲנָפָיו מְרֻבִּים וְשָׁרָשָׁיו מֻעָטִים וְהָרוּחַ

בָּאָה וְעוֹקַרְתּוֹ וְהוֹפַכְתּוֹ עַל פָּנָיו • שֶׁנֶּאֱמַר וְהָיָה כְּעַרְעָר

they have that whereon they can rely. The judgment is a judgment of truth. The penalty is a just one, determined by the person's actions. "This affirmation of the absolute justice of God is one of the unshakable foundations of the Jewish religion throughout its history." (Herford).

everything is prepared for the feast. If a man made use of his opportunities, he is destined to participate in " Thy goodness which Thou hast laid up for them that fear Thee " (Psalm 31. 20). But even the sinner may, after repentance, or retribution at the hands of Heaven, join the " banquet ". The figure of a banquet for the happiness of the righteous in the Hereafter is, of course, pure symbolism ; and the details in regard to the feast—*e.g.* Leviathan—are folk-lore. Rabh (160-247), the renowned pupil of Rabbi Judah the Prince, declared, " In the World to come, there is neither eating nor drinking nor marrying; no envy, emulation or strife; but the righteous sit, with crowns on their heads, and feast on the splendour of the Divine Presence."

21. Elazar, the son of Azaryah. He lived from 70 to 135. Succeeded Rabban Gamaliel II as the Nasi of the Yavneh Sanhedrin, when the latter was deposed. On the restoration of Gamaliel to office, Elazar became Av Beth-Din. He came from an ancient family and was a man of wealth. He accompanied Joshua ben Chananya and Akiba on their mission to Rome. One of his noble sayings—that has become authoritative in Judaism—is : " Only sins against God does the Day of Atonement remove. Sins against man are not forgiven, unless the offended party has first been reconciled ".

and they have that whereon they can rely in their demand ; and the judgment is a judgment of truth ; and everything is prepared for the feast.

21. R. Elazar, the son of Azaryah, said, Where there is no Torah, there are no manners ; where there are no manners, there is no Torah : where there is no wisdom, there is no fear of God ; where there is no fear of God, there is no wisdom : where there is no knowledge, there is no understanding ; where there is no understanding, there is no knowledge : where there is no meal, there is no Torah ; where there is no Torah, there is no meal.

22. He used to say, He whose wisdom exceeds his deeds, to what is he like ? To a tree whose branches are many, but whose roots are few ; and the wind comes and plucks it up *Jeremiah* 17 6 and overturns it upon its face; as it is said, And he shall be like a lonely juniper tree in the desert, and shall not see when good cometh ; but shall inhabit the parched places in the wilderness, a salt land and not inhabited. But he whose

no Torah . . . no manners. Derech eretz, here translated "manners", means "practical life". Without Religion, such practical life is the existence of a heathen or an animal, degraded from its true meaning and dignity.

no manners . . . no Torah. Without practical life and in the absence of social relationship, religious learning is futile piety, instead of a living, beneficent influence.

no fear of God . . . no wisdom. Moral insensibility and religious nihilism are in Scripture the marks of the "fool".

no knowledge . . . no understanding. Without knowledge, the faculty of understanding is left with nothing on which to work.

no understanding . . . no knowledge. Knowledge is the accumulation of data, and is sterile without the "understanding" which enables it to be fully grasped and applied.

no meal . . . no Torah. Unless the body is adequately nourished, the brain will not function properly, and study will be ineffective.

no Torah . . . no meal. Man's duty is to feed his mind and spirit, as well as his body. " Man doth not live by bread alone, but by every thing that proceedeth out of the mouth of the Lord doth man live " (Deuteronomy 8. 3).

22. *He whose wisdom exceeds his deeds.* R. Elazar takes up the saying of R. Chanina ben Dosa (mishna 12), and illustrates it with the aid of Biblical texts.

בַּעֲרָבָה וְלֹא יִרְאֶה כִּי־יָבוֹא טוֹב וְשָׁכַן חֲרֵרִים בַּמִּדְבָּר אֶרֶץ
מְלֵחָה וְלֹא תֵשֵׁב · אֲבָל כֹּל שֶׁמַּעֲשָׂיו מְרֻבִּים מֵחָכְמָתוֹ
לְמָה הוּא דוֹמֶה · לְאִילָן שֶׁעֲנָפָיו מְעָטִים וְשָׁרָשָׁיו מְרֻבִּים
שֶׁאֲפִילוּ כָּל־הָרוּחוֹת שֶׁבָּעוֹלָם בָּאוֹת וְנוֹשְׁבוֹת בּוֹ אֵין מְזִיזִים
אוֹתוֹ מִמְּקוֹמוֹ · שֶׁנֶּאֱמַר וְהָיָה כְּעֵץ שָׁתוּל עַל־מַיִם וְעַל־יוּבַל
יְשַׁלַּח שָׁרָשָׁיו וְלֹא יִרְאֶה כִּי־יָבֹא חֹם וְהָיָה עָלֵהוּ רַעֲנָן
וּבִשְׁנַת בַּצֹּרֶת לֹא יִדְאָג וְלֹא יָמִישׁ מֵעֲשׂוֹת פֶּרִי : (כג) רַבִּי
אֶלְעָזָר חִסְמָא אוֹמֵר · קִנִּין וּפִתְחֵי נִדָּה הֵן הֵן גּוּפֵי
הֲלָכוֹת · תְּקוּפוֹת וְגִמַטְרִיָּאוֹת פַּרְפְּרָיוֹת לַחָכְמָה :

רַבִּי חֲנַנְיָא בֶּן־עֲקַשְׁיָא וכו'

פֶּרֶק רְבִיעִי :

כָּל־יִשְׂרָאֵל וכו'

(א) בֶּן־זוֹמָא אוֹמֵר · אֵיזֶהוּ חָכָם · הַלּוֹמֵד מִכָּל־אָדָם ·

---

23. *Elazar Chisma.* A disciple of R. Joshua ben Chananya and
R. Akiba. He was renowned for his knowledge of astronomy.

laws concerning the sacrifice of birds. Heb. *kinnin*, the name of a
Mishna tractate dealing with the Biblical regulations concerning the
offering of birds in circumstances enumerated in Leviticus, chapters 12,
13 and 15.

purification of women. Heb. *niddah*, also the name of a tractate
expounding the laws of Leviticus 15. 19f.

ordinances of moment. i.e. essential laws of Judaism. These two are
specified because, superficially considered, they would appear to be
subjects of minor importance. They are, however, ordinances of the
Torah, and as such should receive close study.

deeds exceed his wisdom, to what is he like ? To a tree whose branches are few, but whose roots are many, so that even if all the winds in the world come and blow upon it, it *Jeremiah* 17. 8 cannot be stirred from its place; as it is said, And he shall be as a tree planted by the waters ; and that spreadeth out its roots by the river, and shall not perceive when heat cometh, but his leaf shall be green ; and shall not be troubled in the year of drought, neither shall cease from yielding fruit.

23. R. Elazar Chisma said, The laws concerning the sacrifices of birds and the purification of women are ordinances of moment ; astronomy and geometry are the after-courses of wisdom.

" Rabbi Chananya," etc., p. 627.

CHAPTER IV

"All Israel," etc., p. 613.

1. Ben Zoma said, Who is wise ? He who learns from *Psalm* 119. 99 all men ; as it is said, From all my teachers I have gotten

astronomy. lit. " revolutions " of the heavenly bodies. Astronomical knowledge was held in high esteem by the Rabbis. Bar Kappara, a friend of Rabbi Judah the Prince, declared, " He who knows how to compute the course of the sun and the revolution of the planets and neglects to do so, of him Scripture says, ' They regard not the work of the Lord, neither consider the operation of His hands ' " (Isaiah 5. 12).

geometry. The Heb. is a transliteration of the Greek word from which *geometry* is derived. Here it means mathematics in general. " Gematria " also denotes an arithmetical method of exegesis, in which the numerical values of the Hebrew letters in a word are taken into account. Thus, " Satan has no power on the Day of Atonement, because the numerical value of the letters in ‏השטן‎ is only 364 ".

after-courses of wisdom. Important as these studies are, it is the Torah which is the beginning and the foundation of Jewish education. They are the auxiliaries to Wisdom, which is Torah.

CHAPTER IV.

SAYINGS OF YOUNGER CONTEMPORARIES OF RABBI AKIBA.

1. *Ben Zoma*. Simeon ben Zoma, a disciple of R. Joshua ben Chananya. He—together with Ben Azzai, Elisha ben Abuya and Akiba— was attracted by the theosophic speculation of the Gnostics concerning

שֶׁנֶּאֱמַר מִכָּל־מְלַמְּדַי הִשְׂכַּלְתִּי : אֵיזֶהוּ גִבּוֹר • הַכּוֹבֵשׁ אֶת־
יִצְרוֹ • שֶׁנֶּאֱמַר טוֹב אֶרֶךְ אַפַּיִם מִגִּבּוֹר וּמשֵׁל בְּרוּחוֹ מִלֹּכֵד
עִיר : אֵיזֶהוּ עָשִׁיר • הַשָּׂמֵחַ בְּחֶלְקוֹ • שֶׁנֶּאֱמַר יְגִיעַ כַּפֶּיךָ
כִּי תֹאכֵל אַשְׁרֶיךָ וְטוֹב לָךְ • אַשְׁרֶיךָ בָּעוֹלָם הַזֶּה וְטוֹב
לָךְ לָעוֹלָם הַבָּא : אֵיזֶהוּ מְכֻבָּד • הַמְכַבֵּד אֶת־הַבְּרִיּוֹת •
שֶׁנֶּאֱמַר כִּי מְכַבְּדַי אֲכַבֵּד וּבֹזַי יֵקָלּוּ : (ב) בֶּן־עַזַּאי אוֹמֵר •
הֱוֵי רָץ לְמִצְוָה קַלָּה וּבוֹרֵחַ מִן־הָעֲבֵרָה • שֶׁמִּצְוָה גּוֹרֶרֶת

the nature of the Godhead, the process of Creation and the mystery of
Evil. Many lost their way in that jungle of heretical thinking. Ben
Zoma and Ben Azzai died young, in consequence of their assiduous
devotion to those studies ; Elisha ben Abuya became estranged from
Judaism ; and Akiba alone emerged in peace, to become a giant of
religious loyalty and leadership in the annals of Judaism. Ben Zoma's
four questions and answers, sublime in their simplicity, are among
the most noteworthy sayings in religious literature.

he who learns from all men. The wise man has an open mind, and is
willing to learn from anybody. The proof-texts seem to be later editorial
additions.

he who subdues his passions. lit. " his *yetzer* ", his evil inclination ;
see on II, 16, also p. 25. Self-conquest is the highest form of strength.
The story of Samson, who is strong physically but weak morally, and
suffers shipwreck through following " the desire of the eyes ", is the
type of deep tragedy.

Another noble definition of " mighty " given by the Rabbis is, " he
who turns his enemy into a friend ".

he who rejoices in his portion. The Heb. idiom for " he who is content ". The words may also be rendered, " he who is *happy* in his
portion ". Only where there is *happiness* in one's life-work is the greatest
good achieved for self as for others. Rabbi Elimelech, one of the
Chassidic teachers, declared : " Whatever a man's occupation, the
wares in which he deals, or the work he performs ; so long as he respects
his wares, honours his calling and is happy in his work—they will be a
source of sanctification to him, and of usefulness to his fellow-men ".

he who respects his fellow-men. lit. " his fellow-creatures (beriyyoth)",
see on I, 12. This is one of the world's great sayings: it is the key to all
worthy living and beneficent influence in one's human circle. Like
his colleague Ben Azzai, Ben Zoma preached the Brotherhood of man.
And he did this by emphasizing the *interdependence* of men : " not a
mouthful did Adam taste before he ploughed and sowed, cut and bound
the sheaves, threshed and winnowed the grain, ground and sifted the
flour, kneaded the dough and baked it into bread ; but I get up in the

understanding. Who is mighty? He who subdues his
Proverbs
16. 32 passions; as it is said, He that is slow to anger is better than
the mighty, and he that ruleth over his spirit than he that
taketh a city. Who is rich? He who rejoices in his portion;
Psalm 128. 2 as it is said, When thou eatest the labour of thine hands,
happy art thou, and it shall be well with thee : happy art
thou—in this world; and it shall be well with thee—in the
world to come. Who is worthy of honour? He who respects
J. Samuel 2. 30 his fellow-men ; as it is said, For them that honour me I will
honour, and they that despise me shall be held in contempt.

2. Ben Azzai said, Run to do even a slight precept, and
flee from transgression ; for one good deed draws another

morning, and find all this ready before me ". The web of the social
organism was to him more than a mark of civilization ; it was the basis
of practical religion, of the ethical requirement to honour our fellow-
creatures.

2. *Ben Azzai.* Simeon ben Azzai; according to one tradition, he was
martyred with Rabbi Akiba by the Romans in the year 135. Extraordinary assiduity and piety rendered him an outstanding character
among the scholars that gathered round Rabban Yochanan ben Zakkai
at Yavneh. His name ought to be known to every student of Religion.
He is the author of the great saying, *The reward of virtue is virtue, and
the wages of sin is sin*; *i.e.* one good deed leads to another good deed,
and the greatest punishment of evil-doing is that it leads to further
evil-doing. He was a renowned exegete, and it was due to his decisive
voice that the books of Ecclesiastes and Song of Songs were included in
the canon of Scripture (Yadayim III, 5). His was a new conception of
the Golden Rule. When Rabbi Akiba, in the spirit of Hillel, declared
" Thou shalt love thy neighbour as thyself " (Leviticus 19. 18) to be
the great principle in Religion, Ben Azzai maintained that even of more
fundamental importance was the opening verse of the fifth chapter of
Genesis—" This is the book of the generations of man . . . in the
image of God made He him ". For it taught first, the unity of mankind, not merely as members of one race or one people, but as created
in the image of God ; and, secondly, it proclaimed, because of its God-
likeness, the infinite worth of each and every human soul.

run. Show eagerness to perform even a " slight precept ", the same
term as in II, 1 ; but the reason here given is quite different. The
performance of even a slight duty renders easier the performance of the
next, possibly heavier, duty.

good deed. Heb. *mitzvah*, commandment; in later Hebrew, any
good deed is so termed.

flee from transgression. As one should run *to* a good deed, so he
should run *from* a transgression, and remove himself from temptation ;

מִצְוָה וַעֲבֵרָה גּוֹרֶרֶת עֲבֵרָה שֶׁשְּׂכַר מִצְוָה מִצְוָה וּשְׂכַר
עֲבֵרָה עֲבֵרָה : (ג) הוּא הָיָה אוֹמֵר • אַל־תְּהִי בָז לְכָל־אָדָם
וְאַל־תְּהִי מַפְלִיג לְכָל־דָּבָר שֶׁאֵין לְךָ אָדָם שֶׁאֵין לוֹ שָׁעָה
וְאֵין לְךָ דָּבָר שֶׁאֵין לוֹ מָקוֹם : (ד) רַבִּי לְוִיטַס אִישׁ יַבְנֶה
אוֹמֵר • מְאֹד מְאֹד הֱוֵה שְׁפַל רוּחַ שֶׁתִּקְוַת אֱנוֹשׁ רִמָּה :
(ה) רַבִּי יוֹחָנָן בֶּן־בְּרוֹקָה אוֹמֵר • כָּל־הַמְחַלֵּל שֵׁם שָׁמַיִם
בַּסֵּתֶר נִפְרָעִים מִמֶּנּוּ בַּגָּלוּי • אֶחָד בְּשׁוֹגֵג וְאֶחָד בְּמֵזִיד
בְּחִלּוּל הַשֵּׁם : (ו) רַבִּי יִשְׁמָעֵאל בְּנוֹ אוֹמֵר • הַלוֹמֵד עַל־

because each wrongful act dulls the conscience, so that there is weaker moral resistance to the commission of a second offence. The Rabbis explain the opening verse of the Psalms as follows : " He who first *walks* in the counsel of the wicked ", next " *stands* in the way of sinners ", and at length " *sits* in the seat of scoffers ".

one good deed draws another good deed in its train. And so the good life is the result. " The good deed itself is its own complete reward " (Philo). Various philosophers (*e.g.* Spinoza) have quoted and utilized this great saying of Ben Azzai, without mentioning the source.

wages of sin is sin. The human tragedy of sin consists not so much in its punishment as in its progeny. One lie immediately entails another lie to bolster it up, and one crime calls forth a second and a third crime to hide it from the eyes of men.

" This is the curse of every evil deed,
That it begets a further deed of shame."

Furthermore, every evil action leaves in our characters the tendency to commit the same action again. And the predisposition to commit the sin of which we are guilty, does not stop with our lives. *Our* vices may reappear in those that come after us, unto the third and fourth generation.

3. *despise not any man.* All men are equally God's creatures; and the honest toil of the humblest menial is a contribution to the social order. In the words of the Rabbis of Yavneh : " I am a creature of God, and my neighbour is also His creature ; my work is in the city, and his in the field ; I rise early to my work, and he rises early to his. As he cannot excel in my work, so I cannot excel in his work. But perhaps thou sayest, ' I do great things, and he small things ! ' We have learnt that it matters not whether one does much or little, if only he direct his heart to Heaven." " In God's sight it is not the nature of a man's work nor its intrinsic importance that counts, but the whole-heartedness of the thought of God with which it is done " (Moore).

good deed in its train, and one sin, another sin ; for the reward of a good deed is a good deed, and the wages of sin is sin.

3. He used to say, Despise not any man, and carp not at any thing ; for there is not a man that has not his hour, and there is not a thing that has not its place.

4. R. Levitas, of Yavneh, said, Be exceedingly lowly of spirit, since the hope of man is but the worm.

5. R. Yochanan, the son 'of Berokah, said, Whosoever profanes the Name of Heaven in secret, will suffer the penalty for it in public ; and this, whether the Heavenly Name be profaned in ignorance or in wilfulness.

6. R. Ishmael, his son, said, He who learns in order to

---

carp not at anything. This is part of the folk-wisdom of the peoples ; *e.g.* the prince who carps at cobwebs, and in the end is saved by such cobweb when hiding in the hollow of a tree from his mortal enemies. This is told of David when fleeing from Saul, many centuries before Robert Bruce became the hero of a similar legend.

his hour . . . place. Every person or object is sure at some time and in some circumstances to be reckoned with, either for good or for evil (Israelstam).

4. *Levitas.* A contemporary of R. Akiba. Little is known of him.

exceedingly lowly of spirit. Like mishna 24, in which Samuel the Younger took two verses from Proverbs as his motto, Rabbi Levitas' warning seems to be a quotation from Ecclesiasticus 7. 17. " Humble altogether thy pride, for man's expectation is worms ". Though not included in the Canon of the Bible, that book (in Hebrew, " The Wisdom of Joshua ben Sira ") is several times quoted in Rabbinical literature as if it were part of Scripture.

5. *Yochanan, the son of Berokah.* A disciple of R. Joshua ben Chananya.

profanes the name of Heaven. See on i, 11.

in secret. He secretly commits a crime that tarnishes the honour of his Faith and the good name of Israel. Sooner or later, his deed will be exposed, and his true character revealed to the men whose esteem he is anxious to possess.

in ignorance or in wilfulness. Profanation of the Name remains an unforgivable sin, whether the act is unintentional or due to malignity. But the degree of punishment will not be the same, since one is immeasurably more culpable than the other.

6. *Ishmael, his son.* Lived in the latter half of the second century. In his opinion, learning alone is of little value, unless it leads to teaching, and above all else to practice.

he who learns. The Jew is the eternal learner, who is daily to extend

מְנָת לְלַמֵּד מַסְפִּיקִים בְּיָדוֹ לִלְמוֹד וּלְלַמֵּד · וְהַלּוֹמֵד עַל־
מְנָת לַעֲשׂוֹת מַסְפִּיקִים בְּיָדוֹ לִלְמוֹד וּלְלַמֵּד לִשְׁמוֹר
וְלַעֲשׂוֹת : (ז) רַבִּי צָדוֹק אוֹמֵר · אַל־תִּפְרוֹשׁ מִן־הַצִּבּוּר
וְאַל־תַּעַשׂ עַצְמְךָ כְּעוֹרְכֵי הַדַּיָּנִים וְאַל־תַּעֲשֶׂהָ עֲטָרָה
לְהִתְגַּדֶּל־בָּהּ וְלֹא קַרְדֹּם לַחְפָּר־בָּהּ · וְכָךְ הָיָה הִלֵּל אוֹמֵר ·
וְדְאִשְׁתַּמֵּשׁ בְּתָנָא חֲלָף · הָא לָמַדְתָּ כָּל־הַנֶּהֱנֶה מִדִּבְרֵי
תוֹרָה נוֹטֵל חַיָּיו מִן־הָעוֹלָם : (ח) רַבִּי יוֹסֵי אוֹמֵר · כָּל־
הַמְכַבֵּד אֶת־הַתּוֹרָה גּוּפוֹ מְכֻבָּד עַל־הַבְּרִיּוֹת · וְכָל־הַמְחַלֵּל
אֶת־הַתּוֹרָה גּוּפוֹ מְחֻלָּל עַל־הַבְּרִיּוֹת : (ט) רַבִּי יִשְׁמָעֵאל

his knowledge of Torah, the guide to conduct; his mastery of Hebrew, the language of Religion; and his understanding of the everlasting truths enshrined in Israel's Scriptures.

in order to teach. The most sacred task of every Jew is to teach the high and holy truths of Judaism to those who are under his influence.

Heaven will grant him the opportunity. i.e. he is given adequate powers.

in order to practise. The true ultimate purpose of all study; I, 17.

to observe. The Heb. term is often used in connection with negative commandments. It may also be translated, "to defend". He will share in the defence of Judaism against enemies whether from within or without; II, 19.

and to practise. Which is the fruit of learning, and the test of the sincerity of the learner. " Whosoever learns Torah and does not practise it, it were better for him never to have been born " (Midrash).

7. Zadok. Yochanan ben Zakkai successfully interceded for his life with the Romans before the fall of Jerusalem.

separate not thyself. A verbal repetition of Hillel's saying (II, 5); and the next clause is also a repetition of Judah ben Tabbai's saying (I, 8). Some texts omit both, but the remainder of the paragraph is also based on a quotation. These sayings of the eminent Sages who had preceded him, appealed to R. Zadok so strongly that he took them as his motto.

crown. The object of study must not be the desire to receive the deference accorded to scholars. Rabbi Tarfon passing through a garden, ate some figs that had been left behind. The custodians of the garden came up and beat him. When he called out who he was, they let him go. All his days he grieved over this : " Woe is me, for I have used the crown of the Torah for my own benefit ".

teach, Heaven will grant him the opportunity both to learn and to teach ; but he who learns in order to practise, Heaven will grant him the opportunity to learn and to teach, to observe and to practise.

7. R. Zadok said, Separate not thyself from the congregation ; (in the judge's office) act not the counsel's part ; make not of the Torah a crown wherewith to aggrandize thyself, nor a spade wherewith to dig. So also used Hillel to say, He who makes a worldly use of the crown of the Torah shall pass away. Hence thou mayest infer, that whosoever derives a profit for himself from the words of the Torah is helping on his own destruction.

8. R. José said, Whoso honours the Torah will himself be honoured by mankind, but whoso dishonours the Torah will himself be dishonoured by mankind.

9. R. Ishmael, his son, said, He who shuns the judicial

---

nor a spade wherewith to dig. Nor may study of the Torah be turned into a means of support. Neither the Prophets nor the Rabbis accepted payment for their instruction. It was only with the rise of new economic conditions towards the close of the Middle Ages, that Jewish teachers could no longer maintain the old rule of free teaching. Simon ben Zemach Duran (1361–1444)—physician, rabbinical authority and philosopher—was the first rabbi to accept a salary from his congregation in Algiers. In explaining this mishna in his commentary on Aboth, he relates that he had lost all his possessions in the pogrom at Majorca ; that in a Moorish environment he could not derive subsistence from his medical skill; and that a return to European lands was impossible for him, as he was in danger of his life at the hands of the Inquisition. *so also used Hillel to say.* See I, 13.

is helping on his own destruction. lit. " removes his life from the world ". The Torah is a " tree of life " only to them who lay hold of it from love, not to those who pursue their self-interest by its means.

8. *José.* Son of Chalafta. One of the most distinguished of R. Akiba's disciples.

honours the Torah. He reveres the Teaching revealed therein, and accepts it as a guide of life. Such a one—R. José maintains—will command the esteem of fellow-Jews and all fellow-men who respect the consecrated life.

whoso dishonours the Torah. By violating its teachings, his standard of life will become debased, and men will despise him.

9. *Ishmael, his son.* Lived in the latter half of the second century of the Christian era.

בְּנוֹ אוֹמֵר · הַחוֹשֵׂךְ עַצְמוֹ מִן־הַדִּין פּוֹרֵק מִמֶּנּוּ אֵיבָה וְגָזֵל
וּשְׁבוּעַת שָׁוְא · וְהַגַּס לִבּוֹ בְּהוֹרָאָה שׁוֹטֶה רָשָׁע וְגַס רוּחַ :
(י) הוּא הָיָה אוֹמֵר · אַל־תְּהִי דָן יְחִידִי דָן יָחִידִי שֶׁאֵין
אֶלָּא אֶחָד · וְאַל־תֹּאמַר קַבְּלוּ דַעְתִּי שֶׁהֵם רַשָּׁאִים וְלֹא אָתָּה :
(יא) רַבִּי יוֹנָתָן אוֹמֵר · כָּל־הַמְקַיֵּם אֶת־הַתּוֹרָה מֵעֹנִי סוֹפוֹ
לְקַיְּמָהּ מֵעֹשֶׁר · וְכָל־הַמְבַטֵּל אֶת־הַתּוֹרָה מֵעֹשֶׁר סוֹפוֹ לְבַטְּלָהּ
מֵעֹנִי : (יב) רַבִּי מֵאִיר אוֹמֵר · הֱוֵי מְמַעֵט בְּעֵסֶק וַעֲסֹק
בַּתּוֹרָה וֶהֱוֵי שְׁפַל־רוּחַ בִּפְנֵי כָל־אָדָם · וְאִם־בָּטַלְתָּ מִן־הַתּוֹרָה
יֶשׁ־לָךְ בְּטֵלִים הַרְבֵּה כְּנֶגְדֶּךָ · וְאִם־עָמַלְתָּ בַתּוֹרָה יֶשׁ־לוֹ

he who shuns the judicial office. So translated, the saying is advice against the acceptance of judgeship, since it is a thankless task. The Hebrew is lit. "he who withholds himself from (pronouncing) judgment"; and this may mean a judge who is disinclined to give a verdict, and proposes a settlement by compromise.

hatred. By the losing party, either towards the judge or the other litigant. In a compromise, the loss is only partial, and therefore the resentment less deep.

robbery. In the event of the judge passing a wrong judgment, he robs the man of what is his.

vain swearing. Litigation often involves the taking of an oath. This is something sacred, and should only be taken when altogether unavoidable. A compromise would obviate this procedure.

but he who presumptuously lays down decisions. lit, "he who accustoms himself to lay down decisions". If it refers to a judge, it is a condemnation of arrogance. He should be possessed of a spirit of humility and responsibility. The word for "decision" is commonly used of the answer to a question on religious law (shaalah) given by a Rabbi. He, too, when discharging that duty must be humble.

foolish. Over-confidence in a judge may lead to disastrous results. "Seest thou a man wise in his own eyes? There is more hope of a fool than of him" (Proverbs 26. 12).

wicked. Acting in a haughty spirit, he may be guilty of gross injustice as a judge.

of an arrogant spirit. A vice which the Rabbis frequently censured; see III, 1; IV, 4. "Whoever has an arrogant spirit, the Holy One,

office rids himself of hatred, robbery and vain swearing ; but he who presumptuously lays down decisions is foolish, wicked and of an árrogant spirit.

10. He used to say, Judge not alone, for none may judge alone save One ; neither say (to thy judicial colleagues), Accept my view, for the choice is theirs (to concur) ; and it is not for thee (to compel concurrence).

11. R. Jonathan said, Whoso fulfils the Torah in the midst of poverty, shall in the end fulfil it in the midst of wealth ; and whoso neglects the Torah in the midst of wealth, shall in the end neglect it in the midst of poverty.

12. R. Meir said, Lessen thy toil for worldly goods, and be busy in the Torah ; be humble of spirit before all men ; if thou neglectest the Torah, many causes for neglecting it will present themselves to thee, but if thou labourest in the Torah, He has abundant recompense to give thee.

blessed be He, says of him, ' I and he cannot dwell in the world to-gether ' " (Talmud).

10. *judge not alone.* As pointed out on III, 7, at least three judges were required to try a case. Jewish Law, however, allowed a suit in-volving property to be adjudicated by only one, if he was a judicial expert ; but this practice is not recommended by R. Ishmael, because the responsibility is too heavy.

One. God.

for the choice is theirs. The two judges have the right to express their opinion, and the third judge must follow the majority.

11. *Jonathan.* His father's name was Joseph, and he was a disciple of R. Akiba and R. Ishmael ben Elisha.

in the midst of wealth. He neglects his religious duties to devote himself to the care of his possessions. Even in poverty, such a one will find no time for Torah. In either of the two cases mentioned, what is begun in youth is not likely to be altered in age.

12. *Meir.* The most famous of R. Akiba's disciples ; see on VI, 1.

lessen thy toil for worldly goods. Cf. Hillel's saying in II, 6.

humble of spirit. It is remarkable how often the virtue of humility is advocated in Aboth. It is characteristic of Rabbinic teaching.

if thou neglectest. As soon as a person has broken the regular routine of study, he will find many pretexts for further neglect. " Forsake the Torah a single day, and it will forsake thee two days " (Talmud).

abundant recompense. Cf. II, 19, 21.

שְׂכַר הַרְבֵּה לְתֶן־לָהּ : ‏(יג) רַבִּי אֱלִיעֶזֶר בֶּן־יַעֲקֹב אוֹמֵר ‏·
הָעוֹשֶׂה מִצְוָה אַחַת קוֹנֶה לוֹ פְּרַקְלִיט אֶחָד ‏· וְהָעוֹבֵר עֲבֵרָה
אַחַת קוֹנֶה לוֹ קַטֵּגוֹר אֶחָד ‏· תְּשׁוּבָה וּמַעֲשִׂים טוֹבִים
כִּתְרִיס בִּפְנֵי הַפֻּרְעָנוּת : ‏(יד) רַבִּי יוֹחָנָן הַסַּנְדְּלָר אוֹמֵר ‏·
כָּל־כְּנֵסִיָּה שֶׁהִיא לְשֵׁם שָׁמַיִם סוֹפָהּ לְהִתְקַיֵּם ‏· וְשֶׁאֵינָהּ לְשֵׁם
שָׁמַיִם אֵין סוֹפָהּ לְהִתְקַיֵּם : ‏(טו) רַבִּי אֱלְעָזָר בֶּן־שַׁמּוּעַ
אוֹמֵר ‏· יְהִי כְבוֹד תַּלְמִידָךְ חָבִיב עָלֶיךָ כְּשֶׁלָּךְ וּכְבוֹד
חֲבֵרָךְ כְּמוֹרָא רַבָּךְ וּמוֹרָא רַבָּךְ כְּמוֹרָא שָׁמָיִם : ‏(טז) רַבִּי
יְהוּדָה אוֹמֵר ‏· הֱוֵי זָהִיר בְּתַלְמוּד שֶׁשִּׁגְגַת תַּלְמוּד עוֹלָה

13. *Eliezer, the son of Jacob.* Disciple of R. Akiba.

advocate . . . accuser. Before the judgment-throne of God when a
man's life is being assessed. Each act of religious loyalty pleads in his
favour; each act of disloyalty tells against him.

repentance. In Jewish teaching, repentance is the sole, but in-
exorable, condition of God's forgiveness and the restoration of His
favour; and the Divine forgiveness and favour are never refused
to genuine repentance. Countless are the Rabbinic sayings on
repentance. "It was created before the universe, because without it the
world could not endure. Great is repentance, for it brings healing to
the world. Great is repentance, for it reaches to the Throne of God.
There is nothing greater than repentance". See introductory note on
"Repentance" to New Year and the Day of Atonement, pp. 838–840.

deeds of charity. Proof of the sincerity of repentance. The Rabbis
dwell specially on the words describing the repentance of the men of
Nineveh, "And God saw their works, that they turned from their evil
way; and God relented of the evil, which He said He would do unto
them; and He did it not" (Jonah 3. 10)--not their fasting and
sack-cl th, but their "works", *i.e.* good deeds, secured their pardon;
see p. 928.

14. *Yochanan, the sandal maker.* Born in Alexandria. He was a
disciple of R. Akiba.

every assembly. It may be a general reflection like that of v, 20.
Modern commentators assert that it was suggested by prevailing
conditions of the day. After the defeat of Bar Cochba in the year 135,
most of the communities were ruined, and had to be recon-
structed. The task was of overwhelming difficulty; and R. Yochanan

13. R. Eliezer, the son of Jacob, said, He who does one good deed has gotten himself one advocate; and he who commits one transgression has gotten himself one accuser. Repentance and deeds of charity are as a shield against punishment.

14. R. Yochanan, the sandal maker, said, Every assembly which is in the naᵢne of Heaven will in the end be established, but that which is not in the name of Heaven will not in the end be established.

15. R. Elazar, the son of Shammua, said, Let the honour of thy disciple be as dear to thee as thine own, and the honour of thine associate be like the reverence for thy master, and the reverence for thy master like the fear of Heaven.

16. R. Judah said, Be cautious in teaching, for an error in teaching may amount to presumptuous sin.

taught that so long as the effort was made " in the name of Heaven ", the results would be enduring. God does not allow wholly to fail what is done for His sake.

15. *Elazar, the son of Shammua.* Disciple of R. Akiba and colleague of R. Meir.

honour of thy disciple. The duty of respect from the pupil to the master occurs several times in Aboth; here the teacher is bidden equally to esteem his disciple who is devoting himself to study.

associate. i.e. colleague.

reverence for thy master like the fear of Heaven. A much misunderstood clause. It does not mean that the teacher is made equal to God. It means, "that there was a reverence due to the teacher of Torah (by reason of the sacredness of the Torah) and a reverence due to God, the Giver of the Torah; and that to pay that reverence was an equal obligation in each case " (Herford).

16. *Judah.* The son of Ilai; a disciple of R. Akiba and a teacher of great distinction.

presumptuous sin. Although the teacher may have erred unintentionally, the effect may be so serious in spreading false doctrine, that his guilt is equal to the commission of an intentional sin. To cause others to do wrong, the Rabbis emphasized, was much worse than himself to do wrong.

זָדוֹן : (יז) רַבִּי שִׁמְעוֹן אוֹמֵר · שְׁלשָׁה כְתָרִים הֵן · כֶּתֶר תּוֹרָה

וְכֶתֶר כְּהֻנָּה וְכֶתֶר מַלְכוּת · וְכֶתֶר שֵׁם טוֹב עוֹלֶה עַל

גַּבֵּיהֶן : (יח) רַבִּי נְהוֹרַי אוֹמֵר · הֱוֵה גוֹלֶה לִמְקוֹם תּוֹרָה

וְאַל־תֹּאמַר שֶׁהִיא תָבוֹא אַחֲרֶיךָ · שֶׁחֲבֵרֶיךָ יְקַיְּמוּהָ בְּיָדֶךָ ·

וְאֶל־בִּינָתְךָ אַל־תִּשָּׁעֵן : (יט) רַבִּי יַנַּאי אוֹמֵר · אֵין בְּיָדֵינוּ

לֹא מִשַּׁלְוַת הָרְשָׁעִים וְאַף לֹא מִיִּסּוּרֵי הַצַּדִּיקִים : (כ) רַבִּי

מַתִּתְיָה בֶן־חֶרֶשׁ אוֹמֵר · הֱוֵה מַקְדִּים בִּשְׁלוֹם כָּל־אָדָם ·

וֶהֱוֵה זָנָב לָאֲרָיוֹת וְאַל־תְּהִי רֹאשׁ לַשֻּׁעָלִים : (כא) רַבִּי יַעֲקֹב

אוֹמֵר · הָעוֹלָם הַזֶּה דּוֹמֶה לִפְרוֹזְדוֹר בִּפְנֵי הָעוֹלָם הַבָּא ·

17. Simeon. Ben Yochai, see on III, 4. His saying is among the very greatest in Aboth.

crowns. Symbols of dignity.

learning. lit. " Torah ", religious learning.

crown of priesthood. Scripture states, " Thou shalt set the mitre upon his (Aaron's) head, and put the holy crown upon the mitre " (Exodus 29. 6).

a good name. Cf. " a good name is rather to be chosen than great riches " (Proverbs 23. 1) and, " A good name is better than precious oil " (Ecclesiastes 7. 1).

excels them all. Because it alone is the tribute paid to personality and character. " A man attains to priesthood and royalty by heredity, and even learning is not invariably accompanied by nobility of character. Only in the case of a bearer of a good name, do we find outward honour combined with inner worth " (G. Beer).

18. Rabbi Nehorai. A name given to several Rabbis. In this instance it is said to be a pseudonym of R. Elazar ben Arach (II, 10).

a home of the Torah. A place where eminent teachers reside, so that one may benefit from their instruction ; see VI, 9.

the Torah will come after thee. If the author is R. Elazar ben Arach, he may have had his own experience in mind. On the death of his teacher, Rabban Yochanan, he left his associates to live in Emmaus which was not " a home of the Torah ", and he forgot his learning. To the Jew of to-day, this mishna is a warning to live in, or near, a Jewish community.

for there thy associates. True knowledge is the result of contact with other minds ; see I, 16.

upon thine own understanding. To unravel difficulties in one's studies, instead of resorting to guidance from a competent teacher.

17. R. Simeon said, There are three crowns : the crown of learning, the crown of priesthood, and the crown of royalty ; but the crown of a good name excels them all.

18. R. Nehorai said, Wander forth to a home of the Torah—and say not that the Torah will come after Thee—for there thy associates will establish thee in the possession of it ; and lean not upon thine own understanding.

19. R. Yannai said, It is not in our power to explain either the prosperity of the wicked or the afflictions of the righteous.

20. R. Mattithya, the son of Cheresh, said, Be beforehand in the salutation of peace to all men ; and be rather a tail to lions than a head to foxes.

21. R. Jacob said, This world is like an ante-chamber to the world to come ; prepare thyself in the ante-chamber, that thou mayest enter into the hall.

Your own unguided mind may lead to error, heresy, apostasy. The words, "lean not upon thine understanding", are a quotation from Proverbs 3. 5.

19. *Yannai.* His identity is uncertain. He may be the father of R. Dostai in III, 10 ; if so, he was a contemporary of R. Meir.

it is not in our power to explain. Man can answer neither the question, Why do the wicked flourish ? nor, Why do the righteous suffer ? "This saying may be an explanatory comment on the words from Proverbs with which the last mishna closes" (Hoffmann). It might also be translated, "There is not in our hands the security of the wicked, nor the chastisements of the righteous ". This would then describe the political status of the Jews in the days of the author : neither hopelessly bad nor wholly good (Graetz).

20. *Mattithya, the son of Cheresh.* A disciple of R. Eliezer, who fled from the Holy Land after the defeat of Bar Cochba, and lived in Rome.

beforehand in the salutation. A counsel of prudence, especially to a Jew in an unfriendly environment.

be rather a tail to lions. Evidently formulated in opposition to a proverb current both in Rome and Palestine : "Better be a head of foxes, than a tail among lions ".

21. *Jacob.* See III, 9.

prepare thyself. For life in the Hereafter, by good actions and repentance for misdeeds. "Prepare to meet thy God, O Israel" (Amos 4. 12).

the hall. The Heb. is a transliteration of a Greek word for a dining

הַתְקֵן עַצְמְךָ בִּפְרוֹזְדּוֹר כְּדֵי שֶׁתִּכָּנֵס לַטְּרַקְלִין : (כב) הוּא

הָיָה אוֹמֵר · יָפָה שָׁעָה אַחַת בִּתְשׁוּבָה וּמַעֲשִׂים טוֹבִים

בָּעוֹלָם הַזֶּה מִכָּל־חַיֵּי הָעוֹלָם הַבָּא · וְיָפָה שָׁעָה אַחַת שֶׁל־

קֹרַת רוּחַ בָּעוֹלָם הַבָּא מִכָּל־חַיֵּי הָעוֹלָם הַזֶּה : (כג) רַבִּי

שִׁמְעוֹן בֶּן־אֶלְעָזָר אוֹמֵר · אַל־תְּרַצֶּה אֶת־חֲבֵרְךָ בִּשְׁעַת

כַּעֲסוֹ וְאַל־תְּנַחֲמֶנּוּ בְּשָׁעָה שֶׁמֵּתוֹ מֻטָּל לְפָנָיו וְאַל־תִּשְׁאַל

לוֹ בִּשְׁעַת נִדְרוֹ וְאַל־תִּשְׁתַּדֵּל לִרְאוֹתוֹ בִּשְׁעַת קַלְקָלָתוֹ :

(כד) שְׁמוּאֵל הַקָּטָן אוֹמֵר · בִּנְפֹל אוֹיִבְךָ אַל־תִּשְׂמָח וּבִכָּשְׁלוֹ

אַל־יָגֵל לִבֶּךָ · פֶּן־יִרְאֶה יְיָ וְרַע בְּעֵינָיו וְהֵשִׁיב מֵעָלָיו אַפּוֹ :

ה) אֱלִישָׁע בֶּן־אֲבוּיָה אוֹמֵר · הַלּוֹמֵד יֶלֶד לְמָה הוּא דוֹמֶה ·

hall, and may have been chosen because the happiness of the World to come is conceived under the image of a banquet (III. 20).

22. better is one hour. A non-Jewish commentator on Aboth writes:—" This mishna is one of the noblest pearls in the whole realm of religious proverb-lore. Its first half rests on the contrast between this life and the Hereafter. This life is the world of toil and sowing; the Hereafter the world of reaping and reward. Therefore, this life is the superior. For the happiness experienced in performing good deeds, exceeds the joy felt in the reward offered for those good deeds " (Beer). In the midst of time and mortality the performance of good deeds bestows eternal life and everlasting happiness.

blissfulness of spirit. In life upon earth, man is engaged in a continuous struggle between his higher and lower self. Even if his better nature gains the mastery, he feels the strain of the contest, and must be ever watchful to maintain the victory. In the Hereafter, the struggle is over, and he enjoys a tranquility which is impossible in his lifetime (A. Cohen).

23. Simeon, the son of Elazar. A disciple of R. Meir. Advises utmost tact in approaching a man under a strain. His saying proves him to have been a man of exceptional delicacy of feeling and deep knowledge of human nature. Another of his notable sayings is : " If the young tell thee, Build, and the old tell thee, Destroy, follow the counsel of the elders ; for the destruction of the elders is construction, and the construction of the young is destruction ".

do not appease. Do not try to pacify him while his anger is hot. Your interference might only render his fury more uncontrollable.

22. He used to say, Better is one hour of repentance and good deeds in this world than the whole life of the world to come ; yet better is one hour of blissfulness of spirit in the world to come than the whole life of this world.

23. R. Simeon, the son of Elazar, said, Do not appease thy fellow in the hour of his anger, and comfort him not in the hour when his dead lies before him, and question him not in the hour of his vow, and strive not to see him in the hour of his disgrace.

Proverbs
24 17, 18

24. Samuel the Younger used to quote, Rejoice not when thine enemy falleth, and let not thine heart be glad when he stumbleth : lest the Lord see it and it displease him, and he turn away his wrath from him [unto thee].

25. Elisha, the son of Abuya, said, If one learns as a

---

when his dead lies before him. His grief is then so poignant that silence is the greatest kindness. According to Jewish custom, condoling with the mourner begins *after* the burial.

in the hour of his vow. A man makes a vow under the stress of emotion ; and, if he is questioned on its extent at the time it is made, he may only commit himself more deeply.

in the hour of his disgrace. Do not force yourself upon him in the hour of his humiliation.

24. *Samuel the Younger.* He lived in the first century, at Yavneh. He is the author of the Twelfth Benediction ("against heretics") in the Amidah; see p. 143.

used to quote. lit. "says", but his saying consists only of two Biblical verses (Proverbs 24. 17, 18). Among the sins solemnly repudiated in Job 31. 29 ("If I rejoiced at the destruction of him that hated me, or exulted when evil found him") is joy at the misfortune of an enemy. Like Job, Samuel the Younger ranks rejoicing over your enemy's woes as a grave sin. Some commentators connect Samuel's favourite verses with the last mishna. To force your presence upon a person in the hour of his disgrace, is like gloating over his misfortune. Others take his citation as a warning to the Jews, when they rejoiced over a set-back to their enemies during the revolt against Rome (I. H. Weiss).

25. *Elisha, the son of Abuya.* The Faust of Talmudic literature. Despite his learning, he broke away from Judaism, and became "Acher", *i.e.* another man. Rabbi Meir, his one time disciple, remained his friend throughout life. It was probably due to this friendship that Elisha's words were admitted into Aboth. Indeed, it is missing in some Prayer Books. ·

לְדָיוֹ כְּתוּבָה עַל־נְיָר חָדָשׁ · וְהַלוֹמֵד זָקֵן לְמָה הוּא דוֹמֶה ·
לְדָיוֹ כְּתוּבָה עַל־נְיָר מָחוּק : (כו) רַבִּי יוֹסֵי בַּר יְהוּדָה אִישׁ
כְּפַר הַבַּבְלִי אוֹמֵר · הַלוֹמֵד מִן־הַקְּטַנִּים לְמָה הוּא דוֹמֶה ·
לְאוֹכֵל עֲנָבִים קֵהוֹת וְשׁוֹתֶה יַיִן מִגִּתּוֹ · וְהַלוֹמֵד מִן־הַזְּקֵנִים
לְמָה הוּא דוֹמֶה · לְאוֹכֵל עֲנָבִים בְּשׁוּלוֹת וְשׁוֹתֶה יַיִן יָשָׁן :
(כז) רַבִּי מֵאִיר אוֹמֵר · אַל־תִּסְתַּכֵּל בְּקַנְקַן אֶלָּא בְּמַה שֶּׁיֵּשׁ
בּוֹ · יֵשׁ קַנְקַן חָדָשׁ מָלֵא יָשָׁן וְיָשָׁן שֶׁאֲפִילוּ חָדָשׁ אֵין בּוֹ :
(כח) רַבִּי אֶלְעָזָר הַקַּפָּר אוֹמֵר · הַקִּנְאָה וְהַתַּאֲוָה וְהַכָּבוֹד
מוֹצִיאִים אֶת־הָאָדָם מִן הָעוֹלָם : (כט) הוּא הָיָה אוֹמֵר ·
הַיִּלּוֹדִים לָמוּת וְהַמֵּתִים לְהֵחָיוֹת וְהַחַיִּים לִדּוֹן לֵידַע

clean paper. lit. "new paper". What is written upon it remains clearly legible. The mind is similarly fresh to receive impressions in youth.

blotted paper. lit. "rubbed paper". The material was the papyrus leaf. Owing to its costliness, it was sometimes used more than once, the writing being rubbed out with stone. The new writing was not clear, because the original script remained, faintly visible. In like manner, new instruction in old age leaves a blurred impression on the mind. Therefore, the study of Torah should begin in youth. Obviously, this saying dates from before Ben Abuya's fall.

26. *José, the son of Judah of Kephar Babli.* A disciple of R. Elazar ben Shammua (mishna 15) and older contemporary of R. Judah the Prince.

unripe grapes. Which set the teeth on edge.

wine from the vat. The wine is not matured, and leads to intoxication. In like manner, the teaching by the young is liable to be immature, inexact, and leading to error.

old wine. Which is a source of health and festive joy. A simile for ripe knowledge, which only the experience of years can supply.

27. *Meir.* See on VI, 1. Some manuscripts omit "Meir", and the author is then "Rabbi", *i.e.* R. Judah the Prince. He disagreed with the preceding dictum. The age of a teacher is no criterion of the soundness and value of his scholarship. Unripeness in judgment is not the exclusive possession of the young; nor is wisdom, of the old.

child, what is it like ? Like ink written on clean paper. If
one learns as an old man, what is it like ? Like ink written
on blotted paper.

26. R. José, the son of Judah, of Kephar Babli, said,
He who learns from the young, to what is he like ? To one
who eats unripe grapes, or drinks wine from the vat. And
he 'who learns from the old, to what is he like ? To one who
eats ripe grapes, or drinks old wine.

27. R. Meir said, Look not at the flask, but at what it
contains :- there may be a new flask full of old wine, and an
old flask that has not even new wine in it.

28. R. Elazar Ha-kappar said, Envy, desire and ambition drive a man out of the world.

29. He used to say, They that are born are destined to
die ; and the dead to be brought to life again ; and the
living to be judged, to know, to make known, and to be
made conscious that he is God, he the Maker, he the Creator,

---

28. *Elazar Ha-kappar.* An associate of R. Judah the Prince. " Kap-
par " may mean, " the man from Cyprus ".

envy. This is distinct from emulation, which increases skill and
wisdom.

desire. Unbridled hankering after pleasure.

ambition. lit. " lust of honour ". Three anti-social qualities are
enumerated which are a hindrance to harmonious relations with our
fellow-men ; cf. II, 16.

drive a man . . . world. " They break the ties which should unite
a man to his fellow-man ; and, whether or not they lead to physical
death, they destroy his higher life as a moral being, made in the likeness of God " (Herford).

29. A meditation on Human Destiny and the Judgment Day.

the dead to be brought to life again. The clear teaching of the Rabbis,
in opposition to contemporary schools of thought that denied the
Resurrection. It was their firm conviction that "if what never before
existed, exists; why cannot that which once existed, exist again?"
See p. 255.

and the living. i.e. Those who have been brought to life again.

to know . . . made conscious. i.e. that one may know from others,
that one may make others know, and that one may know of himself.
" Truths which in this world men are *taught*, will in the world to come
be known without a teacher " (Taylor).

the Maker. lit. " the Fashioner ".

וּלְהוֹדִיעַ וּלְהִוָּדַע שֶׁהוּא אֵל הוּא הַיּוֹצֵר הוּא הַבּוֹרֵא הוּא

הַמֵּבִין הוּא הַדַּיָּן הוּא הָעֵד הוּא בַּעַל דִּין הוּא עָתִיד לָדוּן

בָּרוּךְ הוּא שֶׁאֵין לְפָנָיו לֹא עַוְלָה וְלֹא שִׁכְחָה וְלֹא מַשּׂוֹא

פָנִים וְלֹא מִקַּח שֹׁחַד · וְדַע שֶׁהַכֹּל לְפִי הַחֶשְׁבּוֹן · וְאַל־

יַבְטִיחֲךָ יִצְרָךְ שֶׁהַשְּׁאוֹל בֵּית מָנוֹס לָךְ · שֶׁעַל כָּרְחֲךָ אַתָּה

נוֹצָר וְעַל כָּרְחֲךָ אַתָּה נוֹלָד וְעַל כָּרְחֲךָ אַתָּה חַי וְעַל

כָּרְחֲךָ אַתָּה מֵת וְעַל כָּרְחֲךָ אַתָּה עָתִיד לִתֵּן דִּין וְחֶשְׁבּוֹן

לִפְנֵי מֶלֶךְ מַלְכֵי הַמְּלָכִים הַקָּדוֹשׁ בָּרוּךְ הוּא :

רַבִּי חֲנַנְיָא בֶּן־עֲקַשְׁיָא וכו׳

פֶּרֶק חֲמִישִׁי :

כָּל־יִשְׂרָאֵל וכו׳

(א) בַּעֲשָׂרָה מַאֲמָרוֹת נִבְרָא הָעוֹלָם · וּמַה־תַּלְמוּד לוֹמַר

וַהֲלֹא בְּמַאֲמָר אֶחָד יָכוֹל לְהִבָּרְאוֹת · אֶלָּא לְהִפָּרַע מִן־

הָרְשָׁעִים שֶׁמְּאַבְּדִים אֶת־הָעוֹלָם שֶׁנִּבְרָא בַּעֲשָׂרָה מַאֲמָרוֹת

the Complainant. Heb. *baal-din* ; opposite of the defendant.

taking of bribes. Cf. II Chronicles 19. 7. The medieval commentators explain that no unrepented misdeed will be overlooked, because of good actions.

respect of persons. Partiality.

everything is according to the reckoning. Continues the thought of the preceding clause. Cf. III, 19 and 20.

imagination. i.e. " thy (evil) inclination " ; see II, 16. It overcomes scruples by suggesting that wrong can be done with impunity ; but there is no escape from the justice of God.

a place of refuge. In the belief that there is no Hereafter.

perforce thou wilt die. No person can escape death which is the fore-runner of the Judgment.

to give account and reckoning. As in III, 1. This solemn admonition fittingly concludes the chapter, with which possibly the whole of Aboth at one time closed.

he the Discerner, he the Judge, he the Witness, he the Complainant ; he it is that will in future judge, blessed be he, with whom there is no unrighteousness, nor forgetfulness, nor respect of persons, nor taking of bribes : know also that everything is according to the reckoning : and let not thy imagination give thee hope that the grave will be a place of refuge for thee ; for perforce thou wast formed, and perforce thou wast born, and thou livest perforce, and perforce thou wilt die, and perforce thou wilt in the future have to give account and reckoning before the Supreme King of kings, the Holy One, blessed be he.

"R. Chananya," etc., p. 627.

CHAPTER V

"All Israel," etc., p. 613.

1. With ten Sayings the world was created. What does this teach us ? Could it not have been created with one Saying ? It is to make known the punishment that will befall the wicked who destroy the world that was created

CHAPTER V.

ANONYMOUS AND NUMBER-SAYINGS.

The sayings in this chapter are nearly all of them anonymous. In form, they consist of a series of groups of ten, seven, four and three things. In substance, they touch upon cosmogony, speculation, sacred history, and the varieties of men, minds and motives. While the preceding chapters are predominantly ethical, this chapter is largely haggadah, folk-lore.

1–18. Number-Groups.

The idea of tabulating things according to number, is found as early as, e.g., Isaiah 17. 6, Amos 1. 3 and Proverbs 6. 16. In oral teaching, number-schemes are a valuable aid to memory.

1–9. Groups of ten.

1. The importance of God's work of Creation is enhanced by the fact that it was created by ten Sayings, instead of one single fiat. This is evidence—humanly speaking—of continuous and careful planning in Creation and its marvels. Great, therefore, is the merit of those who by their lives help to maintain the moral nature of that Creation ; and terrible is the responsibility of those who would destroy it.

וְלִתֵּן שָׂכָר טוֹב לַצַּדִּיקִים שֶׁמְּקַיְּמִים אֶת־הָעוֹלָם שֶׁנִּבְרָא
בַּעֲשָׂרָה מַאֲמָרוֹת : (ב) עֲשָׂרָה דוֹרוֹת מֵאָדָם וְעַד נֹחַ
לְהוֹדִיעַ כַּמָּה אֶרֶךְ אַפַּיִם לְפָנָיו ׳ שֶׁכָּל־הַדּוֹרוֹת הָיוּ מַכְעִיסִים
לְפָנָיו עַד שֶׁהֵבִיא עֲלֵיהֶם אֶת־מֵי הַמַּבּוּל : (ג) עֲשָׂרָה
דוֹרוֹת מִנֹּחַ וְעַד אַבְרָהָם לְהוֹדִיעַ כַּמָּה אֶרֶךְ אַפַּיִם לְפָנָיו ׳
שֶׁכָּל־הַדּוֹרוֹת הָיוּ מַכְעִיסִים לְפָנָיו עַד שֶׁבָּא אַבְרָהָם אָבִינוּ
וְקִבֵּל שָׂכָר כֻּלָּם : (ד) עֲשָׂרָה נִסְיוֹנוֹת נִתְנַסָּה אַבְרָהָם
אָבִינוּ וְעָמַד בְּכֻלָּם לְהוֹדִיעַ כַּמָּה חִבָּתוֹ שֶׁל־אַבְרָהָם אָבִינוּ :
(ה) עֲשָׂרָה נִסִּים נַעֲשׂוּ לַאֲבוֹתֵינוּ בְּמִצְרַיִם וַעֲשָׂרָה עַל
הַיָּם : (ו) עֲשֶׂר מַכּוֹת הֵבִיא הַקָּדוֹשׁ בָּרוּךְ הוּא עַל
הַמִּצְרִיִּים בְּמִצְרַיִם וְעֶשֶׂר עַל הַיָּם : (ז) עֲשָׂרָה נִסְיוֹנוֹת
נִסּוּ אֲבוֹתֵינוּ אֶת־הַקָּדוֹשׁ בָּרוּךְ הוּא בַּמִּדְבָּר ׳ שֶׁנֶּאֱמַר וַיְנַסּוּ

ten Sayings. In the first chapter of Genesis, the formula, "And
God said", is repeated nine times ; and once, implicitly in the words
which preface the Divine institution of marriage, Genesis 2. 18. In
later times, the Jewish Mystics spoke of creation as a series of ten
emanations (sefiroth) from the Infinite (En Sof). The En Sof and
the emanations, however, were conceived as an absolute Unity,
even as the flame and the colours of the flame are latent in the coal.

2 and 3. These two mishnas emphasize the patience of God in
His dealings with sinning mankind.

2. ten generations. See Genesis, chapter 5.

continued provoking him. Wickedness was rife before the generation
that was destroyed by the Flood, and those evil-doers merited a like fate.
Only the long-suffering mercy of God, by waiting for their repentance,
saved them from their deserved doom.

3. from Noah to Abraham. Enumerated in Genesis 11. 10f. Noah
is excluded from the number, for he is the tenth in the earlier series.

received the reward. Which the intermediate generations forfeited by
their sinfulness.

4. The strength of Abraham's Faith, and his steadfastness during
many trials.

with ten Sayings, as well as the goodly reward that will be bestowed upon the just who preserve the world that was created with ten Sayings.

2. There were ten generations from Adam to Noah, to make known the patience of God, seeing that all those generations continued provoking him, until he brought upon them the waters of the Flood.

3. There were ten generations from Noah to Abraham, to make known the patience of God, seeing that all those generations continued provoking him, until Abraham our father came, and received the reward they should all have earned.

4. With ten trials our father Abraham was tried, and he stood firm in them all, to make known how great was the love of our father Abraham.

5. Ten miracles were wrought for our fathers in Egypt, and ten at the Sea.

6. Ten plagues did the Holy One, blessed be he, bring upon the Egyptians in Egypt, and ten at the Sea.

7. With ten trials did our fathers try the Holy One, blessed be he, in the wilderness; as it is said, And they have put me to the proof.these ten times, and have not hearkened to my voice.

Numbers 14. 22

love. That the Patriarch's obedience of God was the outcome of his love of God is expressly stated in Scripture; cf. "Abraham My friend", lit. " who loved Me " (Isaiah 41. 8).

5 and **6.** Two other Scriptural examples in the ten-group.

5. *ten miracles . . . for our fathers.* Each plague which afflicted the Egyptians was at the same time a miracle for the Israelites ; *e.g.* when darkness descended upon Egypt, " all the children of Israel had light in their dwellings " (Exodus 10. 23).

6. *ten at the sea.* Deduced from the varying phrases in the Song of Moses, Exodus 15; *e.g.* " the horse and his rider hath He thrown into the sea "; and " Pharaoh's chariots and his host hath He cast into the sea ". The Passover Haggadah quotes comments of several Rabbis who magnified the number considerably.

As in the mishna preceding, commentators endeavour to find in the Biblical text ten instances of miracles and plagues.

7. *trials . . . try.* Such as the murmuring, in Exodus 14. 11, the making of the Golden Calf, and the report of the Spies. " There is a

אֹתִי זֶה עֶשֶׂר פְּעָמִים וְלֹא שָׁמְעוּ בְּקוֹלִי : (ח) עֲשָׂרָה

נִסִּים נַעֲשׂוּ לַאֲבוֹתֵינוּ בְּבֵית הַמִּקְדָּשׁ ׳ לֹא הִפִּילָה אִשָּׁה

מֵרֵיחַ בְּשַׂר הַקֹּדֶשׁ ׳ וְלֹא הִסְרִיחַ בְּשַׂר הַקֹּדֶשׁ מֵעוֹלָם ׳

וְלֹא נִרְאָה זְבוּב בְּבֵית הַמַּטְבָּחַיִם ׳ וְלֹא אֵרַע קֶרִי לְכֹהֵן

גָּדוֹל בְּיוֹם הַכִּפֻּרִים ׳ וְלֹא כִבּוּ הַגְּשָׁמִים אֵשׁ שֶׁל־עֲצֵי

הַמַּעֲרָכָה ׳ וְלֹא נִצְּחָה הָרוּחַ אֶת־עַמּוּד הֶעָשָׁן ׳ וְלֹא נִמְצָא

פְּסוּל בָּעֹמֶר וּבִשְׁתֵּי הַלֶּחֶם וּבְלֶחֶם הַפָּנִים ׳ עֹמְדִים צְפוּפִים

וּמִשְׁתַּחֲוִים רְוָחִים ׳ וְלֹא הִזִּיק נָחָשׁ וְעַקְרָב בִּירוּשָׁלַיִם

מֵעוֹלָם ׳ וְלֹא אָמַר אָדָם לַחֲבֵרוֹ צַר לִי הַמָּקוֹם שֶׁאָלִין

בִּירוּשָׁלָיִם : (ט) עֲשָׂרָה דְבָרִים נִבְרְאוּ בְּעֶרֶב שַׁבָּת בֵּין

certain daring simplicity, which perhaps only a Jew can fully appreciate, in this linking together of the trials which God and Israel brought on each other " (Herford).

8. Ten Wonders associated with the Temple in Rabbinic literature. It is an attempt to magnify the holiness of the Temple in terms of miracle. These wonders are not in the Bible, but are due to the pious love of both people and priest for the Central Sanctuary, and especially after its destruction by the Romans.

the holy flesh. Of the sacrifices. The flesh could only be eaten by the priests ; but no harmful effect occurred to any one in whom the odour created a longing to partake of it.

never became putrid. Although it often remained in a heated atmos phere for several days.

no unclean accident. Which would have rendered him unfit to officiate on that Sacred Day in the Sanctuary.

wood-pile. The altar was in an uncovered court, open to the sky.

column of smoke. In ordinary circumstances the wind would at times have blown the smoke downwards, and inconvenienced the priests.

the omer. See Leviticus 23. 19f. The sheaf of barley was cut on the second night of Passover for the wave-offering, and prepared for presentation the following day. If any defect had been discovered in the flour, there would not have been time to provide another supply.

the two loaves. See Leviticus 23. 17. They had to be baked before the commencement of the Festival, and no substitute could be found if at the last moment they were disqualified by a defect.

8. Ten miracles were wrought for our fathers in the Temple : no woman miscarried from the scent of the holy flesh ; the holy flesh never became putrid ; no fly was seen in the slaughter house ; no unclean accident ever befell the high priest on the Day of Atonement ; the rain never quenched the fire of the wood-pile on the altar ; neither did the wind overcome the column of smoke that arose therefrom ; nor was there ever found any disqualifying defect in the omer, or in the two loaves (on Pentecost), or in the shewbread ; though the people stood closely pressed together, they found ample space to prostrate themselves ; never did serpent or scorpion injure anyone in Jerusalem ; nor did any man ever say to his fellow, The place is too narrow for me to lodge over night in Jerusalem.

9. Ten things were created on the eve of Sabbath in the

---

the shewbread. See Leviticus 24. 5f. It was changed each Sabbath, and the fresh supply baked before the Holy Day. The stale bread would have had to remain a second week, contrary to the statute, if anything was wrong with the new.

closely pressed together. On the Festivals and Day of Atonement the precincts of the Temple were thronged to their utmost capacity.

prostrate themselves. On the Day of Atonement, as the High Priest pronounced the Divine Name in the Confession.

serpent or scorpion. Although they were to be found in the city.

to lodge over night. Even on the Festivals, when every Israelite made a pilgrimage to Jerusalem, there was sufficient accommodation for the multitudes. Josephus gives fabulous figures of those who came to celebrate Passover in the Holy City. These last two miracles which, as the Talmud points out, relate not to the Temple but to Jerusalem, are capable of telling homiletic application, especially in regard to the broad tolerance of Israel's teaching. Thus, neither serpent-bite nor scorpion-sting was prevalent in Jerusalem: there have been no Inquisitions in Judaism. Nor has any man reason to say, "Judaism is too narrow for me to find spiritual lodgment therein ".

9. " All phenomena that seemed to partake at once of the natural and the supernatural, were conceived as having had their origin in the interval between the close of the work of Creation and the commencement of the Sabbath " (Singer). In this way, the Rabbis gave expression to their conception of the miraculous in the scheme of things. Miracles, they held, were not interruptions of Nature's laws : at Creation, God had provided for them in advance, as part of the cosmic plan. " The Fathers of the Mishna, who taught that Balaam's ass was created in

הַשָּׁמָשׁוֹת וְאֵלּוּ הֵן · פִּי הָאָרֶץ פִּי הַבְּאֵר פִּי הָאָתוֹן
הַקֶּשֶׁת וְהַמָּן וְהַמַּטֶּה וְהַשָּׁמִיר הַכְּתָב וְהַמִּכְתָּב וְהַלֻּחוֹת ·
וְיֵשׁ אוֹמְרִים אַף הַמַּזִּיקִין וּקְבוּרָתוֹ שֶׁל־מֹשֶׁה וְאֵילוֹ שֶׁל־
אַבְרָהָם אָבִינוּ · וְיֵשׁ אוֹמְרִים אַף צְבָת בִּצְבַת עֲשׂוּיָה :

the eve of the Sabbath, in the twilight, were not fantastic fools, but
subtle philosophers, discovering the reign of universal law through the
exceptions, the miracles that had to be created specially and were
still a part of the order of the world, bound to appear in due time much
as apparently erratic comets are " (I. Zangwill).

eve of the Sabbath. At the end of the sixth day of Creation.

mouth of the earth. Which engulfed Korah and his associates;
Numbers 16. 32.

mouth of the well. Tradition relates that this well, named after
Miriam, accompanied the Israelites in the journey through the wilderness; Numbers 21. 16.

mouth of the ass. Which spoke to Balaam; Numbers 22. 28. See
" Balaam and the Ass ", *Numbers,* 237 (one vol. ed., 671).

the rainbow. See Genesis 9. 13f. According to the Rabbis, the
rainbow existed since the very dawn of Creation. The rainbow—that
everlasting symbol of Hope—was thus created contemporaneously
with the appearance of man. Hope springs eternal in the human
breast, and is an essential part of human nature. Man enters the world
with hope; he bears up against all toils and sorrows through hope;
and when his days on earth are nearing their end, he plants Hope on
the grave. Every item in this wonderful mishna is a spiritual hiero-
glyph; see " Man's Spiritual Equipment " in Hertz, *Sermons* I, 170f.

the manna. See Exodus 16. 14f.

the rod. Wherewith Moses performed God's signs in Egypt;
Exodus 4. 17. According to legend, it belonged to Adam, and was
handed down through the generations to Moses.

the Shamir. The Altar had to be built of rough and unhewn stones;
no sword or iron—symbols of violence and discord—could be lifted up
in connection with the Altar which stood for peace, unity, and reconciliation. As no hammer or axe was used, how were the stones fitted
together ? the people asked. And Jewish folk-belief answered by telling
that Solomon in his wisdom came into possession of a wonderful worm,
one of the marvels of creation, the Shamir, which when placed upon
even the hardest stones would instantly cleave them as desired, and all
as easily and noiselessly as the leaves of a book open. Many were the
miraculous deeds—legend tells—that were performed by its help, till,
with the destruction of the Temple, the Shamir disappeared from earth.

the writing on the tables. Of the Decalogue delivered by God
to Moses, which are described as " written on both their sides "

twilight : the mouth of the earth ; the mouth of the well ;
the mouth of the ass ; the rainbow ; the manna ; the rod
of Moses ; the Shamir ; the writing on the tables ; the
instrument of writing, and the tables of stone : some say,
the destroying spirits also, and the sepulchre of Moses, and
the ram of Abraham our father ; and others say, tongs also
made with tongs.

(Exodus 32. 15). Traditionally, the letters were cut through the stone,
so that the words were legible on both sides ; and letters thus cut would
have fallen out but were held in place in a miraculous manner.
    instrument of writing. Engraving tool.
    tables of stone. " The tables were the work of God " (Exodus 32. 16)
i.e. miraculously made. This was one way of teaching the pre-existence
and eternal validity of the Decalogue.
    destroying spirits. Demons figure in Rabbinic folk-lore, and
belief in their reality was widespread; but, as here, they are held
to be absolutely the *creatures* of God; see p. 264. Later Jewish teachers
—the Gaon Samuel ibn Chofni (died 1034), and Abraham ibn Ezra (1104–
1167)—are among the first in the history of the world to deny the existence of demons. Not the least meaning-laden among the things here
enumerated, is the thought that " demons ", *e.g.* the forces of temptation and unrest in man, date from the dawn of Creation, and are part
of the equipment of the human soul from its birth. It is true that, when
these forces dominate us, they are " destroying spirits ". But when
these instincts are properly controlled, when we rule *them*, they are the
driving-forces in life. It is the capacity to fight evil, or to succumb to
evil, that distinguishes man from the brute. And it is because of evil and
suffering and temptation, that life is the glorious battlefield it is. We
are at once the combatants and the combat and the field that is torn
with strife. But in this struggle we are not left groping in the dark.
Simultaneously with the destroying passions of man, the " Tables of
the Law " together with " the Writing on the Tables " were created.
As those instincts towards evil are part of the original constitution of
man, so also are conscience and the holy laws of right and wrong, that
are to control those instincts.
    sepulchre of Moses. Deuteronomy 34. 6. As no man knows its loca-
tion, it must have been made by God. Its pre-existence teaches, "Moses
died : who shall not die ? "
    ram of Abraham. Genesis 22. 13. It was pre-ordained that the ram,
in connection with the sacrifice of Isaac, be at hand in the thicket at
that time. In this way, the whole idea of sacrifice and martyrdom
was conceived as part of the Divine Plan. On the ideal of martyrdom
in Judaism, see p. 256.
    tongs also made with tongs. This mishna attempts to solve the prob-
lem, Who made the tongs which held the first tongs whilst they were
being made ?

(י) שִׁבְעָה דְבָרִים בְּגֹלֶם וְשִׁבְעָה בְּחָכָם · חָכָם אֵינוֹ
מְדַבֵּר לִפְנֵי מִי שֶׁגָּדוֹל מִמֶּנּוּ בְּחָכְמָה · וְאֵינוֹ נִכְנָס
לְתוֹךְ דִּבְרֵי חֲבֵרוֹ · וְאֵינוֹ נִבְהָל לְהָשִׁיב · שׁוֹאֵל כָּעִנְיָן
וּמֵשִׁיב כַּהֲלָכָה · וְאוֹמֵר עַל־רִאשׁוֹן רִאשׁוֹן וְעַל־אַחֲרוֹן
אַחֲרוֹן · וְעַל מַה־שֶּׁלֹּא שָׁמַע אוֹמֵר לֹא שָׁמָעְתִּי · וּמוֹדֶה
עַל־הָאֱמֶת · וְחִלּוּפֵיהֶם בְּגֹלֶם : (יא) שִׁבְעָה מִינֵי פֻּרְעָנִיּוֹת
בָּאִים לָעוֹלָם עַל־שִׁבְעָה גּוּפֵי עֲבֵרָה : מִקְצָתָם מְעַשְּׂרִים
וּמִקְצָתָם אֵינָם מְעַשְּׂרִים רָעָב שֶׁל־בַּצֹּרֶת בָּא מִקְצָתָם רְעֵבִים
וּמִקְצָתָם שְׂבֵעִים · גָּמְרוּ שֶׁלֹּא לְעַשֵּׂר רָעָב שֶׁל־מְהוּמָה וְשֶׁל־
בַּצֹּרֶת בָּא · וְשֶׁלֹּא לִטּוֹל אֶת־הַחַלָּה רָעָב שֶׁל־כְּלָיָה בָּא ·
דֶּבֶר בָּא לָעוֹלָם עַל־מִיתוֹת הָאֲמוּרוֹת בַּתּוֹרָה שֶׁלֹּא נִמְסְרוּ

10–11. Two seven-groups of Sayings.

10. Enumerates the distinguishing marks of the " wise man " in his conversation, this being the mirror of a man's inner refinement.

uncultured. Heb. *golem*; lit. " the embryo ". Here the word is used of a man with an undeveloped mentality. In later legends, *golem* means a clay or wooden figure endowed with life by mystic use of the Divine Name.

wise man. Heb. *chochom*, the man reared in the Torah.

does not break in. He waits until the other has finished what he had to say, before commenting upon his statement.

not hasty to answer. He deliberates, before raising an objection to a statement.

according to the subject matter. Relevant to the theme under discussion.

first thing first. His mind works in orderly sequence.

not understood. Or, " not heard "; *i.e.* if he has no tradition regarding a matter, he states it.

he acknowledges the truth. One of the crowning signs of true culture : if another's argument is more cogent than his own, or if he has been shown his error, he readily admits it.

11. Seven Forms of Retribution for seven Chief Transgressions.

It is not a philosophy of suffering, but a rough-and-ready way of accounting for evils by the principle of " measure for measure ". The transgressions are ritual, ethical, juristic, and social; and thus cover the whole sphere of the religious life.

10. There are seven marks of an uncultured, and seven of a wise man. The wise man does not speak before him who is greater than he in wisdom ; and does not break in upon the speech of his fellow ; he is not hasty to answer ; he questions according to the subject matter, and answers to the point ; he speaks upon the first thing first, and the last last ; regarding that which he has not understood he says, I do not understand it ; and he acknowledges the truth. The reverse of all this is to be found in an uncultured man.

11. Seven kinds of punishment come into the world for seven important transgressions. *(a)*If some give their tithes and others do not, a dearth ensues from drought, and some suffer hunger while others are full. *(b)*If they all determine to give no tithes, a dearth ensues from tumult and drought. *(c)*If they resolve not to give the dough-cake, an exterminating dearth ensues. *(d)*Pestilence comes into the world to fulfil those death penalties threatened in the Torah, the execution of which, however, is not within the function of a human tribunal ; and for the violation of the law regarding the

the world. Here it means, as in 1, 2, the Jewish People.
important transgressions. Or, " categories of transgression ".

(a), (b) and (c) Dearth : for Withholding of tithes to priest and poor.
dearth ensues from drought. The punishment corresponds to the offence. Those who cause priest, widow and the poor to hunger will themselves suffer hunger.
tumult. Of war, which will prevent them from gathering the harvest.
resolve not to give. i.e. in addition to withholding the tithe.
dough-cake. Heb. חלה ; if even the women refuse to do their duty in holy things, the drought will be complete. Cf. Leviticus 26. 9. It was the special obligation of woman to carry out the precept in Numbers 15. 20. For its observance at the present day, see *Numbers*, 158 (one vol. ed., 632).

(d) Pestilence : for Failure to punish crime and Callousness towards the poor.
death penalties. They were crimes to be punished by " death at the hands of Heaven ", and were to be expiated by means of such pestilence. Or, the guilty were not discovered and, if discovered, could not be punished for technical reasons.

לְבֵית דִּין וְעַל פֵּרוֹת שְׁבִיעִית · חֶרֶב בָּאָה לָעוֹלָם עַל־עִנּוּי

הַדִּין וְעַל־עִוּוּת הַדִּין וְעַל־הַמּוֹרִים בַּתּוֹרָה שֶׁלֹּא כַּהֲלָכָה ·

חַיָּה רָעָה בָּאָה לָעוֹלָם עַל־שְׁבוּעַת שָׁוְא וְעַל־חִלּוּל הַשֵּׁם ·

גָּלוּת בָּאָה לָעוֹלָם עַל־עֲבוֹדַת אֱלִילִים וְעַל־גִּלּוּי עֲרָיוֹת וְעַל־

שְׁפִיכוּת דָּמִים וְעַל־שְׁמִטַּת הָאָרֶץ : (יב) בְּאַרְבָּעָה פְרָקִים

הַדֶּבֶר מִתְרַבֶּה · בָּרְבִיעִית וּבַשְּׁבִיעִית וּבְמוֹצָאֵי שְׁבִיעִית

וּבְמוֹצָאֵי הֶחָג שֶׁבְּכָל־שָׁנָה וְשָׁנָה : בָּרְבִיעִית מִפְּנֵי מַעְשַׂר

עָנִי שֶׁבַּשְּׁלִישִׁית · בַּשְּׁבִיעִית מִפְּנֵי מַעְשַׂר עָנִי שֶׁבַּשִּׁשִּׁית ·

בְּמוֹצָאֵי שְׁבִיעִית מִפְּנֵי פֵרוֹת שְׁבִיעִית · בְּמוֹצָאֵי הֶחָג

---

seventh year. Commanded to be observed as a Sabbath-year of the field (Leviticus 25. 1-7). No agricultural work was to be undertaken. What the soil produced had to be eaten by the owner's household, or by the poor, but it was not to be bartered ; *Leviticus,* 266 (one vol. ed., 531). Callousness towards the poor is deemed as grievous a moral calamity as failure to punish capital offenders; see next mishna.

(e) The Sword : for Delay and Perversion of Justice.

delay of justice. More than the proverbial " law's delay " ; *undue* postponement of a judicial decision.

perversion of justice. Condemning the innocent, and freeing the guilty—an infamy denounced by the Prophets as the cardinal sin in any human society.

interpret the Torah . . . sense. Forbidding what is permitted, and permitting what is forbidden.

If justice is the foundation of a nation and of its friendly relations with other nations, then the breakdown of the machinery of justice or its perversion, necessarily leads sooner or later to armed conflict with other peoples. Since the days of Amos, it was the repeated warning of Prophecy that the sword is the Divine punishment for injustice (Beer).

(f) Wild Beasts : for Perjury and Chillul Hashem.

The nation's disintegration becomes greater, as the crimes become more unpardonable. In time of warfare, when the land is desolated, wild beasts multiply. Throughout the Biblical period, the country was at no time so settled that the jungle lay beyond the range of ordinary experience ; so much so, that the promise of the wild beasts being tamed was one of the elements in the Messianic age. Wild beasts must have increased after the devastations of the land under Titus and Hadrian.

fruits of the seventh year. ⁽ᵉ⁾The sword comes into the world for the delay of justice, and for the perversion of justice, and on account of the offence of those who interpret the Torah not according to its true sense. ⁽ᶠ⁾Wild beasts come into the world for perjury, and for the profanation of the Divine Name. ⁽ᵍ⁾Captivity comes into the world on account of idolatry, immorality, bloodshed, and the neglect of the year of rest for the soil.

12. At four periods pestilence grows apace : in the fourth year, in the seventh, at the conclusion of the seventh year, and at the conclusion of the Feast of Tabernacles in each year : in the fourth year, for default of giving the tithe to the poor in the third year ; in the seventh year, for default of giving the tithe to the poor in the sixth year ; at the conclusion of the seventh year, for the violation of the law regarding the fruits of the seventh year, and at the conclusion of the Feast of Tabernacles in each year, for robbing the poor of the grants legally assigned to them.

profanation of the Name. Homiletically, this saying contains a grave warning : Wherever Jews treat the Oath of Sinai as a vain oath ; that is, wherever Jews are guilty of conduct unworthy of their Faith, there the wild beast in man—blind prejudice and causeless hatred—is unchained against Israel.

(g) Exile and captivity : For Idolatry, Immorality and Bloodshed.

These crimes bring with them the crowning catastrophe. The total uprooting of the nation by transportation to a distant foreign land. Each of these three sins the Jew is forbidden to commit, even if threatened with death for his refusal.

year of rest for the soil. The Sabbatical year when the earth lies fallow ; see Leviticus 25. 3f.

12–18. Seven four-groups of Sayings.

12. *pestilence.* This paragraph amplifies what had been stated in the preceding mishna : " Pestilence comes into the world . . . for the violation of the law regarding the fruits of the seventh year ".

robbing the poor. The Torah prescribed that the poor were to receive the gleanings, the corners of the field, and forgotten sheaves (Leviticus 19. 9, Deuteronomy 24. 19). The Feast of Tabernacles was harvesting time. It was then that most of these offences were committed ; therefore, punishment was experienced at that period of the year.

שֶׁבְּכָל־שָׁנָה וְשָׁנָה מִפְּנֵי גֵזֶל מַתְּנוֹת עֲנִיִּים : (יג) אַרְבַּע
מִדּוֹת בָּאָדָם · הָאוֹמֵר שֶׁלִּי שֶׁלִּי וְשֶׁלְּךָ שֶׁלָּךְ זוֹ מִדָּה
בֵּינוֹנִית וְיֵשׁ אוֹמְרִים זוֹ מִדַּת סְדוֹם · שֶׁלִּי שֶׁלָּךְ וְשֶׁלְּךָ
שֶׁלִּי עַם הָאָרֶץ · שֶׁלִּי שֶׁלָּךְ וְשֶׁלְּךָ שֶׁלָּךְ חָסִיד · שֶׁלָּךְ
שֶׁלִּי וְשֶׁלִּי שֶׁלִּי רָשָׁע : (יד) אַרְבַּע מִדּוֹת בַּדֵּעוֹת · נוֹחַ
לִכְעוֹס וְנוֹחַ לִרְצוֹת יָצָא הֶפְסֵדוֹ בִּשְׂכָרוֹ · קָשֶׁה לִכְעוֹס
וְקָשֶׁה לִרְצוֹת יָצָא שְׂכָרוֹ בְּהֶפְסֵדוֹ · קָשֶׁה לִכְעוֹס וְנוֹחַ
לִרְצוֹת חָסִיד · נוֹחַ לִכְעוֹס וְקָשֶׁה לִרְצוֹת רָשָׁע : (טו) אַרְבַּע
מִדּוֹת בְּתַלְמִידִים · מָהִיר לִשְׁמוֹעַ וּמָהִיר לְאַבֵּד יָצָא שְׂכָרוֹ
בְּהֶפְסֵדוֹ · קָשֶׁה לִשְׁמוֹעַ וְקָשֶׁה לְאַבֵּד יָצָא הֶפְסֵדוֹ בִּשְׂכָרוֹ ·
מָהִיר לִשְׁמוֹעַ וְקָשֶׁה לְאַבֵּד זֶה חֵלֶק טוֹב · קָשֶׁה לִשְׁמוֹעַ
וּמָהִיר לְאַבֵּד זֶה חֵלֶק רָע : (טז) אַרְבַּע מִדּוֹת בְּנוֹתְנֵי
צְדָקָה · הָרוֹצֶה שֶׁיִּתֵּן וְלֹא יִתְּנוּ אֲחֵרִים עֵינוֹ רָעָה בְּשֶׁל־
אֲחֵרִים · יִתְּנוּ אֲחֵרִים וְהוּא לֹא יִתֵּן עֵינוֹ רָעָה בְּשֶׁלּוֹ · יִתֵּן

The connection between transgression and such scourges as famine and pestilence was a settled belief of the Talmudic teachers. Moderns may scoff at this belief; yet it is a sound instinct which in all ages has felt that retribution must follow, in some form, upon all transgression. "In the economy of the universe there may be ends of a purely physical kind served by such disasters, apart altogether from their meaning to man. But man at least learns from them that nature does not exist solely for feeding, clothing, and keeping him wealthy " (G. A. Smith).

13. Four types of Men.

neutral character. Some consider such an attitude to be unethical. It resembles that of Sodom, whose motto seems to have been, "each man for himself "; cf. Ezekiel, 16. 49, " Behold this was the iniquity of thy sister Sodom . . . neither did she strengthen the hand of the poor and the needy ". What a man has is not entirely his own. He should recognize the claims of charity.

boor. Heb. *am ha-aretz*; see on II, 6. Social stability is impossible upon his theory.

13. There are four characters among men : he who says, What is mine is mine and what is thine is thine, his is a neutral character (some say, this is a character like that of Sodom) ; he who says, What is mine is thine and what is thine is mine, is a boor ; he who says, What is mine is thine and what is thine is thine, is a saint ; he who says, What is thine is mine and what is mine is mine, is a wicked man.

14. There are four kinds of tempers : he whom it is easy to provoke and easy to pacify, his loss disappears in his gain ; he whom it is hard to provoke and hard to pacify, his gain disappears in his loss ; he whom it is hard to provoke and easy to pacify is a saint ; he whom it is easy to provoke and hard to pacify is a wicked man.

15. There are four qualities in disciples : he who quickly understands and quickly forgets, his gain disappears in his loss ; he who understands with difficulty and forgets with difficulty, his loss disappears in his gain ; he who understands quickly and forgets with difficulty, his is a good portion ; he who understands with difficulty and forgets quickly, his is an evil portion.

16. As to almsgiving there are four dispositions : he who desires to give, but that others should not give, his eye is evil towards what appertains to others ; he who desires that others should give, but will not give himself, his eye is

---

saint. He asks nothing of others, and is ready to give what he has to help the poor.

wicked man. His temperament is that of a robber.

14. Four different dispositions.

saint. It should be noted that he is " hard ", not *impossible*, " to provoke ". Even the best men occasionally give way to anger ; and always to *indignation* at an outrage against decency and right.

15. Four types of students. As no ethical principle is involved, the terms " saint " and " wicked " are not used in this estimate of the intellectual qualities of the student.

16. Four kinds of almsgivers.

his eye is evil. Cf. II, 14. He does not like to see others gain merit and blessing by their charitable acts.

וְיִתְּנוּ אֲחֵרִים חָסִיד · לֹא יִתֵּן וְלֹא יִתְּנוּ אֲחֵרִים רָשָׁע :

(יז) אַרְבַּע מִדּוֹת בְּהוֹלְכֵי בֵית הַמִּדְרָשׁ · הוֹלֵךְ וְאֵינוֹ עֹשֶׂה

שְׂכַר הֲלִיכָה בְּיָדוֹ · עֹשֶׂה וְאֵינוֹ הוֹלֵךְ שְׂכַר מַעֲשֶׂה בְּיָדוֹ ·

הוֹלֵךְ וְעֹשֶׂה חָסִיד · לֹא הוֹלֵךְ וְלֹא עֹשֶׂה רָשָׁע : (יח) אַרְבַּע

מִדּוֹת בְּיוֹשְׁבִים לִפְנֵי חֲכָמִים · סְפוֹג וּמַשְׁפֵּךְ מְשַׁמֶּרֶת וְנָפָה ·

סְפוֹג שֶׁהוּא סוֹפֵג אֶת-הַכֹּל · וּמַשְׁפֵּךְ שֶׁמַּכְנִיס בְּזוֹ וּמוֹצִיא

בְזוֹ · מְשַׁמֶּרֶת שֶׁמּוֹצִיאָה אֶת-הַיַּיִן וְקוֹלֶטֶת אֶת-הַשְּׁמָרִים ·

וְנָפָה שֶׁמּוֹצִיאָה אֶת-הַקֶּמַח וְקוֹלֶטֶת אֶת-הַסֹּלֶת : (יט) כָּל

אַהֲבָה שֶׁהִיא-תְלוּיָה בְדָבָר בָּטֵל דָּבָר בְּטֵלָה אַהֲבָה ·

וְשֶׁאֵינָהּ תְּלוּיָה בְדָבָר אֵינָהּ בְּטֵלָה לְעוֹלָם · אֵיזוֹ הִיא

אַהֲבָה שֶׁהִיא-תְלוּיָה בְדָבָר זוֹ אַהֲבַת אַמְנוֹן וְתָמָר · וְשֶׁאֵינָהּ

תְּלוּיָה בְדָבָר זוֹ אַהֲבַת דָּוִד וִיהוֹנָתָן : (כ) כָּל-מַחֲלֹקֶת

---

against what is his own. He begrudges himself the acquisition of merit.

a saint. He evinces the right ethical spirit.

a wicked man. He has no sympathy for the needy in their distress.

17. Four classes of those who attend in the Beth Hamidrash, to learn their religious duty or some spiritual lesson.

does not practise. The moral lessons which he heard expounded.

reward for going. His attendance was at least proof of a desire to learn, and he received his reward for that.

he who practises. By copying the example of the pious man, but without obtaining his inspiration from hearing the exposition of the Torah.

18. Four kinds of disciples, and their capacity to distinguish between good doctrine and bad, between what is of primary and secondary importance. The distinction applies also to schoolchildren of all times.

sucks up everything. Absorbs the true and the false, the sublime and the trivial.

lets in at one end and out at the other. Typifies the student or child that forgets everything, though he learns readily.

retains the lees. He remembers only the worst of whatever he hears or reads.

evil against what is his own ; he who gives and wishes others to give, is a saint ; he who will not give and does not wish others to give, is a wicked man.

17. There are four characters suggested by those who attend the house of study : he who goes and does not practise, secures the reward for going ; he who practises but does not go, secures the reward for practising; he who goes and practises, is a saint; he who neither goes nor practises, is a wicked man.

18. There are four qualities among those that sit before the wise : they are like a sponge, a funnel, a strainer, or a sieve : a sponge, which sucks up everything ; a funnel, which lets in at one end and out at the other ; a strainer, which lets the wine pass out and retains the lees ; a sieve, which lets out the bran and retains the fine flour.

19. Whenever love depends upon some material cause, with the passing away of that cause, the love too passes away ; but if it be not dependent upon such a cause, it will not pass away for ever. Which love was that which depended upon a material cause ? Such was the love of Amnon and Tamar. And that which depended upon no such cause ? Such was the love of David and Jonathan.

---

lets out the bran. He lets go the worthless and retains the good. Like Rabbi Meir, who stated of his relations to Acher (see IV, 25) that he ate the fruit of his learning—its Jewish content—and threw away the husk. " The sieve spoken of, is one which retains the fine flour in a receptacle attached to the machine, and is so constructed that the coarse grain passes out at the end of the sieve " (Taylor).

19–22. General Moral Reflections.
19. Two kinds of love.
material cause. Such love only seeks gratification of self, and passes away with the attainment of that gratification.
Amnon and Tamar. See II Samuel 13.
David and Jonathan. The most sublime story of disinterested friendship, based on unselfish mutual affection. " The soul of Jonathan was knit with the soul of David, and Jonathan loved him as his own soul " (I Samuel 18. 1), although he knew that David stood between him and the throne.

שֶׁהִיא לְשֵׁם שָׁמַיִם סוֹפָהּ לְהִתְקַיֵּם וְשֶׁאֵינָהּ לְשֵׁם שָׁמַיִם
אֵין סוֹפָהּ לְהִתְקַיֵּם ׳ אֵיזוֹ הִיא מַחֲלֹקֶת שֶׁהִיא לְשֵׁם שָׁמַיִם
זוֹ מַחֲלֹקֶת הִלֵּל וְשַׁמַּי ׳ וְשֶׁאֵינָהּ לְשֵׁם שָׁמַיִם זוֹ מַחֲלֹקֶת
קֹרַח וְכָל־עֲדָתוֹ : (כא) כָּל־הַמְזַכֶּה אֶת־הָרַבִּים אֵין חֵטְא
בָּא עַל־יָדוֹ וְכָל־הַמַּחֲטִיא אֶת־הָרַבִּים אֵין־מַסְפִּיקִין בְּיָדוֹ
לַעֲשׂוֹת תְּשׁוּבָה ׳ מֹשֶׁה זָכָה וְזִכָּה אֶת־הָרַבִּים זְכוּת הָרַבִּים
תָּלוּי בּוֹ ׳ שֶׁנֶּאֱמַר צִדְקַת יְיָ עָשָׂה וּמִשְׁפָּטָיו עִם־יִשְׂרָאֵל׳ יָרָבְעָם
בֶּן־נְבָט חָטָא וְהֶחֱטִיא אֶת־הָרַבִּים חֵטְא הָרַבִּים תָּלוּי בּוֹ ׳
שֶׁנֶּאֱמַר עַל־חַטֹּאות יָרָבְעָם אֲשֶׁר חָטָא וַאֲשֶׁר הֶחֱטִיא אֶת־
יִשְׂרָאֵל : (כב) כָּל־מִי שֶׁיֶּשׁ־בּוֹ שְׁלֹשָׁה דְבָרִים הַלָּלוּ הוּא
מִתַּלְמִידָיו שֶׁל־אַבְרָהָם אָבִינוּ ׳ וּשְׁלֹשָׁה דְבָרִים אֲחֵרִים הוּא
מִתַּלְמִידָיו שֶׁל־בִּלְעָם הָרָשָׁע ׳ עַיִן טוֹבָה וְרוּחַ נְמוּכָה וְנֶפֶשׁ

20. On religious controversy : honest and dishonest.

controversy that is in the name of Heaven. Cf. IV, 14. The discussion is conducted with a sincere desire to reach the truth.

Hillel and Shammai. They and their Schools differed on many points that were keenly debated between them. Since their aim was nothing else than the correct exposition of the Torah, the Talmud related that a *Bath-kol* (see VI, 2) proclaimed, " They both speak the words of the living God ".

Korah and his company. Numbers 16. Their controversy with Moses and Aaron was merely a rebellion against authority, and due to their ambition to supplant these leaders. It met with a tragic end.

21. On moral leaders and misleaders.

to be righteous. To lead lives dominated by Religion, Worship and Beneficence.

no sin shall be brought about. The righteousness of the many that they have learned from him, acts as a defence to him, and he does not become the cause of sin.

shall not have the means to repent. It would be unjust if he escaped punishment by means of penitence, while those whom he had misled suffered. The sins he led others to commit rise in judgment against him, and these sins are beyond the remedial action of his own repentance; see Yoma 87a. " There is a fine chivalry in this Jewish doctrine.

20. Every controversy that is in the name of Heaven, shall in the end lead to a permanent result; but every controversy that is not in the name of Heaven, shall not lead to a permanent result. Which controversy was that which was in the name of Heaven? Such was the controversy of Hillel and Shammai. And that which was not in the name of Heaven? Such was the controversy of Korah and all his company.

21. Whosoever causes many to be righteous, through him no sin shall be brought about; but he who causes many to sin, shall not have the means to repent. Moses was righteous and made many righteous; the righteousness of the many was laid upon him, as it is said, He executed the justice of the Lord, and his judgments with Israel. Jeroboam, the son of Nebat, sinned and caused many to sin; the sin of the many was laid upon him, as it is said, For the sins of Jeroboam which he sinned, and wherewith he made Israel to sin.

Deuteronomy 33. 21

I. Kings 15. 30

22. Whosoever has these three attributes, is of the disciples of Abraham our father; but whosoever has three other attributes, is of the disciples of Balaam the wicked. A good eye, a humble mind and a lowly spirit (are the tokens) of the disciples of Abraham our father; an evil eye,

Jewish teachers alone have had the moral insight to discern, and the wisdom to teach, this lesson " (Herford).

causes many to sin. The climax in the Confession on the Atonement Day is, *we have led astray.*

22. *disciples of Abraham . . . . Balaam.* By the time this mishna was composed, the figure of Balaam had come to typify low heathen viciousness of thought and action; see *Numbers*, 228 (one vol. ed., 668). Note that the contrast is not between Abraham and Balaam, but between their *disciples:* a religious system is judged not by its founders, but by the lives that their followers after them lead. The purpose of this mishna seems to stress the fact that selfishness, pride and haughtiness are un-Jewish vices. The characterization of the followers of Balaam is harsh, but—as a Christian commentator admits— so were the attacks on Jews by contemporaries of the author of this saying.

שֶׁפֶּלָה מִתַּלְמִידָיו שֶׁל־אַבְרָהָם אָבִינוּ ׳ עַיִן רָעָה וְרוּחַ גְּבוֹהָה
וְנֶפֶשׁ רְחָבָה מִתַּלְמִידָיו שֶׁל־בִּלְעָם הָרָשָׁע : מַה בֵּין תַּלְמִידָיו
שֶׁל־אַבְרָהָם אָבִינוּ לְתַלְמִידָיו שֶׁל־בִּלְעָם הָרָשָׁע ׳ תַּלְמִידָיו
שֶׁל־אַבְרָהָם אָבִינוּ אוֹכְלִים בָּעוֹלָם הַזֶּה וְנוֹחֲלִים הָעוֹלָם
הַבָּא ׳ שֶׁנֶּאֱמַר לְהַנְחִיל אֹהֲבַי יֵשׁ וְאֹצְרֹתֵיהֶם אֲמַלֵּא ׳
תַּלְמִידָיו שֶׁל־בִּלְעָם הָרָשָׁע יוֹרְשִׁים גֵּי־הִנֹּם וְיוֹרְדִים לִבְאֵר
שַׁחַת ׳ שֶׁנֶּאֱמַר וְאַתָּה אֱלֹהִים תּוֹרִדֵם לִבְאֵר שַׁחַת אַנְשֵׁי
דָמִים וּמִרְמָה לֹא־יֶחֱצוּ יְמֵיהֶם וַאֲנִי אֶבְטַח־בָּךְ : (נג) יְהוּדָה
בֶּן־תֵּימָא אוֹמֵר ׳ הֱוֵי עַז כַּנָּמֵר וְקַל כַּנֶּשֶׁר רָץ כַּצְּבִי וְגִבּוֹר
כָּאֲרִי לַעֲשׂוֹת רְצוֹן אָבִיךְ שֶׁבַּשָּׁמָיִם : הוּא הָיָה אוֹמֵר ׳
עַז פָּנִים לְגֵי־הִנֹּם וּבוֹשׁ פָּנִים לְגַן עֵדֶן : יְהִי רָצוֹן מִלְּפָנֶיךָ
יְיָ אֱלֹהֵינוּ וֵאלֹהֵי אֲבוֹתֵינוּ שֶׁיִּבָּנֶה בֵּית הַמִּקְדָּשׁ בִּמְהֵרָה
בְיָמֵינוּ וְתֵן חֶלְקֵנוּ בְּתוֹרָתֶךָ : (כד) הוּא הָיָה אוֹמֵר ׳ בֶּן־
חָמֵשׁ שָׁנִים לַמִּקְרָא בֶּן־עֶשֶׂר שָׁנִים לַמִּשְׁנָה בֶּן־שְׁלֹשׁ עֶשְׂרֵה

proud spirit. An ambitious nature.
what is the difference? In the fate which is in store for them.
that love me. Said of Abraham in the Hebrew of Isaiah 41. 8.
substance. In a spiritual sense of the Hereafter.
treasuries. The boon of this world.
Gehinnom. See on 1, 5.
blood-thirsty and deceitful men. According to tradition, it was
Balaam's sinister counsel that was responsible for the death of 24,000
(Numbers 25. 9).

23–26. Close of the Tractate.
23. *Judah, the son of Tema.* It is unknown in which century he lived,
or who his teacher was.

bold as a leopard. As this animal is fearless and cannot be turned
aside from stalking its prey, so the Israelite should permit nothing to
stand in the way of the carrying out of his Jewish and human duties.

light as an eagle. This phrase and " strong as a lion " are taken
from II Samuel 1. 23.

a haughty mind and a proud spirit (are the signs) of the disciples of Balaam the wicked. What is the difference between the disciples of Abraham our father and those of Balaam the wicked ? The disciples of Abraham our father enjoy this world and inherit the world to come ; as it is said, *Proverbs* 8. 21 That I may cause those that love me to inherit substance, and may fill all their treasuries. The disciples of Balaam the wicked inherit Gehinnom and descend into the pit of *Psalm* 55. 24 destruction ; as it is said, But thou, O God, wilt bring them down into the pit of destruction : blood-thirsty and deceitful men shall not live out half their days ; but I will trust in thee.

23. Judah, the son of Tema, said, Be strong as a leopard, light as an eagle, fleet as a hart, and strong as a lion, to do the will of thy Father who is in heaven. He used to say, The bold-faced are for Gehinnom, the shame-faced for the Garden of Eden. (He said further) May it be thy will, O Lord our God and God of our fathers, that the Temple be speedily rebuilt in our days, and grant our portion in thy Torah.

24. He used to say, At five years the age is reached for the study of the Scripture, at ten for the study of the

fleet as a hart. Cf. " I made haste, and delayed not, to observe Thy commandments " (Psalm 119. 60) ; see IV, 2.

thy Father who is in heaven. The term, " Our Father Who is in Heaven " or " My Father Who is in Heaven " is frequent in Rabbinic literature ; see p. 32.

bold-faced. The Heb. expression for "impudent" ; see the prayer of R. Judah the Prince, p. 26.

shame-faced. Those sensitive to public opinion. " Anyone who has a sense of shame will not readily sin " (Talmud).

Garden of Eden. The Heb. term for the abode of the righteous in the World to come.

may it be thy will. This prayer, added after the Amidah (p. 156), at one time closed Chapter V, and therefore the whole of Aboth. The remaining mishnas are later supplements.

24. The Ages of man—a favourite theme of all moralists. Leopold Löw, one of the great Jewish scholars of the nineteenth century, wrote a notable book on "The Ages of Man in Jewish Literature". In this

לְמִצְוֹת בֶּן־חָמֵשׁ עֶשְׂרֵה לַתַּלְמוּד. בֶּן־שְׁמֹנֶה עֶשְׂרֵה לַחֻפָּה
בֶּן־עֶשְׂרִים לִרְדוֹף בֶּן־שְׁלֹשִׁים לַכֹּחַ בֶּן־אַרְבָּעִים לַבִּינָה בֶּן־
חֲמִשִּׁים לְעֵצָה בֶּן־שִׁשִּׁים לְזִקְנָה בֶּן־שִׁבְעִים לְשֵׂיבָה בֶּן־
שְׁמוֹנִים לִגְבוּרָה בֶּן־תִּשְׁעִים לָשׁוּחַ בֶּן־מֵאָה כְּאִלּוּ מֵת וְעָבַר
וּבָטֵל מִן הָעוֹלָם : (כה) בֶּן־בַּג בַּג אוֹמֵר · הֲפָךְ־בַּהּ וַהֲפָךְ־
בַּהּ דְּכֹלָּא בַהּ וּבַהּ תֶּחֱזֵא וְסִיב וּבְלֵה בַהּ וּמִנַּהּ לָא תְזוּעַ
שֶׁאֵין לָךְ מִדָּה טוֹבָה הֵימֶנָּה : (כו) בֶּן־הֵא הֵא אוֹמֵר ·
לְפֻם צַעֲרָא אַגְרָא :

רַבִּי חֲנַנְיָא בֶּן־עֲקַשְׁיָא וכו׳

---

post-Talmudic saying, man's life is divided into three periods—preparation, till twenty ; activity, from twenty to sixty ; and decline, from sixty and beyond.

fulfilment of the commandments. See p. 1043.

for seeking a livelihood. lit. "for pursuing". The "school-leaving" age in this scheme of instruction is twenty. After five years of Talmud study, he is free to devote himself to earning a livelihood. During the first years of marriage, the student-husband usually lived with, and was maintained by, his wife's parents.

thirty. The prime of physical vigour.

fifty. Based on the statement with regard to the Levites. On reaching the age of fifty, they were considered as no longer fit for heavy work, but continued to act as guides and counsellors to the younger Levites (Numbers 8. 25f).

seventy. It was said of David, " he died in a good old age " (I Chronicles 29. 28), and he was seventy at his death.

strength. He must have possessed great natural strength and vigour to have reached that age. Commentators refer to Psalm 90. 10. E. N. Adler suggested that probably it is a euphemism (לשון סגי נהור), and the meaning is "increasing weakness". Such seems to have been the opinion of Abraham Ibn Ezra, when in his poem on this theme he describes the man of eighty as a burden to himself and others.

he bends beneath the weight of years. lit. " to sink down ".

hundred. The limit for a person to retain his faculties, and so to be said at all as living.

Mishna, at thirteen for the fulfilment of the commandments, at fifteen for the study of the Talmud, at eighteen for marriage, at twenty for seeking a livelihood, at thirty for entering into one's full strength, at forty for understanding, at fifty for counsel, at sixty a man attains old age, at seventy the hoary head, at eighty the gift of special strength, at ninety he bends beneath the weight of years, at a hundred he is as if he were already dead and had passed away from the world.

25. Ben Bag Bag said, Turn it (the Torah) and turn it over again, for everything is in it, and contemplate it, and wax grey and old over it, and stir not from it, for thou canst have no better rule than this.

26. Ben Hai Hai said, According to the labour is the reward.

"Rabbi Chananya," etc., p. 627.

---

25. *Ben Bag Bag.* His full name was Yochanan ben Bag Bag. The latter name is said to indicate that he was a descendant of proselytes (בג בב is an abbreviation of *Ben Ger* and *Bath Ger*, " son of a proselyte " and " daughter of a proselyte "). An ingenious suggestion is that his name, and Ben Hai Hai, mentioned in the next mishna, belonged to the same man; and that he was the would-be proselyte who asked Hillel to teach him the whole Torah.

turn it. Study the Torah over and over again, study it from all sides.

everything is in it. It is a complete guide to life. " In it, without doubt, are history and tale; proverb and enigma; correction and wisdom; knowledge and discretion; poetry and word-play; conviction and counsel: dirge, entreaty, prayer, praise, and every kind of supplication; and all this in a Divine way superior to all the prolix benedictions in human books; to say nothing of containing in its depths the Names of the Holy One, blessed is He, and secrets of being without end " (Lev Aboth).

wax grey and old over it. Do not think, on arriving at old age, that its guidance is no longer required.

stir not from it. Do not deviate from the path of life which it lays down; or, do not leave it for extraneous studies.

rule. The Heb. may also denote "standard, or principle, of conduct ".

26. *according to the labour is the reward.* A popular proverb which is here applied to the Torah. What a man derives from it, is proportionate to the devotion he pays it. This and the preceding mishna are in Aramaic.

פֶּרֶק שִׁשִּׁי :

כָּל־יִשְׂרָאֵל וכו'

שָׁנוּ חֲכָמִים בִּלְשׁוֹן הַמִּשְׁנָה בָּרוּךְ שֶׁבָּחַר בָּהֶם וּבְמִשְׁנָתָם:

(א) רַבִּי מֵאִיר אוֹמֵר ׳ כָּל־הָעוֹסֵק בַּתּוֹרָה לִשְׁמָהּ זוֹכֶה לִדְבָרִים
הַרְבֵּה וְלֹא עוֹד אֶלָּא שֶׁכָּל־הָעוֹלָם כֻּלּוֹ כְּדַי הוּא לוֹ ׳ נִקְרָא
רֵעַ אָהוּב אוֹהֵב אֶת־הַמָּקוֹם אוֹהֵב אֶת־הַבְּרִיּוֹת ׳ וּמְשַׂמֵּחַ אֶת־הַמָּקוֹם

CHAPTER VI.

"ON THE ACQUISITION OF TORAH."

This chapter does not form part of the Sayings of the Fathers, or of the official Mishna. When custom assigned a chapter of Aboth for the Sabbaths between Passover and Pentecost, a reading was required for the sixth Sabbath. This "Chapter on the Acquisition of the Torah", was selected for the purpose, because its contents harmonized so well with the spirit of Aboth. It opens with a saying of R. Meir, and there‹ fore came to be known as the "Boraitha of Rabbi Meir". *Boraitha* is the name for the teachings next in authority to those that form part of the Mishna.

the sages taught. In the Talmud this formula is in Aramaic, and introduces a quotation from a source which has not been included in the Mishna.

blessed be he. "He" most probably means God; but some refer it to any student who chooses this chapter for study, or to the compiler who had "chosen" the ancient teachers and their words for his great Eulogy on the Torah.

their Mishna. i.e. their teaching.

1. *Rabbi Meir.* Also known as Nehorai, is the most famous disciple of Rabbi Akiba. Through his dialectical skill he attained eminence in juristic discussion, and high place in the Sanhedrin. He was also great as an exegete, and renowned as a fabulist. Among his teachings are, "Scripture tells us (Deuteronomy 14. 1), *You are children of the Lord your God*—whether we act as children should towards their Father, or whether we do not, He ever remains our Father Who is in Heaven". Equally wonderful is his religious universalism. "Whence do we know that even a heathen, if he obeys the Law of God, thereby attains the same spiritual communion with God as the High Priest? Scripture says (Leviticus 18. 5) 'Mine ordinances which if a man do, he shall live by them'—it does not say, If priest, Levite, or Israelite do God's ordinances, he shall attain life; but it says, if a *man* do them!"

CHAPTER VI

"All Israel," etc., p. 613.

The sages taught the following in the style of the Mishna, —Blessed be he that made choice of them and their Mishna.

EULOGY ON THE TORAH

1. R. Meir said, Whosoever labours in the Torah for its own sake, merits many things ; and not only so, but the whole world is indebted to him : he is called friend, beloved, a lover of the All-present, a lover of mankind : it clothes him in meekness and reverence ; it fits him to become just,

Like his teacher Akiba, he preached the widest optimism. "And God saw everything that He had made, and, behold it was *very good*" (Genesis 1. 31). On this R. Meir's comment was, that even suffering, evil, nay, *death itself*, have a rightful and beneficent place in the Divine scheme. The following are examples of his maxims and parables." Love thy friend who admonishes thee, and hate the one who flatters thee". "Man comes into the world with closed hands—ready to grasp at the world and its possessions. He departs with hands limp and open—he takes nothing with him ". Rabbi Meir was the husband of the wise Beruria ; see p. 588. He was a scribe by trade, and his life was full of trouble and misfortune. He died in his native city in Asia Minor. " Bury me by the sea shore ", was his last wish, " that the waves which wash the Land of my Fathers, may wash also my bones " ; see IV, 12 and 27, and concluding note to VI, p. 721.

whosoever labours in the Torah. Study of the Torah is a supreme religious duty ; see p. 15. And like every other religious duty, it must be pursued " for its own sake ".

for its own sake. From disinterested love, *lishmoh*, not for the sake of any profit or honour to be derived from it. The one true motive is the love of God. The doctrine of disinterested love of God and His Torah holds an important place in Rabbinical ethics, and has been called " the great creation of the Rabbis ". However, knowing human nature, they did not discourage doing right even from an imperfect motive, because it oftens ends in doing right for its own sake.

All-present. See on II, 14.

lover of mankind. The Torah scholar is no cloistered student who flees from his fellow-men, nor is he a cynic.

meekness. He walks humbly with God ; not ostentatiously, but with noiseless acts of love. The insistence on humility distinguishes Jewish, from Greek or pagan, ethics. A great Jewish philosopher declares, " Everything heroic in man is insignificant and perishable, and all his wisdom and virtue unable to stand the crucial test, unless they are the fruits of humility. In this regard there is no exception, neither for any man, any people, nor any age " (Hermann Cohen).

reverence. Of God.

עֲנָוָה וְיִרְאָה וּמַכְשַׁרְתּוֹ לִהְיוֹת צַדִּיק חָסִיד יָשָׁר וְנֶאֱמָן
וּמְרַחַקְתּוֹ מִן־הַחֵטְא וּמְקָרַבְתּוֹ לִידֵי זְכוּת וְנֶהֱנִין מִמֶּנּוּ עֵצָה
וְתוּשִׁיָּה בִּינָה וּגְבוּרָה ׳ שֶׁנֶּאֱמַר לִי עֵצָה וְתוּשִׁיָּה אֲנִי בִינָה
לִי גְבוּרָה ׳ וְנוֹתֶנֶת לוֹ מַלְכוּת וּמֶמְשָׁלָה וְחִקּוּר דִּין וּמְגַלִּים
לוֹ רָזֵי תוֹרָה וְנַעֲשֶׂה כְּמַעְיָן שֶׁאֵינוֹ פוֹסֵק וּכְנָהָר שֶׁמִּתְגַּבֵּר
וְהוֹלֵךְ וְהֹוֶה צָנוּעַ וְאֶרֶךְ רוּחַ וּמוֹחֵל עַל־עֶלְבּוֹנוֹ וּמְגַדַּלְתּוֹ
וּמְרוֹמַמְתּוֹ עַל כָּל־הַמַּעֲשִׂים : (ב) אָמַר רַבִּי יְהוֹשֻׁעַ בֶּן־לֵוִי
בְּכָל־יוֹם וָיוֹם בַּת־קוֹל יוֹצֵאת מֵהַר חוֹרֵב וּמַכְרֶזֶת וְאוֹמֶרֶת
אוֹי לָהֶם לַבְּרִיּוֹת מֵעֶלְבּוֹנָהּ שֶׁל־תּוֹרָה ׳ שֶׁכָּל־מִי שֶׁאֵינוֹ עוֹסֵק
בַּתּוֹרָה נִקְרָא נָזוּף ׳ שֶׁנֶּאֱמַר נֶזֶם זָהָב בְּאַף חֲזִיר אִשָּׁה יָפָה

virtue. lit. " merit ", *i.e.* conduct which earns him God's approval.
counsel is mine. The speaker is Wisdom, identified with Torah.
sovereignty and dominion. The general meaning is that knowledge
of Torah endows one with a commanding personality. But the author
has more particularly in mind, " By me (Torah) princes rule and nobles,
even all the judges of the earth " (Proverbs 8. 16).
  discerning judgment. This is based upon the last words of the verse.
  secrets of the Torah are revealed. By God ; cf. " The counsel (lit.
secret) of the Lord is with them that fear Him " (Psalm 25. 14).
  a never-failing fountain. Cf. II, 11, where R. Elazar ben Arach is
described as a " spring flowing with ever-sustained vigour ".
  modest. The same word as in " walk humbly with thy God " (Micah
6. 8).

  This mishna—which describes the perfect man as conceived by the
Rabbis—enumerates the blessings that attend the study of the Torah,
and the virtues which such study fosters in him who consecrates his days
to it. To some people, the perfection of mind and soul presented in
this mishna appears incomplete. Precious as the religious and ethical
excellencies here given may be, they do not include physical qualities
that made such a strong appeal to the ancient Greeks, as well as to
many moderns. However, competent judges, both Jewish and non-
Jewish, agree that the type of character described is both beautiful and
saintly—a type of character produced by Rabbinism, and only by
Rabbinism.

pious, upright and faithful ; it keeps him far from sin, and brings him near to virtue : through him the world enjoys counsel and sound knowledge, understanding and strength ; Proverbs 8. 14 (as it is said, Counsel is mine, and sound knowledge ; I am understanding ; I have strength) : and it gives him sovereignty and dominion and discerning judgment : to him the secrets of the Torah are revealed ; he is made like a never-failing fountain, and like a river that flows on with ever-sustained vigour ; he becomes modest, patient, and forgiving of insults ; and it magnifies and exalts him above all things.

2. R. Joshua, the son of Levi, said, Every day a Bath-kol goes forth from Mount Sinai, proclaiming these words, Woe to mankind for contempt of the Torah, for whoever does not labour in the Torah is said to be under Proverbs 9. 22 the divine censure ; as it is said, As a ring of gold in a swine's snout, so is a fair woman who turneth aside from Exodus 32. 16 discretion : and it says, And the tables were the work of

---

2. The Supreme Revelation of God is set at naught by neglect and ignorance. Such ignorance is a form of moral bondage.

Joshua, the son of Levi. A foremost exponent of the Haggadic element in Jewish lore, lived in the middle of the third century c.e.

Bath-kol. A heavenly voice. lit. " daughter of the voice " This was held by many to be a form of Divine announcement to man in the later days when Prophecy had ceased.

Mount Sinai. Heb. " Mount Horeb ", the scene of the Revelation of the Torah.

mankind. Heb. *beriyyoth*, which denotes the whole human race. The Gentile world too suffers when the ethical teachings of the Torah are flouted.

contempt of the Torah. Manifested by the neglect of its study and practice.

under the divine censure. lit. " is called rebuked (*nazuf*) ".

as it is said. The proof-text is used to produce a *notarikon* (from Latin *notarius*, " a shorthand writer ") ; *i.e.* letters are selected to form the required word. Thus, *zaken* (old) is explained to mean *zeh shekonoh chochmah*, *i.e.* only he can be called *old* and entitled to all the respect due to the aged, who *has acquired wisdom*—irrespective of his years. These word-plays can be fully appreciated only by those familiar with the Hebrew original and with Rabbinic methods of exegesis.

וְסָרַת מֵעָם : וְאוֹמֵר ' וְהַלֻּחֹת מַעֲשֵׂה אֱלֹהִים הֵמָּה וְהַמִּכְתָּב
מִכְתַּב אֱלֹהִים הוּא חָרוּת עַל־הַלֻּחֹת ' אַל־תִּקְרָא חָרוּת אֶלָּא
חֵרוּת שֶׁאֵין לְךָ בֶּן־חוֹרִין אֶלָּא מִי שֶׁעוֹסֵק בְּתַלְמוּד תּוֹרָה '
וְכָל־מִי שֶׁעוֹסֵק בְּתַלְמוּד תּוֹרָה הֲרֵי זֶה מִתְעַלֶּה ' שֶׁנֶּאֱמַר
וּמִמַּתָּנָה נַחֲלִיאֵל וּמִנַּחֲלִיאֵל בָּמוֹת : (ג) הַלּוֹמֵד מֵחֲבֵרוֹ פֶּרֶק
אֶחָד אוֹ הֲלָכָה אַחַת אוֹ פָּסוּק אֶחָד אוֹ דִבּוּר אֶחָד אוֹ אֲפִילוּ
אוֹת אַחַת צָרִיךְ לִנְהָג בּוֹ כָּבוֹד ' שֶׁכֵּן מָצִינוּ בְּדָוִד מֶלֶךְ
יִשְׂרָאֵל שֶׁלֹּא לָמַד מֵאֲחִיתֹפֶל אֶלָּא שְׁנֵי דְבָרִים בִּלְבָד קְרָאוֹ
רַבּוֹ אַלּוּפוֹ וּמְיֻדָּעוֹ ' שֶׁנֶּאֱמַר וְאַתָּה אֱנוֹשׁ כְּעֶרְכִּי אַלּוּפִי וּמְיֻדָּעִי :
וַהֲלֹא דְבָרִים קַל וָחֹמֶר ' וּמַה דָּוִד מֶלֶךְ יִשְׂרָאֵל שֶׁלֹּא לָמַד
מֵאֲחִיתֹפֶל אֶלָּא שְׁנֵי דְבָרִים בִּלְבָד קְרָאוֹ רַבּוֹ אַלּוּפוֹ וּמְיֻדָּעוֹ '
הַלּוֹמֵד מֵחֲבֵרוֹ פֶּרֶק אֶחָד אוֹ הֲלָכָה אַחַת אוֹ פָּסוּק אֶחָד אוֹ
דִבּוּר אֶחָד אוֹ אֲפִילוּ אוֹת אַחַת עַל־אַחַת כַּמָּה וְכַמָּה שֶׁצָּרִיךְ
לִנְהָג בּוֹ כָּבוֹד ' וְאֵין כָּבוֹד אֶלָּא תוֹרָה ' שֶׁנֶּאֱמַר כָּבוֹד חֲכָמִים

read not. A formula of Rabbinic exegesis. It does not imply a doubt
as to the correctness of the Text. In this instance, only a change in a
vowel is suggested to produce a fine homiletic thought.

no man is free. He alone is truly free who knows and obeys the laws
of God. This is echoed in Milton's lines :

" Licence they mean when they cry Liberty ;
For who loves that, must first be wise and good."

Mattanah . . . Nachaliel . . . Bamoth. As words these place-names
mean " gift, heritage of God, heights ". The verse is thus interpreted :
" From the gift of the Torah, man gains a Divine heritage, and that
leads him to the heights of lofty ideals ".

3. *a single chapter.* Of the Bible or Mishna. This does not mean the
chapters into which the Text is now divided in printed Bibles. Those
are not older than the thirteenth century. The original chapter
division was more according to theme and subject matter.

rule. A statutory decision in Jewish Law.

verse. The shortest section of Scripture. Verse-division goes back
to antiquity.

God, and the writing was the writing of God, graven upon the tables. Read not *charuth* (graven) but *cheruth* (freedom), for no man is free but he who labours in the Torah. But whosoever labours in the Torah, behold he shall be exalted, as it is said, And from Mattanah to Nachaliel, and from Nachaliel to Bamoth.

Numbers
21 19

3. He who learns from his fellow a single chapter, a single rule, a single verse, a single expression, or even a single letter, ought to pay him honour; for so we find with David, King of Israel, who learnt only two things from Ahitophel, and yet regarded him as his master, his guide and his familiar friend, as it is said, But it was thou, a man, mine equal, my guide, and my familiar friend. Now, is it not an argument from minor to major? If David, the King of Israel, who learned only two things from Ahitophel, regarded him as his master, guide and familiar friend, how much more ought one who learns from his fellow a chapter, rule, verse, expression, or even a single letter, to pay him honour? And honour is nothing but Torah; as it is said,

Psalm 55. 14

expression. Whether it be in Biblical or rabbinical literature:

letter. In the case of a word concerning which there is a doubt in regard to spelling, or meaning.

only two things. The word *only* is puzzling, so is the peculiar argument. Commentators differ as to the two things which David learnt from Ahitophel, and their explanations are forced. Joseph Jaabez (fifteenth century), Midrash Shemuel (sixteenth century) and Chaim Walosin (nineteenth century) remarked on the logical incoherence of the reasoning. However, by a simple emendation, *shne debarim*, "two things", become one word, *shenidbarim*, which yields the meaning, "who only conversed together". According to the amended text, the reasoning is plain. If David the King showed honour to one of his subjects from whom he learnt nothing, but merely conversed with him, how much more is it the duty of an ordinary person to show honour to an equal from whom he *has* learnt aught of Torah. Strack, Oesterley, and Herford endorse the emendation, and declare that in this way all difficulties disappear; see Hertz, *Sermons* III, pp. 261–265.

and my familiar friend. The next verse continues; "we took sweet counsel together" (Psalm 55. 15).

argument from minor to major. The first of the thirteen exegetical rules of Rabbi Ishmael, p. 42.

יִנְחֲלוּ וּתְמִימִים יִנְחֲלוּ טוֹב ׳ וְאֵין טוֹב אֶלָּא תוֹרָה ׳ שֶׁנֶּאֱמַר

כִּי לֶקַח טוֹב נָתַתִּי לָכֶם תּוֹרָתִי אַל־תַּעֲזֹבוּ : (ד) כַּךְ הִיא

דַּרְכָּהּ שֶׁל־תּוֹרָה ׳ פַּת בְּמֶלַח תֹּאכֵל וּמַיִם בִּמְשׂוּרָה תִּשְׁתֶּה

וְעַל הָאָרֶץ תִּישָׁן וְחַיֵּי צַעַר תִּחְיֶה וּבַתּוֹרָה אַתָּה עָמֵל ׳ אִם־

אַתָּה עֹשֶׂה כֵּן אַשְׁרֶיךָ וְטוֹב לָךְ ׳ אַשְׁרֶיךָ בָּעוֹלָם הַזֶּה וְטוֹב

לָךְ לָעוֹלָם הַבָּא : (ה) אַל־תְּבַקֵּשׁ גְּדֻלָּה לְעַצְמֶךָ וְאַל־תַּחְמֹד

כָּבוֹד ׳ יוֹתֵר מִלִּמּוּדְךָ עֲשֵׂה ׳ וְאַל־תִּתְאַוֶּה לְשֻׁלְחָנָם שֶׁל־מְלָכִים ׳

שֶׁשֻּׁלְחָנְךָ גָּדוֹל מִשֻּׁלְחָנָם וְכִתְרְךָ גָּדוֹל מִכִּתְרָם ׳ וְנֶאֱמָן הוּא

בַּעַל מְלַאכְתְּךָ שֶׁיְּשַׁלֶּם לָךְ שְׂכַר פְּעֻלָּתֶךָ : (ו) גְּדוֹלָה תוֹרָה

יוֹתֵר מִן־הַכְּהֻנָּה וּמִן־הַמַּלְכוּת ׳ שֶׁהַמַּלְכוּת נִקְנֵית בִּשְׁלֹשִׁים

מַעֲלוֹת וְהַכְּהֻנָּה בְּעֶשְׂרִים וְאַרְבַּע וְהַתּוֹרָה נִקְנֵית בְּאַרְבָּעִים

וּשְׁמוֹנָה דְבָרִים ׳ וְאֵלּוּ הֵן ׳ בְּתַלְמוּד בִּשְׁמִיעַת הָאֹזֶן ׳ בַּעֲרִיכַת

---

4. *this is the way.* Such, this anonymous mishna declares is what
may have to be endured by those who devote themselves to its study.
This is asceticism, and the ascetic note is rare in Jewish literature.
Judaism preaches self-control, and not refusal to make moderate use
of the good things in life; see mishna 8.

morsel of bread with salt. Mentioned in the Talmud as the meal of the
poor.

of hardship. Or, " of privation ".

the while thou toilest in the Torah. Devoting most of his energies to
study, he earns only enough for his barest necessities. A man with
means, on the other hand, was not expected to impoverish himself and
live an ascetic life, while pursuing study.

happy shalt thou be. As in IV, 1.

5. On unworldly ambition.

seek not greatness for thyself. Cf. I, 10.

let thy deeds exceed thy learning. Cf. I, 17 ; III, 12.

table of kings. Laden though it be with costly foods.

thy table is greater than theirs. Because it is hallowed by the conversation on sacred themes ; see III, 4.

thy crown. Of the Torah (IV, 17). By his unworldly devotion to
the Torah, the pious increases reverence for it among men, and thus
spreads true religion and morality. Such a one is free from all lust for
personal glory and reputation (Beer).

Proverbs 3. 35 The wise shall inherit honour ; and the perfect shall inherit
Proverbs good. And good is nothing but Torah; as it is said, For I
28. 10
Proverbs 4. 2 give you good doctrine, forsake ye not my Torah.

4. This is the way that is becoming for the study of the
Torah : a morsel of bread with salt thou must eat, and water
by measure thou must drink; thou must sleep upon the
ground, and live a life of trouble the while thou toilest in
Psalm 128. 2 the Torah. If thou doest thus, Happy shalt thou be, and it
shall be well with thee; happy shalt thou be—in this world,
and it shall be well with thee—in the world to come.

5. Seek not greatness for thyself, and court not honour ;
let thy deeds exceed thy learning ; and crave not after the
table of kings ; for thy table is greater than theirs, and thy
crown is greater than theirs, and thy Employer is faithful
to pay thee the reward of thy work.

ACQUISI- 6. The Torah is greater than the priesthood and than
TION OF
THE royalty, seeing that royalty demands thirty qualifications,
TORAH the priesthood twenty-four, while the Torah is acquired by
forty-eight. And these are they : [1]By audible study ; by
distinct pronunciation ; by understanding and discernment
of the heart ; [5]by awe, reverence, meekness, cheerfulness ;

6. The Student of Religion.
demands thirty qualifications. Enumerated in tractate Sanhedrin ;
while those of the priesthood are deduced from Numbers 18. 8f.
[1]*audible study.* lit. " study with hearing of the ear ". Silent meditation would not leave the same imprint on the memory.
distinct pronunciation. Rehearsing the lessons aloud; the characteristic method of Torah-study among Jews.
understanding. See on III, 21 ; and on the wider meaning of "heart,"
II, 13.
discernment of the heart. Indicates a mind capable of grasping ideas,
and drawing fine distinctions.
[5]*awe.* In the disciple's attitude towards his master.
reverence. Of God, on the principle that " fear (reverence) of the
Lord is the beginning of wisdom " ; Psalm 111. 10.
meekness. See on VI, 1.
cheerfulness. In the performance of the commandments—*simchah
shel mitzvah.*

שְׂפָתַיִם • בְּבִינַת הַלֵּב • בְּשִׁכְלוּל הַלֵּב • בְּאֵימָה • בְּיִרְאָה •
בַּעֲנָוָה • בְּשִׂמְחָה • בְּשִׁמּוּשׁ חֲכָמִים • בְּדִבּוּק חֲבֵרִים • בְּפִלְפּוּל
הַתַּלְמִידִים • בְּיִשּׁוּב • בְּמִקְרָא וּבְמִשְׁנָה • בְּמִעוּט סְחוֹרָה •
בְּמִעוּט דֶּרֶךְ אֶרֶץ • בְּמִעוּט תַּעֲנוּג • בְּמִעוּט שֵׁנָה • בְּמִעוּט
שִׂיחָה • בְּמִעוּט שְׂחוֹק • בְּאֹרֶךְ אַפַּיִם • בְּלֶב־טוֹב • בֶּאֱמוּנַת
חֲכָמִים • בְּקַבָּלַת הַיִּסּוּרִים • הַמַּכִּיר אֶת־מְקוֹמוֹ • וְהַשָּׂמֵחַ
בְּחֶלְקוֹ • וְהָעוֹשֶׂה סְיָג לִדְבָרָיו • וְאֵינוֹ מַחֲזִיק טוֹבָה לְעַצְמוֹ •
אָהוּב • אוֹהֵב אֶת־הַמָּקוֹם • אוֹהֵב אֶת־הַבְּרִיּוֹת • אוֹהֵב אֶת־
הַצְּדָקוֹת • אוֹהֵב אֶת־הַמֵּישָׁרִים • אוֹהֵב אֶת־הַתּוֹכָחוֹת •
וּמִתְרַחֵק מִן־הַכָּבוֹד • וְלֹא־מֵגִיס לִבּוֹ בְּתַלְמוּדוֹ • וְאֵינוֹ שָׂמֵחַ
בְּהוֹרָאָה • נוֹשֵׂא בְּעֹל עִם־חֲבֵרוֹ • וּמַכְרִיעוֹ לְכַף זְכוּת •
וּמַעֲמִידוֹ עַל־הָאֱמֶת • וּמַעֲמִידוֹ עַל־הַשָּׁלוֹם • וּמִתְיַשֵּׁב

ministering to the sages. Heb. *shimmush*; close personal contact with an officiating Rabbi in order to learn religious practice.

[10]*attaching oneself to colleagues.* Studying with other disciples, and not alone; cf. I, 6.

sedateness. Calm and deliberate approach to study.

Scripture . . . Mishna. The essential foundation upon which Jewish religious knowledge is based. Ignorance of either disqualifies a teacher.

moderation in business. Cf. II, 6; IV, 12.

[15]*intercourse with the world.* Heb. *derech eretz* (II, 2).

pleasure. Cf. VI, 4.

sleep. See III, 14.

laughter. Cf. III, 17.

[20]*patience.* An indispensable requirement in all intellectual work.

good heart. Cf. II, 13.

faith in the wise. Confidence in the soundness of their instruction.

resignation under affliction. His sufferings do not weaken his faith in God and his devotion to the Torah. He realizes that the heart is purified, and the character uplifted, by sorrow; and that, far from being a sign of God's displeasure, affliction may be a proof of God's love (יסורין של אהבה).

by ministering to the sages, [10]by attaching oneself to colleagues, by discussion with pupils; by sedateness; by knowledge of the Scripture and of the Mishna; by moderation in business, [15]in intercourse with the world, in pleasure, in sleep, in conversation, in laughter; [20]by patience; by a good heart; by faith in the wise; by resignation under affliction; by recognising one's place, [25]rejoicing in one's portion, putting a fence to one's words, claiming no merit for oneself; by being beloved, loving the All-present, [30]loving mankind, loving just courses, rectitude and reproof; by keeping oneself far from honour; not boasting of one's learning, [35]nor delighting in giving decisions; by bearing the yoke with one's fellow, judging him favourably, and leading him to truth and peace; by [40]being composed in one's study;

Therefore must affliction be received in resignation; and the true Israelite blesses the Name of God for weal and for woe; see p. 87.

recognizing one's place. Inducing in him a spirit of humility. Cf. III, 1; IV, 4.

[25]*rejoicing in one's portion.* He is *happy* in his vocation, despite the privations of a student's life.

putting a fence to one's words. Cf. " Ye sages, be heedful of your words " (I, 11).

claiming no merit for oneself. Cf. II, 9.

being beloved. His character arouses affection in his fellow men; see III, 13.

loving the All-present. Only by loving the Giver of the Torah can he love the Torah itself.

[30]*loving mankind.* For this and the preceding two phrases, see VI, 1.

rectitude. Uprightness.

and reproof. Derived from Proverbs 9. 8, " Reprove a wise man, and he will love thee ".

far from honour. He shuns worldly fame.

not boasting of one's learning. One of the tests of humility. " Let another man praise thee, and not thine own mouth " (Proverbs 27. 2).

[35]*nor delighting in giving decisions.* Cf. IV, 9.

yoke with one's fellow. He can work *with* others, and helps his fellow in the acquisition of Torah and the performance of its duties.

judging him favourably. lit. " in the scale of merit "; see I, 6.

leading him to truth and peace. By helping his colleague to arrive at a just decision, not only is truth vindicated but peace is promoted.

[40]*composed in one's study.* He is calm and deliberate when acquiring knowledge.

בְּתַלְמוּדוֹ ‧ שׁוֹאֵל ‧ וּמֵשִׁיב ‧ שׁוֹמֵעַ וּמוֹסִיף ‧ הַלּוֹמֵד עַל־מְנָת

לְלַמֵּד ‧ וְהַלּוֹמֵד עַל־מְנָת לַעֲשׂוֹת ‧ הַמַּחְכִּים אֶת־רַבּוֹ ‧ וְהַמְכַוֵּן

אֶת־שְׁמוּעָתוֹ ‧ וְהָאוֹמֵר דָּבָר בְּשֵׁם אוֹמְרוֹ ‧ הָא לָמַדְתָּ כָּל־

הָאוֹמֵר דָּבָר בְּשֵׁם אוֹמְרוֹ מֵבִיא גְאֻלָּה לָעוֹלָם ‧ שֶׁנֶּאֱמַר וַתֹּאמֶר

אֶסְתֵּר לַמֶּלֶךְ בְּשֵׁם מָרְדֳּכָי : (ז) גְּדוֹלָה תוֹרָה שֶׁהִיא נוֹתֶנֶת

חַיִּים לְעוֹשֶׂיהָ בָּעוֹלָם הַזֶּה וּבָעוֹלָם הַבָּא ‧ שֶׁנֶּאֱמַר כִּי־חַיִּים

הֵם לְמֹצְאֵיהֶם וּלְכָל־בְּשָׂרוֹ מַרְפֵּא ‧ וְאוֹמֵר רִפְאוּת תְּהִי לְשָׁרֶּךָ

וְשִׁקּוּי לְעַצְמוֹתֶיךָ ‧ וְאוֹמֵר עֵץ־חַיִּים הִיא לַמַּחֲזִיקִים בָּהּ

וְתֹמְכֶיהָ מְאֻשָּׁר ‧ וְאוֹמֵר כִּי לִוְיַת חֵן הֵם לְרֹאשֶׁךָ וַעֲנָקִים

לְגַרְגְּרֹתֶךָ ‧ וְאוֹמֵר תִּתֵּן לְרֹאשְׁךָ לִוְיַת־חֵן עֲטֶרֶת תִּפְאֶרֶת

תְּמַגְּנֶךָ ‧ וְאוֹמֵר כִּי בִי יִרְבּוּ יָמֶיךָ וְיוֹסִיפוּ לְךָ שְׁנוֹת חַיִּים ‧

וְאוֹמֵר אֹרֶךְ יָמִים בִּימִינָהּ בִּשְׂמֹאולָהּ עֹשֶׁר וְכָבוֹד ‧ וְאוֹמֵר

כִּי אֹרֶךְ יָמִים וּשְׁנוֹת חַיִּים וְשָׁלוֹם יוֹסִיפוּ לָךְ : (ח) רַבִּי

---

asking and answering. To be understood as in v, 10, " he questions
according to the subject matter, and answers to the point ".

adding thereto. The same word as in " he who does not increase his
knowledge, decreases it " (i, 13).

⁴⁵*teaching . . . practising.* See IV, 6.

making one's master wiser. On the principle expressed in the saying
of Rabbi Judah the Prince, " Much have I learned from my teachers,
more from my colleagues, and most of all from my pupils ".

fixing attention upon his discourse. Since instruction was oral, it
was of the utmost importance that the pupil should have an exact
report of it in his memory, otherwise he would transmit it to others in
an inaccurate version.

in the name of. Unless he did so, he would be credited with a
statement which he had not originated, and thereby he would be
" *stealing* the good opinion of men ". Verify your citations, and
acknowledge your indebtedness to your sources—is the counsel to
modern students.

in the name of Mordecai. The fact that Mordecai's name had been
mentioned in Esther's report of the plot to assassinate the king, had a

by asking and answering, hearing and adding thereto; by learning with the object of teaching, and [45]by learning with the object of practising ; by making one's master wiser, fixing attention upon his discourse, and reporting a thing in the name of him who said it. So thou hast learnt, Whosoever reports a thing in the name of him that said it brings

Esther 2. 22 deliverance into the world; as it is said, And Esther told the king in the name of Mordecai.

7. Great is the Torah which gives life to those that practise it in this world and in the world to come, as it is

Proverbs 4. 22 said, For they are life unto those that find them, and health

Proverbs 3. 8 to all their flesh ; and it says, It shall be health to thy navel,

Proverbs 3. 18 and marrow to thy bones ; and it says, It is a tree of life to them that grasp it, and of them that uphold it every one is

Proverbs 1. 9 rendered happy ; and it says, For they shall be a chaplet of grace unto thy head, and chains about thy neck ; and it

Proverbs 4. 9 says, It shall give to thine head a chaplet of grace; a crown

Proverbs 9. 11 of glory it shall deliver to thee ; and it says, For by me thy days shall be multiplied, and the years of thy life shall be

Proverbs 3. 16 increased ; and it says, Length of days is in its right hand ;

Proverbs 3. 2 in its left hand are riches and honour ; and it says, For length of days, and years of life, and peace shall they add to thee.

determining influence upon subsequent events; Esther 6. 2f. It led to the fall of Haman, and the salvation of the Jews in Persia.

This mishna, a continuation of the panegyric in praise of Torah in the opening mishna of this chapter, gives in essence the noblest ethical ideals of Aboth. Alongside the formal qualifications of the student—which shows how serious and sacred a thing was religious study to the Rabbis of old—"magnanimous" virtues are proclaimed as essential qualities, and these are such as are to be desired by all men, whatever their creed. Among these qualities are, love of God and man, cheerfulness, love of mercy, truthfulness, humility, peacefulness ; in a word, " a good heart " (II, 9).

7. A continuation of the theme in the preceding mishna.

they are life. Referring to the words of wisdom, *i.e.* Torah. Similarly in the other quotations from Proverbs, Wisdom and Torah are identified.

24

שִׁמְעוֹן בֶּן־יְהוּדָה מִשֵּׁם רַבִּי שִׁמְעוֹן בֶּן־יוֹחַי אוֹמֵר ' הַנּוֹי
וְהַכֹּחַ וְהָעֹשֶׁר וְהַכָּבוֹד וְהַחָכְמָה וְהַזִּקְנָה וְהַשֵּׂיבָה וְהַבָּנִים
נָאֶה לַצַּדִּיקִים וְנָאֶה לָעוֹלָם ' שֶׁנֶּאֱמַר עֲטֶרֶת תִּפְאֶרֶת שֵׂיבָה
בְּדֶרֶךְ צְדָקָה תִּמָּצֵא ' וְאוֹמֵר תִּפְאֶרֶת בַּחוּרִים כֹּחָם וַהֲדַר
זְקֵנִים שֵׂיבָה ' וְאוֹמֵר עֲטֶרֶת חֲכָמִים עָשְׁרָם ' וְאוֹמֵר עֲטֶרֶת
זְקֵנִים בְּנֵי בָנִים וְתִפְאֶרֶת בָּנִים אֲבוֹתָם ' וְאוֹמֵר וְחָפְרָה
הַלְּבָנָה וּבוֹשָׁה הַחַמָּה כִּי־מָלַךְ יְיָ צְבָאוֹת בְּהַר צִיּוֹן וּבִירוּשָׁלַם
וְנֶגֶד זְקֵנָיו כָּבוֹד : רַבִּי שִׁמְעוֹן בֶּן־מְנַסְיָא אוֹמֵר ' אֵלּוּ שֶׁבַע
מִדּוֹת שֶׁמָּנוּ חֲכָמִים לַצַּדִּיקִים כֻּלָּם נִתְקַיְּמוּ בְּרַבִּי וּבְבָנָיו :

(ט) אָמַר רַבִּי יוֹסֵי בֶּן־קִסְמָא ' פַּעַם אַחַת הָיִיתִי מְהַלֵּךְ בַּדֶּרֶךְ
וּפָגַע בִּי אָדָם אֶחָד וְנָתַן־לִי שָׁלוֹם וְהֶחֱזַרְתִּי לוֹ שָׁלוֹם ' אָמַר
לִי ' רַבִּי מֵאֵי־זֶה מָקוֹם אָתָּה ' אָמַרְתִּי לוֹ־מֵעִיר גְּדוֹלָה שֶׁל־
חֲכָמִים וְשֶׁל־סוֹפְרִים אָנִי ' אָמַר לִי ' רַבִּי רְצוֹנְךָ שֶׁתָּדוּר עִמָּנוּ
בִּמְקוֹמֵנוּ וַאֲנִי אֶתֵּן לְךָ אֶלֶף אֲלָפִים דִּינְרֵי זָהָב וַאֲבָנִים טוֹבוֹת
וּמַרְגָּלִיּוֹת ' אָמַרְתִּי לוֹ־אִם אַתָּה נוֹתֵן לִי כָּל־כֶּסֶף וְזָהָב וַאֲבָנִים
טוֹבוֹת וּמַרְגָּלִיּוֹת שֶׁבָּעוֹלָם אֵינִי דָר אֶלָּא בִּמְקוֹם תּוֹרָה ' וְכֵן
כָּתוּב בְּסֵפֶר תְּהִלִּים עַל־יְדֵי דָוִד מֶלֶךְ יִשְׂרָאֵל ' טוֹב לִי תוֹרַת

8. *Simeon, the son of Judah.* A disciple of R. Simeon ben Yochai
(III, 4; IV, 17). This mishna presents the life of the righteous under an
aspect quite different from that in mishna 4.

beauty . . . children. Eight adornments are enumerated, whereas
the number is given as seven at the end of the paragraph. Elijah, the
Gaon of Wilna, omits "wisdom", because it is not referred to in the
Biblical quotations. The Palestinian Talmud omits "old age".

Simeon, the son of Menasya. Contemporary of R. Simeon ben Judah.
9. The incomparable worth of the Torah.

José, the son of Kisma. Colleague of R. Chananya ben Teradyon
(III, 3). He did not join in the revolt under Bar Cochba, and remained
undisturbed by the Roman authorities in the terrible persecutions that

8. R. Simeon, the son of Judah, in the name of R. Simeon, the son of Yochai, said, Beauty, strength, riches, honour, wisdom, (old age,) a hoary head, and children, are comely to the righteous and comely to the world ; as it *Proverbs* 16. 31 is said, The hoary head is a crown of glory, if it be found in *Proverbs* 20. 29 the way of righteousness ; and it says, The glory of young men is their strength, and the adornment of old men is the *Proverbs* 14. 24 hoary head ; and it says, A crown unto the wise is their *Proverbs* 17. 6 riches ; and it says, Children's children are the crown of old men, and the adornment of children are their fathers , *Isaiah* 24. 23 and it is said, Then the moon shall be confounded and the sun ashamed ; for the Lord of hosts shall reign in Mount Zion and in Jerusalem, and before his elders shall be glory.

R. Simeon, the son of Menasya, said, These seven qualifications which the sages enumerated as becoming to the righteous, were all realised in Rabbi Judah the Prince, and in his sons.

9. R. José, the son of Kisma, said, I was once walking by the way, when a man met me and greeted me, and I returned his greeting. He said to me, Rabbi, from what place art thou ? I said to him, I come from a great city of sages and scribes. He said to me, If thou art willing to dwell with us in our place, I will give thee a thousand thousand golden dinars and precious stones and pearls. I said to him, Wert thou to give me all the silver and gold and precious stones and pearls in the world, I would not dwell anywhere but in a home of the Torah ; and thus it is written in the

followed. His saying is the only personal experience related in the first person in the six chapters (1, 17 is only an apparent exception).
   greeted me. lit. " gave me peace ". The Jewish greeting is *sholom aleychem,* " Peace be unto thee " ; and the reply is *aleychem sholom,* " unto thee be peace ".
   great city. Probably Yavneh.
   willing to dwell with us. The man was anxious to secure the Rabbi as a teacher to his community. The phrase, " a thousand thousand golden dinars " is equivalent to, " Ask whatever you wish ".
   home of the Torah. As in IV, 18. José was evidently not the *born* teacher or missionary ; he was purely the student and scholar type.

פִּיד מֵאַלְפֵי זָהָב וָכֶסֶף ' וְלֹא עוֹד אֶלָּא שֶׁבִּשְׁעַת פְּטִירָתוֹ שֶׁל

אָדָם אֵין מְלַוִּים לוֹ לְאָדָם לֹא כֶסֶף וְלֹא זָהָב וְלֹא אֲבָנִים טוֹבוֹת

וּמַרְגָּלִיּוֹת אֶלָּא תוֹרָה וּמַעֲשִׂים טוֹבִים בִּלְבָד ' שֶׁנֶּאֱמַר

בְּהִתְהַלֶּכְךָ תַּנְחֶה אֹתָךְ בְּשָׁכְבְּךָ תִּשְׁמֹר עָלֶיךָ וַהֲקִיצוֹתָ הִיא

תְשִׂיחֶךָ ' בְּהִתְהַלֶּכְךָ תַּנְחֶה אֹתָךְ בָּעוֹלָם הַזֶּה בְּשָׁכְבְּךָ

תִּשְׁמֹר עָלֶיךָ בַּקֶּבֶר וַהֲקִיצוֹתָ הִיא תְשִׂיחֶךָ לָעוֹלָם הַבָּא '

וְאוֹמֵר לִי הַכֶּסֶף וְלִי הַזָּהָב נְאֻם יְיָ צְבָאוֹת : (י) חֲמִשָּׁה

קִנְיָנִים קָנָה לוֹ הַקָּדוֹשׁ בָּרוּךְ הוּא בְּעוֹלָמוֹ וְאֵלוּ הֵן ' תוֹרָה

קִנְיָן אֶחָד שָׁמַיִם וָאָרֶץ קִנְיָן אֶחָד קִנְיָן אַבְרָהָם קִנְיָן אֶחָד יִשְׂרָאֵל

קִנְיָן אֶחָד בֵּית הַמִּקְדָּשׁ קִנְיָן אֶחָד : תוֹרָה מִנַּיִן ' דִּכְתִיב יְיָ

קָנָנִי רֵאשִׁית דַּרְכּוֹ קֶדֶם מִפְעָלָיו מֵאָז : שָׁמַיִם וָאָרֶץ מִנַּיִן '

דִּכְתִיב כֹּה אָמַר יְיָ הַשָּׁמַיִם כִּסְאִי וְהָאָרֶץ הֲדֹם רַגְלָי אִי-זֶה

בַיִת אֲשֶׁר תִּבְנוּ-לִי וְאִי-זֶה מָקוֹם מְנוּחָתִי ' וְאוֹמֵר מָה רַבּוּ

מַעֲשֶׂיךָ יְיָ כֻּלָּם בְּחָכְמָה עָשִׂיתָ מָלְאָה הָאָרֶץ קִנְיָנֶךָ : אַבְרָהָם

the silver is mine. The meaning is : All the treasures of the world are at God's disposal. If He wills me to have a share in them, He will bestow them upon me while I reside in the home of the Torah.

10. An anonymous number-saying, like those in Chapter v. It is included here because the Torah is one of the special Possessions mentioned herein.

made especially his own. While He created the universe in its entirety, the claim is made in Rabbinic literature that there are certain things which " He made especially His own ". In one version, the number is three : Torah, Israel and the Sanctuary ; here, " Abraham " and " heaven and earth " are added. Nowhere else is the total increased to five.

Abraham. The Gaon of Wilna deleted the word, since the corresponding proof-text (see below) is not suitable.

Psàlm 119. 72 Book of Psalms by the hands of David, King of Israel, The law of thy mouth is better unto me than thousands of gold and silver ; and not only so, but in the hour of man's departure neither silver nor gold nor precious stones nor pearls accompany him, but only Torah and good works, as it is *Proverbs* 4. 22 said, When thou walkest it shall lead thee ; when thou liest down it shall watch over thee ; and when thou awakest it shall talk with thee :—when thou walkest it shall lead thee— in this world ; when thou liest down it shall watch over thee—in the grave ; and when thou awakest it shall talk *Haggai* 2. 8 with thee—in the world to come. And it says, The silver is mine, and the gold is mine, saith the Lord of hosts.

10. Five ‚possessions the Holy One, blessed be he, made especially his own in his world, and these are they, The Torah, heaven and earth, Abraham, Israel, and the Holy Temple. Whence know we this of the Torah ? *Proverbs* 8. 22 Because it is written, The Lord possessed me as the beginning of his way, before his works, from of old. Whence of *Isaiah* 66. 1 heaven and earth ? Because it is written, Thus saith the Lord, The heaven is my throne, and the earth is my footstool : what manner of house will ye build unto me ? and *Psalm* 104. 24 what manner of place for my rest ? and it says, How manifold are thy works, O Lord ! In wisdom hast thou made them all : the earth is full of thy possessions. Whence *Genesis* 14. 19 of Abraham ? Because it is written, And he blessed him, and said, Blessed be Abram of the Most High God, Master of heaven and earth. Whence of Israel ? Because it is *Exodus* 15. 16 written, Till thy people pass over, O Lord, till the people *Psalm* 16. 3 pass over which thou hast acquired ; and it says, As for

---

possessed me. Wisdom, *i.e.* Torah.

how manifold are thy works. A second text is added, because it includes the keyword " possession ", which is absent in the first.

and he blessed him. According to the Gaon of Wilna, this provides a third proof-text for " heaven and earth " as a " possession ".

מִנַּיִן ' דִּכְתִיב וַיְבָרֲכֵהוּ וַיֹּאמַר בָּרוּךְ אַבְרָם לְאֵל עֶלְיוֹן קֹנֵה

שָׁמַיִם וָאָרֶץ : יִשְׂרָאֵל מִנַּיִן ' דִּכְתִיב עַד־יַעֲבֹר עַמְּךָ יְיָ עַד־

יַעֲבֹר עַם־זוּ קָנִיתָ ' וְאוֹמֵר לִקְדוֹשִׁים אֲשֶׁר־בָּאָרֶץ הֵמָּה וְאַדִּירֵי

כָּל־חֶפְצִי בָם : בֵּית הַמִּקְדָּשׁ מִנַּיִן ' דִּכְתִיב מָכוֹן לְשִׁבְתְּךָ

פָּעַלְתָּ יְיָ מִקְדָשׁ אֲדֹנָי כּוֹנֲנוּ יָדֶיךָ ' וְאוֹמֵר וַיְבִיאֵם אֶל־גְּבוּל

קָדְשׁוֹ הַר זֶה קָנְתָה יְמִינוֹ : (יא) כֹּל מַה־שֶׁבָּרָא הַקָּדוֹשׁ בָּרוּךְ

הוּא בְּעוֹלָמוֹ לֹא בְרָאוֹ אֶלָּא לִכְבוֹדוֹ ' שֶׁנֶּאֱמַר כֹּל הַנִּקְרָא

בִשְׁמִי וְלִכְבוֹדִי בְּרָאתִיו יְצַרְתִּיו אַף עֲשִׂיתִיו : וְאוֹמֵר ' יְיָ ׀

יִמְלֹךְ לְעֹלָם וָעֶד :

רַבִּי חֲנַנְיָא בֶּן־עֲקַשְׁיָא וכו׳

עָלֵינוּ, *p.* 550.

קַדִּישׁ יָתוֹם, *p.* 554.

---

the saints. lit. " holy ones ", denoting Israel as the people hallowed
by the Torah, and sanctified by its commandments.

11. *whatsoever the Holy One, blessed be he, created.* This final paragraph supplements the preceding. Not only the things there specified
were created by God for His purpose. The *whole* universe is a witness
to God's greatness and glory, and the Selection of Israel was for the
accomplishment of a design which embraced the entire human race ;
viz., the acknowledgment of the Divine Sovereignty by all His creatures.
In the Prayer Book, this sublime aspiration is uttered at the conclusion
of each Service, when the verse, " The Lord shall reign for ever and
ever ", is followed by the Prophet's declaration : " The Lord shall be
King over all the earth ; in that day shall the Lord be One, and His
name One " ; (see p. 210).

the saints that are in the earth, they are the noble ones in whom is all my delight.   Whence of the Holy Temple ?

Exodus 15. 17 Because it is written, The place, O Lord, which thou hast made for thee to dwell in, the sanctuary, O Lord, which *Psalm* 71 54 thy hands have prepared ; and it says, And he brought them to the border of his sanctuary, to this mountain which his might had acquired.

11. Whatsoever the Holy One, blessed be he, created *Isaiah* 43. 7 in his world he created but for his glory, as it is said Everything that is called by my Name, it is for my glory I have created it, I have formed it, yea, I have made it ; and *Exodus* 15. 18 it says, The Lord shall reign for ever and ever.

"Rabbi Chananya," etc., p. 627.

Oleynu, p. 551.

Mourner's Kaddish, p. 555.

OLEYNU. The reading of one of the chapters of Aboth in the synagogue precedes Oleynu and Mourner's Kaddish in the Sabbath Afternoon Service.

In many manuscripts of Aboth, as well as in early editions, there are additional endings, either in this chapter or the preceding one. The most beautiful of these, and especially appropriate because chapter VI opens with a saying of Rabbi Meir, is the following : "When Rabbi Meir concluded the reading of the Book of Job, he said, ' It is the destiny of man to die, and of cattle to be slaughtered; and all are doomed to death. Happy is he who was reared in Torah, and who toils in Torah ; who by his life causes joy of spirit to his Maker ; who advances in good repute, and departs this world with a good name " (Talmud).

FROM THE JEWISH MORALISTS—SECOND SELECTION.

Extracts from Jewish ethical literature have formed a favourite reading of the devout on Sabbaths and Festivals even more than on weekdays ; see pp. 260–263 and 1112–1115. The following selections are from :

   V.   *A Father's Admonition,* by Moses Maimonides (died 1204) ;
   VI.   *Sefer Chassidim,* by R. Judah the Pious (died 1217) ;
   VII. *Rokëach,* by R. Elazar of Worms (died 1238) ;
   VIII. *Semag,* by R. Moses of Coucy (13th century) ; and
   IX.   *Orchoth Tzaddikim* (" The Way of the Righteous "), a Book of
         Morals (15th century).

V.

Fear the Lord the God of thy Fathers and serve Him in love, for fear only restrains a man from sin, while love stimulates him to good. Accustom thyself to habitual goodness, for a man's character is what habit makes it.

If thou find in the Torah or the Prophets or the Sages a hard saying which thou canst not grasp, stand fast by thy faith and attribute the fault to thine own intelligence. Place it in a corner of your heart for future consideration, but despise not thy Religion because thou art unable to understand one difficult matter.

Love truth and uprightness—the ornaments of the soul—and cleave unto them ; prosperity so obtained is built on a sure rock. Keep firmly to thy word ; let not a legal contract or witnesses be more binding than thine verbal promise, whether in public or in private. Disdain reservations and subterfuges, evasions and sharp practices. Woe to him who builds his house upon them. Abhor inactivity and indolence, the causes of bodily destruction, of penury, of self-contempt—the ladders of Satan and his satellites.

Defile not your souls by quarrelsomeness and petulance. I have seen the white become black, the low brought still lower, families driven into exile, princes deposed from their high estate, great cities laid in ruins, assemblies dispersed, the pious humiliated, the honourable held lightly and despised—all on account of quarrelsomeness. Glory in forbearance, for in that is true strength and victory.

VI.

Mislead no one through thy actions designedly, be he Jew or non-Jew. Injustice must be done to none, whether he belong to our Religion or to another.

If thou seest a strange man of another Faith about to commit sin, prevent its coming to pass if it be in thy power, and herein let the prophet Jonah be thy model.

No blessing rests on the money of people who clip coin, make a practice of usury, use false weights and measures, and are in general not honest in business ; their children lose their homes at last, and have to beg for bread. Worthy of punishment is he, too, who heaps excessive burdens on the carryirfg beast, beats and tortures it. A sick or breeding beast should be tenderly dealt with.

When thou findest thyself among people who jeer and gibe, leave them as quickly as thou canst ; for mockery leads to want of respect for one's self and others, and that is the high road to an unchaste life.

Parents must on no account whatever strike a grown-up son, curse him, or so move him to wrath that he forget himself and with whom he is dealing.

On the Day of the Judgment, those who are of kindred virtue and merit, will find themselves in lasting companionship with one another. The father then ceases to mourn and grieve over the son that had left him ; for the ineffable delight felt in the radiance of God's countenance, will send into oblivion all the anguish of earthly life.

VII.

My son, wholly incompatible with a humble spirit is loud and passionate talk, falsehood, uttering of oaths, mockery, unrestrained desire, vengefulness.

Cease to exalt thyself in thine own estimation; and let none of thy failings appear small or trifling in thine own eyes, but all of them weighty and great.

Keep far from all unseemly things ; close thine eyes, thy ears to them with stern decision ; for there be desires which cause the soul to be apostate from God. Therefore, in the days when thou art still young, think of the Heavenly Father who created thee, supported thee, clothed thee ; and requite Him not, ungrateful, by delivering up thy soul to impurity.

Remain faithful to the Torah : deny thyself even many things that are permitted ; be, so far as thou canst, ever of cheerful and joyous temper ; and forget not that it is to God, God Eternal, God the Only One, to Whom thy soul returns in death.

VIII.

Those who lie freely to non-Jews and steal from them, are worse than ordinary criminals. They are *blasphemers* ; for it is due to their guilt, that some say, " Jews have no binding law, no moral standards."

He who is but a novice in the fear of God will do well to say audibly each day, as he rises :

" This day will I be a faithful servant of the Almighty ; be on my guard against wrath, falsehood, hatred, quarrelsomeness ; will look not too closely at women, and forgive those who wound me ". For whoso forgives is forgiven in turn. Hard-heartedness and a temper that will not make up quarrels, are a heavy burden of sin, unworthy of an Israelite.

IX.

The thread on which the different good qualities of human beings are strung as pearls, is the fear of God. When the fastenings of this fear are unloosed, the pearls roll in all directions, and are lost one by

עַרְבִית לְמוֹצָאֵי שַׁבָּת:

תהלים קמ'ד

לְדָוִד ׀ בָּרוּךְ יְהֹוָה צוּרִי הַמְלַמֵּד יָדַי לַקְרָב
אַצְבְּעוֹתַי לַמִּלְחָמָה: חַסְדִּי וּמְצוּדָתִי מִשְׂגַּבִּי וּמְפַלְטִי־
לִי מָגִנִּי וּבוֹ חָסִיתִי הָרוֹדֵד עַמִּי תַחְתָּי: יְהֹוָה מָה־
אָדָם וַתֵּדָעֵהוּ בֶּן־אֱנוֹשׁ וַתְּחַשְּׁבֵהוּ: אָדָם לַהֶבֶל דָּמָה
יָמָיו כְּצֵל עוֹבֵר: יְהֹוָה הַט־שָׁמֶיךָ וְתֵרֵד גַּע בֶּהָרִים
וְיֶעֱשָׁנוּ: בְּרוֹק בָּרָק וּתְפִיצֵם שְׁלַח חִצֶּיךָ וּתְהֻמֵּם:

one. Even a single grave moral fault may be the ruin of all other
advantages; as when, for example, one is always setting off his own
excellence by bringing into prominence his neighbour's failings. Never
put in words anything which can call up a blush on thine own cheek
or make another's grow pale.

Be not blind, but open-eyed, to the great wonders of Nature, familiar,
everyday objects though they be to thee. But men are more wont
to be astonished at the sun's eclipse than at his unfailing rise.

SERVICE FOR THE CONCLUSION OF THE SABBATH

Long before Gaonic times, the service for the Conclusion of the
Sabbath seems to have been preceded by the reading of Psalms. Just
as the coming of Queen Sabbath was welcomed with psalmody and

SERVICE FOR THE CONCLUSION OF SABBATH

Psalm cxliv. [1]A Psalm of David.

GOD'S
BLESSINGS
IN WAR
AND
PEACE

Blessed be the Lord my rock, who teacheth my hands to war, and my fingers to fight : [2]my lovingkindness, and my fortress, my stronghold, and my deliverer ; my shield, and he in whom I take refuge : who subdueth peoples under me. [3]Lord, what is man, that thou regardest him ? or the son of man, that thou takest account of him ? [4]Man is like to vanity : his days are as a shadow that passeth away. [5]Bow thy heavens, O Lord, and come down : touch the mountains, and they shall smoke. [6]Flash forth lightning, and scatter them ; send out thine arrows, and

sacred song, even so she was accompanied on her outgoing. In our Rite, Psalms 144 and 67 are chanted.

The Evening Service is read at a later hour than usual, in order " to add from the profane to the holy ". Folk-lore supplied a touching reason for such delay. The wicked are released from Hell with the coming of the Sabbath : by delaying the official ending of the Sabbath, we prolong the freedom of the forlorn souls from the torments to which they are doomed ! We may regret the superstition evidenced by such belief, but must admire the kindliness and deep humanity it evidences.

PSALM 144.

This Psalm, sung to a joyful traditional tune in a major key, " typifies the joy in work, characteristic of Judaism. It invokes God's protecting hand in the imminent week-day struggle that follows the Sabbath calm " (Abrahams).

1–2. God's protection in War and Peace.

2. *subdueth peoples.* lit. " subdueth my people ". According to the Massorah, this is one of the three places in Scripture where *ammi* ("my people ") is written, whilst *ammim*, " peoples " is expected. Targum and most Jewish commentators translate it as a plural.

3–4. Man's transitoriness only renders God's gracious care more wonderful ; cf. Psalm 8, p. 319.

4. *vanity.* lit. " a breath ".

as a shadow that passeth away. " Life is a passing shadow, says Scripture. Is it the shadow or of a tower, or of a tree ? A shadow that prevails for a while ? No, it is the shadow of a bird in its flight—away flies the bird, and soon there is neither bird nor shadow " (Midrash).

5–8. Prayer that God appear in His majesty and deliver him from his enemies.

שְׁלַח יָדֶיךָ מִמָּרוֹם פְּצֵנִי וְהַצִּילֵנִי מִמַּיִם רַבִּים מִיַּד

בְּנֵי־נֵכָר : אֲשֶׁר־פִּיהֶם דִּבֶּר־שָׁוְא וִימִינָם יְמִין שָׁקֶר :

אֱלֹהִים שִׁיר חָדָשׁ אָשִׁירָה לָּךְ בְּנֵבֶל עָשׂוֹר אֲזַמְּרָה־

לָּךְ : הַנּוֹתֵן תְּשׁוּעָה לַמְּלָכִים הַפּוֹצֶה אֶת־דָּוִד עַבְדּוֹ

מֵחֶרֶב רָעָה : פְּצֵנִי וְהַצִּילֵנִי מִיַּד בְּנֵי־נֵכָר אֲשֶׁר־

פִּיהֶם דִּבֶּר־שָׁוְא וִימִינָם יְמִין שָׁקֶר : אֲשֶׁר בָּנֵינוּ

כִּנְטִעִים מְגֻדָּלִים בִּנְעוּרֵיהֶם בְּנוֹתֵינוּ כְזָוִיּוֹת מְחֻטָּבוֹת

תַּבְנִית הֵיכָל : מְזָוֵינוּ מְלֵאִים מְפִיקִים מִזַּן אֶל זַן

צֹאונֵנוּ מַאֲלִיפוֹת מְרֻבָּבוֹת בְּחוּצוֹתֵינוּ : אַלּוּפֵינוּ מְסֻבָּלִים

אֵין פֶּרֶץ וְאֵין יוֹצֵאת וְאֵין צְוָחָה בִּרְחֹבֹתֵינוּ : אַשְׁרֵי

הָעָם שֶׁכָּכָה לּוֹ אַשְׁרֵי הָעָם שֶׁיְהוָה אֱלֹהָיו :

8. *their right hand.* Their hand uplifted to swear·an oath, is a perjured hand (Rashi).

9–11. Repeated prayer and praise. Whatever comes to man in his warfare, is of God's doing.

9. *a harp of ten strings.* He would give God a *full* sound of praise, even as in the psalm welcoming the Sabbath, 92. 4.

10. *salvation.* Victory.

hurtful sword. lit. " the evil sword ", the sword which is in service of evil men.

12–15. His prayerful hope ; Israel, blessed of the Lord, recognizes that all victory and prosperity comes from God.

12. *our sons . . . as plants.* Rooted in their own land, and carefully trained from youth.

corner-pillars. The poet compares tall and slender young womanhood to palace-cornices adorned with artistically carved work, richly coloured.

14. *our princes.* Heb. אלופינו. This is Rashi's translation followed by many moderns, Jewish and non-Jewish ; cf. Genesis 36. 15 and

confuse them. ⁷Stretch forth thine hands from above ; rescue me, and deliver me out of great waters, out of the hand of strangers ; ⁸whose mouth speaketh deceit, and their right hand is a right hand of falsehood. ⁹I will sing a new song unto thee, O God : upon a harp of ten strings will I sing praises unto thee. ¹⁰It is he that giveth salvation unto kings : who rescueth David his servant from the hurtful sword. ¹¹Rescue me, and deliver me out of the hand of strangers, whose mouth speaketh deceit and their right hand is a right hand of falsehood :—¹²That our sons shall be as plants grown tall in their youth, and our daughters as corner-pillars hewn after the fashion of a palace ; ¹³when our garners are full, affording all manner of store, and our sheep bring forth by thousands, yea, are multiplied by tens of thousands in our fields ; ¹⁴when our princes bear their burdens ; when there is no breach and no surrender, and no lamentation in our streets ; ¹⁵happy is the people, that is thus favoured : yea, happy is the people whose God is the Lord.

Exodus 15. 15. The Rabbis refer it to the *spiritual leaders* of the generation.

bear their burden. Cf. Numbers 11, 11 where Moses speaks to God, " Thou layest the burden of all this people upon me ".

no breach. In the city-walls : or, " no breaking-in·"—no raids by the enemy.

no surrender. Or, " going forth into captivity ". Under strong and loyal rulers, the nation will be safe. Tradition gives a purely religious explanation of these two Heb. phrases ; namely, there will be no moral revolt (פְּרִיצוֹת) among the young.

no lamentation. Of the women and children at the departure of fathers and husbands ; or " no panic ", at surprise by the enemy.

15. *happy is the people.* To whom God shows such token of His love.

whose God is the Lord. The acme of Israel's good fortune is the spiritual blessing of its existence as a holy nation, blessed in the knowledge that the God of Justice, Mercy and Truth, is Israel's God.

תהלים ס'ז

לַמְנַצֵּחַ בִּנְגִינֹת מִזְמוֹר שִׁיר : אֱלֹהִים יְחָנֵּנוּ וִיבָרְכֵנוּ

יָאֵר פָּנָיו אִתָּנוּ סֶלָה : לָדַעַת בָּאָרֶץ דַּרְכֶּךָ בְּכָל־

גּוֹיִם יְשׁוּעָתֶךָ : יוֹדוּךָ עַמִּים ׀ אֱלֹהִים יוֹדוּךָ עַמִּים כֻּלָּם :

יִשְׂמְחוּ וִירַנְּנוּ לְאֻמִּים כִּי־תִשְׁפֹּט עַמִּים מִישֹׁר וּלְאֻמִּים

בָּאָרֶץ תַּנְחֵם סֶלָה · יוֹדוּךָ עַמִּים ׀ אֱלֹהִים יוֹדוּךָ עַמִּים

כֻּלָּם : אֶרֶץ נָתְנָה יְבוּלָהּ יְבָרְכֵנוּ אֱלֹהִים אֱלֹהֵינוּ :

יְבָרְכֵנוּ אֱלֹהִים וְיִירְאוּ אוֹתוֹ כָּל־אַפְסֵי־אָרֶץ :

For מַעֲרִיב see pp. 302—316. עֲמִידָה, pp. 274—294. חֲצִי קַדִּישׁ, p. 422.

Should a Festival occur on any work-day of the following week, וִיהִי נֹעַם and וְאַתָּה קָדוֹשׁ are not said. If ט' בְּאָב commences at the termination of the Sabbath, וִיהִי נֹעַם is omitted. In the house of an אָבֵל begin יֵשֵׁב בְּסֵתֶר .

וִיהִי נֹעַם אֲדֹנָי אֱלֹהֵינוּ עָלֵינוּ וּמַעֲשֵׂה יָדֵינוּ כּוֹנְנָה

עָלֵינוּ וּמַעֲשֵׂה יָדֵינוּ כּוֹנְנֵהוּ :

PSALM 67.
THANKSGIVING TO GOD.

God's hand is traced both in the nation's History, and in the processes of Nature ; and He is praised as the God of the whole earth, as well as of Israel.

2. *gracious . . . bless . . . cause to shine.* These phrases are taken from the Priestly Blessing.

3. *salvation among all nations.* The sight of Israel's blessedness will gently bring the other nations to the true Religion. " If Israel has the light of God's face, the world cannot remain in darkness. Israel can show that he possesses this light by the manner in which he bears himself during the days of business and activity that are ensuing " (Abrahams).

Psalm lxvii. [1]For the Chief Musician ; on Neginoth. A Psalm. A Song.

THANKS-
GIVING
TO GOD
BY ALL
THE
NATIONS

[2]May God be gracious unto us, and bless us ; may he cause his face to shine upon us. (Selah.) [3]That thy way may be known upon the earth, thy salvation among all nations. [4]Let the peoples give thanks unto thee, O God ; let all the peoples give thanks unto thee. [5]O let the nations rejoice and exult : for thou wilt judge the peoples with equity, and lead the nations upon the earth. (Selah.) [6]Let the peoples give thanks unto thee, O God ; let all the peoples give thanks unto thee. [7]The earth hath yielded her increase : God, even our God, shall bless us. [8]God shall bless us ; and all the ends of the earth shall fear him.

For Evening Service see pp. 303–317.

Amidah, pp. 275–295.

Kaddish, p. 423.

Should a Festival occur on any work-day of the following week, the passages from " And let the graciousness " to " and to glorify it " p. 735 are not said. If the Fast of the Ninth of Av commences at the termination of the Sabbath, the first of these passages is omitted. In a house of mourning begin, " He that dwelleth," etc. p. 731.

Psalm 90. 17

And let the graciousness of the Lord our God be upon us : and establish thou the work of our hands upon us ; yea, the work of our hands do thou establish.

---

5. *wilt judge.* God will act as the final universal Judge, and rescue the peoples from the injustice that is rife in the world.

lead. All nations are under the Providential guidance of God.

7. *yielded her increase.* The Psalm was suggested by a prosperous harvest. With the Psalmist, prosperity lifts the eye from earth to heaven, and Israel's blessing is to be a blessing for all men.

The ordinary week-day Evening Service now follows. The only change occurs in Benediction IV of the Eighteen Benedictions. This incorporates a farewell greeting to the departed Sabbath. It stresses the " separation " between holy and profane, light and darkness, Israel and heathen nations, the Sabbath and work-days ; and continues with a prayer that the coming week may be passed in peace, in freedom from sin, and in attachment to the fear of God ; see p. 278.

צ׳א יֵשֵׁב בְּסֵתֶר עֶלְיוֹן בְּצֵל שַׁדַּי יִתְלוֹנָן : אֹמַר לַיהוָֹה
מַחְסִי וּמְצוּדָתִי אֱלֹהַי אֶבְטַח־בּוֹ : כִּי הוּא יַצִּילְךָ מִפַּח
יָקוּשׁ מִדֶּבֶר הַוּוֹת : בְּאֶבְרָתוֹ יָסֶךְ לָךְ וְתַחַת כְּנָפָיו
תֶּחְסֶה צִנָּה וְסֹחֵרָה אֲמִתּוֹ : לֹא־תִירָא מִפַּחַד לָיְלָה
מֵחֵץ יָעוּף יוֹמָם : מִדֶּבֶר בָּאֹפֶל יַהֲלֹךְ מִקֶּטֶב יָשׁוּד
צָהֳרָיִם : יִפֹּל מִצִּדְּךָ אֶלֶף וּרְבָבָה מִימִינֶךָ אֵלֶיךָ לֹא
יִגָּשׁ : רַק בְּעֵינֶיךָ תַבִּיט וְשִׁלֻּמַת רְשָׁעִים תִּרְאֶה : כִּי־
אַתָּה יְהוָֹה מַחְסִי עֶלְיוֹן שַׂמְתָּ מְעוֹנֶךָ : לֹא־תְאֻנֶּה אֵלֶיךָ
רָעָה וְנֶגַע לֹא־יִקְרַב בְּאָהֳלֶךָ : כִּי מַלְאָכָיו יְצַוֶּה־לָּךְ
לִשְׁמָרְךָ בְּכָל־דְּרָכֶיךָ : עַל־כַּפַּיִם יִשָּׂאוּנְךָ פֶּן תִּגֹּף בָּאֶבֶן
רַגְלֶךָ : עַל־שַׁחַל וָפֶתֶן תִּדְרֹךְ תִּרְמֹס כְּפִיר וְתַנִּין : כִּי
בִי חָשַׁק וַאֲפַלְּטֵהוּ אֲשַׂגְּבֵהוּ כִּי־יָדַע שְׁמִי : יִקְרָאֵנִי
וְאֶעֱנֵהוּ עִמּוֹ אָנֹכִי בְצָרָה אֲחַלְּצֵהוּ וַאֲכַבְּדֵהוּ : אֹרֶךְ
יָמִים אַשְׂבִּיעֵהוּ וְאַרְאֵהוּ בִּישׁוּעָתִי : *Repeat the last verse.*

וְאַתָּה קָדוֹשׁ יוֹשֵׁב תְּהִלּוֹת יִשְׂרָאֵל : וְקָרָא
זֶה אֶל־זֶה וְאָמַר קָדוֹשׁ קָדוֹשׁ קָדוֹשׁ יְיָ צְבָאוֹת
מְלֹא כָל־הָאָרֶץ כְּבוֹדוֹ : וּמְקַבְּלִין דֵּן מִן־דֵּן וְאָמְרִין

PSALM 91.

This Psalm was known as מזמור של ברכה, the Psalm of Blessing;
hence its selection as the inaugural Psalm for the new week. It is preceded by verse 17 of Psalm 90, the traditional verse with which Moses
blessed the workers when the Tabernacle had been completed. Some
consider the reading of Psalm 91, to be a survival of the Scriptural
Readings and Discourses at the Conclusion of the Sabbath that were at
one time the rule. Hence the repetition of the *Kedusha-dε-Sidra* ("But
thou art holy," see p. 203).

Psalm xci.

ASSUR-
ANCE OF
DIVINE
PROTEC-
TION
[1]He that dwelleth in the shelter of the Most High abideth under the shadow of the Almighty. [2]I say of the Lord, He is my refuge and my fortress; my God, in whom I trust. —[3]For he shall deliver thee from the snare of the fowler, and from the noisome pestilence. [4]He shall cover thee with his pinions, and under his wings shalt thou take refuge : his truth shall be a shield and armour. [5]Thou shalt not be afraid of the terror by night, nor of the arrow that flieth by day ; [6]of the pestilence that stalketh in darkness, nor of the destruction that ravageth at noonday. [7]A thousand may fall at thy side, and ten thousand at thy See p. 71 right hand, yet it shall not come nigh unto thee. [8]Only with thine eyes shalt thou look on, and see the retribution of the wicked.—[9]For thou, O Lord, art my refuge.—Thou hast made the Most High thy dwelling place ; [10]there shall no evil befall thee, neither shall any scourge come nigh thy tent. [11]For he shall give his angels charge over thee, to keep thee in all thy ways. [12]They shall bear thee upon their hands, lest thou strike thy foot against a stone. [13]Thou shalt tread upon the lion and the adder ; upon the young lion and the serpent shalt thou trample.—[14]Because he hath set his love upon me, therefore will I deliver him : I will set him on high, because he knoweth my Name. [15]When he calleth upon me, I will answer him ; I will be with him in trouble : I will deliver him and honour him. [16]With length of days will I satisfy him, and will let him see my salvation.

Repeat the last verse.

Psalm 22. 4

Isaiah 6. 3

A KE-
DUSHAH

See p. 203

Ezekiel 3. 12
But thou art holy, O thou that dwellest amid the praises of Israel. And one cried unto another, and said, Holy, holy, holy is the Lord of hosts : the whole earth is full of his glory. *And they receive sanction the one from the other, and say, Holy in the highest heavens, the place of his divine abode ; holy upon earth, the work of his might ; holy for ever and to all eternity is the Lord of hosts ; the whole earth is full of the radiance of his glory. Then a wind lifted me up, and I heard behind me

*The Aramaic paraphrase of the preceding verse.

קַדִּישׁ בִּשְׁמֵי מְרוֹמָא עִלָּאָה בֵּית שְׁכִינָתֵהּ · קַדִּישׁ עַל־
אַרְעָא עוֹבַד גְּבוּרְתֵּהּ · קַדִּישׁ לְעָלַם וּלְעָלְמֵי עָלְמַיָּא · יְיָ
צְבָאוֹת מַלְיָא כָל־אַרְעָא זִיו יְקָרֵהּ : וַתִּשָּׂאֵנִי רוּחַ וָאֶשְׁמַע
אַחֲרַי קוֹל רַעַשׁ גָּדוֹל בָּרוּךְ כְּבוֹד־יְיָ מִמְּקוֹמוֹ : וּנְטָלַתְנִי
רוּחָא וְשִׁמְעֵת בַּתְרַי קָל זִיעַ שַׂגִּיא דִּי מְשַׁבְּחִין וְאָמְרִין ·
בְּרִיךְ יְקָרָא דִי יְיָ מֵאֲתַר בֵּית שְׁכִינָתֵהּ : יְיָ ׀ יִמְלֹךְ לְעֹלָם
וָעֶד : יְיָ מַלְכוּתֵהּ קָאֵם לְעָלַם וּלְעָלְמֵי עָלְמַיָּא : יְיָ אֱלֹהֵי
אַבְרָהָם יִצְחָק וְיִשְׂרָאֵל אֲבוֹתֵינוּ · שָׁמְרָה־זֹּאת לְעוֹלָם
לְיֵצֶר מַחְשְׁבוֹת לְבַב עַמֶּךָ וְהָכֵן לְבָבָם אֵלֶיךָ : וְהוּא רַחוּם
יְכַפֵּר עָוֹן וְלֹא יַשְׁחִית וְהִרְבָּה לְהָשִׁיב אַפּוֹ וְלֹא יָעִיר כָּל־
חֲמָתוֹ : כִּי־אַתָּה אֲדֹנָי טוֹב וְסַלָּח וְרַב־חֶסֶד לְכָל־קֹרְאֶיךָ :
צִדְקָתְךָ צֶדֶק לְעוֹלָם וְתוֹרָתְךָ אֱמֶת : תִּתֵּן אֱמֶת לְיַעֲקֹב
חֶסֶד לְאַבְרָהָם אֲשֶׁר־נִשְׁבַּעְתָּ לַאֲבֹתֵינוּ מִימֵי קֶדֶם : בָּרוּךְ
אֲדֹנָי יוֹם ׀ יוֹם יַעֲמָס־לָנוּ הָאֵל יְשׁוּעָתֵנוּ סֶלָה : יְיָ צְבָאוֹת
עִמָּנוּ מִשְׂגָּב־לָנוּ אֱלֹהֵי יַעֲקֹב סֶלָה : יְיָ צְבָאוֹת אַשְׁרֵי
אָדָם בֹּטֵחַ בָּךְ : יְיָ הוֹשִׁיעָה · הַמֶּלֶךְ יַעֲנֵנוּ בְיוֹם־קָרְאֵנוּ ·

בָּרוּךְ אֱלֹהֵינוּ שֶׁבְּרָאָנוּ לִכְבוֹדוֹ וְהִבְדִּילָנוּ מִן־הַתּוֹעִים
וְנָתַן לָנוּ תּוֹרַת אֱמֶת וְחַיֵּי עוֹלָם נָטַע בְּתוֹכֵנוּ · הוּא
יִפְתַּח לִבֵּנוּ בְּתוֹרָתוֹ וְיָשֵׂם בְּלִבֵּנוּ אַהֲבָתוֹ וְיִרְאָתוֹ
וְלַעֲשׂוֹת רְצוֹנוֹ וּלְעָבְדוֹ בְּלֵבָב שָׁלֵם · לְמַעַן לֹא נִיגַע לָרִיק
וְלֹא נֵלֵד לַבֶּהָלָה : יְהִי רָצוֹן מִלְּפָנֶיךָ יְיָ אֱלֹהֵינוּ וֵאלֹ

the voice of a great rushing (saying), Blessed be the glory of the Lord from his place. *Then a wind lifted me up, and I heard behind me the voice of a great rushing, of those who uttered praises, and said, Blessed be the glory of the Lord from *Exodus* 15. 18 the region of his divine abode. The Lord shall reign for ever and ever. *The kingdom of the Lord endureth for ever and to all eternity.

PRAYER
FOR
FIDELITY
TO GOD

O Lord, the God of Abraham, of Isaac and of Israel, our fathers, keep this for ever as the inward thought in the *II Chronicles* heart of thy people, and direct their heart unto thee. 29. 18
Psalm 78. 38 And he, being merciful, forgiveth iniquity and destroyeth not : yea, many a time he turneth his anger away, and doth *Psalm* 86. 5 not stir up all his wrath. For thou, O Lord, art good and forgiving, and abounding in lovingkindness to all them that *Psalm* 119. 142 call upon thee. Thy righteousness is an everlasting right-*Micah* 7. 20 eousness, and thy Torah is truth. Thou wilt show truth to Jacob and lovingkindness to Abraham, according as thou *Psalm* 68. 20 hast sworn unto our fathers from the days of old. Blessed be the Lord, day by day he beareth our burden, even the *Psalm* 46. 8 God who is our salvation. (Selah.) The Lord of hosts is with us ; the God of Jacob is our stronghold. (Selah.) *Psalm* 84, 13 O Lord of hosts, happy is the man who trusteth in thee. *Psalm* 21. 10 Save, Lord : may the King answer us on the day when we call.

AND
LOYALTY
TO THE
TORAH

Blessed is our God, who hath created us for his glory, and hath separated us from them that go astray, and hath given us the Torah of truth and planted everlasting life in our midst. May he open our heart unto his Teaching, and place his love and fear within our hearts, that we may do his will and serve him with an undivided heart, that we may not labour in vain, nor bring forth for confusion. May it be thy will, O Lord our God and God of our fathers, that we may keep thy statutes in this world, and be worthy to live to witness and inherit happiness and blessing in the days of the Messiah *Psalm* 30. 13 and in the life of the world to come. To the end that my glory may sing praise unto thee, and not be silent : O Lord

*The Aramaic paraphrase of the preceding verse.

אֲבוֹתֵינוּ · שֶׁנִּשְׁמוֹר חֻקֶּיךָ בָּעוֹלָם הַזֶּה · וְנִזְכֶּה וְנִחְיֶה
וְנִרְאֶה וְנִירַשׁ טוֹבָה וּבְרָכָה לִשְׁנֵי יְמוֹת הַמָּשִׁיחַ וּלְחַיֵּי
הָעוֹלָם הַבָּא : לְמַעַן יְזַמֶּרְךָ כָבוֹד וְלֹא יִדֹּם · יְיָ אֱלֹהַי
לְעוֹלָם אוֹדֶךָּ : בָּרוּךְ הַגֶּבֶר אֲשֶׁר יִבְטַח בַּיְיָ וְהָיָה יְיָ
מִבְטַחוֹ : בִּטְחוּ בַיְיָ עֲדֵי־עַד כִּי בְּיָהּ יְיָ צוּר עוֹלָמִים :
וְיִבְטְחוּ בְךָ יוֹדְעֵי שְׁמֶךָ כִּי לֹא־עָזַבְתָּ דֹרְשֶׁיךָ יְיָ :
יְיָ חָפֵץ לְמַעַן צִדְקוֹ יַגְדִּיל תּוֹרָה וְיַאְדִּיר :

קַדִּישׁ תִּתְקַבֵּל, p. 206.

During סְפִירָה, *the Omer is counted here*; *and on* חֲנֻכָּה, *the lights are
here kindled by the Reader.*

וְיִתֶּן־לְךָ הָאֱלֹהִים מִטַּל הַשָּׁמַיִם וּמִשְׁמַנֵּי הָאָרֶץ וְרֹב דָּגָן
וְתִירֹשׁ : יַעַבְדוּךָ עַמִּים וְיִשְׁתַּחֲווּ לְךָ לְאֻמִּים הֱוֵה גְבִיר
לְאַחֶיךָ וְיִשְׁתַּחֲווּ לְךָ בְּנֵי אִמֶּךָ אֹרְרֶיךָ אָרוּר וּמְבָרֲכֶיךָ
בָּרוּךְ : וְאֵל שַׁדַּי יְבָרֵךְ אֹתְךָ וְיַפְרְךָ וְיַרְבֶּךָ וְהָיִיתָ לִקְהַל
עַמִּים : וְיִתֶּן־לְךָ אֶת־בִּרְכַּת אַבְרָהָם לְךָ וּלְזַרְעֲךָ אִתָּךְ
לְרִשְׁתְּךָ אֶת־אֶרֶץ מְגֻרֶיךָ אֲשֶׁר־נָתַן אֱלֹהִים לְאַבְרָהָם :
מֵאֵל אָבִיךָ וְיַעְזְרֶךָּ וְאֵת שַׁדַּי וִיבָרֲכֶךָּ בִּרְכֹת שָׁמַיִם מֵעָל
בִּרְכֹת תְּהוֹם רֹבֶצֶת תָּחַת בִּרְכֹת שָׁדַיִם וָרָחַם : בִּרְכֹת
אָבִיךָ גָּבְרוּ עַל־בִּרְכֹת הוֹרַי עַד־תַּאֲוַת גִּבְעֹת עוֹלָם תִּהְיֶיןָ,

everlasting rock. Lit. " rock of ages."

AND GOD GIVE THEE. This is a collection of joyful assurances of
Divine blessing, deliverance, peace and consolation—all of them words
of happy augury with which to begin the new week of toil and labour.

(a) Verses of BLESSING. Taken from the blessings bestowed by
Isaac on Jacob; from Jacob's blessing of Joseph and his brethren;
and from Moses' Farewell Address and Song to Israel.

Jeremiah 17. 7 my God, I will give thanks unto thee for ever. Blessed is the
man that trusteth in the Lord, and whose trust the Lord is.
Isaiah 26. 4 Trust ye in the Lord for ever ; for the Lord is God, an
Psalm 9. 11 everlasting rock. And they that know thy Name will put
their trust in thee ; for thou hast not forsaken them that
Isaiah 42. 21 seek thee, Lord. It pleased the Lord,·for his righteousness'
sake, to magnify the Torah and to glorify it.

Kaddish, p. 207.

SCRIP-   *During Sephirah, the Omer is counted here ; and*
TURAL   *on Chanukah, the lights are here kindled by the Reader.*
VERSES
OF "BLESS-   And God give thee of the dew of heaven, and of the fatness of
ING"   the earth, and plenty of corn and wine : let peoples serve thee, and
Genesis   nations bow down to thee : be lord over thy brethren, and let thy
27. 28, 29   mother's sons bow down to thee : cursed be every one that curseth
Genesis 28. 3, 4 thee, and blessed be every one that blesseth thee. And God Almighty
                  bless thee, and make thee fruitful, and multiply thee, that thou
ASSUR-   mayest be a company of peoples ; and give thee the blessing of
ANCE OF
DIVINE   Abraham, to thee, and to thy seed with thee ; that thou mayest
PROTEC-   inherit the land of thy sojournings, which God gave unto Abraham.
TION
Genesis   From the God of thy father—may he help thee,—and the Almighty
49. 25, 26   —may he bless thee with blessings of the heavens above, blessings
                  of the deep that coucheth beneath, blessings of the breasts and the
                  womb. The blessings of thy father are mighty beyond the blessings
                  of my progenitors unto the utmost bound of the everlasting hills :
Deuteronomy   may they be on the head of Joseph, and on the crown of the head
7. 13–15   of him that is prince among his brethren. And he will love thee, and
                  bless thee, and multiply thee : he will also bless the fruit of thy
                  body and the fruit of thy ground, thy corn and thy wine and thine

> *dew of heaven and . . . fatness of the earth.* Note that the heavenly
> blessings *precede* those of earth. In our weekday life, men too often
> invert the order, or even altogether confine their efforts to toil for the
> fat things of earth.
> *blessing of Abraham.* Which was first of all a spiritual blessing, *i.e.*
> whole-souled surrender to the will of God.
> *blessings of thy father.* The blessings received by Jacob greatly sur-
> passed those that were bestowed on his father ; it is the enhanced
> blessings that Jacob bestowed on **Joseph.**

לְרֹאשׁ יוֹסֵף וּלְקָדְקֹד נְזִיר אֶחָיו : וַאֲהֵבְךָ וּבֵרַכְךָ וְהִרְבֶּךָ
וּבֵרַךְ פְּרִי־בִטְנְךָ וּפְרִי־אַדְמָתֶךָ דְּגָנְךָ וְתִירֹשְׁךָ וְיִצְהָרֶךָ שְׁגַר־
אֲלָפֶיךָ וְעַשְׁתְּרֹת צֹאנֶךָ עַל הָאֲדָמָה אֲשֶׁר־נִשְׁבַּע לַאֲבֹתֶיךָ
לָתֶת לָךְ : בָּרוּךְ תִּהְיֶה מִכָּל־הָעַמִּים לֹא־יִהְיֶה בְךָ עָקָר
וַעֲקָרָה וּבִבְהֶמְתֶּךָ : וְהֵסִיר יְיָ מִמְּךָ כָּל־חֹלִי וְכָל־מַדְוֵי
מִצְרַיִם הָרָעִים אֲשֶׁר יָדַעְתָּ לֹא יְשִׂימָם בָּךְ וּנְתָנָם בְּכָל־
שֹׂנְאֶיךָ :

הַמַּלְאָךְ הַגֹּאֵל אֹתִי מִכָּל־רָע יְבָרֵךְ אֶת־הַנְּעָרִים וְיִקָּרֵא בָהֶם
שְׁמִי וְשֵׁם אֲבֹתַי אַבְרָהָם וְיִצְחָק וְיִדְגּוּ לָרֹב בְּקֶרֶב הָאָרֶץ : יְיָ
אֱלֹהֵיכֶם הִרְבָּה אֶתְכֶם וְהִנְּכֶם הַיּוֹם כְּכוֹכְבֵי הַשָּׁמַיִם לָרֹב :
יְיָ אֱלֹהֵי אֲבוֹתֵכֶם יֹסֵף עֲלֵיכֶם כָּכֶם אֶלֶף פְּעָמִים וִיבָרֵךְ אֶתְכֶם
כַּאֲשֶׁר דִּבֶּר לָכֶם :

בָּרוּךְ אַתָּה בָּעִיר וּבָרוּךְ אַתָּה בַּשָּׂדֶה : בָּרוּךְ אַתָּה בְּבֹאֶךָ
וּבָרוּךְ אַתָּה בְּצֵאתֶךָ : בָּרוּךְ טַנְאֲךָ וּמִשְׁאַרְתֶּךָ : בָּרוּךְ פְּרִי־
בִטְנְךָ וּפְרִי אַדְמָתְךָ וּפְרִי בְהֶמְתֶּךָ שְׁגַר אֲלָפֶיךָ וְעַשְׁתְּרוֹת
צֹאנֶךָ : יְצַו יְיָ אִתְּךָ אֶת־הַבְּרָכָה בַּאֲסָמֶיךָ וּבְכֹל מִשְׁלַח יָדֶךָ
וּבֵרַכְךָ בָּאָרֶץ אֲשֶׁר־יְיָ אֱלֹהֶיךָ נֹתֵן לָךְ : יִפְתַּח יְיָ לְךָ אֶת־
אוֹצָרוֹ הַטּוֹב אֶת־הַשָּׁמַיִם לָתֵת מְטַר־אַרְצְךָ בְּעִתּוֹ וּלְבָרֵךְ אֵת
כָּל־מַעֲשֵׂה יָדֶךָ וְהִלְוִיתָ גּוֹיִם רַבִּים וְאַתָּה לֹא־תִלְוֶה : כִּי־
יְהוָה אֱלֹהֶיךָ בֵּרַכְךָ כַּאֲשֶׁר דִּבֶּר־לָךְ וְהַעֲבַטְתָּ גּוֹיִם רַבִּים

---

let my name be named on them. May they be worthy of having their
names coupled with the name of Israel ; see note p. 402.

oil, the offspring of thy kine and the young of thy flock in the land which he sware unto thy fathers to give thee. Thou shalt be blessed above all peoples : there shall not be male or female barren among you, or among your cattle. And the Lord will take away from thee all sickness ; and he will put none of the evil diseases of Egypt, which thou knowest, upon thee, but will lay them upon all them that hate thee.

Genesis 48. 16 The angel who hath redeemed me from all evil, bless the lads ; and let my name be named on them, and the name of my fathers Abraham and Isaac ; and let them grow into a multitude in the

Deuteronomy 1. 10, 11 midst of the earth. The Lord your God hath multiplied you, and behold ye are this day as the stars of heaven for multitude. The Lord, the God of your fathers, make you a thousand times so many more as you are, and bless you, as he hath promised you.

Deuteronomy 28. 3
Deuteronomy 28. 6
Deuteronomy 28. 5
Deuteronomy 28. 4
Deuteronomy 28. 8
 Blessed shalt thou be in the city, and blessed shalt thou be in the field. Blessed shalt thou be when thou comest in, and blessed shalt thou be when thou goest out. Blessed shall be thy basket and thy kneading-trough. Blessed shall be the fruit of thy body, and the fruit of thy ground, and the fruit of thy cattle, the offspring of thy kine, and the young of thy flock. The Lord shall command the blessing upon thee in thy barns, and in all that thou puttest thine hand unto ; and he shall bless thee in the land which the Lord thy

Deuteronomy 28. 12 God giveth thee. The Lord shall open unto thee his good treasury, the heavens, to give the rain of thy land in its season, and to bless all the work of thy hand : and thou shalt lend unto many nations,

Deuteronomy 15. 6 but thou shalt not borrow. For the Lord thy God will bless thee, as he promised thee : and thou shalt lend unto many nations, but thou shalt not borrow ; and thou shalt rule over many nations, but

Deuteronomy 33. 29 they shall not rule over thee. Happy art thou, O Israel : who is

blessed shalt thou . . . goest out. These are six forms of blessing, covering crops, cattle and daily bread, as well as the blessing of safety in all the manifold activities of daily life. " Mayest thou at thy going out from the world be as sinless as thou wast at thy coming into the world " (Rashi).

lend unto many nations. A sign of power and of independence, and yet not the highest of blessings. Israelites began to engage in commerce in the days of King Solomon. Through no fault of their own, Jews have been divorced from agriculture and confined to commerce for over

וְאַתָּה לֹא תֵעָזֵב וּמָשַׁלְתָּ בְּגוֹיִם רַבִּים וּבְךָ לֹא יִמְשֹׁלוּ:
אַשְׁרֶיךָ יִשְׂרָאֵל מִי כָמוֹךָ עַם נוֹשַׁע בַּיְיָ מָגֵן עֶזְרֶךָ וַאֲשֶׁר־
חֶרֶב גַּאֲוָתֶךָ וְיִכָּחֲשׁוּ אֹיְבֶיךָ לָךְ וְאַתָּה עַל־בָּמוֹתֵימוֹ תִדְרֹךְ:
מָחִיתִי כָעָב פְּשָׁעֶיךָ וְכֶעָנָן חַטֹּאתֶיךָ שׁוּבָה אֵלַי כִּי
גְאַלְתִּיךָ: רָנּוּ שָׁמַיִם כִּי־עָשָׂה יְיָ הָרִיעוּ תַּחְתִּיּוֹת אָרֶץ פִּצְחוּ
הָרִים רִנָּה יַעַר וְכָל־עֵץ בּוֹ כִּי־גָאַל יְיָ יַעֲקֹב וּבְיִשְׂרָאֵל יִתְפָּאָר:
גֹּאֲלֵנוּ יְיָ צְבָאוֹת שְׁמוֹ קְדוֹשׁ יִשְׂרָאֵל:

יִשְׂרָאֵל נוֹשַׁע בַּיְיָ תְּשׁוּעַת עוֹלָמִים לֹא־תֵבֹשׁוּ וְלֹא־תִכָּלְמוּ
עַד־עוֹלְמֵי עַד: וַאֲכַלְתֶּם אָכוֹל וְשָׂבוֹעַ וְהִלַּלְתֶּם אֶת־שֵׁם יְיָ
אֱלֹהֵיכֶם אֲשֶׁר־עָשָׂה עִמָּכֶם לְהַפְלִיא וְלֹא־יֵבֹשׁוּ עַמִּי לְעוֹלָם:
וִידַעְתֶּם כִּי בְקֶרֶב יִשְׂרָאֵל אָנִי וַאֲנִי יְיָ אֱלֹהֵיכֶם וְאֵין עוֹד וְלֹא־
יֵבֹשׁוּ עַמִּי לְעוֹלָם: כִּי־בְשִׂמְחָה תֵצֵאוּ וּבְשָׁלוֹם תּוּבָלוּן הֶהָרִים
וְהַגְּבָעוֹת יִפְצְחוּ לִפְנֵיכֶם רִנָּה וְכָל־עֲצֵי הַשָּׂדֶה יִמְחֲאוּ־כָף:
הִנֵּה אֵל יְשׁוּעָתִי אֶבְטַח וְלֹא אֶפְחָד כִּי עָזִּי וְזִמְרָת יָהּ יְיָ
וַיְהִי־לִי לִישׁוּעָה: וּשְׁאַבְתֶּם־מַיִם בְּשָׂשׂוֹן מִמַּעַיְנֵי הַיְשׁוּעָה:
וַאֲמַרְתֶּם בַּיּוֹם הַהוּא הוֹדוּ לַיְיָ קִרְאוּ בִשְׁמוֹ הוֹדִיעוּ בָעַמִּים
עֲלִילֹתָיו הַזְכִּירוּ כִּי נִשְׂגָּב שְׁמוֹ: זַמְּרוּ יְיָ כִּי גֵאוּת עָשָׂה
מוּדַעַת זֹאת בְּכָל־הָאָרֶץ: צַהֲלִי וָרֹנִּי יוֹשֶׁבֶת צִיּוֹן כִּי־גָדוֹל
בְּקִרְבֵּךְ קְדוֹשׁ יִשְׂרָאֵל: וְאָמַר בַּיּוֹם הַהוּא הִנֵּה אֱלֹהֵינוּ זֶה

1,500 years. However, commerce is not their native bent; as is
evidenced by the fact that, in recent generations, leadership has almost
everywhere been wrested from them by the non-Jewish newcomers in
industrial and financial enterprise.

(b) Verses of REDEMPTION AND SALVATION, expressing joy over
Divine help to Israel.

as a cloud. Symbol of transitoriness.

like unto thee, a people saved by the Lord, the shield of thy help, and that is the sword of thy majesty! And thine enemies shall yield feigned obedience unto thee ; and thou shalt tread upon their high places.

Isaiah 44. 22, 23

VERSES OF "REDEMP-TION AND SALVA-TION"

Isaiah 47. 4

Isaiah 45. 17

Joel 2. 26, 27

Isaiah 55. 12

Isaiah 12. 2-6

Isaiah 25. 9

I have blotted out, as a cloud, thy transgressions, and, as a mist, thy sins ; return unto me, for I have redeemed thee. Sing, O ye heavens, for the Lord hath done it ; shout, ye nethermost parts of the earth ; break forth into singing, ye mountains, and forest, and every tree therein ; for the Lord hath redeemed Jacob, and will glorify himself in Israel. Our Redeemer, the Lord of hosts is his Name, the Holy One of Israel.

Israel is saved by the Lord with an everlasting salvation : ye shall not be put to shame nor confounded for ever and ever. And ye shall eat in plenty and be satisfied, and shall praise the Name of the Lord your God, that hath dealt wondrously with you : and my people shall never be put to shame. And ye shall know that I am in the midst of Israel, and that I am the Lord your God, and there is none else : and my people shall never be put to shame. For ye shall go out with joy, and be led forth with peace : the mountains and the hills shall break forth before you into singing, and all the trees of the field shall clap their hands. Behold, God is my salvation ; I will trust, and will not be afraid; for the Lord God is my strength and song ; and he is become my salvation. Therefore with joy shall ye draw water out of the wells of salvation. And in that day shall ye say, Give thanks unto the Lord, call upon his Name, declare his doings among the peoples, make mention that his Name is exalted. Sing unto the Lord ; for he hath done excellent things : this is made known in all the earth. Cry aloud and shout, thou inhabitant of Zion : for great is the Holy One of Israel in the midst of thee. And one shall say in that day, Lo, this is our God ; we have waited

sing, O ye heavens. The Prophet in a transport of jubilation calls on heaven and earth to rejoice over the marvellous redemption of Israel.

Holy One of Israel. This is Isaiah's favourite designation of God. It became the favourite term for God on the lips of the people down to this day—הקדוש ברוך הוא, "the Holy One, blessed be He". It admirably expresses the fundamental nature of the God Whom Israel proclaimed to the children of men.

shall clap their hands. See p. 56..

קִוִּינוּ לוֹ וְיוֹשִׁיעֵנוּ זֶה יְיָ קִוִּינוּ לוֹ נָגִילָה וְנִשְׂמְחָה בִּישׁוּעָתוֹ:

בֵּית יַעֲקֹב לְכוּ וְנֵלְכָה בְּאוֹר יְיָ: וְהָיָה אֱמוּנַת עִתֶּיךָ

חֹסֶן יְשׁוּעֹת חָכְמַת וָדָעַת יִרְאַת יְיָ הִיא אוֹצָרוֹ: וַיְהִי

דָוִד לְכָל־דְּרָכָו מַשְׂכִּיל וַיְיָ עִמּוֹ: פָּדָה בְשָׁלוֹם נַפְשִׁי מִקְּרָב־

לִי כִּי־בְרַבִּים הָיוּ עִמָּדִי: וַיֹּאמֶר הָעָם אֶל־שָׁאוּל הַיוֹנָתָן

יָמוּת אֲשֶׁר עָשָׂה הַיְשׁוּעָה הַגְּדוֹלָה הַזֹּאת בְּיִשְׂרָאֵל חָלִילָה

חַי־יְיָ אִם־יִפֹּל מִשַּׂעֲרַת רֹאשׁוֹ אַרְצָה כִּי־עִם־אֱלֹהִים עָשָׂה

הַיּוֹם הַזֶּה וַיִּפְדּוּ הָעָם אֶת־יוֹנָתָן וְלֹא־מֵת: וּפְדוּיֵי יְיָ יְשֻׁבוּן

וּבָאוּ צִיּוֹן בְּרִנָּה וְשִׂמְחַת עוֹלָם עַל־רֹאשָׁם שָׂשׂוֹן וְשִׂמְחָה

יַשִּׂיגוּ וְנָסוּ יָגוֹן וַאֲנָחָה: הָפַכְתָּ מִסְפְּדִי לְמָחוֹל לִי פִּתַּחְתָּ

שַׂקִּי וַתְּאַזְּרֵנִי שִׂמְחָה: וְלֹא־אָבָה יְיָ אֱלֹהֶיךָ לִשְׁמֹעַ אֶל־

בִּלְעָם וַיַּהֲפֹךְ יְיָ אֱלֹהֶיךָ לְּךָ אֶת־הַקְּלָלָה לִבְרָכָה כִּי אֲהֵבְךָ

יְיָ אֱלֹהֶיךָ: אָז תִּשְׂמַח בְּתוּלָה בְּמָחוֹל וּבַחֻרִים וּזְקֵנִים יַחְדָּו

וְהָפַכְתִּי אֶבְלָם לְשָׂשׂוֹן וְנִחַמְתִּים וְשִׂמַּחְתִּים מִיגוֹנָם:

בּוֹרֵא נִיב שְׂפָתָיִם שָׁלוֹם שָׁלוֹם לָרָחוֹק וְלַקָּרוֹב אָמַר יְיָ

וּרְפָאתִיו: וְרוּחַ לָבְשָׁה אֶת־עֲמָשַׂי רֹאשׁ הַשָּׁלִישִׁים לְךָ דָוִיד

וְעִמְּךָ בֶן־יִשַׁי שָׁלוֹם שָׁלוֹם לְךָ וְשָׁלוֹם לְעֹזְרֶךָ כִּי עֲזָרְךָ

אֱלֹהֶיךָ וַיְקַבְּלֵם דָוִיד וַיִּתְּנֵם בְּרָאשֵׁי הַגְּדוּד: וַאֲמַרְתֶּם כֹּה

לֶחָי וְאַתָּה שָׁלוֹם וּבֵיתְךָ שָׁלוֹם וְכֹל אֲשֶׁר־לְךָ שָׁלוֹם:

יְיָ עֹז לְעַמּוֹ יִתֵּן יְיָ יְבָרֵךְ אֶת־עַמּוֹ בַשָּׁלוֹם:

in the light of the Lord. In the light of His revelation and teaching.
abundance . . . treasure. "A right religious attitude is the true
strength of the nation, and the pledge of its deliverance from all dangers"
(Skinner).

(c) Verses of RESCUE AND "TURNING OF FORTUNE".

and the rescued. This is the culminating verse of a beautiful prophecy
of Restoration from exile.

for him that he should save us : this is the Lord ; we have waited for him, let us be glad and rejoice in his salvation.

Isaiah 2. 5   O house of Jacob, come ye, and let us walk in the light of the
Isaiah 33. 6   Lord. And abundance of salvation, wisdom and knowledge shall be the stability of thy times : the fear of the Lord is his treasure.
I. Samuel 18. 14   And David prospered in all his ways ; and the Lord was with him.
Psalm 55. 12   He hath rescued my soul in peace so that none might come nigh
I. Samuel 14. 45   me, for they were many that were striving with me. And the people
VERSES OF said unto Saul, Shall Jonathan die who hath wrought this great
"RESCUE salvation in Israel ? Far be it ; as the Lord liveth, there shall not
AND *TURNING* one hair of his head fall to the ground ; for he hath wrought with
OF *FORTUNE"* God this day. So the people rescued Jonathan that he died not.
Isaiah 35. 10 And the rescued of the Lord shall return, and come with singing unto Zion ; and everlasting joy shall be upon their heads : they shall obtain gladness and joy, and sorrow and sighing shall flee
Psalm 30. 12   away. Thou hast turned for me my mourning into dancing ; thou
Deuteronomy 18. 6   hast loosed my sackcloth and girded me with gladness. And the Lord thy God would not hearken unto Balaam ; but the Lord thy God turned the curse into a blessing unto thee, because the Lord
Jeremiah 31. 13   thy God loved thee. Then shall the virgin rejoice in the dance, and the young men and the old together ; for I will turn their mourning into joy, and will comfort them, and make them rejoice from their sorrow.

Isaiah 57. 19   He createth the fruit of the lips : Peace, peace to him that is far off and to him that is near, saith the Lord, and I will heal him.
I. Chronicles 12. 18   Then the spirit came upon Amasai, who was chief of the captains (and he said), Thine are we, David, and on thy side, O son of Jesse ;
OF *"PEACE"*   peace, peace be unto thee, and peace be to him that helpeth thee ; for thy God helpeth thee. Then David received them, and made
I. Samuel 25. 6   them chiefs of the band. And thus ye shall say, All hail, and peace be unto thee, and peace be to thy house, and peace be unto all that
Psalm 29. 11   thou hast. The Lord will give strength unto his people ; the Lord will bless his people with peace.

(d) Verses of Peace.
fruit of the lips. Praise and thanksgiving.
all hail. Heb. כה לחי. According to Isaiah Trani, a renowned thirteenth century exegete, לחי is an abbreviation of לאחי, " to my brother ".

אָמַר רַבִּי יוֹחָנָן בְּכָל־מָקוֹם שֶׁאַתָּה מוֹצֵא גְּדֻלָּתוֹ שֶׁל־
הַקָּדוֹשׁ בָּרוּךְ הוּא שָׁם אַתָּה מוֹצֵא עַנְוְתָנוּתוֹ ׳ דָּבָר זֶה
כָּתוּב בַּתּוֹרָה ׳ וְשָׁנוּי בַּנְּבִיאִים ׳ וּמְשֻׁלָּשׁ בַּכְּתוּבִים: כָּתוּב
בַּתּוֹרָה כִּי יְיָ אֱלֹהֵיכֶם הוּא אֱלֹהֵי הָאֱלֹהִים וַאֲדֹנֵי הָאֲדֹנִים
הָאֵל הַגָּדֹל הַגִּבֹּר וְהַנּוֹרָא אֲשֶׁר לֹא־יִשָּׂא פָנִים וְלֹא יִקַּח
שֹׁחַד: וּכְתִיב בַּתְרֵהּ עֹשֶׂה מִשְׁפַּט יָתוֹם וְאַלְמָנָה וְאֹהֵב
גֵּר לָתֶת לוֹ לֶחֶם וְשִׂמְלָה: שָׁנוּי בַּנְּבִיאִים דִּכְתִיב כִּי כֹה
אָמַר רָם וְנִשָּׂא שֹׁכֵן עַד וְקָדוֹשׁ שְׁמוֹ מָרוֹם וְקָדוֹשׁ אֶשְׁכּוֹן
וְאֶת־דַּכָּא וּשְׁפַל־רוּחַ לְהַחֲיוֹת רוּחַ שְׁפָלִים וּלְהַחֲיוֹת לֵב
נִדְכָּאִים: מְשֻׁלָּשׁ בַּכְּתוּבִים דִּכְתִיב שִׁירוּ לֵאלֹהִים זַמְּרוּ
שְׁמוֹ סֹלּוּ לָרֹכֵב בָּעֲרָבוֹת בְּיָהּ שְׁמוֹ וְעִלְזוּ לְפָנָיו: וּכְתִיב
בַּתְרֵהּ אֲבִי יְתוֹמִים וְדַיַּן אַלְמָנוֹת אֱלֹהִים בִּמְעוֹן קָדְשׁוֹ:
יְהִי יְיָ אֱלֹהֵינוּ עִמָּנוּ כַּאֲשֶׁר הָיָה עִם־אֲבֹתֵינוּ אַל־יַעַזְבֵנוּ
וְאַל־יִטְּשֵׁנוּ: וְאַתֶּם הַדְּבֵקִים בַּיְיָ אֱלֹהֵיכֶם חַיִּים כֻּלְּכֶם הַיּוֹם:
כִּי־נִחַם יְיָ צִיּוֹן נִחַם כָּל־חָרְבֹתֶיהָ וַיָּשֶׂם מִדְבָּרָהּ כְּעֵדֶן
וְעַרְבָתָהּ כְּגַן־יְיָ שָׂשׂוֹן וְשִׂמְחָה יִמָּצֵא בָהּ תּוֹדָה וְקוֹל זִמְרָה:
יְיָ חָפֵץ לְמַעַן צִדְקוֹ יַגְדִּיל תּוֹרָה וְיַאְדִּיר:

תהלים קכ״ח

שִׁיר הַמַּעֲלוֹת אַשְׁרֵי כָּל־יְרֵא יְיָ הַהֹלֵךְ בִּדְרָכָיו: וְגִיעַ
כַּפֶּיךָ כִּי תֹאכֵל אַשְׁרֶיךָ וְטוֹב לָךְ: אֶשְׁתְּךָ כְּגֶפֶן פֹּרִיָּה
בְּיַרְכְּתֵי בֵיתֶךָ בָּנֶיךָ כִּשְׁתִלֵי זֵיתִים סָבִיב לְשֻׁלְחָנֶךָ: הִנֵּה

RABBI YOCHANAN SAID. A Talmudic discourse on Humility by R. Yochanan bar Nappacha (died 279).

(e) Verses of CONSOLATION.

Writings. The third division of the Holy Scriptures, the first two being the Torah and the Prophets.

HAGGADIC DISCOURSE

Rabbi Yochanan said, In every passage where thou findest the greatness of God mentioned, there thou findest also his humility. This is written in the Torah, repeated in the Prophets, and a third time stated in the Writings. It is written in the Torah, For the Lord your God, he is God of gods, and Lord of lords, the great mighty and revered God, who showeth no partiality, nor taketh a bribe. And it is written afterwards, He doth execute justice for the fatherless and widow, and loveth the stranger, in giving him food and raiment. It is repeated in the Prophets, as it is written, For thus saith the high and lofty One that inhabiteth eternity, and whose name is Holy, I dwell in the high and holy place, with him also that is of a contrite and humble spirit, to revive the spirit of the humble, and to revive the heart of the contrite ones. It is a third time stated in the Writings, Sing unto God, sing praises to his Name: extol ye him that rideth upon the heavens whose name is the Lord, and rejoice before him. And it is written afterwards, A father of the fatherless, and a judge of the widows, is God in his holy habitation. The Lord our God be with us, as he was with our fathers : let him not leave us, nor forsake us. And ye that cleave unto the Lord your God are alive every one of you this day. For the Lord hath comforted Zion : he hath comforted all her waste places, and hath made her wilderness like Eden, and her desert like the garden of the Lord ; joy and gladness shall be found therein, thanksgiving and the voice of melody. It pleased the Lord for his righteousness' sake, to magnify the Torah and to glorify it.

Deuteronomy 10. 17, 18

Isaiah 57 15

Psalm 68. 5, 6

1. Kings 8. 57

Deuteronomy 4. 4

Isaiah 51. 3

VERSES OF "CONSOLA-TION"

Isaiah 42. 21

Psalm cxxviii. A Pilgrim Song.

A BLESSED HOME

Happy is every one that feareth the Lord, that walketh in his ways. When thou shalt eat the labour of thine hands, happy shalt thou be, and it shall be well with thee. Thy wife shall be as a fruitful vine, in the recesses of thine house : thy children like olive plants, round about thy table.

In view of the week of toil which now opens, Plsam 128, a eulogy of the. hard-working breadwinner, is recited before *Oleynu*. For an explanation of the psalm, see p. 601.

כִּי־כֵן יְבֹרַךְ גָּבֶר יְרֵא יְהֹוָה : וִיבָרֶכְךָ יְהֹוָה מִצִּיּוֹן וּרְאֵה בְּטוּב
יְרוּשָׁלָם כֹּל יְמֵי חַיֶּיךָ : וּרְאֵה־בָנִים לְבָנֶיךָ שָׁלוֹם עַל־יִשְׂרָאֵל :

The Reader says הַבְדָּלָה, p. 746, omitting the Introductory Verses.

קַדִּישׁ יָתוֹם, p. 554.   עָלֵינוּ, p. 550.

סֵדֶר הַבְדָלָה :

*At the conclusion of Festivals, only the Blessings marked with an
asterisk * are recited.*

A cup of wine is taken in the right hand, and the following is said :—

הִנֵּה אֵל יְשׁוּעָתִי אֶבְטַח וְלֹא אֶפְחָד כִּי עָזִּי וְזִמְרָת
יָהּ יְיָ וַיְהִי־לִי לִישׁוּעָה : וּשְׁאַבְתֶּם מַיִם בְּשָׂשׂוֹן מִמַּעַיְנֵי

HAVDOLAH.

The HAVDOLAH, the religious ceremony that marks the outgoing of
the Sabbath, is the counterpart of the Kiddush that consecrates its
coming in. By means of this ceremony, one deliberately declares that the
Sabbath is actually over and night has set in, before returning to a work-
day week. It is of great antiquity ; and, like the Kiddush, its institution
is ascribed to.the Men of the Great Assembly. The word *havdolah*
means "separation", and Jewish law prohibits the resumption of
ordinary work after a holy day, before such formal act of "separation"
has been pronounced.

The idea of "separation" is not confined to that between blissful
Sabbath rest and the hurly-burly of the work-a-day world, but is
extended to embrace the separation between holy and profane, between
light and darkness, between Israel and the heathen peoples. The
deeper meaning of the ceremony is thus to impress upon us *the reality
of moral distinctions* in the universe. Wherever men are blind to such
distinctions, or even deny their existence, we have religious chaos and
immoralism. Illustrations of such immoralism abound in the story of
many a strange sect, both in Jewish and non-Jewish history.

Behold thus shall the man be blessed that feareth the Lord. May the Lord bless thee out of Zion : mayest thou see the good of Jerusalem all the days of thy life. Yea, mayest thou see thy children's children. Peace be upon Israel.

The Reader says Havdolah, p. 747, omitting the Introductory Verses.
" It is our duty," p. 551. Mourner's Kaddish, p. 555.

THE HAVDOLAH SERVICE.

At the conclusion of Festivals, only the Blessings marked with an asterisk * are recited.

A cup of wine is taken in the right hand, and the following is said :—

Isaiah 12. 2, 3   Behold, God is my salvation ; I will trust, and will not be afraid : for God the Lord is my strength and song, and he is become my salvation. Therefore with joy shall ye

Psalm 3. 9   draw water out of the wells of salvation. Salvation

It is this final paragraph of the Havdolah which enumerates in pairs the realms to be distinguished, that is the essential portion of the ceremony. It originally formed part of the fourth Benediction of the evening Amidah on the outgoing of the Sabbath. But, "for the sake of the children " (Jerusalem Talmud), the Havdolah early became a home ceremony by itself. At first only supplementary to its mention in the Amidah of that evening, it soon became independent and of equal importance with the Benediction.

I will trust. Since the days of Rashi, introductory Scriptural verses precede the ceremonial in the domestic service. In our Rite, the first of these verses is from a joyful thanksgiving of the faithful for the mercies of God. It emphasises that confidence in God is the primary requisite in the struggle that the coming week may bring us.

salvation. Here primarily in the sense of deliverance and preservation from calamity.

with joy. The duty of cheerfulness is a commonplace in Jewish ethics and life.

הַיְשׁוּעָה ؛ לַיָי הַיְשׁוּעָה עַל־עַמְּךָ בִרְכָתֶךָ סֶּלָה ؛ יְיָ
צְבָאוֹת עִמָּנוּ מִשְׂגָּב־לָנוּ אֱלֹהֵי יַעֲקֹב סֶלָה ؛ לַיְּהוּדִים
הָיְתָה אוֹרָה וְשִׂמְחָה וְשָׂשׂוֹן וִיקָר ؛ כֵּן תִּהְיֶה לָּנוּ ؛
כּוֹס יְשׁוּעוֹת אֶשָּׂא וּבְשֵׁם יְיָ אֶקְרָא ؛

*בָּרוּךְ אַתָּה יְיָ אֱלֹהֵינוּ מֶלֶךְ הָעוֹלָם · בּוֹרֵא פְּרִי הַגָּפֶן ؛

The spice-box is taken, and the following is said :—

בָּרוּךְ אַתָּה יְיָ אֱלֹהֵינוּ מֶלֶךְ הָעוֹלָם · בּוֹרֵא מִינֵי
בְשָׂמִים ؛

The hands are spread towards the light, and the following is said :—

בָּרוּךְ אַתָּה יְיָ אֱלֹהֵינוּ מֶלֶךְ הָעוֹלָם · בּוֹרֵא מְאוֹרֵי
הָאֵשׁ ؛

is our refuge. This is the closing verse of Psalm 46 that opens, "God is our refuge and strength, a very present help in trouble. Therefore will we not fear, though the earth be moved, and though the mountains be carried into the midst of the seas ".

the Jews had light. This is the only quotation from the Book of Esther in the Prayer Book. Hence the exceptional use of the word " Jews " ; see p. 13.

cup of salvation. This verse from the Hallel is a transition to the opening Benediction over wine.

fruit of the vine. Even as the coming in of Sabbath is hallowed by a Benediction over a cup of wine, so is its going out sanctified by wine. In the absence of wine, any other beverage—except water—may be used, with the blessing appropriate to it. When the wine is poured into the cup, it is allowed to flow over, as a symbol of the abounding Divine blessing that we hope for in the coming week.

Psalm 46. 12 belongeth unto the Lord : thy blessing be upon thy people. (Selah.) The Lord of hosts is with us ; the God of Jacob *Esther* 8. 16 is our refuge. (Selah.) The Jews had light and joy and *Psalm* 116. 13 gladness and honour. (So be it with us.) I will lift the cup of salvation, and call upon the Name of the Lord.

*Blessed art thou, O Lord our God, King of the universe, who createst the fruit of the vine.

The spice-box is taken, and the following is said :—

Blessed art thou, O Lord our God, King of the universe, who createst divers kinds of spices.

The hands are spread towards the light, and the following is said :—

Blessed art thou, O Lord our God, King of the universe, who createst the light of the fire.

spices. There are various explanations for this Benediction. According to Saadya, the principal meal in olden days used to be taken about sunset. Burning incense was deemed an essential element of an ancient festive meal; and, as on Sabbath this could not be had, it was brought in immediately after the going out of the Sabbath. Incense as an accompaniment of a festive meal ceased after Mishna days, and even the partaking of food in the Sabbath afternoon twilight was discouraged ; but the incense feature survived in the Havdolah. Later, this Benediction received another, a poetical interpretation. It was held that the Sabbath endowed man with a " higher soul " (נשמה יתרה), traces of which are left on the departure of Sabbath and are symbolized by the fragrance of the spices.

the light of the fire. lit. " the lights of the fire ". Because of the plural form of the Hebrew word, suggesting a double flame, custom decreed a specially-woven Havdolah candle, or two lit candles to be held together, so as to give the light a torch-like appearance. While this Blessing is recited, the hands are spread toward the light, so as to make some *use* of the light. and thereby justify the reciting of a Benediction

The cup is again taken in the right hand, and the following is said:—

‏*בָּרוּךְ אַתָּה יְיָ אֱלֹהֵינוּ מֶלֶךְ הָעוֹלָם · הַמַּבְדִּיל

‏בֵּין קֹדֶשׁ לְחוֹל בֵּין אוֹר לְחְשֶׁךְ בֵּין יִשְׂרָאֵל לָעַמִּים ·

‏בֵּין יוֹם הַשְּׁבִיעִי לְשֵׁשֶׁת יְמֵי הַמַּעֲשֶׂה · בָּרוּךְ אַתָּה

‏יְיָ · הַמַּבְדִּיל בֵּין־קֹדֶשׁ לְחוֹל :

over it. It is for this reason, also, that the spice-box is smelt. Otherwise, it would be a ברכה לבטלה, a Blessing " spoken in vain."

Why this Benediction over the light ? Some explain that light was brought in, together with the incense, whenever the olden Sabbath-meal extended beyond night-fall. Another reason given is that, as light was the first thing created by God, it is proper that we begin our week with a Benediction over it. Still another explanation is, that fire is the symbol of civilization. The use of fire raises a man above the brutes, none of them employing it. With its aid, he dissipates darkness, overcomes cold, prepares food, and shapes instruments of labour. Greek mythology represents Prometheus *stealing* fire from the jealous gods, and secretly giving it to man ; for which act Prometheus was chained to a rock, and tortured for endless ages. Quite other is Jewish legend concerning the origin of fire: it declares fire to be a Heavenly gift to man. When Adam saw for the first time the sun go down, say the Rabbis, and an ever-deepening gloom enfold creation, his mind was filled with terror. God then took pity on him, and endowed him with the intuition to take two stones—the name of one was Darkness, and the name of the other Shadow of Death—and rub them against each other, and so discover fire. Thereupon Adam exclaimed with grateful joy : " Blessed be the Creator of Light." Man had thus no need to steal it, as in the Greek legend ; and, far from punishing the inventor of fire, his act was represented as a Divine prompting. Even the names of the stones—Darkness and Shadow of Death—by means of which, according to the Rabbis, fire was first produced, are of profound significance. Because man is created in the image of God, he can overcome darkness and evil, and turn suffering, and even death itself, into light and lasting spiritual good.

The cup is again taken in the right hand, and the following is said:—

*Blessed art thou, O Lord our God, King of the universe, who makest a distinction between holy and profane, between light and darkness, between Israel and the heathen nations, between the seventh day and the six working days. Blessed art thou, O Lord, who makest a distinction between holy and profane.

A modern teacher points out that in the Havdolah ceremony, we *see* the symbols before us ; we *taste* the wine ; we *smell* the fragrant things ; we *feel* the heat of the flame ; and we *hear* the solemn words of Benediction. We thus consecrate our five senses for labour and duty during the coming week (H. P. Mendes).

HAMAVDIL. This hymn seems originally to have formed part of a Neilah Service. It is attributed to Isaac ibn Chayyat (1030–1089). The translation is by Mrs. Alice Lucas. The following version appeared in *The Jewish Encyclopedia :*

> He who parteth sacred and profane,
> To forgive our sins may He deign,
> As the sands our stock increase again,
> And as the myriad stars of night.
>
> Lord, on Thee I call, O save Thou me !
> And the path of life make me see ;
> From the clutch of sickness set me free,
> And lead me forth to day from night ;
>
> In Thy hand, O Lord, are we but clay !
> Light or grave, our faults do not weigh ;
> Then shall day pour forth the word to day,
> And night declare the truth to night.

Hamavdil is only one of a large number of Zemiroth prayers and for the domestic leave-taking of the Sabbath. The most touching of the latter is the brief, simple Prayer spoken to this day by pious Jewish women in, or hailing from, Slavonic lands. It is accompanied by a soul-stirring chant :

> " Gott vun Avruhom, Yitzchok un Yaakov,
> Der heiliger Shabbos koidesh geht ahin " . . .

> (God of Abraham, Isaac and Jacob,
> The holy Sabbath passes away ;
> May the new week come to us
> For health, life and all good ;
> May it bring us sustenance, good tidings,
> Deliverances and consolations, Amen).

הַמַּבְדִּיל בֵּין קֹדֶשׁ לְחוֹל · חַטֹּאתֵינוּ יִמְחֹל · זַרְעֵנוּ וְכַסְפֵּנוּ
יַרְבֶּה כַחוֹל · וְכַכּוֹכָבִים בַּלָּיְלָה :

יוֹם פָּנָה כְּצֵל תֹּמֶר · אֶקְרָא לָאֵל עָלַי גֹּמֵר · אָמַר שׁוֹמֵר ·
אָתָא בֹקֶר וְגַם-לָיְלָה :

צִדְקָתְךָ כְּהַר תָּבוֹר · עַל חֲטָאַי עָבוֹר תַּעֲבוֹר · כְּיוֹם אֶתְמוֹל
כִּי יַעֲבוֹר · וְאַשְׁמוּרָה בַלָּיְלָה :

חָלְפָה עוֹנַת מִנְחָתִי · מִי יִתֵּן מְנוּחָתִי · יָגַעְתִּי בְאַנְחָתִי ·
אַשְׂחֶה בְכָל לָיְלָה :

קוֹלִי שִׁמְעָה בַּל יֻנְטַל · פְּתַח לִי שַׁעַר הַמְנֻטָּל · שֶׁרֹּאשִׁי
נִמְלָא טָל · קְוֻצּוֹתַי רְסִיסֵי לָיְלָה :

הֵעָתֵר נוֹרָא וְאָיוֹם · אֲשַׁוֵּעַ תְּנָה פִדְיוֹם · בְּנֶשֶׁף בְּעֶרֶב יוֹם ·
בְּאִישׁוֹן לָיְלָה :

קְרָאתִיךָ יָהּ הוֹשִׁיעֵנִי · אֹרַח חַיִּים תּוֹדִיעֵנִי · מִדַּלָּה
תְבַצְּעֵנִי · מִיּוֹם עַד לָיְלָה :

טַהֵר טִנּוּף מַעֲשַׂי · פֶּן יֹאמְרוּ מַכְעִיסַי · אַיֵּה נָא אֱלוֹהַּ עֹשָׂי ·
נֹתֵן זְמִירוֹת בַּלָּיְלָה :

נַחְנוּ בְיָדְךָ כַּחֹמֶר · סְלַח נָא עַל קַל וָחֹמֶר · יוֹם לְיוֹם
יַבִּיעַ אֹמֶר · וְלַיְלָה לְלָיְלָה :

הַמַּבְדִּיל בֵּין קֹדֶשׁ לְחוֹל · חַטֹּאתֵינוּ יִמְחֹל · זַרְעֵנוּ וְכַסְפֵּנוּ
יַרְבֶּה כַחוֹל · וְכַכּוֹכָבִים בַּלָּיְלָה :

Verse eight is not translated in Mrs. Lucas' version. De Sola Pool
translates it thus :
  "From sin's dark stain my way be free,
   Lest foes should say in harsh despite
   'Where is the God created thee,
   Who gives His songs by night?' "

The last line is an echo of Job 35. 10 *who giveth songs in the night* ;
i.e. joyful sense of sudden deliverance in the very darkest hour of
tribulation.

HAMAV-
DIL

May He who sets the holy and profane
Apart, blot out our sins before His sight,
And make our numbers as the sand again,
    And as the stars of night.

The day declineth like the palm-tree's shade,
I call on God, who leadeth me aright.
The morning cometh—thus the watchman said—
    Although it now be night.

Thy righteousness is like Mount Tabor vast;
O let my sins be wholly put to flight,
Be they as yesterday, for ever past,
    And as a watch at night.

The peaceful season of my prayers is o'er,
Would that again had rest my soul contrite,
Weary am I of groaning evermore,
    I melt in tears each night.

Hear thou my voice, be it not vainly sped,
Open to me the gates of lofty height ;
For with the evening dew is filled my head,
    My locks with drops of night.

O grant me Thy redemption, while I pray,
Be Thou entreated, Lord of power and might,
In twilight, in the evening of the day,
    Yea, in the gloom of night.

Save me, O Lord, my God, I call on Thee !
Make me to know the path of life aright,
From sore and wasting sickness snatch Thou me,
    Lead me from day to night.

We are like clay within Thy hand, O Lord,
Forgive us all our sins both grave and light,
And day shall unto day pour forth Thy word,
    And night declare to night.

רִבּוֹן הָעוֹלָמִים אַב־הָרַחֲמִים וְהַסְּלִיחוֹת · הָחֵל עָלֵינוּ
אֶת־יְמֵי הַמַּעֲשֶׂה הַבָּאִים לִקְרָאתֵנוּ לְשָׁלוֹם · חֲשׂוּכִים מִכָּל־
חֵטְא וָפֶשַׁע וּמְנֻקִּים מִכָּל־עָוֹן וְאַשְׁמָה וָרֶשַׁע · וּמְדֻבָּקִים
בְּתַלְמוּד תּוֹרָה וּבְמַעֲשִׂים טוֹבִים · וְתַשְׁמִיעֵנוּ בָהֶם שָׂשׂוֹן
וְשִׂמְחָה וְלֹא תַעֲלֶה קִנְאָתֵנוּ עַל־לֵב אָדָם וְלֹא קִנְאַת אָדָם
תַעֲלֶה עַל־לִבֵּנוּ : מַלְכֵּנוּ אֱלֹהֵינוּ הָאָב הָרַחֲמָן · שִׂים בְּרָכָה
וּרְוָחָה וְהַצְלָחָה בְּכָל־מַעֲשֵׂה יָדֵינוּ · וְכָל־הַיּוֹעֵץ עָלֵינוּ וְעַל־
עַמְּךָ בֵּית יִשְׂרָאֵל עֵצָה טוֹבָה וּמַחֲשָׁבָה טוֹבָה אַמְּצוֹ וּבָרְכוֹ
גַּדְּלוֹ וַהֲקֵם עֲצָתוֹ · וְכָל־הַיּוֹעֵץ עָלֵינוּ וְעַל־עַמְּךָ בֵּית
יִשְׂרָאֵל עֵצָה שֶׁאֵינָהּ טוֹבָה תּוֹפֵר עֲצָתוֹ · כַּדָּבָר שֶׁנֶּאֱמַר
עֻצוּ עֵצָה וְתֻפָר דַּבְּרוּ דָבָר וְלֹא יָקוּם כִּי עִמָּנוּ אֵל : וּפְתַח
לָנוּ יְיָ אֱלֹהֵינוּ אַב־הָרַחֲמִים אֲדוֹן הַסְּלִיחוֹת בָּזֶה הַשָּׁבוּעַ
וּבְכָל שָׁבוּעַ · שַׁעֲרֵי אוֹרָה וּבְרָכָה · שַׁעֲרֵי גִילָה וִישׁוּעָה ·
שַׁעֲרֵי סִיַּעְתָּא דִי־שְׁמַיָּא וְשִׂמְחָה · שַׁעֲרֵי קְדֻשָּׁה וְשָׁלוֹם ·
שַׁעֲרֵי תוֹרָה וּתְפִלָּה · וְקַיֶּם־לָנוּ יְיָ אֱלֹהֵינוּ מִקְרָא שֶׁכָּתוּב
מַה־נָּאווּ עַל־הֶהָרִים רַגְלֵי מְבַשֵּׂר · מַשְׁמִיעַ שָׁלוֹם מְבַשֵּׂר
טוֹב מַשְׁמִיעַ יְשׁוּעָה · אֹמֵר לְצִיּוֹן מָלַךְ אֱלֹהָיִךְ · אָמֵן סֶלָה :

The Prayer for the Coming Week, " Sovereign of the Universe," is
partly of Talmudic origin. It is found in the Sephardi Rite, and in
the larger Ashkenazi Prayer books. Its culminating note is Messianic.
    In the Zemiroth, the Prophet Elijah figures prominently. He
was, according to legend, expected to appear as the forerunner of the
Messiah, on a Saturday night, at the beginning of a new week. The
best known of these hymns, is the prayer that God send speedily Elijah
the Prophet, the Tishbite, the Gileadite as the forerunner of the
Redemption of Israel. This hymn forms part of the Sephardi Synagogue service; but, in the Ashkenazi Rite it is voluntary and relegated
to home chanting. Some multiply these hymns at a special *melaveh
malkah* meal in honour of the departing Queen Sabbath.

Sovereign of the Universe, Father of mercy and forgiveness, grant that we begin the working days which are drawing nigh unto us, in peace; freed from all sin and transgression; cleansed from all iniquity, trespass and wickedness; and clinging to the study of thy Teaching, and to the performance of good deeds. Cause us to hear in the coming week tidings of joy and gladness. May there not arise in the heart of any man envy of us, nor in us envy of any man. O, our King, our God, Father of mercy, bless and prosper the work of our hands. And all who cherish towards us and thy people Israel thoughts of good, strengthen and prosper them, and fulfil their purposes ; but all who devise against us, and thy people Israel, plans which are not for good, Oh frustrate them and make

Isaiah 8. 10 their designs of none effect ; as it is said, " Take counsel together, and it shall be brought to nought; speak the word, and it shall not stand; for God is with us ". Open unto us, Father of mercies and Lord of forgiveness, in this week and in the weeks to come, the gates of light and blessing, of redemption and salvation, of heavenly help and rejoicing, of holiness and peace, of the study of thy Torah and of prayer. In us also let the Scripture be fulfilled:

Isaiah 52. 7 How beautiful upon the mountains are the feet of him that bringeth good tidings, that announceth peace, the harbinger of good tidings, that announceth salvation ; that saith unto Zion, Thy God reigneth ! Amen. (Selah.)

סדר נטילת לולב:

On סֻכּוֹת, *previous to* הַלֵּל, *p. 756, being said, the* לוּלָב *is taken,*
and the following Meditation and Benedictions are said :—

הֲרֵינִי מוּכָן וּמְזֻמָּן לְקַיֵּם מִצְוַת בּוֹרְאִי שֶׁצִּוָּנוּ בְּתוֹרָתוֹ
וּלְקַחְתֶּם לָכֶם בַּיּוֹם הָרִאשׁוֹן פְּרִי עֵץ הָדָר כַּפֹּת תְּמָרִים
וַעֲנַף עֵץ־עָבֹת וְעַרְבֵי־נָחַל · וּבְנַעֲנוּעִי אוֹתָם יַשְׁפִּיעַ עָלַי
שֶׁפַע בְּרָכוֹת וּמַחֲשָׁבוֹת קְדוֹשׁוֹת שֶׁהוּא אֱלֹהֵי הָאֱלֹהִים
וַאֲדוֹנֵי הָאֲדוֹנִים שַׁלִּיט בְּמַטָּה וּבְמַעַל וּמַלְכוּתוֹ בַּכֹּל מָשָׁלָה ·
וּתְהֵא חֲשׁוּבָה מִצְוַת אַרְבָּעָה מִינִים כְּאִלּוּ קִיַּמְתִּיהָ בְּכָל־
פְּרָטֶיהָ וְדִקְדּוּקֶיהָ · וִיהִי נֹעַם יְיָ אֱלֹהֵינוּ עָלֵינוּ וּמַעֲשֵׂה
יָדֵינוּ כּוֹנְנָה עָלֵינוּ וּמַעֲשֵׂה יָדֵינוּ כּוֹנְנֵהוּ · בָּרוּךְ יְיָ לְעוֹלָם ·
אָמֵן וְאָמֵן :

בָּרוּךְ אַתָּה יְיָ אֱלֹהֵינוּ מֶלֶךְ הָעוֹלָם · אֲשֶׁר קִדְּשָׁנוּ
בְּמִצְוֹתָיו וְצִוָּנוּ עַל־נְטִילַת לוּלָב :

בָּרוּךְ אַתָּה יְיָ אֱלֹהֵינוּ מֶלֶךְ הָעוֹלָם · שֶׁהֶחֱיָנוּ
וְקִיְּמָנוּ וְהִגִּיעָנוּ לַזְּמַן הַזֶּה :

שֶׁהֶחֱיָנוּ *is said on the First Day of the Festival only. Should the First
Day, however, fall on Sabbath,* שֶׁהֶחֱיָנוּ *is said on the Second Day.*

The Benediction over the Lulav, recited during the Festival of
Tabernacles, is an ancient rabbinic ordinance. For the Benediction,
and during the Hallel, the esrog is taken in the left hand, and then the
Lulav in the right. In the synagogue, this is done immediately
preceding the chanting of Hallel.

ON TAKING THE LULAV

On Tabernacles, previous to Hallel, p. 757, being said, the Lulav is taken, and the following Meditation and Benedictions are said :—

MEDITA-
TION
Leviticus
23. 40

Psalms 19. 17

Lo, I am prepared and ready to fulfil the command of my Creator, who hath commanded us in the Torah, And ye shall take you on the first day the fruit of goodly trees, branches of palm trees, myrtle branches, and willows of the brook. While I wave them, may the stream of blessings flow in upon me, together with holy thoughts which tell that he is the Great God and Supreme Lord, governing below and above, whose kingdom ruleth over all. May this observance of the precept of the Four Species be accounted as though I had fulfilled it in all its details and particulars. And let the graciousness of the Lord our God be upon us ; and establish thou the work of our hands upon us ; yea, the work of our hands do thou establish. Blessed be the Lord for ever. Amen, and Amen.

BENE-
DICTIONS

Blessed art thou, O Lord our God, King of the universe, who hast hallowed us by thy commandments, and hast given us command concerning the taking of the Lulav.

The following Blessing is said on the First Day of the Festival only. Should the First Day, however, fall on Sabbath, it is said on the Second Day.

Blessed art thou, O Lord our God, King of the universe, who hast kept us in life, and hast preserved us, and enabled us to reach this season.

Lo, I am . . . stream of blessings. This prayer is a beautiful spiritualization of a ceremonial act. It is of modern date (1662), and by R. Nathan Hanover, the author of the Meditation on p. 479.

fruit of goodly trees. The *esrog.*

branches of palm trees. The *lulav.*

kept us in life. This Blessing, *shehechyonu,* is the Benediction of thanksgiving for attaining any valued new possession, or for being spared to fulfil the observance of any sacred rite at a festive, recurrent occasion. It is a hallowing of Time, and of the soul's landmarks of joy in human life.

סֵדֶר הַלֵּל:

הַלֵּל *is said on* רֹאשׁ חֹדֶשׁ, שָׁלֹשׁ רְגָלִים *and* חֲנֻכָּה. *On* חוֹל הַמּוֹעֵד סֻכּוֹת,
חוֹל הַמּוֹעֵד פֶּסַח *and* רֹאשׁ חֹדֶשׁ *on* הַלֵּל; *the* תְּפִלִּין *are removed before*
מוּסָף. *In the house of an* אָבֵל, *Hallel is not recited on.* רֹאשׁ חֹדֶשׁ
and חֲנֻכָּה.

בָּרוּךְ אַתָּה יְיָ אֱלֹהֵינוּ מֶלֶךְ הָעוֹלָם · אֲשֶׁר קִדְּשָׁנוּ
בְּמִצְוֹתָיו וְצִוָּנוּ לִקְרוֹא אֶת־הַהַלֵּל:

HALLEL.

A dominant note of praise and thanksgiving is characteristic of the
Jewish Liturgy. This note is clearest in the Hallel Service, which
distinguishes the supreme occasions of Israel's rejoicing. "Hallel is
the Jewish song of jubilation that has accompanied our wanderings of
thousands of years, keeping awake within us the consciousness of our
world-historical mission, strengthening us in times of sorrow and
suffering, and filling our mouths with song of rejoicing in days of
deliverance and triumph. To this day, it revives on each Festival
season the memory of Divine redemption, and our confidence in future
greatness" (S. R. Hirsch).

Hallel ("Hymns of Praise") is the name especially applied to
Psalms 113–118. The fuller title of this group of psalms is "the Hallel
of Egypt", because of the reference in them to the Exodus.

Originally the Hallel psalms (113–118) were the spontaneous thanksgiving for some signal deliverance, as appears from the verse, "This is
the day which the Lord hath made ; we will rejoice and be glad in it"
(118. 24). But in time the Rabbis made the reading of these Psalms
obligatory on the Three Festivals ; and, since the Maccabean days,
Chanukah is likewise marked by the reading of Hallel ; but not Purim,
because the Scroll of Esther is considered its Hallel. The reading of
Hallel on New Moon started as a *minhag* of Babylonian Jewry in the
second century ; and is thus the free outcome of the people's religious
feeling of gratitude for the perennial wonder of Israel's redemption.
On Rosh Hashanah and Yom Kippur, the Hallel psalms of jubilation
and rejoicing are not recited ; because of the solemnity of those
occasions, when the issues of destiny and pardon are being decided

HALLEL

Hallel is said on New Moon, on Passover, Pentecost and Tabernacles, and on Chanukah.

On the Intermediate Days of Festivals, the Tefillin are removed before Hallel ; on New Moon and the Intermediate Days of Passover, before Mussaf.

In the House of Mourning, Hallel is not recited on New Moon and Chanukah.

BENEDIC-
TION
Blessed art thou, O Lord our God, King of the universe, who hast hallowed us by thy commandments, and hast commanded us to read the Hallel.

for mortals. For somewhat similar considerations, these Psalms are omitted in a house of mourning on New Moon and Chanukah during the week of Shivah. And the *complete* Hallel is not said during the last six days of Passover, because of the calamity that then befell the Egyptian host pursuing the Israelites ! Jewish feeling held that there could not be *full* rejoicing, if victory was accompanied by much human suffering, even though the suffering be that of the enemy. " The ministering angels ", say the Rabbis, " were about to chant songs of praise as the Egyptians were drowning. The Almighty rebuked them, " My creatures are perishing in the sea, and ye are ready to sing ! "

On the last six days of Passover, therefore, one-half of Psalms 115 and 116 are omitted. The same is done on New Moon, that being only a minor Festival. Twice in the year, Hallel is recited in the evening : it forms part of the Seder Service on Passover. Various parts are sung antiphonally by Reader and Congregation (118. 1–4), and some verses are repeated (118. 21–24). On the Festival of Tabernacles, the lulav is waved during the refrains of Psalm 118, verses 1–4, 25, 29.

" The Hallel, sounding the whole gamut of trust and despair, dejection and triumph, agony and release, with praise running through the whole, retells to Israel the story of his chequered national life—rejected by the builders, yet become the corner-stone of God's house ; taunted as a people God-forsaken, yet secure in God's love ; drinking the dregs of affliction, yet bearing the cup of salvation to his lips " (Abrahams).

hast commanded us. There is in the Torah no command to read the Hallel. It is an early Rabbinic institution. However, in carrying out what our religious Teachers prescribed, we obey an express injunction of the Torah ; see the note, " given us command ", p. 11.

תהלים קי״ג

הַלְלוּיָהּ ׀ הַלְלוּ עַבְדֵי יְיָ הַלְלוּ אֶת־שֵׁם יְיָ : יְהִי
שֵׁם יְיָ מְבֹרָךְ מֵעַתָּה וְעַד־עוֹלָם : מִמִּזְרַח־שֶׁמֶשׁ עַד־
מְבוֹאוֹ מְהֻלָּל שֵׁם יְיָ : רָם עַל־כָּל־גּוֹיִם ׀ יְיָ עַל
הַשָּׁמַיִם כְּבוֹדוֹ : מִי כַּיְיָ אֱלֹהֵינוּ הַמַּגְבִּיהִי לָשָׁבֶת :
הַמַּשְׁפִּילִי לִרְאוֹת בַּשָּׁמַיִם וּבָאָרֶץ : מְקִימִי מֵעָפָר דָּל
מֵאַשְׁפֹּת יָרִים אֶבְיוֹן : לְהוֹשִׁיבִי עִם־נְדִיבִים עִם נְדִיבֵי
עַמּוֹ : מוֹשִׁיבִי ׀ עֲקֶרֶת הַבַּיִת אֵם־הַבָּנִים שְׂמֵחָה ·
הַלְלוּיָהּ :

PSALM 113.
THE GREATNESS AND CONDESCENSION OF GOD.

God the Deliverer.

1–3. Summons to praise God.

1. *praise ye the Lord.* Heb. *Hallelujah* (the *j* is pronounced *y*); it introduces and closes the psalm, showing that it was written for use in the Temple Service; see p. 73.

servants of the Lord. All those who revere God.

the Name of the Lord. His nature and character as disclosed in His revelation to Israel—the God of Righteousness and Mercy.

2. *this time . . . . evermore.* His praise is destined to fill all time and space.

3. *from the rising of the sun.* From East to West, throughout the world.

is to be praised. Or, " is praised." This wonderful thought is also found in Malachi 1. 11. Both Psalmist and Prophet declare that even the heathen who adore heavenly bodies, really *aim* to worship the Divine Ruler. And God·looks on the heart of the worshippers; see *Deuteronomy*, 54 (759).

Psalm cxiii.

GREAT-
NESS AND
CONDES-
CENSION
OF GOD

¹Praise ye the Lord. Praise, O ye servants of the Lord, praise the Name of the Lord. ²Let the Name of the Lord be blessed from this time forth and for evermore. ³From the rising of the sun unto the going down thereof, the Lord's Name is to be praised. ⁴The Lord is high above all nations, and his glory above the heavens. ⁵Who is like unto the Lord our God, that dwelleth so high ; ⁶that looketh down so low upon the heavens and the earth ? ⁷He raiseth up the lowly out of the dust, and lifteth up the needy from the dunghill ; ⁸that he may set him with princes, even with the princes of his people. ⁹He maketh the barren woman dwell in her house as a joyful mother of children. Praise ye the Lord.

4–8. Why God should be praised.
4. *above the heavens.* *i.e.*, more glorious than the heavens. The heavens declare His glory, but that glory far transcends sun and moon and stars.
5. *dwelleth so high.* Enthroned in the highest heavens, He yet stoops to regard the most lowly on earth. " Rabbi Yochanan said, In every Scriptural passage where thou findest the greatness of God mentioned, there thou findest mention also of His humility " (see p. 478). He is not to be measured by man's finitude.
6. *looketh down.* Judaism emphasizes not only the greatness and omnipotence of God, but also His *nearness* to man ; Psalm 145. 18.
7. *dunghill.* Of his poverty ; an emblem of extreme misery.
8. *with princes.* With nobles.
9. *dwell in her house.* If God bestows children upon the barren woman, He by that very fact makes her full mistress of her home, firmly rooted in her husband's house. Rashi, following Targum and Midrash, takes the once childless wife, gladdened with a family of sons, to mean bereft Zion ; and he considers this psalm as the expression of Israel's gratitude for the Restoration from Babylonian captivity.

תהלים קי׳ד

בְּצֵאת יִשְׂרָאֵל מִמִּצְרָיִם בֵּית יַעֲקֹב מֵעַם לֹעֵז :

הָיְתָה יְהוּדָה לְקָדְשׁוֹ יִשְׂרָאֵל מַמְשְׁלוֹתָיו : הַיָּם רָאָה

וַיָּנֹס הַיַּרְדֵּן יִסֹּב לְאָחוֹר : הֶהָרִים רָקְדוּ כְאֵילִים

גְּבָעוֹת כִּבְנֵי־צֹאן : מַה־לְּךָ הַיָּם כִּי תָנוּס הַיַּרְדֵּן תִּסֹּב

לְאָחוֹר : הֶהָרִים תִּרְקְדוּ כְאֵילִים גְּבָעוֹת כִּבְנֵי־צֹאן :

מִלִּפְנֵי אָדוֹן חוּלִי אָרֶץ מִלִּפְנֵי אֱלוֹהַּ יַעֲקֹב : הַהֹפְכִי

הַצּוּר אֲגַם־מָיִם חַלָּמִישׁ לְמַעְיְנוֹ־מָיִם :

On רֹאשׁ חֹדֶשׁ *and the last Six Days of* פֶּסַח, *omit the next*
eleven verses :—

תהלים קט׳ו

לֹא לָנוּ יְהֹוָה לֹא לָנוּ כִּי לְשִׁמְךָ תֵּן כָּבוֹד עַל־

PSALM 114.
THE MARVELS OF THE EXODUS.

One of the finest lyrics in literature. Nowhere do we find a more
exquisite picture of the Liberation from Egypt, or a more poetic repre-
sentation of the birth of Israel. In inimitably vivid manner, it sketches
the three most wonderful events in Israel's history : the Exodus, the
Revelation, and Israel's Sustenance in the Wilderness.

1–4. Nature amazed.

1. *a people of strange language.* " A barbaric people " (Targum,
Cheyne), with whom we could only communicate by signs. Or, " of
stammering language "—an apt description of Egypt and the Egyptians
from the spiritual angle. In all higher things, those animal-worshippers
were " stammerers ". Their glimpses into eternal truths were like
flashes of light for one brief moment in the night-time, leaving greater
darkness, Egyptian darkness, behind ; see *Exodus*, 63 (396).

Psalm cxiv.

¹When Israel went forth out of Egypt, the house of Jacob from a people of strange language ; ²Judah became his sanctuary, Israel his dominion. ³the sea saw it, and fled ; Jordan turned back. ⁴The mountains skipped like rams, the hills like lambs. ⁵What aileth thee, O thou sea, that thou fleest ? thou Jordan, that thou turnest back ? ⁶Ye mountains, that ye skip like rams ? Ye hills, like lambs ? ⁷At the presence of the Lord tremble, O earth, at the presence of the God of Jacob ; ⁸who turned the rock into a pool of water, the flint into a fountain of waters.

On New Moon and the last Six Days of Passover, omit the next eleven verses :—

Psalm cxv.

¹Not unto us, O Lord, not unto us, but unto thy Name

2. *Judah . . . Israel.* No contrast is intended.

his sanctuary. God's sanctuary ; " Ye have seen what I did unto the Egyptians, and how I bore you on eagle's wings, and brought you unto Myself. Now, therefore, if ye will hearken unto My voice indeed, and keep My covenant, then ye shall be Mine own treasure from among all peoples ; for all the earth is Mine ; and ye shall be unto Me a kingdom of priests, and a *holy* nation " (Exodus 19. 6).

3. *sea . . . Jordan.* The sea and river are personified. As soon as they saw the Almighty at the head of His people, the poet represents them hastening to facilitate Israel's exit from Egypt and entry into the Promised Land ; Exodus 14 and Joshua 3.

4. *mountains . . . . hills.* The poet has in mind the earthquake at the Revelation on Sinai ; Exodus 19. 19.

skipped. i.e., trembled.

5–8. " What aileth thee ? " Nature is challenged to explain its consternation.

7. *tremble, O earth.* Instead of a direct answer to the question, the poet bids the earth tremble still, even as it trembled then, before its Maker.

8. *turned the rock.* Made the water flow from the rock at Rephidim ; Exodus 17. 6 ; Numbers 20. 8–11.

חַסְדְּךָ עַל־אֲמִתֶּךָ : לָמָּה יֹאמְרוּ הַגּוֹיִם אַיֵּה־נָא אֱלֹהֵיהֶם :

וֵאלֹהֵינוּ בַשָּׁמָיִם כֹּל אֲשֶׁר־חָפֵץ עָשָׂה : עֲצַבֵּיהֶם כֶּסֶף

וְזָהָב מַעֲשֵׂה יְדֵי אָדָם : פֶּה־לָהֶם וְלֹא יְדַבֵּרוּ עֵינַיִם

לָהֶם וְלֹא יִרְאוּ : אָזְנַיִם לָהֶם וְלֹא יִשְׁמָעוּ אַף לָהֶם

וְלֹא יְרִיחוּן : יְדֵיהֶם וְלֹא יְמִישׁוּן רַגְלֵיהֶם וְלֹא יְהַלֵּכוּ

לֹא־יֶהְגּוּ בִּגְרוֹנָם : כְּמוֹהֶם יִהְיוּ עֹשֵׂיהֶם כֹּל אֲשֶׁר־בֹּטֵחַ

בָּהֶם : יִשְׂרָאֵל בְּטַח בַּיהֹוָה עֶזְרָם וּמָגִנָּם הוּא : בֵּית

אַהֲרֹן בִּטְחוּ בַיהֹוָה עֶזְרָם וּמָגִנָּם הוּא : יִרְאֵי יְהֹוָה

בִּטְחוּ בַיהֹוָה עֶזְרָם וּמָגִנָּם הוּא :

יְיָ זְכָרָנוּ יְבָרֵךְ יְבָרֵךְ אֶת־בֵּית יִשְׂרָאֵל יְבָרֵךְ אֶת־

בֵּית אַהֲרֹן : יְבָרֵךְ יִרְאֵי יְיָ הַקְּטַנִּים עִם־הַגְּדֹלִים :

יֹסֵף יְיָ עֲלֵיכֶם עֲלֵיכֶם וְעַל־בְּנֵיכֶם : בְּרוּכִים אַתֶּם לַיְיָ

PSALM 115.
IN DEFIANCE OF HEATHENISM.

A song of confidence in time of tribulation and danger to Israel.

1–3. Israel is reviled by idolaters, and appeals to God to vindicate His honour.

1. *not unto us.* We seek Thy aid, not that glory may come to us by the resulting victory, but that Thy lovingkindness and faithfulness to Thine own may be displayed (Davies). This verse expresses the true hero's repudiation of honour to himself.

DEFIANCE
OF
HEATHEN-
ISM

give glory, for thy lovingkindness and for thy truth's sake.
²Wherefore should the nations say, Where, now, is their
God ? ³But our God is in the heavens, he doeth whatsoever he pleaseth. ⁴Their idols are silver and gold, the work
of men's hands. ⁵They have mouths, but they speak not ;
eyes have they, but they see not. ⁶They have ears, but they
hear not ; noses have they, but they smell not. ⁷As for
their hands, they handle not ; as for their feet, they walk
not ; they give no sound through their throat. ⁸They that
make them shall be like unto them ; yea, every one that
trusteth in them. ⁹O Israel, trust thou in the Lord : he is
their help and their shield. ¹⁰O house of Aaron, trust in the
Lord : he is their help and their shield. ¹¹Ye that fear the
Lord, trust in the Lord : he is their help and their shield.

THE GLORY
OF GOD
UPON HIS
WORSHIP-
PERS

¹²The Lord hath been mindful of us ; he will bless, he will
bless the house of Israel ; he will bless the house of Aaron.
¹³He will bless them that fear the Lord, both small and

lovingkindness . . . truth's sake. If God were not to interfere on
behalf of His people, it would seem as if His fundamental attributes of
love and faithfulness (Exodus 34. 6, see p. 479) had vanished.

2. *the nations.* The heathen.

3. *in the heavens.* He is neither visible nor of bodily form ; He is a
spiritual Being.

4–8. Dead idols. Fetishism degrades its followers.

4. *silver and gold.* Usually only covered with silver and gold.

8. *shall be.* Shall become.

like unto them. Such gods drag down their worshippers to their
level of inane stupidity.

9–11. Trust in the Lord ! People, priests and proselytes are addressed.

9. *their help . . . shield.* These words are the answer of the choir
to the preceding, " O Israel, trust thou in the Lord " ; similarly in the
two following verses.

10. *house of Aaron.* The priests.

11. *that fear the Lord.* The proselytes (Rashi). It includes all those
of whatever nation, who are filled with the fear of God (Ibn Ezra).

12. *mindful of us.* By redeeming us from misfortune.

עֹשֵׂה שָׁמַיִם וָאָרֶץ : הַשָּׁמַיִם שָׁמַיִם לַיָי וְהָאָרֶץ נָתַן
לִבְנֵי־אָדָם : לֹא־הַמֵּתִים יְהַלְלוּ־יָהּ וְלֹא כָּל־יֹרְדֵי דוּמָה :
וַאֲנַחְנוּ נְבָרֵךְ יָהּ מֵעַתָּה וְעַד־עוֹלָם · הַלְלוּיָהּ :

On רֹאשׁ חֹדֶשׁ and the last Six Days of פֶּסַח, omit the next
eleven verses :—

תהלים קט"ז

אָהַבְתִּי כִּי־יִשְׁמַע ׀ יְיָ אֶת־קוֹלִי תַּחֲנוּנָי : כִּי־הִטָּה
אָזְנוֹ לִי וּבְיָמַי אֶקְרָא : אֲפָפוּנִי חֶבְלֵי־מָוֶת וּמְצָרֵי
שְׁאוֹל מְצָאוּנִי צָרָה וְיָגוֹן אֶמְצָא : וּבְשֵׁם־יְיָ אֶקְרָא
אָנָּה יְיָ מַלְּטָה נַפְשִׁי : חַנּוּן יְיָ וְצַדִּיק וֵאלֹהֵינוּ מְרַחֵם :
שֹׁמֵר פְּתָאיִם יְיָ דַּלּוֹתִי וְלִי יְהוֹשִׁיעַ : שׁוּבִי נַפְשִׁי
לִמְנוּחָיְכִי כִּי יְיָ גָּמַל עָלָיְכִי : כִּי חִלַּצְתָּ נַפְשִׁי מִמָּוֶת
אֶת־עֵינִי מִן־דִּמְעָה אֶת־רַגְלִי מִדֶּחִי : אֶתְהַלֵּךְ לִפְנֵי

16. *heavens of the Lord.* His peculiar dwelling, as opposed to the earth, the habitation of man.

17. *the dead praise not God.* This is a rhetorical reason for praising God *now.* Praising God means here, to make His mighty deeds of deliverance known to the family of nations. Such praise can only be rendered by the living, and not by the dead, even on the plane of immortality.

go down into silence. They do not join in public worship. The netherworld was, in ancient Semitic thought, a gloomy region where the disembodied spirits led a shadowy existence. This view of Life after death, long survived in the minds of some of the Biblical writers. In

great. [14]May the Lord increase you, you and your children. [15]Blessed are ye of the Lord, who made heaven and earth. [16]The heavens are the heavens of the Lord ; but the earth hath he given to the children of men. [17]The dead praise not the Lord, neither any that go down into silence ; [18]but we will bless the Lord from this time forth and for evermore. Praise ye the Lord.

On New Moon and the last Six Days of Passover omit the next eleven verses :—

Psalm cxvi.

THANKS-GIVING FOR DELIVER-ANCE

[1]I love the Lord, because he heareth my voice and my supplications. [2]Because he hath inclined his ear unto me, therefore will I call upon him as long as I live. [3]The snares of death had encompassed me, and the anguish of the grave had come upon me : I found trouble and sorrow. [4]Then I called upon the Name of the Lord : O Lord, I beseech thee, deliver my soul. [5]Gracious is the Lord and righteous : yea, our God is merciful. [6]The Lord preserveth the simple : I was brought low, and he saved me. [7]Return unto thy rest, O my soul ; for the Lord hath dealt bountifully with thee. [8]For thou hast delivered my soul from death, mine

time, the full hope of immortality was shared by everyone of Israel's sages and singers. It is at its clearest in Psalm 16. 10, 11 : " Thou wilt not abandon my soul to the grave . . . . Thou wilt make known to me the path of life ; in Thy presence is fulness of joy ; at Thy right hand, bliss for evermore ".

PSALM 116.

THANKSGIVING FOR DELIVERANCE.

1–6. Saved from death.

3. *snares* . . . . *anguish*. lit. " cords . . . straits ". Death is represented as a hunter lying in wait with nooses, and driving his prey into a narrow defile from which escape is difficult.

4. *my soul.* Here equivalent to " me ".

6. *simple.* Those who, without guile or experience, are especially exposed to danger.

7–9. Confidence in the future.

יְיָ בְּאַרְצוֹת הַחַיִּים : הֶאֱמַנְתִּי כִּי אֲדַבֵּר אֲנִי עָנִיתִי
מְאֹד : אֲנִי אָמַרְתִּי בְחָפְזִי כָּל־הָאָדָם כֹּזֵב :

מָה־אָשִׁיב לַיְיָ כָּל־תַּגְמוּלוֹהִי עָלָי : כּוֹס־יְשׁוּעוֹת
אֶשָּׂא וּבְשֵׁם יְיָ אֶקְרָא : נְדָרַי לַיְיָ אֲשַׁלֵּם נֶגְדָה־נָּא
לְכָל־עַמּוֹ : יָקָר בְּעֵינֵי יְיָ הַמָּוְתָה לַחֲסִידָיו : אָנָּה
יְיָ כִּי־אֲנִי עַבְדֶּךָ אֲנִי עַבְדְּךָ בֶּן־אֲמָתֶךָ פִּתַּחְתָּ לְמוֹסֵרָי :
לְךָ אֶזְבַּח זֶבַח תּוֹדָה וּבְשֵׁם יְיָ אֶקְרָא : נְדָרַי לַיְיָ
אֲשַׁלֵּם נֶגְדָה־נָּא לְכָל־עַמּוֹ : בְּחַצְרוֹת בֵּית יְיָ בְּתוֹכֵכִי
יְרוּשָׁלַ͏ִם · הַלְלוּיָהּ :

תהלים קי"ז

הַלְלוּ אֶת־יְיָ כָּל־גּוֹיִם שַׁבְּחוּהוּ כָּל־הָאֻמִּים : כִּי גָבַר
עָלֵינוּ חַסְדּוֹ וֶאֱמֶת־יְיָ לְעוֹלָם · הַלְלוּיָהּ :

9. *land of the living.* lit. " lands of the living "—taken by the Rabbis as a confident assumption of immortality.

10—11. The delusiveness of human help.

11. *haste.* Alarm.

all men are liars. The meaning is, Man (not, *every* man) is unreliable. In his distress, man failed the psalmist, but he never lost faith in God.

12. *what shall I render.* That is, How can I requite ?

13. *cup of salvation.* A figure of speech, " cup of deliverance ".

15. *precious.* " God willeth not to let the righteous die before their time " (Ibn Ezra). Their death is not a matter of indifference to Him.

16. *loosed my bonds.* Freed me from captivity.

eyes from tears, my feet from falling. ⁹I shall walk before the Lord in the land of the living. ¹⁰I kept my faith in God even when I spake, I am greatly afflicted ; ¹¹even when I said in my haste, All men are liars.

¹²What can I render unto the Lord for all his benefits towards me ? ¹³I will lift the cup of salvation, and call upon the Name of the Lord. ¹⁴I will pay my vows unto the Lord, yea, in the presence of all his people. ¹⁵Precious in the sight of the Lord is the death of his loving ones. ¹⁶Ah, Lord, truly I am thy servant : I am thy servant, the son of thy handmaid ; thou hast loosed my bonds. ¹⁷I will offer to thee the sacrifice of thanksgiving, and will call upon the Name of the Lord. ¹⁸I will pay my vows unto the Lord, yea, in the presence of all his people ; ¹⁹in the courts of the Lord's house, in the midst of thee, O Jerusalem. Praise ye the Lord.

Psalm cxvii.

UNIVER-SAL PRAISE OF GOD   ¹O praise the Lord, all ye nations ; laud him, all ye peoples. ²For his lovingkindness is mighty over us ; and the truth of the Lord endureth for ever. Praise ye the Lord.

17. *sacrifice of thanksgiving.* Leviticus 7. 11.

18. *pay my vows.* The vows I have made I will pay *in the presence of all* His people. There will be public confession of gratitude.

PSALM 117.

UNIVERSAL PRAISE OF GOD.

The shortest of the Psalms, it is yet one of the grandest, and rightly spoken of as Messianic. It restates the ultimate Hope of Israel that all the children of men shall one day be united in the pure worship of God.

*The following four verses are chanted by the Reader, the Congregation
responding* 'הודו וגו *at the end of each verse.*

תהלים קי״ח

הוֹדוּ לַיְיָ כִּי־טוֹב   כִּי לְעוֹלָם חַסְדּוֹ:

יֹאמַר־נָא יִשְׂרָאֵל   כִּי לְעוֹלָם חַסְדּוֹ:

יֹאמְרוּ נָא בֵית אַהֲרֹן כִּי לְעוֹלָם חַסְדּוֹ:

יֹאמְרוּ נָא יִרְאֵי יְיָ   כִּי לְעוֹלָם חַסְדּוֹ:

מִן־הַמֵּצַר קָרָאתִי יָּהּ עָנָנִי בַמֶּרְחַבְיָה: יְיָ לִי לֹא
אִירָא מַה־יַּעֲשֶׂה לִי אָדָם: יְיָ לִי בְּעֹזְרָי וַאֲנִי אֶרְאֶה
בְשֹׂנְאָי: טוֹב לַחֲסוֹת בַּיְיָ מִבְּטֹחַ בָּאָדָם: טוֹב
לַחֲסוֹת בַּיְיָ מִבְּטֹחַ בִּנְדִיבִים: כָּל־גּוֹיִם סְבָבוּנִי בְּשֵׁם
יְיָ כִּי אֲמִילַם: סַבּוּנִי גַם־סְבָבוּנִי בְּשֵׁם יְיָ כִּי אֲמִילַם:
סַבּוּנִי כִדְבֹרִים דֹּעֲכוּ כְּאֵשׁ קוֹצִים בְּשֵׁם יְיָ כִּי אֲמִילַם:
דָּחֹה דְחִיתַנִי לִנְפֹּל וַיְיָ עֲזָרָנִי: עָזִּי וְזִמְרָת יָהּ וַיְהִי־

PSALM 118.

THANKSGIVING FOR VICTORY.

The last and most jubilant of the Hallel psalms. Its first half
(verses 1–18) is the song of a procession of pilgrims on their way to the
Temple.

1–4. All Israel are bidden to join in thanksgiving for God's
marvellous deliverance of Israel from surrounding enemies.

1. The words are ancient, and seem to have been a popular refrain
on the lips of the worshippers in the Temple; II Chronicles 20. 21.

The following four verses are chanted by the Reader, the Congregation at the end of each verse repeating, " O give thanks," etc., to " for ever."

Psalm cxviii.

¹O give thanks unto the Lord ; for he is good : for his lovingkindness endureth for ever.

²So let Israel now say, that his lovingkindness endureth for ever.

³So let the house of Aaron say, that his lovingkindness endureth for ever.

⁴So let them that fear the Lord say, that his lovingkindness endureth for ever.

⁵Out of my distress I called upon the Lord : the Lord answered me with enlargement. ⁶The Lord is for me, I will not fear : what can man do unto me ? ⁷The Lord is for me as my helper ; therefore shall I see the defeat of them that hate me. ⁸It is better to take refuge in the Lord than to trust in man. ⁹It is better to take refuge in the Lord than to trust in princes. ¹⁰All heathens compassed me about : in the Name of the Lord I surely cut them down. ¹¹They compassed me about ; yea, they compassed me about : in the Name of the Lord I surely cut them down. ¹²They compassed me about like bees ;—they were extinguished as a fire of thorns :—in the Name of the Lord I surely cut them down. ¹³Thou didst thrust sore at me that I might fall : but the Lord helped me. ¹⁴The Lord is my strength and song ; and he is become my deliverance. ¹⁵The voice o

5. *distress.* lit. " straitness ". Israel had been hemmed in by enemies. It is now free to move and act without hindrance.

I called. The speaker is Israel.

7. *as my helper.* Literally, " among them that help me " ; but thi is a peculiar Heb. idiom to designate not one of many helpers, but On who sums up in Himself a host of helpers.

see the defeat. Cf. Psalm 92. 12, p. 361.

13. *thou didst thrust sore.* The enemy is addressed.

14. Taken from the Song of Moses, Exodus 15. 2.

לִי לִישׁוּעָה: קוֹל רִנָּה וִישׁוּעָה בְּאָהֳלֵי צַדִּיקִים יְמִין

יְיָ עֹשָׂה חָיִל: יְמִין יְיָ רוֹמֵמָה יְמִין יְיָ עֹשָׂה חָיִל:

לֹא־אָמוּת כִּי־אֶחְיֶה וַאֲסַפֵּר מַעֲשֵׂי יָהּ: יַסֹּר יִסְּרַנִּי יָּהּ

וְלַמָּוֶת לֹא נְתָנָנִי: פִּתְחוּ־לִי שַׁעֲרֵי־צֶדֶק אָבֹא־בָם

אוֹדֶה יָהּ: זֶה־הַשַּׁעַר לַיְיָ צַדִּיקִים יָבֹאוּ בוֹ:

אוֹדְךָ כִּי עֲנִיתָנִי וַתְּהִי־לִי לִישׁוּעָה:

Repeat this and the next three verses.

אֶבֶן מָאֲסוּ הַבּוֹנִים הָיְתָה לְרֹאשׁ פִּנָּה:

מֵאֵת יְיָ הָיְתָה זֹּאת הִיא נִפְלָאת בְּעֵינֵינוּ:

זֶה־הַיּוֹם עָשָׂה יְיָ נָגִילָה וְנִשְׂמְחָה בוֹ:

Reader and Congregation :—

אָנָּא יְיָ הוֹשִׁיעָה נָּא: אָנָּא יְיָ הוֹשִׁיעָה נָּא:

אָנָּא יְיָ הַצְלִיחָה נָא: אָנָּא יְיָ הַצְלִיחָה נָא:

15. *the right hand.* The might.

doeth valiantly. " Carries the day " (Moffatt) in the battle against Israel's enemies.

19. *open to me.* The procession has now arrived at the Temple gates.

gates of righteousness. The gates to the abode of the righteous God.

20. *the righteous may enter.* And *only* the righteous. Judaism deems all worship offered by wicked or cruel men—unless it be prayer of repentance—an insult to God.

Talmudic legend relates that Alexander the Great, in his travels to the ends of the earth, arrived at the gate of Paradise. He knocked, and the guardian Angel asked, " Who is there " ? " Alexander ", was the answer. " Who is Alexander " ? came the further question. " Alexander, you know—*the* Alexander—Alexander the Great—Conqueror of the World ". " We know him not ", was the reply ; " he cannot enter

exulting and deliverance is in the tents of the righteous : the right hand of the Lord doeth valiantly. [16]The right hand of the Lord is exalted : the right hand of the Lord doeth valiantly. [17]I shall not die, but live, and recount the works of the Lord. [18]The Lord hath chastened me sore : but he hath not given me over unto death. [19]Open to me the gates of righteousness : I will enter into them. I will give thanks unto the Lord. [20]This is the gate of the Lord ; the righteous may enter into it.

[21]I will give thanks unto thee, for thou hast answered me and art become my deliverance. (*Repeat this and the next three verses.*)

[22]The stone which the builders rejected is become the chief cornerstone.

[23]This was the Lord's doing ; it is marvellous in our eyes.

[24]This is the day which the Lord hath made ; we will be glad and rejoice thereon.

Reader and Congregation :—

[25]Save, we beseech thee, O Lord.

Save, we beseech thee, O Lord.

We beseech thee, O Lord, make us now to prosper.

We beseech thee, O Lord, make us now to prosper

here. This is the gate of the Lord : only the righteous may enter into it "

The Midrash too has the following saying : " In the Hereafter a man is asked, What was thine occupation ? If he reply, ' I fed the hungry,' he is answered : ' *That* is the gate of the Lord : enter, thou who didst feed the hungry.' Similar is the greeting to one who clothed the naked, or devoted parental care upon an orphan "

21–24. The grateful people renew their praises for the deliverance

22. *the stone.* Israel, rejected by the nations, is destined to be the foundation-stone of, and attain to the most honourable place in, the Kingdom of God.

cornerstone. Of the foundation of the building.

23. *marvellous.* Nothing less than a miracle.

25–29. Vows and prayers, blessings and praises.

בָּרוּךְ הַבָּא בְּשֵׁם יְיָ בֵּרַכְנוּכֶם מִבֵּית יְיָ:

Repeat this and the next three verses.

אֵל יְיָ וַיָּאֶר לָנוּ אִסְרוּ־חַג בַּעֲבֹתִים עַד קַרְנוֹת
הַמִּזְבֵּחַ:

אֵלִי אַתָּה וְאוֹדֶךָ אֱלֹהַי אֲרוֹמְמֶךָ:
הוֹדוּ לַיְיָ כִּי־טוֹב כִּי לְעוֹלָם חַסְדּוֹ:

יְהַלְלוּךָ יְיָ אֱלֹהֵינוּ כָּל מַעֲשֶׂיךָ · וַחֲסִידֶיךָ צַדִּיקִים
עוֹשֵׂי רְצוֹנֶךָ וְכָל עַמְּךָ בֵּית יִשְׂרָאֵל בְּרִנָּה יוֹדוּ וִיבָרְכוּ
וִישַׁבְּחוּ וִיפָאֲרוּ וִירוֹמְמוּ וְיַעֲרִיצוּ וְיַקְדִּישׁוּ וְיַמְלִיכוּ אֶת
שִׁמְךָ מַלְכֵּנוּ · כִּי לְךָ טוֹב לְהֹדוֹת וּלְשִׁמְךָ נָאֶה לְזַמֵּר
כִּי מֵעוֹלָם וְעַד עוֹלָם אַתָּה אֵל · בָּרוּךְ אַתָּה יְיָ · מֶלֶךְ
מְהֻלָּל בַּתִּשְׁבָּחוֹת:

(רֹאשׁ חֹדֶשׁ טֵבֵת *p*. 206; *but on* חֲנֻכָּה (*excepting* קַדִּישׁ תִּתְקַבֵּל),
חֲצִי קַדִּישׁ, *p*. 422.

---

26. *cometh.* Entereth. This is the greeting extended to the pilgrims
by Priests and Levites.

27. *given us light.* This has been made to refer to Chanukah. It
has an even wider meaning. Abrahams aptly remarks : " The first
word of God in the Creation story was *Let there be light*; and "light"
has been, throughout the world's spiritual progress under the leadership
of Israel, a symbol of the regeneration of humanity with God's spirit,
so that " the path of the righteous is as the light of dawn, that shineth
more and more unto the perfect day " (Proverbs 4. 18).

[26]Blessed be he that cometh in the Name of the Lord : we bless you out of the house of the Lord. (*Repeat this and the next three verses.*)

[27]The Lord is God, he hath given us light : order the festal procession with boughs, even unto the horns of the altar.

[28]Thou art my God, and I will give thanks unto thee : thou art my God, I will exalt thee.

[29]O give thanks unto the Lord ; for he is good : for his lovingkindness endureth for ever.

CON-CLUDING BENEDIC-TION

All thy works shall praise thee, O Lord our God, and thy pious ones, the just who do thy will, together with all thy people, the house of Israel, shall with exultation thank, bless, praise, glorify, exalt, reverence, sanctify and ascribe sovereignty unto thy Name, O our King ; for it is good to give thanks unto thee, and becoming to sing praises unto thy Name, because from everlasting to everlasting thou art God. Blessed art thou, O Lord, a King extolled with praises.

Kaddish, p. 207 ; but on Chanukah (excepting the New Moon of Teveth), Half-Kaddish, p. 423.

---

order the festal procession. Heb. *issru-chag* ; later this Hebrew term became the name for the day *after* a Festival. *Chag*, the word for " festival ", here means, " festal procession ".

with boughs. See Leviticus 23. 40. Refers to the Temple procession with the Lulav-cluster (palm branch, willow, myrtle twigs and esrog).

28. *will give thanks.* It is impossible to determine for which occasion this anonymous psalm was composed. The great scholar S. I. Rapaport undertook to prove that it was composed by King Hezekiah after his illness ; and others hold that it was the psalm sung at the dedication of the Altar in the time of Nehemiah. Still others maintain—quite untenably—that it is Maccabean in origin. But, as the Midrash rightly declares, it fits every great national redemption in Israel, and—we may add—in the life of the nations.

ALL THY WORKS. This doxology, mentioned in the Talmud, is the concluding benediction of Hallel, just as the *yishtabbach* (" Praised be thy Name ", p. 105) is the concluding benediction of the Psalms recited in the first part of the daily Morning Service.

For סֵדֶר קְרִיאַת הַתּוֹרָה *on* רֹאשׁ חֹדֶשׁ *and* חוֹל הַמּוֹעֵד *see pp.* 188–196; *on* יָמִים טוֹבִים *and* שַׁבָּת וְרֹאשׁ חֹדֶשׁ *see pp.* 472–522.

On רֹאשׁ חֹדֶשׁ *and* חוֹל הַמּוֹעֵד *say* אַשְׁרֵי, *p.* 198, וּבָא לְצִיּוֹן, *p.* 570, חֲצִי קַדִּישׁ, *p.* 428.

On רֹאשׁ חֹדֶשׁ *continue with the following* עֲמִידָה.

On יָמִים טוֹבִים *and* חוֹל הַמּוֹעֵד *say the appropriate* מוּסָפִים.

ROSH CHODESH—NEW MOON.

In early Bible times, Rosh Chodesh, New Moon, was a solemn convocation, with special sacrifices, and the sounding of the trumpet in the Sanctuary. It was a day of rejoicing and family festivity; but it had also its solemn aspects, and on it the people sought religious instruction. In the course of the centuries, and especially since the destruction of the Temple, it lost its festive character; and only the following features in the Service distinguish the New Moon from the ordinary weekday :

(a) Yaaleh v'yovo (p. 149) is introduced into the Amidah, and in the Grace after Meals.

(b) The recitation of the Hallel-psalms, 113–118.

(c) Torah-reading (Numbers 28. 1–15), four being called to the Law; but there is no Haftorah. On the Sabbath, the Torah Reading for Rosh Chodesh is *added* to the ordinary Sabbath Reading; but another Haftorah replaces the Sabbath Haftorah, whenever New Moon is on the Sabbath (Isaiah 66), or on Sunday (I Samuel 20. 18–42). On Mondays and Thursdays, Numbers 28. 1–15 is alone read.

(d) Mussaf Amidah. It resembles the Amidah of the Sabbath Additional Service, and goes back to the days of Hillel. God is implored to make the coming month one of happiness and blessing, of deliverance and forgiveness ; so that " it be the end of all our sorrows, and the beginning of our soul's salvation " (Sephardi Prayer Book).

(e) The reading of Psalm 104 (p. 582)—which glorifies Creation, and makes special mention of the Moon as marking the time for Festivals (v. 19) ; and

(f) the omission of all supplicatory prayers (*e.g. tachanun*, pp. 169–182) in the Morning and Afternoon Services.

For Order of Service at the Reading of the Torah on New Moons and the Intermediate Days of Festivals, see pp. 189–197 *(four men are called to the Torah). On Festivals and on New Moons falling on Sabbaths, see pp.* 473–523.
On New Moons and the Intermediate Days of Festivals :—
" Happy are they," p. 199.
" And a redeemer," p. 571, *to " glorify it," p.* 573.
Half-Kaddish, p. 423.
On a Festival and on the Intermediate Days of Festivals, say the Amidah of the Mussaf Service.
On New Moons continue with the following Amidah.

On the Sabbath preceding Rosh Chodesh, there is an announcement of the day or days of the coming New Moon (see p. 507). This prevented in ancient times uncertainty in regard to the proper date of the sacred Festivals. Their observance on different days would have destroyed the religious unity of Israel. Rabban Gamaliel, the Patriarch of Palestine Jewry at the beginning of the second century, was therefore fully justified when he ordered his colleague, R. Joshua ben Chananya, (who was of opinion that Rabban Gamaliel had fixed Rosh Chodesh on the wrong day,) to appear before him in traveller's attire and workday outfit on the day which, according to R. Joshua's reckoning, should have been the Day of Atonement. Fully understanding the vital importance of religious authority in Judaism, Rabbi Joshua obeyed, and thus saved Israel from calamitous religious confusion. That was still a real peril as late as the days of Saadya Gaon (882–942). It was Saadya who at last banished the danger of rival calendars in the camp of Traditional Jews.

Because the proclamation of the New Moon made by the Sanhedrin could not reach in time the Jewish communities outside Palestine, these kept *two days* of the Festivals, so as to be certain of not violating the proper day. This became the established custom in those communities. Even when the calendar was fixed, the Second Day continued to remain a permanent institution of Judaism in the Dispersion, and has now been hallowed by over fifteen centuries' observance. It has thereby attained the force of religious law, and cannot be abrogated by any individual community or Jewry.

תְּפִלַּת מוּסָף לְרֹאשׁ חוֹדֶשׁ בְּחוֹל:

אֲדֹנָי שְׂפָתַי תִּפְתָּח וּפִי יַגִּיד תְּהִלָּתֶךָ:

בָּרוּךְ אַתָּה יְיָ אֱלֹהֵינוּ וֵאלֹהֵי אֲבוֹתֵינוּ · אֱלֹהֵי
אַבְרָהָם אֱלֹהֵי יִצְחָק וֵאלֹהֵי יַעֲקֹב · הָאֵל הַגָּדוֹל הַגִּבּוֹר
וְהַנּוֹרָא אֵל עֶלְיוֹן · גּוֹמֵל חֲסָדִים טוֹבִים וְקוֹנֵה הַכֹּל ·
וְזוֹכֵר חַסְדֵי אָבוֹת וּמֵבִיא גוֹאֵל לִבְנֵי בְנֵיהֶם לְמַעַן שְׁמוֹ
בְּאַהֲבָה ·

מֶלֶךְ עוֹזֵר וּמוֹשִׁיעַ וּמָגֵן · בָּרוּךְ אַתָּה יְיָ · מָגֵן אַבְרָהָם:
אַתָּה גִבּוֹר לְעוֹלָם אֲדֹנָי מְחַיֵּה מֵתִים אַתָּה רַב לְהוֹשִׁיעַ ·

From רֹאשׁ חֹדֶשׁ חֶשְׁוָן inclusive, say :— רֹאשׁ חֹדֶשׁ נִיסָן until רֹאשׁ חֹדֶשׁ חֶשְׁוָן From
מַשִּׁיב הָרוּחַ וּמוֹרִיד הַגָּשֶׁם :

מְכַלְכֵּל חַיִּים בְּחֶסֶד מְחַיֵּה מֵתִים בְּרַחֲמִים רַבִּים · סוֹמֵךְ
נוֹפְלִים וְרוֹפֵא חוֹלִים וּמַתִּיר אֲסוּרִים וּמְקַיֵּם אֱמוּנָתוֹ
לִישֵׁנֵי עָפָר · מִי כָמוֹךָ בַּעַל גְּבוּרוֹת וּמִי דּוֹמֶה לָּךְ ·
מֶלֶךְ מֵמִית וּמְחַיֶּה וּמַצְמִיחַ יְשׁוּעָה ·

In its Mussaf prayer, Rosh Chodesh is designated as "a season of atonement"—a reminder of its solemn aspect which, has, at times, been deeply stressed. In Judaism, all beginnings are holy; and the beginning of the month would, in the minds of many, call forth serious reflections for a better life in the future. In ancient days, these reflections on the New Moon largely had reference to unconscious sins, especially those in connection with the Sanctuary. The devout in the Middle Ages took a more general view. "What occasion could be more appropriate", they asked, "for amendment of life and reconciliation with God"? Moreover, the waxing and the waning of the moon

MUSSAF SERVICE FOR THE NEW MOON

Psalm 51. 17 O Lord, open thou my lips, and my mouth shall declare thy praise.

I. THE
GOD OF
HISTORY Blessed art thou, O Lord our God and God of our fathers, God of Abraham, God of Isaac, and God of Jacob, the great, mighty and revered God, the most high God, who bestowest lovingkindnesses, and art Master of all See p. 131 things ; who rememberest the pious deeds of the patriarchs, and in love wilt bring a redeemer to their children's children for thy Name's sake.

O King, Helper, Saviour and Shield. Blessed art thou, O Lord, the Shield of Abraham.

II. THE
GOD OF
NATURE Thou, O Lord, art mighty for ever, thou revivest the dead, thou art mighty to save.

From the New Moon of Cheshvan until the New Moon of Nisan inclusive, say :—

Thou causest the wind to blow and the rain to fall.

See p. 133 Thou sustainest the living with lovingkindness, revivest the dead with great mercy, supportest the falling, healest the sick, freest the bound, and keepest thy faith to them that sleep in the dust. Who is like unto thee, O King, who orderest death and restorest life, and causest salvation to spring forth?

was to them a symbol of spiritual renewal, and reminded them of the changing fortunes of Israel. See the Benediction to be said on the appearance of the New Moon (p. 995).

The mystic conception of Rosh Chodesh was at last crystallized into a solemn observance. This was done by R. Moses Cordovero (1522–1570), leader of the Safed mystics. He inaugurated the practice of celebrating the day preceding Rosh Chodesh (except at the end of Nisan, Ellul, Tishri, and Kislev) as a *Yom Kippur Koton*, a minor Day of Atonement. His followers fasted that day till the Afternoon Service, when they met in synagogue ; and, arrayed in tallith and tefillin, read the Fast-day Scriptural Lessons, penitential hymns, and confessions. " Following the custom of the very pious, one must repent of his ways, and make restitution both by mouth and personal acts, in order that

וְנֶאֱמָן אַתָּה לְהַחֲיוֹת מֵתִים · בָּרוּךְ אַתָּה יְיָ · מְחַיֵּה הַמֵּתִים :

[*When the Reader repeats the* עֲמִידָה, *the following* קְדוּשָׁה *is said and* הָאֵל הַקָּדוֹשׁ *till* אַתָּה קָדוֹשׁ *omitted.*

Reader. נְקַדֵּשׁ אֶת שִׁמְךָ בָּעוֹלָם כְּשֵׁם שֶׁמַּקְדִּישִׁים אוֹתוֹ

בִּשְׁמֵי מָרוֹם כַּכָּתוּב עַל יַד נְבִיאֶךָ · וְקָרָא זֶה אֶל זֶה וְאָמַר ·

Cong. קָדוֹשׁ קָדוֹשׁ קָדוֹשׁ יְיָ צְבָאוֹת · מְלֹא כָל הָאָרֶץ

כְּבוֹדוֹ : *Reader.* לְעֻמָּתָם בָּרוּךְ יֹאמֵרוּ · *Cong.* בָּרוּךְ כְּבוֹד

יְיָ מִמְּקוֹמוֹ : *Reader.* וּבְדִבְרֵי קָדְשְׁךָ כָּתוּב לֵאמֹר ·

Cong. יִמְלֹךְ יְיָ לְעוֹלָם אֱלֹהַיִךְ צִיּוֹן לְדֹר וָדֹר · הַלְלוּיָהּ :

Reader. לְדוֹר וָדוֹר נַגִּיד גָּדְלֶךָ · וּלְנֵצַח נְצָחִים

קְדֻשָּׁתְךָ נַקְדִּישׁ · וְשִׁבְחֲךָ אֱלֹהֵינוּ מִפִּינוּ לֹא יָמוּשׁ

לְעוֹלָם וָעֶד · כִּי אֵל מֶלֶךְ גָּדוֹל וְקָדוֹשׁ אָתָּה · בָּרוּךְ

אַתָּה יְיָ · הָאֵל הַקָּדוֹשׁ :]

אַתָּה קָדוֹשׁ וְשִׁמְךָ קָדוֹשׁ וּקְדוֹשִׁים בְּכָל־יוֹם יְהַלְלוּךָ

סֶּלָה · בָּרוּךְ אַתָּה יְיָ · הָאֵל הַקָּדוֹשׁ :

רָאשֵׁי חֳדָשִׁים לְעַמְּךָ נָתַתָּ זְמַן כַּפָּרָה לְכָל־

תּוֹלְדוֹתָם · בִּהְיוֹתָם מַקְרִיבִים לְפָנֶיךָ זִבְחֵי רָצוֹן

he may enter the new month as pure as a new-born infant " (Sheloh). This institution soon spread far beyond Safed and the Holy Land, but always remained a voluntary observance. Some congregations in England hold a Yom Kippur Koton service.

IV. The special New Moon portion of this Amidah, consists of an

Yea, faithful art thou to revive the dead. Blessed art thou, O Lord, who revivest the dead.

III.
KĔDUSHA :
SANCTIFI-
CATION

Isaiah 6. 3

See p. 135

[*When the Amidah is repeated the following Sanctification is said.*

Reader.—We will sanctify thy Name in the world even as they sanctify it in the highest heavens, as it is written by the hand of thy prophet :

And they called one unto the other and said,

Ezekiel 3. 12

Cong.—HOLY, HOLY, HOLY IS THE LORD OF HOSTS : THE WHOLE EARTH IS FULL OF HIS GLORY.

Reader.—Those over against them say, Blessed—

Psalm 146. 10

Cong.—BLESSED BE THE GLORY OF THE LORD FROM HIS PLACE.

Reader.—And in thy Holy Words it is written, saying,

Cong.—THE LORD SHALL REIGN FOR EVER ; THY GOD, O ZION, UNTO ALL GENERATIONS. PRAISE YE THE LORD.

Reader.—Unto all generations we will declare thy greatness, and to all eternity we will proclaim thy holiness ; and thy praise, O our God, shall not depart from our mouth for ever, for thou art a great and holy God and King. Blessed art thou, O Lord, the holy God.]

Whenever the above Sanctification is recited, the following, till "the holy God", is omitted.

Thou art holy, and thy Name is holy, and holy beings praise thee daily. (Selah.) Blessed art thou, O Lord, the holy God.

IV.
FESTIVE
RETRO-
SPECT

The beginnings of the months thou didst assign unto thy people for a season of atonement throughout their generations. While they offered unto thee acceptable sacrifices,

introduction, a prayer for restoration of the Temple Service, and a petition for blessing of the month. The introduction is relatively young, and is largely allusive, embodying various rabbinic interpretations of the New Moon offerings.

a season of atonement. See p. 776.

while they offered. See Numbers 10. 10. Hence, with the cessation of the sacrificial system, Rosh Chodesh has ceased to be " a season of atonement ".

וּשְׂעִירֵי חַטָּאת לְכַפֵּר בַּעֲדָם · זִכָּרוֹן לְכֻלָּם יִהְיוּ ·
וּתְשׁוּעַת נַפְשָׁם מִיַּד שׂוֹנֵא : מִזְבֵּחַ חָדָשׁ בְּצִיּוֹן
תָּכִין · וְעוֹלַת רֹאשׁ חֹדֶשׁ נַעֲלֶה עָלָיו · וּשְׂעִירֵי עִזִּים
נַעֲשֶׂה בְרָצוֹן · וּבַעֲבוֹדַת בֵּית הַמִּקְדָּשׁ נִשְׂמַח כֻּלָּנוּ ·
וּבְשִׁירֵי דָוִד עַבְדָּךְ הַנִּשְׁמָעִים בְּעִירֶךְ הָאֲמוּרִים
לִפְנֵי מִזְבְּחֶךָ : אַהֲבַת עוֹלָם תָּבִיא לָהֶם · וּבְרִית
אָבוֹת לַבָּנִים תִּזְכּוֹר : וַהֲבִיאֵנוּ לְצִיּוֹן עִירְךָ בְּרִנָּה
וְלִירוּשָׁלַיִם בֵּית מִקְדָּשֶׁךָ בְּשִׂמְחַת עוֹלָם · וְשָׁם נַעֲשֶׂה
לְפָנֶיךָ אֶת־קָרְבְּנוֹת חוֹבוֹתֵינוּ תְּמִידִים כְּסִדְרָם וּמוּסָפִים
כְּהִלְכָתָם : וְאֶת־מוּסַף יוֹם רֹאשׁ הַחֹדֶשׁ הַזֶּה נַעֲשֶׂה
וְנַקְרִיב לְפָנֶיךָ בְּאַהֲבָה כְּמִצְוַת רְצוֹנֶךָ כְּמוֹ שֶׁכָּתַבְתָּ
עָלֵינוּ בְּתוֹרָתֶךָ עַל־יְדֵי מֹשֶׁה עַבְדָּךְ מִפִּי כְבוֹדֶךָ
כָּאָמוּר :

וּבְרָאשֵׁי חָדְשֵׁיכֶם תַּקְרִיבוּ עֹלָה לַיְיָ פָּרִים בְּנֵי־
בָקָר שְׁנַיִם וְאַיִל אֶחָד כְּבָשִׂים בְּנֵי־שָׁנָה שִׁבְעָה
תְּמִימִם : וּמִנְחָתָם וְנִסְכֵּיהֶם כַּמְדֻבָּר שְׁלֹשָׁה עֶשְׂרֹנִים

acceptable sacrifices. They rendered Israel acceptable to their Heavenly Father, because of the yearning for God's favour that was manifested in bringing them ; see *Leviticus*, 8 (411).

remembrance for them all. Those sacrifices were defrayed from the half-shekels contributed by everyone in Israel; see Exodus 30. 16, *Exodus*, 358 (352).

and goats for a sin offering to atone for them, these were to be a remembrance for them all, and the salvation of their soul from the hand of the enemy. O do thou establish a new altar on Zion, and we will offer upon it the burnt offering of the New Moon, and prepare he-goats for thine acceptance ; while we all of us rejoice in the service of the sanctuary, and in the songs of David thy servant, which shall then be heard in thy city and chanted before thine altar. O bestow upon them everlasting love, and the covenant of the fathers remember unto the children. Bring us with exultation to Zion thy city, and to Jerusalem thy sanctuary with everlasting joy, and there will we prepare unto thee the offerings that are obligatory for us, the daily offerings according to their order, and the additional offerings according to their enactment ; and the additional offering of this New Moon we will prepare and offer unto thee in love according to the precept of thy will, as thou hast prescribed for us in thy Torah through the hand of Moses thy servant, from the mouth of thy glory, as it is said :

*Numbers
28. 11*
     And in your new moons ye shall offer a burnt offering unto the Lord ; two young bullocks and one ram, seven he-lambs of the first year without blemish. And their meal offering and their drink offerings as hath been ordained, three tenth parts of an ephah of fine flour for each bullock, two tenth parts for the ram, one tenth for

---

hand of the enemy. In War ; Numbers 10. 9. The New Moon clarions were sounded in War. That music, by invoking both courage and cheerfulness in the hearers, was a symbol of the Divine aid against the foe ; and thus was Israel, in the hour of danger, remembered of God and saved. This is the original meaning of the phrase ; but the later commentators understand " the enemy " to mean man's Evil Inclination (yetzer hara) and everything that tarnishes our purity of soul.

a new altar. Ezekiel 46. 1, 6. Here begins the petition for the rebuilding of the Sanctuary.

לַפָּר וּשְׁנֵי עֶשְׂרֹנִים לָאַיִל וְעִשָּׂרוֹן לַכֶּבֶשׁ וְיַיִן כְּנִסְכּוֹ
וְשָׂעִיר לְכַפֵּר וּשְׁנֵי תְמִידִים כְּהִלְכָתָם :

אֱלֹהֵינוּ וֵאלֹהֵי אֲבוֹתֵינוּ · חַדֵּשׁ עָלֵינוּ אֶת-הַחֹדֶשׁ
הַזֶּה לְטוֹבָה וְלִבְרָכָה · לְשָׂשׂוֹן וּלְשִׂמְחָה · לִישׁוּעָה
וּלְנֶחָמָה · לְפַרְנָסָה וּלְכַלְכָּלָה · לְחַיִּים וּלְשָׁלוֹם ·
לִמְחִילַת חֵטְא וְלִסְלִיחַת עָוֹן [in Leap Year add וּלְכַפָּרַת
פָּשַׁע] · כִּי-בְעַמְּךָ יִשְׂרָאֵל בָּחַרְתָּ מִכָּל-הָאֻמּוֹת · וְחֻקֵּי
רָאשֵׁי חֳדָשִׁים לָהֶם קָבָעְתָּ · בָּרוּךְ אַתָּה יְיָ · מְקַדֵּשׁ
יִשְׂרָאֵל וְרָאשֵׁי חֳדָשִׁים :

רְצֵה יְיָ אֱלֹהֵינוּ בְּעַמְּךָ יִשְׂרָאֵל וּבִתְפִלָּתָם · וְהָשֵׁב
אֶת-הָעֲבוֹדָה לִדְבִיר בֵּיתֶךָ וְאִשֵּׁי יִשְׂרָאֵל וּתְפִלָּתָם
בְּאַהֲבָה תְקַבֵּל בְּרָצוֹן · וּתְהִי לְרָצוֹן תָּמִיד עֲבוֹדַת
יִשְׂרָאֵל עַמֶּךָ ·

וְתֶחֱזֶינָה עֵינֵינוּ בְּשׁוּבְךָ לְצִיּוֹן בְּרַחֲמִים · בָּרוּךְ אַתָּה
יְיָ · הַמַּחֲזִיר שְׁכִינָתוֹ לְצִיּוֹן :

מוֹדִים אֲנַחְנוּ לָךְ
שָׁאַתָּה הוּא יְיָ אֱלֹהֵינוּ
וֵאלֹהֵי אֲבוֹתֵינוּ לְעוֹלָם
וָעֶד · צוּר חַיֵּינוּ מָגֵן

The Congregation, in an undertone—
מוֹדִים אֲנַחְנוּ לָךְ שָׁאַתָּה
הוּא יְיָ אֱלֹהֵינוּ וֵאלֹהֵי אֲבוֹתֵינוּ
אֱלֹהֵי כָל-בָּשָׂר · יוֹצְרֵנוּ יוֹצֵר
בְּרֵאשִׁית · בְּרָכוֹת וְהוֹדָאוֹת

each lamb, and wine according to the drink offering thereof, a goat for atonement, and two daily offerings according to their enactment.

NEW MOON PRAYER Our God and God of our fathers, renew this month unto us for good and for blessing, for joy and gladness, for salvation and consolation, for support and sustenance, for life and peace, for pardon of sin and forgiveness of iniquity, (*in Leap Year add*, and for atonement of transgression) ; for thou hast chosen thy people Israel from all nations, and hast appointed unto them statutes for the new moons. Blessed art thou, O Lord, who hallowest Israel and the new moons.

V. FOR RESTORA-TION OF TEMPLE SERVICE

See p. 149 Accept, O Lord our God, thy people Israel and their prayer ; restore the service to the inner sanctuary of thy house ; receive in·love and favour both the offerings of Israel and their prayer ; and may the worship of thy people Israel be ever acceptable unto thee.

And let our eyes behold thy return in mercy to Zion. Blessed art thou, O Lord, who restorest thy divine presence unto Zion.

VI. THANKS-GIVING FOR GOD'S UNFAIL-ING MERCIES

See p. 157

We give thanks unto thee, for thou art the Lord our God and the God of our fathers for ever and ever ; thou art the Rock of our lives, the Shield of our salvation through every generation. We will give thanks unto thee and declare thy praise for our lives

The Congregation, in an undertone—

We give thanks unto thee, for thou art the Lord our God and God of our fathers, the God of all flesh, our Creator and the Creator of all things in the beginning. Blessings and thanksgivings

OUR GOD . . . FATHERS. The twelve terms for a prosperous month refer to ordinary years. A thirteenth term was added later, to correspond to the intercalated, thirteenth month in the Jewish leap year.

יְשׁוּעֵנוּ אַתָּה הוּא לְדוֹר לְשִׁמְךָ הַגָּדוֹל וְהַקָּדוֹשׁ · עַל
וָדוֹר · נוֹדֶה לְּךָ וּנְסַפֵּר שֶׁהֶחֱיִיתָנוּ וְקִיַּמְתָּנוּ · כֵּן תְּחַיֵּנוּ
תְּהִלָּתֶךָ עַל חַיֵּינוּ וּתְקַיְּמֵנוּ · וְתֶאֱסוֹף גָּלֻיּוֹתֵינוּ
הַמְּסוּרִים בְּיָדֶךָ וְעַל לְחַצְרוֹת קָדְשֶׁךָ לִשְׁמֹר חֻקֶּיךָ
נִשְׁמוֹתֵינוּ הַפְּקוּדוֹת לָךְ וְלַעֲשׂוֹת רְצוֹנֶךָ וּלְעָבְדְּךָ בְּלֵבָב
שָׁלֵם עַל שֶׁאֲנַחְנוּ מוֹדִים לָךְ ·
בָּרוּךְ אֵל הַהוֹדָאוֹת :

וְעַל נִסֶּיךָ שֶׁבְּכָל־יוֹם עִמָּנוּ וְעַל נִפְלְאוֹתֶיךָ וְטוֹבוֹתֶיךָ
שֶׁבְּכָל־עֵת עֶרֶב וָבֹקֶר וְצָהֳרָיִם · הַטּוֹב כִּי לֹא־כָלוּ
רַחֲמֶיךָ · וְהַמְרַחֵם כִּי לֹא־תַמּוּ חֲסָדֶיךָ · מֵעוֹלָם קִוִּינוּ
לָךְ :

On חֲנֻכָּה *add* עַל הַנִּסִּים *p.* 150.

וְעַל־כֻּלָּם יִתְבָּרַךְ וְיִתְרוֹמַם שִׁמְךָ מַלְכֵּנוּ תָּמִיד לְעוֹלָם
וָעֶד :

וְכֹל הַחַיִּים יוֹדוּךָ סֶּלָה · וִיהַלְלוּ אֶת־שִׁמְךָ בֶּאֱמֶת ·
הָאֵל יְשׁוּעָתֵנוּ וְעֶזְרָתֵנוּ סֶלָה · בָּרוּךְ אַתָּה יְיָ · הַטּוֹב
שִׁמְךָ וּלְךָ נָאֶה לְהוֹדוֹת :

At the repetition of the עֲמִירָה *by the Reader, the following is
introduced :—*

אֱלֹהֵינוּ וֵאלֹהֵי אֲבוֹתֵינוּ · בָּרְכֵנוּ בַבְּרָכָה הַמְשֻׁלֶּשֶׁת בַּתּוֹרָה ·
הַכְּתוּבָה עַל יְדֵי מֹשֶׁה עַבְדֶּךָ · הָאֲמוּרָה מִפִּי אַהֲרֹן וּבָנָיו
כֹּהֲנִים · עַם קְדוֹשֶׁךָ כָּאָמוּר · יְבָרֶכְךָ יְיָ וְיִשְׁמְרֶךָ : יָאֵר יְיָ פָּנָיו
אֵלֶיךָ וִיחֻנֶּךָּ : יִשָּׂא יְיָ פָּנָיו אֵלֶיךָ וְיָשֵׂם לְךָ שָׁלוֹם :

שִׂים שָׁלוֹם טוֹבָה וּבְרָכָה חֵן וָחֶסֶד וְרַחֲמִים עָלֵינוּ

which are committed unto thy hand, and for our souls which are in thy charge, and for thy miracles, which are daily with us, and for thy wonders and thy benefits, which are wrought at all times, evening, morn and noon. O thou who art all-good, whose mercies fail not ; thou, merciful Being, whose lovingkindnesses never cease, we have ever hoped in thee.

be to thy great and holy Name, because thou hast kept us in life and hast preserved us : so mayest thou continue to keep us in life and to preserve us. O gather our exiles to thy holy courts to observe thy statutes, to do thy will, and to serve thee with a perfect heart ; seeing that we give thanks unto thee. Blessed be the God to whom thanksgivings are due.

On Chanukah add " We thank thee," p. 151, to " great Name."

For all these things thy Name, O our King, shall be continually blessed and exalted for ever and ever.

And everything that liveth give thanks unto thee for ever, and shall praise thy Name in truth, O God, our salvation and our help. Blessed art thou, O Lord, whose Name is All-good, and unto whom it is becoming to give thanks.

At the repetition of the Amidah by the Reader, the following is introduced :—

Our God and God of our fathers, bless us with the three-fold blessing of thy Torah written by the hand of Moses thy servant, which was spoken by Aaron and his sons, the priests, thy holy people, as it is said, THE LORD BLESS THEE, AND KEEP THEE : THE LORD MAKE HIS FACE TO SHINE UPON THEE, AND BE GRACIOUS UNTO THEE : THE LORD TURN HIS FACE UNTO THEE, AND GIVE THEE PEACE.

Numbers 6. 24–26

VII. FOR PEACE

Grant peace, welfare, blessing, grace, lovingkindness and mercy unto us and unto all Israel, thy people. Bless us, O our Father, even all of us together, with the light

וְעַל כָּל־יִשְׂרָאֵל עַמֶּךָ · בָּרְכֵנוּ אָבִינוּ כֻּלָּנוּ כְּאֶחָד בְּאוֹר
פָּנֶיךָ · כִּי בְאוֹר פָּנֶיךָ נָתַתָּ לָּנוּ יְיָ אֱלֹהֵינוּ תּוֹרַת חַיִּים
וְאַהֲבַת חֶסֶד וּצְדָקָה וּבְרָכָה וְרַחֲמִים וְחַיִּים וְשָׁלוֹם ·
וְטוֹב בְּעֵינֶיךָ לְבָרֵךְ אֶת־עַמְּךָ יִשְׂרָאֵל בְּכָל־עֵת וּבְכָל־
שָׁעָה בִּשְׁלוֹמֶךָ ·

בָּרוּךְ אַתָּה יְיָ · הַמְבָרֵךְ אֶת־עַמּוֹ יִשְׂרָאֵל בַּשָּׁלוֹם :

אֱלֹהַי · נְצוֹר לְשׁוֹנִי מֵרָע וּשְׂפָתַי מִדַּבֵּר מִרְמָה ·
וְלִמְקַלְלַי נַפְשִׁי תִדּוֹם וְנַפְשִׁי כֶּעָפָר לַכֹּל תִּהְיֶה : פְּתַח
לִבִּי בְּתוֹרָתֶךָ וּבְמִצְוֹתֶיךָ תִּרְדּוֹף נַפְשִׁי · וְכֹל הַחוֹשְׁבִים
עָלַי רָעָה מְהֵרָה הָפֵר עֲצָתָם וְקַלְקֵל מַחֲשַׁבוֹתָם · עֲשֵׂה
לְמַעַן שְׁמֶךָ עֲשֵׂה לְמַעַן יְמִינֶךָ עֲשֵׂה לְמַעַן קְדֻשָּׁתֶךָ עֲשֵׂה
לְמַעַן תּוֹרָתֶךָ · לְמַעַן יֵחָלְצוּן יְדִידֶיךָ הוֹשִׁיעָה יְמִינְךָ
וַעֲנֵנִי : יִהְיוּ לְרָצוֹן אִמְרֵי־פִי וְהֶגְיוֹן לִבִּי לְפָנֶיךָ יְיָ צוּרִי
וְגֹאֲלִי : עֹשֶׂה שָׁלוֹם בִּמְרוֹמָיו הוּא יַעֲשֶׂה שָׁלוֹם עָלֵינוּ
וְעַל כָּל־יִשְׂרָאֵל · וְאִמְרוּ אָמֵן :

יְהִי רָצוֹן לְפָנֶיךָ יְיָ · אֱלֹהֵינוּ וֵאלֹהֵי אֲבוֹתֵינוּ שֶׁיִּבָּנֶה בֵּית
הַמִּקְדָּשׁ בִּמְהֵרָה בְיָמֵינוּ · וְתֵן חֶלְקֵנוּ בְּתוֹרָתֶךָ : וְשָׁם נַעֲבָדְךָ
בְּיִרְאָה כִּימֵי עוֹלָם וּכְשָׁנִים קַדְמוֹנִיּוֹת : וְעָרְבָה לַייָ מִנְחַת
יְהוּדָה וִירוּשָׁלַ͏ִם כִּימֵי עוֹלָם וּכְשָׁנִים קַדְמוֹנִיּוֹת :

קַדִּישׁ יָתוֹם p. 582. , בָּרְכִי נַפְשִׁי p. 206. , תִּתְקַבַּל p. 208. , עָלֵינוּ p. 212.

See p. 154 of thy countenance ; for by the light of thy countenance thou hast given us, O Lord our God, the Torah of life, lovingkindness and righteousness, blessing, mercy, life and peace ; and may it be good in thy sight to bless thy people Israel at all times and in every hour with thy peace.

Blessed art thou, O Lord, who blessest thy people Israel with peace.

CONCLUD-MEDITA-TION O my God ! guard my tongue from evil and my lips from speaking guile ; and to such as curse me let my soul be dumb, yea, let my soul be unto all as the dust. Open my heart to thy Torah, and let my soul pursue thy com- *See p.* 156 mandments. If any design evil against me, speedily make their counsel of none effect, and frustrate their designs. Do it for the sake of thy Name, do it for the sake of thy power, do it for the sake of thy holiness, do it for the sake *Psalm* 60. 7 of thy Torah. In order that thy beloved ones may be *Psalm* 19. 15 delivered, O save with thy right hand, and answer me. Let the words of my mouth and the meditation of my heart be acceptable before thee, O Lord, my Rock and my Redeemer. He who maketh peace in his high places, may he make peace for us and for all Israel, and say ye, Amen.

May it be thy will, O Lord our God and God of our fathers, that the temple be speedily rebuilt in our days, and grant our portion in thy Torah. And there we will serve thee with awe, as *Malachi* 3. 4 in the days of old, and as in ancient years. Then shall the offering of Judah and Jerusalem be pleasant unto the Lord, as in the days of old, and as in ancient years.

Kaddish, p. 207.
" *It is our duty," etc., p.* 209.
Mourner's Kaddish, p. 213.
Psalm civ:, *p.* 583.

THE FESTIVALS

ימים טובים

The Jewish Festivals are, like the Sabbath, supreme examples of the hallowing of life under the influence of Religion. They fall into two groups—the *Solemn*, *i.e.* New Year and Day of Atonement; and the *Joyous*, *i.e.* Passover, Pentecost and Tabernacles. For the Solemn Festivals, see p. 838; in this place we deal with the JOYOUS FESTIVALS, the three Pilgrim Festivals of Temple days. As in the case of the Sabbath, the coming in of Festivals is consecrated by the *Kiddush* prayer, praising God for the gift of the Festival; and their going out is marked by the *Havdolah* blessing, proclaiming the everlasting distinction between light and darkness, between the sacred and the profane, in life. Maimonides comprehends the various duties in connection with Sabbath and Festivals under the following four terms: " We are bidden to *remember*, *keep*, *honour*, and *delight* in them. We ' remember ' the Festivals by means of Kiddush and Havdolah; we ' keep ' them, by refraining from all work forbidden on the Sabbath, except labour for the preparation of food (Exodus 12. 16); we ' honour ' them by festive lights, meals and garments; and we find congenial, happy and cheerful ' delight ' in their observance." Even clearer is the principle of Festival observance that was laid down by the Rabbis: חציו לד׳ וחציו לכם. " Half of it is unto the Lord, and half unto yourselves ". Therefore, the joy and gladness that mark the Festivals are bound up with religious worship and instruction, the strengthening of man's soul-life in God being an essential part of the Holy Day. And each of these Holy Days has its individual Liturgy, as well as its Lesson from the Torah and the Prophets, to be explained by the religious teacher, and applied to man's tasks and duties in life.

I

PASSOVER begins on the fifteenth of Nisan, and extends to the twenty-second of that month. It is the Festival of Spring, of the annual renewal of Nature's life. Passover's human appeal, therefore, is as perennial as Spring. But it is also an historical festival, and commemorates an event —the redemption of Israel from Egyptian slavery—that has changed the destinies of humanity. The story of that event, as recorded in the first fifteen chapters of the Book of Exodus, has become one of the parables of mankind; and has been a light to the Western peoples in their long and weary warfare for liberty. It taught them that God, Who in Egypt espoused the cause of brick-making slaves against a royal oppressor, was a God of Justice and Freedom; and that destruction awaited every dominion of iniquity which denied justice and freedom to the children of men. Thus, the most Jewish of the Festivals, Israel's birthday, is as timely to-day as it was thousands of years ago, and has a message for men of all creeds and all races.

The Rabbis deemed it a sacred task to spread a full understanding of the eternal significance of Passover. And in the performance of this task, led by sound psychological insight, they began with the mind of the young. Out of a single verse in the Biblical Text, they evolved the wonderful Seder Service, with its appeal to the interest of the intelligent

PASSOVER

child. That appeal began in connection with the most distinguishing feature of the Festival, the stern prohibition of eating any leavened food and its total removal from the house ; for the child was associated with it through the ceremony of the Search for leaven on the night before the Festival. The Seder Service itself is opened by the Questions asked by the youngest at the table, and the answer to those Questions—the *Haggadah shel Pesach*—is a running commentary of prayer and legend and exhortation on the bondage in, and redemption from, Egypt. It especially elucidates the terms *pesach*—the paschal offering in the days of old ; *matzah*—the unleavened bread of affliction, the reminder of the readiness with which our fathers in Egypt followed the call to Freedom ; and the *moror*, the bitter herbs, typical of the lot of the Jew in Egypt and in so many other lands after Egypt. The Hallel-psalms early formed part of the Seder; *Nishmas* (p. 417), various hymns, folk-songs and children's rhymes, were added in the course of the centuries.

The Seder Service is a typical example of Jewish education : the ceremonies became object-lessons in religion, sacred history, and morality. At one point in the Seder, it is remarked, " Every Jew should regard himself as if *he* had personally come out of Egypt ". The whole of Jewish ceremonial tends to the self-identification of the child with his fathers, and to fostering in his soul the resolve to take his part in the Jewish present and future.

The Seder in history would require a monograph. In the Middle Ages, the Seder night was a time of terror to the Jewries of Christian Europe. It was on the eve of Passover 1190, that the Jews of York, surrounded by a murderous mob, resolved to anticipate slaughter by suicide, and perished almost to a man. From the twelfth century onwards, the Satanic charge of using human blood on Passover was brought against the Jew by malevolent fanatics, and that foul libel has been responsible for a long series of hideous massacres.

As to the Services on the Joyous Festivals, these contain variations from those of the ordinary Sabbath prayers, as well as numerous additions. The latter are, Hallel, anthems and hymns (piyyutim). The complete Service for each Festival must be sought in the *Machzor*. lit. " cycle of prayers," as the special Prayer Book for Festivals is called. The first printed Ashkenazi *Machzor* appeared in 1521. It has been translated into most European languages, and several times into English.

In general outline, Festival Services and Readings are as follows : On the first two and last two days, the Sabbath Morning Service (pp. 1–104, 416–448) is, with slight modifications, said ; Hallel ; Opening of Ark, with special introductory Prayers ; Scriptural Lesson, Mussaf and concluding Prayers.

During the Intermediate Days—Chol Hammoed—of Passover and Tabernacles, the Weekday and Sabbath services are said on Weekdays and Sabbaths respectively, followed by Hallel, Reading of the Torah and Mussaf. The Kiddush is that of ordinary Sabbaths.

The Scriptural Readings on PASSOVER are :

1st Day, Exodus 12. 21–51 ; Haftorah, Joshua 5. 2–6. 1.

2nd Day, Leviticus 22. 26–23. 44 ; Haftorah, II Kings 23. 1–9, 21–25.

Intermediate Sabbath (Chol Hammoed), Exodus **33**. 12–34. 26 ; Haftorah, Ezekiel **36**. 37–37. 14.

7th Day, Exodus **13**. 17–15. 26 ; Haftorah, II Samuel **22**. 1–51.

8th Day, Deuteronomy **15**. 19–16. 17 ; Haftorah, Isaiah **10**. 32–12. 5.

On each day of the Festival, a few verses from Numbers **28** and a Maftir are read from a second Sefer ; five men are called to the Torah on Festivals, unless it be on a Sabbath day.

THE SONG OF SONGS is read either on the Intermediate Sabbath or on the Seventh and Eighth Day, whichever be a Sabbath. It is a collection of ancient lyrics of the spring-time and youthful love. It centres round a country maiden Sulamith, who is exposed to the blandishments of a Royal wooer, but who remains faithful to her shepherd lover. From an early date, it has been interpreted as an allegory of the mutual love of God and Israel. Israel's Friend is our Heavenly Father, Whom it loves with an undying love, and in fidelity to Whose commandments it is ready to undergo martyrdom—" I am my Beloved's, and my Beloved is mine ".

For the counting of the Omer, see p. 938.

II

The second of the three agricultural festivals, the Festival of the PENTECOST Wheat-harvest, is *Shavuos,* the FEAST OF WEEKS, celebrated on the sixth and seventh of Sivan, seven weeks after the first day of Passover; hence, the name PENTECOST (lit. "fiftieth day "). In Jewish Tradition, however, it is connected with the Covenant on Mount Sinai, and described as זמן מתן תורתנו, " the Season of the Giving of our Torah". This refers to the Proclamation of the Ten Commandments ; see Exodus **19** and **20**. The exact date of that Proclamation is not expressly mentioned in the Torah, but is calculated to have been on the sixth day of the month of Sivan. Hence, its association with the Feast of Weeks, which thus became the Festival of Revelation. (For the idea of Revelation, see p. 251–253). The Rabbis speak of Shavuos as " the concluding festival " to Passover. For the deliverance from bondage was not an end in itself ; it was the prelude to Sinai (Exodus **3**. 12), where Israel crowned the freedom obtained on Passover with the vow of self-consecration to become a Kingdom of priests and a Holy nation.

The solemn reading of the Ten Commandments in the synagogue constitutes the central part of the Shavuos Service. No religious document has exercised a greater influence on the moral and social life of man than the Divine Summary of Human Duty, known as the Ten Commandments, or the Decalogue. While not presenting the Whole Duty of Man, these brief commands—only 120 Hebrew words in all— lay down in simple, unforgettable form, the *foundations* of Religion and of Right for all time and for all men ; see p. 240–247.

The basic importance of the Ten Commandments was ever recognized in Israel. Their eternal and universal significance were duly emphasized by means of parable, metaphor, and all the rare poetic imagery of Rabbinic legend. The Tables on which the Ten Commandments were written were held to have been prepared at the eve of Creation—thus antedating humanity, and, therefore, independent, of time or place or racial culture; and·they were hewn from the sapphire Throne of Glory—and thus of infinite worth and preciousness. The Revelation at Sinai, it was taught, was given in desert territory, which belongs to no one nation exclusively; and it was heard not by Israel alone, but by the inhabitants of all the earth. The Divine Voice divided itself into the 70 tongues then spoken on earth, so that all the children of men might understand its world-embracing and man-redeeming message. The sixth of Sivan, the day of the Revelation at Mount Sinai, was held to be as momentous as the day of Creation itself; for, without the coming into existence of Moral Law, the creation of the material universe would have been incomplete, nay, meaningless.

It is interesting to note that for many ages the Decalogue was given equal pre-eminence in religion outside the Synagogue. Luther summed up the opinion of Western Christendom for over 1,500 years, when he declared, " Never will there be found a precept preferable or comparable to these commands ". In succeeding centuries, the Humanists, the Deists, and even the Freethinkers, spoke with reverence of the Law of Sinai. Two generations ago, Renan wrote : " The unique distinction which awaited this page of Exodus, namely to become the code of universal ethics, was not unmerited. The Ten Words are for all peoples ; and they will be, during all centuries, the commandments of God ". And historians of civilization are generally agreed that, low as the ethical standards ot the world at present undoubtedly are, it is certain that they would be even lower, but for the supreme influence of the Ten Commandments.

Unlike Passover and Tabernacles, the Feast of Weeks has no distinctive ceremony. In many congregations it is customary to decorate the synagogue with flowers and plants on this Festival, a lingering echo of the ancient agricultural celebration. And in some communities, the pious spend a great part of the first night of Shavuos in self-preparation for the spiritual message of the Festival by reading selections from the books of Scripture, as well as from Rabbinic and Mystical literature. The special Book of Service for this purpose is known as *Tikkun leyl Shavuos*. It was also long customary that the Jewish child be initiated into 'the study of the Jewish religion and the Hebrew language on Shavuos, so that to him too that Festival become the day of Revelation.

The Scriptural Readings are :

1st Day, Exodus 19 and 20 ; Haftorah, Ezekiel 1.

2nd Day, Deuteronomy 15. 19–16. 16 ; Haftorah, Habakkuk 3; and, each day, Numbers 28. 26–31 from a second Sefer.

On the Second Day, THE BOOK OF RUTH is read. It is the story of one who, forsaking idolatry, enters the Covenant of Sinai, and joins the Household of Israel. In this scene of domesticity coming down to us from the stormy days of the Judges, we have a marvellous picture of woman's friendship. Ruth became the ancestress of King David.

III

The Feast of Tabernacles (*Succos*) is primarily the Festival of *TABERNA-*
Thanksgiving for the abundance of the harvest, as well as for the mercies *CLES*
to our ancestors in the Wilderness. To the urban dweller of to-day, it
is a reminder that Israel's story has its idyllic side, and that it has been
the tragedy of the Jew to have been sundered from the soil for nearly
2,000 years. Such resolved memory on the part of an entire people is of
vital importance in its destiny. " The vineyards of Israel have ceased to
exist, but the eternal Law enjoins the children of Israel still to celebrate
the vintage. A race that persist in celebrating their vintage, although
they have no fruits to gather, will regain their vineyards " (Benjamin
Disraeli).

Tabernacles derives its name from the command, " Ye shall dwell
in booths seven days . . . that your generations may know that I
made the children of Israel to dwell in booths, when I brought them out
of the land of Egypt " (Leviticus 23. 42–43). The booth is thus a
reminder that, during all those years of wandering and toil, Divine
Providence surrounded our fathers as with clouds of glory. To the
loyal Israelite in warmer climates, the Succah is during the week of
Tabernacles his home ; he eats, entertains, and even lives in it. Those
of northern countries can, as a rule, only take their meals in the Succah.

The other symbol of Succos as the Feast of Ingathering, is the cluster
of plants—the lulav, esrog, myrtle and willow—with which the worshipper rejoices before God, as he chants praises of gratitude to the Giver
of all good. Many are the symbolizations of the four species in this
festive cluster. They have, for example, been taken to indicate different
human types : the tall palm-branch denoting the men of power and
influence ; the aromatic esrog, the men of saintliness and learning ;
the myrtle, the average men and women of a community ; and the
willow representing the poor and lowly—but all of them forming one
human Brotherhood mutually responsible for the welfare and good
name of the whole.

Every day after the Mussaf Amidah, there are circuits round the
synagogue. With lulav and esrog in the hand, the worshippers chant
anthems and invocations beginning with *Hoshana* (" O, save now ").
On the Seventh Day of Tabernacles, seven such circuits are made,
accompanied by the recital of many *Hoshana* hymns and prayers.
Towards the end of the Middle Ages, with the rise of mysticism, the
Seventh Day — Hoshana Rabba — grew greatly in solemnity. By the
sixteenth century, the day came to be looked upon as a continuation of
the Day of Atonement, giving "another chance" for repentance to those
sinful mortals who had on that Holy Day failed to make full use of the
Divine grace. A symbolical beating of a bundle of willow-branches
closes the Hoshana Rabba service. In some communities, the devout
spend the greater portion of the preceding night in vigil and prayer,
reciting the *Tikkun leyl hoshana rabba*, in anticipation of the morrow.

The two festive days of Succos are followed by five Intermediate Days.
The full Festival is resumed on the Eighth Day of Solemn Assembly
(Shemini Atzeres). Its " second day " is known as Rejoicing of the
Law (Simchas Torah).

SHEMINI ATZERES concludes the Tishri cycle of Festivals. It shares with Tabernacles proper the designation of " Season of our Gladness " in the Liturgy. Joy is a fundamental note of the Jewish religious spirit, and happiness is a duty in Judaism. " The essence of our whole Torah is contained in these three things : reverence, love, joy. They are the way to bring us near to God. Thy contrition on the Day of Fasting is in no wise more pleasing to Him than thy joy on the Sabbath or the Festival, if so be that thy delight comes from a devout and full heart" (Hallevi). And the Shulchan Aruch lays down the following rule for festive seasons. " It is man's duty to be joyful and glad at heart on the Festivals, he and his wife and his children and those dependent on him. Make the children happy by giving them sweets and nuts ; and the womenfolk by buying them gifts, according to your means. It is also a duty to give food to the hungry, to the fatherless, and to the widow, as well as to other poor people ".

No wonder that joyous worship has at all times been the key-note of Tabernacles. Greatly beloved were the singing and chanting round the Altar in Temple days. But the ceremony on the Succos Festival which appears to have aroused the greatest enthusiasm, was the festive procession to and from the spring that supplied the water for the libations in the Sanctuary. The Mishna tells us, " He that hath not beheld the rejoicing at the Drawing of water, hath never seen rejoicing in his life ". There were torch-dances by men of saintliness and renown, and songs and hymns by Levites and people, to the accompaniment of flutes, harps and cymbals. Refrains sung at these festivities have come down to us. Some sang, " Happy was our youth, for it did not disgrace our old age " ; others chanted, " Happy is our old age, for it atones for our youth ".

New forms of festivity developed with the centuries. More than a thousand years ago, the last day of the Festival attained to a character, and even to a name, of its own, SIMCHAS TORAH, Rejoicing of the Law. It arose out of the festivities that attended the completion on that day of the annual reading of the Torah, and the commencement of the new Readings. Since the days of the Gaonim, it has been deemed a great honour to be either *Chosan Torah*, " bridegroom of the Torah ", and be called to the reading of the last section of Deuteronomy ; or to be *Chosan Bereshith*—" bridegroom of Genesis ", and be called to open the reading of the Torah. Even the little boys, all in a group, were called to the Reading, when a special Blessing (Genesis 48. 16) was pronounced upon them, "The angel who hath redeemed me from all evil, bless the lads; and let my name be named in them, and the name of my fathers Abraham and Isaac; and let them grow into a multitude in the midst of the earth ". See pp. 828–833.

And thus, the note of Succos-gladness, which began in primeval days as harvest merrymaking, and then became the joy of Temple-worship, has for a millenium and longer culminated in triumphant rejoicing over the Torah, Israel's inalienable heritage.

סדר המועדים והרגלים:

הדלקת נר של רגלים

Before kindling the lights on the eve of the Festival in the Home, say:

רִבּוֹן הָעוֹלָמִים · הִנֵּה בָאתִי לְהַדְלִיק אֶת הַנֵּרוֹת

לִכְבוֹד הָרֶגֶל: וּבִזְכוּת מִצְוָה זוּ תַשְׁפִּיעַ עָלַי וְעַל בְּנֵי בֵיתִי

שֶׁפַע הַחַיִּים שֶׁתְּחָנֵּנוּ וּתְבָרְכֵנוּ בְּרֹב בְּרָכוֹת · וְתַשְׁכֵּן

שְׁכִינָתְךָ בְּתוֹכֵנוּ:

אַב הָרַחֲמִים · אָנָּא מְשֹׁךְ חַסְדְּךָ עָלַי וְעַל קְרֹבַי

הָאֲהוּבִים (וְזַכֵּנִי לְגַדֵּל בָּנַי וּבְנוֹתַי) לָלֶכֶת בְּדַרְכֵי

יְשָׁרִים לְפָנֶיךָ דְּבֵקִים בַּתּוֹרָה וּבְמַעֲשִׂים טוֹבִים ·

הַרְחֵק מֵעָלֵינוּ כָּל חֶרְפָּה תוּגָה וְיָגוֹן · וְשִׂים שָׁלוֹם

The Scriptural Readings on Tabernacles are :
First Day, Leviticus 22. 26–23. 44 ; Haftorah, Zechariah 14. 1–21.
Second Day, Leviticus 22. 26–23. 44 ; Haftorah, I Kings 8. 2–21.
  Sabbath Chol Hammoed, Exodus 33. 12–34. 26 ; Haftorah, Ezekiel
38. 18–39, 16.
  Atzeres, Deuteronomy 14. 22–16. 17 ; Haftorah, I Kings 8. 54–66.
  Simchas Torah, Deuteronomy 33. 1–34. 12 and Genesis 1. 1–2. 3 ;
Haftorah, Joshua 1. 1–18.
  Each day some verses of Numbers 29 are read from a second Sefer.
  THE BOOK OF ECCLESIASTES is read on the Intermediate Sabbath
or on Shemini Atzeres, if that be on a Sabbath. The author of Ecclesiastes,
Koheleth, is puzzled over the perplexity of life, and is bored by its

SERVICE FOR THE FESTIVALS OF PASSOVER, PENTECOST AND TABERNACLES

THE FESTIVAL LIGHTS

Before kindling the lights on the eve of the Festival in the Home, say :—

MEDITA-TION

Lord of the Universe, I am about to perform the sacred duty of kindling the lights in honour of the Festival. And may the effect of my fulfilling this commandment be that the stream of abundant life and heavenly blessing flow in upon me and mine ; that thou be gracious unto us, and cause thy Presence to dwell among us.

PRAYER

Father of Mercy, O continue thy lovingkindness unto me and my dear ones. Make me worthy to (rear my children so that they) walk in the way of the righteous before thee, loyal to thy Torah and clinging to good deeds. Keep thou far from us all manner of shame, grief, and care ; and grant

Psalm 36. 10

that peace, light, and joy ever abide in our home. For with

vanity. Man, he feels, has nothing, knows nothing, is nothing. " The pre-eminence of man over the beast is nought, for all is vanity ", he bitterly exclaims. Yet, from this dark forest of doubt and despair, Koheleth emerges with the triumphant conviction that to do rightly is the final end of life ; nay, that it constitutes the humanity of man. " Let us hear the conclusion of the whole matter ; all hath been heard ; fear God, and keep His commandments ; for this is the whole duty of man " (Ecclesiastes 12. 13).

THE FESTIVAL LIGHTS.

lights. The Festival light, and the Benediction over it, seem an extension of the Sabbath light institution and are of great antiquity, being mentioned in the Jerusalem Talmud. Light is an even more appropriate symbol of the Festivals than of the Sabbath. In Hebrew, the word אורה (light) is often almost a synonym for שמחה (joy).

אוֹרָה וְשִׂמְחָה בִּמְעוֹנֵנוּ · כִּי עִמְּךָ מְקוֹר חַיִּים בְּאוֹרְךָ

נִרְאֶה־אוֹר · אָמֵן :

בָּרוּךְ אַתָּה יְיָ אֱלֹהֵינוּ מֶלֶךְ הָעוֹלָם · אֲשֶׁר קִדְּשָׁנוּ

בְּמִצְוֹתָיו וְצִוָּנוּ לְהַדְלִיק נֵר שֶׁל (שַׁבָּת וְ) *on Friday add :* יוֹם טוֹב :

The following Blessing is omitted on the last two evenings of Passover

בָּרוּךְ אַתָּה יְיָ אֱלֹהֵינוּ מֶלֶךְ הָעוֹלָם · שֶׁהֶחֱיָנוּ וְקִיְּמָנוּ

וְהִגִּיעָנוּ לַזְּמַן הַזֶּה :

On עֶרֶב יוֹם טוֹב, מִנְחָה *is said as on Fridays ; see pp. 272–294.*
For מַעֲרִיב *see pp. 364–374. Should the evening of the Festival fall on*
Friday, מַעֲרִיב *commences with* מִזְמוֹר שִׁיר לְיוֹם הַשַּׁבָּת, *p. 360.*
The following עֲמִידָה *is said at the Evening, Morning and Afternoon*
Services on פֶּסַח, שָׁבֻעוֹת, סֻכּוֹת, שְׁמִינִי עֲצֶרֶת *and* שִׂמְחַת תּוֹרָה.

אֲדֹנָי שְׂפָתַי תִּפְתָּח וּפִי יַגִּיד תְּהִלָּתֶךָ :

בָּרוּךְ אַתָּה יְיָ אֱלֹהֵינוּ וֵאלֹהֵי אֲבוֹתֵינוּ · אֱלֹהֵ

אַבְרָהָם אֱלֹהֵי יִצְחָק וֵאלֹהֵי יַעֲקֹב · הָאֵל הַגָּדוֹל הַגִּבּוֹר

וְהַנּוֹרָא אֵל עֶלְיוֹן · גּוֹמֵל חֲסָדִים טוֹבִים וְקוֹנֵה הַכֹּל

וְזוֹכֵר חַסְדֵי אָבוֹת וּמֵבִיא גוֹאֵל לִבְנֵי בְנֵיהֶם לְמַעַ

שְׁמוֹ בְּאַהֲבָה ·

who hast kept us in life. See p. 755 ; this Benediction is not said on
the last days of Passover, as the Festival is then no longer new. It is
said on the last days of Tabernacles, because Shemini Atzeres is an
independent Festival.

thee is the fountain of life ; in thy light do we see light. Amen.

BLESSINGS Blessed art thou, O Lord our God, King of the universe, who hast hallowed us by thy commandments, and hast commanded us to kindle [*on Friday add* : the Sabbath and] the Festival light.

The following Blessing is omitted on the last two evenings of Passover.

Blessed art thou, O Lord our God, King of the universe, who hast kept us in life, and hast preserved us, and enabled us to reach this season.

On the Eve of Festivals, Afternoon Service is said as on Fridays ; see pp. 273–295, and 299.

For Evening Service, see pp. 365–375. Should the evening of the Festival fall on Friday, the Evening Service commences with " A Psalm, a Song for the Sabbath Day," p. 361.

The following Amidah is said at the Evening, Morning and Afternoon Services of Passover, Pentecost, Tabernacles, the Eighth Day of Solemn Assembly, and Simchas Torah.

THE FESTIVAL AMIDAH

Psalm 51. 17

O Lord, open thou my lips, and my mouth shall declare thy praise.

I. THE GOD OF HISTORY

Blessed art thou, O Lord our God and God of our fathers, God of Abraham, God of Isaac, and God of Jacob, the great, mighty and revered God, the most high God, who bestowest lovingkindnesses, and art Master of all things ; who rememberest the pious deeds of the patriarchs, and in love wilt bring a redeemer to their children's children for thy Name's sake.

THE AMIDAH.

As on the Sabbath, the Festival Amidah consists of seven Benedictions. In its present form it is held to be the product of the liturgical activity of the Babylonian teachers Rabh and Samuel, in the third century. The middle Benediction is known as " Sanctification of the Day " (קדושת היום). It opens with the assertion of the Selection of Israel, and Israel's privilege as the recipient of God's love.

מֶלֶךְ עוֹזֵר וּמוֹשִׁיעַ וּמָגֵן · בָּרוּךְ אַתָּה יְיָ · מָגֵן אַבְרָהָם :

אַתָּה גִּבּוֹר לְעוֹלָם אֲדֹנָי מְחַיֵּה מֵתִים אַתָּה רַב לְהוֹשִׁיעַ :

say — שִׂמְחַת תּוֹרָה and on שְׁמִינִי עֲצֶרֶת of מוּסָף After the
מַשִּׁיב הָרוּחַ וּמוֹרִיד הַגֶּשֶׁם :

מְכַלְכֵּל חַיִּים בְּחֶסֶד מְחַיֵּה מֵתִים בְּרַחֲמִים רַבִּים · סוֹמֵךְ
נוֹפְלִים וְרוֹפֵא חוֹלִים וּמַתִּיר אֲסוּרִים וּמְקַיֵּם אֱמוּנָתוֹ
לִישֵׁנֵי עָפָר · מִי כָמוֹךְ בַּעַל גְּבוּרוֹת וּמִי דוֹמֶה לָּךְ ·
מֶלֶךְ מֵמִית וּמְחַיֶּה וּמַצְמִיחַ יְשׁוּעָה :

וְנֶאֱמָן אַתָּה לְהַחֲיוֹת מֵתִים · בָּרוּךְ אַתָּה יְיָ · מְחַיֵּה
הַמֵּתִים :

When the Reader repeats the עֲמִידָה in the Morning, the קְדוּשָׁה
of p. 452 is said; in the Afternoon that of p. 576,
and הָאֵל הַקָּדוֹשׁ to אַתָּה קָדוֹשׁ omitted.

אַתָּה קָדוֹשׁ וְשִׁמְךָ קָדוֹשׁ וּקְדוֹשִׁים בְּכָל־יוֹם יְהַלְלוּךָ
סֶּלָה · בָּרוּךְ אַתָּה יְיָ · הָאֵל הַקָּדוֹשׁ :

אַתָּה בְחַרְתָּנוּ מִכָּל־הָעַמִּים · אָהַבְתָּ אוֹתָנוּ · וְרָצִיתָ

THE SELECTION OF ISRAEL.

THOU HAST CHOSEN US. Nowhere is the idea of Israel's Selection so
clearly and jubilantly expressed as in this anthem. Recurring in the
Amidahs of all the Festivals, it expresses an axiomatic conviction that
Israel is the Chosen People, called in a special degree to God's service.
" I the Lord have called thee in righteousness, and have taken hold of
thy hand, and kept thee, and set thee for a covenant of the peoples, for
a light of the nations " (Isaiah 42. 6)—a light supernaturally kindled,
lest darkness become complete—a witness of God's sovereignty and
purity, lest He become utterly unacknowledged in the world He had
made.

O King, Helper, Saviour and Shield. Blessed art thou, O Lord, the Shield of Abraham.

II. THE GOD OF NATURE   Thou, O Lord, art mighty for ever, thou revivest the dead, thou art mighty to save.

[After the Additional Service of the Eighth Day of Solemn Assembly and on Simchas Torah say :—

Thou causest the wind to blow and the rain to fall.]

Thou sustainest the living with lovingkindness, revivest the dead with great mercy, supportest the falling, healest the sick, freest the bound, and keepest thy faith to them that sleep in the dust. Who is like unto thee, Lord of mighty acts, and who resembleth thee, O King, who orderest death and restorest life, and causest salvation to spring forth ?

Yea, faithful art thou to revive the dead. Blessed art thou, O Lord, who revivest the dead.

III. THE SANCTIFI-CATION   Thou art holy, and thy Name is holy, and holy beings praise thee daily. (Selah.) Blessed art thou, O Lord, the holy God.

When the Reader repeats the Amidah in the Morning, the Sanctification of p. 453 is said ; in the Afternoon, that of p. 577.

IV. SELECTION OF ISRAEL   Thou hast chosen us from all peoples ; thou hast loved us and taken pleasure in us, and hast exalted us above

---

Each historic nation points with pride to its own peculiar contribution to the spiritual treasure of mankind, whether in art or science, law or government. Now Israel's contribution to the humanization of man transcends that of all the others in eternal significance. "For only in Israel did an *ethical* monotheism exist; and, wherever else it is found later on, it has been derived directly or indirectly from Israel, and was conditioned by the existence of the people of Israel. Hence the term the *election* of Israel expresses merely an historical fact" (Leo Baeck). When we think of the abominations that were part of human life in Egypt, Canaan, Assyria ; when we recall that in Rome the cruelties of barbarism were combined with shameless indulgence of every vice, there is ample justification for the conviction that Israel was a people " apart ", a little island in a vast ocean of animalism. Modern Jews do not always grasp the full significance of this elementary historical fact. "The proud consciousness shall again be yours that you are members of a People which among all the Peoples that labour

בְּנוּ · וְרוֹמַמְתָּנוּ מִכָּל הַלְּשׁוֹנוֹת · וְקִדַּשְׁתָּנוּ בְּמִצְוֹתֶיךָ ·
וְקֵרַבְתָּנוּ מַלְכֵּנוּ לַעֲבוֹדָתֶךָ · וְשִׁמְךָ הַגָּדוֹל וְהַקָּדוֹשׁ
עָלֵינוּ קָרָאתָ :

On Saturday Night add the following :—

וַתּוֹדִיעֵנוּ יְיָ אֱלֹהֵינוּ אֶת־מִשְׁפְּטֵי צִדְקֶךָ וַתְּלַמְּדֵנוּ לַעֲשׂוֹת
חֻקֵּי רְצוֹנֶךָ · וַתִּתֶּן־לָנוּ יְיָ אֱלֹהֵינוּ מִשְׁפָּטִים יְשָׁרִים וְתוֹרוֹת
אֱמֶת חֻקִּים וּמִצְוֹת טוֹבִים · וַתַּנְחִילֵנוּ זְמַנֵּי שָׂשׂוֹן וּמוֹעֲדֵי
קֹדֶשׁ וְחַגֵּי נְדָבָה · וַתּוֹרִישֵׁנוּ קְדֻשַּׁת שַׁבָּת וּכְבוֹד מוֹעֵד
וַחֲגִיגַת הָרֶגֶל · וַתַּבְדֵּל יְיָ אֱלֹהֵינוּ בֵּין קֹדֶשׁ לְחוֹל בֵּין אוֹר
לְחֹשֶׁךְ בֵּין יִשְׂרָאֵל לָעַמִּים בֵּין יוֹם הַשְּׁבִיעִי לְשֵׁשֶׁת יְמֵי

at the loom of history, is the mightiest among those who have created
the eternal values of life" (Chajes). "While other nations", wrote
Matthew Arnold, "had the misleading idea that this or that, other
than righteousness, is saving, and it is not; that this or that, other than
conduct, brings happiness, and it does not—Israel had the true idea
that Righteousness is saving, and that to conduct belongs happiness.
Herein Israel stood alone, the friend and elect of the Eternal. As long
as the world lasts, all who want to make progress in righteousness will
come to Israel for inspiration, as to the people who have had the sense
for righteousness most glowing and strongest. This does truly constitute
for Israel a most extraordinary distinction".

Israel has not always been faithful to its mission ; all the greater
was then its punishment. "You only I have known (*i.e.* chosen) of all
the families of the earth ; *therefore* I will visit upon you all your iniquities" (Amos 3. 2). But there has always been a "righteous Remnant"
in Israel that continued to subordinate the whole of life to the Divine
Will; and, in defiance of all storms and tempests that assailed them, to
uphold the ideals of Judaism. A learned non-Jewish theologian justly
remarks : "If Israel's privileged position is insisted upon, this but
serves to deepen the sense of present inadequacy of character and
achievement, and gives occasion for the expression of passionate
longing and supplication for the People to be made worthy of its high
vocation and destiny" (Box).

hallowed us by thy commandments. Through obedience to God's will,
we become "holy" ; *i.e.* separated from the things that are ignoble
and vile, and at one with all things that make for righteousness and

all nations ; thou hast hallowed us by thy commandments, and brought us near unto thy service, O our King, and hast called us by thy great and holy Name.

[On Saturday Night add the following :—

VATODI-
ENU

Thou, O Lord our God, hast made known unto us thy righteous laws ; thou hast taught us to perform the statutes of thy will ; thou hast given us, O Lord our God, upright judgments, laws of truth, good statutes and commandments. Thou hast caused us to inherit seasons of joy, holy festivals, and feasts of free will offerings ; and hast given us as heritage the sanctity of the Sabbath, the glory of the holy seasons, and the celebration of festivals. Thou hast made a distinction, O Lord our God, between holy and profane, between light and darkness, between Israel and other nations, between the seventh day and the six working days ;

humanity. The commandments, *mitzvoth*, the ceremonies and practical duties of Jewish religious life are means of such hallowing ; their main purpose being " to purge our being of all moral dross ", train us to God, and keep us God-minded. " The performance of these commandments is regarded as exercising a sanctifying influence on the worshipper ; he feels that he is, by so doing, obeying the Divine voice. In this utter obedience he finds a real satisfaction ; and the practice of it evokes in the breast of a pious Jew a genuine devotional spirit which finds expression in acts of praise and thanksgiving " (Box). In brief, sanctification is achieved through the fulfilment of *specific deeds*. Judaism thus differs from other religions which permit direct access to personal salvation through faith *alone*.

called us by thy . . . . Name. The cause of Religion is intertwined with the teaching and story of Israel. Every profanation of the Divine Name is degrading to Israel, even as the moral triumph of Israel over tyranny and persecution is an exaltation of Righteousness and a Sanctification of the Divine in human life. " The Holy One, Israel, and the Torah form a spiritual unity ", is a deep saying of the Jewish Mystics.

VATODIËNU. *made known unto us.* This prayer by Mar Samuel, the companion of Rabh, is a prayer that, through our observance of the Sabbath, a new realization of the infinite difference between holy and profane, between light and darkness, between Israel and the heathen, abide with us throughout the coming week ; and that such realization lead to peace of soul, freedom from sin, and fervent attachment to the God-fearing life.

הַמַּעֲשֶׂה ּ בֵּין קְדֻשַּׁת שַׁבָּת לִקְדֻשַּׁת יוֹם טוֹב הִבְדַּלְתָּ וְאֶת־
יוֹם הַשְּׁבִיעִי מִשֵּׁשֶׁת יְמֵי הַמַּעֲשֶׂה קִדַּשְׁתָּ ּ הִבְדַּלְתָּ וְקִדַּשְׁתָּ
אֶת־עַמְּךָ יִשְׂרָאֵל בִּקְדֻשָּׁתֶךָ :

On Sabbath add the words in brackets.

וַתִּתֶּן־לָנוּ יְיָ אֱלֹהֵינוּ בְּאַהֲבָה [שַׁבָּתוֹת לִמְנוּחָה וּ]
מוֹעֲדִים לְשִׂמְחָה חַגִּים וּזְמַנִּים לְשָׂשׂוֹן ּ אֶת־יוֹם
[הַשַּׁבָּת הַזֶּה וְאֶת־יוֹם]

On פֶּסַח *say :—*

חַג הַמַּצּוֹת הַזֶּה ּ זְמַן חֵרוּתֵנוּ

On שָׁבֻעוֹת :—

חַג הַשָּׁבֻעוֹת הַזֶּה ּ זְמַן מַתַּן תּוֹרָתֵנוּ

On סֻכּוֹת :—

חַג הַסֻּכּוֹת הַזֶּה ּ זְמַן שִׂמְחָתֵנוּ

holiness of Sabbath . . . and festival. The difference is marked even
in outward observance. On Sabbath *all* work is prohibited (except
where life is in danger, see p. 339); on a Festival, only servile work
forbidden, labour in connection with the preparation of food being
permitted.

Vatitten lonu. And thou hast given us. This paragraph, going back
to Talmudic times, is the formal declaration of holiness of the Festival.

Feast of Unleavened Bread. This is the Biblical name of Passover
used in the Liturgy. It represents the aspect of the Festival that is, since
the destruction of the Temple, uppermost in the people's mind. The

thou hast made a distinction between the holiness of the Sabbath and that of the festival, and hast hallowed the seventh day above the six working days : thou hast distinguished and sanctified thy people Israel by thy holiness.

On Sabbath add the words in brackets.

HOLINESS
OF THE
FESTIVAL

And thou hast given us in love, O Lord our God, [Sabbaths for rest,] appointed times for gladness, festivals and seasons for joy ; [this Sabbath Day, and] this day of—

On Passover say—the Feast of Unleavened Bread, the season of our Freedom

On Pentecost—the Feast of Weeks, the season of the Giving of our Torah

On Tabernacles—the Feast of Tabernacles, the season of our Gladness

laws concerning Passover bread have always been joyously observed, and are held, next only to the fast on the Day of Atonement, as an axiomatic sign of Jewish loyalty. All foods that have *any* admixture of leaven (chometz) are forbidden, and utensils which have been used for leaven are put away during Passover.

season of our Freedom. Israel's departure from Egypt presents the dawn of Freedom, and the rise of a new ideal, for mankind. " Strangest of recorded births ! from the strongest and most splendid despotism of antiquity comes the freest republic. From between the paws of the rock-hewn Sphinx rises the genius of human liberty, and the trumpets of the Exodus throb with the defiant proclamation of the rights of man " (Henry George).

Giving of our Torah. It is the Festival of Revelation ; see p. 790, and pp. 251–253.

our Gladness. " And thou shalt rejoice in thy feast, thou, and thy son, and thy daughter, and thy man-servant, and thy maid-servant, and the Levite, the stranger, and the fatherless, and the widow, that are within thy gates . . . and thou shalt be altogether joyful " (Deuteronomy 16. 14, 15). Succos-gladness is to be a social, not a selfish, gladness. These regulations alone suffice to repel the baseless and senseless libel of Judaism being a Religion of gloom.

שְׁמִינִי עֲצֶרֶת and שִׂמְחַת תּוֹרָה On —:

הַשְּׁמִינִי חַג הָעֲצֶרֶת הַזֶּה · זְמַן שִׂמְחָתֵנוּ

[בְּאַהֲבָה] מִקְרָא קֹדֶשׁ זֵכֶר לִיצִיאַת מִצְרָיִם :

אֱלֹהֵינוּ וֵאלֹהֵי אֲבוֹתֵינוּ · יַעֲלֶה וְיָבֹא וְיַגִּיעַ וְיֵרָאֶה

וְיֵרָצֶה וְיִשָּׁמַע וְיִפָּקֵד וְיִזָּכֵר זִכְרוֹנֵנוּ וּפִקְדוֹנֵנוּ וְזִכְרוֹן

אֲבוֹתֵינוּ · וְזִכְרוֹן מָשִׁיחַ בֶּן־דָּוִד עַבְדֶּךָ · וְזִכְרוֹן יְרוּשָׁלַיִם

עִיר קָדְשֶׁךָ · וְזִכְרוֹן כָּל־עַמְּךָ בֵּית יִשְׂרָאֵל לְפָנֶיךָ ·

לִפְלֵיטָה וּלְטוֹבָה וּלְחֵן וּלְחֶסֶד וּלְרַחֲמִים וּלְחַיִּים

וּלְשָׁלוֹם בְּיוֹם

שָׁבוּעוֹת On —:	On פֶּסַח say :—
חַג הַשָּׁבוּעוֹת	חַג הַמַּצּוֹת
שְׁמִינִי עֲצֶרֶת and שִׂמְחַת תּוֹרָה On	סֻכּוֹת On —:
הַשְּׁמִינִי חַג הָעֲצֶרֶת	חַג הַסֻּכּוֹת

הַזֶּה · זָכְרֵנוּ יְיָ אֱלֹהֵינוּ בּוֹ לְטוֹבָה · וּפָקְדֵנוּ בוֹ לִבְרָכָה ·

וְהוֹשִׁיעֵנוּ בוֹ לְחַיִּים · וּבִדְבַר יְשׁוּעָה וְרַחֲמִים חוּס וְחָנֵּנוּ

וְרַחֵם עָלֵינוּ וְהוֹשִׁיעֵנוּ · כִּי אֵלֶיךָ עֵינֵינוּ · כִּי אֵל

מֶלֶךְ חַנּוּן וְרַחוּם אָתָּה :

eighth day. Separately mentioned, because it is a Festival by itself.
holy convocation. Sacred occasion for worship and public reading of
Scripture

YAALEH. A petition for Divine remembrance, so that it tend to the
deliverance and well-being of Israel and its spiritual treasures. It dates
from the seventh century.

On the Eighth Day of Solemn Assembly, and on Simchas Torah—
the Eighth-day Feast of Solemn Assembly, the season of our Gladness

[in love] ; a holy convocation, as a memorial of the departure from Egypt.

**YAALEH
VE-YOVO**   Our God and God of our fathers ! May our remembrance ascend, come and be accepted before thee, with the remembrance of our fathers, of Messiah the son of David thy servant, of Jerusalem thy holy city, and of all thy people the house of Israel, bringing deliverance and well-being, grace, lovingkindness and mercy, life and peace on this day of—

On Passover :—the Feast of Unleavened Bread.
On Pentecost :—the Feast of Weeks.
On Tabernacles :—the Feast of Tabernacles.
On the Eighth Day of Solemn Assembly, and on Simchas Torah :—
the Eighth-day Feast of Solemn Assembly.

Remember us, O Lord our God, thereon for our well-being ; be mindful of us for blessing, and save us unto life : by thy promise of salvation and mercy, spare us and be gracious unto us ; have mercy upon us and save us ; for our eyes are bent upon thee, because thou art a gracious and merciful God and King.

of Jerusalem. Psalm 137. 4 (in the Midrash taken as spoken by God).
the house of Israel. Jeremiah 2. 2. " I remember for thee the kindness of thy youth . . . . how thou wentest after me in the wilderness ".

וְהַשִּׂיאֵנוּ יְיָ אֱלֹהֵינוּ אֶת־בִּרְכַּת מוֹעֲדֶיךָ לְחַיִּים

וּלְשָׁלוֹם לְשִׂמְחָה וּלְשָׂשׂוֹן כַּאֲשֶׁר רָצִיתָ וְאָמַרְתָּ

לְבָרְכֵנוּ : [אֱלֹהֵינוּ וֵאלֹהֵי אֲבוֹתֵינוּ רְצֵה בִמְנוּחָתֵנוּ] קַדְּשֵׁנוּ

בְּמִצְוֹתֶיךָ וְתֵן חֶלְקֵנוּ בְּתוֹרָתֶךָ · שַׂבְּעֵנוּ מִטּוּבֶךָ וְשַׂמְּחֵנוּ

בִּישׁוּעָתֶךָ · וְטַהֵר לִבֵּנוּ לְעָבְדְּךָ בֶּאֱמֶת · וְהַנְחִילֵנוּ יְיָ

אֱלֹהֵינוּ [בְּאַהֲבָה וּבְרָצוֹן] בְּשִׂמְחָה וּבְשָׂשׂוֹן [שַׁבָּת וְ]

מוֹעֲדֵי קָדְשֶׁךָ · וְיִשְׂמְחוּ בְךָ יִשְׂרָאֵל מְקַדְּשֵׁי שְׁמֶךָ ·

בָּרוּךְ אַתָּה יְיָ · מְקַדֵּשׁ [הַשַּׁבָּת וְ] יִשְׂרָאֵל וְהַזְּמַנִּים :

For the conclusion of the עֲמִידָה *at Evening and Afternoon Service, say* רְצֵה *to* קַדְמוֹנִיּוֹת *on pp. 382–388 ; at Morning Service, pp. 460–466.*

---

bestow upon us. lit. " cause us to carry away ". The worshippers entreat God to cause them carry away with them the true spiritual benefit of the Festivals (Abrahams).
even as thou hast . . . . promised. Deuteronomy 16. 13–17.

FESTIVAL
PRAYER

O Lord our God, bestow upon us the blessing of thy holy festivals for life and peace, for joy and gladness, even as thou hast been pleased to promise that thou wouldst bless us. [Our God and God of our fathers, accept our rest.] Hallow us by thy commandments, and grant our portion in thy Torah ; satisfy us with thy goodness, and gladden us with thy salvation ; purify our hearts to serve thee in truth ; and let us inherit, O Lord our God, [in love and favour,] with joy and gladness thy holy [Sabbath and] festivals ; and may Israel, who sanctify thy Name, rejoice in thee. Blessed art thou, O Lord, who hallowest [the Sabbath and] Israel and the festive Seasons.

For the conclusion of the Amidah at Evening and Afternoon Service, say " Accept " to " as in ancient years," on pp. 383–389 ; at Morning Service, pp. 461–467.

who hallowest Israel. On New Moon and all the Festivals there is, in this ancient concluding benediction, special mention of " Israel ", which is not so in the case of the Sabbath. This is because the Festivals are specifically Israelite, whereas the institution of the Sabbath preceded the Selection of Israel, and its message is universal.

seasons. lit. " times ", not the usual word for " festivals ", probably in order to convey the meaning of " commemorative seasons ".

סדר קדוש לרגלים:

To be said on פֶּסַח, שָׁבְעוֹת *and* סֻכּוֹת.
*On the first two nights of Passover, Kiddush is recited
in the Home only.
When the Festival occurs on* שַׁבָּת *begin here :—*

וַיְהִי־עֶרֶב וַיְהִי־בֹקֶר יוֹם הַשִּׁשִּׁי : וַיְכֻלּוּ הַשָּׁמַיִם וְהָאָרֶץ
וְכָל־צְבָאָם : וַיְכַל אֱלֹהִים בַּיּוֹם הַשְּׁבִיעִי מְלַאכְתּוֹ אֲשֶׁר עָשָׂה
וַיִּשְׁבֹּת בַּיּוֹם הַשְּׁבִיעִי מִכָּל־מְלַאכְתּוֹ אֲשֶׁר עָשָׂה : וַיְבָרֶךְ
אֱלֹהִים אֶת־יוֹם הַשְּׁבִיעִי וַיְקַדֵּשׁ אֹתוֹ כִּי בוֹ שָׁבַת מִכָּל־
מְלַאכְתּוֹ אֲשֶׁר־בָּרָא אֱלֹהִים לַעֲשׂוֹת :

בָּרוּךְ אַתָּה יְיָ אֱלֹהֵינוּ מֶלֶךְ הָעוֹלָם · בּוֹרֵא פְּרִי הַגָּפֶן :

On שַׁבָּת *add the words in brackets.*

בָּרוּךְ אַתָּה יְיָ אֱלֹהֵינוּ מֶלֶךְ הָעוֹלָם · אֲשֶׁר בָּחַר־
בָּנוּ מִכָּל־עָם וְרוֹמְמָנוּ מִכָּל־לָשׁוֹן וְקִדְּשָׁנוּ בְּמִצְוֹתָיו ·
וַתִּתֶּן־לָנוּ יְיָ אֱלֹהֵינוּ בְּאַהֲבָה [שַׁבָּתוֹת לִמְנוּחָה וּ]
מוֹעֲדִים לְשִׂמְחָה חַגִּים וּזְמַנִּים לְשָׂשׂוֹן · אֶת־יוֹם [הַשַּׁבָּת
הַזֶּה וְאֶת־יוֹם]

KIDDUSH.

It was the inspiration of religious genius to ordain the Kiddush and
Havdolah ceremony for the Festivals in the same manner as for Sabbath.
The Kiddush, primarily a home prayer (see p. 407), may be said to be a

KIDDUSH FOR FESTIVALS

To be said on Passover, Pentecost and Tabernacles. On the first two nights of Passover, Kiddush is recited in the Home only.

[*When the Festival occurs on Sabbath begin here* :—
And it was evening and it was morning,—the sixth day.
And the heaven and the earth were finished and all their host. And on the seventh day God had finished his work which he had made : and he rested on the seventh day from all his work which he had made. And God blessed the seventh day, and he hallowed it, because he rested from all his work which God had created and made.]

Blessed art thou, O Lord our God, King of the universe, who createst the fruit of the vine.
On Sabbath add the words in brackets.

Blessed art thou, O Lord our God, King of the universe, who hast chosen us from all peoples, and exalted us above all nations, and hallowed us by thy commandments. And thou hast given us in love, O Lord our God, [Sabbaths for rest,] holy festivals for gladness, and sacred seasons for joy : [this Sabbath day and] this day of—

domestic tribute to the sanctity of God, Israel and the Festivals. The most frequent idea recurring in it is " holy "—its Hebrew root occurs five times in the few lines that compose this prayer.

fruit of the vine. Wine in Jewish thought is symbolic of many things. Life, joy, Torah, Israel, Jerusalem, the Messiah—all are compared to wine. There is thus a halo of poetic association over the goblet of wine used in religious celebration. The fact that wine forms part of almost every Jewish rite, including the Marriage Ceremony, had much to do with the characteristic sobriety of Israel. Wine was associated with religion, and undue indulgence became a sin as well as a vice (Abrahams).

chosen us. The main ideas of the Festival Kiddush are taken from the Amidah, and have been dealt with in the comments therein. See on the Selection of Israel, pp. 798–801.

in love. Because the commandments are a source of joy and blessing to Israel.

On the Friday eve of the Intermediate Days, the ordinary Sabbath Kiddush (p. 408) is said.

say ‎On‎ פֶּסַח חַג הַמַּצּוֹת הַזֶּה · זְמַן חֵרוּתֵנוּ

‎On‎ שָׁבֻעוֹת חַג הַשָּׁבֻעוֹת הַזֶּה · זְמַן מַתַּן תּוֹרָתֵנוּ:—

‎On‎ סֻכּוֹת חַג הַסֻּכּוֹת הַזֶּה · זְמַן שִׂמְחָתֵנוּ:—

‎On‎ שְׁמִינִי עֲצֶרֶת ‎and‎ שִׂמְחַת תּוֹרָה:—

הַשְּׁמִינִי חַג הָעֲצֶרֶת הַזֶּה · זְמַן שִׂמְחָתֵנוּ

[בְּאַהֲבָה] מִקְרָא קֹדֶשׁ זֵכֶר לִיצִיאַת מִצְרָיִם : כִּי בָנוּ

בָחַרְתָּ וְאוֹתָנוּ קִדַּשְׁתָּ מִכָּל־הָעַמִּים [וְשַׁבָּת וּ] מוֹעֲדֵי

קָדְשֶׁךָ [בְּאַהֲבָה וּבְרָצוֹן] בְּשִׂמְחָה וּבְשָׂשׂוֹן הִנְחַלְתָּנוּ ·

בָּרוּךְ אַתָּה יְיָ מְקַדֵּשׁ [הַשַּׁבָּת וְ] יִשְׂרָאֵל וְהַזְּמַנִּים :

On Sabbath Night the following הַבְדָּלָה **is added** :—

בָּרוּךְ אַתָּה יְיָ אֱלֹהֵינוּ מֶלֶךְ הָעוֹלָם · בּוֹרֵא מְאוֹרֵי הָאֵשׁ :

בָּרוּךְ אַתָּה יְיָ אֱלֹהֵינוּ מֶלֶךְ הָעוֹלָם · הַמַּבְדִּיל בֵּין קֹדֶשׁ

לְחוֹל בֵּין אוֹר לְחֹשֶׁךְ בֵּין יִשְׂרָאֵל לָעַמִּים · בֵּין יוֹם הַשְּׁבִיעִי

לְשֵׁשֶׁת יְמֵי הַמַּעֲשֶׂה · בֵּין קְדֻשַּׁת שַׁבָּת לִקְדֻשַּׁת יוֹם טוֹב

הִבְדַּלְתָּ · וְאֶת יוֹם הַשְּׁבִיעִי מִשֵּׁשֶׁת יְמֵי הַמַּעֲשֶׂה קִדַּשְׁתָּ ·

הִבְדַּלְתָּ וְקִדַּשְׁתָּ אֶת עַמְּךָ יִשְׂרָאֵל בִּקְדֻשָּׁתֶךָ · בָּרוּךְ אַתָּה יְיָ ·

הַמַּבְדִּיל בֵּין קֹדֶשׁ לְקֹדֶשׁ :

The following is omitted on the last two nights of פֶּסַח.

בָּרוּךְ אַתָּה יְיָ אֱלֹהֵינוּ מֶלֶךְ הָעוֹלָם · שֶׁהֶחֱיָנוּ

וְקִיְּמָנוּ וְהִגִּיעָנוּ לַזְּמַן הַזֶּה :

On Passover say—the Feast of Unleavened Bread, the season of our Freedom

On Pentecost—the Feast of Weeks, the season of the Giving of our Torah

On Tabernacles—the Feast of Tabernacles, the season of our Gladness

On the Eighth Day of Solemn Assembly and on Simchas Torah— the Eighth-day Feast of Solemn Assembly, the season of our Gladness

[in love] ; a holy convocation, as a memorial of the departure from Egypt ; for thou hast chosen us, and hallowed us above all peoples, and thy holy [Sabbath and] festivals thou hast caused us to inherit [in love and favour] in joy and gladness. Blessed art thou, O Lord, who hallowest [the Sabbath,] Israel and the festive Seasons.

[On Saturday night the following is added :—
Blessed art thou, O Lord our God, King of the universe, who createst the light of the fire.

Blessed art thou, O Lord our God, King of the universe, who makest a distinction between holy and profane, between light and darkness, between Israel and other nations, between the seventh day and the six working days. Thou hast made a distinction between the holiness of the Sabbath and that of the festival, and hast hallowed the seventh day above the six working days ; thou hast distinguished and hallowed thy people Israel by thy holiness. Blessed art thou, O Lord, who makest a distinction between holy and holy.]

The following is omitted on the last two nights of Passover.
Blessed art thou, O Lord our God, King of the universe, who hast kept us in life, and hast preserved us, and enabled us to reach this season.

---

holy convocation. For Worship and religious instruction, that must consecrate the Festival rejoicing.

סדר חג הסכות :

To be said in the Tabernacle on the first night of the Festival.

יְהִי רָצוֹן מִלְּפָנֶיךָ יְיָ אֱלֹהַי וֵאלֹהֵי אֲבוֹתַי שֶׁתַּשְׁרֶה
שְׁכִינָתְךָ בֵּינֵינוּ וְתִפְרוֹשׂ עָלֵינוּ סֻכַּת שְׁלוֹמֶךָ בִּזְכוּת מִצְוַת
סֻכָּה שֶׁאֲנַחְנוּ מְקַיְּמִים לְיַחֵד שִׁמְךָ הַקָּדוֹשׁ בָּרוּךְ הוּא
בְּיִרְאָה וּבְאַהֲבָה · וְתַקִּיף אוֹתָנוּ מִזִּיו כְּבוֹדְךָ הַקָּדוֹשׁ
וְהַטָּהוֹר נָטוּי עַל רָאשֵׁינוּ מִלְמַעְלָה כְּנֶשֶׁר יָעִיר קִנּוֹ ·
וּמִשָּׁם יֻשְׁפַּע שֶׁפַע הַחַיִּים לְעַבְדְּךָ (פ' ב'פ') · (לַאֲמָתְךָ
פ' ב'פ') · וּבִזְכוּת צֵאתִי מִבֵּיתִי הַחוּצָה וְדֶרֶךְ מִצְוֹתֶיךָ
אָרוּצָה יֵחָשֶׁב־לִי בְּזֹאת כְּאִלּוּ הִרְחַקְתִּי נָדוֹד · וְהֶעֱרֵב בְּבַקְּנִי
מֵעֲוֹנִי וּמֵחַטָּאתִי טַהֲרֵנִי · תְּחַיֵּינִי אֲדֹנָי תַּשְׁפִּיעַ לִי רֹב
בְּרָכוֹת · וְלָרְעֵבִים גַּם צְמֵאִים תֵּן לַחְמָם וּמֵימָם נֶאֱמָנִים ·
וְתִתֶּן־לִי זְכוּת לָשֶׁבֶת וְלַחֲסוֹת בְּסֵתֶר צֵל כְּנָפֶיךָ בְּעֵת
פְּטִירָתִי מִן־הָעוֹלָם · וְתֵמִיב לָנוּ הַחֲתִימָה וּתְזַכֵּנוּ לֵישֵׁב יָמִים
רַבִּים עַל הָאֲדָמָה אַדְמַת קֹדֶשׁ · בַּעֲבוֹדָתֶךָ וּבְיִרְאָתֶךָ ·
בָּרוּךְ יְיָ לְעוֹלָם · אָמֵן וְאָמֵן :

בָּרוּךְ אַתָּה יְיָ אֱלֹהֵינוּ מֶלֶךְ הָעוֹלָם · אֲשֶׁר קִדְּשָׁנוּ
בְּמִצְוֹתָיו וְצִוָּנוּ לֵישֵׁב בַּסֻּכָּה :

בָּרוּךְ אַתָּה יְיָ אֱלֹהֵינוּ מֶלֶךְ הָעוֹלָם · שֶׁהֶחֱיָנוּ
וְקִיְּמָנוּ וְהִגִּיעָנוּ לַזְּמַן הַזֶּה :

IN THE TABERNACLE

To be said in the Tabernacle on the first night of the Festival.

MEDITA-TION
May it be thy will, O Lord my God and God of my fathers, to let thy divine Presence abide among us. Spread over us the canopy of thy peace in recognition of the precept of the Tabernacle which we are now fulfilling, and whereby we establish in fear and love the unity of thy holy and blessed Name. O surround us with the pure and holy radiance of thy glory, that is spread over our heads as the eagle over the nest he stirreth up : and thence bid the stream of life flow in upon thy servant (thy handmaid). And seeing that I have gone forth from my house abroad, and am speeding the way of thy commandments, may it be accounted unto me as though *Psalm* 51. 4 I had wandered far in thy cause. O wash me thoroughly from mine iniquity, and cleanse me from my sin. Keep me in life, O Lord ; bestow upon me the abundance of thy blessings ; and to such as are hungry and thirsty give bread and water unfailingly. Make me worthy to dwell trustingly in the covert of thy shadowing wings at the time when I depart this world. O deal graciously with us in the decree to which thou settest thy seal, and make us worthy to dwell many days upon the land, the holy land, ever serving and fearing thee. Blessed be the Lord for ever. Amen and Amen.

BENEDIC-TIONS
Blessed art thou, O Lord our God, King of the universe, who hast hallowed us by thy commandments, and hast commanded us to dwell in the Tabernacle.

Blessed art thou, O Lord our God, King of the universe, who hast kept us in life, and hast preserved us, and enabled us to reach this season.

SUCCAH.

may it be Thy will. There is fine fervour and true mystic touch in this Meditation of R. Nathan Hannover ; cf. pp. 479 and 755.
blessed art thou. This Benediction is of early rabbinic origin.
dwell in the Tabernacle. See p. 792.

תפלת מוסף לרגלים :

To be said on פֶּסַח, שָׁבְעוֹת *and* סֻכּוֹת, *and on* חוֹל הַמּוֹעֵד.

אֲדֹנָי שְׂפָתַי תִּפְתָּח וּפִי יַגִּיד תְּהִלָּתֶךָ :

בָּרוּךְ אַתָּה יְיָ אֱלֹהֵינוּ וֵאלֹהֵי אֲבוֹתֵינוּ · אֱלֹהֵי
אַבְרָהָם אֱלֹהֵי יִצְחָק וֵאלֹהֵי יַעֲקֹב · הָאֵל הַגָּדוֹל הַגִּבּוֹר
וְהַנּוֹרָא אֵל עֶלְיוֹן · גּוֹמֵל חֲסָדִים טוֹבִים וְקוֹנֵה הַכֹּל ·
וְזוֹכֵר חַסְדֵי אָבוֹת וּמֵבִיא גוֹאֵל לִבְנֵי בְנֵיהֶם לְמַעַן שְׁמוֹ
בְּאַהֲבָה ·

מֶלֶךְ עוֹזֵר וּמוֹשִׁיעַ וּמָגֵן · בָּרוּךְ אַתָּה יְיָ ° מָגֵן אַבְרָהָם :

אַתָּה גִבּוֹר לְעוֹלָם אֲדֹנָי מְחַיֵּה מֵתִים אַתָּה רַב לְהוֹשִׁיעַ ·

On פֶּסַח *and the first Day of* שְׂמָחַת תּוֹרָה, שְׁמִינִי עֲצֶרֶת *say :—*
מַשִּׁיב הָרוּחַ וּמוֹרִיד הַגָּשֶׁם :

מְכַלְכֵּל חַיִּים בְּחֶסֶד מְחַיֵּה מֵתִים בְּרַחֲמִים רַבִּים · סוֹמֵךְ
נוֹפְלִים וְרוֹפֵא חוֹלִים וּמַתִּיר אֲסוּרִים וּמְקַיֵּם אֱמוּנָתוֹ
לִישֵׁנֵי עָפָר · מִי כָמוֹךָ בַּעַל גְּבוּרוֹת וּמִי דּוֹמֶה לָּךְ ·
מֶלֶךְ מֵמִית וּמְחַיֶּה וּמַצְמִיחַ יְשׁוּעָה ·

וְנֶאֱמָן אַתָּה לְהַחֲיוֹת מֵתִים · בָּרוּךְ אַתָּה יְיָ · מְחַיֵּה
הַמֵּתִים :

MUSSAF.

The Mussaf prayer corresponded with, accompanied, and later on replaced, the *additional* sacrifices on Sabbaths and Festivals, as described in Numbers 28 and 29.

The central prayer in the Mussaf Amidah goes back to the age of the Gaonim. Its distinguishing features are :

MUSSAF
AMIDAH

Psalm 51. 17

MUSSAF FOR THE FESTIVALS

To be said on Passover, Pentecost and Tabernacles, and on the Intermediate Days of Passover and Tabernacles.

O Lord, open thou my lips, and my mouth shall declare

I. THE
GOD OF
HISTORY

thy praise.

Blessed art thou, O Lord our God and God of our fathers, God of Abraham, God of Isaac, and God of Jacob, the great, mighty and revered God, the most high God,

See p. 131

who bestowest lovingkindnesses, and art Master of all things ; who rememberest the pious deeds of the patriarchs, and in love wilt bring a redeemer to their children's children for thy Name's sake.

O King, Helper, Saviour and Shield. Blessed art thou,

II. THE
GOD OF
NATURE

O Lord, the Shield of Abraham.

Thou, O Lord, art mighty for ever, thou revivest the dead, thou art mighty to save.

[*On the Eighth Day of Solemn Assembly, Simchas Torah, and the First Day of Passover say* :—
Thou causest the wind to blow and the rain to fall.]

Thou sustainest the living with lovingkindness, revivest the dead with great mercy, supportest the falling, healest

See p. 133

the sick, freest the bound, and keepest thy faith to them that sleep in the dust. Who is like unto thee, Lord of mighty acts, and who resembleth thee, O King, who orderest death and restorest life, and causest salvation to spring forth ?

Yea, faithful art thou to revive the dead. Blessed art thou, O Lord, who revivest the dead.

(*a*) Lament for the exile of Israel and the destruction of the Temple. " When the Jew speaks of the ' Destruction of the Temple ', he means the destruction of his homeland, the massacre of his sons and daughters, and the Exile with all its physical pain and spiritual suffering. Similarly, when he prays, ' O that the Temple be built ! ' this is but a short prayer for the ingathering of the exiles, and for complete redemption in his homeland " (W. Yawitz).

(b) literal citation of the Scriptural command regulating the additional sacrifice of the Festival.

When the reader repeats the עֲמִידָה, *the following* קְדוּשָׁה *is said.*

Reader. נַעֲרִיצְךָ וְנַקְדִּישְׁךָ כְּסוֹד שִׂיחַ שַׂרְפֵי קְדֶשׁ הַמַּקְדִּישִׁים שִׁמְךָ בַּקֹּדֶשׁ · כַּכָּתוּב עַל יַד נְבִיאֶךָ · וְקָרָא זֶה אֶל זֶה וְאָמַר ·

Cong. קָדוֹשׁ קָדוֹשׁ קָדוֹשׁ יְיָ צְבָאוֹת · מְלֹא כָל־הָאָרֶץ כְּבוֹדוֹ :

Reader. כְּבוֹדוֹ מָלֵא עוֹלָם מְשָׁרְתָיו שׁוֹאֲלִים זֶה לָזֶה אַיֵּה מְקוֹם כְּבוֹדוֹ · לְעֻמָּתָם בָּרוּךְ יֹאמֵרוּ ·

Cong. בָּרוּךְ כְּבוֹד יְיָ מִמְּקוֹמוֹ ·

Reader מִמְּקוֹמוֹ הוּא יִפֶן בְּרַחֲמִים וְיָחוֹן עַם הַמְיַחֲדִים שְׁמוֹ עֶרֶב וָבְקֶר בְּכָל יוֹם תָּמִיד פַּעֲמַיִם בְּאַהֲבָה שְׁמַע אוֹמְרִים ·

Cong. שְׁמַע יִשְׂרָאֵל יְיָ אֱלֹהֵינוּ יְיָ אֶחָד :

Reader. אֶחָד הוּא אֱלֹהֵינוּ הוּא אָבִינוּ הוּא מַלְכֵּנוּ הוּא מוֹשִׁיעֵנוּ · וְהוּא יַשְׁמִיעֵנוּ בְּרַחֲמָיו שֵׁנִית לְעֵינֵי כָּל־חַי לִהְיוֹת לָכֶם לֵאלֹהִים :

Cong. אֲנִי יְיָ אֱלֹהֵיכֶם :

Reader. אַדִּיר אַדִּירֵנוּ יְיָ אֲדוֹנֵנוּ מָה אַדִּיר שִׁמְךָ בְּכָל הָאָרֶץ · וְהָיָה יְיָ לְמֶלֶךְ עַל כָּל הָאָרֶץ בַּיּוֹם הַהוּא

(c) fervent petition for the restoration of the Service in Israel's ancient Sanctuary.

[When the Reader repeats the Amidah, the following Sanctification is said.

*III.
SANCTIFI-
CATION OF
GOD*

See p. 528

Isaiah 6. 3

Reader.—We will reverence and sanctify thee according to the mystic utterance of the holy Seraphim, who sanctify thy Name in the sanctuary, as it is written by the hand of thy prophet, And they called one unto the other and said,

Cong.—HOLY, HOLY, HOLY IS THE LORD OF HOSTS : THE WHOLE EARTH IS FULL OF HIS GLORY.

Reader.—His glory filleth the universe : his ministering angels ask one another, Where is the place of his glory ? Those over against them say, Blessed—

Ezekiel 3. 12

Cong.—BLESSED BE THE GLORY OF THE LORD FROM HIS PLACE.

Reader—From his place may he turn in mercy and be gracious unto a people who, evening and morning, twice every day, proclaim with constancy the unity of his Name, saying in love, Hear—

*Deuteronomy
6. 5*

Cong.—HEAR, O ISRAEL : THE LORD IS OUR GOD, THE LORD IS ONE.

Reader.—One is our God ; he is our Father ; he is our King ; he is our Saviour ; and he of his mercy will let us hear a second time, in the presence of all living (his promise), " To be to you for a God."

Cong.—" I AM THE LORD YOUR GOD."

(d) prayer for the blessings of life and peace and joy to be inaugurated by the Festival.

When the Temple fell, dismay filled many hearts at the cessation of sacrifice as a means of atonement At the sight of the Temple in ruins, a disciple of Rabbi Yochanan ben Zakkai, exclaimed, " Woe to us, for the place where the iniquities of Israel were atoned for is destroyed ! " Whereupon the Master said, " Do not grieve, my son, for we have an atonement which is just as effective, namely, deeds of mercy ; as Scripture says (Hosea 6. 6), *For I desire mercy, and not sacrifice.*" And this was no revolutionary doctrine. While the Temple was still standing, the principle had been established that, unless accompanied by heartfelt repentance, no sacrificial rites were of any avail. When sacrifices were no more, repentance and good works remained as the sole means for the remission of sins.

יִהְיֶה יְיָ אֶחָד וּשְׁמוֹ אֶחָד : וּבְדִבְרֵי קָדְשְׁךָ כָּתוּב לֵאמֹר ·

Cong
יִמְלֹךְ יְיָ לְעוֹלָם אֱלֹהַיִךְ צִיּוֹן לְדֹר וָדֹר · הַלְלוּיָהּ :

Reader.
לְדוֹר וָדוֹר נַגִּיד גָּדְלֶךָ וּלְנֵצַח נְצָחִים קְדֻשָּׁתְךָ

נַקְדִּישׁ · וְשִׁבְחֲךָ אֱלֹהֵינוּ מִפִּינוּ לֹא יָמוּשׁ לְעוֹלָם וָעֶד ·

כִּי אֵל מֶלֶךְ גָּדוֹל וְקָדוֹשׁ אָתָּה · בָּרוּךְ אַתָּה יְיָ ·

הָאֵל הַקָּדוֹשׁ :]

At the repetition of the עֲמִידָה, *the following two lines are omitted :—*

אַתָּה קָדוֹשׁ וְשִׁמְךָ קָדוֹשׁ וּקְדוֹשִׁים בְּכָל־יוֹם יְהַלְלוּךָ

סֶּלָה · בָּרוּךְ אַתָּה יְיָ · הָאֵל הַקָּדוֹשׁ :

אַתָּה בְחַרְתָּנוּ מִכָּל־הָעַמִּים · אָהַבְתָּ אוֹתָנוּ · וְרָצִיתָ

בָּנוּ · וְרוֹמַמְתָּנוּ מִכָּל הַלְּשֹׁנוֹת · וְקִדַּשְׁתָּנוּ בְּמִצְוֹתֶיךָ ·

וְקֵרַבְתָּנוּ מַלְכֵּנוּ לַעֲבוֹדָתֶךָ · וְשִׁמְךָ הַגָּדוֹל וְהַקָּדוֹשׁ

עָלֵינוּ קָרָאתָ :

On שַׁבָּת *add the words in brackets.*

וַתִּתֶּן־לָנוּ יְיָ אֱלֹהֵינוּ בְּאַהֲבָה [שַׁבָּתוֹת לִמְנוּחָה וּ]

מוֹעֲדִים לְשִׂמְחָה חַגִּים וּזְמַנִּים לְשָׂשׂוֹן · אֶת־יוֹם

[הַשַׁבָּת הַזֶּה וְאֶת־יוֹם]

say :— *On* פֶּסַח חַג הַמַּצּוֹת הַזֶּה   זְמַן חֵרוּתֵנוּ

On שָׁבוּעוֹת חַג הַשָּׁבוּעוֹת הַזֶּה · זְמַן מַתַּן תּוֹרָתֵנוּ :—

On סֻכּוֹת חַג הַסֻּכּוֹת הַזֶּה · זְמַן שִׂמְחָתֵנוּ :—

On שְׁמִינִי עֲצֶרֶת *and* שִׂמְחַת תּוֹרָה :—

הַשְּׁמִינִי חַג הָעֲצֶרֶת הַזֶּה · זְמַן שִׂמְחָתֵנוּ

Zechariah 14.9

Reader.—O thou our most glorious One, O Lord our Lord, how glorious is thy Name in all the earth : And the Lord shall be King over the whole earth ; in that day shall the Lord be One and his Name One. And in thy Holy Words it is written, saying,

Psalm 146. 10

Cong.—THE LORD SHALL REIGN FOR EVER, THY GOD, O ZION, UNTO ALL GENERATIONS. PRAISE YE THE LORD.

Reader.—Unto all generations we will declare thy greatness, and to all eternity we will proclaim thy holiness, and thy praise, O our God, shall not depart from our mouth for ever, for thou art a great and holy God and King. Blessed art thou, O Lord, the holy God.]

*At the repetition of the Amidah, the following lines, till "holy God",
are omitted :—*

Thou art holy, and thy Name is holy, and holy beings praise thee daily. (Selah.) Blessed art thou, O Lord, the holy God.

*IV.
SELECTION
OF ISRAEL*

See pp. 798–800

Thou hast chosen us from all peoples ; thou hast loved us and taken pleasure in us, and hast exalted us above all tongues ; thou hast hallowed us by thy commandments, and brought us near unto thy service, O our King, and hast called us by thy great and holy Name.

On Sabbaths add the words in brackets.

And thou hast given us in love, O Lord our God, [Sabbaths for rest] festivals for gladness, and sacred seasons for joy ; [this Sabbath day and] this day of—

On Passover say—the Feast of Unleavened Bread, the season of our Freedom

On Pentecost say—the Feast of Weeks, the season of the Giving of our Torah

On Tabernacles—the Feast of Tabernacles, the season of our Gladness

On the Eighth Day of Solemn Assembly and on the Simchas Torah—the Eighth-day Feast of Solemn Assembly, the season of our Gladness.

[בְּאַהֲבָה] מִקְרָא קֹדֶשׁ זֵכֶר ־ לִיצִיאַת מִצְרָיִם :

וּמִפְּנֵי חֲטָאֵינוּ גָּלִינוּ מֵאַרְצֵנוּ וְנִתְרַחַקְנוּ מֵעַל

אַדְמָתֵנוּ ־ וְאֵין אֲנַחְנוּ יְכוֹלִים לַעֲלוֹת וְלֵרָאוֹת

וּלְהִשְׁתַּחֲווֹת לְפָנֶיךָ ־ וְלַעֲשׂוֹת חוֹבוֹתֵינוּ בְּבֵית בְּחִירָתֶךָ

בַּבַּיִת הַגָּדוֹל וְהַקָּדוֹשׁ שֶׁנִּקְרָא שִׁמְךָ עָלָיו ־ מִפְּנֵי הַיָּד

שֶׁנִּשְׁתַּלְּחָה בְּמִקְדָּשֶׁךָ : יְהִי רָצוֹן מִלְּפָנֶיךָ יְיָ אֱלֹהֵינוּ

וֵאלֹהֵי אֲבוֹתֵינוּ ־ מֶלֶךְ רַחֲמָן שֶׁתָּשׁוּב וּתְרַחֵם עָלֵינוּ

וְעַל ־ מִקְדָּשֶׁךָ בְּרַחֲמֶיךָ הָרַבִּים ־ וְתִבְנֵהוּ מְהֵרָה וּתְגַדֵּל

כְּבוֹדוֹ : אָבִינוּ מַלְכֵּנוּ ־ גַּלֵּה כְּבוֹד מַלְכוּתְךָ עָלֵינוּ

מְהֵרָה וְהוֹפַע וְהִנָּשֵׂא עָלֵינוּ לְעֵינֵי כָּל ־ חָי ־ וְקָרֵב

פְּזוּרֵינוּ מִבֵּין הַגּוֹיִם וּנְפוּצוֹתֵינוּ כַּנֵּס מִיַּרְכְּתֵי אָרֶץ ־

וַהֲבִיאֵנוּ לְצִיּוֹן עִירְךָ בְּרִנָּה וְלִירוּשָׁלַיִם בֵּית מִקְדָּשְׁךָ

בְּשִׂמְחַת עוֹלָם ־ וְשָׁם נַעֲשֶׂה לְפָנֶיךָ אֶת ־ קָרְבְּנוֹת

חוֹבוֹתֵינוּ תְּמִידִים כְּסִדְרָם וּמוּסָפִים כְּהִלְכָתָם : וְאֶת ־

מוּסַף יוֹם [הַשַּׁבָּת הַזֶּה וְאֶת מוּסַף יוֹם]

חַג הַמַּצּוֹת *say* — On *פֶּסַח* : **חַג הַשָּׁבֻעוֹת** On *שָׁבֻעוֹת*

— On *סֻכּוֹת* : *שִׂמְחַת תּוֹרָה* and *שְׁמִינִי עֲצֶרֶת* On

חַג הַסֻּכּוֹת   **הַשְּׁמִינִי חַג הָעֲצֶרֶת**

הַזֶּה ־ נַעֲשֶׂה וְנַקְרִיב לְפָנֶיךָ בְּאַהֲבָה כְּמִצְוַת רְצוֹנֶךָ

כְּמוֹ שֶׁכָּתַבְתָּ עָלֵינוּ בְּתוֹרָתֶךָ עַל ־ יְדֵי מֹשֶׁה עַבְדֶּךָ

מִפִּי כְבוֹדֶךָ כָּאָמוּר :

[in love] ; a holy convocation, as a memorial of the departure from Egypt.

But on account of our sins we were exiled from our land, and removed far from our country, and we are unable to go up in order to appear and prostrate ourselves before thee, and to fulfil our obligations in thy chosen house, that great and holy temple which was called by thy Name, because of the hand of violence that hath been laid upon thy sanctuary. May it be thy will, O Lord our God and God of our fathers, merciful King, that thou mayest again in thine abundant compassion have mercy upon us and upon thy sanctuary, and mayest speedily rebuild it and magnify its glory. Our Father, our King, do thou speedily make the glory of thy kingdom manifest upon us ; shine forth and exalt thyself upon us in the sight of all living ; bring our scattered ones among the nations near unto thee, and gather our dispersed from the ends of the earth. Lead us with exultation unto Zion thy city, and unto Jerusalem the place of thy sanctuary with everlasting joy ; and there we will prepare before thee the offerings that are obligatory for us, the daily offerings according to their order, and the additional offerings according to their enactment ; and the additional offering of [this Sabbath day with the additional offering of] this—

On Passover say—Feast of Unleavened Bread

On Pentecost—Feast of Weeks

On Tabernacles—Feast of Tabernacles

On the Eighth Day of Solemn Assembly and on Simchas Torah—
Eighth-day Feast of Solemn Assembly

we will prepare and offer unto thee in love according to the precept of thy will, as thou hast prescribed for us in thy Torah through the hand of Moses thy servant, from the mouth of thy glory, as it is said :

וּבְיוֹם הַשַּׁבָּת שְׁנֵי־כְבָשִׂים בְּנֵי־שָׁנָה תְּמִימִם וּשְׁנֵי עֶשְׂרֹנִים]
סֹלֶת מִנְחָה בְּלוּלָה בַשֶּׁמֶן וְנִסְכּוֹ : עֹלַת שַׁבַּת בְּשַׁבַּתּוֹ עַל־
עֹלַת הַתָּמִיד וְנִסְכָּהּ :[

On the first two days of פֶּסַח *say* :—

וּבַחֹדֶשׁ הָרִאשׁוֹן בְּאַרְבָּעָה עָשָׂר יוֹם לַחֹדֶשׁ פֶּסַח לַיהֹוָה :
וּבַחֲמִשָּׁה עָשָׂר יוֹם לַחֹדֶשׁ הַזֶּה חָג שִׁבְעַת יָמִים מַצּוֹת
יֵאָכֵל : בַּיּוֹם הָרִאשׁוֹן מִקְרָא־קֹדֶשׁ כָּל־מְלֶאכֶת עֲבֹדָה לֹא
תַעֲשׂוּ :

וְהִקְרַבְתֶּם אִשֶּׁה עֹלָה לַיהֹוָה פָּרִים בְּנֵי־בָקָר שְׁנַיִם וְאַיִל
אֶחָד וְשִׁבְעָה כְבָשִׂים בְּנֵי שָׁנָה תְּמִימִם יִהְיוּ לָכֶם :

On פֶּסַח, *after the first two days, say the last paragraph only.*

On שָׁבֻעוֹת *say* :—

וּבְיוֹם הַבִּכּוּרִים בְּהַקְרִיבְכֶם מִנְחָה חֲדָשָׁה לַיהֹוָה
בְּשָׁבֻעֹתֵיכֶם מִקְרָא־קֹדֶשׁ יִהְיֶה לָכֶם כָּל־מְלֶאכֶת עֲבֹדָה לֹא
תַעֲשׂוּ : וְהִקְרַבְתֶּם עוֹלָה לְרֵיחַ נִיחֹחַ לַיהֹוָה פָּרִים בְּנֵי־בָקָר
שְׁנַיִם אַיִל אֶחָד שִׁבְעָה כְבָשִׂים בְּנֵי שָׁנָה :

On the first two days of סֻכּוֹת *say* :—

וּבַחֲמִשָּׁה עָשָׂר יוֹם לַחֹדֶשׁ הַשְּׁבִיעִי מִקְרָא־קֹדֶשׁ יִהְיֶה לָכֶם
כָּל־מְלֶאכֶת עֲבֹדָה לֹא תַעֲשׂוּ וְחַגֹּתֶם חַג לַיהֹוָה שִׁבְעַת
יָמִים : וְהִקְרַבְתֶּם עֹלָה אִשֶּׁה רֵיחַ נִיחֹחַ לַיהֹוָה פָּרִים בְּנֵי־
בָקָר שְׁלֹשָׁה עָשָׂר אֵילִם שְׁנַיִם כְּבָשִׂים בְּנֵי־שָׁנָה אַרְבָּעָה עָשָׂר
תְּמִימִם יִהְיוּ :

On all Festivals say :—

וּמִנְחָתָם וְנִסְכֵּיהֶם כִּמְדֻבָּר · שְׁלֹשָׁה עֶשְׂרֹנִים לַפָּר · וּשְׁנֵי

[And on the Sabbath day two he-lambs of the first year without blemish, and two tenth parts of an ephah of fine flour for a meal offering, mingled with oil, and the drink offering thereof ; this is the burnt offering of every Sabbath, beside the daily burnt offering thereof.]

On the first two days of Passover say :—

And in the first month, on the fourteenth day of the month, is the Passover unto the Lord. And on the fifteenth day of this month shall be a feast : seven days shall unleavened bread be eaten. On the first day shall be an holy convocation ; ye shall do no servile work.

And ye shall offer an offering made by fire, a burnt offering unto the Lord : two young bullocks and one ram, and seven he-lambs of the first year ; they shall be unto you without blemish.

On Passover, after the first two days, say the last paragraph only.

On Pentecost say :—

And on the day of the first fruits, when ye offer a new meal offering unto the Lord in your Feast of Weeks, ye shall have an holy convocation ; ye shall do no servile work ; ye shall offer a burnt offering for a sweet savour unto the Lord ; two young bullocks, one ram, seven he-lambs of the first year.

On the first two days of Tabernacles say :—

And on the fifteenth day of the seventh month ye shall have an holy convocation ; ye shall do no servile work, and ye shall keep a feast unto the Lord seven days. And ye shall offer a burnt offering, an offering made by fire, of a sweet savour unto the Lord ; thirteen young bullocks, two rams, fourteen he-lambs of the first year ; they shall be without blemish.

On all Festivals say :—

And their meal offering and their drink offerings as hath been ordained ; three tenth parts of an ephah for each bullock, and two tenth parts for the ram, and one tenth part for each lamb, with wine according to the drink offering thereof, and a he-goat

עֶשְׂרֹנִים לָאֵיל׳ · וְעִשָּׂרוֹן לַכֶּבֶשׁ וְיַיִן נִסְכּוֹ · וְשָׂעִיר לְכַפֵּר ·

וּשְׁנֵי תְמִידִים כְּהִלְכָתָם :

On the First Day of סֻכּוֹת ׳חה׳מ *say* :—

וּבַיּוֹם הַשֵּׁנִי פָּרִים בְּנֵי־בָקָר שְׁנֵים עָשָׂר אֵילִם שְׁנָיִם כְּבָשִׂים

בְּנֵי־שָׁנָה אַרְבָּעָה עָשָׂר תְּמִימִם : כְּהִלְכָתָם *to* וּמִנְחָתָם *Repeat*

וּבַיּוֹם הַשְּׁלִישִׁי פָּרִים עַשְׁתֵּי־עָשָׂר אֵילִם שְׁנָיִם כְּבָשִׂים בְּנֵי־

שָׁנָה אַרְבָּעָה עָשָׂר תְּמִימִם : כְּהִלְכָתָם *to* וּמִנְחָתָם *Repeat*

On the Second Day of חה׳מ סֻכּוֹת—

וּבַיּוֹם הַשְּׁלִישִׁי וגו׳   וּמִנְחָתָם וגו׳

וּבַיּוֹם הָרְבִיעִי פָּרִים עֲשָׂרָה אֵילִם שְׁנָיִם כְּבָשִׂים בְּנֵי־שָׁנָה

אַרְבָּעָה עָשָׂר תְּמִימִם :   וּמִנְחָתָם וגו׳

On the Third Day of חה׳מ סֻכּוֹת—

וּבַיּוֹם הָרְבִיעִי וגו׳   וּמִנְחָתָם וגו׳

וּבַיּוֹם הַחֲמִישִׁי פָּרִים תִּשְׁעָה אֵילִם שְׁנָיִם כְּבָשִׂים בְּנֵי־שָׁנָה

אַרְבָּעָה עָשָׂר תְּמִימִם :   וּמִנְחָתָם וגו׳

On the Fourth Day of חה׳מ סֻכּוֹת—

וּבַיּוֹם הַחֲמִישִׁי וגו׳   וּמִנְחָתָם וגו׳

וּבַיּוֹם הַשִּׁשִּׁי פָּרִים שְׁמֹנָה אֵילִם שְׁנָיִם כְּבָשִׂים בְּנֵי־שָׁנָה

אַרְבָּעָה עָשָׂר תְּמִימִם :   וּמִנְחָתָם וגו׳

On הוֹשַׁעְנָא רַבָּא—

וּבַיּוֹם הַשִּׁשִּׁי וגו׳   וּמִנְחָתָם וגו׳

וּבַיּוֹם הַשְּׁבִיעִי פָּרִים שִׁבְעָה אֵילִם שְׁנָיִם כְּבָשִׂים בְּנֵי־שָׁנָה

אַרְבָּעָה עָשָׂר תְּמִימִם :   וּמִנְחָתָם וגו׳

wherewith to make atonement, and the two' daily offerings according to their enactment.

On the first of the Intermediate Days of Tabernacles say :—

And on the second day ye shall offer twelve young bullocks, two rams, fourteen he-lambs of the first year without blemish. And their meal offering, etc.

And on the third day ye shall offer eleven bullocks, two rams, fourteen he-lambs of the first year without blemish. And their meal offering, etc.

On the second of the Intermediate Days of Tabernacles, say the last paragraph, and continue :—

And on the fourth day ye shall offer ten bullocks, two rams, fourteen he-lambs of the first year without blemish. And their meal offering, etc.

On the third of the Intermediate Days of Tabernacles, say the last paragraph, and continue :—

And on the fifth day ye shall offer nine bullocks, two rams, fourteen he-lambs of the first year without blemish. And their meal offering, etc.

On the fourth of the Intermediate Days of Tabernacles, say the last paragraph, and continue :—

And on the sixth day ye shall offer eight bullocks, two rams, fourteen he-lambs of the first year without blemish. And their meal offering, etc.

On the fifth of the Intermediate Days of Tabernacles (Hoshana Rabba), say the last paragraph, and continue :—

And on the seventh day ye shall offer seven bullocks, two rams, fourteen he-lambs of the first year without blemish. And their meal offering, etc.

On שְׁמִינִי עֲצֶרֶת and שִׂמְחַת תּוֹרָה say :—

בַּיּוֹם הַשְּׁמִינִי עֲצֶרֶת תִּהְיֶה לָכֶם כָּל־מְלֶאכֶת עֲבֹדָה לֹא
תַעֲשׂוּ : וְהִקְרַבְתֶּם עֹלָה אִשֵּׁה רֵיחַ נִיחֹחַ לַיהוָֹה פַּר אֶחָד
אַיִל אֶחָד כְּבָשִׂים בְּנֵי־שָׁנָה שִׁבְעָה תְּמִימִם : וּמִנְחָתָם וגו׳

[וְיִשְׂמְחוּ בְמַלְכוּתְךָ שׁוֹמְרֵי שַׁבָּת וְקוֹרְאֵי עֹנֶג ׳ עַם מְקַדְּשֵׁי
שְׁבִיעִי כֻּלָּם יִשְׂבְּעוּ וְיִתְעַנְּגוּ מִטּוּבֶךָ ׳ וְהַשְּׁבִיעִי רָצִיתָ בּוֹ
וְקִדַּשְׁתּוֹ חֶמְדַּת יָמִים אֹתוֹ קָרָאתָ זֵכֶר לְמַעֲשֵׂה בְרֵאשִׁית:]

אֱלֹהֵינוּ וֵאלֹהֵי אֲבוֹתֵינוּ מֶלֶךְ רַחֲמָן רַחֵם עָלֵינוּ
טוֹב וּמֵטִיב הִדָּרֶשׁ־לָנוּ ׳ שׁוּבָה אֵלֵינוּ בַּהֲמוֹן רַחֲמֶיךָ
בִּגְלַל אָבוֹת שֶׁעָשׂוּ רְצוֹנֶךָ ׳ בְּנֵה בֵיתְךָ כְּבַתְּחִלָּה
וְכוֹנֵן מִקְדָּשְׁךָ עַל־מְכוֹנוֹ ׳ וְהַרְאֵנוּ בְּבִנְיָנוֹ וְשַׂמְּחֵנוּ
בְּתִקּוּנוֹ ׳ וְהָשֵׁב כֹּהֲנִים לַעֲבוֹדָתָם וּלְוִיִּם לְשִׁירָם וּלְזִמְרָם
וְהָשֵׁב יִשְׂרָאֵל לִנְוֵיהֶם ׳ וְשָׁם נַעֲלֶה וְנֵרָאֶה וְנִשְׁתַּחֲוֶה
לְפָנֶיךָ בְּשָׁלֹשׁ פַּעֲמֵי רְגָלֵינוּ ׳ כַּכָּתוּב בְּתוֹרָתֶךָ ׳ שָׁלֹשׁ
פְּעָמִים בַּשָּׁנָה יֵרָאֶה כָל־זְכוּרְךָ אֶת־פְּנֵי יְהוָֹה אֱלֹהֶיךָ
בַּמָּקוֹם אֲשֶׁר יִבְחָר בְּחַג הַמַּצּוֹת וּבְחַג הַשָּׁבֻעוֹת
וּבְחַג הַסֻּכּוֹת וְלֹא יֵרָאֶה אֶת־פְּנֵי יְהוָֹה רֵיקָם : אִישׁ
כְּמַתְּנַת יָדוֹ כְּבִרְכַּת יְיָ אֱלֹהֶיךָ אֲשֶׁר נָתַן־לָךְ :

On the Eighth Day of Solemn Assembly, and on Simchas Torah,
say :—

On the eighth day.ye shall have a solemn assembly ; ye shall do no servile work. And ye shall offer a burnt offering, an offering made by fire, of a sweet savour unto the Lord : one bullock, one ram, seven he-lambs of the first year without blemish. And their meal offering, etc.

[They that keep the Sabbath and call it a delight shall rejoice in thy kingdom ; the people that hallow the seventh day, even all of them shall be satiated and delighted with thy goodness, seeing that thou didst find pleasure in the seventh day, and didst hallow it ; thou didst call it the desirable of days, in remembrance of the creation.]

REBUILD-
ING OF
SANC-
TUARY

Our God and God of our fathers, merciful King, have mercy upon us, O thou who art good and beneficent be thou entreated of us ; return unto us in thy yearning compassion for the fathers' sake who did thy will ; rebuild thy house as at the beginning, and establish thy sanctuary upon this site ; grant that we may see it in its rebuilding, and make us rejoice in its re-establishment ; restore the priests to their service, the Levites to their song and psalmody, and Israel to their habitations : and there we will go up to appear and worship thee at the three periods of our festivals, according as it is written in thy Torah,

Deuteronomy
16. 16, 17

Three times in the year shall all thy males appear before the Lord thy God in the place which he shall choose, on the feast of unleavened bread, and on the feast of weeks, and on the feast of tabernacles : and they shall not appear before the Lord empty. Every man shall bring according as he is able, according to the blessing of the Lord thy God which he hath given thee.

restore the priests. Here on a day when there is a Blessing of the Priests, the priests begin to prepare for the ceremony of *duchan.*

וְהַשִּׂיאֵנוּ יְיָ אֱלֹהֵינוּ אֶת־בִּרְכַּת מוֹעֲדֶיךָ לְחַיִּים

וּלְשָׁלוֹם לְשִׂמְחָה וּלְשָׂשׂוֹן כַּאֲשֶׁר רָצִיתָ וְאָמַרְתָּ

לְבָרְכֵנוּ : [אֱלֹהֵינוּ וֵאלֹהֵי אֲבוֹתֵינוּ רְצֵה בִמְנוּחָתֵנוּ] קַדְּשֵׁנוּ

בְּמִצְוֹתֶיךָ וְתֵן חֶלְקֵנוּ בְּתוֹרָתֶךָ · שַׂבְּעֵנוּ מִטּוּבֶךָ וְשַׂמְּחֵנוּ

בִּישׁוּעָתֶךָ · וְטַהֵר לִבֵּנוּ לְעָבְדְּךָ בֶּאֱמֶת · וְהַנְחִילֵנוּ יְיָ

אֱלֹהֵינוּ [בְּאַהֲבָה וּבְרָצוֹן] בְּשִׂמְחָה וּבְשָׂשׂוֹן [שַׁבָּת וּ]

מוֹעֲדֵי קָדְשֶׁךָ · וְיִשְׂמְחוּ בְךָ יִשְׂרָאֵל מְקַדְּשֵׁי שְׁמֶךָ ·

בָּרוּךְ אַתָּה יְיָ · מְקַדֵּשׁ [הַשַּׁבָּת וְ] יִשְׂרָאֵל וְהַזְּמַנִּים :

For the conclusion of the עֲמִידָה *to* רְצֵה *see pp.* 460–466, קַדְמוֹנִיּוֹת.

קריאת התורה לשמחת תורה

The following verses are said by the Reader and repeated by the Congregation:

אַתָּה הָרְאֵתָ לָדַעַת כִּי יְיָ הוּא הָאֱלֹהִים אֵין עוֹד

מִלְּבַדּוֹ : לְעֹשֵׂה נִפְלָאוֹת גְּדֹלוֹת לְבַדּוֹ כִּי לְעוֹלָם

חַסְדּוֹ : אֵין כָּמוֹךָ בָאֱלֹהִים אֲדֹנָי וְאֵין כְּמַעֲשֶׂיךָ :

יְהִי כְבוֹד יְיָ לְעוֹלָם יִשְׂמַח יְיָ בְּמַעֲשָׂיו : יְהִי שֵׁם

יְיָ מְבֹרָךְ מֵעַתָּה וְעַד עוֹלָם : יְהִי יְיָ אֱלֹהֵינוּ עִמָּנוּ

כַּאֲשֶׁר הָיָה עִם אֲבֹתֵינוּ אַל יַעַזְבֵנוּ וְאַל יִטְּשֵׁנוּ :

PRAYER FOR FESTIVAL JOY   O Lord our God, bestow upon us the blessing of thy festivals for life and peace, for joy and gladness, even as thou hast been pleased to promise that thou wouldst bless us. [Our God and God of our fathers, accept our rest,] Sanctify us by thy commandments, and grant our portion in thy Torah ; satisfy us with thy goodness, and gladden us with thy salvation ; purify our hearts to serve thee in truth ; and let us inherit, O Lord our God, [in love and favour] with joy and gladness thy holy [Sabbath and] festivals ; and may Israel who hallow thy name rejoice in thee. Blessed art thou, O Lord, who hallowest [the Sabbath and] Israel and the sacred Seasons.

For the conclusion of the Amidah, see pp. 461–467, "Accept" to "as in ancient years."

READING OF THE LAW ON SIMCHAS TORAH.

The following verses are said by the Reader, and repeated by the Congregation :

Deuteronomy 4. 35
Psalm 136. 4   Unto thee it was shown that thou mightest know that the Lord he is God : there is none else beside him. O give thanks to him who alone doeth great wonders : for his

Psalm 86. 8   lovingkindness endureth for ever. There is none like unto thee among the gods, O Lord ; neither are there any works

Psalm 104. 31   like unto thine. Let the glory of the Lord endure for ever ;

Psalm 113. 2   let the Lord rejoice in his works. Blessed be the Name

I. Kings 8. 57   of the Lord from this time forth for evermore. The Lord

SIMCHAS TORAH.

The Service for the Opening of the Ark, as well as that for returning the Scrolls to the Ark, are considerably enlarged on the Festival of Rejoicing of the Torah. It became customary to take all the Scrolls from the Ark, both at the Evening and at the Morning Service, and to bear them in seven circuits round the synagogue, Reader and Congregation joining in tuneful and inspiring chants during the procession. The

וְאִמְרוּ הוֹשִׁיעֵנוּ אֱלֹהֵי יִשְׁעֵנוּ וְקַבְּצֵנוּ וְהַצִּילֵנוּ מִן
הַגּוֹיִם לְהוֹדוֹת לְשֵׁם קָדְשֶׁךָ לְהִשְׁתַּבֵּחַ בִּתְהִלָּתֶךָ :

יְיָ מֶלֶךְ יְיָ מָלָךְ יְיָ יִמְלֹךְ לְעוֹלָם וָעֶד :

יְיָ עֹז לְעַמּוֹ יִתֵּן יְיָ יְבָרֵךְ אֶת עַמּוֹ בַשָּׁלוֹם :

וְיִהְיוּ נָא אֲמָרֵינוּ לְרָצוֹן לִפְנֵי אֲדוֹן כֹּל :

וַיְהִי בִּנְסֹעַ הָאָרֹן וַיֹּאמֶר מֹשֶׁה קוּמָה יְיָ וְיָפֻצוּ אֹיְבֶיךָ
וְיָנֻסוּ מְשַׂנְאֶיךָ מִפָּנֶיךָ : קוּמָה יְיָ לִמְנוּחָתֶךָ אַתָּה
וַאֲרוֹן עֻזֶּךָ : כֹּהֲנֶיךָ יִלְבְּשׁוּ צֶדֶק וַחֲסִידֶיךָ יְרַנֵּנוּ :
בַּעֲבוּר דָּוִד עַבְדֶּךָ אַל תָּשֵׁב פְּנֵי מְשִׁיחֶךָ : וְאָמַר
בַּיּוֹם הַהוּא הִנֵּה אֱלֹהֵינוּ זֶה קִוִּינוּ לוֹ וְיוֹשִׁיעֵנוּ זֶה
יְיָ קִוִּינוּ לוֹ נָגִילָה וְנִשְׂמְחָה בִּישׁוּעָתוֹ : מַלְכוּתְךָ
מַלְכוּת כָּל עֹלָמִים וּמֶמְשַׁלְתְּךָ בְּכָל דּוֹר וָדֹר :

כִּי מִצִּיּוֹן תֵּצֵא תוֹרָה וּדְבַר יְיָ מִירוּשָׁלָםִ :

אַב הָרַחֲמִים הֵיטִיבָה בִרְצוֹנְךָ אֶת צִיּוֹן תִּבְנֶה חוֹמוֹת
יְרוּשָׁלָםִ : כִּי בְךָ לְבַד בָּטָחְנוּ מֶלֶךְ אֵל רָם וְנִשָּׂא
אֲדוֹן עוֹלָמִים :

All the Scrolls are taken from the Ark, and are borne seven
times round the Synagogue.

our God be with us, as he was with our fathers : let him
not leave us, nor forsake us. And say ye, Save us, O God
of our salvation, and gather us and deliver us from the
nations, to give thanks unto thy holy Name and to triumph
in thy praise.

I. Chronicles 16. 35

The Lord is King : the Lord was King : the Lord shall
be King for ever and ever.

Psalm 29. 11

The Lord will give strength unto his people ; the Lord
will bless his people with peace. And may our words be
acceptable, we pray, before the Lord of all.

OPENING OF ARK

Numbers 10. 35

The Ark is opened.

And it came to pass when the ark set forward, that
Moses said : Rise up, O Lord, and thine enemies shall be
scattered, and they that hate thee shall flee before thee.

Psalm 132. 8
Psalm 132. 9
Psalm 132. 10

Arise, O Lord, unto thy resting-place ; thou, and the ark
of thy strength. Let thy priests be clothed with righteousness ; and let thy loving ones shout for joy. For the
sake of David thy servant, turn not away the face of thine

Isaiah 25. 9

anointed. And it shall be said in that day, Lo, this is our
God : we have waited for him, and he will save us : this
is the Lord ; we have waited for him : we will be glad

Psalm 145. 13

and rejoice in his salvation. Thy kingdom is an everlasting
Kingdom, and thy dominion endureth throughout all
generations.

Isaiah 2.3

For out of Zion shall go forth the Torah, and the word
of the Lord from Jerusalem.

Father of compassion, do good in thy favour unto Zion ;
build thou the walls of Jerusalem. For in thee alone do
we put our trust, O King, high and exalted God, Lord of
worlds.

little boys followed the circuits with banners and lighted candles ; and
after the Service, fruit and sweets were distributed among the children.
Simchas Torah became for all, young and old alike, *the* Festival of Joy.

Reader and Congregation chant:

אָנָּא יְיָ הוֹשִׁיעָה נָּא ׳ אָנָּא יְיָ הַצְלִיחָה נָא :

אָנָּא יְיָ עֲנֵנוּ בְיוֹם קָרְאֵנוּ :

אֱלֹהֵי הָרוּחוֹת הוֹשִׁיעָה נָא : בּוֹחֵן לְבָבוֹת הַצְלִיחָה נָא :

גּוֹאֵל חָזָק עֲנֵנוּ בְיוֹם קָרְאֵנוּ :

דּוֹבֵר צְדָקוֹת הוֹשִׁיעָה נָא : הָדוּר בִּלְבוּשׁוֹ הַצְלִיחָה נָא :

וָתִיק וְחָסִיד עֲנֵנוּ בְיוֹם קָרְאֵנוּ :

זַךְ וְיָשָׁר הוֹשִׁיעָה נָא : חוֹמֵל דַּלִּים הַצְלִיחָה נָא :

טוֹב וּמֵטִיב עֲנֵנוּ בְיוֹם קָרְאֵנוּ :

יוֹדֵעַ מַחֲשָׁבוֹת הוֹשִׁיעָה נָא : כַּבִּיר וְנָאוֹר הַצְלִיחָה נָא :

לוֹבֵשׁ צְדָקוֹת עֲנֵנוּ בְיוֹם קָרְאֵנוּ :

מֶלֶךְ עוֹלָמִים הוֹשִׁיעָה נָא : נָאוֹר וְאַדִּיר הַצְלִיחָה נָא :

סוֹמֵךְ נוֹפְלִים עֲנֵנוּ בְיוֹם קָרְאֵנוּ :

עוֹזֵר דַּלִּים הוֹשִׁיעָה נָא : פּוֹדֶה וּמַצִּיל הַצְלִיחָה נָא :

צוּר עוֹלָמִים עֲנֵנוּ בְיוֹם קָרְאֵנוּ :

קָדוֹשׁ וְנוֹרָא הוֹשִׁיעָה נָא : רַחוּם וְחַנּוּן הַצְלִיחָה נָא :

שׁוֹמֵר הַבְּרִית עֲנֵנוּ בְיוֹם קָרְאֵנוּ :

תּוֹמֵךְ תְּמִימִים הוֹשִׁיעָה נָא : תַּקִּיף לָעַד הַצְלִיחָה נָא :

תָּמִים בְּמַעֲשָׂיו עֲנֵנוּ בְיוֹם קָרְאֵנוּ :

All but three Scrolls are returned to the Ark.
The Service now continues שְׁמַע, *p.* 480.

All the Scrolls are taken from the Ark, and are borne seven times round the Synagogue, whilst the Reader and Congregation chant :

PROCES-
SION WITH
TORAH
SCROLLS

O Lord, save, we beseech thee. O Lord, prosper us, we beseech thee. O Lord, answer us on the day that we call.

God of spirits, save, we beseech thee. Searcher of hearts, prosper us, we beseech thee. O strong Redeemer, answer us on the day that we call.

Utterer of righteousness, save, we beseech thee. Apparelled in glory, prosper us, we beseech thee. Omnipotent and merciful, answer us on the day that we call.

Pure and Upright, save, we beseech thee. Pitier of the poor, prosper us, we beseech thee. Good and bountiful Lord, answer us on the day that we call.

Diviner of thoughts, save, we beseech thee. Mighty and resplendent, prosper us, we beseech thee. Clad in righteousness, answer us on the day that we call.

King of worlds, save, we beseech thee. Resplendent with light and majesty, prosper us, we beseech thee. Upholder of the falling, answer us on the day that we call.

Helper of the needy, save, we beseech thee. Redeemer and Deliverer, prosper us, we beseech thee. A Rock everlasting, answer us on the day that we call.

Holy and revered, save, we beseech thee. Merciful and compassionate, prosper us, we beseech thee. Keeper of the Covenant, answer us on the day that we call.

Sustainer of the single-hearted, save, we beseech thee. Sovereign of Eternity, prosper us, we beseech thee. Perfect in thy doings, O answer us on the day that we call.

All but three Scrolls are returned to the Ark.
The Service now continues with " Hear, O Israel," p. 481.

O Lord. The words chanted during the circuits are all founded on Scriptural phrases, or on those rendered familiar in the Liturgy. For the songs and hymns when the Scrolls are returned to the Ark at the morning Service, see the Festival Machzor.

סדר נשיאת כפים:

On Festivals, except on Sabbath and שִׂמְחַת תּוֹרָה, *the following*
Order of the Blessing of the Priests is added in the מוּסָף *Service*
after יִשְׂרָאֵל עַמֶּךָ,, *p.* 534.

The Priests ascend the steps of the Ark.

וְתֶעֱרַב לְפָנֶיךָ עֲתִירָתֵנוּ כְּעוֹלָה *Congregation and Reader.*

וּבְקָרְבָּן • אָנָּא רַחוּם בְּרַחֲמֶיךָ הָרַבִּים הָשֵׁב שְׁכִינָתְךָ
לְצִיּוֹן עִירְךָ וְסֵדֶר הָעֲבוֹדָה לִירוּשָׁלָיִם • וְתֶחֱזֶינָה עֵינֵינוּ
בְּשׁוּבְךָ לְצִיּוֹן בְּרַחֲמִים • וְשָׁם נַעֲבָדְךָ בְּיִרְאָה כִּימֵי עוֹלָם
וּכְשָׁנִים קַדְמוֹנִיּוֹת :

Reader. בָּרוּךְ אַתָּה יְיָ • שֶׁאוֹתְךָ לְבַדְּךָ בְּיִרְאָה נַעֲבוֹד :

Continue מוֹדִים, *to* לְהוֹדוֹת, *p.* 536.
The Reader says to וּבָנָיו *in an undertone.*

אֱלֹהֵינוּ וֵאלֹהֵי אֲבוֹתֵינוּ • בָּרְכֵנוּ בַּבְּרָכָה הַמְּשֻׁלֶּשֶׁת
בַּתּוֹרָה הַכְּתוּבָה עַל־יְדֵי מֹשֶׁה עַבְדֶּךָ • הָאֲמוּרָה מִפִּי
אַהֲרֹן וּבָנָיו •

BLESSING OF THE PRIESTS.

The Priestly Blessing was one of the most impressive features of the
Service in the Temple at Jerusalem, and has ever held a cherished
place in the worship of the Synagogue. In the Temple, it was pronounced
from a special tribune (*duchan*, hence the current name " duchaning ")
after the sacrifice of the daily offering, morning and evening. It was
transferred into the daily Service in the synagogue; but is to-day
restricted in Ashkenazi communities to the Mussaf of Festivals, except
when these fall on the Sabbath day. The ancient melody that

THE BLESSING OF THE PRIESTS.

*On all Festivals, except on Sabbath and Simchas Torah, the following
Order of the Blessing of the Priests is added in the Mussaf
Amidah after " acceptable unto thee," p. 535.*

The Priests ascend the steps of the Ark.

" DUCHAN"

Cong. and Reader.—And may our prayer be acceptable
unto thee as burnt offering and as sacrifice. O thou who art
merciful, we beseech thee, in thine abundant mercy to
restore thy divine presence unto Zion, and the ordained
service to Jerusalem. And let our eyes behold thy return
in mercy to Zion, and there will we worship thee in awe,
as in the days of old and as in ancient years.

Reader.—Blessed art thou, O Lord, whom alone we
serve in awe.

*Continue " We give thanks unto thee," to " it is becoming
to give thanks," p. 537.*

The Reader says to " and his sons " in an undertone.

Our God and God of our Fathers, bless us with the
three-fold blessing of thy Torah written by the hand of
Moses thy servant, which was spoken by Aaron and his
sons,

accompanies its pronouncement by the Priests is, in its original form
solemn and most impressive.

The Hebrew text of the Blessing consists of three short verses, o.
three, five, and seven words respectively. " It mounts by gradua
stages from the petition for material blessing and protection, to that
for Divine favour as a spiritual blessing ; and, in beautiful climax
culminates in the petition for God's most consummate gift, *shalom*
peace, the welfare in which all material and spiritual wellbeing is
comprehended " (Kautzsch). The fifteen words that constitute these
three verses are clothed in a rhythmic form of great beauty, and they
fall with majestic solemnity upon the ear of the worshipper.

spoken by Aaron. The blessing was not that *of* Aaron, it was only
spoken by him. In Israel the priest was no Mediator, and no priest
could say, " *I* bless the children of Israel ". God is the Source of the
blessing that is *pronounced* by the priests. They are merely the channe
through which the blessing is conveyed *to* the Israelites.

כֹּהֲנִים • *Reader.*

עַם קְדוֹשְׁךָ כָּאָמוּר : *Congregation.*

The Priests pronounce the following blessing .—

בָּרוּךְ אַתָּה יְיָ • אֱלֹהֵינוּ מֶלֶךְ הָעוֹלָם אֲשֶׁר קִדְּשָׁנוּ
בִּקְדֻשָׁתוֹ שֶׁל אַהֲרֹן וְצִוָּנוּ לְבָרֵךְ אֶת עַמּוֹ יִשְׂרָאֵל בְּאַהֲבָה :

Congregation.   *Reader, followed by the Priests, word by word.*

אָמֵן :   יְבָרֶכְךָ יְיָ וְיִשְׁמְרֶךָ •

אָמֵן :   יָאֵר יְיָ פָּנָיו אֵלֶיךָ וִיחֻנֶּךָ •

אָמֵן סֶלָה :   יִשָּׂא יְיָ פָּנָיו אֵלֶיךָ וְיָשֵׂם לְךָ שָׁלוֹם :

Continue שִׂים שָׁלוֹם, *p.* 538, *to the end of the* עֲמִידָה.

bless thee. With life, health and prosperity.

thee. Why is the singular used ? A current explanation states
that, as the prerequisite of all blessing for Israel is unity, all Israel is
to feel as one organic body.

keep thee. Grant thee His divine protection against evil, sickness
and calamity.

This verse has a positive side—may He bless thee with possessions,
so as to render thee independent of the help of mortals ; and a negative
side—may He save thee from all dangers which threaten that independence. May God guard thee from sin, and shield thee from all destructive influences (מן המזיקין) that so often follow in the wake of prosperity.

cause his face to shine. When God's " face " is said to be turned
towards man and to shine upon him, it implies the outpouring of Divine
love and salvation (Psalm 80. 20). In contrast to this, we have the
prayer, " Hide not Thy face from me ".

Reader.—The priests.

Cong.—Thy holy people, as it is said :

The Priests pronounce the following blessing :

Blessed art thou, O Lord our God, King of the universe,
who hast hallowed us with the sanctity of Aaron and hast
commanded us to bless thy people Israel in love.

Reader, followed by the Priests, word for word.	*Cong.* :
The Lord bless thee and keep thee :	Amen.
The Lord make his face to shine upon thee,	
and be gracious unto thee :	Amen.
The Lord turn his face unto thee,	
and give thee peace.	Amen. Selah.

Continue " Grant peace " p. 539, *to the end of the Amidah.*

The Rabbis interpret the words, "make his face to shine upon thee "
in a purely spiritual sense, to imply the gift of knowledge and moral
insight.   " May He give thee enlightenment of the eyes, the light of
the Shechinah ; may the fire of Prophecy burn in the souls of thy
children ; may the light of the Torah illumine thy home " (Sifri.)

and be gracious. Giving thee the gift of knowledge and moral insight.   The Rabbis understand ויחנך in the sense also of, " May He
give thee grace in the eyes of thy fellowmen " ; see Aboth III, 13. p. 655.

lift up. Turn His loving care unto thee.

give thee. Establish for thee.

peace. The Heb. *shalom* means not only freedom from all disaster ;
but health, welfare, security and tranquility.   Peace is no negative
conception, and is not the equivalent of inactivity.   Whether for the
individual or for society, it is that harmonious co-operation of all human
forces towards ethical and spiritual ends which men call the Kingdom
of God.

THE SOLEMN FESTIVALS

Rosh Hashanah and Yom Kippur

Like lighthouses on the shores of eternity, New Year and Day of Atonement have flashed their message of holiness, and have proved potent agencies for spiritual renewal, to a hundred generations in Israel. They strike the deepest chords of human feeling in the breast of the Jew, and voice the sublimest truths of religion : New Year is the *mind*, and the Day of Atonement is the *heart*, of the Israelite's life. Whatever Judaism has to say on God, man, and duty, is enshrined in the prayers and hymns of the " Days of Awe "—as these Festivals came to be called. Those prayers and hymns are the spiritual epitome of the devotion, of Israel's prophets and psalmists, rabbinic teachers and medieval hymn-writers. Even some of the Solemn Festival Responses—brief, pithy statements designed to be within the grasp of all—are passwords of Religion, presenting in bird's-eye-view the religious outlook of Judaism.

Those who seek a full understanding of the Liturgy of the Solemn Festivals, must go to the Machzor, the Book of Devotion which presents the whole cycle of hymns and anthems that in the course of the ages have grown round the ancient basic prayers. The Daily Prayer Book includes only the Amidahs of the Solemn Festivals; and little more than a brief summary of the religious principles underlying those Amidahs, can here be given. But even such a brief summary offers a general view of the Jewish teaching concerning sin, repentance and forgiveness, and reveals a unique and man-redeeming Message.

I. REPENTANCE

The key to the understanding of that Message, as well as of the two Festivals that proclaim it, is the doctrine of תשובה Repentance. The literal meaning of the Hebrew word is, " Return " ; and denotes that inward change of heart which leads the sinner to turn *from* evil, and return *to* God. Repentance—the Rabbis declare—is one of the Divine things that formed part of the Heavenly plan when man was created, and it lies at the root of his life as a moral being. It is, therefore, essential to realize its implications.

1. The first of these implications is man's *freedom of will* in the choice between good and evil. Man's heart is a battle-field : the leanings of his better nature are constantly opposed by the Evil Inclination—yetzer hara—the wilful impulse that induces to passion, hatred, and selfish desire. But, though the Evil Inclination tempts man to sin, it does not *compel* him to do so. Sin, like some wild beast, crouches at the door of the human heart, ready to spring upon the man who gives it the opportunity; but he can rule over it (Genesis 4. 7). Self-conquest, self-control and self-discipline are primary duties, because man can always do the right by reason *of his free will*.

2. Now as to the nature of Sin. In Hebrew, three terms are used for various grades of wrong-doing :

(*a*) חטא, lit. " missing of the mark ", any wayward action due to carelessness, ignorance or error ;

(b) עוון, lit. " crookedness ", a departure from right conduct by conscious transgression of Divine commandment ; and

(c) פשע, lit. " rebellion ", deliberate persistence in such departure.

Sin may begin as an involuntary lapse into hate or wrongdoing, and gradually harden into open defiance of the laws of holiness and right. For, if a man yields ever so little to the prompting of the Evil Inclination, it soon has him in its power. " The cobweb grows into a cable, the passing stranger becomes the master of the house ". But man need never *assume* sin's yoke. The ancients told of distant islands with mountains of magnet of such power, that ruin befell any ship venturing near. Its iron nails and fastenings would fly out, reducing it to so many planks of wood, bringing death to all on board. Sins there are that, likewise, unhinge all restraints of habit and education, and leave us helpless playthings of temptation. Yet man is the pilot of his life's barque, and can so steer it as never to come near those forces of destruction and death.

3. And if a man *has* assumed sin's yoke, he can throw it off. There is an overcoming of sin. In the domain of the spirit, the Ethiopian *can* change his skin, and the leopard his spots. " The greatest apostasy ", said a Chassidic teacher, " would be the forgetting that we are of God, children of our Father Who is in heaven ", and that, therefore, we are able by repentance to rebuild the broken fabric of character, and regain our pristine purity of soul. However, spiritual regeneration is not the work of a moment ; and many are the steps on the Ladder of Repentance that are to be climbed by the sinner before he beholds the stars of Divine Pardon and Forgiveness.

(a) The first of these steps is the awakening to the fact that our conduct has been a going away from God. Our eyes are then opened to our degradation, and we *confess* to ourselves that sin is leading us into darkness. *Confession* is an essential part of repentance. Not that God the All-knowing requires it ; but it is the sinner to whom an honest and unsparing self-knowledge is indispensable. " The moment a man is willing to see himself as he is, and make the confession ' I have sinned ', from that moment the powers of evil lose their control over him " (Midrash). On the place and nature of Confession (וידוי) in the Atonement Service, see p. 905.

(b) *remorse* (חרטה). The full realization of sin's taint evokes contrition and sorrow. On the Day of Atonement, suppression of all physical cravings accompanies our remorse that finds words in penitential prayer and public confession. " Even though he be the veriest sinner, his supplication fits him to obtain mercy, and so helps him to receive it " (Albo).

(c) *amendment*. But confession is quite unreal, unless it is followed by solemn resolve not to repeat the offence. " Let the wicked *forsake* his way, and the man of iniquity his thoughts ; and let him return unto the Lord, and He will have compassion on him ; and to our God, for He will abundantly pardon " (Isaiah 55. 7). Be it noted, however, that it is the sinner that is forgiven by repentance, *not the sins*. Therefore there must be utmost endeavour to *undo* the guilty action, and every effort made to conciliate him whom we have wronged. Reparation and reconciliation are the tests of our sincerity. Rabbi Elazar ben

Azaryah, (see p. 662) is the author of the sublime saying, " For transgressions against God, the Day of Atonement atones ; but for transgressions against a fellow-man, the Day of Atonement does not atone, so long as the sinner has not redressed the wrong done, and conciliated the man he has sinned against ". This has become the authoritative teaching of the Synagogue.

(d) The crown of Repentance is the *Divine Pardon* (מחילה). The sinner has no *claim* on the Divine forgiveness. It is God's inexhaustible love which desires the repentance of the sinner, even of the most hardened sinner. As we read in the Neilah prayer, God delights in repentance ; His hand is ever outstretched to receive the penitent, and, to the day of the sinner's death, doth the Heavenly Father wait for his return. The Rabbis say, " The gates of Repentance are ever open. As the sea is always accessible, so is the Holy One, blessed be He, always accessible to the penitent. Moreover, the repentant sinner attains to a higher spiritual level than even he who has never succumbed to sin. Better is one hour of repentance and good deeds in this world, than the whole life of the world to come ".

(e) Repentance has been called " the Jewish doctrine of salvation " (Moore) ; and Heiler has rightly declared this spontaneous, spiritual and ethical act of self-condemnation, coupled with the will to do good, as " something infinitely simple ". It is only necessary to add, that the word *salvation* is differently understood by Jews and non-Jews. To the non-Jew, *salvation* means redemption from sin here, and deliverance from its consequences thereafter. For these conceptions, the Jew uses the words " repentance for sin " and " forgiveness of sin ". In Israel's prayers, *salvation* denotes either deliverance from distress and peril, or freedom for the moral expansion of our higher nature. It is something that saves us from our lower self, illumines and regenerates our soul, and makes us willing instruments of God's Eternal plan.

" The whole doctrine of Repentance is emphatically a Jewish teaching, and its full development is purely the work of Rabbinical Judaism " (Montefiore).

II. PREPARATION FOR THE " DAYS OF AWE "

True Repentance requires preliminary purification of heart. " Prepare to meet thy God, O Israel " (Amos 4. 12) is the bidding of the Prophet ; and the pious Israelite has at all times attuned his spirit to the call of the Solemn Season.

In Ashkenazi communities, such attuning of spirit starts with the first day of the month of Ellul. Throughout that month, at the conclusion of the Morning Service, a few Shofar notes are sounded (without benediction preceding), whereupon Psalm 27 is said. And, beginning on the Sunday before Rosh Hashanah (and if this falls on Monday or Tuesday, on the second Sunday before), special prayers for forgiveness —*Selichoth*—are recited prior to the Morning Service. These are continued on the weekdays of the Ten Days of Repentance. Special additions in the Amidah, and (in the Morning and Afternoon Services) Ovinu Malkenu, p. 162, are said during those days.

III. NEW YEAR—ROSH HASHANAH

The New Year Festival is far other than the mere opening day, according to the olden Jewish reckoning, of another year in the flight of time. Even as the seventh day in the week is a holy day, so is the seventh month in the year a holy month ; and its opening day is the Herald of the Day of Atonement. The special symbolic rite for the New Year is the sounding of the Ram's horn, the *Shofar*. The meaning of the ceremony to the worshippers who listen in awe to the notes of this oldest of wind instruments, is as solemn as the sounds themselves are soul stirring.

And on the High Festivals the Jew thinks not only of himself, but of peace and blessedness for all mankind. In the most ancient part of the Amidahs of both the New Year and the Day of Atonement, we pray God to hasten the time when the mighty shall be just, and the just mighty ; when all the children of men shall form one band of brotherhood ; when national arrogance and oppression shall have passed away, like so much smoke, from the earth.

The Hebrew names of New Year emphasize different aspects of the Festival.

1. *Rosh Hashanah.* lit. " the beginning of the Year ", is the name in common use since Mishna times. According to Tradition, the creation of the world took place on Rosh Hashanah ; and the Festival is thus a proclamation that God is the King of the universe, and Ruler of the lives of men and nations.

2. *Yom Teruah,* " the Day of the Sounding of the Ram's horn ", is the Biblical name of the Festival. The sounding of the Shofar is to rouse those who have fallen asleep in life ; remind them of the Law of Truth revealed at Sinai ; and announce the sure advent of the Messianic Redemption, when humanity will be One, even as the God of Righteousness is One ; see p. 864.

3. *Yom Ha-zikaron,* " the Day of Remembrance ". The God adored by Judaism is not a lifeless, nebulous Being chained in mechanical laws, such as has been put forward in some philosophies, ancient and modern. He is a conscious Personality, Who made and knows the human heart, Who hears and answers those who cry unto Him. He is mindful of us, and deals with His creatures in mercy and truth ; and He desires us to be mindful of Him, to remember and obey His precepts of eternal wisdom and salvation.

4. *Yom Ha-din*—the annual " Day of Judgment ", when the children of men are judged according to their actions, when they themselves review their deeds during the year that is past. This aspect of the Festival—" the world's assize "—is fervently dwelt on in the prayers and hymns of the Festival. It stresses the Divine power of moral regeneration with which God has endowed the human soul.

הדלקת נר של ראש השנה ויום הכפורים :

Meditation before kindling the lights :

רִבּוֹן הָעוֹלָמִים · הִנֵּה בָאתִי לְהַדְלִיק אֶת־הַנֵּרוֹת

לִכְבוֹד (הַשַּׁבָּת וְלִכְבוֹד :*On Friday add*)

<table>
<tr><td>*For* יוֹם כִּפּוּר *say* :</td><td>*For* רֹאשׁ הַשָּׁנָה *say* :</td></tr>
<tr><td>יוֹם הַכִּפֻּרִים</td><td>יוֹם ־הַזִּכָּרוֹן</td></tr>
</table>

הַזֶּה : וּבִזְכוּת מִצְוָה זוֹ תַּשְׁפִּיעַ עָלַי וְעַל־בְּנֵי בֵיתִי

שֶׁפַע בְּרָכוֹת שֶׁתִּתְחַנֵּנוּ וְתַשְׁכֵּן שְׁכִינָתְךָ בְּתוֹכֵנוּ :

אַב־הָרַחֲמִים וְהַסְּלִיחוֹת · פְּתַח שַׁעֲרֵי שָׁמַיִם

לִתְפִלָּתֵנוּ · וּמְחַל לַעֲוֹנוֹתֵינוּ : לֵב טָהוֹר בְּרָא לָנוּ

[וְזַכֵּנִי לְגַדֵּל בָּנַי וּבְנוֹתַי] לָלֶכֶת בְּדַרְכֵי יְשָׁרִים לְפָנֶיךָ ·

דְּבֵקִים בַּתּוֹרָה וּבְמַעֲשִׂים טוֹבִים : הַרְחֵק מֵעָלֵינוּ

כָּל־חֶרְפָּה תוּגָה וְיָגוֹן · וּשְׁלַח רְפוּאָה לְכָל־מַכְאוֹבֵינוּ :

זָכְרֵנוּ לַחַיִּים · מֶלֶךְ חָפֵץ בַּחַיִּים · וְכָתְבֵנוּ בְּסֵפֶר

הַחַיִּים · לְמַעַנְךָ אֱלֹהִים חַיִּים · אָמֵן :

בָּרוּךְ אַתָּה יְיָ אֱלֹהֵינוּ מֶלֶךְ הָעוֹלָם · אֲשֶׁר קִדְּשָׁנוּ

בְּמִצְוֹתָיו וְצִוָּנוּ לְהַדְלִיק נֵר שֶׁל־ (שַׁבָּת וְ *On Friday add*)

<table>
<tr><td>*For* יוֹם כִּפּוּר *say* :</td><td>*For* רֹאשׁ הַשָּׁנָה *say* :</td></tr>
<tr><td>יוֹם הַכִּפֻּרִים</td><td>יוֹם טוֹב :</td></tr>
</table>

add : יוֹם כִּפּוּר *and* רֹאשׁ הַשָּׁנָה *For both*

בָּרוּךְ אַתָּה יְיָ אֱלֹהֵינוּ מֶלֶךְ הָעוֹלָם · שֶׁהֶחֱיָנוּ

וְקִיְּמָנוּ וְהִגִּיעָנוּ לַזְּמַן הַזֶּה :

THE FESTIVAL LIGHTS FOR NEW YEAR AND DAY OF ATONEMENT

Before Kindling the Lights say :—

MEDITA-TION   Lord of the Universe, I am about to perform the sacred duty of kindling the lights in honour of the (*on Friday add* : Sabbath and of the)

for Rosh Hashanah say :   *for Yom Kippur say* :
Day of Remembrance.   Day of Atonement.

And may the effect of my fulfilling this commandment be that the stream of heavenly blessing flow in upon me and mine ; that thou be gracious unto us, and cause thy Presence to dwell among us.

SUPPLICA-TION   Father of Mercy and Forgiveness, open the gates of heaven unto our prayers on this Sacred Festival, and pardon our transgressions. Create in us a pure heart ; and make me worthy to (rear my children so that they) walk in the way of righteousness before thee, loyal to thy Torah and clinging to good deeds. Keep far from us all manner of shame, grief and care ; and send healing for all our sorrows. Remember us unto life, O King who delightest in life ; and inscribe us in the Book of life, for thine own sake, O living God. Amen.

BENE-DICTIONS   Blessed art thou, O Lord our God, King of the universe, who hast hallowed us by thy commandments, and hast commanded us to kindle (*on Friday add* : the light of the Sabbath, and)

for Rosh Hashanah :   *for Yom Kippur* :
the Festival light.   the light of the Day of Atonement.

For both Rosh Hashanah and Yom Kippur add :—

Blessed art thou, O Lord our God, King of the universe, who hast kept us in life, and hast preserved us, and enabled us to reach this season.

תְּפִלַּת רֹאשׁ הַשָּׁנָה:

מִנְחָה *as on Fridays.* For מַעֲרִיב *see pp.* 364–374. *Should the first evening of* רֹאשׁ הַשָּׁנָה *fall on Friday,* מַעֲרִיב *commences with* מִזְמוֹר שִׁיר לְיוֹם הַשַּׁבָּת, *p.* 360.

The following עֲמִידָה *is said at the Evening, Morning and Afternoon Services :—*

אֲדֹנָי שְׂפָתַי תִּפְתָּח וּפִי יַגִּיד תְּהִלָּתֶךָ :

בָּרוּךְ אַתָּה יְיָ אֱלֹהֵינוּ וֵאלֹהֵי אֲבוֹתֵינוּ • אֱלֹהֵי אַבְרָהָם אֱלֹהֵי יִצְחָק וֵאלֹהֵי יַעֲקֹב • הָאֵל הַגָּדוֹל הַגִּבּוֹר וְהַנּוֹרָא אֵל עֶלְיוֹן • גּוֹמֵל חֲסָדִים טוֹבִים וְקוֹנֵה הַכֹּל • וְזוֹכֵר חַסְדֵי אָבוֹת וּמֵבִיא גוֹאֵל לִבְנֵי בְנֵיהֶם לְמַעַן שְׁמוֹ בְּאַהֲבָה •

זָכְרֵנוּ לְחַיִּים מֶלֶךְ חָפֵץ בַּחַיִּים • וְכָתְבֵנוּ בְּסֵפֶר הַחַיִּים • לְמַעַנְךָ אֱלֹהִים חַיִּים •

מֶלֶךְ עוֹזֵר וּמוֹשִׁיעַ וּמָגֵן • בָּרוּךְ אַתָּה יְיָ מָגֵן אַבְרָהָם :

אַתָּה גִּבּוֹר לְעוֹלָם אֲדֹנָי מְחַיֵּה מֵתִים אַתָּה רַב לְהוֹשִׁיעַ •

AMIDAH

remember us. This addition to the Amidah goes back to the ninth century. It refers to the Heavenly Judgment—the thought uppermost in the Jewish consciousness during the ten Days of Repentance.

Afternoon Service as on Fridays. For Evening Service, see pp. 365-375. Should the first evening of the New Year fall on Friday, the Evening Service commences with "A Psalm, a Song for the Sabbath Day," p. 361.

The following Amidah is said at the Evening, Morning and Afternoon Services :—

Psalm 51. 17 O Lord, open thou my lips, and my mouth shall declare thy praise.

I. THE GOD OF HISTORY

Blessed art thou, O Lord our God and God of our fathers, God of Abraham, God of Isaac, and God of Jacob, the great, mighty and revered God, the most high God, who bestowest lovingkindnesses, and art Master of all things ; See p. 449 who rememberest the pious deeds of the patriarchs, and in love wilt bring a redeemer to their children's children for thy Name's sake.

Remember us unto life, O King, who delightest in life, and inscribe us in the book of life, for thine own sake, O living God.

O King, Helper, Saviour and Shield. Blessed art thou, O Lord, the Shield of Abraham.

II. THE GOD OF NATURE

Thou, O Lord, art mighty for ever, thou revivest the dead, thou art mighty to save.

---

who delightest in life. This wonderful phrase sums up Judaism's belief in a loving and beneficent God, as well as its optimistic outlook on human existence.

inscribe us. For the idea of *Book of Life*, see p. 165. " In a higher than their literal sense, the words of the Liturgy are true. Our destiny—our spiritual destiny—is written down on New Year's Day, and sealed on the Day of Atonement. We write it down in the penitence with which we greet the dawn of the year ; we seal it with the amendment which we solemnly vow on the Fast of Kippur " (M. Joseph).

for thine own sake. i.e. to fulfil Thy purposes.

מְכַלְכֵּל חַיִּים בְּחֶסֶד מְחַיֵּה מֵתִים בְּרַחֲמִים רַבִּים · סוֹמֵךְ
נוֹפְלִים וְרוֹפֵא חוֹלִים וּמַתִּיר אֲסוּרִים וּמְקַיֵּם אֱמוּנָתוֹ
לִישֵׁנֵי עָפָר · מִי כָמוֹךָ בַּעַל גְּבוּרוֹת וּמִי דוֹמֶה לָּךְ ·
מֶלֶךְ מֵמִית וּמְחַיֶּה וּמַצְמִיחַ יְשׁוּעָה ·

מִי כָמוֹךָ אַב הָרַחֲמִים זוֹכֵר יְצוּרָיו לַחַיִּים בְּרַחֲמִים ·
וְנֶאֱמָן אַתָּה לְהַחֲיוֹת מֵתִים · בָּרוּךְ אַתָּה יְיָ · מְחַיֵּה
הַמֵּתִים :

אַתָּה קָדוֹשׁ וְשִׁמְךָ קָדוֹשׁ וּקְדוֹשִׁים בְּכָל־יוֹם יְהַלְלוּךָ
סֶּלָה :

וּבְכֵן תֵּן פַּחְדְּךָ יְיָ אֱלֹהֵינוּ עַל כָּל־מַעֲשֶׂיךָ וְאֵימָתְךָ

Father of Mercy. In the clause inserted in the preceding Benediction
during the Solemn Season, God is addressed as " King "; here He is
invoked as " Father ". Whenever these two terms are combined, the
order is always, " Our Father, our King ". In all these insertions, there
is a prayer for *life*.

THE DIVINE KINGDOM

The opening paragraphs of the special portion of the New Year
Amidah are noteworthy in the literature of devotion. Nowhere is the
thought of the Divine Kingdom expressed with greater power. These
ancient phrases of great simplicity combine the fervour of the Psalmist
with the soaring of the Prophet when they speak of God's universal
sovereignty over Man and Nature, the coming unification of mankind,
and the disappearance of Iniquity from earth.

These paragraphs are attributed to the Babylonian teacher Abba
Areka, better known as RABH (160–247), a genius in the realm of
prayer. He was a pupil of R. Judah the Prince, the compiler of the

See p. 451

Thou sustainest the living with lovingkindness, revivest the dead with great mercy, supportest the falling, healest the sick, freest the bound, and keepest thy faith to them that sleep in the dust. Who is like unto thee, Lord of mighty acts, and who resembleth thee, O King, who orderest death and restorest life and causest salvation to spring forth ?

Who is like unto thee, Father of mercy, who in mercy rememberest thy creatures unto life ?

Yea, faithful art thou to revive the dead. Blessed art thou, O Lord, who revivest the dead.

**III.
SANCTIFI-
CATION
OF GOD**

Thou art holy, and thy name is holy, and holy beings praise thee daily. (Selah.)

Now, therefore, O Lord our God, impose thine awe

Mishna. When he completed his studies in Palestine, he returned to Babylon and founded the Academy of Sura, which continued to be a seat of Rabbinic knowledge and leadership in Jewry for 800 years. Among his notable sayings are, " The commandments of the Torah were given to purify the life of man : their one aim is to free men from error and sin. The world is a beautiful world, and man will be called to account for every lawful occasion on which he has deprived himself of its goodness. Whosoever is devoid of pity is no child of Abraham. It is well to busy oneself with religious study and good deeds, even when the motives for doing so are not entirely disinterested, for the habit of rightdoing will eventually make the intention pure. Israel's Redemption depends on repentance and good deeds."

impose thine awe. In substance, this idea is found in Ben Sira, four centuries before Rabh :

> Save us, O God of all ;
> Send Thy fear upon the nations .
> And let them see Thy power.
> As Thou wast sanctified in us before them,
> So be Thou glorified in them before us ;
> Let them know Thee as we also have known Thee,
> That there is no God, but only Thou, O God.
> Hasten the end, and ordain the appointed time,
> And give reward unto them that wait for Thee,
> That all the ends of the earth may know
> That Thou art the Lord, the God of the ages.
>   (Ecclesiasticus 36. 1–5, 8, 16 and 17).

The universal recognition of God's kingship will change the hearts and souls of men. " When men find the path to God, they will discover

עַל כָּל־מַה־שֶׁבָּרָאתָ · וְיִירָאוּךָ כָּל־הַמַּעֲשִׂים וְיִשְׁתַּחֲווּ
לְפָנֶיךָ כָּל־הַבְּרוּאִים · וְיֵעָשׂוּ כֻלָּם אֲגֻדָּה אַחַת לַעֲשׂוֹת
רְצוֹנְךָ בְּלֵבָב שָׁלֵם · כְּמוֹ שֶׁיָּדַעְנוּ יְיָ אֱלֹהֵינוּ שֶׁהַשָּׁלְטָן
לְפָנֶיךָ עֹז בְּיָדְךָ וּגְבוּרָה בִּימִינֶךָ וְשִׁמְךָ נוֹרָא עַל
כָּל־מַה־שֶׁבָּרָאתָ :

וּבְכֵן תֵּן כָּבוֹד יְיָ לְעַמֶּךָ תְּהִלָּה לִירֵאֶיךָ וְתִקְוָה
לְדוֹרְשֶׁיךָ וּפִתְחוֹן פֶּה לַמְיַחֲלִים לָךְ · שִׂמְחָה לְאַרְצֶךָ
וְשָׂשׂוֹן לְעִירֶךָ וּצְמִיחַת קֶרֶן לְדָוִד עַבְדֶּךָ וַעֲרִיכַת נֵר
לְבֶן־יִשַׁי מְשִׁיחֶךָ בִּמְהֵרָה בְיָמֵינוּ :

וּבְכֵן צַדִּיקִים יִרְאוּ וְיִשְׂמָחוּ וִישָׁרִים יַעֲלֹזוּ וַחֲסִידִים
בְּרִנָּה יָגִילוּ · וְעוֹלָתָה תִּקְפָּץ־פִּיהָ וְכָל־הָרִשְׁעָה כֻּלָּהּ
כֶּעָשָׁן תִּכְלֶה · כִּי תַעֲבִיר מֶמְשֶׁלֶת זָדוֹן מִן־הָאָרֶץ :

וְתִמְלוֹךְ אַתָּה יְיָ לְבַדֶּךָ עַל כָּל־מַעֲשֶׂיךָ בְּהַר
צִיּוֹן מִשְׁכַּן כְּבוֹדֶךָ וּבִירוּשָׁלַיִם עִיר קָדְשֶׁךָ · כַּכָּתוּב

the path to one another, in the consciousness of equality and community " (Baeck). The recognition of the Divine Sovereignty is the
condition for the fulfilment of the Messianic vision of all mankind
forming one Human Brotherhood.

upon all thy works, and thy dread upon all that thou hast created, that all works may revere thee and all creatures prostrate themselves before thee, that they may all form a single band to do thy will with a perfect heart ; even as we know, O Lord our God, that dominion is thine, strength is in thy hand, and might in thy right hand, and that thy Name is to be revered above all that thou hast created.

Give then glory, O Lord, unto thy people, praise to them that revere thee, hope to them that seek thee, and confidence to them that wait for thee, joy to thy land, gladness to thy city, a flowering of strength unto David thy servant, and a clear shining light unto the son of Jesse, thine anointed, speedily in our days.

Then shall the just also see and be glad, and the upright shall exult, and the pious triumphantly rejoice, while iniquity shall close her mouth, and all wickedness shall be wholly consumed like smoke, when thou makest the dominion of arrogance to pass away from the earth.

And thou, O Lord, shalt reign, thou alone over all thy works on Mount Zion, the dwelling place of thy glory, and

---

give then glory. Like the Prophets before them, the Rabbis who laid the foundations of the Liturgy looked upon religion and ethics as pre-eminently *social;* and society in the ancient world meant national society. But the nationalism of Rabbis, as of the Prophets, was of the spiritual kind; and they prayed for the time when the spiritual values of Israel would govern the lives of all the children of men. This explains the petition in this prayer for the concrete Jewish hopes—the Holy Land, the Holy City, the Messiah.

iniquity shall close her mouth. The man of iniquity who tramples on those who are too weak to defend themselves (like the orphan and the stranger), is in Judaism held to be *the* enemy of God and man. And the final disappearance of iniquity is rightly represented in this prayer as the goal of human history.

the dominion of arrogance to pass away. Then shall oppression, destruction and death, no longer be instruments of government.

בְּדִבְרֵי קָדְשֶׁךָ ‧ יִמְלֹךְ יְיָ לְעוֹלָם אֱלֹהַיִךְ צִיּוֹן לְדֹר וָדֹר ‧
הַלְלוּיָהּ :

קָדוֹשׁ אַתָּה וְנוֹרָא שְׁמֶךָ וְאֵין אֱלֹהַּ מִבַּלְעָדֶיךָ ‧
כַּכָּתוּב ‧ וַיִּגְבַּהּ יְיָ צְבָאוֹת בַּמִּשְׁפָּט וְהָאֵל הַקָּדוֹשׁ נִקְדַּשׁ
בִּצְדָקָה : בָּרוּךְ אַתָּה יְיָ ‧ הַמֶּלֶךְ הַקָּדוֹשׁ :

אַתָּה בְחַרְתָּנוּ מִכָּל־הָעַמִּים ‧ אָהַבְתָּ אוֹתָנוּ ‧ וְרָצִיתָ
בָּנוּ ‧ וְרוֹמַמְתָּנוּ מִכָּל־הַלְּשׁוֹנוֹת ‧ וְקִדַּשְׁתָּנוּ בְּמִצְוֹתֶיךָ ‧
וְקֵרַבְתָּנוּ מַלְכֵּנוּ לַעֲבוֹדָתֶךָ ‧ וְשִׁמְךָ הַגָּדוֹל וְהַקָּדוֹשׁ
עָלֵינוּ קָרָאתָ :

On Saturday Night add the following :—

וַתּוֹדִיעֵנוּ יְיָ אֱלֹהֵינוּ אֶת־מִשְׁפְּטֵי צִדְקֶךָ וַתְּלַמְּדֵנוּ לַעֲשׂוֹת
חֻקֵּי רְצוֹנֶךָ ‧ וַתִּתֶּן־לָנוּ יְיָ אֱלֹהֵינוּ מִשְׁפָּטִים יְשָׁרִים וְתוֹרוֹת
אֱמֶת חֻקִּים וּמִצְוֹת טוֹבִים ‧ וַתַּנְחִילֵנוּ זְמַנֵּי שָׂשׂוֹן וּמוֹעֲדֵי
קֹדֶשׁ וְחַגֵּי נְדָבָה ‧ וַתּוֹרִישֵׁנוּ קְדֻשַּׁת שַׁבָּת וּכְבוֹד מוֹעֵד

thy Holy words. The traditional division of Scripture is into three
parts—the Torah, the Prophets, and the Holy Writings (or, Holy
Words).

the holy God is sanctified in righteousness. Or, " is sanctified by
justice ". This declaration of the Prophet Isaiah is among the sublimest
utterances ever spoken by human lips. To understand the idea of
justice, we must bear in mind the following Biblical teaching. There
is in man, created in the image of God, a Divine spark : each human
life, therefore, is sacred and of infinite worth. Because of that spark, a
human being is far other than a chattel, or a thing ; he is a *personality*,
endowed with the right to life, honour, and the fruits of his labour.
The safeguarding of those rights is called *justice* ; whereas *injustice* is
the trampling underfoot of human dignity, and the treatment of

'salm 146. 10
Isaiah 5. 16

in Jerusalem, thy holy city, as it is written in thy Holy Words, The Lord shall reign for ever, thy God, O Zion, unto all generations. Praise ye the Lord.

Holy art thou, and awesome is thy Name, and there is no God beside thee, as it is written, And the Lord of hosts is exalted in judgment, and the holy God is sanctified in righteousness. Blessed art thou, O Lord, the holy King.

IV. THE SELECTION OF ISRAEL
See pp.798-801

Thou hast chosen us from all peoples, thou hast loved us and taken pleasure in us, and hast exalted us above all tongues ; thou hast hallowed us by thy commandments and brought us near unto ηy service, O our King, and called us by thy great and holy Name.

[On Saturday Night add the following :—

Thou, O Lord our God, has made known unto us thy righteous judgments ; thou hast taught us to perform the statutes of thy will ; thou hast given us, O Lord our God, upright judgments, laws of truth, good statutes and commandments. Thou hast caused us to inherit seasons of joy, appointed times of holiness, and feasts of free will offerings, and hast given us as heritage the sanctity of the Sabbath, the glory of the holy convocations, and the celebration of

human beings as if they were mere chattels, things. Isaiah proclaims justice, *i.e.* respect for elementary human rights, to be a sanctification of the Holy God !

Justice—*i.e.* this reverence for the rights of others—is something more than mere abstaining from injury to our fellow-men. It is a positive conception ; and embraces charity, philanthropy and every endeavour to bring out what is noblest and best in others. And it is not limited to our relations with individuals. It extends to action towards groups ; and asserts the claims of the " lower " upon the "higher" classes ; of the poor and helpless, upon them who possess the means to help. This is called *social* justice. But there is also *international* justice, which demands respect for the rights and personality of national groups ; and proclaims that no people can of right be robbed of its national life or territory, its language or spiritual heritage.

וַחֲגִינֵת הָרֶגֶל · וַתַּבְדֵּל יְיָ אֱלֹהֵינוּ בֵּין קֹדֶשׁ לְחוֹל בֵּין אוֹר
לְחֹשֶׁךְ בֵּין יִשְׂרָאֵל לָעַמִּים בֵּין יוֹם הַשְּׁבִיעִי לְשֵׁשֶׁת יְמֵי
הַמַּעֲשֶׂה · בֵּין קְדֻשַּׁת שַׁבָּת לִקְדֻשַּׁת יוֹם טוֹב הִבְדַּלְתָּ
וְאֶת־יוֹם הַשְּׁבִיעִי מִשֵּׁשֶׁת יְמֵי הַמַּעֲשֶׂה קִדַּשְׁתָּ · הִבְדַּלְתָּ
וְקִדַּשְׁתָּ אֶת־עַמְּךָ יִשְׂרָאֵל בִּקְדֻשָּׁתֶךָ :

On שַׁבָּת add the words in brackets.

וַתִּתֶּן־לָנוּ יְיָ אֱלֹהֵינוּ בְּאַהֲבָה אֶת־יוֹם [הַשַּׁבָּת הַזֶּה
וְאֶת יוֹם] הַזִּכָּרוֹן הַזֶּה · יוֹם [זִכְרוֹן] תְּרוּעָה [בְּאַהֲבָה]
מִקְרָא קֹדֶשׁ זֵכֶר לִיצִיאַת מִצְרָיִם :

אֱלֹהֵינוּ וֵאלֹהֵי אֲבוֹתֵינוּ · יַעֲלֶה וְיָבֹא וְיַגִּיעַ וְיֵרָאֶה
וְיֵרָצֶה וְיִשָּׁמַע וְיִפָּקֵד וְיִזָּכֵר זִכְרוֹנֵנוּ וּפִקְדוֹנֵנוּ וְזִכְרוֹן
אֲבוֹתֵינוּ · וְזִכְרוֹן מָשִׁיחַ בֶּן דָּוִד עַבְדֶּךָ · וְזִכְרוֹן יְרוּשָׁלַיִם
עִיר קָדְשֶׁךָ · וְזִכְרוֹן כָּל־עַמְּךָ בֵּית יִשְׂרָאֵל לְפָנֶיךָ ·
לִפְלֵיטָה לְטוֹבָה לְחֵן וּלְחֶסֶד וּלְרַחֲמִים וּלְחַיִּים וּלְשָׁלוֹם
בְּיוֹם הַזִּכָּרוֹן הַזֶּה · זָכְרֵנוּ יְיָ אֱלֹהֵינוּ בּוֹ לְטוֹבָה · וּפָקְדֵנוּ
בוֹ לִבְרָכָה · וְהוֹשִׁיעֵנוּ בוֹ לְחַיִּים · וּבִדְבַר יְשׁוּעָה
וְרַחֲמִים חוּס וְחָנֵּנוּ וְרַחֵם עָלֵינוּ וְהוֹשִׁיעֵנוּ · כִּי אֵלֶיךָ
עֵינֵינוּ · כִּי אֵל מֶלֶךְ חַנּוּן וְרַחוּם אָתָּה :

אֱלֹהֵינוּ וֵאלֹהֵי אֲבוֹתֵינוּ מְלוֹךְ עַל כָּל־הָעוֹלָם כֻּלּוֹ
בִּכְבוֹדֶךָ · וְהִנָּשֵׂא עַל כָּל־הָאָרֶץ בִּיקָרֶךָ · וְהוֹפַע בַּהֲדַר

the festival. Thou hast made a distinction, O Lord our God, between holy and profane, between light and darkness, between Israel and other nations, between the seventh day and the six working days ; thou hast made a distinction between the holiness of the Sabbath and that of the festival, and hast hallowed the seventh day above the six working days : thou hast distinguished and sanctified thy people Israel by thy holiness.]

On Sabbath add the words in brackets :

And thou hast given us in love, O Lord our God, [this Sabbath Day and] this Day of Remembrance, a day of blowing the Shofar, [*on Sabbath substitute for the last phrase—*a day of remembrance of blowing the Shofar, in love] ; a holy convocation as a memorial of the departure from Egypt.

YAALEH V'YOVO

Our God and God of our fathers ! May our remembrance rise and come and be accepted before thee, with the remembrance of our fathers, of Messiah the son of David thy servant, of Jerusalem thy holy city, and of all thy people the house of Israel, bringing deliverance and well-being, *See p. 461* grace, lovingkindness and mercy, life and peace on this Day of Remembrance. Remember us, O Lord our God, thereon for our well-being ; be mindful of us for blessing, and save us unto life : by thy promise of salvation and mercy, spare us and be gracious unto us ; have mercy upon us and save us ; for our eyes are bent upon thee, because thou art a gracious and merciful God and King.

SUPPLI-CATION THAT ALL MANKIND RECOGNIZE GOD'S SOVE-REIGNTY

Our God and God of our fathers, reign thou in thy glory over the whole universe, and be exalted above all the earth in thine honour, and shine forth in the splendour and

גְּאוֹן עֻזֶּךָ עַל כָּל־יוֹשְׁבֵי תֵבֵל אַרְצֶךָ · וְיֵדַע כָּל־פָּעוּל

כִּי אַתָּה פְעַלְתּוֹ וְיָבִין כָּל־יְצוּר כִּי אַתָּה יְצַרְתּוֹ וְיֹאמַר

כֹּל אֲשֶׁר נְשָׁמָה בְאַפּוֹ יְיָ אֱלֹהֵי יִשְׂרָאֵל מֶלֶךְ וּמַלְכוּתוֹ

בַּכֹּל מָשָׁלָה : [אֱלֹהֵינוּ וֵאלֹהֵי אֲבוֹתֵינוּ רְצֵה בִמְנוּחָתֵנוּ]

קַדְּשֵׁנוּ בְּמִצְוֹתֶיךָ וְתֵן חֶלְקֵנוּ בְּתוֹרָתֶךָ · שַׂבְּעֵנוּ מִטּוּבֶךָ

וְשַׂמְּחֵנוּ בִּישׁוּעָתֶךָ · [וְהַנְחִילֵנוּ יְיָ אֱלֹהֵינוּ בְּאַהֲבָה וּבְרָצוֹן

שַׁבַּת קָדְשֶׁךָ וְיָנוּחוּ־בָהּ יִשְׂרָאֵל מְקַדְּשֵׁי שְׁמֶךָ יְ] וְטַהֵר לִבֵּנוּ

לְעָבְדְּךָ בֶּאֱמֶת · כִּי אַתָּה אֱלֹהִים אֱמֶת וּדְבָרְךָ אֱמֶת

וְקַיָּם לָעַד · בָּרוּךְ אַתָּה יְיָ · מֶלֶךְ עַל כָּל־הָאָרֶץ מְקַדֵּשׁ

[הַשַּׁבָּת וְ] יִשְׂרָאֵל וְיוֹם הַזִּכָּרוֹן :

רְצֵה יְיָ אֱלֹהֵינוּ בְּעַמְּךָ יִשְׂרָאֵל וּבִתְפִלָּתָם · וְהָשֵׁב

אֶת־הָעֲבוֹדָה לִדְבִיר בֵּיתֶךָ · וְאִשֵּׁי יִשְׂרָאֵל וּתְפִלָּתָם

בְּאַהֲבָה תְקַבֵּל בְּרָצוֹן · וּתְהִי לְרָצוֹן תָּמִיד עֲבוֹדַת

יִשְׂרָאֵל עַמֶּךָ :

וְתֶחֱזֶינָה עֵינֵינוּ בְּשׁוּבְךָ לְצִיּוֹן בְּרַחֲמִים · בָּרוּךְ אַתָּה

יְיָ · הַמַּחֲזִיר שְׁכִינָתוֹ לְצִיּוֹן :

Congregation, in an undertone—

	מוֹדִים אֲנַחְנוּ לָךְ
מוֹדִים אֲנַחְנוּ לָךְ שָׁאַתָּה הוּא	שָׁאַתָּה הוּא יְיָ אֱלֹהֵינוּ
יְיָ אֱלֹהֵינוּ וֵאלֹהֵי אֲבוֹתֵינוּ אֱלֹהֵי	וֵאלֹהֵי אֲבוֹתֵינוּ לְעוֹלָם
כָל בָּשָׂר · יוֹצְרֵנוּ יוֹצֵר בְּרֵאשִׁית ·	וָעֶד · צוּר חַיֵּינוּ מָגֵן
בְּרָכוֹת וְהוֹדָאוֹת לְשִׁמְךָ הַגָּדוֹל	יִשְׁעֵנוּ אַתָּה הוּא לְדוֹר
וְהַקָּדוֹשׁ · עַל שֶׁהֶחֱיִיתָנוּ וְקִיַּמְתָּנוּ	וָדוֹר · נוֹדֶה לְּךָ וּנְסַפֵּר
כֵּן תְּחַיֵּנוּ וּתְקַיְּמֵנוּ · וְתֶאֱסוֹף	
גָּלִיּוֹתֵינוּ לְחַצְרוֹת קָדְשֶׁךָ לִשְׁמֹר	

excellence of thy might upon all the inhabitants of thy world, that whatsoever hath been made may know that thou hast made it, and whatsoever hath been created may understand that thou hast created it, and whatsoever hath breath in its nostrils may say, The Lord God of Israel is King, and his dominion ruleth over all. [Our God and God of our fathers, accept our rest.] Hallow us by thy commandments, and

See p. 459

grant our portion in thy Torah ; satisfy us with thy goodness, and gladden us with thy salvation [and in thy love and favour, O Lord our God, let us inherit thy holy Sabbath ; and may Israel, who hallow thy Name, rest thereon]. O purify our hearts to serve thee in truth, for thou art God in truth and thy word is truth, and endureth for ever. Blessed art thou O, Lord, King over all the earth, who hallowest [the Sabbath and] Israel and the Day of Remembrance.

V. FOR RESTORA-TION OF TEMPLE SERVICE.

See p. 461

Accept, O Lord our God, thy people Israel and their prayer ; restore the service to the inner Sanctuary of thy house ; receive in love and favour both the fire offerings of Israel and their prayer ; and may the service of thy people Israel be ever acceptable unto thee.

And let our eyes behold thy return in mercy to Zion. Blessed art thou, O Lord, who restorest thy divine presence unto Zion.

The Congregation, in an undertone—

VI. THANKS-GIVING FOR GOD'S UNFAIL-ING MERCIES

We give thanks unto thee, for thou art the Lord our God and the God of our fathers for ever and ever; thou art the Rock of our lives, the Shield of our salvation through every generation. We will give thanks unto thee and

We give thanks unto thee, for thou art the Lord our God and the God of our fathers, the God of all flesh, our Creator and the Creator of all things in the beginning. Blessings and thanksgivings be to thy great and holy Name, because thou hast kept us in life and hast preserved us : so mayest thou continue to keep us in life and to preserve us. O gather our exiles to

עַל תְּהִלָּתֶךָ חַיֵּינוּ הַפְּקוּדִים וְלַעֲשׂוֹת רְצוֹנֶךָ וּלְעָבְדְּךָ
מוֹדִים שֶׁאֲנַחְנוּ עַל שָׁלֵם בְּלֵבָב וְעַל בְּיָדֶךָ הַמְּסוּרִים
נִשְׁמוֹתֵינוּ הַפְּקוּדוֹת לָךְ ׃ בָּרוּךְ אֵל הַהוֹדָאוֹת ׃

וְעַל נִסֶּיךָ שֶׁבְּכָל יוֹם עִמָּנוּ וְעַל נִפְלְאוֹתֶיךָ וְטוֹבוֹתֶיךָ
שֶׁבְּכָל עֵת עֶרֶב וָבֹקֶר וְצָהֳרָיִם ׃ הַטּוֹב כִּי לֹא כָלוּ רַחֲמֶיךָ ׃
וְהַמְרַחֵם כִּי לֹא תַמּוּ חֲסָדֶיךָ ׃ מֵעוֹלָם קִוִּינוּ לָךְ ׃

וְעַל כֻּלָּם יִתְבָּרַךְ וְיִתְרוֹמַם שִׁמְךָ מַלְכֵּנוּ תָּמִיד לְעוֹלָם
וָעֶד ׃

וּכְתוֹב לְחַיִּים טוֹבִים כָּל בְּנֵי בְרִיתֶךָ ׃

וְכֹל הַחַיִּים יוֹדוּךָ סֶּלָה וִיהַלְלוּ אֶת שִׁמְךָ בֶּאֱמֶת ׃
הָאֵל יְשׁוּעָתֵנוּ וְעֶזְרָתֵנוּ סֶלָה ׃ בָּרוּךְ אַתָּה יְיָ הַטּוֹב
שִׁמְךָ וּלְךָ נָאֶה לְהוֹדוֹת ׃

At the Services at שַׁחֲרִית *and* מוּסָף, *say:—*

שִׂים שָׁלוֹם טוֹבָה וּבְרָכָה חֵן וָחֶסֶד וְרַחֲמִים עָלֵינוּ
וְעַל כָּל יִשְׂרָאֵל עַמֶּךָ ׃ בָּרְכֵנוּ אָבִינוּ כֻּלָּנוּ כְּאֶחָד בְּאוֹר
פָּנֶיךָ ׃ כִּי בְאוֹר פָּנֶיךָ נָתַתָּ לָּנוּ יְיָ אֱלֹהֵינוּ תּוֹרַת חַיִּים
וְאַהֲבַת חֶסֶד וּצְדָקָה וּבְרָכָה וְרַחֲמִים וְחַיִּים וְשָׁלוֹם ׃
וְטוֹב בְּעֵינֶיךָ לְבָרֵךְ אֶת עַמְּךָ יִשְׂרָאֵל בְּכָל עֵת וּבְכָל
שָׁעָה בִּשְׁלוֹמֶךָ ׃

At מַעֲרִיב *and* מִנְחָה *say:—*

שָׁלוֹם רָב עַל יִשְׂרָאֵל עַמְּךָ תָּשִׂים לְעוֹלָם ׃ כִּי אַתָּה
הוּא מֶלֶךְ אָדוֹן לְכָל הַשָּׁלוֹם ׃ וְטוֹב בְּעֵינֶיךָ לְבָרֵךְ אֶת

declare thy praise for our lives which are committed unto thy hand, and for our souls which are in thy charge, and for thy miracles, which are daily with us, and for thy wonders and thy benefits, which are wrought thy holy courts to observe thy statutes, to do thy will, and to serve thee with a perfect heart ; seeing that we give thanks unto thee. Blessed be the God to whom thanksgivings are due.

at all times, evening, morn and noon. O thou who art all-good, whose mercies fail not ; thou, merciful Being, whose lovingkindnesses never cease, we have ever hoped in thee.

For all these things thy Name, O our King, shall be continually blessed and exalted for ever and ever.

O inscribe all thy children of thy covenant for a happy life.

And everything that liveth shall give thanks unto thee for ever, and shall praise thy Name in truth, O God, our salvation and our help. Blessed art thou, O Lord, whose Name is All-good, and unto whom it is becoming to give thanks.

At the Morning and Additional Services say :—

VII. FOR PEACE

Grant peace, welfare, blessing, grace, lovingkindness and mercy unto us and unto all Israel, thy people. Bless us, O our Father, even all of us together, with the light of thy countenance ; for by the light of thy countenance thou hast given us, O Lord our God, the Law of life, loving-kindness and righteousness, blessing, mercy, life and peace ; *See p. 465* and may it be good in thy sight to bless thy people Israel at all times and in every hour with thy peace.

[At the Afternoon and Evening Service say :—

Grant abundant peace unto Israel thy people for ever ; for thou art the sovereign Lord ot all peace ; and may it be good in thy sight to bless thy people Israel at all times and in every hour with thy peace.]

עַמְּךָ יִשְׂרָאֵל בְּכָל־עֵת וּבְכָל־שָׁעָה בִּשְׁלוֹמֶךָ:
בְּסֵפֶר חַיִּים בְּרָכָה וְשָׁלוֹם וּפַרְנָסָה טוֹבָה נִזָּכֵר וְנִכָּתֵב
לְפָנֶיךָ אֲנַחְנוּ וְכָל־עַמְּךָ בֵּית יִשְׂרָאֵל לְחַיִּים טוֹבִים וּלְשָׁלוֹם ·
בָּרוּךְ אַתָּה יְיָ · עוֹשֵׂה הַשָּׁלוֹם:

אֱלֹהַי · נְצוֹר לְשׁוֹנִי מֵרָע וּשְׂפָתַי מִדַּבֵּר מִרְמָה ·
וְלִמְקַלְלַי נַפְשִׁי תִדּוֹם וְנַפְשִׁי כֶּעָפָר לַכֹּל תִּהְיֶה: פְּתַח
לִבִּי בְּתוֹרָתֶךָ וּבְמִצְוֹתֶיךָ תִּרְדּוֹף נַפְשִׁי · וְכֹל הַחוֹשְׁבִים
עָלַי רָעָה מְהֵרָה הָפֵר עֲצָתָם וְקַלְקֵל מַחֲשַׁבוֹתָם · עֲשֵׂה
לְמַעַן שְׁמֶךָ עֲשֵׂה לְמַעַן יְמִינֶךָ עֲשֵׂה לְמַעַן קְדֻשָּׁתֶךָ עֲשֵׂה
לְמַעַן תּוֹרָתֶךָ · לְמַעַן יֵחָלְצוּן יְדִידֶיךָ הוֹשִׁיעָה יְמִינְךָ
וַעֲנֵנִי: יִהְיוּ לְרָצוֹן אִמְרֵי־פִי וְהֶגְיוֹן לִבִּי לְפָנֶיךָ יְיָ צוּרִי
וְגֹאֲלִי: עֹשֶׂה שָׁלוֹם בִּמְרוֹמָיו הוּא יַעֲשֶׂה שָׁלוֹם עָלֵינוּ
וְעַל כָּל־יִשְׂרָאֵל · וְאִמְרוּ אָמֵן:

יְהִי רָצוֹן לְפָנֶיךָ יְיָ אֱלֹהֵינוּ וֵאלֹהֵי אֲבוֹתֵינוּ שֶׁיִּבָּנֶה בֵּית
הַמִּקְדָּשׁ בִּמְהֵרָה בְיָמֵינוּ · וְתֵן חֶלְקֵנוּ בְּתוֹרָתֶךָ: וְשָׁם נַעֲבָדְךָ
בְּיִרְאָה כִּימֵי עוֹלָם וּכְשָׁנִים קַדְמוֹנִיּוֹת: וְעָרְבָה לַיְיָ מִנְחַת
יְהוּדָה וִירוּשָׁלָיִם כִּימֵי עוֹלָם וּכְשָׁנִים קַדְמוֹנִיּוֹת:

The following forms of greeting are used on רֹאשׁ הַשָּׁנָה, the
expression being varied according to the sex and number of the
person or persons addressed:

לְשָׁנָה טוֹבָה תִּכָּתֵב: לְשָׁנָה טוֹבָה תִּכָּתֵבוּ:
לְשָׁנָה טוֹבָה תִּכָּתֵבִי: לְשָׁנָה טוֹבָה תִּכָּתֵבְנָה:

In the book of life, blessing, peace and good sustenance may we be remembered and inscribed before thee, we and all thy people the house of Israel, for a happy life and for peace. Blessed art thou, O Lord who makest peace.

MEDITA-TION

O my God! guard my tongue from evil and my lips from speaking guile ; and to such as curse me let my soul be dumb, yea, let my soul be unto all as the dust. Open

ee pp.464-468 my heart to thy Torah, and let my soul pursue thy commandments. If any design evil against me, speedily make their counsel of none effect, and frustrate their designs. Do it for the sake of thy Name, do it for the sake of thy power, do it for the sake of thy holiness, do it for the

Ssalm 108. 7 sake of thy Torah. In order that thy beloved ones may be delivered, O save with thy power, and answer me.

Psalm 19. 15 Let the words of my mouth and the meditation of my. heart be acceptable before thee, O Lord, my Rock and my Redeemer. He who maketh peace in his high places, may he make peace for us and for all Israel, and say ye, Amen.

May it be thy will, O Lord our God and God of our fathers, that the temple be speedily rebuilt in our days, and grant our portion in thy Torah. And there we will serve thee with awe, as in the days of

Malachi 3. 4 old, and as in ancient years. Then shall the offering of Judah and Jerusalem be pleasant unto the Lord, as in the days of old, and as in ancient years.

The following form of greeting is used on New Year :—

May you be inscribed for a happy year.

סדר קדוש לראש השנה :

[*When New Year occurs on* שַׁבָּת *begin here* :—

וַיְהִי־עֶרֶב וַיְהִי־בֹקֶר יוֹם הַשִּׁשִּׁי : וַיְכֻלּוּ הַשָּׁמַיִם וְהָאָרֶץ
וְכָל־צְבָאָם : וַיְכַל אֱלֹהִים בַּיּוֹם הַשְּׁבִיעִי מְלַאכְתּוֹ אֲשֶׁר עָשָׂה
וַיִּשְׁבֹּת בַּיּוֹם הַשְּׁבִיעִי מִכָּל־מְלַאכְתּוֹ אֲשֶׁר עָשָׂה : וַיְבָרֶךְ
אֱלֹהִים אֶת־יוֹם הַשְּׁבִיעִי וַיְקַדֵּשׁ אֹתוֹ כִּי בוֹ שָׁבַת מִכָּל־
מְלַאכְתּוֹ אֲשֶׁר־בָּרָא אֱלֹהִים לַעֲשׂוֹת :]

בָּרוּךְ אַתָּה יְיָ אֱלֹהֵינוּ מֶלֶךְ הָעוֹלָם · בּוֹרֵא פְּרִי הַגָּפֶן :

On שַׁבָּת *add the words in brackets.*

בָּרוּךְ אַתָּה יְיָ אֱלֹהֵינוּ מֶלֶךְ הָעוֹלָם · אֲשֶׁר בָּחַר־
בָּנוּ מִכָּל־עָם וְרוֹמְמָנוּ מִכָּל־לָשׁוֹן וְקִדְּשָׁנוּ בְּמִצְוֹתָיו ·
וַתִּתֶּן־לָנוּ יְיָ אֱלֹהֵינוּ בְּאַהֲבָה אֶת [יוֹם הַשַּׁבָּת הַזֶּה וְאֶת]
יוֹם הַזִּכָּרוֹן הַזֶּה יוֹם [זִכְרוֹן] תְּרוּעָה [בְּאַהֲבָה] מִקְרָא
קֹדֶשׁ זֵכֶר לִיצִיאַת מִצְרָיִם · כִּי בָנוּ בָחַרְתָּ וְאוֹתָנוּ
קִדַּשְׁתָּ מִכָּל־הָעַמִּים · וּדְבָרְךָ אֱמֶת וְקַיָּם לָעַד · בָּרוּךְ
אַתָּה יְיָ · מֶלֶךְ עַל כָּל־הָאָרֶץ מְקַדֵּשׁ [הַשַּׁבָּת וְ] יִשְׂרָאֵל
וְיוֹם הַזִּכָּרוֹן :

KIDDUSH FOR NEW YEAR

[When New Year occurs on Sabbath begin here :—

Genesis 2. 1-3 And it was evening and it was morning,—the sixth day.

And the heaven and the earth were finished and all their host. And on the seventh day God had finished his work which he had made ; and he rested on the seventh day from all his work which he had made. And God blessed the seventh day, and he hallowed it, because he rested thereon from all his work which God had created and made.]

Blessed art thou, O Lord our God, King of the universe, who createst the fruit of the vine.

On Sabbath add the words in brackets.

Blessed art thou, O Lord our God, King of the universe, who hast chosen us from all peoples and exalted us above all tongues, and hallowed us by thy commandments. And thou hast given us in love, O Lord our God, [this Sabbath day and] this Day of Remembrance, a day of blowing the Shofar [*on Sabbath substitute for the last phrase*—a day of remembrance of blowing the Shofar, in love] ; a holy convocation, as a memorial of the departure from Egypt. For thou hast chosen us and hast hallowed us above all nations ; and thy word is truth and endureth for ever. Blessed art thou, O Lord, King over all the earth, who hallowest [the Sabbath and] Israel and the Day of Remembrance.

On Saturday night the following is added :—

בָּרוּךְ אַתָּה יְיָ אֱלֹהֵינוּ מֶלֶךְ הָעוֹלָם · בּוֹרֵא מְאוֹרֵי הָאֵשׁ :

בָּרוּךְ אַתָּה יְיָ אֱלֹהֵינוּ מֶלֶךְ הָעוֹלָם · הַמַּבְדִּיל בֵּין קֹדֶשׁ לְחוֹל

בֵּין אוֹר לְחֹשֶׁךְ בֵּין יִשְׂרָאֵל לָעַמִּים · בֵּין יוֹם הַשְּׁבִיעִי לְשֵׁשֶׁת

יְמֵי הַמַּעֲשֶׂה · בֵּין קְדֻשַּׁת שַׁבָּת לִקְדֻשַּׁת יוֹם טוֹב הִבְדַּלְתָּ ·

וְאֶת יוֹם הַשְּׁבִיעִי מִשֵּׁשֶׁת יְמֵי הַמַּעֲשֶׂה קִדַּשְׁתָּ · הִבְדַּלְתָּ

וְקִדַּשְׁתָּ אֶת עַמְּךָ יִשְׂרָאֵל בִּקְדֻשָּׁתֶךָ · בָּרוּךְ אַתָּה יְיָ הַמַּבְדִּיל

בֵּין קֹדֶשׁ לְקֹדֶשׁ :

בָּרוּךְ אַתָּה יְיָ אֱלֹהֵינוּ מֶלֶךְ הָעוֹלָם · שֶׁהֶחֱיָנוּ

וְקִיְּמָנוּ וְהִגִּיעָנוּ לַזְּמַן הַזֶּה :

קָדוּשׁ *and* בִּרְכַּת הַמּוֹצִיא *having been said, an apple, dipped in honey, is taken, before partaking of which the following is said :—*

בָּרוּךְ אַתָּה יְיָ אֱלֹהֵינוּ מֶלֶךְ הָעוֹלָם · בּוֹרֵא פְּרִי הָעֵץ :

After having partaken of the apple and honey, say :—

יְהִי רָצוֹן מִלְּפָנֶיךָ יְיָ אֱלֹהֵינוּ וֵאלֹהֵי אֲבוֹתֵינוּ

שֶׁתְּחַדֵּשׁ עָלֵינוּ שָׁנָה טוֹבָה וּמְתוּקָה :

[On Saturday night the following is added :—

Blessed art thou, O Lord our God, King of the universe, who createst the light of the fire.

Blessed art thou, O Lord our God, King of the universe, who makest a distinction between holy and profane, between light and darkness, between Israel and other nations, between the seventh day and the six working days. Thou hast made a distinction between the holiness of the Sabbath and that of the festival, and hast hallowed the seventh day above the six working days ; thou hast distinguished and hallowed thy people Israel by thy holiness. Blessed art thou, O Lord, who makest a distinction between holy and holy.]

Blessed art thou, O Lord our God, King of the universe, who hast kept us in life, and hast preserved us, and enabled us to reach this season.

Kiddush and the Blessing over the Bread having been said, an apple, dipped in honey, is taken, before partaking of which the following is said :—

Blessed art thou, O Lord our God, King of the universe, who createst the fruit of the tree.

After having partaken of the apple and honey, say :—

May it be thy will, O Lord our God, and God of our fathers, to renew unto us a happy and pleasant year.

READINGS

At the conclusion of the Morning Service, and before the Taking out of the Torah, *Ovinu Malkenu*, (p. 162) is recited, except on Sabbaths.

The Scriptural READINGS on Rosh Hashanah are :
New Year I, Genesis 21. 1–34 ; Haftorah, 1 Samuel 1–2. 10.
New Year II, Genesis 22. 1–24 ; Haftorah, Jeremiah 3. 12–20.
On the First Day, the stories of Hagar and Ishmael, Hannah and Samuel are read—manifestations of God's ways in the home-life of those who do justice, love mercy, and walk humbly with Him. On the Second Day, the Binding of Isaac recalls the Jewish ideal of martyrdom (see p. 256), coupled in the Haftorah with the Divine promise of Israel's Redemption.

THE SHOFAR.

Before the Return of the Torah to the Ark, there is the Service of the Sounding of the Shofar ; see the Festival Prayer Book.

The SHOFAR has sacred associations in the Jewish consciousness, and manifold have been the interpretations that our Teachers have given this Divine command. It sets in motion in the souls of the worshipper waves of recollection of Israel's past, as well as of solemn reflections on Life and Death, human duty and destiny.

1. The Shofar is the clarion call to repentance. The three traditional notes issuing from the Ram's horn are *tekiah*,—a long stretched-out sound ; *shevorim*—broken notes ; and *teruah*—staccato notes. These have throughout the ages been interpreted as the summons to spiritual regeneration. Maimonides translates their monition as follows :
" Awake from your slumbers, ye who have fallen asleep in life, and ponder over your deeds. Remember your Creator, and be not of those who miss realities in their pursuit after ephemeral shadows, and waste their years in seeking after vain things which do not profit or deliver. Look well to your souls, and let there be betterment in your acts. Forsake each of you your evil ways and thoughts ".

2. Tradition declares Rosh Hashanah to be the anniversary of Creation, and the Shofar-tones are conceived as sounds of jubilation attendant on the proclamation of the Divine kingship. In fulfilling this command we, so to speak, acclaim God as Ruler of our lives and destinies.

3. The Revelation at Sinai was accompanied by the sound of the Shofar. The Shofar-tones remind us of that turning-point in the spiritual life of humanity, as well as reaffirm the eternal validity of that Revelation in the present and future.

4. The Shofar has been spoken of as the horn of the Heavenly Shepherd recalling those who are straying from Israel's fold. Also as the bugle-note of our Captain on High, warning the Jew never to forsake Israel's Banner.

5. In the days of old, the slave in Israel regained his liberty at the blast of the Shofar. It is thus a symbol of freedom, and bids us free ourselves from everything that enslaves us, that is an entanglement to our feet in our progress towards the Higher Life.

6. In the Jubilee year, the poor man received back the heritage of his fathers at the sounding of the Shofar. It therefore bids us, children of to-day, re-enter upon the full possession of *our* spiritual heritage— our Faith, our Sabbath, our Scriptures.

7. The Ram's horn brings back to memory the ram offered instead of Isaac as a sacrifice, as well as Abraham's unconditional obedience to God. It thus recalls both the martyrdom of the Jew and the Jewish Ideal of Martyrdom, *i.e.* the duty of supreme sacrifice for the sake of conviction.

8. The Prophets picture the Reunion of Israel's scattered children as to be ushered in by the sounding of the Shofar. And they speak of the Shofar of the Messiah that shall inaugurate the time when all tiger-passions in the human breast shall have been tamed, and peace reign on earth ; when " the knowledge of God shall fill the earth, as the waters cover the bed of the ocean " (Isaiah 11. 9). And in the poetic conception of our later Teachers, it was the sound of the Great Shofar that will on the Last Day rend open the graves, and cause the dead to rise. Thus, the Messianic Hope, Resurrection and Immortality of the soul are intertwined with the message of the Shofar.

In brief, the fundamental teachings and ideals of Judaism, and glorious memories and hopes of Israel, are in some way linked with the Shofar. Going back to hoary antiquity, that sound is heard throughout Jewish History, on all national rejoicings, on all national calamities ; and it reaches far down to the end of Time, when the drama of humanity shall have ended.

תִּפְלַת מוּסָף לְרֹאשׁ הַשָּׁנָה:

For the commencement of the עֲמִידָה, see p. 844, from אֲדֹנָי שְׂפָתַי
to קָרָאתָ p. 850. Then continue, on שַׁבָּת adding the words in
brackets.

וַתִּתֶּן־לָנוּ יְיָ אֱלֹהֵינוּ בְּאַהֲבָה אֶת־יוֹם [הַשַּׁבָּת הַזֶּה

וְאֶת יוֹם] הַזִּכָּרוֹן הַזֶּה ∙ יוֹם [זִכְרוֹן] תְּרוּעָה [בְּאַהֲבָה]

מִקְרָא קֹדֶשׁ זֵכֶר לִיצִיאַת מִצְרָיִם :

וּמִפְּנֵי חֲטָאֵינוּ גָּלִינוּ מֵאַרְצֵנוּ וְנִתְרַחַקְנוּ מֵעַל

אַדְמָתֵנוּ ∙ וְאֵין אֲנַחְנוּ יְכוֹלִים לַעֲשׂוֹת חוֹבוֹתֵינוּ בְּבֵית

בְּחִירָתֶךָ בַּבַּיִת הַגָּדוֹל וְהַקָּדוֹשׁ שֶׁנִּקְרָא שִׁמְךָ עָלָיו

מִפְּנֵי הַיָּד שֶׁנִּשְׁתַּלְחָה בְּמִקְדָּשֶׁךָ : יְהִי רָצוֹן מִלְּפָנֶיךָ

יְיָ אֱלֹהֵינוּ וֵאלֹהֵי אֲבוֹתֵינוּ מֶלֶךְ רַחֲמָן שֶׁתָּשׁוּב וּתְרַחֵם

עָלֵינוּ וְעַל מִקְדָּשְׁךָ בְּרַחֲמֶיךָ הָרַבִּים וְתִבְנֵהוּ מְהֵרָה

וּתְגַדֵּל כְּבוֹדוֹ : אָבִינוּ מַלְכֵּנוּ ∙ גַּלֵּה כְּבוֹד מַלְכוּתְךָ

עָלֵינוּ מְהֵרָה וְהוֹפַע וְהִנָּשֵׂא עָלֵינוּ לְעֵינֵי כָּל־חָי ∙ וְקָרֵב

פְּזוּרֵינוּ מִבֵּין הַגּוֹיִם וּנְפוּצוֹתֵינוּ כַּנֵּס מִיַּרְכְּתֵי־אָרֶץ ∙

וַהֲבִיאֵנוּ לְצִיּוֹן עִירְךָ בְּרִנָּה וְלִירוּשָׁלַיִם בֵּית מִקְדָּשְׁךָ

בְּשִׂמְחַת עוֹלָם ∙ וְשָׁם נַעֲשֶׂה לְפָנֶיךָ אֶת קָרְבְּנוֹת חוֹבוֹתֵינוּ

תְּמִידִים כְּסִדְרָם וּמוּסָפִים כְּהִלְכָתָם : וְאֶת מוּסְפֵי יוֹם

ADDITIONAL SERVICE FOR NEW YEAR

For the commencement of the Mussaf Amidah, see p. 845, from
" O Lord, open thou " to " holy Name," p. 851. Then continue
(adding on Sabbath the words in brackets) :—

THE SELECTION OF ISRAEL And thou hast given us in love, O Lord our God, [this Sabbath day and] this Day of Remembrance, a day of blowing the Shofar [*on Sabbaths substitute for the last phrase*—a day of remembrance of blowing the Shofar, in love] ; a holy convocation, as a memorial of the departure from Egypt.

" RENEW OUR DAYS AS OF OLD" But on account of our sins we were exiled from our land, and removed far from our country, and as we were unable to fulfil our obligations in thy chosen house, that great and holy temple which was called by thy Name, because of the hand of violence that hath been laid upon thy sanctuary. May it be thy will, O Lord our God and God of our fathers, merciful King, that thou mayest again in thine abundant compassion have mercy upon us and upon thy sanctuary, and mayest speedily rebuild it and magnify its glory. Our Father, our King, do thou speedily make the glory of thy kingdom manifest upon us ; shine forth and exalt thyself upon us in the sight of all living ; bring our scattered ones among the nations near unto thee, and gather our dispersed from the ends of the earth. Lead us with exultation unto Zion thy city, and unto Jerusalem the place of thy sanctuary with everlasting joy ; and there we will prepare before thee

NEW YEAR MUSSAF

Instead of one Intermediate Benediction, as on Sabbaths and the other Festivals, the Mussaf Amidah of New Year has three, each devoted to the proclamation of a basic idea in Judaism—the Sovereignty of God, Divine Providence, and the Sinaitic Revelation respectively. The authorship of these Benedictions is attributed to Rabh ; but, in substance, they must be much older ; and the original formulation seems to have undergone considerable enlargement. In all probability, only their editing and embodiment in the Liturgy are due to Rabh. Each of the proclamations is followed by ten Scriptural proof-texts, and concludes on a heightened note of adoration.

[הַשַּׁבָּת הַזֶּה וְיוֹם] הַזִּכָּרוֹן הַזֶּה · נַעֲשֶׂה וְנַקְרִיב
לְפָנֶיךָ בְּאַהֲבָה כְּמִצְוַת רְצוֹנֶךָ כְּמוֹ שֶׁכָּתַבְתָּ עָלֵינוּ
בְּתוֹרָתֶךָ עַל יְדֵי מֹשֶׁה עַבְדֶּךָ מִפִּי כְבוֹדֶךָ כָּאָמוּר:

[וּבְיוֹם הַשַּׁבָּת שְׁנֵי־כְבָשִׂים בְּנֵי־שָׁנָה תְּמִימִם וּשְׁנֵי עֶשְׂרֹנִים
סֹלֶת מִנְחָה בְּלוּלָה בַשֶּׁמֶן וְנִסְכּוֹ: עֹלַת שַׁבַּת בְּשַׁבַּתּוֹ עַל־
עֹלַת הַתָּמִיד וְנִסְכָּהּ:]

וּבַחֹדֶשׁ הַשְּׁבִיעִי בְּאֶחָד לַחֹדֶשׁ מִקְרָא־קֹדֶשׁ יִהְיֶה
לָכֶם כָּל־מְלֶאכֶת עֲבֹדָה לֹא תַעֲשׂוּ יוֹם תְּרוּעָה יִהְיֶה
לָכֶם: וַעֲשִׂיתֶם עֹלָה לְרֵיחַ נִיחֹחַ לַיָי פַּר בֶּן־בָּקָר
אֶחָד אַיִל אֶחָד כְּבָשִׂים בְּנֵי־שָׁנָה שִׁבְעָה תְּמִימִם:
וּמִנְחָתָם וְנִסְכֵּיהֶם כִּמְדֻבָּר שְׁלֹשָׁה עֶשְׂרֹנִים לַפָּר וּשְׁנֵי
עֶשְׂרֹנִים לָאַיִל וְעִשָּׂרוֹן לַכֶּבֶשׂ וְיַיִן כְּנִסְכּוֹ וּשְׁנֵי
שְׂעִירִים לְכַפֵּר · וּשְׁנֵי תְמִידִים כְּהִלְכָתָם: מִלְּבַד עֹלַת
הַחֹדֶשׁ וּמִנְחָתָהּ · וְעֹלַת הַתָּמִיד וּמִנְחָתָהּ · וְנִסְכֵּיהֶם
כְּמִשְׁפָּטָם לְרֵיחַ נִיחֹחַ אִשֶּׁה לַיָי:

[יִשְׂמְחוּ בְמַלְכוּתְךָ שׁוֹמְרֵי שַׁבָּת וְקוֹרְאֵי עֹנֶג · עַם מְקַדְּשֵׁי
שְׁבִיעִי כֻּלָּם יִשְׂבְּעוּ וְיִתְעַנְּגוּ מִטּוּבֶךָ · וְהַשְּׁבִיעִי רָצִיתָ בּוֹ
וְקִדַּשְׁתּוֹ חֶמְדַּת יָמִים אוֹתוֹ קָרָאתָ זֵכֶר לְמַעֲשֵׂה בְרֵאשִׁית:]

עָלֵינוּ לְשַׁבֵּחַ לַאֲדוֹן הַכֹּל לָתֵת גְּדֻלָּה לְיוֹצֵר
בְּרֵאשִׁית · שֶׁלֹּא עָשָׂנוּ כְּגוֹיֵי הָאֲרָצוֹת וְלֹא שָׂמָנוּ
כְּמִשְׁפְּחוֹת הָאֲדָמָה · שֶׁלֹּא שָׂם חֶלְקֵנוּ כָּהֶם וְגֹרָלֵנוּ

the offerings that are obligatory for us, the daily offerings according to their order, and the additional offerings according to their enactment ; and the additional offerings of [this Sabbath day and] this Day of Remembrance, we will prepare and offer unto thee in love according to the precept of thy will, as thou hast prescribed for us in thy Torah through the hand of Moses thy servant, from the mouth of thy glory, as it is said :—

Numbers 28. 9   [And on the Sabbath day two he-lambs of the first year without blemish, and two tenth parts of an ephah of fine flour for a meal offering, mingled with oil, and the drink offering thereof ; this is the burnt offering of every Sabbath, beside the daily burnt offering and the drink offering thereof.]

Numbers 29. 1, 2   And in the seventh month, on the first day of the month, ye shall have an holy convocation ; ye shall do no servile work : it shall be a day of blowing the Shofar unto you. And ye shall offer a burnt offering for a sweet savour unto the Lord ; one young bullock, one ram, seven he-lambs of the first year without blemish. And their meal offering and their drink offerings as hath been ordained ; three tenth parts of an ephah for each bullock, and two tenth parts for the ram, and one tenth part for each lamb, with wine according to the drink offering thereof, and two he goats wherewith to make atonement, and the two daily offerings according to their enactment ; beside the burnt offering of the New Moon and the meal offering thereof, and the daily burnt offering and the meal offering thereof, and their drink offerings, according to their ordinance, for a sweet savour, an offering made by fire unto the Lord.

[They that keep the Sabbath and call it a delight shall rejoice in thy kingdom ; the people that hallow the seventh day, even all of them shall be satiated and delighted with thy goodness, seeing that thou didst find pleasure in the seventh day, and didst hallow it ; thou didst call it the desirable of days, in remembrance of the creation.]

MALCHI-YOTH : ISRAEL'S SELECTION TO PROCLAIM GOD AS SUPREME KING OF THE UNIVERSE

  It is our duty to praise the Lord of all things, to ascribe greatness to him who formed the world in the beginning, since he hath not made us like the nations of other lands, and hath not placed us like other families of the earth, since

בְּכָל הֲמוֹנָם • וַאֲנַחְנוּ כֹּרְעִים וּמִשְׁתַּחֲוִים וּמוֹדִים לִפְנֵי
מֶלֶךְ מַלְכֵי הַמְּלָכִים הַקָּדוֹשׁ בָּרוּךְ הוּא • שֶׁהוּא נוֹטֶה
שָׁמַיִם וְיוֹסֵד אָרֶץ • וּמוֹשַׁב יְקָרוֹ בַּשָּׁמַיִם מִמַּעַל וּשְׁכִינַת
עֻזּוֹ בְּגָבְהֵי מְרוֹמִים: הוּא אֱלֹהֵינוּ • אֵין עוֹד • אֱמֶת
מַלְכֵּנוּ • אֶפֶס זוּלָתוֹ • כַּכָּתוּב בְּתוֹרָתוֹ • וְיָדַעְתָּ הַיּוֹם
וַהֲשֵׁבֹתָ אֶל־לְבָבֶךָ כִּי יְיָ הוּא הָאֱלֹהִים בַּשָּׁמַיִם מִמַּעַל
וְעַל־הָאָרֶץ מִתָּחַת אֵין עוֹד :

עַל־כֵּן נְקַוֶּה לְּךָ יְיָ אֱלֹהֵינוּ לִרְאוֹת מְהֵרָה בְּתִפְאֶרֶת
עֻזֶּךָ • לְהַעֲבִיר גִּלּוּלִים מִן הָאָרֶץ וְהָאֱלִילִים כָּרוֹת
יִכָּרֵתוּן • לְתַקֵּן עוֹלָם בְּמַלְכוּת שַׁדַּי וְכָל־בְּנֵי בָשָׂר
יִקְרְאוּ בִשְׁמֶךָ • לְהַפְנוֹת אֵלֶיךָ כָּל־רִשְׁעֵי אָרֶץ: יַכִּירוּ
וְיֵדְעוּ כָּל־יוֹשְׁבֵי תֵבֵל כִּי לְךָ תִּכְרַע כָּל־בֶּרֶךְ תִּשָּׁבַע

I

The first of these Benedictions is known as *Malchiyoth*—lit. "King-ships". Its theme is the recognition of God as Lord of the universe. The Malchiyoth Benediction proper begins with the prayer known as *Oleynu*. This prayer is of such transcendent importance that in time it became the closing adoration of *every* statutory Service throughout the year. The first half of Oleynu is a solemn restatement of the Selection of Israel; while its second half voices Israel's Hope for the day when the human family, having become one brotherhood, shall direct all its activities towards God and His service. And Oleynu is one of the oldest of our prayers; "a proof of its age being the fact that there is no mention in it of the restoration of the Temple and the Jewish State, which would scarcely have been omitted had it been composed after their destruction" (Moses Mendelssohn).

MALCHI-YOTH   he hath not assigned unto us a portion as unto thêm, nor a lot as unto all their multitude. For we bend the knee and offer worship and thanks before the supreme King of kings, the Holy One, blessed be he, who stretched forth the heavens and laid the foundations of the earth, the seat of whose glory is in the heavens above, and the abode of whose might is in the loftiest heights. He is our God ; there is none else : in truth he is our King ; there is none besides him ; as it is written in his Torah, And thou shalt know *Deuteronomy* this day, and lay it to thine heart, that the Lord he is God *4. 39* in heaven above and upon the earth beneath : there is none else.

ISRAEL'S HOPE : We therefore hope in thee, O Lord our God, that we *HUMANITY* may speedily behold the glory of thy might, when thou *UNITED IN RECOGNI-* wilt remove the abominations from the earth, and the idols *TION OF THE ONE* will be utterly cut off, when the world will be perfected *GOD* under the kingdom of the Almighty, and all the children of flesh will call upon thy Name, when thou wilt turn unto thyself all the wicked of the earth. Let all the inhabitants of the world perceive and know that unto thee every knee must bow, every tongue must swear. Before thee, O Lord our God, let them bow and fall ; and unto thy glorious Name let them give honour ; let them all accept the yoke of thy kingdom, and do thou reign over them speedily, and for ever and ever. For the kingdom is thine, and to all

This Adoration has had a strange fate, almost typical of Israel's story. The most universalist of prayers, it has yet been the victim of the slanderous accusation that it was a veiled attack on Christianity, and has at various times been suppressed by Governments. It was again and again pointed out that the misinterpreted passages in it were quotations from Isaiah ; and that Rabh, who edited it, lived in an environment where there were no Christians at all. In vain. As late as 1656, Manasseh ben Israel deemed it necessary to devote a chapter in his *Vindiciae Judaeorum* to its defence. He also relates that the Sultan Selim, on reading Oleynu in a Turkish translation, said : " Truly this prayer is sufficient for all purposes ; there is no need of any other " ; see further p. 551.

כָּל־לָשׁוֹן : לְפָנֶיךָ יְיָ אֱלֹהֵינוּ יִכְרְעוּ וְיִפּוֹלוּ · וְלִכְבוֹד
שִׁמְךָ יְקָר יִתֵּנוּ · וִיקַבְּלוּ כֻלָם אֶת־עֹל מַלְכוּתֶךָ ·
וְתִמְלוֹךְ עֲלֵיהֶם מְהֵרָה לְעוֹלָם וָעֶד · כִּי הַמַּלְכוּת
שֶׁלְּךָ הִיא וּלְעוֹלְמֵי עַד תִּמְלוֹךְ בְּכָבוֹד · כַּכָּתוּב בְּתוֹרָתֶךָ ·
יְהוָה ׀ יִמְלֹךְ לְעוֹלָם וָעֶד :
וְנֶאֱמַר · לֹא־הִבִּיט אָוֶן בְּיַעֲקֹב וְלֹא־רָאָה עָמָל בְּיִשְׂרָאֵל
יְהוָה אֱלֹהָיו עִמּוֹ וּתְרוּעַת מֶלֶךְ בּוֹ : וְנֶאֱמַר · וַיְהִי
בִישֻׁרוּן מֶלֶךְ בְּהִתְאַסֵּף רָאשֵׁי עָם יַחַד שִׁבְטֵי יִשְׂרָאֵל :
וּבְדִבְרֵי קָדְשְׁךָ כָּתוּב לֵאמֹר · כִּי לַיְיָ הַמְּלוּכָה וּמֹשֵׁל

not made us like the nations. In Rabh's time that phrase meant,
" He has not made us heathens ". In our day, it stresses the eternal
difference between Israel's Faith and all others. Such conviction is of
vital importance to the loyal Jew. The power of a Religion does not lie
in what it has in common with others, but in what is peculiar to itself
in its own special Message on the great problems and duties of life.

turn unto thyself all the wicked of the earth. All nations shall abandon
idolatry and wickedness, falsehood and violence, and become united
in the recognition of the sovereignty of the Holy God proclaimed by
Israel. The Messianic Hope is thus not to *destroy* the wicked, but to win
them over to God's service ; see on Psalm 104. 35, p. 588. The later
Jewish Mystics dreamt of the time when Satan himself would be turned
into a good angel.

yoke of thy kingdom. The rule of Thy Kingship.

MALCHI-YOTH eternity thou wilt reign in glory ; as it is written in thy
Exodus 15. 18 Torah, The Lord shall reign for ever and ever.

Numbers 23. 21   And it is said, He hath not beheld iniquity in Jacob, neither hath he seen perverseness in Israel : the Lord his God is with him, and the trumpet call of the King is among *Deuteronomy* them. And it is said, And he became King in Jeshurun, *33. 5* when the heads of the people were gathered, the tribes of Israel together. And in thy Holy Words it is written, say-*Psalm* 22. 29 ing, For the kingdom is the Lord's, and he is ruler over the *Psalm* 93. 1 nations. And it is said, The Lord reigneth ; he hath robed him in majesty ; the Lord hath robed him, yea, he that girded himself with strength : the world also is set firm, that it cannot be moved.

Psalm 24. 7-10   And it is said, Lift up your heads, O ye gates, and be ye lifted up, ye everlasting doors, that the King of glory may come in. Who, then, is the King of glory ? The Lord, strong and mighty, the Lord mighty in battle. Lift up your heads, O ye gates ; yea, lift them up, ye everlasting doors, that the King of glory may come in. Who, then, is the King of glory ? The Lord of hosts, he is the King of glory. (Selah.)

---

not beheld iniquity in Jacob. Even Balaam, an enemy of Israel, testified that Israel had not committed any wrong that would warrant the withdrawal of God's blessing.

trumpet call of the King. Israel is constantly reminded of the dominion of God, and summoned to His worship.

Jeshurun. The poetic name of endearment for " Israel ".

were gathered. At Sinai, to enter into the Covenant.

the Lord reigneth. By some wonderful self-revelation of God in the days of the Psalmist, the nations came to realize the majesty and omnipotence of God.

the world also is set firm. There was an end of anarchy and confusion.

lift up your heads. When David removed the Ark to Mt. Zion, the heavy gates of the old fortress are represented by the poet as unwilling to receive the Ark. A voice summons them to open, so that the King of Glory may come in.

בַּגּוֹיִם : וְנֶאֱמַר · יְיָ מָלָךְ גֵּאוּת לָבֵשׁ לָבֵשׁ יְיָ עֹז
הִתְאַזָּר אַף תִּכּוֹן תֵּבֵל בַּל תִּמּוֹט : וְנֶאֱמַר · שְׂאוּ
שְׁעָרִים רָאשֵׁיכֶם וְהִנָּשְׂאוּ פִּתְחֵי עוֹלָם וְיָבֹא מֶלֶךְ
הַכָּבוֹד : מִי זֶה מֶלֶךְ הַכָּבוֹד · יְיָ עִזּוּז וְגִבּוֹר יְיָ גִּבּוֹר
מִלְחָמָה : שְׂאוּ שְׁעָרִים רָאשֵׁיכֶם וּשְׂאוּ פִּתְחֵי עוֹלָם וְיָבֹא
מֶלֶךְ הַכָּבוֹד : מִי הוּא זֶה מֶלֶךְ הַכָּבוֹד · יְיָ צְבָאוֹת
הוּא מֶלֶךְ הַכָּבוֹד סֶלָה : וְעַל־יְדֵי עֲבָדֶיךָ הַנְּבִיאִים
כָּתוּב לֵאמֹר · כֹּה אָמַר יְיָ מֶלֶךְ־יִשְׂרָאֵל וְגֹאֲלוֹ יְיָ צְבָאוֹת
אֲנִי רִאשׁוֹן וַאֲנִי אַחֲרוֹן וּמִבַּלְעָדַי אֵין אֱלֹהִים : וְנֶאֱמַר ·
וְעָלוּ מוֹשִׁיעִים בְּהַר צִיּוֹן לִשְׁפֹּט אֶת־הַר עֵשָׂו וְהָיְתָה
לַיְיָ הַמְּלוּכָה : וְנֶאֱמַר · וְהָיָה יְיָ לְמֶלֶךְ עַל־כָּל־הָאָרֶץ
בַּיּוֹם הַהוּא יִהְיֶה יְיָ אֶחָד וּשְׁמוֹ אֶחָד : וּבְתוֹרָתְךָ
כָּתוּב לֵאמֹר · שְׁמַע יִשְׂרָאֵל יְיָ אֱלֹהֵינוּ יְיָ אֶחָד :

I am the first, and I am the last. The thought in this concluding
paragraph has found expression in many a hymn of the piyyut-writers
of the Festival Liturgy. Foremost among them is " The Lord is King "
by Kalir, the master-paytan who lived in the eighth century, probably
in Palestine. The translation is by I. Zangwill :—
" The universe throbs with Thy pauseless praise,
    Chorus eternal, the Lord is King.
Thy glory is cried from the dawn of days,
    Worshippers calling the Lord was King.
And ever the Saints who shall witness Thy ways
Shall tell that the Lord shall be King for ever.
The Lord is King, the Lord was King, the Lord
    shall be King for ever and ever ".

MALCHI-YOTH

Isaiah 44. 6

Obadiah 1. 21

Zechariah 14. 9

Deuteronomy 6. 4

And by the hands of thy servants, the prophets, it is written, saying, Thus saith the Lord, the King of Israel and his Redeemer, the Lord of hosts : I am the first, and I am the last ; and beside me there is no God. And it is said, And saviours shall come up on Mount Zion to judge the Mount of Esau, and the kingdom shall be the Lord's. And it is said, And the Lord shall be King over all the earth : in that day shall the Lord be One and his Name One. And in thy Torah it is written saying, Hear, O Israel : the Lord our God, the Lord is One.

saviours shall come. The victorious heroes who saved Israel in its conflict with vindictive Edom, shall establish justice in that and neighbouring lands.

shall the Lord be One. In the undivided and undisputed worship of all men. " The Jews were the only people in their world who conceived the idea of a universal religion " (Moore).

his Name One. His manifold revelations of Himself shall be acknowledged by all to be merely aspects of the one sole Name by which He made Himself known unto Israel. This verse embodies the spiritual goal of human history.

Ten Bible passages—each emphasizing in some way the Kingship of God or its recognition—are cited as proof-texts. Three of the verses are taken from the Torah, three from the Psalms, three from the Prophets, and finally another from the Torah.

After each of the special Mussaf Benedictions, Shofar-notes—tekiah, shevorim, teruah—are sounded ; and the following is said :—

" This day is the world's assize : this day Thou causest all the creatures of the Universe to stand in judgment, as children or as servants. If as children, have pity upon us as a father pitieth his children ; and if as servants, our eyes wait on Thee until Thou be gracious unto us, and bring forth our judgment as the light, O God, awesome and holy ". The translation, " world's assize," instead of the " world's birthday," is that of a renowned medieval authority on the Liturgy—*Shibbuley Leket.*

29

אֱלֹהֵינוּ וֵאלֹהֵי אֲבוֹתֵינוּ · מְלוֹךְ עַל־כָּל־הָעוֹלָם כֻּלּוֹ
בִּכְבוֹדֶךָ · וְהִנָּשֵׂא עַל כָּל־הָאָרֶץ בִּיקָרֶךָ · וְהוֹפַע בַּהֲדַר
גְּאוֹן עֻזֶּךָ עַל כָּל־יוֹשְׁבֵי תֵבֵל אַרְצֶךָ · וְיֵדַע כָּל־פָּעוּל
כִּי אַתָּה פְעַלְתּוֹ וְיָבִין כָּל־יָצוּר כִּי אַתָּה יְצַרְתּוֹ וְיֹאמַר
כֹּל אֲשֶׁר נְשָׁמָה בְאַפּוֹ יְיָ אֱלֹהֵי יִשְׂרָאֵל מֶלֶךְ וּמַלְכוּתוֹ
בַּכֹּל מָשָׁלָה : [אֱלֹהֵינוּ וֵאלֹהֵי אֲבוֹתֵינוּ רְצֵה בִמְנוּחָתֵנוּ]
קַדְּשֵׁנוּ בְּמִצְוֹתֶיךָ וְתֵן חֶלְקֵנוּ בְּתוֹרָתֶךָ · שַׂבְּעֵנוּ מִטּוּבֶךָ
וְשַׂמְּחֵנוּ בִּישׁוּעָתֶךָ · [וְהַנְחִילֵנוּ יְיָ אֱלֹהֵינוּ בְּאַהֲבָה וּבְרָצוֹן
שַׁבַּת קָדְשֶׁךָ וְיָנוּחוּ־בָהּ יִשְׂרָאֵל מְקַדְּשֵׁי שְׁמֶךָ ·] וְטַהֵר לִבֵּנוּ
לְעָבְדְּךָ בֶּאֱמֶת · כִּי אַתָּה אֱלֹהִים אֱמֶת וּדְבָרְךָ
אֱמֶת וְקַיָּם לָעַד · בָּרוּךְ אַתָּה יְיָ · מֶלֶךְ עַל כָּל־
הָאָרֶץ מְקַדֵּשׁ [הַשַּׁבָּת וְ] יִשְׂרָאֵל וְיוֹם הַזִּכָּרוֹן :

אַתָּה זוֹכֵר מַעֲשֵׂה עוֹלָם וּפוֹקֵד כָּל־יְצוּרֵי קֶדֶם ·
לְפָנֶיךָ נִגְלוּ כָּל־תַּעֲלֻמוֹת וַהֲמוֹן נִסְתָּרוֹת שֶׁמִּבְּרֵאשִׁית ·
כִּי אֵין שִׁכְחָה לִפְנֵי כִסֵּא כְבוֹדֶךָ · וְאֵין נִסְתָּר מִנֶּגֶד
עֵינֶיךָ : אַתָּה זוֹכֵר אֶת־כָּל־הַמִּפְעָל · וְגַם כָּל־הַיְצוּר
לֹא נִכְחָד מִמֶּךָּ · הַכֹּל גָּלוּי וְיָדוּעַ לְפָנֶיךָ יְיָ אֱלֹהֵינוּ ·
צוֹפֶה וּמַבִּיט עַד סוֹף כָּל־הַדּוֹרוֹת · כִּי תָבִיא חֹק
זִכָּרוֹן לְהִפָּקֵד כָּל־רוּחַ וָנָפֶשׁ · לְהִזָּכֵר מַעֲשִׂים רַבִּים
וַהֲמוֹן בְּרִיּוֹת לְאֵין תַּכְלִית · מֵרֵאשִׁית כָּזֹאת הוֹדַעְתָּ ·

REITER-
ATED
PRAYER
THAT ALL
MANKIND
RECOGNIZE
SOVE-
REIGNTY
OF GOD
Our God and God of our fathers, reign thou in thy glory over the whole universe, and be exalted above all the earth in thine honour, and shine forth in the splendour and excellence of thy might upon all the inhabitants of thy world, that whatsoever hath been made may know that thou hast made it, and whatsoever hath been created may understand that thou hast created it, and whatsoever hath breath in its nostrils may say, the Lord God of Israel is King, and his dominion ruleth over all. [Our God and God of our fathers, accept our rest.] Hallow us by thy commandments, and grant our portion in thy Torah ; satisfy us with thy goodness, and gladden us with thy salvation : [and in thy love and favour, O Lord our God, let us inherit thy holy Sabbath ; and may Israel, who sanctify thy Name, rest thereon]. O purify our hearts to serve thee in truth, for thou art God in truth, and thy word is truth, and endureth for ever. Blessed art thou, O Lord, King over all the earth, who hallowest [the Sabbath and] Israel and the Day of Remembrance.

*V. ZICH-
RONOTH*
Thou rememberest what was wrought from eternity and art mindful of all that hath been formed from of old : before thee all secrets are revealed, and the multitude of hidden things since the creation ; for there is no forgetfulness before the throne of thy glory, nor is there ought hidden from thine eyes. Thou rememberest every deed that hath been done : not a creature is concealed from thee : all things are manifest and known unto thee, O Lord our God, who lookest and seest to the end of all the ages. For thou wilt bring on the appointed time of remembrance for the judgment of every spirit and soul, and the memory of many actions, and the multitude of hidden things without

II

The second special Benediction is called *Zichronoth,*—lit. " Remembrances ". Written in the same elevated style as the paragraphs that precede the Malchiyoth, it proclaims the Everlasting God, Who in His Divine Providence foresees, remembers, and judges the deeds and thoughts of men from the beginning even to the end of days. This

וּמִלְּפָנִים אוֹתָהּ גִּלִּיתָ.זֶה הַיּוֹם תְּחִלַּת מַעֲשֶׂיךָ זִכָּרוֹן לְיוֹם

רִאשׁוֹן ·כִּי חֹק לְיִשְׂרָאֵל הוּא מִשְׁפָּט לֵאלֹהֵי יַעֲקֹב :

וְעַל הַמְּדִינוֹת בּוֹ יֵאָמֵר · אֵי־זוֹ לַחֶרֶב · וְאֵי־זוֹ

לְשָׁלוֹם · אֵי־זוֹ לָרָעָב · וְאֵי־זוֹ לַשָּׂבַע · וּבְרִיּוֹת בּוֹ

יִפָּקֵדוּ · לְהַזְכִּירָם לַחַיִּים וְלַמָּוֶת : מִי לֹא נִפְקָד

כְּהַיּוֹם הַזֶּה · כִּי זֵכֶר כָּל הַיְצוּר לְפָנֶיךָ בָּא · מַעֲשֵׂה

אִישׁ וּפְקֻדָּתוֹ · וַעֲלִילוֹת מִצְעֲדֵי גָבֶר · מַחְשְׁבוֹת אָדָם

וְתַחְבּוּלוֹתָיו וְיִצְרֵי מַעַלְלֵי אִישׁ : אַשְׁרֵי אִישׁ שֶׁלֹּא

יִשְׁכָּחֶךָ · וּבֶן אָדָם יִתְאַמֶּץ־בָּךְ · כִּי דוֹרְשֶׁיךָ לְעוֹלָם לֹא

יִכָּשֵׁלוּ · וְלֹא יִכָּלְמוּ לָנֶצַח כָּל־הַחוֹסִים בָּךְ : כִּי זֵכֶר

כָּל־הַמַּעֲשִׂים לְפָנֶיךָ בָּא וְאַתָּה דוֹרֵשׁ מַעֲשֵׂה כֻלָּם :

וְגַם אֶת־נֹחַ בְּאַהֲבָה זָכַרְתָּ · וַתִּפְקְדֵהוּ בִּדְבַר

יְשׁוּעָה וְרַחֲמִים בַּהֲבִיאֲךָ אֶת־מֵי הַמַּבּוּל לְשַׁחֵת כָּל־

בָּשָׂר מִפְּנֵי רֹעַ מַעַלְלֵיהֶם · עַל־כֵּן זִכְרוֹנוֹ בָּא לְפָנֶיךָ

יְיָ אֱלֹהֵינוּ לְהַרְבּוֹת זַרְעוֹ כְּעַפְרוֹת תֵּבֵל · וְצֶאֱצָאָיו

כְּחוֹל הַיָּם : כַּכָּתוּב בְּתוֹרָתֶךָ · וַיִּזְכֹּר אֱלֹהִים אֶת־נֹחַ

וְאֵת כָּל־הַחַיָּה וְאֶת־כָּל־הַבְּהֵמָה אֲשֶׁר אִתּוֹ בַּתֵּבָה

וַיַּעֲבֵר אֱלֹהִים רוּחַ עַל־הָאָרֶץ וַיָּשֹׁכּוּ הַמָּיִם : וְנֶאֱמַר ·

וַיִּשְׁמַע אֱלֹהִים אֶת־נַאֲקָתָם וַיִּזְכֹּר אֱלֹהִים אֶת־בְּרִיתוֹ

אֶת־אַבְרָהָם אֶת־יִצְחָק וְאֶת־יַעֲקֹב · וְנֶאֱמַר · וְזָכַרְתִּי

ZICH-
RONOTH

number. From the beginning thou didst make this thy purpose known, and from aforetime thou didst disclose it. This day, on which was the beginning of thy work, is a remembrance of the first day, for it is a statute for Israel, a decree of the God of Jacob.

"THE
WORLD'S
ASSIZE"

Thereon also sentence is pronounced upon countries,— which of them is destined to the sword and which to peace, which to famine and which to plenty ; and each separate creature is judged thereon, and recorded for life or for death. Who is not judged on this day ? For the remembrance of every creature cometh before thee, each man's deeds and destiny, his works and ways, his thoughts and schemes, his imaginings and achievements. Happy is the man who forgetteth thee not, and the son of man who strengtheneth himself in thee ; for they that seek thee shall never stumble, neither shall any be put to shame who trust in thee Yea, the remembrance of all works cometh before thee, and thou enquirest into the doings of them all.

GOD'S
MERCIES

Of Noah also thou wast mindful in thy love, and didst remember him with a promise of salvation and mercy, when thou broughtest the waters of the flood to destroy all flesh on account of their evil deeds. So his remembrance came before thee, O Lord our God, to increase his seed like the

---

prayer helped to give the New Year Festival in the mind of the people a more and more solemn character ; that of a " Day of Judgment ", and of self-judgment. This noble conception is not limited to the life of the individual, but is extended also to that of peoples. It is not blind fate that determines the rise and fall of nations and kingdoms : righteousness exalteth a nation. In the long run, it is well with those that build on moral foundations ; in the long run, robber-states write out their own curse.

thereon also sentence . . countries. The medieval author of the soul-stirring prayer, Unsanneh Tokef, makes use of these phrases in his delineation of the annual judgment of the individual.

Each of the ten proof-texts that follow has, in some way, reference to God's merciful remembrance of His creatures.

Noah. The Rite of Yemen Jews has, " Wert Thou not also mindful of Noah in Thy love " ? Storm-tost in the Deluge, yet he, his family, and even the innocent cattle with him, are remembered by God.

אֶת־בְּרִיתִי יַעֲקוֹב וְאַף אֶת־בְּרִיתִי יִצְחָק וְאַף אֶת־
בְּרִיתִי אַבְרָהָם אֶזְכֹּר וְהָאָרֶץ אֶזְכֹּר : וּבְדִבְרֵי קָדְשְׁךָ
כָּתוּב לֵאמֹר · זֵכֶר עָשָׂה לְנִפְלְאֹתָיו חַנּוּן וְרַחוּם יְיָ :
וְנֶאֱמַר · טֶרֶף נָתַן לִירֵאָיו יִזְכֹּר לְעוֹלָם בְּרִיתוֹ : וְנֶאֱמַר ·
וַיִּזְכֹּר לָהֶם בְּרִיתוֹ וַיִּנָּחֵם כְּרֹב חֲסָדָיו : וְעַל־יְדֵי
עֲבָדֶיךָ הַנְּבִיאִים כָּתוּב לֵאמֹר · הָלֹךְ וְקָרָאתָ בְאָזְנֵי
יְרוּשָׁלַם לֵאמֹר · כֹּה אָמַר יְיָ זָכַרְתִּי לָךְ חֶסֶד נְעוּרַיִךְ
אַהֲבַת כְּלוּלֹתָיִךְ לֶכְתֵּךְ אַחֲרַי בַּמִּדְבָּר בְּאֶרֶץ לֹא
זְרוּעָה : וְנֶאֱמַר · וְזָכַרְתִּי אֲנִי אֶת־בְּרִיתִי אוֹתָךְ בִּימֵי
נְעוּרָיִךְ וַהֲקִמוֹתִי לָךְ בְּרִית עוֹלָם : וְנֶאֱמַר · הֲבֵן
יַקִּיר לִי אֶפְרַיִם אִם יֶלֶד שַׁעֲשׁוּעִים · כִּי־מִדֵּי דַבְּרִי
בּוֹ זָכֹר אֶזְכְּרֶנּוּ עוֹד · עַל־כֵּן הָמוּ מֵעַי לוֹ רַחֵם
אֲרַחֲמֶנּוּ נְאֻם־יְיָ :

אֱלֹהֵינוּ וֵאלֹהֵי אֲבוֹתֵינוּ · זָכְרֵנוּ בְּזִכָּרוֹן טוֹב לְפָנֶיךָ
וּפָקְדֵנוּ בִּפְקֻדַּת יְשׁוּעָה וְרַחֲמִים מִשְּׁמֵי שְׁמֵי קֶדֶם
וּזְכָר־לָנוּ יְיָ אֱלֹהֵינוּ אֶת־הַבְּרִית וְאֶת־הַחֶסֶד וְאֶת־
הַשְּׁבוּעָה אֲשֶׁר נִשְׁבַּעְתָּ לְאַבְרָהָם אָבִינוּ בְּהַר הַמֹּרִיָּה ·

their groaning. Of the enslaved children of Israel in Egypt.

then will I remember. In Exile, when Israel is once again under the
heel of inhuman oppressors.

I remember for thee. The Prophet Jeremiah pictures Israel's loyalty
to God as that of an affectionate bride who follows the chosen of her
heart even into the Wilderness. It was only such love that could
account for Israel's willingness to forget both the grandeur and the

ZICH-RONOTH
Genesis 8. 1

dust of the earth, and his offspring like the sand of the sea : as it is written in thy Torah, And God remembered Noah, and every living thing, and all cattle that were with him in the ark : and God made a wind to pass over the earth, and

Exodus 2. 24

the waters subsided. And it is said, And God heard their groaning, and God remembered his covenant with Abraham,

Leviticus 26. 42

with Isaac, and with Jacob. And it is said, Then will I remember my covenant with Jacob ; and also my covenant with Isaac, and also my covenant with Abraham will I remember ; and I will remember the land. And in thy

Psalm 111. 4, 5

Holy Words it is written saying, He hath made a memorial for his wondrous works : the Lord is gracious and full of compassion. And it is said, He hath given food unto them that fear him : he will ever be mindful of his covenant. And

Psalm 106. 45

it is said, And he remembered for them his covenant, and relented according to the multitude of his lovingkindnesses. And by the hands of thy servants, the prophets, it is written

Jeremiah 2. 2

saying, Go and cry in the ears of Jerusalem, saying, Thus saith the Lord, I remember for thee the kindness of thy youth, the love of thy bridal state ; how thou wentest after me in the wilderness, in a land that was not sown. And

Ezekiel 16, 60

it is said, Nevertheless, I will remember my covenant with thee in the days of thy youth, and I will establish unto

Jeremiah 31.20

thee an everlasting covenant. And it is said, Is Ephraim a precious son unto me ? Is he a caressed child ? As often as I spake against him, I earnestly remembered him ; therefore my heart yearneth for him ; I will surely have mercy upon him, saith the Lord.

Our God and God of our fathers, let us be remembered by thee for good : grant us a judgment of salvation and mercy from thy heavens, the heavens of old ; and remember

---

fleshpots of Egypt, and venture into the Unknown on an unheard of quest of God, that was to give a new meaning to man's existence.

is Ephraim a precious son. In the chapter from which this is taken, Rachel, the Mother of Israel's tribes, is weeping for her children ; and

וְתֵרָאֶה לְפָנֶיךָ עֲקֵדָה שֶׁעָקַד אַבְרָהָם אָבִינוּ אֶת־
יִצְחָק בְּנוֹ עַל גַּב הַמִּזְבֵּחַ וְכָבַשׁ רַחֲמָיו לַעֲשׂוֹת
רְצוֹנֶךָ בְּלֵבָב שָׁלֵם · כֵּן יִכְבְּשׁוּ רַחֲמֶיךָ אֶת־כַּעַסְךָ
מֵעָלֵינוּ וּבְטוּבְךָ הַגָּדוֹל יָשׁוּב חֲרוֹן אַפְּךָ מֵעַמְּךָ וּמֵעִירְךָ
וּמִנַּחֲלָתֶךָ · וְקַיֶּם־לָנוּ יְיָ אֱלֹהֵינוּ אֶת־הַדָּבָר שֶׁהִבְטַחְתָּנוּ
בְּתוֹרָתֶךָ עַל יְדֵי מֹשֶׁה עַבְדְּךָ מִפִּי כְבוֹדֶךָ כָּאָמוּר ·
וְזָכַרְתִּי לָהֶם בְּרִית רִאשֹׁנִים אֲשֶׁר הוֹצֵאתִי־אֹתָם מֵאֶרֶץ
מִצְרַיִם לְעֵינֵי הַגּוֹיִם לִהְיוֹת לָהֶם לֵאלֹהִים אֲנִי יְהֹוָה:
כִּי זוֹכֵר כָּל־הַנִּשְׁכָּחוֹת אַתָּה הוּא מֵעוֹלָם וְאֵין שְׁכָחָה
לִפְנֵי כִסֵּא כְבוֹדֶךָ · וַעֲקֵדַת יִצְחָק לְזַרְעוֹ הַיּוֹם
בְּרַחֲמִים תִּזְכּוֹר: בָּרוּךְ אַתָּה יְיָ · זוֹכֵר הַבְּרִית:

אַתָּה נִגְלֵיתָ בַּעֲנַן כְּבוֹדֶךָ עַל עַם קָדְשְׁךָ לְדַבֵּר
עִמָּם · מִן הַשָּׁמַיִם הִשְׁמַעְתָּם קוֹלֶךָ וְנִגְלֵיתָ עֲלֵיהֶם
בְּעַרְפְלֵי טֹהַר · גַּם כָּל הָעוֹלָם כֻּלּוֹ חָל מִפָּנֶיךָ וּבְרִיּוֹת
בְּרֵאשִׁית חָרְדוּ מִמֶּךָ בְּהִגָּלוֹתְךָ מַלְכֵּנוּ עַל־הַר סִינַי
לְלַמֵּד לְעַמְּךָ תּוֹרָה וּמִצְווֹת · וַתַּשְׁמִיעֵם אֶת־הוֹד

the children (" Ephraim "), *i.e.* the Ten Tribes of Israel who have been
led into captivity for their sin, are repenting their former waywardness.
In answer to this, Jeremiah, the poet of the heart, represents God as
welcoming Ephraim's penitence : and saying, " I yearn for him, even
when I rebuke him ; I will have mercy upon him ".
    oath . . . Mount Moriah. See Genesis 22. 16–18, p. 261.
    binding . . Isaac. For the Akedah, read pp. 256 and 257.

unto us, O Lord our God, the covenant and the loving-kindness and the oath which thou didst sware unto Abraham our father on Mount Moriah : and consider the binding with which Abraham our father bound his son Isaac on the altar, how he suppressed his compassion in order to perform thy will with a perfect heart. So may thy compassion over-bear thine anger against us ; in thy great goodness may thy great wrath turn aside from thy people, thy city and thine inheritance. Fulfil unto us, O Lord our God, the word in which thou hast bidden us trust in thy Torah through the hand of Moses thy servant, from the mouth of *Leviticus* 26.45 thy glory ; as it is said, But I will remember unto them the covenant of their ancestors, whom I brought forth out of the land of Egypt in the sight of the nations, that I might be their God : I am the Lord. For thou art he who remem-bereth from eternity all forgotten things, and before the throne of whose glory there is no forgetfulness. O remember the binding of Isaac this day in mercy unto his seed. Blessed art thou, O Lord, who rememberest the covenant.

VI. SHO-FAROTH   Thou didst reveal thyself in a cloud of glory unto thy holy people in order to speak with them. Out of heaven thou didst make them hear thy voice, and wast revealed unto them in clouds of purity. The whole world trembled at thy presence, and the works of creation were in awe of thee, when thou didst thus reveal thyself, O our King, upon Mount Sinai to teach thy people the Torah and command-ments, and didst make them hear thy majestic voice and thy holy utterances out of flames of fire. Amidst thunders and lightnings thou didst manifest thyself to them, and

III

The third of the special Benedictions is called *Shofaroth*—lit. " Shofar-soundings ". It represents God as the Ruler of history, who revealed Himself to Israel amid Shofar-blasts at Sinai, and in His time will gather all men and nations by the trumpet-blasts of the Judgment Day.

קוֹלֶךָ וְדַבְּרוֹת קָדְשְׁךָ מִלַּהֲבוֹת אֵשׁ · בְּקֹלוֹת וּבְרָקִים

עֲלֵיהֶם נִגְלֵיתָ וּבְקוֹל שׁוֹפָר עֲלֵיהֶם הוֹפָעְתָּ : כַּכָּתוּב

בְּתוֹרָתֶךָ · וַיְהִי בַיּוֹם הַשְּׁלִישִׁי בִּהְיֹת הַבֹּקֶר וַיְהִי

קֹלֹת וּבְרָקִים וְעָנָן כָּבֵד עַל־הָהָר וְקֹל שֹׁפָר חָזָק מְאֹד

וַיֶּחֱרַד כָּל־הָעָם אֲשֶׁר בַּמַּחֲנֶה : וַנֶּאֱמַר · וַיְהִי קוֹל

הַשֹּׁפָר הוֹלֵךְ וְחָזֵק מְאֹד מֹשֶׁה יְדַבֵּר וְהָאֱלֹהִים יַעֲנֶנּוּ

בְקוֹל : וַנֶּאֱמַר · וְכָל־הָעָם רֹאִים אֶת־הַקּוֹלֹת וְאֶת־

הַלַּפִּידִם וְאֵת קוֹל הַשֹּׁפָר וְאֶת־הָהָר עָשֵׁן וַיַּרְא הָעָם

וַיָּנֻעוּ וַיַּעַמְדוּ מֵרָחֹק : וּבְדִבְרֵי קָדְשְׁךָ כָּתוּב לֵאמֹר ·

עָלָה אֱלֹהִים בִּתְרוּעָה יְיָ בְּקוֹל שׁוֹפָר : וְנֶאֱמַר ·

בַּחֲצֹצְרוֹת וְקוֹל שׁוֹפָר הָרִיעוּ לִפְנֵי הַמֶּלֶךְ יְיָ : וְנֶאֱמַר ·

תִּקְעוּ בַחֹדֶשׁ שׁוֹפָר בַּכֶּסֶה לְיוֹם חַגֵּנוּ : כִּי חֹק

לְיִשְׂרָאֵל הוּא מִשְׁפָּט לֵאלֹהֵי יַעֲקֹב : וְנֶאֱמַר · הַלֲלוּיָהּ ·

הַלְלוּ אֵל בְּקָדְשׁוֹ הַלְלוּהוּ בִּרְקִיעַ עֻזּוֹ : הַלְלוּהוּ

בִגְבוּרֹתָיו הַלְלוּהוּ כְּרֹב גֻּדְלוֹ : הַלְלוּהוּ בְּתֵקַע שׁוֹפָר

הַלְלוּהוּ בְּנֵבֶל וְכִנּוֹר : הַלְלוּהוּ בְּתֹף וּמָחוֹל הַלְלוּהוּ

בְּמִנִּים וְעֻגָב : הַלְלוּהוּ בְּצִלְצְלֵי־שָׁמַע הַלְלוּהוּ בְּצִלְצְלֵי

תְרוּעָה : כֹּל הַנְּשָׁמָה תְּהַלֵּל יָהּ · הַלְלוּיָהּ :

וְעַל־יְדֵי עֲבָדֶיךָ הַנְּבִיאִים כָּתוּב לֵאמֹר · כָּל־יֹשְׁבֵי

SHO-
FAROTH
Exodus 19. 16

Exodus 19. 19

Exodus 20. 18

Psalm 47. 6

Psalm 98. 6

Psalm 81. 4

Psalm 150

Isaiah 18. 3

while the Shofar sounded thou didst shine forth upon them ; as it is written in thy Torah, And it came to pass on the third day, when it was morning, that there were thunders and lightnings, and a thick cloud upon the mount, and the sound of the Shofar exceeding loud ; and all the people that were in the camp trembled. And it is said, And the sound of the Shofar waxed louder and louder ; Moses spake, and God answered him by a voice. And it is said, And all the people perceived the thunderings and the lightnings, and the sound of the Shofar, and the mountain smoking : and when the people saw it, they were moved and stood afar off.

And in thy Holy Words it is written, saying, God is gone up with a shout, the Lord with the sound of a Shofar. And it is said, With trumpets and sound of Shofar shout joyously before the King, the Lord. And it is said, Blow the Shofar on the new moon, in the time appointed, for our day of festival: for it is a statute for Israel, a decree of the God of Jacob. And it is said, Praise ye the Lord. Praise God in his sanctuary : praise him in the firmament of his power. Praise him for his mighty acts : praise him according to his abundant greatness. Praise him with the blast of the Shofar: praise him with the harp and the lyre. Praise him with the timbrel and dance : praise him with stringed instruments and the pipe. Praise him with the clear-toned cymbals : praise him with the loud-sounding cymbals. Let everything that hath breath praise the Lord. Praise ye the Lord.

And by the hands of thy servants, the prophets, it is written saying, All ye inhabitants of the world, and ye

---

The proof-texts from the Torah deal with the Giving of the Ten Commandments ; then come psalm-verses in which mention of the Shofar is made ; followed by prophecies from Isaiah and Zechariah concerning the ingathering of Israel and the Messianic days, with which the Shofar-sound is associated.

gone up with a shout. A poetic phrase taken from a psalm recited before the Sounding of the Shofar.

praise God in his sanctuary. Psalm 150, the chorus of jubilant joy with which the Book of Psalms closes, is here given in full.

תֵּבֵל וְשֹׁכְנֵי אָרֶץ כִּנְשֹׂא־נֵס הָרִים תִּרְאוּ וְכִתְקֹעַ
שׁוֹפָר תִּשְׁמָעוּ : וְנֶאֱמַר · וְהָיָה בַּיּוֹם הַהוּא יִתָּקַע בְּשׁוֹפָר
גָּדוֹל וּבָאוּ הָאֹבְדִים בְּאֶרֶץ אַשּׁוּר וְהַנִּדָּחִים בְּאֶרֶץ
מִצְרָיִם וְהִשְׁתַּחֲווּ לַיְיָ בְּהַר הַקֹּדֶשׁ בִּירוּשָׁלָ͏ִם : וְנֶאֱמַר ·
וַיְיָ עֲלֵיהֶם יֵרָאֶה וְיָצָא כַבָּרָק חִצּוֹ וַאדֹנָי יֱהֹוִה בַּשׁוֹפָר
יִתְקָע וְהָלַךְ בְּסַעֲרוֹת תֵּימָן : יְיָ צְבָאוֹת יָגֵן עֲלֵיהֶם :
כֵּן תָּגֵן עַל־ עַמְּךָ יִשְׂרָאֵל בִּשְׁלוֹמֶךָ :

אֱלֹהֵינוּ וֵאלֹהֵי אֲבוֹתֵינוּ · תְּקַע בְּשׁוֹפָר גָּדוֹל
לְחֵרוּתֵנוּ וְשָׂא נֵס לְקַבֵּץ גָּלֻיּוֹתֵינוּ · וְקָרֵב פְּזוּרֵינוּ מִבֵּין
הַגּוֹיִם וּנְפוּצוֹתֵינוּ כַּנֵּס מִיַּרְכְּתֵי אָרֶץ · וַהֲבִיאֵנוּ לְצִיּוֹן
עִירְךָ בְּרִנָּה וְלִירוּשָׁלַיִם בֵּית מִקְדָּשְׁךָ בְּשִׂמְחַת עוֹלָם ·
וְשָׁם נַעֲשֶׂה לְפָנֶיךָ אֶת־קָרְבְּנוֹת חוֹבוֹתֵינוּ כִּמְצֻוָּה
עָלֵינוּ בְּתוֹרָתֶךָ עַל יְדֵי מֹשֶׁה עַבְדְּךָ מִפִּי כְבוֹדֶךָ
כָּאָמוּר · וּבְיוֹם שִׂמְחַתְכֶם וּבְמוֹעֲדֵיכֶם וּבְרָאשֵׁי חָדְשֵׁכֶם
וּתְקַעְתֶּם בַּחֲצֹצְרֹת עַל עֹלֹתֵיכֶם וְעַל זִבְחֵי שַׁלְמֵיכֶם
וְהָיוּ לָכֶם לְזִכָּרוֹן לִפְנֵי אֱלֹהֵיכֶם אֲנִי יְיָ אֱלֹהֵיכֶם :
כִּי אַתָּה שׁוֹמֵעַ קוֹל שׁוֹפָר וּמַאֲזִין תְּרוּעָה וְאֵין
דּוֹמֶה לָּךְ : בָּרוּךְ אַתָּה יְיָ · שׁוֹמֵעַ קוֹל תְּרוּעַת עַמּוֹ
יִשְׂרָאֵל בְּרַחֲמִים :

For the conclusion of the עֲמִידָה, *to* רְצֵה קַדְמוֹנִיּוֹת, *see pp. 854–858.*
For the Blessing of the Priests when רֹאשׁ הַשָּׁנָה *falls on a weekday,*
see pp. 834–836.

SHOFAROTH dwellers on the earth, when an ensign is lifted up on the mountains, see ye, and when the Shofar is blown, hear ye.

Isaiah 27. 13 And it is said, And it shall come to pass on that day, that a great Shofar shall be blown ; and they shall come who were lost in the land of Assyria, and they that were dispersed in the land of Egypt ; and they shall worship the Lord in the *Zechariah* 9. 14 holy mountain at Jerusalem. And it is said, And the Lord shall be seen over them, and his arrow shall go forth as the lightning : and the Lord God shall blow the Shofar, and shall go with the whirlwinds of the south. The Lord of hosts shall be a shield unto them. So be a shield unto thy people Israel with thy peace.

Our God and God of our fathers, sound the great Shofar for our freedom, lift up the ensign to gather our exiles ; bring our scattered ones among the nations near unto thee, and gather our scattered ones from the ends of the earth. Lead us with exultation unto Zion thy city, and unto Jerusalem the place of thy sanctuary with everlasting joy ; and there we will prepare before thee the offerings that are obligatory for us, as is commanded us in thy Torah through the hand of Moses thy servant, from the mouth of thy glory, *Numbers* 10. 10 as it is said, And in the day of your gladness, and in your set feasts, and in the beginnings of your months, ye shall blow with the trumpets over your burnt offerings, and over the sacrifices of your peace offerings ; and they shall be to you for a remembrance before your God : I am the Lord your God. For thou hearest the sound of the Shofar and givest heed to the trumpet-blast, and there is none like unto thee. Blessed art thou, O Lord, who in mercy hearkenest to the Shofar sounds of thy people Israel.

Continue pp. 855–859, *"Accept" to "as in ancient years."*

For the Blessing of the Priests when the New Year falls on a weekday, see pp. 835–837.

when an ensign is lifted up. As signal of the decisive Divine intervention in the life of the nations.

a great Shofar. For the gathering of the scattered sons of Israel; cf. the tenth of the Eighteen Benedictions, p. 142.

888

סדר תשליך :

On the First Day of רֹאשׁ הַשָּׁנָה‎, or, when רֹאשׁ הַשָּׁנָה falls on שַׁבָּת,
on the Second Day, after מִנְחָה, it is customary to go to the banks of
a river, or of any other expanse of water, and to say the following: —

מִי אֵל כָּמוֹךָ נֹשֵׂא עָוֹן וְעֹבֵר עַל־פֶּשַׁע לִשְׁאֵרִית
נַחֲלָתוֹ לֹא־הֶחֱזִיק לָעַד אַפּוֹ כִּי חָפֵץ חֶסֶד הוּא :
יָשׁוּב יְרַחֲמֵנוּ יִכְבֹּשׁ עֲוֹנֹתֵינוּ וְתַשְׁלִיךְ בִּמְצֻלוֹת יָם
כָּל־חַטֹּאתָם : וְכָל־חַטֹּאת עַמְּךָ בֵּית יִשְׂרָאֵל תַּשְׁלִיךְ
בִּמְקוֹם אֲשֶׁר לֹא־יִזָּכְרוּ וְלֹא־יִפָּקְדוּ וְלֹא־יַעֲלוּ עַל־לֵב
לְעוֹלָם : תִּתֵּן אֱמֶת לְיַעֲקֹב חֶסֶד לְאַבְרָהָם . אֲשֶׁר־
נִשְׁבַּעְתָּ לַאֲבֹתֵינוּ מִימֵי קֶדֶם :

TASHLICH

In the afternoon of New Year, on the First Day (or, if that be the Sabbath, on the Second Day), it is the custom in some communities to walk to a river or sea-shore, and recite the above verses from Micah. This is done in order to be reminded that even as the body is purified by water, so ought our souls to be purified by repentance and the appeal to the help and mercy of God " (M. Friedländer).

The custom cannot be traced earlier than the thirteenth century. It came to be known as *Tashlich* from the Hebrew phrase (" Thou shalt cast into the sea ") in the second verse.

The verses recited revel in the thought of the Divine Forgiveness. They are the lyrical epilogue of the Book of Micah, and are most appropriate for the occasion.

The Prophet MICAH was a contemporary of Isaiah, and, like him, dreamt of the time when the nations would learn war no more. He was the champion of the poor, and fearlessly denounced luxury, irreligion and degeneracy. He has given the world the noblest

On the First Day of the New Year, or, when New Year falls on Sabbath, on the Second Day, after the Afternoon Service, it is customary to go to the banks of a river, or of any other expanse of water, and to say the following :—

Micah 7. 18 Who is a God like unto thee, that pardoneth iniquity and passeth by the transgression of the remnant of his heritage ? He retaineth not his anger for ever, because he delighteth Micah 7. 19 in lovingkindness. He will again have mercy upon us ; he will subdue our iniquities. And thou wilt cast all their sins into the depths of the sea.—O mayest thou cast all the sins of thy people, the house of Israel, into a place where they shall be no more remembered or ever again come to mind.— Micah 7. 20 Thou wilt show faithfulness to Jacob, and lovingkindness to Abraham, as thou hast sworn unto our fathers from the days of old.

definition of true religion : "It hath been told thee, O man, what is good, and what the Lord doth require of thee ; only to do justly, and to love mercy, and to walk humbly with thy God ".

18. *like unto thee.* " The Prophet does not mean that other gods have a real existence, but speaks from the point of view of the other nations who believe that they do really exist " (Cheyne) ; Exodus 15. 11.

that pardoneth iniquity. This and other phrases recall the supreme revelation of the Divine Attributes accorded to Moses on Sinai—" merciful and gracious, slow to anger and abounding in lovingkindness and truth ; keeping mercy unto thousands, forgiving iniquity, transgression and sin ". These Thirteen Attributes have always had a deep fascination for the Jew, and are a recurrent refrain of the penitential prayers (Selichoth) whenever these are recited, especially in the Neilah Service on the Day of Atonement.

remnant of his heritage. The Prophets hold fast to the belief in a purified Remnant in Israel, a righteous nucleus that is indestructible. And historic Israel that has suffered all things, endured all things, and survived all things for its Faith, may well speak of itself as that Remnant.

subdue. Or, " suppress " (Kimchi). Sins in Scripture are personified as enemies ; or, as wild animals which man has it in his power to master. *into the depths of the sea.* So as never again to come to mind. The words between v. 19 and 20 are not Biblical.

20. *faithfulness.* lit. " truth ".

Jacob . . . Abraham. In the sight of God, Jacob and Abraham are not dead. The Rabbis declared : " Jacob our father did not die ; seeing that his children are alive, he is alive ". The reference here is, therefore, to the children of Jacob and Abraham.

יוֹם כִּפּוּר:

ויקרא מ"ז, ל' ל"א

כִּי־בַיּוֹם הַזֶּה יְכַפֵּר עֲלֵיכֶם לְטַהֵר אֶתְכֶם מִכֹּל
חַטֹּאתֵיכֶם לִפְנֵי יְיָ תִּטְהָרוּ: שַׁבַּת שַׁבָּתוֹן הִיא לָכֶם
וְעִנִּיתֶם אֶת־נַפְשֹׁתֵיכֶם חֻקַּת עוֹלָם:

DAY OF ATONEMENT

The comments on these Scriptural verses are supplementary to the general remarks on Repentance given on pp. 838–840.

30. *on this day.* Called in the Talmud יומא *the* Day, the most sacred of holy days, that voices the sublimest truths of religion. No other nation, ancient or modern, has an institution approaching the Day of Atonement in religious depth—" a day of purification and of turning from sin, for which forgiveness is granted through the grace of the merciful God, who holds penitence in as high an esteem as guiltlessness " (Philo).

shall atonement be made for you. Hebrew יכפר עליכם; lit. " he shall make atonement for you ". To whom does " he " refer ? As the preceding and following verses describe the duties of the people on the Day, it cannot be the High Priest ; otherwise, he would have been specially mentioned (Büchler). Rabbi Akiba rightly held that " he " refers to God. " Happy Israel "—he exclaimed—" before Whom do ye purify yourselves, and Who is it that purifieth you ? Your Father Who is in Heaven ; as it is said (Ezekiel 36. 25), ' I will sprinkle clean water upon you, and ye shall be clean ' ". This saying of Rabbi Akiba is remarkable in many ways. It proclaims man's direct access to God our Father Who is in Heaven, and repudiates all idea of any mediator. And especially noteworthy is the fact that the words, " before Whom do ye purify yourselves " *precede* the words, " Who is it that purifieth you ". This indicates that the initiative in purification is with the sinner. He cleanses himself by fearless self-examination, open confession, and the resolve not to repeat the transgressions of the past. When our Heavenly Father sees the self-abasement and the penitence, He—and not the High Priest or any other mediator—sprinkles, as it were, the clean waters of pardon and forgiveness upon the sinner. " The whole philosophy of monotheism is contained in this rallying-cry of Rabbi Akiba " (Hermann Cohen).

DAY OF ATONEMENT

Leviticus xvi, 30, 31.

30. For on this day shall atonement be made for you, to cleanse you ; from all your sins shall ye be clean before the Lord. 31. It is a sabbath of rest unto you, and ye shall afflict your souls ; it is a statute for ever.

In the Hebrew name of this most sacred of Festivals, *Yom Ha-Kippurim*, כפורים is the plural form for the abstract noun " atonement ". The Zohar translates it literally as an ordinary plural, " because it represents two streams of love. As soon as the desire for reconciliation has awakened in the sinner's soul, and wings its way Heavenward, God's grace comes down to meet it, calming his breast with the assurance of Divine pardon and forgiveness ".

all your sins. Repentance can give even rebellious sins the character of " errors ". By his penitence, the sinner shows that his wilful sins were committed by him when blinded by delusion and passion. Justice demands the punishment of the sinner; but his repentance is evidence of his having acted בשגגה " in error " at the time of sinning. This renders it possible for forgiveness to be extended to him.

from all your sins before the Lord. On this phrase, Rabbi Elazar ben Azaryah (p. 662) based his teaching that only sins committed *before the Lord* does the Day atone, not those against a fellow-man ; and that the Day of Atonement does not absolve the sinner from the duty of restitution to, and reconciliation with, the person whom he has wronged.

31. *a sabbath of solemn rest.* lit. " a sabbath of sabbaths ". The Israelite rests on that day not only from all manner of work, but from all earthly affairs. The whole day is devoted to prayer, Scripture reading, hymn, anthem and confession of sins.

afflict your souls. i.e. fast. The Hebrew phrase well indicates the spiritual aim of fasting. Fasting not only afflicts the soul, but it strengthens it. Seeing that the main cause of sin is gratification of bodily appetites, the fast proves to the sinner that man can conquer all physical cravings, and that the spirit can always master the body. However, abstention from food and other bodily desires, must be accompanied by deep remorse at having fallen short of what it was in our power to be and to do. Without the solemn resolve to abandon evil ways and unrighteous thoughts, fasting is in itself not the complete fulfilment of the Divine purpose of the Day of Atonement.

a statute for ever. The Day of Atonement survived the High Priesthood ; nay, it gained in inwardness and spiritual power on the passing of the sacrificial system. " The fasting and humiliation before God, the confession of sins and contrition for them, and fervent prayer for forgiveness, were, even before the destruction of the Temple, the reality in regard to the Day of Atonement, of which the rites in the Temple were but a dramatic symbol " (Moore). The Rabbis had stressed the Prophetic teaching that, where there was no repentance, sacrificial rites were of no avail. With the cessation of sacrifice, therefore, repentance was left as the sole means for the remission of sins. " In our time, when there is no Temple and no Altar for atonement, there is Repentance. Repentance atones for all iniquities " (Maimonides). The Day of Atonement, the Rabbis further declare, will never pass away. And indeed as long as Israel does not lose its soul, so long shall the Day of Atonement remain.

Two more things are to be said in any preliminary statement on the Day of Atonement. One is, that this Day of fasting, humiliation and penitential prayer is a *festival*. In many synagogues, worshippers stand attired in white, from evening to evening, during the entire Atonement Day. Those white garments are not worn as reminders of the grave ; they are a sign of the festal character of the Day. " When men are summoned before an earthly ruler ", the Rabbis say, " to defend themselves against some charge, they appear downcast and dressed in black, like mourners. The Israelite appears before God on the Atonement Day dressed in white as if going to a feast; because he is confident that, as soon as he returns penitently to his Maker, He will not condemn, but will abundantly pardon ".

The second comment is on the Declaration, *Col Nidré*, with which the Evening Service opens. Outwardly it is a rescinding of vows. Of what kind are the vows which are thus annulled ? *Not* any obligation that had been made to a fellow-man. Jewish Law declares that a vow or oath which was made to another person, cannot be annulled except in the presence of the person concerned, and only with his consent ; while an oath which a man had taken in a court of justice, *could not be absolved by any other authority in the world* ! Why then was it introduced ? Of the various explanations, two may be mentioned. The first is by the late Dr. M. Friedländer :

1. It arose in connection with those who, in the early Middle Ages, refused to join in communal work, and submit to the laws of the community ; or, who by any heinous action had shocked the Jewish conscience, and were in consequence excommunicated. Still, when Yom Kippur came, they longed to join their brethren in public worship. The religious authorities were loth to repel them ; and by this solemn Declaration, such transgressors, *abaryanim*, were suffered to participate in congregational prayer on the Day of Atonement.

That this was the original object of Col Nidré is rendered plausible by the fact that it is preceded by the announcement, " In the name of God and in the name of the Congregation, with the sanction of the Court Above and that of the Court below, we declare it permitted to pray together with those who are transgressors (abaryanim)."

2. The second explanation is the fruit of recent historical studies. They have shown Col Nidré to be a unique memorial of Jewish suffering

and repentance. It arose in Spain, consequent on the religious persecutions by the West Goths in the seventh century. Entire Jewish
communities were then doomed to torture and the stake, unless they
forswore their Faith, and by the most fearful oaths and abjurations
bound themselves nevermore to practise any Jewish observance. In
this way, when better times came, these unfortunates felt themselves
perjured before God and man, if they returned to their Holy Faith,
or kept even the most sacred of the Festivals. It was to ease the conscience of such crushed and distracted men and women, that the Col
Nidré declaration was formulated. In view of this origin of the prayer—
that has only lately become known, and that alone explains its
signal anomalies—Continental congregations that had formerly abolished the Col Nidré declaration, reintroduced it; realizing that the
awakening of historic memories, and the forging of links with the past,
are vital factors in Jewish traditional life and worship; see "Vows and
Vowing in Judaism ", *Numbers*, 310–314 (Soncino, 730-1).

Col Nidré has been fortunate in the melody to which it is traditionally
chanted. It fulfils the counsel offered by Judah the Pious in the thirteenth century, " chant your supplications to God in a melody that
makes the heart weep, and your praises of Him in one that will make
it sing. ₁Thus you will be filled with love and joy for Him that seeth the
heart ". Its fame has spread far beyond the Synagogue. A noted
non-Jewish poet declared : " Such a mysterious song, redolent of a
People's suffering, can hardly have been composed by one brain,
however much inspired " (Lenau).

The hymns that have been introduced into the Evening Service are
soul-stirring in both wording and melody. Among them is the hymn,
אמנם כן " Forgiven ", by R. Yomtob of York, who was probably one of
the martyrs of the massacre in that city in 1190 ; and the hymn whose
opening verse is :
   " Lo, as the potter mouldeth plastic clay
   To forms his varying fancy doth display ;
   So in Thy hand, O God of love, are we ".

Ovinu Malkenu (p. 162) and the Hymn of Glory (p. 214) conclude the
supplications for forgiveness and the litanies of confession that form
part of the Service.

On עֶרֶב יוֹם כִּפּוּר, מִנְחָה *is said as on Fridays, but earlier than usual.*
After עוֹשֶׂה הַשָׁלוֹם, *p.* 293, *say* אֱלֹהֵינוּ וֵאלֹהֵי אֲבוֹתֵינוּ תָּבֹא לְפָנֶיךָ
to the end of the עֲמִידָה *of* יוֹם כִּפּוּר; *see pp.* 907-923.

קַדִּישׁ יָתוֹם *p.* 213, קַדִּישׁ תִּתְקַבַּל *p.* 207, עָלֵינוּ, *p.* 209.

Before going to Synagogue, the FESTIVAL LAMP *is lighted.* *Say the*
Meditation and Benedictions on p. 842.

תפלת יום כפור

The following עֲמִידָה *is said at the Evening, Morning and Afternoon*
Services:

אֲדֹנָי שְׂפָתַי תִּפְתָּח וּפִי יַגִּיד תְּהִלָּתֶךָ:

בָּרוּךְ אַתָּה יְיָ אֱלֹהֵינוּ וֵאלֹהֵי אֲבוֹתֵינוּ · אֱלֹהֵי
אַבְרָהָם אֱלֹהֵי יִצְחָק וֵאלֹהֵי יַעֲקֹב · הָאֵל הַגָּדוֹל הַגִּבּוֹר
וְהַנּוֹרָא אֵל עֶלְיוֹן · גּוֹמֵל חֲסָדִים טוֹבִים וְקוֹנֵה הַכֹּל ·
וְזוֹכֵר חַסְדֵי אָבוֹת וּמֵבִיא גוֹאֵל לִבְנֵי בְנֵיהֶם לְמַעַן
שְׁמוֹ בְּאַהֲבָה ·

זָכְרֵנוּ לַחַיִּים מֶלֶךְ חָפֵץ בַּחַיִּים · וְכָתְבֵנוּ
(*At* נְעִילָה, *substitute* וְחָתְמֵנוּ *in place of* וְכָתְבֵנוּ)
בְּסֵפֶר הַחַיִּים · לְמַעַנְךָ אֱלֹהִים חַיִּים:

מֶלֶךְ עוֹזֵר וּמוֹשִׁיעַ וּמָגֵן · בָּרוּךְ אַתָּה יְיָ · מָגֵן אַבְרָהָם:
אַתָּה גִבּוֹר לְעוֹלָם אֲדֹנָי מְחַיֶּה מֵתִים אַתָּה רַב

895

SERVICE FOR EREV YOM KIPPUR

*On the day previous to the Fast of Atonement, Afternoon Service is said
as on Fridays, but earlier than usual. After " who makest peace,"
p. 293, say " Our God . . . . let our prayer come," to the end of
the Amidah for the Day of Atonement ; see pp. 907—923.
Kaddish, p. 207. " It is our duty," etc., p. 209. Mourner's Kaddish
p. 213.
Before going to Synagogue, the* FESTIVAL LAMP *is lighted. Say the
Meditation and Benedictions on p. 843.*

AMIDAH FOR THE DAY OF ATONEMENT

*The following Amidah is said at the Evening, Morning and Afternoon
Services.*

Psalm 51. 17 O Lord, open thou my lips, and my mouth shall declare
thy praise.

*I. THE GOD
OF
HISTORY*   Blessed art thou, O Lord our God and God of our
fathers, God of Abraham, God of Isaac, and God of Jacob
the great, mighty and revered God, the most high God,
See p. 449 who bestowest lovingkindnesses, and art Master of all
things ; who rememberest the pious deeds of the patriarchs,
and in love wilt bring a redeemer to their children's children
for thy Name's sake.

Remember us unto life, O King, who delightest in life,
and inscribe

*(At the Conclusion Service, substitute " and seal." in place of
" and inscribe ")*

us in the book of life, for thine own sake, O living God.
O King, Helper, Saviour and Shield. Blessed art thou,
O Lord, the Shield of Abraham.

*II. THE GOD
OF
NATURE*   Thou, O Lord, art mighty for ever, thou revivest the
dead, thou art mighty to save. Thou sustainest the living

לְהוֹשִׁיעַ · מְכַלְכֵּל חַיִּים בְּחֶסֶד מְחַיֵּה מֵתִים בְּרַחֲמִים

רַבִּים · סוֹמֵךְ נוֹפְלִים וְרוֹפֵא חוֹלִים וּמַתִּיר אֲסוּרִים

וּמְקַיֵּם אֱמוּנָתוֹ לִישֵׁנֵי עָפָר · מִי כָמוֹךָ בַּעַל גְּבוּרוֹת

וּמִי דּוֹמֶה לָּךְ · מֶלֶךְ מֵמִית וּמְחַיֶּה וּמַצְמִיחַ יְשׁוּעָה ·

מִי כָמוֹךָ אַב הָרַחֲמִים זוֹכֵר יְצוּרָיו לַחַיִּים בְּרַחֲמִים ·

וְנֶאֱמָן אַתָּה לְהַחֲיוֹת מֵתִים · בָּרוּךְ אַתָּה יְיָ

מְחַיֵּה הַמֵּתִים :

אַתָּה קָדוֹשׁ וְשִׁמְךָ קָדוֹשׁ וּקְדוֹשִׁים בְּכָל־יוֹם

יְהַלְלוּךָ סֶּלָה :

וּבְכֵן תֵּן פַּחְדְּךָ יְיָ אֱלֹהֵינוּ עַל כָּל־מַעֲשֶׂיךָ וְאֵימָתְךָ

עַל כָּל־מַה־שֶּׁבָּרָאתָ · וְיִירָאוּךָ כָּל־הַמַּעֲשִׂים וְיִשְׁתַּחֲווּ

לְפָנֶיךָ כָּל־הַבְּרוּאִים · וְיֵעָשׂוּ כֻלָּם אֲגֻדָּה אַחַת לַעֲשׂוֹת

רְצוֹנְךָ בְּלֵבָב שָׁלֵם · כְּמוֹ שֶׁיָּדַעְנוּ יְיָ אֱלֹהֵינוּ שֶׁהַשִּׁלְטָן

לְפָנֶיךָ עֹז בְּיָדְךָ וּגְבוּרָה בִּימִינֶךָ וְשִׁמְךָ נוֹרָא עַל

כָּל־מַה־שֶּׁבָּרָאתָ :

וּבְכֵן תֵּן כָּבוֹד יְיָ לְעַמֶּךָ תְּהִלָּה לִירֵאֶיךָ וְתִקְוָה

לְדוֹרְשֶׁיךָ וּפִתְחוֹן פֶּה לַמְיַחֲלִים לָךְ · שִׂמְחָה לְאַרְצֶךָ

וְשָׂשׂוֹן לְעִירֶךָ וּצְמִיחַת קֶרֶן לְדָוִד עַבְדֶּךָ וַעֲרִיכַת נֵר

לְבֶן־יִשַׁי מְשִׁיחֶךָ בִּמְהֵרָה בְיָמֵינוּ :

וּבְכֵן צַדִּיקִים יִרְאוּ וְיִשְׂמָחוּ · וִישָׁרִים יַעֲלֹזוּ וַחֲסִידִים

בְּרִנָּה יָגִילוּ · וְעוֹלָתָה תִּקְפָּץ־פִּיהָ וְכָל־הָרִשְׁעָה כֻּלָּהּ

See p. 451

with lovingkindness, revivest the dead with great mercy, supportest the falling, healest the sick, freest the bound, and keepest thy faith to them that sleep in the dust. Who is like unto thee, Lord of mighty acts, and who resembleth thee, O King, who orderest death and restorest to life, and causest salvation to spring forth ?

Who is like unto thee, Father of mercy, who in mercy rememberest thy creatures unto life ?

Yea, faithful art thou to revive the dead. Blessed art thou, O Lord, who revivest the dead.

III.
SANCTIFI-
CATION
OF GOD

Thou art holy, and thy Name is holy, and holy beings praise thee daily. (Selah.)

THE
DIVINE
KINGDOM
See p. 846

Now, therefore, O Lord our God, impose thine awe upon all thy works, and thy dread upon all that thou hast created, that all works may revere thee and all creatures prostrate themselves before thee, that they may all form a single band to do thy will with a perfect heart, even as we know, O Lord our God, that dominion is thine, strength is in thy hand, and might in thy right hand, and that thy Name is to be revered above all that thou hast created.

Give then glory, O Lord, unto thy people, praise to them that revere thee, hope to them that seek thee, and confidence to them that wait for thee, joy to thy land, gladness to thy city, a flowering of strength unto David thy servant, and a clear shining light unto the son of Jesse, thine anointed, speedily in our days.

Then shall the just also see and be glad, and the upright shall exult, and the pious triumphantly rejoice, while iniquity shall close her mouth, and all wickedness shall be

כְּעָשָׁן תִּכְלֶה · כִּי תַעֲבִיר מֶמְשֶׁלֶת זָדוֹן מִן־הָאָרֶץ :

וְתִמְלוֹךְ אַתָּה יְיָ לְבַדֶּךָ עַל כָּל־מַעֲשֶׂיךָ בְּהַר

צִיּוֹן מִשְׁכַּן כְּבוֹדֶךָ וּבִירוּשָׁלַיִם עִיר קָדְשֶׁךָ · כַּכָּתוּב

בְּדִבְרֵי קָדְשֶׁךָ · יִמְלֹךְ יְיָ לְעוֹלָם אֱלֹהַיִךְ צִיּוֹן לְדֹר

וָדֹר · הַלְלוּיָהּ :

קָדוֹשׁ אַתָּה וְנוֹרָא שְׁמֶךָ וְאֵין אֱלֹהַּ מִבַּלְעָדֶיךָ ·

כַּכָּתוּב · וַיִּגְבַּהּ יְיָ צְבָאוֹת בַּמִּשְׁפָּט וְהָאֵל הַקָּדוֹשׁ

נִקְדַּשׁ בִּצְדָקָה · בָּרוּךְ אַתָּה יְיָ · הַמֶּלֶךְ הַקָּדוֹשׁ :

אַתָּה בְחַרְתָּנוּ מִכָּל־הָעַמִּים · אָהַבְתָּ אוֹתָנוּ · וְרָצִיתָ

בָּנוּ · וְרוֹמַמְתָּנוּ מִכָּל הַלְּשׁוֹנוֹת · וְקִדַּשְׁתָּנוּ בְּמִצְוֹתֶיךָ ·

וְקֵרַבְתָּנוּ מַלְכֵּנוּ לַעֲבוֹדָתֶךָ · וְשִׁמְךָ הַגָּדוֹל וְהַקָּדוֹשׁ

עָלֵינוּ קָרָאתָ :

On שַׁבָּת *add the words in brackets.*

וַתִּתֶּן־לָנוּ יְיָ אֱלֹהֵינוּ בְּאַהֲבָה אֶת־יוֹם [הַשַּׁבָּת הַזֶּה

לִקְדֻשָּׁה וְלִמְנוּחָה וְאֶת־יוֹם] הַכִּפֻּרִים הַזֶּה לִמְחִילָה

וְלִסְלִיחָה וּלְכַפָּרָה וְלִמְחָל־בּוֹ אֶת־כָּל־עֲוֹנֹתֵינוּ [בְּאַהֲבָה]

מִקְרָא קֹדֶשׁ זֵכֶר לִיצִיאַת מִצְרָיִם :

אֱלֹהֵינוּ וֵאלֹהֵי אֲבוֹתֵינוּ · יַעֲלֶה וְיָבֹא וְיַגִּיעַ וְיֵרָאֶה

וְיֵרָצֶה וְיִשָּׁמַע וְיִפָּקֵד וְיִזָּכֵר זִכְרוֹנֵנוּ וּפִקְדוֹנֵנוּ וְזִכְרוֹן

אֲבוֹתֵינוּ · וְזִכְרוֹן מָשִׁיחַ בֶּן דָּוִד עַבְדֶּךָ · וְזִכְרוֹן

wholly consumed like smoke, when thou makest the dominion of arrogance to pass away from the earth.

And thou, O Lord, shalt reign, thou alone over all thy works on Mount Zion, the dwelling-place of thy glory, and in Jerusalem, thy holy city, as it is written in thy Holy *Psalm* 146. 10 Words, The Lord shall reign for ever, thy God, O Zion, unto all generations. Praise ye the Lord.

Holy art thou, and awesome is thy Name, and there is *Isaiah* 5. 16 no God beside thee, as it is written, And the Lord of hosts is exalted in judgment, and the holy God is sanctified in righteousness. Blessed art thou, O Lord, the holy King.

IV.
SELECTION
OF ISRAEL
Thou hast chosen us from all peoples, thou hast loved us and taken pleasure in us, and hast exalted us above all tongues ; thou hast hallowed us by thy commandments, *See pp.* 798– and brought us near unto thy service, O our King, and 801 hast called us by thy great and holy Name.

On Sabbath add the words in brackets.

And thou hast given us in love, O Lord our God, [this Sabbath day for holiness and rest, and] this Day of Atonement for pardon, forgiveness, and atonement, that we may [in love] obtain pardon thereon for all our iniquities ; an holy convocation, as a memorial of the departure from Egypt.

YAALEH
VE-YOVO
Our God and God of our fathers ! May our remembrance rise and come and be accepted before thee, with the remembrance of our fathers, of Messiah the son of David thy servant, of Jerusalem thy holy city, and of all thy people the house of Israel, bringing deliverance and well-being

---

atonement. We " pardon " where there are extenuating circum stances for a misdeed ; and we " forgive " something for which the perpetrator is sincerely sorry. *Atonement*, lit. at-one-ment, is the " wiping away " of all guilt through repentance.

יְרוּשָׁלַיִם עִיר קָדְשֶׁךָ · וְזִכְרוֹן כָּל־עַמְּךָ בֵּית יִשְׂרָאֵל
לְפָנֶיךָ · לִפְלֵיטָה וּלְטוֹבָה וּלְחֵן וּלְחֶסֶד וּלְרַחֲמִים
וּלְחַיִּים וּלְשָׁלוֹם בְּיוֹם הַכִּפֻּרִים הַזֶּה · זָכְרֵנוּ יְיָ אֱלֹהֵינוּ
בּוֹ לְטוֹבָה · וּפָקְדֵנוּ בּוֹ לִבְרָכָה · וְהוֹשִׁיעֵנוּ בּוֹ
לְחַיִּים : וּבִדְבַר יְשׁוּעָה וְרַחֲמִים חוּס וְחָנֵּנוּ וְרַחֵם
עָלֵינוּ וְהוֹשִׁיעֵנוּ כִּי אֵלֶיךָ עֵינֵינוּ · כִּי אֵל מֶלֶךְ חַנּוּן
וְרַחוּם אָתָּה :

אֱלֹהֵינוּ וֵאלֹהֵי אֲבוֹתֵינוּ · מְחַל.וּ לַעֲוֹנוֹתֵינוּ בְּיוֹם
[הַשַּׁבָּת חַזֶּה וּבְיוֹם] הַכִּפֻּרִים הַזֶּה · מְחֵה וְהַעֲבֵר פְּשָׁעֵינוּ
וְחַטֹּאתֵינוּ מִנֶּגֶד עֵינֶיךָ · כָּאָמוּר · אָנֹכִי אָנֹכִי הוּא
מֹחֶה פְשָׁעֶיךָ לְמַעֲנִי וְחַטֹּאתֶיךָ לֹא־אֶזְכֹּר : וְנֶאֱמַר ·
מָחִיתִי כָעָב פְּשָׁעֶיךָ וְכֶעָנָן חַטֹּאתֶיךָ שׁוּבָה אֵלַי כִּי
גְאַלְתִּיךָ : וְנֶאֱמַר · כִּי־בַיּוֹם הַזֶּה יְכַפֵּר עֲלֵיכֶם לְטַהֵר
אֶתְכֶם מִכֹּל חַטֹּאתֵיכֶם לִפְנֵי יְיָ תִּטְהָרוּ : [אֱלֹהֵינוּ
וֵאלֹהֵי אֲבוֹתֵינוּ רְצֵה בִמְנוּחָתֵנוּ] קַדְּשֵׁנוּ בְּמִצְוֹתֶיךָ וְתֵן
חֶלְקֵנוּ בְּתוֹרָתֶךָ · שַׂבְּעֵנוּ מִטּוּבֶךָ וְשַׂמְּחֵנוּ בִּישׁוּעָתֶךָ ·
[וְהַנְחִילֵנוּ יְיָ אֱלֹהֵינוּ בְּאַהֲבָה וּבְרָצוֹן שַׁבַּת קָדְשֶׁךָ וְיָנוּחוּ
בָהּ יִשְׂרָאֵל מְקַדְּשֵׁי שְׁמֶךָ] וְטַהֵר לִבֵּנוּ לְעָבְדְּךָ בֶּאֱמֶת ·

I, *even* I. Against Whom you have sinned. "A verse of perfect
tenderness" (Skinner). It is spoken to Israel as a people, but applies
to every individual human soul.

See p. 461

grace, lovingkindness and mercy, life and peace on this Day of Atonement. Remember us, O Lord our God, thereon for our well-being ; be mindful of us for blessing, and save us unto life : by thy promise of salvation and mercy, spare us and be gracious unto us ; have mercy upon us and save us ; for our eyes are bent upon thee, because thou art a gracious and merciful God and King.

ATONE-
MENT
SUPPLICA-
TION

Our God and God of our fathers, pardon our iniquities [on this Sabbath day, and] on this Day of Atonement ; blot out our transgressions and our sins, and make them pass

Isaiah 43. 25

away from before thine eyes ; as it is said, I, even I, am he that blotteth out thy transgressions for mine own sake ;

Isaiah 44. 22

and I will not remember thy sins. And it is said, I have blotted out, as a cloud, thy transgressions, and, as a mist,

Leviticus 16.30

thy sins : return unto me, for I have redeemed thee. And it is said, For on this day shall atonement be made for you, to cleanse you ; from all your sins shall ye be clean before the Lord. [Our God and God of our fathers, accept our rest.] Sanctify us by thy commandments, and grant our portion in thy Torah ; satisfy us with thy goodness, and

See p. 458

gladden us with thy salvation ; [and let us inherit, O Lord our God, in love and favour, thy holy Sabbath ; and may Israel, who

---

for mine own sake. This verse embodies the fundamental proclamation of Judaism that there is no other Saviour beside God. Because God is merciful and gracious, forgiving iniquity, transgression and sin (Exodus 34. 6f), He blots out Israel's transgressions. To Isaiah, God is tender as a mother (chapter 66. 13), whose love is spontaneous, unconditional and unquenchable.

I have blotted out. This is the natural culmination of the Divine promise in the preceding verse quoted from the Prophet.

as a cloud. Which passes away, and leaves a clear sky and sunshine behind.

I have redeemed thee. The perfect tense is used, because the redemption is already accomplished in the decree of God.

Forgiver . . . Pardoner. The Hebrew words are specially coined phrases in the Liturgy, in order to give expression to God's infinite mercy.

כִּי אַתָּה סָלְחָן לְיִשְׂרָאֵל וּמָחֳלָן לְשִׁבְטֵי יְשֻׁרוּן בְּכָל־
דוֹר וָדוֹר · וּמִבַּלְעָדֶיךָ אֵין לָנוּ מֶלֶךְ מוֹחֵל וְסוֹלֵחַ
אֶלָּא אָתָּה · בָּרוּךְ אַתָּה יְיָ · מֶלֶךְ מוֹחֵל וְסוֹלֵחַ
לַעֲוֹנוֹתֵינוּ וְלַעֲוֹנוֹת עַמּוֹ בֵּית יִשְׂרָאֵל · וּמַעֲבִיר
אַשְׁמוֹתֵינוּ בְּכָל־שָׁנָה וְשָׁנָה · מֶלֶךְ עַל כָּל־הָאָרֶץ
מְקַדֵּשׁ [הַשַּׁבָּת וְ] יִשְׂרָאֵל וְיוֹם הַכִּפֻּרִים :

רְצֵה יְיָ אֱלֹהֵינוּ בְּעַמְּךָ יִשְׂרָאֵל וּבִתְפִלָּתָם · וְהָשֵׁב
אֶת־הָעֲבוֹדָה לִדְבִיר בֵּיתֶךָ וְאִשֵׁי יִשְׂרָאֵל וּתְפִלָּתָם
בְּאַהֲבָה תְקַבֵּל בְּרָצוֹן · וּתְהִי לְרָצוֹן תָּמִיד עֲבוֹדַת
יִשְׂרָאֵל עַמֶּךָ : וְתֶחֱזֶינָה עֵינֵינוּ בְּשׁוּבְךָ לְצִיּוֹן בְּרַחֲמִים ·
בָּרוּךְ אַתָּה יְיָ · הַמַּחֲזִיר שְׁכִינָתוֹ לְצִיּוֹן :

מוֹדִים אֲנַחְנוּ לָךְ שָׁאַתָּה הוּא יְיָ אֱלֹהֵינוּ
וֵאלֹהֵי אֲבוֹתֵינוּ לְעוֹלָם וָעֶד · צוּר חַיֵּינוּ מָגֵן יִשְׁעֵנוּ
אַתָּה הוּא לְדוֹר וָדוֹר · נוֹדֶה לְּךָ וּנְסַפֵּר תְּהִלָּתֶךָ
עַל־חַיֵּינוּ הַמְּסוּרִים בְּיָדֶךָ וְעַל נִשְׁמוֹתֵינוּ הַפְּקוּדוֹת
לָךְ · וְעַל נִסֶּיךָ שֶׁבְּכָל־יוֹם עִמָּנוּ וְעַל נִפְלְאוֹתֶיךָ
וְטוֹבוֹתֶיךָ שֶׁבְּכָל־עֵת עֶרֶב וָבֹקֶר וְצָהֳרָיִם · הַטּוֹב
כִּי לֹא־כָלוּ רַחֲמֶיךָ · וְהַמְרַחֵם כִּי לֹא־תַמּוּ חֲסָדֶיךָ
מֵעוֹלָם קִוִּינוּ לָךְ :

sanctify thy Name, rejoice thereon] ; and purify our hearts to serve thee in truth ; for thou art the Forgiver of Israel and the Pardoner of the tribes of Jeshurun in every generation, and beside thee we have no king who pardoneth and forgiveth. Blessed art thou, O Lord, thou King who pardonest and forgivest our iniquities and the iniquities of thy people, the house of Israel, who makest our transgressions to pass away year by year, King over all the earth, who hallowest [the Sabbath and] Israel and the Day of Atonement.

V. FOR THE TEMPLE SERVICE

See p. 461

Accept, O Lord our God, thy people Israel and their prayer ; restore the service to the inner sanctuary of thy house ; receive in love and favour both the fire-offerings of Israel and their prayer ; and may the service of thy people Israel be ever acceptable unto thee. And let our eyes behold thy return in mercy to Zion. Blessed art thou, O Lord, who restorest thy divine presence unto Zion.

VI. THANKS-GIVING FOR GOD'S UNFAIL-ING MERCIES

We give thanks unto thee, for thou' art the Lord our God and the God of our fathers for ever and ever ; thou art the Rock of our lives, the Shield of our salvation through every generation. We will give thanks unto thee and declare thy praise for our lives which are committed unto thy hand, and for our souls which are in thy charge, and for thy miracles, which are daily with us, and for thy wonders and thy benefits which are wrought at all times, evening, morn and noon. O thou who art all-good, whose mercies fail not ; thou, merciful Being, whose lovingkindnesses never cease, we have ever hoped in thee.

For all these things thy Name, O our King, shall be continually blessed and exalted for ever and ever.

O inscribe (*At the Conclusion Service, substitute* " O seal " *in place of* " O inscribe.") all the children of thy covenant for a happy life.

וְעַל־כֻּלָּם יִתְבָּרַךְ וְיִתְרוֹמַם שִׁמְךָ מַלְכֵּנוּ תָּמִיד לְעוֹלָם
וָעֶד :

וּכְתוֹב לְחַיִּים טוֹבִים כָּל־בְּנֵי בְרִיתֶךָ :

At *נְעִילָה*, substitute וַחֲתוֹם *in place of* וּכְתוֹב.

וְכֹל הַחַיִּים יוֹדוּךָ סֶּלָה • וִיהַלְלוּ אֶת־שִׁמְךָ בֶּאֱמֶת •
הָאֵל יְשׁוּעָתֵנוּ וְעֶזְרָתֵנוּ סֶלָה • בָּרוּךְ אַתָּה יְיָ • הַטּוֹב
שִׁמְךָ וּלְךָ נָאֶה לְהוֹדוֹת :

At the Services of שַׁחֲרִית, מִנְחָה, מוּסָף *and* נְעִילָה, *say:—*

שִׂים שָׁלוֹם טוֹבָה וּבְרָכָה חֵן וָחֶסֶד וְרַחֲמִים עָלֵינוּ
וְעַל כָּל יִשְׂרָאֵל עַמֶּךָ • בָּרְכֵנוּ אָבִינוּ כֻּלָּנוּ כְּאֶחָד בְּאוֹר
פָּנֶיךָ • כִּי בְאוֹר פָּנֶיךָ נָתַתָּ לָנוּ יְיָ אֱלֹהֵינוּ תּוֹרַת חַיִּים
וְאַהֲבַת חֶסֶד וּצְדָקָה וּבְרָכָה וְרַחֲמִים וְחַיִּים וְשָׁלוֹם •
וְטוֹב בְּעֵינֶיךָ לְבָרֵךְ אֶת־עַמְּךָ יִשְׂרָאֵל בְּכָל־עֵת וּבְכָל־
שָׁעָה בִּשְׁלוֹמֶךָ :

[*At the* מַעֲרִיב *Service say:—*

שָׁלוֹם רָב עַל יִשְׂרָאֵל עַמְּךָ תָּשִׂים לְעוֹלָם • כִּי
אַתָּה הוּא מֶלֶךְ אָדוֹן לְכָל הַשָּׁלוֹם • וְטוֹב בְּעֵינֶיךָ
לְבָרֵךְ אֶת־עַמְּךָ יִשְׂרָאֵל בְּכָל־עֵת וּבְכָל־שָׁעָה בִּשְׁלוֹמֶךָ •]

בְּסֵפֶר חַיִּים בְּרָכָה וְשָׁלוֹם וּפַרְנָסָה טוֹבָה נִזָּכֵר
וְנִכָּתֵב לְפָנֶיךָ אֲנַחְנוּ וְכָל־עַמְּךָ בֵּית יִשְׂרָאֵל לְחַיִּים
טוֹבִים וּלְשָׁלוֹם • בָּרוּךְ אַתָּה יְיָ • עוֹשֶׂה הַשָּׁלוֹם :

And everything that liveth shall give thanks unto thee for ever, and shall praise thy Name in truth, O God, our salvation and our help. Blessed art thou, O Lord, whose Name is All-good, and unto whom it is becoming to give thanks.

At the Morning, Afternoon, Additional, and Conclusion Services say:—

VII FOR PEACE

Grant peace, welfare, blessing, grace, lovingkindness and mercy unto us and unto all Israel, thy people. Bless us, O our Father, even all of us together, with the light of thy countenance ; for by the light of thy countenance thou hast given us, O Lord our God, the Torah of life, lovingkindness and righteousness, blessing, mercy, life and

See p. 465

peace ; and may it be good in thy sight to bless thy people Israel at all times and in every hour with thy peace.

[*At the Evening Service say :—*

Grant abundant peace unto Israel thy people for ever ; for thou art the sovereign Lord of all peace ; and may it be good in thy sight to bless thy people Israel at all times and at every hour with thy peace.]

In the book of life, blessing, peace and good sustenance may we be remembered and inscribed before thee, we and all thy people the house of Israel, for a happy life and for peace. Blessed art thou, O Lord, who makest peace.

CONFESSION (VIDDUY)

Confession is the characteristic feature of the Atonement Services. It was prescribed to the High Priest (Leviticus 16. 21) in the form of, " I have sinned, I have committed iniquity, I have transgressed ". Equally brief was the form of the Confession when it was first embodied in the Festival Amidah. Best known are the Confessions אבל אנחנו חטאנו (" Verily we have sinned ") by Mar Samuel (165–257); and אתה יודע רזי עולם (" Thou knowest the secrets of eternity ") by his companion Rabh. In time, the views of religious authorities prevailed who demanded an *enumeration* of concrete sins in confession. The prayer of Mar Samuel was then followed by the Shorter Litany of Confession אשמנו (" We are guilt-laden "), p. 907. Rabh's prayer was followed by the Longer Litany על חטא שחטאנו. (" For the sins we have sinned before Thee "), p. 911.

אֱלֹהֵינוּ וֵאלֹהֵי אֲבוֹתֵינוּ ·

תָּבֹא לְפָנֶיךָ תְּפִלָּתֵנוּ · וְאַל תִּתְעַלַּם מִתְּחִנָּתֵנוּ ·

שֶׁאֵין אֲנַחְנוּ עַזֵּי פָנִים וּקְשֵׁי עֹרֶף לוֹמַר לְפָנֶיךָ יְיָ

אֱלֹהֵינוּ וֵאלֹהֵי אֲבוֹתֵינוּ צַדִּיקִים אֲנַחְנוּ וְלֹא חָטָאנוּ

אֲבָל אֲנַחְנוּ חָטָאנוּ :

אָשַׁמְנוּ · בָּגַדְנוּ · גָּזַלְנוּ · דִּבַּרְנוּ דֹפִי :

הֶעֱוִינוּ · וְהִרְשַׁעְנוּ · זַדְנוּ · חָמַסְנוּ · טָפַלְנוּ שֶׁקֶר :

The Confession is part of the *public*, congregational, worship. This fact is of cardinal importance, because it prevented Jewish confession from ending in the establishment of the confessional. Judaism knows not private, auricular, confession to a priest who grants or obtains forgiveness for the sinner. Virtue is victory by the individual himself over temptation that assails him ; therefore, we ourselves must leave our sinful ways behind us and return unto God, and no one else can do it for us. "Judaism does not throw the burden of its sins on other shoulders, and it does not let the innocent expiate the actions of the guilty. In Judaism, there is no vicarious atonement. One's own guilt—one's own punishment ; no pardon, without true repentance" (Nahida Remy).

Furthermore, not only is the Jewish confession of sins on the Day of Atonement public and corporate, but it is phrased *in the plural*. "*We* are guilt-laden ; *we* have been faithless, *we* have robbed and spoken basely". "Why was the Confession arranged in the plural number", asked the great Mystic, Isaac Luria (1534–1572), "so that we say, We are guilt-laden, instead of, I am guilt-laden ? Because all Israel is one body, and every individual Israelite a member of that body. Hence follows mutual responsibility among all the members." In modern language, we associate ourselves in the guilt of forlorn and fallen souls, because we recognize *society* (*i.e.* we ourselves collectively) to be responsible for much of the crime and moral misery of our fellowmen. At any rate, few of us have attempted, or have been able. to prevent crimes and vices from being committed by others.

As to the kinds of sins confessed, he it noted that they are nearly everyone of them transgressions against *our fellow-men*. A large number are evil thoughts, failings, and sins against our *own higher nature*. Both the Shorter and Longer Confessions deal exclusively with ethical lapses.

VIII.
LITANIES
OF CON-
FESSION

Our God and God of our fathers, let our prayer come before thee ; hide not thyself from our supplication, for we are not so arrogant and hardened that we should say before thee, O Lord our God and God of our fathers, we are righteous and are sinless ; but verily, we have sinned.

"OSHAMNU"

SHORTER
CONFES-
SION

WE ARE GUILT-LADEN : WE HAVE BEEN FAITHLESS, WE HAVE ROBBED, AND WE HAVE SPOKEN BASELY ;
WE HAVE COMMITTED INIQUITY, AND CAUSED UN-RIGHTEOUSNESS ; WE HAVE BEEN PRESUMPTUOUS, DONE VIOLENCE, FRAMED FALSEHOOD ;
WE HAVE COUNSELLED EVIL, WE HAVE FAILED IN PROMISE, WE HAVE SCOFFED, REVOLTED, AND BLASPHEMED ;

There are some remarkable omissions. Thus, among the very many moral offences enumerated, no mention is made of brutal assaults, bestial cruelty, or murder. To the creators of these Confessions, as well as to the People who in all the centuries sought reconciliation with their Maker through them, these crimes of violence were in their eyes something so unspeakably horrible, that it appeared inconceivable how any Jew could be guilty of them.

In essence, both Confession prayers seem to date from the third century. The detailed enumerations are arranged alphabetically and eventually came to extend over the alphabet. This has been explained as due to the desire that Confession on behalf of a Community cover the whole gamut of human failing. But, in all probability, the alphabetic arrangement was rendered necessary as an aid to memory, seeing that books were not within the reach of the masses.

OUR GOD . . . *so arrogant.* If we were to declare that we are " righteous " and " sinless ", it would be worse than hypocrisy ; it would be arrogance and effrontery.

verily, we have sinned. " This is the root-phrase of the Confession ", said Mar Samuel. When a man has the courage to utter such words, he is on the road to self-emancipation from sin.

OSHAMNU. *we are guilt-laden.* אשמנו is here equivalent to אשמים ואנחנו . " Guilt " covers both *crime*, which is an assault on the personality of others ; and *vice*, which is an assault on our own personality.

faithless. Includes conduct such as repaying evil for good, or betraying the confidence placed in us.

we have robbed. Covers all manner of trespass on the rights of others.

spoken basely. Especially numerous in the Confessions are sins of the tongue. " Where is the person who could say that his tongue has never been employed in falsehood, slander, or self-praise ? " (Friedländer).

presumptuous. Defiant.

יָעַצְנוּ רָע · כִּזַּבְנוּ · לַצְנוּ · מָרַדְנוּ · נִאַצְנוּ ·

סָרַרְנוּ · עָוִינוּ · פָּשַׁעְנוּ · צָרַרְנוּ · קִשִּׁינוּ עֹרֶף :

רָשַׁעְנוּ · שִׁחַתְנוּ · תִּעַבְנוּ · תָּעִינוּ · תִּעְתָּעְנוּ :

סַרְנוּ מִמִּצְוֹתֶיךָ וּמִמִּשְׁפָּטֶיךָ הַטּוֹבִים וְלֹא שָׁוָה

לָנוּ · וְאַתָּה צַדִּיק עַל כָּל־הַבָּא עָלֵינוּ · כִּי אֱמֶת

עָשִׂיתָ וַאֲנַחְנוּ הִרְשָׁעְנוּ :

מַה־נֹּאמַר לְפָנֶיךָ יוֹשֵׁב מָרוֹם · וּמַה־נְּסַפֵּר לְפָנֶיךָ

שׁוֹכֵן שְׁחָקִים · הֲלֹא כָּל־הַנִּסְתָּרוֹת וְהַנִּגְלוֹת אַתָּה יוֹדֵעַ :

(At נְעִילָה *discontinue here, and proceed with* אַתָּה נוֹתֵן *,p.* 930.)

אַתָּה יוֹדֵעַ רָזֵי עוֹלָם · וְתַעֲלוּמוֹת סִתְרֵי כָל־חָי :

אַתָּה חוֹפֵשׂ כָּל חַדְרֵי בָטֶן וּבוֹחֵן כְּלָיוֹת וָלֵב : אֵין

דָּבָר נֶעְלָם מִמֶּךָּ · וְאֵין נִסְתָּר מִנֶּגֶד עֵינֶיךָ :

וּבְכֵן יְהִי רָצוֹן מִלְּפָנֶיךָ יְיָ אֱלֹהֵינוּ וֵאלֹהֵי אֲבוֹתֵינוּ ·

שֶׁתִּסְלַח־לָנוּ עַל כָּל חַטֹּאתֵינוּ · וְתִמְחָל־לָנוּ עַל כָּל

עֲוֹנוֹתֵינוּ · וּתְכַפֶּר־לָנוּ עַל כָּל פְּשָׁעֵינוּ :

counselled evil. Devised or planned evil.

scoffed. "The scoffer is of those who are not admitted into the presence of the Shechinah" (Talmud). The opening verse of the Book of Psalms declares the man blessed who shuns the company of scoffers.

revolted. Against religious authority and the ideals proclaimed by it.

stiff-necked. Stubborn in the wrong.

done wickedly. Hebrew רשענו ; we have been *reshoim* towards our fellow-men.

WE HAVE BEEN REBELLIOUS, WE HAVE ACTED PERVERSELY, WE HAVE TRANSGRESSED, OPPRESSED, AND BEEN STIFF-NECKED;

WE HAVE DONE WICKEDLY, WE HAVE CORRUPTED OURSELVES AND COMMITTED ABOMINATION; WE HAVE GONE ASTRAY, AND WE HAVE LED ASTRAY.

We have turned aside from thy commandments and good judgments, and it availed us nought. But thou art righteous in all that is come upon us; for thou hast acted truthfully, but we have wrought unrighteousness.

What shall we say before thee, O thou who dwellest on high, and what shall we recount unto thee, thou who abidest in the heavens? dost thou not know all things, both the hidden and the revealed?

(At the Conclusion Service, discontinue here, and proceed with, "Thou dost put forth," p. 931)

Thou knowest the secrets of eternity and the most hidden mysteries of all living. Thou searchest the innermost recesses, and dost test the feelings and the heart. Nought is concealed from thee, or hidden from thine eyes.

THE LONGER CONFES-SION

May it then be thy will, O Lord our God and God of our fathers, to forgive us for all our sins, to pardon us for all our iniquities, and to grant us remission for all our transgressions.

---

gone astray. Wandered, like lost sheep. from the path of rectitude and purity.

we have led astray. The height of iniquity. We have caused others to sin through our example; see on Sayings of the Fathers v, 21, p. 698.

it availed us nought. Or, " it was not meet for us "; *i.e.* it was unworthy of us.

Thou knowest the secrets. This and the following brief paragraphs constituted the Confession of Rabh.

עַל חֵטְא שֶׁחָטָאנוּ לְפָנֶיךָ בְּאֹנֶם וּבְרָצוֹן:

וְעַל חֵטְא שֶׁחָטָאנוּ לְפָנֶיךָ בְּאִמּוּץ הַלֵּב:

עַל חֵטְא שֶׁחָטָאנוּ לְפָנֶיךָ בִּבְלִי דָעַת:

וְעַל חֵטְא שֶׁחָטָאנוּ לְפָנֶיךָ בְּבִטּוּי שְׂפָתָיִם:

עַל חֵטְא שֶׁחָטָאנוּ לְפָנֶיךָ בְּגִלּוּי עֲרָיוֹת:

וְעַל חֵטְא שֶׁחָטָאנוּ לְפָנֶיךָ בְּגָלוּי וּבַסָּתֶר:

עַל חֵטְא שֶׁחָטָאנוּ לְפָנֶיךָ בְּדַעַת וּבְמִרְמָה:

וְעַל חֵטְא שֶׁחָטָאנוּ לְפָנֶיךָ בְּדִבּוּר פֶּה:

עַל חֵטְא שֶׁחָטָאנוּ לְפָנֶיךָ בְּהוֹנָאַת רֵעַ:

וְעַל חֵטְא שֶׁחָטָאנוּ לְפָנֶיךָ בְּהַרְהוֹר הַלֵּב:

עַל חֵטְא שֶׁחָטָאנוּ לְפָנֶיךָ בִּוְעִידַת זְנוּת:

וְעַל חֵטְא שֶׁחָטָאנוּ לְפָנֶיךָ בְּוִדּוּי פֶּה:

AL CHET, *For the sin which.* This Longer Confession consists in our Rite of two clauses for each letter of the Hebrew alphabet.

compulsion . . . our own will. Very often a transgression that begins as a matter of *force majeure*, ends as a voluntary action.

hardening of the heart. When we repress the stirrings of conscience and the nobler promptings of our better nature. Unholy action then becomes habitual, and is soon performed deliberately.

utterance of the lips. Irreverent talk, or words that tarnish the good name of a fellow-being.

in speech. Even though the words spoken may be true.
" A truth that's told with bad intent
  Beats all the lies you can invent " (Blake).

" AL
CHET "

THE
LONGER
CON-
FESSION

For the sin which we have committed before thee under compulsion, or of our own will ;

And for the sin which we have committed before thee in hardening of the heart :

For the sin which we have committed before thee out of ignorance ;

And for the sin which we have committed before thee with utterance of the lips :

For the sin which we have committed before thee by unchastity ;

And for the sin which we have committed before thee openly and secretly :

For the sin which we have committed before thee by deliberate deceit :

And for the sin which we have committed before thee in speech :

For the sin which we have committed before thee by wronging our neighbour ;

And for the sin which we have committed before thee by the sinful meditating of the heart :

For the sin which we have committed before thee by association with impurity ;

And for the sin which we have committed before thee by confession with the mouth alone :

---

wronging our neighbour. Overreaching him. Perhaps the reference is here to wounding a fellow-man's feelings by unkind words or insulting epithets ; see *Leviticus,* 208 (Soncino, 504).

sinful meditating. " Habitual meditation on forbidden things may become as harmful as a casual transgression " (Talmud). Sinful brooding has a most corrupting effect on human character, and may lead to abominable crimes ; see p. 934.

עַל חֵטְא שֶׁחָטָאנוּ לְפָנֶיךָ בְּזִלְזוּל הוֹרִים וּמוֹרִים :

וְעַל חֵטְא שֶׁחָטָאנוּ לְפָנֶיךָ בְּזָדוֹן וּבִשְׁגָגָה :

עַל חֵטְא שֶׁחָטָאנוּ לְפָנֶיךָ בְּחֹזֶק יָד :

וְעַל חֵטְא שֶׁחָטָאנוּ לְפָנֶיךָ בְּחִלּוּל הַשֵּׁם :

עַל חֵטְא שֶׁחָטָאנוּ לְפָנֶיךָ בְּטֻמְאַת שְׂפָתָיִם :

וְעַל חֵטְא שֶׁחָטָאנוּ לְפָנֶיךָ בְּטִפְשׁוּת פֶּה :

עַל חֵטְא שֶׁחָטָאנוּ לְפָנֶיךָ בְּיֵצֶר הָרָע :

וְעַל חֵטְא שֶׁחָטָאנוּ לְפָנֶיךָ בְּיוֹדְעִים וּבְלֹא יוֹדְעִים :

וְעַל כֻּלָּם אֱלוֹהַּ סְלִיחוֹת סְלַח־לָנוּ · מְחַל־לָנוּ · כַּפֶּר־לָנוּ :

עַל חֵטְא שֶׁחָטָאנוּ לְפָנֶיךָ בְּכַחַשׁ וּבְכָזָב :

וְעַל חֵטְא שֶׁחָטָאנוּ לְפָנֶיךָ בְּכַפַּת־שֹׁחַד :

עַל חֵטְא שֶׁחָטָאנוּ לְפָנֶיךָ בְּלָצוֹן :

despising parents. There are few mortals who, on looking back upon their lives, feel that they have worthily repaid the immeasurable debt they owe to their parents.

and teachers. Contempt for religious teachers, past or present, is a stain on the character of him who is guilty of it ; and even more so, when a community is the offender.

by violence. By playing the " strong man " to those who are too weak to defend themselves. The Hebrew term is synonymous with " robbery ", and covers all appropriation of wealth by unlawful means.

profanation of the divine Name. By actions that leave a stain on the fair name of Judaism and the Jew. " Every Israelite holds the honour of his Faith and People in his hands "

For the sin which we have committed before thee by
despising parents and teachers ;

And for the sin which we have committed before thee
presumptuously or in error :

For the sin which we have committed before thee by
violence ;

And for the sin which we have committed before thee by
the profanation of the Divine Name :

For the sin which we have committed before thee by
impurity of lips ;

And for the sin which we have committed before thee by
folly of the mouth :

For the sin which we have committed before thee by the
evil inclination ;

And for the sin which we have committed before thee
wittingly or unwittingly :

FOR ALL THESE, O GOD OF FORGIVENESS, FORGIVE
US, PARDON US, GRANT US REMISSION.

For the sin which we have committed before thee by
deliberate lying ;

And for the sin which we have committed before thee by
bribery :

For the sin which we have committed before thee by
scoffing ;

impurity of lips. Obscene talk is a sign of low morality and mentality.

evil inclination. i.e. our passions. When harnessed to high causes, and
under the restraint and guidance of Religion, the passions lead to
greatness. When they are unharnessed, and have become our masters,
they lead to utter degradation and destruction ; see p. 25. " The
wicked are in the power of their desires ; the righteous have their
desires in their power " (Talmud).

wittingly, unwittingly. The Hebrew wording may mean, with or
without the knowledge of those who suffer through our wrong conduct.

FOR ALL THESE. Only in the Ashkenazi Rite does this Response
divide into three parts the recitation of the Longer Confession.

bribery. Either in taking, or in giving, bribes.

וְעַל חֵטְא שֶׁחָטָאנוּ לְפָנֶיךָ בִּלְשׁוֹן הָרָע:

עַל חֵטְא שֶׁחָטָאנוּ לְפָנֶיךָ בְּמַשָּׂא וּבְמַתָּן:

וְעַל חֵטְא שֶׁחָטָאנוּ לְפָנֶיךָ בְּמַאֲכָל וּבְמִשְׁתֶּה:

עַל חֵטְא שֶׁחָטָאנוּ לְפָנֶיךָ בְּנֶשֶׁךְ וּבְמַרְבִּית:

וְעַל חֵטְא שֶׁחָטָאנוּ לְפָנֶיךָ בִּנְטִיַּת גָּרוֹן:

עַל חֵטְא שֶׁחָטָאנוּ לְפָנֶיךָ בְּשִׂיחַ שִׂפְתוֹתֵינוּ:

וְעַל חֵטְא שֶׁחָטָאנוּ לְפָנֶיךָ בְּשִׁקּוּר עָיִן:

עַל חֵטְא שֶׁחָטָאנוּ לְפָנֶיךָ בְּעֵינַיִם רָמוֹת:

וְעַל חֵטְא שֶׁחָטָאנוּ לְפָנֶיךָ בְּעַזּוּת מֵצַח:

slander. Few escape this sin, or at least that of uncharitable talk against their neighbours. The Rabbis class anyone addicted to slander among those who are almost " beyond repentance ". Others in that group are: " He who says, I will sin and repent, I will sin and repent; he who exalts himself by disgracing others; he who sees his children embracing a depraved life, and he does not protest; he who suspects upright men; and he who misleads the many ". While these delinquencies do not make repentance impossible, they certainly render it improbable.

in business. " On the day of Judgment, the first question to be asked of a man will be, Have thy business dealings been honourable " ? (Talmud). Jewish merchants are, as a rule, no better and no worse than their non-Jewish fellows. But among Jewish merchants there are extremes—those who transcend the letter of the law, and those who fall below it. The doings of the latter class are public knowledge, but little is heard of the former class. Thus, the saintly Russian rabbi known as the " Chofetz Chayim " (1838–1933) earned his living, like the Teachers of old, by following some humble handicraft or avocation. He opened a shop to sell herrings; but, finding that all the people of the village came to buy from *him*, so that the other fishmongers lost their custom, he shut his

LONGER
CON-
FESSION

And for the sin which we have committed before thee by slander :

For the sin which we have committed before thee in business ;

And for the sin which we have committed before thee in meat and drink :

For the sin which we have committed before thee by extortion and usury ;

And for the sin which we have committed before thee by the stretched forth neck of pride ;

For the sin which we have committed before thee by the conversation of our lips ;

And for the sin which we have committed before thee with wanton looks :

For the sin which we have committed before thee with haughty eyes ;

And for the sin which we have committed before thee by effrontery :

---

shop. " It is not fair competition ", he said. He became an itinerant bookseller in distant towns, never making known who he was, so as not to derive material advantage from his vast erudition in the Torah.

extortion and usury. Money transactions were forced upon the Jews in the early Middle Ages, because all other occupations were closed to them. They proved themselves far less guilty of extortion than their non-Jewish competitors. In modern times, they tend more and more to spheres of activity other than those of finance.

pride. Pride easily turns into forms exciting amusement or resentment; such as *vanity* and *conceit* (exaggerated self-esteem), or *arrogance,* (a scorn for all the world beside oneself). The prophet Micah declares " walking humbly with God " to be one-third of religion. "Meekness of spirit is the halo of the wise" (Joseph Kimchi). " Everything heroic in man is insignificant and perishable, and all his wisdom and virtue unable to stand the crucial test, unless they are founded on humility. In this there is no exception—neither for any man, any people, or an age " (Hermann Cohen).

effrontery. Shameless conduct towards others. Rabbi Judah the Prince daily prayed (p. 26) to be saved from insolent men who are devoid of reverence and human decency towards their fellow-men.

וְעַל כֻּלָּם אֱלוֹהַּ סְלִיחוֹת סְלַח־לָנוּ · מְחַל־לָנוּ · כַּפֶּר־לָנוּ ׃

עַל חֵטְא שֶׁחָטָאנוּ לְפָנֶיךָ בִּפְרִיקַת עֹל ׃

וְעַל חֵטְא שֶׁחָטָאנוּ לְפָנֶיךָ בִּפְלִילוּת ׃

עַל חֵטְא שֶׁחָטָאנוּ לְפָנֶיךָ בִּצְדִיַּת רֵעַ ׃

וְעַל חֵטְא שֶׁחָטָאנוּ לְפָנֶיךָ בְּצָרוּת עָיִן ׃

עַל חֵטְא שֶׁחָטָאנוּ לְפָנֶיךָ בְּקַלּוּת רֹאשׁ ׃

וְעַל חֵטְא שֶׁחָטָאנוּ לְפָנֶיךָ בְּקַשְׁיוּת עֹרֶף ׃

עַל חֵטְא שֶׁחָטָאנוּ לְפָנֶיךָ בְּרִיצַת רַגְלַיִם לְהָרַע ׃

וְעַל חֵטְא שֶׁחָטָאנוּ לְפָנֶיךָ בִּרְכִילוּת ׃

עַל חֵטְא שֶׁחָטָאנוּ לְפָנֶיךָ בִּשְׁבוּעַת שָׁוְא ׃

וְעַל חֵטְא שֶׁחָטָאנוּ לְפָנֶיךָ בְּשִׂנְאַת חִנָּם ׃

breaking off the yoke. Revolt against Religion and its discipline.

hasty condemnation. Some translate " contentiousness ". But the word פלילות denotes, " playing the judge ", and delight in passing sentence. Instead of judging our neighbour charitably, " in the scale of merit ", we pronounce hasty condemnation on his life and actions.

envy. A selfish and malevolent emotion. Like jealousy, it means hatred of the person envied, and a desire to harm him. The Hebrew term for envy is עין הרע, " the evil eye," the eye that sees only evil in others. Envy shortens man's life ; see p. 641.

FOR ALL THESE, O GOD OF FORGIVENESS, FORGIVE US, PARDON US, GRANT US REMISSION

For the sin which we have committed before thee by breaking off the yoke of thy commandments ;

And for the sin which we have committed before thee by hasty condemnation :

For the sin which we have committed before thee by ensnaring our neighbour ;

And for the sin which we have committed before thee by envy :

For the sin which we have committed before thee by levity ;

And for the sin which we have committed before thee by being stiff-necked :

For the sin which we have committed before thee by running to do evil ;

And for the sin which we have committed before thee by tale-bearing :

For the sin which we have committed before thee by vain oaths ;

And for the sin which we have committed before thee by causeless hatred :

levity. Serious things should be treated seriously. " Levity is the door to lewdness ", said Rabbi Akiba ; see p. 659.

stiff-necked. The stubborn are often feeble of will in the defence of Faith or principle.

causeless hatred. Wanton hatred—hatred for its own sake—is a mortal sin, especially so when displayed in hating the person whom *we have wronged.*

The first Temple fell because of the sins of idolatry, immorality and bloodshed. The Second Temple, despite the fact that the Torah was studied and good deeds performed in its day, fell on account of causeless hatred. This teaches that causeless hatred is as grievous a sin as idolatry, immorality and bloodshed (Talmud).

עַל חֵטְא שֶׁחָטָאנוּ לְפָנֶיךָ בִּתְשׂוּמֶת יָד:

וְעַל חֵטְא שֶׁחָטָאנוּ לְפָנֶיךָ בִּתִמְהוֹן לֵבָב:

וְעַל כֻּלָּם אֱלוֹהַּ סְלִיחוֹת סְלַח-לָנוּ · מְחַל-לָנוּ · כַּפֶּר-לָנוּ:

וְעַל חֲטָאִים שֶׁאָנוּ חַיָּבִים עֲלֵיהֶם עוֹלָה:

וְעַל חֲטָאִים שֶׁאָנוּ חַיָּבִים עֲלֵיהֶם חַטָּאת:

וְעַל חֲטָאִים שֶׁאָנוּ חַיָּבִים עֲלֵיהֶם קָרְבָּן עוֹלֶה וְיוֹרֵד:

וְעַל חֲטָאִים שֶׁאָנוּ חַיָּבִים עֲלֵיהֶם אָשָׁם וַדַּאי וְתָלוּי:

וְעַל חֲטָאִים שֶׁאָנוּ חַיָּבִים עֲלֵיהֶם מַכַּת מַרְדּוּת:

וְעַל חֲטָאִים שֶׁאָנוּ חַיָּבִים עֲלֵיהֶם מַלְקוּת אַרְבָּעִים:

וְעַל חֲטָאִים שֶׁאָנוּ חַיָּבִים עֲלֵיהֶם מִיתָה בִּידֵי שָׁמָיִם:

וְעַל חֲטָאִים שֶׁאָנוּ חַיָּבִים עֲלֵיהֶם כָּרֵת וַעֲרִירוּת:

וְעַל כֻּלָּם אֱלוֹהַּ סְלִיחוֹת סְלַח-לָנוּ · מְחַל-לָנוּ · כַּפֶּר-לָנוּ:

וְעַל חֲטָאִים שֶׁאָנוּ חַיָּבִים עֲלֵיהֶם אַרְבַּע מִיתוֹת בֵּית דִּין ·

סְקִילָה · שְׂרֵפָה · הֶרֶג · וְחֶנֶק · עַל מִצְוֹת עֲשֵׂה ·

---

breach of trust. As when we fail to hand on to future generations the spiritual treasures that were entrusted to us by our parents to transmit.

confusion of mind. lit. " consternation of the heart " ; *i.e.* cowardice, through lack of conviction. The remedy is, " Provide thyself a teacher " (p. 619), and be quit of doubt and confusion in matters of vital and eternal moment.

For the sin which we have committed before thee by breach of trust ;

And for the sin which we have committed before thee with confusion of mind :

> FOR ALL THESE, O GOD OF FORGIVENESS, FORGIVE US, PARDON US, GRANT US REMISSION.

And also for the sins for which we owe a burnt offering :

And for the sins for which we owe a sin offering :

And for the sins for which we owe an offering, varying according to our means :

And for the sins for which we owe an offering, whether for certain or for doubtful trespass.

And for the sins for which we are liable to the penalty of chastisement :

And for the sins for which we are liable to the penalty of forty stripes :

And for the sins for which we are liable to the penalty of death by the hand of heaven :

And for the sins for which we are liable to the penalty of excision and childlessness :

> FOR ALL THESE, O GOD OF FORGIVENESS, FORGIVE US, PARDON US, GRANT US REMISSION :

And also for the sins for which we are liable to any of the four death penalties inflicted by the court,—stoning, burning, beheading, and strangling ; for the violation of

---

AND ALSO . . . BURNT OFFERING. This enumeration of sins according to the punishments attaching to them, probably goes back to Temple days.

וְעַל־מִצְוַת לֹא תַעֲשֶׂה · בֵּין שֶׁיֶּשׁ־בָּהּ קוּם עֲשֵׂה ·
וּבֵין שֶׁאֵין בָּהּ קוּם עֲשֵׂה · אֶת־הַגְּלוּיִם לָנוּ וְאֶת־
שֶׁאֵינָם גְּלוּיִם לָנוּ : אֶת־הַגְּלוּיִם לָנוּ כְּבָר אֲמַרְנוּם
לְפָנֶיךָ · וְהוֹדִינוּ לְךָ עֲלֵיהֶם · וְאֶת־שֶׁאֵינָם גְּלוּיִם לָנוּ
לְפָנֶיךָ הֵם גְּלוּיִם וִידוּעִים · כַּדָּבָר שֶׁנֶּאֱמַר הַנִּסְתָּרֹת
לַיְיָ אֱלֹהֵינוּ · וְהַנִּגְלֹת לָנוּ וּלְבָנֵינוּ עַד־עוֹלָם · לַעֲשׂוֹת
אֶת־כָּל־דִּבְרֵי הַתּוֹרָה הַזֹּאת : כִּי אַתָּה סָלְחָן לְיִשְׂרָאֵל
וּמְחָלָן לְשִׁבְטֵי יְשֻׁרוּן בְּכָל דּוֹר וָדוֹר · וּמִבַּלְעָדֶיךָ אֵין
לָנוּ מֶלֶךְ מוֹחֵל וְסוֹלֵחַ אֶלָּא אָתָּה :

אֱלֹהַי · עַד שֶׁלֹּא נוֹצַרְתִּי אֵינִי כְדַי · וְעַכְשָׁו שֶׁנּוֹצַרְתִּי
כְּאִלּוּ לֹא נוֹצַרְתִּי · עָפָר אֲנִי בְּחַיַּי · קַל וָחֹמֶר בְּמִיתָתִי ·
הֲרֵי אֲנִי לְפָנֶיךָ כִּכְלִי מָלֵא בוּשָׁה וּכְלִמָּה · יְהִי רָצוֹן
מִלְּפָנֶיךָ יְיָ אֱלֹהַי וֵאלֹהֵי אֲבוֹתַי שֶׁלֹּא אֶחֱטָא עוֹד ·
וּמַה שֶּׁחָטָאתִי לְפָנֶיךָ מָרֵק בְּרַחֲמֶיךָ הָרַבִּים · אֲבָל לֹא
עַל יְדֵי יִסּוּרִים וָחֳלָיִים רָעִים :

---

affirmative . . . negative precepts. 'Thou shalt' and 'Thou shalt
not' commandments.

admit of a remedy. The transgression of some prohibitions cannot be
rectified by any subsequent act of the offender; *e.g.* eating leavened
bread on Passover. Contrariwise, the transgression of a law, such as
Deuteronomy 22. 6, 7, forbidding the rifling of a bird's nest and taking
the mother with the young, can be rectified by letting the mother go
free.

affirmative, or for the violation of negative precepts, whether these latter do, or do not, admit of a remedy by the subsequent fulfilment of an affirmative command ; for all our sins, whether they be or be not manifest to us. Such sins as are manifest to us, we have already declared and confessed unto thee; while such as are not manifest unto us, are manifest and known unto thee, according to the word *Deuteronomy* that hath been spoken, The secret things belong unto 29. 28 the Lord our God ; but the things that are revealed belong unto us and to our children for ever, that we may do all the words of this Torah. For thou art the Forgiver of Israel and the Pardoner of the tribes of Jeshurun in every generation, and beside thee we have no king, who pardoneth and forgiveth.

CLOSING CONFES- SION O my God, before I was formed I was nought; and now that I have been formed, I am but as though I had not been formed. Dust am I in my life : how much more so in my death. Behold I am before thee like a vessel filled with shame and confusion. O may it be thy will, O Lord my God and God of my fathers, that I may sin no more, and as to the sins I have committed, purge them away in thine abounding compassion, though not by means of affliction and sore diseases.

BEFORE I WAS FORMED. This was the formula of Confession used by Rabbi Hamnuna, a Babylonian teacher of the end of the third century. *not by* . . . *sore diseases.* As those would incapacitate us for obeying the will of God in the performance of domestic, communal and civil duties.

אֱלֹהַי · נְצוֹר לְשׁוֹנִי מֵרָע וּשְׂפָתַי מִדַּבֵּר מִרְמָה ·
וְלִמְקַלְלַי נַפְשִׁי תִדּוֹם וְנַפְשִׁי כֶּעָפָר לַכֹּל תִּהְיֶה : פְּתַח
לִבִּי בְּתוֹרָתֶךָ וּבְמִצְוֹתֶיךָ תִּרְדּוֹף נַפְשִׁי · וְכֹל הַחוֹשְׁבִים
עָלַי רָעָה מְהֵרָה הָפֵר עֲצָתָם וְקַלְקֵל מַחֲשְׁבוֹתָם · עֲשֵׂה
לְמַעַן שְׁמֶךָ עֲשֵׂה לְמַעַן יְמִינֶךָ עֲשֵׂה לְמַעַן קְדֻשָּׁתֶךָ
עֲשֵׂה לְמַעַן תּוֹרָתֶךָ · לְמַעַן יֵחָלְצוּן יְדִידֶיךָ הוֹשִׁיעָה
יְמִינְךָ וַעֲנֵנִי : יִהְיוּ לְרָצוֹן אִמְרֵי־פִי וְהֶגְיוֹן לִבִּי
לְפָנֶיךָ יְיָ צוּרִי וְגֹאֲלִי : עֹשֶׂה שָׁלוֹם בִּמְרוֹמָיו הוּא
יַעֲשֶׂה שָׁלוֹם עָלֵינוּ וְעַל כָּל־יִשְׂרָאֵל · וְאִמְרוּ אָמֵן :

יְהִי רָצוֹן לְפָנֶיךָ יְיָ אֱלֹהֵינוּ וֵאלֹהֵי אֲבוֹתֵינוּ שֶׁיִּבָּנֶה בֵּית
הַמִּקְדָּשׁ בִּמְהֵרָה בְיָמֵינוּ · וְתֵן חֶלְקֵנוּ בְּתוֹרָתֶךָ : וְשָׁם נַעֲבָדְךָ
בְּיִרְאָה כִּימֵי עוֹלָם וּכְשָׁנִים קַדְמוֹנִיּוֹת : וְעָרְבָה לַיְיָ מִנְחַת
יְהוּדָה וִירוּשָׁלָָם כִּימֵי עוֹלָם וּכְשָׁנִים הַקַּדְמוֹנִיּוֹת :

During the Evening and Morning Services, אָבִינוּ מַלְכֵּנוּ, *pp.* 163–167,
is said, *except when the Day of Atonement falls on a Sabbath.*

CONCLUD-
ING ME-
DITATION

See p. 466

Psalm 60. 7

Psalm 19. 15

O my God ! guard my tongue from evil and my lips from speaking guile ; and to such as curse me let my soul be dumb, yea, let my soul be unto all as the dust. Open my heart to thy Torah, and let my soul pursue thy commandments. If any design evil against me, speedily make their counsel of none effect, and frustrate their designs. Do it for the sake of thy Name, do it for the sake of thy power, do it for the sake of thy holiness, do it for the sake of thy Torah. In order, that thy beloved ones may be delivered, O save with thy power, and answer me. Let the words of my mouth and the meditation of my heart be acceptable before thee, O Lord, my Rock and my Redeemer. He who maketh peace in his high places, may he make peace for us and for all Israel, and say ye, Amen.

May it be thy will, O Lord our God and God of our fathers that the temple be speedily rebuilt in our days, and grant our portion in thy Torah. And there we will serve thee with awe, as in the days of old, and as in ancient years. Then shall the offering of Judah and Jerusalem be pleasant unto the Lord, as in the days of old, and as in ancient years.

During the Evening and Morning Services, " Our Father, our King," pp. 163–167 is said, except when the Day of Atonement falls on a Sabbath.

SCRIPTURAL READINGS

The Reading in the Morning Service is Leviticus 16, that describes the institution of the Day of Atonement. The Rabbis ordained that the Haftorah be Isaiah 57. 14–58. 14. It is a Prophetic admonition as to the life of righteousness—justice to the oppressed, and kindness to the destitute—that must accompany fasting and worship.

תפלת מוסף ליום כפור:

אֲדֹנָי שְׂפָתַי *For the commencement of the* עֲמִידָה, *see p.* 894, *from* to הַקָּדוֹשׁ, *p.* 898. *Then continue, adding on* שַׁבָּת *the words in brackets.*

וַתִּתֶּן־לָנוּ יְיָ אֱלֹהֵינוּ בְּאַהֲבָה אֶת־יוֹם [הַשַּׁבָּת הַזֶּה

לִקְדֻשָּׁה וְלִמְנוּחָה וְאֶת יוֹם] הַכִּפֻּרִים הַזֶּה לִמְחִילָה

וְלִסְלִיחָה וּלְכַפָּרָה וְלִמְחָל־בּוֹ אֶת־כָּל־עֲוֹנֹתֵינוּ [בְּאַהֲבָה]

מִקְרָא קֹדֶשׁ זֵכֶר לִיצִיאַת מִצְרָיִם :

וּמִפְּנֵי חֲטָאֵינוּ גָּלִינוּ מֵאַרְצֵנוּ וְנִתְרַחַקְנוּ מֵעַל אַדְמָתֵנוּ

וְאֵין אֲנַחְנוּ יְכוֹלִים לַעֲשׂוֹת חוֹבוֹתֵינוּ בְּבֵית בְּחִירָתֶךָ

בַּבַּיִת הַגָּדוֹל וְהַקָּדוֹשׁ שֶׁנִּקְרָא שִׁמְךָ עָלָיו מִפְּנֵי הַיָּד

שֶׁנִּשְׁתַּלְּחָה בְּמִקְדָּשֶׁךָ :

יְהִי רָצוֹן מִלְּפָנֶיךָ יְיָ אֱלֹהֵינוּ וֵאלֹהֵי אֲבוֹתֵינוּ מֶלֶךְ

רַחֲמָן שֶׁתָּשׁוּב וּתְרַחֵם עָלֵינוּ וְעַל מִקְדָּשְׁךָ בְּרַחֲמֶיךָ

הָרַבִּים וְתִבְנֵהוּ מְהֵרָה וּתְגַדֵּל כְּבוֹדוֹ : אָבִינוּ מַלְכֵּנוּ •

גַּלֵּה כְּבוֹד מַלְכוּתְךָ עָלֵינוּ מְהֵרָה וְהוֹפַע וְהִנָּשֵׂא עָלֵינוּ

לְעֵינֵי כָּל־חָי וְקָרֵב פְּזוּרֵינוּ מִבֵּין הַגּוֹיִם וּנְפוּצוֹתֵינוּ כַּנֵּס

מִיַּרְכְּתֵי־אָרֶץ • וַהֲבִיאֵנוּ לְצִיּוֹן עִירְךָ בְּרִנָּה וְלִירוּשָׁלַיִם

בֵּית מִקְדָּשְׁךָ בְּשִׂמְחַת עוֹלָם וְשָׁם נַעֲשֶׂה לְפָנֶיךָ אֶת

קָרְבְּנוֹת חוֹבוֹתֵינוּ תְּמִידִים כְּסִדְרָם וּמוּסָפִים כְּהִלְכָתָם :

וְאֶת מוּסַף יוֹם [הַשַּׁבָּת הַזֶּה וְאֶת מוּסַף יוֹם] הַכִּפֻּרִים

ADDITIONAL SERVICE FOR THE DAY OF ATONEMENT

For the commencement of the Amidah see p. 895, *from " O Lord, open thou my lips " to " holy Name," p.* 899. *Then continue (adding on Sabbath the words in brackets)* :—

FESTIVAL BENEDIC- TION   And thou hast given us in love, O Lord our God, [this Sabbath day for holiness and rest, and] this day of Atonement for pardon, forgiveness and atonement, that we may [in love] obtain pardon thereon for all our iniquities ; a holy con- vocation, as a memorial of the departure from Egypt.

" RENEW OUR DAYS AS OF OLD   But on account of our sins we were exiled from our land, and removed far from our country, and we are unable to fulfil our obligations in thy chosen house, that great and holy temple which was called by thy Name, because of the hand of violence that hath been laid upon thy sanctuary.

  May it be thy will, O Lord our God and God of our fathers, merciful King, that thou mayest again in thine abundant compassion have mercy upon us and upon thy sanctuary, and mayest speedily rebuild and magnify its glory. Our Father, our King, do thou speedily make the glory of thy kingdom manifest upon us ; shine forth and exalt thyself upon us in the sight of all living ; bring our scattered ones among the nations near unto thee, and gather our dispersed from the ends of the earth. Lead us with exultation unto Zion thy city, and unto Jerusalem the place of thy sanctuary, with everlasting joy ; and there we will prepare before thee the offerings that are obligatory for us, the daily offerings according to their order, and the additional offerings according to their enactment ; and the additional offerings of [this Sabbath day and] this Day of

הַזֶּה · נַעֲשֶׂה וְנַקְרִיב לְפָנֶיךָ בְּאַהֲבָה כְּמִצְוַת רְצוֹנֶךָ

כְּמוֹ שֶׁכָּתַבְתָּ עָלֵינוּ בְּתוֹרָתֶךָ עַל יְדֵי מֹשֶׁה עַבְדֶּךָ מִפִּי

כְבוֹדֶךָ כָּאָמוּר :

[וּבְיוֹם הַשַּׁבָּת שְׁנֵי־כְבָשִׂים בְּנֵי־שָׁנָה תְּמִימִם וּשְׁנֵי עֶשְׂרֹנִים

סֹלֶת מִנְחָה בְּלוּלָה בַשֶּׁמֶן וְנִסְכּוֹ : עֹלַת שַׁבַּת בְּשַׁבַּתּוֹ עַל־

עֹלַת הַתָּמִיד וְנִסְכָּהּ :]

וּבֶעָשׂוֹר לַחֹדֶשׁ הַשְּׁבִיעִי הַזֶּה מִקְרָא־קֹדֶשׁ יִהְיֶה לָכֶם

וְעִנִּיתֶם אֶת־נַפְשֹׁתֵיכֶם כָּל־מְלָאכָה לֹא תַעֲשׂוּ : וְהִקְרַבְתֶּם

עֹלָה לַייָ רֵיחַ נִיחֹחַ פַּר בֶּן־בָּקָר אֶחָד אַיִל אֶחָד כְּבָשִׂים

בְּנֵי־שָׁנָה שִׁבְעָה תְּמִימִם יִהְיוּ לָכֶם : וּמִנְחָתָם וְנִסְכֵּיהֶם

כִּמְדֻבָּר שְׁלֹשָׁה עֶשְׂרֹנִים לַפָּר · שְׁנֵי עֶשְׂרֹנִים לָאַיִל ·

וְעִשָּׂרוֹן לַכֶּבֶשׂ · וְיַיִן כְּנִסְכּוֹ וּשְׁנֵי שְׂעִירִים לְכַפֵּר · וּשְׁנֵי

תְמִידִים כְּהִלְכָתָם :

[וְיִשְׂמְחוּ בְמַלְכוּתְךָ שׁוֹמְרֵי שַׁבָּת וְקוֹרְאֵי עֹנֶג · עַם מְקַדְּשֵׁי

שְׁבִיעִי כֻּלָּם יִשְׂבְּעוּ וְיִתְעַנְּגוּ מִטּוּבֶךָ · וְהַשְּׁבִיעִי רָצִיתָ בּוֹ

וְקִדַּשְׁתּוֹ חֶמְדַּת יָמִים אֹתוֹ קָרָאתָ זֵכֶר לְמַעֲשֵׂה בְרֵאשִׁית :]

Continue מָחַל⋯⋯אֱלֹהֵינוּ, עֲמִידָה p. 898, to the end of the p. 922.

For the Blessing of the Priests when יוֹם כִּפּוּר falls on a weekday,

see p. 834.

Atonement we will prepare and offer unto thee in love according to the precept of thy will, as thou hast prescribed for us in thy Torah through the hand of Moses thy servant, from the mouth of thy glory ; as it is said :—

Numbers 28. 9   [And on the Sabbath day two he-lambs of the first year without blemish, and two tenth parts of an ephah of fine flour for a meal offering, mingled with oil, and the drink offering thereof ; this is the burnt offering of every Sabbath, beside the daily burnt offering and the drink offering thereof.]

Numbers 29. 7   And on the tenth day of this seventh month there shall be a holy convocation unto you ; and ye shall afflict your *Numbers* 29. 8 souls, ye shall do no manner of work. And ye shall offer a burnt offering unto the Lord for a sweet savour ; one young bullock, one ram, seven he-lambs of the first year ; they shall be unto you without blemish. And their meal offering and their drink offerings as hath been ordained ; three tenth parts of an ephah for each bullock, and two tenth parts for the ram, and one tenth part for each lamb, with wine according to the drink offering thereof, and two he-goats wherewith to make atonement, and the two daily offerings according to their enactment.

[They that keep the Sabbath and call it a delight shall rejoice in thy kingdom ; the people that hallow the seventh day, even all of them shall be satiated and delighted with thy goodness, seeing that thou didst find pleasure in the seventh day and didst hallow it ; thou didst call it the desirable of days, in remembrance of the creation.]

Continue p. 901, " *Our God . . . . pardon,*" *to the end of the Amidah p.* 923.

For the Blessing of the Priests, when the Day of Atonement falls on a weekday, see p. 835.

תְּפִלַּת מִנְחָה לְיוֹם כִּפּוּר:

For the עֲמִידָה, *see p.* 894.

SCRIPTURAL READINGS.

The Reading for the Afternoon Service is Leviticus 18—the Prohibition of Forbidden marriages and Warnings against heathen, immoral practices. The selection of this chapter was no doubt, " prompted by the desire to inculcate on the most solemn day in the Calendar the paramount duty of purity and self-control. And there is but little doubt that obedience to these behests has been, by Divine Providence, one of the most potent factors in the preservation of Israel " (Hermann Adler).

The Afternoon Haftorah is the Book of Jonah. Its selection was prompted by the need to impress upon the worshipper that there is no escape from God's judgment, and that such judgment may be averted by sincere repentance alone.

The BOOK OF JONAH is one of the most wonderful books in the world. It proclaims two fundamental truths of Religion; one, the omnipotence of repentance; and secondly, that the mercy of God embraces all the children of men. This teaching is conveyed by telling the story of a wilful Prophet who is bidden by God to call the inhabitants of unholy Nineveh, the capital of the tyrannous empire of Assyria, to repentance. Jonah attempts to escape from doing so, but in vain. After he had been saved from storm and sea, the Divine command is repeated to him. He obeys; and scarcely had he proclaimed his message than the inhabitants of Nineveh humiliated themselves before God, and repented of their evil ways. To the disappointment of Jonah, God accepts their penitence, and the threatened punishment is averted from the heathen city. " Should not I have pity on Nineveh "—God asks the Prophet—" that great city, wherein are more than six-score thousand persons that cannot discern between their right hand and their left hand (*i.e.* 120,000 little children), and also much cattle " ?

More simply and more sublimely than in these words the truth has never been uttered, that before God there is no difference of nation or creed; that even the enemy alien is our brother, and certainly his innocent babes, nay even his cattle, have a claim on our humanity.

AFTERNOON SERVICE FOR THE DAY OF ATONEMENT

For the Amidah, see p. 895

NEILAH

The Conclusion Service of the Day of Atonement forms the climax of Jewish devotion. The literal meaning of the word *Neilah* is, " the closing of the gates ". There was in ancient times a daily prayer in the Temple just before the closing of its gates in the evening. Outside the Temple there was a similar closing prayer on public fast-days. With the fall of Jerusalem, it is in the Service of the Day of Atonement alone that such closing prayer has remained. Rabh, who had a decisive influence on the Atonement Liturgy, urged that this special prayer take the form of a new Amidah. When this was done, and a whole Service grew round that Amidah, the word *Neilah* was taken to mean by the worshippers, " closing of the Heavenly Gates ". Thus, in both the Ashkenazi and the Sephardi Rite, we have the prayer, " Open unto us the gates of mercy, and forgive our iniquities, at the time of the closing of the Heavenly Gates ". In the Sephardi Rite, the Neilah service begins with the beautiful hymn—*El Nora Alila.*

> " God that doest wondrously,
> God that doest wondrously,
> Pardon at Thy people's cry,
> As the closing hour draws nigh.

> " Few are Israel's sons, and weak ;
> Thee, in penitence, they speak.
> O regard their anguished cry,
> As the closing hour draws nigh.

> " Souls in grief before Thee poured
> Agonize for deed and word ;
> ' We have sinned. Forgive,' they cry,
> As the closing hour draws nigh."

In the Neilah Amidah, the phrase, " inscribe us " is replaced by " seal us " ; the entry having been made in the Book of Life on the New Year, it is sealed at the conclusion of the Season of Repentance. This is, of course, merely a poetic figure ; for the gates of repentance are ever open.

תפלת נעילה:

חֲצִי קַדִּישׁ p. 422. ,וּבָא לְצִיּוֹן p. 570. ,אֶשְׁרֵי, p. 514.

Begin the עֲמִידָה *as in the Evening Service, see p. 894, to* וְהַגְּלוֹת
אַתָּה יוֹדֵעַ, *p. 908. On Sabbath add the words in brackets :—*

אַתָּה נוֹתֵן יָד לְפוֹשְׁעִים וִימִינְךָ פְּשׁוּטָה לְקַבֵּל שָׁבִים ·
וַתְּלַמְּדֵנוּ יְיָ אֱלֹהֵינוּ לְהִתְוַדּוֹת לְפָנֶיךָ עַל כָּל־עֲוֹנוֹתֵינוּ
לְמַעַן נֶחְדַּל מֵעְשֶׁק יָדֵינוּ וּתְקַבְּלֵנוּ בִּתְשׁוּבָה שְׁלֵמָה
לְפָנֶיךָ כְּאִשִּׁים וּכְנִיחֹחִים לְמַעַן דְּבָרֶיךָ אֲשֶׁר אָמָרְתָּ :
אֵין קֵץ לְאִשֵּׁי חוֹבוֹתֵינוּ וְאֵין מִסְפָּר לְנִיחֹחֵי אַשְׁמוֹתֵינוּ ·
וְאַתָּה יוֹדֵעַ שֶׁאַחֲרִיתֵנוּ רִמָּה וְתוֹלֵעָה לְפִיכָךְ הִרְבֵּיתָ
סְלִיחָתֵנוּ : מָה אֲנַחְנוּ מֶה חַיֵּינוּ מֶה חַסְדֵּנוּ מַה־צִּדְקֵנוּ
מַה־יִּשְׁעֵנוּ מַה־כֹּחֵנוּ מַה־גְּבוּרָתֵנוּ · מַה־נֹּאמַר לְפָנֶיךָ
יְיָ אֱלֹהֵינוּ וֵאלֹהֵי אֲבוֹתֵינוּ · הֲלֹא כָּל־הַגִּבּוֹרִים כְּאַיִן

dost put forth thy hand to transgressors. This prayer again emphasizes
the basic importance of Repentance in the religious life of man. When
God announced the creation of man—says a Talmudic legend—Wisdom
feared that his sinfulness would dishonour God's fair world. But God
reminded Wisdom that Repentance had preceded the creation of man :
that good deeds would be invested with atoning power ; and that,

931

CONCLUSION SERVICE FOR THE DAY OF ATONEMENT

" Happy are they," etc., p. 515. " And a Redeemer," etc., p. 571.
Kaddish, p. 423.

Begin the Amidah as in the Evening Service, see p. 895, to "the hidden and the revealed ? " p. 909. On Sabbath add the words in brackets :—

REPENT-
ANCE THE
BASIS OF
RELIGION

Thou dost put forth thy hand to transgressors, and thy right hand is stretched out to receive the penitent ; thou hast taught us, O Lord our God, to make confession unto thee of all our sins, in order that we may cease from our unrighteous acts, and thou wilt receive us when we come unto thee in whole-hearted repentance, even as upon fire offerings and sweet savours, for thy words' sake which thou hast spoken. Endless would be the fire offerings required for our guilt, and numberless the sweet savours for our trespasses ; but thou knowest that our latter end is the worm, and hast therefore shown us manifold ways of forgiveness.

therefore, even the vilest sinner—because of the free-will with which God had endowed him—would be able to mend his ways and be forgiven. And this in brief—the omnipotence of Repentance—is the message of the Day of Atonement.

stretched out. The poetic figure of God's Outstretched Hand to receive the sinner, is in itself a striking refutation of the abominable slander that Judaism believes in an unforgiving God.

to make a confession. " Whoso confesseth his sins and forsaketh them, shall have mercy " (Proverbs 28. 13).

unrighteous acts. lit. " violence of our hands ". As throughout the Atonement Day services, moral transgressions in our everyday dealings with our fellowmen are once again stressed at its culmination.

for thy words' sake. We cannot now offer sacrifices for our sins, if we would ; and could not in any case offer enough sacrifices to atone for all our sins. But Scripture repeatedly teaches that prayer and penitence take the place of sacrifice ; " the sacrifices of God are a broken spirit " (Psalm 51. 19).

manifold ways of forgiveness. God has shown us many other roads that lead to forgiveness, besides that of sacrifice.

לְפָנֶיךָ וְאַנְשֵׁי הַשֵּׁם כְּלֹא הָיוּ וַחֲכָמִים כִּבְלִי מַדָּע
וּנְבוֹנִים כִּבְלִי הַשְׂכֵּל · כִּי רֹב מַעֲשֵׂיהֶם תְּהוּ וִימֵי חַיֵּיהֶם
הֶבֶל לְפָנֶיךָ · וּמוֹתַר הָאָדָם מִן־הַבְּהֵמָה אָיִן כִּי הַכֹּל
הָבֶל :

אַתָּה הִבְדַּלְתָּ אֱנוֹשׁ מֵרֹאשׁ וַתַּכִּירֵהוּ לַעֲמוֹד לְפָנֶיךָ ·
כִּי מִי יֹאמַר לְךָ מַה־תִּפְעָל וְאִם־יִצְדַּק מַה־יִּתֶּן־לָךְ :
וַתִּתֶּן־לָנוּ יְיָ אֱלֹהֵינוּ בְּאַהֲבָה אֶת יוֹם [הַשַּׁבָּת הַזֶּה וְאֶת
יוֹם] הַכִּפֻּרִים הַזֶּה קֵץ וּמְחִילָה וּסְלִיחָה עַל כָּל־עֲוֹנוֹתֵינוּ
לְמַעַן נֶחְדַּל מֵעֹשֶׁק יָדֵינוּ וְנָשׁוּב אֵלֶיךָ לַעֲשׂוֹת חֻקֵּי
רְצוֹנְךָ בְּלֵבָב שָׁלֵם : וְאַתָּה בְּרַחֲמֶיךָ הָרַבִּים רַחֵם
עָלֵינוּ כִּי לֹא תַחְפּוֹץ בְּהַשְׁחָתַת עוֹלָם · שֶׁנֶּאֱמַר · דִּרְשׁוּ

what are we. Here follows a prayer by Mar Samuel, that found its way also into the Daily Morning Service, p. 27.

NEVERTHELESS. It is not the resemblances between man and animal that are decisive; it is the *differences* between them that constitute the humanity of man.

The translation "nevertheless" is required by the sense; and, indeed, in the Rite of Maimonides, the paragraph begins with the word אבל.

hast set man apart. Heathenism degraded man by causing him to kneel before brutes and the works of his hands. Judaism declared man to be akin to God; and—what is more—that he is *conscious* of his affinity to God, because of the gift of reason and sense of right with which his Heavenly Father had endowed him. "Thou hast made him little less than divine, and didst crown him with glory and majesty" (Psalm 8. 6). It is true that man's passions incline him to

What are we ?   What is our life ?   What is our piety ?
What is our righteousness ?   What our helpfulness ?   What
our strength ?   What our might ?   What shall we say before
thee, O Lord our God and God of our fathers ?   Are not
all the mighty men as nought before thee, the men of
renown as though they had not been, the wise as if without
knowledge, and the men of understanding as if without
discernment ?   For most of their works are void, and the
days of their lives are vanity before thee, and the pre-
eminence of man over the beast is nought, for all is vanity

*PRE-
EMINENCE
OF MAN*   Nevertheless, thou hast from the beginning set man
apart, and made him worthy to stand before thee ;   for who
shall say unto thee, What doest thou ? and if he be righteous,
what can he give thee ?   But thou of thy love hast given
us, O Lord our God, [this Sabbath day and] this Day of
Atonement to be the end of, as well as the season of pardon
and forgiveness for, all our iniquities, that we may cease
from our unrighteous acts, and may return unto thee to do
the statutes of thy will with a perfect heart.   O do thou, in
thy abounding compassion, have mercy upon us, for thou
delightest not in the destruction of the world, as it is said,
Isaiah 55. 5   Seek ye the Lord, while he may be found, call ye upon him

sin, but they do not *force* him to do so.   And if he has stumbled and
fallen on the pathway of life, he can always rise again.   Freedom of
will is his, and the power of repentance.   There is no place in Judaism
for the doctrine of man's innate depravity, Original Sin.   " The soul that
Thou gavest me is pure ;   Thou didst create it,   Thou didst form it,
Thou didst breathe it unto me . . . and Thou wilt restore it unto me
in the Hereafter ".   Such is the pious Jew's daily Morning prayer ;
p. 19.
    made him worthy. This was an outflowing of Divine love ; for the
Omnipotent is *in no need of* mortals, nor is He benefited by their actions,
even if these be righteous.
    perfect heart. With undivided heart, whole-souled obedience.

יְיָ בְּהִמָּצְאוֹ קְרָאֻהוּ בִּהְיוֹתוֹ קָרוֹב׃ וְנֶאֱמַר • יַעֲזֹב רָשָׁע
דַּרְכּוֹ וְאִישׁ אָוֶן מַחְשְׁבֹתָיו וְיָשֹׁב אֶל־יְיָ וִירַחֲמֵהוּ וְאֶל־
אֱלֹהֵינוּ כִּי־יַרְבֶּה לִסְלוֹחַ׃ וְאַתָּה אֱלוֹהַּ סְלִיחוֹת חַנּוּן
וְרַחוּם אֶרֶךְ־אַפַּיִם וְרַב־חֶסֶד וּמַרְבֶּה לְהֵיטִיב • וְרוֹצֶה
אַתָּה בִּתְשׁוּבַת רְשָׁעִים וְאֵין אַתָּה חָפֵץ בְּמִיתָתָם •
שֶׁנֶּאֱמַר • אֱמֹר אֲלֵיהֶם חַי־אָנִי נְאֻם אֲדֹנָי יֱהֹוִה אִם־
אֶחְפֹּץ בְּמוֹת הָרָשָׁע כִּי אִם־בְּשׁוּב רָשָׁע מִדַּרְכּוֹ וְחָיָה •
שׁוּבוּ שׁוּבוּ מִדַּרְכֵיכֶם הָרָעִים וְלָמָּה תָמוּתוּ בֵּית
יִשְׂרָאֵל׃ וְנֶאֱמַר • הֶחָפֹץ אֶחְפֹּץ מוֹת רָשָׁע נְאֻם אֲדֹנָי
יֱהֹוִה הֲלוֹא בְּשׁוּבוֹ מִדְּרָכָיו וְחָיָה׃ וְנֶאֱמַר • כִּי לֹא
אֶחְפֹּץ בְּמוֹת הַמֵּת נְאֻם אֲדֹנָי יֱהֹוִה • וְהָשִׁיבוּ וִחְיוּ׃
כִּי אַתָּה סָלְחָן לְיִשְׂרָאֵל וּמָחֳלָן לְשִׁבְטֵי יְשֻׁרוּן בְּכָל־
דּוֹר וָדוֹר • וּמִבַּלְעָדֶיךָ אֵין לָנוּ מֶלֶךְ מוֹחֵל וְסוֹלֵחַ׃

For the conclusion of the עֲמִידָה, see p. 920, from
אֱלֹהַי עַד שֶׁלֹּא נוֹצָרְתִּי.

while he is near. Really this means, " While we are near Him ", and ready to grasp His outstretched Arm.

man of iniquity his thoughts. Judaism does not confine its guidance to *acts.* " Thou shalt not covet "—checking inmost desires and impulses that are springs of sinful deeds—is part of the Ten Commandments. And '"thou shalt not hate Thy brother *in thy heart* " ; is one of the Holiness Laws of Scripture. The blighting effect of thoughts of hate on man, is well known. The mere sight or thought of Mordecai and his people, poisons Haman's joy of life (Esther 5. 13). So is it with all malice-ridden men.

that the wicked turn from his way. This, and the other two verses from Ezekiel give expression to the moral freedom and independence of the individual soul.

Isaiah 55. 6   while he is near. And it is said, Let the wicked forsake his way, and the man of iniquity his thoughts ; and let him return unto the Lord, and he will have mercy upon him ; and to our God for he will abundantly pardon. But thou art a God ready to forgive, gracious and merciful, slow to anger, plenteous in lovingkindness, and abounding in goodness ; thou delightest in the repentance of the wicked, and

Ezekiel 33. 11   hast no pleasure in their death ; as it is said, Say unto them, As I live, saith the Lord, I have no pleasure in the death of the wicked ; but that the wicked turn from his way and live : turn ye, turn ye from your evil ways ; for why will ye die,

Ezekiel 18. 23   O house of Israel ? And it is said, Have I at all any pleasure in the death of the wicked, saith the Lord God, and not rather that he should return from his way, and live ? And

Ezekiel 18. 32   it is said, For I have no pleasure in the death of him that dieth, saith the Lord God ; wherefore turn yourselves and live. For thou art the Pardoner of Israel and the Forgiver of the tribes of Jeshurun in every generation, and beside thee we have no King who pardoneth and forgiveth.

For the conclusion, see p. 921 from " O my God, before I was formed " to " in ancient years ", p. 923.

The Prophet EZEKIEL was among those who, in the year 597 B.C.E., were carried into exile to Babylon. He became one of the spiritual agencies that kept Israel's soul alive in those years of despair. He was at once priest and prophet, inspirer of the nation and pastor of individual souls. He is the great preacher of Repentance, and of Divine Forgiveness to those who in sincerity seek God's pardon. In these verses he affirmed that the individual is not a mere plaything of fate, hopelessly foredoomed by the deeds of his ancestors. In the long run, it is *his* righteousness that preserves him, and his wickedness that destroys him. Neither does the individual forever lie under the ban of his own sins. He can break with his evil past. Men are not judged by that which they *have* been, by *by that which they are and shall become.*

     no pleasure in their death. God's desire is that man shall *live.* "He is a King who delighteth in life." He has therefore endowed man with power to repent.

     beside thee. For to God alone, and not to any angel or Mediator, does the Israelite look for pardon and forgiveness.

אָבִינוּ מַלְכֵּנוּ. *p.* 160–166, *is said.*

The Reader says the following verse, the Congregation repeating it :—

שְׁמַע יִשְׂרָאֵל יְיָ אֱלֹהֵינוּ יְיָ אֶחָד :

The Reader says the following three times, the Congregation each time repeating it :—

בָּרוּךְ שֵׁם כְּבוֹד מַלְכוּתוֹ לְעוֹלָם וָעֶד :

The Reader says the following seven times. the Congregation each time repeating it:

יְיָ הוּא הָאֱלֹהִים :

The Shofar is sounded.

The Neilah service concludes with three PROFESSIONS OF FAITH, recited by Reader and Congregation. These Professions—prescribed to be spoken by, or to, the dying—are here repeated with special solemnity, so as to indicate that the Israelite should be prepared to lay down his life in their defence.

At first the words, " The Lord, He is God ", were alone said. In that phrase Elijah, the fearless Prophet, triumphantly proclaimed, 2800 years ago before the assembled multitude on Mt. Carmel, the unity and essential righteousness of God—a fitting ending to Israel's unique Festival. In later centuries, the Shema, and its accompanying " Blessed be His Name ", were prefixed to Elijah's Declaration, as equally appropriate for the culmination of Israel's Day of Days.

The Shofar is then sounded. This may be a survival of the ancient Jubilee, which began on the tenth of Tishri and was announced by the Shofar.

The above comments on the Neilah in no way do full justice to the beauty and passionate fervour of that Neilah Service. More could be attempted in an annotated edition of the Yom Kippur machzor. The following extract from Zangwill's " Children of the Ghetto " gives a glimpse of the close of Yom Kippur Service in an East End chevrah, a half-century ago :

" . . . Esther dreamed away the long grey day, only vaguely conscious of the stages of the service—Morning dovetailing into Afternoon service, and Afternoon into Evening ; of the prostrations full-length on the floor ; of the rhyming poems with their recurring burdens

" Our Father, our King," on pp. 163–167, *is said.*

The Reader says the following verse, the Congregation repeating it :—

HEAR, O ISRAEL : THE LORD IS OUR GOD, THE LORD IS ONE.

The Reader says the following three times, the Congregation each time repeating it :—

BLESSED BE HIS NAME, WHOSE GLORIOUS KINGDOM IS FOR EVER AND EVER.

The Reader says the following seven times, the Congregation each time repeating it :—

THE LORD, HE IS GOD.

The Shofar is sounded.

---

shouted in devotional frenzy, with special staccato phrases flung heavenwards ; of the wailing confessions of communal sin, with their accompaniment of sobs and tears and beatings of the breast. . . .

Suddenly there fell a vast silence . . . It was as if all creation paused to hear a pregnant word.

' Hear, O Israel, the Lord our God, the Lord is One ! ' sang the cantor frenziedly.

And all the ghostly congregation answered with a great cry, ' Hear, O Israel, the Lord our God, the Lord is One ! '

They seemed like a great army of the sheeted dead risen to testify to the Unity. The magnetic tremor that ran through the synagogue thrilled the lonely girl to the core, and from her lips came in rapturous surrender to an over-mastering impulse the half-hysterical protestation :

' Hear, O Israel, the Lord our God, the Lord is One ! '

And then in the brief instant while the congregation, with ever-ascending rhapsody, blessed God till the climax came with the seven-fold declaration, ' The Lord, He is God ', the whole history of her strange, unhappy race flashed through her mind in a whirl of resistless emotion. She was overwhelmed by the thought of its sons in every corner of the earth proclaiming to the sombre twilight sky the belief for which its generations had lived and died. The grey dusk palpitated with floating shapes of prophets and martyrs, scholars and sages and poets, full of a yearning love and pity, lifting hands of benediction. By what great high roads and queer byways of history had they travelled hither, these wandering Jews, ' sated with contempt ', these human paradoxes, adaptive to *every* environment, omnipresent like some great natural force, indestructible and almost inconvertible. . . .

The roar dwindled to a solemn silence. Then the ram's horn shrilled —a stern long-drawn-out note, that rose at last into a mighty peal of sacred jubilation. The Atonement was complete."

סֵדֶר סְפִירַת הָעֹמֶר:

The עֹמֶר *is counted from the second night of* פֶּסַח *until the night before* שָׁבֻעוֹת.

הִנְנִי מְכַוֵּן מִצְוַת עֲשֵׂה שֶׁל־סְפִירַת הָעֹמֶר כְּמוֹ שֶׁכָּתוּב בַּתּוֹרָה · וּסְפַרְתֶּם לָכֶם מִמָּחֳרַת הַשַּׁבָּת מִיּוֹם הֲבִיאֲכֶם אֶת־עֹמֶר הַתְּנוּפָה שֶׁבַע שַׁבָּתוֹת תְּמִימֹת תִּהְיֶינָה עַד מִמָּחֳרַת הַשַּׁבָּת הַשְּׁבִיעִית תִּסְפְּרוּ חֲמִשִּׁים יוֹם:

בָּרוּךְ אַתָּה יְיָ אֱלֹהֵינוּ מֶלֶךְ הָעוֹלָם · אֲשֶׁר קִדְּשָׁנוּ בְּמִצְוֹתָיו וְצִוָּנוּ עַל סְפִירַת הָעֹמֶר:

1. הַיּוֹם יוֹם אֶחָד לָעֹמֶר: 2. הַיּוֹם שְׁנֵי יָמִים לָעֹמֶר:

3. הַיּוֹם שְׁלֹשָׁה יָמִים לָעֹמֶר: 4. הַיּוֹם אַרְבָּעָה יָמִים לָעֹמֶר:

5. הַיּוֹם חֲמִשָּׁה יָמִים לָעֹמֶר: 6. הַיּוֹם שִׁשָּׁה יָמִים לָעֹמֶר:

7. הַיּוֹם שִׁבְעָה יָמִים שֶׁהֵם שָׁבוּעַ אֶחָד לָעֹמֶר:

8. הַיּוֹם שְׁמוֹנָה יָמִים שֶׁהֵם שָׁבוּעַ אֶחָד וְיוֹם אֶחָד לָעֹמֶר:

9. הַיּוֹם תִּשְׁעָה יָמִים שֶׁהֵם שָׁבוּעַ אֶחָד וּשְׁנֵי יָמִים לָעֹמֶר:

COUNTING OF THE OMER

We solemnly count the forty-nine days between the First Day of the Festival of Passover and the Feast of Weeks, the anniversary of the Giving of our Torah. "Just as one who awaits a most intimate friend on a certain day, counts in ardent expectation the days and even the hours till his coming, so we count the days from the anniversary of our departure from Egypt till the Festival of the Giving of the Torah. For the latter was the aim and object of the exodus from Egypt" (Maimonides).

In later centuries, these seven weeks came to be full of sad memories to Israel. Dire calamities repeatedly befell the Jewish People at this time. Tradition tells of pestilence that swept away tens of thousands

ORDER OF COUNTING THE OMER

The Omer is counted from the second night of Passover until the night before Pentecost.

Leviticus 23. 15, 16

Lo, I am about to fulfil the affirmative precept of the counting of the Omer, as it is written in the Torah, And ye shall count unto you from the morrow after the day of rest, from the day that ye brought the Omer of the wave-offering, seven complete weeks they shall be ; until the morrow of the seventh week shall ye number fifty days.

Blessed art thou, O Lord our God, King of the universe, who hast hallowed us by thy commandments, and hast given us command concerning the counting of the Omer

1. This is the first day of the Omer.
2. This is the second day of the Omer.
3. This is the third day of the Omer.
4. This is the fourth day of the Omer.
5. This is the fifth day of the Omer.
6. This is the sixth day of the Omer.
7. This is the seventh day, making one week, of the Omer.
8. This is the eighth day, making one week and one day of the Omer.
9. This is the ninth day, making one week and two days of the Omer.

of Rabbi Akiba's followers during the weeks of the Counting of the Omer ; and history records appalling massacres at this season by the Crusaders in the year 1096. These and succeeding sombre events are commemorated by special elegies in the older Prayer Books.

The Omer Season is a period of semi-mourning ; and, during the month of Iyar, Jews abstain from weddings and rejoicings—except on the 18th of Iyar, which is the 33rd day of Omer (Lag b'Omer), when there was a cessation of plague in Akiba's age. This day is observed as a semi-holiday, and in Jewish schools as a whole holiday.

ye shall count. Hebrew *u-sefartem.* Hence the period is called *Sefirah.* The counting is done towards the close of the Evening Service.

unto you. Each Israelite is to count for himself, even after the Omer offering could no longer be brought to the Temple.

10. הַיּוֹם עֲשָׂרָה יָמִים שֶׁהֵם שָׁבוּעַ אֶחָד וּשְׁלֹשָׁה יָמִים לָעֹמֶר:

11. הַיּוֹם אַחַד עָשָׂר יוֹם שֶׁהֵם שָׁבוּעַ אֶחָד וְאַרְבָּעָה יָמִים לָעֹמֶר:

12. הַיּוֹם שְׁנֵים עָשָׂר יוֹם שֶׁהֵם שָׁבוּעַ אֶחָד וַחֲמִשָּׁה יָמִים לָעֹמֶר:

13. הַיּוֹם שְׁלֹשָׁה עָשָׂר יוֹם שֶׁהֵם שָׁבוּעַ אֶחָד וְשִׁשָּׁה יָמִים לָעֹמֶר:

14. הַיּוֹם אַרְבָּעָה עָשָׂר יוֹם שֶׁהֵם שְׁנֵי שָׁבוּעוֹת לָעֹמֶר:

15. הַיּוֹם חֲמִשָּׁה עָשָׂר יוֹם שֶׁהֵם שְׁנֵי שָׁבוּעוֹת וְיוֹם אֶחָד לָעֹמֶר:

16. הַיּוֹם שִׁשָּׁה עָשָׂר יוֹם שֶׁהֵם שְׁנֵי שָׁבוּעוֹת וּשְׁנֵי יָמִים לָעֹמֶר:

17. הַיּוֹם שִׁבְעָה עָשָׂר יוֹם שֶׁהֵם שְׁנֵי שָׁבוּעוֹת וּשְׁלֹשָׁה יָמִים לָעֹמֶר:

18. הַיּוֹם שְׁמוֹנָה עָשָׂר יוֹם שֶׁהֵם שְׁנֵי שָׁבוּעוֹת וְאַרְבָּעָה יָמִים לָעֹמֶר:

19. הַיּוֹם תִּשְׁעָה עָשָׂר יוֹם שֶׁהֵם שְׁנֵי שָׁבוּעוֹת וַחֲמִשָּׁה יָמִים לָעֹמֶר:

20. הַיּוֹם עֶשְׂרִים יוֹם שֶׁהֵם שְׁנֵי שָׁבוּעוֹת וְשִׁשָּׁה יָמִים לָעֹמֶר:

21. הַיּוֹם אֶחָד וְעֶשְׂרִים יוֹם שֶׁהֵם שְׁלֹשָׁה שָׁבוּעוֹת לָעֹמֶר:

22. הַיּוֹם שְׁנַיִם וְעֶשְׂרִים יוֹם שֶׁהֵם שְׁלֹשָׁה שָׁבוּעוֹת וְיוֹם אֶחָד לָעֹמֶר:

23. הַיּוֹם שְׁלֹשָׁה וְעֶשְׂרִים יוֹם שֶׁהֵם שְׁלֹשָׁה שָׁבוּעוֹת וּשְׁנֵי יָמִים לָעֹמֶר:

24. הַיּוֹם אַרְבָּעָה וְעֶשְׂרִים יוֹם שֶׁהֵם שְׁלֹשָׁה שָׁבוּעוֹת וּשְׁלֹשָׁה יָמִים לָעֹמֶר:

25. הַיּוֹם חֲמִשָּׁה וְעֶשְׂרִים יוֹם שֶׁהֵם שְׁלֹשָׁה שָׁבוּעוֹת וְאַרְבָּעָה יָמִים לָעֹמֶר:

26. הַיּוֹם שִׁשָּׁה וְעֶשְׂרִים יוֹם שֶׁהֵם שְׁלֹשָׁה שָׁבוּעוֹת וַחֲמִשָּׁה

10. This is the tenth day, making one week and three days of the Omer.

11. This is the eleventh day, making one week and four days of the Omer.

12. This is the twelfth day, making one week and five days of the Omer.

13. This is the thirteenth day, making one week and six days of the Omer.

14. This is the fourteenth day, making two weeks of the Omer.

15. This is the fifteenth day, making two weeks and one day of the Omer.

16. This is the sixteenth day, making two weeks and two days of the Omer.

17. This is the seventeenth day, making two weeks and three days of the Omer.

18. This is the eighteenth day, making two weeks and four days of the Omer.

19. This is the nineteenth day, making two weeks and five days of the Omer.

20. This is the twentieth day, making two weeks and six days of the Omer.

21. This is the twenty-first day, making three weeks of the Omer.

22. This is the twenty-second day, making three weeks and one day of the Omer

23. This is the twenty-third day, making three weeks and two days of the Omer.

24. This is the twenty-fourth day, making three weeks and three days of the Omer.

25. This is the twenty-fifth day, making three weeks and four days of the Omer.

day of rest. Here it means the first day of the Passover.

sheaf of the wave-offering. An omer (half-gallon) of barley—the first to ripen of the grains sown in winter—was solemnly cut in the field, and the yield of this sheaf was brought to the Sanctuary as a token of gratitude to the Lord of the harvest.

by thy commandments. See pp. 10 and 11.

יָמִים לָעְמֶר:

27. הַיּוֹם שִׁבְעָה וְעֶשְׂרִים יוֹם שֶׁהֵם שְׁלֹשָׁה שָׁבוּעוֹת
וְשִׁשָּׁה יָמִים לָעְמֶר:

28. הַיּוֹם שְׁמוֹנָה וְעֶשְׂרִים יוֹם שֶׁהֵם אַרְבָּעָה שָׁבוּעוֹת
לָעְמֶר:

29. הַיּוֹם תִּשְׁעָה וְעֶשְׂרִים יוֹם שֶׁהֵם אַרְבָּעָה שָׁבוּעוֹת וְיוֹם
אֶחָד לָעְמֶר:

30. הַיּוֹם שְׁלֹשִׁים יוֹם שֶׁהֵם אַרְבָּעָה שָׁבוּעוֹת וּשְׁנֵי יָמִים לָעְמֶר:

31. הַיּוֹם אֶחָד וּשְׁלֹשִׁים יוֹם שֶׁהֵם אַרְבָּעָה שָׁבוּעוֹת וּשְׁלֹשָׁה
יָמִים לָעְמֶר:

32. הַיּוֹם שְׁנַיִם וּשְׁלֹשִׁים יוֹם שֶׁהֵם אַרְבָּעָה שָׁבוּעוֹת
וְאַרְבָּעָה יָמִים לָעְמֶר:

33. הַיּוֹם שְׁלֹשָׁה וּשְׁלֹשִׁים יוֹם שֶׁהֵם אַרְבָּעָה שָׁבוּעוֹת
וַחֲמִשָּׁה יָמִים לָעְמֶר:

34. הַיּוֹם אַרְבָּעָה וּשְׁלֹשִׁים יוֹם שֶׁהֵם אַרְבָּעָה שָׁבוּעוֹת
וְשִׁשָּׁה יָמִים לָעְמֶר:

35. הַיּוֹם חֲמִשָּׁה וּשְׁלֹשִׁים יוֹם שֶׁהֵם חֲמִשָּׁה שָׁבוּעוֹת לָעְמֶר:

36. הַיּוֹם שִׁשָּׁה וּשְׁלֹשִׁים יוֹם שֶׁהֵם חֲמִשָּׁה שָׁבָעוֹת וְיוֹם
אֶחָד לָעְמֶר:

37. הַיּוֹם שִׁבְעָה וּשְׁלֹשִׁים יוֹם שֶׁהֵם חֲמִשָּׁה שָׁבוּעוֹת וּשְׁנֵי
יָמִים לָעְמֶר:

38. הַיּוֹם שְׁמוֹנָה וּשְׁלֹשִׁים יוֹם שֶׁהֵם חֲמִשָּׁה שָׁבוּעוֹת
וּשְׁלֹשָׁה יָמִים לָעְמֶר:

39. הַיּוֹם תִּשְׁעָה וּשְׁלֹשִׁים יוֹם שֶׁהֵם חֲמִשָּׁה שָׁבוּעוֹת
וְאַרְבָּעָה יָמִים לָעְמֶר:

40. הַיּוֹם אַרְבָּעִים יוֹם שֶׁהֵם חֲמִשָּׁה שָׁבוּעוֹת וַחֲמִשָּׁה
יָמִים לָעְמֶר:

41. הַיּוֹם אֶחָד וְאַרְבָּעִים יוֹם שֶׁהֵם חֲמִשָּׁה שָׁבוּעוֹת וְשִׁשָּׁה
יָמִים לָעְמֶר:

26. This is the twenty-sixth day, making three weeks and five days of the Omer.

27. This is the twenty-seventh day, making three weeks and six days of the Omer.

28. This is the twenty-eighth day, making four weeks of the Omer.

29. This is the twenty-ninth day, making four weeks and one day of the Omer.

30. This is the thirtieth day, making four weeks and two days of the Omer.

31. This is the thirty-first day, making four weeks and three days of the Omer.

32. This is the thirty-second day, making four weeks and four days of the Omer.

33. This is the thirty-third day, making four weeks and five days of the Omer.

34. This is the thirty-fourth day, making four weeks and six days of the Omer.

35. This is the thirty-fifth day, making five weeks of the Omer.

36. This is the thirty-sixth day, making five weeks and one day of the Omer.

37. This is the thirty-seventh day, making five weeks and two days of the Omer.

38. This is the thirty-eighth day, making five weeks and three days of the Omer.

39. This is the thirty-ninth day, making five weeks and four days of the Omer.

40. This is the fortieth day, making five weeks and five days of the Omer.

41. This is the forty-first day, making five weeks and six days of the Omer.

42. הַיּוֹם שְׁנַיִם וְאַרְבָּעִים יוֹם שֶׁהֵם שִׁשָּׁה שָׁבוּעוֹת לָעְמֶר:

43. הַיּוֹם שְׁלֹשָׁה וְאַרְבָּעִים יוֹם שֶׁהֵם שִׁשָּׁה שָׁבוּעוֹת וְיוֹם אֶחָד לָעְמֶר:

44. הַיּוֹם אַרְבָּעָה וְאַרְבָּעִים יוֹם שֶׁהֵם שִׁשָּׁה שָׁבוּעוֹת וּשְׁנֵי יָמִים לָעְמֶר:

45. הַיּוֹם חֲמִשָּׁה וְאַרְבָּעִים יוֹם שֶׁהֵם שִׁשָּׁה שָׁבוּעוֹת וּשְׁלֹשָׁה יָמִים לָעְמֶר:

46. הַיּוֹם שִׁשָּׁה וְאַרְבָּעִים יוֹם שֶׁהֵם שִׁשָּׁה שָׁבוּעוֹת וְאַרְבָּעָה יָמִים לָעְמֶר:

47. הַיּוֹם שִׁבְעָה וְאַרְבָּעִים יוֹם שֶׁהֵם שִׁשָּׁה שָׁבוּעוֹת וַחֲמִשָּׁה יָמִים לָעְמֶר:

48. הַיּוֹם שְׁמוֹנָה וְאַרְבָּעִים יוֹם שֶׁהֵם שִׁשָּׁה שָׁבוּעוֹת וְשִׁשָּׁה יָמִים לָעְמֶר:

49. הַיּוֹם תִּשְׁעָה וְאַרְבָּעִים יוֹם שֶׁהֵם שִׁבְעָה שָׁבוּעוֹת לָעְמֶר:

הָרַחֲמָן הוּא יַחֲזִיר עֲבוֹדַת בֵּית הַמִּקְדָּשׁ לִמְקוֹמָהּ: יְהִי רָצוֹן לְפָנֶיךָ יְיָ אֱלֹהֵינוּ וֵאלֹהֵי אֲבוֹתֵינוּ שֶׁיִּבָּנֶה בֵּית הַמִּקְדָּשׁ בִּמְהֵרָה בְיָמֵינוּ וְתֵן חֶלְקֵנוּ בְּתוֹרָתֶךָ: וְשָׁם נַעֲבָדְךָ בְּיִרְאָה כִּימֵי עוֹלָם וּכְשָׁנִים קַדְמוֹנִיּוֹת:

728 *p*, תהלים ס'ז

אָנָּא בְּכֹחַ גְּדֻלַּת יְמִינְךָ תַּתִּיר צְרוּרָה • קַבֵּל רִנַּת עַמְּךָ שַׂגְּבֵנוּ טַהֲרֵנוּ נוֹרָא • נָא גִבּוֹר דּוֹרְשֵׁי יְחוּדְךָ כְּבָבַת שָׁמְרֵם • בָּרְכֵם טַהֲרֵם רַחֲמֵם צִדְקָתְךָ תָּמִיד גָּמְלֵם • חֲסִין קָדוֹשׁ בְּרֹב טוּבְךָ נַהֵל עֲדָתֶךָ • יָחִיד גֵּאֶה לְעַמְּךָ פְּנֵה זוֹכְרֵי קְדֻשָּׁתֶךָ • שַׁוְעָתֵנוּ קַבֵּל וּשְׁמַע צַעֲקָתֵנוּ יוֹדֵעַ תַּעֲלֻמוֹת • בָּרוּךְ שֵׁם כְּבוֹד מַלְכוּתוֹ לְעוֹלָם וָעֶד:

42. This is the forty-second day, making six weeks of the Omer.

43. This is the forty-third day, making six weeks and one day of the Omer.

44. This is the forty-fourth day, making six weeks and two days of the Omer.

45. This is the forty-fifth day, making six weeks and three days of the Omer.

46. This is the forty-sixth day, making six weeks and four days of the Omer.

47. This is the forty-seventh day, making six weeks and five days of the Omer.

48. This is the forty-eighth day, making six weeks and six days of the Omer.

49. This is the forty-ninth day, making seven weeks of the Omer.

May the All-merciful restore the service of the Temple to its place. May it be thy will, O Lord our God and God of our fathers, that the Temple be speedily rebuilt in our days, and grant our portion in thy Torah. And there we will serve thee with awe, as in the days of old, and as in ancient years.

CONCLU-DING SUPPLI-CATION

Psalm lxvii, p. 729.

We beseech thee, release thy captive nation by the mighty strength of thy right hand. Accept the joyful chant of thy people. lift us and purify us, O revered God. O thou mighty One, guard as the apple of the eye them that meditate upon thy Unity. Bless them, purify them, have mercy upon them, ever bestow thy charity unto them. O powerful and holy Being, in thine abounding goodness lead thy congregation. Turn, thou who art the only and exalted God, unto thy people, who are mindful of thy holiness. Accept our prayer and hearken unto our cry, thou that knowest all secrets. Blessed be His Name, whose glorious kingdom is for ever and ever.

restore the service. This prayer was written after the fall of the Jewish State, when there was no more reaping of the harvest in the Land of Israel, and no more bringing of the Omer. It expresses the yearning for the time when the Omer could again be offered.

we beseech thee. This prayer was a great favourite of the Cabalists.

THE MINOR FESTIVALS

Chief among the Minor Festivals of the Jewish Calendar are CHANUKAH and PURIM. They do not partake of the holiness of either the Solemn or of the Joyous Festivals, all manner of work being permitted on them.

Though Chanukah and Purim are " minor " Festivals, their importance should not be underestimated. Man is made man by history, and the Jew is made more truly conscious of his Judaism by those historical Festivals. And their significance is in the highest sense religious. The existence of ethical monotheism, *i.e.* Religion itself, was at stake in the struggle between Jews and Syrians, that culminated in the first Chanukah. Likewise, if it had not been for the frustration of Haman's planned massacre of the Jews throughout the Persian Empire, which then included the Jewries of both Babylon and Judea, Israel and Israel's Message to mankind would have disappeared—with incalculable consequences on the whole course of human destiny.

CHANUKAH

The history of CHANUKAH is given in I and II Maccabees, two books of the Apocrypha, the collection of ancient Jewish writings that have remained outside the Sacred Canon of Scripture.

Twenty-one centuries ago, the Syrian king Antiochus Epiphanes held sway over Palestine, and opened the long and sinister list of religious persecutors. He turned the Temple of Jerusalem into a heathen shrine, and the Jewish population were everywhere ordered to offer public sacrifice to idols. Those who refused to do so, who observed Jewish rites, or were found in possession of books of Scripture, were consigned to torture and death. Israel was to give yet another lesson of infinite worth to the children of men ; viz., the willingness to bear testimony to the truth at whatever cost, the readiness to lay down life itself for a sacred cause ; in a word, *martyrdom*. The Jewish People produced in those days of Terror the first martyrs in history. The story of the martyr Mother and her seven sons, all of whom preferred death to dishonour, reflects the indomitable steadfastness that animated the loyal Remnant in those days. And Judaism will ever cherish the answer of the aged priest Mattathias, the father of the Maccabees, to the Royal representative : " Though all the nations that are under the King's dominion obey him, and fall away every one from the religion of their fathers, yet will I and my sons and my brethren walk in the Covenant of our fathers " (I Maccabees 2. 19, 20). Mattathias and his five sons rallied the faithful around them, and unfurled the standard of revolt. This was in the year 168. Three years to the day on which the Temple was profaned by the blaspheming foe, Kislev the 25th 165, Judah Maccabeus and his brethren triumphantly entered the Holy City.   They purified the Temple ; and their kindling of the lights during the eight-day festival of Dedication—Chanukah—is a telling reminder, year by year, of the rekindling of the Lamp of True Religion in their time.   Theirs was a war for principle and conviction, not for glory and conquest.   Their whole achievement can be summed up in the words of the Haftorah of Sabbath Chanukah, words which proclaim the lesson of all Jewish history—" Not by might, nor by power, but by My spirit, saith the Lord of Hosts " (Zechariah 4. 6). The story of the Maccabean heroes who were " ready to live or die nobly " for Conscience, Faith, Freedom, has been a wonderful inspiration to down-trodden nations and persecuted communities.   It filled them with the conviction that there are stronger things in the world than brute force ; and that men and nations fighting for the spirit, are as indestructible as the spirit.

The Greeks were the exponents of the highest culture in antiquity, but that culture differed widely from the lofty teachings of Judaism in the moral and spiritual sphere.   Many of the Greeks regarded pleasure as the sole aim of life.   This was especially true of the soldiers and rulers who brought Greek ways and practices into Judea in the generation before the Maccabees.   Many of the Jewish upper classes had become *Hellenists, i.e.* imitators of Hellenism (or, Greek culture), and they were pagan not only in outward things but in thought and life as well.   The ancient historian laments : " Many were making of no account the honours of their fathers, and thinking the glories of the Greeks best of all."

It must be added that a century later, there began in Alexandria a fusing of Jewish and Greek thought that resulted in a far higher form of Hellenism than the one which the Maccabees resisted.   The new movement produced men like Philo and the author of the " Wisdom of Solomon," and their lives and writings represent a distinct enrichment of religious thought and experience.

Throughout Chanukah, the complete Hallel is recited in the Morning Service, and the eulogy, *We thank thee also for the miracles,* is inserted in the seventeenth Benediction of every Amidah, (see p. 151,) as well as in the Grace after Meals, see p. 969.

All the Blessings of the kindling of the Lights are of early Rabbinic origin.   The lights were at first kindled only in the home, but later were introduced in the synagogue as well.

סֵדֶר חֲנוּכָה :

The Feast of חֲנֻכָּה lasts eight days. On the first evening a light is
kindled, the number of lights being increased by one on each
consecutive evening. The חֲנֻכָּה lights should be kindled as soon
as possible after nightfall.

On Friday the lights are kindled before the beginning of שַׁבָּת.

Before kindling the lights, the following Blessings are said :—

בָּרוּךְ אַתָּה יְיָ אֱלֹהֵינוּ מֶלֶךְ הָעוֹלָם · אֲשֶׁר קִדְּשָׁנוּ
בְּמִצְוֹתָיו וְצִוָּנוּ לְהַדְלִיק נֵר שֶׁל חֲנֻכָּה :

בָּרוּךְ אַתָּה יְיָ אֱלֹהֵינוּ מֶלֶךְ הָעוֹלָם · שֶׁעָשָׂה נִסִּים
לַאֲבוֹתֵינוּ בַּיָּמִים הָהֵם בַּזְּמַן הַזֶּה :

The following Blessing is said on the first evening only :—

בָּרוּךְ אַתָּה יְיָ אֱלֹהֵינוּ מֶלֶךְ הָעוֹלָם · שֶׁהֶחֱיָנוּ וְקִיְּמָנוּ
וְהִגִּיעָנוּ לַזְּמַן הַזֶּה :

After kindling the first light, the following is said :—

הַנֵּרוֹת הַלָּלוּ אֲנַחְנוּ מַדְלִיקִין עַל הַנִּסִּים וְעַל הַתְּשׁוּעוֹת
וְעַל הַנִּפְלָאוֹת שֶׁעָשִׂיתָ לַאֲבוֹתֵינוּ עַל־יְדֵי כֹּהֲנֶיךָ הַקְּדוֹשִׁים ·
וְכָל־שְׁמֹנַת יְמֵי חֲנֻכָּה הַנֵּרוֹת הַלָּלוּ קֹדֶשׁ וְאֵין לָנוּ רְשׁוּת
לְהִשְׁתַּמֵּשׁ בָּהֶם אֶלָּא לִרְאוֹתָם בִּלְבָד · כְּדֵי לְהוֹדוֹת לְשִׁמְךָ
עַל־נִסֶּיךָ וְעַל־יְשׁוּעָתֶךָ וְעַל־נִפְלְאוֹתֶיךָ :

In the Synagogue, מִזְמוֹר שִׁיר חֲנֻכַּת הַבָּיִת, p. 234, is chanted.

SERVICE FOR CHANUKAH.

The Feast of Dedication lasts eight days. On the first evening a light is kindled, the number of lights being increased by one on each consecutive evening. The Chanukah lights should be kindled as soon as possible after nightfall.

On Friday the lights are kindled before the beginning of the Sabbath.

Before kindling the lights, the following Blessings are said :—

BENE-DICTIONS

Blessed art thou, O Lord our God, King of the universe, who hast hallowed us by thy commandments, and commanded us to kindle the light of Chanukah.

Blessed art thou, O Lord our God, King of the universe, who didst work miracles for our fathers in days of old, at this season.

The following Blessing is said on the first evening only :—

Blessed art thou, O Lord our God, King of the universe, who hast kept us in life, and hast preserved us, and enabled us to reach this season.

After kindling the first light, the following is said :—

We kindle these lights on account of the miracles, the deliverances and the wonders which thou didst work for our fathers, by means of thy holy priests. During all the eight days of Chanukah these lights are sacred, neither is it permitted us to make any profane use of them ; but we are only to look at them, in order that we may give thanks unto thy Name for thy miracles, thy deliverances and thy wonders.

In the Synagogue, Psalm xxx, p. 235 is chanted.

and given us command. See p. 11.

no profane use. Not even for the purpose of kindling the other Chanukah lights. This is done by a light called *shammash (servitor)*, which is usually permitted to burn with the others.

PSALM 30. See p. 234. Not only the title of this psalm, but especially its concluding verses are peculiarly appropriate for the occasion.

In the home the following Hymn is chanted :—

מָעוֹז צוּר יְשׁוּעָתִי · לְךָ נָאֶה לְשַׁבֵּחַ · תִּכּוֹן בֵּית
תְּפִלָּתִי · וְשָׁם תּוֹדָה נְזַבֵּחַ · לְעֵת תָּשׁבִּית מַטְבֵּחַ · וְצַר
הַמְנַבֵּחַ · אָז אֶגְמוֹר · בְּשִׁיר מִזְמוֹר · חֲנֻכַּת הַמִּזְבֵּחַ :

רָעוֹת שָׂבְעָה נַפְשִׁי · בְּיָגוֹן כֹּחִי כָלָה · חַיַּי
מֵרְרוּ בְקוֹשִׁי · בְּשִׁעְבּוּד מַלְכוּת עֶגְלָה · וּבְיָדוֹ הַגְּדוֹלָה ·
הוֹצִיא אֶת־הַסְּגֻלָּה · חֵיל פַּרְעֹה · וְכָל־זַרְעוֹ · יָרְדוּ
כְאֶבֶן מְצוּלָה :

דְּבִיר קָדְשׁוֹ הֱבִיאַנִי · וְגַם שָׁם לֹא שָׁקַטְתִּי · וּבָא
נוֹגֵשׂ וְהִגְלַנִי · כִּי זָרִים עָבַדְתִּי · וְיֵין רַעַל מָסַכְתִּי ·
כִּמְעַט שֶׁעָבַרְתִּי · קֵץ בָּבֶל · זְרֻבָּבֶל · לְקֵץ שִׁבְעִים
נוֹשַׁעְתִּי :

כְּרוֹת קוֹמַת בְּרוֹשׁ בִּקֵּשׁ · אֲגָגִי בֶּן־הַמְּדָתָא · וְנִהְיָתָה
לוֹ לְמוֹקֵשׁ · וְגַאֲוָתוֹ נִשְׁבָּתָה · רֹאשׁ יְמִינִי נִשֵּׂאתָ ·
וְאוֹיֵב שְׁמוֹ מָחִיתָ · רוֹב בָּנָיו · וְקִנְיָנָיו · עַל הָעֵץ תָּלִיתָ :

Mo-oz tzur. This hymn is now often sung also in the synagogue.
It recalls the redemption of Israel from Egypt, the Babylonian Exile,
Haman's threat of extermination, and closes with the rescue from the
Terror of Antiochus Epiphanes. It is by an otherwise unknown hymn-
writer Mordecai, in the middle of the thirteenth century. The rendering
is by Solis-Cohen, and can be sung to the stirring traditional tune.
The literal translation of lines two and three is : " when Thou shalt have
utterly destroyed the blaspheming foe, I will complete with song and
psalm the dedication of the altar." By a slight change, this is now :
" when Thou shalt cause all slaughter to cease, and the blaspheming
foe, I will complete, etc.

"MO-OZ
TZUR"

In the home the following Hymn is chanted :—
Mighty, praised beyond compare,
  Rock of my salvation,
Build again my House of Pray'r
  For thy habitation !
Haste my restoration : let a ransomed nation
    Joyful sing
    To its King
Psalms of dedication !

Woe was mine in Egypt-land
  Tyrant kings enslaved me,
Till Thy mighty, outstretched Hand
  From oppression saved me.
Pharaoh, rash pursuing, vowed my swift undoing ;
    Soon, his host
    That proud boast
'Neath the waves was rueing !

To thy holy Hill, the way
  Mad'st Thou clear before me ;
With false gods I went astray—
  Foes to Exile bore me.
Torn from all I cherished, almost had I perished ;
    Babylon fell,
    Zerubabel
Had'st Thou to restore me !

Then the vengeful Haman wrought
  Subtly to betray me ;
In his snare himself he caught—
  He that planned to slay me.
(Haled from Esther's palace, hanged on his own gallows !)
    Seal and ring
    Persia's king
Gave Thy servant zealous.

Zerubabbel. Governor of the returned exiles in Judah. With the encouragement of Haggai and Zechariah, he completed in the year 520 the rebuilding of the Second Temple that had been begun in 537. *Thy servant zealous.* Mordecai.

יָוָנִים נִקְבְּצוּ עָלַי · אֲזַי בִּימֵי הַשְׁמַנִּים · וּפָרְצוּ
חוֹמוֹת מִגְדָּלַי · וְטִמְּאוּ כָּל הַשְּׁמָנִים · וּמִנּוֹתַר קַנְקַנִּים ·
נַעֲשָׂה נֵס לַשּׁוֹשַׁנִּים · בְּנֵי בִינָה · יְמֵי שְׁמוֹנָה · קָבְעוּ
שִׁיר וּרְנָנִים :

Asmoneans. This seems to have been the original name of the Maccabean family, probably derived from a remote ancestor named Hasmon. " Maccabi " means " the Hammer ", which is a title often given to national heroes (like Charles *Martel,* and Edward I, " the Hammer of the Scots ") who beat back a seemingly irresistible enemy. The name Maccabi has also been held to be formed from the initial Hebrew letters of " Who is like unto Thee among the mighty, O Lord "—stated to have been the inscription on the banner of these Jewish heroes.

Javan. The same word as " Ionia " ; Greece.

PURIM.

PURIM is the yearly commemoration of a signal deliverance of the Jews of the Persian Empire from wholesale extermination at the instigation of Haman, the vizier of King Ahasuerus (Xerxes). The word Purim means " lots ", and the Festival is so called because Haman cast lots to determine which day would be most favourable for his plan. Mordecai's sturdy independence did not permit him to prostrate himself before Haman ; and thereby Haman's wounded vanity was fanned into a demoniac hatred which could only be stilled by the extermination of the entire race to which Mordecai belonged. When Haman attempted to win the weak king's sanction to massacre every Jew in his Empire, he spoke of " certain people scattered abroad and dispersed among the peoples in all the provinces of thy Kingdom ; and their laws are diverse from those of every people " ; and then added, " neither keep they the king's laws " (3. 8). This is a foul untruth. Jews everywhere form an intensely patriotic section of the population. The day preceding Purim is the Fast of Esther, observed in accordance of Esther 4. 16.

The BOOK OF ESTHER gives a vivid account of the events preceding Haman's fiendish plan, as well as of Israel's wonderful escape from utter destruction. Strictures have been passed on the Book on allegedly

When the brave Asmoneans broke
    Javan's chain in sunder,
Through the holy oil, Thy folk
    Didst Thou show a wonder.
Ever full remained the vessel unprofaned :
    These eight days,
    Lights and praise
Therefore, were ordained.

moral grounds, but this has been done largely by those who appear to have greater sympathy with him who planned the general massacre than with his intended victims. Those critics overlook the fact that the Jews acted in self-defence, and that they refrained from all personal *gain* in the retribution which they inflicted upon their mortal enemies : " on the spoil they laid not their hand " (9. 10, 15, 16). In other quarters, much is made of the fact that there are few religious references in the narrative. But the whole Book illustrates the working of Divine Providence in the daily events—the unforeseen chances—of life. A great Anglican divine has well said, " When Esther nerved herself to enter, at the risk of her life, the presence of Ahasuerus—' I will go in unto the King, and if I perish, I perish '— when her patriotic feeling vented itself in that noble cry (8. 6), ' How can I endure to see the evil that shall come unto my people ? Or how can I endure to see the destruction of my kindred ? '—she expressed, although she never named the name of God, a religious devotion as acceptable to Him as that of Moses and David " (Stanley). Again, several nineteenth century critics cast doubts on the historicity of events recorded in the book. But scholars who approached the Book with knowledge and an open mind (Sayce, Cassel, Jampel, Hoschander) have vindicated the truth of the narrative.

The story of Purim has, in one form or another been repeated many times in Jewish history, and there are many local Purims on which Jewish communities commemorate their escape from danger ; *e.g.* the Purim of Saragossa (still observed by the descendants), with a special Megillah giving the narrative of the deliverance in 1380. Three generations ago, Liberal Jews gave up the observance of Purim ; among the reasons that impelled their leaders to do so, was the assumption that there would be no more Hamans in the world. The unwisdom of that action is now patent to all. Haman's fiendish plan has in our own day been carried into effect to an appalling extent.

סֵדֶר פּוּרִים :

Before reading the מְגִלָּה *the following Blessings are said :—*

בָּרוּךְ אַתָּה יְיָ אֱלֹהֵינוּ מֶלֶךְ הָעוֹלָם · אֲשֶׁר קִדְּשָׁנוּ
בְּמִצְוֹתָיו וְצִוָּנוּ עַל מִקְרָא מְגִלָּה :

בָּרוּךְ אַתָּה יְיָ אֱלֹהֵינוּ מֶלֶךְ הָעוֹלָם · שֶׁעָשָׂה נִסִּים
לַאֲבוֹתֵינוּ בַּיָּמִים הָהֵם בַּזְּמַן הַזֶּה :

בָּרוּךְ אַתָּה יְיָ אֱלֹהֵינוּ מֶלֶךְ הָעוֹלָם · שֶׁהֶחֱיָנוּ וְקִיְּמָנוּ
וְהִגִּיעָנוּ לַזְּמַן הַזֶּה :

After reading the מְגִלָּה *say :—*

בָּרוּךְ אַתָּה יְיָ אֱלֹהֵינוּ מֶלֶךְ הָעוֹלָם · הָרָב אֶת רִיבֵנוּ
וְהַדָּן אֶת דִּינֵנוּ וְהַנּוֹקֵם אֶת נִקְמָתֵנוּ וְהַמְשַׁלֵּם גְּמוּל לְכָל
אוֹיְבֵי נַפְשֵׁנוּ וְהַנִּפְרָע לָנוּ מִצָּרֵינוּ : בָּרוּךְ אַתָּה יְיָ · הַנִּפְרָע
לְעַמּוֹ יִשְׂרָאֵל מִכָּל־צָרֵיהֶם · הָאֵל הַמּוֹשִׁיעַ :

The following paragraph is omitted after the Reading of the
מְגִלָּה *in the morning.*

אֲשֶׁר הֵנִיא עֲצַת גּוֹיִם וַיָּפֶר מַחְשְׁבוֹת עֲרוּמִים : בְּקוּם עָלֵינוּ
אָדָם רָשָׁע נֵצֶר זָדוֹן מִזֶּרַע עֲמָלֵק : גָּאָה בְעָשְׁרוֹ וְכָרָה לוֹ בּוֹר

The Torah Reading is Exodus 17. 8–16, being the war against
Amalek, the traditional ancestor of Haman.

Purim, like Simchas Torah, was the occasion of much joyousness
in Jewish life, and of merry-making to both young and old.

Megillah. lit. " scroll "; We also speak as " the scroll of " Song of
Songs, of Ruth, of Lamentations, and of Ecclesiastes. But it is only
" the Scroll of Esther," that came to be known as *the* Megillah.

plead our cause. This Benediction, as well as those preceding, are
of ancient date.

SERVICE FOR PURIM

Before reading the Book of Esther the following Blessings are said :—

BENE-
DICTIONS

Blessed art thou, O Lord our God, King of the universe, who hast hallowed us by thy commandments, and hast given us command concerning the reading of the Megillah.

Blessed art thou, O Lord our God, King of the universe, who wrought wonderful deliverance for our fathers in days of old, at this season.

Blessed art thou, O Lord our God, King of the universe, who hast kept us in life, and hast preserved us, and enabled us to reach this season.

After reading the Book of Esther say :—

Blessed art thou, O Lord our God, King of the universe, who dost contend for us, judge our cause, and avenge our wrong, who renderest retribution to our mortal enemies, and on our behalf dealest out punishment to our adversaries. Blessed art thou, O Lord, who on behalf of thy people Israel dealest out punishment to all their adversaries, O God, the Saviour.

The following paragraph is. omitted after the Reading of the Book of Esther in the morning :—

PURIM
MEDITA-
TION

—Who broughtest the counsel of the heathen to nought, and madest the devices of the crafty of none effect, when a wicked man, an arrogant offshoot of the seed of Amalek, rose up against us. Insolent in his riches, he digged himself a pit, and his own greatness laid him a snare. In his mind he thought to entrap, but was himself entrapped ; he sought to destroy, but was speedily destroyed. Haman displayed the hatred of his fathers, and stirred up ancient

Who broughtest the counsel. This alphabetical poem recounts the story of Purim with poetical and Midrashic embellishments ; and closes with a eulogy of Mordecai and of Esther, " the Jews of Shushan", that forms the beginning of the next paragraph. It is a product of the Gaonic age.

Hadassah. lit. " myrtle ", was the " Jewish " name of Esther. Esther, her court name, is probably derived from Istar, meaning " star ".

וּמְדֻלָּתוֹ יְקָשָׁה לּוֹ לֶכֶד : דִּמָּה בְנַפְשׁוֹ לִלְכּוֹד וְנִלְכָּד בִּקֵּשׁ
לְהַשְׁמִיד וְנִשְׁמַד מְהֵרָה : הָמָן הוֹדִיעַ אֵיבַת אֲבוֹתָיו וְעוֹרֵר
שִׂנְאַת אַחִים לַבָּנִים : וְלֹא זָכַר רַחֲמֵי שָׁאוּל כִּי-בְחֶמְלָתוֹ עַל-
אֲגָג נוֹלַד אוֹיֵב : זָמַם רָשָׁע לְהַכְרִית צַדִּיק וְנִלְכַּד טָמֵא בִּידֵי
טָהוֹר : חֶסֶד גָּבַר עַל-שִׁגְגַת אָב וְרָשָׁע הוֹסִיף חֵטְא עַל-
חֲטָאָיו : טָמַן בְּלִבּוֹ מַחְשְׁבוֹת עֲרוּמָיו וַיִּתְמַכֵּר לַעֲשׂוֹת רָעָה :
יָדוֹ שָׁלַח בִּקְדוֹשֵׁי אֵל כַּסְפּוֹ נָתַן לְהַכְרִית זִכְרָם : כִּרְאוֹת
מָרְדְּכַי כִּי-יָצָא קֶצֶף וְדָתֵי הָמָן נִתְּנוּ בְּשׁוּשָׁן ׳ לָבַשׁ שַׂק וְקָשַׁר
מִסְפֵּד וְנָזַר צוֹם וַיֵּשֶׁב עַל-הָאֵפֶר : מִי זֶה יַעֲמוֹד לְכַפֵּר שְׁגָגָה
וְלִמְחוֹל חַטַּאת עֲוֺן אֲבוֹתֵינוּ : גֵּץ פָּרַח מִלּוּלָב הֵן הֲדַסָּה
עָמְדָה לְעוֹרֵר יְשֵׁנִים : סָרִיסֶיהָ הִבְהִילוּ לְהָמָן לְהַשְׁקוֹתוֹ יֵין
חֲמַת תַּנִּינִים : עָמַד בְּעָשְׁרוֹ וְנָפַל בְּרִשְׁעוֹ עָשָׂה לּוֹ עֵץ וְנִתְלָה
עָלָיו : פִּיהֶם פָּתְחוּ כָּל-יוֹשְׁבֵי תֵבֵל כִּי פוּר הָמָן נֶהְפַּךְ לְפוּרֵנוּ :
צַדִּיק נֶחֱלַץ מִיַּד רָשָׁע אוֹיֵב נִתַּן תַּחַת נַפְשׁוֹ : קִימוּ עֲלֵיהֶם
לַעֲשׂוֹת פּוּרִים וְלִשְׂמוֹחַ בְּכָל-שָׁנָה וְשָׁנָה : רָאִיתָ אֶת-תְּפִלַּת
מָרְדְּכַי וְאֶסְתֵּר ׳ הָמָן וּבָנָיו עַל-הָעֵץ תָּלִיתָ :

שׁוֹשַׁנַּת יַעֲקֹב צָהֲלָה וְשָׂמֵחָה בִּרְאוֹתָם יַחַד תְּכֵלֶת מָרְדְּכָי :
תְּשׁוּעָתָם הָיִיתָ לָנֶצַח וְתִקְוָתָם בְּכָל-דּוֹר וָדוֹר : לְהוֹדִיעַ
שֶׁכָּל-קֹוֶיךָ לֹא יֵבֹשׁוּ וְלֹא יִכָּלְמוּ לָנֶצַח כָּל-הַחוֹסִים בָּךְ :
אָרוּר הָמָן אֲשֶׁר בִּקֵּשׁ לְאַבְּדִי ׳ בָּרוּךְ מָרְדְּכַי הַיְּהוּדִי ׳
אֲרוּרָה זֶרֶשׁ אֵשֶׁת מַפְחִידִי ׳ בְּרוּכָה אֶסְתֵּר מְגִנָּה בַּעֲדִי ׳
וְגַם חַרְבוֹנָה זָכוּר לְטוֹב :

וַיְאַדִּיר, *p.* 730, *to* וְאַתָּה קָדוֹשׁ, *p.* 734. *On Saturday Evening*
begin וִיהִי נֹעַם, *p.* 728. *The Reader says* קַדִּישׁ, *p.* 206, (*omitting*
עָלֵינוּ), *p.* 550. *On Saturday, say* וַיִּתֶּן לְךָ, *p.* 734.

emnity against the children, remembering not the mercy of Saul, through whose compassion for Agag the adversary was born. The wicked plotted to cut off the just, and the unclean was caught in the hands of the pure. (Mordecai's) lovingkindness (to Esther) prevailed, but the wicked (Haman) heaped sin upon sins. In his heart he hid his cunning devices, and sold himself to do wickedness. He stretched forth his hand against God's saints ; he gave his silver to cut off the remembrance of them. When Mordecai saw that wrath had gone forth, and that the decrees of Haman were issued in Shushan, he put on sackcloth and wrapped himself in mourning, ordained a fast and sat upon ashes. Who will rise up to atone for error, and obtain pardon for the sin and iniquity of our fathers ? A flower blossometh from the palm tree : lo ! Hadassah arose to awaken the merit of those that slept in the grave. Her servants hastened to make Haman drink the wine of death. He rose by his riches, but fell in his wickedness ; he made him a gallows, and was himself hanged thereon. All the inhabitants of the world were amazed when the lot that Haman had cast for our destruction was turned in our favour. When the righteous was delivered out of the hand of the wicked, and the enemy was put in his stead, the Jews ordained for themselves to celebrate Purim, and to rejoice thereon every year. Thou didst regard the prayer of Mordecai and Esther : Haman and his sons thou didst hang upon the gallows.

The Jews of Shushan rejoiced and were glad when they all of them saw Mordecai in the purple. Thou hast ever been Israel's salvation, and their hope in every generation, to make known that all who hope in thee shall not be ashamed, neither shall any be confounded who put their trust in thee. Accursed be Haman who sought to destroy me ; blessed be Mordecai the Jew ; accursed be Zeresh. the wife of him that terrified me ; blessed·be Esther my protectress, and may Harbonah also be remembered for good.

" But thou art holy," etc., p. 731, to " glorify it," p. 735. On Saturday Evening begin "And let the graciousness," etc., p. 729. The Reader says Kaddish, p. 207, (omitting "May the prayers," etc.), "It is our duty," etc., p. 551. On Saturday, say the Conclusion Service, p. 735.

The Jews of Shushan. This is usually translated, " the lily of Jacob", but is evidently a poetical term for Shushan Jewry, based on Esther 8. 15. (Weinstock).

NINTH OF AV AND THE MINOR FAST DAYS

To the fast of the Day of Atonement, which is a command of the Torah, Jewish Tradition has added four Fast Days that commemorate events connected with the destruction of the Jewish State—the commencement of the siege of Jerusalem (10th of Teveth); the breach made in the wall (17th of Tammuz); the murder of Gedaliah (3rd of Tishri), see Jeremiah 41. 1, 2; and the burning of the Temple (9th of Av). Whenever these dates fall on a Sabbath, the observance is postponed to Sunday.

These Fasts (and also the Fast of Esther, see p. 952), start at daybreak—except the Ninth of Av, which begins the previous evening and lasts twenty-four hours. Their observance strengthens the historic consciousness of the Jew, and helps to make the Jew of the present a spiritual participant in the calamities that befell his fathers of old.

Special Scriptural Readings, and also special prayers, mark the Fast Day Services in the Synagogue. The Reading from the Torah, both mornings and afternoons, is Exodus 32. 11–14 and 34. 1–10. On the Ninth of Av, this reading is set aside for the Afternoon Service only; instead, Deuteronomy 4. 25–40 and Jeremiah 8. 13–9. 23 are read in the morning. In the Afternoon Service on all Fasts, Isaiah 55. 6–56. 8 is the haftorah.

As to the special prayers, *Selichoth* (Penitential Prayers) are recited on ordinary fast-days, and *Kinnoth* (Elegies) on the Ninth of Av. The custom of reciting Selichoth goes back to Temple times; and some of the ancient supplications that have come down to us are of great beauty. One of the supplications introductory to the recitation of the Divine Attributes (see p. 477) reads :

" God omnipotent, enthroned in mercy, Thou dealest with us in lovingkindness, pardoning the sins of Thy people, causing them to pass away one by one. Thou art ever ready to extend forgiveness to sinners and grant pardon to transgressors, acting in charity towards all flesh and spirit, not requiting them according to the evil which they do. Thou, God, who hast taught us to repeat the Thirteen Attributes of mercy, remember unto us this day the covenant of those Attributes—' The Lord, the Lord, a merciful and gracious God, slow to anger and abounding in lovingkindness and truth, keeping mercy for thousands, forgiving iniquity, transgression and sin, and acquitting '."

The three poetic compositions that are found in each Service at which Selichoth are recited, often reflect the historical background of their age, and the disasters that had overtaken the writer's generation. In the Selichah, the Jew throughout fifteen hundred years, told his woe, confessed his sins, and implored God's mercy and forgiveness.

Excellent examples of these poetic compositions are שומר ישראל "Guardian of Israel", and ד׳ אלהי ישראל שוב מחרון אפך "O Lord God of Israel, turn from Thy fierce wrath," that have been taken over into the Daily Prayer Book (pp. 184 and 182).

The NINTH OF AV is by far the most important of the historical Fasts. On that day, the First Temple was destroyed by the Babylonians in the year 586, before the Christian Era. Tradition states that, 656 years later, the Second Temple was burned on the same day by Titus in the year 70 of the present Era. Likewise, in the year 135 the Second War of Independence against the Romans, under Bar Cochba and Rabbi Akiba, ended with the fall of Bethar on the ninth of Av. It is a tragic coincidence that the expulsion of the Jews from Spain in 1492 also began on this same black-letter day of Jewish history.

No wonder that the Fast of Av is marked by all the rigour of the Day of Atonement. As a sign of mourning, tallith and tefillin are not put on during the Morning Service. The curtain is removed from the Ark; and the worshippers, sitting on the floor or on low benches, chant in the evening the Book of Lamentations. Its authorship is ascribed to the Prophet Jeremiah, who foretold and witnessed the downfall of the Jewish State. In the morning, *kinnoth* are intoned, dirges over the passing of the Temple and the religious and national life of which it was the symbol and embodiment, and elegies over the woes of the Captivity and of the continued martyrdom in the long night of Exile. The closing section of the kinnoth are invocations to Zion (" Zionides ") giving expression to Israel's undying longing for the Holy Land and Holy City. The greatest names in Jewish poetry are among authors of the kinnoth—Elazar Kalir (8th century), Solomon ibn Gabirol (1021-1058), Yehudah Hallevi (.1085-1145) and Rabbi Meir of Rothenburg (1215-1293). Hallevi's *Ode to Zion* is one of the great lyrics in world literature; and Rothenburg's Dirge on the burning of Hebrew books at Paris in 1244, rivals it in depth of feeling.

The Sabbath preceding the Fast of Ab is called *Sabbath Chazon*, and the Sabbath following, *Sabbath Nachamu*, because the Haftorahs on these Sabbaths, Isaiah 1, and Isaiah 40, begin respectively with the words חזון and נחמו ; the one containing arraignment ; the other, a message of comfort.

GRACE BEFORE AND AFTER MEALS

So far the Jewish Prayer Book dealt with Public Prayers—daily, Sabbath and Festival Services. Beginning with the Grace over Meals, we have Private Prayers and Blessings, including those in connection with Birth, Death and Mourning. The aim of this part of the Prayer Book is the sanctification of the whole drama of human life.

DIETARY LAWS

There are few more wonderful things in the history of Religion than the spiritualization of the act of eating achieved by Judaism as part of its hallowing of daily life.

To understand that spiritualization, we must recall the laws of food, and take note of the prayers before and after food.

(a) The laws of food are among the major requirements of Jewish religious practice, and constitute an invaluable training in self-mastery. Their supreme motive is holiness : not as an abstract idea, but as a regulating principle in the every day existence of men, women and children. " Sanctify yourselves, and be ye holy ; for I am holy " (Leviticus 11. 44) was spoken in connection with forbidden foods. " The Dietary Laws ", declares Maimonides, " train us in the mastery over our appetites ; they accustom us to restrain both the growth of desire and the disposition to consider pleasure of eating and drinking as the end of man's existence ". The Maccabean martyrs died rather than transgress them. And at the present day, " it ought to be the pride of the modern Jew—and every child should be taught to feel it— that his religion demands from him a self-abnegation from which other religionists are absolved ; that the price to be paid for the privilege of belonging to the hierarchy of Israel is continuous and conscious self-sacrifice " (M. Joseph). For a brief summary of the Dietary Laws, see M. Friedländer, *The Jewish Religion*, pp. 459–466.

(b) The Dietary Laws have proved an important factor in the survival of the Jewish race in the past ; and are, in more than one respect, an irreplaceable agency for maintaining Jewish identity in the present. An illustrious Jewish scientist wrote :—

" In contrast to not a few of our co-religionists who have no occasion for weeks and months together to bestow a thought on their Creed or their People, the Jew who keeps *Kashrus* has to think of his religious and communal allegiance on the occasion of every meal ; and, on every such occasion, the observance of those laws constitutes a renewal of acquiescence in the fact that he is a Jew, and a deliberate acknowledgment of that fact."

The Rabbis were content to say that these laws must be obeyed, although the reason for them transcends human understanding, and although they may provoke the derision of those who have fallen away from the Torah. One ancient gibe, revived in modern days, and used as the final argument against the dietary laws is " Not what goes into the mouth, but what comes out of it, defileth man ". Now, the State could never endorse the literal meaning of the words, " Not what goes into the mouth defileth a man ". It holds that poison which goes into the mouth, *does* defile, and classes poisoning as a peculiarly detestable kind of murder. Likewise, Science sets its face against unripe fruit, adulterated milk, diseased meat—things that go into the mouth. Even many of the Christian Churches have for over a hundred years waged a bitter warfare against the enemy that men take into the mouth " to steal away their brains "—alcohol. And as to the words, " only that which cometh out of the mouth defileth a man ", one needs but recall the fact that *out of* the mouth come speech which raises man above the brute, prayer that unites man to his Creator, words of cheer and faith spoken to the sorrow-laden.

The great majority of Jews continue to abstain from forbidden food not from personal aversion but because " our Father in Heaven has decreed that we should abstain from it " (Sifra). There are, however, those who see a hygienic purpose in these prohibitions, and hold that the forbidden meats were not prohibited arbitrarily, but because they are unwholesome and repulsive in themselves. Moreover, as it is in the blood that the germs or spores of infectious disease circulate, the flesh of all animals for human consumption must be drained of blood. This is effectively done by *Shechitah*, the Jewish manner of slaughtering animals for food. It alone produces instantaneous insensibility in the animal. And the draining of blood is thoroughly completed by " kashering ", the Traditional treatment of the kosher-killed meat when it is prepared for food. Statistical investigation has demonstrated that Jews as a class are immune from, or less susceptible to, certain diseases ; and competent authorities have not hesitated to attribute these healthy characteristics to the influence of the Dietary Laws.

(*c*) Judaism ordains thanksgiving to God before and after the meal. It thus raises the satisfaction of a physical craving into the realm of the spirit. Eating becomes a religious act.

This is ancient Jewish teaching and practice. We learn from I Samuel 9. 13 that the Prophet pronounced a Blessing over the sacrifice before the people would eat of it. A thousand years later, the sect of Essenes (see p. 480) observed utmost reverence in regard to meals. " They enter the dining room pure, as they would enter a sacred precinct. At the beginning and at the end of the meal, they do honour to God as the supplier of life " (Josephus). This indicates that they observed the washing of hands before eating, and recited Blessings before and after meals. Many centuries before the Essenes, the Men of the Great Assembly had introduced the Benedictions of the Grace ; and, among Mishnic teachers, it was especially Rabbi Simeon ben Yochai (see p. 648), who stressed that eating and drinking must be conducted with seemliness; that at the family table no word of anger, no impurity of speech, no excess of any sort should be tolerated. He said,

סדר סעודה וברכותיה :

On washing the hands, previous to partaking of a Meal, say :—

בָּרוּךְ אַתָּה יְיָ אֱלֹהֵינוּ מֶלֶךְ הָעוֹלָם • אֲשֶׁר קִדְּשָׁנוּ
בְּמִצְוֹתָיו וְצִוָּנוּ עַל נְטִילַת יָדָיִם :

The following Blessing is said over the Bread :—

בָּרוּךְ אַתָּה יְיָ אֱלֹהֵינוּ מֶלֶךְ הָעוֹלָם • הַמּוֹצִיא לֶחֶם
מִן הָאָרֶץ :

" If three have eaten at a table and have spoken there no words of Religion, it is as if they had eaten of sacrifices to dead idols " ; *i.e.* such meal was merely a heathen satisfaction of physical needs, with no sacredness whatever surrounding it. The Grace after Meals—consisting of thanksgiving for food, coupled with historic and religious memories— was soon to become universal Jewish usage, and it is a fitting fulfil- ment of Simeon ben Yochai's demand for sacred discourse at table. Through the Grace, the family table became the family Altar. The Grace recalls Israel's sons and daughters to their Father Who is in Heaven, and also binds them to their People. " It may appear a minute matter to pronounce the Hebrew blessing over bread, and to accustom one's children to do so. Yet if a Jew at the time of partaking of food, remembers the identical words used by his fellow-Jews since time immemorial and the world over, he revives in himself, wherever he be at the moment, communion with his imperishable race " (Haff- kine).

BENEDICTIONS BEFORE THE MEAL

On washing the hands, previous to partaking of a Meal, say ;—

WASHING THE HANDS
Blessed art thou, O Lord our God, King of the universe, who hast hallowed us by thy commandments, and hast given us command concerning the washing of the hands.

The following Blessing is said over the Bread :—

"MOTZI"
Blessed art thou, O Lord our God, King of the universe, who bringest forth bread from the earth.

BEFORE THE MEAL.

washing of the hands. See p. 11.

The term, " washing of the hands " is in Hebrew, " lifting up the hands ". The explanation of this idiom is, either that the hands are raised in the act of pouring water over them ; or, it is connected with a rendering of Psalm 134. 2 (" lift up your hands to the sanctuary, and bless the Lord "), which was used as an invocation while the water was poured on the hands.

Motzi. *bringest forth bread.* The wording is based on Psalm 104. 14. Its ten words are equivalent to the ten Hebrew words of Psalm 145. 15 (" The eyes of all wait upon Thee, and Thou givest them their food in due season "). The Rabbis looked upon this verse as containing the essence of the Grace.

The *Motzi* should preferably be recited over a whole loaf. Bread, as the staff of life must be treated with respect ; children are to be taught that even crumbs are not to be trodden upon.

GRACE AFTER MEALS

On Sabbaths and Holydays, and on those days when תַּחֲנוּן
(see p. 167) is not said, שִׁיר הַמַּעֲלוֹת *is said.*

תהלים קכו

שִׁיר הַמַּעֲלוֹת ׳ בְּשׁוּב יְיָ אֶת־שִׁיבַת צִיּוֹן הָיִינוּ כְּחֹלְמִים :
אָז יִמָּלֵא שְׂחוֹק פִּינוּ וּלְשׁוֹנֵנוּ רִנָּה אָז יֹאמְרוּ בַגּוֹיִם הִגְדִּיל יְיָ
לַעֲשׂוֹת עִם־אֵלֶּה : הִגְדִּיל יְיָ לַעֲשׂוֹת עִמָּנוּ הָיִינוּ שְׂמֵחִים :
שׁוּבָה יְיָ אֶת־שְׁבִיתֵנוּ כַּאֲפִיקִים בַּנֶּגֶב : הַזֹּרְעִים בְּדִמְעָה בְּרִנָּה
יִקְצֹרוּ : הָלוֹךְ יֵלֵךְ וּבָכֹה נֹשֵׂא מֶשֶׁךְ־הַזָּרַע בֹּא־יָבֹא בְרִנָּה
נֹשֵׂא אֲלֻמֹּתָיו :

*The following Introduction is customary if three or more Males,
above the age of thirteen, have eaten at table together :*

He who says Grace commences thus :—

רַבּוֹתַי נְבָרֵךְ :

The others respond :—

יְהִי שֵׁם יְיָ מְבֹרָךְ מֵעַתָּה וְעַד עוֹלָם :

AFTER THE MEAL.

I. On Sabbath, ZEMIROTH are sung during the meal, or before the Grace. These gleeful table-hymns are a unique combination of adoration of God with genial appreciation of good cheer ; see p. 410.

But even in those homes in which Zemiroth are not sung, Psalm 126 has in recent centuries been chanted on Sabbaths and Festivals before the Grace—a keen remembrance of Zion amidst the enjoyment of earthly delights. The ancient author of the psalm starts with the Redemption from the Babylonian Exilè. That Restoration of Zion was a marvel so astonishing to both Jew and non-Jew of those days, that it could

AFTER THE MEAL.

On Sabbaths and Holydays, and on those days when Tachanun (see p. 168) is not said, Psalm cxxvi is said :—

Psalm cxxvi. A Pilgrim Song.

RESTORA-TION

See p. 598

SOWING IN TEARS, REAPING IN JOY

When the Lord restored the prosperity of Zion, we were like unto them that dream. ²Then was our mouth filled with laughter, and our tongue with exultation : then said they among the nations, The Lord hath done great things for them. ³The Lord hath done great things for us ; whereat we rejoiced. ⁴Turn our fortunes, O Lord, as the streams in the south. ⁵They that sow in tears shall reap in joy. ⁶Though he goeth on his way weeping, bearing the store of seed, he shall come back with joy, bearing his sheaves.

[The following Introduction is customary if three or more Males, above the age of thirteen, have eaten at table together :

He who says Grace commences thus :—

Let us say grace.

The others respond :—

INTRO-DUCTION TO GRACE

Blessed be the Name of the Lord from this time forth and for ever.

hardly be credited. But adversity had once more overtaken Israel : may God, therefore, again bless and redeem it. Its concluding thought, " They that sow in tears shall reap in joy "—is a message of consolation and hope in every human generation. In the Sephardi Rite, Psalm 23 (" The Lord is my Shepherd "), p. 1053, is thus sung.

A large number of melodies exist for the singing of this opening psalm of the Festive Grace. " These melodies often remain the treasured memory of a life-time, and parents should train their children to learn them early in life " (Berliner).

II. GRACE IN COMPANY.

The Master of the House usually invites a guest, or a member of the family at table, to lead in the Grace. If the company consists of three or more males of thirteen years of age, he who leads in saying Grace summons the rest to join him in thanking " Him of Whose bounty we have partaken ". This custom is ancient, and the formulae in use to-day are found in the Mishna.

let us say Grace. Among Jews from Central and East European countries, this is often said in Yiddish, " Rabosai, mir wellen benschen " ; the last word is from the Latin *benedicere,* to bless.

He who says Grace proceeds :—

בִּרְשׁוּת רַבּוֹתַי

If there be present ten or more Males above the age of thirteen, the word אֱלֹהֵינוּ *is added.*

נְבָרֵךְ (אֱלֹהֵינוּ) שֶׁאָכַלְנוּ מִשֶּׁלּוֹ :

The others respond :—

בָּרוּךְ (אֱלֹהֵינוּ) שֶׁאָכַלְנוּ מִשֶּׁלּוֹ וּבְטוּבוֹ חָיִינוּ :

He who says Grace replies :—

בָּרוּךְ (אֱלֹהֵינוּ) שֶׁאָכַלְנוּ מִשֶּׁלּוֹ וּבְטוּבוֹ חָיִינוּ :

בָּרוּךְ הוּא וּבָרוּךְ שְׁמוֹ :

If less than three Males above the age of thirteen be present, begin here—

בָּרוּךְ אַתָּה יְיָ אֱלֹהֵינוּ מֶלֶךְ הָעוֹלָם · הַזָּן אֶת־הָעוֹלָם כֻּלּוֹ · בְּטוּבוֹ בְּחֵן בְּחֶסֶד וּבְרַחֲמִים · הוּא נוֹתֵן לֶחֶם לְכָל־בָּשָׂר · כִּי לְעוֹלָם חַסְדּוֹ : וּבְטוּבוֹ הַגָּדוֹל תָּמִיד

with the permission. After having invited the company to say Grace, and by the Response ("Let the Name of the Lord be blessed") having ascertained their readiness to do so, the leader asks permission of the Master of the house and that of the company to proceed with the

He who says Grace proceeds :—

With the sanction of the master of the house and of those present,

If there be present ten or more Males above the age of thirteen, the words " our God " are added :—

We will bless (our God) him of whose bounty we have partaken.

The others respond :—

Blessed be (our God) he of whose bounty we have partaken, and through whose goodness we live.

He who says Grace replies :—

Blessed be (our God) he of whose bounty we have partaken, and through whose goodness we live.

Blessed be he, and blessed be his Name.]

If less than three Males above the age of thirteen be present, begin here :—

THANKS-
GIVING

I. FOR
GOD'S
PROVIDEN-
TIAL CARE

Blessed art thou, O Lord our God, King of the universe, who feedest the whole world with thy goodness, with grace, with lovingkindness and tender mercy ; thou givest food to all flesh, for thy lovingkindness endureth for ever. Through thy great goodness food hath never failed us :

actual Grace. If a scholar or Cohen is present, he is included in the formula of request. A son says, " With the permission of my honoured Father (or, honoured Mother) ". These antiphonal Responses have been invaluable in intertwining religion with home feeling, the love of God with filial piety.

blessed be he, and blessed be his Name. This concluding phrase of the Responses is much later than the other formulae. It dates from the twelfth century.

III. THE GRACE.

The Grace after Meals consists of three ancient Blessings, to which a fourth Blessing was added later, besides Supplementary Petitions. Their authorship and introduction is ascribed to Moses, Joshua, David and Solomon. This is another way of saying that they go back to the beginnings of Israel's life as a nation, and that the Grace reflects the national and spiritual growth of Israel.

לֹא־חָסַר לָנוּ וְאַל יֶחְסַר־לָנוּ מָזוֹן לְעוֹלָם וָעֶד בַּעֲבוּר
שְׁמוֹ הַגָּדוֹל · כִּי הוּא זָן וּמְפַרְנֵס לַכֹּל וּמֵטִיב לַכֹּל
וּמֵכִין מָזוֹן לְכָל־בְּרִיּוֹתָיו אֲשֶׁר בָּרָא · בָּרוּךְ אַתָּה יְיָ ·
הַזָּן אֶת־הַכֹּל :

נוֹדֶה לְךָ יְיָ אֱלֹהֵינוּ עַל שֶׁהִנְחַלְתָּ לַאֲבוֹתֵינוּ אֶרֶץ
חֶמְדָּה טוֹבָה וּרְחָבָה · וְעַל שֶׁהוֹצֵאתָנוּ יְיָ אֱלֹהֵינוּ מֵאֶרֶץ
מִצְרַיִם · וּפְדִיתָנוּ מִבֵּית עֲבָדִים · וְעַל בְּרִיתְךָ שֶׁחָתַמְתָּ
בִּבְשָׂרֵנוּ · וְעַל תּוֹרָתְךָ שֶׁלִּמַּדְתָּנוּ · וְעַל חֻקֶּיךָ שֶׁהוֹדַעְתָּנוּ ·
וְעַל חַיִּים חֵן וָחֶסֶד שֶׁחוֹנַנְתָּנוּ · וְעַל אֲכִילַת מָזוֹן שָׁאַתָּה
זָן וּמְפַרְנֵס אוֹתָנוּ תָּמִיד בְּכָל־יוֹם וּבְכָל־עֵת וּבְכָל־
שָׁעָה :

On חֲנֻכָּה and פּוּרִים add עַל הַנִּסִּים, pp. 150, 151.

וְעַל הַכֹּל יְיָ אֱלֹהֵינוּ אֲנַחְנוּ מוֹדִים לָךְ וּמְבָרְכִים
אוֹתָךְ · יִתְבָּרַךְ שִׁמְךָ בְּפִי כָּל־חַי תָּמִיד לְעוֹלָם וָעֶד :
כַּכָּתוּב · וְאָכַלְתָּ וְשָׂבָעְתָּ וּבֵרַכְתָּ אֶת־יְיָ אֱלֹהֶיךָ עַל־
הָאָרֶץ הַטּוֹבָה אֲשֶׁר נָתַן־לָךְ · בָּרוּךְ אַתָּה יְיָ · עַל־הָאָרֶץ
וְעַל־הַמָּזוֹן :

1. *who feedest.* The first is the oldest Blessing, and gives the essence
of the Grace—thanksgiving for the food partaken. In form and content

O may it not fail us for ever and ever for thy great Name's sake, since thou nourishest and sustainest all beings, and doest good unto all, and providest food for all thy creatures whom thou hast created. Blessed art thou, O Lord, who givest food unto all.

II. FOR LAW, COVE-NANT AND LAND OF ISRAEL We thank thee, O Lord our God, because thou didst give as an heritage unto our fathers a desirable, good and ample land, and because thou didst bring us forth, O Lord our God, from the land of Egypt, and didst deliver us from the house of bondage ; as well as for thy covenant which thou hast sealed in our flesh, thy Torah which thou hast taught us, thy statutes which thou hast made known unto us, the life, grace and lovingkindness which thou hast bestowed upon us, and for the food wherewith thou dost constantly feed and sustain us on every day, in every season, at every hour.

On Chanukah and Purim add, "We thank thee also for the miracles," etc., pp. 152, 153.

Deuteronomy 8. 10 For all this, O Lord our God, we thank and bless thee, blessed be thy Name by the mouth of all living continually and for ever, even as it is written, And thou shalt eat and be satisfied, and thou shalt bless the Lord thy God for the good land which he hath given thee. Blessed art thou, O Lord, for the land and for the food.

it is *universal* (quoting Psalm 136. 28), being fitted for men of all races and creeds so long as they believe in God. It may even be said to be " cosmic ", as it affirms God's loving care of all His creatures.

2. *we thank thee.* After the universal blessing comes the *national* blessing. In it, we thank God for the Land of Israel and the Redemption from Egyptian bondage ; for Israel's Torah and the Commandments that link every moment of the Israelite's life with the past of his People.

On Chanukah and Purim, memories of the historic happenings are recalled by brief accounts of these Festivals inserted in this Blessing.

רַחֵם יְיָ אֱלֹהֵינוּ עַל־יִשְׂרָאֵל עַמֶּךָ · וְעַל יְרוּשָׁלַיִם
עִירֶךָ · וְעַל צִיּוֹן מִשְׁכַּן כְּבוֹדֶךָ · וְעַל מַלְכוּת בֵּית דָּוִד
מְשִׁיחֶךָ · וְעַל־הַבַּיִת הַגָּדוֹל וְהַקָּדוֹשׁ שֶׁנִּקְרָא שִׁמְךָ
עָלָיו : אֱלֹהֵינוּ אָבִינוּ · רְעֵנוּ זוּנֵנוּ פַּרְנְסֵנוּ וְכַלְכְּלֵנוּ
וְהַרְוִיחֵנוּ · וְהַרְוַח־לָנוּ יְיָ אֱלֹהֵינוּ מְהֵרָה מִכָּל־צָרוֹתֵינוּ :
וְנָא אַל־תַּצְרִיכֵנוּ יְיָ אֱלֹהֵינוּ לֹא לִידֵי מַתְּנַת בָּשָׂר וָדָם
וְלֹא לִידֵי הַלְוָאָתָם · כִּי אִם לְיָדְךָ הַמְּלֵאָה הַפְּתוּחָה
הַקְּדוֹשָׁה וְהָרְחָבָה · שֶׁלֹּא נֵבוֹשׁ וְלֹא נִכָּלֵם לְעוֹלָם
וָעֶד :

On שַׁבָּת say :—

רְצֵה וְהַחֲלִיצֵנוּ יְיָ אֱלֹהֵינוּ בְּמִצְוֹתֶיךָ וּבְמִצְוַת יוֹם הַשְּׁבִיעִי

thou shalt eat. The duty of saying Grace is based on this verse of
the Torah.
3. *have mercy.* But Israel's life of security and happiness on the
soil of the Holy Land is, for the overwhelming majority of the Jewish
People, a matter of the distant past, and merely a historic memory.
Since the destruction of the Jewish State, vast multitudes of Israel's
sons and daughters have agonized beyond Palestine's borders ; and
have rarely found lasting security anywhere. Before our very eyes,
great Jewries have been hurled down from the heights into utter degradation, ruin, and annihilation. This portion of the Grace, therefore,
begins with רחם " have mercy " ! It implores God's pity upon the Jewish
People as a whole. The middle of this third Benediction consists of a
fervent petition for food, nourishment and sustenance, coupled with
the heart-stirring supplication that we be never thrown on the mercy
of mortals, never become pauperized by their doles or humiliated by

III. FOR RESTORA-TION AND SUSTEN-ANCE

Have mercy, O Lord our God, upon Israel thy people, upon Jerusalem thy' city, upon Zion the abiding place of thy glory, upon the kingdom of the house of David thine anointed, and upon the great and holy house that was called by thy Name. O our God, our Father, feed us, nourish us, sustain, support and relieve us, and speedily, O Lord our God, grant us relief from all our troubles. We beseech thee, O Lord our God, let us not be in need either of the gifts of mortals or of their loans, but only of thy helping hand, which is ' full, open, holy and ample, so that we may never be put to shame nor humiliated.

[On Sabbath say :—

Be pleased, O Lord our God, to strengthen us by thy commandments, and especially by the commandment of the seventh day, this great and holy Sabbath, since this day is great and holy

their loans ; and that we be saved from the dire poverty which may lead to degradation and dishonour. No other People has known such dire poverty as has Israel, with so large a proportion of its masses on the border-line of starvation. It is true that that same People has shown genius in the creation and administration of charitable institutions. This does not lessen the Jew's longing for the " glorious privilege of being independent " ; to be of those who *give*, not of those who receive, charity.

The third Benediction of Grace ends as it began, with remembrance of Israel's ideals, consolation for Israel's woes, and faith in Israel's triumph.

4. The fourth section of the Grace consisted originally of the eight Hebrew words of the Benediction on the receipt of Good Tidings (" Blessed art thou, O Lord our God, King of the universe, who art kind, and dealest kindly "). We do not know the time when this Benediction was added to the other three of the Grace. It may have been added as an expression of supreme thanksgiving when Caligula's attempt to force Emperor-worship upon the Jewish People was frustrated by his death. At any rate, the fourth Benediction had become statutory part of the Grace by the early years of the second century (Büchler).

הַשַּׁבָּת הַגָּדוֹל וְהַקָּדוֹשׁ הַזֶּה ׀ כִּי יוֹם זֶה גָּדוֹל וְקָדוֹשׁ הוּא

לְפָנֶיךָ לִשְׁבָּת־בּוֹ וְלָנוּחַ בּוֹ בְּאַהֲבָה כְּמִצְוַת רְצוֹנֶךָ ׀ בִּרְצוֹנְךָ

הָנִיחַ לָנוּ יְיָ אֱלֹהֵינוּ שֶׁלֹּא תְהִי צָרָה וְיָגוֹן וַאֲנָחָה בְּיוֹם

מְנוּחָתֵנוּ ׀ וְהַרְאֵנוּ יְיָ אֱלֹהֵינוּ בְּנֶחָמַת צִיּוֹן עִירֶךָ ׀ וּבְבִנְיַן

יְרוּשָׁלַיִם עִיר קָדְשֶׁךָ ׀ כִּי אַתָּה הוּא בַּעַל הַיְשׁוּעוֹת וּבַעַל

הַנֶּחָמוֹת ׃

add :— יוֹם טוֹב and רֹאשׁ חֹדֶשׁ On

אֱלֹהֵינוּ וֵאלֹהֵי אֲבוֹתֵינוּ ׀ יַעֲלֶה וְיָבֹא וְיַגִּיעַ וְיֵרָאֶה וְיֵרָצֶה

וְיִשָּׁמַע וְיִפָּקֵד וְיִזָּכֵר זִכְרוֹנֵנוּ וּפִקְדוֹנֵנוּ ׀ וְזִכְרוֹן אֲבוֹתֵינוּ ׀ וְזִכְרוֹן

מָשִׁיחַ בֶּן דָּוִד עַבְדֶּךָ ׀ וְזִכְרוֹן יְרוּשָׁלַיִם עִיר קָדְשֶׁךָ ׀ וְזִכְרוֹן

כָּל עַמְּךָ בֵּית יִשְׂרָאֵל לְפָנֶיךָ ׀ לִפְלֵיטָה וּלְטוֹבָה וּלְחֵן וּלְחֶסֶד

וּלְרַחֲמִים וּלְחַיִּים וּלְשָׁלוֹם בְּיוֹם

on רֹאשׁ חֹדֶשׁ say :—	on רֹאשׁ הַשָּׁנָה :—	סֻכּוֹת on :—
רֹאשׁ הַחֹדֶשׁ	הַזִּכָּרוֹן	חַג הַסֻּכּוֹת
on		
שִׂמְחַת תּוֹרָה and שְׁמִינִי עֲצֶרֶת:	פֶּסַח on :—	שָׁבוּעוֹת on :—
הַשְּׁמִינִי חַג הָעֲצֶרֶת	חַג הַמַּצּוֹת	חַג הַשָּׁבֻעוֹת

הַזֶּה ׀ זָכְרֵנוּ יְיָ אֱלֹהֵינוּ בּוֹ לְטוֹבָה ׀ וּפָקְדֵנוּ בוֹ לִבְרָכָה ׀

וְהוֹשִׁיעֵנוּ בּוֹ לְחַיִּים ׀ וּבִדְבַר יְשׁוּעָה וְרַחֲמִים חוּס וְחָנֵּנוּ

וְרַחֵם עָלֵינוּ וְהוֹשִׁיעֵנוּ ׀ כִּי אֵלֶיךָ עֵינֵינוּ ׀ כִּי אֵל מֶלֶךְ חַנּוּן

וְרַחוּם אָתָּה ׃

וּבְנֵה יְרוּשָׁלַיִם עִיר הַקֹּדֶשׁ בִּמְהֵרָה בְיָמֵינוּ ׀ בָּרוּךְ

אַתָּה יְיָ ׀ בּוֹנֵה בְרַחֲמָיו יְרוּשָׁלָיִם ׀ אָמֵן ׃

בָּרוּךְ אַתָּה יְיָ אֱלֹהֵינוּ מֶלֶךְ הָעוֹלָם ׀ הָאֵל אָבִינוּ

מַלְכֵּנוּ ׀ אַדִּירֵנוּ בּוֹרְאֵנוּ גֹּאֲלֵנוּ יוֹצְרֵנוּ קְדוֹשֵׁנוּ קְדוֹשׁ

before thee, that we may rest and repose thereon in love in accordance with the precept of thy will. In thy favour, O Lord our God, grant us such repose that there be no trouble, grief or lamenting on the day of our rest. Let us, O Lord our God, behold the consolation of Zion thy city, and the rebuilding of Jerusalem thy holy city, for thou art the Lord of salvation and of consolation.]

[On New Moons and Festivals add :—

Our God and God of our Fathers ! May our remembrance rise and come and be accepted before thee, with the remembrance of our fathers, of Messiah the son of David thy servant, of Jerusalem thy holy city, and of all thy people the house of Israel, bringing deliverance and well-being, grace, lovingkindness and mercy, life and peace on this day of—

On New Moon say—the New Moon.

On New Year—Remembrance.

On Tabernacles—the Feast of Tabernacles.

On the Eighth day of Solemn Assembly and on Simchas Torah—the Eighth-day Feast of Solemn Assembly.

On Passover—the Feast of Unleavened Bread.

On Pentecost—the Feast of Weeks.

Remember us, O Lord our God, thereon for our well-being ; be mindful of us for blessing, and save us unto life : by thy promise of salvation and mercy, spare us and be gracious unto us ; have mercy upon us and save us ; for our eyes are bent upon thee, because thou art a gracious and merciful God and King.]

And rebuild Jerusalem the holy city speedily in our days. Blessed art thou, O Lord, who in thy compassion rebuildest Jerusalem. Amen.

IV. "WHO ART KIND AND DEALEST KINDLY" Blessed art thou, O Lord our God, King of the universe, O God, our Father, our King, our Mighty One, the Holy One of Jacob, our Shepherd, the Shepherd of Israel, O King,

יַעֲקֹב · רוֹעֵנוּ רוֹעֵה יִשְׂרָאֵל · הַמֶּלֶךְ הַטּוֹב וְהַמֵּטִיב
לַכֹּל · שֶׁבְּכָל־יוֹם וָיוֹם הוּא הֵטִיב הוּא מֵטִיב הוּא
יֵיטִיב לָנוּ : הוּא גְמָלָנוּ הוּא גוֹמְלֵנוּ הוּא יִגְמְלֵנוּ
לָעַד · לְחֵן לְחֶסֶד וּלְרַחֲמִים וּלְרֶוַח · הַצָּלָה וְהַצְלָחָה
בְּרָכָה וִישׁוּעָה · נֶחָמָה פַּרְנָסָה וְכַלְכָּלָה · וְרַחֲמִים
וְחַיִּים וְשָׁלוֹם וְכָל־טוֹב · וּמִכָּל־טוּב אַל־יְחַסְּרֵנוּ :
הָרַחֲמָן · הוּא יִמְלוֹךְ עָלֵינוּ לְעוֹלָם וָעֶד : הָרַחֲמָן ·
הוּא יִתְבָּרַךְ בַּשָּׁמַיִם וּבָאָרֶץ : הָרַחֲמָן · הוּא יִשְׁתַּבַּח
לְדוֹר דּוֹרִים · וְיִתְפָּאַר בָּנוּ לָנֶצַח נְצָחִים · וְיִתְהַדַּר
בָּנוּ לָעַד וּלְעוֹלְמֵי עוֹלָמִים : הָרַחֲמָן · הוּא יְפַרְנְסֵנוּ
בְּכָבוֹד : הָרַחֲמָן · הוּא יִשְׁבּוֹר עֻלֵּנוּ מֵעַל צַוָּארֵנוּ ·
וְהוּא יוֹלִיכֵנוּ קוֹמְמִיּוּת לְאַרְצֵנוּ : הָרַחֲמָן · הוּא
יִשְׁלַח בְּרָכָה מְרֻבָּה בַּבַּיִת הַזֶּה · וְעַל שֻׁלְחָן זֶה
שֶׁאָכַלְנוּ עָלָיו : הָרַחֲמָן · הוּא יִשְׁלַח לָנוּ אֶת־אֵלִיָּה
הַנָּבִיא זָכוּר לַטּוֹב · וִיבַשֶּׂר־לָנוּ בְּשׂוֹרוֹת טוֹבוֹת
יְשׁוּעוֹת וְנֶחָמוֹת : הָרַחֲמָן · הוּא יְבָרֵךְ

5. The portions of the Grace that follow are all of much later, some of them of quite recent, date.

who art kind and dealest kindly with all, day by day thou
hast dealt kindly, dost deal kindly, and wilt deal kindly
with us ; thou hast bestowed, thou dost bestow, thou wilt
ever bestow benefits upon us, yielding us grace, lovingkindness, mercy and relief, deliverance and prosperity,
blessing and salvation, consolation, sustenance and support, mercy, life, peace and all good : of no manner of good
let us be in want.

The All-merciful shall reign over us for ever and ever.
The All-merciful shall be blessed in heaven and on earth.
The All-merciful shall be praised throughout all generations, glorified amongst us to all eternity, and honoured
amongst us for everlasting.

May the All-merciful grant us an honourable livelihood.
May the All-merciful break the yoke from off our neck,
and lead us upright to our land. May the All-merciful
send a plentiful blessing upon this house, and upon this
V. SUNDRY table at which we have eaten. May the All-merciful send
SUPPLICA-
TIONS us Elijah the prophet (let him be remembered for good),
who shall bring us good tidings, salvation and consolation.

May the All-merciful. These supplications vary in number in the
different Rites. They are lofty, universal aspirations, intermingled
with individual petitions. Abudarham regards them all as private and
personal, to be added at the need or desire of each individual.
break the yoke. For very many centuries Israel was everywhere
under the yoke. Since 1933, this petition has its tragic appropriateness
in our own generation.
Elijah. In Jewish legend, he is the Herald of the Messianic era of
Freedom and Righteousness ; Malachi 3. 23.
good tidings . . . salvation. The Freedom longed for by the Jew
is not for vengeance, but for deliverance from unrighteousness and
inhuman oppression.
consolation. For cruelties and agonies.

*A child at his parents' table says :**	*A master of the house says .**
אֶת־אָבִי מוֹרִי בַּעַל הַבַּיִת	אוֹתִי (וְאֶת־אִשְׁתִּי וְאֶת־
הַזֶּה · וְאֶת־אִמִּי מוֹרָתִי	זַרְעִי) וְאֶת־כָּל־אֲשֶׁר לִי ·
בַּעֲלַת הַבַּיִת הַזֶּה · אוֹתָם	*At a stranger's table say :**
וְאֶת־בֵּיתָם וְאֶת־זַרְעָם וְאֶת־	אֶת־בַּעַל הַבַּיִת הַזֶּה אוֹתוֹ
כָּל־אֲשֶׁר לָהֶם ·	(וְאֶת־אִשְׁתּוֹ וְאֶת־זַרְעוֹ)
	וְאֶת־כָּל־אֲשֶׁר לוֹ ·

אוֹתָנוּ וְאֶת־כָּל־אֲשֶׁר לָנוּ   כְּמוֹ שֶׁנִּתְבָּרְכוּ אֲבֹתֵינוּ
אַבְרָהָם יִצְחָק וְיַעֲקֹב בַּכֹּל מִכֹּל כֹּל · כֵּן יְבָרֵךְ אוֹתָנוּ
כֻּלָּנוּ יַחַד בִּבְרָכָה שְׁלֵמָה · וְנֹאמַר אָמֵן :

בַּמָּרוֹם יְלַמְּדוּ עֲלֵיהֶם וְעָלֵינוּ זְכוּת שֶׁתְּהִי לְמִשְׁמֶרֶת
שָׁלוֹם · וְנִשָּׂא בְרָכָה מֵאֵת יְיָ וּצְדָקָה מֵאֱלֹהֵי יִשְׁעֵנוּ ·
וְנִמְצָא־חֵן וְשֵׂכֶל טוֹב בְּעֵינֵי אֱלֹהִים וְאָדָם :

On שַׁבָּת *say* :—

הָרַחֲמָן · הוּא יַנְחִילֵנוּ יוֹם שֶׁכֻּלּוֹ שַׁבָּת וּמְנוּחָה לְחַיֵּי
הָעוֹלָמִים :

On רֹאשׁ חֹדֶשׁ :—

הָרַחֲמָן · הוּא יְחַדֵּשׁ עָלֵינוּ אֶת־הַחֹדֶשׁ הַזֶּה לְטוֹבָה וְלִבְרָכָה :

On יוֹם טוֹב, *including Chol Ha-moed* :—

הָרַחֲמָן · הוּא יַנְחִילֵנוּ יוֹם שֶׁכֻּלּוֹ טוֹב :

---

*The wording has to be varied according to circumstances.

my honoured father. lit. " my father, my teacher ".
comprehensive blessing. lit. " with all, from all, all " ; suggested
by three texts in Genesis (24. 1 ; 27. 33 and 33. 11).

May the All-merciful bless

*A child at his parent's table says :—**	*A master of the house says :—**
my honoured father, the master of this house, and my honoured mother, the mistress of this house, them, their household, their children, and all that is theirs ;	me, (and my wife and my children) and all that is mine ; *At a stranger's table say :—** the master of this house (and his wife and his children) and all that is his ;

us also and all that is ours, as our fathers Abraham, Isaac and Jacob were blessed each with his own comprehensive blessing ; even thus may he bless all of us together with a perfect blessing, and let us say, Amen.

Both on their and our own behalf may there be such advocacy on high as shall lead to enduring peace ; and may we receive a blessing from the Lord, and righteousness from the God of our salvation ; and may we find grace and good understanding in the sight of God and man.

On Sabbath :—

May the All-merciful let us inherit the day which shall be wholly a Sabbath and rest in the life everlasting.

On New Moon :—-

May the All-merciful renew unto us this month for good and for blessing.

On Festivals, including the Intermediate Days :—

May the All-merciful let us inherit the day which is altogether good.

---

*The wording has to be varied according to circumstances.

advocacy on high. It is a poetic conception of the Rabbis that angelic hosts plead for mortals.

good understanding. See Proverbs 3. 4. Lack of such understanding on the part of those around us, is often the cause of deepest misery.

Sabbath. The sentences for Sabbath and Festivals are the latest additions to the Grace. For the concept of the Sabbath as " a foretaste of the life which is wholly a Sabbath ", see p. 548.

—:רֹאשׁ הַשָּׁנָה *On*

הָרַחֲמָן · הוּא יְחַדֵּשׁ עָלֵינוּ אֶת־הַשָּׁנָה הַזֹּאת לְטוֹבָה וְלִבְרָכָה:

On חוֹל הַמּוֹעֵד סֻכּוֹת :—

הָרַחֲמָן · הוּא יָקִים לָנוּ אֶת־סֻכַּת דָּוִיד הַנֹּפָלֶת:

הָרַחֲמָן: הוּא יְזַכֵּנוּ לִימוֹת הַמָּשִׁיחַ וּלְחַיֵּי הָעוֹלָם הַבָּא:

On שַׁבָּת, יוֹם טוֹב *and* רֹאשׁ חֹדֶשׁ :— *On Week days :—*

מַגְדִּיל   מִגְדּוֹל

יְשׁוּעוֹת מַלְכּוֹ וְעֹשֶׂה חֶסֶד לִמְשִׁיחוֹ לְדָוִד וּלְזַרְעוֹ
עַד־עוֹלָם: עֹשֶׂה שָׁלוֹם בִּמְרוֹמָיו הוּא יַעֲשֶׂה שָׁלוֹם
עָלֵינוּ וְעַל כָּל־יִשְׂרָאֵל וְאִמְרוּ אָמֵן:

יְראוּ אֶת־יְיָ קְדֹשָׁיו · כִּי אֵין מַחְסוֹר לִירֵאָיו: כְּפִירִים רָשׁוּ
וְרָעֵבוּ · וְדֹרְשֵׁי יְיָ לֹא־יַחְסְרוּ כָל־טוֹב: הוֹדוּ לַיְיָ כִּי־טוֹב ·
כִּי לְעוֹלָם חַסְדּוֹ: פּוֹתֵחַ אֶת־יָדֶךָ · וּמַשְׂבִּיעַ לְכָל־חַי רָצוֹן:
בָּרוּךְ הַגֶּבֶר אֲשֶׁר יִבְטַח בַּיְיָ · וְהָיָה יְיָ מִבְטַחוֹ: נַעַר הָיִיתִי
גַּם־זָקַנְתִּי · וְלֹא־רָאִיתִי צַדִּיק נֶעֱזָב וְזַרְעוֹ מְבַקֶּשׁ־לָחֶם: יְיָ עֹז
לְעַמּוֹ יִתֵּן · יְיָ יְבָרֵךְ אֶת־עַמּוֹ בַשָּׁלוֹם:

fallen Tabernacle of David. Based on Amos 9. 11.
days of the Messiah . . . world to come. See pp. 254 and 255.
Great salvation. Psalm 18. 51 and II Samuel 22 differ in the pointing
of the first word in the last verse. In order to use *both* verses, one was
assigned for weekdays, the other for Sabbaths and Festivals.

On New Year :—

May the All-merciful renew unto us this year for good and for blessing.

On the Intermediate Days of Tabernacles :—

May the All-merciful raise up for us the fallen Tabernacle of David.

May the All-merciful make us worthy of the days of the Messiah, and of the life of the world to come.

On Weekdays :—

Psalm 18. 51   Great salvation giveth he to his king;

On Sabbaths, Festivals, and New Moons :—

II Samuel 22. 51   He is a tower of salvation to his king;

and showeth lovingkindness to his anointed, to David and to his seed, for evermore. He who maketh peace in his high places, may he make peace for us and for all Israel, and say ye, Amen.

Psalm 34. 10, 11   O fear the Lord, ye his holy ones ; for there is no want to them that fear him. Young lions do lack and suffer hunger : but they

Psalm 118. 1   that seek the Lord shall not want any good. O give thanks unto the Lord, for he is good : for his lovingkindness endureth for ever.

Psalm 145. 16   Thou openest thine hand, and satisfiest every thing with favour.

Jeremiah 17. 7   Blessed is the man that trusteth in the Lord, and whose trust the

Psalm 37. 25   Lord is. I have been young and now I am old ; yet have I not seen

Psalm 29. 10   the righteous forsaken, nor his seed begging for bread. The Lord will give strength unto his people ; the Lord will bless his people with peace.

O FEAR THE LORD. These verses are said silently, probably out of regard for the feelings of the poor guests who might be at the table, especially on Sabbaths and Festivals.

not seen the righteous forsaken. The Psalmist is speaking of Jewish social conditions. In a Jewish community, no one who is the innocent victim of untoward fortune is allowed to go under. A helping hand will be extended to him. Jewish orphans need not *beg* for bread.

We thus see the Grace as a development across the ages. Linked with epochal events of Israel's past, it yet bears traces of modern growth. It mirrors Israel's invincible trust in God, its faith in life, and its ardent hope in the triumph of Righteousness.

ברכת המזון בקצרה :

בָּרוּךְ אַתָּה יְיָ אֱלֹהֵינוּ מֶלֶךְ הָעוֹלָם · הַזָּן אֶת הָעוֹלָם כֻּלּוֹ ·
בְּטוּבוֹ בְּחֵן בְּחֶסֶד וּבְרַחֲמִים · הוּא נוֹתֵן לֶחֶם לְכָל בָּשָׂר ·
כִּי לְעוֹלָם חַסְדּוֹ · וּבְטוּבוֹ הַגָּדוֹל תָּמִיד לֹא חָסַר לָנוּ וְאַל
יֶחְסַר לָנוּ מָזוֹן לְעוֹלָם וָעֶד בַּעֲבוּר שְׁמוֹ הַגָּדוֹל · כִּי הוּא
זָן וּמְפַרְנֵס לַכֹּל וּמֵטִיב לַכֹּל וּמֵכִין מָזוֹן לְכָל בְּרִיּוֹתָיו אֲשֶׁר
בָּרָא · בָּרוּךְ אַתָּה יְיָ · הַזָּן אֶת הַכֹּל :

נוֹדֶה לְךָ יְיָ אֱלֹהֵינוּ עַל שֶׁהִנְחַלְתָּ לַאֲבוֹתֵינוּ אֶרֶץ חֶמְדָּה
טוֹבָה וּרְחָבָה · בְּרִית וְתוֹרָה · וְלֶחֶם לָשׂוֹבַע · בָּרוּךְ אַתָּה
יְיָ · עַל הָאָרֶץ וְעַל הַמָּזוֹן :

רַחֵם יְיָ אֱלֹהֵינוּ עַל יִשְׂרָאֵל עַמֶּךָ · וְעַל מַלְכוּת בֵּית דָּוִד
מְשִׁיחֶךָ · וְתַגְדִּיל מְהֵרָה כְּבוֹד הַבַּיִת · וּתְנַחֲמֵנוּ בִּכְפְלָיִם ·
בָּרוּךְ אַתָּה יְיָ · בּוֹנֶה בְרַחֲמָיו יְרוּשָׁלָיִם · אָמֵן :

בָּרוּךְ אַתָּה יְיָ אֱלֹהֵינוּ · הָאֵל אָבִינוּ מַלְכֵּנוּ · הַמֶּלֶךְ הַטּוֹב
וְהַמֵּטִיב לַכֹּל · הוּא הֵטִיב הוּא מֵטִיב הוּא יֵטִיב לָנוּ ·

(say On שַׁבָּת וְיַנְחִילֵנוּ יוֹם שֶׁכֻּלּוֹ שַׁבָּת)

(say On יוֹם טוֹב וְיַנְחִילֵנוּ יוֹם שֶׁכֻּלּוֹ טוֹב)

וִיזַכֵּנוּ לִימוֹת הַמָּשִׁיחַ וּלְחַיֵּי הָעוֹלָם הַבָּא :

עֹשֶׂה שָׁלוֹם בִּמְרוֹמָיו הוּא יַעֲשֶׂה שָׁלוֹם עָלֵינוּ וְעַל כָּל־יִשְׂרָאֵל
וְאִמְרוּ אָמֵן :

SHORTER FORM OF GRACE.

Shorter forms of the Grace have from early times been sanctioned
by high Rabbinic authorities. The best known of these forms, by
Naphtali ben David, appeared in Venice in 1603. Slight modifications
have been made in this version by S. Baer, S. Singer and the editor of
this Prayer Book.

SHORTER FORM OF GRACE

THANKS-GIVING FOR GOD'S PROVIDENTIAL CARE   Blessed art thou, O Lord our God, King of the universe, who feedest the whole world with thy goodness, with grace, with lovingkindness and tender mercy ; thou givest food to all flesh, for thy lovingkindness endureth for ever. Through thy great goodness food hath never failed us : O may it not fail us for ever and ever for thy great Name's sake, since thou nourishest and sustainest all beings, and doest good unto all, and providest food for all thy creatures whom thou hast created. Blessed art thou, O Lord, who givest food unto all.

We thank thee, O Lord our God, because thou didst give us an heritage unto our fathers a desirable, good and ample land, the covenant and the Torah, and food in plenty. Blessed art thou, O Lord, for the land and for the food.

Have compassion, O Lord our God, upon Israel thy people, and upon the kingdom of the house of David thine anointed : speedily magnify the glory of the Temple, and doubly comfort us. Blessed art thou, O Lord, who in thy compassion rebuildest Jerusalem. Amen.

Blessed art thou, O Lord our God, O God, our Father, our King, who art kind and dealest kindly with all ; thou hast dealt kindly, dost deal kindly, and wilt deal kindly with us.

(*On Sabbath say* : Let us inherit the day which shall be wholly a Sabbath ; and)

(*On Festivals say* : Let us inherit the day which is altogether good ; and)

O, make us worthy of the days of the Messiah, and the life of the world to come. He who maketh peace in his high places, may he make peace for us and for all Israel, and say ye, Amen.

The oldest of these prayers is the Aramaic (attributed to an otherwise unknown Benjamin the Shepherd), בריך רחמנא מריה דהאי פיתא. " Blessed be the Merciful, the Giver of this Bread ". Dr. M. Friedländer considered this an ideal prayer for children ; or, the Hebrew words ברוך שאכלנו משלו זבמובו חיינו, " Blessed be He of Whose bounty we have partaken, and through whose goodness we live ". Such prayers may be said in any language.

בִּרְכַּת הַמָּזוֹן לַאֲבֵלִים

In the house of an אָבֵל *the following Introductory Form is used :—*

נְבָרֵךְ מְנַחֵם אֲבֵלִים שֶׁאָכַלְנוּ מִשֶּׁלּוֹ :

The others respond :—

בָּרוּךְ מְנַחֵם אֲבֵלִים שֶׁאָכַלְנוּ מִשֶּׁלּוֹ וּבְטוּבוֹ חָיִינוּ :

He who says Grace repeats the last sentence.

In the house of an אָבֵל *the following is substituted in place of the passage from* וּבְנֵה *p. 972 to* אַל־יְחַסְּרֵנוּ *p. 974.*

נַחֵם יְיָ אֱלֹהֵינוּ אֶת אֲבֵלֵי יְרוּשָׁלַיִם וְאֶת הָאֲבֵלִים
הַמִּתְאַבְּלִים בָּאֵבֶל הַזֶּה · נַחֲמֵם מֵאֶבְלָם וְשַׂמְּחֵם מִיגוֹנָם ·
כָּאָמוּר . כְּאִישׁ אֲשֶׁר אִמּוֹ תְּנַחֲמֶנּוּ כֵּן אָנֹכִי אֲנַחֶמְכֶם וּבִירוּשָׁלַיִם
תְּנֻחָמוּ · בָּרוּךְ אַתָּה יְיָ · מְנַחֵם צִיּוֹן בְּבִנְיַן יְרוּשָׁלָיִם :

בָּרוּךְ אַתָּה יְיָ אֱלֹהֵינוּ מֶלֶךְ הָעוֹלָם · הָאֵל אָבִינוּ מַלְכֵּנוּ ·
בֹּרְאֵנוּ גֹּאֲלֵנוּ קְדוֹשֵׁנוּ קְדוֹשׁ יַעֲקֹב · הַמֶּלֶךְ הַחַי הַטּוֹב וְהַמֵּטִיב ·
אֵל אֱמֶת · דַּיַּן אֱמֶת · שׁוֹפֵט צֶדֶק וְלוֹקֵחַ נְפָשׁוֹת בְּמִשְׁפָּט ·
וְשַׁלִּיט בְּעוֹלָמוֹ לַעֲשׂוֹת בּוֹ כִּרְצוֹנוֹ · כִּי כָל דְּרָכָיו מִשְׁפָּט ·
וַאֲנַחְנוּ עַמּוֹ וַעֲבָדָיו · וְעַל הַכֹּל אֲנַחְנוּ חַיָּבִים לְהוֹדוֹת לוֹ
וּלְבָרְכוֹ · גּוֹדֵר פְּרָצוֹת בְּיִשְׂרָאֵל הוּא יִגְדּוֹר אֶת הַפִּרְצָה הַזֹּאת
מֵעָלֵינוּ לְחַיִּים וּלְשָׁלוֹם · הוּא יִגְמְלֵנוּ לָעַד חֵן וָחֶסֶד וְרַחֲמִים
וְכָל טוֹב · וּמִכָּל טוֹב אַל יְחַסְּרֵנוּ :

MOURNER'S GRACE AFTER MEALS.

In the house of a Mourner the following Introductory Form is used :—
We will bless him that comforteth the mourners, and of whose
bounty we have partaken.

The others respond :—
Blessed be he that comforteth the mourners, of whose bounty
we have partaken, and through whose goodness we live.

He who says Grace repeats the last sentence.

---

*In the house of a Mourner the following is substituted, in place of
the passage from "And rebuild," p. 973 to " in want," p. 975 :—*

Comfort, O Lord our God, the mourners of Jerusalem and
those who share in this present mourning. Do thou give them
comfort in place of their mourning, and gladness instead of
their grief, as it is said, As one whom his mother comforteth, so will
I comfort you, and in Jerusalem shall ye be comforted. Blessed art
thou, O Lord, who comfortest Zion by the rebuilding of Jerusalem.

Isaiah 66. 13

Blessed art thou, O Lord our God, King of the universe, O
God, our Father, our King, our Creator, our Redeemer, our Holy
One, the Holy One of Jacob, the living King, who art kind and
dealest kindly with all, true God and Judge, who judgest with
righteousness, and in justice takest the souls of men unto thyself,
who rulest in thy world, doing therein according to thy will, for all
thy ways are justice. We are thy people and thy servants, and
for all things it is our duty to give thanks unto thee and to bless
thee. O thou who repairest the fortune of Israel, mayest thou also
repair this calamity among us, granting us life and peace. Mayest
thou ever bestow upon us grace, lovingkindness, mercy and all good :
of no manner of good let us be in want.

COMFORT O LORD. At an early time, a special version of the third
Benediction became current for use in a House of Mourning. It
abounds in phrases of great beauty:
as one whom his mother comforteth. One of the most touching verses
in Scripture. As the grown man, coming back with wounds and weari-
ness to be comforted of his mother, finds there the comfort he seeks, so
will He comfort all who mourn. God is our Mother.
according to thy will. The note in this Mourners' Prayer is the same
as in the Burial Service—submission to God's inscrutable will.

סֵדֶר הַבְּרָכוֹת :

For the Blessings on Washing the Hands, and before partaking of Bread, see p. 962.

Before drinking Wine :—

בָּרוּךְ אַתָּה יְיָ אֱלֹהֵינוּ מֶלֶךְ הָעוֹלָם • בּוֹרֵא פְּרִי הַגָּפֶן :

Before partaking of Food, other than Bread, prepared from any of "the five species of Grain" (wheat, barley, rye, oats and spelt):—

בָּרוּךְ אַתָּה יְיָ אֱלֹהֵינוּ מֶלֶךְ הָעוֹלָם • בּוֹרֵא מִינֵי מְזוֹנוֹת :

After any Food, excepting Bread :—

בָּרוּךְ אַתָּה יְיָ אֱלֹהֵינוּ מֶלֶךְ הָעוֹלָם • עַל

After Food prepared as above, and Wine :	After Food prepared as above :	After Grapes, Figs, Olives, Pomegranates or Dates :	After Wine :
הַמִּחְיָה וְעַל	הַמִּחְיָה	הָעֵץ	הַגָּפֶן
הַכַּלְכָּלָה עַל הַגָּפֶן	וְעַל	וְעַל פְּרִי	וְעַל פְּרִי
וְעַל פְּרִי הַגָּפֶן	הַכַּלְכָּלָה	הָעֵץ	הַגָּפֶן

וְעַל תְּנוּבַת הַשָּׂדֶה וְעַל אֶרֶץ חֶמְדָּה טוֹבָה וּרְחָבָה

שֶׁרָצִיתָ וְהִנְחַלְתָּ לַאֲבוֹתֵינוּ לֶאֱכוֹל מִפִּרְיָהּ וְלִשְׂבּוֹעַ

BLESSINGS ON VARIOUS OCCASIONS.

The Benediction (ברכה) is the unit of Jewish Prayer, and is the creation of the Men of the Great Synagogue (see p. xviii). Nearly a hundred ancient Blessings are attributed to them. The greater portion form part of the Daily Prayers, or precede the performance of religious duties. The remaining Blessings are expressive of thanksgiving for personal enjoyments and benefits; are grateful recognition of God's

BLESSINGS ON VARIOUS OCCASIONS

*For the Blessings on Washing the Hands, and before
partaking of Bread, see p. 963.*

Before drinking Wine :—

1. Wine

Blessed art thou, O Lord our God, King of the universe,
who createst the fruit of the vine.

*Before partaking of Food, other than Bread, prepared from any of
" the five species of Grain " (wheat, barley, rye, oats and spelt) :—*

2. Before food other than bread

Blessed art thou, O Lord our God, King of the universe,
who createst various kinds of food.

After any Food, excepting Bread :—

3. After food other than bread

Blessed art thou, O Lord our God, King of the universe,

After Wine :	*After Grapes, Figs, Olives, Pomegranates or Dates :*	*After Food prepared as above :*	*After Food prepared as above and wine :*
for the vine and fruit of the vine ;	for the tree and the fruit of the tree ;	for the sustenance and the nourishment ;	for the sustenance and the nourishment, the vine and the fruit of the vine ;

—for the produce of the field ; for the desirable, good and
ample land which thou wast pleased to give as an heritage

goodness, or adoration on beholding remarkable persons or extraordinary
phenomena in nature. They all attest how vivid in Jewish piety is the
sense of God's providence, and what genuine devotion it evoked.
Through these Benedictions, life became one uninterrupted Service
of God.

1-7. The first seven of these Blessings are modifications of Grace—
before and after enjoyment. Blessing and thanksgiving must accompany every use or enjoyment of God's gifts. " Whoever makes a profane
use of God's gifts (that is, partakes of any worldly joy without thanking
God for it), commits a theft against God " (Talmud).

wine. The duty of pronouncing a Benediction before drinking wine
has had a profound influence in Israel. Drunkenness was never a
Jewish vice. "The sanctified use of wine at every Jewish ceremony
produced a real *instinct* for temperance, without destroying an equally
strong instinct for sociability " (Abrahams).

3. This Benediction is a summary of the long Grace after Meals.

מָטוּבָהּ • רַחֶם יְיָ אֱלֹהֵינוּ עַל יִשְׂרָאֵל עַמֶּךָ וְעַל

יְרוּשָׁלַיִם עִירֶךָ וְעַל צִיּוֹן מִשְׁכַּן כְּבוֹדֶךָ וְעַל מִזְבְּחֶךָ

וְעַל הֵיכָלֶךָ • וּבְנֵה יְרוּשָׁלַיִם עִיר הַקֹּדֶשׁ בִּמְהֵרָה

בְיָמֵינוּ וְהַעֲלֵנוּ לְתוֹכָהּ וְשַׂמְּחֵנוּ בְּבִנְיָנָהּ • וְנֹאכַל

מִפִּרְיָהּ וְנִשְׂבַּע מִטּוּבָהּ וּנְבָרֶכְךָ עָלֶיהָ בִּקְדֻשָּׁה וּבְטָהֳרָה•

(On שַׁבָּת say) וּרְצֵה וְהַחֲלִיצֵנוּ בְּיוֹם הַשַּׁבָּת הַזֶּה •

(On רֹאשׁ חֹדֶשׁ) וְזָכְרֵנוּ בְּיוֹם רֹאשׁ הַחֹדֶשׁ הַזֶּה •

(On פֶּסַח) וְשַׂמְּחֵנוּ בְּיוֹם חַג הַמַּצּוֹת הַזֶּה •

(On שָׁבֻעוֹת) וְשַׂמְּחֵנוּ בְּיוֹם חַג הַשָּׁבֻעוֹת הַזֶּה •

(On סֻכּוֹת) וְשַׂמְּחֵנוּ בְּיוֹם חַג הַסֻּכּוֹת הַזֶּה •

(On שִׂמְחַת תּוֹרָה and שְׁמִינִי עֲצֶרֶת)

וְשַׂמְּחֵנוּ בְּיוֹם הַשְּׁמִינִי חַג הָעֲצֶרֶת הַזֶּה •

(On רֹאשׁ הַשָּׁנָה) וְזָכְרֵנוּ לְטוֹבָה בְּיוֹם הַזִּכָּרוֹן הַזֶּה •

כִּי אַתָּה יְיָ טוֹב וּמֵטִיב לַכֹּל וְנוֹדֶה לְךָ עַל הָאָרֶץ

After Food prepared as above, and Wine:	After Food prepared from any of the "five species of Grain":	After Fruit:	After Wine:
וְעַל הַמִּחְיָה	וְעַל הַמִּחְיָה •	וְעַל הַפֵּרוֹת •	וְעַל פְּרִי
וְעַל פְּרִי	בָּרוּךְ אַתָּה יְיָ	בָּרוּךְ אַתָּה יְיָ	הַגָּפֶן • בָּרוּךְ
הַגָּפֶן • בָּרוּךְ	עַל הָאָרֶץ	עַל הָאָרֶץ	אַתָּה יְיָ עַל
אַתָּה יְיָ עַל	וְעַל הַמִּחְיָה :	וְעַל הַפֵּרוֹת :	הָאָרֶץ וְעַל
הָאָרֶץ וְעַל הַמִּחְיָה וְעַל פְּרִי הַגָּפֶן :			פְּרִי הַגָּפֶן :

unto our fathers, that they might eat of its fruits and be satisfied with its goodness. Have mercy., O Lord our God, upon Israel thy people, upon Jerusalem thy city, upon Zion the abiding place of thy glory, upon thine altar and thy temple. Rebuild Jerusalem, the holy city, speedily in our days ; lead us up thither and make us rejoice in its rebuilding. May we eat of the fruits of the land and be satisfied with its goodness, and bless thee for it in holiness and purity.

(*On Sabbath Day*) Be pleased to strengthen us on this Sabbath Day.

(*On New Moon*) Be mindful of us on this day of the New Moon.

(*On Passover*) Make us rejoice on this Feast of Unleavened Bread.

(*On Pentecost*) Make us rejoice on this Feast of Weeks.

(*On Tabernacles*) Make us rejoice on this Feast of Tabernacles.

(*On the Eighth Day of Solemn Assembly and on Simchas Torah*) Make us rejoice on this Eighth-day Feast of Solemn Assembly.

(*On New Year*) Be mindful of us for good on this Day of Remembrance.

For thou, O Lord, art good and beneficent unto all ; and, we will give thee thanks for the land,

After Wine :	*After Fruit :*	*After Food prepared from any of the "five species of Grain " :*	*After Food prepared as above, and Wine :*
and for the fruit of the vine. Blessed art thou, O Lord, for the land and for the fruit of the vine.	and for the fruits. Blessed art thou, O Lord, for the land and for the fruits.	and for the sustenance. Blessed art thou, O Lord, for the land and for the sustenance.	for the sustenance and for the fruit of the vine. Blessed art thou, O Lord, for the land,

the sustenance and the fruit of the vine.

On eating Fruit which grows on Trees :—

בָּרוּךְ אַתָּה יְיָ אֱלֹהֵינוּ מֶלֶךְ הָעוֹלָם · בּוֹרֵא פְּרִי הָעֵץ :

On eating Fruit which grows on the Ground, Herbage, etc. :—

בָּרוּךְ אַתָּה יְיָ אֱלֹהֵינוּ מֶלֶךְ הָעוֹלָם · בּוֹרֵא פְּרִי הָאֲדָמָה :

*On partaking of Flesh, Fish, Eggs, Cheese, etc., or drinking
any Liquor except Wine :—*

בָּרוּךְ אַתָּה יְיָ אֱלֹהֵינוּ מֶלֶךְ הָעוֹלָם · שֶׁהַכֹּל נִהְיֶה בִּדְבָרוֹ :

*After partaking of any of the foods referred to in the three
preceding Blessings :—*

בָּרוּךְ אַתָּה יְיָ אֱלֹהֵינוּ מֶלֶךְ הָעוֹלָם · בּוֹרֵא נְפָשׁוֹת
רַבּוֹת וְחֶסְרוֹנָן · עַל כָּל־מַה־שֶּׁבָּרֵאתָ לְהַחֲיוֹת בָּהֶם
נֶפֶשׁ כָּל־חָי · בָּרוּךְ חֵי הָעוֹלָמִים :

On smelling Fragrant Woods or Barks :—

בָּרוּךְ אַתָּה יְיָ אֱלֹהֵינוּ מֶלֶךְ הָעוֹלָם · בּוֹרֵא מִינֵי בְשָׂמִים :

On smelling Fragrant Plants :—

בָּרוּךְ אַתָּה יְיָ אֱלֹהֵינוּ מֶלֶךְ הָעוֹלָם · בּוֹרֵא עִשְׂבוֹת
בְשָׂמִים :

On smelling Fragrant Fruits :—

בָּרוּךְ אַתָּה יְיָ אֱלֹהֵינוּ מֶלֶךְ הָעוֹלָם · הַנּוֹתֵן רֵיחַ
טוֹב בַּפֵּרוֹת :

On smelling Fragrant Spices :—

בָּרוּךְ אַתָּה יְיָ אֱלֹהֵינוּ מֶלֶךְ הָעוֹלָם · בּוֹרֵא עֲצֵי בְשָׂמִים :

On eating Fruit which grows on Trees :—

4. Fruit from trees

Blessed art thou, O Lord our God, King of the universe, who createst the fruit of the tree.

On eating Fruit which grows on the Ground, Herbage, etc. :—

5. Fruit from ground

Blessed art thou, O Lord our God, King of the universe, who createst the fruit of the earth.

On partaking of Flesh, Fish, Eggs, Cheese, etc., or drinking any Liquor except Wine :—

6. General benediction : "shehakkol"

Blessed art thou, O Lord our God, King of the universe, by whose word all things exist.

After partaking of any of the foods referred to in the three preceding Blessings :—

7. General benediction after above foods : "bore' nefoshos"

Blessed art thou, O Lord our God, King of the universe, who createst innumerable living beings with their wants. We thank thee for all the means that thou hast created wherewith to sustain the life of each of them. Blessed art thou who art the life of all worlds.

On smelling Fragrant Woods or Barks :—

8–12. Benedictions of fragrance

Blessed art thou, O Lord our God, King of the universe, who createst fragrant woods.

On smelling Fragrant Plants :—

Blessed art thou, O Lord our God, King of the universe, who createst fragrant plants.

On smelling Fragrant Fruits :—

Blessed art thou, O Lord our God, King of the universe, who givest a goodly scent to fruits.

On smelling Fragrant Spices :—

Blessed art thou, O Lord our God, King of the universe, who createst divers kinds of spices.

8–12. These five Benedictions are over objects of fragrance.

On smelling Fragrant Oils :—

בָּרוּךְ אַתָּה יְיָ אֱלֹהֵינוּ מֶלֶךְ הָעוֹלָם · בּוֹרֵא שֶׁמֶן עָרֵב :

On witnessing Lightning, or on seeing Fallen Stars, Lofty Mountains,
or Great Deserts :—

בָּרוּךְ אַתָּה יְיָ אֱלֹהֵינוּ מֶלֶךְ הָעוֹלָם · עֹשֶׂה מַעֲשֶׂה בְרֵאשִׁית :

On hearing Thunder :—

בָּרוּךְ אַתָּה יְיָ אֱלֹהֵינוּ מֶלֶךְ הָעוֹלָם · שֶׁכֹּחוֹ וּגְבוּרָתוֹ מָלֵא עוֹלָם :

At the sight of the Sea :—

בָּרוּךְ אַתָּה יְיָ אֱלֹהֵינוּ מֶלֶךְ הָעוֹלָם · שֶׁעָשָׂה אֶת־הַיָּם הַגָּדוֹל :

On seeing beautiful Trees or Animals :—

בָּרוּךְ אַתָּה יְיָ אֱלֹהֵינוּ מֶלֶךְ הָעוֹלָם · שֶׁכָּכָה לוֹ בְּעוֹלָמוֹ :

On seeing the Rainbow :—

בָּרוּךְ אַתָּה יְיָ אֱלֹהֵינוּ מֶלֶךְ הָעוֹלָם · זוֹכֵר הַבְּרִית וְנֶאֱמָן בִּבְרִיתוֹ וְקַיָּם בְּמַאֲמָרוֹ :

On seeing Trees blossoming the first time in the Year :—

בָּרוּךְ אַתָּה יְיָ אֱלֹהֵינוּ מֶלֶךְ הָעוֹלָם · שֶׁלֹּא חִסַּר בְּעוֹלָמוֹ דָּבָר · וּבָרָא בוֹ בְּרִיּוֹת טוֹבוֹת וְאִילָנוֹת טוֹבִים לְהַנוֹת בָּהֶם בְּנֵי אָדָם :

On smelling Fragrant Oils :—

Blessed art thou, O Lord our God, King of the universe, who createst fragrant oil.

On witnessing Lightning, or on seeing Falling Stars, Lofty Mountains, or Great Deserts :—

13–18. *Natural phenomena*   Blessed art thou, O Lord our God, King of the universe, who hast made the creation.

On hearing Thunder :—

Blessed art thou, O Lord our God, King of the universe, whose strength and might fill the world.

At the sight of the Sea :—

Blessed art thou, O Lord our God, King of the universe, who hast made the great sea.

On seeing beautiful Trees or Animals :—

Blessed art thou, O Lord our God, King of the universe, who hast such as these in thy world.

On seeing the Rainbow :—

Blessed art thou, O Lord our God, King of the universe, who rememberest the covenant, art faithful to thy covenant and keepest thy promise.

On seeing Trees blossoming the first time in the Year :—

Blessed art thou, O Lord our God, King of the universe, who hast made thy world lacking in nought, but hast produced therein goodly creatures and goodly trees wherewith to give delight unto the children of men.

13-18. Sights and sounds of beauty and wonder in Nature.

These Benedictions are especially remarkable. Those who were for ages excluded from the life of Nature, thanked God for everything inspiring, beneficent and beautiful in Nature—thunder, lightning, spring-blossoms, aromatic plants and fruits. A non-Jewish theologian remarks, " Natural phenomena move the pious Jew to praise, thanksgiving and adoration. The realm of Nature is to him nothing distant, strange, cold or uncanny ; it is the workshop of the Almighty, and is ruled by His beneficent will " (Bousset).

spring-blossoms. The author of this beautiful Benediction is Rabbi Judah the Prince, the editor of the Mishna.

In connection with these Benedictions, the word *bless* connotes not thanksgiving only, but also wonder and admiration. " This wonder, this admiration is part of the religious sense ; without it Religion lacks something great " (W. E. Barnes). " Be not blind, but open-eyed, to

On seeing a Sage distinguished for his knowledge of the Torah :—

בָּרוּךְ אַתָּה יְיָ אֱלֹהֵינוּ מֶלֶךְ הָעוֹלָם · שֶׁחָלַק מֵחָכְמָתוֹ
לִירֵאָיו :

On seeing Wise Men distinguished for other than Sacred knowledge :—

בָּרוּךְ אַתָּה יְיָ אֱלֹהֵינוּ מֶלֶךְ הָעוֹלָם · שֶׁנָּתַן מֵחָכְמָתוֹ
לְבָשָׂר וָדָם :

On seeing a King and his Court :—

בָּרוּךְ אַתָּה יְיָ אֱלֹהֵינוּ מֶלֶךְ הָעוֹלָם : שֶׁנָּתַן מִכְּבוֹדוֹ
לְבָשָׂר וָדָם :

On seeing strangely formed Persons, such as Giants or Dwarfs :—

בָּרוּךְ אַתָּה יְיָ אֱלֹהֵינוּ מֶלֶךְ הָעוֹלָם · מְשַׁנֶּה הַבְּרִיּוֹת :

On fixing a Mezuzah :—

בָּרוּךְ אַתָּה יְיָ אֱלֹהֵינוּ מֶלֶךְ הָעוֹלָם · אֲשֶׁר קִדְּשָׁנוּ
בְּמִצְוֹתָיו וְצִוָּנוּ לִקְבּוֹעַ מְזוּזָה :

*On tasting any Fruit for the first time in the season ; on entering
into possession of a new House or Land ; or on using new
Raiment for the first time :—*

בָּרוּךְ אַתָּה יְיָ אֱלֹהֵינוּ מֶלֶךְ הָעוֹלָם · שֶׁהֶחֱיָנוּ וְקִיְּמָנוּ
וְהִגִּיעָנוּ לַזְּמַן הַזֶּה :

On hearing Good Tidings :—

בָּרוּךְ אַתָּה יְיָ אֱלֹהֵינוּ מֶלֶךְ הָעוֹלָם · הַטּוֹב וְהַמֵּטִיב :

19-22. *Extra-ordinary Persons*

On seeing a Sage distinguished for his knowledge of the Torah :—

Blessed art thou, O Lord our God, King of the universe, who hast imparted of thy wisdom to them that revere thee.

On seeing Wise Men distinguished for other than Sacred knowledge :—

Blessed art thou, O Lord our God, King of the universe, who hast given of thy wisdom to mortals.

On seeing a King and his Court :—

Blessed art thou, O Lord our God, King of the universe, who hast given of thy glory to mortals.

On seeing strangely formed Persons, such as Giants or Dwarfs :—

Blessed art thou, O Lord our God, King of the universe, who variest the forms of thy creatures.

On fixing a Mezuzah :—

23. *Mezuzah*

Blessed art thou, O Lord our God, King of the universe, who hast hallowed us by thy commandments, and commanded us to affix the Mezuzah.

On tasting any Fruit for the first time in the season ; on entering into possession of a new House or Land ; or on using a new Raiment for the first time :—

24. *Shehechyonu*

See p. 755

Blessed art thou, O Lord our God, King of the universe, who hast kept us in life, and hast preserved us, and hast enabled us to reach this season.

On hearing Good Tidings :—

25. *Good Tidings*

Blessed art thou, O Lord our God, King of the universe, who art good and dispensest good.

the great wonders of Nature, familiar objects of every day though they be. But men are more wont to be astonished at the sun's eclipse than at its unfailing rise " (Orchoth Tzaddikim, 15th century).

19-22. Benedictions on beholding a Sage, a King or wonderful creature. The Jew had a laudable longing to see extraordinary men, and blessed God for the opportunity. Respect for learning could not be more delicately and reverently expressed and inculcated, than by prescribing a Benediction to be recited on beholding a famous man of learning.

23. *mezuzah.* See p. 121.

This is affixed on the upper portion of the right-hand side of the door, as you enter.

On hearing Evil Tidings, or on performing the rite of Keriah :—

בָּרוּךְ אַתָּה יְיָ אֱלֹהֵינוּ מֶלֶךְ הָעוֹלָם • דַּיַן הָאֱמֶת :

סדר ברכת הלבנה

Read תהלים קמ'ח, *verses* 1–6 (*to* וְלֹא יַעֲבוֹר), *p.*92.

בָּרוּךְ אַתָּה יְיָ אֱלֹהֵינוּ מֶלֶךְ הָעוֹלָם • אֲשֶׁר בְּמַאֲמָרוֹ
בָּרָא שְׁחָקִים • וּבְרוּחַ פִּיו כָּל־צְבָאָם : חֹק וּזְמַן נָתַן
לָהֶם • שֶׁלֹּא יְשַׁנּוּ אֶת־תַּפְקִידָם : שָׂשִׂים וּשְׂמֵחִים
לַעֲשׂוֹת רְצוֹן קוֹנָם • פּוֹעֵל אֱמֶת שֶׁפְּעֻלָּתוֹ אֱמֶת •
וְלַלְּבָנָה אָמַר שֶׁתִּתְחַדֵּשׁ עֲטֶרֶת תִּפְאֶרֶת לַעֲמוּסֵי בָטֶן •
הָעֲתִידִים לְהִתְחַדֵּשׁ כְּמוֹתָהּ • וּלְפָאֵר לְיוֹצְרָם עַל שֵׁם
כְּבוֹד מַלְכוּתוֹ • בָּרוּךְ אַתָּה יְיָ • מְחַדֵּשׁ חֳדָשִׁים :

Read תהלים קכ'א, *p.* 590, *and* ק'נ, *p.* 96.

---

26. *Keriah.* See p. 1066, *the true judge. i.e.* " the righteous Judge ";
it is the formula of submission to God's will. The Benediction is also
spoken on beholding holy places in desolation, such as synagogues in
ruin.

27. NEW MOON. This Benediction has in many Rites grown into a
picturesque Service, with many later accretions. It is recited out of
doors, or at an open window while facing the moon, and preferably in
a company of ten persons.

the moon renew itself. The reappearance of the moon, like that of
everything beneficial to man, such as fruits in their season, calls for
praise and gratitude to God. This Benediction dates from the fourth

On hearing Evil Tidings, or on performing the rite of Keriah :—

26.
Evil Tidings

Blessed art thou, O Lord our God, King of the universe, the true Judge.

BLESSING ON THE APPEARANCE OF THE NEW MOON.

Read Psalm cxlviii, verses 1–6 (to " which none shall transgress ") p. 93.

27. Greeting
the New Moon.

Blessed art thou, O Lord our God, King of the universe, by whose word the heavens were created, and by the breath of whose mouth all their host. Thou didst assign them a statute and a season, that they should not deviate from their appointed charge. They are glad and rejoice to do the will of the Master, the truthful Worker whose work is truth, who bade the moon renew itself, a crown of glory, unto those that have been upborne by him from the womb who in the time to come will themselves be renewed like it, to honour their Creator for his glorious kingdom's sake. Blessed art thou, O Lord, who renewest the months.

Read Psalms cxxi, p. 591, and cl, p. 97.

century. It is recited between the third and the sixteenth day after the New Moon.

themselves be renewed. " The waxing and waning of the moon remind the pious of Israel's renewal. Even in its darkest wanderings, Israel, like the moon itself, is never lost ; and Israel's return into the light is assured, so long as its children loyally cling to the paths which God's word hath shown unto them " (Hirsch) ; see p. 776.

" In the Blessings on Various Occasions we find a very jubilation of life—a spontaneous lyric appreciation of earth ; joy in the fruits of the tree, the vine and the field ; enchantment in the fragrant odours of barks, plants, fruits and spices ; exaltation at the sight of stars, mountain, desert, sea and rainbow. Beautiful trees and animals, spring-blossoms equally with scholars and sages, all evoke their grace of appreciation. For storm and evil tidings, too, have their graces—in fortitude ! The Hebrew genius could find growth through sorrow ; and for the Hebrew, good tidings have their grace, no less than fair sights and experience. Everywhere the infiltration of Earth by Heaven " (Louis Zangwill).

סדר קריאת שמע על המטה:

בָּרוּךְ אַתָּה יְיָ אֱלֹהֵינוּ מֶלֶךְ הָעוֹלָם · הַמַּפִּיל
חֶבְלֵי שֵׁנָה עַל־עֵינַי וּתְנוּמָה עַל־עַפְעַפָּי : וִיהִי רָצוֹן
מִלְּפָנֶיךָ יְיָ אֱלֹהַי וֵאלֹהֵי אֲבוֹתַי שֶׁתַּשְׁכִּיבֵנִי לְשָׁלוֹם
וְתַעֲמִידֵנִי לְשָׁלוֹם · וְאַל יְבַהֲלוּנִי רַעְיוֹנַי וַחֲלוֹמוֹת
רָעִים וְהִרְהוּרִים רָעִים · וּתְהִי מִטָּתִי שְׁלֵמָה לְפָנֶיךָ ·
וְהָאֵר עֵינַי פֶּן־אִישַׁן הַמָּוֶת · כִּי אַתָּה הַמֵּאִיר לְאִישׁוֹן
בַּת־עָיִן · בָּרוּךְ אַתָּה יְיָ · הַמֵּאִיר לָעוֹלָם כֻּלּוֹ
בִּכְבוֹדוֹ :

אֵל מֶלֶךְ נֶאֱמָן :

שְׁמַע יִשְׂרָאֵל יְיָ אֱלֹהֵינוּ יְיָ אֶחָד :

בָּרוּךְ שֵׁם כְּבוֹד מַלְכוּתוֹ לְעוֹלָם וָעֶד :

וְאָהַבְתָּ אֵת יְיָ אֱלֹהֶיךָ בְּכָל־לְבָבְךָ וּבְכָל־נַפְשְׁךָ
וּבְכָל מְאֹדֶךָ : וְהָיוּ הַדְּבָרִים הָאֵלֶּה אֲשֶׁר אָנֹכִי מְצַוְּךָ
הַיּוֹם עַל־לְבָבֶךָ : וְשִׁנַּנְתָּם לְבָנֶיךָ וְדִבַּרְתָּ בָּם בְּשִׁבְתְּךָ
בְּבֵיתֶךָ וּבְלֶכְתְּךָ בַדֶּרֶךְ וּבְשָׁכְבְּךָ וּבְקוּמֶךָ : וּקְשַׁרְתָּם
לְאוֹת עַל־יָדֶךָ וְהָיוּ לְטֹטָפֹת בֵּין עֵינֶיךָ : וּכְתַבְתָּם עַל־
מְזֻזוֹת בֵּיתֶךָ וּבִשְׁעָרֶיךָ :

PRAYERS BEFORE RETIRING TO REST AT NIGHT

NIGHT PRAYER

Blessed art thou, O Lord our God, King of the universe, who makest the bands of sleep to fall upon mine eyes, and slumber upon mine eyelids. May it be thy will, O Lord my God and God of my fathers, to suffer me to lie down in peace and to let me rise up again in peace. Let not my thoughts trouble me, nor evil dreams, nor evil fancies, but let my rest be perfect before thee. O lighten mine eyes, lest I sleep the sleep of death, for it is thou who givest light to the apple of the eye. Blessed art thou, O Lord, who givest light to the whole world in thy glory.

God, faithful King.

Deuteronomy 6. 4

HEAR, O ISRAEL: THE LORD IS OUR GOD, THE LORD IS ONE.

Blessed be His Name, whose glorious kingdom is for ever and ever.

Deuteronomy 6. 5-9

⁵And thou shalt love the Lord thy God with all thine heart, and with all thy soul, and with all thy might. ⁶And these words, which I command thee this day, shall be upon thine heart : ⁷and thou shalt teach them diligently unto thy children, and shalt talk of them when thou sittest in thine house, and when thou walkest by the way, *See pp. 116–123* and when thou liest down, and when thou risest up. ⁸And thou shalt bind them for a sign upon thine hand, and they shall be for frontlets between thine eyes. ⁹And thou shalt write them upon the door-posts of thy house, and upon thy gates.

NIGHT PRAYERS.

In larger Siddurim, the Prayers before Retiring to Rest are often prefaced by a Supplication, " Master of the Universe, behold, I forgive every one who has injured me : and may no one be punished because of his wrong to me ! " This is then followed by the Shorter Confession, p. 906.

The Rabbis ordained that the first paragraph of the Shema be

וִיהִי נֹעַם אֲדֹנָי אֱלֹהֵינוּ עָלֵינוּ וּמַעֲשֵׂה יָדֵינוּ כּוֹנְנָה
עָלֵינוּ וּמַעֲשֵׂה יָדֵינוּ כּוֹנְנֵהוּ :

תהלים צ׳א

יֹשֵׁב בְּסֵתֶר עֶלְיוֹן בְּצֵל שַׁדַּי יִתְלוֹנָן : אֹמַר לַיהֹוָה
מַחְסִי וּמְצוּדָתִי אֱלֹהַי אֶבְטַח־בּוֹ : כִּי הוּא יַצִּילְךָ מִפַּח
יָקוּשׁ מִדֶּבֶר הַוּוֹת : בְּאֶבְרָתוֹ יָסֶךְ לָךְ וְתַחַת כְּנָפָיו
תֶּחְסֶה צִנָּה וְסֹחֵרָה אֲמִתּוֹ : לֹא־תִירָא מִפַּחַד לָיְלָה
מֵחֵץ יָעוּף יוֹמָם : מִדֶּבֶר בָּאֹפֶל יַהֲלֹךְ מִקֶּטֶב יָשׁוּד
צָהֳרָיִם : יִפֹּל מִצִּדְּךָ אֶלֶף וּרְבָבָה מִימִינֶךָ אֵלֶיךָ לֹא
יִגָּשׁ : רַק בְּעֵינֶיךָ תַבִּיט וְשִׁלֻּמַת רְשָׁעִים תִּרְאֶה : כִּי־
אַתָּה יְהֹוָה מַחְסִי עֶלְיוֹן שַׂמְתָּ מְעוֹנֶךָ : לֹא־תְאֻנֶּה אֵלֶיךָ
רָעָה וְנֶגַע לֹא־יִקְרַב בְּאָהֳלֶךָ : כִּי מַלְאָכָיו יְצַוֶּה־לָּךְ
לִשְׁמָרְךָ בְּכָל־דְּרָכֶיךָ : עַל־כַּפַּיִם יִשָּׂאוּנְךָ פֶּן תִּגֹּף בָּאֶבֶן
רַגְלֶךָ : עַל־שַׁחַל וָפֶתֶן תִּדְרֹךְ תִּרְמֹס כְּפִיר וְתַנִּין : כִּי
בִי חָשַׁק וַאֲפַלְּטֵהוּ אֲשַׂגְּבֵהוּ כִּי־יָדַע שְׁמִי : יִקְרָאֵנִי
וְאֶעֱנֵהוּ עִמּוֹ אָנֹכִי בְצָרָה אֲחַלְּצֵהוּ וַאֲכַבְּדֵהוּ : אֹרֶךְ
יָמִים אַשְׂבִּיעֵהוּ וְאַרְאֵהוּ בִּישׁוּעָתִי :

Repeat the last verse.

repeated before retiring to rest, together with a special night prayer.
" All the demons of the night flee from him who recites the Shema on
his bed ", is a Rabbinical saying. It is deep psychological truth. " To
fill one's mind with high and noble thoughts, is a wise preparation for

Psalm 90. 17   And let the pleasantness of the Lord our God be upon us : and establish thou the work of our hands upon us ; yea, the work of our hands establish thou it.

Psalm xci.

ASSUR-
ANCE OF
DIVINE
PROTEC-
TION

¹He that dwelleth in the shelter of the Most High, abideth under the shadow of the Almighty. ²I say of the Lord, He is my refuge and my fortress ; my God, in whom I trust.—³For he shall deliver thee from the snare of the fowler, and from the noisome pestilence. ⁴He shall cover thee with his pinions, and under his wings shalt thou take refuge : his truth shall be a shield and armour. ⁵Thou shalt not be afraid of the terror by night, nor of the arrow that flieth by day ; ⁶of the pestilence that stalketh in darkness, nor of the plague that ravageth at noon day. ⁷A thousand may fall at thy side, and ten thousand at thy

See p. 71   right hand ; it shall not come nigh unto thee. ⁸Only with thine eyes shalt thou look on, and see the retribution of the wicked.—⁹For thou, O Lord, art my refuge.—Thou hast made the Most High thy dwelling place ; ¹⁰there shall no evil befall thee, neither shall any scourge come nigh thy tent. ¹¹For he shall give his angels charge over thee, to keep thee in all thy ways. ¹²They shall bear thee upon their hands, lest thou strike thy foot against a stone. ¹³Thou shalt tread upon the lion and the adder : upon the young lion and the serpent shalt thou trample.—¹⁴Because he hath set his love upon me, therefore will I deliver him : I will set him on high, because he knoweth my name. ¹⁵When he calleth upon me I will answer him ; I will be with him in trouble : I will deliver him and honour him ; ¹⁶With length of days will I satisfy him, and will let him see my salvation. *Repeat the last verse.*

the hours of silent night. The presence of the pure, excludes the impure ; and the meditation over the good, drives out the suggestions of evil " (Abrahams).

PSALM 91. Its appropriateness is obvious.

תהלים ג׳

יְיָ מָה־רַבּוּ צָרָי רַבִּים קָמִים עָלָי : רַבִּים אוֹמְרִים לְנַפְשִׁי אֵין יְשׁוּעָתָה לּוֹ בֵאלֹהִים סֶלָה : וְאַתָּה יְיָ מָגֵן בַּעֲדִי כְּבוֹדִי וּמֵרִים רֹאשִׁי : קוֹלִי אֶל־יְיָ אֶקְרָא וַיַּעֲנֵנִי מֵהַר קָדְשׁוֹ סֶלָה : אֲנִי שָׁכַבְתִּי וָאִישָׁנָה הֱקִיצוֹתִי כִּי יְיָ יִסְמְכֵנִי : לֹא־אִירָא מֵרִבְבוֹת עָם אֲשֶׁר סָבִיב שָׁתוּ עָלָי : קוּמָה יְיָ הוֹשִׁיעֵנִי אֱלֹהַי כִּי־ הִכִּיתָ אֶת־כָּל־אֹיְבַי לֶחִי שִׁנֵּי רְשָׁעִים שִׁבַּרְתָּ : לַיְיָ הַיְשׁוּעָה עַל־עַמְּךָ בִרְכָתֶךָ סֶּלָה :

הַשְׁכִּיבֵנוּ יְיָ אֱלֹהֵינוּ לְשָׁלוֹם וְהַעֲמִידֵנוּ מַלְכֵּנוּ לְחַיִּים · וּפְרוֹשׂ עָלֵינוּ סֻכַּת שְׁלוֹמֶךָ · וְתַקְּנֵנוּ בְּעֵצָה טוֹבָה מִלְּפָנֶיךָ · וְהוֹשִׁיעֵנוּ לְמַעַן שְׁמֶךָ · וְהָגֵן בַּעֲדֵנוּ וְהָסֵר מֵעָלֵינוּ אוֹיֵב דֶּבֶר וְחֶרֶב וְרָעָב וְיָגוֹן · וְהָסֵר שָׂטָן מִלְּפָנֵינוּ וּמֵאַחֲרֵנוּ · וּבְצֵל כְּנָפֶיךָ תַּסְתִּירֵנוּ כִּי אֵל שׁוֹמְרֵנוּ וּמַצִּילֵנוּ אָתָּה כִּי אֵל מֶלֶךְ חַנּוּן וְרַחוּם אָתָּה · וּשְׁמוֹר צֵאתֵנוּ וּבוֹאֵנוּ לְחַיִּים וּלְשָׁלוֹם מֵעַתָּה וְעַד עוֹלָם :

בָּרוּךְ יְיָ בַּיּוֹם · בָּרוּךְ יְיָ בַּלָּיְלָה · בָּרוּךְ יְיָ בְּשָׁכְבֵנוּ · בָּרוּךְ יְיָ בְּקוּמֵנוּ : כִּי בְיָדְךָ נַפְשׁוֹת הַחַיִּים וְהַמֵּתִים : אֲשֶׁר בְּיָדוֹ נֶפֶשׁ כָּל־חָי וְרוּחַ כָּל־בְּשַׂר אִישׁ : בְּיָדְךָ אַפְקִיד רוּחִי פָּדִיתָה אוֹתִי יְיָ אֵל אֱמֶת : אֱלֹהֵינוּ

Psalm iii.

CONFID-
ENCE IN
PERIL

²Lord, how are mine adversaries increased! Many are they that rise up against me. ³Many there are which say of my soul, There is no help for him in God. (Selah.) ⁴But thou, O Lord, art a shield about me ; my glory and the lifter up of mine head. ⁵I cry unto the Lord with my voice, and he answereth me from his holy mountain. (Selah.) ⁶I lay me down and sleep ; I awake, for the Lord sustaineth me. ⁷I will not be afraid of the ten thousands of people, that have set themselves against me round about. ⁸Arise, O Lord ; save me, O my God : for thou hast smitten all mine enemies upon the cheek ; thou hast broken the teeth of the wicked. ⁹Salvation belongeth unto the Lord : thy blessing be upon thy people. (Selah.)

GOD THE
GUARDIAN

Cause us, O Lord our God, to lie down in peace, and raise us up, O our King, unto life. Spread over us the protection of thy peace ; direct us aright through thine own good counsel ; save us for thy Name's sake ; be thou a shield about us ; remove from us every enemy, pestilence, sword, famine and sorrow ; remove also the adversary from before us and from behind us. O shelter us beneath the shadow

See p. 312

of thy wings ; for thou, O God, art our Guardian and our Deliverer ; yea, thou, O God, art a gracious and merciful King ; and guard our going out and our coming in unto life and unto peace from this time forth and for evermore.

PSALM 3. 2. *How are mine enemies increased ?* Or, " how many are mine enemies become " ? The psalm was written when Absalom had rebelled against David, and the general rising forced him to flee for his life ; see II Samuel 15–18.
3. *no help for him.* His enemies were bitter.
6. *lay me down and sleep.* In perfect trustfulness and peace.
8. *broken the teeth.* His foes are strong as lions ; to break their teeth is to destroy their power to do harm.
9. *salvation. i.e.* help, victory. This is the answer to *v.* 2.
CAUSE US, O LORD GOD. The remaining passages were gradually added in medieval times. The first two paragraphs are from the Evening Service, but without the concluding Benedictions.

שֶׁבַּשָּׁמַיִם יַחֵד שִׁמְךָ וְקַיֵּם מַלְכוּתְךָ תָּמִיד וּמְלוֹךְ
עָלֵינוּ לְעוֹלָם וָעֶד :

יִרְאוּ עֵינֵינוּ וְיִשְׂמַח לִבֵּנוּ וְתָגֵל נַפְשֵׁנוּ בִּישׁוּעָתְךָ
בֶּאֱמֶת בֶּאֱמֹר לְצִיּוֹן מָלַךְ אֱלֹהָיִךְ · יְיָ מֶלֶךְ יְיָ מָלָךְ
יְיָ ׀ יִמְלֹךְ לְעֹלָם וָעֶד : כִּי הַמַּלְכוּת שֶׁלְּךָ הִיא וּלְעוֹלְמֵי
עַד תִּמְלוֹךְ בְּכָבוֹד · כִּי אֵין לָנוּ מֶלֶךְ אֶלָּא אָתָּה :

הַמַּלְאָךְ הַגֹּאֵל אֹתִי מִכָּל־רָע יְבָרֵךְ אֶת־הַנְּעָרִים
וְיִקָּרֵא בָהֶם שְׁמִי וְשֵׁם אֲבֹתַי אַבְרָהָם וְיִצְחָק וְיִדְגּוּ
לָרֹב בְּקֶרֶב הָאָרֶץ : וַיֹּאמֶר אִם־שָׁמוֹעַ תִּשְׁמַע לְקוֹל
יְיָ אֱלֹהֶיךָ וְהַיָּשָׁר בְּעֵינָיו תַּעֲשֶׂה וְהַאֲזַנְתָּ לְמִצְוֹתָיו
וְשָׁמַרְתָּ כָּל־חֻקָּיו כָּל־הַמַּחֲלָה אֲשֶׁר שַׂמְתִּי בְמִצְרַיִם
לֹא־אָשִׂים עָלֶיךָ כִּי אֲנִי יְיָ רֹפְאֶךָ : וַיֹּאמֶר יְיָ אֶל
הַשָּׂטָן יִגְעַר יְיָ בְּךָ הַשָּׂטָן וְיִגְעַר יְיָ בְּךָ הַבֹּחֵר
בִּירוּשָׁלָיִם הֲלֹא זֶה אוּד מֻצָּל מֵאֵשׁ : הִנֵּה מִטָּתוֹ
שֶׁלִּשְׁלֹמֹה שִׁשִּׁים גִּבֹּרִים סָבִיב לָהּ מִגִּבֹּרֵי יִשְׂרָאֵל :
כֻּלָּם אֲחֻזֵי חֶרֶב מְלֻמְּדֵי מִלְחָמָה אִישׁ חַרְבּוֹ עַל־
יְרֵכוֹ מִפַּחַד בַּלֵּילוֹת : יְבָרֶכְךָ יְיָ וְיִשְׁמְרֶךָ : יָאֵר יְיָ

into thy hand . . . truth. The Babylonian teacher Abaye (273–339)
looked upon this wonderful verse as a sufficient night-prayer in itself.
THE ANGEL. Here follows a collection of Scriptural verses of

NIGHT
PRAYER
    Blessed be the Lord by day ; blessed be the Lord by
night ; blessed be the Lord when we lie down ; blessed be
See p. 314
the Lord when we rise up. For in thy hand are the souls of
Job 12. 10
the living and the dead, (as it is said), In his hand is the
soul of every living thing, and the spirit of all human flesh.
Psalm 31. 6
Into thy hand I commend my spirit ; thou hast redeemed
me, O Lord, God of truth. Our God who art in heaven,
assert the unity of thy Name, and establish thy kingdom
continually, and reign over us for ever and ever.

    May our eyes behold, our hearts rejoice, and our souls
be glad in thy true salvation, when it shall be said unto Zion,
Thy God reigneth. The Lord is King ; the Lord was
King ; the Lord shall be King for ever and ever : for the
kingdom is thine, and to everlasting thou wilt reign in
glory ; for we have no king but thee.

VERSES
OF MERCY
    The angel who hath redeemed me from all evil bless the
Genesis 48. 16
lads ; and let thy name be named on them, and the name
of my fathers Abraham and Isaac ; and let them grow into
Exodus 15. 26
a multitude in the midst of the earth.—And he said, If
thou wilt diligently hearken to the voice of the Lord thy
God, and wilt do that which is right in his eyes, and wilt
give ear to his commandments, and keep his statutes,
I will put none of the diseases upon thee, which I have
put upon the Egyptians ; for I am the Lord that healeth
Zechariah 3. 2
thee.—And the Lord said unto the adversary, The Lord
rebuke thee, O adversary ; yea, the Lord that hath chosen
Jerusalem rebuke thee. Is not this a brand plucked out of
Song of Solo-
mon 3. 7, 8
the fire ?—Behold the bed of Solomon : threescore mighty
men are about it, of the mighty men of Israel : they all
handle the sword, expert in war : every man hath his sword
Numbers 6. 24
upon his thigh, because of fear in the night.—The Lord

" mercy ", *i.e.* of good omen. The threefold repetition of the verses
after the Priestly Blessing is Cabalistic and optional, and so is the
invocation of the angels.

פָּנָיו אֵלֶיךָ וִיחֻנֶּךָּ : יִשָּׂא יְיָ פָּנָיו אֵלֶיךָ וְיָשֵׂם לְךָ שָׁלוֹם :

הִנֵּה לֹא יָנוּם וְלֹא יִישָׁן שׁוֹמֵר יִשְׂרָאֵל : *To be said three times*

לִישׁוּעָתְךָ קִוִּיתִי יְיָ • קִוִּיתִי יְיָ לִישׁוּעָתְךָ •

יְיָ לִישׁוּעָתְךָ קִוִּיתִי :

בְּשֵׁם יְיָ אֱלֹהֵי יִשְׂרָאֵל מִימִינִי מִיכָאֵל • וּמִשְּׂמֹאלִי גַּבְרִיאֵל •

וּמִלְּפָנַי אוּרִיאֵל • וּמֵאֲחוֹרַי רְפָאֵל • וְעַל רֹאשִׁי שְׁכִינַת

אֵל : *To be said three times.*

תהלים כ"ח, *p. 600.*

רִגְזוּ וְאַל־תֶּחֱטָאוּ • אִמְרוּ בִלְבַבְכֶם עַל־מִשְׁכַּבְכֶם

וְדֹמּוּ סֶלָה : *To be said three times.*

בְּטֶרֶם כָּל־יְצִיר נִבְרָא :	אֲדוֹן עוֹלָם • אֲשֶׁר מָלַךְ •
אֲזַי מֶלֶךְ שְׁמוֹ נִקְרָא :	לְעֵת נַעֲשָׂה בְחֶפְצוֹ כֹּל
לְבַדּוֹ יִמְלוֹךְ נוֹרָא :	וְאַחֲרֵי כִּכְלוֹת הַכֹּל
וְהוּא יִהְיֶה בְּתִפְאָרָה :	וְהוּא הָיָה • וְהוּא הֹוֶה •
לְהַמְשִׁיל לוֹ לְהַחְבִּירָה :	וְהוּא אֶחָד • וְאֵין שֵׁנִי •
וְלוֹ הָעֹז וְהַמִּשְׂרָה :	בְּלִי רֵאשִׁית בְּלִי תַכְלִית •
וְצוּר חֶבְלִי בְּעֵת צָרָה :	וְהוּא אֵלִי • וְחַי גֹּאֲלִי •
מְנָת כּוֹסִי בְּיוֹם אֶקְרָא :	וְהוּא נִסִּי וּמָנוֹס לִי •
בְּעֵת אִישָׁן וְאָעִירָה :	בְּיָדוֹ אַפְקִיד רוּחִי •
יְיָ לִי וְלֹא אִירָא :	וְעִם רוּחִי גְּוִיָּתִי •

bless thee, and keep thee : the Lord make his face to shine upon thee, and be gracious unto thee : the Lord turn his face unto thee, and give thee peace.

Psalm 121. 4   Behold, he that guardeth Israel will neither slumber nor sleep. (*To be said three times.*)

Genesis 49. 18   For. thy salvation I hope, O Lord. I hope, O Lord, for thy salvation. O Lord, for thy salvation I hope.

In the name of the Lord, the God of Israel, may Michael be at my right hand ; Gabriel at my left ; before me, Uriel ; behind me, Raphael ; and above my head the divine presence of God. (*To be said three times.*)

Psalm cxxviii p. 601.

Psalm 4. 5   Stand in awe, and sin not : commune with your own heart upon your bed, and be still. (Selah.) (*To be said three times*).

ADON OLOM
Reigned the Universe's Master,
    Ere were earthly things begun ;
When His mandate all created,
    Ruler was the name He won.
And alone He'll rule tremendous
    When all things are past and gone,

See p. 7
He no equal has, nor consort,
    He, the singular and lone,
Has no end and no beginning ;
    His the sceptre, might and throne.
He's my God and living Saviour,
    Rock to Whom in need I run ;
He's my banner and my refuge,
    Fount of weal when call'd upon.
In His hand I place my spirit,
    At nightfall and at rise of sun,
And therewith my body also ;
    God's my God—I fear no one.

ADON OLOM. The translation is from George Borrow's " Lavengro"

MARRIAGE AND THE POSITION OF WOMAN IN JUDAISM

Marriage is that relationship between man and woman under whose shadow alone there can be true reverence for the mystery, dignity, and sacredness of life. Scripture represents marriage not merely as a Mosaic ordinance, but as part of the scheme of Creation, intended for all humanity.

They do less than justice to this Divine institution who view it in no other light than as a civil contract. In a contract, the mutual rights and obligations are the result of agreement, and their selection and formulation may flow from the momentary whim of the parties. In the marriage relation, however, such rights and obligations are high above the fluctuating will of both husband and wife; they are determined and imposed by Religion, as well as by the Civil Law. The contract view fails to bring out this higher sphere of duty and conscience, which is of the very essence of marriage.

The purpose of marriage is twofold—(a) posterity, and (b) companionship.

(a) The duty of rearing a family figures in the Rabbinic codes as the first of the 613 *Mitzvoth* (ordinances) of the Torah (Genesis 1. 28, *Be fruitful and multiply*). To this commandment is due the sacredness and centrality of the child in Judaism—something which even the enlightened nations of antiquity could not understand. The Roman historian Tacitus deemed it a contemptible prejudice of the Jews that " it is a crime among them to kill any child ". What a lurid flashlight these words throw on Graeco-Roman society! It is in such a society that Judaism proclaimed the Biblical teaching that the child was the highest of human treasures. *O Lord God, what wilt Thou give me, seeing that I go childless?* was Abraham's agonizing cry. Of what value were earthly possessions to him, if he was denied a child who would continue his work after him? This attitude of the Father of the Hebrew people has remained that of his descendants throughout the ages. A childless marriage was deemed to have failed in one of its main purposes. In little children—it was taught—God gives humanity a chance to make good its mistakes. Little children are " the Messiahs of mankind "—the perennial regenerative force in humanity. No wonder that Jewish infant mortality is everywhere lower than the non-Jewish—often only one-half of that among the general population.

(b) Companionship is the other primary end of the marriage institution. Woman is to be the helpmate of man, עֵזֶר כְּנֶגְדּוֹ. A wife is a man's other self, all that man's nature demands for its completion physically, socially, and spiritually. In marriage alone can man's need

MARRIAGE AND POSITION OF WOMAN IN JUDAISM

for physical and social companionship be directed to holy ends. It is this idea which is expressed by the term *kiddushin* (" the sanctities ") applied to Jewish marriage—a term which, aside from its original sacerdotal meaning, signifies the hallowing of two human beings to life's holiest purposes. In married life, man finds his truest and most lasting happiness ; and only through married life does human personality reach its highest fulfilment. *A man shall leave his father, and his mother, and shall cleave unto his wife*, says Scripture (Genesis 2. 24). Note that it is the man who is to cleave to his wife, and not the woman, physically the weaker, who is to cleave to her husband ; because, in the higher sphere of the soul's life, woman is the ethical and spiritual superior of man. " Even as the wife is ", say the Rabbis, " so the husband is ". The celibate life is the unblessed life : Judaism requires its saints to show their saintliness *in* the world, and amid the ties and obligations of family life. " He who has no wife abides without good, help, joy, blessing, or atonement. He who has no wife cannot be considered a whole man " (Talmud). All forms of extra-marital companionship outside the sacred estate of matrimony, unhallowed by Religion and unrestrained by its commandments, Judaism considers an abomination. And such extra-marital relations are prohibited just as sternly with non-Jewish women as with Jewish. Thus, Joseph resists the advances of the *heathen* temptress with the words : *How can I do this great wickedness, and sin against God ?* (Genesis 39. 9) ; and the Book of Proverbs is clear on the attitude of Judaism to the " strange woman "—married or unmarried. No less emphatically than in Scripture is purity of life and thought demanded by the Rabbis. The founders of the Christian Church adopted in its entirety the Jewish view on extra-marital relations.

The Biblical ideal of marriage is monogamy. The Creation story and all the Prophetical portions of Scripture speak of the union of a man with *one* wife. Whenever a Prophet speaks of marriage, he is thinking of such a union—lifelong, faithful, holy. Polygamy seems to have well-nigh disappeared in Israel after the Babylonian Exile ; and early Rabbinic literature presupposes a practically monogamic society. Though the *formal* abolition of polygamy, through Rabbenu Gershom, only took place in the year 1000, monogamy had been the rule in Jewish life long before the rise of Christianity.

For the questions and problems concerning the dissolution of marriage, see *Deuteronomy*, 314–319 (932–4). In this connection, the words of the late Dr. Friedländer should be noted. " We acknowledge the principle laid down in the Talmud, " the law of the Country is binding upon us " (דינא דמלכותא דינא) ; but only in so far as our civil relations are concerned. With regard to religious questions, our own religious Code must be obeyed. Religiously neither civil marriage nor civil divorce can be recognized, unless supplemented by marriage or divorce according to religious forms. Furthermore, marriages allowed by the Civil Law, but prohibited by our Religious Law, cannot be recognized before the tribunal of our Religion ".

סֵדֶר אֵירוּסִין וְנִשּׂוּאִין :

בָּרוּךְ הַבָּא בְּשֵׁם יְיָ בֵּרַכְנוּכֶם מִבֵּית יְיָ :
בֹּאוּ נִשְׁתַּחֲוֶה וְנִכְרָעָה נִבְרְכָה לִפְנֵי יְיָ עוֹשֵׂנוּ :
עִבְדוּ אֶת יְיָ בְּשִׂמְחָה בֹּאוּ לְפָנָיו בִּרְנָנָה :

תהלים ק׳, *p.* 20.

מִי אַדִּיר עַל הַכֹּל ∙ מִי בָּרוּךְ עַל הַכֹּל ∙ מִי גָּדוֹל עַל הַכֹּל ∙
הוּא יְבָרֵךְ הֶחָתָן וְהַכַּלָּה :

תְּפִלָּה אוֹ דְרָשָׁה :

It is astonishing to note the amount of hostile misrepresentation
that exists in regard to woman's position in Jewish life. Yet the
teaching of Scripture is quite clear. *God created man in His own image*;
male and female created He them (Genesis 1. 27)—both man and woman
are in their spiritual nature akin to God, and both are invested with
the same authority to subdue the earth and have domination over it.
The wives of the Patriarchs are the equals of their husbands. Miriam,
alongside her brothers, is reckoned as one of the three emancipators
from Egypt (Micah 6. 4); Deborah is "*Judge*" in Israel, and leader
in the war of independence ; and to Hannah (I Samuel 1. 8) her husband
speaks : "Why weepest thou ? am not I better to thee than ten sons ?"
In later centuries, we find woman among the Prophets—Huldah ; and
in the days of the Second Temple, on the throne—Queen Salome
Alexandra. Nothing can well be nobler praise of woman than Proverbs
31 (see p. 404) ; and, as regards the reverence due to her from her
children, the mother was placed on a par with the father in the Decalogue, Exodus 20. 12 ; and before the father, in Leviticus 19. 3. A
Jewish child would not have spoken to his grief-stricken mother as did
Telemachus, the hero's son in the Odyssey : "Go to thy chamber,
and mind thine own housewiferies. Speech shall be for man, for all,
but for me in chief ; for mine is the lordship in the house ".

1009

THE MARRIAGE SERVICE.

Psalm 118. 26   Blessed be he that cometh in the name of the Lord: we bless you out of the house of the Lord.

Psalm 95. 6   O come, let us worship and bow down; let us kneel before the Lord our Maker.

Psalm 100. 2   Serve the Lord with joy; come before him with exulting.

Psalm c, *p.* 61.

He who is mighty, blessed and great above all beings, may he bless the bridegroom and the bride.

PRAYER OR ADDRESS.

The property rights of woman became clearly defined in the Talmudic period. Her legal status under Jewish law " compared to its advantage with that of contemporary civilizations " (G. F. Moore). " In respect to possessing independent estate, the Jewish wife was in a position far superior to that of English wives before the enactment of recent legislation " (I. Abrahams).

A conclusive proof of woman's dominating place in Jewish life is the undeniable fact, that the hallowing of the Jewish home was her work; and that the laws of chastity were observed in that home, both by men and women, with a scrupulousness that has hardly ever been equalled. The Jewish Sages duly recognized her wonderful spiritual influence, and nothing could surpass the delicacy with which respect for her is inculcated : "Love thy wife as thyself, and honour her more than thyself. Be careful not to cause woman to weep, for God counts her tears. Israel was redeemed from Egypt on account of the virtue of its women. He who weds a good woman is as if he had fulfilled all the precepts of the Torah " (Talmud).

---

blessed be he that cometh. The singing of these verses, followed by Psalm 100, and a short invocation (" He who is mighty ") from a medieval wedding-hymn, form the musical prelude to the Service. They are purely optional.

The Marriage Service proper is usually preceded by a special Prayer offered by the minister, or by a brief address on the sacredness of the occasion and the solemn duties of Holy Wedlock. The readiness of the bridegroom and the bride to assume those duties is sufficiently indicated by their presence for the marriage ceremony. Still, there are those who desire verbally to declare their consent, and their acceptance of

ברכת אירוסין :

בָּרוּךְ אַתָּה יְיָ אֱלֹהֵינוּ מֶלֶךְ הָעוֹלָם · בּוֹרֵא פְּרִי הַגָּפֶן :

בָּרוּךְ אַתָּה יְיָ אֱלֹהֵינוּ מֶלֶךְ הָעוֹלָם · אֲשֶׁר קִדְּשָׁנוּ

בְּמִצְוֹתָיו · וְצִוָּנוּ עַל הָעֲרָיוֹת · וְאָסַר לָנוּ אֶת הָאֲרוּסוֹת ·

וְהִתִּיר לָנוּ אֶת הַנְּשׂוּאוֹת לָנוּ עַל יְדֵי חֻפָּה וְקִדּוּשִׁין · בָּרוּךְ

אַתָּה יְיָ · מְקַדֵּשׁ עַמּוֹ יִשְׂרָאֵל עַל יְדֵי חֻפָּה וְקִדּוּשִׁין :

*The Bridegroom places the ring upon the forefinger of the right hand
of the Bride, and says :—*

הֲרֵי אַתְּ מְקֻדֶּשֶׁת לִי בְּטַבַּעַת זוֹ כְּדַת מֹשֶׁה וְיִשְׂרָאֵל :

the undertaking set forth in the Kesubah. To them the minister may
put the following questions, either before or after his address :—

Minister—" You (A) and (B) are about to be wedded according to the Law of Moses and of Israel."

" Will you (A) take this woman (B) to be your wedded wife ?
Will you be a true and faithful husband unto her ? Will you
protect and support her ? Will you love, honour and cherish her "?

Bridegroom—" I will."

Minister—" Will you (B) take this man (A) to be your
wedded husband ? Will you be a true and faithful wife unto him ?
Will you love, honour and cherish him ? "

Bride—" I will."

fruit of the vine. Both parts of the Marriage Service open with the
Benediction over a cup of wine. (See note p. 809.) Wine is a symbol
of joy, and joyousness at a wedding is a religious duty. The couple both
drink from both cups of wine—an indication of their resolve henceforth
to share whatever destiny Providence may allot to them.

given us command. This ancient Benediction over the institution
of marriage is known as the "Benediction of Betrothal". Originally

PRE-LIMINARY BENEDIC-TIONS

Blessed art thou, O Lord our God, King of the universe, who createst the fruit of the vine.

Blessed art thou, O Lord our God, King of the universe, who hast hallowed us by thy commandments, and hast given us command concerning forbidden marriages ; who hast disallowed unto us those that are betrothed, but hast sanctioned unto us such as are wedded to us by the rite of the nuptial canopy and the sacred covenant of wedlock. Blessed art thou, O Lord, who hallowest thy people Israel by the rite of the nuptial canopy and the sacred covenant of wedlock.

The Bridegroom places the ring upon the forefinger of the right hand of the Bride, and says :—

BRIDE-GROOM'S DECLARA-TION

BEHOLD, THOU ART CONSECRATED UNTO ME BY THIS RING, ACCORDING TO THE LAW OF MOSES AND OF ISRAEL.

a considerable time—even a year—intervened between the " Betrothal " (אירוסין), by which the bridal couple became bound for all purposes save living together, and Wedlock (נישואין). Since many centuries, the solemnization of Betrothal is always combined with the solemnization of the complete Nuptials, by reciting the Seven Benedictions that constitute the second part of the Marriage Service.

forbidden marriages. Here the term is equivalent to " the laws of chastity ". For the "List of Forbidden Marriages" see *Leviticus* 186 (Soncino, 559).

canopy. Heb. *chuppah,* symbolic of the home-taking of the bride by the bridegroom.

sacred covenant of wedlock. Heb. *kiddushin,* lit. " the sanctities ". Marriage is thus neither a transaction, nor merely a contractual relation, but a sanctification.

behold, thou art . . . Israel. This Declaration of the bridegroom to the bride is the essence of the ceremony. The officiating minister should translate it to the Bridegroom, who repeats the Hebrew formula, word by word, after him.

consecrated unto me. The literal meaning of the word indicates that she becomes " holy " unto him—an object of reverence and utmost regard. To all other men as well she becomes " holy ", *i.e.* forbidden, in the same way as holy Temple vessels are inviolable for common use.

ring. Need not be of gold, but should be without jewels. Rings have been in use at Jewish weddings since the seventh century.

according to the Law of . . . Israel. This ancient phrase also expresses the resolve of bridegroom and bride to lead their common life according to the rule and manner of Judaism.

The כְּתוּבָה *is read by the Celebrant, after which the*
שֶׁבַע בְּרָכוֹת לְנִשׂוּאִין *are said :—*

בָּרוּךְ אַתָּה יְיָ אֱלֹהֵינוּ מֶלֶךְ הָעוֹלָם ' בּוֹרֵא פְּרִי הַגָּפֶן :

בָּרוּךְ אַתָּה יְיָ אֱלֹהֵינוּ מֶלֶךְ הָעוֹלָם ' שֶׁהַכֹּל בָּרָא לִכְבוֹדוֹ :

בָּרוּךְ אַתָּה יְיָ אֱלֹהֵינוּ מֶלֶךְ הָעוֹלָם ' יוֹצֵר הָאָדָם :

בָּרוּךְ אַתָּה יְיָ אֱלֹהֵינוּ מֶלֶךְ הָעוֹלָם ' אֲשֶׁר יָצַר אֶת הָאָדָם
בְּצַלְמוֹ ' בְּצֶלֶם דְּמוּת תַּבְנִיתוֹ ' וְהִתְקִין לוֹ מִמֶּנּוּ בִּנְיַן עֲדֵי
עַד ' בָּרוּךְ אַתָּה יְיָ ' יוֹצֵר הָאָדָם :

שׂוֹשׂ תָּשִׂישׂ וְתָגֵל הָעֲקָרָה ' בְּקִבּוּץ בָּנֶיהָ לְתוֹכָהּ בְּשִׂמְחָה '
בָּרוּךְ אַתָּה יְיָ ' מְשַׂמֵּחַ צִיּוֹן בְּבָנֶיהָ :

שַׂמֵּחַ תְּשַׂמַּח רֵעִים הָאֲהוּבִים ' כְּשַׂמֵּחֲךָ יְצִירְךָ בְּגַן עֵדֶן
מִקֶּדֶם ' בָּרוּךְ אַתָּה יְיָ ' מְשַׂמֵּחַ חָתָן וְכַלָּה :

בָּרוּךְ אַתָּה יְיָ אֱלֹהֵינוּ מֶלֶךְ הָעוֹלָם ' אֲשֶׁר בָּרָא שָׂשׂוֹן
וְשִׂמְחָה ' חָתָן וְכַלָּה ' גִּילָה רִנָּה דִּיצָה וְחֶדְוָה ' אַהֲבָה
וְאַחֲוָה וְשָׁלוֹם וְרֵעוּת ' מְהֵרָה יְיָ אֱלֹהֵינוּ יִשָּׁמַע בְּעָרֵי יְהוּדָה
וּבְחֻצוֹת יְרוּשָׁלָיִם קוֹל שָׂשׂוֹן וְקוֹל שִׂמְחָה ' קוֹל חָתָן וְקוֹל
כַּלָּה ' קוֹל מִצַּהֲלוֹת חֲתָנִים מֵחֻפָּתָם וּנְעָרִים מִמִּשְׁתֵּה
נְגִינָתָם ' בָּרוּךְ אַתָּה יְיָ ' מְשַׂמֵּחַ חָתָן עִם הַכַּלָּה :

*A glass is broken by the Bridegroom, and the Celebrant pronounces
the Benediction.*

THE KESUBAH, the Hebrew Marriage Document, was introduced by
Simeon ben Shatach (p. 620) as a protection to the wife in the event
of her becoming widowed or divorced. It assigns to her a fixed sum
which remains a prior claim on his estate. This Document testifies that
on such and such a date the Bridegroom said to his Bride : " Be thou my
wife according to the Law of Moses and of Israel. I will work for thee ;
I will honour thee ; I will support and maintain thee, even as it be-
seemeth a Jewish husband to do, who work for their wives, and honour,

The Hebrew Marriage Document is read by the Celebrant, after which
the following Seven Benedictions are said :—

THE SEVEN BENEDIC-TIONS OF WEDLOCK

Blessed art thou, O Lord our God, King of the universe, who createst the fruit of the vine.

Blessed art thou, O Lord our God, King of the universe, who hast created all things to thy glory.

Blessed art thou, O Lord our God, King of the universe, Creator of man.

Blessed art thou, O Lord our God, King of the universe, who hast made man in thine image, after thy likeness, and hast prepared unto him, out of his very self, a perpetual fabric. Blessed art thou, O Lord, Creator of man.

May she who was barren (Zion) be exceeding glad and exult, when her children are gathered within her in joy. Blessed art thou, O Lord, who makest Zion joyful through her children.

O make these loved companions greatly to rejoice, even as of old thou didst gladden thy creature in the garden of Eden. Blessed art thou, O Lord, who makest bridegroom and bride to rejoice.

Blessed art thou, O Lord our God, King of the universe, who hast created joy and gladness, bridegroom and bride, mirth and exultation, pleasure and delight, love, brotherhood, peace and fellowship. Soon may there be heard in the cities of Judah, and in the streets of Jerusalem, the voice of joy and gladness, the voice of the bridegroom and the voice of the bride, the jubilant voice of bridegrooms from their canopies, and of youths from their feasts of song. Blessed art thou, O Lord, who makest the bridegroom to rejoice with the bride.

A glass is broken by the Bridegroom, and the Celebrant pronounces
the Benediction.

support, and maintain them in faithfulness." The Document proceeds to state, " and the Bride plighted her troth unto him, and consented to become his wife". This portion of the Kesubah should either be cited in the address of the minister, or read in the vernacular by him.

The Seven Benedictions of Wedlock that follow the reading of the Kesubah are Talmudic in origin. Through their recital, each new home is brought into relation with the story of Creation, with the whole of Israel's history, and with Israel's Messianic Hope. The opening

ברכת המזון לנשואין :

He who says Grace commences thus :—

דְּוַי הָסֵר וְגַם חָרוֹן ׳ וְאָז אִלֵּם בְּשִׁיר יָרוֹן ׳ נְחֵנוּ בְּמַעְגְּלֵי
צֶדֶק ׳ שְׁעֵה בִּרְכַּת בְּנֵי יְשֻׁרוּן :

בִּרְשׁוּת מָרָנָן וְרַבָּנָן וְרַבּוֹתַי ׳ נְבָרֵךְ אֱלֹהֵינוּ שֶׁהַשִּׂמְחָה
בִּמְעוֹנוֹ ׳ וְשֶׁאָכַלְנוּ מִשֶּׁלּוֹ :

the others respond :—

בָּרוּךְ אֱלֹהֵינוּ שֶׁהַשִּׂמְחָה בִּמְעוֹנוֹ וְשֶׁאָכַלְנוּ מִשֶּׁלּוֹ וּבְטוּבוֹ
חָיִינוּ :

*He who says Grace repeats the last sentence, and continues the Form
of Service, pp. 966–978. At the conclusion of the Grace the
Seven Benedictions, p. 1012, are said.*

Blessing is over the wine; and the second and third Benediction are in
adoration of the Creator of Nature and of man. The fourth, praises
God for the God-likeness of man and for human love. The fifth, prays
that the joy of bridegroom and bride may soon be shared by Zion
Restored; and the sixth, that the happiness of the bridegroom and
bride be comparable to that of the first human pair in Eden. The
seventh Benediction combines the Divine ordering of the joys of
husband and wife with the memory of Zion, in rapturous praise of Him
Who is the creator of joy and gladness, mirth and exultation, love and
brotherhood, and the rejoicing of bridegroom over bride.

glass. Is broken by the bridegroom as a reminder of the Destruction
of Jerusalem (זכר לחורבן). Another symbolization of the rite may be
mentioned : even as one step shatters the glass, so will one act of un-
faithfulness for ever destroy the holiness and happiness of the home.

benediction. In English communities, the ceremony closes with
the Priestly Blessing.

Choral weddings conclude with the singing of Psalm cl. p. 97.

GRACE AFTER THE WEDDING FEAST.

He who says Grace commences thus :—

Banish, O Lord, both grief and wrath, and then the dumb shall exult in song. Guide us in the paths of righteousness. Regard the benediction of grace by the children of Jeshurun.

With the sanction of those present we will bless our God, in whose abode is joy, and of whose bounty we have partaken.

The others respond :—

Blessed be our God in whose abode is joy, and of whose bounty we have partaken, and through whose goodness we live.

He who says Grace repeats the last sentence, and continues the Form of Service, pp. 967—979.

At the conclusion of the Grace the Seven Benedictions, p. 1013, are said.

GRACE AFTER THE WEDDING FEAST.

There are special formulations of the Responses introductory to the Grace, just as there are at the Grace in a House of Mourning (see p. 988) and at an Initiation into the Covenant of Abraham (p. 1031).

banish . . . both grief and wrath. From a poem by Dunash ben Labrat, a renowned grammarian in tenth-century Spain.

in whose abode is joy. A striking phrase, characteristic of Jewish thought. " In Thy presence is fulness of joy ", sings the Psalmist (16. 11).

סדר חנוכת הבית :

תהלים ל׳, *p.* 234

תהלים ט״ו

מִזְמוֹר לְדָוִד ׳ יְהֹוָה מִי־יָגוּר בְּאָהֳלֶךָ מִי־יִשְׁכֹּן בְּהַר קָדְשֶׁךָ : הוֹלֵךְ תָּמִים וּפֹעֵל צֶדֶק וְדֹבֵר אֱמֶת בִּלְבָבוֹ : לֹא־רָגַל עַל־לְשֹׁנוֹ לֹא־עָשָׂה לְרֵעֵהוּ רָעָה וְחֶרְפָּה לֹא־נָשָׂא עַל־קְרֹבוֹ : נִבְזֶה בְּעֵינָיו נִמְאָס וְאֶת־יִרְאֵי יְהֹוָה יְכַבֵּד נִשְׁבַּע לְהָרַע וְלֹא יָמִיר : כַּסְפּוֹ לֹא־נָתַן בְּנֶשֶׁךְ וְשֹׁחַד עַל־נָקִי לֹא לָקַח עֹשֵׂה־אֵלֶּה לֹא יִמּוֹט לְעוֹלָם :

CONSECRATION OF A HOUSE.

Though we have in Scripture references to the dedication of a new-built house (Deuteronomy 20. 5), and even descriptions of the dedication of the Altar and of the Temple (Numbers 8 and I Kings 8), there is no fixed Form of Service for the consecration of a House. In recent centuries, Sephardim had usages of their own for such occasions, but among Ashkenazim the Benediction at the fixing of the *Mezuzah* is often the only prayer recited. Chief Rabbi Hirschell (1762-1842) composed an Order of Service which was at one time widely used ; and Dr. Hermann Adler drew up the Form, and wrote the Prayer, which, with some modification, are reprinted in this edition.

The Consecration Service opens with the affixing of the Mezuzah, if this has not already been done, and the reciting of the Blessing (p. 992), with *shehechyonu* (on the same page).

PSALM 30. " Song at the Dedication of the House." This is obviously an appropriate psalm for a Consecration Service, as it seems to have been recited at the dedication of the Second Temple.

SERVICE AT THE CONSECRATION OF A HOUSE.

Psalm xxx, *p*. 235.

Psalm xv. ¹A Psalm of David.

Lord, who shall abide in thy tent ? Who shall dwell in thy holy mountain ? ²He that walketh blamelessly and worketh righteousness, and speaketh truth in his heart. ³He that slandereth not with his tongue, nor doeth evil to his fellow, nor bringeth reproach upon his neighbour. ⁴In whose eyes a vile person is despised ; but he honoureth them that fear the Lord. He that sweareth to his own hurt, and changeth not. ⁵He that putteth not out his money to usury, nor taketh a bribe against the innocent. He that doeth these things shall never be moved.

PSALM 15. This psalm describes the Jewish ideal of human conduct, and enumerates the qualifications of the worthy worshipper at God's Sanctuary that qualify him for communion with the all holy God. The demands are moral acts of integrity and faithfulness of heart. In Rabbinic literature, this psalm is deemed, alongside of Micah 6. 8, as an embodiment of the 613 Commandments. " It depicts the type of character which Englishmen most admire " (W. R. Inge).

1. *holy.* Unapproachable by sinners.

2. *blamelessly.* Uprightly ; he is the genuine, sincere man.

worketh righteousness. His dealings with his fellowmen are honest and straightforward.

truth in his heart. His is an inward sincerity.

3. *reproach.* Scandal. He is no tale-bearer.

4. *vile . . . despised.* He has a contempt for rogues, whatever their wealth or station ; but he honours the men of piety, learning and noble character, even if they be poor and of low estate.

changeth not. If he made an agreement, he carries it out, though it turn out to his disadvantage.

5. *usury . . . bribe.* Two of the worst lapses from honourable and just dealing ; see *Deuteronomy*, 286–289 (848).

6. *never be moved.* His place in the Divine favour is assured ; see Psalm 16. 8.

אִם־יְיָ לֹא־יִבְנֶה בַיִת שָׁוְא עָמְלוּ בוֹנָיו בּוֹ · אִם־יְיָ לֹא־יִשְׁמָר־עִיר
שָׁוְא שָׁקַד שׁוֹמֵר : אַשְׂכִּילָה בְּדֶרֶךְ תָּמִים מָתַי תָּבוֹא אֵלַי
אֶתְהַלֵּךְ בְּתָם־לְבָבִי בְּקֶרֶב בֵּיתִי : לֹא־אָשִׁית לְנֶגֶד עֵינַי
דְּבַר־בְּלִיָּעַל עֲשֹׂה־סֵטִים שָׂנֵאתִי לֹא יִדְבַּק בִּי : לֵבָב עִקֵּשׁ
יָסוּר מִמֶּנִּי רָע לֹא אֵדָע : עֵינַי בְּנֶאֶמְנֵי־אֶרֶץ לָשֶׁבֶת עִמָּדִי
הֹלֵךְ בְּדֶרֶךְ תָּמִים הוּא יְשָׁרְתֵנִי :

תהלים קי״ט (אותיות ברכה)

ב׳

בְּכָל־לִבִּי דְרַשְׁתִּיךָ אַל־תַּשְׁגֵּנִי מִמִּצְוֹתֶיךָ : בְּלִבִּי צָפַנְתִּי
אִמְרָתֶךָ לְמַעַן לֹא אֶחֱטָא־לָךְ : בְּפִקּוּדֶיךָ אָשִׂיחָה וְאַבִּיטָה
אֹרְחֹתֶיךָ : בְּחֻקֹּתֶיךָ אֶשְׁתַּעֲשָׁ״ע לֹא אֶשְׁכַּח דְּבָרֶךָ :

PSALM 127. 1. House-building and all human undertakings are in
vain, unless God is the Guide and Guardian.
waketh. Keepeth watch.
PSALM 101. 3. *not cleave unto me*. If any base dealing or practice
has seized on him unawares, he would shake it off as an abominable
thing.
set no base thing Avoid every unworthy aim or striving.
will know no evil thing. Be not intimate with, or collaborate with,
anyone for its realization.

Psalm 127. 1   Except the Lord build the house, they labour in vain that build it : except the Lord watch over the city, the watchman waketh but in vain.

Psalm 101. 2, 3, 4, 6   I will give heed unto the upright way : O when wilt thou come unto me ? I will walk within my house in the integrity of my heart. I will set no base thing before mine eyes : I hate the doing of things crooked : it shall not cleave unto me.

A perverse heart shall depart from me : I will know no evil thing. Mine eyes shall be upon the faithful of the land, that they may dwell with me : he that walketh in the way of integrity, he shall minister unto me.

BEROCHAH
VERSES
Psalm 119.
10, 11, 15, 16

BETH.

With my whole heart have I sought thee : O let me not wander from thy commandments. Thy word have I treasured up within mine heart, that I might not sin against thee. I will meditate on thy precepts, and look towards thy paths. I will delight myself in thy statutes : I will not forget thy word.

PSALM 119. Among the noblest of Jewish ideals is the Holiness of Home. To the Jew, his home has been more than " his castle " ; it has been his *sanctuary* ; and by its purity, domestic affection and sanctity, it has at all times compelled the admiration of a hostile world. Now this psalm is especially appropriate for the consecration of a Jewish home, because one of the foundations upon which the Jewish Home rests is loving obedience to the Law of God. And no portion of Scripture gives more wonderful expression to that love of the Torah, and the loyal Israelite's readiness to obey its precepts, than Psalm 119. It is the "Alphabet of Divine Love ", and subordinates the whole of life and conduct to the Will and Commandments of God. It contains 22 stanzas, one stanza for every letter of the Hebrew alphabet ; and each stanza consists of eight verses, everyone of them beginning with the same letter. This elaborate alphabetic arrangement was probably resorted to as an aid to memory. Four verses are here reprinted from those stanzas of Psalm 119 whose initials form the word ברכה, *blessing*.

wander. Through lack of knowledge.

treasured up. As a most precious possession.

delight myself. Meditation on the truths and duties taught by his Sacred Faith is a delight to the faithful Jew.

ר'

רָחוֹק מֵרְשָׁעִים יְשׁוּעָה כִּי־חֻקֶּיךָ לֹא דָרָשׁוּ : רַחֲמֶיךָ רַבִּים ׀
יְהֹוָה כְּמִשְׁפָּטֶיךָ חַיֵּנִי : רָאֵה כִּי־פִקּוּדֶיךָ אָהָבְתִּי יְהֹוָה
כְּחַסְדְּךָ חַיֵּנִי : רֹאשׁ־דְּבָרְךָ אֱמֶת וּלְעוֹלָם כָּל־מִשְׁפַּט צִדְקֶךָ :

כ'

כָּלְתָה לִתְשׁוּעָתְךָ נַפְשִׁי לִדְבָרְךָ יִחָלְתִּי : כָּלוּ עֵינַי לְאִמְרָתֶךָ
לֵאמֹר מָתַי תְּנַחֲמֵנִי : כִּמְעַט כִּלּוּנִי בָאָרֶץ וַאֲנִי לֹא־עָזַבְתִּי
פִקֻּדֶיךָ : כְּחַסְדְּךָ חַיֵּנִי וְאֶשְׁמְרָה עֵדוּת פִּיךָ :

ה'

הוֹרֵנִי יְהֹוָה דֶּרֶךְ חֻקֶּיךָ וְאֶצְּרֶנָּה עֵקֶב : הֲבִינֵנִי וְאֶצְּרָה
תוֹרָתֶךָ וְאֶשְׁמְרֶנָּה בְכָל־לֵב : הַדְרִיכֵנִי בִּנְתִיב מִצְוֹתֶיךָ כִּי־בוֹ
חָפָצְתִּי : הָקֵם לְעַבְדְּךָ אִמְרָתֶךָ אֲשֶׁר לְיִרְאָתֶךָ :

רִבּוֹן הָעוֹלָם הַשְׁקִיפָה מִמְּעוֹן קָדְשְׁךָ וְקַבֵּל בְּרַחֲמִים וּבְרָצוֹן
אֶת תְּפִלַּת בָּנֶיךָ וְתַחֲנוּנָם ׳ אֲשֶׁר הִתְאַסְּפוּ פֹּה לַחֲנֹךְ אֶת
הַבַּיִת הַזֶּה וּלְהַקְרִיב לְפָנֶיךָ אֶת תּוֹדָתָם עַל כָּל הַחֶסֶד

v. 160. *the sum of thy word.* lit. " the head ; " the beginning and
end, the totality.

RESH.

Psalm 119.
v. 155, 156,
159, 160

Salvation is far from the wicked ; for they seek not thy statutes. Great are thy tender mercies, O Lord : quicken me according to thy judgments. See how I love thy precepts : quicken me, O Lord, according to thy lovingkindness. The sum of thy word is truth : and everyone of thy righteous judgments endureth for ever.

CAPH.

v. 81, 82, 87, 88

My soul pineth for thy salvation : I hope for thy word. Mine eyes pine for thy promise, while I say, When wilt thou comfort me ? They have almost made an end of me on earth ; but I forsake not thy precepts. Quicken me according to thy lovingkindness ; so shall I observe the testimony of thy mouth.

HAI.

v. 33–35, 38

Teach me, O Lord, the way of thy statutes ; and I will keep it unto the end. Give me understanding, and I will keep thy Law ; yea, I will observe it with my whole heart. Make me to tread the path of thy commandments ; for therein do I delight. Confirm thy word unto thy servant, which leadeth unto the fear of thee.

CONSECRA-
TION
PRAYER

Sovereign of the universe ! Look down from thy holy habitation, and in mercy and favour accept the prayer and supplication of thy children, who are assembled here to consecrate this dwelling, and to offer their thanksgiving unto thee for all the lovingkindness and truth thou hast shown unto them. We beseech thee, let not thy lovingkindness depart, nor the covenant of thy peace be removed

Beth and Resh. These verses overflow with passionate love of the Divine commandments, which are hailed as the safeguard and joy of life.
Caph and Hai. The psalmist is here the spokesman of Israel, as well as of the individual worshipper in days of persecution. He longs for a deeper understanding of God's Word.

וְהָאֱמֶת אֲשֶׁר עָשִׂיתָ אִתָּם : אָנָּא חַסְדְּךָ מֵאִתָּם אַל יָמוּשׁ ·
וּבְרִית שְׁלוֹמְךָ אַל תָּמוּט : הָגֵן בְּעַד בֵּית מְגוּרָם · לֹא הְאֻנֶּה
אֵלָיו רָעָה · וְנֶגַע וָצֶעַר לֹא יִקְרַב אֵלָיו · וְלֹא יִשָּׁמַע קוֹל צְוָחָה
בְּחוֹמוֹתָיו : זַכֵּה אֶת בְּנֵי הַבַּיִת לָשֶׁבֶת בְּמִשְׁכָּנָם בְּאַחֲוָה
וְרֵעוּת · לְאַהֲבָה וּלְיִרְאָה אוֹתְךָ וּלְדָבְקָה בָּךְ · וְלַהֲגוֹת
בְּתוֹרָתְךָ וּלְקַיֵּם מִצְוֹתֶיהָ :

הָרֵק בִּרְכוֹתֶיךָ עַל בַּעַל הַבַּיִת · בָּרֵךְ יְיָ חֵילוֹ וּפוֹעַל
יָדָיו תִּרְצֶה : הַרְחִיקֵהוּ מִידֵי עֲבֵרָה וְעָוֹן · וִיהִי נוֹעַמְךָ
עָלָיו · וּמַעֲשֵׂה יָדָיו כּוֹנְנֵהוּ : יְהִי נָא חַסְדְּךָ אֶת אִשְׁתּוֹ
צוֹפִיָּה הֲלִיכוֹת בֵּיתָהּ · וְתֵדַע כִּי אִשָּׁה יִרְאַת יְיָ הִיא
תִּתְהַלָּל : *הוֹפַע עַל בְּנֵיהֶם וּבְנוֹתֵיהֶם רוּחַ חָכְמָה
וּבִינָה · הַדְרִיכֵם בִּנְתִיב מִצְוֹתֶיךָ · וְכָל רוֹאֵיהֶם יַכִּירוּם כִּי
הֵם זֶרַע בֵּרַךְ יְיָ · בְּרוּכִים בַּתּוֹרָה וּבְיִרְאָה*: שָׁמְרֵם מִכָּל
רָע · שְׁמוֹר אֶת נַפְשָׁם. וִיקַיֵּם בָּהֶם · בָּרוּךְ אַתָּה בְּבוֹאֶךָ ·
וּבָרוּךְ אַתָּה בְּצֵאתֶךָ : וְכַאֲשֶׁר זָכִינוּ לַעֲשׂוֹת חֲנֻךְ הַבַּיִת
עַתָּה   כֵּן נִזְכֶּה גַם יַחַד לִרְאוֹת חֲנֻכַּת הַבַּיִת הַגָּדוֹל וְהַקָּדוֹשׁ
בִּירוּשָׁלַיִם עִירְךָ קִרְיַת מוֹעֲדֵנוּ בִּמְהֵרָה בְיָמֵינוּ · אָמֵן ·

---

*The words between the asterisks have to be varied, or omitted, according to circumstances.

from them. Shield this their abode that no evil befall it. May sickness and sorrow not come nigh unto it, nor the voice of lamentation be heard within its walls. Grant that the members of the household may dwell together in this their habitation in brotherhood and fellowship, that they may love and fear thee, and cleave unto thee, and may meditate in thy Law, and be faithful to its precepts.

Bestow thy blessings upon the master of this house. Bless, O Lord, his substance, and accept the work of his hands. Keep him far from sin and transgressing. Let thy grace be upon him, and prosper thou his labours and undertakings. May thy lovingkindness be with her who looketh well to the ways of her household, and may she be mindful that the woman who feareth the Lord, she shall be praised.* Bestow upon their sons and daughters the spirit of wisdom and understanding. Lead them in the path of thy commandments, so that all who see them may. acknowledge that they are an offspring blessed of the Lord, blessed with a knowledge of thy Law and with the fear of thee.* Preserve them from all evil ; preserve their lives.

Deuteronomy 28. 6 May thy gracious promise be realised in them, Blessed shalt thou be when thou comest in, blessed when thou goest out. And even as we have been permitted to consecrate this house, so grant that we may together witness the dedication of thy great and holy temple in Jerusalem, the city of our solemnities, speedily in our days. Amen.

The words between the asterisks have to be varied, or omitted, according to circumstances.

סדר ברית מילה:

Upon the arrival of the Child who is to be initiated into the Covenant of Abraham, those present at the Ceremony rise and say :—

בָּרוּךְ הַבָּא:

The Father of the Child says :—

הִנְנִי מוּכָן לְקַיֵּם מִצְוַת עֲשֵׂה שֶׁצִּוָּנוּ הַבּוֹרֵא יִתְבָּרַךְ לָמוּל אֶת בְּנִי • כַּכָּתוּב בַּתּוֹרָה • וּבֶן־שְׁמוֹנַת יָמִים יִמּוֹל לָכֶם כָּל־זָכָר לְדֹרֹתֵיכֶם:

The מוֹהֵל takes the Child and, placing it upon a seat, says :—

זֶה הַכִּסֵּא שֶׁל אֵלִיָּהוּ זָכוּר לַטּוֹב: לִישׁוּעָתְךָ קִוִּיתִי יְיָ: שִׁבַּרְתִּי לִישׁוּעָתְךָ יְיָ • וּמִצְוֹתֶיךָ עָשִׂיתִי: שִׁבַּרְתִּי לִישׁוּעָתְךָ יְיָ: שָׂשׂ אָנֹכִי עַל אִמְרָתֶךָ כְּמוֹצֵא שָׁלָל רָב: שָׁלוֹם רָב לְאֹהֲבֵי תוֹרָתֶךָ וְאֵין לָמוֹ מִכְשׁוֹל: אַשְׁרֵי תִּבְחַר וּתְקָרֵב יִשְׁכֹּן חֲצֵרֶיךָ •

THE COVENANT OF ABRAHAM.

Circumcision is the abiding symbol of the consecration of the Children of Abraham to the God of Abraham. As the sacred rite of the Covenant, it is of fundamental importance for the religious existence of Israel. Unbounded has been the devotion with which it has been kept. Jewish men and women have in all ages been ready to lay down their lives in its observance. The Maccabean martyrs died for it. The officers of King Antiochus, the chronicler tells us, put to death the mothers who initiated their children into the Covenant—" and they hanged their babes about their necks " (I Maccabees 1. 61). We find the same readiness for self-immolation in its defence when the Roman Emperor Hadrian aimed, by prohibiting it, at the destruction of Judaism ; when in the dread days of the Inquisition, obedience to this command meant certain death ; yea, whenever and wherever tyrants

SERVICE AT A CIRCUMCISION.

Upon the arrival of the Child who is to be initiated into the Covenant of Abraham, those present at the ceremony rise and say :—

Blessed be he that cometh.

The Father of the Child says :—

INTRO-
DUCTION

Genesis 17.12

I am here ready to perform the affirmative precept to circumcise my son, even as the Creator, blessed be he, hath commanded us, as it is written in the Torah, And he that is eight days old shall be circumcised among you, every male throughout your generations.

The Mohel takes the Child, and, placing it upon a seat, says :—

This is the throne of Elijah :—may he be remembered for good !

Genesis 49. 18

Psalm 119. 166

Psalm 119. 162

Psalm 119. 165

Psalm 65. 5

For thy salvation I have waited, O Lord, I have hoped, O Lord, for thy salvation ; and have done thy commandments. I have hoped for thy salvation, O Lord. I rejoice at thy word, as one that findeth great spoil. Great peace have they who love thy Torah ; and there is no stumbling for them. Happy is he whom thou choosest, and causest to approach that he may dwell in thy courts.

undertook to uproot the Jewish Faith. So vitally significant has loyalty to this rite proved itself, that even an excommunicated semi-apostate like Benedict Spinoza (1632-1677) declared : " Such great importance do I attach to the sign of the Covenant, that I am persuaded it is sufficient by itself to maintain the separate existence of the nation forever."

blessed . . . cometh. Is the usual Hebrew formula of welcome. The custom is mentioned by Abudarham.

I am here ready. This introduction to the Service is a simplified version of the prefatory meditation provided by the Cabalists to the performance of this precept, as well as to that of other precepts, like Tefillin, Lulav, and Succah.

affirmative. Of the 613 commandments, 248 are affirmative (Thou shalt's) and 365 negative (Thou shalt not's).

throne of Elijah. Many and various are the legends, traditions, and folk-ways that cluster round the ceremony of Initiation. Among the most poetical is the idea that Elijah, Israel's zealous Prophet of Righteousness and Redemption, is in spirit present at every Covenant of circumcision, and is the guardian of the child that is entering the Covenant.

remembered for good. The usual phrase is, " may his memory be for a blessing ".

The occasion is one of great religious joy ; hence the nature of the Scriptural verses selected.

Those present respond :—

נִשְׂבְּעָה בְּטוּב בֵּיתֶךָ קְדוֹשׁ הֵיכָלֶךָ :

The מוֹהֵל *places the Child upon the knees of the* סַנְדְּק *, and before performing the Circumcision, says the following Blessing :—*

בָּרוּךְ אַתָּה יְיָ אֱלֹהֵינוּ מֶלֶךְ הָעוֹלָם · אֲשֶׁר קִדְּשָׁנוּ בְּמִצְוֹתָיו וְצִוָּנוּ עַל הַמִּילָה :

Immediately after the Circumcision, the Father says the following Blessing :—

בָּרוּךְ אַתָּה יְיָ אֱלֹהֵינוּ מֶלֶךְ הָעוֹלָם · אֲשֶׁר קִדְּשָׁנוּ בְּמִצְוֹתָיו וְצִוָּנוּ לְהַכְנִיסוֹ בִּבְרִיתוֹ שֶׁל אַבְרָהָם אָבִינוּ :

Those present respond :—

כְּשֵׁם שֶׁנִּכְנַס לַבְּרִית כֵּן יִכָּנֵס לַתּוֹרָה וּלְחֻפָּה וּלְמַעֲשִׂיב טוֹבִים :

The מוֹהֵל *continues :—*

בָּרוּךְ אַתָּה יְיָ אֱלֹהֵינוּ מֶלֶךְ הָעוֹלָם · בּוֹרֵא פְּרִי הַגָּפֶן :

בָּרוּךְ אַתָּה יְיָ אֱלֹהֵינוּ מֶלֶךְ הָעוֹלָם · אֲשֶׁר קִדֵּשׁ יְדִיד מִבֶּטֶן

---

godfather. Known as *sandek*—probably a Greek word meaning, " companion to the child ".

commanded us. The Benedictions, both of the mohel and of the father, as well as the Response for the welfare of the child, are of Talmudic origin. Those present express the wish that the child may enter upon his heritage of Torah, of (Chuppah) a Jewish home, and of good deeds (*i.e.* human service). It is a noteworthy wish. By entrance into the heritage of

(1) *Torah*, his will be a real, as opposed to a nominal, membersnip in the House of Israel. The sacred symbols and observances of his Faith will then dominate his earliest years ; so that the foundation of his character-training will be a firm grasp of the teachings and institutions of his Faith, and of the broad facts of Israel's story and achievement, together with acquaintance with the Sacred Language and the ideals of

Those present respond :—

Psalm 65. 5
O let us be satisfied with the goodness of thy house, thy holy temple.

The Mohel places the Child upon the knees of the Godfather, and before performing the Circumcision says the following Blessing :—

BENEDIC-TION BY MOHEL
Blessed art thou, O Lord our God, King of the universe, who hast hallowed us by thy commandments, and hast given us command concerning the Circumcision.

Immediately after the Circumcision, the Father says the following Blessing :—

BENEDIC-TION BY FATHER
Blessed art thou, O Lord our God, King of the universe, who hast hallowed us by thy commandments, and hast commanded us to make our sons enter into the covenant of Abraham our father.

Those present respond :—

Even as this child has entered into the covenant, so may he enter into the Torah, the nuptial canopy, and into good deeds.

The Mohel continues :—

See p. 809
Blessed art thou, O Lord our God, King of the universe, who createst the fruit of the vine.

Blessed art thou, O Lord our God, King of the universe, who didst sanctify Isaac the well-beloved from birth setting thy statute

Jewish worship. In that way alone will he be endowed with the Jewish outlook and the Jewish consciousness ; see p. 120.

(2) *nuptial canopy.* It should be made the aim of every Jewish child to remain part of Israel, to continue the work of Israel, and build a home *in* Israel. Judaism expects that its sons and daughters should feel themselves bound, even though the duty might involve the sacrifice of precious affections, to refrain from courses of conduct—such as marrying out of the Faith—that undermine the stability of Israel. " It is true that occasional unions between Jew and Gentile do no appreciable harm to the Jewish cause, however much mischief they may lay up, in the shape of jealousy and dissension, for those who contract them, and of religious confusion for the children. But a general practice begins as a rule by being occasional. Every Jew who contemplates marriage outside the pale must regard himself as paving the way to a disruption which would be the final, as it would be the culminating, disaster in the history of his People " (M. Joseph).

(3) *good deeds.* Education is not a process that shall train the child more adroitly to snatch at place or power in a world where men

וְחוֹק בִּשְׁאֵרוֹ שָׂם וְצֶאֱצָאָיו חָתַם בְּאוֹת בְּרִית קֹדֶשׁ · עַל
כֵּן בִּשְׂכַר זֹאת · אֵל חַי חֶלְקֵנוּ צוּרֵנוּ · צַוֵּה לְהַצִּיל יְדִידוּת
שְׁאֵרֵנוּ מִשַּׁחַת · לְמַעַן בְּרִיתוֹ אֲשֶׁר שָׂם בִּבְשָׂרֵנוּ · בָּרוּךְ
אַתָּה יְיָ · כּוֹרֵת הַבְּרִית :

אֱלֹהֵינוּ וֵאלֹהֵי אֲבוֹתֵינוּ · קַיֵּם אֶת-הַיֶּלֶד הַזֶּה לְאָבִיו וּלְאִמּוֹ ·
וְיִקָּרֵא שְׁמוֹ בְּיִשְׂרָאֵל (פְּלוֹנִי בֶּן פְּלוֹנִי)· יִשְׂמַח הָאָב בְּיוֹצֵא
חֲלָצָיו · וְתָגֵל אִמּוֹ בִּפְרִי בִטְנָהּ · כַּכָּתוּב · יִשְׂמַח אָבִיךָ וְאִמֶּךָ
וְתָגֵל יוֹלַדְתֶּךָ · וְנֶאֱמַר · וָאֶעֱבֹר עָלַיִךְ וָאֶרְאֵךְ מִתְבּוֹסֶסֶת
בְּדָמָיִךְ וָאֹמַר לָךְ בְּדָמַיִךְ חֲיִי · וָאֹמַר לָךְ בְּדָמַיִךְ חֲיִי :
וְנֶאֱמַר · זָכַר לְעוֹלָם בְּרִיתוֹ · דָּבָר צִוָּה לְאֶלֶף דּוֹר : אֲשֶׁר
כָּרַת אֶת-אַבְרָהָם וּשְׁבוּעָתוֹ לְיִצְחָק : וַיַּעֲמִידֶהָ לְיַעֲקֹב לְחֹק
לְיִשְׂרָאֵל בְּרִית עוֹלָם · וְנֶאֱמַר · וַיָּמָל אַבְרָהָם אֶת-יִצְחָק בְּנוֹ
בֶּן-שְׁמוֹנַת יָמִים כַּאֲשֶׁר צִוָּה אֹתוֹ אֱלֹהִים : הוֹדוּ לַיְיָ כִּי-
טוֹב כִּי לְעוֹלָם חַסְדּוֹ : זֶה הַקָּטוֹן (פְּלוֹנִי) גָּדוֹל יִהְיֶה · כְּשֵׁם
שֶׁנִּכְנַס לַבְּרִית כֵּן יִכָּנֵס לַתּוֹרָה וּלְחֻפָּה וּלְמַעֲשִׂים טוֹבִים :

The סַנְדָּק *drinks of the Wine ; a few drops are given to the Infant,
and the Cup of Blessing being sent to the Mother, she also
partakes thereof.*

in his flesh, and sealing his offspring with the sign of the holy covenant. On this account, O living God, our Portion and our Rock, give command to deliver from destruction thy dearly beloved People, for the sake of the covenant thou hast set in our bodies. Blessed art thou, O Lord, who dost establish thy covenant.

PRAYER FOR THE CHILD

Our God and God of our fathers, preserve this child to his father and to his mother, and let his name be called in Israel —— the son of ——. Let the father rejoice in his offspring, and the mother be glad with the fruit of her body ; as it is written, Let thy father and thy mother rejoice, and let her that bare thee be glad : and it is said, And I passed by thee, and I saw thee weltering in thy blood, and I said unto thee, In thy blood live. Yea, I said unto thee, In thy blood live. And it is said, He hath remembered his covenant for ever, the word which he commanded to a thousand generations ; (the covenant) which he made with Abraham, and his oath unto Isaac, and established it unto Jacob for a statute to Israel for an everlasting covenant. And it is said, And Abraham circumcised his son Isaac when he was eight days old, as God had commanded him. O give thanks unto the Lord ; for he is good ; for his lovingkindness endureth for ever. This little child ——, may he become great. Even as he has entered into the covenant, so may he enter into the Torah, the nuptial canopy, and into good deeds.

Proverbs 23. 25

Ezekiel 16. 6

Psalm 105. 8–10

Genesis 21. 4

Psalm 118. 1

The Godfather drinks of the Wine ; a few drops are given to the Infant, and the Cup of Blessing being sent to the Mother, she also partakes thereof.

strive and struggle for mean prizes, where each is seeking his own profit and pleasure, and every man's hand is against his neighbour. Quite the contrary. The most sacred aim of education is to plant within the heart practical sympathy with those in suffering. A child should be trained to look for opportunities to " do a mitzvah ", *i.e.* show lovingkindness to anyone in distress, so as to make his life a blessing to his fellow men.

rejoice . . . . be glad. In case one of the parents is no longer alive, the words, בגן עדן " in Paradise ", are here added.

in thy blood, live. Cf. Ezekiel 16. 6.

ברכת המזון לברית מילה :

He who says Grace begins thus :—

רַבּוֹתַי נְבָרֵךְ :

The others respond :—

יְהִי שֵׁם יְיָ מְבוֹרָךְ מֵעַתָּה וְעַד עוֹלָם :

He who says Grace repeats the last sentence, and continues :—

נוֹדֶה לְשִׁמְךָ בְּתוֹךְ אֱמוּנַי ׳ בְּרוּכִים אַתֶּם לַיְיָ :

*The last sentence is repeated by the company present, who also make
the same response after each of the following stanzas :—*

בִּרְשׁוּת אֵל אָיוֹם וְנוֹרָא ׳ מִשְׂגָּב לְעִתּוֹת בַּצָּרָה ׳ אֵל נֶאְזָר
בִּגְבוּרָה ׳ אַדִּיר בַּמָּרוֹם יְיָ :

בִּרְשׁוּת הַתּוֹרָה הַקְּדוֹשָׁה ׳ טְהוֹרָה הִיא וְגַם פְּרוּשָׁה ׳ צִוָּה
לָנוּ מוֹרָשָׁה ׳ מֹשֶׁה עֶבֶד יְיָ :

בִּרְשׁוּת הַכֹּהֲנִים הַלְוִיִּם ׳ אֶקְרָא לֵאלֹהֵי הָעִבְרִיִּים ׳ אֲהוֹדֶפּוּ
בְּכָל אִיִּים ׳ אֲבָרְכָה אֶת־יְיָ :

בִּרְשׁוּת מָרָנָן וְרַבָּנָן וְרַבּוֹתַי ׳ אֶפְתַּח בְּשִׁיר פִּי וּשְׂפָתַי ׳
וְתֹאמַרְנָה עַצְמוֹתַי ׳ בָּרוּךְ הַבָּא בְּשֵׁם יְיָ :

Then proceed נְבָרֵךְ, *p.* 966.

GRACE AFTER THE MEAL FOLLOWING
A CIRCUMCISION

He who says Grace begins thus :—
Let us say grace.

The others respond :—
Blessed be the Name of the Lord from this time forth and
for ever.

He who says Grace repeats the last sentence, and continues :—
We will give thanks unto thy Name in the midst of the
faithful : blessed are ye of the Lord.

The last sentence is repeated by the company present :—
With the sanction of the awful and revered God, who is a refuge
in times of trouble, the God girt with strength, the Lord mighty
on high, we will give thanks unto thy Name in the midst of the
faithful : blessed are ye of the Lord.

With the sanction of the holy Torah, pure and clear, which
Moses the servant of the Lord commanded us to be an heritage, we
will give thanks unto thy Name in the midst of the faithful : blessed
are ye of the Lord.

With the sanction of the priests and Levites I will call upon
the God of the Hebrews, I will declare his glory in every region,
I will bless the Lord. We will give thanks unto thy Name in the
midst of the faithful : blessed are ye of the Lord.

With the sanction of those present I will open my lips with song,
yea, my whole body shall declare, Blessed is he that cometh in the
Name of the Lord. We will give thanks unto thy Name in the
midst of the faithful : blessed are ye of the Lord.

Then proceed as on p. 967, "We will bless," etc.

GRACE AFTER THE MEAL. FOLLOWING.

As at a Wedding, and in the House of a Mourner, both the introductory and the supplementary portions of the Grace are enlarged and
adapted to the celebration. The poetical introduction is by a French
author of the early 13th century ; and the six additional passages
towards the end, come from the days of the First Crusade.

After בְּעֵינֵי אֱלֹהִים וְאָדָם, p 976, *the following is introduced :—*

הָרַחֲמָן הוּא יְבָרֵךְ אֲבִי הַיֶּלֶד וְאִמּוֹ · וְיִזְכּוּ לְגַדְּלוֹ וּלְחַנְּכוֹ
וּלְחַכְּמוֹ · מִיּוֹם הַשְּׁמִינִי וָהָלְאָה יֵרָצֶה דָמוֹ · וִיהִי יְיָ אֱלֹהָיו
עִמּוֹ :

הָרַחֲמָן הוּא יְבָרֵךְ בַּעַל בְּרִית הַמִּילָה · אֲשֶׁר שָׂשׂ לַעֲשׂוֹת
צֶדֶק בְּגִילָה · וִישַׁלֵּם פָּעֳלוֹ וּמַשְׂכֻּרְתּוֹ כְּפוּלָה · וְיִתְּנֵהוּ לְמַעְלָה
לְמָעְלָה :

הָרַחֲמָן הוּא יְבָרֵךְ רַךְ הַנִּמּוֹל לִשְׁמוֹנָה · וְיִהְיוּ יָדָיו וְלִבּוֹ
לָאֵל אֱמוּנָה · וְיִזְכֶּה לִרְאוֹת פְּנֵי הַשְּׁכִינָה · שָׁלֹשׁ פְּעָמִים
בַּשָּׁנָה :

If the מוֹהֵל *says Grace, one of the Company present says the following
paragraph :—*

הָרַחֲמָן הוּא יְבָרֵךְ הַמָּל בְּשַׂר הָעָרְלָה · וּפָרַע וּמָצַץ דְּמֵי
הַמִּילָה · אִישׁ הַיָּרֵא וְרַךְ הַלֵּבָב עֲבוֹדָתוֹ פְּסוּלָה · אִם־שְׁלָשׁ־
אֵלֶּה לֹא יַעֲשֶׂה לָהּ :

הָרַחֲמָן הוּא יִשְׁלַח לָנוּ מְשִׁיחוֹ הוֹלֵךְ תָּמִים · בִּזְכוּת חַתְנֵי
מוּלוֹת דָּמִים · לְבַשֵּׂר בְּשׂוֹרוֹת טוֹבוֹת וְנִחוּמִים · לְעַם אֶחָד
מְפֻזָּר וּמְפוֹרָד בֵּין הָעַמִּים :

הָרַחֲמָן הוּא יִשְׁלַח לָנוּ כֹּהֵן צֶדֶק אֲשֶׁר לֻקַּח לְעֵלוֹם · עַד
הוּכַן כִּסְאוֹ כַּשֶּׁמֶשׁ וְיַהֲלוֹם · וַיָּלֶט פָּנָיו בְּאַדַּרְתּוֹ וַיִּגְלוֹם ·
בְּרִיתִי הָיְתָה אִתּוֹ הַחַיִּים וְהַשָּׁלוֹם :

Continue הָרַחֲמָן הוּא יְזַכֵּנוּ, *etc., p.* 978.

After " in the sight of God and man," p. 977, the following is introduced :—

May the All-merciful bless the father and mother of the child ; may they live to rear him, to initiate him in the precepts of the Torah, and to train him in wisdom : from this eighth day and henceforth his entrance into the covenant finds acceptance, and may the Lord his God be with him.

May the All-merciful bless the master of this festivity who has observed the covenant of Circumcision, and rejoiced exceedingly to perform this deed of piety ; may God reward and advance him for his act with a full recompense.

May the All-merciful bless the tender infant that has been circumcised on his eighth day ; may his hands and heart be firm with God, and may he live to appear before the Divine Presence three times in the year.

If the Mohel says Grace, another of those present says the next paragraph :—

May the All-merciful bless him who has performed the circumcision, duly fulfilling each part of the precept.—The service would be invalid of one who is timid and faint-hearted, or who failed to carry out the three essentials of the ceremony.

May the All-merciful, regardful of the merit of them that are akin by the blood of the circumcision, send us the righteous anointed one to bring good tidings and consolation to the people that is scattered and dispersed among the nations.

May the All-merciful send us the righteous priest, who remains withdrawn in heaven until a throne, bright as the sun and radiant as the diamond, shall be prepared for him, the Prophet who covered his face with his mantle and wrapped himself therein, with whom is God's covenant of life and of peace.

Continue, "May the All-merciful make us worthy," etc., p. 979.

---

master of this festivity. Hebrew, *baal beriss ha-milah.* This term is used, so as to include the godfather, if the father is not alive.

righteous anointed one. Elijah, identified in Rabbinic legend with Phineas, the zealous priest.

heaven. The Heb. word is irregular, occurring only in II Chronicles 88. 7. Some translate it, " concealment ".

Prophet. Elijah, conceived as the herald of the Messiah.

covered his face. I Kings 19. 13.

covenant of life. Numbers 25. 12 ; Malachi 2. 5.

סדר פדיון הבן:

The first-born Child, if a male, must be redeemed on the thirty-first day of his birth. If, however, the Father be a Cohen or a Levite, or the Mother the daughter of a Cohen or a Levite, they are exempt from the duty of Redemption. Should the thirty-first day fall on a Sabbath or Holyday, the ceremony is postponed until the day following.

The Father, presenting his Child to the Cohen, makes the following declaration :—

זֶה בְּנִי בְכוֹרִי הוּא פֶּטֶר רֶחֶם לְאִמּוֹ ∙ וְהַקָּדוֹשׁ בָּרוּךְ הוּא צִוָּה לִפְדּוֹתוֹ ∙ שֶׁנֶּאֱמַר וּפְדוּיָו מִבֶּן חֹדֶשׁ תִּפְדֶּה בְּעֶרְכְּךָ כֶּסֶף חֲמֵשֶׁת שְׁקָלִים בְּשֶׁקֶל הַקֹּדֶשׁ עֶשְׂרִים גֵּרָה הוּא ∙ וְנֶאֱמַר קַדֶּשׁ־לִי כָל־בְּכוֹר פֶּטֶר כָּל־רֶחֶם בִּבְנֵי יִשְׂרָאֵל בָּאָדָם וּבַבְּהֵמָה לִי הוּא :

The Father then places before the Cohen silver to the amount of five selaim or shekels (fifteen shillings), and the Cohen asks :—

מַאי בָּעִית טְפֵי לִתֵּן לִי בִּנְךָ בְכוֹרְךָ שֶׁהוּא פֶּטֶר רֶחֶם לְאִמּוֹ ∙ אוֹ בָּעִית לִפְדּוֹתוֹ בְּעַד חָמֵשׁ סְלָעִים כִּדְמְחַיַּבְתְּ מִדְּאוֹרַיְתָא :

The Father replies :—

חָפֵץ אֲנִי לִפְדּוֹת אֶת־בְּנִי ∙ וְהֵילָךְ דְּמֵי פִדְיוֹנוֹ כִּדְמְחַיַּבְתִּי מִדְּאוֹרַיְתָא :

REDEMPTION OF FIRST-BORN

It was the usage in ancient Israel that the first-born son in each household was devoted to the service of God. Rabbinic tradition teaches that, till the completion of the Sanctuary, the duties of

1035

SERVICE FOR THE REDEMPTION OF THE FIRST-BORN (PIDYON HA-BEN)

The first-born Child, if a male, must be redeemed on the thirty-first day of his birth. If, however, the Father be a Cohen or a Levite, or the Mother the daughter of a Cohen or a Levite, they are exempt from the duty of Redemption. Should the thirty-first day fall on a Sabbath or Holyday, the ceremony is postponed until the day following.

The Father, presenting his Child to the Cohen, makes the following declaration :—

This my first-born son is the first-born of his mother, and the Holy One, blessed be he, hath given command to redeem him, as *Numbers* 18. 16 it is said, And those that are to be redeemed of them from a month old shalt thou redeem, according to thine estimation, for the money of five shekels, after the shekel of the sanctuary, the shekel being *Exodus* 13. 2 twenty gerahs ; and it is said, Sanctify unto me all the first-born, whatsoever openeth the womb among the children of Israel, both of man and of beast : it is mine.

The Father then places before the Cohen silver to the amount of five selaim or shekels (fifteen shillings), and the Cohen asks :—

Which wouldst thou rather, give me thy first-born son, the first-born of his mother, or redeem him for five selaim, which thou art bound to give according to the Torah ?

The Father replies :—

I desire rather to redeem my son, and here thou hast the value of his redemption, which I am bound to give according to the Torah.

priesthood were confined to them ; and the descendants of Aaron who thereafter performed all priestly functions, were acting merely in place of the first-born. In order both morally and legally to set each first-born male child free from this service, it was to be redeemed, and the redemption-money paid over to a Cohen. The Benedictions are of Talmudic origin.

wouldst thou rather have. The question is not entirely in Hebrew, and may be said in any language.

34

The Cohen receives the redemption money, and returns the Child to his Father, whereupon the latter says the following Blessing :—

בָּרוּךְ אַתָּה יְיָ אֱלֹהֵינוּ מֶלֶךְ הָעוֹלָם · אֲשֶׁר קִדְּשָׁנוּ בְּמִצְוֹתָיו
וְצִוָּנוּ עַל פִּדְיוֹן הַבֵּן :

בָּרוּךְ אַתָּה יְיָ אֱלֹהֵינוּ מֶלֶךְ הָעוֹלָם · שֶׁהֶחֱיָנוּ וְקִיְּמָנוּ
וְהִגִּיעָנוּ לַזְּמַן הַזֶּה :

The Cohen then takes the redemption money, and, holding it over the head of the Child, says :—

זֶה תַּחַת זֶה · זֶה חִלּוּף זֶה · זֶה מָחוּל עַל זֶה · וְיִכָּנֵס
זֶה הַבֵּן לַחַיִּים לַתּוֹרָה וּלְיִרְאַת שָׁמַיִם : יְהִי רָצוֹן שֶׁכְּשֵׁם
שֶׁנִּכְנַס לַפִּדְיוֹן כֵּן יִכָּנֵס לַתּוֹרָה וּלְחֻפָּה וּלְמַעֲשִׂים טוֹבִים ·
אָמֵן :

The Cohen places his hand upon the head of the Child, and pronounces the following Benediction :—

יְשִׂמְךָ אֱלֹהִים כְּאֶפְרַיִם וְכִמְנַשֶּׁה : יְבָרֶכְךָ יְיָ וְיִשְׁמְרֶךָ :
יָאֵר יְיָ פָּנָיו אֵלֶיךָ וִיחֻנֶּךָּ : יִשָּׂא יְיָ פָּנָיו אֵלֶיךָ וְיָשֵׂם לְךָ
שָׁלוֹם :

יְיָ שׁוֹמְרֶךָ יְיָ צִלְּךָ עַל־יַד יְמִינֶךָ : כִּי אֹרֶךְ יָמִים וּשְׁנוֹת
חַיִּים וְשָׁלוֹם יוֹסִיפוּ לָךְ : יְיָ יִשְׁמָרְךָ מִכָּל־רָע יִשְׁמֹר אֶת־
נַפְשֶׁךָ · אָמֵן :

Torah, nuptial canopy, good deeds. See p. 1026.
As Ephraim and Manasseh. See p. 402.
thy shade. Thy protection.
thy soul. Thy life.

*The Cohen receives the redemption money, and returns the Child to his
Father, whereupon the latter says the following Blessing :—*

**FATHER'S
BENEDIC-
TION**
Blessed art thou, O Lord our God, King of the universe, who
hast hallowed us by thy commandments, and given us command
concerning the redemption of the first-born son.

Blessed art thou, O Lord our God, King of the universe, who
hast kept us in life, and hast preserved us, and enabled us to reach
this season.

*The Cohen then takes the redemption money, and, holding it over the
head of the Child, says :—*

This is instead of that, this in commutation for that, this in
remission of that. May this child enter into life, into the Torah
and the fear of Heaven. May it be God's will that even as he has
been admitted to redemption, so may he enter into the Torah, the
nuptial canopy, and into good deeds. Amen.

*The Cohen places his hand upon the head of the Child, and pronounces
the following Benediction :—*

Genesis **48**. 20
Numbers **6**. 24
God make thee as Ephraim and Manasseh. The Lord bless thee,
and keep thee : the Lord make his face to shine upon thee, and be
gracious unto thee : the Lord turn his face unto thee, and give thee
peace.

Psalm **121**. 5
Proverbs **3**. 2
Psalm **121**. 6
The Lord is thy guardian : the Lord is thy shade upon thy right
hand. For length of days, and years of life and peace shall they
add to thee. The Lord shall guard thee from all evil ; he shall
guard thy soul. Amen.

תְּפִלָּה לְיוֹלֶדֶת :

On entering the Synagogue say :—

וַאֲנִי בְּרֹב חַסְדְּךָ אָבוֹא בֵיתֶךָ אֶשְׁתַּחֲוֶה אֶל־הֵיכַל
קָדְשְׁךָ בְּיִרְאָתֶךָ :

אָהַבְתִּי כִּי־יִשְׁמַע | יְיָ אֶת־קוֹלִי תַּחֲנוּנָי : כִּי־הִטָּה
אָזְנוֹ לִי וּבְיָמַי אֶקְרָא : אֲפָפוּנִי חֶבְלֵי־מָוֶת וּמְצָרֵי
שְׁאוֹל מְצָאוּנִי צָרָה וְיָגוֹן אֶמְצָא : וּבְשֵׁם־יְיָ אֶקְרָא אָנָּה
יְיָ מַלְּטָה נַפְשִׁי : חַנּוּן יְיָ וְצַדִּיק וֵאלֹהֵינוּ מְרַחֵם :
שֹׁמֵר פְּתָאיִם יְיָ דַּלּוֹתִי וְלִי יְהוֹשִׁיעַ : שׁוּבִי נַפְשִׁי
לִמְנוּחָיְכִי כִּי יְיָ גָּמַל עָלָיְכִי : כִּי חִלַּצְתָּ נַפְשִׁי מִמָּוֶת
אֶת־עֵינִי מִן־דִּמְעָה אֶת־רַגְלִי מִדֶּחִי : אֶתְהַלֵּךְ לִפְנֵי יְיָ
בְּאַרְצוֹת הַחַיִּים :

מָה־אָשִׁיב לַיְיָ כָּל־תַּגְמוּלוֹהִי עָלָי : לְךָ־אֶזְבַּח זֶבַח
תּוֹדָה וּבְשֵׁם יְיָ אֶקְרָא : נְדָרַי לַיְיָ אֲשַׁלֵּם נֶגְדָה־נָּא
לְכָל עַמּוֹ : בְּחַצְרוֹת בֵּית יְיָ בְּתוֹכֵכִי יְרוּשָׁלָ͏ִם הַלְלוּיָהּ :

The following Blessing is then said :—

בָּרוּךְ אַתָּה יְיָ אֱלֹהֵינוּ מֶלֶךְ הָעוֹלָם • הַגּוֹמֵל
לְחַיָּבִים טוֹבוֹת • שֶׁגְּמָלַנִי כָּל־טוֹב :

The Minister responds :—

מִי שֶׁגְּמָלֵךְ כָּל טוֹב הוּא יִגְמָלֵךְ כָּל טוֹב סֶלָה :

PRAYER OF THANKSGIVING FOR WOMEN AFTER RECOVERY FROM CHILDBIRTH

On entering the Synagogue say :—

Psalm 5. 8　As for me, in the abundance of thy lovingkindness will I come into thy house : I will worship toward thy holy temple in the fear of thee.

Psalm 116.1–9　I love the Lord, because he heareth my voice and my supplications. Because he hath inclined his ear unto me, therefore will I call upon him as long as I live. The snares of death had surrounded me, and the anguish of the grave had come upon me : distress and sorrow were mine. Then I called upon the Name of the Lord : O Lord, I beseech thee, deliver my soul. Gracious is the Lord and righteous :

See p. 762　yea, our God is merciful. The Lord guardeth the simple : I was brought low, and he saved me. Return unto thy rest, O my soul ; for the Lord hath dealt bountifully with thee. For thou hast delivered my soul from death, mine eyes from tears, my feet from falling. I shall walk before the Lord in the land of the living.

Psalm 116. 12, 17–19　What can I render unto the Lord for all his benefits towards me ? I will offer to thee the sacrifice of thanksgiving, and will call upon the Name of the Lord. I will pay my vows unto the Lord, yea, in the presence of all his people ; in the courts of the Lord's house, in the midst of thee, O Jerusalem. Praise ye the Lord.

THANKSGIVING AFTER CHILDBIRTH.

Prayers of thanksgiving must have accompanied the sacrifice offered by the mother after the birth of the child (Leviticus 12. 6–8). The later custom of the mother visiting the synagogue, seems to have arisen in medieval Germany. Girl infants are sometimes named during such visit ; but usually this is done on the Sabbath after the birth, when the father is " called up " to the Torah ; see p. 490.

The Service was arranged by Dr. Nathan M. Adler in 1880, and is here reprinted with slight changes.

אָנָּא הָאֵל הַגָּדוֹל הַגִּבּוֹר וְהַנּוֹרָא · בְּרוֹב חַסְדְּךָ
אָבוֹא בֵיתֶךָ לִזְבּוֹחַ לְךָ זֶבַח תּוֹדָה עַל כָּל הַטּוֹבוֹת
אֲשֶׁר גְּמַלְתָּ עָלָי : אֲפָפוּנִי חֲבָלִים וְצִירִים אֲחָזוּנִי ·
בַּצַּר לִי קָרָאתִי אֵלֶיךָ וַתִּשְׁמַע מֵהֵיכָלֶךָ קוֹלִי וְהָיִיתָ
בְּעֶזְרִי · רָפֵאתָ לְכָל תַּחֲלוּאַי עֲטַרְתַּנִי חֶסֶד וְרַחֲמִים :
עַד הֵנָּה עֲזָרוּנִי רַחֲמֶיךָ · אָנָּא אַל תִּטְּשֵׁנִי לָנֶצַח ·
הוֹאֵל אֱלוֹהַּ וּבָרֵךְ אֶת אֲמָתֶךָ · חַזְּקֵנִי וְאַמְּצֵנִי אוֹתִי
וְאֶת בַּעֲלִי וּנְגַדֵּל אֶת הַיֶּלֶד אֲשֶׁר יָלַד לָנוּ לְיִרְאָתֶךָ
וּלְעָבְדְּךָ בֶּאֱמֶת וְלָלֶכֶת אֹרַח מֵישָׁרִים : שְׁמוֹר אֶת
הַיֶּלֶד הָרַךְ בְּכָל דְּרָכָיו · חָנֵּנוּ דֵעָה בִּינָה וְהַשְׂכֵּל ·
וְתֵן חֶלְקוֹ בְּתוֹרָתֶךָ וִיקַדֵּשׁ אֶת שִׁמְךָ הַגָּדוֹל · וְהָיָה
לְמֵשִׁיב נֶפֶשׁ לָנוּ בִּימֵי שִׂיבָתֵנוּ :
וַאֲנִי תְפִלָּתִי לְךָ יְיָ עֵת רָצוֹן אֱלֹהִים בְּרָב חַסְדֶּךָ
עֲנֵנִי בֶּאֱמֶת יִשְׁעֶךָ · אָמֵן :

*If the Infant is brought into the Synagogue, the Minister is to
pronounce the Benediction over it :—*

יְבָרֶכְךָ יְיָ וְיִשְׁמְרֶךָ : יָאֵר יְיָ פָּנָיו אֵלֶיךָ וִיחֻנֶּךָּ :
יִשָּׂא יְיָ פָּנָיו אֵלֶיךָ וְיָשֵׂם לְךָ שָׁלוֹם :

The following Blessing is then said :—

MOTHER'S
BENEDIC-
TION Blessed art thou, O Lord our God, King of the universe, who doest good unto the undeserving, and who hast dealt kindly with me.

The Minister responds :—

See p. 487 He who hath shown thee kindness, may he deal kindly with thee for ever.

AND
PRAYER O God, great, mighty and revered, in the abundance of thy lovingkindness I enter thy house to offer unto thee the sacrifice of thanksgiving for all the benefits thou hast bestowed upon me. Travail beset me ; pains seized upon me ; but in my distress I cried unto thee, and from thine habitation thou didst hear my voice, and didst help me. Thou didst heal all my sickness, and crown me with loving-kindness and tender mercy.

Hitherto thy mercy hath helped me. I beseech thee, O God, forsake me not ever. Bestow thy blessing upon thy handmaid ; strengthen and uphold me together with my husband, that we may rear the child that has been born unto us to fear thee and to serve thee in truth, and to walk in the path of righteousness. Keep the tender babe in all his (her) ways. Favour him (her) with knowledge, understanding and discernment, and let his (her) portion be in thy Torah, so that he (she) may sanctify thy great Name, and become a comfort to us in our old age.

Psalm 69. 14 May my prayer unto thee, O Lord, be in an acceptable time ; O God, in the abundance of thy lovingkindness, answer me with thy sure salvation. Amen.

If the Infant is brought into the Synagogue, the Minister is to pronounce the Benediction over it :—

Numbers 6. 24 The Lord bless thee, and keep thee : the Lord make his face to shine upon thee, and be gracious unto thee : the Lord turn his face unto thee, and give thee peace.

תפלה ליום בר מצוה :

Prayer recited by the בַּר מִצְוָה, *when called to the Torah, before the Blessing ; or after his being addressed by the Minister.*

אֱלֹהַי וֵאלֹהֵי אֲבוֹתַי · בֶּאֱמֶת וּבְתָמִים אֶשָּׂא אֵלֶיךָ
אֶת עֵינַי בַּיּוֹם הַגָּדוֹל וְהַקָּדוֹשׁ הַזֶּה לֵאמֹר · הִנֵּה
יַלְדוּתִי חָלְפָה הָלְכָה לָּהּ וְאָנֹכִי הָיִיתִי לְאִישׁ · עָלַי
לִשְׁמוֹר אֶת חֻקֵּי רְצוֹנֶךָ · וְעָלַי לַעֲנוֹת בְּיוֹם פְּקוּדָתִי
כַּאֲשֶׁר תִּגְמוֹל לִי כִפְרִי מַעֲלָלַי : מִיּוֹם הִוָּלְדִי בֶּן
יִשְׂרָאֵל אָנִי · אָמְנָם בַּיּוֹם הַזֶּה בָּאתִי שֵׁנִית בַּקָּהָל
לָךְ · וְלִפְנֵי כָל־הָעַמִּים אֶתְפָּאֵר עַל שִׁמְךָ אֲשֶׁר נִקְרָא
עָלֵינוּ :

וְעַתָּה אָבִי שֶׁבַּשָּׁמַיִם · שְׁמַע אֶל הַתְּפִלָּה וְאֶל
הַתְּחִנָּה הַזֹּאת · שְׁלַח עָלַי שִׁפְעַת בִּרְכוֹתֶיךָ · גֶּשֶׁם
נְדָבוֹת וּבִרְכוֹת הָנֵף עָלָי · לְמַעַן יָמַי יִשְׂבְּעוּן וְיִרְוְיוּן
מִדֶּשֶׁן עֲדָנֶיךָ : הוֹרֵנִי נָא דֶרֶךְ חֻקֶּיךָ · הַדְרִיכֵנִי
בִנְתִיב מִצְוֹתֶיךָ : תֵּן בְּלִבִּי לְאַהֲבָה וּלְיִרְאָה אֶת
שְׁמֶךָ · הַחֲזֵק בְּיָדִי וְאַל תַּרְפֵּנִי · וְלֹא אֶכָּשֵׁל עַל
דַּרְכִּי אֲשֶׁר אָנֹכִי הוֹלֵךְ עָלֶיהָ הַיּוֹם בָּרִאשׁוֹנָה :
הַצִּילֵנִי מִיֵּצֶר הָרָע · וְתֶן בִּי כֹחַ לִשְׁמוֹר אֶת תּוֹרָתְךָ
הַקְּדוֹשָׁה וְאֶת פִּקּוּדֶיךָ אֲשֶׁר יַעֲשֶׂה אוֹתָם הָאָדָם וָחַי
בָּהֶם : וּבְכָל־יָמַי אֶקְרָא בְּקוֹל גָּדוֹל וְלֹא אֵבוֹשׁ ·
שְׁמַע יִשְׂרָאֵל יְיָ אֱלֹהֵינוּ יְיָ אֶחָד :

BAR MITZVAH PRAYER

Prayer recited by the Bar Mitzvah, when called to the Torah, before the Blessing, or after his being addressed by the Minister.

My God, God of my fathers! On this solemn and sacred day, which marks my passage from boyhood to manhood, I humbly raise my voice unto thee in fervent prayer that I ever walk the way of the upright before thee.

In my earliest infancy I was brought within thy sacred covenant with Israel ; and to-day I again enter thine elect congregation as an active member, bearing the full responsibility for all my doings, and under the sacred obligation to sanctify thy holy Name before all the world. Do thou, O heavenly Father, hearken unto my prayer, and bestow upon me thy gracious blessings, so that my earthly life may be sustained and made happy by thine ineffable mercies. O bend my will to thine, that I may obey thy statutes and faithfully carry out thine ordinances. Dispose my heart to love and fear thy holy Name, and grant me thy support and the strength necessary to avoid the worldly dangers which beset the path lying before me. Save me from temptation, so that I may observe thy holy Torah, and those precepts on which human happiness and eternal life depend. Thus I will throughout the days of my *Deuteronomy* pilgrimage on earth trustfully and gladly proclaim : *6 4* " HEAR, O ISRAEL : THE LORD IS OUR GOD, THE LORD IS ONE ! "

BAR MITZVAH.

On the words spoken by the father of the lad, when the latter concludes the Blessing at the Reading of the Torah, see p. 491.

The term *bar mitzvah* is now colloquially restricted to the lad entering upon his religious majority on his thirteenth birthday. Adequate preparation of the lad in Jewish and religious knowledge has always been deemed an essential prerequisite of the celebration. The Bar-mitzvah is usually the *maftir* on the Sabbath when he is called to the Torah. The above Prayer by Chacham Artom is in use in Sephardi synagogues; and was, with some modifications, included in the Authorised Prayer Book in 1923.

תְּפִלַת הַדֶּרֶךְ :

יְהִי רָצוֹן מִלְּפָנֶיךָ יְיָ אֱלֹהֵינוּ וֵאלֹהֵי אֲבוֹתֵינוּ שֶׁתּוֹלִיכֵנוּ
לְשָׁלוֹם וְתַצְעִידֵנוּ לְשָׁלוֹם וְתִסְמְכֵנוּ לְשָׁלוֹם וְתַנְחֵנוּ אֶל־מְחוֹז
חֶפְצֵנוּ לְחַיִּים וּלְשִׂמְחָה וּלְשָׁלוֹם · וְתַצִּילֵנוּ מִכַּף כָּל־אוֹיֵב
וְאוֹרֵב וְאָסוֹן בַּדֶּרֶךְ וּמִכָּל־מִינֵי פֻּרְעָנִיּוֹת הַמִּתְרַגְּשׁוֹת לָבוֹא
לָעוֹלָם · וְתִשְׁלַח בְּרָכָה בְּמַעֲשֵׂה יָדֵינוּ · וְתִתְּנֵנוּ לְחֵן וּלְחֶסֶד
וּלְרַחֲמִים בְּעֵינֶיךָ וּבְעֵינֵי כָל־רוֹאֵינוּ · וְתִשְׁמַע קוֹל תַּחֲנוּנֵינוּ ·
כִּי אֵל שׁוֹמֵעַ תְּפִלָּה וְתַחֲנוּן אָתָּה · בָּרוּךְ אַתָּה יְיָ · שׁוֹמֵעַ
תְּפִלָּה :

וְיַעֲקֹב הָלַךְ לְדַרְכּוֹ וַיִּפְגְּעוּ־בוֹ מַלְאֲכֵי אֱלֹהִים : וַיֹּאמֶר יַעֲקֹב
כַּאֲשֶׁר רָאָם מַחֲנֵה אֱלֹהִים זֶה וַיִּקְרָא שֵׁם־הַמָּקוֹם הַהוּא
מַחֲנָיִם : הִנֵּה אָנֹכִי שֹׁלֵחַ מַלְאָךְ לְפָנֶיךָ לִשְׁמָרְךָ בַּדָּרֶךְ
וְלַהֲבִיאֲךָ אֶל־הַמָּקוֹם אֲשֶׁר הֲכִנֹתִי : יְבָרֶכְךָ יְיָ וְיִשְׁמְרֶךָ : יָאֵר
יְיָ פָּנָיו אֵלֶיךָ וִיחֻנֶּךָּ : יִשָּׂא יְיָ פָּנָיו אֵלֶיךָ וְיָשֵׂם לְךָ שָׁלוֹם :

Then say תהלים צ״א *and* וִיהִי נֹעַם, *p. 70.*

אַתָּה סֵתֶר לִי מִצַּר תִּצְּרֵנִי · רָנֵּי פַלֵּט תְּסוֹבְבֵנִי סֶלָה :
בִּטְחוּ בַיְיָ עֲדֵי־עַד · כִּי בְּיָהּ יְיָ צוּר עוֹלָמִים : יְיָ עֹז לְעַמּוֹ
יִתֵּן · יְיָ | יְבָרֵךְ אֶת־עַמּוֹ בַשָּׁלוֹם : יְיָ צְבָאוֹת עִמָּנוּ · מִשְׂגָּב־
לָנוּ אֱלֹהֵי יַעֲקֹב סֶלָה : יְיָ צְבָאוֹת אַשְׁרֵי אָדָם בֹּטֵחַ בָּךְ :
יְיָ הוֹשִׁיעָה · הַמֶּלֶךְ יַעֲנֵנוּ בְיוֹם קָרְאֵנוּ :

Then say תהלים קכ״א, *p. 590.*

PRAYER TO BE SAID WHEN GOING ON A JOURNEY OR VOYAGE

May it be thy will, O Lord my God and God of my fathers, to conduct me in peace, to direct my steps in peace, to uphold me in peace, and to lead me in life, joy and peace unto the haven of my desire. O deliver me from every enemy, ambush and hurt by the way, and from all afflictions that visit and trouble the world. Send a blessing upon the work of my hands. Let me obtain grace, lovingkindness and mercy in thine eyes and in the eyes of all who behold me. Hearken to the voice of my supplications; for thou art a God who hearkenest unto prayer and supplication. Blessed art thou, O Lord, who hearkenest unto prayer.

Genesis 32. 2 And Jacob went on his way, and the angels of God met him. And when Jacob saw them, he said, This is the camp of God : and he called the name of that place Mahanaim (a double camp).

Exodus 23. 20 Behold, I send an angel before thee, to keep thee by the way, and *Numbers 6. 24* to bring thee into the place which I have prepared. The Lord bless thee, and keep thee : the Lord make his face to shine upon thee, and be gracious unto thee : the Lord turn his face unto thee, and give thee peace.

Then say, "And let the pleasantness," etc., and Psalm xci, p. 71.

Psalm 32. 7 Thou art my shelter ; thou wilt preserve me from trouble ; thou wilt compass me about with songs of deliverance. (Selah.)

Isaiah 26. 4 Trust ye in the Lord for ever ; for the Lord is God, an everlasting *Psalm 29. 10* Rock. The Lord will give strength to his people, the Lord will *Psalm 46. 8* bless his people with peace. The Lord of hosts is with us : the God *Psalm 84. 13* of Jacob is our stronghold. (Selah.) O Lord of hosts, happy is the *Psalm 20. 10* man that trusteth in thee. Save, Lord : may the King answer us on the day when we call.

Then say Psalm cxxi, p. 591.

PRAYER FOR TRAVELLERS.

The Prayer is ancient. The Scriptural verse and additional selections are very much later, and vary in different Rites. Psalm 91 is the Psalm of Divine guardianship (p. 71) ; and 121, the Psalm of God's Providential care (p. 591 .

סדר ליום אשר בו יתנדבו
לבתי חולים :

אַשְׁרֵי מַשְׂכִּיל אֶל־דָּל בְּיוֹם רָעָה יְמַלְּטֵהוּ יְיָ :
יְיָ יִשְׁמְרֵהוּ וִיחַיֵּהוּ וְאֻשַּׁר בָּאָרֶץ :
הִגִּיד לְךָ אָדָם מַה־טּוֹב וּמָה יְיָ דּוֹרֵשׁ מִמְּךָ כִּי
אִם־עֲשׂוֹת מִשְׁפָּט וְאַהֲבַת חֶסֶד וְהַצְנֵעַ לֶכֶת עִם־אֱלֹהֶיךָ :

COLLECTION FOR HOSPITALS.

At one time all hospitals in England were dependent on the voluntary support of the public, and they are still very largely so dependent. This fact necessitated regular appeals to the public. These appeals began to be made in many Anglo-Jewish congregations three generations ago at an annual Synagogue Service. For use at these special occasions, Dr. N. M. Adler composed a Form of Service which is here republished, with changes in the selection of Scriptural verses. To the Prayer for those who help maintain the hospitals, there is now added a Prayer for those who *receive* healing within them.

The religious significance of such Hospital support cannot be overstated. The pillars of Religion are three : the Torah—God's word to man ; worship—man's response to God ; and charity—man's love of fellow-man. And Judaism not only preached this fundamental duty of man's humanity to man, but translated it into permanent institutions. It has been claimed that the first hospitals in the world were erected in Jerusalem (" houses of separation " for lepers, II Kings 15. 5), and that the Hospital is a Jewish contribution to human civilization. Thus, the Church Father Jerome praises the lady who opened the first hospital in Rome, " because she transplanted the terebinth of Abraham to Ausonian shores "—*terebinth of Abraham*, being the Jewish term for a hostel and hospital. It is also significant that the medieval Hebrew term for hospital, *hekdesh*, is from the same root as, and almost identical in meaning with, the Hebrew word for " sanctuary," *mikdash*. As if to say : even as the Sanctuary causes heavenly influences to descend upon the worshipper, and is the door to

SERVICE ON THE OCCASION OF MAKING
COLLECTIONS FOR HOSPITALS

Psalm 41. 2–3   Happy is he that wisely considereth the poor : the Lord will deliver him in the day of misfortune. The Lord will preserve him, and keep him alive, and he shall be made happy in the land.

Micah 6. 8   He hath shewed thee, O man, what is good, and what doth the Lord require of thee, but to do justly, and to love mercy and to walk humbly with thy God ?

holy living, so wherever human suffering is alleviated, *we stand on holy ground* and are face to face with a sanctifying Source, blessing those who give and those who receive.

The Rabbis made the alleviation of suffering an obligation incumbent upon all men, and to be observed towards all men *because of their humanity*. These Jewish Teachers lived in the days of the later Roman Empire, when human beings were " butchered to make a Roman holiday " ; yet they declared it a primary duty of the Israelite to visit and help the sick of his heathen neighbours, and bury their friendless dead, just as much as it was his duty to help the Jewish sick, or bury the friendless dead of his own People.

The first modern hospitals for Jewish sick were erected by the Sephardim of France, somewhat earlier than the opening of the London Beth Holim in 1747. Most Anglo-Jewish communities have made the necessary arrangements for the supply of Kosher food to Jewish patients in the General hospitals, though a few specifically Jewish hospitals also exist. These are open to Jew and non-Jew alike.

who wisely considereth. Treatment of the poor requires wisdom. Helping others—Philanthropy—is seen to be a study ! Helping the poor calls for knowledge of the material conditions of the case to be helped, and for understanding of the moral issues involved, as well as delicacy of feeling, if our help is to uplift and not degrade.

MICAH 6. 8. *hath shewed thee.* This sublime utterance of the Prophet is rightly held by many to be the noblest summary of Religion.

to do justly. For the basic importance of justice, see p. 850.

to love mercy. The true Jew has a passion for pity, he *loves* mercy. The Rabbis denied that anyone who was devoid of *rachmonus* could be a descendant of Abraham. " He who makes the sorrowful rejoice will partake of life everlasting " (Talmud).

to walk humbly with thy God. In fellowship and communion with our Heavenly Father; not ostentatiously, but with inward devotion and noiseless acts of love.

הֲלוֹא פָרֹס לָרָעֵב לַחְמֶךָ וַעֲנִיִּים מְרוּדִים תָּבִיא בָיִת
כִּי־תִרְאֶה עָרֹם וְכִסִּיתוֹ וּמִבְּשָׂרְךָ לֹא תִתְעַלָּם:
כִּי אַעֲלֶה אֲרֻכָה לָךְ וּמִמַּכּוֹתַיִךְ אֶרְפָּאֵךְ נְאֻם יְיָ:
יִשְׁלַח דְּבָרוֹ וְיִרְפָּאֵם וִימַלֵּט מִשְּׁחִיתוֹתָם: יוֹדוּ
לַיְיָ חַסְדּוֹ וְנִפְלְאוֹתָיו לִבְנֵי אָדָם:

ד ר ש ה:

מִי שֶׁבֵּרַךְ אֲבוֹתֵינוּ אַבְרָהָם יִצְחָק וְיַעֲקֹב הוּא יְבָרֵךְ
אֶת־כָּל־אֲשֶׁר נְשָׂאָם לִבָּם לְהָבִיא נְדָבוֹת לְבָתֵּי
חוֹלִים בָּעִיר הַזֹּאת · הַקָּדוֹשׁ בָּרוּךְ הוּא יְשַׁלֵּם שְׂכָרָם
וְיַצִּילֵם מִכָּל צָרָה וְצוּקָה וְיָסִיר מֵהֶם כָּל מַחֲלָה
וְיִשְׁלַח בְּרָכָה וְהַצְלָחָה בְּכָל מַעֲשֵׂה יְדֵיהֶם:
אָנָּא הָרוֹפֵא לְכָל בָּשָׂר וּמְחַבֵּשׁ לְעַצְּבוֹת בְּנֵי אָדָם ·
שְׁלַח רְפוּאָה שְׁלֵמָה מִן הַשָּׁמַיִם · רְפוּאַת הַנֶּפֶשׁ
וּרְפוּאַת הַגּוּף · לְכָל הַשּׁוֹכְבִים עַל עֶרֶשׂ דְּוָי בְּעִירֵנוּ:

Isaiah 58. 7   Is it not to break thy bread to the hungry, and that thou bring the wandering poor into thy house? When thou seest the naked, that thou cover him, and that thou hide not thyself from thine own flesh?

Jeremiah 30. 17   I will restore health unto thee, and I will heal thee

Psalm 107. 20   of thy wounds, saith the Lord. He sendeth his word, and healeth them, and delivereth them from their destructions.

Psalm 107. 21   Oh that men would praise the Lord for his goodness, and for his wonderful works to the children of men!

SERMON.

INVOCA-TION FOR THOSE HELPING HOSPITALS   May he who blessed our fathers, Abraham, Isaac, and Jacob, bless all those whose heart stirreth them up to bring free-will offerings for the support of the hospitals of this city. May the Holy One, blessed be he, give them their recompense, deliver them from all trouble and distress, remove from them all sickness, and send blessing and prosperity upon all the work of their hands.

FOR THOSE WHO RECEIVE HEALING IN HOSPITALS   O thou who art the Healer of all flesh and bindest up their wounds, send a perfect healing from heaven, a healing of soul and body, unto all who lie on a bed of pain in our

---

to break thy bread. These two verses are from the Haftorah on the Day of Atonement, on the acts of lovingkindness and pity that must accompany true devotion.

חַזְּקֵם וְאַמְּצֵם וּבְחַלּוּיֵן עֲצָמוֹת תְּבָרְכֵם · וְהַאֲרֵךְ יְמֵיהֶם

וּשְׁנוֹתֵיהֶם בְּטוֹב וּבַנְּעִימִים · וְנֹאמַר אָמֵן :

תהלים קי'ב

הַלְלוּיָה · אַשְׁרֵי־אִישׁ יָרֵא אֶת־יְיָ בְּמִצְוֹתָיו חָפֵץ

מְאֹד : גִּבּוֹר בָּאָרֶץ יִהְיֶה זַרְעוֹ דּוֹר יְשָׁרִים יְבֹרָךְ :

הוֹן־וָעֹשֶׁר בְּבֵיתוֹ וְצִדְקָתוֹ עֹמֶדֶת לָעַד : זָרַח בַּחֹשֶׁךְ

אוֹר לַיְשָׁרִים חַנּוּן וְרַחוּם וְצַדִּיק : טוֹב־אִישׁ חוֹנֵן

וּמַלְוֶה יְכַלְכֵּל דְּבָרָיו בְּמִשְׁפָּט : כִּי־לְעוֹלָם לֹא־יִמּוֹט

לְזֵכֶר עוֹלָם יִהְיֶה צַדִּיק : מִשְּׁמוּעָה רָעָה לֹא יִירָא

נָכוֹן לִבּוֹ בָּטֻחַ בַּיְיָ : סָמוּךְ לִבּוֹ לֹא יִירָא עַד אֲשֶׁר־

יִרְאֶה בְצָרָיו : פִּזַּר נָתַן לָאֶבְיוֹנִים צִדְקָתוֹ עֹמֶדֶת לָעַד

קַרְנוֹ תָּרוּם בְּכָבוֹד : רָשָׁע יִרְאֶה וְכָעַס שִׁנָּיו יַחֲרֹק

וְנָמָס תַּאֲוַת רְשָׁעִים תֹּאבֵד : הַלְלוּיָה :

PSALM 112.

THE SOURCE OF ALL HAPPINESS.

1. *delighteth greatly in his commandments.* "And not in the *reward* which their observance brings," add the Rabbis. He is not like a servant who serves his master for a wage: he is filled with the love of right for its own sake. "He who desires to serve God from Love

city. Turn their weakness into strength, and bless them with bodily vigour; restore them to perfect health, and prolong their days in happiness and well-being; and let us say, Amen.

Psalm cxii.

THE
SOURCE
OF ALL
HAPPINESS

[1]Praise ye the Lord. Happy is the man that feareth the Lord, that delighteth greatly in his commandments. [2]His seed shall be mighty upon earth; the generation of the upright shall be blessed. [3]Wealth and riches are in his house: and his righteousness endureth for ever. [4]Unto the upright there dawneth light in the darkness, unto him that is gracious and full of compassion and righteous. [5]It is well with the man who dealeth graciously and lendeth; he shall maintain his cause in judgment. [6]For he shall never be moved: the righteous shall be had in everlasting remembrance. [7]He shall not be afraid of evil tidings: his heart is steadfast, trusting in the Lord. [8]His heart is established, he shall not be afraid, until he see the defeat of his enemies. [9]He hath dispersed, he hath given to the needy; his righteousness endureth for ever; his might shall be exalted in glory. [10]The wicked shall see it, and be grieved, he shall gnash with his teeth, and melt away: the desire of the wicked shall perish. Praise ye the Lord.

must not serve Him because of the reward in the World to come. But he does right and eschews wrong because he is a man, and owes it to his manhood to strive towards perfection " (Maimonides).

4. *in the darkness.* Even in direst misfortune, his faith remains unshaken.

תפלה לחולה:

תהלים כ'ג

מִזְמוֹר לְדָוִד · יְהוָֹה רֹעִי לֹא אֶחְסָר : בִּנְאוֹת דֶּשֶׁא
יַרְבִּיצֵנִי עַל־מֵי מְנוּחֹת יְנַהֲלֵנִי : נַפְשִׁי יְשׁוֹבֵב יַנְחֵנִי
בְמַעְגְּלֵי־צֶדֶק לְמַעַן שְׁמוֹ : גַּם כִּי־אֵלֵךְ בְּגֵיא צַלְמָוֶת
לֹא־אִירָא רָע כִּי־אַתָּה עִמָּדִי שִׁבְטְךָ וּמִשְׁעַנְתֶּךָ הֵמָּה

PRAYERS IN SICKNESS.

The duty of visiting and helping the sick extends, as we have seen, to Jew and non-Jew alike. Such visiting is deemed a great *mitzvah*. " He who visits the sick may be the cause of his recovery ; and he who does not visit the sick may be the cause of his death " (Talmud). This is especially true of the sick of the poor and friendless. Among the tokens of lovingkindness to be shown, is prayer for the recovery of the patient. The prayer in our Siddur is *by*, and not *for*, the sufferer. ' A short supplication *for* an ill person found its way in medieval times into the daily Amidah (p. 141), and there are invocations (*mi-sheberachs*) on behalf of the sick after the Reading of the Torah on Sabbath, p. 493. In the Sephardi Rite, the following is a part of the set prayer offered for one who is seriously ill :

" God, the Divine Ruler enthroned in mercy, who created His world with His attribute of mercy, His are lovingkindness and mercy. He is nigh to them who call upon Him ; in times of distress He answers their cry. May His tender mercy overflow towards all pious communities in trouble and distress. Among them may He remember in pity and tenderness, and give compassionate deliverance, saving healing and relief to . . . who lies afflicted on a bed of sickness, entreating the Lord his God to grant him grace, tender compassion, and perfect healing.

PRAYER IN SICKNESS

Psalm xxiii. [1]A Psalm of David.

GOD THE
SHEPHERD

The Lord is my shepherd; I shall not want. [2]He maketh me to lie down in green pastures : he leadeth me beside the still waters. [3]He restoreth my soul : he guideth me in the paths of righteousness for his Name's sake. [4]Yea, though I walk through the valley of the shadow of death. I will fear no evil ; for thou art with me : thy rod

" May the supreme King of kings have pity on him, pardon all his sins and transgressions, assuage his pain, remove all disease from him, and lengthen the years of his life.
" May the supreme King of kings in His mercy grant him complete restoration to health, even as it is written, ' When he calleth upon me, I will answer him ; I will be with him in trouble : I will deliver and honour him. With length of days will I satisfy him, and will let him see my salvation ' ".

In our Form of Prayer, based on that arranged by Dr. H. Adler, the person afflicted recites Psalm 23, a portion of Psalm 139, and a personal prayer for healing, including a brief confession of sin and resolve of repentance.

PSALM 23. THE GOOD SHEPHERD. The most beloved of all psalms. It is an unrivalled expression of perfect trust in God.

2. *in green pastures.* In lands where grass is short-lived, the shepherd must find fresh meadows for his flock ; and this involves wanderings with their attendant dangers.

3. *restoreth.* Refresheth his soul with rest and food.

for his Name's sake. Because His Name is Righteous, and His nature loving and merciful.

4. *valley of the shadow of death.* The shepherd in his wanderings must take his flock past many a ravine and rugged precipice—ready hiding-places for wild beasts or lawless men.

art with me. In the darkness where unseen foes may attack him.

rod. The psalmist continues to think of God under the image of the shepherd who defends his flock with the *rod*, *i.e.* the club, against wild beasts or human enemies, and leads it with the shepherd's *staff*.

יְנַחֲמֵנִי : תַּעֲרֹךְ לְפָנַי שֻׁלְחָן נֶגֶד צֹרְרָי דִּשַּׁנְתָּ בַשֶּׁמֶן
רֹאשִׁי כּוֹסִי רְוָיָה : אַךְ טוֹב וָחֶסֶד יִרְדְּפוּנִי כָּל־יְמֵי חַיָּי
וְשַׁבְתִּי בְּבֵית יְהֹוָה לְאֹרֶךְ יָמִים :

תהלים ק״ג

לְדָוִד ׀ בָּרְכִי נַפְשִׁי אֶת־יְהֹוָה וְכָל־קְרָבַי אֶת־שֵׁם
קָדְשׁוֹ : בָּרְכִי נַפְשִׁי אֶת־יְהֹוָה וְאַל־תִּשְׁכְּחִי כָּל־גְּמוּלָיו :
הַסֹּלֵחַ לְכָל־עֲוֺנֵכִי הָרֹפֵא לְכָל־תַּחֲלוּאָיְכִי : הַגּוֹאֵל
מִשַּׁחַת חַיָּיְכִי הַמְעַטְּרֵכִי חֶסֶד וְרַחֲמִים : הַמַּשְׂבִּיעַ בַּטּוֹב
עֶדְיֵךְ תִּתְחַדֵּשׁ כַּנֶּשֶׁר נְעוּרָיְכִי : עֹשֵׂה צְדָקוֹת יְהֹוָה
וּמִשְׁפָּטִים לְכָל־עֲשׁוּקִים : יוֹדִיעַ דְּרָכָיו לְמֹשֶׁה לִבְנֵי
יִשְׂרָאֵל עֲלִילוֹתָיו : רַחוּם וְחַנּוּן יְהֹוָה אֶרֶךְ אַפַּיִם וְרַב־
חָסֶד : לֹא לָנֶצַח יָרִיב וְלֹא לְעוֹלָם יִטּוֹר : לֹא כַחֲטָאֵינוּ
עָשָׂה לָנוּ וְלֹא כַעֲוֺנֹתֵינוּ גָּמַל עָלֵינוּ : כִּי כִגְבֹהַּ שָׁמַיִם
עַל־הָאָרֶץ גָּבַר חַסְדּוֹ עַל־יְרֵאָיו : כִּרְחֹק מִזְרָח מִמַּעֲרָב
הִרְחִיק מִמֶּנּוּ אֶת־פְּשָׁעֵינוּ : כְּרַחֵם אָב עַל־בָּנִים רִחַם
יְהֹוָה עַל־יְרֵאָיו : כִּי הוּא יָדַע יִצְרֵנוּ זָכוּר כִּי־עָפָר

---

5. *a table.* Instead of Shepherd, God is now pictured as Host Who
protects the wayfarer, against the fierce rays of the sun, and gives him,
famishing with thirst, life-refreshing water to drink.

6. *dwell . . . forever.* A glimpse of immortal life.

and thy staff, they comfort me. ⁵Thou preparest a table before me in the presence of mine enemies : thou hast anointed my head with oil ; my cup runneth over. ⁶Surely happiness and lovingkindness will follow me all the days of my life ; and I shall dwell in the house of the Lord for evermore.

Psalm ciii. ¹A Psalm of David.

THE
FATHERLY
LOVE OF
GOD
Bless the Lord, O my soul ; and all that is within me, bless his holy Name. ²Bless the Lord, O my soul, and forget not all his benefits : ³who forgiveth all thine iniquity ; who healeth all thy diseases : ⁴who redeemeth thy life from the pit ; who crowneth thee with lovingkindness and tender mercies : ⁵who satisfieth thy years with good things ; so that thy youth is renewed like the eagle's. ⁶The Lord executeth righteous acts, and judgments for all that are oppressed. ⁷He made known his ways unto Moses, his doings unto the children of Israel. ⁸The Lord is merciful and gracious, slow to anger, and abounding in lovingkindness. ⁹He will not always contend ; neither will he keep his anger for ever. ¹⁰He hath not dealt with us after our sins, nor requited us after our iniquities. ¹¹For as the heaven is high above the earth, so ·mighty is his lovingkindness over them that fear him. ¹²As far as the east is from the west, so far hath he removed our transgressions from us. ¹³Like as a father hath mercy upon his children, so the Lord hath mercy upon them that fear him. ¹⁴For he knoweth our frame ; he remembereth that we are dust.

PSALM 103. The Fatherly Love of GOD.
    5. *like the eagle's.* The strength and longevity of the eagle gave rise to the popular belief in its power periodically to renew its youth.
    10. *not . . . after our sins.* He punished less than our iniquities deserved.
    14. *our frame.* Our formation ; Gen. 2. 7.

אֱנוֹשׁ כֶּחָצִיר יָמָיו כְּצִיץ הַשָּׂדֶה כֵּן יָצִיץ : כִּי אֲנַחְנוּ :
רוּחַ עָבְרָה־בּוֹ וְאֵינֶנּוּ וְלֹא־יַכִּירֶנּוּ עוֹד מְקוֹמוֹ : וְחֶסֶד
יְהֹוָה מֵעוֹלָם וְעַד־עוֹלָם עַל־יְרֵאָיו וְצִדְקָתוֹ לִבְנֵי בָנִים :
לְשֹׁמְרֵי בְרִיתוֹ וּלְזֹכְרֵי פִקֻּדָיו לַעֲשׂוֹתָם : יְהֹוָה בַּשָּׁמַיִם
הֵכִין כִּסְאוֹ וּמַלְכוּתוֹ בַּכֹּל מָשָׁלָה : בָּרְכוּ יְהֹוָה מַלְאָכָיו
גִּבֹּרֵי כֹחַ עֹשֵׂי דְבָרוֹ לִשְׁמֹעַ בְּקוֹל דְּבָרוֹ : בָּרְכוּ יְהֹוָה
כָל־צְבָאָיו מְשָׁרְתָיו עֹשֵׂי רְצוֹנוֹ : בָּרְכוּ יְהֹוָה כָּל־מַעֲשָׂיו
בְּכָל־מְקֹמוֹת מֶמְשַׁלְתּוֹ בָּרְכִי נַפְשִׁי אֶת־יְהֹוָה :

תהלים קל׳ט

לַמְנַצֵּחַ לְדָוִד מִזְמוֹר · יְהֹוָה חֲקַרְתַּנִי וַתֵּדָע : אַתָּה
יָדַעְתָּ שִׁבְתִּי וְקוּמִי בַּנְתָּה לְרֵעִי מֵרָחוֹק : אָרְחִי וְרִבְעִי
זֵרִיתָ וְכָל־דְּרָכַי הִסְכַּנְתָּה : כִּי אֵין מִלָּה בִּלְשׁוֹנִי הֵן
יְהֹוָה יָדַעְתָּ כֻלָּהּ : אָחוֹר וָקֶדֶם צַרְתָּנִי וַתָּשֶׁת עָלַי

15–18. Man is fleeting : God's mercy everlasting.

16. *the wind.* Reference is here to the dry *sirocco* coming from the Arabian desert and withering up all vegetation.

17. *them that fear him.* Cf. Exodus 20. 6 ; p. 243.

19–22. The supreme sovereignty of God should be acclaimed by the whole universe.

20. *angels.* lit. " messengers " ; any being or natural force—wind or lightning—that fulfils the bidding of God is a " messenger of God " ; see p. 583.

¹⁵As for man, his days are as grass ; as the flower of the field, so he flourisheth. ¹⁶For the wind passeth over it, and it is gone ; and the place thereof shall know it no more. ¹⁷But the lovingkindness of the Lord is from everlasting to everlasting upon them that fear him, and his righteousness unto children's children, ¹⁸to such as keep his covenant, and to those that remember his precepts to do them. ¹⁹The Lord hath established his throne in the heavens ; and his kingdom ruleth over all. ²⁰Bless the Lord, ye his angels : ye mighty in strength, that fulfil his word, hearkening unto the voice of his word. ²¹Bless the Lord, all ye his hosts ; ye ministers of his, that do his will. ²²Bless the Lord, all ye his works, in all places of his dominion : bless the Lord, O my soul.

GOD THE ALL-SEEING

Psalm cxxxix. ¹For the Chief Musician. A Psalm of David.

O Lord, thou hast searched me, and knowest me. ²Thou knowest my downsitting and mine uprising, thou understandest my thoughts afar off. ³Thou siftest my path and my lying down, and art familiar with all my ways. ⁴For while there is not yet a word on my tongue, lo, thou, O Lord, knowest it all. ⁵Thou hast beset me

PSALM 189. One of the most magnificent of the psalms. It is a supreme expression of the omnipresence of God, as of the intimate personal relation between man and his Maker.

1–6. God knows all man's thoughts and actions.

2. *downsitting . . . uprising.* My whole existence.

afar off. See on *v.* 4.

3. *siftest.* Subjecting my life and doings to closest examination.

4. *not yet on my tongue.* The same thought as in the lines of the English poet :

" The rose whose beauty glads thine eye to see,
Blossomed in God ere time began to be."

5. *beset.* Surrounded.

כְּפֶּכָה : פְּלִיאָה דַעַת מִמֶּנִי נִשְׂגְּבָה לֹא־אוּכַל לָהּ :
אָנָה אֵלֵךְ מֵרוּחֶךָ וְאָנָה מִפָּנֶיךָ אֶבְרָח : אִם־אֶסַּק
שָׁמַיִם שָׁם אָתָּה וְאַצִּיעָה שְּׁאוֹל הִנֶּךָ : אֶשָּׂא כַנְפֵי־
שַׁחַר אֶשְׁכְּנָה בְּאַחֲרִית יָם : גַּם־שָׁם יָדְךָ תַנְחֵנִי
וְתֹאחֲזֵנִי יְמִינֶךָ : וָאֹמַר אַךְ־חֹשֶׁךְ יְשׁוּפֵנִי וְלַיְלָה אוֹר
בַּעֲדֵנִי : גַּם־חֹשֶׁךְ לֹא־יַחְשִׁיךְ מִמֶּךָ וְלַיְלָה כַּיּוֹם יָאִיר
כַּחֲשֵׁיכָה כָּאוֹרָה : אוֹדְךָ עַל כִּי נוֹרָאוֹת נִפְלֵיתִי
נִפְלָאִים מַעֲשֶׂיךָ וְנַפְשִׁי יֹדַעַת מְאֹד : וְלִי מַה־יָּקְרוּ
רֵעֶיךָ אֵל מֶה עָצְמוּ רָאשֵׁיהֶם : אֶסְפְּרֵם מֵחוֹל
יִרְבּוּן הֱקִיצֹתִי וְעוֹדִי עִמָּךְ : חָקְרֵנִי אֵל וְדַע לְבָבִי
בְּחָנֵנִי וְדַע שַׂרְעַפָּי : וּרְאֵה אִם־דֶּרֶךְ־עֹצֶב בִּי וּנְחֵנִי
בְּדֶרֶךְ עוֹלָם :

אָנָּא יְיָ רוֹפֵא כָל בָּשָׂר · רַחֵם עָלַי וּסְעָדֵנִי בְּחַסְדֶּךָ
הַגָּדוֹל עַל עֶרֶשׂ דְּוָי : שְׁלַח לִי תְּרוּפָה וּתְעָלָה בְּתוֹךְ
שְׁאָר חוֹלֵי בָנֶיךָ : רְפָא אֶת־מַכְאֹבִי וְחַדֵּשׁ כַּנֶּשֶׁר
נְעוּרָי : חָן בִּינָה לְרוֹפֵא וְיִגְהֶה מִמֶּנִּי מְזוֹרִי · וַאֲרוּכָתִי
מְהֵרָה תִצְמָח :

7–12. God's omnipresence.

9. *take the wings of morning, i.e.* follow the first rays of dawn in the distant East.

behind and before, and laid thine hand upon me. ⁶Such knowledge is too wonderful for me : it is too high, I cannot attain unto it. ⁷Whither can I go from thy spirit? or whither can I flee from thy presence? ⁸If I ascend into heaven, thou art there ; or if I make the grave my bed, behold thou art there. ⁹If I take the wings of the morning, and dwell in the uttermost parts of the sea, ¹⁰even there shall thy hand lead me, and thy right hand shall hold me. ¹¹If I say, Let deep darkness cover me, and the light about me be night ; ¹²even the darkness darkeneth not from thee, but the night is light as the day—the darkness is as the light. ¹⁴I will give thanks unto thee, for that I am fearfully and wonderfully made : wonderful are thy works ; and that my soul knoweth right well. ¹⁷How precious unto me are thy thoughts, O God ! How great is the sum of them ! ¹⁸If I would count them, they are more in number than the sand : when I awake, I am still with thee. ²³Search me, O God, and know my heart : try me, and know my thoughts : ²⁴and see if there be any way of sorrow in me, and lead me in the way everlasting.

GOD'S OMNI- PRESENCE

SUPPLICA- TION

I beseech thee, O Lord, Healer of all flesh, have mercy on me, and support me in thy grace upon my bed of sickness. Send me, and all who are sick among thy children, relief and cure. Assuage my pain, and renew my youth as the eagle's. Bestow wisdom upon the physician

---

9. *uttermost parts of the sea.* Or, " uttermost regions of the West ".

14–24. Nor is it surprising that man cannot escape his Maker, Who with unsearchable wisdom had moulded man's frame of life.

18. *when I awake.* In the world to come (Targum).

24. *way of sorrow.* Way of error.

lead me in the way everlasting. A perfect prayer.

SUPPLICATION. *Bestow wisdom upon the physician.* It was a long time before man recognized that Providence worked through natural laws, and by means of human agencies. Even in the camp of Judaism, there were those who looked upon the art of healing as an

אֱלוֹהַּ סְלִיחוֹת חַנּוּן וְרַחוּם אֶרֶךְ אַפַּיִם וְרַב־חֶסֶד ·
מוֹדֶה אֲנִי לְפָנֶיךָ בְּלֵב נִשְׁבָּר וְנִדְכֶּה כִּי חָטָאתִי וְהָרַע
בְּעֵינֶיךָ עָשִׂיתִי : הִנֵּה נִחַמְתִּי עַל רָעָתִי · וְאָשׁוּב בִּתְשׁוּבָה
שְׁלֵמָה לְפָנֶיךָ : עָזְרֵנִי אֱלֹהֵי יִשְׁעִי · וְלֹא אָשׁוּב לְכִסְלָה
וְאֶתְהַלֵּךְ לְפָנֶיךָ בֶּאֱמֶת וּבְתָמִים : שְׁמַע תְּפִלָּתִי וְהוֹסֵף
יָמִים עַל יָמָי וַאֲכַלֶּה שְׁנוֹתַי בַּנְּעִימִים · לְמַעַן אוּכַל
לַעֲבוֹד עֲבוֹדָתֶךָ וְלִשְׁמוֹר פִּקּוּדֶיךָ בְּלֵב שָׁלֵם : אָמֵן
וְאָמֵן :

תפלה קצרה על ערש דוי

אַל־תַּסְתֵּר פָּנֶיךָ מִמֶּנִּי · בְּיוֹם צַר לִי הַטֵּה־אֵלַי אָזְנֶךָ ·
בְּיוֹם אֶקְרָא מַהֵר עֲנֵנִי : כִּי אַעֲלֶה אֲרֻכָה לָךְ ·
וּמִמַּכּוֹתַיִךְ אֶרְפָּאֵךְ נְאֻם־יְיָ :

רְפָאֵנִי יְיָ וְאֵרָפֵא · הוֹשִׁיעֵנִי וְאִוָּשֵׁעָה · כִּי תְהִלָּתִי
אָתָּה · וִיהִי רָצוֹן מִלְּפָנֶיךָ יְיָ אֱלֹהַי וֵאלֹהֵי אֲבוֹתַי שֶׁתִּשְׁלַח
לִי מְהֵרָה רְפוּאָה שְׁלֵמָה מִן הַשָּׁמַיִם · רְפוּאַת הַנֶּפֶשׁ
וּרְפוּאַת הַגּוּף · בָּרוּךְ אַתָּה   יְיָ רוֹפֵא נֶאֱמָן וְרַחֲמָן
לְכָל בָּשָׂר :

that he may cure my wound, so that my health may spring forth speedily.

CON-FESSION

O God of forgiveness, who art gracious and merciful, slow to anger and abounding in lovingkindness, I confess unto thee with a broken and contrite heart that I have sinned, and have done that which is evil in thy sight. Behold, I repent me of my evil way, and return unto thee with perfect repentance. Help me, O God of my salvation, that I may not again turn unto folly, but walk before thee in truth and uprightness. Hear my prayer, prolong my life, let me complete my years in happiness, that I may be enabled to serve thee and keep thy statutes with a perfect heart. Amen, and Amen.

A SHORT PRAYER ON A BED OF SICKNESS

Psalm 102. 3

Hide not thy face from me in the day when I am in trouble; incline thine ear unto me: in the day when I call answer me speedily.

Jeremiah 30. 17

I will restore health unto thee, and I will heal thee of thy wounds, saith the Lord.

Jeremiah 17. 14

Heal me, O Lord! and I shall be healed; save me and I shall be saved; for thou art my praise. May it be thy will, O Lord my God, and the God of my fathers, speedily to send from heaven a perfect cure, both spiritual and physical, unto my sickness. Blessed art thou, O Lord, who art the faithful and merciful Healer of all flesh. Amen.

impious interference with the plans of an all-wise Dispenser of Destinies. Indeed, so deep-rooted was religious hesitancy towards the physician, that the *permissibility* to make use of the physician had to be distinctly pointed out. Our Teachers also warned against so-called " faith " healings. אין סומכין על הנס " Miracles are not of every day occurrence," was one of their sayings. " The wise man, the God-fearing man ", they laid it down as a principle of conduct, " will not dwell in a place where there is no physician ".

תפלה לעומד מחליו

Read תהלים כ׳ג and ק׳נ, pp. 1052–6. Then continue :—

אָנָּא הָאֵל הַגָּדוֹל הַגִּבּוֹר וְהַנּוֹרָא · בְּרֹב חַסְדְּךָ אָבוֹא
לְפָנֶיךָ לְהוֹדוֹת לְךָ עַל כָּל הַטּוֹבוֹת אֲשֶׁר גָּמַלְתָּ עָלָי :
מִן הַמֵּצַר קְרָאתִיךָ וַתַּעֲנֵנִי · מֵעֶרֶשׂ דְּוַי שִׁוַּעְתִּי אֵלֶיךָ
וַתִּשְׁמַע אֶת־קוֹלִי תַחֲנוּנָי : יַסֹּר יִסַּרְתַּנִי יָהּ וְלַמָּוֶת לֹא
נְתַתָּנִי · בְּאַהֲבָתְךָ וּבְחֶמְלָתְךָ הֶעֱלִיתָ מִן שְׁאוֹל נַפְשִׁי ·
כִּי רֶגַע בְּאַפֶּךָ חַיִּים בִּרְצוֹנֶךָ בָּעֶרֶב יָלִין בֶּכִי וְלַבֹּקֶר
רִנָּה : חַי חַי הוּא יוֹדֶךָ כָּמוֹנִי הַיּוֹם · וְנַפְשִׁי אֲשֶׁר פָּדִית
תְּסַפֵּר נִפְלְאוֹתֶיךָ לִבְנֵי אָדָם · בָּרוּךְ אַתָּה רוֹפֵא נֶאֱמָן
לְכָל בָּשָׂר :

אֵל רַחוּם וְחַנּוּן הַגּוֹמֵל לְחַיָּבִים טוֹבוֹת · קָטֹנְתִּי מִכֹּל
הַחֲסָדִים אֲשֶׁר עָשִׂיתָ עִמָּדִי עַד הֵנָּה · אָנָּא טַהֵר לְבָבִי
וְזַכֵּנִי לָלֶכֶת בְּדֶרֶךְ יְשָׁרִים לְפָנֶיךָ וּמְשֹׁךְ עֶזְרְךָ
לְעָבְדֶּךָ : חַזְּקֵנִי וְאַמְּצֵנִי מֵרָפְיוֹן וּבְחִלּוּץ עֲצָמוֹת תְּבָרְכֵנִי :
הַרְחֵק מֵעָלַי כָּל צָרָה וְתוּגָה · שָׁמְרֵנִי מִכָּל רָע וּבַעֲצָתְךָ
תַנְחֵנִי · וְזָרְחָה לִי תָּמִיד שֶׁמֶשׁ צְדָקָה וּמַרְפֵּא בִּכְנָפֶיהָ ·
יִהְיוּ לְרָצוֹן אִמְרֵי פִי וְהֶגְיוֹן לִבִּי לְפָנֶיךָ יְיָ
צוּרִי וְגוֹאֲלִי · אָמֵן :

PRAYER ON RECOVERY FROM SICKNESS

Read Psalms xxiii and ciii, pp. 1053–5. *Then continue :—*

O God, great, mighty, and revered, in the abundance of thy lovingkindness I come before thee to render thanks for all the benefits thou hast bestowed upon me. In my distress I called upon thee and thou didst answer me ; from my bed of pain I cried unto thee and thou didst hear the voice of my supplication. Thou hast chastened me sore, O Lord, but thou didst not give me over unto death. In thy love and pity thou didst bring up my soul from the grave. For thy anger is but for a moment ; thy favour is for a lifetime : weeping may tarry for the night, but joy cometh in the morning. The living, the living, he shall praise thee, as I do this day, and my soul that thou didst redeem shall tell thy wonders unto the children of men. Blessed art thou, the faithful Physician unto all flesh.

O God, merciful and gracious, who dispensest kindnesses to the undeserving, I am indeed unworthy of all the mercies thou hast hitherto shewn unto me. O purify my heart that I may be fitted to walk in the way of the upright before thee ; and continue thy help unto thy servant. Restore me to perfect health, and with bodily vigour bless thou me. Remove from me all sorrow and care, preserve me from all evil, and guide me with thine own counsel ; so shall the sun of righteousness arise unto me with healing in its wings.

Psalm 19. 15 Let the words of my mouth and the meditation of my heart be acceptable before thee, O Lord, my Rock and my Redeemer. Amen.

PRAYER ON RECOVERY.

Was first produced by author of this commentary, for the Soldier's Prayer Book in 1915, and became part of the Authorised Prayer Book in 1916.

וִדּוּי שְׁכִיב מְרַע :

מוֹדֶה אֲנִי לְפָנֶיךָ יְיָ אֱלֹהַי וֵאלֹהֵי אֲבוֹתַי שֶׁרְפוּאָתִי
וּמִיתָתִי בְּיָדֶךָ : יְהִי רָצוֹן מִלְּפָנֶיךָ שֶׁתִּרְפָּאֵנִי רְפוּאָה
שְׁלֵמָה ∙ וְאִם הַמָּוֶת כָּלָה וְנֶחֱרַץ מֵעִמְּךָ אֲקַחֶנּוּ מִיָּדְךָ
בְּאַהֲבָה ∙ וּתְהִי מִיתָתִי כַּפָּרָה עַל כָּל חֲטָאִים וַעֲוֹנוֹת
וּפְשָׁעִים שֶׁחָטָאתִי וְשֶׁעָוִיתִי וְשֶׁפָּשַׁעְתִּי לְפָנֶיךָ ∙ וְתַשְׁפִּיעַ
לִי מֵרַב טוּב הַצָּפוּן לַצַּדִּיקִים ∙ וְתוֹדִיעֵנִי אֹרַח חַיִּים
שֹׂבַע שְׂמָחוֹת אֶת פָּנֶיךָ נְעִימוֹת בִּימִינְךָ נֶצַח :

אֲבִי יְתוֹמִים וְדַיַּן אַלְמָנוֹת ∙ הֲגֵן בְּעַד קְרוֹבַי הַיְקָרִים
אֲשֶׁר נַפְשִׁי קְשׁוּרָה בְנַפְשָׁם : בְּיָדְךָ אַפְקִיד רוּחִי
פָּדִיתָה אוֹתִי יְיָ אֵל אֱמֶת ∙ אָמֵן וְאָמֵן :

בִּשְׁעַת יְצִיאַת הַנְּשָׁמָה :

יְיָ מֶלֶךְ ∙ יְיָ מָלָךְ ∙ יְיָ׀ יִמְלֹךְ לְעוֹלָם וָעֶד :

(To be said three times.)

בָּרוּךְ שֵׁם כְּבוֹד מַלְכוּתוֹ לְעוֹלָם וָעֶד :

(To be said three times.)

יְיָ הוּא הָאֱלֹהִים :

(To be said seven times.)

שְׁמַע יִשְׂרָאֵל יְיָ אֱלֹהֵינוּ יְיָ אֶחָד :

CONFESSION ON A DEATH BED.

I acknowledge unto thee, O Lord my God and God of my fathers, that both my cure and my death are in thy hands. May it be thy will to send me a perfect healing. Yet if my death be fully determined by thee, I will in love accept it at thy hand. O may my death be an atonement for all the sins, iniquities and transgressions of which I have been guilty against thee. Bestow upon me the abounding happiness that is treasured up for the righteous. Make known to me the path of life : in thy presence is fulness of joy ; at thy right hand bliss for evermore.

Thou who art the father of the fatherless and judge of the widow, protect my beloved kindred with whose soul *Psalm 31. 6* my own is knit. Into thy hand I commend my spirit ; thou hast redeemed me, O Lord God of truth. Amen, and Amen !

When the end is approaching :—

THE LORD IS KING ; THE LORD WAS KING ; THE LORD SHALL BE KING FOR EVER AND EVER. (*To be said three times.*)

BLESSED BE HIS NAME, WHOSE GLORIOUS KINGDOM IS FOR EVER AND EVER. (*To be said three times.*)

THE LORD HE IS GOD. (*To be said seven times.*)

HEAR, O ISRAEL : THE LORD IS OUR GOD, THE LORD IS ONE.

CONFESSION ON A DEATH BED.

" He who confesses and forsakes his sins, will obtain mercy " (Proverbs 28. 13). Hence the solemn duty, and the atoning effect, of confession on the death-bed, if repentance had been delayed till then. The Yom Kippur Confessions, in the singular, are recited when the dying man retains consciousness and strength to do so.

No one special form of death-bed confession existed in ancient times. The above Prayer, edited by Dr. H. Adler is largely from Shulchan Aruch, and embodies the traditional phrases in use since Nachmanides (1194–1270). It is a sublime document of Religion.

PRINCIPAL LAWS OF MOURNING

The Laws of Mourning apply in the case of the death of seven relatives—father, mother, husband, wife, child, brother and sister (including half-brother or half-sister).

Immediately *before* the Funeral, there is the rite of KERIAH, the rending of the garment. This is to be performed standing. At the death of a parent, the rent is made in the clothes on the left side, opposite the˙heart. At the death of the other relatives (husband, wife, child, brother or sister), the rent is made in one outer garment only, and on the right side. The Blessing recited is ברוך דיין האמת " Blessed be the righteous Judge " (p. 994), a pious submission to the all-just will of God. *KERIAH*

In the event of the news of the death and burial of a relative, other than a parent, not reaching the Mourner until after the lapse of thirty days, there is no *Keriah*. In the case of a parent, however, *Keriah* is obligatory even if years have elapsed since the death.

Immediately after the Funeral, SHIVAH begins. The day of burial is counted as the first day of the Seven Days of Mourning; and the Shivah ends on the morning of the seventh day, one hour on that morning being deemed a full day. *SHIVAH*

The Mourners remain in their homes during the weekdays of the Shivah; and, as they enter the synagogue on Friday eve, a special Greeting is extended to them by the worshippers; see p. 358. On the weekdays, Mourners sit on low stools, and felt (or cloth, or rubber) shoes are worn by them. They abstain from following their usual avocations; and Morning and Evening Services are held in the home, with appropriate additional Psalms and Mourning Prayer (pp. 1089–1099) added to the ordinary Week-day service. A light (symbolical of the soul) is kept burning in the House of Mourning during the Shivah.

The Mourners do not take part in any festivity or amusement during thirty days (the SHELOSHIM), reckoning from the day of the Funeral; and during twelve months, in the case of a parent's death. The period of˙the SHELOSHIM ends on the morning of the thirtieth day after the Funeral. *SHELO-SHIM*

If news of the death of a relative reaches the Mourner *within* thirty days after the Funeral, Shivah is observed and the Sheloshim are reckoned from the day on which the information is received. If news of the death of even a parent arrives after the expiration of thirty days, neither the week of Shivah nor the period of Sheloshim is observed; but the Mourners should sit on the floor, or on a low stool, for one hour.

FESTIVALS AND MOURNING   As on the Sabbath, there is no Mourning on Festivals, individual sorrows being submerged in the spiritual rejoicing of the House of Israel. Therefore, if the rites prescribed for Mourners have been observed even for one hour prior to the advent of a Festival, *the period of Shivah is held to have terminated.* And as to the Sheloshim, if that be either Passover or Pentecost, fifteen days only need then be kept. In the case of Tabernacles, only eight days.

If the Shivah was *completed* prior to the commencement of these Festivals, the period of Sheloshim is considered to have ended. In the case of the New Year, if one hour's Mourning had been kept before the advent of the Festival, Shivah is at an end; and the period of Sheloshim continues only to the succeeding Day of Atonement. If the mourning commenced before Yom Kippur, that Day ends Shivah, and Tabernacles terminates the Sheloshim.

If a Funeral has taken place *during* Chol ha-moed, the Intermediate Days of Passover and Tabernacles, both the Shivah and the Sheloshim commence at its termination, the last day of the Festival, however, being counted as one of the days of Shivah and Sheloshim.

YAHRZEIT   The anniversary of a parent's death is solemnly observed. All amusements are avoided, and a Memorial (Yahrzeit) Light is kindled, and remains burning until sunset the next day. Every effort should be made to say Kaddish at the congregational services that day. Some observe the anniversary as a fast day.

In a case where three days or longer elapse between the death and the burial of a parent, the *first* Yahrzeit is on the anniversary of the day of burial; and, in all subsequent years, on the anniversary of the day of death.

תפלה קודם הלוית המת

Read either (I.) תהלים כ'ג, *p.* 1052, *and* ק'ל, *p.* 602 ; *or* (II.) *the Scriptural Selections following. Then continue with* אֱנוֹשׁ כֶּחָצִיר.

אֲדֹנָי מָעוֹן אַתָּה הָיִיתָ לָּנוּ בְּדֹר וָדֹר : בְּטֶרֶם הָרִים יֻלָּדוּ וַתְּחוֹלֵל אֶרֶץ וְתֵבֵל וּמֵעוֹלָם עַד־עוֹלָם אַתָּה אֵל : תָּשֵׁב אֱנוֹשׁ עַד־דַּכָּא וַתֹּאמֶר שׁוּבוּ בְנֵי־אָדָם : כִּי אֶלֶף שָׁנִים בְּעֵינֶיךָ כְּיוֹם אֶתְמוֹל כִּי יַעֲבֹר וְאַשְׁמוּרָה בַלָּיְלָה : יְמֵי שְׁנוֹתֵינוּ בָהֶם שִׁבְעִים שָׁנָה וְאִם בִּגְבוּרֹת שְׁמוֹנִים שָׁנָה וְרָהְבָּם עָמָל וָאָוֶן כִּי גָז חִישׁ וַנָּעֻפָה : לִמְנוֹת יָמֵינוּ כֵּן הוֹדַע וְנָבִא לְבַב חָכְמָה :

דִּרְשׁוּ יְיָ בְּהִמָּצְאוֹ קְרָאֻהוּ בִּהְיוֹתוֹ קָרוֹב : יַעֲזֹב רָשָׁע דַּרְכּוֹ וְאִישׁ אָוֶן מַחְשְׁבֹתָיו וְיָשֹׁב אֶל־יְיָ וִירַחֲמֵהוּ וְאֶל־ אֱלֹהֵינוּ כִּי־יַרְבֶּה לִסְלוֹחַ : כִּי לֹא מַחְשְׁבוֹתַי מַחְשְׁבוֹתֵיכֶם וְלֹא דַרְכֵיכֶם דְּרָכָי נְאֻם יְיָ : כִּי גָבְהוּ שָׁמַיִם מֵאָרֶץ כֵּן גָּבְהוּ דְרָכַי מִדַּרְכֵיכֶם וּמַחְשְׁבֹתַי מִמַּחְשְׁבֹתֵיכֶם :

אֱנוֹשׁ כֶּחָצִיר יָמָיו כְּצִיץ הַשָּׂדֶה כֵּן יָצִיץ : כִּי רוּחַ עָבְרָה־בּוֹ וְאֵינֶנּוּ וְלֹא־יַכִּירֶנּוּ עוֹד מְקוֹמוֹ : וְחֶסֶד יְיָ מֵעוֹלָם

HOME SERVICE PRIOR TO FUNERAL.

This special Service, drawn up by the author of this Commentary in 1919, was included in the Authorised Prayer Book in 1922.

PSALM 90. "The World's Great Funeral Psalm." Nowhere is there a nobler realization that everything human is transitory, and that God alone is everlasting.

HOME SERVICE PRIOR TO FUNERAL

Read either (I.) *Psalms xxiii, p.* 1053, *and cxxx, p.* 603 ; *or* (II.) *the Scriptural Selections following. Then continue with "As for man."*

Psalm 90. 1–4   O Lord, thou hast been a dwelling-place unto us in all generations. Before the mountains were brought forth, or ever thou gavest birth to the earth and the world, even from everlasting to *See p.* 68   everlasting thou art God. Thou turnest man back to dust, and sayest, Return, ye children of men. For a thousand years in thy sight are but as yesterday when it is past, and as a watch in the *Psalm* 90. 10, 12   night. The days of our years are threescore years and ten, or even by reason of strength fourscore years ; yet is their pride but travail and nothingness ; for it is soon gone by, and we fly away. So teach us to number our days, that we may get us a heart of wisdom.

Isaiah 55. 6–9   Seek ye the Lord while he may be found, call ye upon him while he is near ; let the wicked forsake his way, and the unrighteous man his thoughts ; and let him return unto the Lord, and he will have mercy upon him ; and to our God, for he will abundantly pardon. For my thoughts are not your thoughts, neither are your ways my ways, saith the Lord. For as the heavens are higher than the earth, so are my ways higher than your ways, and my thoughts than your thoughts.

Psalm 103. 15–17   As for man, his days are as grass ; as the flower of the field, so he flourisheth. For the wind passeth over it, and it is gone ; and

a dwelling-place unto us in all generations.
　　　　" O God, our help in ages past,
　　　　　　Our hope for years to come,
　　　　　　Our shelter from the stormy blast,
　　　　　　And our eternal home " (Watts).
　　return, ye children of men. Unto Me, the Judge of the human spirit. God, the unchanging, is the Refuge of changing and erring man.
　　so teach us. Give us that discernment which we lack.
　　Isaiah 55. 6–9. The great Call to Repentance, which forms the Prophetic Reading on every Fast-day.
　　when he is near. In hours of grief and sorrow, the human heart often feels itself nearer to God than in days of heedless prosperity.
　　let the wicked forsake. Such forsaking is itself a seeking of God, and a finding of Him.

וְעַד־עוֹלָם עַל־יְרֵאָיו וְצִדְקָתוֹ לִבְנֵי בָנִים : בְּאֹרַח צְדָקָה חַיִּים

וְדֶרֶךְ נְתִיבָה אַל־מָוֶת : וְיָשֹׁב הֶעָפָר עַל הָאָרֶץ כְּשֶׁהָיָה

וְהָרוּחַ תָּשׁוּב אֶל הָאֱלֹהִים אֲשֶׁר נְתָנָהּ : מִי לִי בַשָּׁמַיִם

וְעִמְּךָ לֹא־חָפַצְתִּי בָאָרֶץ : כָּלָה שְׁאֵרִי וּלְבָבִי צוּר־לְבָבִי

וְחֶלְקִי אֱלֹהִים לְעוֹלָם : מַה־יָּקָר חַסְדְּךָ אֱלֹהִים וּבְנֵי אָדָם

בְּצֵל כְּנָפֶיךָ יֶחֱסָיוּן : כִּי עִמְּךָ מְקוֹר חַיִּים בְּאוֹרְךָ נִרְאֶה־אוֹר :

Read the selections FOR A MAN *or* FOR A WOMAN, *and then continue*
with אֵל מָלֵא רַחֲמִים, *on* 1072.

FOR A MAN.

מִי־יַעֲלֶה בְהַר יְיָ וּמִי־יָקוּם בִּמְקוֹם קָדְשׁוֹ : נְקִי כַפַּיִם וּבַר

לֵבָב אֲשֶׁר לֹא נָשָׂא לַשָּׁוְא נַפְשִׁי וְלֹא נִשְׁבַּע לְמִרְמָה : יִשָּׂא

בְרָכָה מֵאֵת יְיָ וּצְדָקָה מֵאֱלֹהֵי יִשְׁעוֹ :

סוֹף דָּבָר הַכֹּל נִשְׁמָע אֶת הָאֱלֹהִים יְרָא וְאֶת מִצְוֹתָיו

שְׁמוֹר כִּי זֶה כָּל הָאָדָם :

הַיּוֹם קָצֵר וְהַמְּלָאכָה מְרֻבָּה וְהַפּוֹעֲלִים עֲצֵלִים וְהַשָּׂכָר

הַרְבֵּה וּבַעַל הַבַּיִת דּוֹחֵק : לֹא עָלֶיךָ הַמְּלָאכָה לִגְמוֹר וְלֹא

אַתָּה בֶן־חוֹרִין לְהִבָּטֵל מִמֶּנָּה : נֶאֱמָן הוּא בַּעַל מְלַאכְתְּךָ

שֶׁיְּשַׁלֶּם לְךָ שְׂכַר פְּעֻלָּתֶךָ • וְדַע שֶׁמַּתַּן שְׂכָרָם שֶׁל־צַדִּיקִים

לֶעָתִיד לָבוֹא :

PROVERBS 12. *there is no death.* Companionship with the Eternal
is eternal companionship.

ECCLESIASTES 12. *returneth unto God who gave it.* This is embodied
in the Morning Prayer, p. 19. " The soul which thou gavest me is
pure ; thou didst create it, thou didst form it, thou didst breathe it
unto me. Thou preservest it within me, and thou wilt take it from
me."

PSALM 73. Wonderful is the triumphant faith, which surrenders
all to God, and the pure love which counts all in the universe as

the place thereof shall know it no more. But the lovingkindness of the Lord is from everlasting to everlasting upon them that fear

Proverbs 12. 28 him, and his righteousness unto children's children. In the way of righteousness is life ; and in the pathway thereof there is no

Ecclesiastes 12. 7 death. And the dust returneth to the earth as it was, but the spirit

Psalm 73. 25, 26 returneth unto God, who gave it. Whom have I in heaven but thee ? And there is none upon earth that I desire beside thee. My flesh and my heart faileth : but God is the strength of

Psalm 35. 9, 10 my heart and my portion for ever. How precious is thy lovingkindness, O God ! And the children of men take refuge under the shadow of thy wings. For with thee is the fountain of life : in thy light do we see light.

Read the selections FOR A MAN *or* FOR A WOMAN *and then continue, with " O Lord, who art full of compassion," on p.* 1073.

FOR A MAN.

Psalm 24. 3–5 Who may ascend the mountain of the Lord ? And who may stand in his holy place ? He that hath clean hands and a pure heart ; who hath not set his desire upon vanity, and hath not sworn deceitfully. He shall receive a blessing from the Lord, and righteousness from the God of his salvation.

Ecclesiastes 12. 13 Let us hear the conclusion of the whole matter : Fear God, and keep his commandments : for this is the whole duty of man.

Daniel 12. 3 And they that be wise shall shine as the brightness of the firmament ; and they that turn many to righteousness, as the stars for ever and ever.

See p. 643 The day is short, and the work is great, and the labourers are sluggish, and the reward is much, and the Master of the house is urgent. It is not thy duty to complete the work, but neither art thou free to desist from it. Faithful is thy Employer to pay thee the reward of thy labour ; and know that the grant of reward unto the righteous will be in the time to come.

nothing in comparison with Him. One radical Bible critic, who was rarely fair to Judaism, felt compelled to state, " We mortals are not fit to pronounce words of such wonderful sublimity "

FOR A MAN. Psalm 24. " Who will be God's welcome guest ? "

not set his desire upon vanity. Not striving after empty and frivolous things. The translation is based on this Kethiv.

righteousness. *i.e.* the reward of his righteousness.

FOR A WOMAN.

The portions in brackets to be omitted according to circumstances.

אֵשֶׁת חַיִל מִי יִמְצָא וְרָחֹק מִפְּנִינִים מִכְרָהּ : [בָּטַח בָּהּ לֵב
בַּעְלָהּ וְשָׁלָל לֹא יֶחְסָר : גְּמָלַתְהוּ טוֹב וְלֹא־רָע כֹּל יְמֵי
חַיֶּיהָ :] כַּפָּהּ פָּרְשָׂה לֶעָנִי וְיָדֶיהָ שִׁלְּחָה לָאֶבְיוֹן : עֹז וְהָדָר
לְבוּשָׁהּ וַתִּשְׂחַק לְיוֹם אַחֲרוֹן : פִּיהָ פָּתְחָה בְחָכְמָה וְתוֹרַת־
חֶסֶד עַל־לְשׁוֹנָהּ : [צוֹפִיָּה הֲלִיכוֹת בֵּיתָהּ וְלֶחֶם עַצְלוּת לֹא
תֹאכֵל : קָמוּ בָנֶיהָ וַיְאַשְּׁרוּהָ בַּעְלָהּ וַיְהַלְלָהּ : רַבּוֹת בָּנוֹת
עָשׂוּ חָיִל וְאַתְּ עָלִית עַל־כֻּלָּנָה :] תְּנוּ־לָהּ מִפְּרִי יָדֶיהָ
וִיהַלְלוּהָ בַשְּׁעָרִים מַעֲשֶׂיהָ :

יְשַׁלֵּם יְיָ פָּעֳלֵךְ וּתְהִי מַשְׂכֻּרְתֵּךְ שְׁלֵמָה מֵעִם יְיָ
אֱלֹהֵי יִשְׂרָאֵל אֲשֶׁר בָּאת לַחֲסוֹת תַּחַת כְּנָפָיו :

אֵל מָלֵא רַחֲמִים שׁוֹכֵן בַּמְּרוֹמִים· אֵלֶּה סְלִיחוֹת חַפּוּן
וְרַחוּם אֶרֶךְ אַפַּיִם וְרַב חֶסֶד · הַמְצֵא כַפָּרַת פֶּשַׁע וְהַקְרָבַת
יֶשַׁע וּמְנוּחָה נְכוֹנָה תַּחַת כַּנְפֵי הַשְּׁכִינָה בְּמַעֲלוֹת קְדוֹשִׁים
וּטְהוֹרִים כְּזֹהַר הָרָקִיעַ מַזְהִירִים · אֶת נִשְׁמַת
שֶׁהָלְכָה (שֶׁהָלְכוּ) לְעוֹלָמוֹ (לְעוֹלָמָהּ) : אָנָּא בַּעַל הָרַחֲמִים
זָכְרָה לוֹ (לָהּ) לְטוֹבָה כָּל זְכִיּוֹתָיו (זְכִיּוֹתֶיהָ) וְצִדְקוֹתָיו
(וְצִדְקוֹתֶיהָ) בְּאַרְצוֹת הַחַיִּים · וּפְתַח לוֹ (לָהּ) שַׁעֲרֵי צֶדֶק
וְאוֹרָה שַׁעֲרֵי חֶמְלָה וַחֲנִינָה · בְּסֵתֶר כְּנָפֶיךָ תַּסְתִּירֵהוּ
(תַּסְתִּירֶהָ) לְעוֹלָמִים · וּצְרוֹר בִּצְרוֹר הַחַיִּים אֶת נִשְׁמָתוֹ
(נִשְׁמָתָהּ) · יְיָ הוּא נַחֲלָתוֹ (נַחֲלָתָהּ) · וְיָנוּחַ (וְתָנוּחַ) בְּשָׁלוֹם
עַל מִשְׁכָּבוֹ (מִשְׁכָּבָהּ) וְנֹאמַר אָמֵן :

FOR A WOMAN.

The portions in brackets to be omitted according to circumstances.

Proverbs 31.
10–12   A woman of worth who can find ? For her price is far above
rubies. [The heart of her husband trusteth in her ; and he shall
have no lack of gain. She doeth him good, and not evil all the
Proverbs 31. 20 days of her life.] She stretcheth out her hand to the poor ; yea,
Proverbs 31.   she putteth forth her hands to the needy. Strength and majesty
25–29   are her clothing ; and she laugheth at the time to come. She
openeth her mouth with wisdom ; and the law of lovingkindness is
on her tongue. [She looketh well to the ways of her household, and
See p. 404   eateth not the bread of idleness. Her children rise up and call her
happy ; her husband also, and he praiseth her, saying : Many
Proverbs 31. 31 daughters have done worthily, but thou excellest them all.] Give
her of the fruit of her hands ; and let her works praise her in the
gates.
Ruth 2. 12   The Lord recompense thy works, and a full reward be given
thee of the Lord God of Israel, under whose wings thou art come
to trust.

EL MOLEY   O Lord, who art full of compassion, who dwellest on high—
RACHA-
MIM   God of forgiveness, who art merciful, slow to anger and abounding
in lovingkindness—grant pardon of transgressions, nearness of
salvation, and perfect rest beneath the shadow of thy divine presence,
in the exalted places among the holy and pure, who shine as the
brightness of the firmament, to _____ who hath gone to
his [her] eternal home. We beseech thee, O Lord of compassion,
remember unto him [her] for good all the meritorious and pious
deeds which he [she] wrought while on earth. Open unto him [her]
the gates of righteousness and light, the gates of pity and grace.
O shelter him [her] for evermore under the cover of thy wings ;
and let his [her] soul be bound up in the bond of eternal life. The
Lord is his [her] inheritance ; may he [she] rest in peace. And let
us say, Amen.

FOR A WOMAN.
10. *who can find ? i.e.* is not easily found.
11. *trust in her.* She is her husband's counsellor. She is kind to
the poor and gentle to all ; self-respecting and dignified.
EL MOLEY RACHAMIM. The usual Memorial Prayer, enlarged by
inclusion of a few phrases from the Sephardi Rite.

צדוק הדין :

The verses, אֱנוֹשׁ כֶּחָצִיר יָמָיו, *p.* 1068, *may be read prior to* הַצוּר תָּמִים.

On those days on which תַּחֲנוּן (*p.* 168) *is not said,* מִכְתָּם לְדָוִד (*p.* 1080) *is read instead of the following* :—

הַצוּר תָּמִים פָּעֳלוֹ · כִּי כָל־דְּרָכָיו מִשְׁפָּט · אֵל
אֱמוּנָה וְאֵין עָוֶל · צַדִּיק וְיָשָׁר הוּא ;

הַצוּר תָּמִים בְּכָל־פֹּעַל · מִי־יֹאמַר לוֹ מַה־תִּפְעָל ·
הַשַּׁלִּיט בְּמַטָּה וּבְמַעַל · מֵמִית וּמְחַיֶּה · מוֹרִיד שְׁאוֹל
וַיָּעַל :

הַצוּר תָּמִים בְּכָל־מַעֲשֶׂה · מִי־יֹאמַר אֵלָיו מַה־תַּעֲשֶׂה ·

THE BURIAL SERVICE.

Five fundamental teachings of the Jewish Faith are emphasized in this ancient and solemn Service.

I. The first teaching of the Burial Service is, *Resignation to the will of God.* In the very moment of the death of a loved one, when grief is most poignant, the survivors are to assert their faith in the absolute and unfathomable justice of Providence.

> " Thou Power Supreme, Whose mighty scheme
> These woes of mine fulfil.
> Here firm I rest, they must be best,
> Because they are Thy will."

And so the Burial Service is called in Hebrew *Tzidduk Ha-din,* " The justification of the Judgment ". Its basic thought is brought out in the following paraphrase :

> " Righteous art Thou, O God, and ever just,
> And none can question, none withstand Thy will ;
> And though our hearts be humbled to the dust,
> Teach us, through all, to see Thy mercy still.

> " Our life is measured out by Thee above,
> And to Thy will each human heart must bow.
> No frail remonstrance mars our perfect love,
> No man shall say to Thee, ' What doest Thou ? ' "

THE BURIAL SERVICE

The verses "As for man, p. 1069, may be read prior to "The Rock, his work."

On those days on which Tachanun (p. 169) is not said, Psalm xvi (p. 1081) is read instead of the following :—

Deuteronomy 32. 4

ADORATION OF GOD AND RESIGNATION TO HIS WILL

The Rock, his work is perfect, for all his ways are judgment : a God of faithfulness and without iniquity, just and right is he.

The Rock, perfect in every work, who can say unto him, What workest thou ? He ruleth below and above ; he ordereth death and restoreth to life : he bringeth down to the grave, and bringeth up again.

The Rock, perfect in every deed, who can say unto him, What doest thou ? O thou who speakest and doest, of thy grace deal kindly with us, and for the sake of him who was bound like a lamb, O hearken and do.

" When suffering to human fault is due,
Forgive, O Lord, and stay Thine hand, we pray :
And when it brings but trial of faith anew,
Turn Thou the night of gloom to trustful day ".
(A. A. Green).

This teaching " His will, not ours, be done " is but a restatement of the Kaddish; see pp. 269–271. Portions of the *Tzidduk Ha-din* are found in the Talmud. It was formulated in Gaonic times, with rhymed additions in later centuries.

THE ROCK. The opening verse of this Adoration is taken from the Farewell Song of Moses, and is a solemn affirmation of the ethical perfection of God in the moral government of the universe. The simile of " Rock " stresses the unchangeableness of God, as well as denoting Him as the Refuge to the children of men. The waves may beat for ages against the rock, yet it remains a place of safety in time of storm and flood.

perfect. Irreproachable.

a God of faithfulness. " Faithful to give the righteous his due reward in the life after death " (Rashi).

iniquity. Better, *injustice.* Maimonides declares the recognition of the justice of God to be one of the fundamental principles of the Jewish Faith.

הָאֹמֵר וְעֹשֶׂה · חֶסֶד חִנָּם לָנוּ תַעֲשֶׂה · וּבִזְכוּת הַנֶּעֱקָד
כְּשֶׂה · הַקְשִׁיבָה וַעֲשֵׂה :

צַדִּיק בְּכָל־דְּרָכָיו · הַצּוּר תָּמִים · אֶרֶךְ אַפַּיִם וּמָלֵא
רַחֲמִים · חֲמָל־נָא וְחוּס־נָא עַל־אָבוֹת וּבָנִים · כִּי לְךָ
אֲדֹן הַסְּלִיחוֹת וְהָרַחֲמִים :

צַדִּיק אַתָּה יְיָ לְהָמִית וּלְהַחֲיוֹת · אֲשֶׁר בְּיָדְךָ
פִּקְדוֹן כָּל־רוּחוֹת · חָלִילָה לְךָ זִכְרוֹנֵנוּ לִמְחוֹת ·
וְיִהְיוּ־נָא עֵינֶיךָ בְּרַחֲמִים עָלֵינוּ פְּקוּחוֹת · כִּי לְךָ אֲדֹן
הָרַחֲמִים וְהַסְּלִיחוֹת :

אָדָם אִם בֶּן־שָׁנָה יִהְיֶה · אוֹ אֶלֶף שָׁנִים יִחְיֶה ·
מַה־יִּתְרוֹן לוֹ · כְּלֹא־הָיָה יִהְיֶה · בָּרוּךְ דַּיַּן הָאֱמֶת
מֵמִית וּמְחַיֶּה :

בָּרוּךְ הוּא · כִּי אֱמֶת דִּינוֹ · וּמְשׁוֹטֵט הַכֹּל בְּעֵינוֹ ·
וּמְשַׁלֵּם לְאָדָם חֶשְׁבּוֹנוֹ וְדִינוֹ · וְהַכֹּל לִשְׁמוֹ הוֹדָיָה יִתֵּנוּ :

יְדַעֲנוּ יְיָ כִּי צֶדֶק מִשְׁפָּטֶיךָ · תִּצְדַּק בְּדָבְרֶךָ · וְתִזְכֶּה
בְשָׁפְטֶךָ · וְאֵין לְהַרְהֵר אַחַר מִדַּת שָׁפְטֶךָ · צַדִּיק
אַתָּה יְיָ וְיָשָׁר מִשְׁפָּטֶיךָ :

דַּיַּן אֱמֶת · שׁוֹפֵט צֶדֶק וֶאֱמֶת · בָּרוּךְ דַּיַּן הָאֱמֶת ·
שֶׁכָּל־מִשְׁפָּטָיו צֶדֶק וֶאֱמֶת :

נֶפֶשׁ כָּל־חַי בְּיָדֶךָ · צֶדֶק מָלְאָה יְמִינְךָ וְיָדֶךָ ·
רַחֵם עַל־פְּלֵיטַת צֹאן יָדֶךָ · וְתֹאמַר לַמַּלְאָךְ · הֶרֶף יָדֶךָ :

*ADORA-
TION OF
GOD AND
RESIGNA-
TION TO
HIS WILL*

Just in all thy ways art thou, O perfect Rock, slow to anger and full of compassion. Spare and have pity upon parents and children, for thine, Lord, is forgiveness and compassion.

Just art thou, O Lord, in ordering death and restoring to life, in whose hand is the charge of all spirits ; far be it from thee to blot out our remembrance : O let thine eyes mercifully regard us; for thine, Lord, is compassion and forgiveness.

If a man live a year or a thousand years, what profiteth it him? He shall be as though he had not been. Blessed be the true Judge, who ordereth death and restoreth to life.

Blessed be he, for his judgment is true, and his eye discerneth all things, and he awardeth unto man his reckoning and his sentence, and all must render acknowledgment unto him.

We know, O Lord, that thy judgment is righteous : thou art justified when thou speakest, and pure when thou judgest, and it is not for us to murmur at thy method of judging ; just art thou, O Lord, and righteous are thy judgments.

O true and righteous Judge ! Blessed be the true Judge, all whose judgments are righteous and true.

The soul of every living thing is in thy hand ; thy might is full of righteousness. Have mercy upon the remnant of the flock of thy hand, and say unto the destroying angel, Stay thy hand.

bound like a lamb. A reference to the Akedah, the Binding of Isaac ; cf. p. 256.

hearken and do. Hearken to our prayer, and save from further calamity.

stay thy hand. Cf. II Samuel 24. 16.

גְּדוֹל הָעֵצָה וְרַב הָעֲלִילִיָּה · אֲשֶׁר־עֵינֶיךָ פְקֻחוֹת

עַל־כָּל־דַּרְכֵי בְּנֵי אָדָם · לָתֵת לְאִישׁ כִּדְרָכָיו וְכִפְרִי

מַעֲלָלָיו: לְהַגִּיד כִּי־יָשָׁר יְיָ · צוּרִי וְלֹא־עַוְלָתָה בּוֹ :

יְיָ נָתַן · וַיְיָ לָקַח · יְהִי שֵׁם יְיָ מְבֹרָךְ : וְהוּא רַחוּם

יְכַפֵּר עָוֹן וְלֹא יַשְׁחִית · וְהִרְבָּה לְהָשִׁיב אַפּוֹ · וְלֹא יָעִיר

כָּל־חֲמָתוֹ :

the Lord gave . . . of the Lord. The sublimest expression of resignation to the will of God ever uttered by human lips. An unforgettable application of these words in overwhelming sorrow was made by Beruria, the brilliant wife of Rabbi Meir, see p. 270. (The poet Coleridge has introduced this soul-stirring story into English literature ; it is quoted, among other tales from the Talmud, in the *A Book of Jewish Thoughts.*) The BOOK OF JOB, the source from which these wonderful words are taken, is a dramatic poem grappling with the problem, Why do the righteous suffer ? It is based on the story of an upright and universally revered man who is suddenly overwhelmed by direst misfortune. He is stunned and overwhelmed by his undeserved misery ; but he unswervingly clings to God. " Though He slay me, yet will I trust in Him." At first he vehemently demands an explanation of the agony that had befallen him ; but gradually he perceives that the whole universe is an unfathomable mystery, and the evil and suffering in it are not more mysterious than the good and the great. Moreover, he comes to see that suffering gives mortals an opportunity for disinterested goodness, for loving God even when they are not rewarded for it. Wisely did, Resh Lakish, one of the old Rabbis, teach, " Job is not so much history, as it is a parable of human life ".

No more appropriate culmination to the *Tzidduk ha-din* could have been conceived than this verse from Job.

II. The second note of the Burial Service is its message of *the Immortality of the Soul.* The body dies, decays, and is no more. But the soul—a spark of the Divine Being—is *immortal.* God's protection does not cease at the portals of the grave. And the dead do not merely merge into the All, or become absorbed into the Divine Source of all being. There is continued, separate existence of the soul after death. Triumphantly both Mourner and congregation repeat the Psalmist's conviction,

"Thou wilt not abandon my soul to the grave.
Thou wilt make known to me the path of life :
In thy presence is fulness of joy ;
At thy right hand, bliss forevermore."

*Jeremiah
32. 19*
ADORA-
TION
AND
Psalm 92. 16
RESIGNA-
TION

Thou art great in counsel and mighty in deed ; thine eyes are open upon all the ways of the children of men, to give unto every one according to his ways, and according to the fruit of his doings. To declare that the Lord is upright ; he is my Rock, and there is no unrighteousness in him.

Job 1. 21

Psalm 78. 38

The Lord gave, and the Lord hath taken away ; blessed be the Name of the Lord. And he, being merciful, forgiveth iniquity and destroyeth not : yea, many a time he turneth his anger away, and doth not stir up all his wrath.

This world is but the ante-chamber to the Future Life—man's true Home ; and that is a spiritual universe. " In the World to come," declared Rabh, " there is no eating or drinking, no marrying or bartering, no envy, hatred or contention ". And yet that Life is not one of mere passivity ; for in it man's immortal spirit continues its moral progress and tasks of holiness. " There is no rest for the righteous ", is a deep spiritual paradox of our Teachers ; " they proceed from strength to strength in the World to come, even as they did in their earthly days ".

III. The third ground-note of the Burial Service is the cardinal principle of Judaism, *There is a Judge and a Judgment Day.* Because of its basic beliefs in a God of justice, and in the Free-will of man, Judaism declares that every human soul appears in Judgment before the God of Right. God cannot be indifferent to human conduct ; and man's behaviour affects man's future destiny. " All thy deeds are written in a book." *In what form* reward and punishment are meted out, it is not given mortals fully to understand. See pp. 253–255, and ' Reward and Punishment in Judaism ", p. 121.

Our Teachers declare that Immortality is the lot of all—Jew and non-Jew alike—who in their earthly days do justly, love mercy, and walk in humility with their Maker ; and, furthermore, that even the tarnished soul will not forever be denied spiritual bliss. Beyond this, they maintain with the Prophet (Isaiah 64. 3) that no human eye hath seen, nor can mortal fathom, what awaiteth us in the Hereafter. Moses Mendelssohn (1729–1786) gave noble expression to the attitude of the loyal Jew on this question. " As for myself, I am contented with the conviction that God's eyes are ever upon me ; that His Providence and justice will follow me into the Future Life, as it has protected me in this life ; and that my true happiness consists in the development of the powers of my soul. It is such felicity that awaits me in the Life to come. More I do not desire to know ".

תהלים ט'ז

מִכְתָּם לְדָוִד · שָׁמְרֵנִי אֵל כִּי־חָסִיתִי בָךְ : אָמַרְתְּ
לַיְיָ אֲדֹנָי אָתָּה · טוֹבָתִי בַּל־עָלֶיךָ : לִקְדוֹשִׁים אֲשֶׁר־
בָּאָרֶץ הֵמָּה · וְאַדִּירֵי כָּל־חֶפְצִי־בָם : יִרְבּוּ עַצְּבוֹתָם
אַחֵר מָהָרוּ · בַּל־אַסִּיךְ נִסְכֵּיהֶם מִדָּם · וּבַל־אֶשָּׂא אֶת־
שְׁמוֹתָם עַל־שְׂפָתָי : יְיָ מְנָת־חֶלְקִי וְכוֹסִי · אַתָּה תּוֹמִיךְ
גּוֹרָלִי : חֲבָלִים נָפְלוּ־לִי בַּנְּעִמִים · אַף־נַחֲלַת שָׁפְרָה
עָלָי : אֲבָרֵךְ אֶת־יְיָ אֲשֶׁר יְעָצָנִי · אַף־לֵילוֹת יִסְּרוּנִי
כִלְיוֹתָי :

שִׁוִּיתִי יְיָ לְנֶגְדִּי תָמִיד · כִּי מִימִינִי בַּל־אֶמּוֹט :
לָכֵן שָׂמַח לִבִּי וַיָּגֶל כְּבוֹדִי · אַף־בְּשָׂרִי יִשְׁכֹּן
לָבֶטַח : כִּי לֹא־תַעֲזֹב נַפְשִׁי לִשְׁאוֹל · לֹא־תִתֵּן חֲסִידְךָ

PSALM 16. The serenity of peace that accompanies communion with God.

1. *michtam.* lit. " a golden " psalm, rich in spiritual thought.

in thee do I take refuge. The Psalmist may refer to an aspect of God as Rock other than that of permanence. He may have in mind " a rock pierced with caves, as in the limestone rocks of Palestine. The psalmist takes refuge in God, as a fugitive might take refuge in one of these caves " (Barnes).

2. *I say.* In the Hebrew this is expressed, " Thou, O my soul, hast said "—as if the poet conversed with himself.

but in thee. No higher good than Thee. " Master of the Universe", exclaimed one of the Chassidic teachers, " I desire neither Thy Paradise nor the bliss in the Life to come ; I desire Thee, and Thee alone " (Rabbi Elimelich of Lisansk).

3. *my delight.* The psalmist's delight is in the saints, the noble ones, and not in those great in the world's esteem, who are iniquitous idolaters. *Their* sorrows will be many, and he will have no dealings with them.

Psalm xvi. 'Michtam of David.

Guard me, O God, for in thee do I take refuge. ²I say
unto the Lord, Thou art my lord : I have no good but in
thee. ³As for the saints that are in the earth, they are the
noble ones in whom is all my delight. ⁴Their sorrows
will be multiplied that have gotten unto themselves
another god : their drink offerings of blood will I not
pour out, nor take their names upon my lips. ⁵The Lord
is the portion of mine inheritance and of my cup : thou
maintainest my lot. ⁶The lines are fallen unto me in
pleasant places ; yea, I have a delightsome heritage. ⁷I
will bless the Lord, who hath given me counsel : yea, my
reins admonish me in the night seasons.

⁸I have set the Lord always before me ; because he is
at my right hand, I shall not be moved. ⁹Therefore my
heart rejoiceth and my glory is glad : my flesh also dwelleth

4. *their drink offerings of blood.* A probable explanation of this
difficult verse is : the psalmist is gravely ill ; and those surrounding
him would, in such extremity of danger, resort to magic, invoke occult
powers of healing, and perform their foul ritual (" drink offerings of
blood ") to effectuate such healing. But the psalmist clings to God
alone (*v.* 1). As for the gods of the heathen, they shall receive no
offerings from him, neither will he as much as mention their names ;
the God of his fathers is his strength and joy forever.
5. *my inheritance.* My riches and treasures.
my cup. The sustenance of my life.
maintainest my lot. " My welfare is in Thy hand."
6. *lines.* The land was divided among the tribes of Israel by *lines*
and apportioned by *lot.* The psalmist's portion—his fellowship with
God in heaven—is his *delightsome heritage.*
7. *reins.* They were deemed in ancient times to be the seat of
emotion and affection ; almost equivalent to " conscience ".
8. *I have set . . . me.* This great text is in many synagogues inscribed over the Ark, or over the Reader's desk.
at my right hand. The position of a protector.
9. *my heart . . . glory . . . flesh.* His whole being.
my glory. My soul ; man's spiritual nature.

לִרְאוֹת שָׁחַת : תּוֹדִיעֵנִי אֹרַח חַיִּים · שְׂבַע שְׂמָחוֹת
אֶת־פָּנֶיךָ · נְעִימוֹת בִּימִינְךָ נֶצַח :

*The Coffin is borne from the Hall to the Burial Ground. Those who
have not visited the Burial Ground for thirty days, say the
following :—*

בָּרוּךְ אַתָּה יְיָ אֱלֹהֵינוּ מֶלֶךְ הָעוֹלָם · אֲשֶׁר־יָצַר
אֶתְכֶם בַּדִּין · וְזָן וְכִלְכֵּל אֶתְכֶם בַּדִּין · וְהֵמִית אֶתְכֶם
בַּדִּין · וְיוֹדֵעַ מִסְפַּר כֻּלְּכֶם בַּדִּין · וְעָתִיד לְהַחֲזִיר
וּלְהַחֲיוֹתְכֶם בַּדִּין : בָּרוּךְ אַתָּה יְיָ מְחַיֵּה הַמֵּתִים :

אַתָּה גִּבּוֹר לְעוֹלָם אֲדֹנָי · מְחַיֵּה מֵתִים אַתָּה רַב לְהוֹשִׁיעַ :
מְכַלְכֵּל חַיִּים בְּחֶסֶד · מְחַיֵּה מֵתִים בְּרַחֲמִים רַבִּים · סוֹמֵךְ
נוֹפְלִים · וְרוֹפֵא חוֹלִים · וּמַתִּיר אֲסוּרִים · וּמְקַיֵּם אֱמוּנָתוֹ
לִישֵׁנֵי עָפָר · מִי כָמוֹךָ בַּעַל גְּבוּרוֹת וּמִי דּוֹמֶה לָּךְ · מֶלֶךְ
מֵמִית וּמְחַיֶּה וּמַצְמִיחַ יְשׁוּעָה · וְנֶאֱמָן אַתָּה לְהַחֲיוֹת מֵתִים :

10. *thy loving one.* The pious worshipper.

11. *path of life.* Eternal life ; that life in the Divine Presence
which is joy forever.

at thy right hand. Or, " in thy right hand ", as the sole Dispenser
of all lasting good.

IV. A fourth note of the Burial Service is the doctrine of the
Resurrection of the Dead. In its literal meaning, Resurrection is an
unfathomable mystery ; but not much more so than birth, or the

in safety. ¹⁰For thou wilt not abandon my soul to the grave : neither wilt thou suffer thy loving one to see destruction. ¹¹Thou wilt make known to me the path of life : in thy presence is fulness of joy ; at thy right·hand bliss for evermore.

The Coffin is borne from the Hall to the Burial Ground. Those who have not visited the Burial Ground for thirty days, say the following :—

Blessed be the Lord our God, King of the universe, who formed you in judgment, who nourished and sustained you in judgment, who brought death on you in judgment, who knoweth the number of you all in judgment, and will hereafter restore you to life in judgment. Blessed art thou, O Lord, who revivest the dead.

Thou, O Lord, art mighty for ever, thou revivest the dead, thou art mighty to save.

See p. 133

Thou sustainest the living with lovingkindness, revivest the dead with great mercy, supportest the falling, healest the sick, loosest the bound, and keepest thy faith to them that sleep in the dust. Who is like unto thee, Lord of mighty acts, and who resembleth thee, O King, who orderest death and restorest life, and causest salvation to spring forth ? Yea, faithful art thou to revive the dead.

stupendous miracle of the annual resurrection of plant-life after winter. It is not any more difficult for the Almighty to reconstruct a body after its dissolution than to create a universe out of nothing. The Talmud records the following argument in favour of Resurrection. " If what never before existed, exists, why cannot that which once existed, exist again ? " Resurrection of the Dead does not necessarily imply identity with the material composing the body when alive ; rather that the sum-total of all our deeds and thoughts, habits and character, does not vanish into nought at the moment of death. There is for the soul in the World-to-come identity of personality with the soul in the earthly life.

*When the Coffin is lowered into the Grave, the following is said, the
sentence being varied according to the sex of the departed :—*

עַל מְקוֹמוֹ יָבֹא בְשָׁלוֹם :

עַל מְקוֹמָה תָּבֹא בְשָׁלוֹם :

*On quitting the Burial Ground it is customary to pluck some grass,
and to say one of the following sentences :—*

וְיָצִיצוּ מֵעִיר כְּעֵשֶׂב הָאָרֶץ :

זָכוּר כִּי־עָפָר אֲנָחְנוּ :

*All those who have been present at the Interment wash their hands,
and say :—*

בִּלַּע הַמָּוֶת לָנֶצַח • וּמָחָה אֲדֹנָי אֱלֹהִים דִּמְעָה מֵעַל כָּל־

פָּנִים • וְחֶרְפַּת עַמּוֹ יָסִיר מֵעַל כָּל־הָאָרֶץ • כִּי יְיָ דִּבֵּר :

They then return to the Hall, and say וִיהִי נֹעַם p. 70.

*The following Kaddish is said by Children after the Burial of their
Parents. On those days on which* תַּחֲנוּן (p. 168) *is not said,
the Kaddish, p. 1098, is substituted.*

Mourners. יִתְגַּדַּל וְיִתְקַדַּשׁ שְׁמֵהּ רַבָּא בְּעָלְמָא דִּי הוּא

עָתִיד לְאִתְחַדָּתָא וּלְאַחֲיָאָה מֵתַיָא וּלְאַסָּקָא יָתְהוֹן

לְחַיֵּי עָלְמָא • וּלְמִבְנֵא קַרְתָּא דִּי־יְרוּשְׁלֵם וּלְשַׁכְלֵל הֵיכְלֵהּ

like the grass. The custom of plucking grass on leaving the burial
ground is of medieval origin. The two texts " are emblematic at
once of the frailty of life, and the certain hope of immortality "
(Abrahams).

V. The fifth note of the Burial Service is the message of *the
immortality and resurrection of Israel,* with which the salvation of the
individual is indissolubly bound up. To the Rabbis, religion and
society were pre-eminently social, and society in the ancient world

When the Coffin is lowered into the Grave, the following is said, the
sentence being varied according to the sex of the departed :—

May he come to his place in peace.

May she come to her place in peace.

On quitting the Burial Ground it is customary to pluck some grass,
and to say one of the following sentences :—

Isaiah 26. 19   And they of the city shall flourish like the grass of the
earth.

Psalm 103. 14   He remembereth that we are dust.

[All those who have been present at the Interment wash their hands,
and say :—

Isaiah 25. 8   He maketh death to vanish in life eternal ; and the
Lord God wipeth away tears from off all faces ; and the

See p. 1099   reproach of his people shall he take away from off the
earth : for the Lord hath spoken it.]

They then return to the Hall, and say, "And let the graciousness of the
Lord our God be upon us," p. 71.

The following Kaddish is said by Children after the Burial of their
Parents. On those days on which Tachanun is not said (p. 169),
the Kaddish, p. 1099, is substituted.

BURIAL
KADDISH   *Mourners.*—May his great Name be magnified and
sanctified in the world that is to be created anew, where
he will revive the dead, and raise them up unto life eternal ;
will rebuild the city of Jerusalem, and establish his temple

meant national society. But the nationalism of the Rabbis was of the
spiritual kind ; and the doctrine of the Messianic Kingdom includes all
the larger ideals of humanity—universal peace, the reign of righteousness, and the sure coming of an era in which all men will recognize
that God is One and His Name One. But this glorious age will come
about through the vindication and regeneration of the Jewish People.
The salvation of Israel will usher in the triumph of justice and the
fullest consummation of God's purposes for all the children of men.
For the concept of the Messiah, see p. 254. All this teaching is
embodied in the Burial Kaddish.

בִּגְנוּהּ · וּלְמֶעְקַר פָּלְחָנָא נֻכְרָאָה מֵאַרְעָא וְלַאֲתָבָא פָּלְחָנָא

דִי־שְׁמַיָּא לְאַתְרֵהּ · וְיַמְלִךְ קֻדְשָׁא בְּרִיךְ הוּא בְּמַלְכוּתֵהּ

וִיקָרֵהּ בְּחַיֵּיכוֹן וּבְיוֹמֵיכוֹן וּבְחַיֵּי דִי־כָל־בֵּית יִשְׂרָאֵל

בַּעֲגָלָא וּבִזְמַן קָרִיב · וְאִמְרוּ אָמֵן :

Cong. and Mourners יְהֵא שְׁמֵהּ רַבָּא מְבָרַךְ לְעָלַם וּלְעָלְמֵי

עָלְמַיָּא :

Mourners. יִתְבָּרַךְ וְיִשְׁתַּבַּח וְיִתְפָּאַר וְיִתְרֹמַם וְיִתְנַשֵּׂא

וְיִתְהַדָּר וְיִתְעַלֶּה וְיִתְהַלָּל שְׁמֵהּ דִי־קֻדְשָׁא · בְּרִיךְ הוּא ·

לְעֵלָּא מִן־כָּל־בִּרְכָתָא וְשִׁירָתָא תֻּשְׁבְּחָתָא וְנֶחֱמָתָא דִי

אֲמִירָן בְּעָלְמָא · וְאִמְרוּ אָמֵן :

יְהֵא שְׁלָמָא רַבָּא מִן־שְׁמַיָּא וְחַיִּים עָלֵינוּ

וְעַל־כָּל־יִשְׂרָאֵל · וְאִמְרוּ אָמֵן :

עֹשֶׂה שָׁלוֹם בִּמְרוֹמָיו הוּא יַעֲשֶׂה שָׁלוֹם

עָלֵינוּ וְעַל־כָּל־יִשְׂרָאֵל · וְאִמְרוּ אָמֵן :

אָנָּא, *p.* 1094, *and* קַדִּישׁ יָתוֹם, *p.* 1098.

in the midst thereof ; and will uproot all alien worship from the earth, and restore the worship of the true God. O may the Holy One, blessed be he, reign in his sovreignty and glory during your life and during your days, and during the life of all the house of Israel, even speedily and at a near time, and say ye, Amen.

Cong. and Mourners.—Let his great Name be blessed for ever and to all eternity.

Mourners.—Blessed, praised and glorified, exalted, extolled and honoured, magnified and lauded be the Name of the Holy One, blessed be he ; though he be high above all blessings and hymns, praises and consolations, which are uttered in the world ; and say ye, Amen.

May there be abundant peace from heaven, and life for us and for all Israel ; and say ye, Amen.

He who maketh peace in his high places, may he make peace for us and for all Israel ; and say ye, Amen.

"O Lord and King," p. 1095, and Mourner's Kaddish, p. 1099.

―――――――

For the history and significance of the Burial Kaddish see the notes on the Half-Kaddish, p. 106 ; and especially on the Mourner's Kaddish, pp. 269–271. The Burial Kaddish too was in origin a closing doxology pronounced after a homiletic discourse, and gave expression to the yearning for the rebuilding of the Temple and realization of the Messianic Hope.

תפלה בבית האבל:

After the ordinary Daily Service, the following Psalm (מ׳ט) is read in the House of a Mourner. On those days on which תַּחֲנוּן (p. 168) is not said, תהלים ט׳ז, p, 1080, is substituted for Psalm מ׳ט.

תהלים מ׳ט

לַמְנַצֵּחַ לִבְנֵי־קֹרַח מִזְמוֹר: שִׁמְעוּ־זֹאת כָּל־הָעַמִּים

הַאֲזִינוּ כָּל־יֹשְׁבֵי הֶלֶד: גַּם־בְּנֵי אָדָם גַּם־בְּנֵי־אִישׁ יַחַד

עָשִׁיר וְאֶבְיוֹן: פִּי יְדַבֵּר חָכְמוֹת וְהָגוּת לִבִּי תְבוּנוֹת:

אַטֶּה לְמָשָׁל אָזְנִי אֶפְתַּח בְּכִנּוֹר חִידָתִי: לָמָּה אִירָא

בִּימֵי רָע עֲוֹן עֲקֵבַי יְסֻבֵּנִי: הַבֹּטְחִים עַל־חֵילָם וּבְרֹב

עָשְׁרָם יִתְהַלָּלוּ: אָח לֹא־פָדֹה יִפְדֶּה אִישׁ לֹא־יִתֵּן

לֵאלֹהִים כָּפְרוֹ: וְיֵקַר פִּדְיוֹן נַפְשָׁם וְחָדַל לְעוֹלָם: וִיחִי־

עוֹד לָנֶצַח לֹא יִרְאֶה הַשָּׁחַת: כִּי יִרְאֶה חֲכָמִים יָמוּתוּ

יַחַד כְּסִיל וָבַעַר יֹאבֵדוּ וְעָזְבוּ לַאֲחֵרִים חֵילָם: קִרְבָּם

בָּתֵּימוֹ לְעוֹלָם מִשְׁכְּנֹתָם לְדוֹר וָדֹר קָרְאוּ בִשְׁמוֹתָם עֲלֵי

אֲדָמוֹת: וְאָדָם בִּיקָר בַּל־יָלִין נִמְשַׁל כַּבְּהֵמוֹת נִדְמוּ:

IN THE HOUSE OF MOURNING.

PSALM 49. The author calls it a *parable, i.e.* didactic meditation; and a *dark saying, i.e.* the exposition, in this instance, of a deep moral problem. Why do the wicked prosper. The psalmist's answer is that the injustices and inequalities of human existence are corrected in a Life Hereafter.

1–5. Let all listen, as the theme concerns the whole of humanity.

IN THE HOUSE OF MOURNING

After the ordinary Daily Service, the following Psalm (xlix) is read in the House of a Mourner. On those days on which Tachanun (p. 169) is not said, Psalm xvi, p. 1081, is substituted for Psalm xlix.

Psalm xlix. ¹For the Chief Musician.

A Psalm of the Sons of Korah.

INEQUALI-TIES OF LIFE

²Hear this, all ye peoples ; give ear, all ye inhabitants of the world : ³both low and high, rich and poor, together. ⁴My mouth shall speak wisdom ; and the meditation of my heart shall be of understanding. ⁵I will incline my ear to a parable : I will open my dark saying to the lyre. ⁶Wherefore should I fear in the days of evil, when the iniquity of them that would supplant me surroundeth me, ⁷even of them that trust in their wealth, and boast themselves in the multitude of their riches ? ⁸None of them can by any means redeem his brother, nor give to God a ransom for him : ⁹(for the redemption of their soul is costly, and must be let alone for ever :) ¹⁰that he should still live always, that he should not see the pit. ¹¹For he will see that wise men die, the fool and the brutish together perish, and abandon their wealth to others. · ¹²Their inward thought is that their houses shall continue for ever, and their dwelling-places to all generations ; they call their lands after their own names. ¹³But man that is in glory abideth not : he

6–13. Though men idolize riches, these must be surrendered on, and cannot save from, death.

6. *in days of evil.* When evil men seem to have the upper hand.

iniquity . . . surroundeth me. Unscrupulous neighbours were eager to get him into their power.

8. *redeem his brother.* How powerless is their wealth ! They cannot thereby deliver their dearest friend from death.

9. *costly.* All the world's treasure will not suffice.

11. *together perish.* All alike come to the grave—rich and poor, wise and foolish.

12. *call their lands.* They name their estates after themselves.

13. *abideth not.* But earthly magnificence abideth not. What seems to mortal eyes permanent, vanishes like mist.

זֶה דַרְכָּם כֵּסֶל לָמוֹ וְאַחֲרֵיהֶם בְּפִיהֶם יִרְצוּ סֶלָה: כַּצֹּאן
לִשְׁאוֹל שַׁתּוּ מָוֶת יִרְעֵם וַיִּרְדּוּ בָם יְשָׁרִים לַבֹּקֶר וְצוּרָם
לְבַלּוֹת שְׁאוֹל מִזְּבֻל לוֹ: אַךְ־אֱלֹהִים יִפְדֶּה־נַפְשִׁי מִיַּד
שְׁאוֹל כִּי יִקָּחֵנִי סֶלָה: אַל־תִּירָא כִּי־יַעֲשִׁר אִישׁ כִּי־
יִרְבֶּה כְּבוֹד בֵּיתוֹ: כִּי לֹא בְמוֹתוֹ יִקַּח הַכֹּל לֹא־יֵרֵד
אַחֲרָיו כְּבוֹדוֹ: כִּי־נַפְשׁוֹ בְּחַיָּיו יְבָרֵךְ וְיוֹדֻךָ כִּי־תֵיטִיב
לָךְ: תָּבוֹא עַד־דּוֹר אֲבוֹתָיו עַד־נֵצַח לֹא יִרְאוּ־אוֹר:
אָדָם בִּיקָר וְלֹא יָבִין נִמְשַׁל כַּבְּהֵמוֹת נִדְמוּ:

תהלים ל״ט

לַמְנַצֵּחַ לִידוּתוּן מִזְמוֹר לְדָוִד: אָמַרְתִּי אֶשְׁמְרָה דְרָכַי
מֵחֲטוֹא בִלְשׁוֹנִי אֶשְׁמְרָה לְפִי מַחְסוֹם בְּעוֹד רָשָׁע לְנֶגְדִּי:
נֶאֱלַמְתִּי דוּמִיָּה הֶחֱשֵׁיתִי מִטּוֹב וּכְאֵבִי נֶעְכָּר: חַם־לִבִּי
בְּקִרְבִּי בַּהֲגִיגִי תִבְעַר־אֵשׁ דִּבַּרְתִּי בִּלְשׁוֹנִי: הוֹדִיעֵנִי יְיָ
קִצִּי וּמִדַּת יָמַי מַה־הִיא אֵדְעָה מֶה־חָדֵל אָנִי: הִנֵּה

14–21. The fate of the worldly wicked and of the righteous.
14. *foolish.* In the Bible sense of " sinner ".
15. *in the morning.* The poet conceives the wicked perishing in the night—" death is their shepherd ". The righteous awake triumphant over their oppressors.
16. *he will receive me.* This is a clear hope of new life with God.
19. *blessed his soul.* Congratulated himself on his good fortune.
20. *go to the . . . fathers.* The more usual phrase is, " he shall be gathered to his fathers ", and shall nevermore see the light.

*FATE OF
WICKED
AND
RIGHTEOUS
CON-
TRASTED* is like the beasts that perish. ¹⁴This is the way of them that are foolish, and of their followers who take pleasure in their speech. (Selah.) ¹⁵Like sheep they are laid in the grave ; death shall be their shepherd : but the upright shall have dominion over them in the morning ; and their form shall be for the grave to consume, that there be no habitation for it. ¹⁶But God will redeem my soul from the grasp of the grave : for he will receive me. (Selah.) ¹⁷Be not thou afraid when a man becometh rich, when the glory of his house is increased : ¹⁸for at his death he shall carry nothing away ; his glory shall not descend after him. ¹⁹Though while he lived he blessed his soul, and though mèn praise thee that thou doest well unto thyself, ²⁰he shall go to the generation of his fathers, who shall never see the light. ²¹Man that is in glory, but without understanding, is like the beasts that perish.

*THE
PATHOS
OF LIFE*
Psalm xxxix.

¹For the Chief Musician, for Jeduthun.   A Psalm of David.

²I said, I will take heed to my ways, that I sin not with my tongue : I will keep my mouth with a bridle, while the wicked is before me. ³I was dumb, and kept silence, I held my peace, and had no comfort : and my sorrow was stirred. ⁴My heart was hot within me ; while I was musing the fire kindled : then spake I with my tongue ﹕ ⁵Lord, make me to know mine end, and the measure of

---

21. *glory.* Pomp, worldly magnificence. Not what a man *has,* but what he *is,* matters.

PSALM 39. On the Pathos of Life by a Sufferer who is near to Death.

1. *Jeduthun.* One of the directors of Temple music.

2-4. He is silent, when tempted to murmur at the prosperity of the wicked.

2. *with a bridle.* I will put a muzzle to my mouth.

4. *kindled.* The flame of feeling could not be restrained.

טְפָחוֹת נָתַתָּה יָמַי וְחֶלְדִּי כְאַיִן נֶגְדֶּךָ אַךְ כָּל־הֶבֶל כָּל־
אָדָם נִצָּב סֶלָה : אַךְ־בְּצֶלֶם יִתְהַלֶּךְ־אִישׁ אַךְ־הֶבֶל יֶהֱמָיוּן
יִצְבֹּר וְלֹא־יֵדַע מִי־אֹסְפָם : וְעַתָּה מַה־קִּוִּיתִי אֲדֹנָי תּוֹחַלְתִּי
לְךָ הִיא : מִכָּל־פְּשָׁעַי הַצִּילֵנִי חֶרְפַּת נָבָל אַל־תְּשִׂימֵנִי :
נֶאֱלַמְתִּי לֹא אֶפְתַּח־פִּי כִּי אַתָּה עָשִׂיתָ : הָסֵר מֵעָלַי
נִגְעֶךָ מִתִּגְרַת יָדְךָ אֲנִי כָלִיתִי : בְּתוֹכָחוֹת עַל־עָוֹן יִסַּרְתָּ
אִישׁ וַתֶּמֶס כָּעָשׁ חֲמוּדוֹ אַךְ הֶבֶל כָּל־אָדָם סֶלָה :
שִׁמְעָה תְפִלָּתִי יְיָ וְשַׁוְעָתִי הַאֲזִינָה אֶל־דִּמְעָתִי אַל־
תֶּחֱרַשׁ כִּי גֵר אָנֹכִי עִמָּךְ תּוֹשָׁב כְּכָל־אֲבוֹתָי : הָשַׁע
מִמֶּנִּי וְאַבְלִיגָה בְּטֶרֶם אֵלֵךְ וְאֵינֶנִּי :

*The officiating Minister may here select one of the "Readings in the
House of Mourning" (pp. 1100–1105) for each Evening Service
during the Shivah-week.*

5–7. Prayer to understand how transitory and vain is human life.
6. *handbreadths.* A handbreadth equals to four fingers, less than
half a span.
8–10. Life being thus transient, God alone is the one sure stay in
life.
9. *from all my transgressions.* From the guilt and the consequences
of his transgressions.
of the foolish. Who regard the sufferings of the godly as a mark of
God's wrath, and taunt him accordingly.
10. *I am dumb . . . it.* An expression of perfect resignation to the
will of God.

my days, what it is ; let me know how fleeting I am. ⁶Behold, thou hast made my days as handbreadths ; and my lifetime is as nothing before thee : surely every man, though he stand firm, is but a breath. (Selah.) ⁷Surely as a mere semblance every man walketh to and fro : surely they are disquieted for vanity : one heapeth up riches and he knoweth not who shall gather them. ⁸And now, Lord, what wait I for ? My hope is in thee. ⁹Deliver me from all my transgressions ; make me not the reproach of the foolish. ¹⁰I am dumb, I open not my mouth ; because thou hast done it. ¹¹Remove thy stroke away from me : I am consumed by the blow of thine hand. ¹²When thou with rebukes dost chasten man for iniquity, thou makest his beauty to waste away like a moth : surely every man is a breath. (Selah.) ¹³Hear my prayer, O Lord, and give ear unto my cry ; hold not thy peace at my fears ; for I am a stranger with thee, a sojourner, as all my fathers were. ¹⁴O spare me, that I may again be glad, before I go hence, and be no more.

The officiating Minister may here select one of the " Readings in the House of Mourning " (pp. 1100–1105) for each Evening Service during the Shivah-week.

11–14. Prayer for relief and respite.
12. *rebukes.* Not in words merely, but through affliction.
his beauty. All that a man takes pleasure in.
13. *stranger with thee.* The Heb. word is *ger* : the psalmist claims that, as a stranger, he is the guest of God, and as such entitled to His special care.

Wherever possible there should be at a Shivah Evening Service, either a brief address, or a Reading from Scripture, the Rabbinical Writings, and the Moralist literature.

תפלה בעד המת

אָנָּא יְיָ מֶלֶךְ מָלֵא רַחֲמִים · אֱלֹהֵי הָרוּחוֹת לְכָל־
בָּשָׂר · אֲשֶׁר בְּיָדְךָ נַפְשׁוֹת הַחַיִּים וְהַמֵּתִים · אָנָּא
קַבֵּל בְּחַסְדְּךָ הַגָּדוֹל אֶת־נִשְׁמַת־

For a Woman, say :—	*For a Man, say :—*
אֲשֶׁר נֶאֶסְפָה אֶל עַמָּה :	אֲשֶׁר נֶאֶסַף אֶל עַמּוֹ :
In the case of a young child omit from חוּם *to* לְפָנֶיהָ	*In the case of a young child omit* from חוּם *to* לְפָנָיו
חוּם וַחֲמוֹל עָלֶיהָ ·	חוּם וַחֲמוֹל עָלָיו · סְלַח
סְלַח וּמְחַל לְכָל־פְּשָׁעֶיהָ ·	וּמְחַל לְכָל־פְּשָׁעָיו · כִּי אָדָם
כִּי אָדָם אֵין צַדִּיק בָּאָרֶץ	אֵין צַדִּיק בָּאָרֶץ אֲשֶׁר יַעֲשֶׂה־
אֲשֶׁר יַעֲשֶׂה־טּוֹב וְלֹא	טוֹב וְלֹא יֶחֱטָא : זְכוֹר
יֶחֱטָא : זְכוֹר לָה צִדְקָתָה	לוֹ צִדְקָתוֹ אֲשֶׁר עָשָׂה
אֲשֶׁר עָשְׂתָה וִיהִי שְׂכָרָה	וִיהִי שְׂכָרוֹ אִתּוֹ וּפְעֻלָּתוֹ
אָתָּה וּפְעֻלָּתָה לְפָנֶיהָ :	לְפָנָיו :
אָנָּא הַסְתֵּר אֶת־נִשְׁמָתָה	אָנָּא הַסְתֵּר אֶת־נִשְׁמָתוֹ

MEMORIAL PRAYER.

"Unless we are prepared to maintain that at his death the fate of
man is fixed irretrievably and for ever ; that, therefore, the sinner who

MEMORIAL PRAYER.

MEMORIAL PRAYER O Lord and King, who art full of compassion, God of the spirits of all flesh, in whose hand are the souls of the living and the dead, receive, we beseech thee, in thy great lovingkindness the soul of_____.

For a Man, say :—	*For a Woman, say :—*
who hath been gathered unto his people.	who hath been gathered unto her people.
In the case of a young child, omit from "Have mercy" to "before him."	*In the case of a young child, omit from "Have mercy" to "before her."*
Have mercy upon him ; pardon all his transgressions, for there is none righteous upon earth, who doeth only good, and sinneth not. Remember unto him the righteousness which he wrought, and let his reward be with him, and his recompense before him.	*Have mercy upon her ; pardon all her transgressions, for there is none righteous upon earth, who doeth only good, and sinneth not. Remember unto her the righteousness which she wrought, and let her reward be with her, and her recompense before her.*
Oh shelter his soul in the shadow of thy wings. Make	Oh shelter her soul in the shadow of thy wings. Make

Ecclesiastes 7. 20

rejected much of God's love during a brief lifetime, has lost all of it eternally—prayer for the peace and salvation of the departed soul commends itself as one of the highest religious obligations " (Singer). Forms of such prayer have been known since the eleventh century. The Prayer in use in Anglo-Jewish congregations, admirably edited by Dr. Nathan M. Adler, embodies the main ideas of the older forms. Some modifications and expansions have been made by the author of this commentary.

בְּצֵל כְּנָפֶיךָ ·   הוֹדִיעֵהוּ אֹרַח | בְּצֵל כְּנָפֶיךָ ·   הוֹדִיעָהָ אֹרַח

חַיִּים שְׂבַע שְׂמָחוֹת אֶת־ | חַיִּים שְׂבַע שְׂמָחוֹת אֶת־

פָּנֶיךָ נְעִימוֹת בִּימִינְךָ נֶצַח · | פָּנֶיךָ נְעִימוֹת בִּימִינְךָ נֶצַח ·

וְתַשְׁפִּיעַ לוֹ   מֵרַב   טוּב | וְתַשְׁפִּיעַ לָהּ   מֵרַב   טוּב

הַצָּפוּן לַצַּדִּיקִים · | הַצָּפוּן לַצַּדִּיקִים ·

כְּמוֹ שֶׁכָּתוּב   מָה   רַב   טוּבְךָ   אֲשֶׁר־צָפַנְתָּ לִּירֵאֶיךָ פָּעַלְתָּ
לַחוֹסִים בָּךְ נֶגֶד בְּנֵי אָדָם :

אָנָּא יְיָ   הָרוֹפֵא   לִשְׁבוּרֵי   לֵב   וּמְחַבֵּשׁ לְעַצְּבוֹתָם ·
שַׁלֵּם נִחוּמִים לָאֲבֵלִים ·

[In the case of a female child include the following :— | *[In the case of a male child, include the following :—*

וּתְהִי   פְּטִירַת   הַיַּלְדָה | וּתְהִי פְּטִירַת הַיֶּלֶד הַזֶּה

הַזֹּאת קֵץ לְכָל־צָרָה וְצוּקָה | קֵץ לְכָל־צָרָה וְצוּקָה לְאָבִיו

לְאָבִיהָ וּלְאִמָּהּ :] | וּלְאִמּוֹ :]

חַזְּקֵם וְאַמְּצֵם בְּיוֹם אָבְלָם וִיגוֹנָם וְזָכְרֵם [וּבְנֵי בֵיתָם]
לְחַיִּים טוֹבִים וַאֲרֻכִּים : תֵּן בְּלִבָּם יִרְאָתְךָ וְאַהֲבָתָךְ
לְעָבְדְךָ בְּלֵבָב שָׁלֵם : וּתְהִי אַחֲרִיתָם שָׁלוֹם · אָמֵן :

כְּאִישׁ אֲשֶׁר אִמּוֹ תְּנַחֲמֶנּוּ כֵּן אָנֹכִי אֲנַחֶמְכֶם וּבִירוּשָׁלַםִ

known to him the path of
life : in thy presence is fulness of joy; at thy right hand,
bliss for evermore. Bestow
upon him the abounding
happiness that is treasured
up for the righteous,

known to her the path of
life : in thy presence is fulness of joy; at thy right hand,
bliss for evermore. Bestow
upon her the abounding
happiness that is treasured
up for the righteous,

Psalm 31. 20   as it is written, Oh how great is thy goodness, which thou
has laid up for them that fear thee, which thou hast wrought
for them that trust in thee before the children of men !

*CLOSING
SUPPLICA-
TION*

O Lord, who healest the broken-hearted and bindest up
their wounds, grant thy consolation unto the mourners.

[*In the case of a male child,
include the following :—*

May the death of this
child mark the end of all anguish and tribulation unto
his parents.]

[*In the case of a female child,
include the following :—*

May the death of this
child mark the end of all anguish and tribulation unto
her parents.]

Oh strengthen and support them in the day of their grief
and sorrow ; and remember them (and their children)
for a long and good life. Put into their hearts the fear
and love of thee, that they may serve thee with a perfect
heart ; and let their latter end be peace. Amen.

Isaiah 66. 13   Like one whom his mother comforteth, so will I
comfort you, (saith the Lord), and in Jerusalem shall ye

Isaiah 60. 20   be comforted. Thy sun shall no more go down, neither
shall thy moon withdraw itself ; for the Lord shall be

---

whom his mother comforteth. God's is more than a father's love.
That is sometimes hard and confined to the successful child. Not so a
mother's. With an instinct that is almost divine, she feels that the
erring child, the unfortunate child has the greatest need of love. And
such is God's love.

    in Jerusalem . . . comforted. In the salvation and triumph of Israel
over all forces of evil, will you find your highest comfort.

תְּנָחֵמוּ : לֹא־יָבֹא עוֹד שִׁמְשֵׁךְ וִירֵחֵךְ לֹא יֵאָסֵף · כִּי יְיָ

יִהְיֶה־לָּךְ לְאוֹר עוֹלָם · וְשָׁלְמוּ יְמֵי אֶבְלֵךְ : בִּלַּע הַמָּוֶת

לָנֶצַח · וּמָחָה יְיָ אֱלֹהִים דִּמְעָה מֵעַל כָּל־פָּנִים · וְחֶרְפַּת

עַמּוֹ יָסִיר מֵעַל כָּל־הָאָרֶץ · כִּי יְיָ דִּבֵּר :

קַדִּישׁ יָתוֹם

Mourner. יִתְגַּדַּל וְיִתְקַדַּשׁ שְׁמֵהּ רַבָּא בְּעָלְמָא דִּי־בְרָא

כִרְעוּתֵהּ · וְיַמְלִיךְ מַלְכוּתֵהּ בְּחַיֵּיכוֹן וּבְיוֹמֵיכוֹן וּבְחַיֵּי

דִי־כָל־בֵּית יִשְׂרָאֵל בַּעֲגָלָא וּבִזְמַן קָרִיב · וְאִמְרוּ אָמֵן :

Cong. and Mourner. יְהֵא שְׁמֵהּ רַבָּא מְבָרַךְ לְעָלַם וּלְעָלְמֵי

עָלְמַיָּא ·

Mourner. יִתְבָּרַךְ וְיִשְׁתַּבַּח וְיִתְפָּאַר וְיִתְרוֹמַם וְיִתְנַשֵּׂא

וְיִתְהַדָּר וְיִתְעַלֶּה וְיִתְהַלָּל שְׁמֵהּ דְּיִקֻדְשָׁא · בְּרִיךְ הוּא ·

לְעֵלָּא מִן־כָּל־בִּרְכָתָא וְשִׁירָתָא תֻּשְׁבְּחָתָא וְנֶחֱמָתָא דִּי־

אֲמִירָן בְּעָלְמָא · וְאִמְרוּ אָמֵן :

יְהֵא שְׁלָמָא רַבָּא מִן־שְׁמַיָּא וְחַיִּים עָלֵינוּ

וְעַל־כָּל־יִשְׂרָאֵל · וְאִמְרוּ אָמֵן :

עֹשֶׂה שָׁלוֹם בִּמְרוֹמָיו הוּא יַעֲשֶׂה שָׁלוֹם

עָלֵינוּ וְעַל־כָּל־יִשְׂרָאֵל · וְאִמְרוּ אָמֵן :

thine everlasting light, and the days of thy mourning shall be ended. He maketh death to vanish in life eternal; and the Lord God wipeth away tears from off all faces; and the reproach of his people shall he take away from off all the earth : for the Lord hath spoken it.

MOURNER'S KADDISH.

KADDISH

Mourner.—Magnified and sanctified be his great Name in the world which he hath created according to his will. May he establish his kingdom during your life and during your days, and during the life of all the house of Israel, even speedily and at a near time, and say ye, Amen.

Congregation and Mourner.—Let his great Name be blessed for ever and to all eternity.

Mourner.—Blessed, praised and glorified, exalted, extolled and honoured, magnified and lauded be the Name of the Holy One, blessed be he ; though he be high above all the blessings and hymns, praises and consolations, which are uttered in the world ; and say ye, Amen.

May there be abundant peace from heaven and life for us and for all Israel ; and say ye, Amen.

He who maketh peace in his high places, may he make peace for us and for all Israel ; and say ye, Amen.

---

death to vanish in life eternal. Other translations of this difficult phrase are, "He will destroy death forever," and, "He will swallow up death in victory" (A. V.).

tears from off all faces. This verse is taken from Isaiah's Vision of Universal Brotherhood, in which God invites the peoples of earth to a feast. They come in the garb of mourning and with faces veiled. When God removes the veil, He sees the eyes dim with tears, and He wipes away the tears and all traces of past sorrow !

reproach of his people. The Jews in the Dispersion suffered much from the taunts and dislikes of their heathen neighbours. The Prophet foretells that, in the regeneration awaiting humanity, even this malignant hatred—never more malignant than in our day—would cease.

READINGS IN THE HOUSE OF MOURNING.

It is an ancient pious custom that religious study and meditation on Sacred themes form part of the Service of Mourning. Religious study has in Israel always been looked upon as worship; and, when part of a Mourning Service, such study is deemed to have an atoning efficacy on behalf of the deceased. That is to say, such study is a testimony to the identification of the deceased in his life with the fount of living Judaism, and is thus accounted to his merit before the Heavenly Judge.

One of the five following Readings in the House of Mourning may be recited by the officiating Minister before the Memorial Prayer, p. 1095.

I

" The Lord gave, and the Lord hath taken away; blessed be the Name of the Lord."
SCRIPTUR-AL VERSES
Job 1. 21

" Restore unto me the joy of Thy salvation; and uphold me with Thy willing spirit. Whom have I in heaven but Thee? and there is none upon earth that I desire beside Thee."
Psalm 51. 14
Psalm 73. 25

" Yea, thou I walk through the valley of the shadow of death, I will fear no evil, for Thou art with me; Thy rod and thy staff, they comfort me. I shall behold Thy face in righteousness; I shall be satisfied, when I awake, with Thy likeness."
Psalm 23. 4
Psalm 17. 15

" They that are born are destined to die; and the dead to be brought to life again; and the living to be judged, to know, to make known, and to be made conscious that He is God, He the Maker, He the Creator, He the Discerner, He the Judge, He the Witness, He the Complainant. He it is that will in future judge, blessed be He, with Whom there is no unrighteousness, nor forgetfulness, nor partiality, nor taking of bribes; know also that everything is according to the reckoning. And let not thy imagination give thee to hope that the grave will be a place of refuge for thee; for perforce thou wast formed, and perforce thou wast born, and thou livest perforce, and perforce thou wilt die, and perforce thou wilt in the future have to give account and reckoning before the Supreme King of kings, the Holy One, blessed be He."
RABBINI-CAL SAYINGS

" When a person enters the world, his hands are clenched; as though to say, ' The whole world is mine, I shall inherit it '. But when he takes his leave of it, his hands are spread open; as though to say, ' I have inherited nothing from the world '."

" The righteous are called living, even in their death; the wicked are called dead, even while they are alive."

The Minister may here give a brief address, or the following admonition of Rabbi Bachya may be read :—
" My soul, look carefully back—on thy pilgrim's track; all cometh from the dust—and thither return it must. Whatever has been moulded and built, when its time is fulfilled, must go back to the ground, where its material was found. Death is life's brother; they keep fast to one
ADMONI-TION.

another, each taking hold of one end of their plunder, and none can tear them asunder. Soon thou wilt come—to thy eternal home, where thou must show thy work and receive thy wages—on rightful scales and gauges—or good or bad, according to the worth—of thy deeds on earth.

" Therefore get thee up, and to thy Master pray—by night and day. Seek the Lord, thy Light, with all thy might ; walk in meekness, pursue the right ; so that with His mercy-screen the Master—hide thee in the day of disaster. Then thou shalt shine like the heavens bright, and like the sun when going forth in might ; and o'er thy head —shall be spread—the rays—of the sun of grace—that brings—healing and joy in his wings."

May our prayers, readings and meditations in memory of the departed be acceptable before our Father who is in Heaven, the Great Comforter, who sends His divine consolation to all who mourn for the loss of those dear unto them.

Memorial Prayer, p. 1095, *and Mourner's Kaddish, p.* 1099.

II

SCRIPTUR-AL VERSES Psalm 16. 8–11   " I have set the Lord always before me ; surely He is at my right hand, I shall not be moved. Therefore, my heart is glad, and my glory rejoiceth ; my flesh also dwelleth in safety. For thou wilt not abandon my soul to the grave ; neither wilt Thou suffer Thy loving one to see destruction. Thou makest me to know the path of life ; in Thy presence is fulness of joy ; at Thy right hand, bliss for evermore."

Ecclesiastes 7. 1, 2   " A good name is better than precious oil ; and the day of death than the day of one's birth. It is better to go to the house of mourning than to go to the house of feasting ; for that is the end of all men, and the living will lay it to his heart."

Proverbs 12. 28   " In the way of righteousness is life ; and in the pathway thereof, there is no death."

RABBINI-CAL SAYINGS   " Reflect upon three things, and thou wilt not come within the power of sin ; know whence thou camest, and whither thou art going, and before Whom thou wilt in future have to give account and reckoning."

" The day is short, and the work is great, and the labourers are sluggish, and the reward is much, and the Master of the House is urgent. It may not be given thee to complete the work, but thou art not at liberty to desist from it.

" R. Eliezer said, ' Repent one day before thy death '. His disciples asked him, ' Does anyone know on what day he will die ' ? He replied, ' All the more reason that he repent to-day, lest to-morrow he die. Let his whole life, therefore, be spent in repentance '."

" Render the soul back to God in the same state that He gave it to thee : as He gave it to thee in a state of purity, return it to Him in a state of purity."

" The souls of the righteous are in the hand of God, and no torment shall touch them. In the eyes of the foolish they seemed to have died ; but they are in peace. Their hope is full of immortality." (Wisdom of Solomon 3. 1–4).

The Minister may here give a brief address, or the following may be read :—

An old Saxon chieftain on a wintry day was revelling with his warriors in the banqueting hall, when he noticed a sparrow fly in at one door, hover a moment over the light and warmth of the hearth-fire, fly across the hall to the other door, and vanish into the night whence it came. " So seems the life of man ", he exclaimed. " Out of the darkness we come, we enjoy for a while the warmth and sunshine of the world, and then again into darkness we lapse ". This is strikingly beautiful, but heathen, gloomy, false. Man's life is not a journey from darkness to darkness. There is within us a divine spark. We come from God, and we go back to God. " The dust returneth to the earth as it was, but the spirit returneth unto God who gave it ". If we have lived justly, loved mercy and walked in humility with God and man, then the end of our toil is not a flight into darkness ; but to that life which is wholly a Sabbath—rest with God, peace everlasting.

May our prayers, readings and meditations in memory of the departed be acceptable before our Father who is in Heaven, the Great Comforter, who sends His divine consolation to all who mourn for the loss of those dear unto them.

Memorial Prayer, p. 1095, and Mourner's Kaddish, p. 1099.

III

" As for man, his days are as grass ; as the flower of the field, so he flourisheth. For the wind passeth over it, and it is gone ; and the place thereof shall know it no more. But the lovingkindness of the Lord is from everlasting to everlasting upon them that fear Him, and His righteousness unto children's children. How precious is Thy lovingkindness, O God ! And the children of men take refuge under the shadow of Thy wings. For with Thee is the fountain of life : in Thy light do we see light." *SCRIPTURAL VERSES Psalm 103. 15–17* *Psalm 36. 8, 10*

" Life is a passing shadow, says the Scripture. Is it the shadow of a tower, of a tree ? A shadow that prevails for a while ? No, it is the shadow of a bird in its flight— away flies the bird, and there is neither bird nor shadow." *RABBINICAL SAYINGS*

" Those who endure evil without returning wrong for wrong, who hear insults and answer not, who do good in a spirit of love, and accept suffering in a spirit of glad resignation—of such Scripture says : ' They that love Him shall be as the sun when he goeth forth in his might ' ".

" It is better to be of the persecuted than those that persecute, to be accursed rather than he who curses. He who judges his neighbour charitably, will himself be judged in charity. Despise no man, and hold nothing to be impossible. For there is not a man that has not his hour, and there is not a thing that has not its place."

" Do not unto others what thou wouldst not have others do unto thee. That is the whole Torah. The rest is commentary."

" Wouldst thou glorify God ? Seek to be like Him—just, loving, compassionate, merciful."

" Though at the Last Judgment there appeared nine hundred and ninety-nine accusers against a man, and but one advocate, yet shall that man be deemed meritorious. And who are the advocates of man ? Repentance and good works."

The Minister may here give a brief address, or the following may be read :—

A certain man had three friends, two of whom he loved dearly, the other he but lightly esteemed. It happened one day that the king commanded his presence at court, at which he was greatly alarmed, and wished to procure an advocate. Accordingly he went to the two friends whom he loved ; one flatly refused to accompany him, the other offered to go with him as far as the king's gate, but no farther. In his extremity, he called upon the third friend, whom he least esteemed; and that friend not only went willingly with him, but so ably defended him before the king that he was acquitted.

In like manner, every man has three friends when Death summons him to appear before his Creator. His first friend, whom he loves most, namely, his money, cannot go with him a single step ; his second, relations and neighbours, can only accompany him to the grave, but cannot defend him before the Judge : while his third friend, whom he does not highly esteem—his good works—goes with him before the King, and obtains his acquittal.

May our prayers, readings and meditations in memory of the departed be acceptable before our Father who is in Heaven, the Great Comforter, who sends His divine consolation to all who mourn for the loss of those dear unto them.

Memorial Prayer, p. 1095, and Mourner's Kaddish, p. 1099.

36*

IV

SCRIPTUR-
AL VERSES
" The Lord is nigh unto all them that call upon Him, To all that call upon Him in truth." *Psalm* 145. 18

" He that walketh in darkness and hath no light, let him trust in the name of Lord, and put his confidence in his God." *Isaiah* 50. 10

" Cast thy burden upon the Lord, and He shall sustain thee." *Psalm* 55. 22

" For He doth not afflict willingly, nor grieve the children of men." *Lamentations* 3. 33

" A man should ever school himself to say : " Whatever God doeth, He doeth for the best." *RABBINI-
CAL
SAYINGS*

" The Surgeon that has made the wound, knows best how to heal it."

" Suffering leads men's hearts to God."

" Whatever measure He metes out to thee, be it joy or sorrow, thou shalt love Him. Let thy conduct be such, that men will come to love God through thee."

" The aim and end of all wisdom are repentance and good works. Even the most righteous shall not attain so high a place in Heaven as the truly repentant. Blessed is he that repents while still in the full vigour of manhood. Blessed is he whose noble deeds go as mourners behind his bier. Blessed is he who, on departing from this earth, bequeaths a good name to his children."

" This world is like a vestibule before the world to come ; prepare thyself in the vestibule, that thou mayest enter into the presence-chamber."

" There are those who gain Eternity in a lifetime, others who gain it in one brief hour."

" Better is one hour of repentance and good deeds in this world than the whole life of the World to come ; and better is one hour of blissful-ness of spirit in the World to come than the whole life in this world."

The Minister may here give a brief address, or the following may be read :—

According to ancient Jewish custom, the ceremony of rending our garments when our nearest and dearest on earth is lying dead before us, is to be performed *standing up*. This teaches : Meet all sorrow standing upright. The future may be dark, veiled from the eye of mortals—but not the manner in which we are to meet the future. We cannot lay down terms to life. Life must be accepted on its own terms. But hard as life's terms may be, life never dictates unrighteousness, unholiness, dishonour.

May our prayers, readings and meditations in memory of the departed be acceptable before our Father who is in heaven, the Great Comforter, who sends His divine consolation to all who mourn for the loss of those dear unto them.

Memorial Prayer, p. 1095, and Mourner's Kaddish, p. 1099.

V

SCRIPTUR-
AL VERSES
Jeremiah
9. 23, 24 "Let not the wise man glory in his wisdom, neither let the mighty man glory in his might, let not the rich man glory in his riches; but let him that glorieth glory in this, that he understandeth and knoweth Me, that I am the Lord who exercise lovingkindness, judgment, and righteousness in the earth : for in these things I delight, saith the Lord."

Ecclesiastes
12. 1, 2, 7, 13 "Remember also thy Creator in the days of thy youth, or ever the evil days come, and the years draw nigh, when thou shalt say, I have no pleasure in them ; or ever the sun and the light, and the moon and the stars be darkened, and the clouds return after the rain ; and the dust return to the earth as it was, and the spirit return to God who gave it."

"This is the end of the matter ; all hath been heard ; fear God and keep His commandments, for this is the whole duty of man."

RABBINI-
CAL
SAYINGS "Fear God, as much as you fear man", said Rabbi Yohanan ben Zakkai. 'Not more ? ' asked his pupils in surprise. 'If you would but fear Him as much ! ' said the dying sage."

"The righteous are masters of their passions. Not so the wicked : they are the slaves of their desires. The righteous need no monuments : their deeds are their monuments. Let thy yea be yea, and thy nay be nay. The righteous promise little, and do much ; the wicked promise much, and do not perform even a little. Accustom thyself to complete any good work thou hast undertaken."

The Minister may here give a brief address, or the following may be read :—

Jewish men and women must learn once more the Jewish view of death, the Jewish view of life. The Jew never *feared* death ; frankly and manfully did he face it. "Do not act as if the lease of eternity were thine", was the warning of our Sages. "Live as if this hour were thy last ; and ask thyself : Should I care to be surprised by death in what I am now doing ? "

To those who gave heed to these words, death was an inspiration to holy living. Our Sages rightly viewed This life as a preparation to the Life to come. The hour of death was the entrance to that Coming Life. In that hour—they held—infinity touches infinity ; and a mortal in his death-agony is a being that is about to cast off the shell which on earth enveloped the imperishable soul. The hour of death, therefore, was to our fathers the most solemn in all human existence. Such must it also become to us. Once more would then every Jew in that hour proclaim his spiritual identity with all the preceding generations in Israel by repeating the great Professions of his Sacred Faith, culminating in the Shema Yisroel. The desire of each and every Israelite would then be, תמות נפשי מות ישרים "May I die the death of the righteous " ; and he would so live as not to be ashamed to meet his fathers in the World to come.

May our prayers, readings and meditations in memory of the departed be acceptable before our Father who is in Heaven, the Great Comforter, who sends His divine consolation to all who mourn for the loss of those dear unto them.

Memorial Prayer, p. 1095, and Mourner's Kaddish, p. 1099.

הַזְכָּרַת נְשָׁמוֹת :

The following is recited on the Eighth day of Passover and Taber-
nacles, on the Second day of Pentecost, and on the Day of Atonement.

יְיָ מָה־אָדָם וַתֵּדָעֵהוּ בֶּן־אֱנוֹשׁ וַתְּחַשְּׁבֵהוּ : אָדָם לַהֶבֶל
דָּמָה יָמָיו כְּצֵל עוֹבֵר : בַּבֹּקֶר יָצִיץ וְחָלָף לָעֶרֶב יְמוֹלֵל
וְיָבֵשׁ : לִמְנוֹת יָמֵינוּ כֵּן הוֹדַע וְנָבִא לְכַב חָכְמָה : שְׁמָר־
תָּם וּרְאֵה יָשָׁר כִּי אַחֲרִית לְאִישׁ שָׁלוֹם : אַךְ־אֱלֹהִים יִפְדֶּה־
נַפְשִׁי מִיַּד שְׁאוֹל כִּי יִקָּחֵנִי סֶלָה : כָּלָה שְׁאֵרִי וּלְבָבִי צוּר
לְבָבִי וְחֶלְקִי אֱלֹהִים לְעוֹלָם : וְיָשֹׁב הֶעָפָר עַל־הָאָרֶץ כְּשֶׁהָיָה
וְהָרוּחַ תָּשׁוּב אֶל־הָאֱלֹהִים אֲשֶׁר נְתָנָהּ : אֲנִי בְּצֶדֶק אֶחֱזֶה
פָנֶיךָ אֶשְׂבְּעָה בְהָקִיץ תְּמוּנָתֶךָ :

יִזְכּוֹר אֱלֹהִים נִשְׁמַת אָבִי מוֹרִי (פ׳ בן פ׳) (אִמִּי מוֹרָתִי)
(פ׳ בת פ׳) שֶׁהָלַךְ לְעוֹלָמוֹ (שֶׁהָלְכָה לְעוֹלָמָהּ) אָנָּא תְּהִי
נַפְשׁוֹ (נַפְשָׁהּ) צְרוּרָה בִּצְרוֹר הַחַיִּים וּתְהִי מְנוּחָתוֹ
(מְנוּחָתָהּ) כָּבוֹד שֹׂבַע שְׂמָחוֹת אֶת פָּנֶיךָ נְעִימוֹת בִּימִינְךָ
נֶצַח • אָמֵן :

אַב הָרַחֲמִים אֲשֶׁר בְּיָדְךָ נַפְשׁוֹת הַחַיִּים וְהַמֵּתִים •
תַּנְחוּמֶיךָ יְשַׁעַשְׁעוּ נַפְשֵׁנוּ בְּזָכְרֵנוּ (בַּיּוֹם הַקָּדוֹשׁ הַזֶּה) אֶת־
קְרוֹבֵינוּ הָאֲהוּבִים וְהַנִּכְבָּדִים אֲשֶׁר הָלְכוּ לִמְנוּחָתָם • אֶת־
תוֹרֵינוּ הַיְקָרִים עֲטֶרֶת רֹאשֵׁנוּ וְתִפְאַרְתֵּנוּ אֲשֶׁר כָּל־מַעֲמָתָם
לְהַדְרִיכֵנוּ בְּדֶרֶךְ הַטּוֹב וְהַיָּשָׁר וְהַיָּשָׁר לְלַמְּדֵנוּ חֻקָּיו וּמִצְוֹתֶיךָ
וּלְהוֹרוֹתֵנוּ עֲשׂוֹת צְדָקָה וְאַהֲבַת חֶסֶד : אָנָּא יְיָ אַמְּצֵנוּ לִשְׁמוֹר

YIZKOR—MEMORIAL SERVICE FOR PARENTS

*The following is recited on the eighth day of Passover and Tabernacles,
on the Second day of Pentecost, and on the Day of Atonement.*

Psalm 144. 3, 4   Lord, what is man, that thou regardest him ? or the son of man, that thou takest account of him ? Man is like

Psalm 90. 6   to vanity ; his days are as a shadow that passeth away. In

Psalm 90. 12   the morning he flourisheth, and sprouteth afresh ; in the evening he is cut down, and withereth. So teach us to number our days that we may get us a heart of wisdom.

Psalm 37. 37   Mark the innocent man, and behold the upright : for the

Psalm 49. 16   latter end of that man is peace. But God will redeem my soul from the grasp of the grave : for he will receive me.

Psalm 73. 26   My flesh and my heart faileth : but God is the strength

Ecclesiastes 12. 17   of my heart and my portion for ever. And the dust returneth to the earth as it was, but the spirit returneth

Psalm 17. 15   unto God who gave it. I shall behold thy face in righteousness ; I shall be satisfied, when I awake, with thy likeness.

For a Father :—	*For a Mother :—*
May God remember the soul of my revered father who has gone to his repose. May his soul be bound up in the bond of life. May his rest be glorious, with fulness of joy in thy presence, and bliss for evermore at thy right hand.	May God remember the soul of my revered mother who has gone to her repose. May her soul be bound up in the bond of life. May her rest be glorious, with fulness of joy in thy presence, and bliss for evermore at thy right hand.

Father of mercy, in whose hand are the souls of the living and the dead, may thy consolation cheer us as we

MEMORIAL SERVICE FOR THE DEAD.

It has for several centuries been customary to commemorate the dead (הזכרת נשמות) on the last day of Festivals, and especially on the Day of Atonement. In recent generations, such prayers have become an important feature of the Festival Service. Chief Rabbi Hermann Adler arranged the above Service, and composed the special Prayer which is also often recited at Yahrzeit services.

אֶת פְּקוּדָתָם כָּל עוֹד נִשְׁמָתֵנוּ בְּקִרְבֵּנוּ ' וְנַפְשָׁם תָּנוּחַ בְּאֶרֶץ
הַחַיִּים לַחֲזוֹת בְּנֹעֲמְךָ וּלְהִתְעַנֵּג מִטּוּבֶךָ :

וְעַתָּה הָאֵל הַטּוֹב וְהַמֵּטִיב מַה־נֹּאמַר וּמַה־נְּדַבֵּר ' צְרָכֵינוּ
מְרֻבִּים וְדַעְתֵּנוּ קְצָרָה : בֹּשֶׁת פָּנִים פְּקַדְתָּנוּ מִדֵּי עֲלוֹת
עַל־לִבֵּנוּ זֵכֶר כָּל־הַטּוֹבָה שֶׁגְּמַלְתָּ עָלֵינוּ : אָנָּא פְּנֵה הַיּוֹם
בְּחֶסֶד וּבְרַחֲמִים אֶל תְּפִלַּת עֲבָדֶיךָ הַשּׁוֹפְכִים אֶת־נַפְשָׁם
לְפָנֶיךָ : אָנָּא חַסְדְּךָ מֵאִתָּנוּ אַל־יָמוּשׁ : הַטְרִיפֵנוּ לֶחֶם
חֻקֵּנוּ וְאַל תַּצְרִיכֵנוּ לִידֵי מַתְּנַת בָּשָׂר וָדָם : הָסֵר
מֵעָלֵינוּ כָּל־דְּאָגָה וְתוּגָה כָּל־צָרָה וָפַחַד כָּל־חֶרְפָּה וָבוּז :
בְּיִרְאָתְךָ הַטְּהוֹרָה תְּחַזְּקֵנוּ וּבְתוֹרָתְךָ הַתְּמִימָה תְאַמְּצֵנוּ :
זַכֵּנוּ לְגַדֵּל אֶת־בָּנֵינוּ וּבְנוֹתֵינוּ לִשְׁמֹר מִצְוֹתֶיךָ וְלַעֲשׂוֹת
רְצוֹנֶךָ כָּל־יְמֵי חַיֵּיהֶם : אֵל נָא אַל תַּעֲלֵנוּ בַּחֲצִי יָמֵינוּ
וּנְמַלֵּא בְשָׁלוֹם אֶת מִסְפַּר יָמֵינוּ : יָדַעְנוּ אַף יָדַעְנוּ כִּי
חָדֵל לַחְנוּ וּטְפָחוֹת נָתַתָּ יָמֵינוּ : עָזְרֵנוּ אֱלֹהֵי יִשְׁעֵנוּ לְהִתְנַהֵג
בֶּאֱמֶת וּבְתָמִים יְמֵי שְׁנֵי חַיֵּי מְגוּרֵנוּ : וְכַאֲשֶׁר יַגִּיעַ קִצֵּנוּ
לְהִפָּרֵד מִן הָעוֹלָם חֵיֶה אַתָּה עִמָּנוּ וְנִשְׁמָתֵינוּ תִּהְיֶינָה
צְרוּרוֹת בִּצְרוֹר הַחַיִּים עִם נִשְׁמוֹת אֲבוֹתֵינוּ וְנִשְׁמוֹת
הַצַּדִּיקִים הָעוֹמְדִים לְפָנֶיךָ ' אָמֵן וְאָמֵן :

remember (on this holy day) our beloved parents, the crown of our head and our glory, whose desire it was to train us in the good and righteous way, to teach us thy statutes and commandments, and to instruct us to do justice and to love mercy. We beseech thee, O Lord, grant us strength to be faithful to their charge while the breath of life is within us. And may their souls repose in the land of the living, beholding thy glory and delighting in thy goodness.

And now, O good and beneficent God, what shall we say, what shall we speak unto thee ? Our needs are many, our knowledge slender. Shame covers us as often as the remembrance of all thy love for us rises within our minds. O turn this day in lovingkindness and tender mercy to the prayers of thy servants who pour out their souls before thee. May thy lovingkindness not depart from us. Give us our needful sustenance, and let us not be in want of the gifts of mortals. Remove from us care and sorrow, distress and fear, shame and contempt. Strengthen us in our reverence for thee, and fortify us to keep thy perfect Torah. Let thy grace be with us, that we may rear our children to keep thy commandments, and to fulfil thy will all the days of their life. O God, take us not hence in the midst of our days. Let us complete in peace the number of our years. Verily we know that our strength is frail, and that thou hast made our days as handbreadths. Help us, O God of our salvation, to bear ourselves faithfully and blamelessly during the years of our pilgrimage. And when our end draws nigh and we depart this world, be thou with us, and may our souls be bound up in the bond of life with the souls of our parents and of the righteous who are ever with thee. Amen, and Amen.

סדר תפלה בהקים מצבה לקרוביו:

תהלים א׳

אַשְׁרֵי הָאִישׁ אֲשֶׁר לֹא הָלַךְ בַּעֲצַת רְשָׁעִים וּבְדֶרֶךְ
חַטָּאִים לֹא עָמָד וּבְמוֹשַׁב לֵצִים לֹא יָשָׁב: כִּי אִם־בְּתוֹרַת
יְיָ חֶפְצוֹ וּבְתוֹרָתוֹ יֶהְגֶּה יוֹמָם וָלָיְלָה: וְהָיָה. כְּעֵץ שָׁתוּל
עַל־פַּלְגֵי־מָיִם אֲשֶׁר פִּרְיוֹ יִתֵּן בְּעִתּוֹ וְעָלֵהוּ לֹא יִבּוֹל וְכֹל
אֲשֶׁר־יַעֲשֶׂה יַצְלִיחַ: לֹא כֵן הָרְשָׁעִים כִּי אִם־כַּמֹּץ אֲשֶׁר־
תִּדְּפֶנּוּ רוּחַ: עַל כֵּן לֹא יָקֻמוּ רְשָׁעִים בַּמִּשְׁפָּט וְחַטָּאִים
בַּעֲדַת צַדִּיקִים: כִּי־יוֹדֵעַ יְיָ דֶּרֶךְ צַדִּיקִים וְדֶרֶךְ רְשָׁעִים
תֹּאבֵד :

Read   מִי יַעֲלֶה   or   אֵשֶׁת חַיִל   on p. 1070-1072 for a Man or a
Woman respectively ;   תהלים ט״ו   p. 1080;   כ״ג   p. 1052 ; and
מִפַּחַד בַּלֵּילוֹת to אֲדֹנִי מָעוֹן   on p. 1068 ; then continue :—

אֱנוֹשׁ כֶּחָצִיר יָמָיו כְּצִיץ הַשָּׂדֶה כֵּן יָצִיץ : כִּי רוּחַ
עָבְרָה־בּוֹ וְאֵינֶנּוּ וְלֹא־יַכִּירֶנּוּ עוֹד מְקוֹמוֹ : וְחֶסֶד יְיָ מֵעוֹלָם
וְעַד־עוֹלָם עַל־יְרֵאָיו וְצִדְקָתוֹ לִבְנֵי בָנִים : שׁמְרָ־תָם וּרְאֵה

TOMBSTONE SETTING.

The Service is modern.

PSALM 1. " The Two Ways ", forms an appropriate opening of the
Book of Psalms. It strikes the fundamental note of the Psalter and
the Wisdom Books of Scripture, proclaiming that it is well with the
righteous, and ill with the wicked. " It is a paean on the eternal
righteousness of God " (Barnes).

1. *walketh not.* The man who begins by *walking* in the counsel of
the wicked (*i.e.* following their counsel) will soon *stand* in the way of
sinners, and will end by *sitting* in the company of scoffers.

SERVICE AT THE SETTING OF A TOMBSTONE

Psalm i

THE RIGHT-EOUS MAN

¹Happy is the man that walketh not in the counsel of the wicked, nor standeth in the way of sinners, nor sitteth in the seat of scoffers. ²But his delight is in the law of the Lord ; and in his law doth he meditate day and night. ³And he shall be like a tree planted by the streams of water, that bringeth forth its fruit in its season, whose leaf also doth not wither ; and whatsoever he doeth shall prosper. ⁴The wicked are not so ; but are like the chaff which the wind driveth away. ⁵Therefore the wicked shall not stand in the judgment, nor the sinners in the congregation of the righteous. ⁶For the Lord knoweth the way of the righteous, but the way of the wicked shall perish.

Read " Who may ascend " or "A woman of worth " on p. 1071 and 1073, for a Man or Woman respectively ; Psalms xvi, p. 1081 ; xxiii, p. 1053 ; and "O Lord, thou hast " to " than your thoughts," p. 1069. Then continue :—

Psalm 103. 15-17

As for man, his days are as grass ; as the flower of the field, so he flourisheth. For the wind passeth over it, and it is gone ; and the place thereof shall know it no more. But the lovingkindness of the Lord is from everlasting to everlasting upon them that fear

scoffer. Those who make what is good and holy the object of ridicule.

2. *delight.* His Faith is a joy to him : he is happy in his Judaism.

meditate day and night. " In the hours of his leisure, whether day or night " (Kimchi). He is the eternal learner of Torah and Religion.

3. *like a tree . . . planted . . . his fruit.* Whose roots have unfailing supply of water, and whose branches and leaves afford shelter and food to present and future. The righteous life has both permanence and productivity.

4. *chaff.* In sharp contrast is the impermanence and unproductivity of the wicked life : it is like the chaff on the ancient threshing floor, where the wheat was winnowed by throwing it up against the wind.

5. *judgment.* In the Day of Judgment. There is a moral government in the world, and God's judgment will be such a winnowing-process to the wicked.

6. *shall perish.* The Heb. suggests the idea of losing itself as in the sands of the desert.

יָשָׁר כִּי אַחֲרִית לְאִישׁ שָׁלוֹם : בְּאֹרַח צְדָקָה חַיִּים
וְדֶרֶךְ נְתִיבָה אַל־מָוֶת : פּוֹדֶה יְיָ נֶפֶשׁ עֲבָדָיו וְלֹא
יֶאְשְׁמוּ כָּל־הַחוֹסִים בּוֹ : וְיָשֹׁב הֶעָפָר עַל הָאָרֶץ כְּשֶׁהָיָה
וְהָרוּחַ תָּשׁוּב אֶל הָאֱלֹהִים אֲשֶׁר נְתָנָהּ : מִי לִי בַּשָּׁמַיִם
וְעִמְּךָ לֹא־חָפַצְתִּי בָאָרֶץ : כָּלָה שְׁאֵרִי וּלְבָבִי צוּר־לְבָבִי
וְחֶלְקִי אֱלֹהִים לְעוֹלָם : מַה־יָּקָר חַסְדְּךָ אֱלֹהִים וּבְנֵי אָדָם
בְּצֵל כְּנָפֶיךָ יֶחֱסָיוּן : כִּי עִמְּךָ מְקוֹר חַיִּים בְּאוֹרְךָ נִרְאֶה־אוֹר :

קַדִּישׁ יָתוֹם p. 1098. ;אָנָּא וכו׳ p. 1094; p. 70 תהלים צ"א

FROM THE JEWISH MORALISTS—THIRD SELECTION

For earlier extracts from Jewish ethical literature, see pp. 260–3
and 722–4.

X.   From *Rokëach*, by R. Elazar of Worms (died 1238) ;
XI.   From *Sefer Chassidim*, by R. Judah the Pious (died 1217) ;
XII.   From *Col Bo* by R. Moses of Evreux (1240).
XIII.   From *the Book of Fables* by Berachyah Ha-nakdan
            (probably Benedict of Oxford) 1260.
XIV.   From *the Ethical Will* of Asher ben Yechiel (13th century).
XV.   From *Orchoth Tzaddikim* (" The Ways of the Righteous "),
            (15th century).

X.

The pious Jew bears unrepiningly the burden of his People's Faith,
holds worldly delights in contempt, is master of his passions, and, in
sooth, has God continually before his eyes. The path which his feet
tread is straightforward, and the words he utters soft and gentle.
He rears his children to a worthy life, and sees that they have
betimes homes of their own. He is of a contented mind, and rejoices
when the world goes well with others. He loves his neighbours and
friends, lends to the needy, gives alms secretly, and does good purely
for God's sake. Men of this sort do not exalt themselves above others,
indulge in no idle talk, long not wretchedly for the love in woman's
eyes, are silent when blame is poured on them ; for their thoughts
are ever with Him Whose praises are sung by their faithful lips.

Psalm 37. 37   him, and his righteousness unto children's children. Mark the
innocent man, and behold the upright , for the latter end of that
Proverbs 12.28   man is peace. In the way of righteousness is life ; and in the path-
Psalm 34. 23   way thereof there is no death. The Lord setteth free the soul of his
servants ; and none that take refuge in him shall be condemned.
Ecclesiastes   And the dust returneth to the earth as it was, but the spirit returneth
12. 7
Psalm 73. 25,   unto God, who gave it. Whom have I in heaven but thee ? And
26   there is none upon earth that I desire beside thee. My flesh and
my heart faileth : but God is the strength of my heart and my
Psalm 36. 8,   portion for ever. How precious is thy lovingkindness, O God ! And
10   the children of men take refuge under the shadow of thy wings.
For with thee is the fountain of life : in thy light do we see light.
Psalm xci, *p.* 71 ; *"O Lord and King, who art full of compassion,"*
p. 1095 ; *Mourner's Kaddish, p.* 1099.

My son, free thyself from passion and desire before thy light is
quenched, before thy soul is required of thee, before the Book of thy
deeds is opened for Judgment. Let the fear of God breed in thee the
habit of silence, for much speech can hardly be without sin. And when
thou dost speak, speak truth only, never praise of thyself, but moderate
thought in modest words.

XI.

Be honourable in thy business dealings. Do not say that such and
such a price has been offered thee for thy wares, when the thing is not
true ; and do not act as though thou hadst a desire to sell what thou
possessest, when there is in thy mind no serious thought of doing so
Such things are unworthy of an Israelite.

On the worldly possessions of those who oppress the workman,
or who buy stolen goods, rests no blessing. They or their children will
lose all they have. Let no one be troubled in mind or take up wrong
ideas because of the prosperity of wicked people, or of such as hold
parents in little honour ; their end is evil.

In thy intercourse with non-Jews, be careful to be as wholly sincere
as in that with Jews. In most places, Jews are not unlike Christians in
their morals and usages.

If an assassin take refuge with thee, give him no protection, even though he be a Jew. If one who bears a heavy burden on his shoulders meet thee on a narrow and difficult path, make way for him, even though he be a non-Jew.

To him who is merciful, God is merciful. The pitiless man is like the cattle of the field that are indifferent to the sufferings of their kind.

There are three sorts of people for whom we ought to feel especial sympathy : a reasonable, prudent creature subjected to a capricious fool ; a good man who has to take orders from a base man ; and a noble being dependent upon one of vulgar nature. There are three to whom we should sternly close our hearts : a cruel person who commits vile things ; the fool who rushes into ruin in spite of warning ; and the ingrate. Ingratitude is the blackest of faults ; it is not to be shown even towards the dumb creatures that we use.

XII.

Above all, let a man be on his guard against wrath ; for the powers of hell do what they will with the blindly angry man. Busy thyself as oft and as much as possible with the study of Divine things, not to know them only, but to perform the duties they inculcate ; and when thou closest the book, look within thee to see if there is aught for thee to carry out answering to what thou hast learned.

XIII.

Sooner be a servant among the noble-minded than a leader among the vulgar ; for some of the honour of the former will remain with thee, while thou must share the contempt of thy unworthy followers. If thou too earnestly seek pre-eminence and power, be sure that they will flee from thee ; but if thou bearest thyself in this world like a guest receiving its hospitality, men will try to find for thee a place of honour.

If, because of beauty or riches that are thine, thou raisest thy head above neighbour or brother, thou feedest hateful envy, and the beggar whom thou despisest may yet triumph over thee. Better enough in freedom, than plenty at the table of another.

Love thy children with an impartial love ; the hope oft errs that you place on the more promising, and all the joy may come from him that thou hast kept in the background.

XIV.

Take pleasure in being warned against wrong and set right, and seek for good counsel and instruction cheerfully. Hunt not for honours, and force not thyself into any place that belongs not to thee. Never cease to acquire friends ; avoid making even one enemy. When a companion is of approved truth, spare no pains in attaching him to thee and cherish him carefully; but flatter him not and say no untrue word to him. Strive not to screw out the secrets of others. See that thou cause not those of thy household to stand in dread of thee: much misery and wrong have sprung ere now therefrom.

XV.

It is wretched pride when one is always thinking others as lower than himself, and that his own opinion is always better than that of others. All moral advance is thereby made impossible; such a one is always seeking thanks for what he does, and takes delight in others crouching as inferiors before him.

Let a man be never ashamed to carry out the commands of Religion, even though he be mocked therefor; and never be ashamed to confess the truth. But let a man be well on his guard against putting others to shame. Let him take heed not to lay bare wantonly the failings of a neighbour, or of giving him a dishonourable nickname. Be tender-hearted towards servants who are not Jews. Make not their labour too heavy for them: treat them not as though they were of no account whatever. Even in dispute with a serving man, speak affably, and listen to what he has to say.

Genuine compassion and pity become and highly adorn the Israelite; be pitiful, therefore, even to thy cattle, and give them food even before thou thyself eatest. The words of Scripture, " The tender mercies of the wicked are cruel ", refer to such as exact heavy returns from poor men for favours received.

Let thy trust and dependence be placed on God alone. Thy business affairs are nothing more than the means He applies to thy support. It is not the iron, but the force that moves the iron, that fells the tree.

Be grateful for, not blind to the many, many sufferings which thou art spared; thou art no better than those who have been searched out and racked by them.

Hurt no one's feelings who has any bodily defect, or on whose family rests a stain. If thou sittest next to such a one, speak not of such deficiency or fault, even in reference to others than himself. Touch not the subject of a quarrel that is ended, lest thou fan the dying embers afresh. Luxury, idleness and good living lead to unrestraint of soul, and so to evil speaking and mockeries. Keep thy soul always pure; thou knowest not the moment when it may be required of thee. Many a young and strong man has gone before thee to his eternal Home. Thou puttest thyself in fine garments to please men; forget not that God looks on the heart, and adorn that well in honour of Him.

תְּפִלַת שַׁחֲרִית לִילָדִים:

1. בָּרוּךְ אַתָּה יְיָ אֱלֹהֵינוּ מֶלֶךְ הָעוֹלָם · הַמַּעֲבִיר
שֵׁנָה מֵעֵינַי וּתְנוּמָה מֵעַפְעַפָּי:

2. מוֹדֶה אֲנִי לְפָנֶיךָ מֶלֶךְ חַי וְקַיָּם שֶׁהֶחֱזַרְתָּ בִּי
נִשְׁמָתִי בְּחֶמְלָה · רַבָּה אֱמוּנָתֶךָ:

3. שְׁמַע יִשְׂרָאֵל יְיָ אֱלֹהֵינוּ יְיָ אֶחָד:
בָּרוּךְ שֵׁם כְּבוֹד מַלְכוּתוֹ לְעוֹלָם וָעֶד:
וְאָהַבְתָּ אֵת יְיָ אֱלֹהֶיךָ בְּכָל־לְבָבְךָ וּבְכָל־נַפְשְׁךָ
וּבְכָל־מְאֹדֶךָ:

4. תּוֹרָה צִוָּה־לָנוּ מֹשֶׁה מוֹרָשָׁה קְהִלַּת יַעֲקֹב:

5. שְׁמַע בְּנִי מוּסַר אָבִיךָ · וְאַל תִּטֹּשׁ תּוֹרַת אִמֶּךָ ·
וּמְצָא חֵן וְשֵׂכֶל טוֹב בְּעֵינֵי אֱלֹהִים וְאָדָם:

6. אֱלֹהַי · נְצוֹר לְשׁוֹנִי מֵרָע וּשְׂפָתַי מִדַּבֵּר מִרְמָה:
אַל תְּבִיאֵנִי לִידֵי נִסָּיוֹן · הַרְחִיקֵנִי מֵאָדָם
רַע וּמֵחָבֵר רָע · וְתִגְמְלֵנִי חֲסָדִים טוֹבִים:

7. בָּרוּךְ אַתָּה יְיָ אֱלֹהֵינוּ מֶלֶךְ הָעוֹלָם · שֶׁעָשַׂנִי
יִשְׂרָאֵל:

*For Infants, I, 3, 7.

MORNING PRAYER FOR YOUNG CHILDREN.

1. Blessed art thou, O Lord our God, King of the universe, who removest sleep from mine eyes, and slumber from mine eyelids.

2. I give thanks unto thee, O living and eternal King who hast restored my soul unto me in mercy : great is thy faithfulness.

3. HEAR, O ISRAEL : THE LORD IS OUR GOD, THE LORD IS ONE.
Blessed be His Name, whose glorious kingdom is for ever and ever.
And thou shalt love the Lord thy God with all thine heart, and with all thy soul, and with all thy might.

4. Moses commanded us the Torah as an inheritance of the congregation of Jacob.

5. Hearken, my child, to the instruction of thy father ; and despise not the teaching of thy mother. Then shalt thou find grace and good repute in the eyes of God and man.

6. O my God, guard my tongue from evil and my lips from speaking guile. O lead me not into temptation ; keep me far from a bad man and a bad companion ; and bestow thy lovingkindnesses upon me.

7. Blessed art thou, O Lord our God, King of the universe, who hast made me an Israelite.

*For Infants, 1, 3, 7.

תְּפִלַּת לַיְלָה לִילָדִים:

1. בָּרוּךְ אַתָּה יְיָ אֱלֹהֵינוּ מֶלֶךְ הָעוֹלָם · בּוֹרֵא יוֹם וָלַיְלָה · גּוֹלֵל אוֹר מִפְּנֵי־חֹשֶׁךְ וְחֹשֶׁךְ מִפְּנֵי־אוֹר · בָּרוּךְ אַתָּה יְיָ · הַמַּעֲרִיב עֲרָבִים:

2. שְׁמַע יִשְׂרָאֵל יְיָ אֱלֹהֵינוּ יְיָ אֶחָד: בָּרוּךְ שֵׁם כְּבוֹד מַלְכוּתוֹ לְעוֹלָם וָעֶד:

3. וְאָהַבְתָּ אֵת יְיָ אֱלֹהֶיךָ בְּכָל־לְבָבְךָ וּבְכָל־נַפְשְׁךָ וּבְכָל־מְאֹדֶךָ:

4. בָּרוּךְ אַתָּה יְיָ אֱלֹהֵינוּ מֶלֶךְ הָעוֹלָם · הַמַּפִּיל חֶבְלֵי שֵׁנָה עַל עֵינַי וּתְנוּמָה עַל עַפְעַפָּי:

5. וִיהִי רָצוֹן מִלְּפָנֶיךָ יְיָ אֱלֹהַי וֵאלֹהֵי אֲבוֹתַי · שֶׁתַּשְׁכִּיבֵנִי לְשָׁלוֹם וְתַעֲמִידֵנִי לְשָׁלוֹם:

6. בָּרוּךְ יְיָ בַּיּוֹם · בָּרוּךְ יְיָ בַּלַּיְלָה · בָּרוּךְ יְיָ בְּשָׁכְבֵנוּ · בָּרוּךְ יְיָ בְּקוּמֵנוּ:

7. בְּיָדְךָ אַפְקִיד רוּחִי פָּדִיתָה אוֹתִי יְיָ אֵל אֱמֶת:

*For Infants, 2, 4, 7.

NIGHT PRAYER FOR YOUNG CHILDREN.

1. Blessed art thou, O Lord, our God, King of the universe, who createst day and night ; thou rollest away the light from before the darkness, and the darkness from before the light. Blessed art thou, O Lord, who bringest on the evening twilight.

2. HEAR, O ISRAEL : THE LORD IS OUR GOD, THE LORD IS ONE.
Blessed be His Name, whose glorious kingdom is for ever and ever.

3. And thou shalt love the Lord thy God with all thine heart, and with all thy soul, and with all thy might.

4. Blessed art thou, O Lord our God, King of the universe, who makest the bands of sleep to fall upon mine eyes, and slumber upon mine eyelids.

5. May it be thy will, O Lord my God and God of my fathers, to let me lie down in peace, and to let me rise up again in peace.

6. Blessed be the Lord by day ; blessed be the Lord by night ; blessed be the Lord when we lie down ; blessed be the Lord when we rise up.

7. Into thy hand I commend my spirit ; thou hast redeemed me, O Lord God of truth.

*For Infants, 2, 4, 7.

INDEX TO PSALMS